Im Banne des Unheimlichen

# EURO GOTHIC

# classics of continental horror cinema

# EURO GOTHIC

## classics of continental horror cinema

### JONATHAN RIGBY

SIGNUM BOOKS

*In memoriam Victor Rigby (1924-2016), who introduced me to horror films and was still watching them in his nineties.*

This edition published in Great Britain
in 2021 by Signum Books, an imprint of
Flashpoint Media Ltd
208 Mill Road
Cambridge
CB1 3NF

A CIP catalogue record for this book is
available from the British Library.

ISBN 9780957648159

Edited by Marcus Hearn
Designed by Peri Godbold

Printed and bound in China by
1010 Printing International Ltd.

## PICTURE CREDITS

**Front endpaper**
*Totentanz* (1919): Sascha Gura
*Dr Mabuse, der Spieler* (1921): Rudolf Klein-Rogge,
   Gertrude Welker
*Alraune* (1929 talkie version): Brigitte Helm
*La Charrette fantôme* (1939): Pierre Fresnay, Louis Jouvet
*Le Corbeau* (1943): Pierre Fresnay
*Der Verlorene* (1950): Peter Lorre
*Torticola contre Frankensberg* (1951): Michel Piccoli,
   Véra Norman
*Les Sorcières de Salem* (1956): Mylène Demongeot
*Faust* (1960): Will Quadflieg
*La settima tomba* (1965): Bruna Baini, Nando Angelini
*Necronomicon* (1967): Américo Coimbra, Janine Reynaud
*Im Banne des Unheimlichen* (1968): Peter Mosbacher

**Half-title page**
*Nosferatu Eine Symphonie des Grauens* (1921): Max Schreck

**Frontispiece**
*Les Diaboliques* (1954): Simone Signoret, Paul Meurisse

**Contents page**
*Der Student von Prag* (1926): Conrad Veidt
*I tre volti della paura* (1963): Boris Karloff
*Miss Muerte* (1965): Guy Mairesse
*Pánico en el Transiberiano* (1971): Juan Olaguivel, Silvia Tortosa
*Lèvres de sang* (1975): Catherine and Marie-Pierre Castel
*Quella villa accanto al cimitero* (1981): Giovanni De Nava

**Back endpaper**
*De Sade 70* (1969): Jack Taylor, Uta Dahlberg
*Nella stretta morsa del ragno* (1971): Karin Field
*Antefatto* (1971): Brigitte Skay
*La venganza de la momia* (1973): Rina Ottolina, Paul Naschy
*Magdalena, vom Teufel besessen* (1974): Dagmar Hedrich
*Les Week-ends maléfiques du Comte Zaroff* (1974):
   Robert de Laroche, Nathalie Zeiger
*La Bête de Gévaudan* (1973): Sirpa Lane
*Sette note in nero* (1976): Jennifer O'Neill, Gianni Garko
*Le notti del terrore* (1980): unknown zombies
*Sobrenatural* (1980): Cristina Galbó
*Lo squartatore di New York* (1981): Alexandra Delli Colli
*Dèmoni 2... l'incubo ritorna* (1986): Coralina Cataldi Tassoni

# Contents

# Author's note

It began in a black-tiled bathroom in Brussels – to be precise, the bathroom attached to the Royal Suite at the Astoria Hotel on Rue Royale. It was May 2012 and, after decades of absorbing horror films of every nationality, I was amazed to find myself in the very room where one of the key scenes in Harry Kümel's *Les Lèvres rouges* had been filmed 42 years earlier. Sadly, as part of the hotel's decade-long refurbishment, that ebony bathroom was soon to be ripped out and lost forever. Indeed, the building itself was closed and, for all its fin-de-siècle grandeur, looked somewhat forlorn – exactly the "sinister, deserted caravanserai" referred to in the film.

With Mark Gatiss, John Das and Matthew Thomas I was working on the feature-length BBC special *Horror Europa* at the time. We'd already visited the Thermae Palace in Ostend, the colonnade and stained-glass restaurant of which were instantly recognisable from Kümel's film. Now we were interviewing Kümel himself prior to meeting Édith Scob, star of the 1959 film *Les Yeux sans visage*, at her apartment in Paris. The whole experience inspired me to act, at long last, on a notion I'd had many years before – the notion that something called *Euro Gothic* would be a natural successor to my previous books *English Gothic* and *American Gothic*.

As you might expect, this new book functions in much the same way as its predecessors. While discussing scores of other films in less detail, I've chosen to focus on 113 representative titles, providing each one with credits – several of the cast lists, by the way, are the most complete yet published, certainly in English – and a couple of quotes, generally a contemporary review and a comment from a participant. (In a few instances a comment, one worth quoting anyway, proved elusive, so for those films you get two contemporary reviews instead.) The criteria involved in selecting films, major or minor, are also as before, with animation, shorts, comedies, science fiction, amateur productions and films featuring only isolated moments of horror being, for the most part, ruled out. Experimental or avant-garde films have been treated selectively as well.

Whenever possible, the years attached to films in this book are those of production, not necessarily release; you'll therefore find numerous dates that differ from the standard ones given in other sources. Titles are generally those by which the films were known in their native countries, though with *Flesh for Frankenstein* and *Blood for Dracula* I've opted for English titles given that both films appeared in English well before being seen in Italian. I've also, where possible, ignored the many temporary pseudonyms used by actors and technicians, preferring to use their real names instead; the excellent Roberto Curti book *Italian Gothic Horror Films, 1957-1969* was especially useful in this regard. Other exceptional books that help map out the terrain of continental horror include Pete Tombs' and Cathal Tohill's trailblazing *Immoral Tales: Sex and Horror Cinema in Europe 1956-1984*, Antonio Lázaro-Reboll's *Spanish Horror Film* and various in-depth director studies by such writers as Tim Lucas, Stephen Thrower and Troy Howarth. My chief confederate where original research was concerned was the indefatigable Kevin Lyons, who fielded literally hundreds of arcane queries (and was almost never stumped), furnished me with oodles of films to watch, and provided the majority of the credits contained in the box-outs.

My thanks are also due to my multilingual friends Sergio Angelini, Josephine Botting and Uwe Sommerlad; any errors in translation are, of course, my own. For generous provision of illustrations I have to thank Dima Ballin, James Blackford, Paul J Brown (Midnight Media), Steve Fenton, Troy Howarth, Peter Jilmstad, Denis Meikle, Marc Morris, Josh Saco, Silver Ferox Design, the Alan Y Upchurch Collection and BFI Stills. Stuart Hall, meanwhile, loaded me with yet more films to watch. Others whose help proved invaluable include Darrell Buxton, Roberto Curti, Eugenio Ercolani, José Luis Salvador Estébenez, Carl Ford, Elric Fraumeni, Sebastian Haselbeck, Simon Hitchman, Uwe Huber, Anastasia Kerameos, Robert James Kiss, Tim Lucas, Elena Marcarini, Kim Newman, Mark Thompson-Ashworth and the BFI's indispensable librarians.

My designer, Peri Godbold, worked her customary magic in making the book look extra-special, while my publisher, Marcus Hearn, enabled the whole project in the first place. Many thanks, also, to my wife Claire, who for much of the last two years has had to put up with my total absorption in continental ghastliness. Nobody will be happier to see the published book than she.

*Jonathan Rigby*
*London*
*July 2016*

# Introduction

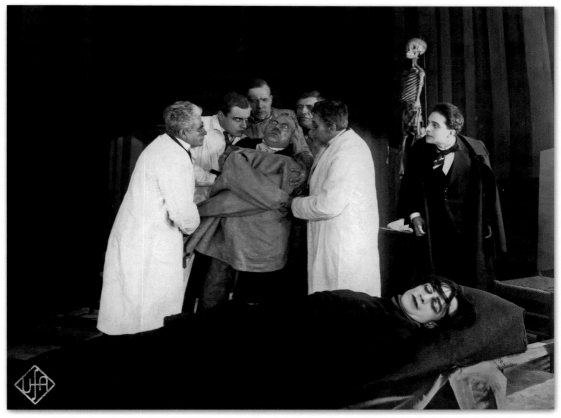

Conrad Veidt reclines, Friedrich Fehér (far right) recoils and Werner Krauss gets firmly straitjacketed in *Das Cabinet des Dr Caligari* (1919)

The European horror film, seething with transgressive imagery and narrative irrationality, has often posed a problem for more literal-minded, English-speaking audiences. The thinking seems to go roughly like this: Give us a good dose of horror, by all means, but please retain at least a smidgen of plot coherence and don't surrender completely to the destabilising illogic of nightmare. Yet European filmmakers pay heed to such literary niceties only when it suits them, and the perplexity of 'foreigners' when faced with these lurid and provocative films can be traced right back to the beginning of cinema.

In the silent era, for example, Agnes Smith was among the best of the many writers working on America's lavishly produced fan publications, eventually becoming editor of *Motion Picture Magazine*

in 1926. Yet it was for the rival *Picture-Play* that, some five years earlier, she had been required to get to grips with *Das Cabinet des Dr Caligari* (The Cabinet of Dr Caligari). In addition to welcoming what she called this "strange, new type of picture" and claiming that action-fixated Hollywood directors could learn a lot from "its weird and terrible story … because it brings to the screen a third dimension that it has hitherto lacked," Smith candidly admitted that "I am somewhat baffled by it. I know what I personally think of it, but what the motion-picture public will think of it is another matter. If I come right out and say that it is one of the most important and significant productions of the year, some *Picture-Play* reader is likely to misunderstand me and ask the editor to have me committed to an insane asylum."[1]

In the wake of the First World War, the avant-garde 'otherness' of *Caligari* made a phenomenal impact, and Agnes Smith was by no means the only commentator left shattered by its artistic innovations and Grand Guignol tone. Acknowledging its effectiveness as a horror story, she concluded with a traditional warning: "If you take the children to see *Doctor Caligari* just because I have said it is an interesting picture, don't blame me if they have nightmares." She also immediately co-opted the film as a facetious yardstick by which to judge more conventional products appealing to more 'normally' constituted picturegoers, pointing out on the very next page that "If you don't like [the J M Barrie adaptation] *Sentimental Tommy*, you ought to join *Doctor Caligari*'s cute little insane asylum, because something is wrong with your finer feelings." Though coming so early in the game, Smith's confused response – fair-mindedly recognising the film's importance yet shrinking from being identified as a horror fan in case this might qualify her for a straitjacket – remains typical of the uneasy relationship between film critics and the horror genre, particularly the extremes of European horror.

For those lured in by the hype created by Smith and other critics, *Caligari*'s New York showcase at the Capitol Theatre in April 1921 was masterminded by S L 'Roxy' Rothafel, who cannily set the film to themes by Stravinsky and Schoenberg that were at least as alien to American punters as the film itself. "The music had, as it were, to be made eligible for citizenship in a nightmare country,"[2] he sagely pointed out. He was referring, of course, to the geography of an unbalanced mind, but that Germany was itself a 'nightmare' country in the early 1920s was soon borne out by the flood of macabre films produced by German studios. And that these films were a response to the trauma of a hideously destructive war wasn't hard to work out; indeed, they offered a modern variant on a tendency observed by the Marquis de Sade as long ago as 1800.

Assessing the recent proliferation of Gothic novels centred on "sorcery and phantasmagoria," de Sade maintained that "this style ... was the inevitable fruit of the revolutionary shocks felt by the whole of Europe," on the principle that only by invoking Hell and venturing into "the country of chimeras" could writers hold the attention of a public that had "experienced more misfortune in four or five years than the most famous novelist in literature could paint in a century."[3] De Sade's idea, hatched in the wake of the French Revolution, that horror fictions provide a therapeutic outlet at times of distress and deprivation has long since become a critical commonplace, and

in European horror cinema it's substantiated not just by the nightmares of Weimar Germany but also by the kind of nervy French *fantastique* produced during the Second World War.

One of the contrary delights of European horror, however, is its explosive emergence at times when distress and deprivation are, superficially at least, in short supply. Just as Britain's revolutionary revival of Gothic horror was played out against a late-1950s backdrop of 'you've never had it so good' affluence, so Italy's resultant horror boom arose in the midst of that country's economic post-war miracle. Spain's attempts at horror may have been hamstrung, initially, by the looming presence of a Fascist dictator, yet the country's own economic boom triggered a belated flood of horror product, with the atavistic, blood-bolted archetypes of Gothic horror offering, as in Italy, a subversive counterpoise to an apparently forward-thinking national outlook. This was a dichotomy neatly expressed by Barbara Steele, the British-born star of some of the most indelible Italian horrors, who described 1960s Italy as "pure rapture: blazing, ripe, passionate, overfed, oversexed, feral, fecund," with "everybody there caught up in a collective thrall in this period of electrifying optimism" – yet producing a series of morbid films that "were both baroque and romantic ... [speaking] to a part of us that we don't consciously like to look at. The inevitability of death; sex and rage; beauty and the beast."[4]

Agnes Smith's guarded welcome to Dr Caligari also included the claim that "It is an excellent example of the workings of a morbid, scientific Teutonic mind." National stereotyping is certainly a temptation when assessing European horror; it's hard, for example, to miss the poetic debts to surrealism characteristic of France, the fascinated yet fearful emphasis on seductive women typical of Italy, and the monstrous parallels to Fascist overlords, past and present, exploited in Spain. But, again, another of the contrary delights of the form is the cultural shape-shifting encouraged by post-war co-productions, whereby films might be attributable, according to which country happened to provide the majority share of financing, to Italy-Spain or France-Italy or Spain-France or West Germany-Italy or any number of other permutations.

In this hydra-headed form European horror responded not just to the fluctuating fortunes of the industry but also to the social upheavals beyond it, in particular the erosion of censorship in the late 1960s. Coupled, ironically, with the rise of the women's movement, the countercultural call to tune in, turn on, drop out and disrobe was a gift to

A capering demon and a grisly assemblage of murdered wives in Georges Méliès' version of the Bluebeard legend, *Barbe-bleue* (1901)

exploitation filmmakers everywhere, providing a field day, among audiences, for dirty old men and goggle-eyed teenage boys alike – and the fusions of sex and horror perfected in mainland Europe were more outrageous and provocative than anywhere else. Loosening the stays of censorship also brought with it a revolutionary new emphasis on blood and viscera, with the Kensington Gore that streamed from Christopher Lee's eye in Britain's *The Curse of Frankenstein* – considered so shockingly gruesome in 1957 – appearing almost anaemic when compared, 20-odd years later, to the cannibalistic eviscerations of Italian horror.

The present book takes the story up to 1983, for reasons that will become clear at the end, together with a brief indication of what happened to the main players after that point. It also confines itself, in the main, to examining the output of Germany, Italy, Spain and France – though the boundary-blurring nature of international co-production means that I've been able to include some French-speaking Belgian films and German-speaking Swiss ones too. Generally speaking the majority finance behind a film indicates what I consider to be its chief nationality – Mario Bava's *La frusta e il corpo* (The Whip and the Body), for example, is essentially an Italian film despite input from France. Occasionally, however, I've permitted myself a more subjective view, as in the case of Jorge Grau's *No profanar el sueño de los muertos*, which may have been chiefly financed by Italian producer Edmondo Amati but seems to me, thanks to Grau's crucial contribution as an unusually inspirational director, an essentially Spanish film. Thus I do not call it *Non si deve profanare il sonno dei morti* in these pages, though both titles basically mean the same thing: Do Not Profane the Sleep of the Dead.

Finally, in focusing on Germany, Italy, Spain and France, my aim has been, not only to emphasise the countries most often involved in mutually beneficial co-productions, but also, more prosaically, to keep the book to a manageable length. It certainly doesn't imply any disrespect towards the remarkable horror films emanating from other parts of Europe. It was tempting to cover such directors as Denmark's Benjamin Christensen, Sweden's Victor Sjöström and Calvin Floyd, Poland's Wojciech Has and Janusz Majewski, Czechoslovakia's Juraj Herz and Jaromil Jireš, not forgetting a couple of personal favourites from opposite ends of the 1950s – Erik Blomberg's Finnish *Valkoinen peura* (The White Reindeer) and Kåre Bergstrøm's Norwegian *De dødes tjern* (The Lake of the Dead). There's also the small matter of Károly Lajthay's 1921 release *Drakula halála* (Dracula's Death), a Hungarian production that ranks as the first film to present Bram Stoker's vampire on screen – albeit in the person of a *Caligari*-style mental patient who only *thinks* he's Dracula.

But to add that lot to the mix would have resulted in a book of seriously unwieldy proportions. Maybe some other time.

# Part One

The developing drama of the soul: Conrad Veidt in the Austrian production *Orlacs Hände* (1924)

## *Warning Shadows* 1896-1954

In August 1807 a four-volume publication called *Feudal Tyrants*, freely adapted by Matthew 'Monk' Lewis from an original by Benedikte Naubert, was given a resounding thumbs-down by *The Monthly Review*, whose critic complained that "never was heard any thing so dismal as the direful croaking of this German raven!"

The book had been examined at much greater length, but no more encouragingly, in the previous month's issue of *The Critical Review*: "We well know what we are to expect in a German work of imagination: ghosts, bones, chains, dungeons, castles, forests, murders, and rapine pass before us in long order, till sated with horrors and habituated to their view we regard them with as much composure as an undertaker contemplates the last melancholy rites of his mortal brethren." The verdict was brutal, with the reviewer pointing out that "we are greatly at a loss to assign any plausible reason for the author ransacking the repositories of German literature to produce nothing better than this."

Responsible in 1796 for a scandalously transgressive Gothic novel called *The Monk*, Lewis

neglected to credit Naubert on the title page of *Feudal Tyrants*, contenting himself with the decorous subtitle *A Romance, taken from the German*. In this Lewis was echoing many other subtitles of the day, with the phrase 'from the German' quickly becoming a kind of code for 'irrational thrills and lurid horrors will be found within'. As late as 1839, the identification of Germany with Gothic excess was still marked enough for the American writer Edgar Allan Poe to preface his first anthology, *Tales of the Grotesque and Arabesque*, with a very firm rebuttal. "If in many of my productions terror has been the thesis," he wrote, "I maintain that terror is not of Germany, but of the soul."

Back in the 1760s the high-minded arbiters of the Age of Reason, complacently rejecting all taint of atavism and superstition, had themselves been rejected by a new generation dedicated to creating, as the English novelist Mrs Radcliffe put it, "a sensation of sublimity rising into terror." Intellectuals and potboiling hacks alike were gripped by the desire to induce in their audiences the "suspension of mingled astonishment and awe" prescribed by Radcliffe, to luxuriate in what the poet Shelley, adapting her words, called "the tempestuous loveliness of terror." And much of the 'sublime' iconography of the great Gothic novels had been put in place by German authors. The cemetery tryst of Burger's *Lenore*, the satanic pact of Goethe's *Faust* and the Sicilian necromancer of Schiller's *Der Geisterseher* (The Ghost Seer) had been followed by a long line of writers trading in the uncanny and ineffable, among them Ludwig Tieck, E T A Hoffmann, Adalbert von Chamisso and the Brothers Grimm. Of these, von Chamisso's *Peter Schlemihls wundersame Geschichte* (Peter Schlemihl's Wondrous Story) and Hoffmann's *Der Sandmann* (The Sand Man), published in 1814 and 1817 respectively, were classic expressions of the German preoccupation with doppelgängers and human simulacra.

These and other preoccupations were transmitted to France by Charles Nodier, who, as well as writing many striking fictions of his own, also composed an 1820 stage adaptation of Polidori's *The Vampyre*, a story that had been conceived at the same Geneva house party that sired Mary Shelley's *Frankenstein*. Nodier's heirs included Honoré de Balzac, Prosper Mérimée, Théophile Gautier and Charles Baudelaire; the latter not only translated Poe into French but claimed to address his morning prayers to him. There were also Alexandre Dumas and Eugène Sue, masters of the roman-feuilleton, serialised sensation novels that entranced a mass audience. (Dumas was the author, too, of another stage adaptation of *The Vampyre*, some 30 years after Nodier's original.) Prefiguring all of them was the Marquis de Sade, an admirer of Mrs Radcliffe and 'Monk' Lewis whose obsessive works, almost exclusively written in prison, far exceeded even the grossest transgressions of Lewis' most famous book.

With this kind of pedigree, it was quite natural, at the end of the 19th century, for the weird and uncanny to intrude into the developing film industries of France and Germany. Their near neighbours, Spain and Italy, had far less in the way of a Gothic literary tradition and would be correspondingly slow to exploit the cinema's potential for the dreamlike and horrific – though, when they finally did, they would dominate the field with a veritable tidal wave of horror product. For the time being, however, the genre belonged to France and Germany, particularly the latter. There, the trauma of the First World War would catalyse an extraordinary boom in morbid and macabre films; as Lotte Eisner memorably put it, "the ghosts which had haunted the German Romantics revived, like the shades of Hades after draughts of blood."[1]

But there was plenty of horror available to filmgoers even before that sudden 1920s efflorescence, and the majority of it came from France.

## FIRST STIRRINGS, MAINLY FRENCH

When cinema began, the field was occupied, not by moguls, but by mavericks and magicians. The moguls' turn would come when motion picture production was converted into a fully fledged industry. In the meantime, Georges Méliès had his small studio in Montreuil and, a little later, Spain's Segundo de Chomón set up shop in Paris. These and other like-minded visionaries conjured from the fledgling medium a dazzling host of hallucinatory images, from ghosts and shape-shifters to demons and even outer-space aliens.

With their pioneering use of special effects, Méliès and Chomón grasped the dream potential of cinema long before the surrealists. Méliès portrayed a shape-shifting Satan in *Le Manoir du diable* (The House of the Devil) as early as 1896, subsequently astonishing his patrons by unleashing disembodied heads, turning women into skeletons, turning money bags into women, showing Belphegor dipping the damned in a giant cauldron, reducing a young woman to instant decrepitude – and, of course, creating the indelible image of a spacecraft buried in the eye of a pizza-faced moon in the 1902 release *Le Voyage dans la lune* (A Trip to the Moon). Chomón's films for the Pathé Frères company began in 1905, offering such phantasmagorical delights as a horde of scythe-wielding devils in *La Légende du fantôme* (The Legend of a Ghost) or a cloaked skeleton showing off his magical powers in *Le Spectre rouge* (The Red Spectre). As well as being obsessed with adding aesthetically pleasing colour effects to his films, he also returned with amazing regularity to the theme of meddlesome ghosts, proving that he could haunt houses (*La Maison hantée*), castles (*Le Château hanté*), hotels (*L'Hôtel hanté*), cottages (*Le Cottage hanté*), even kitchens (*Cuisine hantée*).

Not surprisingly, early filmmakers frequently turned to literature as a means of satisfying the insatiable demands of the nickelodeons – and also to give their films a little cachet in a burgeoning industry deemed disreputable by many. Victor Hugo was a frequent source, with the French pioneer Alice Guy directing *La Esmeralda* for the Gaumont company as early as 1905, another version of which appeared under Hugo's original title, *Notre-Dame de Paris*, in 1911; the hunchback Quasimodo was played in the first by Henri Vorins and in the second by Henri Krauss.

Lucien Bataille as *Balaoo* (1913), advertised by the Éclair company with the subtitle 'ou des pas au plafond' (or the footprints on the ceiling)

Edgar Allan Poe was also turned to on a regular basis. Henri Desfontaines, for example, handled *Le Puits et le pendule* (The Pit and the Pendulum) and *Hop-Frog* in 1909 and 1910 respectively, adding *La Momie* (based on *Some Words with a Mummy*) and *Le Scarabée d'or* in 1911 – though some doubt exists as to whether the latter was based on Poe's *The Gold Bug* or not.

A combined scarab and mummy featured in the 1912 Gaumont production *The Vengeance of Egypt*. "The story," claimed a US trade advertisement, "is that of a pursuing Nemesis which rises from its spirit sepulchre to avenge the stealing of a ring from a mummy. For a century's length it brings violent death to the successive holders of the ring, operating through agencies of plague, poison, strangler, bullet, aeroplane and automobile."[2] Unfortunately, this smorgasbord of supernatural retribution may not have been French at all. Over a century later it remains unclear whether the film was made by Gaumont's Paris or New York branches; that no French title for it has turned up suggests the latter possibility.

Maurice Renard, a writer whose fascination with the revolutionary technique of grafting would eventually sire the much-filmed novel *Les Mains d'Orlac*, made his debut in 1908 with *Docteur Lerne, sous-dieu* (Dr Lerne, Under-God), a book that poet and proto-surrealist Guillaume Apollinaire pronounced superior to its inspiration, H G Wells' *The Island of Dr Moreau*. The Eclipse company made a film version in 1913, *L'Île d'épouvante* (The Island of Terror), though they almost entirely scrapped Renard's bizarre story of a mad scientist transplanting the hero's brain into a bull (and vice versa) prior to projecting his own soul into the hero's automobile. The Eclipse version appears to have been an exotic adventure story, transferring the action from Renard's castle to a Moreau-like Pacific island and with the washed-up hero frustrating the mad Dr Wagner's plans to use him as a surgical guinea pig. The show-stopper, apparently, was a scene of blood washing under the hero's bedroom door.

Perhaps also inspired by H G Wells, man-into-ape scenarios were popular, generally for comic rather than Darwinian purposes, though a 1908 film called *L'Homme-singe* (The Man Monkey) added the gruesome touch of brain transplantation. Five years later, Victorin Jasset's March 1913 release *Balaoo* featured Dr Coriolis (Henri Gouget) losing control of his humanised baboon (Lucien Bataille) to a brutal poacher (Camille Bardou). Dodging the opportunity to focus on a manipulative mad scientist, the scenario instead has a manipulative mad poacher who cajoles Balaoo into committing a murder but faces rebellion when proposing to kidnap the doctor's niece (Madeleine Grandjean). The motif of an artificial creature being used as a killer but softening in the face of beauty was to have any number of repercussions.

*Balaoo* was the first film based on a story by Gaston Leroux, France's master of mystery fiction. In 1919 Leroux would get together with writer Arthur Bernède and actor René Navarre to form the Société des Cinéromans company in Nice, though it was Universal in the USA who, not long before Leroux's death in 1927, brought him his greatest fame with a lavish film version of *The Phantom of the Opera*. Both Bernède and Navarre were associates of the visionary writer-director Louis Feuillade, who had succeeded Alice Guy as Gaumont's artistic director in January 1907 and had supervised around 80 pictures a year prior to finding his true métier in 1913. With Navarre in the title role, Feuillade's five *Fantômas* films were based on a character featured in no fewer than 32 books by Pierre Souvestre and Marcel Allain; they led, first, to Feuillade's classic wartime serial *Les Vampires* (The Vampires, 1915-16) and then to a joint venture with Bernède called *Judex*. Having begun shooting *Judex* in June 1916, Feuillade released the first of its 12 instalments the following January. It immediately proved just as phenomenally popular as its predecessors, eventually siring another dozen episodes collectively entitled *La Nouvelle mission de Judex* (Judex's New Mission).

In *Fantômas* and *Les Vampires* Feuillade had spun an alluring gauze of glamour and fantasy around first a masked master criminal and then a whole gang of thrillingly anarchic crooks, the titular 'Vampires'. Faced with complaints about the potentially corrupting influence of these films, Feuillade and Bernède had crafted, in *Judex*, a do-gooding avenger, the disguised Comte de Trémeuse, who nevertheless retained all the enigmatic, cloak-twitching charisma of Feuillade's criminals. In the anagrammatic villainess Irma Vep (incarnated by the voluptuous Musidora), *Les Vampires* launched a 'vamp' icon to rival America's Theda Bara, and, in his combination of fantasticated pulp plots with spectral views of suburban Paris, Feuillade won the posthumous adulation of the surrealists. He left his mark, too, on future French fantasists like Georges Franju and Jean Rollin.

Another early stylist was Maurice Tourneur, who would be sent by Éclair to the USA in 1914 but rounded off his work for the company's French operation with a couple of brief horror films. *Le Système du docteur Goudron et du professeur Plume* (The System of Dr Goudron and Professor Plume) was released on Boxing Day 1913, with *Figures de cire* (Wax Figures) following in March 1914. The first, exported as *The Lunatics*, was a storm-racked 'lunatics taking over the asylum' scenario in which the director (Henri Gouget, from Jasset's *Balaoo*) devises a therapy involving eye-gouging and throat-slitting. The result was described in *Moving Picture World* as "weird and awe-inspiring," "artistic, real and gripping" and "not a picture good for three-year-olds to see just before going to bed at night; but for grown folks it is a strong offering."[3] *Figures de cire*, which survives, is a one-reel 'foolhardy gent challenged to spend the night in a wax museum' story, with a delightful lead performance from Henry Roussel and plenty of charming shadowplay as "the darkness lends the motionless figures an alarming and mysterious appearance," eventually driving Roussel insane. The waxworks proprietor (Gouget again) is introduced with a skull superimposed over his head.

This was an appropriate optical trick, given that Gouget was a regular player at the Théâtre du Grand Guignol in Paris. Indeed, both these Tourneur films were founded on Grand Guignol plays written by the theatre's master dramatist André de Lorde. (The first play was itself modelled on the Poe story *The System of Dr Tarr and Prof Fether*.) A former convent forming a cul de sac at the end of the Rue Chaptal, the Grand Guignol opened in April 1897, and a year after Tourneur's film the directorship passed from Max Maurey to Camille Choisy, both of whom were dedicated to maintaining the establishment's blood-bolted notoriety as a theatre of horror. The uninhibited as-it-happens sadism of the Grand Guignol was a precious commodity to thrill-hungry Parisians and curious tourists alike, and it couldn't possibly be replicated on screen until

Britain's Hammer Film Productions came along in the late 1950s, hastening the theatre's eventual closure in November 1962.

In the meantime, the cultivated André de Lorde became known as 'Prince de la Terreur', his plays often being set in operating theatres or lunatic asylums and frequently performed with nurses standing by, thanks to the high rate of fainting among audiences. De Lorde happily dovetailed his Grand Guignol commitments with plenty of film adaptations, the toothsome titles ranging from *Terrible angoisse* (Terrible Anguish, 1906) and *Le Cercueil de verre* (The Glass Coffin, 1912) to *La Double existence du docteur Morart* (Dr Morart's Double Life, 1920) and *Le Château de la mort lente* (The Castle of Slow Death, 1925). As late as 1933, Maurice Tourneur, having returned from Hollywood, also returned to the world of De Lorde for the striking featurette *L'Homme mystérieux* (The Mysterious Man), in which the venal Charles Vanel has his paranoid brother released from confinement with hair-raising consequences.

## THE DOUBLE AND THE DESPOT

Germany's early filmmakers only dabbled in macabre subjects, among them the gypsy curse of the Deutsche Bioscop production *Gräfin Ankarström* (Countess Ankarström, 1910) and the figure of Death appearing to pre-war megastar Henny Porten in the December 1912 release *Der Schatten des Meeres* (The Shadow of the Sea). After a halting start, the German industry only really came into its own with the introduction of the so-called Autorenfilm, a concept aimed squarely at breaking down the resistance of the bourgeoisie. To this end, properties from literature or, better still, famous literary personalities of the day were pressed into service in order to raise the tone of a medium considered irredeemable by the intelligentsia.

Kowtowing to celebrated figures from the worlds of literature and theatre was, of course, a sign of the nascent industry's identity crisis – and, appropriately enough, the very first Autorenfilm was about a split personality. Max Mack's Vitascope production *Der Andere* (The Other) reached Berlin audiences in January 1913 and was scripted by Paul Lindau, septuagenarian author of the 20-year-old play on which it was based. With Albert Bassermann as a vaunted attorney who unwittingly consorts with low-lifes in the person of a nocturnal other self, the film alluded to the enduring German fascination with the doppelgänger, or double; not only that, it was respectfully noticed in the quality press (an achievement in itself). Very soon afterwards came a Deutsche Bioscop production that outstripped it in both departments, splitting its protagonist

Paul Wegener broods and Lyda Salmonova dances unavailingly
in a publicity shot for *Der Student von Prag* (1913)

quite literally into two entities, thus invoking the supernatural, and also becoming the first German film to attract international attention.

The prime movers behind *Der Student von Prag* (The Student of Prague) were an interesting trio. The director was Stellan Rye, a Danish playwright who, as recently as November 1911, had been imprisoned for 100 days for so-called 'gross indecency' (ie, homosexuality). Traumatised by the experience, he had deserted Copenhagen for Berlin and was establishing himself in the local film industry. The leading man was Paul Wegener, a successful theatre actor who was increasingly fascinated by the cinema's potential for creating images that were unrealisable on stage. (He was just one of many big names supplied to German cinema by Max Reinhardt, director of Berlin's Deutsches Theater, who would also influence future films through his revolutionary stage effects and chiaroscuro lighting.) The writer, Hanns Heinz Ewers, shared Wegener's unfashionable enthusiasm for cinema but came from very different climes. He was the decadent author of a particularly lurid brand of sex-horror fiction, having placed a surrogate of himself – one Frank Braun – at the heart of the 1909 novel *Der Zauberlehrling* (The Sorcerer's Apprentice) and its 1911 follow-up *Alraune*; a third Braun adventure, *Vampir*, would follow in 1922.

Ewers' script, which Rye shot on location in Prague in May 1913, was theoretically a screen original, yet it came with a formidable list of derivations. To the source actually mentioned on screen, a poem by Alfred de Musset, could be added Poe's short story *William Wilson* and a dash of Wilde's *The Picture of Dorian Gray*. In addition there were German sources – Adalbert von Chamisso's *Peter Schlemihls wundersame*

*Geschichte* (Peter Schlemihl's Wondrous Story), about a man who sells his own shadow, and E T A Hoffmann's development of the same character in *Die Abenteuer der Silvester-Nacht* (The New Year's Eve Adventure). The new story that resulted – apparently based on an idea of Wegener's – is set in 1820 and involves the entrapment of a penniless student, Balduin, by an eccentric emissary of the Devil called Scapinelli. Balduin is infatuated with a beautiful young Countess and, in return for giving up his mirror image to Scapinelli, he receives more than enough money to court her. But his liberated 'other' self dogs his footsteps at every turn, precipitating disaster.

After a very brief prologue in which Ewers and Wegener are seen, as themselves, taking a stroll by the Vltava River in Prague, the realisation of the story is very much of its time; there's not a single close-up to be had, for example. Wegener, at this early stage, is a rather stolid screen presence (the fact that Rye doesn't allow us a close look at either of his faces doesn't help), but John Gottowt is a charmingly skittish Devil's agent. Rye stumbles when called upon to stage an action sequence, with Balduin's rescue of the Countess from a lake proving conspicuously low on excitement, but he gets the most out of the classic sequence in which the student's image steps out of a full-length mirror and calmly melts from the room alongside the jubilant Scapinelli. Its subsequent appearances are equally otherworldly, whether manifesting itself on a colonnaded balcony at a society ball, emerging from behind a monument in Prague's Jewish cemetery, or contemptuously wiping its sword, having killed a love rival whom Balduin had promised to spare. In scenes like these Guido Seeber's photographic effects go a long way to justifying Ewers' and Wegener's faith in cinema's magical potential, remaining eerie over 100 years on.

*Der Student von Prag* held contemporary audiences spellbound, and not just in Germany; it also did good business in the US and UK under the catchpenny title *A Bargain with Satan*. Such was its success that Deutsche Bioscop themselves sponsored a one-reel spoof wittily entitled *Die andere Student von Prag* (The Other Student of Prague). That the film had touched a nerve was demonstrated in a very different way by Otto Rank, a colleague of Sigmund Freud's whose viewing of the film prompted him to write the innovative 1914 study *Der Doppelgänger Eine psychoanalytische Studie* (The Double: A Psychoanalytic Study).

Pressing on without Wegener, Ewers and Rye had another film ready for showing by November 1913, though the necrophile theme of *Die Eisbraut* (The Ice Bride) entailed a ban from the German censor. Based on an old Ewers story, it concerned an artist who becomes romantically obsessed by the ice-bound corpse of a 20,000-year-old woman, eventually axeing the ice away only for the naked figure to decompose in the yucky style of Poe's *The Facts in the Case of M Valdemar*. (The star, incidentally, was Theodor Loos, who 22 years later would play the Scapinelli figure in a talkie remake of *Der Student von Prag*.) Ewers and Rye also collaborated on *Die Augen des Ole Brandis* (The Eyes of Ole Brandis), a precursor of the 1963 film *X The Man with the X-Ray Eyes*, and Rye went it alone for *Das Haus ohne Tür* (The House Without a Door), whose serial-style thrills included a scything pendulum straight out of Poe. Though Danish, Rye joined the German army in July 1914 and was dead by mid-November.

Paul Wegener, meanwhile, pursued his interest in the transmigration of souls by starring in and, with Emil Albes, co-directing *Die Rache des Blutes* (The Revenge of the Blood), in which a transfusion from a Death Row criminal triggers an alarming personality change; a similar story would be told in Maurice Renard's 1920 novel *Les Mains d'Orlac* (The Hands of Orlac). In due course Wegener would handle a fanciful 'invisible man' scenario in the 1916 film *Der Yoghi* prior to striking a couple more deals with the Devil – first by directing himself in *Hans Trutz in Schlaraffenland* (Hans Trutz in the Land of Plenty; with future director Ernst Lubitsch as a goat-horned tempter) and then by reverting to a straight adaptation of the *Peter Schlemihl* story for Rochus Gliese's 1920 production *Der verlorene Schatten* (The Lost Shadow).

In the meantime Wegener had hit upon his signature role, and the inspiration for it wound right back to the location filming of *Der Student von Prag* in the summer of 1913. In Prague, he and his actress wife Lyda Salmonova heard the 16th century legend of the Golem, a statue fashioned from clay and given life by Rabbi Loew. A year later Wegener was making a film about it – *Der Golem* (The Golem).

The 16th century setting, however, was not to Deutsche Bioscop's budget-conscious taste, so Wegener reluctantly arranged for his Golem to be rediscovered and revived in the present day. With the cobweb-strewn statue being discovered in a subterranean vault by workmen digging a well, the film set a plot precedent for future horror pictures as diverse as *The Return of the Vampire* and *Quatermass and the Pit*. The eccentric Jewish antiques vendor who buys the statue and succeeds in resurrecting it was played by Henrik Galeen, who also co-wrote and co-directed the film with Wegener; another Reinhardt associate, he would graduate to several other classic horror titles, though never again as an actor. As she had in *Der Student von Prag*, Lyda Salmonova added romantic complications as the antiquarian's daughter.

Among contemporary estimates, a critic in *Der Kinematograph* pointed out that "The action stands or falls on whoever assumes the title role – and no better man could have been chosen for it than Paul Wegener, whose emphatic and consistent performance lends gripping conviction to the spooky, otherworldly apparition."[4] The picture appears to have been completed just before the Great War began, reaching cinemagoers in January 1915; hostilities prevented its export to Britain, but it eventually reached the US as *The Monster of Fate*. It has since become lost, though a few fragmentary minutes remain, including the Golem's climactic plunge from a high tower. Curiously, in 1917 Wegener gave his blessing to a self-reflexive send-up by actually writing and directing one himself. *Der Golem und die Tänzerin* (The Golem and the Dancer), also lost, was made for the PAGU company and set in its own studio, with Wegener assuming his Golem guise to take mischievous advantage of a Golem-fixated dancer (Salmonova). Producer Paul Davidson and designer Rochus Gliese also seem to have put in personal appearances.

The Great War began on 28 July 1914, and within two years Deutsche Bioscop had put a majestic six-part serial called *Homunculus* into production. In doing so, they offered a fantasticated premonition of the ungovernable forces that the conflict would unleash. Written by Robert Reinert and directed by Otto Rippert, *Homunculus* began shooting at the beginning of May 1916 and had its first one-hour instalment on view at Berlin's Marmorhaus before the end of June. In it, the Danish star Olaf Fønss laments that "The crib in which I was born was a chemical laboratory," exacting his revenge by turning himself into "a terrible scourge

Olaf Fønss perfects his "exceptional leadership qualities" in the Deutsche Bioscop serial *Homunculus* (1916)

of hate and destruction." In the course of his travels he cures a north African king purely through "his willpower, created by science," creates a revolutionary explosive, becomes a despotic captain of industry, foments revolution by disguising himself as a rabble-rouser (this involves removing his cloak and mussing his hair a bit), unleashes a devastating war, and finally has to do battle with a lab-created doppelgänger of himself. Though he prevails, he's then extinguished by a bolt of lightning, an act of God that takes out a whole mountain crag at the same time.

As a charismatic combination of Byronic anti-hero and Nietzschean Übermensch, Homunculus is said to possess "exceptional leadership qualities" – a touch of the Führers that lends a prophetic charge to his scheme for bringing about "die Vernichtung der Menschheit" (the destruction of Mankind). As played by Fønss, he provides another kind of forecast too. There are the attenuated eyebrows, the handsome but ashen countenance, a "mouth as cold as death [that] knows not how to kiss," and an all-black uniform of frock coat, felt hat and silk-collared cloak – and on top of all this comes an extremely telling moment when a female admirer ventures into his bedroom, pulling aside the bed curtains to find him in a rigid, death-like sleep, completing his resemblance to future screen vampires. Rippert's serial remains a marvel of 'cast of thousands' grandeur, with especially striking contributions from cinematographer Carl Hoffmann and designer Robert A Dietrich. As well as inspiring an immediate parody – a sex-switched one-off spoof called Homunkulieschen – it also sparked a craze for similarly macabre serials, starting with Robert Heymann's Die Memoiren des Satans (The Memoirs of Satan) in 1917.

In the wake of Homunculus, Otto Rippert stuck with cameraman Carl Hoffmann for the 1918 release Das verwunschene Schloß (The Bewitched Castle), soon afterwards getting together with the fledgling screenwriter Fritz Lang for such 1919 titles as the Fatal Woman intrigue Totentanz (Dance of Death) and the historical epic Die Pest in Florenz (The Florentine Plague). In 1917, an earlier mentor of Lang's, producer-director Joe May, had cast his wife, Mia May, and Georg John in the title roles of the mystical, Lang-scripted drama Hilde Warren und der Tod (Hilde Warren and Death). These and other early titles were quickly forgotten, yet May and Rippert had kick-started a career that would elevate Lang to a key position among German directors of the 1920s.

## FIGURES OF THE NIGHT

In the 1910s, Paul Wegener was the most prominent figure in a burgeoning genre that boasted plenty of other practitioners, though the majority of the films produced are now lost. In 1915, for example, Ernst Mátray made the first film version of a perennial favouite, Das Phantom der Oper (The Phantom of the Opera), and the following year writer-director Arthur Robison featured an ape-suited multiple murderer in Nächte des Grauens (Night of Horror). Arthur Wellin's Pique Dame (The Queen of Spades) followed in March 1918, an adaptation of Pushkin's ghost story that eventually sired a 1927 remake under the elaborated title Pique-Dame Das Geheimnis der alten Gräfin (The Queen of Spades: The Mystery of the Old Countess).

Quite often, however, come-hither titles could prove deceptive. Ernst Lubitsch's Die Augen der Mumie Ma (The Eyes of the Mummy Ma) appeared in 1918, with just an early scene in an Egyptian tomb to semi-justify the title, the remainder involving a burly hypnotist in blackface (Emil Jannings) stalking his liberated former slave (Pola Negri) through German high society. For Lubitsch, a horror picture (albeit a bogus one) was an anomaly in any case; originally an actor for Reinhardt, his lavish German costume pictures, also showcasing Negri, would take him to Hollywood for a series of sophisticated comedies displaying the celebrated 'Lubitsch touch'.

Much the most ubiquitous of 1910s horror merchants was a 30-something Austrian-born entrepreneur called Richard Oswald. Initially an actor, Oswald joined the script department of Vitascope in 1914 and immediately wrote Rudolf Meinert's very loose but highly successful Conan Doyle adaptation Der Hund von Baskerville (The Hound of the Baskervilles). Meinert's Sherlock Holmes was Alwin Neuß, who had played Jekyll and Hyde for the Danish company Nordisk back in 1910 and for whom Oswald accordingly wrote a new version, Ein seltsamer Fall (A Strange Case), directed by Max Mack and put before the public in December 1914. Oswald then wrote the first three in a long line of Hund sequels – Das einsame Haus (The Empty House), Das unheimliche Zimmer (The Eerie Room) and a 'back-story' entry called Die Sage vom Hund von Baskerville (The Saga of the Hound of the Baskervilles), making early forays into direction with the last two.

Thereafter Oswald signed his name to a variety of wartime creepers, mostly for his own production company, among them Die Rache der Toten (Revenge of the Dead), Der lebende Leichnam (The Living Corpse), Die seltsame Geschichte des Baron Torelli (The Strange Story of Baron Torelli) and a three-part item called Das unheimliche Haus (The Eerie House). He also turned to literature for the February 1916 release Hoffmanns Erzählungen (Tales of Hoffmann) and, the following year, Das Bildnis des Dorian Gray (The Picture of Dorian Gray).

Massively industrious, Oswald was responsible, too, for some of the earliest showcases for Conrad Veidt, a young Reinhardt actor who, having been discharged from the army in January 1917, increasingly devoted himself to film engagements. For Oswald, Veidt played the heroic Phileas Fogg in *Die Reise um die Erde in 80 Tagen* (Around the World in 80 Days) and the sinister, soul-collecting Button Moulder in a film version of Ibsen's *Peer Gynt*. Veidt was also featured in Oswald's controversial series of Aufklärungsfilme (enlightening films), which juggled exploitation and 'education' in titles like *Es werde Licht!* (Let There Be Light!), *Die Prostitution* (Prostitution) and *Anders als die Andern* (Different from the Others). It was clear, however, that Veidt's magnetic personality and gaunt, imposing frame were ideally suited to disquieting roles of the Button Moulder variety. In fact, veteran producer Oskar Messter got to Veidt even before Oswald did, casting him in the September 1917 release *Furcht* (Fear). Vaguely reminiscent of Conan Doyle's *The Sign of Four*, the film features Veidt as an Indian priest avenging a German aristocrat's theft of a statue of Buddha; the writer-director was Robert Wiene, a man Veidt would encounter again.

Having used the word 'unheimlich' in at least two earlier films, Richard Oswald had yet another 'uncanny' title ready for German picturegoers at the beginning of November 1919. For *Unheimliche Geschichten* (Uncanny Tales) he put his regular star triumvirate of Conrad Veidt, Reinhold Schünzel and Anita Berber into a five-part portmanteau, complete with "a fantastic preface in an antiquarian bookshop" that proceeds to link the disparate stories together. The film provided a blueprint for the anthology horrors that would become popular in future decades, notably the 1945 film *Dead of Night* and several produced by Amicus in the 1960s and '70s – the last of which, *From Beyond the Grave*, would be set, coincidentally, in a curio shop not unlike the one in *Unheimliche Geschichten*.

*After-hours, the figures in three paintings step down from their canvases and inspect the bookshop in which they're housed. They are the Devil, Death and a high-class 18th century prostitute, and, browsing through the books, they stumble upon five creepy stories. One concerns a young woman's disappearance, another a vengeful ghost, yet another a drunken wife killer, the fourth a police inspector investigating a cult leader, and the last a light-hearted case of trumped-up supernatural manifestations.*

At the outset the film introduces us to a conspicuously strange bookseller, driving out his customers, hopping about the premises, and alternately caressing and flinging the merchandise. We also meet Schünzel's Devil (who looks more like a boxing coach in a cloak) and Veidt's very scary-looking personification of Death. The 20-year-old Berber was already notorious for her nude cabaret appearances and is here cast, rather pointedly, as 'The Harlot'; she's absent,

## UNHEIMLICHE GESCHICHTEN

Germany 1919
Richard-Oswald-Produktion
112 minutes b/w
released 5 November 1919
. . . . . . . . . . . . . . . . . . . . . . . . . . . . . . . . . .
Director of Photography: Karl Hoffmann; Design: Julius Hahlo [uncredited]; Stories: *Die Erscheinung* by Anselma Heine, *Die Hand* by Robert Liebmann, *Die schwartze Katze* (The Black Cat) by Edgar Allan Poe, *Der Selbstmörderklub* (The Suicide Club) by

Robert Louis Stevenson, *Der Spuk* by Richard Oswald; Producer-Director: Richard Oswald

Anita Berber (courtesan, woman, girlfriend, wife of drunk, sister of club president, wife); Conrad Veidt (Death, stranger, assassin, traveller, club president, husband); Reinhold Schünzel (the Devil, former husband, murderer, drunk, Artur Silas, travelling Baron); Hugo Döblin; Paul Morgan; uncredited: Bernhard Goetzke (medium); Georg John; Richard Oswald (himself)

**Richard Oswald, to whom, in part, the German film industry already owes its revitalisation, has now created the film of the uncanny. His 'five eerie stories' are definitely a significant advance in the cinematic conquest of uncharted territory, and one can only applaud this effort to open up the picture houses to new material ... Schünzel, Veidt and Anita Berber could be his foundation stones for a new type of film, which also calls for a new style.**
*Lichtbild-Bühne 15 November 1919*

Conny and I started together and appeared in many pictures. We became a well-known team. We had fun and never quarrelled. When we met after years of separation we joked and laughed. The fact that we saw little of one another lately could not destroy this pleasant comradeship. Now death has definitely separated us. With Conny a part of my life has gone.
*Reinhold Schünzel [letter of condolence to Lily Veidt, April 1943]*

Conrad Veidt recoils and Reinhold Schünzel pleads for mercy in the corpse-uncovering climax of *Die schwartze Katze*, the third of five segments in *Unheimliche Geschichten* (1919)

however, from a brief, self-congratulatory prologue in which Veidt, Schünzel and Oswald appear smilingly as themselves.

The first story, *Der Erscheinung* (The Phenomenon), is based on an Anselma Heine original, with Schünzel as a lunatic stalker offering violence to his ex-wife. Schünzel's bug-eyed performance is a sort of panto prefiguring of Peter Lorre in Fritz Lang's 1931 film M, yet the ex-husband quickly turns out to be an irrelevance, for the story is really about Veidt, as the woman's rescuer, losing track of her at an hotel and then discovering that she's contracted the plague. This was to become an extremely well-worn plot – resurfacing, for example, in the American *Midnight Warning* (1932), Germany's *Verwehte Spuren* (Scattered Traces, 1938) and the British *So Long at the Fair* (1949) – and it's intriguing to see it in embryo here.

*Die Hand* (The Hand) is attributed to Oswald's co-screenwriter, Robert Liebmann, and is an efficient 'retribution from Beyond' story, with Veidt and Schünzel vying for Berber's affections and Schünzel finally, in a notably intense scene, strangling his rival. Veidt's spectral hand then appears among the several splayed round a table at a seance, only for his ghost to turn up in its entirety and administer poetic justice, leaving bloody fingermarks on Schünzel's neck. Veidt's disembodied hand here is an intriguing touch, given that Freud published *Das Unheimliche* in the same year *Unheimliche Geschichten* came out, with severed hands included among his inventory of classic 'uncanny' images.

*Die schwartze Katze* is based on Poe's *The Black Cat*, with all three stars on top form and a powerful climax in which Veidt smashes down Schünzel's cellar wall to let loose a pet cat and disclose Berber's corpse. Actually, Oswald shrinks from showing us the body itself, an omission he'd put right 13 years later when making another film called *Unheimliche Geschichten*. Fourth in line is *Der Selbstmörderklub*, based on R L Stevenson's *The Suicide Club*, which benefits from some interesting location work as Schünzel's investigator prowls about outside a suburban Berlin mansion, coupled with witty interior design for the weird secret society presided over by a white-haired Veidt. Veidt's self-satisfied intertitle – "Der Schreck hat ihn getötet" (Fear killed him) – is trumped by Schünzel, who of course isn't dead at all and smartly turns the tables on Veidt. Unfortunately, the final story, Oswald's own *Der Spuk* (The Haunting), is a boring trifle, with intertitles archly written in verse and an 18th century grandee (Veidt) faking some extremely feeble poltergeist activity to scare off a love rival.

The wrap-up to the framing story is perfunctory too, though a lame final reel did little to dent the film's success. According to *Illustrierter Film-Kurier*,

Oswald's own cinema, the Richard-Oswald-Lichtspiele on Berlin's Kantstraße, was besieged by eager punters for at least three weeks, to the extent that "The police have had to come to regulate traffic."[5] Calls for a sequel went unheeded, though a send-up quickly appeared, *Ganz unheimliche Geschichten* (Completely Creepy Stories), courtesy of star comedian Gerhard Dammann. Oswald's film would resurface in the 1920s under such reissue titles as *Grausige Nächte* (Grisly Nights) and, as noted, he finally got round to mounting a remake of sorts in 1932.

That Conrad Veidt wasn't appearing in macabre films by accident – that he had, in other words, a personal leaning towards this sort of material – is indicated by his establishment in 1919 of Veidt-Film (Berlin). The company made just two pictures, both of them apparently lost, with Veidt directing as well as starring in both. The second one, *Die Nacht auf Goldenhall* (The Night at Golden Hall) seems to have been a romantic melodrama with a murder thrown in, but the first, *Wahnsinn* (Madness), featured an equivocal gypsy prophecy and Veidt's increasingly crazed determination to make it come true.

Veidt's workload during this period was intense, and Richard Oswald, anticipating the success of *Unheimliche Geschichten*, added to it by immediately getting Veidt together again with Anita Berber and Reinhold Schünzel for another now-lost film, *Nachtgestalten* (Figures of the Night), though the showiest character – a lonely billionaire seeking world domination – was reserved for Paul Wegener. Then in 1920 Oswald cast Veidt again in a satirical item, also lost, called *Kurfürstendamm*, in which Veidt's Satan found himself unable to compete with the corrupt denizens of the titular Berlin thoroughfare, especially when trying his hand at being a film producer. Given the recent and very brief career of Veidt-Film, it's possible that Veidt approached this particular section of Oswald's script with some cynical feelings of his own.

## TILL THE BREAK OF DAWN

In December 1919 Robert Reinert's *Nerven* (Nerves) opened in Munich, making its way to Berlin the following month. Writer of *Homunculus*, Reinert here concocted an unrelenting phantasmagoria, nominally about the nervous breakdown of a bigshot captain of industry and his convoluted circle but in fact offering a hair-raising image of the communal breakdown afflicting society as a whole

For the efflorescence of German cinema in the immediate post-war period was played out against a truly catastrophic backdrop. The punitive reparations imposed by the Treaty of Versailles and the state of virtual civil war that existed in Germany in 1919 were the beginning of a downward spiral which by November 1923 saw the dollar equivalent to 4,200,000,000,000 marks. (Where cinema admission was concerned, the hand-over of a lump of coal became an accepted substitute for cash.) Despite these circumstances, Germany's film industry grew rapidly during this period, becoming the envy even of all-powerful Hollywood. The jewel in the industry's crown was Ufa (Universum Film Aktien Gesellschaft), an initially state-owned production combine, founded in December 1917, that in due course would acquire state-of-the-art facilities at Berlin-Tempelhof and Neubabelsberg.

In the meantime, the crowds flocking to see Richard Oswald's *Unheimliche Geschichten* in November 1919 made it abundantly clear that there was money to be made from horror. Indeed, Erich Pommer – later the influential production head of Ufa, but at this stage running his own company, Decla-Film – was preparing an eerie subject of his own even as Oswald's film went on release. "The mysterious and macabre atmosphere of Grand Guignol was at the time in vogue in German films," Pommer later pointed out, "and this story was perfectly full of it. They [the writers] saw in their script an 'experiment' – I saw a comparatively inexpensive production."[6]

Pommer had bought the script for *Das Cabinet des Dr Caligari* (The Cabinet of Dr Caligari) back on 19 April, but only in December was Decla ready to put it into production. The script's origins and inspiration exist now in a swirl of legend and speculation, with one of the writers, Hans Janowitz, claiming to have witnessed a sex murder in Hamburg, near the Holstenwall, in 1913, and the other, Carl Mayer, having apparently engaged in psychological warfare with an army psychiatrist during the recent conflict. Both, in any case, were concerned to allegorise "the authoritative power of an inhuman state gone mad"[7] in their gruesome story of a deranged tyrant inducing a sleepwalking young man to go out to kill – and, like so many millions in the war, be killed.

In pre-production, however, Mayer and Janowitz were outraged by two things. First, a frame was attached to their story, making it clear that it was

the fantasy of a madman. Second, the Decla design team decided to underline this by devising stridently unrealistic sets, complete with painted shadows, sets that could only be the distorted vision of a mental patient – an approach enthusiastically endorsed by the film's director, Robert Wiene. The chosen mode was Expressionism, an exaggerated means of rendering psychological states that had been around in most of the arts for a good 15 years but was only now coming to the cinema.

Unconcerned by the writers' objections, Pommer and his associate Rudolf Meinert put the film into production at the Lixie-Atelier, Berlin-Weissensee in the closing weeks of 1919. The three leading actors – Werner Krauss, Conrad Veidt and Lil Dagover – were all familiar from Max Reinhardt's Deutsches Theater, and Veidt of course had already proven his suitability for macabre roles several times over. Quoting the maniacal delusions of its chief character, the completed film was advertised with the legend 'Du musst Caligari werden' (You must become Caligari) and opened at Berlin's Marmorhaus on 26 February 1920. Its impact was immediate, and only intensified when it crossed the Atlantic, opening in New York on 13 April 1921; the Los Angeles premiere on 15 May actually provoked an anti-German riot. The *New York Times* critic, borrowing a nasty word popularised by President Harding just the year before, stated the obvious when saying that "There is nothing of normalcy about it"[8] – and that was one of the milder responses by far.

*Two haunted-looking men are sitting in a garden, with the younger one, Francis, telling his companion of a strange experience he had in Holstenwall. There, a carnival mountebank calling himself Dr Caligari exhibited an eerie, black-clad somnambulist, Cesare, who foretold the death of Francis' friend Alan. Sure enough, Alan was murdered that same night. When Cesare abducted the beautiful Jane, a chase ensued and the fleeing Caligari was traced to a nearby insane asylum...*

*Caligari* begins with a weirdly chilling little tableau – a pallid young man and a beetle-browed older one sitting in a semi-circular garden, autumn leaves underfoot and the old man muttering, "There are

Expressionist artist Josef Fenneker created this memorable manifestation of post-war hysteria for the Berlin premiere of *Nerven* (1919)

Three archetypes brought together at the Holstenwall fair: Werner Krauss, Conrad Veidt and Lil Dagover in *Das Cabinet des Dr Caligari* (1919)

## DAS CABINET DES DR CALIGARI

Germany 1919
UK / US: **The Cabinet of Dr Caligari**
Decla-Film / Holz & Co
71 minutes b/w
in production December 1919
· · · · · · · · · · · · · · · · · · · · · · · · · · · · ·
Director of Photography: Willy Hameister;
Design: Hermann Warm, Walter Reimann,
Walter Röhrig; Assistant Director: Rochus
Gliese [uncredited]; Music [at premiere]:
Giuseppe Becce; Special Optical Effects:
Ernst Kunstmann [uncredited]; Story and

Screenplay: Carl Mayer, Hans Janowitz;
Producers: Erich Pommer, Rudolph Meinert
[both uncredited]; Director: Robert Wiene

*Werner Krauss (Dr Caligari); Conrad Veidt*
*(Cesare); Friedrich Fehér (Francis); Lil*
*Dagover (Jane); Hans Heinrich v Twardowski*
*(Alan); Rudolf Lettinger (Dr Olsen);*
*uncredited: Rudolf Klein-Rogge (criminal);*
*Hans Lanser-Rudolff (old man); Henri*
*Peters-Arnolds (young doctor); Ludwig Rex*
*(town clerk); Elsa Wagner (landlady)*

**Das Kabinett [sic] des Dr Caligari, rolling across the Marmorhaus screen, is an
experiment that can be called successful right down to the smallest details.
Whereas, in Nachtgestalten, Richard Oswald attempted the spooky film in
naturalistic mode, Robert Wiene has called on Expressionism's aid, powerfully
underscoring the action in conjunction with his splendid artistic consultants
Hermann Warm, Walter Reimann and Walter Röhrig ... The impact of the
piece was intense and sparked off well-deserved applause, for the director
in the first instance then all the others too.** Der Abend (Berlin) 27 February 1920

In the late summer of 1919 it so happened that Dr Robert Wiene offered me
a leading role in a film called Das Cabinet des Dr Caligari ... [which] was to be
produced with completely new artistic means ... The time around 1919 was a
veritable breeding ground for Expressionism, as was seen in the film. Aren't
all standards to be reassessed in times of chaos and disorientation?
Lil Dagover [Ich war die Dame, 1979]

penetrating. That the film turns out to be a 'lunatics taking over the asylum' scenario, vaguely recalling the 1845 story *The System of Dr Tarr and Prof Fether*, was probably the only crumb of comfort it offered to English-speaking critics at the time. Struggling to convey some idea of the film's twisted narrative, alien atmosphere and crazily Expressionist sets, they could invoke the familiar name of Edgar Allan Poe – as they did, almost to a man – and leave it at that.

"It is almost impossible to convey to those who did not see this picture when it first was shown," wrote Gilbert Seldes in 1937, "the astonishing and almost catastrophic effect which it had. It is one of the few pictures which I have ever heard hissed – not for political but for aesthetic reasons."[9] This was just the kind of headline-grabbing controversy the Decla executives had counted on when approving the modish abstractions of the production designers. For underneath all the decorative flourishes they had a horror story of classic simplicity, so much so that it laid down a precise blueprint for a nascent genre. In Werner Krauss' Caligari – a demented psychiatrist who has assumed that name in tribute to an 18th century Italian mesmerist – it had the prototype mad scientist. And in Conrad Veidt's Cesare – a willowy, black-clad somnambulist whom Caligari sends out on errands of murder – it had the prototype misunderstood monster.

The performances in each case burned themselves indelibly into the iconography of horror. Krauss'

spirits all around us. They have driven me from hearth and home, from wife and child..." Then a beautiful young woman in white sails past them, seemingly hypnotised and parting spindly overhanging tree branches as she passes. "That's my fiancée," the young man points out. The sense of dislocation, of minds irretrievably out of joint, is immediate and

Caligari is a shabby-genteel sociopath (emphasis on the 'shabby') who, in his distressed Beidermeier threads and absurd top hat, looks resplendently scuzzy – probably evil-smelling and slimy to the touch. And when we discover his true vocation late in the film, his absurd gait – half-mincing, half-military, with a Napoleonic hand thrust firmly under his lapel – is a brilliant portrait of bureaucracy run mad. Veidt, meanwhile, lends his mastery of mime and angular 6'3" frame to a zombie slave more profoundly pitiful than any that was to follow. When Cesare – who's only 23, we're told – is first awoken from his trance, the titanic struggle to open his kohl-rimmed eyes is among the most riveting long-held close-ups in cinema; the look of unfathomable horror he finally directs at us is unforgettable too. And as he stalks his victims he fulfils exactly the Expressionist ideal, seeming like an automated outgrowth of the distorted landscapes through which he moves. The scene in which he appears at Jane's window, literally taking the frame apart in order to make his entrance, may have been dulled by repetition but almost certainly had contemporary audiences screaming.

*Caligari*'s other set-pieces are just as archetypal, and a sense of creeping dread still clings to them – Caligari urging Cesare to step forward from his upended coffin and "awaken for a moment from your dark night," Alan's foolhardy query of "How long will I live?" and the somnambulist's prophetic utterance of "Till the break of dawn," the subsequent murder of the young man in knife-wielding shadowplay. Then, the abduction of Lil Dagover's white-robed ingenue from her midnight bedroom and, finally, the big reveal when Caligari is located at a nearby madhouse and turns out to be the man in charge.

Coming after the breathless pursuit and ignominious death of Cesare, the flashback to the origins of Caligari's mania might seem like an anti-climactic narrative necessity. But it's nothing of the sort. The recreational courtyard of the asylum, with its weathered but comfy armchairs and strange 'sunburst' floor design, is fascinating. And the glimpse we get of Caligari's inner sanctum as he pores excitedly over a treasured book called *Somnambulismus* – and his distracted foray into a nearby park, where he is assailed by animated thought bubbles spelling out "Du musst Caligari werden" – are among the most horribly gripping vignettes in the film. (They also confirm the double-meaning in the film's title, for the 'cabinet' of Caligari refers not just to Cesare's coffin but to the doctor's study.) And, once Caligari is apprehended and put into a straitjacket of his own, Francis' story climaxes with a spectacle unsurpassed for hideous grotesquerie – the baffled Caligari, prone on a couch, struggling against his imprisoning bonds, black eyes burning malignantly in the sluglike face, a thick stream of spittle coursing over his chin and down his neck.

This, however, is not the end. We return to the garden and our suspicions are immediately confirmed, for Francis gets up and accompanies the old man into the sunburst courtyard we've already seen. A bearded dotard rants unheeded, a woman plays an imaginary piano, two others vie for ownership of a doll, Jane is seen wearing a queenly tiara, and Cesare passes through with a small bunch of flowers. When Francis identifies Cesare as the killer from his story, his crazy old companion (brilliantly played by Hans Lanser-Rudolff) obviously decides that Francis is too mad to be seen with and beats a diplomatic retreat. Caligari then makes his entrance, looking like a normal middle-aged alienist, and Francis screams, "You all think I'm insane. It's not true. It's the director who's insane!"

This, of course, is the point at which Mayer and Janowitz decided that their original concept had been unforgivably betrayed. So Francis was mad all along, rendering the writers' anti-war allegory 'mad' as well and therefore neutralising it. But in their indignation Mayer and Janowitz failed to notice that the ending imposed on their story made it *more* subversive, not less. It introduces a Chinese Box effect that is the film's final masterstroke, for a viewer would have to be very credulous and conformist indeed to find Caligari's third identity in any way reassuring. "Now I know exactly how to cure him," he says, smoothing a stray wisp of hair in a curiously narcissistic gesture as the camera irises in on his self-satisfied but otherwise unreadable face. Suggesting that, in the aftermath of war, sane men are still in the grip of state-sanctioned egomaniacs, it's a deeply chilling shot, and it brings the film to a close. Yet Mayer and Janowitz couldn't see it.

One of the stranger outcomes of *Caligari*'s notoriety was a loose stage adaptation by André de Lorde and Henri Bauche, which appeared at the Théâtre du Grand Guignol in 1925; entitled *Le cabinet du Dr Caligari*, it fused Cesare and Francis into one by having Caligari hypnotise Francis into a somnambulant state. The film itself was to be discussed and debated for decades to come, and within the film industry some of those discussions focused on proposed remakes and sequels, making for a very tangled web indeed.

In Paris exile in 1934, Robert Wiene reportedly had Jean Cocteau in mind to play Cesare for Wiene's own Camera Films outfit. He then decamped to London and in 1935 Bela Lugosi was approached to play Caligari on behalf of Concordia Films, a company set up by the exiled Friedrich Fehér, who had played the whey-faced Francis in Wiene's original. By Christmas that year *Motion Picture Daily* was reporting that matinée idol Ramon Novarro had dropped out of the projected Concordia version, yet Wiene was still confident that the film would be on the floor in mid-March 1936. It didn't happen, and by June 1937 the same trade paper mentioned that Fehér had turned his attention to an American version. In the following decade the film's original co-writer, Hans Janowitz, was behind a proposed sequel called variously *Caligari II* or *The Return of Caligari*, and finally an Americanised 'in name only' remake was produced in 1962.

By the time Janowitz was pushing his sequel idea, another world war had come and gone and Siegfried Kracauer was preparing to publish his landmark study *From Caligari to Hitler*, in which, as David Robinson puts it, "Decla's novelty horror film was made to carry a massive weight of significance."[10] Kracauer's thesis, that the "cortege of tyrants and monsters"[11] initiated by *Caligari* reflected Germany's deep-rooted susceptibility to real tyrants, was schematic but alluring, and it identified Dr Caligari's most virulent descendant as Dr Mabuse, a hypnotic Weimar super-criminal created by novelist Norbert Jacques.

Scripted by Fritz Lang's wife Thea von Harbou, Lang's two-part epic *Dr Mabuse, der Spieler* (Dr Mabuse, the Gambler) reached German cinemas in May 1922, with its first section pointedly subtitled *Ein Bild der Zeit* (A Picture of the Times); the second concluded with the monstrous crime lord going insane and hallucinating the shades of his victims. Ten years later, alarmed by the inexorable rise of the Nazis, Lang concocted a sequel, *Das Testament des Dr Mabuse* (The Will of Dr Mabuse), in which the director of the asylum in which Mabuse was incarcerated is possessed by

Conrad Veidt as the unauthorised Jekyll and Hyde figure in *Der Januskopf* (1920)

Mabuse's bug-eyed spirit. That Germany had indeed moved from Caligari to Hitler by that stage was demonstrated when the Nazis banned the film outright.

## REACTIVATED HULK

For Conrad Veidt, his breathrough role in *Caligari* was sandwiched between two films for F W Murnau, both photographed by Karl Freund and both now lost. Shot in August 1919, *Satanas* was written by *Caligari*'s director Robert Wiene, casting Veidt as the Devil, a role he would play again in Oswald's *Kurfürstendamm*; here, he wearily traversed three historical epochs in the style of Charles Maturin's Gothic classic *Melmoth the Wanderer*.

The second film, *Der Januskopf* (The Head of Janus), was given an exhibitors' preview – under the title *Schrecken* (Terror) – in April 1920. The loss of this one is especially tantalising given its unauthorised source in R L Stevenson's *Strange Case of Dr Jekyll and Mr Hyde*; screenwriter Hans Janowitz, another *Caligari* graduate, changed the protagonists' names to Warren and O'Connor. Subtitled *Eine Tragödie am Rande der Wirklichkeit* (A Tragedy on the Brink of Reality), the film's interest isn't confined to the Murnau-Janowitz-Veidt combination, for Veidt's manservant was an early credit for the Hungarian actor Bela Lugosi.

Robert Wiene, meanwhile, had another film on show at Berlin's Marmohaus a little over six months after *Caligari* opened there. For *Genuine Die Tragödie eines seltsamen Hauses* (Genuine: The Tragedy of a Strange House) he retained screenwriter Carl Mayer, cinematographer Willy Hameister, actor Hans Heinrich von Twardowski and designer Walter Reimann, with the Expressionist painter César Klein drafted in to add spice to a further round of so-called Caligarism.

In Mayer's scenario Fern Andra's Genuine conforms exactly to the Fatal Woman template, consumed by "the desire to practice her irresistible wiles" and coaxing a beau into suicide because it would be "a beautiful proof of love." Discovered among bare-breasted slave girls in the marketplace, she's taken home by a palsied old aristocrat and placed under glass for observation. Escaping, she cajoles Twardowski into cutting the old man's throat but expires before the soon-to-be traditional angry mob can get at her. Of the design peculiarities, the presence of a mounted skeleton with a clockface rather than a skull is a memorable touch. Unfortunately, *Genuine* was too flimsy a vehicle to withstand charges that Wiene's use of freakish settings was already degenerating into affectation.

No trace of freakish affectation marred Paul Wegener's latest film, *Der Golem Wie er in die Welt kam* (The Golem: How He Came Into the World), in which architect Hans Poelzig's staggering reproduction of

Ernst Deutsch shrinks from Paul Wegener's stony countenance
in *Der Golem Wie er in die Welt Kam* (1920)

## DER GOLEM WIE ER IN DIE WELT KAM

Germany 1920
US: **The Golem**
Projektions-AG Union [PAGU]
85 minutes b/w
in production May 1920
·······················
Director of Photography: Karl Freund;
Art Directors: Hans Poelzig, Kurt Richter;
Costumes: Rochus Gliese; Music [at
premiere]: Hans Landsberger; Effects
Photography: Guido Seeber [uncredited];
Scenario: Henrik Galeen, Paul Wegener;

Producer: Paul Davidson; Directors: Carl
Boese, Paul Wegener

Paul Wegener (the Golem); Albert Steinrück
(Rabbi Loew); Lyda Salmonova (Miriam, his
daughter); Ernst Deutsch (Famulus, his servant);
Hanns Sturm (Rabbi Jehuda, the council elder);
Max Kronert (temple servant); Otto Gebühr
(Emperor); Dore Paetzold (Emperor's mistress);
Lothar Müthel (Florian, the knight); uncredited:
Greta Schroeder (girl with rose); Loni Nest
(little girl)

old Prague benefited from Ufa's extensive facilities and
a budget considerably larger than Wegener's previous
attempt at the story. This time round Wegener retained
Henrik Galeen as co-writer but, for the co-director
slot, Galeen made way for Carl Boese, who focused
chiefly on the special effects sequences. For Wegener
the updating of the story in his 1914 version had been
an awkward compromise; now he had the chance to
dramatise the original legend as he'd always intended,
with shooting getting under way in May 1920.

> In 16th century Prague, the Jewish leader Rabbi Loew
> consults the stars and is warned of dire danger to his
> people. Sure enough, an edict from the Emperor is soon
> handed down, insisting on the expulsion of the Jews
> from their ghetto. While the Emperor's messenger,
> Florian, strikes up a romance with the Rabbi's daughter
> Miriam, Loew is fashioning a huge clay statue,
> telling himself that "I must wrest from the dread spirit
> Astaroth the life-giving word..."

The Golem [is] the latest motion picture to come from the explorative
innovators of Germany. The photoplay gives the impression of some
fabulous old tale of strange people in a strange world, fascinating, exciting
to the imagination, and yet so unfamiliar in all of its aspects that it always
seems remote, elusive even, when one would like to get closer to its meaning
... The most impressive performance is that of Mr Wegener as the Golem.
New York Times 20 June 1921

I met [F W] Murnau's closest friend, Rochus Gliese, a wonderful stage designer
and a motion-picture director. He and Paul Wegener were planning to make a
picture called The Golem ... When summer came it meant no work for us at the
[Deutsches] theatre because we were laid off for two months. Gliese said, "Why
don't you come and work on the picture?" ... Two weeks later I was building
sets. Edgar G Ulmer [interviewed by Peter Bogdanovich in Kings of the Bs, New York 1975]

Still impressive, the grandeur of *Der Golem* made
a considerable impact on release and, along with
spectaculars like Ernst Lubitsch's *Madame DuBarry*,
it may well have been an inspiration for Universal's
mega-production of *The Hunchback of Notre Dame*,

which followed in 1922. The American film, however,
substituted elephantiasis for grandeur and quasi-
literary stuffiness for the obvious sincerity and tightly
controlled narrative of Wegener's film. Poelzig's
Expressionist settings, beautifully photographed
by Karl Freund, manage to be at once twisted and
dreamlike yet practical and livable in, in sharp

contrast to the jagged abstractions of *Caligari*. As a result the film creates an entirely convincing impression of time and place without recourse to 'cast of thousands' Hollywood pomposity.

The early going is problematic, with Wegener opening on a view of stars in the night sky, conferring cosmic significance on a story that then takes a detour into court intrigue and romantic bathos. As played by Lothar Müthel, the imperial envoy is a ridiculously effete figure, twirling a flower non-stop during his initial appearances; we're then treated to some gruesome scenes of tremulous eroticism as he and Miriam grope gauchely towards each other. (Wegener's then wife, Lyda Salmonova, remained a fixture in his productions of the period, yet she makes no particular mark here. Intriguingly, Greta Schroeder appears briefly in the Rose Festival sequence; not just the future female lead of *Nosferatu*, she was also a future Mrs Wegener.) Fortunately, we also get intercut scenes of the Rabbi consulting his design sketches for the work-in-progress Golem, after which the central section of the film becomes a sustained tour de force, starting with a thrilling incantation sequence in which the Rabbi informs his assistant that "The hour has come. The position of the stars is favourable to our spell."

The maelstrom that ensues still grips – the magic circle that turns to a ring of fire, the smoke arising as will o'the wisps dart around above the practitioners' heads, and finally the mask-like face of Astaroth, floating anti-clockwise through the murk and exhaling plumes of ectoplasm from its stony mouth, ectoplasm that literally smokes up the crucial word 'Aemaet'. As co-director Carl Boese explained to Lotte Eisner, to obtain these effects "the whole laboratory had been built on scaffolding. Technicians, installed in a kind of underground passage, sent smoke and blazing matter up through the slits."[12] Boese's ingenious manipulation of practical and in-camera effects gives the scene an arcane, elemental charge that no doubt struck awe into its original spectators.

The film's demands clearly posed major headaches for Boese, yet disarming simplicity was more often than not the solution. When, for example, the Rabbi is preparing to affix the life-giving amulet to the Golem's chest, he walks into colossal close-up, his hands filling the screen as they fumble nervously with the paper bearing the magic word. Though striking and unusual in itself, this close-up was obviously designed to allow Wegener to substitute for the dummy Golem without interrupting the shot, literally stepping into place behind the Rabbi before the latter walks back into mid-shot. The dummy Golem, however, remains one of the film's few mis-steps; it

looks nothing like Wegener and particularly so when it alternates with him in successive shots. Even so, Wegener himself is every bit as awe-inspiring as the invocation sequence, his eyes illuminating strangely as the amulet is applied and his face turning, again in colossal close-up, to face the audience.

The wonder of Wegener's performance is the granite sort of wit that he brings to this monolithic figure; he's so completely confident in his effects that he can apply absurd humour to the role within seconds of first appearing. Not long after that massive close-up we get an intertitle reading "Golem's first errand" – and off he goes to the shops with a very domestic shopping bag on his arm and a childlike look of glee on his stony face. (The dislocation here recalls that peculiar moment in Stoker's *Dracula* when, in the midst of his castle ordeal, Harker spots the servantless Count making the beds and laying the table.) Yet touches like this do nothing to reduce the impact of the Golem's appearance at the Rose Festival, when his Samson-like support for a collapsing roof guarantees the Emperor's undying gratitude. Nor does it dilute the extraordinary moment when the Golem suddenly rebels, his face contorting, again in massive close-up, into a hate-filled mask as he surveys the alarmed Rabbi.

Wegener also excels in conveying the creature's gradual softening into tenderness and finally grief when he comprehends his non-human origin; that the film, in this and many other ways, provided a model for Universal's future Frankenstein pictures is by now, of course, a critical commonplace. And when the Golem fulfils the destiny laid down for him by Astaroth – that he will finally turn on his master and prove impossible to control – we're given a slam-bang finale that future scenes of monster mayhem would emulate a thousand times over. Whether smashing down doors, dragging the unconscious Miriam by her lengthy pigtails, flinging the cowardly Florian (not before time) from a high tower, or putting a large section of the ghetto to the torch, Wegener's Golem is a sight to behold.

Then comes the ironic ending, in which the proud Jewish automaton is inadvertently undone by a flaxen-haired little girl and his deactivated hulk is swarmed over by a horde of similarly Aryan little monsters. *Der Golem* has inspired some debate regarding its attitude to Judaism; the Emperor's racist decree, for example, accuses Jews of practicing the Black Arts and we then see Rabbi Loew doing exactly that in order to vivify the Golem. On the 'have your cake and eat it too' principle, the Jews are presented as oppressed underdogs yet their leader turns to a trusty recipe book entitled *Necromancie* to remedy the situation.

Wegener and his collaborators – several of whom were themselves Jewish – no doubt allowed their flair for theatrical effect to smother any consideration of what now looks pretty clearly like confusion of intent.

In 1922 Wegener wrote and directed another historical spectacle, *Herzog Ferrantes Ende* (The End of Duke Ferrante), reuniting with cinematographer Karl Freund and also reconvening such *Golem* actors as Hans Sturm, Ernst Deutsch and, of course, Lyda Salmonova. Playing a 15th century Neapolitan grandee who lined his basement with the petrified corpses of his enemies, Wegener may have provided a cue here for the dungeon stalkings of Conrad Veidt's Ivan the Terrible in *Das Wachsfigurenkabinett* (Waxworks). It's hard to say, however, since *Herzog Ferrantes Ende* is now lost. Another Wegener release in 1922 was Arthur von Gerlach's *Vanina*, based by Carl Mayer on a Stendhal story, with Wegener as yet another heartless tyrant – a disabled Italian governor who orders the execution of his daughter's insurrectionist sweetheart. Von Gerlach's oneiric sequence of the lovers traversing seemingly interminable corridors in an attempt to flee the dungeons, only to emerge in the execution yard, indicated not merely the inescapability of fate but also a potentially significant talent. Sadly, he died not long after the release of his second film, a lavishly brooding Gothic romance called *Zur Chronik von Grieshuus* (Concerning the Chronicle of the Grey House).

## THE MONSTER IN THE BEDROOM

Lil Dagover – who, like Conrad Veidt, was a graduate of *Caligari* – was also to acquire a reputation for macabre subjects, though by no means as wide-ranging as Veidt's. In fact, she'd met Death himself in Carl Froelich's *Der Tänzer* (The Dancer) even before her shock encounter with Veidt's eerie somnambulist. In 1921 she was faced with another personification of Death, this time in the person of Bernhard Goetzke. This sepulchral-looking actor had initiated a seance in Oswald's *Unheimliche Geschichten* with the euphemistic dialogue title "Wir wollen tisch rücken" (let's move the table). Now he essayed the title role in Fritz Lang's Decla production *Der müde Tod* (The Weary Death), a film that combined heavy Nordic mysticism with humour and spectacle, and thus proved one of Germany's first breakout hits internationally.

Buying a plot of land next to a provincial graveyard, Goetzke's Death erects a vast, impenetrable wall around it and spirits away Dagover's young sweetheart. Searching for him, Dagover sees a small army of transparent dead people passing through the wall, prompting her to take a drug-induced dream journey into Death's domain. The cold, screen-

Lil Dagover makes the ultimate sacrifice, with Bernhard Goetzke as Death, in *Der müde Tod* (1921)

encompassing wall is a breathtaking image, and it's paralleled by the sumptuous darkness beyond it, a darkness pierced by a forest of tall candles which Death identifies as an assemblage of souls awaiting their time. This Death is extremely reasonable as well as jaded, for he offers the girl three goes at proving that "love is as strong as death." It's at this point that the film turns into a portmanteau, with three exotic stories that occasionally touch on horror – a dead man buried up to his neck in the first and, in the third, a briefly glimpsed humanoid cactus (rather different from the one seen 30-odd years later in *The Quatermass Xperiment*). And the melodramatic conclusion inevitably involves the girl's self-sacrifice, complete with a baleful end title indicating that "He who loses his life shall gain it."

Known for export purposes as plain *Destiny*, *Der müde Tod* went out in October 1921, just as another film involving a heroine's self-sacrifice was winding up production. Here, however, was a picture that replaced Lang's mystic Volkslied (folk song) with an extremely heavy dose of unadulterated skin-crawling horror. Happily, the come-hither advertising tag-lines devised for *Nosferatu Eine Symphonie des Grauens* (Nosferatu: A Symphony of Horror) contained no phrases as ponderous and sententious as "He who loses his life shall gain it." Instead viewers were offered a challenge: 'So you want to see a symphony of horrors? You may get more than you bargained for. Watch out. *Nosferatu* isn't something to be taken lightly. Once again: beware.'

The publicity campaign for *Nosferatu*'s 1922 premiere – which, after a gala preview on 4 March, took place at Berlin's Primus-Palast on the 15th – reportedly cost more than the film itself. But that chilling admonition to prospective patrons was soon to appear ironic, for the people who *really* needed to watch out, and who certainly got more than they bargained for, were the personnel of the one-shot company Prana-Film. It's an oft-told story: Prana's failure to clear copyright on *Dracula*, Bram Stoker's indignant widow going on the warpath, the apparent destruction of all prints in July 1925. Then the film's vampire-like resurrection as an art-house attraction in London and New York, followed by an iconic afterlife as the mouldering, rat-faced ancestor of all vampire films.

*1830s Wisborg. An occultist estate agent called Knock sends his assistant, Hutter, on a trip to Transylvania to meet a prospective client called Graf Orlok. Hutter's wife Ellen foresees disaster but he sets out regardless. Discomfited en route by the locals' talk of werewolves, Hutter finally meets Orlok and discovers that his host is a centuries-old vampire. He is powerless, however, to stop Orlok from setting out on a journey of his own...*

Prana's name alluded to the Buddhist principle of 'breath-as-life', yet the company's own life was extremely short. Inaugurated on 31 January 1921 by artist Albin Grau and businessman Enrico Dieckmann, it oversaw the production of *Nosferatu* between August and October of that year, with interiors shot at Berlin's Jofa-Atelier and locations ranging from the Upper Tatras to Rostock and Lübeck and, for the vampire's stronghold, Oravský Castle in Slovakia. Yet by June 1922 the company had gone into receivership, abandoning such mooted follow-ups as *Hollentraume* (Infernal Dreams) and *Der Stumpfteufel* (Swamp Devil).

Albin Grau was a prominent occultist and the three projected Prana films were conceived with that agenda in mind; something of *Nosferatu*'s importance to Grau is indicated by the fact that he managed, consciously or not, to get his surname into the film's subtitle. Contributing much more than the costumes and sets he's credited for, he was careful, in preparing the film, to choose the right collaborators. As well as having directed Conrad Veidt in both *Satanas* and *Der Januskopf*, F W Murnau had also made a couple of murder stories, *Der Bucklige und die Tänzerin* (The Hunchback and the Dancer) and *Schloß Vogeloed Die Enthüllung eines Geheimnisses* (Castle Vogeloed: The Revelation of a Mystery); boasting a few dashes of hallucinatory horror, the latter had been completed as recently as March 1921. Screenwriter Henrik Galeen, meanwhile, had been involved in both the 1914 and 1920 versions of *Der Golem*.

The shade of the Golem hovered over *Nosferatu* in another important way. A 1915 novel by Gustav Meyrink, though unrelated to Galeen's first Golem film, nevertheless bore the same title; it came with illustrations by Hugo Steiner-Prag that impressed Grau deeply, providing him with a cadaverous model for the hideous prosthetics he would devise for *Nosferatu*'s star, Max Schreck. Faced with Stoker's story Galeen made some significant alterations. Among other things, he shifted the setting from 1890s London to 1830s Wisborg, thus evoking the Biedermeier atmosphere of E T A Hoffmann, and changed all the characters' names, starting with Count Dracula himself, who became Graf Orlok. This dissimulation was made rather redundant by the film's premiere brochure, which admitted *Dracula* as the source and thus aroused the attentions of Florence Stoker.

In 1967, one of horror's first notable historians, Carlos Clarens, dismissed *Nosferatu* as "a blurry Gothic romance," also branding it "crude, unsubtle and illogical."[13] Yet blurry, crude, unsubtle and illogical are all words applicable to the worst kind of nightmare. In creating the film's uniquely disturbing imagery, Murnau offered visual echoes of such Romantic painters as Friedrich and Kersting, together with the slightly later Böcklin; as Siegfried Kracauer observed with a small shock of highbrow puzzlement, "It is noteworthy that such an amount of picture sense and technical ingenuity served the sole purpose of rendering horrors."[14] Such artful flourishes were aimed at recreating something vividly present in Stoker's novel yet so far ignored in German horror pictures – the intrusion of the abnormal into the normal, the dislocating secret of all the most effective nightmares. *Nosferatu*'s predecessors had been so stridently Expressionist that everything seemed abnormal from the word go. Murnau, however, used real locations and insinuated the hideous Orlok into them like a manifestation of Death itself.

The domestic detail in the film is carefully observed to this end. At the beginning, Ellen plays with a pet cat; her faintly silly young husband, the estate agent Hutter, runs in with a bunch of flowers; their bright young friends play croquet. All seems right with the world, though the dark-eyed Ellen is already conscious of a lurking disquiet, an approaching shadow. Like Lucy in the book (like *Caligari*'s Cesare for that matter), she's a sleepwalker – and like Stoker's Mina, she will later reveal a psychic link with the monster. Solemn though Ellen may be, the grotesque only rears its head in the person of Hutter's gurning employer, Knock. It's easy to laugh at this baroquely overstated version of Stoker's fly-eating Renfield character, but that's precisely what Murnau intended. He rather resembles Orlok and is there to channel audience laughter away from his appalling master.

Max Schreck exhales an icy draught from Doomsday
in *Nosferatu Eine Symphonie des Grauens* (1921)

For Orlok, exhaling over audiences what the Hungarian critic Béla Balász called "an icy draught from Doomsday,"[15] is nothing less than plague and pestilence personified. There were hints of plague imagery in the original book, and Stoker – whose obsession with what he called plague-spots finally reached demented proportions in his final novel, *The Lair of the White Worm* – would surely have approved of Orlok's mastery over rats and the fact that people drop like flies wherever he goes.

Stoker's Dracula starts out as an ancient and disagreeable aristocrat prior to getting younger and (a bit) more presentable as the story progresses. Interestingly, Orlok does the reverse. He quickly discards the curious silk hat he wore as (somewhat inadequate) camouflage when first greeting Hutter, becoming less and less socially acceptable, and more and more hideous, as he roams abroad. (The inspiration here may have been John Barrymore's recent performance as *Dr Jekyll and Mr Hyde*, which exactly anticipated Orlok's elongated fingers, phallic head and gradually worsening countenance.) Which is the vampire's most appalling manifestation is hard to say – as a nocturnal, bald-domed apparition framed in his guest's doorway ... a sliver of gimlet-eyed face glimpsed through a rent in his coffin lid ... a casket-toting phantom proudly surveying his new domain ... or a long-clawed silhouette that climactically swarms up to the heroine's bedroom.

Thanks to Murnau's extensive location work, the elemental power of landscape becomes a significant presence in the film, suggesting that a hideous supernatural threat can exist quite comfortably amid the beauty of nature. Underlining this, Stoker's scientific trappings are dropped and the Van Helsing character almost erased – but his surrogate, Professor Bulwer, still finds time to give an illuminating lecture on Venus fly-traps and tentacled polyps, describing the latter as "transparent, nearly weightless, no more than phantoms." Murnau cuts straight from this to Knock in his asylum cell, gazing hungrily at a spider devouring a paralysed fly. This echoes Dr Seward's theory, in the book, that Renfield is part of an elaborate food-chain, an idea expressed by Murnau in the simplest images,

# NOSFERATU
# EINE SYMPHONIE DES GRAUENS

*Germany 1921*
*UK / US:* **Nosferatu**
*Prana-Film*
*94 minutes b/w*
*production began August 1921*

. . . . . . . . . . . . . . . . . . . . . . . . . . . . .

Director of Photography: F A Wagner; Sets: Albin Grau; Camera assistant: Günther Krampf [uncredited]; Music [at premiere]: Hans Erdmann; Freely composed by Henrik Galeen, after the novel *Dracula* by Bram Stoker [uncredited on original prints]; Producers: Enrico

Dieckmann, Albin Grau; Director: F W Murnau

Max Schreck (Graf Orlok); Gustav von Wangenheim (Thomas Hutter); Greta Schroeder (Ellen, Hutter's wife); G H Schnell (Harding, a ship-owner); Alexander Granach (Knock); Ruth Landshoff (Ruth Harding); John Gottowt (Professor Bulwer); Gustav Botz (Dr Sievers); Max Nemetz (captain); Wolfgang Heinz (first mate); Guido Herzfeld (innkeeper); Karl Etlinger, Albert Venohr, Heinrich Witte (sailors); Hardy von François (doctor in hospital)

**Nosferatu is a sensational film, mainly because it departs so radically from the well-worn paths of a hundred highly polished romances and machine-made adventure stories ... Max Schreck's Nosferatu is brilliant both in make-up and movement. Henrik Galeen's scenario provides a firm framework. And in staging it, F W Murnau has created a masterpiece.** Lichtbild-Bühne 11 March 1922

**The terror of war is gone from men's eyes, but it has left something behind: the desire, probably unconscious in many cases, to understand what lay behind this monstrous event that swept over us like a cosmic vampire, drinking the blood of millions.** Albin Grau [writing in Bühne und Film # 21, 1921] strongly suggesting that vampirism is a fundamental, maybe *the* fundamental, rule of nature.

In opposition the film offers only the power of love. In a self-sacrificial echo of Wagner's *Der fliegende Holländer* (The Flying Dutchman), Ellen realises that to vanquish Orlok she must welcome him with open arms and thus detain him till dawn. It's a simplistic solution but makes sense given the way this Teutonic makeover of *Dracula* strips away Stoker's documentary nuts-and-bolts to expose the myth at its core. It's a solution, too, that is filled with horror, for Orlok has reached his peak of physical repulsiveness just in time for this weirdly erotic tryst. Arguably more disturbing, however, is an earlier moment when the vampire's voyage across the Black Sea comes to an end and the Death Ship noses its way into Wisborg harbour. Emerging from the hold, Orlok permits himself a fanged half-smile as he clamps one taloned hand on the ledge – not just for leverage, but as an arrogant gesture of total dominion. It's an image worthy of Bruegel's 16th century phantasmagoria *The Triumph of Death*, particularly the inhuman spark of anticipation in Orlok's eyes – coldly jubilant at the prospect of being let loose among the living.

Ruth Weyher, the aristocratic focus of maniacal jealousy in *Schatten* (1923)

Despite the collapse of Prana-Film and the cancellation of *Nosferatu*'s two proposed follow-ups, the company's prime movers weren't done with the film business quite yet. Re-emerging as Pan-Film, Grau and Dieckmann put Arthur Robison's *Schatten* (Shadows) before Berlin picturegoers in October 1923, with Dieckmann producing and Grau taking credit not just for design but also the basic 'idea', something he'd modestly neglected to do on *Nosferatu*. Carried over from that film were actors Alexander Granach and Gustav von Wangenheim, together with cinematographer Fritz Arno Wagner. The result, according to Wagner, "only found response from the film aesthetes, making no impression on the general public."[16] Indeed, *Schatten* was an art film through and through, with its art-house credentials confirmed during limited export engagements as *Warning Shadows*.

A couple of years before, Lupu Pick's *Scherben* (Shattered) had elucidated its Carl Mayer scenario with recourse to just one intertitle – Werner Krauss, as a disintegrating railway signalman, confessing that "Ich bin ein Mörder" (I am a murderer). *Schatten* went

one better by excluding intertitles altogether, telling an archetypal story of a Beidermeier-period aristocrat (Fritz Kortner) consumed with jealousy regarding his flirtatious wife (Ruth Weyher) and a handsome young suitor (Wangenheim). Going steadily berserk in the style of Leontes in *The Winter's Tale*, he gives admittance to a capering showman (Granach), who promptly converts the proceedings into a shadowplay 'happening', drawing off the shadows of the assembled company and thus allowing them to act out their owners' baser instincts. When their shadows are reinstated, it's revealed that the company have effectively been watching a film-within-a-film played out on the blank wall of the banqueting room. The aristocrat and his entourage are suitably chastened by this glimpse into their souls and normality is restored.

As perhaps the ultimate expression of the Teutonic fixation on shadow selves, *Schatten* gains a great deal from the seething atmosphere of suppressed sex with which Robison imbues it. The wife has no fewer than four tongue-lolling admirers and even the cadaverous young footman is caught sneaking a look up the chambermaid's rather 1920s-looking skirts. The aristocrat's mental collapse is signalled when he spies a canteen of rapiers and literally sees red; the swords blur into a crimson haze and before long he has his wife tethered to the banqueting table. The sadism reaches a high pitch when he forces the quailing suitors to ritually sacrifice her, with Robison offering a silhouetted view of their rapiers lancing phallically towards her quivering bosom. But, aside from touches such as these, a certain preciousness clings to the enterprise, a tendency flagged up right at the beginning, when Robison has the characters introduce themselves under a proscenium arch and takes nearly five extremely laborious minutes to do it.

Dieckmann having abandoned the film industry after *Schatten*, Grau took on a few more design jobs prior to following suit in 1925. Yet a strange echo of their efforts came round at the dawn of the 1930s, when the arrival of sound resulted in a brief fad for repurposing old silent films via the addition of dialogue and sound effects. Presumably aware that Universal's *The Phantom of the Opera* had enjoyed a talkie revival in January 1930,

Waldemar Ronger of the one-shot Berlin company Deutsch-Film-Produktion took *Nosferatu* and came up with *Die zwölfte Stunde Eine Nacht des Grauens* (The Twelfth Hour: A Night of Horror), getting it into theatres in May. In converting the film to sound Ronger not only changed all the names again (Graf Orlok became Fürst Wolkoff, for example), he also shot new scenes and had recourse to Murnau's out-takes – yet he omitted all mention of Murnau from the credits.

Murnau's original had already been screened by London's Film Society and New York's Film Guild, in December 1928 and June 1929 respectively, so Ronger's resurrection of it in a new guise was just another indication that Florence Stoker's campaign to destroy *Nosferatu* had failed.

# VEIDT FRIGHT

In June 1923 the Joe May Studios in Berlin played host to a film in which no fewer than three tyrannical figures were showcased, with at least one of them fitting neatly into Siegfried Kracauer's "cortege of tyrants and monsters." The timing was appropriate, given that Germany's post-war hyper-inflation was just then reaching its peak, destroying the economy and impoverishing the middle class. The Dawes Plan would help to put Germany back on an even keel the following year, but the seething discontent engendered in this period needed only another economic crisis, at the turn of the 1930s, to ensure the ascendancy of Adolf Hitler.

In Paul Leni's *Das Wachsfigurenkabinett* (Waxworks) Emil Jannings' rotund Haroun al Raschid and Werner Krauss' spectral Jack the Ripper are positioned either side of Conrad Veidt's gimlet-eyed Ivan the Terrible. Designing the sets himself in collaboration with Alfred Jünge, Leni took Henrik Galeen's portmanteau script, itself modelled on Lang's *Der müde Tod*, and infused it with a heavy dose of Caligarism. Alluring imagery aside, the Haroun al Raschid story is an over-extended comic divertissement and the Ripper segment a mere cough-and-a-spit at the very end. It doesn't even qualify as a discrete episode, instead rounding off Galeen's linking story, in which a young poet goes in search of copywriting work at a local carnival. Though the Ripper's climactic pursuit

Conrad Veidt's demented Ivan the Terrible, centrepiece of the second story in *Das Wachsfigurenkabinett* (1923)

of the boy and his sweetheart is a hallucinatory riot of mismatched superimpositions, one can't help feeling that poor Werner Krauss was grievously short-changed. It's possible that budget over-runs were responsible for this curtailment, given that a mooted fourth episode didn't get filmed at all. No matter, for the framing story is engaging and the Ivan the Terrible episode a mini-masterpiece.

The elderly waxworks proprietor (John Gottowt) gets the episode under way by inserting a key into Ivan's chest, cranking up the figure's left arm in an eerie approximation of life. The fact that the figures are automata as well as mere effigies is never alluded to again; instead, we're transported to the bowels of the Kremlin in the 16th century, where Ivan and his wizened astrologer creep through oppressively low-ceilinged caverns "to gloat," as an intertitle puts it, "over the dying agonies of his poisoned victims." With eyes swivelling watchfully from side to side and his tongue forever flickering in sadistic anticipation, Veidt's Ivan is a masterful study in paranoia. And that he's just another grotesque emanation of the film's wildly Expressionist decor is made clear when double doors, each adorned with a saintly icon, swing open to reveal a third – the sumptuously gilded Czar all dressed up for a wedding. In a truly chilling endgame, he finishes by obsessively turning and re-turning an hour-glass for the remainder of his life, insanely determined to prove that "the Czar is mightier than Death."

The film's German release was delayed until November 1924; to compensate, its eventual appearance in the USA – variously titled *The Three Wax Works* or *The Three Wax Men* – ensured Leni's transferral to Hollywood. There, his visual genius illuminated the Universal 'Jewels' *The Cat and the Canary* and *The Last Warning* plus the grandiose 'Super Jewel' *The Man Who Laughs* (starring Veidt), prior to his early death in 1929. His assistant director on *Das Wachsfigurenkabinett*, Wilhelm Dieterle, also played the young poet; his own directorial career in Hollywood yielded such evergreens as *The Hunchback of Notre Dame* and *All That Money Can Buy*.

By the time Veidt's Ivan the Terrible reached German audiences, a subsequent Veidt vehicle called *Orlacs Hände* (The Hands of Orlac) had already received

Alexandra Sorina comforts the post-operative
Conrad Veidt in *Orlacs Hände* (1924)

# ORLACS HÄNDE

Austria 1924
UK / US: **The Hands of Orlac**
Pan-Film
112 minutes b/w
*previewed 24 September 1924 (Berlin),
30 September 1924 (Vienna)*
. . . . . . . . . . . . . . . . . . . . . . . . . . . .
Directors of Photography: Günther Krampf,
Hans Androschin; Design: Stefan Wessely;

Design Assistants: Hans Rouc, Karl Exner
[both uncredited]; Adapted by: Louis
Nerz, from the novel by Maurice Renard;
Director: Robert Wiene

Conrad Veidt (Orlac); Alexandra Sorina (Yvonne
Orlac); Fritz Strassny (Orlac's father); Paul
Askonas (servant); Carmen Gartellieri (Regine);
Hans Homma (Dr Serral); Fritz Kortner (Nera)

**Conrad Veidt ... gave a splendid virtuoso performance, a virtuosity perhaps
to be classified among the truly great achievements of this artist. The
book certainly has strong cinematic qualities, very well brought out by the
director, Dr R Wiene ... The end comes as a big surprise, a switch from the
unreal-fantastic to the realist-criminal. The film's artistic consistency is
disrupted, certainly, but it's hard to believe this conclusion will detract from
its public appeal – rather the reverse.** *Lichtbild-Bühne 7 February 1925*

> I was in the theatre on the opening night, and I have never seen such
> an astonishing scene. All over the theatre there were shouts and cries;
> women fainted; men shouted, "It is terrible to show a film like this."
> ... I went in front of the curtain ... [and] spoke a few words, telling
> them about the making of the picture, my own feelings. I tried to
> smooth them down. And, to my own surprise, I succeeded.
> *Conrad Veidt ['The Story of Conrad Veidt', Sunday Dispatch 28 October 1934]*

*Having been involved in a train wreck, celebrated concert
pianist Paul Orlac is left with crushed and useless hands
that are subsequently amputated. A doctor grafts a pair
of donor hands onto Orlac's stumps, but the recipient is
horrified when he learns that they came from an executed
murderer called Vasseur. Unable to play and refusing
to touch his wife Yvonne, Orlac then discovers that his
miserly father has been stabbed to death...*

A bizarre fusion of forward-looking science fiction
(transplanted hands) and virtually mediaeval mysticism
(the idea that they retain their murderous impulses),
*Orlac* reunited Veidt with Robert Wiene, director of
*Caligari*. The company that achieved this remarkable
coup was Pan-Film of Austria, meaning that Vienna,
already the birthplace of psychoanalysis, became the
progenitor of 'body horror' too. Whether the world
was ready for it or not is hard to say; by Veidt's own
account, the first night audience met the film with
undisguised revulsion, yet film critics of the day greeted
it warmly as a major work from a major director.

Getting Veidt and Wiene back together resulted in
a film well away from the heavy stylisation of *Caligari* –
the settings range across realistic convalescent homes,
suburban villas and low-life taverns – but in many
ways just as compellingly strange. Again, Veidt's very

its premiere engagements. Shot in the summer of
1924, this was based on *Les Mains d'Orlac*, a four-year
old French novel by Maurice Renard that had recently
been translated into German by Norbert Jacques,
creator of Dr Mabuse. Both men were writing long
before transplant surgery became feasible but a
number of years after neurologists had identified
so-called Alien Hand Syndrome.

identity is at stake, and the crux of his mental crisis is played out in a cavernous midnight bedroom in which he stares fixedly at his outstretched hands. Suddenly starting to walk forward, his spatted feet seem to move not of their own volition but that of the hands. Crisped into talons, the hands convey him into the next room, where he retrieves a concealed dagger, frenziedly stabs at thin air and narrowly avoids cutting off his left hand at the wrist.

In scenes like these, Veidt's mask-like face and precisely controlled movements, making Orlac's mental state manifest through his whole body, evoke a Kabuki dance drama, inspiring a contemporary critic in *Film-Kurier* to offer a fine summation of this exemplar of the Expressionist ideal: "The play of his hands is full of absolute genius. Their movements alone are sufficient to portray psychological states, to unfold the developing drama of the soul."[17] And not just his hands, for Veidt was reputed to be able to act even with the veins in his forehead. In *Orlacs Hände* you can see this in action in a whole series of incredible hallucinatory set-pieces; in a famous still (which Pan-Film converted into an extremely striking poster), it's clear that Veidt's pulsing brow is doing just as much work as his burning eyes and upheld hands. "Remove them now!" Orlac urges his surgeon, succumbing to a gruesomely literal case of transplant rejection. "I don't want them – these wretched things! I'm telling you ... they demand blood ... crimes ... murder ..." The overall effect is to show a highly strung man, possessed by post-operative trauma, sliding inexorably into an abyss of madness and despair.

Despair is the keynote of this lengthy and sombre film, with Wiene dwarfing his puppet characters in sparsely furnished, heavily shadowed rooms, also excelling himself in the truly nightmarish nocturnal train wreck that destroys Orlac's original hands. Here, the abstracted bails of barbed wire that witnessed the death of *Caligari*'s somnambulist are exchanged for a more forthright echo of the Great War, with running stretcher bearers, mangled carriages heaped up on the horizon and clouds of apocalyptic smoke.

Elsewhere, a seam of twisted eroticism is brought tantalisingly to the surface. Right at the start, Yvonne reads a letter from her husband promising that "my hands will glide over your hair and I'll feel your body beneath my hands." Later she yearns to re-encounter his "beautiful, tender hands" and is mortified when he decrees that "These hands will never be allowed to touch another person." In the USA a few years later, Tod Browning would make *The Unknown* for M-G-M, in which Joan Crawford's luminous Nanon is the exact opposite of Yvonne, her pathological fear of

men's hands prompting Lon Chaney to an appalling sacrifice. The two films would make a neat double-bill for fans of kinky dismemberment melodramas from the Roaring Twenties.

After Orlac's decision to keep away from Yvonne, the suppressed eroticism is underlined when Fritz Kortner's conniving blackmailer urges Orlac's maid to "seduce his hands," leading to a highly charged sequence between master and maid. Eventually Kortner masquerades as Vasseur with black leather gauntlets apparently replacing his lost hands, showing them off to Orlac with fetishistic pride under the glare of an overhead lamp. Striking though this image is, it's part and parcel of the film's disappointingly humdrum explanation of Orlac's fears. This last-reel rationalisation aside, *Orlacs Hände* remains a genuinely unnerving tour de force. Small wonder that, in addition to numerous disguised ones, it has sired several official remakes, from *Mad Love* in 1935 and *Les Mains d'Orlac* in 1960 to Philippe Setbon's gender-switched TV movie *Les Mains de Roxana* in 2012.

The hints of possession contained in *Orlacs Hände* indicated that Germany's interest in demonic doubles was undimmed. A number of other films had gone the doppelgänger route more directly, notably Urban Gad's January 1921 release *Ich – bin – Du...* (I – Am – You...), in which Hans Mierendorff was an eminent Egyptologist whose identity is assumed by a criminal double. Mierendorff's own company, the aptly named Lucifer-Film, was also responsible in its brief life for titles like *Teufelskirche* (The Devil's Church, 1919), in which a pastor (Mierendorff) encounters Satan (Paul Rehkopf), and *Die Maske des Todes* (The Mask of Death, 1920), in which Mierendorff was a combined aristocrat-criminal and yet another double role was reserved for Margit Barnay.

## GAMBLING WITH EVIL

By the summer of 1926, long after the dissolution of Lucifer-Film, a new Berlin company, Sokal-Film, had decided to resurrect German cinema's original phantom double. To realise this ambitious scheme, the young producer Harry Sokal put together a truly remarkable package, with Conrad Veidt and Werner Krauss in the leads, Henrik Galeen as director and co-writer, settings by *Caligari*'s Hermann Warm, and cinematography by Günther Krampf, who had been Fritz Arno Wagner's operator on *Nosferatu*. The icing on the cake was that all these talents were brought together for a reworking of Hanns Heinz Ewers' 13-year-old Faust variant, *Der Student von Prag* (The Student of Prague). A few years later the youthful British filmmaker Paul Rotha, in his landmark book *The Film Till Now*, eulogised the

# DER STUDENT VON PRAG

Germany 1926
UK / US: **The Student of Prague**
Sokal-Film
91 minutes b/w
censor date 19 October 1926

· · · · · · · · · · · · · · · · · · · · · · · · · ·

Director of Photography: Günther Krampf;
Art Director: Hermann Warm; Assistant
Director: Erich Kober [uncredited];
Production Manager: Max Maximilian
[uncredited]; Camera Operator: Erich
Nitzschmann [uncredited]; Music [at

premiere]: Willy Schmidt-Gentner; Scenario:
Henrik Galeen, based on a novella [sic] by
Hanns Heinz Ewers; Producer: H R Sokal;
Director: Henrik Galeen

*Conrad Veidt (Balduin, a student); Werner Krauss
(Scapinelli); Elizza la Porta (Liduschka); Fritz
Alberti (Graf Schwarzenberg); [Gräfin] Agnes
Esterhazy (Margit, his daughter); Ferdinand v
Alten (Baron Waldis-Schwarzenberg, her cousin
and fiancé); Erich Kober, Max Maximilian (two
students); uncredited: Marian Alma; Silvia Torff*

Are we really in the era of reprints and new editions of old movies already?
... Sixteen years ago [sic] Wegener was this sinister, nihilistic Student
of Prague ... Today it's Conrad Veidt. And he's at least as splendid as his
predecessor, without a doubt ... The overall effect is magnificent. Of all the
German films this season, this one deserves to be a popular success.
*Film-Kurier 26 October 1926*

What does the old 'fantastic' fairytale world of the Brothers Grimm and
Wilhelm Hauff, of E T A Hoffmann and even, perhaps, of Edgar Allan Poe mean
to us and our children today? Today's reality has become the equivalent of
yesterday's fantasy. In our films, therefore, we had to look for new problems
in this field. What can we still call 'fantastic' today? Everything that seems
possible in our unconscious, although it is not to be found in our common
everyday reality. Henrik Galeen [speaking in 1929; reprinted in Prawer, Caligari's Children, 1980]

Conrad Veidt with a cruciform keepsake in the Sokal-Film
version of *Der Student von Prag* (1926)

result for its "open spaciousness and dark psychology,
wild poetic beauty and a deeply dramatic theme" and
for utilising "Conrad Veidt at his best; a performance
that he has never equalled before or since." Going
further, Rotha concluded that "all these [elements]
entitled the film to rank as great."[18]

*1820. Though famed throughout Prague for his prowess as
a fencer, Balduin is chiefly preoccupied with his dwindling
finances. An enigmatic figure called Scapinelli visits him
in his shabby student digs and offers him a King's ransom
in exchange for an item of Scapinelli's choice contained
within the room. Sadly, Balduin has accepted the cascade
of gold pieces before Scapinelli reveals what his chosen
item actually is – Balduin's mirror image.*

With a reputed budget of 360,000 marks this new
*Student* was a deluxe affair and proved a big hit with
German audiences. Carlos Clarens would later
bracket the film with *Orlacs Hände*, calling them "the
last gleams of the Romantic revival"[19] – and clearly
Galeen went all out to confer a Hoffmann-like
lustre on this latest iteration of the age-old German
obsession with the doppelgänger.

There are signs, too, that Galeen and his colleagues
were well aware that this film marked a kind of end
point for the shadowy nightmares that had prevailed
since *Caligari*. To underline the fact, the re-teaming of
the erstwhile somnambulist and his insane master,
Veidt and Krauss, was no doubt considered de rigueur.
Rather like Karloff and Lugosi or Lee and Cushing in
later years, it was a casting combination that already
conjured images of a cinematic tradition; after all, the
American critic Gilbert Seldes was referring to "the
almost legendary *Cabinet of Dr Caligari*"[20] as early as
1925. So potent was the combination that, if Galeen
ever entertained any notions of casting his longtime
friend and brother-in-law John Gottowt (who had
played Scapinelli in the 1913 original), he quickly
thought better of them.

By this stage, however, Veidt, as a screen presence,
has clearly outdistanced Krauss. This Scapinelli –
notably younger than the one played by Gottowt
13 years before – is a wink-tipping, lip-smacking
trickster who may as well have a neon sign over his
stovepipe hat reading 'agent of the Devil'. In a famous
shot echoing Caspar David Friedrich, he stands on the
brow of a hill overseeing a chaotic fox hunt, with his
furled umbrella at a conveniently quirky angle – and
Krauss is very obviously striking a pose rather than
inhabiting a character. Veidt, by contrast, was capable
of fusing the Expressionist 'pose' with naturalistic
subtlety and a carefully controlled use of the silent

screen's gestural eloquence. In particular, his double-performance at the film's climax is among the greatest in the genre, alternating huge-eyed close-ups of Balduin's mounting hysteria with the truly chilling spectacle of the remorseless doppelgänger standing in front of fluttering drapes at Balduin's window. "Certainly," observed a US critic in 1929, "the final sequence of his vain flight from his ever-pursuing image and the life and death climax before the shattered mirror is one of the finest achievements of screen pantomime and camera magic."[21]

The tragic inevitability of the action is made clear right from the beginning, with the opening shot disclosing Balduin's headstone, complete with the legend 'He gambled with Evil and lost.' That the film's final shot will itself be a doppelgänger of this first one is a foregone conclusion. In the meantime Galeen discreetly improves on the 1913 film in several respects. Balduin's skill as a fencer is actually shown to us this time (bringing Veidt some flattering comparisons in the press to Douglas Fairbanks), and Galeen replaces the older film's faintly ridiculous scene of Paul Wegener splashing about in a lake with an earthbound but thrillingly edited struggle to rescue a young Countess from a runaway horse. Here is evidence of the profound impact made by the 'entfesselte Kamera' (unchained camera), a technique pioneered by F W Murnau and his cinematographer Karl Freund in the 1924 classic *Der letzte Mann* (The Last Man) – a film that, having been exported as *The Last Laugh*, led to Murnau's departure for Hollywood.

In Galeen's film, the technique recurs during a striking sequence in which the dissipated Balduin trashes a low-life public house, a scene in which Krampf's woozily slurring camera achieves so hallucinatory an effect that the viewer becomes unsure who's doing the damage – Balduin or his demonic other self. When the story's originator, Hanns Heinz Ewers, wrote a belated novelisation in 1930, he added a rather pompous introduction in which he conceded that "this second film is much superior to the first, namely in all the things that can be had for money and time" – but regretted the addition of this scene because it "does not sit comfortably at all with the style of the rest of the film."[22] (He also complained, more reasonably, that the new film wasn't actually shot in Prague.) On the contrary, the decorous 'style' of the film is here seen to craze and disintegrate just as Balduin himself is doing, and the effect is spellbinding.

The film's other memorable images include Scapinelli's shadow, projected enormously onto a blank wall above which Balduin and the Countess are trysting on a balcony, and a nostalgic touch in which

Scapinelli, reading over the terms of the fateful deal, applies to it the same myopic scrutiny that *Nosferatu*'s vampire gave to a similar document. Above all, however, there's the hair-raising flight from Balduin's malevolent stalker, climaxing with the wind-swept Balduin seeking refuge at an isolated house only to have the door answered by himself.

After ten years as the gaunt-faced embodiment of German post-war fragmentation, Veidt had perfected a theory of acting that, perhaps inevitably, made reference to the many doppelgängers he had played. He finally elucidated it in 1940 when asked about his abandonment of the stage, maintaining that "in films I have found a new dope – the fascinating, if playful, concept of a double personality. It intrigues me to think that there is another man abroad in the world who resembles me, that I may sit in this hotel room with a Scotch-and-soda talking of him and yet that shadow of me is somewhere, swaying audiences in darkened theatres with an impression of love, or hate, or deceit. There, too, is the actor's sense of power and one feels it as surely as any heard applause."[23]

After the doppelgänger apotheosis of *Der Student von Prag*, however, Veidt started to move away from otherworldly subjects. In the late 1920s German filmmakers were beginning to follow the lead of director G W Pabst, relinquishing exaggerated fantasy in favour of 'die neue Sachlichkeit' (new objectivity), leading Paul Rotha to identify *Der Student* itself as a stand-out title in "the transition period when the decorative art film was being succeeded by the naturalistic film."[24] It was a timely moment, then, for John Barrymore to ask Veidt over to Hollywood, with Veidt beginning his journey in mid-September 1926. As well as playing opposite Barrymore in *The Beloved Rogue*, Veidt enjoyed a few grotesque and-or sinister roles during his stay, notably in Paul Leni's *The Man Who Laughs* and Paul Fejos' *The Last Performance*, on top of which he was reported, in September 1928, to be front-runner for the title role in Universal's projected film version of *Dracula*. But with talkies rapidly becoming omnipresent he decided to go back home and perfect his English, returning to Germany in February the following year.

Back in 1926, Werner Krauss' skittish Scapinelli wasn't the only demonic tempter on show that year, for the new version of *Der Student von Prag* came out less than a fortnight after the October premiere of a lavish Ufa super-production dramatising the myth from which *Student* originated. The idea of synthesising Goethe, Christopher Marlowe and other sources into an epic film version of *Faust* had been toyed with by D W Griffith in the USA and, in Germany, the ubiquitous Richard Oswald. Revived at Ufa, the

Emil Jannings gurns his way past Gösta Ekman's defences
in *Faust Eine deutsche Volkssage* (1926)

project was handed to F W Murnau, whose six months' toil on *Faust Eine deutsche Volkssage* (Faust: A German Folk Tale) began in October 1925. The result was a puzzling contradiction: a dazzling display of the high artistry of which silent cinema was now capable, but also a bloated pomposity shading from sanctimonious mawkishness into low comedy and finally outright kitsch. The project's elephantine pretentions were expertly skewered after the war by Siegfried Kracauer, who observed coolly that "Ufa seemed determined to make this film a cultural monument."[25]

Yet as a showcase for state-of-the-art special effects the film had no peer. The first image is of a bunch of Toytown apocalyptic horsemen suggesting that Ufa's experts had got no further than Méliès, but this proves deceptive. The horned Devil, hissing "Mein ist die Erde!" (the Earth is mine!) from a realm of stygian darkness, reappears as an enveloping shroud of pestilence, literally squirting black smoke from under his enormous cloak as poisoned villagers run in horror from the plague. Keen to help them, Faust obtains "the potent threefold key to controlling spirits" and

conjures up a peasant Mephisto with luminous eyes who magically reappears wherever Faust goes. The terms of their pact are literally smoked up from the parchment in Mephisto's hands, after which the soot-blackened demon conjures an inferno of belching flame while regressing the doctor to his youthful self; the first vision he tempts Faust with, plainly identifying sex as an instrument of evil, is a naked girl.

Unfortunately, the arrival of the androgynous new Faust (Gösta Ekman) is matched by Mephisto's transformation into a bulbous, mincing low comic, with Emil Jannings' ludicrously overblown performance making much of the remainder unwatchable. There are still some striking moments, particularly when Faust's abandoned sweetheart (Camilla Horn) is discovered iced over in a snowdrift. But the bathos of the ending – in which an absurd winged angel vanquishes the Devil with the shimmering, one-word intertitle "Liebe" (love) – prefigures the kind of manipulative use of volkssagen that the Nazis would master.

As both "a cultural monument" and an effects showcase Murnau's film had a precedent in Fritz Lang's *Die Nibelungen* (The Nibelung Saga), the two-part Decla super-production with which Lang and Thea von Harbou had followed the success of *Dr Mabuse, der Spieler*. Complete with an opening rubric dedicating the proceedings to the German people, this was one of Hitler's favourite films, reportedly having caused him to weep on first viewing it. A genuinely titanic rendering of Germany's national epic, it was first seen in February 1924 and in the following decade would be reissued by the Nazis – but only the first film, *Siegfried*, with all its sword-forging, dragon-slaying and fortune-gathering Aryan heroics. The second film, *Kriemhilds Rache* (Kriemhild's Revenge), in which Lang allowed the heroic image to disintegrate into madness while the terrifying Margarethe Schön presides over scenes of untold carnage, was suppressed.

## UNHOLY ALLIANCES
While Murnau's *Faust* was in its lengthy post-production phase and Conrad Veidt was making the revamped *Student von Prag*, a more monolithic representative of German horror, Paul Wegener, was working on a US production at the Victorine facility in Nice. Rex Ingram's *The Magician* was based on a Somerset Maugham novel pretty clearly intended as a lampoon of Aleister Crowley, with Wegener cast as the insane Dr Oliver Haddo, whose interest in "the creation of human beings by alchemistry" is bad news for heroine Alice Terry. The result proved of great

interest to James Whale, who would quote from the film quite liberally when making *Frankenstein* in 1931.

One of Ingram's assistants on *The Magician* was the young Michael Powell, whose impression of Wegener was not favourable. "I feel sure that Rex would have played Conrad Veidt in the part if he had not recently seen *The Golem*," he wrote 60 years later. "But Wegener was chosen, and so we were saddled with a pompous German whose one idea was to pose like a statue and whose one expression to indicate magical powers was to open his huge eyes even wider, until he looked about as frightening as a bullfrog."[26] Powell's view notwithstanding, *The Magician* came as a boost to Wegener, whose career had been somewhat stalled for a few years but who now picked up a number of weird showcases in the film's wake. By May 1927 he was playing the title role, opposite Anita Dorris' mesmerised Trilby, in Gennaro Righelli's *Svengali*, and soon afterwards he starred as a reverted-to-savagery Arctic aviator in Max Reichmann's *Ramper, der Tiermensch* (Ramper, the Beast Man). By the latter part of the year he was ready for a rematch with Hanns Heinz Ewers, author of the pre-war Wegener vehicle *Der Student von Prag*. The new film was called *Alraune* and the writer-director was the ubiquitous Henrik Galeen.

In Ewers' original novel, a scientist is inspired to create life by the legend of the mandrake root, which reputedly bears a humanoid appearance because it's fertilised by the ejaculate left behind by hanged felons. Uniting a depraved Berlin whore and a notorious sex criminal via artificial insemination, he comes up with a soulless and destructive beauty whom he calls Alraune.

This lurid and frankly misogynist stuff, first published in 1911 as *Alraune Die Geschichte eines lebenden Wesens* (Alraune: The Story of a Living Being), already had a rather confusing track record as a cinema property. A Hungarian version from 1918 is reputed to have been directed by Mihály Kertész, later to find fame in Hollywood as Michael Curtiz; unconfirmed reports suggest that there may have been a German adaptation that year too. To obfuscate matters still further, yet another 1918 film, Eugen Illés' clumsily titled *Alraune, die Henkerstochter, genannt die rote Hanne* (Alraune the Hangman's Daughter, known as Red Hanna), bore no relation to Ewers' book, instead turning on a motif that would be repeated many times in future decades – a modern woman haunted by a long-dead ancestor who was burned at the stake, complete with an elaborate mediaeval flashback. To top it all off, something called *Alraune und der Golem* was announced with much fanfare during the same period but appears not to have gone into production. Had it done so, it would have headed a long line of

monster-mashes stretching from *Frankenstein Meets the Wolf Man* to *Alien vs Predator* and beyond.

By 1927, however, all this was ancient history. Galeen's film of *Alraune* is a lavish affair, back-pedalling in a big way on the more intractable aspects of Ewers' book (notably its scenes of sex-vampirism) and even, for the purposes of a barely credible happy ending, keeping Alraune alive at the end. But in Wegener, as the formidable Professor ten Brinken, and Brigitte Helm, as the adamantine Fatal Woman par excellence, it has a pair of charismatic actors who hold the attention in a story shadowed by the oncoming threat of Nazi eugenics. The Professor affirms his support for Serge Voronoff's real-life research into gland-grafting, simultaneously handing out baby rabbits to his listeners for no discernible reason. Alraune herself, prior to the flickers of redemption permitted at the end, appears to be exactly what the Professor was warned he would get – "a living creature lacking the warmth of life yet carrying the chill of death." In short, a remorseless female counterpart to *Homunculus*.

Her early experiences at a convent, in scenes anticipating Leontine Sagan's classic 1930 film *Mädchen in Uniform*, involve a Mother Superior who appears to be played by a man. As a timid indication of the depraved depths Galeen otherwise withholds from us, Alraune places a stag beetle on the Mother Superior's back. Later, her realisation of her true origin is powerfully done – "What place have I, a child of vice and crime, among human beings?" – and her vengeful seduction of her so-called 'father' crackles with the kind of forbidden perversity that was an Ewers trademark. Here, Helm smoulders and shimmers in skimpy silver lamé, simultaneously resurrecting and transcending the 'vamp' archetype

Brigitte Helm exudes the chill of death as the alluring *Alraune* (1927)

Captain of industry
Alfred Abel and
insane inventor
Rudolf Klein-Rogge
in *Metropolis* (1926)

established by Theda Bara a decade earlier. Visually, Galeen is content to reference his own work (*Alraune*'s shadowed hands hover over the Professor's sleeping breast in a sex-switched quote from *Nosferatu*), while offering a mediaeval gallows tableau that may have provided another source of inspiration for James Whale's *Frankenstein*. Unfortunately, *Alraune*'s impact is blunted by Galeen's semi-absorption of the 'new objectivity' then gaining momentum in Germany, making the film a 'neither fish nor fowl' compromise.

As the former artificial man of *Der Golem*, Wegener was a natural choice for the creator in *Alraune*. Helm's casting, too, was a waggish reference to another picture, albeit a much more recent one. Making her film debut as the dazzling Robot Maria in Fritz Lang's *Metropolis*, she had been the weirdly glamorous centrepiece of a film that set the pattern for an entire genre. Imagining a workers' insurrection in the year 2000, the film's astonishing visuals resonate to this day, though its philosophical banality – which also set a pattern – was lambasted even at the time. H G Wells himself entered the fray, noting the film's indebtedness to Karel Čapek, Mary Shelley and, indeed, H G Wells, enumerating its catalogue of "every possible foolishness, cliché, platitude, and muddlement about mechanical progress" and making the shrewd observation that Rudolf Klein-Rogge's insane inventor,

Rotwang, "occupies a small old house, embedded in the modern city, richly adorned with pentagrams and other reminders of the antiquated German romances out of which its owner has been taken. A quaint smell of Mephistopheles is perceptible for a time. So even at Ufa, Germany can still be dear old magic-loving Germany."[27]

Ufa, however, had greater problems to contend with than the disapproval of H G Wells, for the unprecedented extravagance of *Metropolis* succeeded in crippling the conglomerate's finances. Lang's ambitious vision of the future was shot at Neubabelsberg from May 1925 to October 1926, reputedly employed 36,000 people in front of the cameras, and left Ufa owing 40 million marks to the Deutsche Bank. Though bailed out initially by the American studios M-G-M and Paramount, Ufa's troubles reached a head in March 1927 (just a couple of months after *Metropolis* was finally released), making it vulnerable to a successful takeover bid by the Prussian media magnate Alfred Hugenberg, whose nationalist agenda set the scene for a further film industry takeover six years down the line, that of the Nazis.

In the meantime, Germany's virtual abandonment of fantastic subjects – prompted in part by the trend towards streetwise realism and in part, perhaps, by the damage wrought by *Metropolis* – may also have been encouraged by a newly vigilant 'zensur'.

As Rudolf Leonhard, screenwriter of G W Pabst's *Tagebuch einer Verlorenen* (Diary of a Lost Girl), explained to Lotte Eisner in 1953: "The German censor, who had blithely slept his way through the period of dreams and fantasies, seems to have woken up at the neue Sachlichkeit (the 'new objectivity') and realism which emerged around 1927-28."[28]

Shot in summer 1929, *Tagebuch* was one of two Pabst films that enshrined the gamine beauty of the American actress Louise Brooks; it was preceded, in the closing months of 1928, by *Die Büchse der Pandora* (Pandora's Box). Frank Wedekind's turn-of-the-century Lulu plays, previously filmed with Erna Morena in 1917 and Asta Nielsen in 1922, enshrined the 'guileless femme fatale' figure that was later given a misogynist, proto-Nazi makeover by the Ewers novel *Alraune* – the same image, in fact, that had found its way, in robotic form, into *Metropolis*. The atmospheric beauty of Pabst's take on Lulu, heavily adulterated by censorship, ends in a pall of East End fog as Brooks' Lulu encounters Gustav Diessl's mournful Jack the Ripper. The sparkle of her teeth, the phosphorescence in his eye, the gleam of the blade behind his back – these rhyming images culminate in a discreet shot of her convulsing hand, indicating that symbolic retribution has been visited on a free spirit that transgressed society's bounds.

Despite the fall-off in fantasy subjects, in 1930 both Brigitte Helm and Paul Wegener would make return trips to the weird world of Hanns Heinz Ewers. The presumed-lost silent melodrama *Fundvogel* (Foundling Bird) was a May 1930 release in which Wegener's barking-mad Dr Reutlinger proposed to turn the beauteous Camilla Horn into a man. Deviating, spoilsport-fashion, from Ewers' overwrought sex-change novel, the action appears to have wound up with Reutlinger's great experiment being averted. Directed by Wolfgang Hoffmann-Harnisch, the film reached picturegoers a few months after a sound remake of *Alraune* that brought back Brigitte Helm but replaced Wegener with Albert Bassermann; it also had the clever idea of casting Helm not just as Alraune but as her demi-monde mother. Put together by the indefatigable Richard Oswald, this film formed part of the early talkie period's knee-jerk mania for remaking silent films of extremely recent vintage, yet it was to prove a worthwhile venture, improving on the silent in several respects.

A smaller (and presumably far cheaper) production, Oswald's film nevertheless manages to follow the novel much more closely. There are no blood-drinking sex sessions, of course, but at least Ewers' textbook 'destroyer of men' actually gets to do some destroying this time, while the Professor's arrogance and financial corruption are given much more of an airing. Alraune is passed off here, not as ten Brinken's daughter, but as his niece, allowing him to actually kiss her when provoked. Treating her to some stunning close-ups, cinematographer Günther Krampf increases Helm's luminosity 100 per cent, while Oswald indulges in a breathtakingly fast-cut runaway-car sequence. Once the Professor has killed himself, however, the film marks time rather boringly until Alraune finally follows suit. The beginning, too, is disfigured by dreary scenes of hearty students singing a vaguely misogynist song.

This queasy kind of material points forward to Ewers' future role as the Hitler-commissioned biographer of the youthful Nazi 'martyr' Horst Wessel – who, coincidentally, had been a teenage extra in the 1926 version of *Der Student von Prag*. Ewers also wrote a propagandist biopic of Wessel, but his romance with National Socialism didn't last long. Deemed suspiciously decadent (and also pro-Jewish), his books were proscribed and, on his death in 1943, he had become a septuagenarian 'unperson'.

## LIFE EBBING NEAR THE LOIRE

With his personal interest in the doppelgänger theme – what he called "that shadow of me" – Conrad Veidt may well have been amused by an important casting decision made by the French writer-director Jean Epstein in the early weeks of 1928. To play Roderick Usher in an upcoming Poe adaptation, Epstein cast Jean Debucourt, whose features may have been a trifle softer, less gaunt, than Veidt's, but whose noble brow and haunted countenance made him in all other respects a dead ringer.

For contemporary audiences a hint of Conrad Veidt in Epstein's protagonist may as well have been code for 'macabre'. Yet Epstein himself deplored what he saw as the pasted-on Expressionism of *Caligari*, calling it "nothing but a still life, all the living elements killed by a [paint] brush."[29] As a prominent member of a group of avant-garde cinéastes loosely dubbed French Impressionists, Epstein was able to turn *La Chute de la maison Usher* (The Fall of the House of Usher) into a kind of screen poetry entirely different to the angular extremities of *Caligari* – hazy and evanescent, soft like Debucourt's face rather than sharp like Veidt's, precisely attuned to the suppressed emotions of its characters, and steeped in what an intertitle calls "the overpowering melancholy of the Usher environs."

*When an elderly friend of Roderick Usher's arrives at the isolated and inhospitable Usher mansion, he finds that the younger man is obsessively devoted to painting*

Marguerite Gance lies 'dead' among virgin crants and maiden strewments in *La Chute de la maison Usher* (1928)

## LA CHUTE DE LA MAISON USHER

*France 1928*
UK / US: **The Fall of the House of Usher**
*63 minutes b/w*
*Les Films Jean Epstein [uncredited]*
*production began February 1928*
. . . . . . . . . . . . . . . . . . . . . . . . . . .

Director of Photography: [Georges] Lucas; Art Director: Pierre Kéfer; Assistant Director: Luis Buñuel [uncredited]; Camera Operator: Jean Lucas [uncredited];

Costumes: Fernand Osché [uncredited]; Special Effects: Ruggieri [uncredited]; Screenplay: Jean Epstein [uncredited], based on a story by Edgar Allan Poe; Director: Jean Epstein

*Marguerite Gance (Lady Madeline Usher); Jean Debucourt (Roderick Usher); Charles Lamy (Allan); Fournez-Goffard (doctor); Luc Dartagnan (servant); Pierre Kéfer; Pierre Hot; Halma*

Jean Epstein has in this film, suggested by Poe's fantastic story, achieved much of the gruesome mystery and horror of the original, and ... the interior scenes in the doomed house, and the remarkable scene where Madeleine's coffin is carried along the marshes to the family vault, are full of mystery and imagination ... It is a production of striking and highly artistic execution.
*The Bioscope* 27 November 1929

Along with Abel Gance and Marcel L'Herbier, Epstein, originally from Russia, was one of the best-known directors of the French cinema ... He took me on as second assistant, in charge of the interiors ... "You be careful," he said to me. "I see surrealistic tendencies in you. If you want my advice, you'll stay away from them." Luis Buñuel [*My Last Breath*, 1982]

reading 'Usher', the fog and damp of "the Usher environs" seem to permeate the very image. In fact, the sign only partially reads 'Usher' because, in a telling symbol of the family's creeping malaise, the sign is worm-eaten and the name half obliterated. The atmosphere of disquiet intensifies when the old man leaves a local inn. At an upper window, framed by straggling vines, appears the frightened, distorted face of a barmaid, presumably anxious to issue a warning but unable to articulate it.

After this, the reunion of the old friends at the Usher mansion sees them utterly dwarfed by a cold and cavernous hallway marked by a few sticks of widely spaced furniture. The dominant feature, though placed so far back as to almost disappear in the murk, is a massive fireplace with sculpted boars' heads adorning the chimney breast. And it's in this forbidding space that we get a first real frisson of alarm – as Roderick applies himself to a portrait of his wife, she flinches at the first stroke of his brush, as if cut. This small moment brings to mind Epstein's critique of *Caligari* – that it killed all its "living elements" with a paint brush.

Usher's obsessive painting of his wife, and its vampire-like effect on her ebbing life force, is a device borrowed from another Poe story, *The Oval Portrait*. Just as Roger Corman would incorporate *Hop-Frog* into his 1963 film *The Masque of the Red Death*, Epstein found it necessary to bulk up the action with nods to other Poe motifs. We glimpse, for example, a portrait marked 'Ligeia Lady Usher 1717', together with a swinging clock pendulum and a black cat nestled between the feet of a suit of armour. Though superficially faithful to Poe, Epstein was nevertheless intent on repurposing the story for his own ends. Usher's friend, for example, is no longer a contemporary but a whiskery dotard who has to resort to eye glasses and ear trumpets, suggesting that his perceptions may be just as out-of-whack as Usher's. More significantly, Epstein dispenses with Poe's whiff of incest by turning Madeline into Usher's wife rather than his sister. Yet this adjustment lends weight to Epstein's portrayal of Madeline as an objectified cipher, prey to the frankly sadistic whims of a husband who feels compelled, no matter what, to keep on objectifying her via his canvas.

*portraits of his ailing wife Madeline – despite obvious indications that the process is draining her of life. When she dies and is interred in the family vault, Roderick becomes convinced that she's actually still alive...*

In addition to Debucourt, Epstein cast Marguerite Gance (wife of his fellow Impressionist, Abel Gance) as Madeline; he then shot *La Chute de la maison Usher* at the Studios d'Epinay in Île-de-France, venturing to Brittany and the foggy marshlands of the Sologne, south-east of Blois, for some truly haunting location work. As the elderly traveller contemplates a sign

The poetic imagery used to underscore this is as bizarre as it is memorable. Standing beside Madeline as she poses is a strangely phallic pedestal decorated with a small forest of candles; drizzling white sperm, they flame into life even as she fades steadily away. Madeline finally swoons in a beautiful series of double exposures and is consigned to the family vault by a three-man funeral cortege, struggling in laborious slow motion between clumps of trees while those same candles are superimposed giant-size at either side of the frame. Also attending the interment are a bristling owl and, in slimy mockery of Roderick's sexual repression, a pair of copulating toads.

Though it stands well outside the parameters of commercial cinema, Epstein's film nevertheless provides several clues to the fact that he knew his horror pictures. Poe's story begins with the narrator's arrival at the Usher house, gloomily surveying "the bleak walls," "rank sedges" and "white trunks of decayed trees" that Epstein so atmospherically conjures up in the film. Yet Epstein adds a prologue in which the traveller stops for directions at a local inn. Its fearful occupants – complete with horrified intertitle exclamations of "Usher??!!" – are clearly borrowed from Murnau's *Nosferatu*, and before that, of course, Stoker's *Dracula*. Later, the equivocal family doctor has a bespectacled death's-head look recalling Lon Chaney's Erik in *The Phantom of the Opera*, while the Usher corridors pulsate with wind-agitated drapes very similar to the ones featured in Paul Leni's recently released *The Cat and the Canary*.

The agitation of those drapes is so constant it verges on the risible, though in the end they become just another feature of the fusillade of effects that forms the film's climax. Delving into Roderick's disintegrating mind, Epstein scrutinises the inner workings of the fateful clock in forensic detail; meanwhile Roderick's guitar strings snap of their own accord and a tree in the park is struck by lightning in a shower of sparks. Autumn leaves scurry away down the corridors, fanned onward by a rapidly oncoming camera. Stacked-up books tumble down and the suit of armour topples over in the rising tempest, gouts of flame rise up from the baronial fireplace and, as the revived Madeline approaches, Roderick utters the immortal line, "Nous l'avons mise vivante dans la tombe!" – We have put her living in the tomb!

At the height of the maelstrom we notice yet more intriguing peculiarities. The watchful owl, for example, is optically erased from the screen at the moment of impact, while a deliberately phoney starscape stands in for what Poe called "the entire orb of the satellite." Madeline's ordeal seems to have turned her hair black rather than white, and at the very end Epstein contradicts Poe a final time by allowing everyone, including Roderick and Madeline, to get out of the stricken building with no difficulty at all. Though anticlimactic, this act of authorial mercy rounds off an assemblage of eerie imagery that has few peers.

Epstein's assistant on *Usher* was the young Spaniard Luis Buñuel – though only early on, for the pair soon fell out and by 19 March Buñuel was starting production at the Studios de Billancourt on a short film he'd devised in conjunction with Salvador Dalí. The surrealists of 1920s Paris valued cinema for its potential to blur the boundaries between dream and reality, and in offering a practical demonstration of this *Un Chien andalou* (An Andalusian Dog) threw up shocking and horrific imagery that commercial filmmakers could never have countenanced.

Already, Germaine Dulac's 1927 film *La Coquille et le clergyman* (The Seashell and the Clergyman) had offered, among other seemingly irrational elements, a screen-filling view of Genica Athanasiou's naked breasts (shock) and a vision of Lucien Bataille's head splitting asunder (horror). But now Buñuel and Dalí went further, crafting an astounding series of provocations – a woman's eye bisected by a razor in close-up; a man's stigmata-pierced hand disgorging a horde of ants; the man wiping his mouth and thus erasing it (the woman's armpit hair magically takes its place); a pair of eyeless, decomposing donkeys draped over grand pianos; a severed hand being poked at on a Paris street; the man drooling blood as he fondles the woman's bare breasts and bottom; the man shooting his own doppelgänger to death... All in 16 minutes, and all demonstrating that the visceral outrages of the Paris Grand Guignol could pass seamlessly into the realm of surrealist dream logic.

Buñuel's controversial 1930 follow-up, *L'Age d'or* (The Golden Age), ended with a provocative vignette referencing "la plus bestiale des orgies" from the Marquis de Sade's *Les 120 journées de Sodome* (The 120 Days of Sodom). This second film was sponsored by the Vicomte de Noailles, who also backed Jean Cocteau's *Le Sang d'un poète* (The Blood of a Poet) the same year. In this 55-minute reverie Cocteau replaced the confrontational shock tactics of *Un Chien andalou* with a balletic, nearly weightless attempt "to avoid," as he put it, "the deliberate manifestations of the unconscious in favour of a kind of half-sleep through which I wandered as though in a labyrinth."[30]

In Cocteau's hands the erased mouth of Buñuel's film leaps from a portrait sketch to inhabit the artist's palm, then migrates to a statue that immediately starts talking. These classic images of the uncanny are joined by another – the mirror, made so familiar by the German fantasies of the silent era, which in this instance the artist hero plunges into as though it were a swimming pool. Admitted to the zone between dream and reality, he encounters a child with bells on who swarms across walls and ceilings, a snowball that kills, and a chaise longue that assembles its own reclining statue piece by piece. He finally shoots himself, in a copious gore effect that Cocteau uses twice, and is himself turned into a statue.

The impalpable flow of dreams and nightmares wasn't confined to the surrealists, nor did they have a monopoly on aristocratic sponsors. For, just as Cocteau and Buñuel turned to a Viscount for support, so the Danish director Carl Theodor Dreyer turned to a Baron. In 1927 he'd made *La Passion de Jeanne d'Arc* (The Passion of Joan of Arc) for the Société Générale des Films, an arrangement that

Enrique Riveros undergoes an early gore effect in *Le Sang d'un poète* (1930)

was terminated on the film's commercial failure the following year. Finance for Dreyer's next feature came from the 25-year-old Baron Nicolas de Gunzburg, with whom he set up a one-shot Paris production company called Film-Production Carl Dreyer. The Baron's one stipulation was that he should play the lead; all but three of the remaining actors were amateurs too.

These anomalous features were joined by others. Though in essence a silent film, *Vampyr* was produced around Courtempierre during the summer months of 1930, when the whole world was going crazy for talkies. And by the time it was given a belated release in May 1932, Bela Lugosi's epicene *Dracula* and Boris Karloff in *Frankenstein* had long since branded themselves on the public mind, ensuring that the miasmic strangeness of Dreyer's film was met with perplexity and outright hostility.

*Holidaying in Courtempierre, David Gray encounters an old man who mutters obscurely about an impending death. Unable to sleep, David wanders into an outhouse and sees strange visions, together with an imperious elderly lady and a shabby-genteel doctor. Moving on to a nearby château, David meets the old man again, who is shot dead almost instantly. Of the dead man's two daughters, the elder, Leone, is succumbing to a wasting disease...*

An opening title card points out that our protagonist is "a dreamer for whom the line between the real and the supernatural became blurred." The blurring of the real and the unreal, of life and death, will turn out to be the film's governing theme, and in the meantime this opening statement is blurry and non-specific in itself. Is David in this state of uncertainty from the outset or is it the upcoming sequence of events that are to compromise his vision? Is he, in short, the classic unreliable narrator?

Even his name is in question; in German prints he's referred to, for some reason, as Allan rather than David. As for the original screenplay, he's referred to there as Nicolas – suggesting, at the very least, a close kinship between the character and the actor playing him. To confuse matters further, the noble moniker of Nicolas de Gunzburg was dropped in the film's credits in favour of a pseudonym – Julian West. So a kind of dreamlike uncertainty is encoded in the film at its very core. Though he later decamped to New York to become a fashion editor at *Vogue*, De Gunzburg was at this time a prominent patron of the Ballets Russes, making it strangely appropriate that the film he financed plays out like an underwater ballet. The man himself drifts through the story like a somnambulist, observing an outbreak of vampirism in Courtempierre as if he's of the action yet somehow not in it. It therefore seems perfectly logical when his astral body gets loose in the film's latter stages. Maybe David, or Allan, was himself a phantom all along.

Everyone else moves through the all-pervading haze like inscrutable marionettes, their fragments of dialogue hard to make out and confined, in any case, to gnomic non-sequiturs. (Perhaps the strangest of these comes when David, mid-transfusion, says, "I'm losing blood." "Nonsense," replies the doctor from the next room. "Your blood's right here.") The creeping sense of dislocation is in place from the very moment David arrives at his riverside hotel. A scythe-bearing peasant sits placidly in a crudely fashioned ferry boat. A painting depicting the triumph of Death decorates David's bedroom, and when a strange babbling issues from outside, David's candlelit investigation reveals a horribly disfigured old man emerging from the attic.

(This character never reappears.) Thereafter, keys turn by themselves, silhouetted clods of earth leap backwards onto a gravedigger's spade, mounted baby skeletons decorate a dilapidated library, and a phantom band serenades a group of dancing shadows in an outhouse, only to be halted by an electrifying cry of "Silence!" from a white-haired old woman far below.

The cumulative effect is that of a dream on the edge of consciousness – not a fully fledged nightmare, but the strangling sensation of swimming up from the depths while not quite managing to surface. We get the vivid impression that, in crossing the river to get to his destination, David has slipped unknowingly into limbo. The oneiric haze perfected by Dreyer and cinematographer Rudolph Maté was laid down on the opening page of the script – "The landscape is bathed in a grey, dim twilight"[31] – and, as was the case in Epstein's *Usher*, it seems to impregnate the very film stock. Anaemic and impalpable, it parallels the ebbing life of the vampire's victim, particularly in a stunning shot, reminiscent of Fuseli's *The Nightmare*, in which the old lady hovers over the swooned heroine in a stretch of parkland outside the château.

*Vampyr*'s most famous set-pieces are three in number. First, the ailing Leone, infected with vampirism, suddenly stares at her uncomprehending sister with a shockingly feral intensity – a powerful, long-held moment which is a small tour de force for Sybille Schmitz. (Schmitz, incidentally, was one of the three professionals in the film; the others were Maurice Schutz and Albert Bras.) Second, David dreams his own death, looking out from the window in his coffin lid to see first a peg-legged policeman screwing it down, then, in an indelibly eerie shot, the vampire woman leaning in for a closer look. Finally, the doctor, who of course is the vampire's Renfield-like familiar, becomes trapped in a flour mill and is suffocated in a remorseless cascade of white powder. (Brutally, Dreyer keeps on cutting back to this terrible inundation, resulting in the scene being severely abbreviated for German audiences.) But the film is just as powerful in its quieter moments, some of which are so quiet they're virtually subliminal. When, for example, David is recovering from giving blood to Leone, it may, or may not, be the vampire's voice that can be heard crooning, "Follow me. Death is waiting..."

Roundly dismissed on its initial release (a rejection that precipitated a nervous breakdown for Dreyer), *Vampyr* would nevertheless exercise a powerful influence on other filmmakers. As early as 1934, a funeral sequence in the American film *The Crime of Dr Crespi*, together with a pygmy skeleton decorating the mad doctor's office, seem to have been drawn direct from Dreyer's film; later on *Vampyr* would be quoted on a regular basis in Italian horror films, in particular. In putting together the script with theatre director Christen Jul, Dreyer's own inspiration was Sheridan Le Fanu's 1872 anthology *In a Glass Darkly*, with the finished product containing stray fragments of the stories *Carmilla* (girls in a château falling prey to a female vampire) and *The Room in the Dragon Volant* (the hero's all-too-sentient premature burial). But Dreyer's real intent, it seems, was to translate, not the

## VAMPYR OU L'ÉTRANGE AVENTURE DE DAVID GRAY

*France 1930*
US: *Castle of Doom*
*Film-Production Carl Dreyer*
*83 minutes b/w*
*production began 1 April 1930*

............................................

Director of Photography: Rudolf Maté; Artistic Advisor: Hermann Warm; Editor: Tonka Taldy [uncredited]; Sound: Hans Bittmann; Dialogue Director / Sound Editor: Paul Falkenberg; Music: Wolfgang Zeller; Screenplay: Christen Jul, Carl Th Dreyer, freely based on the novel [sic] *In a Glass Darkly* by J Sheridan Le Fanu; Producer: Nicolas de Gunzburg [uncredited]; Director: Carl Th Dreyer

Julian West [Nicolas de Gunzburg] (David Gray) [German version: Allan Gray]; Maurice Schutz (the father); Rena Mandel (Gisèle); Sybille Schmitz (Léone); Jan Heronimko (the village doctor Marc); Henriette Gérard (the old woman in the graveyard [Marguerite Chopin]); Albert Bras (the old servant); N Babanini (his wife); Jane Mora (the nurse)

Although in many ways it was one of the worst films I have ever attended, there were some scenes in it that gripped with a brutal directness ... They have depth and a simplicity of style which is seldom achieved in the hurried world of the film studio. But, for all that, it was a peculiarly irritating picture. The scenario was so bad that the author had to excuse it by pretending it was a dream. *New York Times 31 July 1932*

At one of the first screenings of rushes we noticed that one of the takes was grey. We asked ourselves why, then we realised it was caused by a misplaced light shining on the lens. The film's producer and Rudolf Maté and I thought about the take in relation to the style we were seeking ... From then on, and for every shot, we projected a false light on the lens through a veil. *Carl Dreyer [interviewed by Michel Delahaye in Cahiers du Cinéma September 1965]*

Nicolas de Gunzburg (aka Julian West) experiences his own interment in *Vampyr* (1930)

book, but its title. Taking the eerily diffused light of the French countryside as his medium, he conjured from it an alluring paradox – a netherworld that is simultaneously luminous and impenetrably dark.

## SHADOWS OF THE PAST

The early 1930s was the halcyon period for Hollywood horror, with Tod Browning's *Dracula* and James Whale's *Frankenstein* both coming out in 1931 and siring a long line of Universal thrillers – Robert Florey's *Murders in the Rue Morgue*, Karl Freund's *The Mummy*, Whale's *The Old Dark House* and *The Invisible Man*, Edgar Ulmer's *The Black Cat* and more. On top of this, M-G-M offered such titles as *Freaks* and *The Mask of Fu Manchu*, Paramount had *Dr Jekyll and Mr Hyde* and *Island of Lost Souls*, Warners chipped in with *Doctor X* and *Mystery of the Wax Museum*, and RKO crafted jungle thrillers both small (*The Most Dangerous Game*) and colossal (*King Kong*). To say nothing of the slew of similar offerings from lesser studios.

Many of the films were stylistically indebted to their German antecedents of the 1920s, an indebtedness confirmed by the presence of many German refugees among their technical personnel. To take just two conspicuous examples, Karl Freund and Edgar Ulmer had worked together on the 1920 version of *Der Golem*, as cinematographer and design assistant respectively, while Universal's *Rue Morgue* film – directed by a Frenchman and photographed by Freund – was effectively *Caligari* with an ape instead of Conrad Veidt. Perhaps conscious of this migration, and maybe

Mirror-gazing serial killer with an actor's personality: Peter Lorre in *M* (1931)

feeling that Hollywood's new-found horror expertise couldn't be competed with anyway, filmmakers in Germany, and Europe generally, made few attempts at macabre subjects during this period.

In May 1930, however – just ahead of the Hollywood horror boom – *Caligari* director Robert Wiene was at work on his first sound film, *Der Andere* (The Other), in which Fritz Kortner is a distinguished lawyer whose other self consorts with the very people he condemns. The part had been played by Albert Bassermann in Max Mack's famous version of 1912; in the changed circumstances of 1930, Wiene's sponsors were

canny enough to have him make a French version simultaneously, in which Jean-Max was cast as *Le Procureur Hallers* (Prosecutor Hallers). That this strictly psychological riff on the time-honoured doppelgänger theme was a popular subject was reaffirmed in 1933 by an entirely separate Italian remake, Alessandro Blasetti's *Il caso Haller* (The Haller Case). Other durable motifs were on show in Erich Engels' *Geheimnis des blauen Zimmers* (Secret of the Blue Room), which started shooting at Halloween 1932 and was in theatres, with remarkable speed, by mid-December. Mixing 'old dark house' atmospherics with a classic 'locked room' mystery, this was picked up by Universal and as a result enjoyed no fewer than three American remakes between 1933 and 1944.

After Wiene's *Der Andere*, the split-personality motif reappeared in Fritz Lang's first sound film, *M*. This was made amid the violent political upheavals that marked the beginning of 1931; just a few months beforehand, the onset of the Depression, bringing with it bank failures, industrial collapse and mass unemployment, had seen a dramatic rise in support for Adolf Hitler's National Socialists. In this powderkeg atmosphere Lang and Thea von Harbou crafted a documentary-style portrait of the civic paranoia set in train by a rash of child murders, a portrait that would win the film rave reviews all around the world. The economy of the opening is remarkable – a trilby-hatted shadow falling across the Gothic script of a 'wanted' poster, a mother's unavailing cries of "Elsie," a child's ball rolling from under a bush, a discarded balloon bobbing against telegraph wires. The killer, meanwhile, is identifiable only by sound – by his ominous whistling of an air by Grieg or by such pronouncements as "What a pretty ball you have there."

With the Weimar serial killers Carl Grossmann and Fritz Haarmann referenced in the dialogue, few viewers could doubt that this was a story torn from the proverbial headlines, an impression underlined by the realistic street sets constructed at the Staaken facility in Spandau. Yet our first actual view of the killer stirs memories of the shadowy split personalities of the silent period. Cutting straight from a graphologist theorising that the killer's writing might "reveal an actor's personality," Lang suddenly shows us two images of the killer, one of them reflected in a mirror he's scrutinising himself in. Later, the killer – brilliantly played by the young Reinhardt actor Peter Lorre – is apprehended by a kangaroo court composed of the Berlin underworld and presided over by a grim-faced, leather-jacketed gangster (Gustav Gründgens). The killer's final breakdown is expressed in exactly the language of the doppelgängers so recently abdicated from German cinema. "It's there all the time," he gasps, "following me silently. It's me, pursuing myself … I want to escape, to escape from myself. But it's impossible: I have to obey it." In this way Lang mapped a deep-rooted German obsession onto the no-nonsense, up-to-the-minute genre of the police procedural.

Richard Oswald, meanwhile, was offering rather different echoes of the local industry's halcyon period – echoes, in fact, of his own achievements in the 1910s. In the summer of 1928 he had directed a new, and reportedly faithful, version of *Der Hund von Baskerville* (The Hound of the Baskervilles) for producer F W Kraemer. Then, going on release in September 1932, came a film recalling Oswald's 1919 hit *Unheimliche Geschichten*. Indeed, the collective title and two of the three source stories were the same, with Poe's *The Black Cat* and Stevenson's *The Suicide Club* flanking an all-new version of Poe's *The System of Dr Tarr and Prof Fether*. The choice of this new tale was possibly motivated by the French feature version of the same story, *L'Étrange fiancée* (The Strange Fiancée), that Georges Pallu had made just a couple of years earlier. That may have been one inspiration; another, perhaps, was the story's 'the lunatics have taken over the asylum' motif, a timely one given the inexorable rise of the Nazis.

> When an inventor murders his young wife, reporter Frank Briggs is around to hear the screams. Unsatisfied by his tense interview with the inventor, Briggs gets the police involved and, on discovery of the wife's walled-up corpse, a manhunt begins. Briggs himself pursues the killer to a waxworks museum and then to a lunatic asylum. After another six months' search, Frank finds that the killer has reinvented himself as the leader of a suicide cult.

With Paul Wegener as his star, Oswald built around this formidable figure a story structure that remains quite unusual in the field of horror portmanteaux – the 'uncanny tales' aren't compartmentalised but instead become part of a free-flowing narrative in which Wegener (billed only as 'Der Mörder') is pursued and eventually outwitted by a smoothie newshound played by Harald Paulsen. In a smart

## UNHEIMLICHE GESCHICHTEN

Germany 1932
US: *Ghastly Tales* / *The Living Dead*
Richard Oswald-Film / Roto-GP-Films
89 minutes b/w
censor date 24 August 1932

. . . . . . . . . . . . . . . . . . . . . . . . . . . . .

Director of Photography: Heinrich Gärtner; Art Directors: Franz Schroedter and [uncredited] Walter Reimann; Editors: Max Brenner, Friedel Buckow [both uncredited]; Sound: Fritz Seeger; Music: Rolf Marbot, Bert Reisfeld [both uncredited]; Make-up: Adolf and Emma Doelle [uncredited]; Screenplay: Heinz Goldberg, Eugen Szatmári, based on stories by Edgar Allan Poe and Robert Louis Stevenson; Producers: Richard Oswald, Gabriel Pascal [both uncredited]; Director: Richard Oswald

Paul Wegener (the killer); Harald Paulsen (Frank Briggs); Eugen Klöpfer ('chief physician'); Roma Bahn (killer's wife); Gretl Berndt (singing woman in asylum); Blandine Ebinger (young woman in suicide club); Ilse Fürstenberg (woman in asylum); Maria Koppenhöfer ('Her Highness'); Gerhard Bienert (police superintendent); Karl-Heinz Charrell (asylum porter); Paul Henckels (hospital doctor); Erwin Kalser (asylum orator); uncredited: Hans Behall (bankrupt); Fred Goebel (second editor); John Gottowt (museum curator); Ferdinand Hart (Jon); Heinrich Heilinger (Baptist); Victor de Kowa (young man in suicide club); Karl Meinhard, Michael von Newlinski (players); Mary Parker (Briggs' fiancée); Natascha Silvia (girl); Franz Stein ('spinning top' inmate)

**[This] Film is the occasion of a comeback by Richard Oswald … [who] has succeeded in creating an effectively gruesome picture … Effect is intensified by excellent acting. Sound and photography excellent. Settings of Walter Reimann and Franz Schroedter are first rate. A film which resembles *Caligari* and for a long time to come will enjoy success.** *Variety 27 September 1932*

**At one point my father received the title of Staatsschauspieler, roughly State Actor, an honour that included a life-sized bust of Goebbels' head. My father promptly placed this gold-painted work of art in the downstairs lavatory, and many a guest was startled on entering the room.** *Peter Wegener [reprinted in Nicolella / Soister, Many Selves: The Horror and Fantasy Films of Paul Wegener, 2012]*

Paul Wegener as the combined wife killer, asylum director and cult leader of *Unheimliche Geschichten* (1932)

in-joke, Paulsen's character, Frank Briggs, may well have been named in reference to the 'Frank Braun' he'd played in Oswald's talkie remake of *Alraune*. Wegener, of course, was a monumental reminder of the silent era, and for maximum nostalgia John Gottowt was cast opposite him as a museum curator, the same role he'd played for Paul Leni in *Das Wachsfigurenkabinett*. Gottowt had also appeared in *Nosferatu* and *Genuine*, winding right back to his role as satanic tempter to Wegener's *Student von Prag* in 1913.

Gottowt's museum is lined, not just with wax figures, but with robots, all of them clearly played by actors. Also on display is a dummy ape with conspicuously projectile nipples and an effigy of Fritz Haarmann, the homosexual serial killer who had been executed in Hanover as recently as April 1925 and who was previously alluded to in *M*. Wegener's deranged inventor stumbles into the museum in flight from the police, after a rather hurried précis of *The Black Cat* in which, betraying the teething troubles of sound pictures, an unusual amount of extraneous noise from the crew can be heard. Even so, the yowling of the imprisoned cat and discovery of Wegener's walled-up, white-faced wife are powerfully done, and in the museum a tremendous dust-up ensues between Wegener and Paulsen, with Walter Reimann (formerly co-designer of *Caligari*) adding an outré touch of his own by sending a wire-borne stuffed crocodile sailing over the melée.

There follows a highly effective retelling of Poe's lunatic asylum story, with terrific shots of the incarcerated staff members pleading to be let out and a splendid gallery of eccentrics entertaining the perplexed Paulsen at dinner. Paulsen's dawning realisation, as a small ensemble serenades the twitching diners with Strauss' *Blue Danube* waltz, is played for something very close to the Absurdist comedy Poe intended. This section also contains an intriguing forecast of another world war, with a female inmate obsessively repeating, "They're coming! The planes! They're dropping bombs! Hurry to the basement!" Finally, a rather dull rendition of *The Suicide Club* sees Wegener poised between Dr Mabuse and a James Bond villain; as metal rings leap out to restrain Paulsen in his Art Deco chair, one half expects Wegener to say, "No, Mr Briggs, I expect you to die." With Wegener as a murderous lunatic who has reinvented himself as the slick-haired mastermind of a society that persuades people to kill themselves, the story offers a further presentiment of Nazi domination. In the end, of course, Wegener is hoist by his own petard, mugs for all he's worth in a series of remarkable close-ups, and in due course is added to the dummies in Gottowt's Chamber of Horrors.

A slightly lumpen but otherwise beguiling attempt to revive an outmoded genre, *Unheimliche Geschichten* was described by *Variety*'s local correspondent as "trash, but very well-done trash which promises to become a world success."[32] Unsurprisingly, this prediction proved unfounded. In December 1940, when the film finally arrived in New York as *The Living Dead*, critic Bosley Crowther dismissed it as "a nightmare reminder of the old pre-Nazi macabre school of German films, which did all right by such things as *M* but apparently had its bad moments, too."[33] That the film was indeed a relic, representing a long-lost, pre-Nazi Germany, was underlined by the grim fact that it was John Gottowt's last screen credit. As a Jew he had been banned from acting by the Nazis; in August 1942 he would be murdered by the SS.

Back in November 1931, a little before Wegener and Gottowt got back together for *Unheimliche Geschichten*, another horror veteran, Conrad Veidt, found himself playing an ambiguous personage of very recent vintage in Adolf Trotz's *Rasputin, Dämon der Frauen* (Rasputin, Demon with Women). The Rasputin story had already been filmed on several occasions, three times in Germany alone, and would later provide grandstanding showcases for such actors as Lionel Barrymore, Harry Baur, Pierre Brasseur, Edmund Purdom, Christopher Lee, Gert Fröbe and Tom Baker. In the meantime, Veidt's characteristically mesmeric version was reputedly ordered destroyed by Hitler's propaganda minister, Joseph Goebbels, in April 1933, the same month in which Veidt sensibly decided to move to England. Happily, like *Nosferatu*, the film survived.

## ANOTHER STUDENT, ANOTHER STRANGER

Adolf Hitler had been appointed Germany's Chancellor at the end of January 1933, enabling Goebbels to take over the Reichsfilmstelle (National Film Agency), carefully policing the content of German films on the twin principles of devotion to the Fatherland and unthinking obeisance to charismatic leaders. In addition, a process of Arisierung (Aryanisation) was applied to the film industry as to all other walks of life. In this sterile atmosphere of propagandist airbrushing there was no room for the unheimlich gloom and doom of the previous decade, given that the chief message to be got across was one of hearty Aryan optimism, that all was unquestionably right with the National Socialist world.

Yet there were very occasional exceptions, among them an anodyne 1935 remake of the Murnau picture *Schloß Vogelöd* and yet another go, in 1936, at that old standby *Der Hund von Baskerville*, a film that would reportedly be found in Hitler's bunker after his suicide. A little later came Heinz Hilpert's *Die unheimlichen Wünsche* (The Unholy Wishes, 1939), a dressy adaptation of *Le Peau de chagrin* that supplemented Balzac's 'be careful what you wish for' parable with a happy ending. More significantly, there were two films that referred back to eerie classics directed in the Weimar period by Henrik Galeen and Fritz Lang.

Shot in the summer of 1935, a third version of *Der Student von Prag* was produced by Cine-Allianz Tonfilm but with no input from the company's newly marginalised founders, Arnold Pressburger and Gregor Rabinovitch, both of whom were Jewish. For much of the early going this new reading threatens to turn into a Nazi operetta, with an overdose of student roistering and plenty of warbling from Balduin's sweetheart, who is now an opera star rather than a Countess. (She's played by the formidable Dorothea Wieck, which is a bonus.) Then Scapinelli arrives – or rather Dr Carpis, as he's now called – and with him comes a rationalisation of the plot that, paradoxically, renders it nonsensical. "In olden days

Adolf Wohlbrück made it onto the cover of *Illustrierter Film-Kurier* in the third version of *Der Student von Prag* (1935)

the Devil purchased the poor student's soul," Carpis explains, adding conceitedly that that isn't the case any more. Though played by Conrad Veidt lookalike Theodor Loos, complete with a devilish widow's peak and constant spooky underlighting, this tempter is clearly mortal – he even has unrequited feelings for the beautiful diva – and how on earth he (a) imprisons the "sentimental dreamer" that is Balduin's better self in a mirror and (b) confers on Balduin the gift of winning at cards is never explained.

That Balduin's doppelgänger should be imprisoned rather than liberated (no literal stepping out of the mirror here) is an interesting twist given the repressive circumstances in which the film was made. Even so, director Arthur Robison – who had been responsible 12 years previously for *Schatten* – succeeds in reclaiming some of the hallucinatory grandeur of the 1926 film when Balduin starts to imagine his embodied conscience popping up at inopportune moments, with a cold, quiet eeriness attaching to the scenes in which Balduin recoils from his phantom double. The excellent

sets are by *Caligari* veteran Hermann Warm, who also worked on the 1926 version. But much of the film's success is down to Adolf Wohlbrück, who descends into hysteria in fine style prior to a moving exit line, murmuring "There he is again: the sentimental dreamer" while looking in the shattered mirror.

Sadly, Robison died shortly before the film was released. In his *Spectator* review Graham Greene described him as "one of the few directors who could mark a picture with his own personality," while calling the film itself "dull" – "a curiosity, a relic of the classical German film of silent days."[34] Adolf Wohlbrück left Germany soon afterwards, sensibly changing his name to Anton Walbrook, and in 1948 he essayed a very Balduin-type role in the exceptional British ghost story *The Queen of Spades*.

That the all-new student of Prague recalled the mysticism of silent cinema was obvious, given the film's remake status. *Fährmann Maria* (Ferryman Maria) went into release a month later, in January 1936, yet its throwback credentials will only have been spotted by filmgoers who remembered the conflict between love and a very literal Death in Lang's 15-year-old *Der müde Tod*. It was made by Frank Wysbar, who had upset the Nazi regime in only his second film as director, the insufficiently 'uplifting' *Anna und Elisabeth*, in which Dorothea Wieck and Hertha Thiele played a disabled aristocrat and a peasant faith healer respectively. Undaunted, Wysbar ramped up the doom-laden mysticism yet further when setting up his cameras on the Lüneburg Heath, near Hamburg, in mid-August 1935. In a canny bit of casting, he'd given the role of Maria to Sybille Schmitz, who a few years earlier had been in Dreyer's *Vampyr* – a film Wysbar also echoed in his atmospheric use of lonely waterways, shadowed by Death.

*An elderly ferryman drops dead while transporting a black-clad stranger from one side of the river to the other, and word soon gets round that the ferry has a curse on it. The young Maria is new to the area, however, and happily takes on the job. On her first night she rescues a traumatised young man from*

## FÄHRMANN MARIA

Germany 1935
US: *Death and the Maiden*
*Die Terra presents a Pallas Film*
85 minutes b/w
production began 15 August 1935
· · · · · · · · · · · · · · · · · · · · · · · · · · · · ·
Director of Photography: Franz Weihmayr;
Art Directors: Bruno Lutz and [uncredited]
Fritz Maurischat; Editor: Lena Neumann
[uncredited]; Sound: Hans Grimm

[uncredited]; Music: Herbert Windt;
Screenplay: Hans-Jürgen Nierentz, Frank
Wysbar; Producer-Director: Frank Wysbar

Sybille Schmitz (Maria); Aribert Mog (the man
from the other shore); Peter Voss (the stranger);
Carl de Vogt (the minstrel); Karl Platen (the
old ferryman); Gerhard Bienert (the laird);
Eduard Wenck (the mayor); uncredited: Ernst
Stimmel (schoolteacher)

**[Franz Weihmayr] has created marvellous chiaroscuro images brimming with atmosphere. The picture is a triumph of photography, so artistic and so powerful that the actors are made to look like phantoms ... At times words and sound effects are given undue emphasis, placing a heavy load on the players ... [while] both realism and logic have a tendency of compromising the fantastical narrative.** *Berliner Volkszeitung* 8 February 1936

*Fährmann Maria ... is symbolical of the triumph (sometimes) of faith over desperation ... The brunette Sybille Schmitz of Vienna manages to put considerable conviction into the difficult character of Maria, despite her predilection for more sophisticated roles ... Based on an ancient legend, the simple story is developed so deliberately that it seems to drag occasionally, but spectators must not expect Hollywood tempo in screen efforts of this nature.* New York Times 24 December 1938

*pursuing horsemen. Her passenger the following evening is the black-clad stranger...*

David Stewart Hull, one of the earliest historians of Third Reich cinema, was well aware of stating the obvious when he pointed out that *Fährmann Maria* "has nothing in common with any [other] films of the National Socialist epoch." He even went so far as to call it "one of the high points of the German

"I'm a stranger here. I have no home."
Sybille Schmitz as *Fährmann Maria* (1935)

sound cinema."[35] Wysbar's film is perhaps too modestly conceived to support such a high claim, but it still casts an extraordinary spell. It creates a brooding atmosphere of impending disaster in its first few minutes and, except for a rather indulgently developed romance in its middle section, sustains this fatalistic mood right to the end. It also boasts excellent performances from Sybille Schmitz and, as her implacable passenger, Peter Voss.

The key to Wysbar's achievement is his use, in concert with cinematographer Franz Weihmayr, of his chief location. According to Hull, Wysbar was familiar with the Lüneburg Heath having been there in 1934 to start shooting an aborted film called *Der Werwolf*. Here, the heath's ghostly environs become the film's fourth major character, alongside Maria, the fugitive young man she tends, and the baleful figure billed only as 'der Fremde' (the stranger). This stranger is carefully situated within the landscape right from the beginning. In answer to the nocturnal summons of a bell on the opposite bank, the old ferryman casts off on his clumsy conveyance – the ferry is of the arduous rope-and-pulley variety – and squints enquiringly at the trees on the other side for some sign of his prospective passenger. Only at the last minute does the stranger become visible, stepping forward as if disgorged from a dark copse of trees.

Wysbar balances ominous views of the landscape with daytime shots of natural beauty – dewy flowers, floating blossom, waving corn, sparkling waters – and at the very end he comes up with maybe the only moment in the whole film that pleased Goebbels, when the young man surveys the countryside, newly purged of Death, and beamingly says, "Die Heimat!" (the motherland). Yet so strongly imagined are Wysbar's nocturnal scenes that the primeval gloom lingers when the Aryan uplift is long forgotten.

In a place and period when female characters were relegated to obedient homemakers and helpmeets, Sybille Schmitz's dark-eyed Maria is an anomaly – an independent woman, with no family ties, who calmly announces to the Mayor that "I'm a stranger here. I have no home." So she too is an interloper and therefore equipped to deal on a roughly equal footing with the Death figure on the other bank. The latter is determined to claim the young man at any cost, and the contest involves an echo of *Nosferatu* when Maria sprawls in the church, subsumed by the shadow of the cross, and makes a selfless appeal. "Dear Lord," she pleads. "Save him. Take me instead." This comes after a thrilling section in which the stranger accompanies her to the village dance, with all the locals, crouched at their trestle tables, recoiling from the stranger's sweeping gaze; anxious to distract him from his mission, Maria persuades him to partner her in a swirling Totentanz.

The film is set quite deliberately in a kind of timeless limbo, with Wysbar confusing the viewer by dressing Maria in a vaguely Elizabethan gown of watered silk for the romantic scenes while giving the stranger a caped Napoleonic frock coat on his first appearance. Later, however, he discards the frock coat and awaits Maria in martial pose, arms akimbo, while wearing a belted black tunic and riding boots. His resemblance to a Nazi storm trooper couldn't be clearer. The horsemen that pursued the boy earlier are similarly attired, and their supernatural role as Death's outriders goes hand in hand with a more earthbound reading of them as Fascist agents hunting down a young dissident. Of course, in Wysbar's nifty little allegory Fascist agents and Death's outriders are one and the same anyway. One wonders how he thought he'd ever get away with it.

As it turned out, Goebbels waved the film through over the panicked misgivings of his advisory panel, presumably so as not to give it the unwarranted exposure a ban would entail. And perhaps, ten years later, Wysbar felt a twinge of schadenfreude when his main location, the Lüneburg Heath, became the site of the German forces' unconditional surrender at the end of World War II. By then he'd long since fled to the USA, where in August 1945 – as Frank 'Wisbar' – he concocted a studio-bound, but still extremely eerie, reimagining of *Fährmann Maria* for the Poverty Row studio PRC. The title was *Strangler of the Swamp* and the emphasis was radically altered, with the emblematic Death figure changed to a revenge-driven ghost. Ironically, in Rosemary LaPlanche the film boasted a former Miss America who was much more Aryan-looking than the dark and angular Sybille Schmitz – though by that time Goebbels was in no position to care one way or the other.

## HISTORY REPEATING

Frank Wysbar's departure for America was typical of the severe haemorrhaging of talent suffered by the German industry during the Nazi era, though there were a number of other distinguished names who elected to stay put.

As early as September 1933 Werner Krauss – Dr Caligari himself – was given a dramatic indication of what the latter choice might mean on an international level. Having recently become vice-president of the Reichstheaterkammer, he ventured into London's West End to star in Gerhart Hauptmann's *Before Sunset*. "Hardly had the curtain risen before the Shaftesbury [Theatre] was in uproar, leaflets showering, stink-bombs bursting,"[36] recalled theatre historian J C Trewin. Krauss nevertheless became a Staatsschauspieler (Actor of the State) the following year, eventually consenting to play multiple anti-semitic roles in Veit Harlan's notorious 1940 film *Jud Süß* (Jew Süss). As a result, history repeated itself post-war, when his December 1950 appearance in Ibsen's *John Gabriel Borkman* at Berlin's Theater am Kurfürstendamm involved punch-ups in the auditorium and street demonstrators being subdued by water cannon.

The fate of Caligari's hapless minion, Conrad Veidt, was very different. Settling in Hampstead, he became one of Britain's most popular stars, first under the patronage of Michael Balcon and later Alexander Korda. His mastery of weird roles was by no means forgotten; in April 1938, for example, he visited France to star in Jean Dréville's *Le Joueur d'échecs* (The Chess Player), portraying the 18th century robot inventor 'Baron' von Kempelen. "In the hands of Mr Conrad Veidt," observed the *New Statesman*, "Kempelen is a bizarre character who seems to have stepped out of the silent world of *Dr Caligari* and *The Student of Prague*."[37] And the following year Veidt headlined Korda's Technicolor super-production *The Thief of Bagdad*, in which his hypnotic Grand Vizier gave a very good indication of what his unrealised Count Dracula might have been like. There followed a second Hollywood stint, yielding such deluxe titles as *A Woman's Face* and *Casablanca*, prior to his early death, aged 50, in April 1943.

Dréville's *Le Joueur d'échecs* was a remake of a Raymond Bernard film dating back to 1926. Both versions were essentially glamorous costume pictures with a few weird asides provided by the titular, chess-playing robot, typifying France's cautious attitude to fantastic subjects. For, with the exception of Epstein's *Usher* and various André de Lorde projects, the country's horror output in the 1920s and '30s was slim.

Pierre Marodon had made the Maeterlinck adaptation *Les Morts parlent* (The Dead Speak) as far back as 1920, following it in 1921 with the 12-part serial *Le Château des fantômes* (The Château of Ghosts). A few years later cinema pioneer Alfred Machin made *Le Manoir de la peur* (The Mansion of Fear), detailing a Provençal crime wave and reserving a major role for his pet chimpanzee, Augustus, while in 1927 Henri Desfontaines, prime Poe purveyor of the 1910s, made a film version of Arthur Bernède's novel *Belphégor*, a lurid crime story involving a supposed ghost in the Louvre. By 1933 Maurice Champreux, son-in-law of the late Louis Feuillade, was remounting an old

Feuillade-Bernède subject as a talkie, *Judex 34*, echoing another Feuillade resurrection that had been made two years earlier, the Paul Fejos film *Fantômas*. Yet another recycling surfaced in 1937. Fedor Ozep's *La Dame de pique* (The Queen of Spades), based on a Pushkin story already filmed in Russia and twice in Germany, boasts a hurtling-to-camera vision of veteran actress Marguerite Moreno, as a ghostly 19th century Countess who knew the secret of winning at cards, but otherwise has about 75 per cent less supernatural content than the classic British version of 1948.

Another director signing his name to a couple of 1930s reimaginings of silent films was Julien Duvivier. One of the great stylists of the period, Duvivier had evinced an interest in horror subjects as early as 1922, when a two-reeler called *Le Logis de l'horreur* (The House of Horror) involved a honeymooning couple being cursed on the Riviera by a black-clad old lady and then delivered to a castle tenanted by a homicidal maniac. By 1935 he was at the Barrandov Studios in Prague for a Czech co-production called *Golem*, which – with the ancient Rabbi Loew deceased and his place taken by the callow Rabbi Jacob – functions as a loose sequel to the famous German film of 1920. The main figure is the crazed Emperor Rudolf II (ripely played by Duvivier's

Ferdinand Hart as the granite-faced title character of *Le Golem* (1935)

regular collaborator, Harry Baur), over whom hovers a charming threat voiced by the young Rabbi – that the immobilised Golem will revive in order to "give your gold to the poor and your bodies to the beasts."

Duvivier was obviously intoxicated by the extensive resources at his disposal, for *Le Golem*, as it was known in France, is a historical blockbuster of impressive breadth and grandeur. The convoluted court intrigues aren't unduly engaging, however, and interest is eked out initially by some torture in the stews, a humanoid mandrake root having a bird's blood drizzled onto it when Rudolf inspects the work of multiple alchemists, and a splendid scene in which the desolate Emperor confides his insecurities to the massive, and impassive, Golem.

Yet, when the statue is finally activated, the film too sparks into life, and in grand style, with a final reel of palace-collapsing mayhem that bears the stamp of *King Kong*. Ferdinand Hart's Golem is little more than a robot but he's truly impressive when his eyes suddenly light up and his massive chest takes reviving breaths. Liberating the Jewish underdogs, he treads on one courtier's head with his Karloff boots and calmly defenestrates another. (The latter plunges to a courtyard below where he's promptly devoured by a horde of uncaged lions.) It's tough, too, not to sympathise with the Golem when the Rabbi summarily disposes of him just moments after he's done his civic-destruction stuff; his now-tenantless Dracula cloak collapses in a heap, prefiguring many a subsequent vampire film.

After *Golem*, Duvivier made the classic proto-noir *Pepé le moko*, which reached French audiences in January 1937 and became a crucial title, alongside such films as Jean Renoir's *La Grande illusion* and Marcel Carné's *Le Jour se lève*, in the new French vein of poetic realism. Taking the same oxymoronic approach – a studio-constructed reality with symbolist underpinnings – to a story with pronounced fantastic elements, Duvivier turned in May 1939 to an old Selma Lagerlöf novel, *Körkarlen*, already brilliantly filmed as a silent by Victor Sjöström and, in Duvivier's hands, becoming *La Charrette fantôme* (The Phantom Carriage). Revolving around a Salvation Army soup kitchen, this has terrific performances from fatalistic vagrants Pierre Fresnay and Louis Jouvet, together with ravishing photography by Jules Krüger and striking optical effects co-ordinated by none other than Jean Epstein. Yet, try as one might to be gripped by the travails of an ailing social worker played by the luminous Micheline Francey, the action drags and only the scattered supernatural elements hold the attention.

These are of an extremely high standard, however, starting with an old lady (Mme Lherbay) who is bedevilled by the phantom grating of "a noisy cart" and eventually encounters the conveyance itself in a snowy wasteland. Jouvet subsequently meets his end, in a tour de force sequence, on snow-covered rooftops; the fact that he dies at the very moment New Year's Day arrives ensures that he will be the driver of the fateful carriage for the next 12 months. Jouvet, a titan of French theatre whose gallows countenance perfectly suits this mournful embodiment of the Grim Reaper, finally catches up with Fresnay's alcoholic semi-lunatic in a desolate graveyard. "So," he murmurs, "it's *you* I have to collect..." The funereal atmosphere of these scenes, brilliantly achieved, is compromised only by the warblings of a heavenly choir.

While Duvivier was making *La Charrette fantôme*, the outbreak of another world war was looking inevitable. Abel Gance, director in 1918 of arguably the world's first pacifist feature film, *J'Accuse* (I Accuse), had been far-sighted enough to make another film of the same name in 1937. The original version, released in April 1919, had culminated with a scene of overwhelming emotional impact

A memorial statue stirs eerily into life during the shattering climax of *J'Accuse* (1937)

– a maddened veteran, recounting his vision of the war dead arising to verify "if their sacrifice and their death had been to any purpose." To realise this "innombrable troupeau" (numberless horde), swarming down rustic lanes and beckoning at the windows of their loved ones, Gance cast 2000 soldiers who were on eight-day passes from Verdun. "They played the dead knowing that in all probability they'd be dead themselves before long," Gance recalled. "Within a few weeks of their return, 80 per cent had been killed."[38]

Among Gance's previous credits were a few titles in which he'd used macabre imagery to far less sombre ends. His earliest efforts included a couple of vehicles for the famous actor Édouard de Max, both in 1912 – *Une vengeance d'Edgar Poë* (Edgar Poe's Revenge), directed by Gérard Bourgeois and written by Gance, and a miniature Gance Grand Guignol called *Le Masque d'horreur* (The Mask of Horror), in which Max played a deranged sculptor. After the first *J'Accuse*, and as a kind of battery-charging divertissement

between his massive productions of *La Roue* (The Wheel) and *Napoléon*, Gance made a two-reel horror-comedy in 1923 for the dapper comic star Max Linder. Theoretically, *Au Secours!* (Help!) was just another entry in the already well-worn 'comedians plus ghosts' sub-genre. But Harold Lloyd, in *Haunted Spooks*, or Buster Keaton, in *The Haunted House*, hadn't been faced with Gance's playfully bizarre camera experimentation, nor had they descended into weeping hysteria to the borderline-disturbing degree Linder does here.

By 1937 Gance was well aware of another impending disaster, prompting him, in his new version of *J'Accuse*, to focus on a war veteran who goes mad when his pacifist inventions are diverted to military ends. Desperate to convince mankind of its folly, he repairs to the national cemetery at Douaumont and addresses "my 12 million comrades killed in the war, you who were ignored and trampled on for 20 years. Arise, all of you! The living are going to war once again."

The long-drawn sequence that climaxes the film, for which the phrase 'tour de force' seems inadequate, is a hair-raising melange of withering flowers, gathering storms, pounding seas, fleeing citizens, and memorial statues that come eerily to life. Skull-faced aviators in bi-planes are seen in the skies, while below, in a series of nightmarish superimpositions, the dead rise from their graves. This time, Gance turned to members of the Union des Gueules Cassées (Union of Broken Mugs), genuine war veterans whose shattered faces form the vanguard of this spectral army. The result is a phantasmagoria more horrific, and moving, than anything in a bona-fide horror film of the period, and it's given maximum impact by Victor Francen's truly stupendous performance. "Fill your eyes with this horror," he shrieks, "and the weapons will fall from your hands."

The call went unheeded, of course. Germany invaded Poland on 1 September 1939 and Britain and France declared war two days later.

## ESCAPE INTO FANTASY

On the fall of France in mid-June 1940, Marshal Philippe Pétain, 84-year-old hero of the Great War and newly invested Chief of State, relocated the government to Vichy while Paris became part of a Nazi-occupied zone. As of November 1942 that zone was extended to the entire country, with Pétain's regime becoming little more than a tool of the Germans; the liberation of Paris, and expulsion of Pétain, followed in August 1944.

In these circumstances many local filmmakers, mindful of the German censors' constant vigilance, turned to the neglected field of French fantastique, on the principle that adhering to strict realism was by now too risky a proposition. The veteran director Marcel L'Herbier led the way with the whimsical confusions of dream and reality featured in the not especially popular *La Nuit fantastique* (The Fantastic Night, 1942), but the supremely elegant film that set the seal on this new approach did so, at least in part, by virtue of its massive success. Released in December 1942, Marcel Carné's *Les Visiteurs du soir* (The Night Visitors), a 15th century fairy tale in which Satan intervenes when two of his agents become entangled in human affairs, provided an excellent smokescreen for anti-Nazi sentiment; tellingly, the Devil (brilliantly played by Jules Berry) proves incapable of diverting the path of true love. Carné insisted that the film's message of resistance was unintentional, but audiences knew better – and their Nazi overseers were put off the scent, in any case, by Carné's mythic setting.

The Devil also appeared, albeit in a very different guise, in a film directed by Maurice Tourneur, who 30 years earlier had made a couple of France's earliest Grand Guignol adaptations. The Faustian fable *La Main du diable* (The Devil's Hand) started shooting on Friday 21 August 1942 – coincidentally the very same day that Tourneur's son Jacques completed production on *Cat People* in Hollywood. That a picture charting a deal with the Devil should be produced by Continental Films, the French company established during the Occupation by Joseph Goebbels, makes Tourneur's film an unusually poignant treatment of the Faust story. Continental's German overseer, Alfred Greven, presumably turned a blind eye to the implications, just as he ignored the fact that Tourneur's screenwriter, Jean-Paul Le Chanois, was (a) a member of the Resistance and (b) Jewish.

*At the Hôtel de l'Abbaye, a mountain hostelry filled with boisterous trippers, a nervous man wearing a black glove on one hand explains that he was once an artist, getting nowhere by painting dogs and vegetables yet desperate to impress his girlfriend Irène. So when offered a talismanic severed hand, guaranteed to bring wealth and prestige, he agreed to pay the asking price (one sou), unaware that the final cost would be infinitely higher.*

Loosely derived from a 19th century story by Gérard de Nerval, *La Main du diable* begins with an agreeably sinister flourish – a huge, taloned hand swiping the title card from the screen. Then a mysterious stranger arrives, rather like the title character in James Whale's *The Invisible Man*, at a remote inn nestled in a mist-wreathed valley. The back-story provided for failed artist Roland Brissot is studded with sinister little foreshadowings, among them the fact that his high-maintenance sweetheart works in a glove shop; deciding to paint a pair of gloves, he assures her that "Each finger will appear animated."

But Tourneur only shifts into a darker mode when Brissot encounters an agitated restaurateur, Mélisse (Noël Roquevert), who takes him to an upper room and reveals the grisly, five-fingered talisman that will assure Brissot of worldly success. As he does so, a human silhouette emerges from the restaurant's shadowy stairwell, anxiously crying out "Ne l'acheter pas!" (Don't buy it!). Armand Thirard's chiaroscuro lighting and several further wails of "Ne l'acheter pas!" give this section a queasy atmosphere akin to the obscure hotel gibberings of Dreyer's *Vampyr*. Mélisse, having gone into motor-mouthed overdrive in his desperation to clinch the sale, screams in agony when the exchange is effected; in an unusually gruesome touch, relinquishing the talisman causes him to lose his own left hand.

Brissot, it transpires, is just the latest custodian of a hand that belonged in life to the mediaeval monk Maximus Léo, and in Tourneur's ultimate tour de force he meets its six previous owners at a Monte Carlo carnival. They include a musketeer, a boxer, an illusionist, a surgeon, a juggler and a chef (the last is Mélisse, of course); all are weirdly masked (as pigs, pharaohs, lions, skulls etc) and all are conspicuously hook-handed. The rueful reminiscences they share with Brissot are staged with dazzling economy and include a shadow-play decapitation.

Equally chilling is the film's Devil figure, a snickering, bowler-hatted civil servant who could just as easily be a representative of the collaborationist Vichy government as an emissary of Hell. Played by the actor-playwright Palau and described as "a sort of provincial notary ... plump, with a head like a sugar-loaf," he's framed at one point underneath a huge, cartoon-like rendition of Goya's 'Satan Devouring His Son'. In the end he insists on repayment of a six-million-franc debt and is only seen off by the climactic resurrection of Maximus Léo himself.

Amid the gathering darkness, the film has quite a lot of incidental fun at the expense of contemporary art and its vacuous hangers-on; it also enjoys a deluxe

Pierre Fresnay
painting with
another man's hand
in *La Main
du diable* (1942)

cast headed by Pierre Fresnay, whose progress from feckless bohemian to overweening art hero and finally to a hollow man all too aware of his hollowness is brilliantly achieved. As a Faust variant with a severed hand as its centrepiece, the film inevitably recalls the old *Hands of Orlac* story, especially when Brissot laments that "This hand of mine – this hand I did all my paintings with – it's not my hand. It's another man's." But this hand pointed forward as well as back. The image of Maximus Léo's delicate fingers, flexing themselves in the recesses of its miniature casket, no doubt made an impact on Tourneur's fellow Frenchman Robert Florey, who in 1945 would make *The Beast with Five Fingers* for Warner Bros.

Gripping and elegant in equal measure, *La Main du diable* makes no direct reference to the Nazis; how could it? Yet its present-day setting made 'interpreting' the film after the war a very simple matter. In 1947, for example, the *New York Times* critic Bosley Crowther noted that "There may be some hidden significance in this film which is applicable to those citizens of France who bartered their souls during the Nazi Occupation."[39] And Faustian fables continued to resonate with French audiences for some time to come, presumably because of festering resentments regarding collaboration. René Clair, for example, made *La Beauté du diable* (The Beauty of the Devil) in 1949 as a spry and waggish vehicle for Gérard Philipe and Michel Simon.

## LA MAIN DU DIABLE

France 1942
UK: **The Devil's Hand**
US: **Carnival of Sinners**
Tobis presents a Continental Films production
82 minutes b/w
production began 21 August 1942
......................................
Director of Photography: Armand Thirard;
Art Director: André Andrejew; Editor:
Christian Gaudin [uncredited]; Sound:
William Robert Sivel [uncredited]; Music:
Roger Dumas; Special Effects: Nicolas
Wilcke [uncredited]; Screenplay: Jean-Paul
Le Chanois, based on *La Main enchantée* by
Gérard de Nerval [uncredited]; Producers:
Maurice Tourneur, Alfred Greven [both
uncredited]; Director: Maurice Tourneur

Pierre Fresnay (Roland Brissot); Josseline Gaël
(Irène); Noël Roquevert (Mélisse); Guillaume
de Sax (Gibelin); [Pierre] Palau (the little
man); Pierre Larquey (Ange); [André] Gabriello
(diner); Antoine Balpêtré (Denis); [Marcelle]
Rexiane (Mme Denis); André Varennes (colonel);
Georges Chamarat (Duval); Jean Davy
(musketeer); Jean Despeaux (boxer); uncredited:
André Bacqué (Maximus Léo); René Blancard
(surgeon); Georges Chamarat (Duval); Jean
Coquelin (notary); Jacques Courtin (policeman);
Georges Douking (pickpocket); Charlotte
Ecard (guest); Gabrielle Fontan (palm reader);
Garzoni (juggler); Albert Malbert (Verdure);
Paul Marcel (illusionist); Roland Milès (guest);
Clary Monthal (cleaning lady); Marcelle
Monthil (colonel's wife); Colette Régis (Mme
Duval); Jacques Roussel (art critic); Louis Salou
(casino director); Renée Thorel (lady who's
cold); Robert Vattier (Perrier); Henri Vilbert
(brigadier); Georges Vitray (doctor); Henry
Gerrar; Roger Vincent

**Carnival of Sinners ... is a worthy contribution to the art-house trade. Macabre aspects of its basic theme and frequent use of symbolism make it unlikely for the run-of-mill film patronage ... One scene in particular, in which Fresnay's predecessors in the possession of the hand are gathered at a banquet table, has a ballet-like quality that moves with poetic motion.** *Variety 2 April 1947*

**As conceived by its enterprising author – and as written by him, no doubt – the story of this strange and grotesque picture was probably a quite convincing tale ... But the mere illustration of it, as the idea becomes more involved and the imagery drifts into phantasms, inevitably tends to look absurd ... The film is intended as weird diversion. It succeeds in part and for a while but not enough.** *New York Times 8 April 1947*

Then in 1955 Claude Autant-Lara's *Marguerite de la nuit*, a lavishly coloured showcase for Michèle Morgan and Yves Montand, had the self-reflexive wit to cast Palau

Gabrielle Dorziat and Pierre Renoir, inheritors of a wolfish legacy in *Le Loup des Malveneur* (1942)

as the elderly Dr Faust, 13 years after his turn as the Devil in *La Main du diable*.

The ambiguity of *La Main du diable* was clearly a good way of slipping coded messages past the Nazi regime – though keeping things ambiguous had its dangers where non-Nazi viewers were concerned, with the deliberate haziness of some films being seen as collaborationist rather than embodying resistance. In March 1943 Jean Cocteau deputed his script for *L'Éternel retour* (The Eternal Return) to director Jean Delannoy. Unfortunately, this modern-dress variation on the Tristan and Isolde legend, featuring a love potion and a hair-raisingly malignant dwarf, laid itself open to post-war misinterpretation, particularly in the UK. Elizabeth M Harris of the Academy on London's Oxford Street – the country's first art-house cinema – bracketed the film with Carné's *Les Visiteurs du soir* when discussing "films directed under German supervision, emphasising the Nordic race theory and with a distinctly unwholesome flavour."[40] Richard Winnington, meanwhile, noted that Delannoy's "trance-like atmosphere of doom and despair swept me into a nightmare of Teutonic mysticism" and suggested that it must have been "a pleasure for the Nazis to give permission for the production as well as to view the picture."[41]

This kind of misinterpretation was bad enough, but a worse fate was in store for a filmmaker who forsook fantasy altogether and opted for a warts'n'all snapshot of contemporary France. On 10 May 1943 Henri-Georges Clouzot began shooting *Le Corbeau*

(The Crow) in the Île-de-France community of Montfort-l'Amaury. Made, like *La Main du diable*, for Continental, this retained at least four of the earlier film's actors – Pierre Larquey, Noël Roquevert, Palau and, in the lead once again, the exceptional Pierre Fresnay. Here, a provincial town is riven by an epidemic of 850 poison-pen letters within two months, with the townspeople descending into a denunciation-crazed form of collective insanity. In charting the grisly consequences of "l'encre qui fait couler de sang" (the ink that spills blood), Clouzot gave an early indication of the misanthropy that would seep through later titles like *Les Diaboliques*.

*Le Corbeau* is by no means a conventional horror film, yet the genre's first British historian, Ivan Butler, nevertheless made the accurate claim that "as a black study of a communal nightmare it is technically brilliant and disturbingly convincing."[42] Though applicable in any age and clime, Clouzot's mordant view of the human condition was of obvious significance in the paranoid atmosphere of the Occupation, and the Germans lost no time in advertising the film as an illustration of a specifically French malaise. Tarred with this brush, the picture was execrated on all sides after the war and Clouzot and his screenwriter Louis Chavance were temporarily banned from making films; leading actors Pierre Fresnay and Ginette Leclerc were briefly interned. "Of all the crimes committed by the film industry during the Occupation," Evelyn Ehrlich has observed, "seemingly the most serious was working on *Le Corbeau*."[43]

A number of other titles, safely concealed under the cloak of fantasy, made capital of the vogue for the fey and macabre. Among these, Guillaume Radot's *Le Loup des Malveneur* (The Wolf of the Malveneurs) is as close to contemporary Hollywood horror as occupied France ever got. Radot began shooting the film at the Studios des Buttes-Chaumont on Monday 27 July 1942; by a curious coincidence, a rather similar Hollywood product, John Brahm's Fox B-movie *The Undying Monster*, got under way in California exactly a week later, on 3 August. Where the family curse of lycanthropy in Brahm's film eventually resolves itself into a crude shot of fur-faced John Howard shinning up a cliff, in Radot's hands the curse winds up in the subterranean lab of a presumed-missing researcher, with Pierre Renoir lending a kind of dead-eyed authority to such generic pronouncements as "I am the greatest scientist of the century!"

Throughout, Radot has fun with the name 'Malveneur' (literally, evil huntsman), emphasising that the locals are beset by "peur des Malveneur" and having a truculent carter tell the heroine that "I go no further" prior to muttering "Malveneur? Malheur!" Eccentric, insular and aristocratic, the Malveneurs are excluded from the local cemetery, cursed by a legendary ancestor who was "man by day, wolf by night," and now, in the 20th century, are presided over by the haughty Magda (Gabrielle Dorziat). Renoir's Reginald, meanwhile, has a pretty young wife with a weak heart and tells her, rather disturbingly, that "It's *your* blood I see in my test tubes." The wife is played, incidentally, by Marie Olinska, one of the notorious 'Comtesses de la Gestapo'; the couple's daughter is Olinska's own four-year-old daughter Bijou, who looks rather like Donnie Dunagan in *Son of Frankenstein*.

The film is ham-fisted here and there, as when model shots of the castle turrets fail to match the location used elsewhere. And that Reginald's wolf serum (or whatever it is) is intended to keep the family bloodline going is rather vaguely elucidated, which is a shame given that Radot's purpose was (presumably) to excoriate the French upper classes. But the burgeoning romance between the young leads, Madeleine Sologne and Michel Marsay, is sweetly done, and to underline it Radot has some nifty tricks up his sleeve, as when he shoots them in close-up through the rungs of a postcard carousel outside a newsagent. Radot excels himself, too, in a striking funeral procession obviously inspired by *Vampyr*, complete with indoor mist giving place to outdoor fog and weirdly canted shots of a cross under a roiling sky. And, because Reginald serenades his experiments by playing a pump organ, the final conflagration is accompanied, rather unexpectedly, by a jaunty air on the harmonium.

Another 1942 film, Serge de Poligny's *Le Baron fantôme* (The Phantom Baron), is mainly given over to a four-pronged 19th century romance, with droll asides from its top-billed actor, the lugubrious character star André Lefaur, as a bogus Dauphin. But

Jean Cocteau as the corridor-hopping title character in *Le Baron fantôme* (1942)

in the opening reel, and at select moments thereafter, de Poligny engages the full battery of Gothic effects. In 1826, a widowed Countess (Gabrielle Dorziat again) arrives at a dilapidated castle with her young charges; her progress to the main door is marked by a sign warning against 'Wolf Traps', the buffeting of a preternatural gale, the watchful presence of a black cat and the eventual arrival of a peg-legged old retainer. In flashback we learn of the somnambulant Baron's unaccountable disappearance, with Jean Cocteau, no less, hopping strangely down the nocturnal corridors as the old retainer looks on fearfully. (Though responsible for the film's dialogue, Cocteau conspicuously wrote none for himself.) The sequence ends with the retainer concluding his story and identifying the black cat as the Baron reincarnated. "This fellow is totally insane," gasps the Countess.

Later on, Jany Holt (familiar from Duvivier's 1935 *Golem*) proceeds down secret passageways to find the Baron's concealed corpse in the lower depths. Clearly a seated dummy rather than Cocteau, it crumbles to nothing when she snatches its last will and testament from its taloned hands. Incorporating an explicit nod to Sleeping Beauty, de Poligny intensifies the fairy-tale atmosphere by means of a dreamy set-piece in which the white-robed Holt is carried by Alain Cuny across a glimmering studio pond. Lavishly appointed in every department, *Le Baron fantôme* also marked one of the first film credits for couturier Christian Dior. Indeed, the film's Gothic lavishness is sufficiently intense to suggest that Cocteau's involvement went beyond just acting and dialogue-writing. The man himself might possibly have been dropping a hint when, in his production diary for the later *La Belle et la Bête*, he noted that "I've got the same unit that we used in *Baron fantôme*, willing and helpful."[44] In another suggestive touch, the film's last line – "Il était une fois..." (Once upon a time...) – was to become the crucial introductory line of *La Belle et la Bête*.

In 1944, de Poligny and Jany Holt were reunited, this time in Carcassonne, for a modern-dress, and much less effective, Gothic romance called *La Fiancée des ténèbres* (The Bride of Darkness). Here, Holt's whey-faced Sylvie is haunted by a long-ago romp in a hayloft which resulted in the boy's death; a shot of a scythe accidentally slicing the back of his neck is surprisingly bloody. Now she eschews romance in favour of tending to her elderly guardian (Édouard Delmont). The old man is obsessed with reviving the 13th century Cathari sect, with an ancient parchment and an unearthed funerary statue finally giving entrance to an Albigensian sanctuary. "We have found the portal to the other world!" he exults.

Thirty years later, *Les Cahiers de la cinémathèque* pointed out that *La Fiancée* "is widely regarded today as the first and only film of Cathar inspiration. On its original release it was sneered at amid almost total incomprehension, thanks to the labyrinthine complexity of a scenario loaded with cultural references."[45] Sadly, the surfeit of cultural references is garbled rather than gripping, eventually causing the film to collapse into soft-focus whimsy and making the Cathar survival, in particular, seem strangely unconnected to the remainder. The cathedral-like grotto is an impressive creation, however, and a scene in which the local archivist (Line Noro) drops dead in front of Sylvie is powerfully done. Though the film was based on a story by Gaston Bonheur, one of de Poligny's co-scenarists on *La Fiancée* was, not Jean Cocteau, but the rising playwright Jean Anouilh – and Sylvie, cursed by "this terrifying thing that I carry inside me: death," is certainly very like the fatalistic heroines of Anouilh's plays.

Renée Faure, Roger Pigaut and a dead man's hand advertising the atmospheric *Sortilèges* (1944)

The rather scholarly and otherworldly tone of *La Fiancée* was conspicuously absent from Christian-Jaque's *Sortilèges* (Spells), a really grim rural tragedy in which a hermit diabolist seeks to engage the affections of a sickly young woman; he does this by drizzling the blood of a dove over her throat. The result is highly reminiscent of Victor Sjöström's 1927 M-G-M classic *The Wind*, exchanging Sjöström's smouldering Mojave Desert for the snow-covered expanses of the Massif Central, and a runaway black horse for the demonic white one of the earlier film. It benefits from a compellingly nasty performance by Lucien Coëdel, who confesses that "it's in my

nature to frighten people," plus the ghoulish image of a dead man's clutching hand protruding from the snow. Complete with further echoes of Chaplin's *The Gold Rush*, the film is extremely atmospheric but also over-long. Shot in March 1944, it had to wait until December 1945 to go on release.

By then, of course, the war was over.

## RIPPLES FROM A HAUNTED LAKE

The Gothic route taken by German filmmakers during the 1920s, and to a lesser extent by French ones in the 1940s, was not replicated in Italy or Spain – and in both cases prohibitive censorship and the influence of the Catholic church was a significant factor in suppressing macabre urges. Lack of a strong literary tradition may have played a part too. Italy, for example, had been the exotic setting of several of the early Gothic fictions, with villains routinely bearing such names as Schedoni or Montoni before German names like Frankenstein became fashionable. But the Gothic mode was only assimilated by native writers – among them Inigio Ugo Tarchetti, Antonio Fogazzaro, Matilde Serao and Italo Svevo – in the latter part of the 19th century.

In the early days of cinema, Arturo Ambrosio produced adaptations of *The Pit and the Pendulum* and *Hop-Frog* in 1910, following them a year later by adapting *The Masque of the Red Death* as *La maschera tragica* (The Tragic Mask). Ambrosio's associate Luigi Maggi also made such disparate titles as *La ballata della strega* (The Witch's Ballad, 1910) and *Satana* (Satan, 1912), having previously been Ambrosio's co-director on the 1908 hit *Gli ultimi giorni di Pompeii* (The Last Days of Pompeii). This film helped to define a genre which the Italians pretty much invented, a genre that, in the 1910s, formed the basis of the local industry's international success. Historical or mythological epics, massive in scope, reached their zenith with Giovanni Pastrone's *Cabiria*, which proved such a smash in 1914 that even D W Griffith was influenced by it. The film not only introduced Bartolomeo Pagano's 'strong man' character Maciste, who would be spun off into a long series of personalised vehicles; it also had Segundo de Chomón collaborating on cinematography and special effects with Eugenio Bava, whose son Mario would later play a key role in Italian horror.

Before *Cabiria*, however, came the 1911 release *L'Inferno* (Hell), a three-years-in-the-making phantasmagoria in which Virgil takes Dante on a guided tour of the infernal regions. The sustained barrage of horrific imagery in Dante's 14th century epic poem was here conveyed in unsparing detail. Among the hordes of virtually naked damned souls, the film offers heretics writhing in fiery grave plots, traitors immersed in lakes of ice, a view of the winged monster Geryon, a headless sinner flourishing his own head like a lantern, legions of bat-winged demons wielding whips and tridents, even Count Ugolino chewing obsessively on his betrayer's skull. The pièce-de-résistance, which is granted the film's single close-up, is a shaggy-sided, three-mouthed Lucifer munching enthusiastically on Brutus and Cassius.

*L'Inferno* was lucky, perhaps, to come out when it did. Later on, a censorship code initiated in 1913 and formalised in 1920 ensured a rough passage for such titles as Mario Roncoroni's loose H G Wells adaptation *Il giustiziere invisibile* (The Invisible Avenger, 1915), Domenico Gaido's *La maschera dello scheletro* (The Mask of the Skeleton, 1919) and Arnaldo Frateili's *La rovina della casa degli Usher* (The Fall of the House of Usher, 1920), a Poe adaptation also known, less provocatively, as *Una notte romantica* (A Romantic Night). Less contentious titles included a couple that took advantage of the cult of 'Borellismo' – ie, they starred the sumptuous icon Lyda Borelli. Nino Oxilia's *Rapsodia satanica* (Satanic Rhapsody, 1915) is a gender-swapped version of *Faust* in which an old lady, consumed with "nostalgia for things past," has her youth restored by a leering, purple-gowned Mephisto (Ugo Bazzini). And Carmine Gallone's *Malombra* (1916) is an adaptation of Antonio Fogazzaro's celebrated 1881 novel, with Borelli playing a young aristocrat haunted by "creatures of the past that rise from the shadows" in a lakeside villa.

Another touchy subject, however, arose in 1920 in the shape of Eugenio Testa's *Il mostro di Frankenstein* (Frankenstein's Monster). Confusingly, this film appears to have been made in Italy by an Italian crew for a German company set up by the film's Italian star, Luciano Albertini. Whether of German or Italian parentage, the film qualifies as the world's third Frankenstein film, after the US productions *Frankenstein* and *Life Without Soul*. As a bonus, its colossal monster, Umberto Guarracino, was cast

in 1921 as the most prominent creature in Urban Gad's *Die Insel der Verschollenen* (The Isle of the Lost), a German variant on H G Wells' *The Island of Dr Moreau*.

Back in Italy, Guarracino also turned up as a massively hirsute Pluto in Guido Brignone's *Maciste all'inferno* (Maciste in Hell), a film presented to the censor board in October 1925 and initially vetoed. Here, Bartolomeo Pagano's well-muscled Maciste is transported to a sulphuric Hell modelled carefully on Gustave Doré's 19th century illustrations, just as *L'Inferno* had been 14 years before. As in *Cabiria*, the Spanish pioneer Segundo de Chomón was entrusted with the effects, which include flying demons, disembodied heads, and (again) a giant, bat-winged Lucifer visibly devouring the damned. Faced with the scantily clad temptresses Proserpina (Elena Sangro) and Luciferina (Lucia Zanussi), even Maciste himself becomes a demon for a while. "Oh, what joy!" exults the irresistible Proserpina. "You kissed me and now you will remain in Hell for eternity!" With those words Sangro prefigures the numerous fatal women that will take centre stage when Italian Gothic comes into its own.

Benito Mussolini's National Fascist Party had risen to power in October 1922 and naturally deemed horror and fantasy films inimical to a suitably rose-tinted view of Italian life, a view endorsed via a propaganda machine at stark variance with the brutal reality. Horror therefore came through only in fragmentary form and only very occasionally, as in Nunzio Malasomma's 1934 film *La cieca di Sorrento* (The Blind Girl of Sorrento), in which the title character is threatened by her mother's killer. There were also a few very mild murder-mysteries inspired by Edizione Mondadori's 'I Libri Gialli', a popular series of 'yellow books' initiated in 1929. With its catchpenny title, Mario Camerini's lighthearted *Giallo* (Yellow, 1933) was based by screenwriter Mario Soldati on a play by the phenomenally successful crime writer Edgar Wallace, whose name would crop up again decades later when the giallo became an identifiable, and much nastier, sub-genre.

Real horror, however, was only available to the very few who caught a couple of Milanese student films, both silent and both based on Poe – *Il cuore rivelatore* (The Tell-Tale Heart, 1934) and *Il caso Valdemar* (The Valdemar Case, 1936). The first – directed by Alberto Mondadori, with future giants Mario Monicelli and Alberto Lattuada as co-writer and set designer respectively – features paranoid visions of eyeballs spinning in space, Cocteau style, plus another one sitting on a dinner plate, and finally a frantic axe murder when the protagonist's compulsion overwhelms him. The second, co-directed by Gianni

Hoepli and Ubaldo Magnaghi, is grimily disturbing, boasting canted shots of a sinister mesmerist looming into camera and, when his 'suspended' subject is finally allowed to die, a staggeringly gruesome decomposition scene which hardly needs the explanatory intertitle referring to 'una massa semiliquida, una abominevole putrefazione'. The scene anticipates the graphic make-up effects of Giannetto De Rossi by over 40 years.

For a country that was later to be so fertile in lurid horrors, Italy's conspicuous tardiness in developing the form is striking. With Gothic themes having to make do with getting in by the back door in non-horror pictures, Ferdinando Maria Poggioli directed two brooding period pieces – *Gelosia* (Jealousy) in 1942 and, the following year, *Il cappello da prete* (The Priest's Hat) – that touched on the theme, derived pretty equally from Shakespeare and Poe, of foul deeds inducing first obsessive guilt and finally madness. Roldano Lupi was the aristocratic and steadily disintegrating lead in these pictures, murdering an innocent farmer in the first and a money-lending cleric in the second. Any hopes of Poggioli pursuing this Gothic path were scotched when, just three months after the second picture's delayed release in November 1944, he killed himself.

These two Poggioli films were based on classic novels by Luigi Capuana and Emilio De Marchi respectively. But it was Antonio Fogazzaro's *Malombra*, already filmed in 1916, that was to provide a seedbed for the Gothics to come by means of a lavish new film version made in 1942. Oozing prestige from every pore, and as sumptuous-looking a production as any country made during the 1940s, Mario Soldati's film was an early producer credit for a future titan of the industry, Dino De Laurentiis. The breathtaking location photography was focused on the Villa Pliniana on Lake Como (the reputedly haunted mansion that was Fogazzaro's original inspiration) while interiors were shot at Cinecittà, the massive production facility in Rome that had been opened by Mussolini just five years before.

Haunted aristocrat Isa Miranda and faithful lady's maid Doretta Sestan in the lavishly appointed *Malombra* (1942)

The luminous Isa Miranda is Marina di Malombra, a haughty noblewoman who is delivered to a lakeside mansion under the tight control of her inflexible uncle, Count d'Ormengo (Gualtiero Tumiati). There she comes under the influence of a dead ancestor, Donna Cecilia, whose wings were similarly clipped in the very same villa. She also becomes obsessed by a novel called *Fantasmi del passato* (Ghosts of the Past), whose handsome young author just happens to have been engaged by the uncle as his amanuensis.

"My house," the impressively bearded Count observes, "is a shell in which many molluscs have lived." The Gothic lavishness is thickly spread by art director Gino Brosio and beautifully photographed by Massimo Terzano, and a genuine chill of unease attaches to the stand-out scene in which Marina discovers a lock of Cecilia's hair concealed under the keys of a spinet. Effective, too, are the exhortations of Cecilia's ghostly voice, telling Marina that "The moment of vengeance has come. Il Conte d'Ormengo is your enemy!" Unfortunately, at over two hours the film becomes seriously over-extended; Fogazzaro's novel is the kind of sprawling saga best suited to a TV mini-series, a treatment it duly received in 1974. Even so, the plot convolutions build to a brilliantly staged crime of passion in which Andrea Checchi, as the unlucky young author, is outstanding. Coincidentally, 18 years later a more grizzled Checchi would appear in *La maschera del demonio* (The Mask of the Demon), the film that got Italian Gothic up and running. Along with many other pictures it inherited the reincarnation and doppelgänger themes so elegantly suggested in *Malombra*.

Post-war came another significant pointer to the Italian horrors of the 1960s. As Roberto Curti has noted, the opening reel of the 1949 release *Il Trovatore* (The Troubadour) provides a tantalising blueprint for several future Gothics, prefiguring, in particular, *La maschera del demonio* again. Directed by the veteran Carmine Gallone (who had made the original *Malombra* over 30 years earlier), this adaptation of Verdi's opera begins with a murky, nocturnal view through the colonnaded arches of the Palace of Aljafería, with an off-screen narrator alluding to the "atmosphere of tragedy" that clings to the place, prior to cutting to a tumbril bearing an accused witch to the stake. The attendant mob, the officers with pikes, the executioners putting their torches to the pyre, the distraught daughter screaming from the sidelines – they're all here but are somewhat diluted by inappropriately jaunty music.

By 1949, of course, the war was long over, the hated Mussolini had long since been shot and the King who had sanctioned the Mussolini regime had died in exile, a republic having been established in mid-1946. Torn apart during the war and subject to several years of considerable hardship in its aftermath, Italy would be utterly transformed in the 1950s by an unprecedented economic boom. On the way to this consumerist miracle, films like Roberto Rossellini's *Roma citta aperta* (Rome Open City), Luchino Visconti's *La terra trema* (The Earth Trembles) and Vittorio De Sica's *Ladri di biciclette* (Bicycle Thieves) gained international acclaim, yet local audiences weren't especially interested in the unflinching glare of neo-realism, preferring the exact opposite.

Their taste for escapism did not, however, extend to horror. In this atmosphere a 1951 comedy like Giorgio Simonelli's *La paura fa 90* (Fear Scores 90) was just the ticket. Its 'theatre troupe in a haunted house' scenario was derived from the 'film crew in a haunted house' of Mario Baffico's 1940 film *Incanto di mezzanotte* (Midnight Magic), and precisely the same narrative would recur in a number of full-on Italian Gothics a decade hence. Also in the early 1950s, the murder-mystery *Delitto al Luna Park* (Crime in Luna Park) offered another very mild foretaste of the giallo mode, as well as being one of the earliest films directed by Renato Polselli, who would later be responsible for Italy's first straight-faced vampire film.

## SLIM PICKINGS IN SPAIN

In Spain, the reluctance to embrace horror was even more marked than in Italy, with the all-encompassing power of Catholicism discouraging any forays into the so-called dark side. Another stumbling block, as in Italy, was Spain's relative paucity of a literary background in the genre. Despite an abundance of Spanish myths and legendry, the only substantial literary source was the post-Romantic poet Gustavo Adolfo Bécquer, author of the Poe-like *Leyendas* (Legends), and even he would go pretty much untapped until 1971.

In the silent period, and for a good 30 years thereafter, the pickings were decidedly slim. In 1919, *El otro* (The Other) led the way with a story of a widow

and her lover being haunted by the dead husband, one Dr Riaza; it was co-directed by Joan María Codina and Eduardo Zamacois, author of the source novel, who also cast himself in it. The following year the same producers made *El espectro del castillo* (The Castle Spectre), which the Australian film star Aurele Sidney directed just before his untimely death, and a trickle of other titles followed from other companies – the castle-dwelling sorceress of Maximiliano Thous' *La bruja* (The Witch, 1923), the criminal mesmerist of Benito Perojo's *Más allá de la muerte* (Beyond Death, 1924), the premature burial of Miguel Ballesteros' *Fue un pesadilla* (It Was a Nightmare, 1925) and the Devil visiting Bilbao in Benjamín Núñez's *Mefistófeles en el infierno* (Mephistopheles in Hell, also 1925).

With the arrival of the talkies came the famous monsters unleashed by Hollywood, but Spain's only response was Eduardo García Maroto's two-reel 'old dark house' parody *Una de miedo* (Scary Movie, 1935), whose narrator made the rather forlorn assertion that "We can do invisible men in Spain, too." Twenty years later, however, Spanish horror hadn't got much further when Maroto went the same parodic route in his three-part comedy portmanteau *Tres eran tres* (Three Were Three), in which a Frankenstein segment – *Una de monstruos* (Monster Movie) – was joined by send-ups of Westerns and musicals.

Having begun in July 1936, the cataclysm of the Spanish Civil War finally ended with the flight of the Republican government and the occupation of Madrid by Francisco Franco's Nationalist forces in March 1939. The military dictatorship that ensued would last for over 35 years, with media censorship and curbs on freedom of speech joined, as before, by the supreme power of the Catholic church. In this repressive climate historical epics, parochial musicals, costume melodramas and phoney religious biopics formed the chief cinematic diet, with filmmakers encouraged to toe the government line by the promise of state subsidies. Horror, naturally, had no place.

Even so, the Madrid playwright Enrique Jardiel Poncela provided a few scraps of fantasy in his 1935 comedy *Las cinco advertencias de Satanás* (Satan's Five Warnings), telling of an ageing roué whose attempts to settle down are complicated by the Devil himself. This was filmed by Isidro Socías in 1937, then again in Mexico in 1945 prior to returning to Spain in a mod 1969 version directed by José Luis Merino. Poncela also wrote the 1942 play *Los habitantes de la casa deshabitada* (The Inhabitants of the Uninhabited House), a mixture of crooks and spooks that was duly filmed four years later and again, as *Fantasmas en la casa* (Ghosts in the House), in 1961.

Antonio Casal listens enraptured to 'la Bella Medusa' in La torre de los siete jorobados (1944)

# LA TORRE DE LOS SIETE JOROBADOS

Spain 1944
US: *The Tower of the Seven Hunchbacks*
Judez-Films | España Films
85 minutes b/w
in production July 1944

Director of Photography: Henri Barreyre; Art Directors: Pierre Schild, Francisco Escriñá, Antonio Simont; Editor: Sara Ontañón; Sound: Enrique Dominguez; Music: [José Ruiz de] Azagra; Make-up: [Antonio] Florido; Adaptation and Dialogue: José Santugini, Edgar Neville, based on the novel by Emilio Carrere; Producers:

Luis Judez, Germán López Prieto; Director: Edgar Neville

Antonio Casal (Basilio Beltrán); Isabelita de Pomés (Inés); Guillermo Marín (Dr Sabatino); Félix de Pomés (Don Robinson de Mantua); Julia Lajos (Bella Medusa's mother); Manolita Morán (Bella Medusa); Julia Pachelo (Braulia); Antonio Riquelme (Don Zacarías); Manuel Miranda; Emilio Barta; [Antonio L] Estrada; [Luis] Ballester; [Luis] Latorre; Rosario Rollo; Julia García; uncredited: Inocencio Barbán (night watchman); José Marco (ghost of Napoléon)

This Spanish picture, opening at the Capitol, demonstrates that no type of film is beyond the grasp of our directors and actors … Santugini has crafted a good script from the fantasy by Carrere, and director Edgar Neville has pulled off a deft production that … sustains the viewer's interest, with the intrigue and mystery not dropping off even for a moment … Barreyne's [sic] camerawork is exceptional. ABC Madrid 28 November 1944

Comic actor Antonio Casal returns to the Cine Alcázar [Barcelona] today in the 'premiere' screening of *La torre de los siete jorobados* … Edgar Neville has stamped the famous novel by Emilio Carrere, in its screen version, with all the dexterity a good film requires, taking advantage of all the most refined resources of cinematic technique and highlighting the many attractions of humour, excitement and interest contained in the original work.
La Vanguardia 13 December 1944

anomaly as Carrere's novel had 20-odd years earlier, for this charming hybrid of romance and detective story contained enough grotesque and spectral elements to fulfil a long-felt want.

> Turn-of-the-century Madrid. Wondering how to pay for his next date with a beautiful cabaret artiste, Basilio Beltrán tries his luck at roulette, winning a sizable sum through the guidance of a cadaverous-looking man with only one eye. The man later reveals himself as the eminent archaeologist Professor Robinson de Mantua. Dead for a year, he now enlists Basilio's aid in protecting his niece Inés from the secret society responsible for his death.

Neville's film begins with an absurd little musical number by 'la Bella Medusa', the flighty cabaret star Basilio has his eye on. She's a hearty Hispanic counterpart to the vulpine character played by Linda Darnell in the contemporaneous Hollywood thriller *Hangover Square*, and the theme of her song is superstition. Sure enough, a black cat darts past our doting hero, who will quickly prove not just superstitious but also psychic.

Neville loses little time in playing his trump card. For barely has Basilio moved from cabaret to casino when the camera tracks unfussily towards a large, square mirror at the rear of the lobby. Fronds from a plant display are visible at its foot, a distant sofa is reflected in its surface, and suddenly a black-clad figure becomes visible, grinning ambiguously as it steps out of the mirror and into the lobby. The top hat, caped frock-coat and blacked-out monocle stir memories of Dr Caligari or Scapinelli from *Der Student von Prag*; the emergence from a mirror alludes to that film, too, and also, perhaps, to the mirrored portal featured in Cocteau's *Le Sang d'un poète*. Strikingly realised, this image has since acquired a kind of symbolic significance – for Professor Mantua's spectral entrance into that lobby represents the intrusion into Spanish cinema of all the irrational elements that had previously been suppressed.

The Professor, Basilio later points out, is "a tall thin man dressed like a Lutheran with one eye." He's played by the former Olympic fencer Félix de Pomés, an aristocratic figure who looks splendidly ghoulish yet turns out to be on a benevolent mission. Part of

In the early 1930s, with the advent of talkies requiring that Spanish-speaking versions be made in parallel with major Hollywood films, Poncela had enjoyed a spell in California, an experience shared by Poncela's half-English friend Edgar Neville. It was Neville who, in the summer of 1944, made a film of the 1920 novel La torre de los siete jorobados (The Tower of the Seven Hunchbacks), in which the bohemian poet and theosophist Emilio Carrere had situated a Gaston Leroux-style intrigue in the heart of Madrid. In 1944, Neville's film seemed just as much of an the genius of the film is that Mantua is so engagingly humanised – he explains, for example, that he misses his beloved statuette of the Venus de Milo because "she was my type" – yet his reappearances are never allowed to lose the icy thrill that attended his arrival. Neville chances his arm slightly by including a scene in Basilio's bedroom in which Mantua is briefly joined by none other than Napoléon, who complains about being "always on the go" thanks to the summonses of over-zealous spiritualists. Yet Mantua's otherworldly charisma survives even a vignette as skittish as this.

In the casino Basilio indulges in further superstition by rubbing the hump of a passing hunchback – an ironic gesture, not only because the hunchback will turn out to be part of the conspiracy Basilio later gets involved in, but also because the person who really brings him luck is Professor Mantua. Basilio cleans up at the tables (another echo of *Der Student von Prag*) and then the plot is set in train by Mantua's offhand reveal of the grisly rent in his neck. "It's an old wound," he smiles. "It brought about my death." The intrigue that develops includes Basilio's 'meet cute' encounter with the Professor's niece (played by Félix de Pomés' real-life daughter Isabel), the discovery of a set of cabalistic instructions in the Professor's inner sanctum, and a trip to a condemned house that gives access to a subterranean city beneath Old Madrid.

This underground complex was constructed, we're told, by Jews in flight from the 15th century Expulsion laws, a telling historical detail given the persecution being undergone by Jews at the time the film was made. Now it houses a counterfeiting operation staffed exclusively by hunchbacks. In an off-colour moment, their oleaginous boss, Sabatino, describes his acquisition of a distorting mirror as "a little bit of vanity" – reflected in it, his back becomes straight. These are not, however, the scuttling, doubled-over hunchbacks of horror movie tradition; they're everyday guys with relatively discreet humps who just happen to be set down in the film's extraordinary Gothic environment of huge, honeycombed stairwells and cobwebbed subterranean crypts. Among the items on display in the lower depths are plenty of cowled skeletons and even one or two mummified Knights Templar, eerily anticipating the 1970s horror pictures of Amando de Ossorio. As well as being reached via a fireplace in the condemned house, the underground city also communicates directly with the Professor's own apartment, in which the beautiful Inès now lives – thus conforming to the time-honoured Gothic theme of bourgeois façades underpinned by atavistic layers stretching back, in this instance, to the horrors of the Inquisition.

The film's crepuscular lighting and old-fashioned *misterioso* score explicitly recall the eeriness of silent cinema, and with the added bonus of Antonio Casal's charming performance as Basilio it's a delightful entertainment on all counts. And its suggestive possibilities weren't lost on contemporary observers. One Barcelona critic, for example, commended Neville's film for "opening up a new stylistic path for our cinema."[46]

Yet after it that stylistic path was abandoned for some 17 years. Admittedly, a film on release at the same time as Neville's, Rafael Gil's highly successful *El clavo* (The Nail), displayed touches of graveyard Gothic in a costume melodrama based on Pedro Antonio de Alarcón's Poe-influenced novel. In 1947, Carlos Serrano de Osma's *La sirena negra* (The Black Siren) focused on Fernando Fernán Gómez's obsessive love for the dead Isabel de Pomés and her living lookalike, and the following year Antonio del Amo's straightforward biopic, *El huésped de las tinieblas* (The Guest of Darkness), was spiced with "a fantastic interpretation of the sublime and tormented dreams" of Gustavo Adolfo Bécquer. And among the small crumbs to be had in the following decade were the guilty nightmares suffered in 1951 by murderous María Félix in Luis Saslavsky's *La corona negra* (The Black Crown, based on a Jean Cocteau outline), together with J L Sáenz de Heredia's colourful comedy *Faustina* (1956), which matched Félix with Fernando Fernán Gómez and Fernando Rey in an 'old lady granted her youth by Mephistopheles' story, recalling Italy's ancient *Rapsodia satanica*.

Another borderline title was brought about by the single-minded drive of Daniel Mangrané to get Wagner on film, which he finally did in the summer of 1951 when co-directing *La montaña sagrada* (The Holy Mountain) with Carlos Serrano de Osma. Released under Wagner's original title, *Parsifal*, this mega-budget folly, completely divorced from Spanish cinema's usual fare, was a commercial disaster. It was sufficiently phantasmagoric, however – particularly when the Grail-questing hero is trapped in an alluring Jardín de los Pecados Capitales (Garden of Deadly Sins) – to be retitled *The Evil Forest* for US audiences. Sensibly, Mangrané chose the imposing Félix de Pomés, erstwhile spectre of *La torre de los siete jorobados*, to play the villainous sorcerer Klingsor.

These films, however, weren't much for Spanish horror fans to chew on. Only in the latter part of the 1950s, when Spain's isolation began to be eroded by tourism and glimpses of exciting new forms of popular culture, did the iron hand of censorship start to loosen. As a result, Spanish cinema's first bikinis –

an absurd landmark showcased in Joan Bosch's *Bahía de Palma* (Palma Bay) – were put on camera in the same year, 1961, as Spain's first out-and-out horror film.

## THE BEAST, THE WITCH AND THE LIQUID MIRROR

The devastation of the Second World War brought with it – both during its course and in the immediate aftermath – an interest in using ghosts as an emotionally cathartic glimpse into the afterlife. In the USA the trend resulted in such titles as *Happy Land* and *Between Two Worlds*, while Britain had *The Halfway House* and *Blithe Spirit*; post-war came such Hollywood evergreens as *The Ghost and Mrs Muir* and *Portrait of Jennie*. France was no exception, with a number of titles perpetuating the vein of fantastic whimsy that had been popular during the Occupation.

In January 1945, for example, Claude Autant-Lara started production on the delightful *Sylvie et le fantôme* (Sylvie and the Phantom), in which Odette Joyeux is beguiled by the ghost of Jacques Tati, in his feature debut. Other fantastic emanations included the hints of witchcraft in Serge Debecque's 1946 romance *Coïncidences* or, the following year, the existential afterlife seen in Jean Delannoy's *Les Jeux sont faits* (The Die is Cast). The latter's screenwriter, Jean-Paul

Sartre, had recently created a more baleful view of the afterlife – Hell, in fact – in the stage play *Huis clos* (In Camera), which was belatedly opened out for the screen by Jacqueline Audry in 1954.

The greatest flowering of French *fantastique*, post-war, remains Jean Cocteau's entrancingly strange *La Belle et la Bête* (Beauty and the Beast), the embattled production of which stretched from the last week of August 1945 to the first week of January 1946. Returning to direction after 15 years and shooting with meagre resources at Senlis and Rochecorbon, Cocteau engaged designer Christian Bérard and cinematographer Henri Alekan to help create the cinema's most convincing fairy-tale environment. Appealing to the viewer to surrender to "un peu de cette naïveté" – ie, the naïveté of children – Cocteau took Mme de Beaumont's 18th century rendering of the story and contrived the ideal showcase for his surreal, and disarmingly simple, special effects. He also discreetly foregrounded the tale's subtext regarding male-female relations, with Mila Parély's scheming Félicie observing that "There are plenty of other husbands with heads and horns" and Josette Day's luminous Belle informing the Beast that "There are men far more monstrous than you, though they conceal it well."

In the USA, playwright Tennessee Williams was unequivocal, hailing *La Belle et la Bête* as "one of the great films to come out of Europe since the war" and encapsulating its curious spell in words Cocteau himself couldn't have bettered. "Visually," he wrote, "it has an extraordinary luster which I suppose some people would define as 'the phosphorescence of decay'. I prefer to think of it as the remembered radiance of that state of innocence in which fairy tales were read and which they wear in our recollection."[47] That radiance illuminates, not just Belle, but also the Beast, played with a tense mixture of ferocity and romantic resignation by Jean Marais and sporting a brilliant make-up reportedly modelled on Marais' own dog. Make-up man Hagop Arakelian here outdid anything lycanthropic so far produced in Hollywood, with the Beast's grimly beautiful visage in fact appearing more leonine than canine. The moment when he appears at Belle's door at dead of night, snarling and literally smoking with spilt blood after a kill, underlines the tragedy as much as the horror.

*La Belle et la Bête* was to exercise a powerful influence in decades to come. That it was a crucial source for Jacques Demy's Perrault-derived 1970 musical *Peau d'ane* (Donkey Skin) is obvious; Demy even cast Jean Marais as Catherine Deneuve's regal father. Yet the film's influence reached beyond the standard fairy-tale canon and deep into Gothic

Smoking with spilt blood: Jean Marais in *La Belle et la Bête* (1945)

Frédéric Rey of the Folies Bergère
dances with a half-naked celebrant in
*Le Destin exécrable de Guillemette Babin* (1947)

horror. As early as 1962 the youthful editors of *Midi-Minuit Fantastique* made a photographic comparison between Marais' Beast in his blood-streaked Hamlet shirt and Oliver Reed wearing an exactly similar garment in Terence Fisher's then-recent Hammer production *The Curse of the Werewolf*. In Italy, too, Mario Bava would reference Cocteau's floating supernatural beings and bizarrely outfitted castle interiors in such 1960s films as *La maschera del demonio* and *Operazione paura*. As recently as 2013, however, Marina Warner separated Cocteau's masterpiece from the antiseptic vacuities of CGI with the observation that "In many ways the film's influence has not been deep enough and much more could still be learned from it."[48]

In the wake of *La Belle et la Bête* – and five years after directing *Le Loup des Malveneur* – Guillaume Radot returned to horror with an extraordinary film called *Le Destin exécrable de Guillemette Babin* (The Execrable Fate of Guillemette Babin). Starting production in mid-August 1947 at the Buttes-Chaumont studio, this was based on a novel by Maurice Garçon, a celebrated barrister recently elected to the Académie Française. Garçon's novel dated back to 1926 and was actually called *La Vie exécrable de Guillemette Babin, sorcière* (The Execrable Life of Guillemette Babin, Sorceress); the small title adjustment was presumably meant to remind patrons of Sacha Guitry's 1942 film *Le Destin fabuleux de Désirée Clary*.

*In the late 16th century, Guillemette Babin's birth is attended by bad omens. Her mother, Radegonde, is burnt at the stake as a witch and Guillemette is taken on as a servant by the elderly Pierre Pasquier. Guillemette precipitates the deaths of Pasquier's wife and son, after which Pasquier loses no time in getting married to her. On the wedding night, however, she ventures into the woods and attends a wild and uninhibited Sabbat...*

## LE DESTIN EXÉCRABLE DE GUILLEMETTE BABIN

France 1947
Union Générale Cinématographique
97 minutes b/w
production began 18 August 1947

. . . . . . . . . . . . . . . . . . . . . . . . . . . . . .

Director of Photography: Paul Cotteret; Art Director: Marcel Magniez; Editors: Pierre Caillet, Suzanne Lafaye; Sound: [Louis] Perrin; Music: Maurice Thiriet; Make-up: Louis Bonnemaison; Adaptation and Dialogue: Yves Brainville, Guillaume Radot, inspired by the novel by Maurice Garçon; Producer-Director: Guillaume Radot

Héléna Bossis (Guillemette Babin); Jean Davy (Prosecutor Salavert); Édouard Delmont (Pierre Pasquier); Jacky Flynt (Mathilde); Germaine Kerjean (Radegonde); Paul Demange (Master Nicolas); Michel Barbey (Jean-François Pasquier); Renaud Mary (Charles Perrin); Robert Seller (Louis Le Noble); Colette Fleuriot (Clotilde); Léone Nogarède (unknown role); [Jacques] Dufilho (monk); [Grégoire] Gromoff ç(unknown role); Jean Heuzé (prior of St-Geniest); Jacques Torrens (Fouquembières); Jean Carmet (Étienne); Frédéric Rey (Devil at the sabbath); Christine Vallendier (Marie); Mathevet (school child); Sylvain (unknown role); Francette Vernillat (Guillemette as a child); uncredited: Alfred Baillou (gaoler); Palmyre Levasseur (Dame Pasquier); Christine Pallendier (Marie); Simone Bogarde

Set at the end of the 16th century, this film is made up of numerous beautiful exteriors, recreating the earthiness of the period along with its wild passions and superstitions ... True to the spirit of the picture, Guillaume Radot has staged a Sabbat sequence which is remarkable ... The film is illuminated by some very pretty location photography, the music is excellent and the settings especially well designed. *La Cinématographie Française* 20 November 1948

Promisingly, for the first scene Guillaume Radot recaptures the atmosphere of strangeness that made his *Loup des Malveneur* a success. After that, everything takes a turn for the worse ... The scenes are stitched together without continuity, without spirit, without precision. As for the highlight of the film, the famous Sabbat, wishing to achieve a climax Radot merely achieves the ridiculous ... There was a good idea here, alas poorly exploited. *L'Écran Français* 5 April 1949

Radot's film is an odd one in that it takes witchcraft, the 1500s variety anyway, as a palpable fact, but in doing so treats the subject in a bewildering variety of styles, not all of them harmonious. Paul Cotteret's photography, meanwhile, turns a caressing eye on the countryside of the Dordogne, yet Radot doesn't fully exploit the contrast between sylvan beauty and the grimy human depravities played out against it. The period detail is accurate enough but somewhat

squeaky clean; the men model the doublet-and-hose look as if for a 16th century fashion catalogue, and Guillemette's glossy lipstick remains unsmirched even when she's slung into a dungeon.

And yet the film exercises a strange fascination, if only because the clash of styles makes it a constantly surprising experience. It begins on a fine note of foreshadowing, with a toad dropping unexpectedly from a pitcher of wine on the night of Guillemette's birth. Then the tone begins to wander, starting with a magical scene of the child Guillemette, sent out by her mother to gather herbs, encountering a black-clad old woman in the ruined hulk of a castle. Cackling, the woman vanishes into thin air, leaving the girl with her staff. Amid heavenly voices and a sudden attack of slow motion, the girl appears transfigured, ascending stone steps prior to pitching backwards in a faint. The action then leaps forward 12 years to a scene of outright whimsy – Guillemette's mother bedevilling a couple of foolish young men by flinging sulphurous powders at the feet of one and turning the other into a donkey. Then Guillemette is seen sitting anxiously at the hearth, flickering flames obstructing our view of her as a gentle means of indicating that (a) her mother is about to be incinerated and (b) that Guillemette will eventually go the same way.

Radot is much better with disquieting details than silly donkey-morphing interludes. Having seen a vision of herself in the woods, robed in white amid plumes of mist, Guillemette returns home to find that her hairline has started to bleed; pressing a flower to it to staunch the blood, the flower wilts on the instant, and her little black kitten, on nuzzling the polluted petals, drops dead. Radot is just building up, however, to his major production number, a Sabbat set-piece that still startles today. On her wedding night, Guillemette leaves her drunken old husband passed out on the bed – no consummation has taken place – and wanders into the forest in a conspicuously see-through nightdress. Quoting from Rex Ingram's 1926 film *The Magician*, Radot reveals a mob of rustic worshippers presided over by a lithe young semi-nude Devil. It's actually the famous Folies Bergère dancer Frédéric Rey, and his writhing routine involves a courtly female celebrant slipping out of her dress to reveal nothing underneath but a thong and silver high heels.

As satanic rituals go, there's little here of the carnivalesque obscenity that marked Benjamin Christensen's *Häxan*, nor even the oiled-up hedonism of *The Magician*. The mood is more like a diabolist-kitsch version of *Seven Brides for Seven Brothers*. Nevertheless, the amount of bare breasts and bottoms on display adds to the genuine head of steam that Radot works up, as huge dishes of unholy water emit clouds of sulphur and the tempo of the celebrants' carousing grows increasingly frenzied. The scene could be read as the sexual fantasy of an unsatisfied bride on her wedding night, yet Radot appears to take it quite literally. Elsewhere he makes no bones about the fact that Guillemette is a genuine witch; her use of a voodoo doll to get rid of her benefactor's elderly wife, for example, couldn't be clearer, and when a well-intentioned lawyer suggests at the end that she's

"the victim of too rich an imagination," he just sounds ridiculous. And yet, unlike her persecutors in the film, Radot passes no judgment on her, leaving us to read the placid features of Héléna Bossis as best we can.

"Convicted of sorcery, magic, murder, adultery and bestiality," Guillemette finally ends up in prison. Having been flogged, she makes the very nasty weals on her back magically fade away. When a priest points a crucifix at her they suddenly reappear, bleeding profusely against a mass of blackened bruising; the cut in her hairline re-opens too. The film provides a forecast, then, not just of the witchy eroticism that Euro horror would embrace some 20 years later, but also of the higher level of gruesomeness that accompanied it. By coincidence, Guillemette's diminutive gaoler is Alfred Baillou, who in 1970 would play a major role in *Morgane et ses nymphes*, one of the softcore extravaganzas sired by Radot's film.

None of the transgressive weirdness of *Guillemette Babin* found its way into the last 1940s example of French fantastique. Jean Faurez's portmanteau film *Histoires extraordinaires* (Extraordinary Stories) was made at the Studios Photosonor in Faurez's native Courbevoie and was released to French cinemagoers at Halloween 1949. The film's on-screen subtitle – *à faire peur ou à faire rire* (to frighten or amuse) – gives a clue to its light-hearted lack of impact, despite the abundant promise of getting together three Poe stories and prefacing them with one by Thomas de Quincey. The connective tissue involves a bunch of garrulous, tale-spinning French gendarmes, laborious scenes that were dropped entirely when Armor Films marketed the four segments as short subjects in the 1950s.

*Invitation à la valse* (Invitation to the Waltz) is a trifle in which a homicidal pianist (Roger Blin) serenades his girl victims with Chopin's Funeral March. *Le Cœur révélateur* (The Tell-Tale Heart) is a scrupulously faithful rendering; it even begins with the killer insisting, true to Baudelaire's translation of Poe's original, "Vrai! – je suis très nerveux, épouvantablement nerveux..." The killer is played by Faurez's co-scenarist Guy Decomble, but the effect of the adaptation is ruined by constantly cutting back to Decomble's confession in the police station. At least Faurez is brave enough to give us several close-ups of the victim's 'vulture' eye. *La Barrique d'amontillado* (The Cask of Amontillado) is the one undoubted success in the film, with Jules Berry and Fernand Ledoux beautifully matched as the drunken Harlequin and the man who proposes to immure him; their interplay gives queasy life to the sadistic impulse behind Poe's "bonne plaisanterie." *La Résurrection de Barnabé* (Barnaby's Resurrection), based on Poe's

*Thou Art the Man*, is the longest story and has a nice Jack-in-the-Box effect when the dead man pops up at dinner. Otherwise it's only memorable for Martial Rèbe's cockney-accented French in the title role.

When *Histoires extraordinaires* reached Paris cinemas in October 1949, Jean Cocteau was mid-way through filming *Orphée*, which in due course was put before British cinemagoers in May 1950 – several months, curiously enough, before its Paris premiere at the Colisée Gaumont in September. "*Orpheus*," observed London critic Virginia Graham, "is M Jean Cocteau at his most eerie, abstruse and symbolic."[49] Here, Cocteau set his characteristic stamp on Orpheus' trip to the Underworld by updating the story to the bohemian milieu of post-war Paris, casting Jean Marais as a conflicted poet who receives messages that come literally from Beyond (ie, via a radio transmitter) and then introducing a chillingly matter-of-fact pair of Death figures in Heurtebise (François Périer) and the Princess (María Casares).

Here, too, Cocteau served up a simple yet still-astonishing display of optical effects. Echoing the Beast's magic gauntlet in *La Belle et la Bête*, there are surgical gloves that snap onto the poet's hands by themselves, allowing him to pass through a mirror as if it were a rippling lake; there's also "the usual route" taken by the deathly chauffeur, a route that, in a nod to *Nosferatu*, suddenly turns to negative through his windshield. Together with slow motion, reverse filming and entrancing scenes of apparent weightlessness, these are the touches characterised by another contemporary critic, Elizabeth Frank, as "moments of great atmospheric beauty of an intensely sinister kind."[50] Just as sinister is the prolonged tribunal scene in which Casares is arraigned by her superiors for calling Orpheus' wife Eurydice before her time, together with the mordant conclusion of Heurtebise when the lovers are reunited on the earthly plane – "We had to return them to their swamp." The film was advertised in Britain as 'An Immortal Thriller', and it has proved exactly that.

In late 1959, exactly ten years after making *Orphée*, Cocteau made *Le Testament d'Orphée ou ne me demandez pas pourquoi* (The Testament of Orpheus, or: Don't Ask Me Why). The film was shot in the wake of Marcel Camus' *Orfeu negro* (Black Orpheus), an Oscar-winning French-Italian-Brazilian co-production with touches of voodoo and riotously colourful scenes of the Rio carnival. Cocteau's coldly contemplative envoi couldn't be more different, with constant self-referential allusions to "mon film *Orphée*" and even an on-screen acknowledgment that this latest work was to be "mon film d'adieu" (my farewell film). There are arresting

Jean Marais embraces the portal to the otherworld in *Orphée* (1949)

moments, of course; the 70-year-old Cocteau, effectively playing himself and longing for rebirth, is a time traveller who meets his own doppelgänger, encounters a humanoid horse and later gasps "Quelle horreur!" when impaled by a rubber-clad living statue. And this time the plank-like resurrection of *Nosferatu*, which he'd quoted before, is enacted by Cocteau himself. But as a summation of Cocteau's lifelong preoccupations the film substitutes surrealist obfuscation for the barest glimmer of narrative, and it's hobbled in particular by an interminable repetition of the earlier film's tribunal sequence, with Casares and Périer as the judges this time and Cocteau himself in the spotlight.

Back at the beginning of the 1950s, and back in the realm of slickly packaged commercial cinema, France produced one of the greatest black comedies in any language with Claude Autant-Lara's *L'Auberge rouge* (The Red Inn). Making the most of a hilariously inventive script by Jean Aurenche and Pierre Bost, Autant-Lara began shooting in March 1951 and on the film's release just before Halloween faced a firestorm of controversy, particularly from affronted Catholics. Based on a hideous, Sweeney Todd-style case of serial-killing innkeepers in 1830s Peyrebeille, the key to the film's success, in addition to the script and Autant-Lara's deft direction, is the dazzling interplay between comic star Fernandel, as a well-meaning, camel-faced Capuchin monk adrift in the snowy wastes of the Ardèche, and the vulgar opportunism of Françoise Rosay and Julien Carette as the monstrous publicans he encounters. Entirely studio-bound, the film rejoices in such ridiculous contrivances as a runaway monkey (played by a tiny actor) and macabre ones like the looming snowman that encases the latest murder victim. The scene in which Rosay confesses her sins to the hyperventilating Fernandel ("Well, if you must know, tonight's murder was the 102nd") is a classic.

Arguably the most unusual French product of the period was shot, like *Histoires extraordinaires*, at the Studios Photosonor. Paul Paviot's *Torticola contre Frankensberg* (Torticola versus Frankensberg) was first reviewed in December 1951 and turned out to be a 36-minute monster parody with future star Michel Piccoli as the titular Torticola. The uncredited make-up artist was *La Belle et la Bête*'s Hagop Arakelian, with other distinguished contributors ranging from designer Alexandre Trauner and composer Joseph Kosma to actors Roger Blin and Héléna Manson (both of whom had been among the victims of Clouzot's *Le Corbeau* in 1943). Even Pierre Brasseur and Daniel Gélin pop up, both of them uttering the same abominable gag: "Have you seen the Invisible Man?"

Torticola – "a bloodthirsty monster spun from the brain of a lunatic" – is shown reading Freud and grunts "See how brainy I am?" Frankensberg's other experimental subjects include a man with a cat's brain (he's called Meusenberg and mews a lot) and a corresponding cat with the man's brain. The latter gives the heroine directions to the Brittany castle that dominates the action, outside which cowled cultists drone their way through 'Frère Jacques'. Riffing on old-time movie serials by dividing itself into three episodes, Paviot's film plays for the most part like a surrealist student skit, with distant echoes of Britain's *Goon Show*. Featured in the May 1964 issue of *Famous Monsters of Filmland* under the ambiguous title 'The Most Horrible Frankenstein', the film remains interesting for sending up a form in which France had no real track record.

Among other shorts from the period was an experimental and highly atmospheric version of Poe's *Bérénice*, made in 1954 by writer-director Éric Rohmer (who cast himself as Poe's deranged, teeth-pulling obsessive) and strikingly photographed by Jacques Rivette; both men were to become key figures in France's Nouvelle Vague. But the closest French filmmakers got to a bona-fide horror feature in the early 1950s was Robert Darène's first film *Le Chevalier de la nuit* (The Knight of the Night). With frustrating

timidity, however, the subject was smothered in an excess of Belle Époque frou-frou. The film's interest lies in its script by playwright Jean Anouilh, whose fatalistic heroines had been reflected in his 'additional scenes' engagement on *La Fiancée des ténèbres* in 1944. He was also fond of 'two sides of the same coin' male characters, whether played by different actors, as in his post-war masterpiece *La Répétition*, or by the same, quick-changing performer, as in *L'Invitation au château*. Hence *Le Chevalier*'s potentially intriguing venture into Jekyll and Hyde territory.

Shot at the Studios de Billancourt in May and June 1953, *Le Chevalier* involves a 19th century aristocrat (Jean-Claude Pascal) being coaxed into splitting himself into good and evil entities. Unfortunately, the man's sweetheart (Renée Saint-Cyr) is a celebrated ballerina, inspiring Darène to squander a fusillade of agreeable Gothic effects on tediously extended ballet sequences. 'Two men, an angel and a demon, struggled within him,' panted the tag-line. 'Which one has vanquished the other?' Despite these echoes of the doppelgänger theme from Poe's *William Wilson*, most of the fun is provided by Pascal's Mephistophelean tempter, brilliantly portrayed by Jean Servais – the Belgian actor who not long before had played the malevolent side of the coin in the original staging of *La Répétition*.

## OLD WOUNDS

During the war, Hollywood horror films – long influenced by their German models – had acquired a German flavour of a different kind. In *Man Made Monster* (1940), Lionel Atwill could be heard invoking 'Destiny' while planning "a race of superior men." Similarly, John Carradine described his "dreams of creating a race of supermen" as "a laudable intent" in *Captive Wild Woman* (1942). Creepiest of all, Erich von Stroheim, in *The Lady and the Monster* (1943), observed that "When you try to solve the mysteries of nature, it doesn't matter whether you experiment with guinea pigs or human beings."

These and many other unhinged doctors, though not actually portrayed as Nazis, were certainly intended to be read as such. But when the war ended with the apocalyptic shocks of Hiroshima and Nagasaki, together with profoundly horrifying documentary evidence of Nazi war crimes, the behaviour of movie mad scientists suddenly seemed at best trivial, at worst tasteless, helping to send the traditional horror film into temporary eclipse.

Germany itself was in ruins, split into sections by the Allies, and – with an economic miracle akin to Italy's still some way off – its people were left to contemplate what Carl Jung controversially dubbed 'collective guilt'. So December 1950 was a very strange moment for Peter Lorre to return to Germany for his one and only attempt at direction, providing visual echoes of M in a film called *Der Verlorene* (The Lost One). M itself had been remade in Los Angeles that summer by Joseph Losey, but Lorre – who also co-wrote the script – went a different route with *Der Verlorene*, re-opening old sores by playing a Nazi research scientist whose betrayal by his fiancée triggers homicidal urges. A few years later a more traditional serial killer – disfigured, black-garbed – stalked a circus in Paul May's *Phantom des großen Zeltes* (Phantom of the Big Top). This Christmas 1954 release not only recalled the brief Jack the Ripper section of the 30-year-old *Das Wachsfigurenkabinett*, it also prefigured the Edgar Wallace adaptations that were soon to become so popular in Germany. The film's co-writer, Egon Eis, had not only scripted the 1931 release *Der Zinker* (The Squeaker),

Erich von Stroheim with Hildegard Knef's all-new incarnation of *Alraune* (1952)

one of a handful of pre-war Wallace subjects, but would also partake in the Wallace bonanza to come.

A more fantastical echo of Germany's Weimar horrors was provided by director Arthur Maria Rabenalt, whose new version of the Hanns Heinz Ewers chestnut *Alraune* was shot in Munich in June 1952. Again, it was a strange moment to revive memories of a lurid eugenics fantasy that, in retrospect, seemed to predict the work of Nazi scientists, especially because none other than the above-mentioned Erich von Stroheim was starring as Professor ten Brinken. Presumably with this in mind, a process of post-war softening was introduced, turning Alraune into an introspective beauty who, though responsible for her share of deaths, finally confesses that "There is an evil force I can't fight against that has a strange power over me" – a line that, in the aftermath of the Nazis, sounds rather like "I was only obeying orders."

Unfortunately, Hildegard Knef is unable to transfuse into Alraune even a fraction of the adamantine charisma of Brigitte Helm. Confounding the producers' hopes of smuggling "something a little bit risqué" past the censors, she reportedly refused to play a heartless monster on the principle that "I want to be allowed to love."[51] Von Stroheim apparently had ideas of his own too, and screenwriter Kurt Heuser eventually claimed to recognise just one sentence from his 276-page script. Trying to reconcile these four conflicting pressures, Rabenalt ended up, perhaps unsurprisingly, with a dog's dinner. There are felicitous moments, however, including the orgasmic rush of natural

resources when Alraune sniffs out a valuable spring on the Professor's land and the climactic scene in which the girl is shot down by her creator, who (in a tame nod to the incestuous passions of the silent version) explains that "I didn't want anybody else to have her." The first appearance of Alraune, singing a siren song and being spotted in different oneiric guises by her three suitors, is beautifully done too, and it's cleverly reversed at the end when she has brief visions of them – all now dead – as she runs headlong through the Professor's snow-covered estate.

"Bull-necked, with the baleful eye of the alchemists," observed *Der Spiegel*, "Erich von Stroheim plays the mandrake-father as a late flowering of the Middle Ages."[52] An old hand at glowering mad-scientist melodramatics, von Stroheim is always good value, and a charming reminder of his Hollywood horrors is provided here by another of the Professor's creations, a ridiculous caged gorilla in front of which Alraune poses demurely. The film also contains a pointer to the future in the form of romantic lead Karlheinz Böhm, who at the end of the decade would play the film-studio psychopath in Michael Powell's *Peeping Tom*.

By the time Powell's film went into production in October 1959, post-war European horror had finally begun to take on cohesive life, engendered in the main by a money-spinning burst of activity in British studios. But an internationally successful French film had played its part too, a film whose bitter and bilious tone owed something to enmities stirred up during the war and still reverberating ten years on.

# Part Two

## *Experiments in Evil* 1954-1963

Just as Germany had been responsible for the efflorescence of continental Gothic in the aftermath of World War I, so France and Italy would between them bring about its delayed reappearance after World War II. It was a strange state of affairs, with one industry, the French one, stumbling into the genre more or less by chance and then showing a high-minded disinclination to stay there, and the other, in Italy, rolling up its sleeves to apply itself to a form that held only marginal interest for local filmgoers but could be very profitably exported.

In between the French and Italian breakthroughs came the revolutionary charge provided by Great Britain, where a small company called Hammer Film Productions revived the genre with spectacular international success. Italy's subsequent enthusiasm for horror made perfect commercial sense in view of this startling development, but France, disdaining the vulgar lure of exploitation, held stubbornly aloof. This despite the fact that French filmmakers had produced two of the most brutally effective horror pictures of the 1950s. Indeed, the first of them, *Les Diaboliques*, had been matched in the UK with one of Hammer's

early forays into SF-Gothic, *X the Unknown*, a double-bill that, according to the young novelist and horror fan Kingsley Amis, "took days off my life."[1] Yet no flood of French fantastique resulted.

Italy's burgeoning horror expertise was particularly remarkable given the industry's almost total lack – Soldati's wartime version of *Malombra* notwithstanding – of any background in the genre. In the 1950s, Italian cinema could boast not only such internationally fêted talents as Fellini, De Sica, Antonioni, Rossellini and Visconti, but also a wealth of activity focused on popular genres, ensuring an extraordinary box-office high of 819 million admissions in 1955. Yet horror was a conspicuous absentee among the crowd-pleasing filoni ('streams') so energetically exploited by local producers.

Even so, the country's peplum (sword-and-sandal) pictures and other swashbuckling costume dramas frequently provided an outlet for suppressed sadism, and even Totò, the delightfully lugubrious comic star whose 1950s output was prodigious, was transported mid-decade from a monochrome Italy to a luridly coloured Underworld in Camillo Mastrocinque's *Totò* all'*inferno* (Totò in Hell). Otherwise, De Sica could be seen loosening the stays of neo-realism with the spectral fantasy of *Miracolo a Milano* (Miracle in Milan) and future horror specialist Piero Regnoli was co-writer of Filippo Walter Ratti's *Non è mai troppo tardi* (It's Never Too Late), a version of *A Christmas Carol* with Paolo Stoppa as the Scrooge equivalent. But that was about it.

France, too, maintained a healthy popular industry as well as nurturing such major names as René Clément, Jacques Becker, Claude Autant-Lara, André Cayatte and Max Ophüls. It was a period that, in 1954, would be savaged by François Truffaut for its rather stuffy adherence to "la tradition de qualité," an adherence that, in Truffaut's view, qualified the majority of France's output as "le cinéma de Papa."[2] Ossified or not, it was certainly a period that had no use for horror. Yet among the major names that could rank with Becker and company was a man whose bleak view of humanity embraced bourgeois squalor, post-war guilt and violent death. Even while the shock waves from Truffaut's notorious broadside were still fresh, Henri-Georges Clouzot was preparing the black-hearted provincial nightmare that would help to shorten Kingsley Amis' life.

## VULGAR, NASTY – AND FRENCH

When Clouzot made *Les Diaboliques*, he was fresh from a huge hit that had finally established his name internationally – not that this did anything to brighten the near-nihilistic world view expressed in his films. Shooting on *Le Salaire de la peur* (The Wages of Fear) had occupied him from August 1951 to September 1952; on its release in April 1953 it was recognised instantly as a grimy, sweat-stained masterwork of the thriller genre. With four jaded men driving two trucks of nitroglycerine across a hazard-strewn South American landscape, the film was aptly apostrophised on its US release by critic Bosley Crowther: "You sit there waiting for the theatre to explode."[3]

Clouzot turned next to a novel, *Celle qui n'était plus* (She Who Was No More), by the ace writing team of Pierre Boileau and Thomas Narcejac, commencing production in July 1954 on a screen adaptation announced as *Les Veuves* (The Widows). The book's narrative, in which a salesman plots with his mistress to kill his domineering wife, was departed from in many ways, but its mood of gathering hysteria – and the threat of a return from the grave by the murdered person – was adhered to so brilliantly that it was decided to beef up the title, hence *Les Diaboliques* (The Diabolical Ones). Recompensing Clouzot for the film's gruelling 16-week shoot, the film rapidly became a smash hit in France, also becoming a crossover success in the UK (as *The Fiends*) and the US

(as plain *Diabolique*). Writing in the highbrow British magazine *Tribune*, R D Smith not only deplored the film's "fever of calculated perversion"[4] but also headed his review 'Vulgar, nasty – and French'. Publicity of this sort didn't harm the film's prospects one iota.

> *Christina Delasalle and Nicole Horner are wife and mistress, respectively, to the tyrannical and penny-pinching headmaster of a down-at-heel boys' school in Saint-Cloud. Michel is equally abusive to both women, and they eventually hatch an elaborate plot to kill him. Luring him to Nicole's place in Niort, they dose him with drugged whisky and drown him in the bath. Unhappily, his waterlogged remains proceed to go nerve-shatteringly astray...*

*Les Diaboliques* has been so widely imitated that repetition and familiarity seem to have called in question the film's status as horror, with the debate stretching right back to horror's first historians, both of whom were writing as early as 1967. According to Carlos Clarens, "*Les Diaboliques* is a pure puzzle, a thriller (however black) that employs the apparatus of terror in the context of a detective story."[5] Ivan Butler, however, was unequivocal. "In *Le Salaire de la peur* and even in *Le Corbeau*," he wrote, "horror is an incidental ingredient. In *Les Diaboliques* it is almost the entire recipe."[6] Significantly, critics during the film's original run sided pretty squarely with Butler. Under the heading *A Diabolical Horror Film*, *Life* magazine noted in March 1956 that "All this winter a French horror movie called *Diabolique* has been scaring the wits out of Americans in a few small art theaters. But now, booked for release in big movie houses and even drive-in theaters, it will start spreading its sensational shocks and shudders on a grand scale."[7]

That *Les Diaboliques* does indeed function as a horror film is clear, not just from the squalid and prolonged murder sequence, but from the script's central conceit – that a man appears to have cheated death and is bedevilling his killers from beyond the grave. That the resolution turns out to be an earthbound one is neither here nor there, given the stand-out horror sequence that immediately precedes it. This scene, echoing the initial murder in that it too is staged in the clinical whiteness of a bathroom, involves an apparition so horrific it slams the most sensitive of the two women against the wall and induces heart failure. A horror set-piece timed to the agonising rhythm of a prolonged death rattle, it climaxes with a uniquely cruel juxtaposition – the victim's eyes rolling up into her head and, a moment later, the 'apparition' apparently popping its own eyes from their sockets.

The preceding action, even in its most humdrum details, is queasily horrific too; as Dilys Powell so

Simone Signoret
and Véra Clouzot,
jittery post-war
conspirators in *Les
Diaboliques* (1954)

# LES DIABOLIQUES

France 1954
UK: *The Fiends*
US: *Diabolique*
Filmsonor Société Anonyme / Véra Films
114 minutes b/w
production began 18 July 1954
. . . . . . . . . . . . . . . . . . . . . . . . . . . . . .
Director of Photography: Armand Thirard;
Art Director: Léon Barsacq; Editor: Madeleine
Gug; Sound: William Robert Sivel; Music:
Georges Van Parys; Make-up: Anatole Paris;
Screenplay: H G Clouzot, Jérôme Geronimi,
in collaboration with René Masson, Frédéric
Grendel, from the novel *Celle qui n'était plus* by
Boileau-Narcejac; Production Manager: Louis
de Masure; Producer-Director: H G Clouzot

Simone Signoret (Nicole Horner); Véra Clouzot
(Christina Delasalle); Paul Meurisse (Michel

Delassalle); Charles Vanel (Commissaire
Alfred Fichet); Pierre Larquey (M Drain);
Michel Serrault (M Raymond); Jean Brochard
(Plantiveau); Noël Roquevert (M Herboux);
Thérèse Dorny (Mme Herboux); Georges
Chamarat (Dr Loisy); Robert Dalban
(mechanic); Camille Guérini (photographer);
Jacques Hilling (morgue attendant); Henri
Coutet (second morgue attendant); Jean
Lefebure (soldier); Aminda Montserrat (Mme
Plantiveau); Jean Témerson (bellboy); Jacques
Varennes (M Bridoux); Georges Poujouly
(Soudieu); Yves-Marie Maurin (Moinet);
uncredited: Robert Acon Rodrigo (José); Henri
Humbert (Patard); Michel Dumur (Ritberger);
Jean-Pierre Bonnefous (De Gascuel); Johnny
Hallyday (student); Madeleine Suffel
(dry-cleaning woman); Georges Béver;
Dominique Brun; Jean Clarieux; Jimmy Urbain

Since there seems to be a vogue at the moment for the horrid in
entertainment, Henri-Georges Clouzot's *Les Diaboliques* is likely to do well. It
is an extremely clever film, and very horrid indeed ... Clouzot's juggling with
delayed horror is brilliant; Armand Thirard's black and white photography a
thing of subtle lights and unholy shadows. The horridest shock of all is kept
for the very end. *The Observer* 4 December 1955

When I said 'yes' that splendid afternoon in July 1954 to his [Clouzot's]
offer to play in *Les Diaboliques*, I knew that I was letting myself in for a hell
of a time. I had no idea that it was going to be as wretched as it was for
16 weeks ... [by the end of which] the director, his wife and I were no
longer on speaking terms. Thank God, Meurisse and Vanel were on that set.
Simone Signoret [*La Nostalgie n'est plus ce qu'elle était*, 1976]

eloquently put it at the time, "Clouzot fixes you, not
with a glittering eye but with the eye of a mackerel two
days dead; you cannot escape the dreadful hypnosis."[8]
The clamminess begins right away, with Clouzot's

recurrent water imagery introduced by an opening
image of scum on the surface of a neglected swimming
pool. Moments later the tyres of the Delasalles' 2CV
Camionette splash their way through a dirty puddle
(symbolically crushing a child's paper boat in the
process); later still we have watered wine, rain-dripping
school gates, bathroom trauma, an anonymous body
fished out of the Seine, even a pool of piss left in
the 2CV by an inebriated soldier. "You do seem to
have water very much on your minds in this house,"
deadpans a grizzled detective in the latter stages.

The grim atmosphere of the school, meanwhile,
is memorably sketched in. Michel, played by the
splendidly reptilian Paul Meurisse, is a shabby Little
Hitler with delusions of grandeur represented by his
bamboo cigarette holder and Prince of Wales suit.
Among his incidental pleasures are feeding rotten
fish to the entire establishment and, as is pretty
unmistakably indicated, an occasional afternoon
devoted to marital rape. That the women, brilliantly
played by the birdlike Véra Clouzot and statuesque
Simone Signoret, are in a desperate situation, and that
they have opted for a drastic solution, is made clear
when Nicole stares impassively at Michel's retreating
back and says coolly, "I shan't have any regrets."

The murder in Niort, replete with suspense, is made
all the queasier by Clouzot's judicious introduction of
incongruous humour. Straying into the film from some
black farce by Jean Anouilh, Nicole's fussy boarders

include Monsieur Herboux, the kind of bespectacled Frenchman who wears his beret even in bed. Setting his watch by the popular radio comedian Zappy Max, he's horrified by the pipe-rattling disturbances coming from the room above. "Midnight baths?" he fumes. "The decline of Rome!" Little does he realise that these ill-timed ablutions are the cover for a hideous murder.

Pushed beneath the water, Michel becomes an inhuman, slick-haired husk within seconds, and it's this ghastly image that will resonate throughout the remainder of the film. His body, stashed in a large wicker basket, is dumped in the school's brackish swimming pool at the film's halfway point, and after that the heart-in-mouth horror that Michel might have transcended death is sustained with spider-like cunning. As *Time* magazine put it, the film comes complete "with a moral: you can lead a corpse to water, but you can't make it sink."[9]

What with stressful visits to the morgue to inspect 'number 4702' and Michel's face apparently materialising in the annual school photograph, the nail-biting tension inevitably involves the gradual breakdown of Christina and Nicole's relationship. Ironically, this breakdown goes hand in hand with intimations that their collusion may have had a lesbian aspect, an aspect that was made quite plain with their counterparts in the novel. It's also during this section that we're introduced to the cigar-chewing and creepily persistent detective, Commissaire Fichet, charmingly played by Charles Vanel. As an aside, it's worth noting that Fichet is an obvious precursor to the Lieutenant Columbo character later popularised on US television; coincidentally or otherwise, Columbo's creators originally called the character Lieutenant Fisher.

Abetted by the sumptuously inky images of his regular cinematographer Armand Thirard, Clouzot makes brilliant use in the final stretch – never bettered, in fact – of several apparent clichés of the 'old dark house' thriller. The pathetically vulnerable heroine, backlit in her white nightdress; the gloved hand gliding up a banister; the creaking door; the panicked cry of "Qui est là?" and the endless, darkened corridor with light spilling from a distant doorway – all these are supplemented by such novel touches as a sudden burst of typing, a view of Michel's hat and gloves propped against the typewriter, and the freshly typed paper that reads 'Michel Delasalle' over and over. And then the lights go out. "The terrors mount to the satisfying crescendo of a Gothic nightmare,"[10] noted one reviewer, after which we get the much-imitated twist and finally a playful suggestion that yet another ghost might be at large.

The film as a whole, however, is the exact opposite of playful. It seems steeped in the mood of festering recrimination that followed the war – an unsurprising mood, perhaps, given that Clouzot himself had been unjustly banned from filmmaking when *Le Corbeau* was assumed to be collaborationist.

European horror may have gone quiet again for a while after *Les Diaboliques*, but its flinty, cold-hearted example would be by no means forgotten. Quite apart from its enduring power as a well-nigh perfect horror-thriller, the film remains significant for the impact it had on Alfred Hitchcock. The film's English-language reviews contained several remarks calculated to sting Hitchcock's pride, from "Hitchcock is suaver; but this Frenchman is joltier"[11] to "Mr Hitchcock, if he is not being displaced from his throne, will at least have to move over."[12] Matters became worse when Hitchcock's own Boileau-Narcejac adaptation, *Vertigo*, bombed both critically and commercially. No less a game-changing horror classic than *Psycho* can therefore be seen as Hitchcock's means of 'getting even' with Clouzot, sharing with *Les Diaboliques* such features as a seedy provincial setting, glacial monochrome photography, murder in a boarding house, desperate female leads, a fleabitten detective who shows up in the final act, an appeal to cinemagoers not to reveal the story's shattering twist – and, above all, horrible events staged in bathrooms.

The film's influence extended well beyond *Psycho*, however. Not only would its plot mechanics be replicated all over the world, but its sleazy, verging on fly-blown, atmosphere would sink deep into the fabric of European horror. France itself may have made no special effort to replicate its success, but in Italy, for example, the black gloves worn by Clouzot's nocturnal interloper during the film's climax would become an inescapable signifier of the giallo sub-genre, while the bilious view of marital relations contained in the film became a staple feature of Italy's Gothic horrors.

While making *Les Diaboliques*, Simone Signoret was getting ready to play the lead, opposite her husband Yves Montand, in a French adaptation of Arthur Miller's explosive play *The Crucible*. *Les Sorcières de Salem* (The Witches of Salem), as it was retitled, duly opened at the Théâtre Sarah Bernhardt in December 1954 and ran for a year. By August 1956, the original stage director, Raymond Rouleau, was making a controversial film version, with the gamine Mylene Demongeot added to the Signoret-Montand star-power and a screenplay in which Jean-Paul Sartre, no less, put his own spin on Miller's political reading of the 17th century witch trials. The result – which, unusually, was an East German co-production – is as powerful, austere and moving as André Michel's similarly titled *La Sorcière* (The Witch) is vapid, pretty and uninvolving. Begun in August 1955, the film has Maurice Ronet, as a boorish French engineer billeted in Sweden, inexplicably forsaking Nicole Courcel's interesting and tough local businesswoman for Marina Vlady's ridiculous 'wild child' and suspected witch. This Swedish co-production got plenty of mileage from Vlady's provocative (and absurdly airbrushed) performance, but it only really comes alive when Ronet is trapped in quicksand. Its supernatural content, in any case, is almost zero.

While Simone Signoret plunged, post-*Diaboliques*, into the world of trumped-up New England witchcraft trials, her *Diaboliques* co-star Paul Meurisse was responsible for a few touches of diabolism in Henri Decoin's *L'Affaire des poisons* (The Affair of the Poisons). With Meurisse a stand-out as the satanic Abbé Guibourg, this grim reconstruction of the 17th century 'inheritance powders' scandal was made in the summer of 1955 and paired Meurisse with France's premier femme fatale, Viviane Romance. The writers of *Les Diaboliques*, meanwhile, took a little longer to follow it up. Finally, Boileau and Narcejac provided the source novel and script for Luis Saslavsky's *Les Louves* (The She-Wolves). Shot at

US import Anthony Quinn and Italian bombshell Gina Lollobrigida in the underwhelming *Notre-Dame de Paris* (1956)

the end of 1956, this announces its nerve-jangling intentions with the screaming of a siren in its very first shot. The intrigue that develops when escaped POW François Périer assumes the identity of a dead colleague, taking refuge with the dead man's doting pen-friend (Micheline Presle), is expertly contrived, leading to a typically ingenious twist as Presle screams at Périer to stay alive from the opposite side of a locked door. Jeanne Moreau is also involved, conducting a moodily lit communal seance, and the film's kinship with *Les Diaboliques* was emphasised by its US title, *Demoniac*.

In the mid-1950s, French filmmakers' reluctance to venture further into horror may have been aggravated by the elephantine misfire that was *Notre-Dame de Paris*, a new version of the Victor Hugo novel previously filmed as *The Hunchback of Notre Dame* – and duly acquiring that title in its export version. This French-Italian co-production, scheduled to start in early March 1956, was delayed until 17 April in order for the US star Anthony Quinn to complete work in California on *Man from Del Rio*. The wait was hardly worth it, given that Quinn's Quasimodo, sporting the most inconspicuous hump imaginable, is a negligible presence relative to the Quasimodos played previously by Lon Chaney and Charles Laughton. The focus is really on the Italian bombshell Gina Lollobrigida, who was at the height of her 'La Lollo' celebrity and here plays a truly sumptuous Esmeralda. The film's deadening attempt at epic sweep was the work of old-school director Jean Delannoy. One of the prime bêtes noires of the up-and-coming generation of French cineastes, he proved here that Truffaut's 'cinéma de Papa' jibe had some validity.

## FREDA? BUT IT'S ITALIAN!

Two years after Clouzot made *Les Diaboliques*, Riccardo Freda initiated a project in Rome that reproduced much of Clouzot's noirish post-war modernity – but with added supernatural and science-fiction overtones.

When pitching *I vampiri* (The Vampires) to producers Luigi Carpentieri and Ermanno Donati in 1956, the 47-year-old Freda was well known for such costume spectaculars as *Il cavaliere misterioso* (The Mysterious Rider) and *La vendetta di Aquila Nera* (Revenge of the Black Eagle). Another title, *Il conte Ugolino* (Count Ugolino), came out in 1949 and was derived from Dante's account of a 13th century nobleman who, having been walled up in a tower by a conniving Archbishop, may or may not have resorted to cannibalism. There's nothing here, of course, resembling the Count's obsessive head-chewing as seen in the 1911 film *L'Inferno*.

But there's an abundance of dungeon atmospherics and a particularly grim ending, with the bricks sealing up the Count's prison being smashed down and his daughter (played by Freda's wife, Gianna Maria Canale) venturing inside. The final shot shows her recoiling in close-up from whatever it is she finds there and letting loose a bloodcurdling scream.

Despite this highly suggestive moment, full-on Gothic horror remained uncharted territory to Italian filmmakers, but that didn't prevent Freda from telling Carpentieri and Donati that he could have a treatment ready in 24 hours and make the picture itself in a fortnight. (Italian trade papers of the period indicate that the actual shooting of the film in December 1956 took at least twice as long, but it was a bold claim either way.) The screenplay, eventually thrown together by Freda in collaboration with Piero Regnoli, looted any number of previous films but owed its chief inspiration to the legend of Countess Erszébet Báthory, the 16th century 'Blood Countess' who went to extreme lengths to preserve her youth. Freda listed German Expressionism and, more specifically, Dreyer's *Vampyr* among his personal influences while stoutly maintaining that "The kind of creatures invented by Bram Stoker don't interest me. Yet I know that modern vampirism exists, draining the vitality of the person sitting next to you."[13]

*Paris, 1957. Over a six-month period, four young women have been discovered drained of blood, prompting journalist Pierre Lantin to vie with Inspector Chantal in tracking down the killer. Lantin has a beautiful admirer in Gisèle du Grand, yet he's as indifferent to her as his father was, 30 years earlier, to Gisèle's now elderly aunt, the Duchesse du Grand. Lantin's instinctive dislike is explained when the two women turn out to be one and the same.*

"Hey, you guys! There's a woman drowned over here!" So begins *I vampiri*, with a group of workmen discovering a corpse in the Aniene (doubling as the Seine). The quarry, the mechanical digger, the all-round matter-of-factness – all these situate Freda's film very firmly in the modern world. But as the newspaper montages and bantering exchanges between reporters and policemen pile up, the strongest echo is of an earlier modern world, the inter-war one captured in the Michael Curtiz films *Doctor X* and *Mystery of the Wax Museum*.

The aggressively contemporary setting of those films – though not in itself a deterrent to Gothic effects – was mandated by a nervous Warner Bros management unwilling to fully embrace the horror craze set off by Universal. *I vampiri* ended up similarly compromised. Wary of censorship, Freda's producers dropped all his nastier conceits, several of which he claimed to have actually filmed. A drug addict called Joseph Signoret (the surname a nod, perhaps, to one of the leading ladies of *Les Diaboliques*) is the robotic pawn who supplies the Duchesse du Grand and her scientist cousin with the victims they need; scenes in which he was guillotined, put back together by the mad Professor, and literally lost his transplanted head while under police interrogation were all deleted. Similarly, the imprisoned heroine, Lorette, wasn't rescued in Freda's original draft, but found hanged. These changes, plus a general drift towards making *I vampiri* into a standard police procedural, presumably explain why Freda – always a tempestuous kind of director – stormed off the set towards the end of production. His gifted cinematographer, Mario Bava, took over direction for the remainder of the schedule.

Though blunted somewhat as a horror film, *I vampiri* nevertheless bristles with suggestive possibilities. Of the many contemporary Gothics that had preceded it, Freda and co-writer Regnoli seem to have fixed, plot-wise, on *The Corpse Vanishes*, a Monogram potboiler made in the spring of 1942 in which Bela Lugosi was a mad doctor draining young brides of spinal fluid (or something) in order to preserve the youth of his wife, a Countess.

Yet, in terms of Gothic atmosphere, *I vampiri* echoes a much more distinguished film made seven years later. "No one's seen her face in years," remarks Lantin's ill-fated friend of the permanently veiled Duchesse du Grand. "She was a beautiful woman who never adjusted to growing old," he adds. And when Bava's camera glides down from a chandelier to reveal a string quartet, a group of ossified dancers and a massive stone-flagged ballroom, the aroma of Billy Wilder's *Sunset Blvd* is confirmed. A couple of elderly socialites debate whether the Duchess' last ball was held in 1925 or 1929, the very era in which Wilder's deluded Norma Desmond was in her movie-star prime. In the same way, Lantin himself becomes identified with Wilder's Joe Gillis character and the elderly Professor du Grand with Norma's devoted butler, Max von Mayerling.

That *Sunset Blvd* was itself a disguised updating of *Dracula* made it a natural for reinterpretation as a horror film, and Freda garnishes the resultant blend of ancient and modern with many telling details. Standard-issue scenes in which Lantin confers with a pathologist and a newspaper editor (cameo roles played by Freda and Regnoli respectively) are yoked together with an extraordinary funeral for the Professor, allowing production designer Beni Montresor to lay down a

# I VAMPIRI

*Italy 1956*
UK: *Lust of the Vampire*
US: *The Devil's Commandment*
Titanus / Athena Cinematografica
81 minutes b/w
production began late November 1956

Director of Photography: Mario Bava; Art
Director: Beni Montresor; Editor: Roberto
Cinquini; Sound: Mario Messina; Music:
Roman Vlad; Make-up: Franco Freda; Special
Effects: Mario Bava [uncredited]; Screenplay:
Piero Regnoli, Rijk Sijöstrom, Riccardo
Freda; Story: Piero Regnoli, Rijk Sijöstrom;
Producers: Ermanno Donati, Luigi Carpentieri,
Piero Donati; Director: Riccardo Freda

*Gianna Maria Canale (Gisèle du Grand);
Carlo D'Angelo (Inspector Santel); Dario
Michaëlis (Pierre Lantin); Wandisa Guida
(Lorette Robert); Antoine Balpêtré (Professor
Julien du Grand); Paul Muller (Joseph
Signoret); Angiolo Galassi (Ronald Fontaine);
Renato Tontini (Rinaldo, du Grand's
assistant); Charles Fawcett (Lorette's father);
Miranda Campa (Lorette's mother); Gisella
Mancinotti (Lorette's friend); uncredited:
Barbara Wohl (Lisette); Ronny Holliday
(Nora); Joy Holliday (Anita); Riccardo Freda
(doctor); Piero Regnoli (M Bourgeois, editor);
Emilio Petacci (antiques dealer); Armando
Annuale (mourner)*

Touted as the 'first Italian horror film', this piece by Freda goes over
material that isn't especially original, not so much in story terms but more
in the way the various situations are resolved. The film can't, therefore,
be called a complete success, though it doesn't lack for sequences that are
pretty shocking. *Intermezzo* 30 June 1957

Setting my film in the 1950s meant that I could avoid the expense of
period recreation and also make my story more credible. I wanted
the audience to leave the cinema thinking to themselves, 'That could
happen right here, it could happen right now!'
Riccardo Freda [quoted in Poindron, *Riccardo Freda: Un pirate à la caméra*, 1994]

A veiled, aristocratic crone in the midst of Beni Montresor's
extraordinary mausoleum set in *I vampiri* (1956)

we later discover, has concealed lights in its eyes that
pulse out a warning when the police descend on the
Château du Grand. For the Professor's funeral was only
a ruse to offset suspicion; his ultra-modern laboratory,
with its all-important blood-transfusion apparatus,
is still up and running in the castle's crumbling
basement. The abducted Lorette, meanwhile, wakes
in a shadowy lumber room in the attic, finding herself
eyed by a dangling fruit bat and discovering three
skeletal corpses in the next room.

Early on, the film boasts a classic suspense
sequence in which showgirl Nora is waylaid in her
dressing room by the looming drug addict – an early
role for the Swiss actor Paul Muller, who would
become a ubiquitous figure in Euro horror. Yet the
show-stopping moment in which it's revealed that
Gisèle and her aunt are the same person is seriously
muffed. To age Gianna Maria Canale before our
very eyes, Bava – a special effects expert as well as
a brilliant cameraman – used the same process of
graduated filters that Karl Struss had devised for the
silent version of *Ben-Hur*. It's a terrific effect in itself,
but the make-up it reveals is entirely inadequate.
Given that the Duchess was rebuffed by Lantin's

blueprint for the crumbling, skull-and-crossbones
magnificence that would predominate in future Italian
Gothics. Reconfiguring ancient architecture for a
specifically modern purpose, one of the stone skulls,

father only 30 years before, she could feasibly be around 50. Unfortunately, the veiled, shuffling creature seen in the funeral sequence has suggested a hideous crone, as does the horrified recoil of the young man who's privy to Gisèle's transformation. What we get, however, is by no means a crone. Canale herself was only 29 at the time, and a few crude pencil marks, together with a silver wig that fails to match her hairstyle of only a few seconds before, aren't enough to 'sell' this crucial moment.

Though poorly motivated, the young man's horrified recoil on seeing the 'real' Gisèle says a lot about *I vampiri*'s positioning of a blood-lusting, megalomaniac female at the centre of the action. This dominating figure, a classic example of what Barbara Creed has dubbed the 'monstrous-feminine', was to arouse conflicting feelings of fear and desire, attraction and repulsion in any number of Italian horror films to come. In this first attempt, the dichotomy is reflected in Montresor's beautifully designed castle interior by statuesque gryphons sporting grotesquely enlarged breasts. It's just one more way in which *I vampiri* established itself as a trailblazer.

The film was to have its effect by stealth, however, for it made little impact on first release, grossing just 125,300,000 lire – in stark contrast to a contemporaneous British film that succeeded in turning the genre on its head overnight. And, in this instance, the word 'contemporaneous' is pretty much exact. *I vampiri* is first mentioned in the 'film in lavorazione' (films in production) column of the fortnightly trade paper *Cinema Nuovo* on 1 December 1956, a date neatly corresponding with the calendar – open at 'Dicembre 1956' – that hovers above Piero Regnoli's head in the newspaper office scene. Clearly, then, Freda's film was in production at the same time as Terence Fisher's *The Curse of Frankenstein*, which had begun at Bray Studios near London on 19 November. In due course, *I vampiri* would receive its censorship visa on Wednesday 3 April 1957 (opening in Italian theatres two days later), while Fisher's film had its 'X' certificate approved by the British Board of Film Censors on Monday the 8th.

Though nearly four weeks would elapse before *The Curse of Frankenstein* opened in the UK, it proceeded to smash attendance records throughout the country and did similarly phenomenal business in the USA, causing Hammer Film Productions to turn their thoughts, not unnaturally, to adapting *Dracula* as a follow-up. Freda, meanwhile, was left to puzzle over why *I vampiri* failed to make much impression even on Italian audiences. "I was in San Remo," he recalled. "And I found myself outside a cinema where *I vampiri* was playing. At that time I'd sometimes go

into the auditorium to study an audience's reaction. I don't know why, but the theatre was almost empty ... Anyway, plenty of people were attracted by the posters, which were extremely beautiful. The people would read *I vampiri* ... *I vampiri* ... And that appeared to tempt them. Then at the very last moment they'd notice the name Freda. The reaction was kind of automatic. 'Freda? But it's Italian – it must be terrible. Italians can't make this kind of movie.'"[14]

While Freda contemplated the future ruse of giving himself a British-sounding pseudonym, the open door represented by *I vampiri* appeared to have closed already. Italy's nascent Gothic strain would therefore go into hibernation for a couple of years, to be dusted off only when *The Curse of Frankenstein* and particularly *Dracula* did excellent business at Italian box-offices.

## MESSIEURS OPALE ET DORMEUIL

While Italian Gothic hibernated, so did continental horror in general. It returned in the opening months of 1959 with two films shot in Paris – the real Paris, not the fake one created for *I vampiri* by Mario Bava's camera trickery. The first of these pictures was directed by a grand master of French cinema, Jean Renoir. Seeking to reconcile the rivalry between cinema and television, the 64-year-old writer-director of such classics as *La Grande illusion* and *La Règle du jeu* had come up with a trailblazing concept – a film that could play on TV and enjoy a theatrical release at the same time.

Trailblazing it may have been, but the concept was decidedly unwelcome. Made in January 1959 and showcased at the Venice Film Festival on 8 September, *Le Testament du docteur Cordelier* was held up – for both TV and cinema audiences – by a dispute with the Federation of French Film Exhibitors, who considered it unfair competition on the grounds that it was made for the state-subsidised Radiodiffusion-Télévision Française. "French exhibs," noted *Variety* in October 1960, "also have called on foreign colleagues to boycott the pic."[15] As a result, the hoped-for simultaneous premiere only took place on 16 November 1961. Renoir's experimental hybrid has suffered something of an identity crisis ever since, which is perhaps appropriate given its source in R L Stevenson's 1886 novella *Strange Case of Dr Jekyll and Mr Hyde*.

*Maître Joly, solicitor to the distinguished psychiatrist Dr Cordelier, is disconcerted when his client makes out a will leaving everything to an unknown quantity called Monsieur Opale. Soon afterwards, Joly witnesses a little girl being attacked in the street; giving chase, he's horrified when the thuggish culprit admits himself (with a key) into Cordelier's suburban home. Then, as*

Pillar of society: Jean-Louis Barrault as a Parisian Dr Jekyll in *Le Testament du docteur Cordelier* (1959)

*Opale's outrages accumulate and a manhunt ensues, Cordelier arranges to give his arch rival, Séverin, a private demonstration of his latest experiment...*

Over a ten-day shooting period Renoir utilised multiple cameras and lengthy takes, having diligently rehearsed his actors beforehand as if for a stage play. The results aren't uniformly satisfactory. With the exception of the great Jean-Louis Barrault, the actors have trouble infusing life into several overly talky sequences, the interior sets struggle to attain much atmosphere, and a combination of uneven pacing and superfluous scenes needlessly inflates the running time to 95 minutes. (That Cordelier is a pillar of the community is quite obvious without the insertion of a rather thinly populated soirée for the Canadian ambassador.) On top of this, Joseph Kosma's music – except for the creepy little xylophone cues accompanying Opale – is a trial to listen to. As if to offset such objections, Renoir himself shows up at the beginning, introducing "this evening's programme" from the set of a mythical TV show called *Jean Renoir présente* – presumably a waggishly competitive nod to the very real *Alfred Hitchcock Presents*.

The film remains valuable, however, not just for Barrault's remarkable performance but also for its unusual fidelity to the Stevenson original – though, perversely, Renoir told Jean-Luc Godard at the time that "I had no intention of doing an adaptation. Let's say, if you will, that it was in a sense memories of reading Stevenson's book that gave Jean Serge and me the idea for *Cordelier*. But there was on our part absolutely no attempt at or preconceived idea of transposition, in the real sense of the word. I feel very strongly about this."[16]

If so, Renoir's 'memories' were far more focused than the direct observation of most other Stevenson adapters. Using a complex flashback structure, Renoir attempts to rehabilitate the story as the 'who is that appalling creature?' mystery it once was. He does, however, fill in some of the gaps left by Stevenson,

## LE TESTAMENT DU DOCTEUR CORDELIER

France 1959
UK / US: **Experiment in Evil**
RTF / SOFIRAD / Compagnie Jean Renoir
95 minutes b/w
in production January-February 1959
..................................................
Director of Photography: Georges Leclerc; Art Director: Marcel-Louis Dieulot; Editor: Renée Lichtig; Sound: Joseph Richard; Music: Joseph Kosma; Make-up: Anatole Paris, Igor Keldich; Special Effects: Lax; Screenplay: Jean Renoir; Artistic Collaborator: Jean Serge; based on *Strange Case of Dr Jekyll and Mr Hyde* by Robert Louis Stevenson [uncredited]; Production Manager: Jacques Hollebeke; Director: Jean Renoir

Jean-Louis Barrault (Dr Cordelier / Opale); Teddy Bilis (Maître Joly); Michel Vitold

(Dr Séverin); Jean Topart (Désiré); Micheline Gary (Marguerite); Jaques Dannouille (Commissaire Lardaut); André Certes (Inspector Salbris); Jean-Pierre Granval (hotelier); Gaston Modot (Blaise); Céline Sales (girl); Sylviane Margolle (little girl); Jacqueline Morane (Alberte); Ghislaine Dumont (Suzy); Madeleine Marion (Juliette); Didier d'Yd (Georges); Primerose Perret (Mary); Raymond Jourdan (disabled man); uncredited: Jacque Catelain (ambassador); Régine Blaess (ambassador's wife); Raymone (Mme des Essarts); Dominique Dangon (mother); Claudie Bourlon (Lise); Jacqueline Frot (Isabelle); Françoise Boyer (Françoise); Monique Theffo (Annie); Annick Allières (neighbour); Jean Bertho, Jacques Ciron, Emile Genevois (passers-bye); Jean Renoir, Jean Serge, Renée Lichtig (themselves)

Jean-Louis Barrault does some fine pantomiming as the clownish monster who is the evil in the doctor ... But other actors are left to fend for themselves. Direction is simple and unassuming which makes the film lag and lose tempo at times. Renoir has tried to make a pic to please both mediums and hasn't quite brought it off ... It lacks the weight and technical standards for art [art-house] chances. *Variety* 16 September 1959

At all periods people have jumped from one art to another ... So why should anyone try to force me to shoot *Cordelier* at the Boulogne or Saint-Maurice studios instead of in those of RTF? ... It seems there is a move to prevent my film from being shown in cinemas on the pretext that it will have been shown on television. But they forget that ultimately the only judge is the public. *Jean Renoir* [speaking in 1959; quoted in *Godard on Godard*, 1972] giving Opale a bolt-hole in the sleazy Pigalle district, a frightened girlfriend and an extensive collection of whips to brutalise her with. ("Poor Suzy," a friend points out. "She can't even stand up straight.") He also sketches in Cordelier's hypocrisy with an unusually frank back-story. Clucking publicly over other people's "unwholesome taste for amorous escapades," he meanwhile ignores the heavy-breathing entreaties of willing female patients, instead rendering them unconscious with a hypodermic and interfering with them in semi-necrophile fashion – all in the name of avoiding scandal.

Perhaps the most telling detail lifted from Stevenson's original is the fact that Opale, as an emanation of Cordelier, is clearly a smaller man; indeed, he looks horribly absurd in Cordelier's too-large clothing. In another Stevenson touch, witnesses find it hard to describe what he looks like. "All I know is that he was dreadful," a traumatised young woman stammers out to the police. This indefinable air of 'wrongness' is brilliantly sustained by Barrault, for whom the bristling unibrow and simian knuckle fur devised by the make-up man were mere accessories. Though gauche and unco-ordinated, the liberated Opale is also, by his own admission, light as air. With twitching shoulders and a lolloping gait he 'dances' down the wintery Paris boulevards like some brutish, conscienceless teenager. Contemporary audiences may well have perceived him as a kind of mutant Teddy Boy.

All this, of course, makes Opale comical as well as creepy, complete with a pronounced echo of cinema's most famous comedian of all. That Barrault's skittish mime work is Chaplinesque must have seemed especially obvious to the French audiences who venerated the great 'Charlot', yet Kim Newman has noted that the other side of Chaplin is deconstructed by Barrault too: "The dignified, dapper, white-haired Dr Cordelier is the image of the offscreen Chaplin of later years."[17] Yet the Cordelier-Opale schism can be applied to the whole range of conflicted comic performers, not just the specific one intended by Renoir and Barrault. Cordelier, for example, bears a striking physical resemblance to another British actor, Kenneth Williams, in whom a pinched, high-toned aestheticism was at constant war with anarchic impulses of a brazenly vulgar, supposedly lower-class kind.

Making Opale a comedian as well as a killer is perhaps the film's most disconcerting achievement. Elsewhere, Renoir balances the rather arid interiors with some memorably atmospheric location work, whether in Opale's semi-improvised abominations in Paris back streets or in a tense nocturnal sequence in the grounds of Cordelier's mansion at Marnes-la-Coquette.

And the sophistication of Renoir's adaptation is signalled from the very outset by naming Cordelier after an order of Franciscan monks and by the use of a schizoid word in the title, 'testament' meaning both a will and a confession. But, for all its ponderings on "the problem of evil" and what Opale dubs "the framework of your society," the film survives in the main as a dazzling showcase for Jean-Louis Barrault.

When Renoir was making *Le Testament*, French cinephiles were just beginning to absorb the first wave of startlingly gruesome new horror pictures from England – in particular, from Hammer Film Productions. In April 1957 Paris cinemagoers had been offered Val Guest's *The Quatermass Xperiment*, with Terence Fisher's *The Curse of Frankenstein* following in November and Guest's *Quatermass 2* in December. *The Revenge of Frankenstein* and *The Abominable Snowman*, directed by Fisher and Guest respectively, appeared in September 1958, then Fisher's magisterial *Dracula* premiered on 2 February 1959.

Just eight days later, Georges Franju, co-founder of the Cinémathèque Française, started shooting *Les Yeux sans visage*, a film that not only featured a two-faced doctor, like Renoir's, but also his two-faced daughter. On top of this it would vie with the British boom in sheer gruesomeness while incorporating a vein of surrealist poetry, as if André de Lorde had forged an unholy alliance with Jean Cocteau. "The French have always admired the English penchant for horror stories," wrote Raymond Durgnat several years later, "and imagined that the land of Mary Shelley, Bram Stoker, Jack the Ripper and Terence Fisher would appreciate an artistically made horror film."[18]

Yet the grue, rather than the poetry, was all that most reviewers could see – particularly in Britain. The fashionable young novelist John Braine, moonlighting as film critic for the *Daily Express*, pointed out that "*Eyes Without a Face* ... proves one thing. The French are thorough. Someone had the idea of making a horror film even nastier than anything Hammer Films could do; and they succeeded."[19] Braine's headline was similarly terse and to the point: 'This One is Revolting'.

*Paris, February 1959. The celebrated plastic surgeon Dr Génessier identifies a dead body as that of his missing daughter Christiane, burying it in the family vault and later telling Christiane – who in reality is neither missing nor dead – that 'killing' her was a necessary measure in order to complete her treatment. For she has been appallingly disfigured in a car crash caused by her father. Now, Louise, a former patient of the doctor's, lures pretty students to his château in order for their faces to be removed...*

# LES YEUX SANS VISAGE

France-Italy 1959
*Italy: Occhi senza volto*
UK: *Eyes Without a Face*
US: **The Horror Chamber of Dr Faustus**
Champs-Élysées Productions / Lux-Film
90 minutes b/w
production began 10 February 1959

Director of Photography: Eugen Schüfftan;
Art Director: Auguste Capelier; Supervising
Editor: Gilbert Natot; Sound: Antoine
Archimbaud; Music: Maurice Jarre; Make-
up: Georges Klein; Special Effects: Henri
Assola; Adapted by Boileau-Narcejac, Jean
Redon, Claude Sautet and [uncredited]
Georges Franju, from the novel by Jean
Redon; Dialogue: Pierre Gascar; Production

Manager: Pierre Laurent; Producer: Jules
Borkon; Director: Georges Franju

*Pierre Brasseur (Dr Génessier); Alida Valli
(Louise); Édith Scob (Christiane Génessier);
Juliette Mayniel (Edna Gruberg); François
Guerin (Dr Jacques Vernon); Alexandre Rignault
(Inspector Parot); Béatrice Altariba (Paulette
Merodon); René Génin (Henri Tessot); [Charles]
Blavette (kennel employee); Claude Brasseur
(police inspector); Michel Etcheverry (Dr
Lherminier); Yvette Etiévent (mother of sick child);
Marcel Pères (first man at cemetery); Lucien
Hubert (second man at cemetery); uncredited:
Birgitta Juslin (Juliette); Gabrielle Doulcet
(Génessier's admirer); France Asselin; Conrado
Guarducci; Charles Lavialle; Max Montavon*

**Eyes Without a Face is a piece of revolting, pandering, evil rubbish. I wonder
what the censor was up to, the day he gave this film an X certificate. He
should have ordered it to be publicly burned in the Charing Cross-road.
And, on top of the fire, he should have thrown the makers of the film, and
the people who saw fit to release it in Britain.** *Daily Herald 29 January 1960*

**I did not read Jean Redon's novel, which was just a starting block for the
film. The real job was done by Boileau & Narcejac and Franju. I know that, at
one point, Boileau & Narcejac considered having [Pierre] Brasseur or me fall
into a vat of cement, but Franju preferred the ending to be more dreamlike
... I had such admiration for Franju. He had this vision, and my task was to
get into his world.** *Édith Scob [quoted in Video Watchdog May 2004]*

Édith Scob drifts doll-like through the lower
depths in *Les Yeux sans visage* (1959)

Though listed as a source in the film's credits, Jean
Redon's novel *Les Yeux sans visage* didn't come out until
the summer of 1959, several months after the film
was completed; issued by Fleuve Noir with Pierre
Brasseur (Génessier) and Alida Valli (Louise) on
the cover, it may in reality have been a novelisation.
Whatever the truth of this, the script, concocted
by the ace *Diaboliques* team of Pierre Boileau and
Thomas Narcejac, gave plenty of scope for the kind of
material that would excite bloodthirsty audiences and
scandalise high-minded critics.

The basic storyline – transparently based on the
pulp potboilers made by Hollywood's Poverty Row
companies in the 1940s, particularly the above-
mentioned Bela Lugosi vehicle *The Corpse Vanishes* –
allowed for a surgical centrepiece of unprecedented
explicitness, a literal 'face lift' echoed at the end by
a face-ripping attack by a pack of ravening dogs. Yet
the deepest impression left by the film is of a glacial,
hard-to-define dread, a creeping sense of dislocation
that led Franju to describe *Les Yeux* as "an anguish film
... a quieter mood than horror."[20] It was appropriate,
then, that Fleuve Noir assigned Redon's novel to their
'Collection Angoisse' series.

The anxiety is brilliantly encapsulated right at the
start, with the camera flashing past the ghostly limbs
of gnarled roadside trees as Louise's Citroën 2CV
speeds towards a darkened tributary of the Seine.
A figure in a man's trilby and trenchcoat lurches
drunkenly – lifelessly? – in the back seat, and the
viewer's stomach turns over with a little flutter of

unspecified apprehension. Moments later comes the graceless struggle to dump the body, clearly a young woman, in the river. And the whole sequence is scored with Maurice Jarre's spidery little waltz, which, along with the rest of Jarre's music, endures as one of the great horror scores by virtue of its jaunty incongruity.

Franju follows this with the first of several subversive touches that depart from the template laid down in 1940s Hollywood. Pierre Brasseur's fleshy Dr Génessier gives a speech to a conspicuously well-heeled gathering, with a young Jesuit priest included among the fawning society ladies and other grandees. His talk of radiation and exsanguination is greeted with rapturous cries of "What a wonderful future you've opened up for us," in sharp contrast to the career-destroying ridicule that was routinely heaped on Boris Karloff and Bela Lugosi in similar situations. So the hideous experimentation in Génessier's subterranean laboratory, covert though it is, is conducted by a man fêted by his peers and society in general, rather than a misunderstood renegade who's been marked out as a dangerous lunatic.

With its series of hexagonal iron doors and hordes of caged, angry dogs, Génessier's basement resembles an underground bunker, underlining his resemblance to the kind of Nazi scientists Franju's producers had explicitly warned him not to invoke. (As well as being told not to offend Germans by using a mad scientist, he was also urged to placate Spain by avoiding sacrilege and Britain by excluding animal experimentation – all of which stipulations he blithely ignored.) We're given many hints as to the doctor's overweening arrogance, most tellingly Christiane's testimony, apropos the fateful car crash, that "He always has to dominate, even on the road. He was driving like a demon."

To further illustrate Génessier's megalomania, and his almost complete detachment from other people's suffering, we're given a subdued scene that is nevertheless one of the film's most horrifying. In it he confers outside the morgue with an elderly man whose daughter, Simone Tessot, has been missing for ten days. We don't know it yet but poor Simone was the experimental subject Louise dumped in the Seine at the beginning, so by callously identifying Simone as Christiane the doctor denies the old man any chance of 'closure'. Beautifully played by René Génin, Tessot appeals to Génessier, father to father, for reassurance that he identified the body correctly, to which Génessier gives the utterly loathsome reply, "It seems curious to me that I should have to comfort you. After all, *you* still have some hope." He then temporarily blinds Tessot in his headlight beams as he glides away in a sleek and shimmeringly black Citroën DS.

Whether Citroën were aware of it or not, the fact that Franju has the mad scientist drive a stately DS and his mad procurer, Louise, a humble 2CV was maybe not an ideal form of product placement. The 2CV, in particular, acquires a genuinely sinister aura as Louise ferries a new victim, Edna, to Génessier's looming mansion in the Paris banlieues. The two have met in a ticket queue outside the Théâtre des Champs-Élysées on Avenue Montaigne, indicating that, when offered free tickets by mysterious women, pretty young college students ought really to turn them down. The advertised play, incidentally, was indeed running at the time – it was Jacques Mauclair's studio revival of the 1953 Ionesco play *Victimes du devoir*. Though presumably a happy accident, the play's title – 'Victims of Duty' – applies quite precisely to Génessier and Louise, who are enslaved by guilt in the doctor's case and gratitude in Louise's, given that her flawless face is one of Génessier's success stories.

The scene that follows in Génessier's drawing room, in which Edna becomes thoroughly spooked by the stiff formality of her peculiar hosts, is one of the queasiest in the genre and superlatively played by Brasseur, Valli and Juliette Mayniel. It ends with Génessier offering Edna a port but instead clamping a chloroform pad to her nose. The scene also contains a small gag typical of the film's grim sense of humour: Génessier's name may echo 'genesis' but his chosen alias on receiving Edna is Dormeuil, suggesting the word 'dormir' (to sleep). When Edna emerges from her chloroform-induced slumber, she finds herself strapped to an operating table and catches a glimpse of the looming Christiane without her mask. Through Edna's tranquillised haze, Franju gives us only an occluded view of Christiane's 'real' face; the same effect was used 30-odd years earlier in *The Phantom of the Opera*, though what we can see of Georges Klein's remarkable make-up more closely resembles Lionel Atwill's in *Mystery of the Wax Museum*. Already we've heard from a police doctor about the terrible burns and water saturation that affected Christiane's face, to which an inspector has cheerfully added, "Let's not forget the rats." So we don't have to be shown this horror in suppurating detail, as Franju fully realised.

As well as being genuinely ghastly, Edna's hazy vision increases our compassion for the film's haunting central figure. Played with eerie delicacy by the 21-year-old Édith Scob, Christiane appears briefly with her 'true' face (albeit lifted from the hapless Edna), contemplating her new life and asking the loaded question, "First I need to come back from the dead. How am I to do that?" But necrosis quickly sets in (economically chronicled via a nasty series of worsening portrait shots) and Christiane returns to the spectral half-life she knew before. As she drifts doll-like through the massive house in a smoothly featureless mask, the pallid latex not only echoes the silvery satin of her bat-collared Givenchy housecoat, it also raises fundamental questions about how far a person's identity is vested in their facial features.

The enduring power of the film is its piquant suggestion that, faceless or not, Christiane retains a purity of soul belying her robotic appearance. Indeed, the real robots, with their mechanised, obsessive and inhuman behaviour patterns, are Génessier and Louise, whose faces are intact. Significantly, Christiane reasserts her humanity at the end by revolting against Génessier's patriarchal cruelty, freeing Paulette (the latest experimental subject), stabbing the uncomprehending Louise in the throat, and unleashing the dogs on Génessier himself. She then liberates her caged doves and floats into the surrounding darkness, the birds fluttering serenely around her retreating figure. And up comes the FIN title.

The film recalls *I vampiri* in small ways, from the Paris setting and rejuvenating experiments by a mad doctor to a predictably functional police investigation – though even here Franju betters Freda with more engaging and recognisable characters. (Alexandre Rignault's no-nonsense Inspector Parot is a pleasantly droll presence in these scenes.) In any case, having been released in both France and Britain in January 1960, Franju's film would go on to exercise a profound influence over future continental horrors, an influence far exceeding its own magpie borrowings.

In the meantime, Franju was given an early warning of the short-term antagonism *Les Yeux* would arouse when it was previewed at the 1959 Edinburgh Film Festival. Accompanied by Juliette Mayniel, he arrived in Edinburgh on Tuesday 1 September for a press conference organised by Tony Tenser, publicity manager of the film's UK distributor, Miracle. The screening itself apparently caused no fewer than seven audience members to faint. It was at this point that Franju made a not especially tactful observation to the effect that he realised now why Scotsmen wore skirts.

## REAL BUTCHERS, THESE MEDICS

Oddly enough, the 'no mad scientists because of Germany' warning, given to Franju while he was preparing *Les Yeux sans visage*, was ignored in West Germany itself, where a similar film was in production at exactly the same time.

*Die Nackte und der Satan* (The Nude and the Devil) was apparently intended by the 62-year-old

writer-director Victor Trivas as a comeback. A former associate of G W Pabst, Trivas had directed the 1931 anti-war classic *Niemandsland* (No Man's Land) prior to fleeing the Nazis at the outbreak of World War II and earning Hollywood script credits on *The Stranger* and *Where the Sidewalk Ends* (gaining an Oscar nomination for the former). Now he was finally back in Germany and assuming the director's chair for the first time in nearly 25 years.

When starting work on *Die Nackte* in February 1959, Trivas was no doubt aware that a rather grander prodigal son, Fritz Lang, had released a colourfully exotic adventure called *Der Tiger von Eschnapur* (The Tiger of Eschnapur) just the previous month, with an equally escapist follow-up, *Das indische Grabmal* (The Indian Tomb), due out in March. Where Lang proposed to reassert his position by crafting a couple of commercial hits bathed in glorious Technicolor, Trivas went the opposite route, resurrecting the monochrome, angst-ridden Expressionism of which Lang himself had been a key architect back in the 1920s. But after making *Die Nackte und der Satan* – a film featuring a sentient severed head and a hunchbacked nurse being given the shapely body of a stripper – Trivas found further directing assignments impossible to come by.

*Using his revolutionary Serum Z, the ailing Professor Abel has succeeded in reviving the head of a dog. When he succumbs to a heart condition, his mentally unstable assistant Dr Ood preserves Abel's head in the same way. The disembodied Professor then becomes an unwilling witness to Ood's unholy fusion of his deformed assistant Irene and a glamorous stripper called Lily…*

Wolfgang C Hartwig, head of the Munich company Rapid-Film, was an anomaly in a sedate post-war industry devoted to the idealised rural sagas of the so-called Heimatfilme and similarly manipulated views of World War II. Hartwig, by contrast, was the kind of producer whose first fiction feature would be announced in *Der Spiegel* like this: "The findings of the late sexual statistician Alfred C Kinsey will be utilised in the German feature film *Liebe, wie die Frau sie wünscht* (Love, the Way the Woman Wants It)"[21] – an announcement made, what's more, less than a fortnight after Kinsey's death. In December 1958, when Hartwig's latest film, *Mit Eva fing die Sünde an* (Sin Began with Eve), was doing the rounds in German cinemas, he paid a visit to Paris and was profoundly affected by a trip to the Grand Guignol in Rue Chaptal. So much so that after the performance he became convinced that films fusing sex and horror would go down a storm.

The insane Horst Frank reduces Michel Simon to a living head in *Die Nackte und der Satan* (1959)

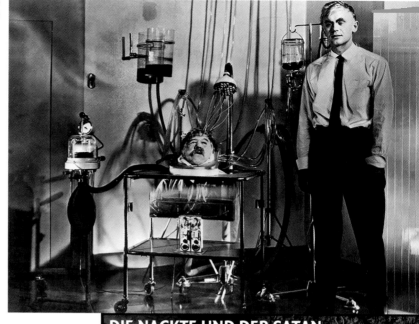

*Die Nackte und der Satan* was the first fruit of this thinking, with a central gimmick identical to René Berton's 1928 Grand Guignol play *L'Homme qui a tué la mort* (The Man who Killed Death). There, Professor Fargus revived the guillotined head of a supposed murderer and the prosecutor lost his mind when the head continued to plead its innocence. Here, the remorseless Dr Ood (memorably played by Horst Frank) has himself been the subject of a brain operation, claiming that "The price of my genius was madness" while indulging in familiar mad scientist rhetoric like "I'm not bound by their [society's] rules. No, I'm above all their laws!"

Like *Les Yeux sans visage*, Trivas' basic scenario might have fitted snugly into PRC's potboiler schedules of, say, 1942 – though, where Franju subverted the template with unexpected lyricism, Trivas does so with a strong whiff of perversion. For as the film progresses we see the youthful Ood growing in sexual confidence – of the 'control freak verging on rapist' variety – the more he invades people's bodies on the operating table. "Are you an undertaker?" asks striptease artiste Lily while dancing with him at the seedy Tam Tam Club, adding: "You hold me like I was dead." Later, in a very funny shot, she excitedly kicks her legs up on Professor Abel's sofa while Ood, waiting for his craftily administered sedative to take effect, dispassionately takes her pulse. But Ood's apparent indifference is discarded once Irene's head has been put onto Lily's shoulders. Indeed, he starts touching her up the minute she emerges from her 117 days of post-operative suspension, making constant reference to her beautiful new body and acclaiming her as "my creation."

His desperation to get inside the new Irene is made all the more queasily repugnant by the fact that he's already been 'inside' her for the purposes of the transplant. At first, Irene echoes the hunchbacked nurse played by Jane Adams in the 1945 film *House of Dracula*; later she stumbles woozily, and heavily bandaged, around Ood's shadowy laboratory exactly like Juliette Mayniel's Edna in *Les Yeux sans visage*. Perversely, she only surrenders to Ood sexually when he makes it clear to her just how insane he is, taking Trivas' echoes of

## DIE NACKTE UND DER SATAN

West Germany 1959
US: **The Head**
Rapid-Film
96 minutes b/w
production began late February 1959
. . . . . . . . . . . . . . . . . . . . . . . . . . . . .
Director of Photography: Georg Krause;
Art Directors: Hermann Warm, Bruno Monden; Editor: Friedl Buckow-Schier; Sound: Rudolf Kaiser; Music: Willi Mattes; Make-up: Karl Hanoszek, Susanne Krause; Special Effects: Theo

Nischwitz; Production Manager: Ludwig Spitaler; Producer: Wolf C Hartwig; Writer-Director: Victor Trivas

Horst Frank (Dr Ood); Michel Simon (Professor Abel); Paul Dahlke (Commissioner); Karin Kernke (Irene); Helmut Schmid (Bert, lab assistant); Christiane Maybach (Lily); Dieter Eppler (Paul); Kurt Müller-Graf (Dr Burke); uncredited: Maria Stadler (Frau Schneider); Otto Storr (bartender); Barbara Valentin (dance partner in club); Herb Beschanner

**The Head** is a tedious and tasteless horror film of German origin ... Its box-office fortunes depend upon the impact of exploitation measures, to which the film most provocatively lends itself ... Trivas' direction is heavy, choppy and disjointed, but there are one or two passages endowed with a desirably eerie quality via the art, music and photography department contributions. *Variety* 18 October 1961

Dieter Eppler and Michel Simon [were] both excellent actors, though Simon was a strange guy who shared his home with monkeys ... The severed head trick was done with mirrors. Under the table in which Simon was embedded they mounted a mirror which reflected a similar table. The fascinating thing about the picture was that all the equipment was genuine ... so our film was based on medical developments that were already anticipated.
Horst Frank [quoted in *Splatting Image* June 1999]

*Pygmalion* and *Alraune* to another, kinkier level. The film's poisonous eroticism is founded on a sexualised view of surgery echoed in several other pictures of the period, notably the lurid British shocker *Circus of Horrors*. In a roundabout way it would lead to the freak extremes of 21st century films like *The Human Centipede*.

Trivas decorates the film's pulpily transgressive details with a doom-laden luxuriance that's much enhanced by the eerie atonalities of composer Willi Mattes and, particularly, Georg Krause's chiaroscuro cinematography. The film's Expressionist credentials are confirmed by the participation of production designer Hermann Warm; having worked on such classics as *Caligari*, *Der müde Tod* and *Vampyr*, he gave Abel and Ood the most strikingly realised environment since the modernist perfection of the 1934 chiller *The Black Cat*. The film also boasts unusually good effects work to realise its other source of surgical horror – Professor Abel's terrible predicament, a predicament that earned the film the no-nonsense export title *The Head*.

The 'revived head' motif was a popular one in the late 1950s; from Britain came *The Man Without a Body*, from Mexico *La cabeza viviente* (The Living Head), and from the USA *The Thing that Couldn't Die* and the similarly titled Z-grade classic *The Brain that Wouldn't Die*. Made some six months after Trivas' film, the last of these is extremely similar in plot, though for talking-head purposes director Joseph Green used the glacially angular beauty of Virginia Leith rather than the lived-in, hangdog dewlaps of the legendary French star Michel Simon. (It's one of those curious cinematic coincidences that, mere weeks after his old colleague Jean Renoir transposed Jekyll and Hyde to Paris, Simon should find himself playing a severed head in Munich.) Abel's plight is rammed home by a terrific tracking shot into his horrified face when the flash of Ood's scalpel announces the Lily-Irene body-swapping operation, and it also gives Trivas the chance to include some discussion of medical ethics. "Did you ask the *dog* permission before you operated?" sneers the unrepentant Ood, a loaded question balanced later by the man-in-the-street observation of a passing police inspector: "Real butchers, these medics."

*Die Nackte und der Satan* opened in West Germany in late July 1959, though by that time Wolf Hartwig had been involved in a court case brought against him by actress Kai Fischer, who had been assured on 23 February that her role as Lily wouldn't involve any nudity or toplessness. Having replaced her on the day before production began with the more amenable Christiane Maybach, Hartwig was obliged to pay Fischer 4000 marks in compensation. "It was perfectly obvious she wasn't going to be prancing around

French advertising for the lurid Yugoslavian-shot exploiter *Ein Toter hing im Netz* (1959)

dressed as Joan of Arc," he pointed out. "We didn't hire her for her acting ability."[22] This little skirmish is instructive, given that within ten years full nudity, never mind toplessness, was to become commonplace in Euro horror, and in exploitation generally.

Undaunted, Hartwig put another sex-horror subject into production in September, this time showcasing Barbara Valentin. This curvaceous beauty queen had celebrated her 18th birthday by accompanying Hartwig on his seminal visit to the Grand Guignol; in the meantime she'd made a 'blink and you'll miss it' appearance in *Die Nackte*. The new film was *Ein Toter hing im Netz* (A Corpse Hangs in the Web), which used sylvan locations in Porec, Yugoslavia to suggest the tropical island on which a group of exotic dancers become stranded after a plane crash. Their boss Gary (Alex D'Arcy) goes for a nocturnal walk and is attacked by an oversized but entirely ridiculous spider, turning him into an arachnid-human hybrid in a halfway effective make-up.

The film's focus, however, is so firmly on the barely clad, in-fighting dancers that it becomes an ersatz nudie-cutie, ineptly directed by Fritz Böttger and (uncredited) Hartwig himself – also by D'Arcy, if his own account is to be believed. Indeed, for export, two versions were prepared, *It's Hot in Paradise* and *Horrors of Spider Island*, the latter back-pedalling on the salacious content and emphasising horror. Screamed the tag-line for the first: 'Seven showgirls crashed on a diabolical island and fought passionately for the ultimate prize ... A MAN!!' And for the second: 'One bite from a giant spider turned him into THE WORLD'S MOST HIDEOUS MONSTER with a diabolical lust to KILL!'

Cinematographer Georg Krause, fresh from *Die Nackte und der Satan*, does what he can with Gary's infrequent arachnid manifestations, and there's an almost imaginative moment when one of the women addresses him by name and he retreats, shame-faced, into shadow. Beyond stray touches like this it's hard to disagree with the tidal wave of critical execration that greeted the film's Paris release, as *Le Mort dans le filet* (The Corpse in the Web), in February 1961. A fairly typical response came from *Cinéma 61*, official journal of the Fédération française des ciné-clubs:

"Dread and eroticism that'll have you falling about with laughter."[23] Conversely, Ado Kyrou (author of *Le Surréalisme au cinéma*) urged the highbrow readers of *Positif* to "rush down to the Midi-Minuit cinema" to catch "the stuff that dreams are made on" in "this masterwork of Dadaism."[24]

Despite this lofty endorsement, Hartwig would subsequently steer clear of horror subjects, making a borderline exception for *Der Turm der verbotenen Liebe* (The Tower of Forbidden Love), which he put into production in March 1968. Directed by Franz Antel and Fritz Umgelter, this was a lurid adaptation of the classic Alexandre Dumas melodrama *La Tour de Nesle* (The Tower of Nesle), previously filmed under its original title by Abel Gance in 1954. There, the eye-popping Gevacolor nudity was provided by Silvana Pampanini and her handmaidens; in the new version, Teri Tordai and hers were just as uninhibited in Eastmancolor. This swashbuckling saga of Marguerite, 14th century Queen of France, who exhausts her lovers prior to killing them, features the fetishistic image of Tordai as a hooded, topless archer within its first few minutes. Released as *Tower of Screaming Virgins* in the US, it acquired the frankly unbelievable title *She Lost Her ... You Know What* in the UK. After it, Hartwig was tempted down the sex-horror route again by the vogue for slasher films in 1980. In the interim he hit very big indeed with a baker's dozen of pseudo-sexological *Schulmädchen-Report* (Schoolgirl Report) films, which cleaned up at German box-offices throughout the 1970s.

## A BLOB AND THREE VAMPIRES

Preceding their epoch-making plunge into costume Gothic, Hammer Films had scored their first horror smash with the 1955 release *The Quatermass Xperiment*, a film that kicked off a vogue for rampaging, gelatinous threats from outer space. It was released in Italy as *L'astronave atomico del dottor Quatermass* (The Atomic Spaceship of Dr Quatermass), a title that in due course would be echoed by Riccardo Freda when he made *L'orribile segreto del Dr Hichcock* (The Horrible Secret of Dr Hichcock). Before that, however, Freda had made the kind of fully fledged rip-off that Italian genre cinema would come to specialise in. *Caltiki il mostro immortale* began production on 4 May 1959 and would be profitably exported as *Caltiki the Immortal Monster*. On home ground, however, it was greeted with indifference, as when a critic in *Schermi* dismissed it as "Banal science fantasy. The fantasy is feeble and the science took a vacation."[25]

'Based,' according to the credits, 'on an ancient Mexican legend,' *Caltiki* involves a standard-issue

True Brit import John Merivale encounters a marauding blob in *Caltiki il mostro immortale* (1959)

archaeological expedition investigating the site of an abandoned Mayan city, discovering a shrine to Caltiki ("a goddess who hungered for blood") and awakening a 2,000,000-year-old organism that lurks in a subterranean lake. The banality referred to by *Schermi's* critic is provided in abundance by the dreary human dramas that clog Filippo Sanjust's script, whereas the marauding-blob highlights are brilliantly achieved via miniature sets and yards and yards of tripe, the intricate effects work falling to Mario Bava and his father Eugenio. Writing in 1984, Freda was magnanimous enough to point out that the film "should be considered his [Mario Bava's] first true venture as a director, as I abandoned the film for the last two weeks of production after arguing with the producers."[26]

Whatever the truth behind this directorial hand-over, there can be little doubt that the film's horror highlights bear the stamp that Bava would soon make his own. A scuba diver finding skeletal remains and scattered treasure at the bottom of the lake, the same diver's helmet being removed to reveal a fleshless yet still sentient skull, a crazed expedition member subsumed screaming amid the creature's oleaginous folds – these and other ghastly moments more than justify sitting through the banal stuff. And, among many nods to *The Quatermass Xperiment*, Freda repeats the earlier picture's extremely creepy 'rediscovered film detailing what happened to the expedition' section – anticipating, as US critic Tim Lucas has noted, the found-footage sub-genre by 40 years.

After his 'Italians can't do horror' experience with *I vampiri*, Freda was careful to credit himself this time as Robert Hamton (modified in subsequent films to

Hampton) – and also to engage a rather incongruous-looking British lead, the true-blue John Merivale. This faux-Anglo touch was made particularly apposite, not so much by Hammer's blob-spawning Quatermass success, but by *The Curse of Frankenstein* and *Dracula*, both of which (retitled *La maschera di Frankenstein* and *Dracula il vampiro*) made a major impact on local audiences.

Yet the Italian industry's initial response wasn't to plunge straight into the darkest depths of Gothic horror. Instead, Maxima Film engaged comedy specialist Stefano Vanzina (aka Steno) to concoct a lusciously coloured Ultrascope divertissement called *Vita dura per i vampiri* (A Hard Life for Vampires), a title changed during production to *Tempi duri per i vampiri* (Hard Times for Vampires). Here, a downtrodden little aristocrat sees his castle converted into a jet-setters' hotel, incurring the wrath of his undead Bavarian uncle – and the masterstroke in an otherwise inauspicious project was to import Hammer's Dracula, Christopher Lee, to play the uncle. Lee duly flew into Rome on 30 July 1959, the film having already been under way at Sestri Levante for several weeks. Concerned about typecasting, he agreed to appear on condition that his character was clearly signposted as, not Dracula, but Baron Roderico.

Indeed, he looks

Christopher Lee in a hedge (bottom right) in the Renato Rascel vehicle *Tempi duri per i vampiri* (1959)

magnificent as a vampire subtly different from his grey-haired, black-garbed Count – ashen-faced, much more gaunt, sporting significantly bigger fangs, with jet-black hair plastered to his head and the red flanges of his cloak swept dramatically over each shoulder. He also experiments with demonic facial expressions absent from his first attempt at Dracula, expressions that would profitably resurface in the 1965 film *Dracula Prince of Darkness* and its follow-ups. And whatever the indignities inflicted on him (among them, falling into a hedge at sight of a cruciform coat-hanger, then, at cock-crow, dashing wildly past gaily coloured beach umbrellas in search of sanctuary), he plays the part entirely straight and remains splendidly scary.

The joke of the film, such as it is, is that Lee's Baron gets to bite only his unappetising nephew Oswaldo (played by pint-sized singer-comedian Renato Rascel), leaving Oswaldo to nuzzle all the film's resplendent

beach beauties in a single night. (In addition to Sylva Koscina, Lia Zopelli and Susanne Loret, the glamorous victims include German actress Kai Fischer, fresh from making her compensation claim against Wolf Hartwig.) The film is significant for marking Lee's advent into Italian exploitation; also for its use of Bruno Martino's catchy hit, 'Dracula Cha-Cha-Cha', a song underlining the vampire's incompatibility with the on-the-make Italy of Fellini's *La dolce vita*, which was in production at the same time. The humour, however, stubbornly fails to translate. Even Italian critics were unamused when the film opened in Rome in October. "The director tries to disguise the flimsiness of the comedy with a parade of beautiful women," carped one. "But even the participation of specialist Christopher Lee doesn't produce the desired result."[27]

By December, writer-director Renato Polselli was shooting something considerably stronger for the Consorzio Italiano company. Using the Castello di Passerano, near Palestrina, for his exteriors and the Palazzo Borghese in Artena for interiors, Polselli collaborated with debutant screenwriters Giuseppe Pellegrini and Ernesto Gastaldi on *L'amante del vampiro* (The Vampire's Lover). "I had been favourably impressed by [Terence] Fisher's *Dracula*," Polselli reflected later, "and I tried to update the story, putting in beat dancers and such."[28]

*When dancers Luisa and Francesca, together with Francesca's boyfriend Luca, seek refuge from a storm in Damian Castle, they meet the regal Countess Alda (who looks strikingly like a portrait of a supposedly 400-years-dead ancestor) and her manservant Herman. When Luisa is attacked by Herman in his grotesque vampire form, Luca and Luisa's boyfriend Giorgio take steps to ensure that Francesca doesn't meet the same fate.*

*L'amante del vampiro* kicks off with a sequence realised by Polselli with enormous brio, conferring freshness and surprise on an otherwise standard scenario. He stresses the natural world at its simplest – cows, a waterfall, a pretty dairy maid sent to fetch water – prior to insinuating the supernatural via a pursuing

Maria Luisa Rolando rises from the grave in *L'amante del vampiro* (1959)

silhouette. One composition is especially striking, with the waterfall smoothly frothing like the head on a pint of Guinness, a grimly spiked picket fence looming above and the already spooked Brigita dwarfed in between them. Once the girl has been attacked, she's delivered by her rescuers to a local dance school, allowing Polselli to introduce the unfettered eroticism that would predominate in the Italian horrors to come. The awakened dancers come running en masse in their barely-there baby-doll nighties, with one of them (Luisa's) conspicuously more transparent than the others.

Though it was to be exactly ten years before the British censor would allow Hammer the same kind of imagery in the similarly titled *The Vampire Lovers*, it's easy enough to tick off Polselli's numerous nods to Fisher's *Dracula* as the film proceeds. From the threatening male vampire framed in a French window to the Countess appearing (with, sadly, zero impact) on the castle's staircase, and from there to a climax in which Luca uses crossed candlesticks against Herman (who dutifully chucks things at his pursuer, Christopher Lee-style, before being reduced, like the Countess, to a pile of empty clothes and boots), the derivation is clear. There's even an echo of *The Curse of Frankenstein* when Francesca's curiosity leads to her being locked in a mausoleum with the monstrous Herman. But Polselli is at

## L'AMANTE DEL VAMPIRO

*Italy 1959*
US: **The Vampire and the Ballerina** / **The Vampire's Lover**
*Consorzio Italiano Films*
*85 minutes b/w*
*production ended 24 December 1959*
. . . . . . . . . . . . . . . . . . . . . . . . . . . . . . .
Director of Photography: Angelo Baistrocchi; Art Director: Amedeo Mellone; Editor: Renato Cinquini; Sound: Raffaele Del Monte, Leopoldo Rosi; Original Music: Aldo Piga; Choreographer: Maria Ciampaglia; Make-up: Gaetano Capogrosso; Story and

Screenplay: Renato Polselli, Giuseppe Pellegrini, Ernesto Gastaldi; Production Manager: Umberto Borsato; Producer: Bruno Bolognesi; Director: Renato Polselli

*Hélène Remy (Luisa); Tina Gloriani (Francesca); Walter Brandi (Herman); Maria Luisa Rolando (Contessa Alda); Isarco Ravaioli (Luca); Gino Turini (Giorgio); Ugo Cragnani (professor); Bava Sanni (Brigita); Giorgio Braccesi (doctor); Ombretta Ostenda, Marisa Quattrini, Titti Valeri, Stefania Sabatini, Franca Licastro (dancers); Brigitte Castor; Lut Maryk*

**Many more chills but also less decorum can be found in Renato Polselli's *L'amante del vampiro*, which isn't a parody of the vampire genre but, alas, a serious bid by our cinema to take on this lucrative showbiz subject, or at any rate it would like to be ... It's done in the style of a fairground show, with some well-judged horror effects and plot developments that are anything but dull.** *La Stampa* 24 May 1960

**I guess that was the first Italian film on vampires, and it came about through a meeting with producer [Bruno] Bolognesi. Knowing I'd had experience of giallo literature, he asked me if I'd be willing to make a horror movie ... I shot the film at two different castles: the one in Passerano, one wing of which was later bought by the English politician [John] Profumo ... and the one in Artena (again, near Rome), owned by Prince Borghese.** *Renato Polselli* [quoted in Bruschini, *Horror all'italiana 1957-1979*, 1996]

his strongest when he departs from his Hammer models entirely.

Again, it's Brigita who is the focus of Polselli's best scenes. In a playful echo of Dreyer's *Vampyr*, she experiences her own funeral, cypress trees looming overhead, dirt hammering down onto the window in

L'ULTIMA PREDA
DEL VAMPIRO

LYLA ROCCO · WALTER BRANDI
MARIA GIOVANNINI · ALFREDO RIZZO
TILDE DAMIANI · ANTOINE NICOS
CORINNE FONTAINE · ERIKA DI CENTA
MARISA QUATTRINI · LEONARDO BOTTA
Regia di PIERO REGNOLI
produzione NORD FILM ITALIANA

Vietato ai minori di 16 anni

Showgirls Corinne Fontaine and Lyla Rocco, either one of whom might become L'ultima preda del vampiro (1960)

her coffin lid, her eyes staring and weirdly luminous; the effect is spellbinding. In the second scene she rises from the grave and the conniving Herman, having given her a honeyed promise of "life without end," tricks her into lying in her coffin again. He then, shockingly, slams a stake into her with a maniacal yell of "This time you'll die with no chance of waking again, because I am, and must remain, master of my world." Those cypresses, a recurrent image in the film, oscillate in alarm.

The sexual emphasis provided by Polselli begins with Luisa venturing into a massive walk-in closet at the castle, relishing the sensual thrill of the assembled velvets and furs prior to clutching her heart in ecstasy when assaulted by Herman. Later, her appeals to Francesca to go looking for the errant Luca carry a subdued lesbian undertow that was to be much expanded in future films. The whiff of perversity surrounding the sexually dependent relationship between Herman and the Countess was a trailblazer too, with the partners alternating in the master-servant roles and the Countess making a point of only drinking from Herman himself. He tops himself up with the blood of others while the Countess expresses a kind of fascinated repulsion for the monster he becomes at her blood-lusting instigation. ("I need you," she breathes. "But I can't look at you...") The transformed Herman's prosthetics are rubbery and ineffective, but the sausage fingers and thickly swollen facial features do suggest that, in surrendering to vampire lust, he becomes a kind of grotesquely distended phallus.

The film has a few drawbacks, including the sexy dance troupe's spontaneous, yet all too obviously rehearsed, dance routines, which have kitsch value but little else. The Countess, maintaining her youth via Herman's blood donations, is an obvious nod to the smouldering template provided by Gianna Maria Canale in I vampiri, but Maria Luisa Rolando is too callow an actress to convince in the role. She has the capacious bosom already deemed indispensable to an undead seductress ("You could've studied geography on her breasts,"[29] observed co-writer Gastaldi) but no Gothic presence whatsoever. And Walter Brandi's rather stodgy Herman leaves the viewer in no doubt that Italian filmmakers would have to do a hell of a lot better if they wanted to find an effective competitor for Christopher Lee; no wonder Brandi was given a horror make-up to sustain him through his vampiric moments.

L'amante del vampiro having wrapped on Christmas Eve, Brandi had another go at playing a vampire the following year. Going on release in November 1960, L'ultima preda del vampiro (The Vampire's Final Victim) was written and directed by Piero Regnoli, with Brandi cast in the dual role of modern-day Count Gabor Kernassy and his centuries-old vampire ancestor.

Unencumbered by horror make-up this time, Brandi tries instead to shape his blandly unthreatening features into the sexy-stern mould perfected by Christopher Lee. He fails.

Worse still, he's completely upstaged by Maria Giovannini's revived Katia, one of five stranded burlesque dancers who've sought refuge at Kernassy's ancestral castle. (For interiors this was actually the Palazzo Borghese again: same location, same vampire, same plot.) Attacking her former employer, Giovannini is clearly nude – indeed, a topless shot emerges from Aldo Greci's chiaroscuro photography to prove the point – and later she's nude again when doing battle with her vampire master in the Kernassy crypt. She finally succumbs to a flaming stake that, in an audacious shot, sends streams of blood pouring down her bare legs. Nude or not, Giovannini is a fang-baring sight to behold.

Releasing the film in the US as *The Playgirls and the Vampire*, the London-born distributor Richard Gordon put together a trailer that promised patrons a dose of 'raw, naked terror!' With Giovannini around, at least the adjectives were accurate. On top of this, soulful heroine Lyla Rocco (whose husband, Alberto Lupo, was simultaneously starring in a horror film of his own: *Seddok*) spends much of her screen time in a fetchingly transparent negligée, just as Hélène Remy did in *L'amante del vampiro*. Elsewhere, however, the film's idea of eroticism is on the sniggering-schoolboy level – though sniggering of a different kind is reserved for the burlesque troupe's dance routines, which are significantly worse than those in *L'amante*.

The film's mixture of Gothic atmosphere and cheesecake titillation is crystallised in its first two scenes. In one, the vampire's hand gropes its way out of a stone sepulchre; in the second Katia's hand travels languorously up her right leg before adjusting her stocking top. Four years earlier, Regnoli had been co-writer of *I vampiri*, but none of that film's sophistication bleeds through into *L'ultima preda*. The only flash of wit comes when the girls' manager (Alfredo Rizzo) settles down in bed to drool over the October 1959 issue of *Frolic*. The nude Katia appears on cue and frightens him out of his wits, which may or may not have been Regnoli's judgment on his 'all mouth and no trousers' target audience.

## LITERARY SOURCES
## REAL AND UNREAL

In May 1959, no fewer than 16 French directors were photographed sitting in serried ranks on the steps of the Palais du Festival at Cannes, among them François Truffaut, Jean-Luc Godard, Claude Chabrol, Robert Hossein, Roger Vadim and Édouard Molinaro. The photo announced the arrival of France's so-called Nouvelle Vague (new wave), an influx of young talent offering a provocative challenge to what Truffaut, five years earlier, had called "une certaine tendance du cinéma français"[30] (ie, a tendency towards literary stuffiness and production-line vacuity). Like fellow filmmakers Jacques Rivette and Éric Rohmer, Truffaut, Chabrol and Godard were all key contributors to the magazine *Cahiers du Cinéma*, which advanced 'la politique des auteurs' as a means of identifying film as the artistic vision of just one person – the director.

Yet the Nouvelle Vague was hardly a unified movement, as the disparate filmmakers in that famous photo attest. Vadim and Molinaro, for example, were already comfortably ensconced in the commercial sector. Molinaro, later to specialise in boisterous comedy, was currently making his name with lean thrillers, while Vadim had scored a money-spinning triumph as far back as 1956, launching his then-wife, Brigitte Bardot, as the original 'sex kitten' in *Et Dieu ... créa la femme* (And God ... Created Woman). Both men would also flirt with horror. Whereas Molinaro waited until March 1976 before making a vampire film, Vadim got to work on one as early as January 1960.

> Carmilla Karnstein comes of an old Austrian family that, some 200 years ago, was reputed to harbour vampires. Her Italian cousin, Leopoldo, is set to marry Carmilla's childhood friend Georgia Monteverdi, and stages a spectacular fireworks display as part of a pre-nuptial Bal Masque – in the process inadvertently detonating a hidden cache of Nazi munitions. Wandering the estate, Carmilla discovers that the explosives have uncovered the crypt of her vampiric ancestor, Millarca.

Echoing his famous Bardot hit, the title of Vadim's vampire film was *...Et mourir de plaisir* (...And Die of Pleasure), and while making it at Rome's Cinecittà facility he enjoyed the significant luxury of a $750,000 budget. A radical modernisation of J S Le Fanu's 1871 novella *Carmilla*, this French-Italian co-production weaves a sophisticated spell of ambiguity around its leading character, leaving viewers to decide for themselves whether Carmilla genuinely becomes a vampire or – reeling from the psychological shock of her cousin marrying her friend – merely imagines herself as one. All this, of course, was predictably junked for the purposes of US distribution, where the film's title became *Blood and Roses*. As well as excising over ten minutes' footage, Paramount added an intrusive narration purportedly spoken by the undead Millarca, thus eliminating the un-American 'taint' of

## ...ET MOURIR DE PLAISIR

France-Italy 1960
Italy: *Il sangue e la rosa*
UK / US: **Blood and Roses**
Les Films EGE / Documento Film
87 minutes colour
production began 4 January 1960

. . . . . . . . . . . . . . . . . . . . . . . . . . . . .

Director of Photography: Claude Renoir;
Art Directors: Jean André, Robert Guisgand;
Editors: Victoria Mercanton, Maurice Lucidi;
Sound: Robert Biart, Julien Coutellier; Music:
Jean Prodromidès; Make-up: Amato Garbini;
Screenplay: Claude Martin, Claude Brûlé;

Roger Vadim, Roger Vailland, from the story
*Carmilla* by J Sheridan Le Fanu; Producer:
Raymond Eger; Director: Roger Vadim

*Mel Ferrer (Leopoldo de Karnstein); Elsa Martinelli
(Georgia Monteverdi); Annette Vadim (Carmilla
de Karnstein); Alberto Bonucci (Carlo Ruggieri);
René-Jean Chauffard (Dr Verari); Gaby Farinon
(Lisa); Serge Marquand (Giuseppe); Edith Arlène
Peters Catalano (cook); Nathalie Lafaurie (Marie);
Camilla Stroyberg (Martha); Marc Allégret (Judge
Monteverdi); uncredited: Renato Speziali (Guido
Naldi); Gianni Di Benedetto (policeman)*

**Filmed at the Emperor Hadrian's villa outside Rome under the direction
of Roger Vadim (*And God Created Woman*), this eerie tale of a lady vampire is
the most subtle, careful and beautiful of the current crop of chillers.**
*Time* 8 September 1961

**I adore the fantastic. Carmilla, the young vampire in Sheridan Le Fanu's
novel, always had a special position in my own personal mythology ... But,
despite the success of my last film, persuading a producer and distributors
to put their money into a film about a female vampire was no easy matter in
an age of jet planes and television. It was madness, I was told ... *Et mourir de
plaisir* was a fine film, but ahead of its time.** Roger Vadim (*Mémoires du Diable*, 1975)

Annette Stroyberg (then known as Annette Vadim) ventures into the
ancestral crypt in the *Carmilla* adaptation *...Et mourir de plaisir* (1960)

uncertainty. They also referred to the film, in a trailer
scored with heavily doom-laden library music, as
'The ultimate in adult and unadulterated horror!'

That ominous library music would acquire a
notorious afterlife when recycled in George Romero's
*Night of the Living Dead*, whereas the plangent score in

Vadim's film, composed by Jean Prodromidès, relies
largely on rippling harps. (Irish harps, to be precise
– possibly in tribute to the nationality of *Carmilla*'s
author.) Everything else about the film is similarly
top-drawer, in particular the truly sumptuous
Technicolor photography by Claude Renoir. Together
with the contemporaneous work being done for
Hammer by Jack Asher, Renoir's imagery here provided
a template for the lushly coloured experimentalism
that would predominate in later horrors. On top of
this, Vadim's use of a modern setting, plus his discreet
emphasis on aberrant sexuality, would have a decisive
effect on the development of continental Gothic.
Though France would remain curiously reticent and
relatively unproductive in the area of cinema horror, it
nevertheless provided – in *Les Diaboliques*, *Les Yeux sans
visage* and finally *...Et mourir de plaisir* – three of the most
massively influential titles in a still-coalescing genre.

Appropriately, it's the bespectacled Vadim himself
who sets the narrative going. "I bet you have a story to
tell us," he says to a bearded doctor as they relax in an
ultra-modern Caravelle jet airliner. Indeed the doctor
does, alluding to "une histoire curieuse" and beginning
with a couple of little shepherdesses venturing into a
sunlit graveyard. The looming Karnstein headstones
accord well with their fearful talk of vampires, though
Mel Ferrer's Leopoldo soon reassures us that "We
[Karnsteins] stopped being vampires in 1775."

The Carmilla we're presented with here – played
by Vadim's then-wife, Annette Stroyberg – at first
appears thoroughly up to date, gyrating to her
Dansette record player rather than participating in
the folk dancing at the party. The nocturnal fireworks
display over the cemetery is a riot of dazzling colours
interspersed with plumes of explosive fog, and a
sickly yellow glow pulses from the ruined abbey as
Carmilla ventures near. A flurry of bats precedes her
descent into the crypt and, very subtly, Vadim irises in
on the entranced girl as the risen Millarca – apparently
– approaches, with only the revenant's laboured
breathing heard on the soundtrack.

Later in the film Vadim works the first of two
intriguing variations on the Le Fanu scene in which
the heroine sees "Carmilla standing near the foot of
my bed, in her white night-dress, bathed, from her
chin to her feet, in one great stain of blood." For
Vadim this becomes a white ball gown stained at the
bosom with red candle-wax, causing Carmilla to flee
through lilac-hued corridors to a cheval glass, which
to her horror discloses a yet bigger splotch. Yet from
our viewpoint Carmilla's dress is still pure white, a
detail that makes her subsequent tearing of the dress
– exposing her naked and blood-covered right breast

– all the more startling. Needless to say, she destroys the illusion by shattering the mirror.

As well as giving himself a small role in the film, Vadim also cast his mentor, writer-director Marc Allégret, as Georgia's father. It was Allégret who had introduced Vadim to Jean Cocteau; in fact, Vadim and Stroyberg had both appeared in Cocteau's 1959 film *Le Testament d'Orphée* just a couple of months before embarking on *...Et mourir de plaisir*. The shade of Cocteau hovers over Vadim's most striking achievement in the film, when Carmilla pricks the neck of her sleeping friend with an ornamental ring and the image immediately drains to monochrome.

The dream sequence that ensues picks up a trick from William Castle's recently released shocker *The Tingler*, with stridently red blood seeping from Carmilla's black-and-white throat; this is followed by Georgia's plunge into the swimming pool of the unconscious (the oscillating waters are accessed via her bedroom window) and finally by a surgery sequence in which silver-faced nurses sporting crimson gloves hover over a topless subject on the operating table. David Pirie has suggested that this unnerving tableau is an "echo [of] the analytical reading of *Dracula* as a memory of a child's trauma at the hands of surgeons."[31] Whatever it may be, it constitutes the most memorable moment in a consistently provocative film.

For all its luscious imagery, the film remains somewhat inert in terms of pacing and incident, suffering too from strangely robotic protagonists and a too-pat ending. Also, the erotic content that would be magnified so greatly in future films is, at this early stage, merely sketched. Vadim, for example, reduces Le Fanu's pronounced lesbian subtext to an ambiguous kiss between Georgia and Carmilla in a rain-streaked greenhouse, a kiss that leaves the tiniest red stain on Georgia's lower lip. Among the future directors who would do most to eroticise the vampire myth was another Frenchman, Jean Rollin, much of whose imagery is telegraphed here by the scene in which Carmilla walks among the crumbling masonry of the abbey. Intriguingly, Rollin would work with R J Chauffard – the narrator-doctor in Vadim's film – in his 1969 picture *La Vampire nue*, later casting the Karnsteins' groundsman, Serge Marquand, in a similarly rustic role in *Les Raisins de la mort*.

Having been seen playing the piano in *...Et mourir de plaisir*, there was more of the same for Mel Ferrer when he took the lead in Edmond T Gréville's *Les Mains d'Orlac* (The Hands of Orlac). This Anglo-French co-production, shot at both Shepperton Studios and the Studios de la Victorine in Nice, began shooting on 16 May 1960, revisiting the classic Maurice Renard

novel that inspired Robert Wiene's *Orlacs Hände* in 1924 and Karl Freund's *Mad Love* in 1935. In order to accrue tax benefits at both ends of the co-production deal, the British crew were excluded from the French credits just as their French counterparts went unmentioned in the UK version, a subterfuge bolstered by Gréville's dual nationality.

The bones of the story are as before – renowned concert pianist Steven Orlac loses his hands in a plane crash and comes close to losing his mind when he suspects that the hands of executed murderer Vasseur have been grafted on in their place. But here the blackmailer buzzing round him is a down-at-heel burlesque illusionist called Néron, a role that provides a splendid showcase for Christopher Lee in the 'seedy spiv' mode he briefly specialised in post-*Dracula*. Indeed, he cuts a delightfully hateful figure, making it clear that Néron isn't merely opportunistic but certifiably insane, and in the process wiping the floor with the rather listless Ferrer.

Unlike the other British character players who pass through, Lee provided his own French dialogue; Dany Carrel, cast as Néron's pixie-like assistant Li-Lang, was also heard in both versions. Sadly, some of Gréville's visual affectations were cut from the UK edit, notably a dissolve from a maid's foot poised on an Electrolux vacuum cleaner to the shapely ankle of a Marseilles prostitute. Several of the refinements in Gréville's dialogue were also dispensed with, as when Orlac's fiancée Louise points out that "When the Mistral rises, it's as if the Devil is breathing." Presumably a nod to Gréville's 1947 picture *Le Diable souffle*, this line comes out very differently in English. "It's probably this

Certifiably insane: Christopher Lee hatches an elaborate blackmail plot in *Les Mains d'Orlac* (1960)

wretched Mistral," she observes. "It's true, you know – it does get on one's nerves sometimes." Whatever the language, the film is finally somewhat bland, crucially lacking the wild, hallucinatory edge common to the two earlier versions of the story.

Contributing a spot of off-hand toplessness to *Orlac*'s French cut, Dany Carrel was fresh from doing something similar in Giorgio Ferroni's *Il mulino delle donne di pietra* (The Mill of the Stone Women), which she made at the same time Mel Ferrer was making *...Et mourir de plaisir*. Like the Vadim film, this too was a collaboration between Italy and France, though this time the majority contributor was Italy. In due course, French critic Michel Caen would extol the result as "a film of immense beauty," drawing attention to "the numerous charms of the [Terence] Fisher aesthetic ... [with] some scenes apparently drawn direct from *Dracula* or *The Brides of Dracula*." In more general terms, Caen gave the film an enthusiastic thumbs-up on the grounds that it "has everything: chained-up girls, needles, scalpels..."[32]

> *Holland, 1892. Charged with reporting on the upcoming centenary celebrations for Professor Gregorius Wahl's so-called Mill of the Stone Women, Hans von Armin meets Wahl's beautiful daughter Elfy. After a night of love, he decides to return to his childhood sweetheart Liselotte; on being told the news, Elfy becomes distraught, collapses and apparently dies. When she turns up alive, Hans determines to find out how Wahl and his shifty associate Dr Bohlem brought her back.*

In fact, Ferroni's film couldn't quote directly from Fisher's *The Brides of Dracula*, given that the latter began shooting eight days later, on Tuesday 26 January 1960. But the two films share a likeness that goes beyond the gorgeous colour effects achieved by Jack Asher at Bray and Pier Ludovico Pavoni at Cinecittà. For, by a pretty remarkable coincidence, both film's blood-red end titles are superimposed over model shots of a windmill engulfed in purifying flames.

Discounting Steno's inane comedy *Tempi duri per i vampiri*, *Il mulino* was Italy's third Gothic horror and the first to be made in colour. Visually it remains very much in line with what Caen called "the Fisher aesthetic," though for its plot mechanics it turned to other sources. According to the credits, the script was based on a Pieter van Weigen story contained in *Flemish Tales*. Both author and anthology were bogus, however – an unnecessary little fiction designed to gentrify the film for a target audience that wouldn't have given a toss either way. The real derivations are plain. Dr Bohlem's job, as becomes clear in the third

act, is to exsanguinate healthy young women in order to keep the ailing Elfy alive, while Wahl petrifies the discarded bodies for use in his "macabre carousel" of female martyrs and murderers. (And extremely macabre it is, too.) So *House of Wax* is invoked by Wahl and *Les Yeux sans visage* by Bohlem. Given that the latter film opened in Paris only a week before *Il mulino* started production, it seems likely that somebody involved – maybe Ferroni himself – had attended the film's screening at the 1959 Edinburgh Film Festival.

The look of *Il mulino* is consistently beautiful though never flashy; the action is too sombre for that, whipping up a brooding atmosphere of Lowlands mystery rivalled only by the later *Les Lèvres rouges*. (And that film had the advantage of actually being directed by a Belgian.) An opening quote from Carl Dreyer's *Vampyr*, in the form of a gibbet-mounted bell overlooking a dreary waterway, is succeeded by a host of arresting effects, from the delicate green that dapples the mill's alabaster statuary to the gossamer tracery of cobwebs through which Elfy beckons in Hans' drug-induced hallucinations. The startling depth and clarity of Pavoni's photography, particularly when we're guided through the various sculptures displayed in Wahl's study, somehow achieves the 3-D effect of *House of Wax* without recourse to 3-D.

The prevailing hue is a funereal blue, but when strong colours do intrude they're used for discreetly poetic purposes. Hans, for example, returns from his night of passion with the scarlet-robed Elfy to find a red rose mysteriously displayed on his desk; after taking a moment's interest in it, he tosses it carelessly aside en route to a tryst with Liselotte. This callous gesture acts as a cue for the operatic emotions that precipitate Elfy's collapse. Hovering in the upper reaches of the mill, she watches Hans and Liselotte kissing below; behind her, the wooden turbines grind inexorably as an index to her roiling anger. Because Elfy is afflicted "with the same malady that proved fatal to her mother" (as Wahl rather vaguely puts it), emotional upheavals are likely to be fatal. And so it proves in an extraordinary confrontation scene that ends with Elfy's unconscious face magically acquiring a stony pallor together with several livid cuts and bruises. The overwrought emotional pitch, coupled with the sumptuous imagery, would prove a cornerstone of Italian Gothic.

Though the film replaces the plastic surgery of *Les Yeux sans visage* with blood transfusions, the statuesque Scilla Gabel was nevertheless an apt choice for Elfy; a former stand-in for Sophia Loren, she had reportedly undergone plastic surgery in order to look less like her. Professor Wahl's face belongs to Herbert Böhme, a monolithic German tragedian reminiscent

Scilla Gabel
succumbs to high
emotion, with grisly
consequences, in
*Il mulino delle donne
di pietra* (1960)

of Donald Wolfit in the non-Hammer British horror
*Blood of the Vampire*. Like that 1957 film, the script
of *Il mulino* is clotted with a good deal of scientific
mumbo-jumbo about blood cells. The mumbo-jumbo
here is put into the mouth of Wahl's colleague
Dr Bohlem, played by an actor who was just months
away from recreating Fritz Lang's Dr Mabuse –
Wolfgang Preiss. The choice of German actors to play
the villains is intriguing, given that the film's other
leads were provided by France (hero Pierre Brice,
heroine Dany Carrel) and Italy (tragic femme fatale
Gabel). To what degree national stereotyping might
have been involved is up to the viewer.

The film takes its time getting round to identifying
Wahl and Bohlem as the villains (not that we're
ever in much doubt about it), since the second act is
mainly given over to Hans' trauma regarding what's
real and what's merely imagined. Did Elfy not actually
die? If so, did he not actually brush the yellow tulips
from the glass panel in her coffin and see her dead
face underneath? – an image so beautifully rendered
by Ferroni and Pavoni that it could easily count as a
hallucination. It turns out, of course, that Bohlem has
given Hans hallucinogenic drugs to induce exactly
this uncertainty, but in the meantime Hans' teetering
on the edge of madness prefigures the crazed hero
of Ferroni's only other horror film, *La notte dei diavoli*

## IL MULINO DELLE DONNE DI PIETRA

Italy-France 1960
France: **Le Moulin des supplices**
UK: **Drops of Blood**
US: **Mill of the Stone Women**
Galatea / Wanguard Film / Faro Film / Explorer
    Film (Rome) / Comptoir d'Expansion
    Cinématographique
95 minutes colour
production began 18 January 1960
. . . . . . . . . . . . . . . . . . . . . . . . . . . . .
Director of Photography: Pier Ludovico
Pavoni; Art Director: Arrigo Equini; Editor:
Antonietta Zita; Music: Carlo Innocenzi;
Make-up: Franco Palombi; Screenplay:

Remigio Del Grosso, Giorgio Ferroni,
Ugo Liberatore, Giorgio Stegani; Story:
Remigio Del Grosso, Giorgio Ferroni,
from the short story of the same name in
*Flemish Tales* by Pieter Van Weigen [sic];
Producer: Giorgio Venturini; Director:
Giorgio Ferroni

Pierre Brice (Hans von Arnim); Scilla Gabel (Elfy
Wahl); Dany Carrel (Liselotte); Herbert Boehme
(Professor Gregorius Wahl); Wolfgang Preiss
(Dr Bohlem); Liana Orfei (Annelore); Marco
Guglielmi (Ralf); Olga Solbelli (Selma); Alberto
Archetti (Conrad)

Diligently patterned on models both ancient and modern, *Il mulino delle donne
di pietra* aims for horror effects in a variation on the 'waxworks museum'
theme ... Giorgio Ferroni has directed with skill and a degree of well-honed
technique, but to induce shivers he has contented himself with the standard
paraphernalia of coffins, cadavers, shrieks and creaks. As a result, the
shivers, through force of habit, are fewer than expected. *La Stampa 9 March 1961*

Ferroni was a splendid 'Film-Italiener', with everything going swiftly and
smoothly and for whom nothing was a problem. Later on I visited him in
Yugoslavia when he was shooting something there. [Probably *La notte dei
diavoli*, 1971.] Now, I don't want to be unfair but I'd call him a lovable hack.
If a scene wasn't quite as good as he wanted it to be he'd just say, "We'll
use it anyway!" *Wolfgang Preiss* [quoted in *Splatting Image* June 2003]

(Night of the Devils), which would follow in 1971. Of
course, Hans is a pretty shabby sort of hero anyway
– the kind of man who beds a woman one night
and tries to slide out of any commitment the next
morning. Yet the film also invites us to share in his

panic at Elfy's hysterical response, as if to suggest the only real mistake he made was sleeping with a woman who's not quite right in the head.

After Hans' travails in the second act, the tension between Wahl and Bohlem, belying the efficiency with which they work together, dominates the film's final third. As they fuss over the blood transfer between Elfy and artists' model Annelore, a pair of dish-mounted torches blaze at either side of the screen, giving their procedures an almost hieratic solemnity. (These same torches will later be overturned by Wahl to bring on the climactic inferno.) But underneath they thoroughly despise each other. The artist Wahl, with his aristocratic monocle, sneers at the ex-con scientist Bohlem, who wears bourgeois pince-nez, and loudly mocks his aspirations to marry Elfy. "The only face my daughter will see when she returns to life will be mine," he seethes, with just the merest hint of incestuous innuendo.

For his part, Bohlem calls Wahl "a sadistic mummifier of women" – and there is indeed a charming irony when Wahl pompously identifies himself as a representative of "decent society." For just moments before we've seen him fitting a latex mask over Annelore's dead face, a moment so horrible it seems to anticipate *The Texas Chain Saw Massacre*. It's a flash of genuine grotesquerie in a film that's otherwise among the most elegant horrors Italy ever produced.

# A SIGHT TO DREAM OF, NOT TO TELL

By the late summer of 1959, Mario Bava was indulging his passion for Russian literature by concocting a screen treatment of Gogol's 1830s story *Viy*. After numerous salvage jobs on other directors' work, including Freda's *I vampiri*, he was at last preparing to make his fully fledged directorial debut with a Galatea project called *La maschera del demonio* (The Mask of the Demon). His chosen story was one he was in the habit of recounting to his children at bedtime, though in the eventual scripting process not a great deal of it survived. "Such was the ingenuity of the scriptwriters – myself included – that precisely nothing was left of Gogol's story," Bava quipped several years later.[33]

The title of the project was a frank attempt to cash in on *House of Wax* and *The Curse of Frankenstein*, which in Italy had been titled *La maschera di cera* and *La maschera di Frankenstein* respectively. The real template, however, was the provocative fusion of sex and horror in Fisher's *Dracula il vampiro*, and in searching for a female counterpart to Christopher Lee the debutant director stumbled across a 22-year-old actress hailing from Birkenhead, near Liverpool.

Barbara Steele had already followed Lee's example in one crucial respect – as a Rank contract artiste, her progress had been impeded by her exotic and, to casting directors, faintly sinister appearance. Having been offloaded onto 20th Century-Fox, her Hollywood chances were similarly stymied by a Screen Actors Guild strike that kicked off on 7 March 1960. On this cue she decamped to Europe and exactly three weeks later – on the 28th – the shooting of *La maschera del demonio* began at Titanus. Her availability may have been a happy accident, but she proved the ideal figurehead for the film that finally made Italian Gothic a going concern.

*Moldavia, 1830. Dr Kruvajan and his young assistant Dr Gorobec are bound for a Moscow symposium when they pause to inspect the tomb of Asa, a witch put to death 200 years before. At the same time, they encounter Asa's lookalike descendant, Katia Vajda, with whom Gorobec is smitten. Unknown to Kruvajan, his blood, accidentally shed over the sarcophagus, partially revives Asa. To complete her regeneration, she wills her vampire cohort, Javutich, to rise from the grave too...*

Few horror films have begun with the literally bludgeoning impact achieved by Bava's debut. The introductory alfresco witch trial, with the accused spitting out a baneful curse on her accusers, was to be repeated many times over the following years, with only minor variations. (Curiously, the scene had an almost exact precedent in a British film called *The City of the Dead*, made at Shepperton six months before *La maschera* – though the likelihood of Bava having seen it is almost non-existent, given that it didn't even appear in the UK until September 1960.) The sinister iconography here is expertly co-ordinated by Bava – the beetling trees, the black-cowled Inquisitors bearing flaming tapers, the upright beams to which Asa and Javutich are tethered, the smouldering brazier in which a branding iron is prepared. And, shockingly, barely a minute has passed when the 'S' brand is applied to Asa's naked back; the effect, achieved with what looks like suppurating plasticine, would be repeated far less convincingly in any number of future films.

Only now does Asa turn to show her face, with Bava tracking in smoothly to give us a good look at Steele's smouldering, teeth-clenched glare of defiance. We notice, too, that Javutich is immobile on his beam with the titular mask of Satan already riveted to his face – for Bava's primary focus, inevitably, will be the torture of the beautiful woman rather than that of the negligible male. To put us in Asa's position, Bava pulls off a brilliantly disconcerting POV shot in which

Barbara Steele mourns her supposedly deceased father
(Ivo Garrani) in *La maschera del demonio* (1960)

## LA MASCHERA DEL DEMONIO

*Italy* 1960
UK: *Revenge of the Vampire* / *The Mask of Satan*
US: **Black Sunday**
Galatea / Jolly Film
85 minutes b/w
production began 28 March 1960
. . . . . . . . . . . . . . . . . . . . . . . . . . . . .
Director of Photography: Mario Bava;
Art Director: Giorgio Giovannini; Editor:
Mario Serandrei; Music: Roberto Nicolosi;
Music [AIP version]: Les Baxter; Special
Effects: Mario Bava, Eugenio Bava [both
uncredited]; Screenplay: Ennio de Concini,

Mario Serandrei, with [uncredited] Mario
Bava, Marcello Coscia, Dino De Palma, from
a story by Nikolai Gogol; Producer: Massimo
De Rita; Director: Mario Bava

Barbara Steele (Princess Asa Vajda / Katia Vajda);
John Richardson (Andrej Gorobec); Andrea Checchi
(Dr Choma Kruvajan); Ivo Garroni (Prince
Vajda); Arturo Dominici (Javutich); Enrico Olivieri
(Constantine); Antonio Pierfederici (priest); Tino
Bianchi (Ivan); Clara Bindi (innkeeper); Mario
Passante (coachman); Renato Terra (Boris);
Germana Dominici (innkeeper's daughter)

There is sufficient cinematographic ingenuity and production flair in
*Black Sunday* to keep an audience pleasantly unnerved. This in spite of a
screenplay that reads, in translation from the original Italian, like a grade
school imitation of Poe ... Barbara Steele, in the dual role of the witch and
her intended victim, ... bears a strong resemblance to Jackie Kennedy and
manages to be attractive in both parts, which may not have been the original
intention. *Variety* 22 February 1961

We sat in a [Rome] screening room, as I recall, at 9.00 in the morning and,
because of the high ceilings and marble floors, it was as cold as a sonofabitch!
And then this picture started. It was terrific! ... Bava himself arrived towards
the end of the screening ... [and] was happy that we liked the film and that
we were quite effusive about it. But he was very modest. I thought Bava was
a great artist. *Samuel Z Arkoff* [US distributor, quoted in *Metro* # 110, 1997]

the spikes lining the inside of the mask seem to float
towards the viewer. Then, with a tremendous mallet
blow from a brawny, cowled executioner, the mask is
fixed in place. A sudden welter of blood and Roberto
Nicolosi's ominous strings and brass introduce the
opening credits.

If Bava wanted to eclipse the shatteringly gruesome
Grand Guignol effects featured in Hammer's
*The Curse of Frankenstein*, he'd certainly made a good
start – though, to some extent, he neutered the
effect by insisting on black-and-white photography.
(Galatea were reportedly keen to use blood-bolted,
Hammer-style colour, but Bava was mindful of the
'instant ageing' special effects he wanted to use later
in the film; previously seen in *I vampiri*, they were
reliant on coloured filters that couldn't be used in
a colour context.) The monochrome, however,
allowed him to combine the all-new grue of Hammer
with the misty ambience of Universal, creating a
truly startling hybrid that left audiences of the day –
particularly American ones – agog.

When the action moves forward to the 200th
anniversary of Asa's execution, Bava exploits this fusion
of old and new in a sustained barrage of crepuscular
imagery. He's happy to quote from distinguished

forebears, as when Katia's fearful father hallucinates
the demon mask in the surface of his mulled wine,
echoing *White Zombie*. Similarly, Kruvajan is lured to
Asa's resting place by a strange keening noise that, as
in *Sunset Blvd*, turns out to be the wind playing tricks

with a dilapidated pipe organ; soon afterwards, the risen Javutich commandeers a coach that plunges forward in eerie slow motion, neatly reversing the speeded-up conveyance of *Nosferatu*. In addition to these elegant quotations Bava crafts such stunning sequences as the earth mound heaving obscenely over Javutich's grave, chairs and suits of armour being overturned as an unseen presence gains entrance to Katia's home, and Kruvajan's journey through subterranean corridors to a sarcophagus that literally explodes in order to disclose the half-revived Asa. Such set-pieces, intensely imagined and flawlessly executed, make it very clear that Bava – though motivated in the first instance by the commercial imperative to echo a successful import – had found his true metier.

Bava also gave his father Eugenio the opportunity to indulge in squishy special effects that go further than the pre-credits sequence in physical horror – the mask, removed from Asa's eyeless face, revealing tiny scorpions rioting in the sockets; the same sockets bubbling up with what look like (and actually were) poached eggs; a newly turned vampire having a spike thrust into its left eye in a nasty geyser of monochrome gore. Added to the spiked mask looming towards the spectator at the beginning and the witch's eyeless sockets in the crypt, this winceable moment inaugurated an Italian tradition of eye violence that would reach its apotheosis in Lucio Fulci's *Zombi 2* nearly 20 years later.

Though in its essentials the film plays like a children's fairy story, the effect is subverted, not just by horrid moments such as these, but by the undercurrent of tainted sexuality that would give Italian Gothic its distinctive flavour. We notice, for example, that Gorobec's interest in the living Katia is exactly paralleled by Kruvajan's unhealthy fascination for her dead ancestor. A whiff of incest is unmistakable when Katia's transmogrified father rises from his coffin to assail her. When an imposing portrait of Javutich is revealed to be a concealed entrance to the castle's murky lower depths, a further portrait, more deeply buried still, acts as a portal to the crypt itself – it depicts Asa, entirely nude save for a crystal ball and a serpent coiled around her wrist. And Asa's gimlet-eyed intensity turns to orgasmic breast-heaving when she finally has Katia in her clutches and starts to drain her youth.

Katia herself is a rather pallid heroine even before being drained, though, when trysting with Gorobec, she demonstrates a morbid awareness of how quickly the bloom can turn to decay. "Here is the image of my life," she frowns. "Look at it. It's being consumed day by day, just like this garden." Embodying the doppelgänger figure that was once so popular in

Germany and would now turn up time and again in Italy, Steele inevitably makes a far greater impact as the voracious Asa, hissing out malign instructions to Kruvajan while crisping her taloned fingers against the jagged edge of her sarcophagus. It's perhaps a weakness of the film, however, that Asa is kept supine for so long. Worse: rather in the manner of Christopher Lee's upcoming *Dracula* sequels, she doesn't even last very long when she finally gets up – about a minute, in fact. In the process she risks being upstaged by Arturo Dominici's splendidly scary (and far more active) Javutich, or by the tragic desolation that Andrea Checchi brings to the vampirised Kruvajan.

Even so, the moment that seals the upright Asa's fate remains a classic of sexual horror, with the appalled Gorobec catching a glimpse of a fleshless rib cage beneath her enveloping black cloak. It's a truly hideous spectacle, lashing together desire and disgust while recalling a key image in Coleridge's *Christabel*. (There, the vampiric Lady Geraldine unbinds "The cincture from beneath her breast: / Her silken robe, and inner vest, / Dropt to her feet, and full in view, / Behold! her bosom and half her side, / Hideous, deformed, and pale of hue – / A sight to dream of, not to tell!") The scene's impact was memorably encapsulated by Jean-Paul Török in *Positif*, whose July 1961 issue honoured Bava's film with a cover photo. "Under the flowing robes of this strikingly beautiful young woman," Török wrote, "the tattered fragments of a skeleton come shuddering into view. But is she any the less desirable?"[34]

Clearly, then, it wasn't just US baby-boomers, traumatised by the film's local release as *Black Sunday*, who fell under Steele's spell. Back in Europe, thoughtful French cinephiles, enraptured by *Le Masque du démon*, also surrendered themselves at the altar of the baleful Barbara, with Török's loaded question growing ever more pertinent as film after film consolidated her cult status.

Advertised in Italy as 'La più terrificante, obsessiva e allucinante creazione della fantasia di Gogol' (The most terrifying, obsessive and hallucinatory creation of Gogol's imagination), the film was duly picked up for US distribution by Samuel Z Arkoff and James H Nicholson of American International (AIP). Having forked out a very reasonable $100,000 to acquire it, they prepared a variant cut, the above-mentioned *Black Sunday*, and in the process changed Bava's vision in several ways, most conspicuously by replacing the Nicolosi score with an alternative one by Les Baxter. Released in February 1961, this US version was bizarrely coupled in some of its original play-dates with the British comedy *Carry On Nurse*; despite this, it went on to become a huge hit and kindled AIP's interest in more direct Bava collaborations. Indeed, even before releasing the film they brought Barbara Steele back to Hollywood in January 1961 for a small but showy role in Roger Corman's *Pit and the Pendulum*.

Bava's film fared less happily in Britain, where it was submitted to the censor by Anglo Amalgamated and effectively banned. Explaining his decision in 1973, BBFC secretary John Trevelyan gave a good indication of the extraordinary rapidity of change that marked the 1960s. The film, he wrote, "was refused a certificate in 1961 on grounds of disgust, but was eventually passed by the Board in 1968 because by this time it looked rather ridiculous: it was then distributed under the title of *Revenge of the Vampire*."[35]

While the BBFC were recoiling in disgust from his first feature, Mario Bava was moving on undaunted to his second. Prior to *La maschera del demonio*, he'd proved his mettle, not just by completing *I vampiri* and *Caltiki*, but also by directing, uncredited, large chunks of Pietro Francisci's *Le fatiche di Ercole* (The Labours of Hercules) and *Ercole a la regina di Lidia* (Hercules and the Queen of Lidia). As *Hercules* and *Hercules Unchained*, these had been two of Italy's biggest international moneyspinners, setting the style for the extremely lucrative peplum genre – otherwise known as 'sword and sandal' pictures. In 1961 a third Hercules film was entrusted to Bava alone, and with it he set aside the queasy monochrome of *La maschera*, experimenting instead with the abstract use of vividly coloured gel lighting. *Ercole al centro della terra* (Hercules in the Centre of the Earth) began filming at Cinecittà on 29 May and pitted South African muscleman Reg Park against Christopher Lee, aptly cast as Lico, demonic ruler of the Underworld. The result, as Antonio Bruschini pointed out, is "a sort of horror-vampire movie in which only by chance is the hero named Hercules."[36]

Utilising the bare bones of a temple set familiar from numerous Italian epics, Bava smothered it in smoke and bold splotches of colour with results

Muscleman Reg Park and intended sacrifice Leonora Ruffo in *Ercole al centro della terra* (1961)

that are strikingly handsome. Lico's palace resides in a strange landscape stained crimson and blue, its apparently lavish throne room open to a blood-red sky. "Evil shall triumph, even over the Gods, to dominate the Earth," he intones – whereupon Bava inserts some memorably creepy shots of groping zombie hands and grating sarcophagus lids. Lico has Hercules' lover Daianara in his thrall; at one point she responds to his summons by rising from a slab in the plank-like fashion patented by *Nosferatu*. Advised by a Sibylline oracle to "take into your veins the blood of Daianara" in order to "gain eternal life," Lico limbers up by killing the beautiful Helena, then makes ready to sacrifice Daianara by the light of the moon.

The demented resurrection sequence that follows reintroduces those shrouded zombies and hurls them at the camera in vast numbers. Though the flying ghouls are fitted with visible wires, their ensuing battle with Hercules – simultaneously ridiculous and disturbing – remains one of the most remarkable scenes in Bava's portfolio. Indeed, for all its comic-book accoutrements *Ercole al centro della terra* is a dark and doom-laden picture through which all the actors pass with a kind of deathly serenity. The blank-faced beauties are Leonora Ruffo (Daianara) and Rosalba Neri (Helena); the latter, only 21 at the time, would later become arguably the sultriest of all Italy's horror heroines. As well as providing an early showcase for Neri, *Ercole al centro della terra* also gave a tantalising glimpse of what Bava's colour effects might achieve when let loose on a full-blown Gothic.

Given their loose foundations in mythology, there were several other pepla that flirted with horror elements – among them the hirsute horned beast of Silvio Amadio's 1960 release *Teseo contro il Minotauro* (Theseus versus the Minotaur), or three years later a dog-masked deity demanding sacrificial victims in Giorgio Ferroni's *Ercole contro Moloch* (Hercules versus Moloch) and the undead legions summoned by a necromancer in Giuseppe Vari's *Roma contro Roma*

(Rome versus Rome). Proving that the word 'contro' was almost omnipresent in this sub-genre, the best remembered of these films is *Maciste contro il vampiro* (Maciste versus the Vampires); directed by Giacomo Gentilomo in 1961, this one features sadism galore as Maciste allies himself with a race of blue-faced men against the hideous vampire Kobrak, who climactically turns himself into a Maciste doppelgänger. This was followed by two films boldly dropping the word 'contro'. As well as taking its title from a celebrated 1925 original, Riccardo Freda's *Maciste all'inferno* (Maciste in Hell, 1961) transports the hero, rather oddly, to 16th century Scotland and thence to Hell, and in Alberto De Martino's *Perseo l'invincibile* (Perseus the Invincible, 1962) the hero's quest involves an aquatic dragon and a highly peculiar Medusa, both designed by effects guru Carlo Rambaldi.

The Perseus film and the two Maciste titles have been identified as belonging to what Tim Lucas calls 'Mario Bava's secret filmography', in that Bava contributed optical effects to them between other assignments. Of the three, it's Freda's phantasmagoric *Maciste all'inferno* in which the intimate interconnections between the two sub-genres are most marked. Co-scripted, like *La maschera del demonio*, by Ennio De Concini, the Freda film was given a title by its American distributor, Medallion Pictures, that unconsciously foregrounded the similarities between the two pictures. They called it *The Witch's Curse*.

## VAMPIRES ATOMIC AND OPERATIC

While ...*Et mourir de plaisir* and *La maschera del demonio* turned to literature for inspiration, *Seddok "l'erede di Satana"* (Seddok, "Successor to Satan") followed the lead of *Il mulino delle donne di pietra* by echoing an up-to-the-minute film – the same up-to-the-minute film, in fact, namely Franju's *Les Yeux sans visage*. For director Anton Guilio Majano, *Seddok* would remain a once-only crack at horror, though one of his co-writers, Alberto Bevilacqua, later collaborated on a couple of Bava films prior to becoming a prominent novelist, filmmaker and poet in his own right. Yet, where *Il mulino* supplanted Franju's pulp poetry with a lusciously Eastmancolored poetry of its own, *Seddok* stripped away all forms of poetry and left just the pulp behind.

*Jeanette Morineau is a high-class French stripper whose boyfriend Pierre disapproves of her job. When he goes off to sea she crashes her car and is disfigured. She then falls into the hands of Professor Albert Levin, whose groundbreaking serum, Derma 28, "removes every trace of degeneration of cell structure." Its effects are only temporary, however, and the supply quickly runs out. Distilling more entails a series of ghastly murders, perpetrated by Levin in a hideously deformed state triggered by exposure to radiation.*

Majano was a specialist in stately TV adaptations of literary classics; prior to *Seddok*, his recent assignments for RAI (Radiotelevisione italiana) had included versions of *Jane Eyre* and *Treasure Island*. Available for many years only in a savagely truncated American print, *Seddok* proves, even in its uncut Italian version, that horror was by no means Majano's forte. What style the film possesses is almost solely attributable to the fetching chiaroscuro effects of cinematographer Aldo Giordani, whose fondness for rippling, reflected water is carried over from the strip club (with its small ornamental pool) to a nocturnal quayside murder and finally a moody, fog-shrouded shot of Pierre's hulking ship at anchor. Beyond that, the film remains interesting as a thoroughly garbled compilation of newly emerging horror motifs, thrown together on the 'everything but the kitchen sink' principle and making very strange bedfellows indeed.

The film's indebtedness to *Les Yeux sans visage* is as blatant as they come, right down to its setting in the ever-popular France. In addition, the stripclub ambience of recent films from Britain (*Beat Girl*) and Germany (*Die Nackte und der Satan*) is much in evidence, with the latter film supplying the warped imperative to get the shapely stripper onto the operating table as rapidly as possible. Susanne Loret, one of the glamorous bathing beauties from the previous year's *Tempi duri per i vampiri*, performs a conspicuously clunky strip routine right at the outset, a routine easily outclassed later on by a specialist, Glamor Mora.

The theme of facial disfigurement and corrective surgery was similarly fashionable, as seen in the twisted faces of Susan Travers in *Peeping Tom* and Erika Remberg in *Circus of Horrors*, though Loret's scaly cheek and cascading curtain of hair is closer to the make-up seen in a later British film, *Frankenstein Created Woman*. This theme was a grim hangover from the war, a nightmare only gaining prurient expression via exploitation cinema some 15 years later – and given tasteless application here when it's revealed that Levin has done research work in Hiroshima and brought back with him a photo album of genuine deformities, which we're shown. This plot point entails some dialogue suggesting the killer might (very loosely) be termed a "vampiro atomico," which in turn led to the film's enticing US title, *Atom Age Vampire*.

Co-existing with all these modish themes is a much more ancient motif, though it may well have

Susanne Loret recoils as Alberto Lupo and Sergio Fantoni fight it out in Seddok "l'erede di Satana" (1960)

## SEDDOK "L'EREDE DI SATANA"

Italy 1960
UK: *Seddok*
US: *Atom Age Vampire*
Lion's Films
107 minutes b/w
visa date 11 August 1960

Producer: Mario Fava*; Director: Anton Giulio Majano

. . . . . . . . . . . . . . . . . . . . . . . . . . . . .

Director of Photography: Aldo Giordani; Art Director: Walter Martigli; Editor: Gabriele Varriale; Sound: Ivo Benedetti; Music: Armando Trovajoli; Choreographer: Marisa Cianpaglia; Make-up: Euclide Santoli; Special Effects: Ugo Amadoro; Screenplay: Gino de Sanctis, Alberto Bevilacqua, Anton Giulio Majano; Story [and Assistant Director]: Piero Monviso; Production Manager: Elio Ippolito Mellino;

Alberto Lupo (Professor Levin); Susanne Loret (Jeannette); Sergio Fantoni (Pierre); Franca Parisi (Monique); Andrea Scotti (gardener); Rina Franchetti (nurse); Roberto Bertea (Sacha); Ivo Garroni (Commissioner); Gianni Loti; Tullio Altamura; Gianna Piaz; Francesco Sormano; Nicoletta Varé; Cartei Appio; Bruno Benedetti; Silvano Marabotti; Alfredo Mariotti; Glamor Mora ('performing her original Afro-Cuban dance with the Complesso 5 Diavoli')

* this credit, included on both domestic and export prints, does not refer to the similarly named Mario Bava

Ignoring the biased view that filmmakers working in the giallo, science fiction and horror genres aren't up to much, this horror film by Anton Giulio Majano can stand proudly beside the ones made by foreign directors ... The ingredients are the same and the variations minimal, with no truly original idea to mark it out. *Rivista del Cinematografo* 7 June 1961

Glimpses of the torrid night life that have made Rome the night life center of the European continent are featured in Atom Age Vampire ... Susanne Loret, the blonde star who plays the part of an exotic dancer who comes under the spell of a mad scientist, is starred in several dances, while other dancers are also featured in specialities that rival the now popular bossa nova.
*from the original Topaz Film Corporation pressbook*

been included merely as a nod to the ageing effects recently showcased in *I vampiri*. For reasons that are inadequately explained, Levin turns into a Hyde-like monster whenever a killing spree is in view. The lap-dissolve effects here are no more convincing than the same technique as used in *The Wolf Man* nearly 20 years before, though they're supplanted by a rather beguiling bit of stop-motion animation in the later stages. Similarly impressive is an effects sequence in which Jeanette's deformity magically disappears from her face.

Unfortunately, Levin's fully realised monster make-up is less than scary and his plight is decidedly unengaging, given that he's a tight-lipped, monomaniac version of Pygmalion who knows exactly where his mad love for Jeanette comes from. "It's only a compulsion," he maintains, outlining the unhealthy motivations of scores of sexual tyrants to come. "I want to dominate the girl. To possess her." Worse, our heroes, Jeanette and Pierre, are almost as unappealing, one thoroughly self-absorbed, the other priggish and perpetually miserable. The only sympathetic characters are Levin's devoted assistant Monique, though even she is undone by the soapy melodramatics of a predictable love triangle subplot, and his mute manservant Sacha, touchingly played by Roberto Bertea. At one point, Ivo Garrani's charming police inspector refers to this long-suffering character as a classic giallo stereotype.

Surprisingly, the Italian cut is just as lumpy and sluggish as the cut-down export version, and to make matters worse it runs for a seriously taxing 107 minutes. Among the film's incidental crudities is a copy of *Éclair Soir* in which the headline, inexplicably, is in Italian. 'La città in allarme: Un gorilla fugge dallo zoo' refers to the fact that Levin's murders are at first attributed to a fugitive ape. Yet the thing never puts in an appearance. Had it done so, the film could have added *Murders in the Rue Morgue* to its many unashamed borrowings. Contemptuously, *La Stampa* headed its brief review 'Horror-Comic with a Fake Gorilla'.[37]

In a big month for Italian horror films, *Seddok* opened in Rome on 18 August 1960, exactly a week after *La maschera del demonio*. Renato Polselli's *L'amante del vampiro* had beaten them both, arriving in late May, and Piero Regnoli's *L'ultima preda del vampiro* would follow all of them, appearing in November. On release at the same time was Regnoli's *Ti aspetterò all'inferno* (I'll Be Waiting for You in Hell), in which John Drew Barrymore is a paranoid bank robber succumbing to spectral visions. This kind of noir-horror mix was unusual in an industry that, despite the best efforts of Bava and company, was still happier with a timid combination of horror motifs and comedy.

Marino Girolami, for example, was writer-director of *Il mio amico Jekyll* (My Friend Jekyll). Released, like *La maschera del demonio*, on 11 August 1960, this matched Ugo Tognazzi and Raimondo Vianello (stars of the popular TV sketch show *Un due tre*) with the US actress-singer Abbe Lane. The title is a cheat, given that the plot involves a grotesque-looking, and grotesquely horny, professor (Vianello) implanting his own lustful drives into the mind of a prim and proper young reform school teacher (Tognazzi). Even in a climate of music-hall ribaldry, however, the explosive release of sexual inhibitions is still the theme, just as in Italy's more sober Gothics. The following year Tognazzi and Vianello were the draws in Steno's *Psycosissimo*, playing unwilling hired killers whom Edy Vessel proposes to make mincemeat of – literally, by ensnaring them in a sausage factory. 'Più agghiacciante di ... *Psyco*! Più diabolico dei ... *Diabolici!*' screamed the posters, acknowledging the spoof's sources in *Psycho* and *Les Diaboliques*, though there was little realistic prospect of the film being more chilling or diabolical than either.

The prolific Tognazzi had previously appeared in a supporting role in Giorgio Simonelli's haunted house comedy *Fantasmi e ladri* (Ghosts and Robbers, 1958), while Girolami was later responsible for the haunted castle comedy *La ragazza sotto il lenzuolo* (The Girl Beneath the Sheet, 1961). Tognazzi's TV colleague Raimondo Vianello graduated to ghost comedy too, playing the castle spectre of Simonelli's *Gerarchi si muore* (Fascist Bosses Till Death), also in 1961. This was one of the films that introduced the comic team of Franco Franchi and Ciccio Ingrassia to an inexplicably delighted Italian audience; also in the cast was the French ingenue Yvonne Monlaur, fresh from appearing in Britain's *Circus of Horrors*, *The Brides of Dracula* and *The Terror of the Tongs*. A couple of years later, Franchi and Ingrassia were the draws in Steno's 1963 Frankenstein parody *Un mostro e mezzo* (A Monster and a Half), though they were only brought on board after Steno's original plan – to match Boris Karloff with the veteran comic Totò – was abandoned.

By far the classiest of these fantasy comedies is Antonio Pietrangeli's *Fantasmi a Roma* (Ghosts in Rome), written in part by Fellini collaborator Ennio Flaiano and future director Ettore Scola, and boasting a truly deluxe ensemble headed by Marcello Mastroianni, Vittorio Gassman, Sandra Milo and Britain's Belinda Lee. (Tragically, the latter was killed in a car crash just a few weeks before the film's April 1961 premiere.) Best of all is the brilliant Neapolitan actor-playwright Eduardo De Filippo, who potters around his sprawling haunted palazzo while stoutly resisting corporate efforts to convert the place into a 20-storey supermarket. "If something's old, leave it the way it is," he harrumphs. "How would I look with a Teddy Boy hairdo?" The film loses something after De Filippo makes a fatal effort to mend the building's faulty plumbing, but it's consistently charming and, courtesy of cinematographer Giuseppe Rotunno, looks absolutely gorgeous. It hit London in August 1964, playing at the La Continentale on Tottenham Court Road under the more come-hither title *Phantom Lovers*.

Other Italian curiosities opted to incorporate horrific elements into non-comedy scenarios. Romano Ferrara's 1961 production *I pianeti contro di noi* (The Planets Against Us) presented Michel Lemoine as the multiple faces of an alien force cloned from the same man. (Along with producer Robert de Nesle, Lemoine represented French co-production money, while the film itself represented the first of many ventures into horror for both men.) At the same time, Franco Prosperi, Gualtiero Jacopetti and Paolo Cavara scored a worldwide hit with *Mondo cane* (Dog World), initiating a series of prurient 'shockumentaries' with dubious claims to authenticity. Among the films that flowed from it were *Mondo cane n.2*, which features a vignette devoted to the burgeoning vogue for sexy-sadistic *fotoromanzi* (photo novels), while both *Sexy proibitissimo* and *Supersexy '64* confronted their top-drawer strippers with cheesy monsters.

Looking around himself at all these developments, Renato Polselli, director of the groundbreaking *L'amante del vampiro*, seems to have determined not to be outdone. Accordingly, he returned to the vampire theme in 1961 with a picture called *Il vampiro dell'opera* (The Vampire of the Opera). Again, he wrote the script in tandem with Giuseppe Pellegrini and Ernesto Gastaldi (though the latter claimed only to have provided an outline), and this time he journeyed to Umbria in order to take advantage of the 105-year-old Teatro Comunale at Narni. The result ran into financial difficulties and wasn't released until 1964, when it went out as

*Il mostro dell'opera* (The Monster of the Opera). So Polselli had missed the boat after all, and he wouldn't make another horror picture until shooting *La verità secondo Satana* (The Truth According to Satan) in September 1970.

Maybe this was just as well, because in *Il mostro dell'opera* he gives every indication of a filmmaker for whom the 1970s couldn't come soon enough. The kinky asides of *L'amante del vampiro* are inflated into a wildly incoherent stew of fetishistic imagery, but a stew still constrained to some degree by 1960s censorship. The tone is set right at the beginning, as a beautiful dancer in a backlit nightie is pursued into the theatre flies, then, disorientatingly, through a basement lumber room (which Polselli shows us upside-down). She finally comes up against an invisible wall as a tuxedoed vampire threatens her with, of all things, a colossal pitchfork. It's a nightmare, of course, and it's succeeded by a very dreary replication of various 'backstage musical' clichés. Marco Mariani's young director is so invincibly enthusiastic that he entirely ignores the sombre warnings of a liveried caretaker (Alberto Archetti) that "No company has dared perform here for years." Amid all the leeringly photographed dance routines it comes as a relief when the vampire, Stefano, finally reappears in the aisle and announces himself as "an admirer of old-fashioned theatre."

Giuseppe Addobbati takes centre stage as *Il vampiro dell'opera* (1961), belatedly released as *Il mostro dell'opera*

Later, Stefano is briefly seen in doublet and hose in a Renaissance flashback, making it clear that the contemporary leading lady is a reincarnation of the lover who betrayed him. But Polselli's real interest is in the hints of lesbianism among the dancers ("friendship between two women is purer," one of them suggests), and in the S&M stylings of Stefano's alternate reality, in which a bunch of barely clad harpies are chained to a wall amid swathes of ground fog and try to get their plastic fangs into the heroine. Polselli also goes for broke in a ridiculously extended scene of the company dancing insanely under Stefano's baleful influence. Character actor Giuseppe Addobbati isn't exactly Christopher Lee but he looks very effective when snarling in a harsh glare of underlighting. He was, to put it mildly, a much better choice than Walter Brandi, vampire star of *L'amante del vampiro* and *L'ultima preda del vampiro*.

## HIER SPRICHT EDGAR WALLACE!

While full-blown Gothic horror was getting into gear in Italy, the same couldn't be said for Germany, where the proto-sleaze contained in Victor Trivas' *Die Nackte und der Satan* had been met with disgust and sired no followers. But a modified, more audience-friendly form of German Gothic was just around the corner, albeit a form of German Gothic heavily informed by a slightly outmoded German notion of what English Gothic should look like. And it was initiated by a picture that went on release just six weeks after the Trivas film.

Thanks to Harald Reinl's *Der Frosch mit der Maske* (The Masked Frog), Edgar Wallace, the phenomenally successful British author of sometimes macabre crime thrillers, enjoyed a massive resurgence of popularity in Germany 27 years after his death. Viewing Guy Hamilton's *The Ringer*, a 1952 Wallace adaptation from the UK, the Danish producer Preben Philipsen and his German associate Waldfried Barthel had elected not to release it in Germany, embarking instead on a Wallace film of their own. *Der Frosch* accordingly began shooting in Copenhagen on 24 April 1959. On its release in early September, it was successful enough to trigger a long-running series under the Rialto Film banner, the sequence only petering out in 1972.

The creepy, bug-eyed criminal mastermind of *Der Frosch mit der Maske* was followed by similar threats in *Der rote Kreis* (The Red Circle), *Die Bande des Schreckens* (The Gang of Terrors) and *Der grüne Bogenschutze* (The Green Archer). In the course of this intial quartet of Krimi (Kriminalfilme), such series regulars as Joachim Fuchsberger, Eddi Arent and Karin Dor all made their debuts. By January 1961 it was the turn of *Die toten Augen von London* (The Dead Eyes of London), the first of 14 Wallace pictures directed by Alfred Vohrer and effectively a remake of the 1939 British film *The Dark Eyes of London*. There, Bela Lugosi had played a duplicitous insurance broker and his other self, the supposedly saintly superintendent of a home for the blind. Reverting to Wallace's original, the

# DIE TOTEN AUGEN VON LONDON

West Germany 1961
US: **Dead Eyes of London**
Prisma / Rialto Film
98 minutes b/w and colour
production began 16 January 1961
. . . . . . . . . . . . . . . . . . . . . . . . . . .
Director of Photography: Karl Löb;
Art Directors: Mathias Matthies, Ellen
Schmidt; Editor: Ira Oberberg; Sound:
Werner Schlagge; Music: Heinz Funk;
Make-up: Walter Wegener, Gerda
Wegener; Screenplay: Trygve Larsen [Egon
Eis], from the novel by Edgar Wallace;
Dialogue Collaborator: Wolfgang Lukschy;
Production Manager: Herbert Sennewald;
Producer: Horst Wendlandt; Director:
Alfred Vohrer

Joachim Fuchsberger (Inspector Larry Holt); Karin
Baal (Eleanor Ward); Dieter Borsche (David Judd /
Paul Dearborn); Wolfgang Lukschy (Stephan Judd);
Eddi Arent (Inspector Harvey); Anneli Sauli (Fanny
Weldon); Klaus Kinski (Edgar Strauss); Bobby
Todd (Lew Norris); Franz Schafheitlin (Sir John
Archibald); Harry Wüstenhagen (Fred); Ady Berber
(Jacob Farrell); Rudolf Fenner (Matthew Blake);
Hans Paetsch (Gordon Stuart); Fritz Schröder-
Jahn (Chief Inspector); Ida Ehre (Ella Ward);
Walter Ladengast (porter); Joseph Offenbach
(gravedigger); Gertrud Prey (Mrs Brooks);
Kurt A Jung (Jones); Max Walter Sieg (chauffeur);
Horst Schweimler (midget); Joachim Wolff (Mr
Jenkins); Günther Jerschke (coroner); Erich Weiher
(Richard Porter); Hans Irle (policeman); Rolf
Mittmann; Joachim Rake; Manfred Steffen

**The agreeable 'English' atmosphere applied by director Alfred Vohrer to
this celebrated Wallace-Krimi is gripping yet still tips the occasional wink.
Joachim Fuchsberger and Karin Baal head an excellent ensemble, with Dieter
Borsche as the surprise baddie.** *Hamburger Abendblatt 31 May 1961*

**My favourite scene in** Die toten Augen von London **was Ady Berber stalking me
as 'Blind Jake', with his scary white contact lenses. His wife always had to put
these in before each scene, because she was the only one he trusted. His hands
were made up with sticky fake hair and ... we had to do different takes because
the hair got stuck to my face, leaving me looking like a bearded lady. In real
life Ady was the sweetest, gentlest soul.** *Karin Baal [speaking in Hallo, hier spricht Karin
Baal! – bonus feature on the Tobis-Universum release Edgar Wallace Blu-Ray Edition 1, 2016]*

Ady Berber gropes blindly for Karin Baal in *Die toten Augen von London* (1961)

Rialto version separated these characters, making
them brothers and instead turning the focus onto
their monstrous henchman, Blind Jake.

> *Australian impresario Richard Porter is waylaid on
> a foggy London street by a hulking blind brute. The
> subsequent discovery of his apparently drowned corpse
> makes Porter just the latest of several wealthy men
> who've turned up dead after taking out policies with the
> same Greenwich insurance firm. With the help of Braille
> specialist Nora Ward, Scotland Yard's Inspector Holt
> realises that an institute for the blind might provide the
> key to the mystery...*

That Vohrer's first Wallace film is to be steeped in
atmosphere is obvious from the very beginning. Using
an iris effect that will be repeated several times later
on, Vohrer reveals the glow of a street lamp prior to
panning down to a large, bald-headed figure lurking on
a flight of steps just below pavement level. As fog horns
resonate from the nearby river, we note with a chill of
unease the figure's unseeing eyes and unusually hairy
hands, together with the broad leer stretched across his
unshaven face. A muffled old man emerges through
fog, fog that's clearly the cold and clammy kind given
that he takes out a handkerchief to wipe his spectacles.
Seizing the old man by the ankles, the crouching
figure rises up and deposits him in the back of a van.
Then crimson splotches of animated blood usher in
the credit titles. They too are vividly red against an
otherwise monochrome backdrop – initiating a vogue
for colour credits that would become a series staple
until the Wallace films moved into full colour in 1966.

Like so many European chillers to follow, the
Wallace pictures would display a rather sketchy grasp
of London geography – what Kim Newman has called
"the Through a *London A to Z* Darkly effect."[38] Yet in this
enticing opening – and throughout *Die toten Augen* – the
darkened streets of Hamburg's Speicherstadt district
double very convincingly for London's unreconstructed
Docklands. This is a largely mythical London,
nevertheless; it's the same London perpetuated in any
number of fog-laden Gothics, the Ripper territory that
was set in cobbled stone by John Brahm's 1943 classic
*The Lodger*. Yet Vohrer proves he can induce the same
atmospheric chill even in the shadowed stairwell of
a bland and functional apartment building. As Nora
advances apprehensively up the stairs, we hear from
above the sound of a lightbulb being smashed – a
sure indicator that the hulking Blind Jake is on the
premises. Then, just as Vohrer exploited the childhood
fear of having one's ankles grabbed in the prologue,
he touches another deep-rooted nerve when Nora's

hand slides up the banister and makes unexpected contact with the hairy digits of her assailant.

Blind Jake is played by the former wrestler Ady Berber, whose monolithic presence is arguably more effective than the elaborately made-up Wilfrid Walter in the 1939 version. He's written out about two-thirds of the way through, shot to death by his master and tumbling down a muddy incline, a striking close-up disclosing his dead stare of disbelief and hirsute hands that now clutch his *own* throat for a change. Vohrer reels off a series of other terrific set-pieces with consummate skill – a blackmailing prostitute being strangled as her pet parrot shrieks on its perch, the attempted incineration of Nora's elderly guardian in an underground room, and an old-fashioned climax in which Inspector Holt is restrained, Nora is imprisoned in a glass-panelled chamber that fills inexorably with water, and a bogus priest proves himself alarmingly handy with a blowtorch.

Vohrer indulges himself, too, with numerous skittish affectations – among them, a morgue scene beginning on a huge close-up of the corpse's feet, a minor crook whose mirrored shades reflect the image of his spiv-like interlocutor, and a mouthwash scene viewed, bizarrely, from behind the subject's teeth. The minor crook is played by the young Klaus Kinski, an actor who would loom large not just in subsequent Wallace films but in European horror generally. He ends up being spectacularly defenestrated, with Vohrer plunging precipitously into a huge close-up of a screaming onlooker's mouth as Kinski hurtles to the cobbles below. The spiv-like associate, meanwhile, is given a similarly memorable exit, straight down a lift shaft.

The mixture of visual pyrotechnics with garbled plotting and imaginatively staged murders in this and other Wallace films was to exercise a decisive influence on the giallo thrillers soon to emerge in Italy. Here, the prostitute murderer wears the sinister black gloves that were to become a key signifier of the Italian strain, and a scene in which a doorman (Walter Ladengast) looks through a spyhole only to be shot through the eye was memorably reprised by Dario Argento in the 1987 film *Opera*. The police procedural aspect of the gialli is foreshadowed too, and in *Die toten Augen* it's done more engagingly than usual, with Joachim Fuchsberger's Holt and Karin Baal's Nora making an appealing romantic team.

The success of this new strain of Krimi had an obvious effect on other German filmmakers. In May-June 1960, for example, Artur Brauner's CCC Filmkunst staged the revival of a classic Weimar supercriminal via Fritz Lang's last film, *Die 1000 Augen des Dr Mabuse* (The Thousand Eyes of Dr Mabuse), following up in 1961 with Harald Reinl's *Im Stahlnetz des Dr Mabuse* (In the Steel Net of Dr Mabuse); in these and three further films, Mabuse was played by the cold-eyed Wolfgang Preiss. There were also rival Wallace films. By June 1960 producer Kurt Ulrich had got *Der Rächer* (The Avenger) into production, and at the end of the following year CCC started work on a series of films based on the works of the writer's son, Bryan Edgar Wallace. These would include such choice titles as *Das Phantom von Soho* (The Phantom of Soho, 1963) and *Das Ungeheuer von London-City* (The Monster of London City, 1964).

Undaunted by this hydra-like growth of competitors, the Rialto series picked up several distinguished contributors in the wake of *Die toten Augen von London*. The next entry, shot in April 1961, was a British co-production in which Christopher Lee appeared in both the UK version, *The Devil's Daffodil*, and the German one, *Das Geheimnis der gelben Narzissen* (The Mystery of the Yellow Daffodils). At the end of the year Lee turned up again, this time in the gangster thriller *Das Rätsel der roten Orchidee* (The Puzzle of the Red Orchid); in the interim Rialto had churned out both *Der Fälscher von London* (The London Forger) and *Die seltsame Gräfin* (The Strange Countess). The latter is an 'old dark house' mystery in which the title role was assigned to Lil Dagover, 42 years after her appearance in *Das Cabinet des Dr Caligari*. Sadly, her character's name – Gräfin Eleanora Moron – doesn't play quite as well in English as it does in German.

In February 1962 Rialto brought back Alfred Vohrer to direct *Die Tür mit den 7 Schlössern* (The Door with Seven Locks), an entry that saw the series sliding more than ever into playful skittishness as well as featuring a mad scientist intent on forging an ape-human hybrid.

Brigitte Grothum in the clutches of creepy Klaus Kinski in *Die seltsame Gräfin* (1961)

(The property had previously been filmed in 1940 by the same British team responsible for the Lugosi version of *The Dark Eyes of London*.) Next, a submersible killer with wetsuit and spear gun appeared in Vohrer's *Das Gasthaus an der Themse* (The Guest House on the Thames), after which Vohrer kicked off 1963 with the black mamba poisonings of *Der Zinker* (The Squeaker). Beginning with *Das Gasthaus*, the series' distinctive credits sequences were enhanced with a disembodied voice intoning the imperishable catchphrase, "Hallo. Hier spricht Edgar Wallace!"

Not content with having originated Rialto's Wallace series, in 1962-63 Harald Reinl also made *Der Teppich des Grauens* (The Carpet of Horror) and *Die weiße Spinne* (The White Spider), inaugurating a brief run of creepy mysteries based on the works of Wallace's German contemporary, Louis Weinert-Wilson. To add to the confusion, Reinl had barely finished making *Die weiße Spinne* when he was called upon, in April 1963, to direct one of Artur Brauner's Bryan Edgar Wallace titles, *Der Würger von Schloß Blackmoor* (The Strangler of Blackmoor Castle). Reinl's wife, Karin Dor, starred in all three.

The bona-fide Rialto series, meanwhile, showed no let-up in popularity. After the completion of Alfred Vohrer's *Der Zinker* in February 1963, 'old dark house' atmospherics had been the draw in both Franz Josef Gottlieb's *Der schwarze Abt* (The Black Abbot) and Vohrer's *Das indische Tuch* (The Indian Scarf). Following these, Harald Reinl's *Zimmer 13* (Room 13) coupled a series of razor murders with a topical plot point referencing Britain's Great Train Robbery, which wasn't yet four months old when the film went into production. One of the killings, in which Elfi Estell's undercover policewoman poses as a stripper and has her throat slashed directly on finishing her act, offers a glimpse of nudity and a surprisingly graphic gush of arterial blood – a timely innovation, given that the film began shooting on 25 November 1963, the day before Mario Bava started shooting the seminal giallo *6 donne per l'assassino* (Six Women for the Killer) in Rome.

After this, the Rialto team rattled through *Die Gruft mit dem Rätselschloss* (The Vault with the Puzzle Padlock), *Der Hexer* (The Sorcerer) and *Das Verrätertor* (The Traitor) in 1964, followed in 1965 by *Neues vom Hexer* (News from the Sorcerer) and *Der unheimliche Mönch* (The Sinister Monk). The last of these, directed once again by Harald Reinl, was an adaptation of the same Wallace property, *The Terror*, that Warner Bros had made into the world's second all-talking picture in 1928. The story inspired Rialto, too, to come up with an innovation – the inclusion of a colour sequence, heralding the series' move into Eastmancolor throughout with *Der Bucklige von Soho*.

Directed by Alfred Vohrer in June 1966, this one is set in a girls' reformatory shadowed by a hunchback who strangles escapees but turns out not to be a hunchback at all. In its wake, the series' second colour film, *Das Geheimnis der weißen Nonne* (The Mystery of the White Nun), was shot by Cyril Frankel in August 1966 and was made available in a variant English-speaking cut called *The Trygon Factor*.

Using a British director wasn't a first for the series, given that the earlier *Das Verrätertor* had been directed by Freddie Francis. On top of this, at least one British entrepreneur was keenly aware of Rialto's success. Always keen to exploit a popular trend, Harry Alan Towers not only turned to Wallace's contemporary, Sax Rohmer, for a series of Anglo-German Fu Manchu films; he also set up several Wallace-derived pictures in cahoots with Germany's Constantin-Film. Chief among these was *Circus of Fear*, directed by John Moxey at Bray Studios in December 1965. Released in Germany as *Das Rätsel des silbernen Dreieck* (The Puzzle of the Silver Triangle), this dull crime thriller involves Krimi veterans Christopher Lee, Heinz Drache, Eddi Arent and Klaus Kinski rubbing shoulders with Suzy Kendall, Leo Genn and Cecil Parker in the unlikely environs of Winkfield in Berkshire.

## BLACK GLOVES, GRASPING HEIRS

Beyond Edgar Wallace and Dr Mabuse, German filmmakers in the early 1960s acknowledged their shadowy Weimar roots only sporadically. Representing high culture, the celebrated actor Gustaf Gründgens, already a long-time Mephistopheles, crowned his career with a 1957 revival of Goethe's *Faust* at the Hamburg Schauspielhaus; a film version, with some discreetly cinematic flourishes added, started shooting at the Schauspielhaus at the end of May 1960. Directed, like the stage production, by Peter Gorski, the result picked up a Deutsche Filmpreis. (A little over 20 years later, István Szabó's *Mephisto*, based on a controversial novel obviously modelled on Gründgens, would pick up the Academy Award for Best Foreign Film.) Representing light-hearted comedy aimed at kids, Kurt Hoffmann's charming *Das Spukschloß im Spessart* (The Haunted Castle in Spessart) followed the Gründgens-Gorski Faust into German cinemas at Christmas 1960. Recipient of several awards of its own, this so-called 'grusical' features a baker's dozen of musical numbers while mixing up the gamine Liselotte Pulver with a Schlossful of do-gooding spooks.

The satirical comedy of Hoffmann's film gave it a parochial feel, whereas the success of Rialto's

Edgar Wallace pictures was by no means confined to Germany. Indeed, in summer 1961 director Paolo Heusch infused something of a Krimi atmosphere into an Italian-Austrian co-production called *Lycanthropus*. The convoluted plotting was attributable in this instance, not to Wallace, but to Ernesto Gastaldi, here writing his first solo horror script and focusing on what might loosely be termed a 'medical' lycanthrope – presiding over a girls' reform school, the mystery assailant suffers from an aberrant pituitary gland that acts up at the time of the full moon. The film was acquired by Compton-Cameo for UK distribution and renamed *I Married a Werewolf*, whereas in America it formed part of an M-G-M double-bill with the British film *Corridors of Blood* and was given the euphonious new title *Werewolf in a Girls' Dormitory*. Yet it's a good deal grimmer and more straight-faced than such ridiculous export titles might suggest.

> When inmate Mary Smith is murdered in the grounds
> of a girls' reformatory, suspicion falls on several people
> in turn – among others, shifty caretaker Walter, upright
> superintendent Mr Swift, just-arrived biology teacher
> Julian Olcott and philandering benefactor Sir Alfred
> Whiteman. The plot thickens when Julian reveals
> his specialist area of research – the "psycho-physical
> transformation" undergone by the so-called Lycanthropus.

Recalling the previous year's Hammer production *The Brides of Dracula*, the girls' school setting of *Lycanthropus* is a potent one but is handled by Heusch with none of the unbridled eroticism that Renato Polselli and Piero Regnoli had brought to their recent vampire films. Indeed, in only one shot – a fulsome blonde writhing erotically on her bed – does Heusch even nod to the Polselli-Regnoli approach. Heusch's reticence isn't a problem, but trying to work out where the reformatory is located most definitely is, given that English postage stamps and pound notes share screen time with letters from Boston and characters hailing from Vermont.

The confusion is made worse by a cast assembled from Austria, Poland, France, Prussia and Italy who for the most part seem to be acting in English yet are subjected, in the export version, to a truly excruciating dub. These drawbacks do serious damage to an otherwise nicely knotted murder mystery, focusing attention more firmly on the film's visual qualities, which are its strongest suit in any case.

Heusch's key collaborator here was cinematographer George Patrick – pretty obviously a pseudonym, though even Italian sources don't seem to know who for. The

## LYCANTHROPUS

Italy-Austria 1961
Austria: **Bei Vollmond Mord**
UK: **I Married a Werewolf**
US: **Werewolf in a Girls' Dormitory**
Royal Film
83 minutes b/w
visa date 18 October 1961

· · · · · · · · · · · · · · · · · · · · · · · · · · ·

Director of Photography: Renato Del Frate; Art Director: Piero Filippone; Editor: Giuliana Attenni; Sound: Aldo De Martino; Music: Armando Trovajoli; Make-up: Raffaele Cristini, Franco Palombi, Emilia Pomilia, Aldo Ascenzi; Story and Screenplay: Ernesto Gastaldi; Production Manager: Jone Tuzi; Producer:

Guido Giambartolomei; Director: Paolo Heusch

Barbara Lass (Brunhilde); Carl Schell (Julian Olcott); Donatella Mauro (Sandy); Luciano Pigozzi (Walter); Anna Degli Uberti (Sheena Whiteman); Bianca Maria Roccatani (Mary Smith); Maurice Marsac (Sir Alfred Whiteman); Curt Lowens (Mr Swift); Grazia Fachini (Leonor MacDonald); Giuseppe Mancini (porter); Liliana Rondoni (Miss Schultz); Giuseppe Transocchi (police inspector); Anna Maria Aveta, Lucia Cera, Luciana Fratini, Marta Melocco (schoolgirls); Rossana Canghiari; Francesca Dolbecco; Liliana Rondoni; uncredited: John Karlsen (old man)

**The film manages to make the majority of its visual imagery more grotesque than terrifying. The actors do a good enough job ... [among them] the expressive Polish actress Barbara Lass and Carl Schell. Good photography in black and white.** *Intermezzo* 28 February 1962

> We literally shot in five different languages ... Carl Schell and I performed well in German. Barbara [Lass] and Carl acted in French. Maurice Marsac would act in French with Barbara, or English with Carl and me. And the Italians would do their stuff in Italian. The original script was in English, and I tried to stick to English whenever possible. Curt Lowens [quoted in *Ultra Filmfax* July-August 1998]

Curt Lowens as the self-loathing shape-shifter of *Lycanthropus* (1961) duo's first big showcase is Mary's nocturnal tryst with her "middle-aged, over-sexed phoney" of a lover, Sir Alfred. The night photography here is exceptional, particularly when Mary flees hell-for-leather through the woods with a slavering humanoid creature sprinting at her heels. We finally see her in the clutches of a pair of hairy hands, which are preparing to tear open her blouse when Heusch tactfully cuts to the full moon, then to a shot of Mary's corpse being unceremoniously dumped in a lake. Armando Trovajoli's music, engagingly spooky throughout, incorporates a metronomic 'death toll' motif as the grief-stricken girls gather in the courtyard the following morning.

Mary's death is pretty brutal stuff, and Heusch similarly pulls no punches when she's seen laid out on a slab, her face marked by livid gashes, her eyelids pulled back from glassily popping eyes. Happily, the wilfully obtuse police inspector introduced in this scene is soon eclipsed by Mary's investigative friend Brunhilde (renamed Priscilla in the export version), who's given a charmingly gamine appeal by the huge-eyed Polish star Barbara Lass. Heusch screws the suspense admirably tight when she keeps a fact-finding date with Sir Alfred at his customary woodland outhouse. Assailed by wolfish snarling in the darkened interior, Brunhilde is only temporarily relieved when Sir Alfred's vengeful wife Sheena emerges from the gloom, toting a pair of threatening hounds on a leash.

Unfortunately, the Sheena character comes off by far the worst of anyone in the dub track, making the film hard to take seriously until she's definitively silenced by a lethal injection administered by black-gloved hands. *Lycanthropus* thus marks the point at which this creepy signifier of the German Krimis was transferred to Italy, later becoming an equally creepy signifier of the giallo sub-genre.

After her encounter with Sheena, Brunhilde is herself attacked by the werewolf against the bars of the school gates, its presence announced by a vast close-up of its watchful left eye and then by a similarly alarming view of its yawning, drooling maw and impressively large fangs. Brunhilde is rescued by the caretaker's pet dog (aptly named Wolf), and if the film's preponderance of dogs seems like a tribute to *Les Yeux sans visage*, the reference is then made explicit in its best and craziest scene. The ingredients here – female scientist removing the pituitary from a doped-up dog, her werewolf lover writhing in chains as she administers the antidote, another dog leaping from its confinement to savage the woman, the restored lover struggling to free himself and help her – make for a memorably perverse brew, all the more so when the man finally gets free and, in a hysterical frenzy

of self-loathing, belabours the dog with an iron bar. Quite apart from the scene's heady mixture of science-fiction and inter-species romance, the dog's ferocious revenge on the whole principle of animal experimentation is a startling one.

Later in 1961, Julien Duvivier – whose distinguished back catalogue included such fantastic subjects as *Golem*, *La Charrette fantôme* and, in Hollywood, *Flesh and Fantasy* – went about adapting a famous 1937 mystery novel by John Dickson Carr. *The Burning Court* demonstrated Carr's unrivalled mastery of the 'locked room' mode but its ambiguous ending ruffled rationalist feathers with (God forbid!) intimations of the supernatural. To overhaul the book, Duvivier got together with his old colleague Charles Spaak, the Belgian screenwriter whose credits included Renoir's *La Grande illusion*. Their radical adaptation, *La Chambre ardente* (The Burning Chamber), transferred the action from Philadelphia to Bavaria and attracted such fashionable young names as Jean-Claude Brialy, Perrette Pradier and (representing German co-production money) Nadja Tiller.

*The 75-year-old Mathias Desgrez lives in a rambling Black Forest château and has invited historian Michel Boissard to inspect the family papers relating to the executed 17th century poisoner Marquise de Brinvilliers. Along with Boissard comes his wife Marie d'Aubray, who, as a descendant of the Marquise, is of particular interest to Mathias, himself descended from the Marquise's chief accuser. Other members of the Desgrez family show up and before long Mathias is dead – in impossibly mysterious circumstances.*

Completing production on 15 October, the result was released five months later and was dismissed by one French critic, with reference to Jean Epstein's 1928 Poe adaptation, as "a poor man's *House of Usher*."[39] This must have been a galling verdict for Duvivier, whose supernatural mystery was clearly conceived as deluxe in every department, bolstered by top-drawer contributions from composer Georges Auric and cinematographer Roger Fellous, together with separate credits for 'gowns' and even 'lingerie'. On top of this, Duvivier's traditional old dark house wasn't a poor man's anything, being a fabulously grand and airy Bavarian château, and his characters, though in essence the grasping relatives featured in any number of ossified mystery-thrillers, had been carefully updated as flash and facile Frenchmen of the modern day.

These are the kind of young jet-setters who dismiss the magnificent family seat as a "white elephant,"

Jean-Claude Brialy,
Claude Piéplu
and Claude Rich
inspect the skull
of the Marquise
de Brinvilliers in
*La Chambre ardente*
(1961)

"house of death" or "dilapidated rat hole," expressing a preference for Deauville and Saint-Tropez. (Why the ancestral home is in the Black Forest is never explained – though, again, the film's German co-finance presumably had something to do with it.) Into their midst comes the historian's wife Marie, who, in a nod to the French fantastique of Franju, is played by Édith Scob. Whether recollecting her mediumistic mother or the Black Masses she witnessed as a child, Marie is an ethereal presence and finds a receptive ear in the shadowy Dr Hermann. Played by the distinguished veteran Antoine Balpêtré (previously seen in *La Main du diable* and *I vampiri*), he's an old friend of Mathias, now living in a lodge in the grounds and discussing with Marie "the living dead, existing beyond the arcane and impenetrable mysteries of death."

Yet, like Carr's novel, *La Chambre ardente* remains a hybrid, with the supernatural hovering on the fringes and both Marie and Dr Hermann becoming slightly lost in the shuffle. In Scob's case this is a great shame, as the narrative involves the hinted-at reincarnation of the real-life Marquise de Brinvilliers, a plot point that deserved more than just a written account, post-credits, of her 1676 trial in the 'chambre ardente' and subsequent execution. Here, surely, was an opportunity to stage the kind of 'curse uttered at the stake' flashback so recently immortalised in Bava's *La maschera del demonio*, with Scob as a blonde, porcelain counterpoint to the raven-haired exoticism of Barbara

## LA CHAMBRE ARDENTE

France-Italy-West Germany 1961
Italy: *I peccatori della foresta nera*
West Germany: *Das brennende Gericht*
UK: *The Curse and the Coffin*
US: *The Burning Court*
International Productions / Comacico (Paris) / Taurus Film (Rome) / Laura-Film (Munich)
113 minutes b/w
production began 16 August
. . . . . . . . . . . . . . . . . . . . . . . . . . . . . .
Director of Photography: Roger Fellous; Art Director: Willy Schatz; Editors: Paul Cayatte, Nicole Colombier; Sound: Guy Chichignoud; Music: Georges Auric; Make-up: Yvonne Fortuna; Special Effects: Lax; Screenplay and Adaptation: Julien Duvivier,

Charles Spaak, from the novel *The Burning Court* by John Dickson Carr; Dialogue: Charles Spaak; Producer: Yvon Guézel; Director: Julien Duvivier

Nadja Tiller (Myra Schneider); Jean-Claude Brialy (Marc Desgrez); Perrette Pradier (Lucy Desgrez); Édith Scob (Marie Boissard); Antoine Balpêtré (Dr Hermann); Claude Rich (Stéphane Desgrez); Walter Giller (Michel Boissard); [Frédéric] Duvallès (Mathias Desgrez); Héléna Manson (Mme Henderson, housekeeper); René Génin (M Henderson, caretaker); Claude Piéplu (Inspector Krauss); Dany Jacquet (midwife); Gabriel Jabour (jeweller); Laurence Belval; uncredited: Carl Brake (Dr Baxter); Cathérine Thévenin (Frieda, maid)

Given that this concoction ... serves only as an excuse to display obscene, libidinous, sadistic and suchlike elements, we're within our rights to object ... The whole thing reeks of manufacture to the point of being almost comical. Strange, this indulgence in the sordid that has swallowed up some of our ageing directors. *Télérama* 15 April 1962

Then there was *La Chambre ardente*, directed by Julien Duvivier, in which I played a character who had a kind of magnetic power. It was a story that could have been interesting, a whodunit 'fantastique' ... But I've not done much cinema, in all honesty. I don't understand why, now. I was a very introverted person. *Édith Scob* [quoted in *L'Écran Fantastique* November 1979]

Steele. At one point the doddery Mathias reads a letter purportedly written by the Marquise to the man who betrayed her, containing a curse that Scob would no doubt have relished: "I am guilty of abominable crimes but your betrayal of love is a worse sin. To you and all your line come darkness and atrocious death!"

Omitting such a bloodcurdling scene was perhaps an error of good taste, though elsewhere

Duvivier proves that his knack for conjuring spooky atmosphere was second to none. The fateful night of the old man's death involves a cowled female figure in 17th century garb gliding up the baronial staircase and later disappearing – or so it seems – through a solid wall. Later, a nocturnal descent into the crypt for an unofficial autopsy is attended by the hooting of owls, the croaking of frogs and – as the coffin is unscrewed – the persistent, low-level moaning of the wind. Marie, meanwhile, hovers above, watching an extremely eerie, apparently sentient pall of mist curling its way around the shrubbery. The coffin, of course, turns out to be empty, containing only a knotted twine identified by Dr Hermann as a witch's ladder. Later still the elderly caretaker is beset by a gale so intense it seems like the work of a poltergeist. Venturing outside, he notices a light in the private chapel and, through the cobwebbed wrought-iron gates, glimpses the apparently dead Mathias sitting placidly at the altar.

*La Chambre ardente* is superlatively acted, with Claude Rich a stand-out as the feckless Stéphane. The kind of young aristocrat whose Porsche actually belongs to a client, he contributes a moment of genuine grotesquerie when dragging up as the Marquise de Brinvilliers for a costume ball. Best of all is Claude Piéplu, whose fabulously inscrutable Inspector Krauss only arrives, *Les Diaboliques* style, in the final act. "In modern houses," he deadpans, "walking through walls is simple: they're made of cardboard." And, sorting through the occult artefacts in Mathias' concealed closet, he finds not only the Marquise's skull but also what he tactfully calls "a rare volume for randy old men."

In addition to his expert direction of an excellent cast, Duvivier also pulls off a couple of deliriously bizarre set-pieces. In the first, the old man's lying-in-state involves family members pirouetting around the open casket to the strains of a Strauss waltz; the lid is sealed in place just seconds after a fly has settled on the corpse's nose. The funeral procession is arguably even stranger, with a long line of mourners shrouded in fog as an oompah band belts out *Stars and Stripes Forever*. Sadly, dazzling moments like these cut no ice with the unforgiving arbiters of the Nouvelle Vague, who considered the sexagenarian Duvivier an anachronism and his choice of a spooky 'old dark house' thriller even more so. Indeed, the satirical weekly *Le Canard enchaîné* dismissed the film as "grandpa's cinema"[40] while likening Duvivier himself to the Citroën floating engine of 1932.

*La Chambre ardente* is certainly superior, however, to a rather similar film made by Georges Franju some

12 months earlier. In September 1960, with the shock waves from *Les Yeux sans visage* still reverberating, Franju had gone to a moated pile in the Loire valley to make *Le Château de mystère* (The Castle of Mystery). Retaining screenwriters Boileau and Narcejac together with composer Maurice Jarre, the result was subsequently given the unalluring release title *Pleins feux sur l'assassin* (Spotlight on the Killer).

The pile in question, the Château de la Bretesche at Missillac, is the star attraction in a surprisingly staid update of the ossified 'creepy castle' routine, with Pierre Brasseur popping up right at the beginning to conceal himself behind a mirror, and there die, in order to confound his greedy heirs. After this pronounced echo of the wartime Gothic romance *Le Baron fantôme*, various deaths ensue – "the last one standing will inherit the lot," somebody mutters – and Franju sprinkles a few grace notes over the material, among them a dead crow flung onto a dinner table, a homicidal owl, a tenantless rocking chair, a nude bathing scene for Dany Saval, and a spectacular death plunge for Pascale Audret. But the film remains stubbornly inert. Giving a clue as to why, Franju described it, not just as "a ghost story without a ghost," but also, production-wise, as "an avalanche of concessions."[41]

## FASCINATING SKIN

If Duvivier's *La Chambre ardente* was a modern streamlining of ageing 'old dark house' motifs, it was paralleled by a Spanish-French co-production that looted an impressively varied array of horror conventions. Starting production around the time Duvivier's film ended, *Gritos en la noche* (Screams in the Night) was written and directed by the 31-year-old Jesús Franco – and, like *La Chambre ardente*, inspired grudging critical references to Epstein's *La Chute de la maison Usher*. Reviewers in both *La Cinématographie Française* and Britain's *Monthly Film Bulletin* made the Epstein connection, with the MFB critic sounding mightily perplexed. "This film is at once appalling and unique," he noted, "so bad as to be almost enjoyable for its ludicrous qualities, so singular that curiosity hunters are likely to look at it agog," before adding in rising puzzlement: "An occasional shot or two is worthy of James Whale or Epstein," and concluding with an utterly defeated three-word summation: "Really most extraordinary."[42]

*France, November 1912. Five women have disappeared in the last three months and Inspector Tanner is assigned to the case. It transpires that a former prison doctor called Orlof is using a supposedly executed young murderer, the blind and robotic Morpho Lautner, to*

Ricardo Valle and
Howard Vernon
contemplate a
new experimental
subject (Mara Laso)
in *Gritos en la noche*
(1961)

abduct the women, after which Orlof experiments on
them in his château laboratory. His avowed aim? To
restore the beauty of his catatonic daughter Melissa, who
was disfigured in a laboratory fire.

"Really most extraordinary" seems, in retrospect,
a reasonable epitaph for Jesús Franco's mind-
boggling career, which between 1959 and 2013
encompassed over 170 films. (Incidentally, of his
several pseudonyms, Jess Franco was the most
straightforward and that's what we shall call him
from here on.) As far as horror is concerned, *Gritos en
la noche* was Franco's starting point. Before it he had
directed a quartet of early features in comic, musical
and thriller modes, the first of which, *Tenemos 18 años*
(We're 18), featured an intriguing interlude in which
a couple of teens stumble upon a masked aristocrat
who turns out to be a hideously disfigured strangler.

Yet the notion of making a fully fledged Spanish
horror film – the first since *La torre de los siete jorobados*
17 years before – only arose out of a crisis. According
to Franco chronicler Stephen Thrower, a proposed
film about a Mexican workers' revolt, *Los Avengadores*
(The Avengers), was all set to go but was cancelled at
the last minute thanks to a threatened ban from the
Spanish censor board. It was a screening in Nice of
Terence Fisher's *The Brides of Dracula* that suggested a

## GRITOS EN LA NOCHE

Spain-France 1961
France: **L'Horrible Docteur Orlof**
UK: **The Demon Doctor**
US: **The Awful Dr Orlof**
Hispamer Films / Eurociné
93 minutes b/w
in production October-November 1961

· · · · · · · · · · · · · · · · · · · · · · · · · · · · · ·

Director of Photography: Godofredo Pacheco;
Art Director: Antonio Simont; Editor: Alfonso
Santacaña; Music: José Pagán, A Ramírez
Ángel; Make-up: Adolfo Ponte; Screenplay
and Dialogue: Jess Franco, based on a novel
by David Kuhne [sic]; Executive Producer:
Sergio Newman; Producer: Gerardo
Mendiburu; Director: Jess Franco

Conrado San Martín (Inspector Edgar Tanner);
Diana Lorys (Wanda Bronsky / Melissa Orlof);

Howard Vernon (Dr Orlof); Ricardo Valle
(Morpho Lautner); María Silva (Dany); Mara
Laso (Irma Gold); Perla Cristal (Arnette);
Venancio Muro (Jeannot Roussel); Fernando
Calzado (Maurice); Felix Dafauce (Tanner's
boss); Elena María Tejeiro (Ursula Schneider);
Juan A Riquelme (Kraus); Javier Rivera
(M Hogan); Rafael Hernández, Angel Calero,
Fernando Sala, Lali Vincent, José Carlos Arevalo
(witnesses); Sandalio Hernandez (Raimond);
Rafael Ibañez; María de la Riva (Claire); María
Luisa Paredes (Polly); Pilar Gómez Ferrer
(Wanda's aunt); Mercedes Manera (Beth); Juan
Antonio Arévalo (young policeman); Juan García
Tienda (Elias Houseman); Faustino Cornejo (man
in evening dress); Manuel Vázquez (police artist);
Carmen Porcel (Mme Gold); Placido Seqeiros
(coachman); Luis Rico (fingerprint man); Enrique
Ferpi (barman)

**Relying on all the traditional paraphernalia of horror – recalling here Robert
Wiene's *Caligari* and there Jean Epstein's *House of Usher* – the director, Jesús
Franco, has convincingly fleshed out his variation on a well-worn theme.**
La Cinématographie Française 7 March 1964

**There was a producer I knew, Marius Lesoeur, who said, "I want you to meet
this young director. I'm co-producing his picture." I liked him [Franco] from
the beginning, and that film, *The Awful Dr Orlof*, has become a sort of horror
classic. It's shown on TV in America now at 4.00 am, for – for truck drivers.**
Howard Vernon [quoted in *The Dark Side* April 1993]

way out of the impasse. Franco went along to see it
with his producers, Hispamer's Sergio Newman and
Eurociné's Marius Lesoeur, and the idea to make a
Gothic horror film was born. The result did terrific

business, not so much in Spain (where it made under 45,000 pesetas) but certainly internationally. It was made available in France, for example, in a shorter but much racier cut called *L'Horrible Docteur Orlof*, while in America it gained considerable notoriety when distributed by Plaza Films International under the irresistible title *The Awful Dr Orlof*.

That name Orlof is the first of numerous quotations contained within the film. Franco's cultivated tastes extended to an encyclopaedic knowledge of pulp literature and cinema, and the outcome, in *Gritos en la noche*, is a fever-dream gazetteer of horror motifs curated by a connoisseur. Though Orlof sounds a little like Orlok, the cadaverous vampire of *Nosferatu*, the name was actually drawn from *The Dark Eyes of London*, the British Edgar Wallace adaptation that had been remade in Germany only eight months or so before *Gritos* began. In the British version, Bela Lugosi played Greenwich insurance broker Dr Feodor Orloff, whose retinue includes a murderous blind manservant called Jake. The missing 'f' in Orloff's name would be restored on the multiple occasions when Franco resurrected the character in later films. Similarly, Franco's rechristening of Jake as Morpho would prove prophetic, given that this character, too, would 'morph' his way through any number of future Franco scenarios. The dogged but rather dull Inspector Tanner – another name drawn from Edgar Wallace – would also crop up repeatedly in Franco's ever-expanding universe.

Among Franco's other reference points, he ticks off the 'monster in the wardrobe' motif from Robert Siodmak's *The Spiral Staircase* in the opening scene, and soon afterwards positions the shadowy Orlof exactly like the theatre-haunting Dr Gogol from Karl Freund's *Mad Love*. Franco also echoes the showbiz heroines of John Brahm's *The Lodger* and *Hangover Square* while moulding Inspector Tanner into the kind of figure played by George Sanders in both films. Also stirred into the mix were a couple of recent Brahm-style pictures from Britain, *Grip of the Strangler* and *Jack the Ripper*; the second of these was no doubt a particularly strong reference point for Franco's French co-producers, having opened in Paris as recently as August 1960 and become a cornerstone of the French fascination for what Alain Le Bris called "l'horrifique cinéma Anglo Saxon."[43]

Via Morpho, Franco also contrived a two-fold echo of Christopher Lee's performances for Hammer. Ricardo Valle's twitchily robotic mime recalls *The Curse of Frankenstein*, as does his climactic appearance on Orlof's battlements with the unconscious heroine in his arms. And Morpho's black suit and floor-length opera cloak give him the precise silhouette of Lee's Dracula; he also has a habit, for reasons that have nothing to do with narrative sense but everything to do with recalling a major box-office smash, of biting his victims' throats. On top of all this, the basic plot mechanics of Franco's film were obviously derived from the most revered of old-time continental horrors, *Caligari*, and the most transgressive of the 'new' ones, *Les Yeux sans visage*.

The paradoxical thing about this riot of magpie references is that Franco's synthesis of them is entirely unique, a point conceded even by the *Monthly Film Bulletin*. Much of this is due to Franco's quirkily dynamic staging, his penchant for taking the kinky sex implied by previous horror scenarios to unprecedented extremes (though various censor boards ensured that these extremes were only savoured at the time by French audiences), and his passion for avant-garde jazz, which gave the film an extraordinary musique concrète accompaniment that anticipates the aural assault of *Eraserhead* and *Suspiria* by 15 years. Credited to José Pagán and Antonio Ramírez Ángel, the cacophony starts straight away, conferring a genuinely hellish tone on Franco's exhilarating fusillade of images as a tipsy soubrette is assaulted by Morpho in her bedroom. Franco crafts a truly brutal opening here, indicating quite clearly that this is a horror picture with the gloves well and truly off.

Franco's key collaborators in *Gritos* were Spanish cinematographer Godofredo Pacheco, whose doom-laden monochrome explicitly recalls German Expressionism, and Swiss character actor Howard Vernon, whose thin-lipped, faintly reptilian features were perfect for the mournfully elegant sociopath at the film's centre. The magical moment in which we get our first proper look at Orlof involves the doctor presenting María Silva's guileless Dany with a shimmering necklace; as he hovers over her, the brilliance of the gems suddenly lights up Orlof's face in the gloom of his theatre box. "I'm fascinated by your skin," he murmurs. "Oh, what a tragedy that all this youthfulness, this freshness must vanish and never more be seen!" Franco follows this creepy admission with a stunning set-piece in which Dany accompanies Orlof to a derelict mansion on the edge of town, failing to notice the discarded 'For Sale' sign lying amid the autumn leaves outside it. The ensuing chase sequence in the house itself, in which Dany is twice cornered by the remorseless Morpho, is thrillingly staged by Franco, ending on an elegiac note when Orlof inspects Dany's dead body. "Her face is unmarked," he notes. "It has such a lovely pallor, as if it were alabaster..."

Orlof's real base of operations turns out to be the Castillo de la Coracera at San Martín de Valdeiglesias. (Pacheco's exterior shots of this forbidding 15th century edifice were impressive enough to ensure its virtual omnipresence in future Spanish horror films.) There we encounter Perla Cristal's Arnette; she's Orlof's ex-con housekeeper and, in time-honoured fashion, her eventual murder will trigger the sentimental Morpho's climactic rebellion against his cruel master. Cristal's strikingly exotic face is one of several that Franco exploits in the film. Another belongs to the beautiful Diana Lorys, whose plucky heroine, Wanda Bronsky, does much more to solve the mystery than Conrado San Martín's affable but slow-on-the-uptake Inspector Tanner.

Yet another great face belongs to Mara Laso as the ill-fated chanteuse Irma, whose abduction from the Vieux Colombier cabaret constitutes another of Franco's stand-out scenes. When laid out in Orlof's basement operating theatre, Laso gives way to a topless body-double, between whose bare breasts Orlof traces a bloody scalpel line, a procedure owing precious little to facial surgery but quite a lot to a French audience gagging for sadistic thrills. Later – and seemingly using exactly the same body-double – Franco has Wanda's breasts break free in a climactic struggle with Morpho, who takes the opportunity to give them a very thorough grope.

Fernando Delgado discovers the brutalised Gogó Rojo
in *La mano de un hombre muerto* (1962)

Startling moments like this co-exist with more eccentric Franco touches, notably a scene, recalling Poe's *The Murders in the Rue Morgue*, in which a bunch of witnesses are quizzed by Tanner about the two men they saw, both of whom are represented by absurdly cartoonish likenesses that no real police artist would ever draw. The sureness of Franco's approach is better represented by the weirdly poetic asides with which he peppers the action, as when the unfortunate Dany is boxed up in a casket and driven through the night to an out-of-the-way boathouse. The image of

her abductors sculling their way serenely across a darkened lake, with their sinister freight lodged in the boat alongside them, is irresistibly evocative of the mythological descent into Hell via the River Styx. And, once they've alighted on the opposite shore, there's an obvious visual reference to Ingmar Bergman's *The Seventh Seal* when Orlof and Morpho are seen skulking in silhouette across the brow of a hill as they convey Dany to her dreadful destination.

Franco's follow-up, *La mano de un hombre muerto* (The Hand of a Dead Man), was shot late in 1962 and, like *Gritos en la noche*, supposedly took its title from a novel written by Franco's alter ego, David Kuhne – though no novels sporting that name, or any of the variations on it that Franco would offer over the years, have ever been discovered. In any case, the title was changed for French audiences to the more alluring *Le Sadique Baron Von Klaus*, coupling the sadistic Baron rather nicely with his predecessor, *L'Horrible Docteur Orlof*. And in it Franco intensified the startling aroma of perversion first showcased in *Gritos*, as well as retaining Howard Vernon, this time in a secondary role as the protagonist's shifty uncle.

Detailing a murder spree in the fictional Austrian village of Holfen, Franco was able to insinuate not one but two manifestos into this film, foreshadowing his later work first verbally and then visually. Watched over by a suspended skeleton, twitchy young Ludwig (Hugo Blanco), last scion of the ill-famed Von Klaus clan, settles down in the family torture chamber to read the memoirs of his baleful ancestor, which speak of "an initiation into a passionate world of rare and unknown sensations, a seductive and tragic world bred in pain and blood, the tragic eroticism of all the senses, ending finally in death." At the opposite end of the film, the same dungeon is the scene of an eye-popping display of sexual sadism, as Ludwig first ravishes the bare-breasted Margaret

(Gogó Rojo), then whips her and finally strings her up for tortures that mercifully give way to a fade-out. The alluring monochrome softness of Godofredo Pacheco's imagery (much of it seen through a mirror fetishistically fitted into the bed canopy) clashes dissonantly with the grisly subject matter – though, as before, only French filmgoers were privy to this transgressive set-piece at the time.

The film offers yet another forecast in its black-gloved killer, looming at windows as women strip down to their lingerie with ritzy outbreaks of Daniel White jazz on the soundtrack. Together with the charmingly waggish relationship between Inspector Borowsky (Georges Rollin) and crime reporter Karl Steiner (Fernando Delgado), these details indicate that the yet-to-coalesce giallo sub-genre had an important Spanish precedent in addition to the familiar Krimi influence from Germany. Elsewhere, Franco pulls off several shadowy and brilliantly orchestrated set-pieces, notably when Ludwig's fiancée Karine (Paula Martel) is sent screaming from her bed by the exaggerated ticking of a clock. The climax, too, in which Ludwig is urged by his ancestor to "join me in the eternal peace of the swamps," is exceptional.

Graziella Granata in a Terence Fisher-style composition for *La strage dei vampiri* (1961)

Franco even throws in a playful reference to the biggest art-house enigma of the moment. Written by Alain Robbe-Grillet, Alain Resnais' *L'Année dernière à Marienbad* (Last Year in Marienbad) had been unveiled at the Venice Film Festival in August 1961, immediately provoking intense debate about its precise meaning. What, commentator after commentator mused, was the key to the chicly dreamlike, and ever so slightly menacing, wanderings of Delphine Seyrig, Giorgio Albertazzi and Sacha Pitoëff "along these corridors, across these salons, these galleries, in this edifice from another century"? Did Seyrig meet Albertazzi at the same hotel a year before, or did she not? Was unavoidable fate the governing agent in the inscrutable exchanges between

these statuesque characters – characters that might, in fact, be the "people long dead" referred to in the voice-over? In Franco's transgressive little horror picture, the whole Gothic conundrum of Resnais' film boils down to Howard Vernon searching for enlightenment and asking a passing flunkey, "Where's that book about Marienbad?"

## A COFFIN NAMED DESIRE

Walter Brandi, the unlikely vampire of Polselli's *L'amante del vampiro* and Regnoli's *L'ultima preda del vampiro*, made a third vampire picture at the end of 1961. Roberto Mauri's *La strage dei vampiri* (The Slaughter of the Vampires) reached Italian screens in February the following year and cast Brandi, not as the vampire this time, but as a strangely feminised hero. Having lost his wife to the local bloodsucker, Brandi's Wolfgang takes to his bed to convalesce, wearing a satin nightie with a ruffled collar, and is attacked there by his vampirised maid Corinne (Gena Gimmy). He later toughens up sufficiently to ram a multi-spiked railing through his cloaked nemesis. Overloaded with eye-shadow and blusher, German actor Dieter Eppler is no more convincing a Christopher Lee substitute than Brandi was in the previous two films.

Again, Lee was clearly much on the filmmakers' minds, for this entry, set in the 19th century, shows up even more clearly than its forebears the profound impact made by Terence Fisher's *Dracula*. Among numerous echoes, the vampire stashes his coffin in the hero's wine cellar, while his first victim is called Louise (Lucy) and has a cross thrust provocatively in her face. She also threatens a servant's little daughter, saying to her "I want to show you some wonderful new hiding places" in imitation of Lucy's "I know somewhere nice and quiet where we can play" in Fisher's film. And everything stops for an elaborate blood transfusion presided over by Luigi Batzella's cheroot-chewing Van Helsing surrogate, the oddly named Dr Nietzsche.

The film opens promisingly, with Mauri getting the traditional 'angry villagers' routine out of the way at the beginning rather than the end. (Here, the scriptwriter for the English-language version may have been laughing up his sleeve when the vampire callously abandons his female consort to the villagers' pitchforks with the cowardly line "My life may be at stake!") But soon afterwards the action devolves into a slow and deadening plod notable only for emphasising the victims' orgasmic response to the vampire's attentions. This bold emphasis sorts oddly, though, with some squeamishness elsewhere; as in Renato Polselli's two vampire films, the victims display no bite marks. For the most part, however, Mauri focuses firmly on Graziella Granata (as both the living and undead Louise), in the process making her cleavage the true star of the picture. Aldo Piga offers some competition with a swooning score that matches his work on Brandi's previous vampire titles.

Shortly after *La strage dei vampiri* reached Italian screens, Luigi Carpentieri and Ermanno Donati, who had produced *I vampiri* for Titanus a little over five years earlier, re-entered the field via their own production company, Panda Film. In doing so they adopted the collective pseudonym Louis Mann, in deference to Riccardo Freda's dictum that English names were essential in slipping horror pictures past the Italian public. Indeed, for the new film Freda retained his own Robert Hampton alias while insisting on the Anglicisation of everyone else's names too. Art director Franco Fumagalli, for example, endured a literal translation into Frank Smokecocks.

To bolster the subterfuge, Freda engaged bona-fide Brits as his protagonists, pitting Barbara Steele's eerily imperilled beauty against the brilliantly contained insanity of Robert Flemyng. (Another motive – given Freda's sweeping statement that "Our [Italian] actors are the laziest of all"[44] – may have been the perceived efficiency and discipline of British players.) Explaining his decision to play the title role in *L'orribile segreto del Dr Hichcock* (The Horrible Secret of Dr Hichcock), Flemyng maintained that "I particularly wanted to go to Rome, so I thought, 'What the hell, no one will ever see it.'"[45]

*October 1897. When anaesthetics pioneer Dr Bernard Hichcock returns to London after a 12-year absence, he brings with him a new bride, Cynthia. What Cynthia doesn't know is that Hichcock's previous wife, Margharetha, expired as a result of a 'play dead' sex session in which he administered just a bit too much of his famous anaesthetic. What Hichcock doesn't know*

*is that Margharetha didn't actually die. Having been rescued from premature burial by the Hichcocks' faithful housekeeper, she's still on the premises.*

Freda shot the film in a whirlwind 14 days during April 1962 at the Villa Perucchetti in Rome. The result is as lushly rendered a horror picture as Italy had yet produced, with colour photography by Raffaele Masciocchi that vies for macabre beauty with Claude Renoir's in *...Et mourir de plaisir* and, from Britain, Jack Asher's in *The Brides of Dracula*. Yet, for all its tasteful handling and aspirations to be accepted as a British film, the film's subject matter was more uncompromising than any British shocker of the period could have countenanced. For, in crafting his fourth horror script, 27-year-old screenwriter Ernesto Gastaldi made no bones about the fact that Dr Hichcock's 'orribile segreto' is necrophilia. Explaining his preference for dealing with human monsters, and citing Krafft-Ebing's *Psychopathia Sexualis* into the bargain, Freda pointed out that "It's really interesting to make films like *Hichcock*, where the 'hero' is simultaneously a great surgeon, a respected college professor and a necrophiliac. It's not as unusual as you might think."[46]

The opening recalls the 1958 Hammer production *The Man who Could Cheat Death*, but instead of an elderly gent having his uterparathyroid gland removed in a foggy Paris back street we're shown a young woman's casket being rifled in a London cemetery. Having contemptuously tossed aside a floral tribute, a pair of gloved, claw-like hands feverishly prise up the coffin lid and fondle the face and form of the chalk-faced girl within. The grave-robbing prologue is so familiar a convention that it actually takes a moment to register the fact that this is, to put it mildly, something else again.

There follows a hauntingly strange moment when Hichcock returns to his home and, like a stranger, looks in at the drawing room window. The scene within, in which the voluptuously blonde Margaretha is giving a piano recital to various appreciative guests, is a microcosm of the stiffly formal Victorian society of which the doctor is ostensibly a part, and before heading for the front door Hichcock surveys the tableau with an expression that looks vaguely sour but is otherwise detached and unreadable. Inside, the housekeeper, Martha, tells him that "Everything's ready upstairs." She then gives Margaretha a horribly salacious half-smile, signalling that the recital needs to end so that Hichcock's sexual needs can be met.

The bedroom, of course, looks more like a sepulchre, with a shimmering nude statue in one corner and plenty of sable drapery illumined by a crimson glare from the fireplace. As the ritual begins,

## L'ORRIBILE SEGRETO DEL DR HICHCOCK

Italy 1962
UK: *The Terror of Dr Hichcock*
US: *The Horrible Dr Hichcock* / *Raptus The Secret of Dr Hichcock*
Panda Società per l'Industria Cinematografica
88 minutes colour
in production April 1962

Director of Photography: Raffaele Masciocchi; Art Director: Franco Fumagalli; Editor: Ornella Micheli; Sound: Renato Cadueri; Music: Roman Vlad; Make-up:

Euclide Santoli; Story and Screenplay: Ernesto Gastaldi; Producers: Luigi Carpentieri, Ermanno Donati; Director: Riccardo Freda

Barbara Steele (Cynthia Hichcock); Robert Flemyng (Dr Bernard Hichcock); Silvano Tranquilli (Dr Kurt Lowe); Maria Teresa Vianello (Margaretha Hichcock); Harriet White (Martha); Howard Rubian (laboratory specialist); Neil Robinson, Spencer Williams (hospital assistants); Aldo Cristiani; Evaristo Signorini; Giovanni Querel

Setting aside a somewhat expressionist use of colour, this film seems very English, at once conventional and heavy-handed in treatment, and morbid and obscure in purpose. Despite some naïveties, the degree of sadism attained by certain scenes of necrophilia and torture makes us wonder: to what extent is this an inventory of Psychopathia Sexualis UK? *Cahiers du Cinéma* April 1963

Literally, one rushed from room to room and it was shot at an enormous pace ... I was amazed, to be quite frank. I'd been hoping it would overshoot by two or three months and I'd be stuck in Rome for ages, but no, not at all. I was back in England at the end of two or three weeks. Freda knew how to compose a picture and how to move it, how to cut it and all that. He was a very talented man. Robert Flemyng [quoted in Video Watchdog January–February 1999]

Anaesthetics pioneer Robert Flemyng returns home with new bride Barbara Steele in *L'orribile segreto del Dr Hichcock* (1962)

temptation – to up Margaretha's dose. The effect is spellbindingly horrible. And, when Hichcock realises the fatal consequences of the increased anaesthetic, Flemyng employs a thrillingly melodramatic gesture – hands flung up convulsively to cover his screaming face – that remains one of the great acting moments in Italian horror.

Hichcock's monstrously self-centred procedures demand the ultimate in passivity from the women in his power, taking the traditional 'lie back and think of England' attitude popularly associated with Victorian womanhood and adding to it the grim addendum, '... and while you're at it pretend to be a corpse.' Things are no better when, 12 years having passed, Cynthia arrives on the scene; the relationship between Hichcock and his new bride offers a depressing view of a marriage so starchily passionless it may as well be embalmed. A post-prandial tableau at the fireside speaks volumes – Cynthia watching her husband intently, expectantly; Hichcock obliviously lighting a cigar and finally announcing that "I'd better get back to the clinic." The lure, it transpires, is a recently dead female laid out in the shimmering, white-tiled mortuary.

Roman Vlad's exceptional score slurs into funereal strings. A hypodermic is reverently drawn from a black and red casket, and Vlad introduces a nagging piano motif as Hichcock is consumed by a further

True to the name of its protagonist, the film abounds in references to the works of Alfred Hitchcock. These are mainly visual (the fateful glass of milk from *Suspicion*, a pillowed skull doubling for *Under Capricorn*'s shrunken head), though the situation itself echoes both *Rebecca* and the necrophile subtext of *Vertigo*. But the film's real flavour is derived from a much older source: Edgar Allan Poe, in whose stories an unhealthy whiff of necrophilia is seldom far from the surface. In the unaccustomed role of threatened heroine, Barbara Steele undergoes a long series of nocturnal vicissitudes, including a premature burial and a riveting bedroom set-piece that also springs straight from Poe.

Here, she finds herself laid out, corpse-like, on Hichcock's black-draped bed. Suffused in crimson, her husband's face literally pulsates as he leans over her (an effect achieved by the simple expedient of an inflatable mask). Whether we're to take this literally or interpret it as Cynthia's nightmare vision, it's a truly ghastly externalisation of Hichcock's compulsions, transferring arousal from the groin to his horribly engorged face. And, thanks to Masciocchi's lurid colour effects, it's a nightmare bathed in hues borrowed directly from Poe's *The Masque of the Red Death*, where "the effect of the firelight that streamed upon the dark hangings through the blood-tinted panes was ghastly in the extreme, and produced so wild a look upon the countenances of those who entered..."

The remainder of the film is marked by a few oddities, notably the fact that the risen Margharetha has somehow become a veiled old crone, facilitating an arbitrary echo of *I vampiri* when Hichcock rather unexpectedly proposes to rejuvenate her with Cynthia's blood. The rushed ending is a bit of a let-down all round, featuring an all-too obvious stunt double for Flemyng and a final conflagration that's surprisingly ineffective – particularly when you consider that, in staging it, the capricious Freda reportedly endangered the lives of everyone involved. "Freda came and sat by me," Flemyng recalled, "and I said, 'Well! What about *that*!' He said, 'Oh my dear, you are so nice, so calm, so English! These Italians are so hysterical.' And I said, 'Well, I'm not surprised; there are even people who were actually carried out with their hair taken off!' (Well, not quite, but you know.) So anyway, I asked him, 'Did you get the shot?' And he looked at me rather cunningly, and said, '*Bellissima!*'"[47]

In France, *Cahiers du Cinéma* waggishly conspired in Freda's 'this film isn't Italian' subterfuge by placing *L'effroyable secret du Dr Hichcock*, not in its 'Films italiens'

section, but among the 'Films anglais', where it rubbed shoulders with, of all things, *A Taste of Honey*. In the USA, the film was advertised with such sleazily inspired tag-lines as 'His secret was a coffin named DESIRE!' and 'The candle of his lust burnt brightest in the shadow of the grave!' Retitled *The Horrible Dr Hichcock*, it was aptly coupled in December 1964 with *The Awful Dr Orlof* (ie, Franco's *Gritos en la noche*), both films being dismissed by the *New York Times* in precisely 40 words: "Yesterday, the Palace Theater presented a pair of films on the subject of necrophilia. They were called *The Horrible Dr Hitchcock* and *The Awful Dr Orlof*. For once, the adjectives in the titles were not only descriptive but also accurate."[48]

Back in July 1963 Freda's film had been less auspiciously matched for its UK release as *The Terror of Dr Hichcock*. Having been bought by Compton-Cameo, it went out as support to Compton's self-made 'social problem' sexploiter *The Yellow Teddybears*. Even so, *Hichcock* provided further proof that Italian horror, though not much remarked upon at home, could be lucratively exported.

## PLASTIC SURGERY AND A JOCULAR DUMMY

By the beginning of 1962, the French fascination for the new style of British horror was gaining ground, with a steady stream of Paris releases to sustain the growing cult. In the two-year period starting in December 1959, French audiences had lapped up such titles as *Horrors of the Black Museum*, *The Hound of the Baskervilles*, *The Mummy*, *Blood of the Vampire*, *Jack the Ripper*, *Peeping Tom*, *The Stranglers of Bombay*, *The Flesh and the Fiends*, *The Brides of Dracula*, *Circus of Horrors* and *The Curse of the Werewolf*. The interest was fed by several appreciative articles, written mainly by Ado Kyrou and Jean-Paul Török, in the highbrow journal *Positif* – to such a degree that the magazine's publisher, Eric Losfeld, saw the wisdom in creating a separate publication celebrating horror and fantasy in Britain and beyond.

Thus was born *Midi-Minuit Fantastique*, the brainchild of medical students Michel Caen and Alain Le Bris, with editorial input from the more experienced Jean Boullet and Jean-Claude Romer. Named after the Midi-Minuit, a legendary Boulevard Poissonnière cinema specialising in the outré and offbeat, the magazine kicked off in May 1962 with a Terence Fisher special, eventually chalking up 20 editions (four of them double-issues) and folding at the end of 1970. Featuring such cover stars as Bela Lugosi, Barbara Steele (twice), Raquel Welch and Delphine Seyrig, its contributors ranged from artist

Roland Topor and film director Bertrand Tavernier to novelist Boris Vian and playwright Eugène Ionesco. In this way the magazine applied unprecedented intellectual scrutiny to a genre that was still held at arm's length by France's actual film industry.

In Spain, meanwhile, there was no great rush to build on the success of Jess Franco's *Gritos en la noche*. But a cautious interest in backing homegrown horror was occasionally shown by American production companies, which entered into agreements with local entrepreneurs, themselves well aware of the way Spanish cinema had been enriched in recent years by the trend towards international co-productions. The most visible symbol of the new climate was the 'Hollywood in Madrid' grandiosity of US mogul Samuel Bronston, who worked closely with the Franco regime in making such epics as *King of Kings* and *El Cid* on Spanish soil, building a massive studio complex in Las Rozas to that end. Yet there would be nothing grandiose about Spain's cheaply made horror pictures, and their hybrid nature may even have helped to delay the moment when Spain would plunge headlong into horror in the late 1960s.

With its pronounced echoes of Franju's *Les Yeux sans visage*, *Gritos en la noche* had been out in Spain only a few months when the first of these hybrids, sporting Franju echoes of its own, went into production at the end of July 1962. Isidoro M Ferry's *La cara del terror* (The Face of Terror) enjoyed uncredited financial input from the Los Angeles company Carthay Films and was scripted by Monroe Manning, a writer whose prolific contributions to the anthropomorphic TV adventure series *Lassie* would later see him graduate to another – *Flipper*. Yet in *La cara del terror* he dealt with mental aberration and the after-effects of plastic surgery. Rather than emulating the surrealist poetry of Franju, the result shows inevitable signs of trying to reproduce the slick monochrome sheen of contemporary US thrillers.

*When Dr Charles Taylor applies to the Institute of Neuro-Science for permission to try out his*

Barbara Steele – pictured in *Lo spettro* (see page 114) – made her first appearance on the cover of *Midi-Minuit Fantastique* in December 1964

*revolutionary new form of plastic surgery on one of their patients, the principal, baulking at Taylor's proposal to patent his invention, curtly refuses. One inmate, the disfigured Norma Worden, overhears the altercation and stows away in Taylor's car. Only when he has restored her looks does Taylor realise that she has a history of violence and instability…*

The film's supposed setting in the USA perplexed at least one contemporary reviewer, who noted that "the dialogue fails to match what we see" and enumerated such plainly visible Madrid locations as the Calle de Castelló, the Avenida de José Antonio (now called the Gran Vía), the Calle de Alcalá, and the terrace of the Hotel Felipe II at San Lorenzo de El Escorial "with its view of the monastery."[49] Despite these geographical gaffes, the film's American feel will have been underlined for Spanish audiences by leading lady Lisa Gaye, younger sister of the Hollywood star Debra Paget. Well known too for *Rock Around the Clock* and oodles of TV Westerns, she has a vulpine beauty that suits the unscrupulous Norma extremely well. Her eyebrows are particularly dramatic, a fact capitalised on by make-up man Fernando Martínez, who freezes one of them in an interrogative arch amid the hideous fire damage disfiguring the left side of her face.

Though pretty mild as horror, *La cara del terror* is also strangely forthright in some areas. The excellent make-up is a case in point. Where Franju was careful to occlude the reality of Christiane's face in *Les Yeux sans visage*, Isidoro Ferry shows us Norma's disfigurement unadorned the minute we get a proper look at her. The fact that it occupies the left, or sinister, side of her face handily suggests a personality divided between good and evil, and Manning's script is interesting in that, once beautified, Norma initially makes a sincere attempt to 'go straight', until circumstances – and other people – force her into violence, Frankenstein's monster style. Before Norma's arrival, Dr Taylor has claimed that restoring the appearance of disfigured mental patients can have a beneficial effect on their

Escaped mental patient Lisa Gaye displays
*La cara del terror* (1962)

psyches, a sweeping theory that the script doesn't presume to question. It does, however, link the film to a 1951 Hammer thriller called *Stolen Face*, in which Paul Henreid's plastic surgeon turns a scarred petty criminal into a replica of Lizabeth Scott, with predictably nasty consequences.

The plastic surgeon here is Fernando Rey, who had recently starred in Luis Buñuel's *Viridiana* and confers a lot of class on *La cara* merely by showing up. "You've made a big mistake and I'll prove it, Dr Chambers," he tells the institute's principal, a line straight out of the 'jeered by his peers' mad scientist phrasebook. In addition, Taylor's laboratory features a stuffed crocodile on one wall, a strange bit of interior decoration that Bela Lugosi might have approved. Yet this doctor is eminently sane – indeed, affable. On first seeing Norma's face, he's realistic enough to say, "I've seen worse. War veterans – entirely disfigured." ("They were men," she pointedly replies.) His invention "enables the grafting of plastic materials to living tissue" – a rather literal interpretation of 'plastic' surgery, involving the application of what look like plastic bacon rashers direct to Norma's face. Rey even carries us through a sticky moment when Taylor, having ensured that his plastic is "virtually impervious to heat," realises aghast that "I never thought about *body* temperature."

It's this, of course, that triggers the gradual degeneration we're expecting, and Norma's plight is effectively sketched in. Having coshed the doctor and escaped from his surgery, she reinvents herself as Nora Black, whose written details reveal a birth date – 6 March 1935 – that matches Gaye's own. Taking work as a hotel chambermaid, she encounters a couple of predictably randy types – the hotel manager and a monied playboy who's little better than a rapist. She's eventually compelled to kill them both, and cinematographer José F Aguayo (another veteran of *Viridiana*) gives us a memorable shot of the hotelier lying dusty and broken at the foot of a lift shaft. Norma-Nora's desperate efforts to restore her worsening face with cold cream are truly pitiful. Finally going berserk in the doctor's surgery, she indulges in a cat fight with his assistant Alma ("Let

## LA CARA DEL TERROR

Spain-USA 1962
UK / US: **The Face of Terror**
Documento Film / Izaro Films / Carthay Films [uncredited]
83 minutes b/w
production began 23 July 1962
. . . . . . . . . . . . . . . . . . . . . . . . . . . . . .
Director of Photography: José F Aguayo; Art Director: Sigfrido Burman; Editor: Antonio Ramírez; Sound: Gabriel Basagaña; Music: José Buenagu; Make-up: Fernando Martínez; Story and Screenplay: Monroe Manning; Producer: Gustavo Quintana; Director: I M Ferry

Lisa Gaye (Norma Worden); Fernando Rey (Dr Taylor); Virgilio Teixeira (Matt Wilder); Gérard Tichy (Dr Chambers); Carlos Casaravilla (Dr Reich); Pedro Hurtado (Phillips); Emilio Rodríguez (Inspector Hopkins); Jacinto San Emeterio (Mr Pollack, hotel manager); Conchita Cuetos (Alma); Eduardo Sancho (Mandel); Ana María Custodio (nurse); Miguel del Castillo (police doctor); Guillermo Carmona (Harry); José Martín; Angel Celdrán; José Rein Loring

Few stories have reached the screen that are as disorganised and inexpertly assembled as this. In reality, the story amounts to very little, resulting in stretching and repetition and wildly unlikely situations. If what happens rings false, the characters are no less so. And, given the people who appear in them, the moments that ought to be considered highlights produce diametrically opposite effects to the ones intended. The actors involved can't do much, even those, like Fernando Rey, of proven talent.
ABC Madrid 30 October 1962

When Lisa Gaye turns those deep, wide-set eyes full into the camera, no human male in the audience can truthfully deny the instantaneous surge of a hot little flame, called s-e-x ... For years, Lisa labored under the handicap of being known as 'Debra Paget's sister', but she has finally shaken off the identity-by-association to emerge in her latest film, *Face of Terror*, as a powerful, undeniably individual star in her own right.
*from the original Futuramic Releasing pressbook*

me rearrange your pretty face!") and only gains access to the restorative liquid once she's dead. The smashed beaker dripping fluid onto Norma's lifeless face, magically dissolving the scar tissue, is a moment straight out of a werewolf film, and rather an ingenious touch.

But for the most part the Americanised smoothness of *La cara del terror* renders it rather bland, indicating that this wasn't the way forward for Spanish horror as it took its baby steps. The film does, however, boast a memorably haunting animated title sequence, with a bandaged woman being gradually unravelled to the strains of an eerie torch song. "That mask you wear has turned on you," smoulders actress-singer Sandra le Brocq. "Now you're alone in the dark..."

Subsequent Spanish-American items would come from the itinerant producer Sidney Pink, but in the meantime local writer-director Eugenio Martín made his horror debut at Madrid's CEA facility in October 1962. While *La cara del terror* was going the rounds as a Halloween attraction, Martín was shooting *Hipnosis*, making use of finance from Rome and Bonn as well as Spain's Procusa company.

Massimo Serato and Jean Sorel with the eerie Grog in Hipnosis (1962), known in Germany as 'Only a Dead Witness Keeps Quiet'

Playing like the harder-edged kind of Krimi, this comes complete with a black-gloved menace suggestive of the Italian giallo pictures to come. (The film was made at the same time as Franco's *La mano de un hombre muerto*, which also, as noted above, set a Hispanic precedent for the giallo.) Martín is at his best, however, when alternating huge close-ups of Eleonora Rossi Drago's smouldering eyes with the beady orbs of a ventriloquist's dummy called Grog. Looking like a devilish fusion of Cameron Mitchell and Frankie Howerd, this creature is the film's most memorable presence, though his echoing laughter, hinting at supernatural powers, turns out to be a trick, just another feature of Rossi Drago's elaborate investigation of the ventriloquist's murder. The pretty-boy killer is Jean Sorel, who, in a really striking shot, is seen framed behind the jaws of an oncoming mechanical digger. The action is otherwise a bit humdrum, with Martín sensibly cutting to the watchful Grog as often as he can.

The film made it to Britain as *Dummy of Death*, and indeed Grog inevitably recalls the Hugo character from the British classic *Dead of Night*, though Martín claimed not to have seen that film. "What I do remember," he claimed, "is that [Hipnosis] made a pile of money here in Spain and got great reviews."[50] Yet

Martín would have to wait until the 1970s to develop the macabre flair hinted at by Grog.

## BLOOD ON THE LENS

By the time Riccardo Freda's *L'orribile segreto del Dr Hichcock* appeared in Britain and the US, Freda had long since polished off a quasi-sequel. In December 1962 he reconvened with producers Luigi Carpentieri and Ermanno Donato, cinematographer Raffaele Masciocchi, and actresses Barbara Steele and Harriet White for *Lo spettro* (The Ghost). In most other respects the film was a departure, with an entirely different Dr Hichcock (played, what's more, by an entirely different actor, Elio Jotta) and a plot founded on the already well-established *Les Diaboliques* template.

As well as making more money at the domestic box-office than any other film in the first wave of Italian Gothics, *Lo spettro* also brought forth a lyrical tribute to its star from the normally imperious Freda. "Ah! Barbara Steele," he enthused in the seventh issue of *Midi-Minuit Fantastique*. "She is extraordinary! In *Lo spettro* she has eyes that are metaphysical; they're not real, they're impossible, they're the eyes of a de Chirico painting. Sometimes, under certain lights and combined with certain colours, her face takes on expressions that don't appear quite human, effects that no other actress could obtain."[51]

*Scotland, November 1910. Confined to a wheelchair, Dr John Hichcock indulges his interest in spiritualism while being treated by his younger associate, Dr Charles Livingstone. The latter, however, is having an affair with Hichcock's wife Margaret. Given that Livingstone's treatment involves administering carefully measured doses of poison, their plot to kill Hichcock is easily brought to fruition merely by withholding the antidote. But suppressing the guilty apparitions in the aftermath proves much more difficult.*

Again, Freda focused on human monsters in *Lo spettro*, confining them in a claustrophobic Scottish mansion and bathing their machinations in a crepuscular,

Barbara Steele hesitates over Elio Jotta's throat in Lo spettro (1962)

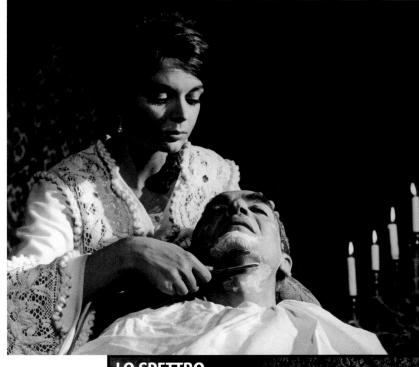

all-pervading blue. Initially the colour signals Hichcock's unhealthily obsessive interest in the afterlife; once he's apparently arrived there, the colour provides a suitably polluted backdrop to the steadily fragmenting relationship of the conspirators. Hichcock's death is a bloodless affair, but a further murder features plenty of gore, prompting Freda to introduce some discreet touches of red in the closing stages – from the red orb of a lamp and the resultant glow on a medium's face to a hitherto unnoticed shade of red in the carpets.

So single-minded is this emphasis on blue with discreet splashes of red that Lo spettro fails to replicate the colourful luxuriance of L'orribile segreto. Its plot, too – lacking the hot-button complication of necrophilia – is more predictable, with no prizes for guessing the climactic outcome as Hichcock's supposed hauntings proceed. Even so, Freda handles the thin material with consummate skill, crafting several memorable set-pieces and going for broke in the third act with a razor murder that outdoes even *Psycho*. Directed, of course, by the real Hitchcock, *Psycho* had made a colossal international impact in 1960. Excepting such direct rip-offs as William Castle's *Homicidal*, Lo spettro was perhaps the first horror film to incorporate the heightened violence pioneered by Hitchcock, and in Technicolor to boot.

That the Hichcock house is steeped in Stygian gloom is an understatement. At the beginning, lightning illuminates the blue-tinted windowpanes while a seance is conducted within. The medium is Hichcock's housekeeper Catherine; as well as having blue hair, she also vomits out cheesecloth ectoplasm. "By means of these seances I can cross the border," Hichcock explains, "the border of the spirit world to which I belong." He proceeds to make two suicide attempts in a single scene while describing himself as "just a living corpse." The morbidity stretches to a rather splendid portrait of the ailing doctor, in which he's depicted standing next to a waist-high plinth with a skull sitting on top. And Freda injects a moment of almost touching tranquillity when Margaret gives

## LO SPETTRO

Italy 1962
UK: *The Spectre*
US: *The Ghost*
Panda Società per l'Industria Cinematografica
93 minutes colour
in production December 1962

Director of Photography: Raffaele Masciocchi; Art Director: Mario Chiari; Editor: Ornella Micheli; Music: Franco Mannino; Make-up: Massimo Giustini;

Screenplay: Oreste Biancoli, Riccardo Freda; Story: Oreste Biancoli; Producer: Luigi Carpentieri; Director: Riccardo Freda

Barbara Steele (Margaret Hichcock); Peter Baldwin (Dr Charles Livingstone); Harriet White (Catherine Wood); Elio Jotta (Dr John Hichcock); Carol Bennet (woman); Carlo Kechler (police superintendent); Umberto Raho (Canon Owens); Reginald Price Anderson (Albert Fisher)

Dr Hichcock (he of the Orribile Segreto) pops up again in a Gothic, skull-festooned and highly unlikely Scotland ... yet it must be admitted that the overall result is a splendid exercise in Grand Guignol ... The absurd plot, and Freda's direction, work themselves out compellingly, the spectral interludes carrying a minatory charge which hasn't perhaps been equalled since the hauntings in [Robert] Florey's *The Beast With Five Fingers*.
Monthly Film Bulletin May 1964

I must say that Freda – in terms of acting – was the best [Italian director] to work with. He really was *there* for everybody. And he loved to work, or rather was obliged to work, under very tight schedules. Both of the Hichcock films were made in ten days ... But Freda had such passion for his work, you could really feel this energy directed right out at you.
Barbara Steele [quoted in Video Watchdog September-October 1991]

her husband a shave, with the razor hovering over his throat while she debates whether to kill him or not. She finally decides against it as a Viennese waltz issues from a music box. Hichcock, meanwhile, is oblivious, reminiscing about their first meeting, 13 years before, in Copenhagen.

That eerie music-box theme will return to haunt the lovers in due course, along with tinkling bells, a howling dog, an apparently self-motivated wheelchair, and yells of "Margaret!" that sound like Hichcock but seem to proceed from the possessed housekeeper. Retrieving an all-important key from the dead man's coffin, Livingstone explains to Margaret that the putrefaction they encounter there is "the effect of the injections – they hasten decay." Then Freda stages a splendidly creepy visitation in Margaret's boudoir. Lugubrious brass and vibes resonate on the soundtrack as Hichcock appears through the blue-gold drapes at her window, his face eerily underlit, several of his teeth missing and with pulpily decayed hands bearing a posy. And Freda doesn't let up. Blood seeps inexplicably from a roof beam onto the white sheets of the lovers' bed, prompting a frantic dash upstairs and a horrifying glimpse – through an attic door that refuses to open properly – of Hichcock's tongue-lolling corpse dangling from another beam.

Freda offers an occasional respite from the blue blanket of dark that he throws over the proceedings; a limpidly beautiful shot of Margaret looking out of a window quotes *L'orribile segreto*, for example, and there's a ravishingly autumnal scene in which the veiled widow goes to lay flowers on Hichcock's grave. But it remains a foregone conclusion that the lovers will devolve into acrimonious in-fighting in response to the supposedly supernatural assaults afflicting them. And when Margaret finally lets rip with the razor she only contemplated using on her husband, the result is as hair-raisingly violent a scene as Italian horror had yet come up with. The blood literally runs down the camera lens.

Under threat in the castle dungeons: Annie Alberti in *Metempsyco* (1962)

This last-minute emphasis on blood brings with it a genuinely inexplicable snuff box that literally oozes the stuff, an effect hard to square with the plot rationalisation provided at the end. There are a few other mis-steps – the creepy housekeeper, for example, indulges in the fagged-out 'clawing hand that turns out to be somebody innocuous' gag not once but twice. But, in addition to boasting more than its share of barnstorming set-pieces, the film builds to a fiendishly sadistic endgame that involves an unsuspected dose of curare, no fewer than five bullets being pumped into a supporting character, and what W C Fields might have called the fatal bottle of gin.

*Lo spettro* was sent out in the UK, like its predecessor, by Compton-Cameo, this time as support to the Robert Hartford-Davis film *Saturday Night Out*. The same month – February 1964 – Compton put another Hartford-Davis picture into production at Shepperton Studios. *The Black Torment* was an obvious attempt to replicate the Freda style, picking up the distinctive hues of *Lo spettro* to such an extent it might better have been called *The Blue Torment*. And, given that Compton was the forerunner of a company called Tigon-British, the result counts as the first in a long line of classic horror pictures that includes *Repulsion*, *Witchfinder General*, *Blood on Satan's Claw* and *The Creeping Flesh*.

If Freda's Hichcock duo represented a lurid apex in Italian Gothic, there were other pictures on offer that represented the bottom of the barrel. Antonio Boccaci's *Metempsyco* – which was released in Italy on 27 March 1963, just three days ahead of *Lo spettro* – is a case in point. Here, the Palazzo Borghese threw open its doors once again, providing the baronial interiors for a dreary, by-the-numbers shocker in which a turn-of-the-century psychiatrist's daughter (Annie Alberti) turns out to be the reincarnation of a 20-years-missing Countess. A lumbering owl-faced mutant with a low-slung left eye is responsible, meanwhile, for the murders of a couple of young girls. At first this creature, gurning and giggling, makes quite an impression. Later on he's seen far too frequently in broad daylight – lurching around outside the film's exterior location, Castello Orsini at Nerola – for any mystique to be retained.

Boccaci was a prolific pulp author who was here directing his one-and-only film. Making the most of the opportunity, he also cast himself in a prominent role, wearing burnt cork and a jewelled turban as the late Countess' Hindu fiancé. The film's paucity of imagination is indicated by the heroine's dream sequence, which is crudely compounded of a cowled skeleton, perambulating suits of armour, a couple of monster-masked creatures recalling a William Castle picture, and a bit of falling masonry. The

Vincent Price closes the door on his former
neighbours in *The Last Man on Earth* (1963)

castle's torture chamber contains
cross-beams for the female victims,
indicating that someone had
recently re-viewed the 1931 version
of *Murders in the Rue Morgue*, while
the usual endless round of corridor-
wandering is here enlivened by
hamsters posing as rats. In a
provocative touch, it's suggested
that the heroine is a nymphomaniac,
while the poor villainess – played
by Boccaci's 30-something wife,
Flora Carosello – is contemptuously
referred to as "that old woman."

Acquired by Richard Gordon for
US distribution, the film was retitled
*Tomb of Torture* and put out alongside
the West German picture *Der Fluch
der grünen Augen* (The Curse of the
Green Eyes), itself retitled *Cave of
the Living Dead*. Circulated mainly to
drive-ins, the double-bill ('Twice the Thrills! Twice the
Chills!!') proved a profitable one, despite the fact that
the Italian half of it was dismal in the extreme.

## RITUAL CLEANSING

While *Metempsyco* was being readied for release,
Vincent Price arrived in Rome for a highly unusual
project whose origins could be traced back to
Anthony Hinds of Hammer Film Productions.

Earmarked for director Val Guest in 1957, *The Night
Creatures* was Richard Matheson's screen adaptation
of his three-year old post-apocalyptic novel *I Am
Legend*, but antipathy from censors in both Britain
and America caused Hinds to offload the rights onto
a former Hammer associate called Robert Lippert. By
January 1963 Lippert had finally got the production
moving as a combined Italian-American effort called
*L'ultimo uomo della terra*, distributed in the US under the
literal translation *The Last Man on Earth*. Lippert was
clearly in a receptive mood where post-apocalyptic
narratives were concerned, because a year later he put
another one, Terence Fisher's *The Earth Dies Screaming*,
into production in England. Both films would
feature siege situations and zombie-like antagonists,
exercising a pretty clear influence on George
Romero's seminal 1968 release *Night of the Living Dead*.

*September 1968. Scientist Robert Morgan is the only
survivor of an unexplained pandemic that wiped out*

## THE LAST MAN ON EARTH

USA-Italy 1963
Italy: *L'ultimo uomo della terra*
*Associated Producers Inc presents / Produzioni
la Regina*
86 minutes b/w
production began 21 January 1963
. . . . . . . . . . . . . . . . . . . . . . . . . . . .
Director of Photography: Franco Delli
Colli; Art Director: Giorgio Giovannini;
Film Editor: Gene Ruggiero; Sound: Enzo
Silvestri, Armando Timpani; Music: Paul
Sawtell, Bert Shefter; Make-up: Piero
Mecacci; Screenplay: Logan Swanson

[Richard Matheson], William F Leicester,
from the novel *I Am Legend* by Richard
Matheson; Producer: Robert L Lippert;
Director (English-language version): Sidney
Salkow; Director: Ubaldo Ragona

Vincent Price (Robert Morgan); Franca Bettoia
(Ruth Collins); Emma Danieli (Virginia Morgan);
Giacomo Rossi Stuart (Ben Cortman); Umberto
Raho (Dr Mercer); Christi Courtland (Kathy
Morgan); Antonio Corevi (governor); Ettore
Ribotta (reporter); uncredited: Giuseppe Mattei
(militia leader); Rolando De Rossi

**Very much of a curate's egg. Both the opening, with some extremely
effective Antonioni-ish shots of deserted streets and buildings, and
the ending are strikingly bold. But in between times, despite Richard
Matheson's intriguing story, the production languishes sadly into crude
effects, erratic editing and silly dialogue. Vincent Price goes through the
motions of a flamboyant performance, but is not really on top of his form.**
Monthly Film Bulletin February 1967

**I thought it was terrible. That's about the only way you can describe it. I had
written a good screenplay but they had someone rewrite it and make it abysmal
... I was told that Fritz Lang was going to direct it, but it turned out otherwise.**
Richard Matheson [quoted in Brosnan, The Horror People, 1976]

*humanity some three years before and created from the
victims a new race of undead ghouls. Though free to
exterminate the creatures during the day, Morgan holes
up in his suburban home at night – which is when his
former friends and neighbours assail his stronghold
in ineffectual but persistent fashion. The deadening
routine is broken, however, when Morgan meets another
apparent survivor called Ruth Collins.*

Directed by Ubaldo Ragona, the film had Sidney Salkow attached in post-production to ensure its suitability for US audiences. Richard Matheson disowned the end result anyway, covering his shame in the opening credits with the pseudonym Logan Swanson. And yet the film remains more faithful than any of the *I Am Legend* adaptations – official and unofficial – that were to follow. In particular it captures a mood of paranoid bleakness and alienation that at the time was more a feature of British science fiction than its American counterpart.

Indeed, the desolation of the opening was soon to be echoed in *The Earth Dies Screaming*, both films presenting the kind of deathly vistas that would still be giving good value in the 2002 hit *28 Days Later*. No doubt Ragona's tableaux here were given added urgency by the Cuban Missile Crisis, during which Russia and America had flirted so terrifyingly with nuclear war just a few months before the film was produced. Not that there's anything literally 'urgent' about these images; quite the opposite. There's a kind of Cold War stasis about the eerily deserted spaces and randomly sprawled bodies, and the quietly resigned tone of Morgan's internal monologue as he goes about his daily business is similarly powerful.

Such a heavy reliance on voice-over narration generally signals a screenplay that doesn't trust the imagery to do the talking, but here the combination of Price's familiar voice with the ritualised banality of his existence makes the opening scenes curiously gripping. There are some delightful contrasts. Moments after donning a gas mask and flinging a dead woman into a sulphurous pit, Morgan is seen jostling his way through discarded trolleys at a deserted supermarket, with only garlic on his shopping list. Later he takes his pick from an abandoned mirror emporium; his vampire-like enemies, it transpires, show up in mirrors all right but they hate what they see. And Price is very good when barricading himself in at night, putting some aggressive jazz on the turntable, and flinging himself disconsolately on the sofa. Outside, a gang of ghouls are gathering in images exactly anticipating *Night of the Living Dead*.

Unfortunately, SF specialist Philip Strick was more or less accurate when pointing out that, after this intriguing first act, "haste has evidently set in, and the whole production gets ugly and banal."[52] Actually, the signs were there already, from the rather listless montage that conveys Morgan's round of daytime stakings to some conspicuously sluggish struggles with the ghouls when he tries to get back into his house, and from there to a glimpse of his home

movies, which include improbable amounts of grainy stock footage. Now the film devolves into a 25-minute flashback that makes it clear Price was grievously miscast as an Everyman figure. Embroiled at the time in Roger Corman's febrile Poe pictures, he was just too baroque a presence to be convincing as a regular 1960s family guy. Somebody a bit more meat and potatoes, a bit less paté de foie gras – say, Martin Balsam or Lee J Cobb – would have fit the bill far better.

Interest picks up again in the third act, when Morgan meets a kind of double-agent representative of a new breed of human – a breed that looks upon the isolated Morgan as a legendary figure, to be feared and destroyed. These new people dress in black turtlenecks, travel around in Jeeps and tote machine-guns, a kind of Fascist chic with special resonance for the country in which the film was made – particularly since much of the modernist location work was done in Rome's Mussolini-sponsored EUR district. But, thanks to the haste referred to by Strick, this theme goes unexplored, as does Morgan's response to the uncomfortable fact that his daily stake-outs have made him the monster. Instead we're reminded that Price was unsuited, not just to being a regular guy, but also to being an action man – flinging home-made bombs at militarist pursuers was not his forte. The film then rushes to a symbolic ending in which our compromised hero is speared to death at a church altar, with the assembled blackshirts standing around rather gormlessly as a baby cries and the end title crashes in.

Also in production during February 1963, Brunello Rondi's *Il demonio* (The Demon) was another film that anticipated a horror classic. In all other respects, however, it was a very different proposition, applying the tenets of Italian neorealism to a true story of apparent demonic possession in Lucania. Daliah Lavi, the 22-year-old Israeli actress cast in the lead, even had the opportunity to meet the girl she was playing. Rondi was riding the crest of a wave at the time; a long-time Fellini collaborator, he was between Oscar nominations for co-writing *La dolce vita* and *8½*. With credentials like these, *Il demonio* was clearly a long way from the average Italian Gothic, yet it dealt with the 'problem' of female sexuality in a similarly ambivalent way. Not only that, the film anticipated much of what happens in *The Exorcist* ten years in advance.

*In the small community of Bolsini, Purificazione – Purif for short – is a farmer's daughter who's never recovered from her relationship with a young man called Antonio. Now that he's about to marry another woman, Purif distils a potion from drops of her own*

Daliah Lavi as the
tragic Purificazione
in *Il demonio* (1963)

*blood and tricks him into drinking it. To no avail,*
*however; the wedding goes ahead. Purif, meanwhile,*
*is submitted to a full-scale exorcism in the local church.*

Rondi shot *Il demonio* in the Sassi section of the
so-called 'subterranean city' of Matera, a settlement
that reputedly dates back to prehistoric times. It's
an appropriate location given the atavistic rituals
indulged in throughout the film, which Rondi
shows us in absorbing ethnographic detail. We see
a bride and groom at the altar, anxiously monitoring
the oscillations of a candle flame as an index to
their future happiness. We see two sets of parents
preparing the bridal chamber for them, putting salt
under the pillow, sprinkling grapes on the bedspread
in the shape of a cross, and secreting an enormous
scythe under the bed to ward off demons. We see a
child's funeral procession that features bare-backed
young men being birched as they walk. And, up in the
mountains, we're shown the villagers trying to turn
back an "ugly black cloud," yelling at the heavens,
jingling cow-bells and stamping the earth.

With its crystalline monochrome photography
and atmosphere of small-town barbarism, the film
prefigures Kaneto Shindō's 1964 film *Onibaba* – a
picture set, not in 'modern' Italy, but mediaeval Japan.

## IL DEMONIO

Italy-France 1963
France: **Le Démon dans la chair**
Titanus / Vox Film / Les Films Marceau Cocinor
100 minutes b/w
production began 18 February 1963

Director of Photography: Carlo Bellero; Set
Decoration: Andrea Fantacci; Editor: Mario
Serandrei; Sound: Aurelio Pennacchia; Music
by: Piero Piccioni; Make-up: Franco Freda;

Screenplay: Ugo Guerra, Luciano Martino,
Brunello Rondi; Story: Brunello Rondi;
Producers: Ugo Guerra, Federico Magnaghi,
Luciano Martino; Director: Brunello Rondi

Daliah Lavi (Purif); Frank Wolff (Antonio); Nicola
Tagliacozzo (Zio Giuseppe); Giovanni Cristofanello
(Father Tommaso); Anna Maria Aveta (Sister
Angela); Tiziana Casetti; Dario Dolci; Franca
Mazzoni; Maria Teresa Orsini; Rossana Rovere

The film's transition from realism to fantasy is all the better for the main role
being played by Daliah Lavi: with her, right away, the demonic theme doubles
up as a sexual theme ... The two dimensions of the film mesh perfectly, but
it's the erotic aspects, in particular, that become almost traumatic. And if
the film gives in to the easy aesthetic effect obtainable from witchcraft, it
still has Daliah Lavi, woman and sorceress. *Cahiers du Cinéma* October 1963

I was very taken by this movie, by this part, and it never happened to me
before or since. I mean, to be almost possessed myself by the movie, by the
girl. She entered my persona. It was frightening! The fact that the atmosphere
had stayed in the village helped a lot. We were not in a studio; we were in
the mountains with those people, and I was affected by this, very sensitive to
that environment. *Daliah Lavi* [quoted in *Video Watchdog* September-October 2012]

Purif (a diminutive of, ironically, the Italian word
for 'purification') is universally reviled as a witch but
seems no more unhinged than the people among
whom she's grown up. The only difference is that the
villagers' ritualistic obsessions are endorsed by the
Church. Yet when another ritual takes place directly
outside the local house of God, Purif's confession of

having conversed with demons actually seems less alarming – because more fanciful – than some of the confessions that the crowd listens to without raising an eyebrow. One middle-aged man confesses to drooling in secret over his naked 16-year-old daughter, another to driving his son out of the house and causing him to starve to death. Yet the community's ingrained sexism ensures that it's Purif who's immediately hauled inside the church and submitted to an impromptu exorcism.

During the ceremony, the local priest repeatedly asks the supposed demon "Chi sei?" (who are you?) – thus anticipating the title of one of *The Exorcist*'s many Italian clones from 1974. The priest does his best, itemising Asmodeus, Leviathan, Balaam, Behemoth, Isacaron and Astaroth as possible identities of the "revolting beast" inhabiting the girl. But the focus is squarely on Purif and Daliah Lavi's extraordinary performance. Fingers crisped into talons, hair matted to her forehead, eyes mad in her mask-like face (with just the tiniest bit of extra make-up shading to suggest a demonic presence), she lewdly waggles her tongue at the crucifix, starts speaking in tongues, and even inverts herself for a protracted 'spider walk' – an effect repeated far less effectively in *The Exorcist* (sufficiently ineffectively, in fact, to be cut from release prints). From Purif's scuttling viewpoint, Rondi gives us a really memorable view of the church's ornate altar – inverted, naturally.

Lavi's performance is startling from first to last, uninhibitedly sensual and, sensibly, never quite clarifying whether Purif is really possessed or just extremely disturbed. She has good reason to be disturbed, since the institutionalised exploitation of young women seems to be a fact of life in Bolsini – and, by implication, southern Italy in general. Purif's own father beats her unmercifully, an elderly shepherd thinks nothing of binding her hands and feet and raping her, while a local faith healer, fondly known as Uncle Giuseppe, interferes with her under the guise of performing a cure. ("You're not breathing hard enough, daughter...") We're also left to infer that Antonio led her on and then dumped her, as he's clearly still strongly attracted to her when not literally casting the first stone.

When Purif is transferred to a convent, Rondi demonstrates that the representatives of conventional Christianity are no more enlightened than the backward villagers. The cry of "The smoke has turned black! It's her guilt!" when the villagers torch Purif's home is little different from the panic displayed by the nuns when she shows an 'unhealthy' interest in a so-called suicide tree. Lest she communicate with the dead soul underneath, they encircle the trunk with bales of barbed wire from which images of the Madonna are hung – as powerful a symbol of the convoluted traps of Christian dogma as can be imagined. And, in a stunningly eerie shot, Purif, like a good martyr, just plunges her way through these defences prior to embracing the tree with blood-streaming hands.

Intriguingly, Rondi sprinkles this tragic drama of superstition and suppressed sexuality with some unequivocally supernatural details. Writhing on her bed in the midst of a thunderstorm, Purif screams her head off and seems to be resisting an invisible aggressor, acquiring mystery scratches on her shoulders and wrists; when her father comes in she's on her front and has somehow been tethered with ropes. (How?) And, in a magical little interlude, she talks happily with a small boy called Salvatore next to a mountain stream. Returning to Bolsini she hears the high-decibel keening of local women and realises the boy was already dead.

# VAMPIRES GO TO THE MOVIES TOO

When Terence Fisher's *Dracula* opened in Italian cinemas at the tail end of 1958, its extraordinary success was exploited by pulp publishers as well as filmmakers. By 17 June the following year, a week or so before the parodic *Tempi duri per i vampiri* began production in Sestri Levante, a new series of lurid paperbacks called *KKK I classici dell'orrore* (KKK Horror Classics) appeared on news-stands courtesy of Edizioni KKK, with the first edition a suitably enticing novella called *Il vampiro* by Leona Celli, writing as Clay O'Neil. Then on 15 December, while *L'amante del vampiro* was being shot at Palazzo Borghese, Editrice Romana Periodici started a series of its own called *I racconti di Dracula* (Tales of Dracula), the first number being devoted to *Uccidono i morti?* (Kill the Dead?) by Max Dave, real name: Pino Belli.

For Celli, Belli and many others the result was a pseudonymous bonanza, and for fans the bonanza was extended by a parallel proliferation of cineromanzi – handy-sized magazines in which individual films were 'narrated' by means of stills. Polselli's *L'amante del vampiro*, for example, was the basis of both *Astro # 39* in October 1960 and the 14th issue of *Malia I fotoromanzi del brivido* (Sorcery: Thrilling Photo Stories) in March 1962. In at least one instance the *Malia* series got to a film long before it came out, with Polselli's *Il mostro dell'opera* being showcased under its working title *Il vampiro dell'opera* in February 1962. Other films were handled somewhat belatedly, notably Duvivier's *La Chambre ardente* – under its Italian title *I peccatori della Foresta*

*Nera* (Sinners of the Black Forest) – in June 1964. On top of this, a new and controversial publishing phenomenon, the *fumetti neri* or 'black' comics, reconfigured Fantômas and similar anti-heroes in a mod and newly eroticised guise, starting with the debut of Diabolik in November 1962 and then such successors as Kriminal and a female variant called Satanik. All three characters would sire cinema spin-offs, two in Kriminal's case.

In this halcyon period for sexed-up mass-market fiction it was perhaps inevitable that those yellow-jacketed crime stories pioneered by Edizioni Mondadori back in 1929 would finally make the transition from page to screen. A new, horror-tinged *filone*, the *giallo*, would take time to coalesce but in its fully developed form would frequently embrace the bizarre and irrational, together with an unflinching emphasis on graphic, often sexualised violence. Just as he would later direct the 1967 film version of *Diabolik*, so Mario Bava would sign his name to the first two bona-fide examples of the nascent *gialli*.

Yet the first of them turned out to be more a whimsical caprice than a headlong plunge into grotesquerie. In the first week of May 1962 Bava began shooting *La ragazza che sapeva troppo* (The Girl Who Knew Too Much), which would fail commercially yet prove one of his most influential films. Here, Letícia Román plays Nora, a plucky American heroine who, self-reflexively, is an avid reader of Italian crime novels. Bava is less at home with the 'meet cute' details of her relationship with a local doctor (John Saxon) than with the Gothic chiaroscuro of their visit to Nora's ailing Aunt Ethel during a thunderstorm. There follows a brilliant set-piece in which Nora witnesses a dead-of-night murder at the foot of the Spanish Steps, and the next day the doctor casts doubt on her experience with a conundrum that was to echo through innumerable *gialli* to come. "Does this look like the kind of place where women get stabbed?" he asks as fashion models parade around the sunlit Piazza di Spagna.

In its essentials the film is a comedy-thriller and, despite Bava's addition of macabre touches here and

In December 1960 Maddalena Gui's novella *La vergine di Norimberga* – subsequently filmed (see page 138) – was showcased in the 23rd issue of KKK *I classici dell'orrore*

there, it's clear that his heart wasn't really in it. Even so, he contrives an intriguing climax that allows Valentina Cortese's splendid villainess to introduce a genuinely sadistic note, saying of her own sister, "I made her suffer a long time before I killed her." Bava also has contradictory fun in this final confrontation by reserving the spooky underlighting for the frightened heroine rather than the killer. For distribution to US teens, AIP ordered a new score, retitled the film *The Evil Eye* and deleted all reference to Nora having inadvertently smoked marijuana.

Bava's next film followed in February 1963 and this time AIP contributed a 'minimo garantito' in advance. As well as consolidating his relationship with Sam Arkoff and Jim Nicholson, the new film also marked Bava's last work for Nello Santi's Galatea outfit, producers of his first official directorial assignment, *La maschera del demonio*. *La paura* (The Fear) was a portmanteau featuring three stories, the first of them enabling Bava to elaborate on the *giallo* mode established in *La ragazza che sapeva troppo*. The film also traded on the current vogue for multi-story pictures, most famously the De Sica-Fellini-Monicelli-Visconti combine *Boccaccio '70*, as well as specifically referencing AIP's own Poe compilation *Tales of Terror*, which Roger Corman had directed back in December 1961.

Released under the expanded title *I tre volti della paura* (The Three Faces of Fear), the result bypassed Poe but showed off its erudition by citing de Maupassant, Tolstoy and Chekhov as its literary antecedents, though the first and last of these attributions were basically bogus and even the second referred to Aleksey Tolstoy rather than his more celebrated second cousin, Leo. Even so, the film offered Bava the opportunity to render his Gothic nightmares in luscious, hallucinatory colour for the first time, while AIP's involvement brought with it a major bonus – the 75-year-old Boris Karloff. At the height of his renewed 'monster boom' celebrity, Karloff had recently fronted the American TV

Mario Bava oversees a ghostly mask-fitting during production of I tre volti della paura (1963)

# I TRE VOLTI DELLA PAURA

Italy 1963
UK / US: *Black Sabbath*
Emmepi Cinematografica / Lyre
 Cinematographique / Galatea
99 minutes colour
production began 4 February 1963

· · · · · · · · · · · · · · · · · · · · · · · · · · · · · · ·

Director of Photography: Ubaldo Terzano; Art
Director: Riccardo Dominici; Editor: Mario
Serandrei; Sound: Mario Messina; Music:
Roberto Nicolosi; Make-up: Otello Fava;
Screenplay: Marcello Fondata in collaboration
with Alberto Bevilacqua and Mario Bava,
freely adapted from three stories by Anton

Chekhov [sic], Aleksey Tolstoi and Guy
de Maupassant [sic]; Director: Mario Bava

*framing sequences* – Boris Karloff (himself);
**Il telefono** – Michèle Mercier (Rosy); Lidia
Alfonsi (Mary); uncredited: Milo Quesada
(Franco); **I wurdulak** – Boris Karloff (Gorka);
Mark Damon (Vladimir); Maria Antonietta
Golgi (Sdenka); Massimo Righi (Pietro); Rica
Dialina (Giorgio's wife); Glauco Onorato
(Giorgio); **La goccia d'acqua** – Jacqueline
Pierreux (Miss Chester); Milly Monti
(housekeeper); Harriet White (Miss Perkins);
Gustavo De Nardo (inspector)

**With its mixture of actual, imagined and fabulous horror this picture has
an obvious market. It will make an all-creepie programme with *The Tomb
of Ligeia*. The three stories are all quite different and vary in entertainment
value ... The most successful episode is undoubtedly *The Wurdalak* [sic] in
which there is a simply lovely glut of murder and vampirism. Appropriately
the head vampire is Boris Karloff.** Kinematograph Weekly 12 November 1964

> **We worked mostly at night, because in *I tre volti della paura* it was the night,
> the dark, that had to stick out ... Our starting point – before we began to
> write – was always some question from Mario. For instance: 'What is the
> scariest thing for the viewer to watch?' ... He had this list of top scares that
> he was constantly updating: 'Now, this is scarier than the other thing.'**
> Alberto Bevilacqua [quoted in Lucas, Mario Bava: All the Colors of the Dark, 2007]

anthology *Thriller* and a British counterpart called
*Out of This World*. Naturally then, Bava cast him
not only in the Tolstoy story but also as the creepily
avuncular front man for the whole enterprise.

> *Boris Karloff introduces three brief tales of terror. In
> the first, a Paris call girl is tormented by threatening
> phone calls coming, apparently, from her vengeful pimp.
> In the second, a rural Russian family is preyed upon
> by a vampire patriarch, who converts them all into*

wurdalaks. Finally, an acquisitive nurse is
charged with laying out the corpse of an elderly
medium; having looted the body, she finds
that the medium has returned home with her.

*I tre volti della paura* opens with Karloff
picked out against a psychedelic backdrop
while waggishly warning us that vampires
"go to the movies too." In his first of
numerous boldly emblematic uses of colour,
Bava floods Karloff's face with candified red
the second he refers to their "strange habit
of drinking blood." And without further
ado we're precipitated into *Il telefono* (The
Telephone), which relies for most of its
nervous horror on the humdrum business of
a constantly ringing phone.

The device itself, however, is a fetching red;
coupled with a black receiver, it announces the chicly
colour-coded fetishism that was to become the sine qua
non of the giallo. It also makes sardonic reference to
the vapid 'telefoni bianchi' (white telephone) films that
had proliferated under Mussolini. Much of the pleasure
in this story derives from Bava's detailed prowling
of Michèle Mercier's exquisite apartment; when her
lesbian lover, Lidia Alfonsi, shows up, we can marvel,
too, at her stylish green outfit with its edgings of black
ermine. The same aesthetic appreciation extends to the
dazzle of a butcher knife when Alfonsi rummages in
the kitchen drawers. That Bava has an utterly negligible
story to work with seems almost beside the point in the
full flood of such stylistic invention.

*I wurdulak* (The Wurdalak) is on an entirely
different level and qualifies as perhaps the best
40-minute Gothic horror film ever made. Here, Susy
Andersen's beautiful Sdenka defines the wurdalak
as the kind of vampires that "yearn for the blood of
those they loved most when they were alive." The
ensuing destruction and rebirth of Sdenka's whole
family is realised with astonishing force by Bava,
building to a genuinely gruelling climax in which a
mother, Maria, stabs her own husband in order to
bring in her little son from the icy wastes outside
the house. The boy has clearly become a vampire,
yet it's Karloff's forbidding Gorca who's actually on
the doorstep when the woman flings open the door.
The beckoning ghost child – made all the creepier
in this instance by its double-meaning wails of "I'm
cold" – would soon become a staple Bava image, as
would the chilling 'face at the window' motif, initially

disclosing just Gorca but finally teaming him with Maria and the boy.

Every feature of this story is beautifully crafted, from a discreet ration of *Nosferatu* quotes to dazzling colour effects that turn the snowy landscapes a deep blue while painting an abandoned convent in hallucinatory shades of green and lilac. Gorca's midnight return – a hunched silhouette, crossing back to the land of the living via a rope bridge – lets us know in starkly poetic terms that he's no less a force of nature than the keening wind and turbulent waters. And the queasy uncertainty of his family as they try to second-guess whether his travels have 'turned' him is memorably conveyed. That the horror stems from a grizzled patriarch, and is enabled in large part by the family's unthinking obeisance to him, is given an added twist by the whiff of paedophilia that hangs over the story. This is a patriarch who looks on his tiny grandson with undisguised gloating fascination, subsequently hovering over his bed before gathering him up and spiriting him away.

The pall of hellish smoke that sweeps over the vampires' faces at the end of *I wurdulak* is a tough act to follow, but in *La goccia d'acqua* (The Drop of Water) Bava contrives a lusciously horrible nightmare from a handful of simple devices – a buzzing fly, the resonant drip-drip of water, the ugly rictus of a deceased medium. "She had no friends other than the ones who made the table shake," we're told, linking Mme Zena to the seance-fixated Dr Hichcock of Freda's *Lo spettro*. Unlike Hichcock, however, her return is no imposture but very much a supernatural-psychological manifestation, building to a really grim final tableau in which Bava zooms into the glassy stare of her dead victim. Again, the compositions here teem with sensuous detail, whether in the victim's flat (fitfully lit by the bilious green of an exterior neon sign) or the medium's cavernous salon, with its purple vaulted ceiling and scattering of abandoned cats. Only the medium herself lets down this otherwise exemplary story. Sculpted by Bava's father Eugenio, she's too obviously a wax dummy (or in some shots a latex mask applied to an uncredited actress) to fully convince.

Nevertheless, Mme Zena scared the wits out of many of the juvenile audiences at whom AIP's standard product was aimed. The rest of the picture, though, was far too adult for AIP's purposes, resulting in a much-adulterated English-language version entitled *Black Sabbath*. The stories were reshuffled (starting with the vengeful medium, moving on to the red telephone and leaving the vampire patriarch till last), and *Il telefono* was crudely recut as a ghost story in an effort to expunge its lesbian overtones. Furthermore,

Karloff was recruited for story introductions that are unique to the American cut and Roberto Nicolosi's score was replaced with a Les Baxter one. Many other, less radical changes were made, including the removal of a shot of Gorca kissing the little boy. Oddly enough, his line "Can't I fondle my own grandson?" – far more explicit than its equivalent in the Italian version – was allowed to remain.

Ironically, another item that was ditched was a coda Bava had inserted in an effort to satisfy AIP's demands for lighter material. As Karloff bids us adieu in his Gorca costume, the camera pulls back to reveal the truncated dummy horse he's sitting on, together with a bunch of Titanus stage hands brandishing tree branches while running in galumphing circles in simulation of a horseback pursuit. But such a funny and brazenly clever demystification of the filmmaking process was far too rich for AIP's blood, so out it went.

Not that these changes guaranteed a hit. As noted by Bava's biographer Tim Lucas, *Black Sabbath* earned just $419,000 in the USA, a significant drop on the take scored by *Black Sunday* in its first year, which stood at $706,000. In Italy, Bava's new film, under its *I tre volti della paura* title, fared even worse, managing a domestic gross of 103.5 million lire (approximately $65,000). Even at this level, however, *I tre volti* was a healthier proposition domestically than the majority of its peers, as is clear from the domestic grosses compiled by film historian Roberto Curti. In the first wave of Italian Gothics, only a select few titles exceeded the 100 million lire mark – *Lycanthropus* (115), *I vampiri* (125), *La maschera del demonio* (139), *L'orribile segreto del Dr Hichcock* (142), *Il mulino delle donne di pietra* (164) and *Lo spettro* (175). At a puny 36 million, *La strage dei vampiri* represented rock-bottom, while the only title to even nip at the heels of the much more lucrative sword-and-sandal genre, or the yet more phenomenal Spaghetti Westerns to come, was the inane comedy *Tempi duri per i vampiri* (385 million).

But the fact that Italian punters showed no great willingness to stand in line for a horror picture, though regrettable, was by no means insurmountable. There was an international market to be tapped too, notably the vast audience that pitched up at US grindhouses and drive-ins. The chance of making money out of them would keep Italian horror afloat for several years to come. Indeed, this strategy, often geared around cost-sharing co-productions with France or Spain and frequently entailing the use of international names, was the beginning of a process that would end with exploitation merchant Joe D'Amato, who in the 1990s admitted quite frankly that most of his films hadn't really been aimed at Italians at all.

# Part Three

Nightmare in a greenhouse: Barbara Steele and faceless monster Paul Muller in *Amanti d'oltretomba* (1965)

## *Angels for Satan* 1963-1966

In the first half of the 1960s, the ongoing economic booms common to Italy, France, Spain and West Germany were reflected in the buoyancy of their local film industries, with Italy leading the way. "Rome has become the new centre of the celluloid universe," asserted British critic F Maurice Speed late in 1962, "[producing] some of the period's most impressive and intellectually stimulating movies – as well as a lot of hammy historical 'epics' heavily dubbed into Americanised-English, which if they make money certainly don't bring prestige!"[1]

A good example of this dichotomy was available three years later, when Italian filmgoers in the autumn of 1965 could choose between seeing Reg Park in a conspicuously feeble fag-end of the peplum genre, *La sfida dei giganti* (Challenge of the Giants), complete with plenty of footage recycled from earlier Hercules pictures, or Giulietta Masina in Fellini's first colour feature, *Giulietta degli spiriti* (Juliet of the Spirits), in which a dazzling range of psychedelic phantoms are unleashed on her at a seance. Fellini had previously experimented with colour, incidentally, in his segment of the portmanteau film *Boccaccio '70*, which

featured a different kind of surrealist spectacle – Anita Ekberg, as the Devil, stepping down from a huge billboard and bestriding Rome like a colossus.

The co-existence of art and commerce wasn't confined, of course, to Italy. Enjoying the fruits of new-found consumerism, Spain was home to the Madrid-based collective Nuevo Cine Español (New Spanish Cinema) and its Catalan counterweight, the Escuela de Barcelona (Barcelona School); other Spanish filmmakers took advantage of the gradual loosening of censorship to make plenty of purely commercial crime thrillers, beach movies and 007-style spy spoofs. (A handful of horror pictures were added to the mix too, and in due course a few members of the Barcelona School would venture into the genre, as we shall see.) In France, policiers and crazy comedies enjoyed a commercial heyday even as the Nouvelle Vague created such world stars as Catherine Deneuve, Jean-Paul Belmondo and Jeanne Moreau. In 1965 Jean-Luc Godard fashioned a playful hybrid of art and exploitation motifs called *Alphaville Une Étrange aventure de Lemmy Caution* (Alphaville: A Strange Adventure for Lemmy Caution), casting Howard Vernon, Jess Franco's Dr Orlof, as

Leonard Nosferatu, creator of the tyrannical super-computer Alpha 60. Two years later, and in very different mood, Godard would add cannibalism to the anarchic riot of carnage in his anti-capitalist road movie *Week-end*.

In Germany, the young signatories of the Oberhausen Manifesto inveighed against 'Papas Kino' (just as Truffaut had skewered le cinéma de Papa nearly ten years before), paving the way for 'das neue Kino' at the end of the decade. Simultaneously, new exploitation franchises were being perfected in order to stave off the defection of audiences to television. Rialto, for example, added to its popular Edgar Wallace series a new sequence of colourful Westerns based on the books of Karl May, a lucrative vein that Artur Brauner's CCC also tried to tap, just as it had with the Wallace films. Where Germany's Westerns looked to Yugoslavia for locations, Italy's Sergio Leone went to Almería for the phenomenal 1964 smash *Per un pugno di dollari* (A Fistful of Dollars), triggering a spate of so-called Spaghetti Westerns and making an international star of Clint Eastwood. Italian filmgoers also responded enthusiastically to a rash of slick sex comedies, larkish espionage romps and the kind of portmanteau pictures popularised by *Boccaccio '70*.

Though Bava's *I tre volti della paura* would remain the only all-horror anthology, several of these portmanteaux were careful to include a horror story in the bill of fare. Gianni Puccini's six-tier black comedy *Io uccido, tu uccidi* (I Kill, You Kill) contrived to put the Sicilian comics Franco e Ciccio into the same film as Jean-Louis Trintignant, Emmanuelle Riva and Eleonora Rossi Drago; it also incorporated a trio of murderous children into its fourth story, *Giochi acerbi* (Immature Games), and featured Rossi Drago's castle-dwelling Black Widow in the fifth, *Il plenilunio* (The Full Moon). Another 1965 comedy, *Thrilling*, boasted three directors and three stories, with the great Alberto Sordi appearing in the third segment, Carlo Lizzani's *L'autostrada del sole* (Highway of the Sun), playing a benighted motorist who puts up at a motel staffed by homicidal maniacs. Yet another 1965 release, *Umorismo in nero* (Black Humour), was an Italian-French-Spanish co-production built on the same multi-director lines as *Thrilling*, devoting its Italian story, Giancarlo Zagni's *La cornacchia* (The Crow), to Folco Lulli's realisation that the beautiful widow he's engaged to (Alida Valli) is none other than Death.

## MOROSE AND DEATH-LIKE

Perhaps the most extraordinary product of the portmanteau trend was the first of three stories contained in the multi-director collection *Amori pericolosi* (Perilous Loves), released in August 1964.

Set in 1912 and directed by Giulio Questi, the story is called *Il passo* (The Footstep) and recalls both Poe's *The Tell-Tale Heart* and Ambrose Bierce's *The Middle Toe of the Right Foot*. It begins with a view of eerily irradiated trees in front of a French château, accompanied by the gnomic inscription, "If your wife's footsteps are too heavy – do not kill her." The boldly experimental 30-odd minute film that unfolds positions Frank Wolff's feckless military man between a barefoot housekeeper (Graziella Granata, from *La strage dei vampiri*) and a clubfoot wife (Juliette Mayniel, from *Les Yeux sans visage*); taking aim at a human silhouette during target practice, the latter explains bitterly that "I prefer the legs." What develops is essentially a sick joke, with Wolff's obsessive horror at the sound of his wife's lurching footfall, coupled with fetishistic views of her built-up shoe, building to a brutally ironic twist ending. The agitated score (Ivan Zandor), the brilliant editing (Franco Arcalli), the queasily sustained hothouse atmosphere – all these made *Il passo* a striking calling card, and Questi's subsequent features would be more arresting still.

Distantly echoed in *Il passo*, Ambrose Bierce had previously formed the basis of a three-part portmanteau from France, Robert Enrico's *Au Coeur de la vie* (In the Midst of Life). One of the Civil War stories contained in it, *La Rivière du hibou* (Owl River), was marketed by itself as a short, winning a 1963 British Academy award as *Incident at Owl Creek* and a 1964 Oscar under Bierce's original title, *An Occurrence at Owl Creek Bridge*. A beautifully observed 27-minute death reverie, its central idea was subsequently spun out to feature length on numerous occasions, from *Jacob's Ladder* to *The Sixth Sense*. Sadly, Enrico himself ventured into the genre only once more, making a highly atmospheric Henry James adaptation, *La Redevance du fantôme* (The Ghostly Rental), for French TV in 1965.

Very rarely adapted, Ambrose Bierce lagged a long way behind his fellow countryman Edgar Allan Poe, who in a roundabout way would trigger the second wave of Italian horror. For, just as the first wave had been set in motion by Hammer Films, the second took its cue from Roger Corman's sequence of Poe adaptations for AIP, specifically his 1961 smash *Pit and the Pendulum*, which made as big an impact on Italian audiences as Fisher's *Dracula* had a few years earlier. Henceforth no Italian Gothic seemed complete without a diseased family at its centre, garnished if possible by torture devices in the basement and prolonged, candlelit corridor-wanderings for the beleaguered heroine. The Corman effect on Italian horror was actually a two-way street, given that an

Mutant aristocrat and sinister housekeeper: the first of numerous genre credits for Helga Liné in the Italian-Spanish co-production *Horror* (1963)

## HORROR

Italy-Spain 1963
US: *The Blancheville Monster*
Film Columbus / Llama Film
90 minutes b/w
Italian visa date 14 May 1963
. . . . . . . . . . . . . . . . . . . . . . . . . . . . .
Director of Photography: Alejandro Ulloa; Art Director: Antonio Simoni; Editor: Otello Colangeli; Music: Carlo Franci; Make-up: Romolo De Martino; Special Effects: Emilio G Ruiz; Screenplay: Gianni

Grimaldi, Sergio Corbucci; Production Manager: Roberto Palaggi; Producers: Italo Zingarelli, Alberto Aguilera; Director: Alberto De Martino

Gérard Tichy (Roderick Blackford); Leo Anchóriz (Dr Atwell); Ombretta Colli (Emily Blackford); Helga Liné (Eleonor); Irán Eory (Alice Taylor); Vanni Materassi (John Taylor); Francisco [Paco] Morán (Alastair); Emilia Wolkowicz (cook); Harry Winter (groundsman)

Another 'haunted castle', as our cinematic summer season demands ... Directed by Martin Herbert [sic], *Horror* adheres exactly to the rules of the terror genre, as well as boasting a vague basis in a story by the great Poe ... Immersed completely in the style of the 19th century 'horror pic', this little film doesn't lack for sinister efficacy, despite entrusting clichéd motifs to rather humble actors whom we've never heard of. *La Stampa* 15 June 1963

Our audience never really believed in the quality of our productions so we had to hide behind pseudonyms. Even Sergio Leone was forced to direct his first Western under a different name. I had to choose Martin Herbert for *Horror* because the producer wanted to give the impression of an American production. I used this name also for several other pictures I did afterwards.
*Alberto De Martino* [quoted in *European Trash Cinema* April 1995]

Italian influence was encoded into *Pit and the Pendulum* itself – for Corman's "blasphemous chamber" in which "the blood of a thousand men and women was spilled" was occupied not just by Vincent Price but also the bewitching Barbara Steele.

Though Freda's *L'orribile segreto del Dr Hichcock* was a film thoroughly steeped in Poe, Freda himself denied that it was in any way influenced by the Corman way of doing things. Among the first of Italy's indisputably Corman-inspired films, then, was Alberto De Martino's baldly titled *Horror*, the advertising for which, on its appearance in the first week of June 1963, billed Edgar Allan Poe above the title as if he were the film's star. (Both title and 'star' were rendered in a suitably glaring yellow.) For export the film retained the title *Horror* in the UK but in America it became *The Blancheville Monster* – a change reflecting some fundamental alterations imposed by the conspicuously bad English-language dub. The Scottish setting, for example, had been transposed to Brittany and the ailing aristocratic line of Blackford was rechristened de Blancheville.

*October 1884. Returning to her Scottish family seat after a period spent studying in London, Emily Blackford is dismayed to find that her saturnine older brother, Roderick, has engaged rather shifty-looking new servants. Worse, she learns that her father is dead and that, according to time-honoured prophecy, the Blackfords will die out should any daughter of the* house turn 21. That's exactly the age Emily is due to reach in five days' time...

De Martino's film begins in grand style, with Carlo Franci's full-blooded score thundering across a scene of a daylight forest lashed by rain and lightning. The camera pans smoothly to a neighbouring mansion that appears to occupy a weird, nocturnal space of its own, focusing first on a family crest above the battlements, then panning up a tall tower to a pair of hands clutching the bars of a lighted window. An animated lightning bolt flashes across to form the word *Horror* and the effect is complete.

The benighted pile divorced from its surroundings, bearing both a noble crest and an incarcerated maniac – this is recognisable Poe territory, and the impression is confirmed when Emily arrives and tells the gloomy Roderick that "I'm 21 now, and I don't have to answer to anyone for my actions." "There's still a week till your birthday," Roderick replies with an enigmatic smile. "And until then your life belongs to me..." The incestuous note here tips us off that Roderick Blackford is really Roderick Usher, and that Emily (or, for argument's sake, Madeline) will in due course find herself submitted to a premature burial. As for the house itself, one of Roderick's guests, in a very Poe-like touch, observes that "Everything here seems morose and death-like," extending this description even to the walls.

In the meantime, De Martino faithfully conforms to the Corman template with a masterfully confected scene in which Emily's college friend, Alice, is disturbed in her bed by distant bellows of agony. Taking up the regulation candelabrum, she ventures out and heads upstairs as midnight strikes. When she throws open a steel door in the tower room, De Martino's camera rattles in for a jarring reveal of the sinister housekeeper, hypodermic in hand, and a deformed nobleman who lurches into frog-faced close-up right on cue. Helga Liné's housekeeper – her first of numerous horror roles – is just one of several indications that *Horror* was actually a co-production with Spain. Others include the Roderick of Gérard Tichy (like Liné, a German-born actor specialising in Spanish films) and the sombre presence of Leo Anchóriz and Paco Morán as Roderick's doctor and butler. On top of this, the Blackford estate is clearly the same castillo lately occupied by Dr Orlof, while the family vaults are located in the nearby Cistercian monastery of Santa María de Valdeiglesias, subsequently to harbour the Blind Dead and numerous other Hispanic monstrosities.

*Horror* is rather lugubriously paced and could have profited from at least ten of its 90 minutes being

shaved off. Gratifyingly, however, De Martino lays the atmosphere on thick. The Blackford patriarch, it transpires, isn't dead after all, for it is he, fire-ravaged and demented, who writhes unhappily in that upper room. When it's Emily's turn to answer his summons, she wanders outside in a nightie even more see-through than Alice's, fetching up at the burial ground as a cowled shadow croons, "Abandon yourself to eternal rest. All torment will end with the sweetness of death..."

Later, a striking nightmare sequence – in which that ominous cowl is occupied first by the doctor, then by the tower mutant, and finally by Roderick – is played out on a Corman-like soundstage thick with ground fog and gnarled trees. There are signs that other influences were at work, too. The icy woodland exteriors, for example, are reminiscent of the loosely Poe-derived Hammer film *The Shadow of the Cat*, as is the rather arbitrary discovery of the butler's corpse under a carpet of autumn leaves. An older derivation is that frequent source, Dreyer's *Vampyr*, which is explicitly invoked when the family members, dwarfed by the monastery's vaulted arches, consign Emily to her premature tomb; in the US version, unfortunately, the girl's panicked interior monologue is rendered ridiculous by the over-enthusiastic dubbing actress.

Roderick, of course, is climactically revealed as the villain, explaining himself with a mad-aristo variation on the standard mad-scientist rationale. "After all," he hisses, "what is the death of a useless creature compared to the life, the future of the Blackfords?" By 'a useless creature' he means poor Emily, regarding whom the film leaves us with a tantalising mystery. When she stumbles from her tomb, causing the horrified Roderick to pitch backwards down a well, we're left entirely unenlightened as to how on earth she got out.

A more radical way of invoking Corman's Poe pictures was to insert Poe himself into the action. This was what Gianni Grimaldi and Bruno Corbucci, the writers of *Horror*, did with their next project, *Danza macabra* (Danse macabre). Originally earmarked for Corbucci's director brother Sergio, the job eventually went to Antonio Margheriti, who polished the film off in a mere two weeks in the second half of March 1963, utilising television's multi-camera method to ensure speed. Though not stinting on the expected crepuscular atmosphere, the result pushed the fusion of horror and eroticism to new extremes.

*On a November night some time in the 1840s, Edgar Allan Poe is witness to a £100 wager between Sir Thomas Blackwood and the young journalist Alan Foster. Foster's challenge is to spend the night at Blackwood's apparently unoccupied country seat. There*

A heart-stopping encounter for
Barbara Steele and Georges Rivière
in *Danza macabra* (1963)

## DANZA MACABRA

Italy-France 1963
France: *Danse macabre*
UK / US: *Castle of Blood*
Era Cinematografica / Leo Lax Films
92 minutes b/w
production began 18 March 1963
. . . . . . . . . . . . . . . . . . . . . . . . . . . .
Director of Photography: Riccardo
Pallottini; Art Director: Ottavio Scotti;
Editor: Otello Colangeli; Music: Riz
Ortolani; Make-up: Sonny Arden;
Screenplay: Gianni Grimaldi, Bruno
Corbucci, from a story by Edgar Allan

Poe [sic]; Production Manager: Alfonso
Donati; Producers: Franco Belotti, Walter
Zarghetta, Marco Vicario; Associate
Director: Sergio Corbucci [uncredited];
Director: Antonio Margheriti

Barbara Steele (Elisabeth Blackwood); Georges
Rivière (Alan Foster); Margarete Robsahm (Julia);
Arturo Dominici (Dr Carmus); Silvano Tranquili
(Edgar Allan Poe); Umberto Raho (Lord Thomas
Blackwood); Sylvia Sorrente (Elsi Perkings);
Giovanni Cianfriglia (killer); Benito Stefanelli
(William); Miranda Poggi

A story of mad love, a recitation of damnation, a necrophile poem – the
chief merit of *Danse macabre* is in maintaining its perilous course throughout,
with no concessions to dilute or circumscribe it: reviving the spectres, a
dark disorientation pervades the film, that neither the coming of dawn, nor
the crowing of the cock (though fatal to vampires), can dissipate for one
moment. This is an adult film that must be seen through the eyes of a child.
*Cahiers du Cinéma* May-June 1965

Danza macabra was the first picture at that time, to my knowledge, to talk
about lesbianism, and it was so well done, so sensitively handled, that even
the terrible censors we had at that time in Italy, guys who used to put on
masks and then take an axe to your film, didn't cut a single frame... And the
rest of the picture in my opinion was very well done. *Antonio Margheriti* [quoted in
*The Dark Side* August 1995]

*Foster meets and falls in love with Blackwood's sister
Elisabeth. But he also encounters the metaphysician
Dr Carmus, who has a chilling theory regarding
Elisabeth and the five other people on the premises.*

The momentous meeting between Poe, Foster and
Blackwood takes place at a public house called The
Four Devils, with Poe reciting his teeth-scattering
horror story *Berenice* and, in the aftermath, claiming this

as his first visit to London. (This Poe
presumably wasn't educated in Stoke
Newington, as the real Poe was.)
Silvano Tranquilli is an unusually
handsome Edgar, the soon-to-be
ubiquitous Umberto Raho is a
refined and watchful Blackwood,
and Georges Rivière uses a donnish
tone and rather florid hand gestures
to suggest that poor Foster will be
ill-equipped to fight off a gang of
blood-lusting spectres.

The trio's discussion of the
afterlife is, truth be told, rather
dull; only when they get into a
coach, bound for Blackwood's
dilapidated mansion, does the
interest quicken. Here, Tranquilli
gets to mouth Poe's famous dictum, "The death of a
beautiful woman is, unquestionably, the most poetical
topic in the world" – as good an indication as any
that Barbara Steele is going to show up in due course.
In the meantime Foster gets to do the stuff that in
Corman films is normally reserved for the damsel
in distress. Leaving his companions at the gate, he
wanders down the driveway, encounters a tiny black
kitten, enters the house, exchanges a flaming taper
for the usual candelabrum, is disturbed by flapping
shutters, a booming clock and a tinkling music-box,
swerves nervously at his own reflection in a full-length
mirror, and even plays the piano. Only then does the
sepulchral Elisabeth reach out and touch his shoulder.

All this gives us ample time in which to admire
Ottavio Scotti's beautiful, cobwebbed interiors and
Riccardo Pallottini's brooding photography of them.
But, for a film made in such haste, the end product
is surprisingly long and one wishes, just as with
*Horror*, that Margheriti could have trimmed – from
here and elsewhere – maybe ten of its 92 minutes.
Even so, with Elisabeth's arrival the tone genuinely
darkens. Foster is something of a stuffed shirt and
clearly inexperienced with women. "To be honest,"
he says with disarming candour, "I've been very
lonely." The couple's love talk is therefore dopey in
the extreme, but Elisabeth's endearments soon take
on a decidedly vampiric tone. "I want to absorb the
warmth of your body," she breathes. "You will give
me life..." Margheriti cuts to a shot of flames leaping
in the grate as they (presumably) make love, then he

floors us (and Foster) with Elisabeth's post-coital pronouncement: "My heart isn't beating, Alan. It hasn't beaten for ten years. I'm dead, Alan. Dead."

The words are hardly out of Elisabeth's mouth when a half-naked bodybuilder type suddenly bursts in upon the couple in a jealous rage. The fleshly nature of the Blackwood apparitions is subsequently explained by the sombre Dr Carmus (splendidly played by Arturo Dominici), who acts as a kind of funereal tour guide to Foster (and us) while pointing out that the revenants are kept alive by their senses rather than their 'spirit'. To prove his point he decapitates a tough-to-kill grass snake (an early instance of the unfaked animal cruelty that will crop up in later Italian films) prior to showing Foster what is effectively a film within a film. As the house's tenants replay their violents deaths, Margheriti ratchets up the already unhealthy erotic atmosphere considerably, moving from implied cunnilingus in the stables to three re-enacted sex murders in as many minutes – all of them focused on Elisabeth's four-poster bed, including a taboo-breaking lesbian interlude for Steele and the glacially blonde Margarete Robsahm.

The phantasmagoric mood intensifies still further with a replay of Carmus' own death, which involves an extremely creepy descent to the Blackwood crypt and a glimpse of the supine, skull-faced bodybuilder heaving reviving breaths in a cloud of unearthly vapour. Finally, Foster's horror is complete with the ghostly appearance of the foolish young newly-weds who accepted Blackwood's wager the previous year. Their re-enacted deaths involve Margheriti pushing the envelope yet again, this time when Sylvia Sorrente appears topless at the fireside.

The crescendo of terror here is expertly contrived. Fleeing from the assembled ghosts' mantra of "Your blood means life a year from now," Foster drags Elisabeth outside; there, Steele has one of her greatest moments, collapsing in the ground fog as her agonised face turns into a skull. The macabre spectacle greeting Poe the following morning doesn't faze the unscrupulous Blackwood one bit; having been aware all along of the bizarre once-a-year time loop that revives his sister and the others, he calmly collects his £100 from Foster's lifeless body and goes on his way. It's a bleak wrap-up to a film that, despite longueurs, fully deserves the "poème nécrophilique"[2] tag bestowed on it by *Cahiers du Cinéma*.

In March 1971, exactly eight years after making *Danza macabra*, Margheriti began shooting a colour remake called *E venne l'alba ma tinta di rosso* (Came the Dawn But Stained Red). Giovanni Addessi, one of several producers on the earlier film, pointed out that a domestic gross of under 101 million lire qualified the original as a financial failure and that it would be worth making a 'bigger and better' version. The result came out as *Nella stretta morsa del ragno* (In the Tight Grip of the Spider) and Margheriti was candid on the subject in later interviews, lamenting that Addessi "spent a lot of money for nothing ... because the colour photography destroyed everything: the atmosphere, the tension."[3]

How right he was. All the incidents from *Danza macabra* are slavishly reproduced, with an approximately 75 per cent reduction in impact in every instance. In the person of Anthony Franciosa, Foster has become an American, the wager has been reduced to a mere £10 (Foster can't afford anything more), the phantom bodybuilder is no longer shirtless, and Franciosa goes more extravagantly mad in the closing stages than Rivière did. Otherwise it's business as usual, though Klaus Kinski is brought in to give a typically Kinskified version of Edgar Allan Poe. The TV movie colour and Franciosa's TV movie face drain interest very rapidly, and all in all it's hard not to concur with Margheriti's contention that "It was stupid to remake it."[4]

## OVERWHELMINGLY ITALIAN

By 1962 the number of continental assignments coming Christopher Lee's way prompted him to move, in March, from Belgravia to the northern shore of Lake Geneva. His first film after the move came round in July and was a German-Italian-French co-production called *Sherlock Holmes und das Halsband des Todes* (Sherlock Holmes and the Deadly Necklace), shot at Artur Brauner's Haselhorst Atelier in Spandau and on location in Dublin.

Christopher Lee uncovers an Egyptian mummy in *Sherlock Holmes und das Halsband des Todes* (1962)

Directed by Hammer's Terence Fisher from a screenplay by old Hollywood hand Curt Siodmak, the result was touted as a 'gruselig-spannenden Leichenrevue' (chiller-thriller corpse-cabaret) but it remains hard to judge thanks to the disastrous dub track applied to Lee's brusque Holmes and Thorley Walters' faithful Watson. The plot involves the theft of an invaluable necklace that once belonged to Cleopatra, with Holmes recovering it from an Egyptian sarcophagus concealed in Moriarty's apartment. An upcoming clash between Holmes and Jack the Ripper having been hinted at in the film's final scene, exactly such a sequel was duly announced in the German tabloid Bild under the title Sherlock Holmes entlarvt Jack the Ripper (Sherlock Holmes Unmasks Jack the Ripper). In the event the film's producer, Henry E Lester, decamped to England and the mooted sequel became A Study in Terror, in which John Neville inherited the Holmes role.

Lee would eventually move back to London in April 1965, but in the meantime nearly half his film output was devoted to full-blown Italian Gothics. The sequence began with a Mario Bava reunion called La frusta e il corpo (The Whip and the Body), which brought Lee to Rome, for what turned out to be a lengthy Italian summer, on 7 May 1963.

After the heavily signposted necrophilia of L'orribile segreto del Dr Hichcock, screenwriter Ernesto Gastaldi here concocted an openly sadomasochistic Gothic romance, with the result that the completed film was charged with obscenity in a Roman court. Strangely, the attendant publicity seems to have entailed the film's failure rather than the queues around the block one might have expected; in Italy La frusta made back less than half of its 150 million lire budget. Happily, distributors in the US and UK expressed an interest. Less happily, the versions released there not only bypassed the recommended export title – The Whip and the Flesh – but were cut to pieces too. In America the film was released, preposterously, as What, while British filmgoers saw it under a more alluring but rather unspecific title, Night is the Phantom.

*Kurt Menliff returns to his ancestral castle to lay claim to his lands and title, despite the fact that his father, the Count, has yet to die. He also re-ignites a smouldering affair with his beautiful sister-in-law Nevenka, who disappears briefly after their passionate tryst on the beach – an interval during which Kurt is mysteriously murdered in his bedroom. After this, Nevenka is haunted and brutally chastised by a whip-wielding apparition bearing Kurt's face.*

In the UK trade paper Daily Cinema, Peter John Dyer would pithily describe Bava's film as "another of Italy's prankish simulations of a British horror movie,"[5] and in this estimate he was at least half right. The simulation extended not merely to the casting of Christopher Lee but also to the phoney Anglicisation of almost everyone else's names; even Bava knuckled under and called himself John M Old. Yet the British ambience of La frusta was ambience only; the film's more precise model was actually a US production, the same one that had already influenced De Martino's Horror and Margheriti's Danza macabra. As Gastaldi admitted 30-odd years later, "The producers, Ugo Guerra and Elio Scardamaglia, showed me an Italian print of Pit and the Pendulum before I started writing it. 'Give us something like this,' they said."[6]

What Gastaldi came up with was a story set rather vaguely around 1825, focusing on a beautiful woman who loses her grip on sanity after having murdered an abusive but demonically irresistible lover. Translating script to screen, Bava turned La frusta e il corpo into arguably the last word in over-ripe Gothic romance, a film so lusciously operatic it seems like one long agonising swoon – forever trembling, like the conflicted Nevenka, on the brink of some otherworldly orgasm. Its scenes of heavy-duty sado-eroticism – among them Kurt's repeated lashing of Nevenka in a blaze of teeth-clenched ferocity – are much enhanced by Carlo Rustichelli's truly rhapsodic score and the disturbingly romantic glow in which Bava bathes them; also by the iconic faces of Lee and Daliah Lavi, who are ideally cast as Kurt and Nevenka.

The physical beauty conferred on the film by Bava and cinematographer Ubaldo Terzano surpasses even that of Bava's previous title, I tre volti della paura. In their hands, and those of art director Ottavio Scotti, even an unremarkable castle hallway set, previously seen in De Martino's Horror, is given a bewitching Technicolor makeover. Repeated views of scarlet roses, the pink-hued surf of the beach at Tor Caldara, the green-hued hand that claws at the heroine from the darkness, the velvety black that obscures all of the supine Nevenka except for her frightened eyes – the visual riches in La frusta verge on cloying, a kind of high-calorie Gothic made all the richer by the constant recourse to Rustichelli's swelling strings and piano.

Like King Lear, the film uses raging, inclement weather as an index to the characters' ungovernable emotions; indeed, Shelley's original Gothic prescription – "the tempestuous loveliness of terror" – has rarely been so vividly realised. In this combustible environment, the sadomasochistic bond between Kurt and Nevenka recalls the whip-lashing histrionics of

The whip (Christopher Lee) and the body (Daliah Lavi) in the sumptuous *La frusta e il corpo* (1963)

the Gainsborough melodramas made in Britain some 20 years before, while simultaneously laying bare the darker undercurrents of such 'respectable' Gothic fictions as *Wuthering Heights* and *Jane Eyre*. As Kurt, Lee has never looked more Byronic. His role is relatively small but, as in *Dracula*, his presence, alternately feared and desired, permeates the entire picture. Kurt's demise calls forth a typically eloquent piece of Lee mime, with Bava's staging suggesting that Kurt has been stabbed in the throat not by a human being but by an enveloping red curtain – a borderline-absurd moment put across by Lee with a brilliant display of death-rattling disbelief.

As a presumed ghost, Kurt first appears to Nevenka at a rain-streaked French window prior to receding solemnly into darkness again. Stunning in itself, this shot is carefully modelled on one of Peter Wyngarde's visitations in Jack Clayton's *The Innocents* – an apt reference, given that, like the heroine of Clayton's film, Nevenka is conjuring this terrifying spectre of sexual torment from her mind. That the ghostly Kurt is a phantom reflection of her own frustration is made plain when, caressing herself longingly in front of a mirror, his grinning face suddenly appears at her shoulder – another heart-stoppingly powerful moment.

Before all this becomes clear, the film teases the viewer with various possibilities, possibilities that Bava doesn't seem especially interested in but which are presumably intended to make up an absorbing mystery – not merely the 'who killed Kurt?' question but also the burgeoning 'perhaps Kurt is still alive?' option. This part of the plot is set up by a manservant spotting inexplicable lights in the Menliffs' crypt-cum-chapel, a plot point seemingly lifted direct from Duvivier's *La Chambre ardente*. (Even the design of the chapel's exterior is more or less the same as in the Duvivier film.) It leads to the final revelation that in her nocturnal fugues Nevenka has actually been dressing up as Kurt – though, unlike Norman Bates' murderous masquerade in *Psycho*, the sight of this potentially silly disguise is

## LA FRUSTA E IL CORPO

Italy-France 1963
France: *Le Corps et le fouet*
UK: **Night is the Phantom**
US: **What** / **The Whip and the Body**
Vox Film / Leone Film / Francinor / Paris International
88 minutes colour
in production May–June 1963

. . . . . . . . . . . . . . . . . . . . . . . . . . . . .

Directors of Photography: Ubaldo Terzano and [uncredited] Mario Bava; Production Designer: Ottavio Scotti; Editor: Renato Cinquini; Music: Carlo Rustichelli; Make-up: Franco Freda; Story and Screenplay: Ernesto Gastaldi, Ugo Guerra, Luciano Martino; Production Manager: Elio Scardamaglia; Producer: Federico Magnaghi; Director: Mario Bava

Daliah Lavi (Nevenka); Christopher Lee (Kurt Menliff); Tony Kendall (Christian Menliff); Ida Galli (Katia); Harriet White (Giorgia); Gustavo De Nardo (Count Menliff); Luciano Pigozzi (Losat); Jacques Herlin (priest)

**Commendably compulsive – if a shade arty – box-office horror attraction ... Unfortunately, the plot is both obscure and far-fetched and the whole thing is on the slow and repetitive side. Nevertheless the acting is an enormous compensation ... Also the darkly Freudian goings-on will strike a chord in the subconscious of more people than would be prepared to admit it.**
Daily Cinema 27 January 1965

**I would say that, outside of De Sica or Fellini, he [Mario Bava] was the best director I worked with. He knew his craft extremely well ... My memories of Christopher Lee are vague; he was pleasant but formal, aloof. His role was also short and he wasn't with us for the entire production. It was a two-week film, I think.** Harriet White [quoted in Video Watchdog March–April 1994] sensibly withheld from us. "I killed him again," she stammers, "and this time for good." In doing so she demonstrates the final fusion of their identities, since in 'killing' him she only succeeds in killing herself. On this tragic note Kurt's improbably decomposed remains are set alight, with Bava closing the proceedings on a cheeky close-up of his still-tumescent whip twitching obscenely in the flaming coffin.

La frusta e il corpo contains a few self-referential witticisms (a concealed doorway in the Count's fireplace is a playful quote from La maschera del demonio), and also places a bit too heavy an emphasis on the absurdly muddy riding boots that are meant to signal Kurt's continued existence. It also doesn't have quite enough script. Killing off Kurt after only 20 minutes leaves Bava slightly adrift, reliant almost exclusively on his visual flair as the haunting gets into gear and – to be frank – making bricks without straw for lengthy periods. There's a protracted sequence, for example, in which Nevenka is seen sitting at the pianoforte and the Count by the fireside, with the housekeeper hovering in the doorway – a sequence in which Bava manages to distract us from the fact that precisely nothing is happening by the sheer romantic intensity of his images. In Britain, Freddie Francis faced a similar 'not enough script' problem in the 1965 film The Skull, choosing, like Bava, to beguile the viewer with visual sleight-of-hand.

But Bava makes the most of the fascinating faces at his disposal – not just Lee and Lavi, but also Ida Galli, Gustavo De Nardo, Harriet White and Luciano Pigozzi. Most importantly, his use of supposedly irrational colour schemes to bring Nevenka's psychosexual trauma to life leaves him without peer in the field of Italian Gothic.

"Very weird some of these Italian projects were,"[7] Lee mused in his autobiography, and the weirdest of the lot was Giuseppe Veggezzi's Katarsis – which for Lee was a quick job slotted in directly after his work on La frusta e il corpo. Shot at the Castello Odescalchi overlooking Lake Bracciano between 14 May and 7 June 1963, Katarsis was first unveiled in September and sank pretty much without trace. A second release followed in August 1965, retitled Sfida al diavolo (Challenge to the Devil) and bolstered with newly shot wraparound material involving gangsters and nightclub

A midnight metamorphosis for Christopher Lee in Katarsis (1963)

performers. These added scenes – sparsely populated and seemingly interminable – feature a tubby young monk explaining to a similarly tubby chanteuse why he turned his back on a life of petty crime.

The lengthy flashback that follows constitutes the original Katarsis, introducing us to half-a-dozen beatniks (the future monk included) who beat up an innocent man at the roadside prior to finding their way into a forbidding castle. "It seemed deserted," the monk tells us in voice-over, "and was eerily silent, like an unreal world." Echoing the Hammer Dracula, they find refreshments laid out on a cobwebbed table; they then dance insanely to a tom-tom beat for what seems like hours. Finally, "a person outside time" (Lee) shows up, claiming to have sold his soul in order to preserve his lover's beauty and persuading the teens to search the castle for her body. Once they've gone, the clock strikes midnight and he turns into a much younger man, beetle-browed, bearded and staring balefully into camera.

After this genuinely chilling moment, we follow the juves as they explore the castle's every Freudian nook and cranny (spiral staircases, lengthy corridors, a glass-partitioned upper room), after which they return downstairs to find that the lover was concealed in the fireside clock all along. This curious foreshadowing of Jean Rollin's 1970 film Le Frisson des vampires is followed by the beatniks burying the woman outdoors, then rediscovering their roadside victim and realising – surprise surprise – that it's Lee, bringing the film's half-baked metaphysical pretensions full circle. Though it often looks and feels like a student film, Katarsis has loads of atmosphere and benefits from a hypnotic Berto Pisano score. According to Lee, director Veggezzi (or Joseph Veg, as the film's publicity material billed him) committed suicide soon after the film wrapped.

Another Italian project, La vergine di Norimberga (The Virgin of Nuremberg), completed filming at De Paolis Studios on 13 July and was released, with remarkable speed, on 15 August. Fresh from directing Barbara Steele in Danza macabra, Antonio Margheriti was here reunited with producer Marco Vicario and leading man Georges Rivière; he also got the chance to shoot a Gothic horror in luscious colour. The film was based on a novella by Maddalena Gui (writing

Mirko Valentin gives
Rossana Podestà
a demonstration
of "the old ways"
in *La vergine di
Norimberga* (1963)

as Frank Bogart), published back in December 1960 as the 23rd instalment of the pulp series *KKK I classici dell'orrore*. Handily, Vicario was publisher of the KKK series and assigned the female lead to his glamorous wife, Rossana Podestà. Lee was retained for a barely speaking, yet oddly touching, red herring role in a film replete with archaic Gothicisms but also a few pointers to the future.

> Mary Hunter is honeymooning at the Rhineland castle that once belonged to her husband's presumed-dead father. Plagued by visions of mutilated women that turn out to be all too real, she discovers that father-in-law is still on the premises, having been turned into a living skull by Nazi surgeons when he participated in a plot to assassinate Hitler. Convinced that "the old ways are still the best," he's now taken on the persona of a mediaeval torturer called the Punisher.

At the time, the commercial hook for *La vergine di Norimberga* was its promise – only half-fulfilled, as it turned out – of a momentous meeting between Lee's *Dracula il vampiro* and the beauteous *Helen of Troy*, as played by Podestà in Robert Wise's multi-national 1955 epic of the same name. But in retrospect the film's significance lies elsewhere, in its modern-day

## LA VERGINE DI NORIMBERGA

Italy 1963
UK: *The Castle of Terror*
US: *Horror Castle*
*Marco Vicario presents / Atlantica Cinematografica*
85 minutes colour
production ended 13 July 1963

Director of Photography: Riccardo Pallottini; Art Director: Riccardo Dominici; Editor: Otello Colangeli; Sound: Alberto Bartolomei; Music: Riz Ortolani; Make-up: Franco Di Girolamo; Special Effects: Antonio Margheriti; Screenplay: Antonio Margheriti,

Edmond T Gréville, Renato Vicario, based on the original story *La vergine di Norimberga* by Frank Bogart [Maddalena Gui]; Producer: Marco Vicario; Director: Antonio Margheriti

Rossana Podestà (Mary Hunter); Georges Rivière (Max Hunter); Christopher Lee (Erich); Jim Dolen (John Selby); Lucille St Simon (Hilde); Luigi Severini (doctor); Anny Degli Uberti (Marta); Luciana Milone (Trude); Mirko Valentin (General Hunter / The Punisher); Consalvo Dell'Arti; James Borden; Bredon Brett; Peter Hardy; Robert Mayor; Rex Vidor; Patrick Walton; Carole Windsor

*The Castle of Terror* is given a flying start by nicely atmospheric sets and tight editing which never gives the action a moment's rest. Stir in a spirited performance by Rossana Podestà, a nice chamber of horrors, a care for detail (the rats swimming round Max in his watery dungeon), a handful of genuinely chilling moments, and an unusually effective denouement, and it all adds up to a highly enjoyable piece of nonsense, marred only by an irritatingly insistent score. *Monthly Film Bulletin March 1964*

I thought of setting the beginning in an out-of-time place, a 16th century castle, even though right after the opening titles, when a jazz number comes in, you realise we're in modern times. This was another film I shot in a few weeks, three to be precise, and with different cameras. It was the challenge of making pictures that were to be sent all over the world, but doing so on a low budget. *Antonio Margheriti [quoted in Bruschini, Horror all'italiana, 1996]*

setting and string of elaborately conceived murders, marking it out as a precursor of the seminal giallo *6 donne per l'assassino*, which Mario Bava began shooting some four months later at the same Roman landmark

– Villa Sciarra. *La vergine* also confirms the intimate relationship between Italy's horror cinema and its indigenous pulp literature. Having originated in *KKK*, the third link in the chain eventually arrived in April 1965, when the film was adapted as the 51st issue of the photo-comic *Malia I fotoromanzi del brivido*.

Except for a few stodgy bits of exposition, the first two-thirds of *La vergine* are a sustained nightmare for damsel-in-distress Mary. Indeed, Podestà doesn't appear in anything other than a nightie until a full hour has elapsed, and the film might well stand as the last word in 'imperilled beauty exploring old castle' scenarios were it not for the fact that so many were to follow. And the grue content is surprisingly high, too. Even before the credits, Mary advances on the Iron Maiden of the title – the dominant feature of the castle's less-than-cheerful torture museum – and finds in it the unfortunate maid Hilde, with bloody cavities where her eyes once were.

The maid is Lucile Saint-Simon, formerly the winsome love interest of *Les Mains d'Orlac* but here subordinated to displaying pierced sockets in the pre-credits sequence. If Saint-Simon's truncated on-screen presence suggests pre-release cutting, it also suggests a mysterious French connection in an otherwise Italian film. Supporting this view are leading man Georges Rivière, first AD Bertrand Blier (later a distinguished director in his own right) and co-writer Edmond T Gréville, director of *Orlac*.

The film is set, however, in Germany, with some curious references to the war and the Nazi period that would be entirely expunged when it was exhibited in that country. Lee's character, Erich, was batman to Max's supposedly deceased father and sports nasty bomb damage on the left side of his face. Max counters this with "The war left my spirit in a worse state than Erich's face," adding rather unconvincingly, "But it doesn't show." Daddy himself, the so-called General, is a crazed subterranean torturer who, in addition to the Iron Maiden horror, muzzles another victim with a wicker cage containing a hungry rat, causing her nose to be partly chewed off in a startlingly graphic scene. "Its use has been forbidden since the 15th century, because it's too barbaric," he says of the face-cage, adding dreamily, "The mind of man is ever at the service of evil…"

Just as grisly as the tortures is Margheriti's coldly stylish monochrome flashback to the General's agonies at the hands of the Nazi surgeons, a sequence that carries a nasty whiff of Franju's *Les Yeux sans visage* while offering a foretaste of Italy's Nazi exploitation films of the 1970s. For all its gruesome details, however, Margheriti succeeds in making the film

strangely moving. Lee's Erich, for example, cuts a very frightening, watchful figure while patrolling the crypt (the same crypt, incidentally, that appeared in *Danza macabra*), but he's actually a gentle soul. Indeed, Lee reported that, though fitted with a prominent facial scar, "It was quite relaxing, for once, to be able to look at somebody else getting the sticky end of the wedge"[8] – referring to Yugoslav actor Mirko Valentin, encased in Franco Di Girolamo's extraordinarily hideous make-up for the skull-faced Punisher. We first see this frightful visage when Mary whips off the General's black hood in a moment worthy of *The Phantom of the Opera*.

Later, Erich cradles the expiring General in his arms as the castle goes up in flames in a pietà reminiscent of Ygor and the Monster in the old Universal horrors. In his final speech the General stammers out his belief that "The war is over and lost but we go on, still sending thousands of men to their deaths. We must stop this slaughter. We'll have peace again, Erich." A fine sentiment, though it does nothing to justify his habit of torturing and killing people.

## GOTHIC OLD AND NEW

British horror fans, picking up a chunky Pan Books anthology called *The Vampire* in 1965, are unlikely to have known that it was actually a truncated version of a massive, 788-page Italian compendium published by Feltrinelli five years earlier. Nor can they have realised that the Feltrinelli version was almost certainly the inspiration for a couple of recent horror pictures.

*I vampiri tra noi* (Vampires Among Us) was compiled by Ornella Volta and Valerio Riva, though great emphasis was placed on the book's brief introduction by Roger Vadim, to the extent that the cover of the French edition, *Histoires de Vampires*, was adorned not with, say, fangs but a photo of Vadim. Among the 37 items included in the Italian original were the Tolstoy story adapted in Bava's *I tre volti della paura*. Also present was Le Fanu's evergreen *Carmilla*. Already filmed by Vadim himself, the latter would receive a slightly more straightforward adaptation in the form of *La maledizione dei Karnstein* (The Curse of the Karnsteins), which brought Christopher Lee back to Rome, for his fourth Italian Gothic in a three-month period, on 17 July 1963. This Spanish co-production would reach Italian cinemas the following spring under the modified title *La cripta e l'incubo* (The Crypt and the Nightmare), carrying with it a typically extravagant tag-line: '95 minuti di inimmaginabile suspense' (95 minutes of unimaginable suspense).

*Count Ludwig von Karnstein lives in castellated seclusion with his daughter Laura while conducting an*

Nela Conjiù involves
Adriana Ambesi in
arcane rituals in
*La cripta e l'incubo*
(1963)

affair with his youthful parlourmaid Annette. Though describing his arcane researches as "idle curiosity," he's haunted by a family curse that suggests one of his descendants will be a reincarnation of an executed witch called Sheena. When the pretty Ljuba is providentially delivered to the castle, he suspects that Laura's interest in the new arrival might be that of a vampire...

Shot at the Castello Piccolomini in Balsorano, *La cripta*, though earmarked for Antonio Margheriti, went instead to the 62-year-old director Camillo Mastrocinque, who appears to have made a poor impression on the film's youthful screenwriters, Ernesto Gastaldi and Tonino Valerii. "Mastrocinque was a director of meagre talent," claimed Gastaldi. "He directed a lot of comic films in which the leading man [Totò] was also the leading man on the set. When he directed *La cripta e l'incubo*, he was embarrassed."[9] Gastaldi's claims notwithstanding, *La cripta* survives as one of Italy's more stylish Gothics of the period, with a cloying vein of suppressed desire running through it and a group of more than competent actors being upstaged by oodles of crepuscular atmosphere.

Cooked up by Mastrocinque and cinematographers Julio Ortas Plaza and Giuseppe Aquari, the claustrophobic gloom gains considerably in impact

## LA CRIPTA E L'INCUBO

Italy-Spain 1963
Spain: **La maldición de los Karnstein**
UK: **Crypt of Horror**
US: **Crypt of the Vampire**
EI Associates Producers / Hispamer Films
82 minutes b/w
production began 17 July 1963

. . . . . . . . . . . . . . . . . . . . . . . . . . . . . .

Directors of Photography: Julio Ortas,
Giuseppe Aquari; Editor: Roberto Cinquini;
Music: Carlo Savina; Make-up: Emilio Trani;
Story and Screenplay: Tonino Valerii, Ernesto

Gastaldi, from *Carmilla* by J S Le Fanu;
Production Manager: Otello Cocchi; Producer:
Mario Mariani; Director: Camillo Mastrocinque

Christopher Lee (Count Ludwig Karnstein);
Adriana Ambesi (Laura); Pier Anna Quaglia
(Lyuba); José Campos (Friedrich Klauss); Véra
Valmont (Annette); Angelo Midlino (hunchback);
Carla Calò (Ljuba's mother); Nela Conjiù
(Rowena); José Villasante (Cedric [butler]); José
Cortés; James Brightman; uncredited: John Karlsen
(Franz Karnstein); Angela Minervini (Tilde)

**This is occasionally quite atmospheric, with an effective climax and some nice shots of the castle battlements by moonlight and so forth. For the rest, though, it is slow and static, indifferently acted and directed, and poorly dubbed.** Monthly Film Bulletin January 1965 [complete review]

My Swiss time became overwhelmingly Italian ... We moved down to a Gothic pile in southern Italy to make *Maledizione dei Karnstein*, a confection of elements of Le Fanu's *Carmilla*, and here it was my pleasure to be Count Ludwig von Karnstein, the noble father of a brood of Lesbian vampires.
Christopher Lee [*Tall, Dark and Gruesome*, London 1977]

from a judicious use of its airy, outdoor opposite. In broad daylight, a young visitor, Friedrich Klauss, almost shares a kiss with the apparently receptive Laura. With immaculate timing, the panicked neighing of a horse disrupts this tremulous moment. Ljuba's coach comes into view, losing a wheel, and once her attractive, 30-something mother has calculatedly left Ljuba behind, the two girls are suddenly framed in a tight, conspiratorial two-shot as they watch her go. That the young man no longer has a chance in the discreetly lesbian atmosphere initiated by Ljuba's arrival couldn't be clearer. To underline the point, we later see Laura and Ljuba giggling together in the castle's sunlit, tree-lined avenues as Karnstein looks on apprehensively from above.

The touches of lesbianism are faithfully imported from Le Fanu, of course, as is the scene of Ljuba's carefully orchestrated coach accident. The nearly 25 minutes preceding this incident are devoted to several non-Le Fanu details, details with which Mastrocinque and the writers firmly wrestle *Carmilla* into the Italian Gothic idiom perfected by Bava and Margheriti. As played by Christopher Lee, Laura's father is converted into a handsome bibliophile, fretting over his lineage and engaging an art specialist to track down a missing portrait of the baleful Sheena. Klauss, the young restorer, points forward to several such characters in future Italian horrors, while an elaborate recreation of Sheena's crucifixion points blatantly backwards, to *La maschera del demonio*. Gastaldi and Valerii also invent a frosty Karnstein housekeeper, whose job is to cajole Laura into participating in weird rites aimed at resurrecting the witch.

The most intriguing deviation from Le Fanu, however, comes later, with Karnstein, and through him the viewer, being misled into thinking that Laura is the resident vampire and Ljuba the victim. The misdirection is reinforced by Laura's fiery, fulsome exoticism and Ljuba's rather bland, pallid good looks. The two are certainly well cast in this respect. Adriana Ambesi, playing Laura, had just appeared with Lee in *Katarsis*, while Pier Anna Quaglia would be retained by Mastrocinque for his second and last horror picture, *Un angelo per Satana*.

Taper held aloft, Karnstein finally leads an expedition into his ancestral crypt and the truth about Ljuba becomes clear. Mastrocinque plays these climactic passages for all they're worth, though he's scored several bullseyes already. First, Laura's nightmare involves four phantom females gliding eerily into her boudoir; one of them, Ljuba, turns into a grinning skull when Laura languorously kisses her hands. (Given that Laura and Ljuba look like sexually awakening adolescents, Laura's subsequent shock at discovering a huge splotch of blood on her bedsheets carries a surprisingly frank Freudian charge.) Later, the housekeeper cuts the hand from a hanged pedlar and – prefiguring an exactly similar five-fingered prop in *The Wicker Man* – presses it into service as a flaming Hand of Glory. This doesn't prevent her from getting murdered, after which the film reaches an early, and agreeably demented, crescendo when Laura imagines her funeral,

with the corpse suddenly sitting up amid relentless booms of thunder and pointing accusingly at her.

Among *La cripta*'s other pleasing curiosities is Karnstein's rather peculiar relationship with his coquettish parlourmaid, scenes that are nicely played by Lee and Véra Valmont. "Why don't we get married?" she asks. "You could be my daughter," he scoffs. "All right then," she replies. "Adopt me." In addition, in a scene roughly analogous to the Le Fanu passage in which Carmilla spots a passing funeral cortège, Ljuba is given a curiously poetic speech as she sits in the open with Laura. "How beautiful it is here," she points out, "as if Nature sets the scene then waits for the actors to enter, unsure whether they're in a farce or a tragedy. It's the ideal place to live – or die."

After *La cripta e l'incubo* Christopher Lee's sustained Italian summer was finally over, allowing him to return to the UK for a couple of Hammer assignments – *The Devil-Ship Pirates* in August and *The Gorgon* in December. Mario Bava, meanwhile, may well have looked at Margheriti's *La vergine di Norimberga*, one of the other products of Lee's Italian phase, and wondered if he'd been guilty of short-changing the nascent giallo mode. First he'd sent it up (in *La ragazza che sapeva troppo*), then he'd subordinated it to the briefest of the three vignettes contained in *I tre volti della paura*. Now, with *La vergine*, a younger director had come along and made a much more full-blooded proto-giallo. Bava's only option was to make a murder thriller so dazzlingly stylish and bloody that the competition was blown out of the water. This he did in *L'atelier della morte* (The Fashion House of Death), which on release acquired the even more explanatory title *6 donne per l'assassino* (Six Women for the Killer) prior to being rebranded in English-speaking territories with the title arguably best suited to its fetishistic handling of sex and death – *Blood and Black Lace*.

*Isabella is one of the glamorous models at Christian Haute Couture in Rome, a fashion house managed by Massimo Morlacchi on behalf of the Contessa Cristiana Cuomo. When Isabella is brutally murdered, her diary is picked up by fellow model Nicole. Proposing to hand it to the police, she instead gets murdered in her turn. As more models die and the available suspects are rounded up, Inspector Silvestri finds himself completely stumped.*

That Bava's film was intended as a sexed-up Eastmancolor riff on the Edgar Wallace Krimis then coming out of West Germany is obvious from just a cursory glance. Bava and screenwriter Marcello Fondato seem also to have picked up some important tips from Arne Mattsson's *Mannekäng i rött* (Mannequin

Lea Lander stumbles on Mary Arden's disfigured corpse in *6 donne per l'assassino* (1963)

in Red), a chic Swedish murder-mystery from 1958. On top of this, Fondato's plot incorporated a few details familiar from *I vampiri* and *Lycanthropus*, together with a last-reel twist that adapts the famous denouement of *Les Diaboliques*. From these disparate strands Bava crafted a film so lusciously savage that it simultaneously defined a genre while making many of the thrillers that followed it appear redundant.

Despite its unprecedentedly brutal murder sequences, *6 donne* opens with some discreet touches of humour. Scored with a memorably funky bossa-nova theme by Carlo Rustichelli, the credits sequence features a blue-wigged, blood-red mannequin that literally points the viewer towards the 14 leading actors, all of whom are themselves posed like mannequins as their names pop up one by one in the candied glow of Ubaldo Terzano's lighting. The film proper begins with a close-up on a storm-buffeted sign in red and gold; advertising 'Christian Haute Couture', it suddenly departs its moorings, with superb comic timing, as Terzano's camera tracks in towards the impressive mansion in which much of the action will take place. But impish touches like this were smothered for most critics by the ghastliness of the killings. The *Hollywood Reporter's* James Powers, for example, was shaken and disturbed by the film's incipient misogyny, noting that "The murders are particularly grisly, and the corpses are lingeringly photographed with overt sexual and sadistic intent."[10]

Or, as Antonio Bruschini put it 30 years later, "even when dead they pose as pin-ups."[11] The murder of Isabella, for example, follows very rapidly on the comic-yet-ominous collapse of that red-and-gold sign. Suffused in an eerie, phosphorescent light piercing through an overarching canopy of trees, Isabella is buffeted by a persistent wind and finally set upon by a white-masked killer who repeatedly bashes her face against a tree trunk. We're even given a hideous sound effect to suggest flesh being ground

## 6 DONNE PER L'ASSASSINO

Italy-France-West Germany 1963
France: *6 Femmes pour l'assassin* / *L'atelier de la peur*
West Germany: *Blutige Seide*
UK / US: *Blood and Black Lace*
Emmepi Cinematografica / Productions Georges de Beauregard / Monachia Film
86 minutes colour
production began 26 November 1963
. . . . . . . . . . . . . . . . . . . . . . . . . . . . .
Director of Photography: Ubaldo Terzano; Art Director: Arrigo Breschi; Editor: Mario Serandrei; Sound: Vittorio Trentino; Music: Carlo Rustichelli; Make-up: Emilio Trani; Story and Screenplay: Marcello Fondato in collaboration with Giuseppe Barilla,

Mario Bava; Production Manager: Armando Govoni; Producers: Massimo Patrizi, Alfredo Mirabile; Director: Mario Bava

Cameron Mitchell (Massimo Morlacchi); Eva Bartok (Countess Cristiana); Thomas Reiner (Inspector Silvestri); Arianna Gorini (Nicole); Dante DiPaolo (Franco); Mary Arden (Peggy); Franco Ressel (Riccardo Mirelli); Claude Dantes (Tao-Li). Luciano Pigozzi (Cesare Lazzarini); Lea Lander (Greta); Massimo Righi (Marco); Francesca Ungaro (Isabella); Giuliano Raffaelli (Inspector Zanchin); Harriet White (Clarice); Mary Carmen (model); Heidi Stroh (blonde model); Enzo Cerusico (garage attendant); Nadia Anty (model)

Visually, the film's a knock-out. Dramatically, it's a let-down. The plot doesn't really add up even at the end ... However, the fashion salon background gives it all an added interest and horror connoisseurs will surely get a kick out of a film that ravishes the eye even if it does offend the ear. *Daily Cinema* 5 January 1966

I came from Germany doing television and was used to, let's say, dull camerawork. It was fascinating for me to see the imaginative ways in which a camera could be used ... I think the secret was that there was no direct sound. In Germany they always spent a lot of time arranging the microphones. Bava didn't have to bother about that, because everything was dubbed in later. *Thomas Reiner [quoted in Lucas, Mario Bava: All the Colors of the Dark, 2007]* against bark, after which the killer's disposal of the body invites us to admire the dead woman's green knickers, exposed stocking tops and almost-escaping right breast. Much later, Bava contrives a kind of funereal beauty from the death of the strikingly exotic Tao-li; in a scene that was presumably a nod to *Psycho* and, again, *Les Diaboliques*, she's more or less nude when drowned in her bathtub, her doll-like features submerged amid a billowing cloud of blood.

The other murders, equally sensational, contain similar quotes. Peggy, for example, is pressed face-first against a white-hot stove, echoing the pièce de résistance of one of André de Lorde's most famous Grand Guignol dramas, the 1925 hit *Un Crime dans une maison de fous* (A Crime in a Madhouse). Her friend Greta, who's compelled through a complicated set of circumstances to hide Peggy's body, is 'merely' smothered by a sofa cushion, yet this comes after a brilliant sequence in which she's alerted to the presence of an intruder by the unexpected sound of a harp. This reference to Jacques Tourneur's *I Walked with a Zombie* acts like an abstract musical cue for a trick performed by a master magician. The trick takes the form of an eerily smooth tracking shot (the film is full of them) in which the camera glides past the foreground harp to close in on Peggy's half-concealed body. A beat, and then the body is slowly dragged into total concealment by an unseen hand – an ingenious touch that's almost off-handedly macabre.

The film is enriched by an unusually eye-catching cast of characters, ranging from the Contessa's craven male hangers-on (epileptic, impotent or drug-addicted) to female beauties so immaculate they're barely distinguishable from the frozen mannequins lining the salon's showrooms. The action is weighed down, however, by the usual rather stolid police investigation, with a supervising officer who theorises lamely that "Perhaps female beauty makes him [the killer] lose control." This theory, and indeed the inspector himself, is forgotten about as the film hastens to its conclusion, in which Fondato's not especially inspired resolution is really 'sold' by Bava's two leads. Having worked earlier in the year with Boris Karloff and Christopher Lee, Bava realised that no such monolithic Gothic personages were necessary for the ultra-modern scenario of *6 donne*. Having woven an almost supernatural aura around his infallible killer, Bava needed actors compelling enough to convince us of a strictly earthbound conspiracy. The slickly contemporary figures of Eva Bartok and Cameron Mitchell were perfect in this regard, and the edgy chemistry between Cristiana and Massimo brings the film to a gripping climax.

Surprisingly, *6 donne* was only a modest success at the Italian box-office, but its alluringly horrible murders ensured that numerous filmmakers would follow its example, gradually lending substance to a form that was to reach its apotheosis in the early 1970s. For the time being, however, several of these early gialli were rather dull and neutered affairs, containing precious little of Bava's high style.

Among the earliest, Jean Josipovici's *Delitto allo specchio* (Murder in the Mirror) actually came out in the same week as Bava's film, with punters further enticed by a parenthetical subtitle: *(Sexy Party)*. The standard gang of vacuous hipsters, led by Michel Lemoine, is here supplemented by John Drew Barrymore's youthful psychic, and the film's sinister castle setting was to be repeated in several other pictures that cross-fertilised clunky murder sprees with random Gothic trappings. Among these were Gastone Grandi's *24 ore di terrore* (24 Hours of Terror), Angelo Dorigo's *Assassino senza volto* (Killer Without a Face) and Cesare Canevari's splendidly titled *Una jena in cassaforte* (A Hyena in the Safe).

Other time-honoured motifs included the fateful will-reading, as featured in Vittorio Sindoni's *Omicidio per vocazione* (Murder by Vocation) and Dorigo's *A ... come assassino* (A ... for Assassin), the latter based on an Ernesto Gastaldi play from 1960. Also familiar was the 'killings in a girls' school' routine of Antonio Margheriti's *Nude ... si muore* (Naked ... You Die), a project intended initially for Bava and based on a script co-written by Tudor Gates, who would thriftily recycle the setting in the 1970 Hammer horror *Lust for a Vampire*. Other films, like Roberto Mauri's *Le notti della violenza* (The Nights of Violence), made the fundamental error of privileging the dull policemen over the marauding killer. And long before all of these, the form was already ripe for parody. The summer 1964 release *Che fine ha fatto Totò baby?* (What Ever Happened to Baby Totò?) turned veteran comic Totò into a marijuana-crazed killer, complete with numerous good-natured quotes from Robert Aldrich's recent hit *What Ever Happened to Baby Jane?*

The most interesting of these early gialli was the work of Ernesto Gastaldi, not just in his usual role as writer but also as director. In spring 1965 he made a modest four-hander called *Libido*, which established the 'primal scene' template of a young man (Giancarlo Giannini, in his film debut) who has been rendered unstable by the boyhood experience of seeing his father commit a murder. In gravitating towards the giallo after writing a long line of lurid Gothics, Gastaldi was following in the footsteps of Hammer screenwriter Jimmy Sangster, who in 1960, tiring of costume Gothic, had turned producer with the psychological thriller *Taste of Fear* – a film that, given their common debt to *Les Diaboliques*, *Libido* somewhat resembles.

Gastaldi's picture abounds in thunder and lightning, mystery footprints, and macabre tableaux (notably the artfully posed corpse of Dominique Boschero). It also boasts a splendidly contrived ending and a terrific Carlo Rustichelli score. On top of this it has Gastaldi's wife, Mara Maryl, as a ditzy blonde who looks at a Renaissance canvas and says "What big arses people used to paint" – a line that, according to Gastaldi, earned the film a prohibitive certificate. Cast as Maryl's husband in the film is Luciano Pigozzi, a prolific character actor, often billed as Alan Collins, who bore a striking resemblance to Peter Lorre. He'd already played shifty caretakers in *Lycanthropus* and *La frusta e il corpo*, together with one of the enfeebled males in *6 donne per l'assassino* and a hateful Harlequin in *Il castello dei morti vivi*, and he would continue in similar roles for years to come.

## POWER-CUTS AND ULTRASONIC JEWELLERY

Though films like Margheriti's *Danza macabra* and Bava's *La frusta e il corpo* retain their fascination decades later, other Italian Gothics are likely to have induced yawns of indifference even at the time.

Gino Mangini's *La jena di Londra* (The Hyena of London) is a good example. Released in June 1964, it may well have been influenced by the 1957 Boris Karloff vehicle *Grip of the Strangler*, with a pre-credits execution for the so-called Hyena of London (called the Haymarket Strangler in the British film) and a denouement in which the most avuncular character turns out to have a split personality. The film is remarkably precise about the date of the Hyena's dispatch (19 December 1883), yet flashes forward to a period loosely described in an on-screen caption as 'some time ago'; it looks like maybe ten years later. The remainder of that on-screen caption will induce hoots of derision from British viewers, given that the action is apparently situated in 'Bradford, a small village near London'. Unfortunately, the film is a rhythmless slog, despite featuring a renewed murder spree that's apparently attributable to the Hyena. There are a few atmospheric moments, as when a hand is found "sprouting from the ground like a mushroom," plus a halfway effective pursuit and murder of Claude Dantes (so recently submitted

The rapidly fragmenting Giancarlo Giannini drags Dominique Boschero down with him in *Libido* (1965)

to a watery death in Bava's *6 donne per l'assassino*). And, almost inevitably, a cameo role for Luciano Pigozzi.

Two months before *La jena*'s Italian release, West German audiences were treated to a distinctive home-grown riposte to Italy's Gothic shockers. Akos von Ratony's *Der Fluch der grünen Augen* (The Curse of the Green Eyes) was a project unique in the Hungarian director's filmography in that he also produced and co-scripted it. For his antagonists he called upon Adrian Hoven, an actor who was soon to loom large in German horror, and the baleful Wolfgang Preiss, who'd recently played CCC's Dr Mabuse no fewer than five times. When distributed in the USA by Richard Gordon, the film's title was changed to *Cave of the Living Dead* – maybe to avoid confusion with the very different British drama *Girl with Green Eyes*.

*Six young women have been killed within six months, their deaths accompanied by inexplicable power-cuts in the near vicinity. When Inspector Frank Doren is sent to solve the mystery, another victim turns up on the very morning after his arrival – a victim whose body subsequently goes missing from her own wake. Doren finds a glamorous ally in Karin Schumann, assistant to the saturnine Professor Van Adelsberg, whose research is focused exclusively on blood...*

Back in 1959 Wolf C Hartwig had transported a troupe of curvaceous dancers to Yugoslavia for the sex-horror cocktail *Ein Toter hing im Netz*, his example being followed when Harald Reinl chose the ideal location for his Karl May-derived Westerns. Von Ratony went the same route, setting up *Der Fluch* as a Yugoslavian co-production, in the process giving his film a rather

Wolfgang Preiss gives Karin Field an insight into his scientific research in *Der Fluch der grünen Augen* (1963)

## DER FLUCH DER GRÜNEN AUGEN

Germany-Yugoslavia 1963
UK / US: *Cave of the Living Dead*
an A v [von] Ratony production for Objektiv-Film
81 minutes b/w
in production December 1963
. . . . . . . . . . . . . . . . . . . . . . . . . . . . .
Director of Photography: Hrvoj Saric;
Art Director: Ivan Pengow; Editor: Klaus
Dudenhöfer; Sound: F Jurjec; Music:
Herbert Jarczyk; Make-up: Irmgard Forster;

Screenplay: Kurt Roecken; Producer-Director:
Akos von Ratony [Ákos Ráthonyi]

Adrian Hoven (Inspector Frank Doren); Carl
Mohner (village doctor); Erika Remberg (Maria);
Wolfgang Preiss (Professor Van Adelsberg); Karin
Field (Karin Schumann); John Kitzmiller (John);
Tito Strozzi (police chief); Emmerich Schrenk
(Thomas); Vida Juvan (Nani); Stane Sever (Stefan
[landlord]); Laci Cigoj, Danilo Turk (policemen)

**The German crime film, when not directed by Lang, is better ignored, while their fantasy films don't even exist. If we were to mix the two genres, this, I suspect, is what we'd get. A few years back, who would have put their money on 'underrated filmmaker' (etc) Akos von Ratony? A joker, that's for sure.** Cahiers du Cinéma June 1967

**I'm ashamed of that film. This Hungarian director, Akos von Ratony, was a confabulator, but absolutely convinced of what he was doing ... I'd made [John Frankenheimer's] The Train in November, and immediately afterwards I travelled to Yugoslavia to do Der Fluch der grünen Augen ... When I left the cinema after watching it, I hid my face to make sure the audience didn't lynch me on the spot.** Wolfgang Preiss [quoted in Splatting Image June 2003]

special flavour. The landscapes through which Hoven's Inspector Doren moves are authentically cold, flinty and arid, while Von Ratony makes great use of local extras who, among other things, gather curiously at the disinterring of a vampire woman from a well. In a community like this it seems almost reasonable to find an elderly sorceress dispensing her

wisdom over a flaming cauldron, a character who, in the Hollywood of 20 years before, might have been played by Maria Ouspenskaya.

Much of *Der Fluch* is indebted to earlier models, with *Nosferatu* explicitly evoked when a balletic shadow swarms across a blank wall at dead of night and a dark figure with taloned fingernails looms over Erika Remberg in her bed. Yet the swarming shadow also recalls a striking nocturnal highlight of a 1932 potboiler called *The Vampire Bat*, a film that shares with *Der Fluch* a fearful community riven by vampire murders, an urbane investigator, flittering bats, a village idiot character who meets his end in a cave, and a mad scientist engaged in arcane experiments up on the hill. Yet Von Ratony and co-writer Kurt Roecken are careful to introduce a few peculiarities of their own, among them vampires who can only operate for 59 minutes per night (and, when they do, cause power-cuts), a snake that dies when vampire blood is poured on it, and a powder distilled from rose thorns that can eradicate freshly inflicted vampire bites and thus rescue the victim – even if, like Karin, they've already sprouted fangs.

All this is explained by the elderly sorceress, who also shows Doren a vision of tiny nude vampires dancing in her cauldron flames. "They live in the loveliest of bodies," she claims. Elsewhere, however, Von Ratony makes little attempt to emulate the sexy bloodsuckers common to Italian shockers. As Karin, Karin Field undresses for bed in a scene shot teasingly from behind, but Remberg's vampire woman is given only one kinky detail, when she pauses to tear open Karin's blouse while attacking her near the end. In Britain Remberg had made a big impression in her husband Sidney Hayers' 1959 film *Circus of Horrors*, but here she suffers from a paucity of screen time.

And she isn't the only one. Though Hoven is an engaging enough presence as the omnipresent Doren, perhaps the major mystery about *Der Fluch* is that Von Ratony got hold of an iconic figure like Wolfgang Preiss yet gave him so little to chew on. The Professor is a sketchy character; engaged in research that's presumably intended to reverse his own vampirism, he never gets the opportunity to elucidate it even slightly. Indeed, Preiss is given only a couple of good scenes, spookily underlit by leaping firelight on both occasions and muttering scraps of dialogue lifted almost verbatim from Stoker's *Dracula*. When failing to show up in a mirror, he tells Karin that "In this house we don't tolerate vanity," later urging Doren to "Please treat the castle as your own" prior to warning him against transgressing locked doors. "In my old age," adds this well-preserved 53-year-old, "I need much less sleep," an observation that must leave even the most inattentive viewer in no doubt that Van Adelsberg is at the root of the recent murders. Yet Preiss has so much less to do than Lionel Atwill, who played the equivalent role in *The Vampire Bat*.

Despite this miscalculation, Von Ratony works up some palpable atmosphere, cutting regularly to speeded-up clouds scudding across a nocturnal moon and lending genuine grandeur to the torch-lit grotto in which Van Adelsberg is finally dispatched. Happily, Van Adelsberg's well-meaning black manservant is spared the comic relief role he would have played in Von Ratony's Hollywood models; that function is fulfilled instead by inept village cops whom Doren describes as "a couple of comedians." Less happily, the intelligent

The Spanish thriller *Fuego* (1963) was known in America as *Pyro* and in Britain as *Wheel of Fire*

and proactive Karin finally defaults to type at the climax, complaining about being cold and submitting to the local doctor's insistence that "This isn't work for women."

In Spain, meanwhile, filmmakers' reluctance to venture into the fantastic was perhaps exacerbated by the financial failure of an ambitious Cold War fable of the 'assorted people waiting for the bomb to drop' variety; this was Mariano Ozores' *La hora incógnita* (The Unknown Hour), a March 1964 release from Hispamex. But, following the Americanised example of *La cara del terror*, foreign producers were still willing to step in and experiment with the occasional horror-hybrid, as demonstrated by the US entrepreneur Sidney Pink.

Having introduced 3-D to the world with *Bwana Devil* in 1952, Pink had travelled to Europe and been behind such oddities as Denmark's 1960 dinosaur folly *Reptilicus*. A few years later he was in Madrid, setting up a new film with director Julio Coll; the result, *Fuego* (Fire), went into production in April 1963. This strange but engaging shocker plays for half its length like the kind of erotic thriller that would become popular in Hollywood some 25 years later, then transforms into a revenge tragedy modelled on *House of Wax*. With this in mind, Pink reportedly had Vincent Price pencilled in for the lead, but settled for Barry Sullivan instead.

Lushly photographed by Manuel Berenguer, the film keeps one's interest through the accumulation of outré detail. Sullivan is Vance Pierson, an architect obsessed by ferris wheels; cue a certain amount of philosophising about "the wheel of life" and a plot structure that spirals back on itself in the name of tragic inevitability. In another odd touch, Laura Blanco (Martha Hyer), the blonde temptress who coaxes Sullivan away from his wife and daughter, says off-handedly of her own daughter, "Her father was my father" – after which the subject is never raised again. Then, at the halfway mark, comes a thrillingly staged sequence in which the jealous Laura torches Vance's mansion, eradicating his family ties at one stroke. Vance, meanwhile, is consigned to hospital, where an attendant doctor (Paco Morán) explains that

"Not even an army of surgeons would be able to make him look human again."

"Run, Laura, run," rasps Vance, swathed in bandages like the Invisible Man. "My breath on your back will be like a cold wind from Hell." After this dire threat (grippingly played by Sullivan), Laura's paranoid agitation offers Coll a nice opportunity to stage the kind of scene that in Val Lewton films like *Cat People* was dubbed a 'Lewton walk'. Apparently pursued by the quickening tattoo of a man's shoes on a nocturnal Spanish street, her terror is defused by the squealing arrival of a car. Vance's murder spree is perhaps less gripping than the build-up, but it does include a bedroom unmasking in which we get to see his convincingly fire-ravaged features. The film is well-tailored (literally – Mitzou of Madrid dressed Hyer while Petrocelli of New York did the same for Sullivan), and includes substantial roles for future Euro-horror staples Fernando Hilbeck and Soledad Miranda.

Miranda would, in due course, be immortalised in the febrile works of Jess Franco. In the meantime, Franco was occupied at the beginning of 1964 by a loose sequel to his breakout hit *Gritos en la noche*, filmed once again at the Castillo de la Coracera. This was *El secreto del doctor Orloff* (The Secret of Dr Orloff), which not only added an 'f' to Orlof's name but also subordinated him (in the person of Javier de Rivera) to not much more than a sick-bed appearance in the opening reel. This was the first example of the remarkable elasticity of Franco's creations; transplanted to the mid-1960s, this Orloff may be elderly but he isn't nearly as old as he'd be were he the same 'Orlof' we last encountered in 1912. For Franco, Orlof (or Orloff) had already become the totemic mad scientist, adaptable to any setting, period or situation – and, in this instance, acting as the catalyst for a story about another mad scientist altogether.

*The marriage of Inglud and Dr Conrad Fisherman is predicated entirely on civilised hatred, as the doctor's niece Melissa finds out when she stays at their Holfen home over Christmas. There she discovers that her late father, Andros, is also in residence. Having had an affair with Inglud the year Melissa was born, Andros was killed by Conrad but has since been revived via a 'secret' imparted by the ailing Dr Orloff...*

As well as the gorgeous chiaroscuro imagery of veteran cinematographer Alfonso Nieva, *El secreto del doctor Orloff* benefits from a variety of eccentric Franco touches – a grimly tragic story incongruously set at Christmas, a heroine whose bedtime reading consists of an Henri-Georges Clouzot profile in the January 1964 edition of *Elle*, a hate-filled dipsomaniac aunt who comes over like a poor man's version of Martha in Edward Albee's 1962 play *Who's Afraid of Virginia Woolf?* The script, written by Franco and his then-wife Nicole, boasts plenty of wit as well as plot mechanics cheerfully lifted from various PRC and Universal potboilers of the 1940s.

Sent out on missions of murder by his vengeful brother, the pitiful Andros is an obvious nod to the hypnotised Cesare from *Das Cabinet des Dr Caligari*. But pulpier sources are at work in Fisherman's method of enabling Andros to identify his female victims. Recalling the aftershave perfected by Bela Lugosi in *The Devil Bat* and George Zucco's plucked feathers in *The Flying Serpent*, Fisherman uses a trigger mechanism based on ultrasonic transmitters contained in the women's necklaces – all of them personal gifts from Fisherman himself. At the outset Orloff explains to his "most devoted disciple" how ultrasonics are capable of "provoking different kinds of cellular reactions," but this aspect of the plot never rises above gobbledegook. More damagingly, why Fisherman wants these women dead in the first place is a question Franco seems blithely unconcerned about. We're left to infer that they're transient mistresses of his from the nearby town but beyond that we remain resolutely unenlightened.

Yet from such pulpy and loosely motivated devices Franco crafts an unusually haunting film, shadowed in particular by the enmity between Fisherman and Inglud, together with the forlorn figure who came between them and who is now confined to Fisherman's secret lab. The pre-credits sequence immediately arrests the viewer's attention, setting up this triangular relationship in stark, ambiguous images smoked up from Fisherman's mind as he lolls dreamily on the marital bed. Into this combustible ménage steps Melissa with all the guileless innocence of the classic horror heroine. (She's played by the 19-year-old French actress Agnès Spaak, daughter of Charles Spaak – screenwriter of, among others, *La Chambre ardente*.) Soon enough, she gets to meet the father she never knew in a masterful little sequence involving a nocturnal search of the castle. Opening a wardrobe in Andros' long abandoned bedroom, Melissa reverently smoothes the lapel of an old sports jacket before turning to find the man himself staring down at her from the darkness.

As Andros, Hugo Blanco has the intense stare and papery make-up of an earlier mind-control victim, the title character in *The Mad Ghoul* – by coincidence, another old George Zucco vehicle. Blanco achieves memorable moments of weird pathos when visiting

## EL SECRETO DEL DOCTOR ORLOFF

Spain-France 1964
France: *Les Maîtresses du docteur Jekyll*
UK: *Dr Jekyll's Mistresses*
US: *The Secret of Dr Orloff*
Leo Films / Eurociné
91 minutes b/w
production began 28 January 1964

Director of Photography: Alfonso Nieva;
Art Director: José María de la Guerra;
Editor: Ángel Serrano; Sound: Jesús
Jiménez; Music: Daniel White; Make-up:
José Echevarria; Special Effects: Castro;
Story and Screenplay: Nicole Guettard, Jess
Franco, from a novel by David Khune [sic];

Production Manager: Fernando Somoza;
Producer: Leo Lax, Marius Lesoeur [both
uncredited]; Director: Jess Franco

Agnès Spaak (Melissa); José Rubio (Juan
Manuel); Perla Cristal (Rosa); Pastor
Serrador (Inspector Díaz); Hugo Blanco
(Andros Fisherman); Marcelo Arroita-Jáuregui
(Professor Conrad Fisherman); Luisa Sala
(Inglud Fisherman); Daniel Blumer (Carlos
Serrano); Juan Antonio Soler (Siegfried); Magda
Maldonado (Rosa's friend); Manuel Gitián
(Cicero); Javier de Rivera (Dr Orloff); Milagros
Giujarro (Orloff's wife); uncredited: Jess Franco
(nightclub pianist)

El secreto del doctor Orloff [is] directed by Jesús Franco, from whom, after
his most recent productions, we expected a project on a higher level than
horror, monsters, angst and diabolical experiments ... accompanied by
'scary music' and the obligatory trip to a cemetery. Among the performers,
Agnès Spaak, José Rubio and Perla Cristal stand out, along with other
characters well suited to the grisly theme. *La Vanguardia* 25 February 1965

I think, once you've got to know your characters and have told people
something about them, it's occasionally worth deepening, broadening and
adding to them ... I always come back to Orloff, to Radeck, to Pereira. It's
a kind of iconography that surrounds me and I like it ... In that sense you
could say I have done just one, extremely long, film.
Jess Franco [quoted in *Cinefantástico y de terror español 1900-1983*, 1999]

In Italy, *El secreto del doctor Orloff* (1964) was issued as
'Dr Jekyll's Lovers', an appropriation of the Jekyll name that
also applied to the French and British releases

Melissa's bedroom on Christmas Eve and stroking
her hair with his black-gloved hands, or (in a really
striking shot) looking down at his own grave under
a bleakly threatening sky. Climactically gunned down
in the town square, his dying words are "¿Por qué?"
(Why?) – a line arbitrarily changed to "Thank you" in
the English dub. Unfortunately, Fisherman himself
– as played by the poet and film critic Marcelo Arroita-
Jáuregui – is a bearded, bovine, unthreatening hulk far
removed from the elegant villainy of Howard Vernon,
whom Franco's producers apparently couldn't afford.

For all the Expressionist gloom in which the main
narrative is steeped, one of the chief pleasures of
El *secreto* is the idiosyncratic humour that courses
through the film. The romance between Melissa and
José Rubio's charmingly unconventional hero, Juan
Manuel, starts from a standard 'meet cute' situation
and rapidly progresses to some above-average
badinage. "You go for gloomy castles the same way
I go for Sophia Loren," observes Juan Manuel.
"I guess we both like national monuments." Inside
the castle the Fishermans are attended by a crazy old
retainer called Cicero, who explains that he failed to
sleep well because he forgot to go to bed and accounts
for the castle's dilapidation with "The more I let it
slide the less I feel like cleaning it." And the requisite
police investigation – so often the pace-slackening
bane of films like this – is given a boost by the cop
on the case, Inspector Díaz, who suavely skewers the

imprecise accounts of various murder witnesses and
is excellently played by Pastor Serrador.

Confusingly, Eurociné's French version of the
film changed Fisherman's name to Jekyll in order to
facilitate the title *Les Maîtresses du docteur Jekyll*, as well
as adding a couple of rather jarring nude scenes. It's
this slightly compromised edit that remains the most
readily available today.

Having played Dr Fisherman (or, if you prefer,
Dr Jekyll) at the beginning of 1964, Marcelo

Arroita-Jáuregui found himself acting at the very end of the year in a lame 'old dark house' murder-mystery that indicated just how reluctant Spanish filmmakers were to follow Jess Franco into the realms of all-out horror. Pedro Lazaga's El rostro del asesino (The Face of the Killer) slathers the relevant house – the 12th century Monasterio de Piedra in Zaragoza – in plenty of thunder and fog, and gets a bit of mileage out of the interesting faces among the suspects: Jorge Rigaud, Perla Cristal, Fernando Sancho. But, as a mark of its utter failure, it only went out in Spain two years later (in November 1966) as support feature to the 16-year-old Gary Cooper vehicle Bright Leaf.

Another Lazaga film, Un vampiro para dos (A Vampire for Two), made it into cinemas a year earlier, in November 1965. Here, the popular comic duo of Gracita Morales and José Luis López Vázquez become domestic servants to the mild-mannered Baron de Rosenthal (Fernando Fernán Gómez) and his voracious sister Nosferata (Trini Alonso). In addition to the standard vampire gags (with garlic in abundance), this one announces its satirical intent via protagonists who would rather go to Germany to work for genuine bloodsuckers than continue toiling on the Madrid Metro.

## PETRIFIED PLAYERS, BURNING EFFIGIES AND BOGUS RATS

When David Greene's production of Spoon River opened at London's Royal Court Theatre on 13 February 1964, the 28-year-old Canadian actor Donald Sutherland can hardly have imagined it would lead to his first credited film appearance – playing a doltish policeman and a hook-nosed witch in the same film. Two Americans, writer-director Warren Kiefer and fledgling producer Paul Maslansky, had $116,000 to spend on an Italian-French co-production called Il castello dei morti vivi (The Castle of the Living Dead). They saw Greene's production, signed up Sutherland on the spot and flew him to Rome at the end of April.

Curiously, Sutherland would continue in similar vein for the remainder of the year. By late May he found himself at Shepperton for the Amicus picture Dr Terror's House of Horrors and as of September he was at Elstree for the Hammer thriller Fanatic. Once 1964 was out of the way, however, he had no trouble breaking free of the horror mould – unlike the lordly star attraction of both Il castello and Dr Terror. For Christopher Lee, the role of Count Drago in Warren Kiefer's film no doubt seemed like business as usual, though it carried distant echoes of Edgar Allan Poe that, so far, were unique in his career. Kiefer also provided him with some agreeably ominous dialogue,

including such Gothic bon mots as "Many men waste their lives searching for the secret of life. It is the secrets of death that interest me..."

*France, circa 1820. Bruno, leader of an itinerant Commedia dell'Arte troupe, is assaulted by his resident Harlequin and is rescued by a former cavalry captain called Eric. At a loose end, Eric takes over the Harlequin role in time for the company's command performance at the castle of Count Drago. The Count appreciates theatre but has his own peculiar concept of it – a still-life version in which the players are frozen into permanent immobility by "an aqueous secretion of a tropical plant."*

For Italian quota purposes, poor Warren Kiefer had to adopt a pseudonym on Il castello and, thanks to decades of misinformation, was finally subsumed in many reference works by his own alias. Yet, by yoking together such disparate influences as Ligeia, Psycho, House of Wax, The Seventh Seal and The Most Dangerous Game, this native of New Jersey had created one of the most engaging and imaginative of all Italian horror pictures. In particular, his use of Italy's time-honoured Commedia dell'Arte – with its characteristic use of masks and recourse to instantly recognisable archetypes like Columbina, Pulcinella and Pantalone – was a perfect fit for the stock characters and reiterated situations of Gothic horror.

According to contemporary press coverage, "Kiefer had originally written [the film] as a comedy-horror picture. When the American film team brought in Italian co-producers, Serena Films, officials there wanted a straight horror picture ... Now, he feels, they have a picture true horror fans will enjoy and one which should 'give some laughs' to a more sophisticated audience."[12] In making this major adjustment Kiefer had some highly distinguished collaborators. The film's limpid monochrome imagery was captured by Fellini's sometime cinematographer Aldo Tonti, whose operator, Luigi Kuveiller, was soon to become a distinguished cinematographer himself. The interior of the oft-used Castello Odescalchi was transformed by art director Carlo Gentili into a bizarre gallery of petrified falcons, eagles and even pelicans, arranged artfully on indoor trees. Angelo Francesco Lavagnino, taking a break from a long stream of pepla, Spaghetti Westerns and space operas, came up with a lyrical yet at times strangely funky score. And Christopher Lee, who had just returned from making his Hollywood debut in an episode of The Alfred Hitchcock Hour, was brought in for ten of the schedule's 24 days to star as necrophile aesthete par excellence, Count Drago.

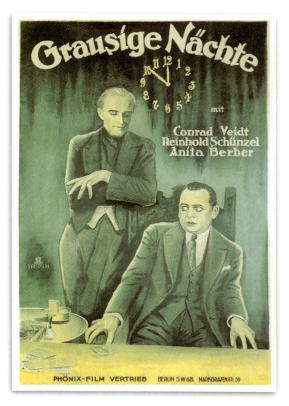

TOP: The early portmanteau film *Unheimliche Geschichten* (1919) was reissued as *Grausige Nächte*

TOP RIGHT: Striking Josef Fenneker artwork for the barely disguised Jekyll and Hyde adaptation *Der Januskopf* (1920)

ABOVE: As well as designing and producing *Nosferatu Eine Symphonie des Grauens* (1921), Albin Grau was also responsible for the advertising art

RIGHT: Conrad Veidt once more, this time striking a Faustian bargain in *Der Student von Prag* (1926)

ABOVE LEFT: The second *Unheimliche Geschichten* (1932) gave greater prominence in its advertising to producer-director Richard Oswald than to star Paul Wegener

ABOVE: Another Faustian bargain, this time in occupied France – *La Main du diable* (1942)

LEFT: Costume Gothic – whimsical but highly atmospheric – was the main ingredient of *Le Baron fantôme* (1942)

BELOW: The ninth issue of the wartime magazine *Grandi film illustrati* focused on the sumptuous Isa Miranda vehicle *Malombra* (1942)

A postwar remake of a peculiar 1920s favourite: *Alraune* (1952)

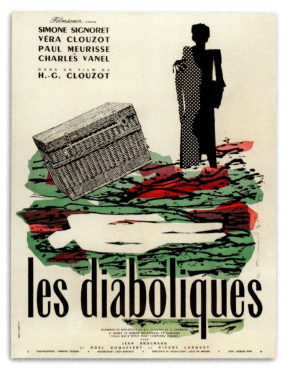

Raymond Gid's classic poster design for *Les Diaboliques* (1954)

Without exaggerating, director Riccardo Freda called
the posters for *I vampiri* (1956) "extremely beautiful"

Italy's response to the success of Hammer's *Dracula*
was *L'amante del vampiro* (1959)

ABOVE: Ambiguous intimacy for Elsa Martinelli and Annette Stroyberg in ...*Et mourir de plaisir* (1960)

ABOVE RIGHT: Mel Ferrer, male lead of ...*Et mourir de plaisir*, moved straight on to the transplant melodrama *Les Mains d'Orlac* (1960)

RIGHT: Mad artist Herbert Boehme, mad scientist Wolfgang Preiss and experimental subject Liana Orfei in *Il mulino delle donne di pietra* (1960)

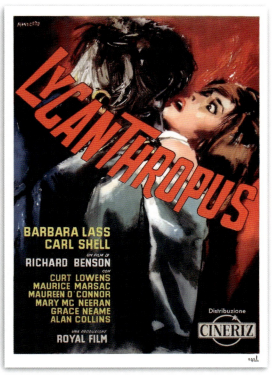

A resurrected witch and a 'medical' werewolf featured in, respectively, *La maschera del demonio* (1960) and *Lycanthropus* (1961)

Jean-Claude Brialy and Nadja Tiller, plus veteran character actor René Génin, appeared in
*La Chambre ardente* (1961, also available in Belgium as 'The Cadaver in the Crypt')

ABOVE: 'If you have nerves of steel ... here's the film that will shatter them.' Mexican advertising for *Gritos en la noche* (1961)

RIGHT: Strikingly macabre locandina for the necrophile shocker *L'orribile segreto del Dr Hichcock* (1962)

FAR RIGHT: Barbara Steele takes aim at a boudoir apparition in the second 'Hichcock' film, *Lo spettro* (1962)

ABOVE: 'A message from beyond opens up *The Crypt of Terror*.' Another Mexican lobby card, this time for *La cripta e l'incubo* (1963)

LEFT: The German release of *La frusta e il corpo* (1963) was delayed until 1967; the poster tag-line became the title of a homegrown shocker the same year

BELOW: Six women, five graves – a fashion house of death was the scene of the trailblazing giallo *6 donne per l'assassino* (1963), while the Barbara Steele vehicle *5 tombe per un medium* (1965) was seen in France as 'Cemetery of the Living Dead'

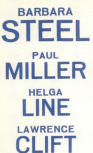

BARBARA
STEEL

PAUL
MILLER

HELGA
LINE

LAWRENCE
CLIFT

JOHN
MC. DOUGLAS

e con
RIK
BATTAGLIA

REGIA:
ALLAN
GRÜNEWALD

UNA PRODUZIONE E DISTRIBUZIONE
CINEMATOGRAFICA "EmmeCi", ROMA

MUSICHE DEL
M. ENNIO MORRICONI

GIRATO SU PELLICOLA
FERRANIA P 30

Vendite all'Estero
FONO ROMA
Via Maria Cristina, 5 - Roma
Tel. 383634

PRINTED IN ITALY BY POLICROM S.p.A.
Roma - Via Tiburtina Km. 14,300

AMANTI D'OLTRETOMBA

ABOVE: Barbara Steele (not Steel) and Paul Muller (not Miller) adorned the lavish fold-out pressbook for *Amanti d'oltretomba* (1965)

LEFT AND BELOW: The eerie ghost girl of Mario Bava's *Operazione paura* (1966) was rapidly co-opted by Federico Fellini for the *Toby Dammit* episode of *Histoires extraordinaires* (1967), in which she was played by Marina Yaru

Yugoslavia's Mirko Valentin, Italy's Gaia Germani, France's Philippe Leroy and Britain's Christopher Lee starred in _Il castello dei morti vivi_ (1964), a film made by Americans in Rome

As equal parts mad artist and mad scientist, Drago is a compound of numerous characters – Zaroff from _The Most Dangerous Game_ (he actually refers to humans as "the most interesting and most dangerous animal of all" at one point), Franco's Dr Orlof (caressing the heroine's face and murmuring, "You should never grow old; you should stay like this forever"), any number of Poe protagonists (he waves drink away with "My health forbids it" and keeps his perfectly preserved wife in a massively cobwebbed four-poster), and the deranged sculptors of _Mystery of the Wax Museum_ and its remake _House of Wax_. In the latter guise, he finally reveals a creepy hidden room worthy of Bluebeard himself, peopled with humans who have been calcified rather than merely stuffed. And given that Lee is playing the role – "made up," as one British reviewer put it, "to look like a walking cadaver"[13] – there are also the expected echoes of Dracula, from a castle approach in which no bird sings to an opening line that runs, predictably, "Welcome to my home."

But as the panda-eyed Drago, Lee is more than his usual frosty self. His delighted laughter and applause during the troupe's command performance is truly manic, and at the end, when stabbed with his own embalming scalpel by a vengeful witch, he enjoys one of his most memorable screen deaths – bent double, hair flopping forward, face frozen into a disbelieving scream. As for Donald Sutherland, his turn as a local

## IL CASTELLO DEI MORTI VIVI

Italy-France 1964
France: _Le Château des morts vivants_
UK / US: _The Castle of the Living Dead_
Serena Film / Filmsonor
90 minutes b/w
production began 27 April 1964
. . . . . . . . . . . . . . . . . . . . . . . . . . . .
Director of Photography: Aldo Tonti; Art Director: Carlo Gentili; Editor: Mario Serandrei; Music: Angelo Francesco Lavagnino; Make-up: Guglielmo Bonotti; Story

and Screenplay: Warren Kiefer; Production Manager: Renato Dandi; Producer: Paul M Maslansky; Director: Warren Kiefer

Christopher Lee (Count Drago); Gaia Germani (Laura); Philippe Leroy (Eric); Mirko Valentin (Sandro); Donald Sutherland (Sergeant Paul / witch); Renato Terra Caizzi (Forge); Antonio De Martino (Neep); Luciano Pigozzi (Dart); Ennio Antonelli (Gianni); Jacques Stany (Bruno); Luigi W Bonos (Marc, policeman)

Utterly unbelievable, of course, but a smashing chiller-diller of the Germanic sick school ... In style it reminds me strongly of the original and horrifying tales by the Brothers Grimm ... Not for those whose taste is for the subtleties of the psychological thriller, but a feast of the macabre for those who enjoy an out and out weirdie. _Daily Cinema_ 23 February 1968

It's a fairy tale for grown-ups ... The co-operation we got from everyone couldn't have been more excellent. Without it we wouldn't have had a prayer of achieving what we did ... It pays off, because if you can make a good film for less than $150,000 you've got half the battle won. _Warren Kiefer_ [quoted in _Daily American_ 30-31 August 1964]

policeman is an engaging echo of Kiefer's original comic intentions, while his contorted witch is as outré a cross-dressing casting choice as Elspeth Dudgeon's centenarian patriarch in _The Old Dark House_.

_Il castello_ has much else to commend it, notably an unusual setting in the Napoleonic era and some extremely atmospheric scenes set in the sunlit Parco dei Mostri at Bomarzo, complete with Pirro Ligorio's monstrous 16th century sculptures. There,

Drago officiates at a lugubrious funeral ceremony and his homicidal manservant pursues the troupe's resourceful dwarf around the massive stone beasts. (The manservant, Sandro, is played by the cadaverous Mirko Valentin – reversing the master-servant relationship he and Lee had played out in *La vergine di Norimberga*.) And the final tableau – as hero, heroine and dwarf ride off into the sunset – is as conventional a happy ending as could be imagined, but it's movingly played by Philippe Leroy, Gaïa Germani and Antonio De Martino. The last of these actors, incidentally, has since fallen prey to the identity crises that seem to dog this film, with various commentators claiming that he's the same actor as Skip Martin, who played dwarfs in such British films as *The Masque of the Red Death* and *Vampire Circus*. He isn't.

While filming *Il castello dei morti vivi*, Christopher Lee told a 23-year-old film journalist called Dario Argento that his next project was to be another Italian one – an AIP-sponsored adaptation of H P Lovecraft's *The Dunwich Horror*, to co-star Boris Karloff and to be directed by Mario Bava. Sadly, this didn't come to pass; the project would be handed on to Dean Stockwell, Ed Begley and Daniel Haller when the film was finally made in California in 1969. Argento would go on to become a major director in his own right, assuming Bava's mantle throughout the 1970s. But while Lee was talking to Argento, an even younger director-to-be, the monied 20-year-old Englishman Michael Reeves, was making an early foray into the film industry by directing bits and pieces of second-unit work on *Il castello dei morti vivi*. He would later direct *The Sorcerers* and *Witchfinder General* back in the UK; indeed, for the latter he borrowed *Il castello*'s use of a 'time-and-place' opening narration.

In the meantime, screenwriters Ernesto Gastaldi and Tonino Valerii, having adapted Le Fanu's *Carmilla* as *La cripta e l'incubo*, resurrected the baleful Karnstein name in 1964 for what could loosely be considered a prequel, investigating what happened to the family in the dying days of the 15th century. Producer Felice Testa Gay (making his one-and-only Gothic) crushed Valerii's ambitions to direct, selecting the reliable Antonio Margheriti instead. Shot in three weeks using Margheriti's time-saving multi-camera method, the film reunited him with Barbara Steele, whose first Gothic this was since Margheriti's *Danza macabra* some 18 months before. According to Steele, the director was "very assertive, emotional and aggressive. I liked him very much, but I had such enormous collisions with Margheriti it's very strange that I worked with him twice. I don't know whether you felt it or not in those films, but we had total conflict

all the way. I guess he wanted a certain kind of rage and energy from me."[14]

This time round, those enormous collisions helped produce a film that seems to have held more appeal for Italian audiences than most Gothics. Sporting a promisingly creepy title – *I lunghi capelli della morte* (The Long Hair of Death) – Margheriti's latest made 321,000,000 lire, more than three times the amount earned by *Danza macabra*.

*September 1499. Feckless aristocrat Kurt Humboldt marries Elizabeth Karnstein, the daughter of a woman burned at the stake several years previously for murdering Kurt's uncle. Kurt was the real murderer, and now – as the plague prophesied by Elizabeth's mother sweeps through the surrounding area – he plans to kill Elizabeth too. For he has since fallen in love with the beautiful Mary, unaware that she is the fleshly shade of Elizabeth's vengeful stepsister, Helen Rochefort.*

'At the end of the 15th century, cruelty, superstition and frightful evils loomed over mankind.' So reads an opening title card, rooting the action in a period not often visited in horror pictures. The era is recreated with some fidelity, helped considerably by Riccardo Pallottini's atmospheric photography of the imposing Castello Massimo overlooking Arsoli. That the period was important was confirmed by Margheriti in 1995. "That was a different kind of picture [to *Danza macabra*]," he pointed out. "They wanted to do more of a historical picture with horror elements. I don't know if that was the right idea. It's not a bad picture, but it's not *Danza macabra* – that's a ten times better picture."[15]

Margheriti wasn't far off in this estimate, for *I lunghi capelli della morte* fails to live up to its title. Aside from a few well-realised set-pieces, and a conspicuously grim case of poetic justice at the climax, the action tends to be rather stiff and somnolent, as if the perpetually busy Margheriti was feeling a bit burned out and couldn't muster the requisite enthusiasm. The late-mediaeval setting was mandated, in any case, by a new phase in the Italian reliance on Roger Corman's Poe pictures. The usual suspect, *Pit and the Pendulum*, is quoted in Kurt's ironic fate at the end, but a more recent Corman entry, *The Masque of the Red Death*, accounts for the entire subplot about a castle stronghold that's seemingly impervious to the pestilence raging outside.

Even so, when *I lunghi capelli* works up its intermittent heads of steam, the results are memorable. The witch burning at the beginning echoes *La maschera del demonio* yet again, but with an intriguing variation in that poor Adele Karnstein is boxed in behind a strange

Laura Nucci checks
on Barbara Steele's
nocturnal activities
in *I lunghi cappelli
della morte* (1964)

construction of thatched ramparts that are then set
ablaze. Her dying curse has a pleasingly apocalyptic
ring, too – "You'll suffer this death of mine on the
last day of this century!" A visit to the Humboldt
vaults produces a nice shudder of revulsion when
the murdered uncle, who's little more than a tattered
skeleton, appears to stir into life – but only because rats
are rioting in his empty chest cavity. The resurrection
of Helen is impressively done too, with a lightning
bolt striking her rain-lashed grave in a welter of mud –
though the lap-dissolves that show her skull gradually
taking on boggle-eyed flesh are clumsy in the extreme.

That an apocalyptic tone was sought by the
filmmakers is confirmed when Helen makes her
subsequent entrance in the Humboldt chapel;
moments earlier, Umberto Raho's sanctimonious
priest was quoting the lines in the Book of Revelation
regarding the Seventh Seal. (Perhaps it was no
coincidence that Ingmar Bergman's film of that title
was one of Corman's inspirations when making *The
Masque of the Red Death*.) After this, however, the action
devolves into yet another replay of *Les Diaboliques*,
with the repugnant Kurt murdering his wife and
being driven to hysteria by reports that she's still
alive. At least Giorgio Ardisson gives his all to these
scenes, and they wind up with a particularly explicit
restatement of the now-familiar 'you've been sleeping
with a corpse' theme. "Look inside that sarcophagus,

# I LUNGHI CAPELLI DELLA MORTE

*Italy* 1964
UK / US: **The Long Hair of Death**
*Cinegay*
100 minutes b/w
*visa date* 29 December 1964
. . . . . . . . . . . . . . . . . . . . . . . . . .
Director of Photography: Riccardo
Pallottini; Art Director: Giorgio Giovannini;
Editor: Mario Serandrei; Sound: Giulio
Tagliacozzo; Music: Carlo Rustichelli;
Make-up: Euclide Santoli; Story : Ernesto

Gastaldi; Screenplay: Tonino Valerii,
Antonio Margheriti; Production Manager:
Ferruccio De Martino; Producer: F Testa
Gay; Director: Antonio Margheriti

Barbara Steele (Helen Karnstein / Mary
Karnstein); Giorgio Ardisson (Kurt Humboldt);
Halina Zalewska (Elizabeth Karnstein); Umberto
Raho (Von Klage); Laura Nucci (Grumalda);
Giuliano Raffaelli (Count Humboldt); Giovanni
Pazzafini (friar); Jeffrey Darcey (messenger)

The effort to lend conviction to the gloomy atmosphere of this dark witchcraft
story is basically useless, because the clunky plot ends in tedium, failing even
to elicit laughter with its awkward resolutions. Both direction and acting are
on the same, very mediocre level. *Segnalazioni cinematografiche* Vol 57, 1965

The screenplay we had was very badly written ... On the set, a lot of things
turned out to be stupid or impossible, so we had to invent a lot and improvise
every day ... There was hardly any time to think, to invent, or write something
down properly, because we had to shoot, shoot and shoot. Something is
wrong with that film. Antonio Margheriti [quoted in *Video Watchdog* May-June 1995]

Kurt," grins Steele's ghostly Helen. "Go on. Take a
look at the woman you devoted all your embraces to."
Sure enough, inside the casket is a mass of hair and
a suppurating, worm-crawling face that forces a very
satisfying scream from the traumatised Kurt.

Elizabeth and her dead stepsister's concerted
revenge on the rotten-to-the-core patriarchy that Kurt
represents is satisfying all round. ("You can't refuse,"
he told the reticent Elizabeth on their wedding night.
"I am your master.") The film also gains interest

from some curious coincidences. Kurt, for example, finds the supposedly dead Elizabeth's hair in her hairbrush, an incident also present in the film Roger Corman was making at exactly the same time, *The Tomb of Ligeia*. And, having featured a Hand of Glory in *La cripta e l'incubo*, this time Gastaldi and Valerii predicted another major prop from *The Wicker Man*, consigning Kurt to a fiery death in a grotesque wicker effigy at the end. Not only that; by showing Kurt's viewpoint from inside it, Margheriti anticipated the skull's-eye-view shots featured in the 1965 film *The Skull*.

*I lunghi capelli della morte* reached Italian cinemas on the penultimate day of 1964. The following week the American actor Peter Baldwin, last seen being razor-slashed by Barbara Steele in *Lo spettro*, was back in Italy to make *La donna del lago* (The Lady of the Lake). This exceptional collaboration between Luigi Bazzoni and Franco Rossellini, in which Baldwin's world-weary novelist arrives in an isolated backwater in quest of a mysterious hotel waitress, has latterly been claimed as a proto-giallo, though in fact there's little to identify it as such. It mainly qualifies as horror thanks to the extraordinary climate of unspecified menace that Bazzoni and Rossellini conjure up from almost nothing. Snow, ice and plenty of queasily irradiated monochrome switch the viewer from past to present, passing through dreams en route, and finally bringing Baldwin, as he puts it, "to the point of almost losing touch with reality."

Virna Lisi, hovering on the brink of international stardom, is the unattainable female, seen only in abstracted lovemaking flashbacks in which the lover might be the town's hotelier, or his son, or both – and with only the muted cawing of a bird on the soundtrack as Baldwin tries to make sense of his memories. Salvo

Virna Lisi as the unattainable lover in the quietly menacing *La donna del lago* (1965)

Randone is splendid as the simultaneously affable and sinister hotelier, and as the mystery of the woman's death – was it murder or suicide? – approaches its resolution, Baldwin receives one of the most alarmingly worded notes in the genre: "I'll meet you in the slaughterhouse at 11." Renzo Rossellini's excellent music sets the doom-laden tone, and the denouement, though slightly rushed and rather pat, is nevertheless a great showcase for the always watchable Valentina Cortese. Looking back to Resnais' *L'Année dernière à Marienbad*, the film also points forward to Bazzoni's cult 1974 film *Le orme* (Footsteps), in which the Baldwin role was taken on by Florinda Bolkan.

Another film made right at the beginning of 1965 – Garibaldi Serra Caracciolo's *La settima tomba* (The Seventh Grave) – demonstrated the wide differential in quality that Italian horror was capable of. This one began production in February and proves two things. First, that the proprietors of the Castello Piccolomini at Balsorano would let just about anybody shoot there. Second, that any film in which a hamster is cast as a rat is likely to reside at the very bottom of the Italian Gothic barrel. The last film guilty of the hamster-rat confusion was *Metempsyco*, and that was quite bad enough. *La settima tomba* is even worse, an on-the-cheap retread of every 'will reading at midnight' plot ever devised, unmarked by any trace of style, atmosphere or even incident, and a film so ossified it could have been made 40 years earlier.

Set in 'Old Scotland' (wherever that may be), the action plays out at Nofis Castle, once home, apparently, to Sir Francis Drake. Its most recent incumbent died of leprosy, "so disfigured by the disease that an autopsy wasn't possible." In fact he's still alive, leprous but not disfigured at all, and intent on transfusing the taint into the psychic heroine via some unspecified blood transfer. "Leprosy can heal, I assure you," he raves. "You'll be like me. Soon!" The film has a halfway decent seance sequence, in which Stefania Menchinelli's striking face and intense performance are used to good effect. But the rest is tedium.

## STOPPED CLOCKS, DEAD LOVERS AND SPACE VAMPIRES

In 1965, Massimo Pupillo directed three horror pictures in rapid succession prior to disappearing from the horror scene as rapidly as he'd arrived. Trained in France by Marcel Pagnol, he concentrated

Faithless wife Barbara Steele and duplicitous solicitor Riccardo Garrone in *5 tombe per un medium* (1965)

on documentary shorts prior to being engaged by the US producer Ralph Zucker for the first two films in this unexpected horror triptych. These were *5 tombe per un medium* (Five Graves for a Medium) and *Il boia scarlatto* (The Crimson Executioner), which in due course would form a memorable US double-bill as *Terror-Creatures from the Grave* and *Bloody Pit of Horror*. For the first, which began production in January 1965, Zucker shot a couple of extra gore scenes for the American market, prompting Pupillo, perversely, to grant him full director credit in all territories. "I didn't give a fuck,"[16] he explained some 30 years later.

> Spring 1911. When solicitor Josef Morgan is summoned by Jeronimus Hauff to his secluded villa, Morgan's younger colleague, Albert Kovac, goes in his place – only to find that Hauff has been dead for very nearly a year. Hauff, it transpires, was a necromancer who claimed to have established contact with the area's 500-years-dead plague victims. Now he proposes to use their spirits in avenging his own murder.

Reserved for US viewers, Zucker's gruesome highlights included a pre-credits sequence in which a man is trampled by his own horse, and later a wheelchair-bound paraplegic impaling himself on a sabre. Though only in black-and-white, the first gave gorehounds an exposed eyeball to savour, the second nothing less than a lapful of heaving intestines. The film is certainly better off without these scenes, though the impalement is arguably more plausible than the old man's death in the Italian version, in which he somehow contrives to hang himself from a sitting position.

With or without gore scenes, the real selling point of *5 tombe* was Barbara Steele, who, according to Pupillo, behaved like a diva on set until given a directorial talking-to in front of the entire crew on the fourth day. She may have had good reason to be a bit impatient by this stage; the unrewarding

## 5 TOMBE PER UN MEDIUM

Italy-USA 1965
UK / US: **Terror-Creatures from the Grave**
MBS Cinematografica | GIA Cinematografica | International Entertainment
90 minutes b/w
in production January-February 1965
· · · · · · · · · · · · · · · · · · · · · · · · · · ·
Director of Photography: Carlo Di Palma; Art Director: Gabriele Crisanti; Editor: Mariano Arditi; Sound: Goffredo Salvatori; Music: Aldo Piga; Make-up: Vittorio Biseo; Screenplay: Romano Migliorini,

Roberto Natale; Producers: Francesco Merli, Ralph Zucker, Massimo Pupillo; Associate Director: Ralph Zucker; Director: Massimo Pupillo

Barbara Steele (Clio Hauff); Walter Brandi (Alfred Kovac); Mirella Maravidi (Corinna Hauff); Alfredo Rizzo (Dr Nemek); Riccardo Garrone (Josef Morgan); Luciano Pigozzi (Kurt); Ennio Balbo (Oscar Stinner); Tilde Dall'Aglio (Louise); Ignazio Dolce; Armando Guarnieri; Pietro Sartori; Lucio Zarini

Lightning flashes and booming thunder set the stage for the more supernatural phases of this macabre drama ... Fortunately, in what is otherwise a rather routine and stilted exercise in horror, more grisly fare is provided in the form of a collection of mummified limbs on permanent exhibition at the sinister villa, in which the ever-dependable Barbara Steele seems comfortably at home. *Monthly Film Bulletin* November 1968

> To check if the [special] effects were working I attended a screening in a very popular movie theatre in Rome on Via Prenestina. I sat behind a big guy who was almost bald, and I waited for the thumping heart scene. As the scene progressed I could see drops of sweat slowly dripping from this guy's head and he mumbled to himself, "Fucking son of a bitch." To me that was the best compliment!
> Massimo Pupillo [quoted in *Shock: The Essential Guide to Exploitation Cinema*, 1996]

role of Jeronimus Hauff's faithless widow could have been played by anybody. Looking more gaunt than ever in this film, she was presumably hired to give the character a Morticia Addams look that would pep up the posters. Perhaps echoing Steele's own disenchantment, Clio Hauff is portrayed as an aspirant aristocrat who was formerly on the stage. Prior to her show-stopping death, Clio's self-pitying account of being set down by her husband in a provincial backwater ("among wolves," as she puts it) is Steele's only good scene, though it's cut short rather acidly when Clio's stepdaughter Corinne says, "Don't forget what a bad actress you were..."

The film is a strange mixture of familiar and unfamiliar elements, and it's rather listlessly paced until the final outbreak of post-mortem revenge in the final reel. Among the familiar elements are a Harker-like solicitor being engaged by a dead man, a secretary who points out fearfully that "Bregoville is a town forgotten by God, a cursed place," a storm intervening to force Kovac into staying the night, and the recurrent Italian emphasis on marital infidelity being punished from beyond the grave. Indeed, Steele was due to go through the whole routine again in Mario Caiano's *Amanti d'oltretomba* just a few months later.

Among less time-honoured devices are a dead owl rammed into the engine of the solicitor's motor car, a villa built on the site of a 15th century lazar house in which "hundreds of people died," an extensive collection of clocks that stopped at the moment of their owner's death, plus a display cabinet at Villa Hauff featuring half-a-dozen severed hands and another crammed with skulls and unspecified organs in glass jars. "An eccentric sort, this Jeronimus Hauff," muses Kovac. "Clearly a scientist, or at any rate someone who enjoyed upsetting his guests." Hauff was also given to recording his experiments on a phonograph, and when Kovac listens to the dead man's mutterings on the wax cylinders the film exactly anticipates a key scene in Sam Raimi's *The Evil Dead*.

At dinner on his first night, Kovac makes a ridiculous social gaffe when he assumes Corinne is the daughter, rather than stepdaughter, of the conspicuously youthful-looking Clio. He's an uninspiring character throughout, and Walter Brandi – the sometime vampire of *L'amante del vampiro* and *L'ultima preda del vampiro* – isn't the kind of actor to lift him off the page. Alfredo Rizzo, another veteran of *L'ultima preda*, is much more fun as the pragmatic Dr Nemek. At one point, while piecing together the details of the curse Nemek consults a town clerk who perches at a high desk as if imported direct from *Das Cabinet des Dr Caligari*. In an elementary continuity blunder, this lank-haired pen-pusher tells Nemek that Hauff died in May 1910, contradicting the date carved on Hauff's gravestone.

Cinematographer Carlo Di Palma – who at the time was between jobs for Michelangelo Antonioni on *Il deserto rosso* and *Blow Up* – lends icy atmosphere to a daytime exhumation scene, including a striking coffin-POV shot of Hauff's black-clad widow and daughter wearing elaborate hats at the graveside. And Steele lends a characteristically perverse touch to a lovemaking scene in which she bites her own arm rather than her partner's. But things only really hot up in the flashback to Hauff's murder, when Pupillo treats us to weird close-ups of the conspirators' insane laughter, after which Hauff's clocks suddenly reanimate themselves and the eerie creaking of an invisible plague wagon announces the so-called "night of revenge". The severed hands start flexing, the bottled organs begin to pulse, and the victims acquire nasty plague sores prior to slumping dead beside globes, harps and grandfather clocks. It's a barnstorming climax but perhaps not quite enough to justify the build-up. Even so, *5 tombe* was confidently advertised to Italian cinemagoers as 'un film fatto su misura per chi ama divertisi con il cuore in gola' – roughly speaking, 'a picture tailor-made for people who like heart-in-mouth entertainment'.

While Barbara Steele was playing Clio Hauff in February 1965, a uniquely tantalising prospect arose – a proposed teaming of Steele with Christopher Lee. The film, *Diabolica* (aka *Trance*), was to be directed by Fulvio Tului but sadly went unmade. Over in the UK, the distribution arm of Tigon British was well aware of the value such a teaming might have; in February 1968 they put *Il castello dei morti vivi* and *5 tombe per un medium* together 'in a big Double X programme' and splashed the pressbook with the banner headline 'Lee & Steele! – Names That Spell Terror!' Unfortunately, Tigon's production arm wasn't quite so astute. The Tigon film *Curse of the Crimson Altar* was just being completed at the time, with Lee, Steele and none other than Boris Karloff in the cast – but the finished product kept Steele strictly segregated from her male co-stars.

Back in spring 1965, soon after the disappearance of the *Diabolica* project, Steele found herself cast instead in Mario Caiano's *Amanti d'oltretomba* (Lovers from Beyond the Grave). Italy's Gothic horrors were now becoming so self-referential that it was time for a kind of 'Barbara Steele's Greatest Hits' package; the only significant omission from Caiano's script was an introductory witch-burning, its place being taken by an extended torture scene for a faithless wife and her lover. Caiano shot the film in a mere 18 days in the Villa Parisi at Frascati, and he was enough of a Gothic aficionado to craft his pseudonym – Allan Grünewald – from a combination of Edgar Allan Poe and the German Renaissance artist Matthias Grünewald. To underline the point, he decorated the film's opening credits with a particularly grim painting, attributed to Grünewald, called *The Dead Lovers*.

Lovers from beyond the grave: Barbara Steele and Rik Battaglia materialise in the upper reaches of Villa Parisi in *Amanti d'oltretomba* (1965)

1872. Dr Stephen Arrowsmith affects to leave for a symposium in Edinburgh but instead interrupts the lovemaking between his wife Muriel and their groundsman, David. Having tortured the pair to death, he uses Muriel's electrified blood to restore the beauty of the withered housekeeper, Solange, who becomes his mistress. He then marries Muriel's monied stepsister Jenny – whose history of mental imbalance he exploits without mercy. But the shades of Muriel and David step in to thwart him.

According to the film's English-language trailer, the ever-calculating Dr Arrowsmith is "a merciless and diabolical sadist." True enough; of all the Sadean figures proliferating in Italian horror, Arrowsmith was arguably the nastiest yet. Unfortunately, he also remains the most one-dimensional. Paul Muller was returning to horror for the first time since appearing in the pioneering *I vampiri* and would soon become one of the most ubiquitous presences in the genre. Yet there's not a lot he can do with Dr Arrowsmith other than knit his satanic brows together under a conspicuously bad wig. He's doing exactly that in the film's opening shot – an extreme close-up in which hellish plumes of smoke waft over his face while he tortures a spread-eagled frog. But at no point do we get any insight into the man, a failing that gives the film a rather mechanical feel

## AMANTI D'OLTRETOMBA

Italy 1965
UK: *The Faceless Monster*
US: *Nightmare Castle*
Cinematografica EmmeCi
104 minutes b/w
in production April-May 1965

......................................

Director of Photography: Enzo Barboni; Art Director: Massimo Tavazzi; Editor: Renato Cinquini; Sound: Bernardino Fronzetti; Music:

Ennio Morricone; Make-up: Duilio Giustini; Story and Screenplay: Mario Caiano, Fabio De Agostini; Production Manager: Carlo Caiano; Producer-Director: Mario Caiano

Barbara Steele (Muriel Arrowsmith / Jenny Arrowsmith); Paul Muller (Dr Stephen Arrowsmith); Helga Liné (Solange); Marino Masé (Dr Derek Joyce); Giuseppe Addobbati (Jonathan, butler); Rik Battaglia (David)

**Barbara is both brunette and blonde; there are dream sequences (overexposed, just as they should be); the disrobings and amorous delights have been abbreviated by the French censor. In short, it's all very enjoyable, despite some longueurs and the first reel playing like a small scrap from a portmanteau movie.** *Cahiers du Cinéma June 1966*

**That's a film I really love ... The only flaw the film had, in my opinion, was that it was made in black and white at a time when audiences wanted to see films in colour. Actually, in the beginning I'd intended it to be made in three colours: black, white and red ... But the process would have meant expenses that my producer wasn't prepared to meet and so nothing came of the idea.** *Mario Caiano [quoted in Palmerini / Mistretta, Spaghetti Nightmares, 1996]*

as Arrowsmith's one-note schemes wind their way to an eventual running time of 104 minutes.

Among Italian Gothics, this makes *Amanti d'oltretomba* almost as long as the bloated *Seddok*, and while watching the film it's sometimes hard to suppress a twinge of sympathy for the film's UK distributors, New Realm, who in 1969 drastically reduced it to a mere 73 minutes. They also changed the title to *The Faceless Monster*, presumably in reference to one of the stand-out scenes that make the film worth watching. Here, the beleaguered Jenny is woken by a booming clock and rushing wind, together with the combined sounds of her predecessor, Muriel, sighing in orgasm and shrieking in agony. She then 'dreams' a genuinely eerie greenhouse scene. Foggily occluded in an unearthly white light, she re-enacts Muriel's tryst with the gardener prior to the intervention of the poker-wielding Arrowsmith, whose face is rendered a featureless blur by the simple expedient of a stocking mask.

The opening, too, is powerful stuff. With cinematographer Enzo Barboni sending her shadow soaring into the upper reaches of the Villa Parisi, Steele's raven-haired Muriel is a truly imposing figure. The surging rhapsody of Ennio Morricone's score (his first for a horror film) is ideally suited to the tainted romance that develops, with the hunky David clumping his way up the stairs as Muriel slowly disrobes in her boudoir. Wrapped in his embrace, she tells him that "I'm going to rid you of your vulgar ways and replace them with others much more subtle and refined" – an extremely odd pre-coital pronouncement that, sadly, is typical of the film's clunking English dialogue track.

The ensuing torture sequences are pretty extreme for 1965, with David belaboured by a flaming poker, Muriel anointed with acid via a specially rigged pipette, and the pair of them finally electrocuted on the marital bed in a grotesque parody of orgasm – perhaps accounting for the film's provocative working title, *Orgasmo*. Through it all the weakened Muriel denounces Arrowsmith with teeth-baring relish, seeming to draw strength from her pain – a sadomasochist detail made explicit at the end when the risen Muriel tells her husband that "Now I'm going to reward you with that same pleasure." Though it takes a very long time for them to reappear, the rising of the lovers makes for a scintillating climax, with their ghosts – as obstinately corporeal as those featured in *Danza macabra* – called into being when a young doctor finds their extracted hearts on a kind of kebab skewer and un-transfixes them. Arrowsmith is messily incinerated in his own torture chair and the young doctor consoles Jenny with the virtually parodic curtain line, "Don't worry, Jenny. Now all of your nightmares are over and done with forever."

After its opening reference to *Lady Chatterley's Lover*, the film subsequently recalls such 'haunted second wife' narratives as *Rebecca* and *Ligeia* while reserving its loudest echoes of all for the Patrick Hamilton play *Gas Light*. The laboratory rejuvenation of Solange, meanwhile, is lifted direct from *I vampiri*. Sadly,

Helga Liné, so icily beautiful in her revived form, looks ridiculous in a pie-faced old-age make-up that makes her resemble a 32-year-old with severe burns. And, between the barnstorming book-ends at beginning and end, we're stuck in the remainder of the film with the conspicuously drippy Jenny and the pretty but uninspired young hero. Indeed, sustenance is provided only by Barboni's consistently beautiful tours of the villa and by such agreeably outré details as a suspiciously fleshy pot-plant that seemingly weeps blood.

While Mario Caiano was perfecting the high Gothic of *Amanti d'oltretomba* in Frascati, Mario Bava was at Cinecittà, splicing Gothic with space opera in *Terrore nello spazio* (Terror in Outer Space), his first venture into SF since rescuing Freda's *Caltiki il mostro immortale* in 1959. In the interim, the wavering line of Italian science fiction had largely been perpetuated by Antonio Margheriti, among whose earliest films was the pulpy 1960 release *Space Men*. In 12 weeks in 1964 Margheriti made a quartet of cheap and cheerful space operas back to back for the TV series *Fantascienza*, though in the event all four went out to cinemas. All set on the same space station, they're chiefly distinguished by Angelo Francesco Lavagnino's thrillingly strange scores, though the first film, *I criminali della galassia* (Criminals of the Galaxy), became a camp US hit for M-G-M as *Wild, Wild Planet*.

It was in April 1965 that the colourful, cut-price kitsch of Margheriti's space operas found a sombre Gothic addendum in *Terrore nello spazio*. This was the only film that emerged from a projected slate of five SF subjects proposed to Bava by Arkoff and Nicholson of AIP. Very loosely based on a 1960 story by Renato Pestriniero called *Una notte di 21 ore* (One Night of 21 Hours), the script passed through the hands of five Italian writers, including Bava himself, before AIP called on SF specialist Ib Melchior to salvage it. "I was given no input, no special requests," he recalled. "I knew Bava was going to direct it. I had seen his work. I was thinking absolutely along the lines of Bava."[17] Hardly surprisingly, the result is a roiling vision of Hell decked out in Space Age camouflage.

*Lured to the planet Aura by a mysterious distress signal, the crew members of the spaceships Galliot and Argos are driven murderously insane on landing. Mark Markary, captain of the Argos, resists the madness and is thus able to rescue his fellows. Venturing onto the planet's hellish surface, they find that the Galliot crew, including Markary's brother, destroyed each other. They also find that the planet is infested with formless aliens intent on inhabiting the bodies of the dead.*

Possessed astronaut
Federico Boido,
stranded on the
'planet of the
vampires' in *Terrore
nello spazio* (1965)

Sporting the come-hither title *Planet of the Vampires*,
the film was released in the US in September 1965
as support to a British-made AIP shocker called *Die,
Monster, Die!* It was an appropriate pairing, given the
British film's loose foundation in H P Lovecraft and
the fact that the Bava picture boasts a Lovecraftian
flavour of its own.

This isn't just a matter of its scenes of undead
revenants roaming an alien landscape, but also
its intimations of a dormant, demonic civilisation
waiting patiently for the opportunity to gain dominion
over humanity. The contest is vividly outlined in some
memorable Melchior dialogue towards the end, when
the converted commander of the Galliot explains to
his opposite number that "We have been attempting
to summon you here for centuries." "We'll never
submit to a breed of parasites," retorts Markary.
Moments before, the Galliot captain has been exposed
as a mere shell, inhabited by an alien force, when
the vinyl sheen of his space tunic falls open to reveal
a sudden glimpse of red-raw innards and rib cage
– a charming Bava touch, quoting directly from *La
maschera del demonio*.

Just as he had manipulated a few basic props to
create the colour-saturated underworld of *Ercole al centro
della terra*, so in *Terrore nello spazio* Bava created a Stygian
inferno from not much more than a few studio rock

## TERRORE NELLO SPAZIO

*Italy-USA-Spain* 1965
Spain: *Terror en el espacio*
UK / US: *Planet of the Vampires*
Italian International / American International
   Pictures / Castilla Cooperativa Cinematográfica
88 *minutes colour*
*production began* 22 *March* 1965
. . . . . . . . . . . . . . . . . . . . . . . . . . . . .
Director of Photography: Antonio Rinaldi;
Art Director: Giorgio Giovannini; Editors:
Antonio Gimeno, Romana Fortini; Sound:
Eugenio Fiori, Mario Ronchetti, Paolo Ketoff;
Music Instrumentation and Electronic
Effects: Gino Marinuzzi Jr; Head Make-up:

Amato Garbini; Special Effects: Mario Bava
[uncredited]; Special Models: Carlo Rambaldi
[uncredited]; Screenplay: Ib J Melchior,
Alberto Bevilacqua, Castillo Cosulich, Antonio
Román, Mario Bava, Rafael J Salvia, based
on a story by Renato Pestriniero; Producer:
Fulvio Lucisano; Director: Mario Bava

Barry Sullivan (Captain Mark Markary); Norma
Bengell (Sonya); Ángel Aranda (Wess); Evi
Marandi (Tiona); Stelio Candelli (Brad); Franco
Andrei (Bert); Fernando Villena (Dr Karan);
Mario Morales (Eldon); Ivan Rassimov (Carter);
Rico Boido (Keir); Alberto Cevenini (Toby)

**Planet of the Vampires is pretty far out. Plot is punctuated with gore, shock,
eerie music and wild optic and special effects that can be exploited by
American International for okay biz in nabe [neighbourhood] spots. Color
camera work and production value are smooth and first class ... Actors rush
about with unrelieved solemnity and at times appear as confused as the
audience at what is happening.** Variety 1 December 1965

For *Terrore nello spazio* I had nothing, I mean nothing, to work with. There
was a sound stage but it was empty and derelict and there was no money
and it was supposed to represent a planet. So what did I do? There were
these big plastic rocks on the stage next door ... I took them and placed
them in the middle of my set ... and then I used smoke bombs to fog up the
background. Then, moving the rocks around, I shot the film.
Mario Bava [quoted in *Profondo Rosso Speciale* August 1991]

formations and a smoke machine. To showcase the
uniquely inhospitable Auran atmosphere, he specially
requested the insertion of an eerie resurrection
sequence. The result is a real show-stopper, with three

spindly menhirs collapsing in the Cinecittà mists and the metal slabs underneath them grating open to reveal the dead Galliot astronauts scrabbling their way out of transparent plastic shrouds. The scene is made all the weirder by Gino Marinuzzi's astonishing electronic music and sound, which confer an ominous otherworldliness on the entire film by means of unceasing wind effects.

In 1979, *Cinefantastique*'s Jeffrey Frentzen stirred up a minor controversy by giving his review of Ridley Scott's *Alien* the provocative title 'It! The Terror from Beyond the Planet of the Vampires'.[18] Indeed, that *Alien* hashed together the plot of Edward L Cahn's *It! The Terror from Beyond Space* with some of the imagery and ideas of the Bava film seems indisputable. As well as echoing Melchior's contamination theme and the film's strangely organic spaceship designs (notably the fleshy portals through which the crew issue onto Aura's surface), *Alien* also has its equivalent of Bava's most disturbing sequence, in which Markary and his communications officer, Sanya, venture into the control room of a horribly barnacled alien spacecraft. Having found one giant, horse-like skeleton slumped in the mists outside, they find another poised at a console, reverberating with a centuries-old recorded message – presumably a warning of some kind, but now just a forlorn torrent of indecipherable burbling.

As usual, Bava himself was responsible for the film's special effects. Most of them quite literally done with mirrors, they're occasionally of only Toy Town authenticity; the shots of the Argos in flight are especially unconvincing, as is the visualisation of the Aurans as "little globes of light, something fleeting, nothing definite." Even so, the effects give the film a children's theatre aspect that is beguilingly surreal. In creating something out of (almost) nothing, Bava was also helped by Gabriella Mayer's stylish space wear, which earned the distinction of being copied in the 1982 Disney film *Tron*, and by the brilliant set designer Giorgio Giovannini, whose cavernous spaceship interiors are just as unwelcoming as the planet outside.

In this kind of environment the actors might be expected to count for little, but Norma Bengell, glamorous star of Brazil's Cinema Novo movement, is suitably chilling when Sanya exhorts the last survivor to embrace "this wonderful new complexity," a line explicitly echoing Don Siegel's *Invasion of the Body Snatchers*. And, though looking almost as craggily sinister as the alien landscape, US import Barry Sullivan is a reassuring central presence, anchoring a production that was presumably just as incomprehensible to make as it sometimes is to watch. As Philip Strick put it in 1986, Sullivan's "resistance to the chaotic forces around him personifies both Bava's attitude as director and ours as audience."[19]

## PROGRAMMED KILLERS AND BRETON GHOSTS

After making *El secreto del Dr Orloff* early in 1964, Jess Franco became preoccupied with Orson Welles' embattled Shakespeare adaptation *Chimes at Midnight*, on which he served as second-unit director; simultaneously he assisted Welles on an aborted version of *Treasure Island*. As a result there was a conspicuous pause in Franco's personal output, a pause that would turn out to be highly uncharacteristic for so wildly prolific a filmmaker. But, at the behest of Hesperia Films producer Carlos Couret, he came back in May 1965 to make one of his strongest films, the Spanish-French co-production *Miss Muerte*.

> Explaining his research into isolating "the physical centres of good and evil" in man, Dr Zimmer receives so hostile a reception at a neurologists' symposium that he succumbs to heart failure. In response, his vengeful daughter Irma fakes her own death, sustaining facial burns in the process. Having rectified these surgically, she submits nightclub performer Nadia, the so-called 'Miss Death', to Zimmer's conditioning process. The brainwashed Nadia is then sent out to kill three doctors – Vicas, Moroni and Kallman.

*Miss Muerte* – known in France as *Le Diabolique Docteur Z* – is pulp horror put over with enormous flair and conviction. Utilising the basic plot mechanics of the Cornell Woolrich classic *The Bride Wore Black*, the story was devised by Franco under his usual David Kuhne alias but the screenplay was provided by Jean-Claude Carrière, who had recently embarked on a six-film collaboration with Luis Buñuel. Exactly two years later, in May 1967, François Truffaut would begin shooting the elegant Hitchcock pastiche *La Mariée était en noir*, an official adaptation of the Woolrich original; in the meantime, Franco's typically idiosyncratic take on the material grips the viewer from the first frames, only letting up at judiciously timed moments en route to a creepily ambiguous final shot.

Expertly setting the tone, the seven-minute pre-credits sequence is a dizzying pile-up of bizarre imagery and incident. A storm-racked gaol break; an elderly, wheelchair-bound man in strange goggles; caged owls, monkeys, foxes and rabbits among the retorts of a private laboratory; a ludicrous machine with hydraulic arms that pinion experimental subjects into position. Finally a rod is inserted into the escaped killer's left temple and comes out the other side. In a film in which virtually every scene is a set-piece, it's fortunate that the next one does a good job of elucidating what we've just been shown, as well as being thoroughly gripping in its own right. Dr Zimmer explains to his peers his indebtedness to the infamous Dr Orloff (a single reference that arguably qualifies this as yet another Orloff film), after which his plans to effectively lobotomise dangerous criminals are greeted with cries of "Nazi bastard," causing him to expire in the arms of his devoted daughter.

Incongruously, there follows the kinky nightclub act that, with variations, will recur so often in Franco's later films. Though brief, it's memorably disconcerting, with the lithe Miss Muerte wrestling a male, swivel-eyed mannequin onto a giant spider's web and donning a skull mask as the lights blink out. Appropriately, her fate is later sealed in an empty theatre, where Franco's hysterical staging of her pursuit and abduction is so brilliantly achieved the word 'bravura' seems barely adequate.

Franco is so much master of his material in *Miss Muerte* that he can even make a sinister highlight of a supposedly idyllic scene in which two young women take an impromptu swim. Thereafter he deals with Irma's restoration of her fire-damaged face with admirable succinctness; a really striking overhead shot of Irma on the operating table failed to distract the BBFC from a close-up of a scalpel piercing her (rather crude) burns make-up, adding to the nearly eight minutes of cuts inflicted on the film for its British release. In the aftermath, Irma's face seems superficially revived, yet she suffers from a persistent, post-operative sheen of oily sweat throughout the remainder of the action, a neat image of the suppurating corruption into which her vendetta plunges her.

For the title role of *Miss Muerte* is actually split between two characters. To the guileless Nadia the name merely denotes her nightclub alter ego, whereas Irma orchestrates real murder with the cold-eyed enthusiasm of a hardened sociopath. As these two contrasting faces of death, Estella Blain and Mabel Karr are equally riveting and put the rest of the

cast in the shade. The supposed hero, for example, is a rather dodgy fellow in a bad hairpiece, dallying with both women and needing to be rescued at the end, while the three guilty doctors are only there to be the focus of the film's stalking sequences.

The first – played by the reliable Howard Vernon in his third of more than 30 Franco appearances – is seduced by Nadia in a train's dining car, with

## MISS MUERTE

Spain-France 1965
France: *Le Diabolique docteur Z / Dans les griffes du maniaque*
UK / US: *The Diabolical Dr Z*
Hesperia Films / Speva Films / Ciné Alliance
86 minutes b/w
production began 3 May 1965

. . . . . . . . . . . . . . . . . . . . . . . . . . . . . .

Director of Photography: Alejandro Ulloa; Art Director: Antonio Cortés; Editors: Jean Feyte, Marie-Louise Barberot; Sound: Louis Hochet [credited only on French version]; Music: Daniel White; Make-up: Francisco Ramón Ferrer; Adaptation and Dialogue: Jean-Claude Carrière; Story: David Kuhne [Jess Franco]; Production Manager: Henri

Baum; Producers: Michel Safra, Serge Silberman; Director: Jess Franco

Estella Blain (Nadia, 'Miss Muerte'); Mabel Karr (Irma Zimmer); Howard Vernon (Professor Vicas); Fernando Montés (Dr Philippe Brighthouse); Marcelo Arroita-Jáuregui (Dr Moroni); Cris Huerta (Dr Kallman); Antonio Giménez Escribano (Dr Zimmer); Guy Mairesse (Hans Bergen); Ángela Tamayo (June); Mer Casas (Sandra Moroni); Lucía Prado (Barbara); Albert Bourbón (policeman); uncredited: Jess Franco (Inspector Tanner); Rafael Hernández (Green's assistant); Vicente Roca (police doctor); Nieves Salcedo (MC); José Villasante (driver); Daniel White (Inspector Green)

**Miss Muerte is one of this director's most skilful productions, ... getting together a number of typical horror movie effects and mixing them with some bashful outbreaks of erotica ... The acting isn't of a remarkable standard, maybe because the characters offer few opportunities to shine.** ABC Madrid 16 August 1966

**Curiously, Miss Muerte is one of the very few co-productions of mine that was untouched by censorship. They didn't touch a single shot, despite it being a very erotic picture ... I thought that at last the censors were beginning to understand eroticism, but I was wrong. They'd just taken it for another innocuous horror movie.** Jess Franco [quoted in *Cinefantástico y de terror español 1900-1983*, 1999]

Estella Blain catches up with Marcelo Arroita-Jáuregui in a deleted scene from *Miss Muerte* (1965)

cinematographer Alejandro Ulloa turning her into a seeming emanation of his dreams via amazing alternations of light and shadow. The second doctor-victim is pursued through cramped, foggy alleyways in which everything – including a laughing, barely glimpsed prostitute – suddenly becomes nightmarish. (For good measure, this doctor's blameless wife has her head smashed through a leaded window.) And the dispatching of the third doctor leads to a spirited and wholly unexpected fight sequence among suits of armour, and finally to the teasing last shot referred to above.

Central to the effect of that last shot are Nadia's fingernails, which, though dipped in curare, are quite long and sharp enough to be fatal in themselves. We've already seen them do their worst in a really hair-raising sequence in which Irma's female assistant was slashed to death. Yet, if *Miss Muerte* has a significant flaw, it's that the pitifully conflicted Nadia only dispatches the first of the three doctors; the other two are killed by Irma's obedient henchman and by Irma herself. Despite this mis-step, Franco had stumbled on a truly powerful image – the robotic, smoulderingly beautiful and heavily eroticised killer – and would exploit it much more thoroughly in future projects.

Antonio Casas, clawed to bits by an invisible entity in *El sonido de la muerte* (1965)

Just before Franco got to work on *Miss Muerte*, José Antonio Nieves Conde started directing *El sonido de la muerte* (The Sound of Death) on 26 April 1965. Here was a rarity twice over – not merely a Spanish monster movie but, in deference to a conspicuously threadbare budget, a Spanish *invisible* monster movie. It's the standard Americanised siege situation, very vaguely recalling *The Thing from Another World* as a group of boorish treasure-seekers disturb an age-old amorphous entity in a Greek cave. Manuel Berenguer's classy monochrome photography, some surprisingly grisly clawings inflicted on the expedition members, another early role for Soledad Miranda, and a first ever appearance from the Polish actress Ingrid Pitt – none of these things quite compensates for the turgid pace and the swelling tide of verbal diarrhoea in the dialogue. Indeed, the Andalucian edition of *ABC* accurately complained that "everything about this overblown and artificial film rings false ... demonstrating our filmmakers' pronounced uneasiness with the science fiction genre."[20]

A much better Spanish title from 1965 rejected lurid shock or zero-budget effects, opting instead for spectral chills. After his collaboration with Julio Coll on *Fuego*, US producer Sidney Pink turned to writer-director Javier Setó, with whom he'd made the 1963 costume picture *El valle de las espadas* (The Valley of Swords). Setó's new project, *La llamada* (The Calling), was very different; a limpid reflection on love after death, the result was aptly described by Pink as "an excellent horror film that was built around a warm and sensitive love story."[21] He was so pleased with it that he took out a full-page ad in the 20 October edition of *Variety* to announce its completion.

> *Pablo is a 22-year-old Spanish medical student who is in love with a Breton beauty called Dominique Monceau. When she's killed in a plane crash, her promise to remain true to him after death proves to have been all too literal. The rest of the Monceau clan are dead too, as Pablo finds out when visiting the family seat in Brittany.*

In *La llamada* Setó sets out his stall with uncluttered ease. What starts as a simple romance, rendered in the social-realist monochrome familiar from any number of Nouvelle Vague items, rapidly darkens in tone, with the relationship between Pablo and Dominique revealing disturbing undercurrents even before the latter dies. "I've heard that you Bretons act more like ghosts than humans sometimes," suggests Pablo, prefiguring his end within the film's first few minutes.

Emilio Gutiérrez Caba mourns the loss of Dyanik Zurakowska in the eerie Spanish ghost story *La llamada* (1965)

The couple's favoured day out takes them to a cold, flat landscape bisected by spindly tree branches; a chill wind is audible on the soundtrack and there's an ominous downturn in Gregorio García Segura's score when a spartan building appears on the horizon. It looks rather like a prison but turns out to be a cemetery. Its interior inspires the luminous Dominique to express a death wish. Calling death "the state of perfection for all men," she surveys the gravestones and exults in being "surrounded by the most important and most enduring things in the whole world – love and death."

So far, Setó and cinematographer Francisco Sánchez have woven a coolly mesmerising spell around the young lovers, much enhanced by the truthful performances of Emilio Gutiérrez Caba and 18-year-old Dyanik Zurakowska. Having concentrated on Eros, Setó now moves the focus onto Thanatos in a striking scene – striking for, among other things, its simplicity – in which Pablo takes a nocturnal drive around Madrid. We've just admired a large hoarding for David Lean's *Lawrence of Arabia* when suddenly Segura's jazzy score cuts out. Pablo puzzles over his car radio, then realises – as do we – that all extraneous sound has gone, not just the music. He then raises his hands despairingly to his ears as the noise of a plane crash is forced on him telepathically. Rarely has a director created the impression of a different 'zone' so effectively – and all Setó has done is cut the soundtrack.

The same level of eeriness is maintained throughout the remainder of the film. Dominique goes with Pablo on a return visit to the windswept cemetery, taking the opportunity to tell him that, despite appearances, she's dead. He doesn't believe her and there follows a painfully credible scene in which he tries to convince the aviation company that her inclusion on their list of crash victims is wrong. Now, at the halfway mark, Setó cleverly shifts focus again, introducing a new character in the form of Pablo's concerned Professor (Carlos Lemos). Calling Pablo "son," he agrees to join the boy at Dominique's funeral in Brittany, where Pablo claims to see Dominique among the mourners. Lemos creates a frisson all his own merely by a

## LA LLAMADA

Spain 1965
US: **The Sweet Sound of Death**
*Sidney W Pink presents a Hermic production*
88 minutes b/w
production completed by October 1965
. . . . . . . . . . . . . . . . . . . . . . . . .
Director of Photography: Francisco Sánchez; Art Director: José Antonio de la Guerra; Editor: Antonio Ramírez de Loaysa; Music: Gregorio García Segura; Make-up: Adolfo Ponte; Original Story

and Screenplay: Paulino Rodrigo Díaz, Javier Setó; Producer: Sidney W Pink [uncredited]; Director: Javier Setó

Emilio Gutiérrez Caba (Pablo); Carlos Lemos (Professor); Dyanik Zurakowska (Dominique); Paco Morán (Jacques); Tota Alba (Mme Monceau); Sun De Sanders (Claudia); Víctor Israel (caretaker); Joe and Angie Gordon (children); Jorge Alsina; Daniel Blum; Ana Godoy; José María Shelly

**Javier Setó has skilfully told this tale of a couple of student sweethearts whose love propels them to the boundaries of the supernatural ... The atmosphere [is] highly successful; the background music and black-and-white photography contribute in a big way to creating the climate of mystery appropriate to the plot.** ABC Andalucía 20 October 1967

*La llamada ... was very well made and starred two reliable young actors; its only drawback was Setó's insistence on making it in black and white. The picture, which we retitled* Sweet Sound of Death, *never reached its full audience potential because of the black and white, but I am proud to have my name on the quality film.*
Sidney Pink [So You Want to Make Movies: My Life as an Independent Film Producer, 1989]

disquieted furrowing of his brow – for the Professor, of course, can't see her at all.

It remains only for us to visit Dominique's ancestral château, mindful of her warning, early in the film, that "My family are set in their ways. We're almost a feudal clan." The Professor's daytime reconnoitre has revealed only a deserted hulk, but when Pablo calls after dark the door is answered by a creepily handsome man in uniform (Paco Morán). The vast vaultedness of the interior, the tiny figures gathered at tea within, the rain driving against the casements as Pablo sits down to a non-existent dinner with them, the grim pleasantries of the military man ("We have a higher incidence of fog than anywhere else in Europe") as he shows Pablo to his bedroom – these simple effects induce a profound chill of unease. And when Pablo goes exploring, discovering a family album revealing that his three hosts all died between 1944 and 1947, Setó shows us the eerily underlit faces of all three as they emerge watchfully from the gloom; the soldier's face is heralded by the ghostly flare of his cigarette.

As the Professor goes in search of the missing Pablo, *La llamada* reaches a predictably tragic conclusion, proving itself worthy of standing alongside such far better-known ghost films as America's *The Uninvited*, Britain's *The Haunting* and Canada's *The Changeling*. The crepuscular atmosphere wrought by Setó even survives the dubbed and abbreviated export version prepared by Pink under the title *The Sweet Sound of Death*. The film's spell-stopped delicacy also provides a striking contrast with the lurid Spanish horrors that would follow it, particularly since Dyanik Zurakowska went on to become a staple of such films as *La marca del hombre lobo* and *La orgía nocturna de los vampiros*.

In the wake of *La llamada*, Sidney Pink put José María Elorrieta's *Una bruja sin escoba* (A Witch Without a Broom) into production in mid-April 1966. A limp,

The 'carnivorous tree' melodrama *La isla de la muerte* (1966) reached French audiences as 'The Vampire Baron'

time-hopping, *Bewitched*-style caprice, it kicked off a final phase of comedies, action films and Westerns preceding Pink's retirement in 1970. Among these last films was the Italian-Spanish farce *Madigan's Millions*, in which Pink gained the distinction of giving Dustin Hoffman his first film role.

Another American working in mainland Europe was Mel Welles, who, having starred opposite a man-eating plant in Roger Corman's *The Little Shop of Horrors*, directed a Spanish-German co-production in 1966 involving a man-eating tree. Later to gain the distinction of being banned in Finland, *La isla de la muerte* (The Island of Death) was known in Germany as *Das Geheimnis des Todesinsel* (The Mystery of Death Isle). Exploiting Spain's burgeoning tourist industry, the film sends a half-dozen trippers and their guide to a supposed "earthly paradise" and "horticultural wonderland" where they meet an insane, Zaroff-like botanist. Echoing the crazed botanists played by Gale Sondergaard in *The Spider Woman Strikes Back* and George Coulouris in *Womaneater*, Cameron Mitchell wears donnish pince-nez to coo over his assembled shrubs, finally going berserk in a thunderstorm and accidentally axeing his own creation. "I'm sorry, my dearest – my darling," he babbles. "I didn't mean it." He also relishes dialogue that could have come straight from the pen of Barry Took and Marty Feldman, as when he admonishes an amorous guest (Kai Fischer) with "You were about to touch my giant – [pause] – gardenias."

For what it's worth, this rather dull *Ten Little Indians* plot is enlivened at the end by the gruesome, slime-drooling tree, which fully bears out an Andalucian critic's observation that "Welles has achieved some special effects of undoubted horror."[22] And there's a great, grisly, final shot of Mitchell when he's absorbed – as we all knew he would be – into the expiring tree.

## TOURISTS AND TAXIDERMISTS

Among several lost opportunities for Barbara Steele in the mid-1960s was Nicholas Ray's proposed film of Dylan Thomas' long-mothballed Burke and Hare script, *The Doctor and the Devils*; others reportedly cast were Laurence Harvey, Geraldine Chaplin, Susannah York and Barry Foster. This ill-fated project was set for September 1965, not long after Steele had spent a day (a very *long* day) on a peculiar film directed by the 21-year-old Michael Reeves. Impressed by the second-unit work Reeves had done on *Il castello dei morti vivi*, producer Paul Maslansky offered Reeves the opportunity to make his directorial debut in Italy – though a sizable portion of the £15,000 budget had to be supplied by Reeves himself, who luckily had a private income. The result therefore qualifies as an

Anglo-Italian co-production, known in Italy as either *Il lago di Satana* or *La sorella di Satana*, giving viewers a choice between Satan's lake or Satan's sister. In the UK it acquired the ridiculous title *Revenge of the Blood Beast*.

Sadly, Reeves' first film is a pretty tough watch, giving only very minor indications of his later work on *The Sorcerers* and *Witchfinder General*. The main trouble is that the script – written by Reeves himself under the intriguing pseudonym Mike Byron – is intended as a horror-comedy, yet Reeves clearly didn't have a comic bone in his body. He was at least aware of this deficiency, as when Steele's Veronica says "What a strange place; it's all so full of weirdies and werewolves" and receives the tart reply, "Terrible line, darling." The respondent is Veronica's husband Philip, played by Reeves' boyhood friend Ian Ogilvy. They're honeymooning in 'Transylvania – Today' according to an opening title card, though Reeves diverts briefly to a witch-hunting flashback set exactly 200 years earlier, on 18 July 1765. The witch's curse and 200th anniversary motif are references to *La maschera del demonio*, though other details – scattered sheep, villagers on the brow of a hill, a massive ducking engine – point forward to *Witchfinder*.

The witch, Vardella, was played by a male actor-dancer, Jay 'Flash' Riley, in a conspicuously ugly mask. There's a joltingly hysterical edge to his performance that translates into some frenzied scenes of violence, in which Reeves' mania for personally flinging fake blood – a mania attested to by Ogilvy, among others – gets an early airing. But much of the action, rather windily shot in Scope, devolves into painfully unfunny comedy, with a quirky local savant called Count 'Von' Helsing and a Communist hotelier played with zero wit by Mel Welles. The film at least gives Steele the unaccustomed opportunity to look chic in shades and trilby, as well as driving around the Roman countryside in a black VW Beetle, though at the end she signs off in her usual possessed mode with "I'll be back..."

For US release as *The She Beast*, Reeves' film was coupled with *The Embalmer*, the export version of a 'submersible taxidermist' curio called *Il mostro di Venezia* (The Monster of Venice). Directed and co-written by Dino Tavella, this one squanders a neat idea – a necrophile serial killer emerges from the canals of Venice to snatch his prey – on a great deal of dreary travelogue material and horror imagery modelled on Germany's Krimi style. The killer is a potentially interesting mix of ancient and modern,

Jay 'Flash' Riley as the hideous Vardella in *Il lago di Satana* (1965), released in America as *The She Beast*

changing from a wet suit into a skull mask and monk's habit when returning to the catacombs. But his embalmed victims, arranged upright in separate cubicles in a forlorn echo of the 1934 classic *The Black Cat*, are serenaded in standard-issue speeches that give no clue to his motivation. "How lovely you are, like alabaster goddesses," he tells them. "No living woman possesses your mysterious fascination or your sweet repose. You shall stay here with me always; no one shall have you..." And so on and so forth.

In addition to location work in Venice, Tavella shot his interiors at Trieste's Ceria Studios, and the dankness of the killer's subterranean lair is effectively suggested, particularly during a brief scene in which he blends seamlessly into a group of mouldering monastic corpses. The hero (Luigi Martocci) is a well-groomed newspaper man but at the climax he fails to save his girlfriend from a horrible death. This downbeat detail might be said to forecast the nihilism of later films like *Witchfinder General* and *Night of the Living Dead*, but in context it seems merely arbitrary. There are a few other peculiarities – a hatchet-faced old lady doing the Twist, for example, and Tavella's curious affectation of freeze-framing on each of the prospective victims when we first meet them. But none of these things helps relieve the deadening familiarity of the basic material. The British trade paper *Kinematograph Weekly* opted to be charitable, however, noting that "a few well-laid red herrings help to hold interest" and describing the film as a "handy support [feature] for the not-too-critical."[23]

Psychiatrist William Berger, nurse Barbara Wilson and blood-dripping patient Massimo Righi in *La lama nel corpo* (1965)

The Villa Parisi in Frascati, having accommodated *Amanti d'oltretomba* in the spring of 1965, would provide the setting for two further Italian Gothics later in the year. For *La lama nel corpo* (The Blade in the Body), Elio De Scardamaglia, co-producer of the similarly titled *La frusta e il corpo*, retained the services of the American actress Harriet White, who in *La frusta* and Freda's two *Hichcock* films had proved herself the ideal creepy housekeeper. According to co-writer Ernesto Gastaldi, the author of the film's source story, Lionello De Felice, was also the director, prior to walking out at the eleventh hour and being replaced by De Scardamaglia. The result is a precise fusion of Italy's well-worn Gothic conventions with the emergent clichés of the giallo; to this end, the regulation cowled silhouette wields a straight razor not in a super-chic fashion house but a gloomy pile situated (apparently) in 1870s Norfolk.

Exported as *The Murder Clinic*, this tale of a lunatic asylum beset by razor killings is rather dreary stuff until the Nouvelle Vague star Françoise Prévost shows up in the second act. Unfortunately she remains confined to the middle section – but she cuts a formidable figure in red tartan while attempting to blackmail the twitchy asylum director (William Berger). Commendably, the plucky housemaid manages not to drop the breakfast tray on discovering Prévost's body, after which we're treated to a flashback explaining how the doctor's unlucky sister-in-law plunged into a vat of quicklime. "Her presence was like a gentle and capricious breeze," we've been told; now, in time-honoured *Les Yeux sans visage* fashion, "she's monstrous" and is awaiting a skin graft in her garret hideaway. The disfigurement applied to Delfi Mauro is of Halloween mask crudity but, as the film's spirited climax kicks in, it still proves horribly effective.

The third Villa Parisi film of 1965 featured a far more presentable taxidermist-cum-serial killer than the one seen in *Il mostro di Venezia*. When making *Il terzo occhio* (The Third Eye) that summer, former avant-garde painter Mino Guerrini was poised between co-writing Bava's *La ragazza che sapeva troppo* and directing a quartet of lowbrow 1970s comedies featuring Jacques Dufilho's Colonel Buttiglione. With *Il terzo occhio*, however, he crafted an extremely classy riposte to the Hitchcock films *Vertigo* and *Psycho*, while attributing the original story, rather loosely, to the 15th century reputed serial killer Gilles de Rais.

*Mino Alberti is a mother-fixated aristocrat well versed in taxidermy. His housekeeper, Marta, wants to marry him and therefore engineers the deaths of Mino's mother and his fiancée Laura on the same day. Something snaps in Mino and he starts inviting young women back to his villa, only to kill them when they realise that Laura's preserved corpse is in the neighbouring bed. Marta, meanwhile, happily connives in his crimes. But then Laura's eerily similar sister arrives...*

For their second necrophile Gothic, Panda producers Luigi Carpentieri and Ermanno Donati again employed the collective pseudonym Louis Mann. Yet *Il terzo occhio* is very different to the florid 19th century canvas of *L'orribile segreto del Dr Hichcock*. Shot in limpid black-and-white by Allesandro D'Eva, the film is set in a slickly contemporary Italy that nevertheless harbours sociopathic killers amid its rapidly fading aristocracy. And to play the lead Guerrini chose a handsome 23-year-old who was very much the man of the moment. Not long after completing *Il terzo occhio*, Franco Nero signed on to play the coffin-dragging anti-hero of Sergio Corbucci's *Django* – a film that, in the event, was put before Italian audiences two months before Guerrini's film, which had been held up by some pretty rough censorship negotiations.

These difficulties were hardly surprising, given the combustible nature of what Guerrini had put on screen. "You're like a child," Laura tells Mino early on. "You can't handle rejection." Perceptive though this observation is, it merely scratches the surface of an extremely troubled soul. Mino's cloistered existence in the crumbling family seat is persuasively sketched in during the film's first act, with the hothouse atmosphere of southern Italy echoing the sweltering Deep South melodramatics of *Cat on a Hot Tin Roof* and other Tennessee Williams plays. The claustrophobia is almost palpable, with Guerrini making telling use of the four faces at his disposal – the chiselled Nero, porcelain Erika Blanc, sultry Gioia Pascal and, pre-eminently, the Zero Mostel-like features of Olga Solbelli as Mino's monstrous mother. Solbelli provides the cue for the most effective of Guerrini's many stylish touches – cutting away from her to a startling, screen-filling close-up of a stuffed owl, for example, or positioning her in dominating profile with Laura framed between proscenium-like curtains in the background.

The tensions, both sexual and class-based, simmer away nicely, finally exploding when Marta precipitates the mother down a flight of stairs prior to stamping on her head, after which Mino's repeated cries of "No!" bring this section to a suitably operatic close. The spectacle prompting Mino's outburst – Laura dangling from a crashed car with her dead face submerged under the water – sets the coldly necrophile tone for the remainder of the film. Telling him "You'll always need new sacrifices," Marta forms an unholy alliance with Mino that leads to three deaths, the last of which is her own. The first is that of a high-class nightclub performer, played by the future RAI television personality Marina Morgan; she does a decorous strip to the most doleful jazz imaginable prior to fetching up at Mino's villa and encountering Laura's corpse. This and Mino's subsequent murder of a prostitute are masterfully contrived by Guerrini, with the victims' screaming horror juxtaposed with Mino's snivelling abjection in the aftermath.

Throughout, Guerrini emphasises his suspended animation motif, not just by recourse to Mino's stuffed birds, but also by the profusion of strange statuettes in the house, statuettes that are frequently seen reflected in mirrors. At length the ultimate mirror image turns up – Erika Blanc again, this time as Daniela – and Marta attacks her

## IL TERZO OCCHIO

*Italy 1965*
*US: **The Third Eye***
*Panda Cinematografica*
*98 minutes b/w*
*in production June–July 1965*
...........................

Director of Photography: Alessandro D'Eva; Art Director: Mario Chiari; Editor: Ornella Micheli; Assistant Director: Ruggero Deodato; Music: Francesco De Masi; Make-up: Giuliano Laurenti; Screenplay: Piero Regnoli, Mino

Guerrini; Story by Ermanno Donati, 'freely adapted from a story by Gilles de Reys' [sic]; Production Manager: Alfonso Donati; Producers: Luigi Carpentieri, Ermanno Donati; Director: Mino Guerrini

*Franco Nero (Mino Alberti); Gioia Pascal (Marta); Erika Blanc (Laura / Daniela); Olga Solbelli (Mino's mother); Marina Morgan (nightclub performer); Richard Hillock (doctor); uncredited: Luciano Foti (policeman)*

**It's pointless to demand credibility in a story naïvely imported from the Anglo-Saxon 'Gothic' novel, and just as naïvely compounded of ingredients lifted from 'gialli' via horror pictures and vestiges of the 'sexy' genre. And yet cinema has such suggestive power that, through visual eloquence, it can dignify hotchpotches even more ridiculous than this. Sadly this doesn't apply to *Terzo occhio*, where ... the viewer struggles between a smidgen of fear and a big impulse to laugh.**
La Stampa 29 July 1966

**Guerrini was a very strange guy. Crazy, in fact ... One day we were filming a scene at the Villa Parisi in Frascati, in the bathroom, with Franco Nero and Erika Blanc, and at a certain point Guerrini took a shit in front of the entire crew! ... I called the producers ... and Ermanno Donati slapped him in the face ... He was talented, though.**
*Ruggero Deodato [quoted in Nocturno August 2008]*

Gioia Pascal assumes total control of Franco Nero – for a while at least – in *Il terzo occhio* (1965)

with a peculiarly monstrous knife when it becomes clear that Mino has confused Daniela with Laura. The climax is bleak and powerful. Totally unhinged, Mino turns the knife on Marta herself and abducts Daniela in his Fiat, explaining that "I love white more than any other colour. It reminds me of newly fallen snow, before anyone has defiled it. It's beautiful, and so virginal..." Eventually parking by the ghostly hulk of a Martello tower, he subjects Daniela to a garbled version of Macbeth's "It is a tale / Told by an idiot" speech before being apprehended by the police.

Though Mino's arrest comes as something of an anti-climax, Daniela's sufferings on the beach, exquisitely played by Blanc, are truly grim to watch – and at the fade-out we're invited to consider whether the still-screaming Daniela has been driven insane by her experience. Ultimately, the film's power derives from the contrast between Guerrini's coolly classy direction and the unhealthily twisted drives compelling its characters. Mino's derangement is obvious. "It's as if I had a third eye suddenly," he laments, "and it always stares in the same direction." But Marta's motivations are arguably even more chilling – to satisfy a lust not merely for Mino but for social advancement, she arranges two killings herself prior to cajoling an uncontrollable serial killer into marriage. Her agonising death scene (in which, suffering from multiple stab wounds, she drags herself towards a ringing telephone) is one of the most protracted in the genre.

Having given the killer his own name (Mino), it was under his real forename, Giacomo, that Guerrini received a story credit on the 1979 film *Buio omega*, which was exported as *Beyond the Darkness*. Directed by sleazemeister Joe D'Amato, this loose remake of *Il terzo occhio* junks all that was most interesting about its progenitor (ie, the first act) and literalises everything else, using the freedoms of a new era to turn an elegant piece of psychodrama into a childishly explicit gorefest.

Mino is now called Frank, while Marta is an eerie-looking older woman, Iris, who suckles him at her breast. When eviscerating his dead lover, Frank slings her innards into a bucket and actually chews on her heart. ("The embalming scene shocked everyone," noted D'Amato. "It was so stomach-churning and realistic many thought we had used real autopsy footage. It was all faked."[24]) Frank subsequently kills a British hitchhiker, though not before pincering off her fingernails for no particular reason. Iris then chops up the body preparatory to an acid bath. Later still Frank bites a chunk out of a jogger's neck and consigns her body to the furnace. "No one will touch your baby doll," Iris assures Frank prior to stabbing

him in the crotch and putting out one of his eyes. With all those added entrails the film runs over ten minutes longer than the original, and the result is as revolting as it sounds.

## PREENING MUSCLEMEN AND CONNIVING SERVANTS

Though professing no great interest in the horror genre, Massimo Pupillo followed *5 tombe per un medium* with two further Gothics made in 1965. In later years he claimed to have finished making *5 tombe* on a Saturday and plunged straight into *Il boia scarlatto* (The Scarlet Executioner) the following Monday, taking actors Walter Brandi and Alfredo Rizzo with him. Yet he seems to have misremembered the order of events, for *5 tombe* was completed in March and *Il boia scarlatto* didn't follow until the summer, with *La Stampa* noting the film's completion in mid-July while trumpeting one of Pupillo's beautiful starlets, "executioner's girl" and "former Miss Piedmont" Luisa Baratto.[25]

For Brandi and Rizzo – stars, five years previously, of *L'ultima preda del vampiro* – the set-up must have been eerily familiar. Not only were they back in that film's chief location, the Palazzo Borghese at Artena, they were working from a script with a virtually identical plot. There was at least one striking innovation, however – the casting of the former Mr Universe, Mickey Hargitay, in the title role.

*When ten interlopers descend on his secluded castle, retired muscleman actor Travis Anderson reluctantly allows them to stay the night. The group are there to shoot sexy and sadistic stills for a forthcoming edition of the Skeletrik comic book, and when Anderson recognises the publisher's mousey secretary as his former fiancée Edith, he suddenly snaps, assuming the guise of the Crimson Executioner – a sadistic madman who was executed on the premises way back in 1648.*

Pupillo certainly proved his versatility with the febrile Eastmancolor histrionics of *Il boia scarlatto*, a film contrasting wildly with the stately monochrome chills of the two films he made either side of it. Romano Migliorini and Roberto Natale's script provided the ideal pretext for satirising three things at once – the kind of formula sexy-Gothics represented by *L'ultima preda*, the fetishised cult of physical perfection enshrined in Italy's sword-and-sandal pictures, and the burgeoning vogue for adults-only fotonovels, many of them based on popular films. Appropriately, *Il boia scarlatto* itself would get the treatment, with the 60th issue of *Malia* being devoted to the film in February 1966.

Crazed muscleman Mickey Hargitay torments visiting glamour model Femi Benussi in *Il boia scalatto* (1965)

The action begins with the by-now familiar 'execution that initiated the curse' routine, set in stone by *La maschera del demonio* and soon to be replicated yet again in the West German picture *Die Schlangengrube und das Pendel*. That the whole film should be considered with tongue firmly in cheek is indicated by the Iron Maiden into which the Crimson Executioner is thrust, a rather flimsy and gaily painted object better suited to a travelling carnival than a 17th century dungeon.

Moving up to the present, three colour-coded cars – red, white and blue – cruise into view; one of the four ill-fated glamour models assesses the familiar Castello di Balsorano (which was used for exteriors) and says tartly, "You'd have to be a creep to live in a place like this!" This is just one of several sassy lines in a reasonably witty opening, though the comedy quickly becomes laboured. The film's US producer, Ralph Zucker, cast as the photographer, is lumbered with a particularly unfunny routine as he tries to 'motivate' the young models. Yet the eroticised sadism here aptly prefigures the tortures to come. One girl, for example, is wearing just a nightie while being throttled by a skull-faced suit of armour; another sports a bikini and wields an axe over a chopping block. Alfredo Rizzo is the self-important publisher – pretty much the same role he played in *L'ultima preda*, only this time with a hairpiece – and the Skeletrik character anticipates by over a year two Titanus films based on the skeletal comic-book character Kriminal.

The central figure, Travis Anderson, is withheld at first. We see plenty of his thuggish goons in their skin-tight T-shirts but the man himself is introduced only in profile, whether brooding over a chess board or communicating with his guests via intercom. Only when he shows up in a flowered kimono with lavender trim does he get a chance to expound his narcissistic philosophy. Explaining his withdrawal from the world, he claims that "Mankind is made up of inferior creatures, spiritually and physically deformed, who would've corrupted the harmony of my perfect body." Rejecting Edith again, he affirms his determination "to

## IL BOIA SCARLATTO

Italy-USA 1965
US: **Bloody Pit of Horror**
MBS Cinematografica / International Entertainment
87 minutes colour
in production June-July 1965
. . . . . . . . . . . . . . . . . . . . . . . . . . . .
Director of Photography: Luciano Trasatti; Art Director: Franco Fontana; Editor: Mariano Arditi; Sound: Goffredo Salvatori; Music: Gino Peguri; Make-up: Diulio Scarrozza; Special Effects: Carlo Rambaldi [uncredited]; Story and Screenplay: Roberto Natale, Romano

Migliorini; Production Manager: Marino Vaccà; Producers: Francesco Merli, Ralph Zucker; Director: Massimo Pupillo

Mickey Hargitay (Travis Anderson); Walter Brandi (Rick); Luisa Baratto (Edith); Ralph Zucker (Dermot); Rita Klein (Nancy); Alfredo Rizzo (Daniel Parks); Barbara Nelli (Susie); Moa Tahi (Kinojo); Femi Benussi (Annie); Nando Angelini (Parry); Albert Gordon (Raoul); Gino Turini (moustachioed bullyboy); Roberto Messina (balding bullyboy)

A more prudent and measured application of Grand Guignol effects, especially towards the end, might have saved *Il boia scarlatto* from a touch of the ridiculous ... It's a rather bargain-basement 'horror movie' that does its best to mix the usual terror scenes with erotica. The protagonist is Mickey Hargitay, ex 'Mister Muscolo'. *La Stampa 26 April 1966*

What I tried to give to the character [of the Crimson Executioner] was a sort of sexual symbology, even though the producers didn't agree. I've always tried to put hints for sophisticated audiences into my movies. In fact, the first time he appears, when he's in front of the fireplace and the other people enter the room, I arranged all those bottles neck down, purely to symbolise sexual impotence. *Massimo Pupillo [quoted in Bruschini, Horror all'italiana, 1996]*

avoid the contagion of human sentiment," adding that "A woman's love would have destroyed me." He says all this while oiling up his impressive pectorals in an ornate mirror. Clearly then, Travis is a grotesque parody of the latent homoeroticism lurking behind the cult of hyper-masculinity. With his male acolytes and secret torture chamber, he comes across like a musclebound twin to Edmond Bancroft, the insane, gay-coded author in the 1958 film *Horrors of the Black Museum*.

Unlike Bancroft, Anderson is also an exemplar of the repressed moral reformer whose prurience curdles into mania. He's convinced that the Crimson Executioner's "noble crusade against sin lives again through me" – an idée fixe recalling the Punisher in Margheriti's *La vergine di Norimberga*. Acting on this conviction, he suits up in his absurd red tights and face mask and descends to the stews to torment his guests. One, Moa Tahi, is suspended semi-naked in a mock-web, complete with a comical motorised spider and cables that trigger a volley of arrows, a fiendish contrivance poised somewhere between silent cliffhangers, James Bond spoof and the 21st century fondness for so-called 'torture porn'. Even in a film as daft as this, however, it's tough to understand how Walter Brandi was considered the kind of hero material capable of besting the Crimson Executioner – unless, as Pupillo claimed, Brandi was also an uncredited co-producer.

With the pulpy, unbridled sadism of *Il boia scarlatto*, it's tempting to think that Pupillo was settling some old scores. He was a 12-year veteran of Italy's censorship committee, which he considered "a very unpleasant, very bad experience."[26] Despite performing well in US grindhouses under the imperishable title *Bloody Pit of Horror*, the film would be rejected outright when presented to the British Board of Film Censors in 1967, a development that may have caused Pupillo some rueful amusement.

Following rapidly on the heels of *Il boia scarlatto*, Pupillo's third Gothic of 1965, *La vendetta di Lady Morgan* (The Vengeance of Lady Morgan), was shot in August. Yet another Italian horror picture purportedly set in Scotland, the film saw Pupillo returning to the sombre monochrome of *5 tombe per un medium* and to the same location, Castello Chigi at Castel Fusano. The film was not, however, a return engagement with producer Ralph Zucker. Indeed, *La vendetta* enjoyed no American financial input at all and was exported only to Germany, falling into such obscurity in subsequent decades that it was assumed to be a lost film. Happily, it survives – and, as a bizarre cross-fertilisation of Patrick Hamilton's *Gas Light* with Margheriti's *Danza macabra*, it makes a considerable impact.

*Scotland, 1865. Wealthy heiress Susan Blackhouse is in love with Pierre Brissac. When he's apparently drowned en route to Paris, she marries another suitor, the titled Harold Morgan, who quickly engages three sinister servants to help him in his scheme to drive his wife to suicide. Their plan succeeds, but she reappears as a ghost and brings about their deaths, a vendetta she recounts to Pierre on his return. But the four deceased schemers return too...*

*La vendetta di Lady Morgan* begins on a romantic note, with two horses (one white, one dark) grazing contentedly as blond Pierre and brunette Susan enjoy a sylvan tryst. Their situation is efficiently sketched in – Pierre is employed on restoration work at Susan's ancestral castle and in order to marry him Susan has to first turn down the saturnine Harold. Along with her kindly Uncle Neville, Susan is the last of the Blackhouses and claims to be six months away from turning 21, a claim contradicted later on by the dates on her gravestone. Either way, when news comes through of Pierre's presumed fate on a cross-channel ferry, she states forlornly that "For me, time stopped at Dover."

What follows is a fairly straightforward replay of the 'young bride with scheming husband' routine common to *Gas Light* and so many others, though here it's spiced up with a trio of shifty domestic servants, one of whom has hypnotic powers. Erika Blanc's Lillian, simultaneously glacial and smouldering, bends Susan to her will even when the latter is alone in her bed. Blanc's hypnotic voice-over is accompanied here by an especially overwrought passage of Piero Umiliani's score; indeed, the music goes into thunderous overdrive when Susan merely gets out of bed and turns up the gas lamp. Elsewhere, Umiliani's music is less obtrusive, though the best bits are strangely identical to the doom-laden sonorities of Angelo Francesco Lavagnino's contemporaneous space-opera scores.

Harold's campaign includes a snake-in-the-bed gag recalling Doyle's *The Speckled Band*, the imprisonment of Uncle Neville in the family dungeon (handily situated beneath the family graveyard), and finally an excitingly staged sequence in which Lillian hypnotises Susan into teetering on the battlements at dead of night. Dreamy shots of the white-robed Susan, wobbling woozily in the wind, are nicely contrasted with Harold, Lillian and the local doctor swarming up a narrow stairwell as they rush to her supposed rescue. Instead, she ends up sprawled amid ground fog in the courtyard below, with the name "Pierre" on her lips as she expires. And here the film dispenses with merely hinting at the supernatural, for the amnesiac Pierre simultaneously wakes in his hospital bed, crying out "Susan!" and regaining his memory.

Pupillo's producer on this occasion was Franco Belotti, who had previously produced *Danza macabra* from a script co-written by Gianni Grimaldi. With Belotti and Grimaldi reunited on *Lady Morgan*, it comes as no great surprise when the film slips into *Danza macabra* mode for its unashamedly supernatural third act. Barbara Nelli's Susan and Michel Forain's Pierre go through exactly the same paces that Barbara

Barbara Nelli breathes her last amid copious ground fog in *La vendetta di Lady Morgan* (1965)

Steele and Georges Rivière did in the earlier film, with Susan telling Pierre she's dead only after they have (by implication) made love. Hovering outside the bedroom door are Harold and his three confederates – and because we've not yet heard Susan's story, we don't realise at first that they too are dead.

In the ensuing flashback, Pupillo is unafraid to embrace the borderline-comic potential of the conspirators being bedevilled by Susan's invisible machinations, among them such hokey devices as guttering candles, an exploding urn, whisky turning to acid and shaving water turning to blood. As guilty hysteria sets in, Pupillo makes great use of the splendid faces at his disposal – Blanc's chiselled beauty as Lillian, Gordon Mitchell's handsome Neanderthal look as the butler Roger, and the surly features of Paul Muller, who's cast here in more or less the same role (while wearing quite possibly the same wig) as the one he recently played in *Amanti d'oltretomba*. And the crescendo of recriminations is well handled too, with one conspirator stabbed behind the arras, another strangled, a third gruesomely trampled by horses' hooves, and Harold himself going flying off the battlements just as Susan did.

Then, in the final reel, a further *Danza macabra* touch is thrown in, revealing the conspirators' ghosts to be remorseless vampires. Having exhausted the supply provided by poor Uncle Neville in the dungeon, they now tell Pierre that "We just need your blood. You'll be our new fountain of life." Pupillo creates some great imagery here – the ghosts lying on the floor to lap up Pierre's spilt blood, four pairs of hands reaching greedily into frame to collar him, even a shot prefiguring *Night of the Living Dead* in which the ghouls

## LA VENDETTA DI LADY MORGAN

*Italy 1965*
*Morgan Film*
*88 minutes colour*
*production began 26 July 1965*
. . . . . . . . . . . . . . . . . . . . . . . . . . .
Director of Photography: Oberdan Trojani; Production Designer: Ugo Pericoli; Editor: Mariano Arditi; Music: Piero Umiliani; Make-up: Massimo Giustini; Story: Edward

Duncan; Screenplay: Gianni Grimaldi; Producer: Franco Belotti; Director: Massimo Pupillo

Gordon Mitchell (Roger); Erika Blanc (Lilian); Paul Muller (Sir Harold Morgan); Barbara Nelli (Lady Susan Morgan); Michel Forain (Pierre Brissac); Carlo Kechler (Sir Neville Blackhouse); Edith MacGoven (Terry);

*La vendetta di Lady Morgan* transports us to an atmosphere in which the dead resurrect ... Max Hunter's [Massimo Pupillo's] direction takes advantage of all the ingredients aimed at an impressionable audience: creaking doors that open and close, flapping curtains, candles that suddenly go out and so on. The actors, their faces lit so ghoulishly, are Gordon Mitchell, Erika Blanc, Paul Muller, Barbara Nelly [sic] and Michel Forain. *Corriere della Sera* 31 March 1966

I wasn't interested in making any more horror films ... In Italy, when you make a certain type of film you become labelled and you can't do anything else. I remember one day, a producer called me to do a film only because the other producers told him he had to get either Mario Bava or me. When I understood this, I felt dead.
*Massimo Pupillo [quoted in* Shock: The Essential Guide to Exploitation Cinema, *1996]*

recoil from fire. The film then screeches to a demented, despairing and, it must be said, extremely abrupt close.

## ALL OF THEM WITCHES

Also in production in August 1965 was *Più tardi Claire, più tardi...* (Too Late Claire, Too Late...), with which Brunello Rondi sought to recover from the commercial failure of the splendid *Il demonio*. It wasn't the right project to accomplish this feat, languishing unreleased until July 1968 and only reaching America as a TV sale with the moronic title *Run, Psycho, Run*. Where *Il demonio* anatomised the survival of barbarism in rural areas of modern Italy, *Più tardi* sought to dramatise the savagery of the contemporary bourgeoisie by examining their forebears of 1912.

There's much Edwardian sea bathing and lawn tennis, plus stuffed shirts talking at inordinate length amid some surprisingly shaky period detail. The story involves a judge's wife and little boy being murdered and the judge returning to the scene 12 months later, rather like Robert Flemyng's Dr Hichcock, with a doppelgänger wife and son to supplant them. There are two really striking scenes – the original murders, in which cinematographer Carlo Bellero's stalking shadowplay works wonders, and a bizarre vignette in which Adriana Asti's disturbed country girl taunts the new son with a butcher knife. The remainder, to put it mildly, is a lot less involving.

By 8 December *Variety* was reporting that Barbara Steele had been cast in yet another costume Gothic, this one entitled *Un angelo per Satana* (An Angel for Satan). Returning to horror after his arresting work on *La cripta e l'incubo*, the venerable Camillo Mastrocinque was in the director's chair and the film went into production in mid-January 1966. Though apparently based on a novel by the Italian screenwriter Luigi Emmanuele, the script is a pretty obvious composite of two 19th century sources, taking the haunted lakeside heroine of Antonio Fogazzaro's *Malombra* and coupling her with the malevolent statue of Prosper Mérimée's *La Vénus d'Ille*. The result would turn out to be Steele's ninth and last Italian Gothic. Yet again she was playing a fiendish split personality, with the old Madonna-Whore equation enshrined even in the film's title.

*Roberto Merigi is a young sculptor engaged by Conte Montebruno to restore a 200-year-old statue of his ancestor Magdalena. Long lost, the statue was recovered from the bottom of a lake, and the decision to refurbish it seems foolhardy given the local superstition that it has a curse attached to it. When the Count's young niece, Harriet, returns from a 15-year stay in England, she forms a bond with Roberto – but also begins to undergo psychic transformations at the stroke of midnight.*

In a straight lift from Mario Soldati's 1942 film version of *Malombra*, *Un angelo per Satana* begins on an exquisitely mournful note – a rowing boat on an expanse of lake, hazy low-lying hills on the horizon, a silhouetted figure waiting on the skeletal jetty. This last detail also recalls the chilly introduction to Ferroni's *Il mulino delle donne di pietra*, though Mastrocinque manages to weave from these borrowings an otherworldly atmosphere of his own. Underscoring this, Francesco De Masi's plangent theme matches the tone exactly, though as yet the viewer has no idea why this pall of misery should hang so heavy over Conte Montebruno's lands.

No sooner has Roberto stepped off the boat and gained audience with the Count than the clues begin to filter in. But as Montebruno explains the curse associated with the recently rediscovered statue of Magdalena, we begin to puzzle over his motivation. Charmingly played by Claudio Gora, he has a frog-like, self-satisfied look, with an inclination towards games-playing indicated by his professed expertise in Machiavelli. But Gora keeps the viewer guessing as to whether this lordly, cheroot-chewing aristocrat is avuncular or unpleasantly venal. And Mastrocinque – co-writing the film as well as directing – takes care to give us similarly vivid characters elsewhere, whether it's Dario the guileless school teacher, Rita the lady's maid who loves him, or Carlo, the resident class-conscious thug who attacks Roberto when he presumes to sketch customers in the local inn. There's also a mentally unstable groundsman, Vittorio, who becomes the first victim of the transmogrified Harriet, seduced by her with such straight-down-to-business lines as "I want to warm myself by your fire" and "Have you ever seen a naked lady?"

Exactly what Harriet becomes possessed by is explained in a memorably weird scene in which Roberto is lured from his bed by orgasmic sighs and a disembodied female voice repeatedly breathing his name. In an attic lumber room a discarded, unframed portrait magically unfurls itself amid lightning flashes and plumes of sulphuric smoke, revealing a 17th century noblewoman whose canvas face bubbles and pulsates as her ghostly voice addresses Roberto. Belinda, it seems, was Magdalena's homely older sister, who "longed to be loved, caressed, kissed, seduced. But men ran away from me; they laughed at me." Nursing a bitter hatred for Magdalena's beauty, she went to a watery grave with her sister's loathed statue. Now she warns Roberto that "If you fall in love with her [Harriet], the curse will fall on you too."

So, when Harriet slips into her midnight fugues, we can assume that she's enacting the suppressed, destructive urges of a Renaissance old maid. Her victims include Vittorio (who attempts to rape a girl and ends up brutally lynched in the market square), Carlo (who torches his own home, thereby incinerating his whole family and himself) and Rita (who rejects Dario at Harriet's prompting, causing the boy to hang himself). "We women are much more beautiful than men," Harriet tells Rita. "We'll have lots of fun together. We'll make men suffer..." The hints of lesbianism contained in Steele's earlier films are foregrounded in Harriet's scenes with Rita, and the moments in which Harriet gazes into a cheval glass, triggering her midnight personality transfers, are among the most erotic Steele ever played. Women are portrayed, once again, as Janus-faced creatures who can't be trusted. In her dealings with the local men, Harriet becomes the ultimate tease; under Belinda's influence she even conforms to the age-old cliché of the woman who entices a man to the point of no return and then screams rape.

Though the Harriet-Belinda role is hardly an enlightened one, Steele is at her most smoulderingly powerful here, looking splendidly crazed when she daubs on heavy make-up (very 1960s-looking make-up, it must be said) during her first transformation. Mastrocinque introduces several other suggestive touches, among them a Magdalena statue that, though pretty obviously a mannequin, looks unpleasantly creepy when festooned with seaweed. Others include a toad that Roberto kicks back into the lake when it appears suddenly on his toecap, and a copy of Voltaire's *La Pucelle d'Orléans* that's positioned by the Count's head when he finally expires.

Just before this, the film has shot itself in the foot with the disappointing revelation that Harriet was subject to hypnosis rather than demonic possession. "This isn't about witches and spells," Roberto tells the villagers. "It's about criminals and murderers." But how did the scheming villains cause that attic portrait to come to suppurating life? This anomaly provides at least a crumb of comfort for those who prefer their explanations supernatural.

And with that, Steele closed the door on her career in Italian horror – sadly, with a film that, maybe because it was shot in suddenly unfashionable monochrome, wasn't widely exported. A quarter of a century later she pointed out that "My major complaint with these movies is they always deal with the same ideas: sadism, necrophilia, demonic possession and victimisation. In my defence I don't think any of the roles I've personally played have reflected a disgust for, or degraded, women. I wouldn't have done them if they had."[27]

Had Steele taken the female lead in Damiano Damiani's *La strega in amore* (The Witch in Love), she might not have been

## UN ANGELO PER SATANA

Italy 1966
UK / US: **An Angel for Satan**
*Discobolo Cinematografica*
93 minutes b/w
production began mid-January 1966
· · · · · · · · · · · · · · · · · · · · · · · · · · · ·
Director of Photography: Giuseppe Aquari; Art Director: Alberto Boccianti; Editor: Gisa Radicchi-Levi; Sound: Fiorenzo Magli; Music: Francesco De Masi; Make-up: Efrade Titi, Giovanni Morosi; Screenplay: Giuseppe

Mangione, Camillo Mastrocinque, from a novel by Luigi Emmanuele; Producer: Liliana Biancini; Director: Camillo Mastrocinque

Barbara Steele (Harriet Montebruno); Anthony Steffen (Roberto Merigi); Claudio Gora (Count Montebruno); Pier Anna Quaglia (Rita); Aldo Berti (Victor); Marina Berti (Ilda); Vassili Karamenisis (Dario); Mario Brega (Carlo Lionesi); Antonio Acqua (gardener); Antonio Corevi; Betty Delon; Giovanna Lenzi; Livia Rossetti; Halina Zalewska

**As far as we're concerned Barbara represents evil and that's all there is to it. Having said that, all we need add is that** Un angelo per Satana **is merely funny, an effect opposite to what the director presumably intended.**
Film Mese September 1967

I was very young when I did those films. You look so absurd being melodramatic when you're young. It can work for Vincent Price – I mean, he's a certain age, and he's got a certain kind of look to crawl around pillars all the time. But it certainly can't work when you're 20. You look totally idiotic, because your face doesn't live up to what you're implying ... Why I became typecast I have no idea. *Barbara Steele* [quoted in *Video Watchdog* September-October 1991]

Barbara Steele as the high-handed Harriet Montebruno in her final Italian Gothic, *Un angelo per Satana* (1966)

Striking Italian artwork for the classy Carlos Fuentes
adaptation *La strega in amore* (1966)

If the film were intended to satirise Logan's craven hypocrisy the effect is undone by the sheer sadistic relish of this 'witch' burning sequence. This ending was devised exclusively by Damiani and his co-writer Ugo Liberatore, having no parallel in Fuentes' original, and the sheer horror of it forms a grim climax to the first wave of Italian Gothic. A half-fascinated ambivalence towards the seductive-destructive female figure had been the dominant motif of so many Italian horror pictures, yet in taking it to its logical conclusion *La strega in amore* seems to invite viewers, not to condemn the man's revulsion, but to share it.

It's a shame the film leaves such a bad taste in the mouth, because it's otherwise a thing of beauty, with crystalline monochrome images by Leonida Barboni and a stunning milieu of faded grandiloquence devised by Luigi Scaccianoce. The dualistic echoes of *La maschera del demonio* and, particularly, *I vampiri* wind right back to *Sunset Blvd*, with Johnson entering the airless atmosphere of the palazzo and fencing verbally with Sarah Ferrati's baleful Consuelo, whose back-story reveals that she's 58 (hardly the ancient crone the film seems to think she is) and was formerly married to the Mexican ambassador, who now lies embalmed in a glass sarcophagus next to the dusty library.

The centrepiece of the palazzo is a circular staircase, emphasising the labyrinthine perplexity into which Logan is plunged, and the film moves smoothly from Rosanna Schiaffino's Aura saying ambiguously that "My mother won't surrender to time" to a really stunning shot of the two women sitting together on a chaise longue, eerily echoing each other's gestures. Apart from the nasty ending, the film's only blunder is the inclusion of a former lover (Gian Maria Volonté) – again, a character not present in Fuentes' novella. He was presumably included to pad out the running time, and that's pretty much all he does.

## MOSS-COVERED GLOOM

The profound disorientation of a man mired in a strange villa that defies the rules of time and space featured, not just in *La strega in amore*, but also in Mario Bava's next film, with Bava making bravura use of a far more nightmarish spiral staircase while entirely excluding the ugly misogyny underlying the Damiani film. If *La strega in amore* was the mod, mean-spirited climax to Italian Gothic's first flood, then Bava's *Operazione paura* (Operation Fear) represents a sublime metaphysical coda.

Surprisingly, its quality was rewarded not just by export audiences but also by local ones; its domestic gross of 201 million lire may have undershot

quite so sanguine about that last sentiment. Starting production on 7 February 1966, this was the first of many Italian assignments for the smooth British actor Richard Johnson, precipitating him into a strange combination of aspirant art movie and moody psychological thriller based on Carlos Fuentes' recent novella *Aura* – which was also the film's working title. In negotiating the transition from Mexican magic realism to Italian Gothic, the film is situated in a beautifully captured modern-day Rome, where Johnson is a womanising writer, Logan, who's so outrageously chauvinist he even baulks at making the bed. ("Who, me?" he says to his long-suffering girlfriend.) Lured into becoming librarian to a reclusive aristocrat, he falls for the woman's beautiful daughter, Aura, but soon discovers that mother and daughter are one and the same. Then, facing the possibility of being usurped by a younger model, he lapses into macho panic and torches the Madonna-Whore figure (currently in her older guise) against the railings of her own palazzo.

*La strega in amore* by a couple of thousand, but Bava's film was nevertheless far more successful than the majority of 'straight' Gothics that had been pouring out of Italy in the preceding six years – including his own. This was presumably good news for the fly-by-night company that made it, a company that mid-way through production ran out of cash and appealed to cast and crew to continue without wages. (A particularly embarrassing moment, no doubt, for Luciano Catenacci, who was not only the project's tyro co-producer but also a prominent cast member.) Yet the film's takings will have been little consolation to Bava himself, who claimed to have received no payment for his contribution at all.

*1907. The superstitious inhabitants of Karmingen live in fear of the Villa Graps, where the Baroness of that name is consumed by grief and rage over the death of her eldest daughter Melissa. The girl lived only from 1880 to 1887 but her ghost is now conjured up by her mediumistic mother as a means of compelling the villagers to take their own lives. Called in to perform an autopsy on the latest victim, Dr Paul Eswai struggles to make sense of the mystery.*

In an opportunist gesture typical of the Italian film industy, Bava's most poetic film – complete with surrealist references to, among others, Jean Cocteau and M C Escher – got its name from the preponderance of larkish spy spoofs of the period that included the word 'operazione' in their titles. Two of these featured the archly named protagonist James Tont, while a third, Osvaldo Civirani's *Operazione poker*, may have been the film that some unsuspecting Italians expected to see when turning up to watch *Operazione paura*. What they got couldn't have been more different. *Le macabre ore della paura* (The Macabre Hours of Fear), as Bava's film was known in production, is more doom-laden than anything Italy's Gothic filone had yet produced. Not a ray of light seems to penetrate the moss-covered gloom of Karmingen, none of the characters so much as cracks a smile (unless to exult over death and destruction), and – as Stuart Byron aptly put it in his *Variety* review – Bava's "main horror character of ghost of a seven-year-old girl raises viewer's hair on cue whenever she appears."[28]

The writers of Bava's new film were Romano Migliorini and Roberto Natale, whose first joint venture had been Pupillo's *5 tombe per un medium* – the plot of which, as Tim Lucas has persuasively argued, was pretty comprehensively recycled for *Operazione paura*. Between them Migliorini and Natale gave Bava the bare bones of arguably his most extraordinary

achievement, a film which scrambles viewers' perceptions as surely as it does those of the rationalist hero, Dr Eswai. Bolstering a flimsy scenario, Bava here concocted some of his eeriest images – a family tomb clogged with cobwebs so big they're slung from the pillars like hammocks; Melissa's ball bouncing in slow motion over the sheeted corpse of one of her victims; the ghost's face, framed by flaxen tresses, staring with placid malevolence through a fogged-up window.

Composited from the bordering municipalities of Faleria and Calcata, the mythical Karmingen is a phantasmagoric landscape in which every interior is stained a sickly amber, every exterior a gangrenous green, and in which every mouldering archway is wreathed in backlit ground fog. On top of this, the place is brooded over by the baneful Villa Graps (itself a fusion of Titanus sets with the Villa Lancelotti in Frascati), a haunted edifice that, thanks to the Baroness' occult tinkerings, has become a nexus of dislocatory supernatural powers, a kind of netherworld limbo in which she finds herself trapped. Rather like the fearful Dr Karswell in the British classic *Night of the Demon*, Baroness Graps exercises only intermittent control over the elemental forces she has conjured up. Sitting in her cobwebbed boudoir she mutters "Leave me alone!" as a chorus of eerily muted 'voices' rise around her, a chorus supplemented by the subliminal giggling of her spectral daughter.

In this bizarre environment the local innkeeper notes the inexplicable tolling of a church bell and claims that "It isn't the wind. It's the hatred; the bell is being moved by the hatred." (Giuseppe Addobbati looks significantly gaunter and more haunted here than he did as the suave vampire of Polselli's *Il mostro dell'opera*.) The disorientation extends, too, to Dr Eswai's beautiful associate, Monika, who falls through space in a doll-infested nightmare only to find one of the sinister-looking dolls propped up at the foot of her bed. In the end even Eswai is forced to abandon his stubborn conviction that the trouble stems purely from "poverty and ignorance combined with superstition." In Villa Graps he responds to Monika's cry for help by running headlong through eight rooms that are really just the first room endlessly repeated, finally 'catching up with himself' in a truly startling doppelgänger pay-off. He then recoils against a massive painting of the villa's façade only to be absorbed into the canvas and somehow deposited outside the *real* façade.

A thrilling revision of a key scene in Corman's version of *The Masque of the Red Death*, Bava's doppelgänger moment was subsequently lifted wholesale in David Lynch's 1991 film *Twin Peaks: Fire Walk with Me*. The list of films and filmmakers

Giacomo Rossi Stuart enmeshed in the web of Villa Graps in *Operazione paura* (1966), which in Germany somehow became 'The Dead Eyes of Dr Dracula'

DIE TOTEN AUGEN DES Dr.DRACULA

## OPERAZIONE PAURA

Italy 1966
UK: *Curse of the Dead*
US: *Kill, Baby... Kill!*
FUL Films
83 minutes colour
in production February-March 1966

. . . . . . . . . . . . . . . . . . . . . . . . . . . .

Director of Photography: Antonio Rinaldi; Art Director: Alessandro Dell'Orco; Editor: Romano Fortini; Music: Carlo Rustichelli [and others, uncredited]; Make-up: Maurizio Giustini; Screenplay: Romano Migliorini,

Roberto Natale, Mario Bava; Story: Migliorini, Natale; Producers: Nando Pisani, Luciano Catenacci; Director: Mario Bava

Giacomo Rossi Stuart (Dr Paul Eswai); Erika Blanc (Monika Schuftan); Fabienne Dalí (Ruth); Giovanna Galletti (Baroness Graps); Piero Lulli (Inspector Krüger); Luciano Catenacci (Karl, Burgomeister); Micaela Esdra (Nadine); Franca Dominici (Martha); Giuseppe Addobbati (landlord); Mirella Pamphili (Irina); Valerio Valeri (Melissa Graps)

A creepy that has some fascinating moments of crawliness ... Mario Bava sets out to give us a spine-chiller in the grand manner. That it doesn't come off is less the fault of the direction, which does wonders in cramped conditions, but the believability of the characters involved ... Despite this, though, there are some quite chilling episodes which should silence the cynics in most audiences, and the photography ... has, at times, a bloodstained beauty.
*Daily Cinema* 26 May 1967

I remember we shot the film very quickly. It was all over in three weeks, maybe less. We'd shoot a scene and after a few minutes' rehearsal we'd shoot the next. It was really hard. But Mario was a great director. I loved the way he worked with actors: so simple, so sweet. There was no screaming on his set. He had a childlike enthusiasm and the beauty of it was that he communicated it to everyone working with him.
*Erika Blanc [quoted in Amarcord March-April 1998]*

influenced by *Operazione paura* is long, extending from Fellini and Scorsese right up to the vengeful, lank-haired ghosts of millennial J-Horror. More generally, the whole paraphernalia surrounding

Melissa – the eerily oscillating swing, the bouncing ball, the girlish giggling – would become foundation stones of the 'ghost child' sub-genre. It's all the more astounding, then, to discover that Bava underlined Melissa's otherworldliness by casting a suitably disguised little boy. "That child was awfully shy and highly suspicious of everyone," recalled Erika Blanc, who played Monika. "His name was Valerio [Valeri]. An extremely serious child whose expression never altered. Impassive. At one point the crew even began to be afraid of him. Superstition, I think."[29]

True to Italian tradition, Melissa is just one side of a double-edged female coin. Her opposite is the innocent Monika, now 21 but six years Melissa's junior and actually, as is revealed in a not especially surprising plot development, the dead girl's long-lost sister. (As Monika, Erika Blanc was here completing a Gothic triptych begun by *Il terzo occhio* and *La vendetta di Lady Morgan*. Slithering away from the above-mentioned bedside doll, she shows a great deal of leg but otherwise the film is remarkable for the way Bava entirely subordinates sex to the supernatural.) The Baroness' dedication to infernal powers has its counterpoise, too. The raven-haired Ruth is a beautiful white witch whose atavistic methods are pooh-poohed by the unbending Eswai. Satisfyingly, it's Ruth who ends up saving his bacon when he descends into the mind-altering maelstrom that is Villa Graps.

Rather less satisfying, however, is the way Ruth does it. The climactic return of Melissa's victims, heavily signposted in advance by the moanings of the damned resonating throughout the villa, never actually transpires. (The film's suddenly truncated budget may well have been to blame here.) Motivated by personal loss, Ruth instead goes to the villa and merely strangles the Baroness, getting reciprocally impaled on a fireside poker for her pains. Had the budget been up to it, the film might have ended with the kind of 'turning the instruments of evil against evil' scene exemplified by Hammer's *The Kiss of the Vampire*, in which the grizzled Professor Zimmer conjures a horde of vampire bats to invade the frightful Château Ravna. As it is, the film winds up with something of an anti-climax.

Perhaps this was appropriate. Italian Gothic, in its first phase at any rate, was here breathing its last. Symbolically, the once-thriving Titanus Appia studio, like the Galatea company that had shaped Bava's first directorial efforts, was on its last legs. *Operazione paura* therefore takes on an elegiac feel, underlined by its use of sets and locations from, among others, *L'ultima preda del vampiro*, *La cripta e l'incubo*, *Il boia scarlatto*, *La lama nel corpo* and *La vendetta di Lady Morgan*, together with a score attributed to Carlo Rustichelli but actually cannibalised from familiar themes by Rustichelli, Vlad, Lavagnino, Masi and Trovajoli. Indeed, the recurrence of well-known themes and images may well put viewers into a disorientating, head-spinning Villa Graps of their own.

Equally symbolically, Bava moved straight from *Operazione paura* to a painful assignment on one of the dumb spy spoofs referred to above. A fiasco featuring Vincent Price as the enervated villain, this was served up to Italians as *Le spie vengono dal semifreddo* (The Spies who Came In from the Semi-Cold) and to AIP audiences as *Dr Goldfoot and the Girl Bombs*. After that, in April 1967 Dino De Laurentiis assigned Bava the film version of the subversive comic-book *Diabolik*, and he wouldn't return to traditional horror for several years thereafter.

A typically attractive Italian locandina for the mod Gothic romance *La lunga notte di Veronique* (1966)

Yet *Operazione paura*, released in July 1966, wasn't quite the last Italian Gothic to reach cinemas during the genre's halcyon period. Made in May and issued on 1 October, Gianni Vernuccio's *La lunga notte di Veronique* (The Long Night of Veronique) opts for a suitably mournful fade-out in which an elderly Count descends into a tomb and reflects sadly on the suicide pact he reneged on some 50 years before. This is entirely in keeping with a film that's by no means a horror story but rather a tragic supernatural romance. "I think there's going to be a big return to romanticism,"[30] Vernuccio stated, rather optimistically, during production, citing the Fogazzaro classic *Malombra* as a model.

The film begins with a folksy ballad by the pop duo Paki e Paki plus the rubric 'It took three generations to seal a love pact'. And later on Vernuccio declares his influences quite clearly when the old man, faced with his previously unsuspected grandson, points out that this wouldn't happen "even in the worst 19th century novels." The ghost of the old man's sweetheart is played by Alba Rigazzi (Miss Italia 1965) and she makes some striking appearances. She's first seen, rather fetchingly, as a reflection in the red sheen of a sports car's bonnet, and she later skips, in a yellow mac, across a lush green sward to hitch a ride in a passing hearse. She also makes phone calls, to both the old man and his grandson. The latter, of course, falls in love with her and actually joins her in death. The film is very pretty, making the most of its bucolic Brianza locations and the Villa Mambretti in Fino Mornasco. But it's only really enlivened by a subplot involving the Count's saucy housekeeper (Maria Ardizzone), who brings the action right up to date with her lingerie-clad seduction of the boy. "If you prefer to do it on the floor," she shrugs, "it's all the same to me."

Vernuccio's underwhelming film was released in the UK under the laughably bald title *But You Were Dead*. And for a while there in the late 1960s it looked as if Italy's Gothic strain might be just that. This at least left the field free for Germany, France and especially Spain to get in on the act.

# Part Four

Dance of the vampire: Julián Ugarte lures Dyanik Zurakowska in *La marca del hombre lobo* (1968)

## *Nights of the Devil* 1967-1971

At Christmas 1966 the splendid Vittorio Gassman was the draw in Ettore Scola's comedy *L'arcidiavolo* (The Arch Devil); he was cast as Belphegor, an agent of Satan sent to sow discord among peace-loving 15th century Italians. Farcical variations notwithstanding, Italy's Gothic horrors were in the process of going underground for a time, given that their already well-worn conventions were beginning to appear quaint – and, more to the point, unprofitable – next to the hardbitten narratives and phenomenal commercial success of the emerging Spaghetti Westerns.

The ritualised violence in Italian westerns was paralleled by the flip, wink-tipping sadism featured in Britain's James Bond films. As Jonathan Rosenbaum has pointed out, these two 1960s phenomena dominated a decade that had begun with the butcher-knife shocks of Alfred Hitchcock's *Psycho* and would end with the balletic slow-motion massacres of Sam Peckinpah's *The Wild Bunch*. The catharsis provided by these films reflected a decade of tumultuous, often violent, social change, a ferment that was reflected back again by the staggering speed with which censorship restrictions were loosened – a loosening

that naturally revolutionised representations of sex as well as violence. The bewilderment attending these seismic shifts was particularly marked, not surprisingly, among the censors themselves. In Britain, for example, John Trevelyan of the BBFC pointed out that "The world is changing; people are changing; ideas are changing. These changes have been so rapid that it is difficult to assess their significance, or even to keep pace with them."[1]

In Italy, the end of the 1960s was marked by the onset of the so-called Years of Lead, a period that was to span a decade and more of social unrest, kidnappings, terrorist bombings and political assassinations. The scintillating years earlier in the 1960s, years during which Italy had exercised worldwide influence as an ultra-chic arbiter of style and fashion, suddenly seemed long gone. In this anxious atmosphere, cinemagoers turned to another new filone, the poliziotteschi. Hard-edged crime thrillers in the mould of Peter Yates' *Bullitt* and Don Siegel's *Dirty Harry*, these films bore titles – *Banditi a Milano* (Bandits in Milan), *Città violenta* (Violent City) – that spoke for themselves. Filmmakers interested in horror found an outlet in the collapse of censorship, which allowed them to mould macabre scenarios into the lascivious shapes demanded by sex films. The sex-horror hybrids that resulted, bringing to the surface all the concealed impulses of the older Gothics, would become omnipresent in the 1970s.

A similar hybrid of sex and horror seemed unlikely to take root in Spain, not merely because, under Franco, censorship still maintained its stranglehold, but also because Spain had barely produced any horror pictures anyway. That, however, was about to change. As a wholly unexpected Spanish horror boom began to manifest itself, the filmmakers involved had to keep on their toes. Not only were they required to make their films in two versions (chastely 'covered' ones for the domestic market, far nuder ones for export), they also had to adhere to the 'such things don't happen here' attitude of the Franco regime, resulting in stories set in Germany, France, Britain, Portugal – anywhere but Spain itself. The resultant flood of films was aimed, in any case, at foreign markets, for whom horror was a saleable genre and the actual nationality of the films immaterial.

The boom was preceded by a rare incursion of Spanish supernatural into the Academy Awards, when Francisco Rovira Beleta's extremely handsome-looking 1967 film *El amor brujo* (Bewitched Love) – depicting a love affair shadowed by a supposedly dead lover, and based on a Manuel de Falla ballet previously filmed in 1949 – was nominated as Best Foreign Language Film. It was a signal honour, and one that wouldn't be repeated.

## BLEACHED BONES, GREEN BLOOD, SPRING-LOADED TALONS

Having been in London in January 1967 to make *The Sorcerers* for producer Tony Tenser and director Michael Reeves, Boris Karloff's next stop, in February, was Torremolinos, the centre of Spain's burgeoning package-holiday industry. There, he was cast as blind sculptor Franz Badulescu in Santos Alcocer's *El coleccionista de cadáveres* (The Corpse Collector), another in the small range of hybrid US co-productions that preceded Spain's horror boom proper. This one would be exported as both *Cauldron of Blood* and *Blind Man's Buff*, though it failed to get a Spanish release until February 1970, exactly a year after Karloff's death. Sadly, its clumsily thrown-together appearance – complete with massively sluggish travelogue longueurs and a bewilderingly fragmented narrative that takes at least half the running time to get to the point – made it an undignified envoi at best.

Even so, the film boasts some pleasantly groovy production design (Gil Parrondo) and a few nuggets of effective horror, glimmering amid the mess rather like the bleached human bones that are exposed when Badulescu's sculptures are smashed. Viveca Lindfors is memorably perverse as his controlling wife Tania, fulfilling the Valli role from *Les Yeux sans visage* as she lures young innocents to the acid vat in her subterranean dungeon. Among her victims is Dyanik Zurakowska from *La llamada*, who is first serenaded on the harp and then killed in a halfway-effective stalking sequence. Similarly arresting are Tania's nightmare flashbacks to a childhood whipping, with the psychedelic visuals accompanied by shots of monocled Nazis and Karloff's goggled head rapidly decomposing via stop-motion.

Badulescu, of course, is in a direct line of descent from Lionel Atwill's Ivan Igor in the 1932 classic *Mystery of the Wax Museum*. Like him, he calls his sculptures "my children" but, unlike Igor, he doesn't know the full story behind the special armatures provided by Tania. "I'm an important artist," he complains to her, "and you treat me as though I were a child." As a result, their final showdown in the dungeon carries unexpected weight. After Tania's hand has been plunged gruesomely into the acid, Badulescu throws himself off a cliff moments before the credits roll. As a final insult, the film's consistently inappropriate score accompanies this moment of self-sacrifice with a comedy music sting.

Spain's Jess Franco, meanwhile, left the stifling restraints of his homeland behind and in the spring of 1967 made *Necronomicon*, a West German production shot in Lisbon and Berlin, with actor Adrian Hoven involved on the production side. It opens with a classic sequence that now ranks as quintessential Franco. In a limbo of impenetrable darkness, a Titian-haired dominatrix chastises a young man and woman, both suspended in rags from crudely fashioned cross-beams. The sado-masochistic content is (for the time) pretty extreme. Then, a nifty piece of rug-pulling – the floor-show ends, the lights come up, the performers take their bows and the well-heeled nightclub punters applaud politely. Unfortunately, the remainder of the film slides into soft-focus obfuscation as dreams merge into reality and back again. Janine Reynaud's dominatrix describes herself as "Lorna the erotic love queen" and ends up blinding Howard Vernon's black-tie-and-tails Admiral with a stiletto (leaving him literally gimlet-eyed) and stabbing her feckless jet-set lover (Jack Taylor) in the back of the neck. In the meantime, Franco nods to Fellini's *La dolce vita* with a thoroughly tiresome high-life party sequence, complete with a tuxedoed dwarf and dog-yapping socialites.

"Films are outmoded, don't you agree?" muses Taylor, excusing Buñuel, Godard and Lang from the charge; presumably flattered, Lang was much taken with the film. Retitled *Succubus* and touted as 'The Sensual Experience of 69', it also went down big in the USA. But, stripped of the shock factor that once attached to its violence and nudity, the film's foggy pretensions look empty and juvenile. Worse, in tune with Franco's recurring mind-control theme the apparently powerful Lorna character is revealed as a mere cipher manipulated by a possible Devil figure (played by Reynaud's husband, Michel Lemoine), who ends the film with a glib voice-over pronouncement of "You, Lorna, are Faustine."

Working with Adrian Hoven again, Franco's subsequent films in 1967 included two further Janine Reynaud vehicles, *Sadisterotica* and *Bésame monstruo* (Kiss Me, Monster), skittish Pop Art divertissements with the lightest of horror flavourings – a hirsute Morpho (Lemoine) in the first, a super-race and secret cult in the second. Then in the latter months of the year Franco was whisked off to Rio de Janeiro at the behest of British producer Harry Alan Towers, leaving Hoven to direct a Franco scenario that eventually saw release as *Im Schloß der blutigen Begierde* (In the Castle of Bloody Lust). The castle in question, though decidedly under-used by Hoven, was Austria's Burg Kreuzenstein, while the team assembled was the by-now familiar one of Reynaud, Lemoine, Vernon and Hoven's co-producer on the Franco films, the playboy and Siemens millionaire Pier A Caminnecci.

The result is a barely comprehensible mess in which a gaggle of hip partygoers fetch up at the home of a grieving Count (Vernon) who's bent on reviving his dead daughter. In his desperation he has set loose a bear in the surrounding countryside, a bizarre detail introduced merely so that Lemoine can later be beaten up by said bear when he tries to escape. It's a man in a bear suit, of course, and this strange echo of *The Winter's Tale* is augmented by other Shakespearean references. King Lear's "Let copulation thrive" speech issues in voice-over during a prolonged flashback to a 17th century gang rape, filmed in soft focus as Reynaud watches from aloft while languorously caressing her bare breasts. And at the end an Ophelia type goes around distributing flowers while quoting from *Hamlet*. There's an unusually graphic sex scene between Reynaud and Caminnecci, but the poverty of the filmmakers' imagination is indicated, not merely by recurrent rape scenes, but also by endless stock footage of genuine open-heart surgery as Vernon and his surgical assistant do their stuff in the basement. It goes on and on and on.

Vladimir Medar, the bearded Croatian actor cast as Vernon's looming manservant, was fresh from a far superior West German chiller shot just a few months

earlier. *Die Schlangengrube und das Pendel* (The Snakepit and the Pendulum) was touted as Germany's first Gothic horror since before the war – rightly so, if we discount *Die Nackte und der Satan* and *Der Fluch der grünen Augen* by virtue of their contemporary settings. Conceived by Constantin-Film as the first in a new line of 'grusenfilme', Harald Reinl's picture brought Christopher Lee to Munich on 19 June 1967, halfway through the schedule. Two days before his arrival, Lee announced in a fan club bulletin that his role was that of "a rather revolting aristocrat." "I really have no idea whether this film will ever be shown outside Europe," he added, "and it is just possible that this might be an advantage."

> *Roger Montelise and Lillian von Brabant receive separate, yet equally mysterious, invitations to visit Castle Andomai on Good Friday. Popularly known as 'das blutige Schloß', Andomai was home to the notorious Count Regula, executed 35 years before for the murder of 12 virgins. After a long and harrowing journey, Roger and Lillian are present for the Count's ritual revival by his undead manservant Anatol, only to learn that they're both descended from Regula's long-ago accusers...*

Though cast as the absurdly named Graf Regula (which sounds like a constipation cure even in German), Lee actually had nothing much to worry about. Advertised as 'Die Reise in das Land des Grauens!' (The Journey into the Land of Horror!), *Die Schlangengrube* is somewhat short on incident but is otherwise a curiously charming film, owing more to Bava's *La maschera del demonio* and Fisher's *Dracula Prince of Darkness* than its supposed source in Edgar Allan Poe.

Fisher liked to refer to his horror pictures as fairy tales for adults, yet Reinl's film resembles, in most of its essentials, a fairy tale for children. There are off-colour details like 12 dead virgins arranged in artistic postures around Regula's torture chamber, or the bloody morsels pecked at by a gaggle of indoor vultures. But otherwise the film is quite family-friendly. It's appropriate, then, that Reinl's opening scenes are played out in the quaintly mediaeval streets of Rothenburg ob der Tauber, the same location in which Robert Helpmann's Child Catcher plies his trade in *Chitty Chitty Bang Bang* – a film that started shooting just ten days after *Die Schlangengrube* finished.

In line with the faintly whimsical atmosphere cooked up by Reinl, Peter Thomas' score ignores all the story's cues for Gothic flamboyance, substituting absurdly rinky-dink themes that are much more Edgar Wallace than Edgar Poe. Similarly, the spiked mask attached to Regula's face in the pre-credits sequence carries

Karin Dor and Lex Barker, trapped in the catacombs of Castle Andomai in *Die Schlangengrube und das Pendel* (1967)

none of the bloody impact contained in the equivalent Bava scene. And when the resurrection ritual finally arrives, Anatol cuts his wrists but the blood exuded is green; furthermore, the blood splashes only onto the glass surface of Regula's casket, not onto Regula's actual remains, making the scene appear positively anaemic when compared with the shower of bright-red Kensington Gore that had recently reactivated *Dracula Prince of Darkness*. That film is also recalled by Medar's gun-toting, pleasure-loving padre (though, unlike Fisher's Father Sandor, he turns out to be an impostor) and by Anatol himself, whose resemblance to Dracula's manservant Klove is emphasised by his similarly staged entrance in the castle.

Where *Die Schlangengrube* scores is in its photography and production design, which between them create an extraordinary concentration of Gothic images. Roger and Lillian's mist-wreathed coach journey to Regula's castle is engagingly eerie; the limbs on the trees are human ones, hanged bodies depend from the branches and corpses are scattered underfoot. And in the castle itself, art directors Gabriel Pellon and Rolf Zehetbauer clearly had a field day. Regula's decorative scheme includes walls studded with human skulls, hellish frescoes

## DIE SCHLANGENGRUBE UND DAS PENDEL

West Germany 1967
UK: *The Blood Demon*
US: *The Torture Chamber of Dr Sadism*
*Constantin Film*
*80 minutes colour*
*production began 16 May 1967*

. . . . . . . . . . . . . . . . . . . . . . . . . . . . . . .

Directors of Photography: Ernst W Kalinke, Dieter Liphardt; Art Directors: Gabriel Pellon and [uncredited] Rolf Zehetbauer; Editor: Hermann Haller; Sound: Hans-Joachim Richter; Music: Peter Thomas; Costumes: Irms Pauli; Make-up: Erich L

Schmekel and [uncredited] Gerda Bublitz; Special Effects: Erwin Lange; Optical Effects: Theo Nischwitz; Screenplay: Manfred R Köhler, from motifs by Edgar Allan Poe; Producer: Erwin Gitt; Director: Harald Reinl

Lex Barker (*Roger Montelise / Roger von Marienberg*); Karin Dor (*Baroness Lilian von Brabant*); Christopher Lee (*Graf Frederic Regula [Graf von Andomai]*); Karl Lange (*Anatol*); Christiane Rücker (*Babette*); Vladimir Medar (*Pater Fabian*); Dieter Eppler (*coachman*)

A surprise packet of deadpan humour deriving from the contrast between the lavish supply of corpses, snakes, rats, tarantulas, scorpions and buzzards, and the tongue-in-cheek banality of the English dialogue ... Weird and wondrously camp, employing every ghoulish trick in the book to provoke more laughs than screams. Enormous fun. *Today's Cinema* 21 November 1969

I much enjoyed my stay in Munich and was pleasantly surprised at what I saw of the film in the projection. The colour is superb, the sets are excellent and the acting more than adequate. So it may not be quite so ineffective as I feared.
Christopher Lee [fan club letter, dated 22 July 1967]

apparently painted by Hieronymus Bosch, skeletons dressed in suits of armour, a scything pendulum that almost cuts Roger in two, and a cavernous snakepit featuring human arms and yet more skulls. Meanwhile, snakes, tarantulas, lizards and scorpions abound, confirming Regula's domain as a nightmare realm from which there appears to be no escape.

Erwin Lange's special effects, however, seem to have been allocated less of the budget. An acid spill and a climactic round of disintegrations are crudely achieved, and Anatol's spontaneously healed bullet wound is done in a stop-motion plasticine style reminiscent, again, of a children's film.

Lex Barker – the former Tarzan and so-called 'Sexy Lexy', who had acquired a huge German following in Reinl's popular Westerns – is a stolid presence as Roger, not making very much of the character's belated quest for his true identity. Reinl's wife, Karin Dor, goes through her Gothic heroine paces with aplomb, while Dieter Eppler, formerly the heavily rouged bloodsucker of *La strage dei vampiri*, is more comfortably cast here as a nervous coachman. (In common with the film's anodyne scheme, he's the only character, apart from the undead ones, who dies – of a heart attack.) As for the weary Regula, the role isn't much more than a glorified cameo, and Lee isn't helped by an unusually greasepaint-heavy make-up job. He's upstaged, in any case, by his own manservant, who has much more screen time and, as played by Carl Lange, is a splendidly ghoulish figure.

"You could, if you wanted to, call the character a living dead but he is *not* a vampire,"[2] Lee observed, rather testily, during production. By this stage Lee had good reason to seem almost as jaded as Graf Regula. As an indication of the interchangeability of his recent roles he had only to look at some of the uninspired dialogue they entailed. Late in 1966 *The Vengeance of Fu Manchu* had required him to say "Now my vengeance is complete," a line echoed in *Die Schlangengrube* when Regula looks up from his retorts and mutters "A few more seconds and my vengeance is complete" – and echoed again in May 1968 by the line "Now my revenge is complete" in *Dracula Has Risen from the Grave*. Yet the only thing that could reasonably be called complete at this period was Lee's disenchantment. Salvation was at hand, however, for an extremely busy 1969 brought with it

an engagement for Billy Wilder in *The Private Life of Sherlock Holmes*. On this cue, Lee's involvement, not just in Euro horror but horror generally, would begin to taper off as a new decade dawned – though not completely, as will be seen.

Like Lee, several of the other cast and crew members assembled for *Die Schlangengrube und das Pendel* were veterans of Rialto's Edgar Wallace pictures, among them Karin Dor, Carl Lange, Dieter Eppler, composer Peter Thomas, cinematographer Ernst W Kalinke and, of course, director Harald Reinl. In 1967 the Wallace films, with their heady mix of fog-shrouded faux-English landscapes, cowled murderers, poisonous aristocratic families and dashing Scotland Yard men, still seemed to be going from strength to strength – though, given the increasingly permissive nature of their competitors, obsolescence was just around the corner.

In February, Lange had played a sinister asylum superintendent in *Die blaue Hand* (The Blue Hand), in which the titular weapon is a metal gauntlet with spring-loaded talons, useful for impaling young men at the organ or slicing through the heroine's lace curtains. Prefiguring his behaviour in *Die Schlangengrube*, Lange arranges for the girl (Diana Körner) to be trapped in a room seething with vermin. Under the heading 'Abominations from the Vaults', a contemporary reviewer noted, tongue firmly in cheek, that director Alfred Vohrer had reverted to "Großvaters Gruselkino" (Grandpa's scary movies), seeking out "Schocker-Schrecks" in a "Mabuse-Milieu" where "skeletons grin in crypts, secret doors creak, and the hooded killer comes at night ... A hideous face slavers around the ghastly loony bin, the psychiatrist lets loose snakes and rats, and out springs: Klaus Kinski. Kinski escalates the film to total terror – he plays a dual role."[3]

Next in line was *Der Mönch mit der Peitsche* (The Monk with the Whip), in which a mad scientist gasses his assistant and then has his own neck

*'London under the spell of uncanny crime.' Advertising for Rialto's 23rd Edgar Wallace film,* Die blaue Hand *(1967)*

broken by the titular whip even before the opening credits are over. *Der Hund von Blackwood Castle* (The Hound of Blackwood Castle) completed the 1967 schedule in October, showcasing a dog fitted with snake-envenomed fake fangs, an underground snake pit, and a supposedly dead sea captain laid out in an ornate sarcophagus. Inspecting the regulation old dark house, Siegfried Schürenberg's delightful Sir John of Scotland Yard makes one of the series' drollest observations when noticing a skull on the mantelpiece. "An example of ancestral worship," he muses. "Did you ever see so many cobwebs? No wonder the sun has set on the British Empire!"

With the three titles concocted in 1968 (all of them directed, like the previous year's trio, by Alfred Vohrer), the series fell into the inevitable trap of cannibalising itself. In February, *Im Banne des Unheimlichen* (Under the Spell of the Uncanny) went through the usual paces but added a hideous, skull-masked villain closely modelled on the 1946 Republic serial *The Crimson Ghost*. *Der Gorilla von Soho* (The Gorilla of Soho) followed in June; more or less a remake of Vohrer's 1961 classic *Die toten Augen von London*, this substituted a lunatic in a ridiculous ape suit for the blind hulk previously played by Ady Berber. Finally, *Der Mann mit dem Glasauge* (The Man with the Glass Eye) opted to retread *Der Bucklige von Soho*, a film released just two years previously, with the white-slavery routine transferred from a reform school to a London burlesque theatre.

*Der Mann* completed shooting just before Christmas 1968, after which there was a long gap before production began in January 1971 on the series' damp-squib final entry, Harald Philipp's *Die Tote aus der Themse* (The Corpse in the Thames). The Rialto series had by this stage numbered no fewer than 29 films – the same score racked up over a rather longer period by Britain's Carry On films, which in their ensemble atmosphere closely resembled the Wallace Krimis.

The long pause between *Der Mann* and *Die Tote* had been filled by Rialto's proxy attempt to keep pace with changing public tastes. Having contributed 30 per cent of the finance to the Riccardo Freda giallo *A doppia faccia* (Double Face), they passed it off in Germany as another Wallace picture under the title *Das Gesicht im Dunkeln* (The Face in the Dark). In 1972 they tried the trick twice more, putting out Massimo Dallamano's *Cosa avete fatto a Solange?* (What Have You Done to Solange?) as *Das Geheimnis der grünen Stecknadel* (The Mystery of the Green Pin) and Umberto Lenzi's *Sette orchidee macchiate di rosso* (Seven Orchids Stained Red) as *Das Rätsel des silbernen Halbmonds* (The Riddle of the Silver Crescents). So Rialto's total, depending

on how you look at it, could be recorded as 32 rather than 29. Either way, these three Italian films had to be extensively trimmed for German release. The Rialto Krimis may have provided a loose blueprint for the Italian gialli, but by the early 1970s they had been far outdistanced by them in gruesome tone, sexual aberration and violent incident.

Even so, the Wallace films soon acquired nostalgic allure, as was amply demonstrated, in a backhanded sort of way, by a couple of ribald 21st century parodies, *Der Wixxer* (The Wanker) and *Neues vom Wixxer* (News from the Wanker). Made in 2003 and 2006 respectively, these two had the good grace to retain a few of the original Rialto veterans, notably, in the second film, Joachim Fuchsberger. To *Der Spiegel*, these films, though utterly puerile, were proof that "Even in the 21st century, it's simply impossible not to be captivated by Edgar Wallace." Or, put more simply: "Wallace ist Kult."[4]

## FRENCH REVOLUTION

In the 1960s France's horror output was decidedly slim, though the looser area of fantastique was better represented, in large part thanks to several rekindlings of the spirit of Louis Feuillade and Arthur Bernède.

Chief among these was Georges Franju's charming 1963 reimagining of *Judex*, co-written by Feuillade's grandson Jacques Champreux, which comes complete with a stunning falcon-masked entrance for the title character, a substantial role for the veteran character actor René Génin, and a fetishistic rooftop battle between Francine Bergé and Sylva Koscina. There's also a scene in which Jacques Jouanneau is seen eagerly reading a Fantômas thriller – the Feuillade subject that Franju frankly admitted he would have preferred to remake. The character fell instead to André Hunebelle, whose mid-decade trilogy of *Fantômas* revivals starred Jean Marais and revelled in hi-tech 007-style extravagance. Eventually, in 1973 Franju would invoke Fantômas by proxy in his final work *L'Homme sans visage* (The Man Without a Face), a TV series later cobbled into a compromised feature called *Nuits rouges* (Red Nights). The writer was Jacques Champreux again, who also starred as the titular super-criminal – boasting, among other accomplishments, a bunch of brain-tampered 'zombies' at his command and a glamorous, rooftop-crawling confederate in Gayle Hunnicutt.

Soon after Franju's *Judex* came another manifestation of the combined shade of Feuillade-Bernède. Claude Barma's four-part Bernède adaptation *Belphégor ou le fantôme du Louvre* (Belphegor or the Phantom of the Louvre) starred the cult chanteuse Juliette Gréco and kept ten million French viewers riveted to their

A masterful creation: Jacqueline Sieger's Queen of the Vampires in *Le Viol du vampire* (1967)

Queen of Spades), shot in early 1965 by Léonard Keigel and marking the last screen appearance of the great 1930s star Dita Parlo. With the ageing Countess taking precedence in this version of the story, the haunting of her inadvertent killer is reduced to the Countess' face appearing briefly in a window pane, though a neat coda shows the now-ghostly protagonists sitting down at a card table prior to a 1960s cleaning lady passing through with a vacuum cleaner.

Beyond these scattered morsels there wasn't much on offer. Yet French fantastique was about to receive an entirely unexpected shot in the arm from the social and political upheavals that marked 1968. On Friday 22 March that year, a student occupation at the recently opened Paris University at Nanterre triggered a sequence of events that was to become, as Steven Erlanger has put it, "a watershed in French life, a holy moment of liberation for many, when youth coalesced, the workers listened and the semi-royal French government of President Charles de Gaulle took fright."[5] After Paris riots on 6 and 10 May, France's workforce showed its solidarity by coming out on strike; within a fortnight a staggering ten million workers had downed tools. On Monday the 27th a momentous meeting of the Union Nationale des Étudiants de France at the Charléty stadium featured explicit calls for revolution. Three days later, de Gaulle called an election and the ironic upshot was that in late June he was swept back to power with a colossal majority.

It was on Monday the 27th, that flashpoint day when the cry for revolution went up at Charléty, that a modest little film called *Le Viol du vampire* (The Rape of the Vampire) opened in Paris. Unsurprisingly, in so volatile an atmosphere a film as uniquely off-kilter as this provoked localised riots of its own. The beleaguered writer-director, not yet 30 and at the time a sound editor for a newsreel company, was Jean Rollin.

Ten years earlier, Rollin's first short, *Les Amours jaunes* (The Yellow Amours), had been derived from the poète maudit Tristan Corbière. His other influences included Feuillade and the surrealist painters Max Ernst, Paul Delvaux and René Magritte; he would pay tribute to yet another inspiration in a two-part *Midi-Minuit Fantastique* article called *Aujourd'hui, Gaston Leroux*. He was ideally placed, then, to answer a call from distributor Jean Lavie, who had acquired the rather brief 1942 potboiler *Dead Men Walk* and needed something to go with it. Financed by the American expatriate Sam Selsky, Rollin concocted a 35-minute featurette called *Le Viol du vampire* for 100,000 francs. Impressed, Selsky suggested making another. With *Les Femmes vampires* (The Vampire Women) in the can, it was decided to fuse the two

television sets throughout March 1965. A film cash-in, *La Malédiction de Belphégor* (The Curse of Belphegor), followed in 1967, with directors Georges Combret and Jean Maley moving the supposed hauntings to the Toulon Opéra, where a decidedly lame body-count mystery develops with no discernible basis in Bernède's original novel. Despite this, in 2000 the TV show's continuing mystique inspired Jean-Paul Salomé's glitzy feature *Belphégor Le fantôme du Louvre*.

Short subjects derived from Poe were sometimes available, as in Robert Lachenay's 1960 version of *Le Scarabée d'or* (The Gold Bug) and Alexandre Astruc's *Le Puits et le pendule* (The Pit and the Pendulum), which appeared on TV in January 1964 as a showcase for Maurice Ronet. Beyond Poe, Guy de Maupassant was the source of Ado Kyrou's *La Chevelure* (The Hair, 1960), with Michel Piccoli driven mad on discovering a strand of hair inside a piece of antique furniture, and Jean-Daniel Pollet's striking 1966 update of *Le Horla*, which arms Laurent Terzieff with microphones and tape recorders as he succumbs to an invisible vampire. Where features were concerned, there was an ornate but timid remake of Pushkin's *La Dame de pique* (The into a feature and advertise the result as 'Le 1er film de Vampire français!' (the first French vampire film!).

Announcing itself as a 'mélodrame en deux parties', the feature version of *Le Viol du vampire* offers a concise preview of Rollin's style right from the outset. We have the limpidly poetic imagery (a white-clad woman reclining against a fungoid tree, with a small bat attached to her chest), the impish humour (a gurning village idiot lurches into camera and collapses directly underneath Rollin's director credit), and the emphasis on luscious eroticism (the first naked breasts appear before five minutes are up). In the first part, four apparent vampire women – calling themselves "damned souls, haunted by our desires" – are pursued by three apparent vampire hunters, with events (apparently) being orchestrated by a crazy old country squire in cravat, blazer and cavalry twills. A duelling scene in Louis Quinze costume ends with a bat efficiently skewered on a rapier; a further duel is a real visual treat, with sparklers, sconces and leaping flames illuminating the façade of the women's château as they fence. A peasant revolt then leads to the beach at Dieppe – a location that had impressed Rollin as a child and would therefore crop up in film after film, making him as much the master of bleak seascapes and groyne-bisected pebbles as M R James.

The 'deuxième partie' is even less comprehensible than the first, though it picks up on the beach with the death of the squire at the hands of the so-called Queen of Vampires and her entourage. (The Queen, played by a young psychiatric nurse called Jacqueline Sieger, is a masterful creation.) The action comprises effective scenes in crypts and operating theatres, plus a clinic where some kind of vampire antidote is being processed; we're also transported to chilly country lanes where cars cruise by in scenes very similar to George Romero's *Night of the Living Dead*, which was released some six months later. Finally, a fully fledged 'happening' at the disused Théâtre du Grand Guignol blooms into all-out insurrection, unconsciously mirroring not only Lindsay Anderson's *If....* but also the riotous scenes in the cinemas in which Rollin's film first played. The two-part structure, pulpy narrative and beautiful black-and-white photography by Guy Leblond echo the movie serials Rollin so admired, and the score by Free Jazz specialist François Tusques is extraordinary. "The world will become a feast of blood," announces the Queen to riotous applause, "and we will have the best seats!" Words that would set the pattern for Rollin's future career.

The countercultural spirit that in part animated Rollin was vividly present, too, in a striking 1968 short called *La Fée sanguinaire* (The Bloodthirsty Fairy),

in which a mysterious young woman is delivered to her victim's door in an industrial barrel. The young man, who thumbs through Georges de Coulteray's *Le Sadisme au cinéma* before getting round to opening the barrel, ends up bloodily emasculated by his naked guest, after which his penis is added to a collection of jam jars containing the members of various assassinated political leaders. (The one marked 'Kennedy' has two; others, such as the one marked 'De Gaulle', are, for the time being at least, empty.) The film has 'Paris 68' stamped right through it and was among the the first of numerous avant-garde provocations from the Belgian experimentalist Roland Lethem. In addition to To Katinaki and Pierre Lampe in the leads, the cast includes the young critic Jean-Pierre Bouyxou and production designer Jio Berk, both of whom would graduate to working with Jean Rollin.

## SUICIDE LEAP

The French upheavals of spring 1968 extended to the film industry too; in fact, it was a series of violent demonstrations related to the Cinémathèque Française that did much to lay the groundwork for the subsequent uprising. In February Henri Langlois, director of the Cinémathèque, was summarily dismissed, a high-handed measure from André Malraux's Ministry of Culture that created an international scandal. Cowed by the ferment, Malraux finally reinstated Langlois in late April, while simultaneously slashing the Cinémathèque's budget. The sequel took place at that year's Cannes Film Festival, where on 18 May the screening of Carlos Saura's *Peppermint frappé* was prevented by Saura himself and his star Geraldine Chaplin; along with Jean-Luc Godard and François Truffaut, they physically prevented the Grande Salle curtains from being opened. The call was to show solidarity with the students and workers of France by cancelling the festival – and the following afternoon, amid rioting, the cancellation duly took place.

Shown the day before the *Peppermint frappé* chaos was a film directed in part by Louis Malle, who happened to be a member of the Cannes jury that year. This was *Histoires extraordinaires* (Extraordinary Stories), an Edgar Allan Poe anthology that arguably lost some commercial momentum thanks to the historic events that upstaged it. A French-Italian co-production masterminded by Raymond Eger and Alberto Grimaldi, the project originated with the announcement of numerous big names, all of them bandied about purely to attract other big names; among them were Visconti, Bergman, Renoir, Losey, Welles and Chabrol. Conceived as a seven-episode affair, the project

Terence Stamp
goes to pieces
at Cinecittà in
the *Toby Dammit*
episode of *Histoires
extraordinaires* (1967)

## HISTOIRES EXTRAORDINAIRES

France-Italy 1967
Italy: *Tre passi nel delirio*
UK / US: *Tales of Mystery and Imagination /
Spirits of the Dead*
Les Films Marceau-Cocinor Paris / Produzioni
Europee Associati Rome
121 minutes colour
production began 20 March 1967 (William
Wilson), May 1967 (Metzengerstein),
October 1967 (Toby Dammit)
. . . . . . . . . . . . . . . . . . . . . . . . . . . .
In Charge of Production: Raymond Eger; Based
on stories by Edgar Allan Poe; **Metzengerstein**
– Director of Photography: Claude Renoir;
Set Decorator: Jean André; Editor: Hélène
Plemiannikov; Costumes: Jacques Fonteray;
Music: Jean Prodromidès; Screenplay: Roger
Vadim, Pascal Cousin, Clement Biddlewood
[English version]; Director: Roger Vadim;
**William Wilson** – Director of Photography:
Tonino Delli Colli; Art Director: Carlo Leva;
Editors: Franco Arcalli, Suzanne Baron;
Costumes: Ghislain Uhry; Music: Diego
Masson; Screenplay: Louis Malle, Clement
Biddlewood [English version]; Director:
Louis Malle; **Toby Dammit** – Director of
Photography: Giuseppe Rotunno; Art
Director: Fabrizio Clerici; Editor: Ruggiero
Mastroianni; Costumes: Piero Tosi; Music:

Nino Rota; Screenplay: Federico Fellini,
Bernardino Zapponi [uncredited on English
print], Co-Producer: Alberto Grimaldi;
Director: Federico Fellini.

**Metzengerstein** – Jane Fonda (Countess
Frederique Metzengerstein); Peter Fonda (Baron
Wilhelm Berlifitzing); James Robertson Justice
(counsellor to the Countess); Françoise Prevost
(friend of the Countess); Georges Douking
(tapestry maker); Philippe Lemaire (Philippe);
Carla Marlier (Claude); Serge Marquand (Hugues);
Marlène Alexandre (courtier); uncredited on
English print: Anny Duperey (courtier); **William
Wilson** – Brigitte Bardot (Giuseppina); Alain
Delon (William Wilson); Katia Christine (woman
on dissection table); Umberto d'Orsi (Hans);
Daniele Vargas (professor); Renzo Palmer (priest);
Marco Stefanelli (young William); uncredited
on English print: John Karlsen (schoolmaster);
**Toby Dammit** – Terence Stamp (Toby Dammit);
Salvo Randone (Padre Spagna); Anne Tonietti
(TV commentator); Marie-Ange Aniés (starlet);
Marina Yaru (child / Devil); David Bresson; Peter
Dane; Monica Pardo; uncredited on English print:
Fabrizio Angeli, Ernesto Colli (film directors);
Andrea Fantasia (film producer); Antonia Pietrosi
(actress); Polidor (old actor); Alfredo Rizzo (irate
motorist); Milena Vukotic (interviewer).

With the exception of original authorship, the three films have nothing in
common. *Toby Dammit*, the first new Fellini to be seen here since *Juliet of the
Spirits* in 1965, is marvelous: a short movie but a major one. The Vadim is as
overdecorated and shrill as a drag ball, but still quite fun, and the Malle, based
on one of Poe's best stories, is simply tedious. New York Times 4 September 1969

He [Fellini] wanted to make one of my stories [into a film], and asked me to
work with him on the script. But soon he found out this was impossible, that
it had to be Poe, and so we turned instead to *Never Bet the Devil Your Head*.
By the time we finished, nothing was left except for the title [sic] and the
ending. Bernardino Zapponi [quoted in Alpert, Fellini: A Life, 1986]

eventually boiled down to just three stories and three
directors – Malle, Roger Vadim and Federico Fellini.

*Three strange tales derived from the works of Edgar Allan
Poe. In Metzengerstein, a vicious young Countess
victimises her ethereal cousin and he returns from the
dead as a vengeful stallion. In William Wilson,
a sadistic military cadet is bedevilled by his own
doppelgänger, eventually killing him and thus killing
himself. And in Toby Dammit a dissipated young
British film star loses his head, quite literally, when
immersed in the hellish phantasmagoria of Cinecittà.*

Even in its less ambitious form, the schedule of
*Histoires extraordinaires* stretched across a nine-month
period. Malle's *William Wilson* was shot in March 1967
and Vadim's *Metzengerstein* in May (immediately before
the 1 June start date of his iconic comic-strip fantasy
*Barbarella*). Fellini, recovering from a serious illness,
only got round to directing *Toby Dammit* in October.
The film's art-house chic was further bolstered by
the prettiest people of the moment – Jane Fonda and
her brother Peter for Vadim, Alain Delon and Brigitte
Bardot for Malle, and Terence Stamp (deputising for
Peter O'Toole) for Fellini. On release, the Italian title
was *Tre passi nel delirio* (Three Steps into Delirium),
while in America AIP distributed the film as *Spirits of
the Dead*, adding a 27-second Poe recitation by Vincent
Price in a cheapjack effort to dovetail the film with
their own Poe franchise.

Despite their impeccably modish credentials, the first two stories, *Metzengerstein* and *William Wilson*, might more aptly be titled *Histoires ennuyeuses*. To listen to and look at, the first is almost as arresting as Vadim's *...Et mourir de plaisir*. It has a similar harp-laden score from Jean Prodromidès plus ravishing views of the Finistère coastline from cinematographer Claude Renoir. Decked out in ridiculous fetish gear by costume designer Jacques Fonteray, Jane Fonda is a mediaeval "petty Caligula" whose equivocal fascination for a neighbouring Baron results in his death and subsequent resurrection as a huge black stallion – which she climactically 'rides' into an orgasmic inferno. The sexual implications are made pretty plain; she "seemed riveted to the saddle," we're told, while incest is added to bestiality by the stunt casting of Peter Fonda as the Baron. Vadim makes the horse, thundering through an archway amid plumes of black smoke, an impressively oneiric figure, but the scenes of Fonda's attendant exquisites, lolling about in a haze of Flower Power decadence, are equal parts rhythmless and risible. There's also an idiot-proof narration that drones on interminably.

Shot in Bergamo, the Malle story is similarly tripped up by its central set-piece, in this case a dreary and suspense-free card game in which Delon's sociopathic cadet humiliates Bardot's sultry card-sharp but is stymied for the umpteenth time by his extremely persistent doppelgänger. For film purposes there's no real story to get to grips with here, though Malle does what he can with a lengthy flashback to Wilson's childhood, including a scene of a fellow schoolboy being dangled over a tub seething with rats. For the rest, Malle pads out the action, rather listlessly, with sexual sadism, most of it directed at Katia Christine. Stretched out topless on a dissection slab, Christine's character is publicly tortured by Wilson and enriches the story with one telling detail. When the protective doppelgänger appears, her confusion and instinctive fear of the uncanny cause her to rush, fatally, into Wilson's arms rather than the double's.

Unsurprisingly, Fellini's *Toby Dammit* – based, just barely, on Poe's *Never Bet the Devil Your Head* – is in a different class altogether. Terence Stamp, made up on Fellini's instructions to look like Edgar Allan Poe, is a fragmenting British film star who is precipitated into a genuinely infernal vision of Rome when signing up for a Vatican-sponsored Catholic Western.

This, eight years on, is the monochrome jet-set satire of Fellini's *La dolce vita* curdled into the hues of a sickly, psychedelic nightmare. The skies are a roiling orange, as if the bomb has just dropped; masked faces, cardboard cut-outs and other bizarre simulacra await Toby at the airport; a gala reception-cum-fashion parade-cum awards ceremony takes place on a strange causeway over a misty, floodlit lake; and his own personal devil, a grinning, flaxen-haired little girl, appears to him with a white, bouncing ball. (The girl, played by Marina Yaru, is a verbatim quote from Bava's recent *Operazione paura*, causing Bava to vacillate between feeling ripped-off and rather flattered.) Hedged about by robotic grotesques from the nethermost regions of Italy's celebrity circuit, the vacuous Toby is clearly embroiled in a Swinging 60s purgatory, so it only remains for him to embark on a suicidal journey in the gratis Ferrari that lured him to Rome in the first place.

The hell-for-leather drive to the collapsed, limbo-locked Ariccia bridge – bristling once more with dummies, face masks and even a flock of fake sheep, to replicate Toby's fragmenting perceptions – is a dazzling tour de force, brought to a calmly disquieting end as his head is plucked from the tarmac and the dawn rises on a vista of utter desolation. The suicide leap and the severed head are pretty much all that remain of Poe's original, yet the film represents a perfect fusion of Fellini's trademark grotesquerie with Poe's own. Helping effect this fusion was co-writer Bernardino Zapponi, who would move on to several other Fellini projects as well as working with Dario Argento, Dino Risi and Juan Buñuel.

Having decapitated Terence Stamp, Fellini planned to do exactly the same to Margaret Rutherford in a proposed sequel to *Toby Dammit* based on Poe's *How to Write a Blackwood's Article*. Sadly, this fascinating idea never came to fruition. In the wake of *Histoires extraordinaires*, France's enduring veneration for Poe, which of course dated right back to Baudelaire, yielded a couple of short subjects – Andrée Girard's *Le Cœur révélateur* (The Tell-Tale Heart) and Robert Lachenay's *Morella*, both in 1971. Another decade on, the TV company FR3 resurrected the collective title *Histoires extraordinaires* for a rather variable series of six star-studded Poe adaptations, comprising Claude Chabrol's *Le Système du docteur Goudron et du professeur Plume*, Alexandre Astruc's *La Chute de la maison Usher*, Ruy Guerra's *La Lettre volée* (The Purloined Letter), Maurice Ronet's *Ligeia* and *Le Scarabée d'or*, and Juan Buñuel's *Le Joueur d'échecs de Maelzel* (Maelzel's Chess Player).

A few months after the Vadim-Malle-Fellini *Histoires extraordinaires* appeared at Cannes and Rollin's *Le Viol du vampire* in Paris, a couple of other French fantasies went into production. Jean-Pierre Bastid's *Hallucinations sadiques* (Sadistic Hallucinations) began in Ainay-le-Château, in the Auvergne, on 12 August 1968 and managed to head its cast with a 'name' –

Daniel Gélin. The co-producer was Robert de Nesle, who had been responsible for Franju's *Judex* and would spend much of the 1970s sponsoring Jess Franco.

Sadly, Bastid's film is a somnolent misfire in which a mentally unstable architect – not only charged with restoring Gélin's country house near Bourges but also doing time as his mistress – is driven to distraction by 'hallucinations' of Gélin's wife. It turns out to be the usual *Diaboliques* conspiracy, this time with an inheritance at stake, and the dialogue abounds in such po-faced utterances as "Trust is like Atlantis: submerged and fading away." R J Chauffard passes through, cast as much the same bearded doctor he played in Vadim's *...Et mourir de plaisir*, and Anouk Ferjac is impressive as the ill-fated heroine. At one point she takes a bath and hallucinates blood coming from the shower, at another a female corpse is nastily 'bottled' in order to disfigure it. Otherwise the characters just play snooker an awful lot.

The obsessively iterated action in Jean-Daniel Verhaeghe's *L'Araignée d'eau* (The Water Spider) is the cutting of bread, which the pasty-faced hero seems even more fascinated by than the mysterious young woman resident in his attic. Starting on 12 November, Verhaeghe polished off this rustic fantasy in a mere four weeks, having co-written the script with Marcel Béalu, author of the original novel. Beginning with a written quote from philosopher Gaston Bachelard – 'Fairy tales are children's fears given life' – the film concerns a 19th century writer who finds a water spider and takes it home with him. What happens next proves his contention that "The supernatural manifests itself to each and every one of us at some time or other."

The spider's transmutation into a beautiful girl (Elisabeth Wiener) is brilliantly done; a pulsing heartbeat on the soundtrack slowly gives way to a sinister bassoon drone while massive close-ups of arachnid body parts suddenly reveal a human eye glimpsing out amid strands of hair. (Though in a much quieter key, this shot anticipates the millennial Japanese ghost story *Ringu*.) There's a magical sequence in which the writer happily liberates all his bottled butterflies, and a decidedly strange one in which he fantasises unleashing a horde of cats in

a church service, with gruesome consequences. The film is beautifully scored by Serge Kaufmann, but the main character (Marc Eyraud) is a disagreeable, under-achieving boor and the film's poetic atmosphere masks a decided lack of incident, with the running time struggling to attain even 80 minutes. That *L'Araignée d'eau* wasn't about to revolutionise French *fantastique* became clear when it took over two years to get a release, only appearing in January 1971.

## ENTER EL HOMBRE LOBO

In July 1968 Spanish audiences were presented with a film that would manage what Jess Franco's *Dr Orlof* had so far failed to do. Smoothly made though it is,

Belgian advertising for *Hallucinations sadiques* (1968), featuring Sabine Sun, Daniel Gélin and Anouk Ferjac

*La marca del hombre lobo* (The Mark of the Wolf Man) isn't important as the one-and-only Gothic horror credit for director Enrique L Eguiluz. It remains significant, instead, for initiating a bona-fide boom in Spanish horror – and for introducing an actor-writer, Paul Naschy, who was to become synonymous with the genre.

"Naschy is an intriguing study," wrote Barrie Pattison several years later. "A barrel-chested former champion weightlifter, he manages to get his shirt off in most productions, usually to be whipped and chained. He also manages to take the leading lady to bed ... Naschy is an actor who manages to stay within his limits and keeps a sincerity needed in such unsophisticated material."[6] Published in 1975, Pattison's *The Seal of Dracula* was perhaps the first English-language book to give Naschy some recognition, though in his native Spain he'd already been hailed as "un mito ibérico" (an Iberian myth)[7] in the 1974 book *Cine de Terror y Paul Naschy* (Horror Cinema and Paul Naschy). Pattison's pithy formulation says a lot about Naschy's enduring appeal; in fact, the words 'sincerity' and 'unsophisticated' cut to the heart of the matter. For Naschy, who was 33 when *La marca* was shot, was essentially a fan. His passion for the old Universal horrors had been kindled at an impressionable age and would profoundly affect much of his work.

Recalling his first exposure to Erle C Kenton's 1942 film *Frankenstein Meets the Wolf Man*, Naschy observed that "I had the good luck to slip into Madrid's old

Iris Cinema and watch this marvellous film that would mark me for life. Lon Chaney [Jr] could never have imagined that his bite on screen would transfer the curse of lycanthropy to a seven-year-old Spanish boy."[8] Naschy had a pronounced talent for mythologising himself, a tendency discernible even in his account of this 'primal' scene – for not only did he specify the Cine Rex in other accounts, but Kenton's film only came out in Spain in 1946, when Naschy was actually 12. Strangely, the film preceding Kenton's, George Waggner's *The Wolf Man*, had been banned by the Spanish authorities, so Naschy experienced the original Universal series out of sequence. The incoherence and non-continuity thus engendered would be preserved in Naschy's own ramshackle yet wildly imaginative scripts.

By his own account, Naschy's casting as the noble werewolf Waldemar Daninsky was a happy accident. Written under Naschy's real name, Jacinto Molina, *La marca* was intended for Lon Chaney Jr himself, but when it became clear that the 62-year-old star was in no condition to take the role, the film's German co-producers prevailed on Naschy to step in. (Similarly, Barbara Steele, pencilled in for the role of a glamorous vampire woman, was replaced by Aurora de Alba.) The German end of the deal also provided the film with the glamorous accoutrements of 3-D, stereo sound and 70mm widescreen. Spanish censors had a predictable impact on *La marca* too. Way back in 1961, Hammer's *The Curse of the Werewolf* failed to get a release in Spain for the simple reason that it was set there; under no circumstances would the repressive functionaries of the Franco regime sanction a film suggesting that their homeland harboured beastly lycanthropes. Mindful of this, Naschy cannily changed his werewolf's nationality from Galician to Polish.

*When Jacinta von Aarenberg meets the enigmatic Waldemar Daninsky, she rapidly throws over her monied fiancé Rudolph Weissman. Taking part in a wolf hunt, Waldemar rescues Rudolph from the clutches of the resurrected Imre Wolfstein, receiving a fateful bite in the process. Desperate to lift the resultant curse of lycanthropy from Waldemar, Jacinta and Rudolph send for Dr Janos Mikhelov, unaware that he and his wife Wandessa are vampires...*

Though conceived in part as a tribute to Lon Chaney Jr, *La marca* begins with a stylish sequence paying unmistakable homage to Lon Chaney Sr. The Red Death's intrusion into the masked ball in Chaney's *The Phantom of the Opera* is given a mod makeover in which Jacinta's 18th birthday party is joined by an enigmatic figure in a blood-red Devil costume. Naschy's Daninsky cuts an impressive figure among the masked and costumed revellers; his black mask gives him a slightly corvine appearance and, whisking Jacinta away amid a hail of confetti, he announces himself as "the spirit of evil: the Devil himself." Photographed in honeyed hues as Eguiluz tracks smoothly past various pieces of glowing statuary, the scene confers satanic glamour on Daninsky but does so purely for effect. After all, Daninsky will turn out to be a reluctant werewolf whose struggles against the forces of evil are heroic rather than satanic. Even so, it makes for an undeniably intriguing entrance. The scene also introduces a touch of self-reflexive wit; the heroine, renamed Janice in the English dub, is actually called Jacinta, the feminine form of Naschy's real name.

Jacinta is played by Dyanik Zurakowska, star of Javier Setó's recent ghost story *La llamada*. Naschy's habit of surrounding himself with beautiful women is already well in evidence in this prentice effort; accompanying Zurakowska are Aurora de Alba as the feral Wandessa and Rosanna Yanni as blonde gypsy Nascha. It's Nascha who initiates the Daninsky curse in the film's all-important replay of a key scene from *Frankenstein Meets the Wolf Man*. Along with a male companion, she ventures into the Wolfstein crypt and drunkenly removes the silver dagger from the remains of Imre Wolfstein. It's this (rather inadequately made-up) lycanthrope that attacks the noble Daninsky during the wolf hunt, leading rapidly to a barnstorming transformation for the victim. Cannily flooding the lens with distorting Vaseline, Eguiluz obviates the need for the kind of crude lap-dissolves used in the Universal films, and Daninsky springs forth fully formed in the first of numerous werewolf make-ups Naschy would sport down the years.

His first foray is bad news for a local peasant couple, introduced peeling potatoes (her) and cleaning a rifle (him). "I'm glad there are no wolves to worry us," mutters the man. Right on cue, the hirsute Daninsky crashes in upon them; the man tumbles into the fire and vomits blood, while the camera lingers momentarily on the woman's savaged body. Naïve throwback though the film may be in its essentials, Naschy was nevertheless well aware that it was 1968, not 1942, making this scene a hair-raisingly violent departure from the Universal originals.

To introduce the third act, Eguiluz comes up with his most arresting visual, an image described by Nigel Andrews on the film's belated UK release as "a de Chirico-like shot of the fog clearing on a windswept station platform"[9] as the duplicitous Mikhelovs come

Paul Naschy
makes his debut
as the lycanthropic
Waldemar Daninsky
in *La marca del
hombre lobo* (1968)

## LA MARCA DEL HOMBRE LOBO

Spain-West Germany 1968
West Germany: **Die Vampire des Dr Dracula**
UK: *Hell's Creatures*
US: **Frankenstein's Bloody Terror**
Maxper PC / [uncredited] Hi-Fi Stereo 70 Munich
88 minutes colour
in production February-March 1968

. . . . . . . . . . . . . . . . . . . . . . . . . . . .

Director of Photography: Emilio Foriscot; Art
Director: José Luis Ferrer; Editor: Francisco
Jaumandreu; Music: Ángel Arteaga; Make-up:
José Luis Ruiz; Special Effects: Molina;
Story and Screenplay: Jacinto Molina [Paul
Naschy]; Executive Producer: Maximiliano
Pérez-Flores; Director: Enrique López Eguiluz

Paul Naschy (Waldemar Daninsky); Dyanik
Zurakowska (Countess Jacinta von Aarenberg);
Manuel Manzaneque (Rudolph Weissmann);
Aurora de Alba (Wandessa Mikhelov); Julián
Ugarte (Dr Janos Mikhelov); José Nieto (Count
Sigmund von Aarenberg); Carlos Casaravilla
(Judge Aarno Weismann); Ángel Menéndez
(Otto [forester]); Antonio Jiménez Escribano;
Rafael Alcantara; Juan Medina; Antonio Orengo
(Otto [butler]); Angela Rhu; Pilar Vela;
Milagros Ceballos (Martha); Beatriz Savón
(Frau Hildegard); María Teresa Torralba;
Victoriano López; Rosanna Yanni (Nascha);
Gualberto Galbán (Gyogyo)

*La marca del hombre lobo* is a film of the 'horror' genre which puts on a
tremendous parade of fantasy, making use, too, of some scary tricks of
the 'vampire' type ... The opening of the film gives you a good idea of the
atmosphere of mystery and horror that unfolds in almost every scene.
Naturally, there are a few surprises. *La Vanguardia* 19 September 1968

As was to be expected, the Spanish critics didn't look kindly on the film.
It was only natural. What did those hacks know about horror-fantasy,
vampirism or lycanthropy? One scathing reviewer, who wrote under the nom
de plume of Bitibinovsky in *La Codorniz* ('the more audacious magazine for
the more intelligent reader'), slagged it off in no uncertain terms, although
he also predicted that it would go down in history. And it undoubtedly did.
Paul Naschy [*Memorias de un hombre lobo*, 1997]

into view. In another striking shot, their departure
from the station is observed from the undercarriage
of a train waiting at the opposite platform. Mikhelov
drops a number of hints – notably, "Our work is such
that we are forced to remain awake at night and to
sleep during the day" – that make it very clear he and

his wife are vampires, and in Julián Ugarte the film
boasts a far more interesting answer to Christopher
Lee than the lumpen actors (Walter Brandi, Dieter
Eppler) so far used in Italian films. Looking rather
like a strawberry-blond Laurence Harvey, Ugarte is
fragile yet strangely magnetic, finally donning the
regulation red-lined cloak and whisking Jacinta away
from her would-be rescuers with balletic ease. Weirdly
balletic, too, is his climactic battle with Daninsky,
a ritualised clash of the titans that would be repeated,
with variations, in numerous Naschy films to come.

For a homegrown product, the colourful production
gloss and concentrated Gothic imagery of *La marca del
hombre lobo* was quite new to Spanish audiences, though
it retained a link to Franco's *Gritos en la noche* by using
the same subterranean Valdeiglesias interiors. For
US audiences, however, the film's sleek elegance was
somewhat compromised by a tacked-on introduction,
lamely justifying the distributor's inexplicable title
change to *Frankenstein's Bloody Terror*. "Now: the most
frightening Frankenstein story of all," rumbles the
voice-over, "as the ancient werewolf curse brands the
family of monster-makers as Wolfstein. Wolfstein!
The inhuman clan of blood-hungry wolf-monsters!"

While trying to get *La marca del hombre lobo* off the
ground, Naschy sought the help of, among others,
writer-director Amando de Ossorio. "After a couple
of whiskies," Naschy recalled, "he told me, in
fatherly fashion, that this horror business was very

appealing but just not viable – that's what Hammer were there for – and a genre picture made in Spain just wouldn't work."[10] By the time *La marca* was being readied for release, Ossorio had clearly changed his tune, for in the early summer of 1968 he made a Spanish-Italian co-production called *Malenka, la sobrina del vampiro* (Malenka, Niece of the Vampire). The idea was to match Swedish sex bomb Anita Ekberg with the venerable Boris Karloff, but when the Karloff offer failed to work out the vampire Count from *La marca*, Julián Ugarte, was the seemingly obvious replacement. (Rosanna Yanni and Carlos Casaravilla were also imported direct from *La marca*.) Unfortunately, Ugarte was only two years Ekberg's senior, making him an odd choice to play her uncle.

Ekberg is Silvia, an Italian fashion model who travels to Germany when informed that she's come into a title. German locations weren't actually involved, of course; the ivy-covered exteriors were the Castillo de Brutón in Vizcaya and for interiors Ossorio defaulted to the usual haunt at San Martín de Valdeiglesias. There, Silvia discovers that she has "the same beauty born of mystery" as her great-grandmother Malenka, whose alchemical experiments in "necrobiology" caused her to be burned at the stake. To pad out his by-the-numbers story, Ossorio plucks a few choice moments from *Dracula*. When the toothy Adriana Ambesi tries to seduce Ekberg in her bed, Ugarte's Graf Wohldruck bursts in in a jealous rage and turfs her out. Later, three men (one of them a worse-for-drink Van Helsing surrogate played by Casaravilla) keep watch in a graveyard and witness the rising of Diana Lorys. Unfortunately, the remainder is crudely strung together and seems unsure of how intentionally funny it's meant to be. Indeed, at times it seems like little more than a hotly contested battle of heaving bosoms, with Yanni bolstering the already pneumatic mix of Ekberg, Ambesi and Lorys.

Echoing the last-minute rationalisations of Tod Browning's *London After Midnight* and *Mark of the Vampire*, the film throws in a ridiculous last-minute twist indicating that Silvia's uncle has trumped up the whole vampire scenario for his own nefarious ends. Yet moments later he receives a burning torch in the chest and crumbles to a skull in a conspicuously crummy effects sequence. This illogical resolution (apparently forced on Ossorio by his producers) at least discloses a spindly skeleton hand, prefiguring the memorable Blind Dead series that Ossorio would initiate three years later.

According to Paul Naschy, in the wake of *La marca del hombre lobo*'s success he was lured over to France to make a second Daninsky film, *Las noches del hombre*

Adriana Ambesi and Julián Ugarte as chic German vampires in *Malenka, la sobrina del vampiro* (1968)

*lobo* (Nights of the Wolf Man). Apparently the film materials disappeared when the director, René Govar, died during post-production, but the fact that Govar appears never to have existed suggests strongly that the film didn't either. Daninsky's next appearance, *Los monstruos del terror* (The Monsters of Terror), wasn't a product of confabulation but of a Spanish-West German agreement brokered by the former Samuel Bronston associate Jaime Prades. Prades' proposed film empire was facing imminent collapse, however. Director Hugo Fregonese walked off the film when money wasn't forthcoming and he was replaced by fellow Argentinian Tulio Demicheli. Hardly surprisingly, the end result is an unfocused mess.

It's also unashamedly childish, splicing Naschy's nostalgia for the Universal monsters with an invasion of alien doppelgängers and making barely a moment's sense. To illustrate the strange dichotomy between Naschy's childhood memories and the commercial requirements of the late 1960s, this parade of monster-mash juvenilia is punctuated by torn flesh and ripped throats, together with much sustained screaming as women are subjected to nasty sound-wave tortures. Daninsky is one of several classic monsters revived by Michael Rennie and his alien cohorts on the principle that mankind can be subjugated by reviving all its most atavistic fears. (The film's working title, referring to Rennie, was *El hombre que vino de Ummo* – The Man who Came from Ummo.) In the end, however, the aliens' plans are scuppered when they discover that human emotions "may be even stronger than their nuclear weapons."

The other menaces are Dracula and Frankenstein's monster (appearing pseudonymously as Janos de

Mielhoff and the Faranchsalen monster), plus a
revived mummy whose exposed, green-hued face looks
agreeably like Paul Wegener's. The Karloff-parody
monster, however, is a complete joke. Felicitous
moments include our hero (Craig Hill) being buzzed
by bats when stretched upright on a rack, the
vampire (Manuel de Blas) getting tangled in a giant
cobweb when staked, and a well-contrived climactic
dynamiting of the trusty castle at Valdeiglesias. Among
Naschy's Universal quotes are the names Maleva and
Ilonka, plus a fairground routine lifted wholesale from
*House of Frankenstein*. Karin Dor and Diana Sorel show
up to prove Rennie's contention that "beautiful women
are like powerful magnets" – but, more importantly,
the film marked the horror debut of Patty Shepard.
Cast untypically as love interest, this 22-year-old native
of South Carolina had sufficient icy allure to become,
in due course, Spain's answer to Barbara Steele.

Curiously, while Naschy was perfecting his
Waldemar Daninsky persona, writer-director
Pedro Olea was working on a project that looked at
lycanthropy as a state of mind. Olea's 1969 film
*El bosque del lobo* (Forest of the Wolf) was showcased at
Cannes the following year, eventually hitting Spanish
cinemas a year after that and amassing numerous
awards – three of them for its leading man, José Luis
López Vásquez. The central figure, Benito Freire, is an
itinerant pedlar given to homicidal fugues, particularly
when escorting defenceless people across country.
A "prudish Englishman" (John Steiner) discusses
lycanthropy with him, citing Ovid, Herodotus, Virgil
and Petronius but having the sense to take to his heels
when Freire goes into one of his fits. In a cautiously
anti-Catholic gesture, Olea portrays the local Abbot
(Antonio Casas) as the least perceptive man around,
telling everyone that Freire is "as good as gold, I know
that for a fact."

Vásquez is really splendid as the cringingly servile
killer, despairingly beating the ground with his fists
after each murder and finally stammering "Thank
you" when apprehended by a torch-bearing mob.
The character is clearly modelled on Manuel Blanco
Romasanta, who in the 1840s became Spain's
first serial killer and at his trial claimed to be a
lycanthrope. He would eventually reappear, under
his own name, in Paco Plaza's 2004 film *Romasanta,
la caza de la bestia* (Romasanta, the Beast Hunt).

## FRANCO-TOWERS, AND OTHER STRANGE PERMUTATIONS

Paul Naschy's ascendancy in Spanish horror was
accompanied by Jess Franco's continuing adventures
with non-Spanish sponsors. Directly after finishing

*Bésame monstruo* in late 1967, Franco parted ways with
Adrian Hoven and entered into partnership with the
British entrepreneur Harry Alan Towers. A former
child actor, radio producer and ATV executive, Towers
had been arrested in the US in 1961, allegedly for
his involvement in a call-girl racket, but apparently
jumped bail and only gave himself up 20 years later,
paying a paltry fine of $4,200. So the numerous films
he produced in the interim were all made while he
was officially on the run.

In November 1967, Towers and Franco began their
association in discouraging style with *The Blood of
Fu Manchu*, known to its West German and Spanish
co-producers as *Der Todeskuß des Dr Fu Man Chu* and
*Fu Manchu y el beso de la muerte*. The 'death kiss' referred
to in these titles not only linked the film to earlier
Franco projects like *Miss Muerte* but also counted as the
latest extravagant plot device in a successful Towers
franchise. Filmed in Dublin, Bray Studios and Hong
Kong respectively, *The Face of Fu Manchu* (1965),
*The Brides of Fu Manchu* and *The Vengeance of Fu Manchu*
(both 1966) had all been Anglo-German co-productions
and all, particularly the first, had several plus points.
With *Blood* the minuses began to proliferate, though
Christopher Lee's Fu, transported to Rio de Janeiro
and sending out a bevy of hypnotised beauties on 'kiss
and kill' missions, appears commendably unruffled.

Franco's Towers collaborations in 1968 included
*Sumuru* (aka *The Girl from Rio*), in which Shirley Eaton
played Sax Rohmer's female Fu Manchu equivalent, and
a film that inaugurated a long-lived strand in Franco's
filmography – the influential 'women in prison'
melodrama *99 mujeres* (99 Women). There followed
*Justine* and *The Castle of Fu Manchu*, which between them
occupied Franco from late May to the end of July.
The second of these was the fifth and final entry in
the Towers series and succeeded in being even more
shambolic than the previous one. *Justine*, however, was
a film that, like *99 mujeres*, would resonate long and
loud in Franco's work – for, in stark contrast to the
inept Fu Manchu fag-end, it was a sprightly and lavishly
appointed adaptation of a Marquis de Sade original.

De Sade had acquired a 1960s vogue via Peter
Weiss' controversial 1963 play *Marat/Sade*, in which
Patrick Magee played the Marquis not only in Peter
Brook's London and New York productions but also
in Brook's baldly theatrical film version. Possibly in
acknowledgment of this (though more likely to keep
costs down while utilising the unpredictable Klaus
Kinski), Franco shot framing scenes for *Justine* in which
the incarcerated de Sade is seen, quill in hand, in a
starkly black limbo bisected by prison bars – a 'fringe
theatre' set-up if ever there was one. The remainder

of the film, though overlong at two hours, dramatises de Sade's picaresque saga of vice and virtue in the style of recent big-studio sex comedies like *The Amorous Adventures of Moll Flanders*, and the result is certainly far superior to the inane AIP-sponsored biopic *De Sade*, made in Germany by Cy Endfield at the same time.

Though decorated by Franco with red-and-green-tinted scenes in the stews featuring plenty of blood and breasts, *Justine* is essentially a piece of costume fol-de-rol, quite distinct from the boldly imaginative modern-dress fever-dreams with which the Franco-Towers combine moved from 1968 into 1969. Both *Venus in Furs* and *De Sade 70* charted areas of sexual decadence and dependency that Franco would develop ever more explicitly in the 1970s. The first was made in October 1968 and, though

Dennis Price and Maria Röhm in the mesmeric, wordless centrepiece of *Venus in Furs* (1968)

opportunistically lumbered by its US sponsors with the famous Leopold von Sacher-Masoch title, tells its own story entirely, following jazz trumpeter James Darren from Istanbul to Rio and back as he conducts an oneiric love affair with the deceased Maria Röhm. Discovering her corpse in the surf, Darren muses that "She was beautiful even though she was dead. There was a connection between us." What that connection is is revealed at the film's doppelgänger climax, which offers a strangely moving echo of Bierce's *An Occurrence at Owl Creek Bridge*, and the journey there is realised by Franco with the kind of intoxicating Pop Art voluptuousness that the more famous *Necronomicon* failed to achieve.

Röhm has been killed in a kinky sex game by three well-heeled decadents (Klaus Kinski, Dennis Price, Margaret Lee), and her ghostly revenge on them is exacted in the requisite fur coat but with no recourse to violence whatever. Her wordless scene with Price is a seven-minute tour de force, a mesmeric triumph not just for Franco but also for the actors and the ominously brilliant score by Mike Hugg and Manfred Mann. The film loses a bit of momentum after this high point, and Franco's frequent use of Rio carnival stock footage grows irksome, but otherwise he's on top form, creating a mood of erotic obsession and deathly limbo that's truly memorable. Even simple touches – like a jet-set party in which the participants are frozen like mannequins – linger in the memory.

*De Sade 70*, a terse and to-the-point working title that would acquire any number of elaborate

alternatives on release, isn't on quite the same level. But in transposing de Sade's *Philosophie dans le boudoir* to a modern setting it still manages some startling effects. Mme Saint-Ange (Maria Röhm) and Mirvel (Jack Taylor) are the conniving decadents who devote themselves to the "education, corruption and destruction" of teenage innocent Eugénie (Marie Liljedahl). Franco contrives to remove the heart from a naked sacrificial model within the first five minutes; elsewhere, the film's red-tinted sex scenes are cumulatively boring and some Sapphic bathtime bonding between Röhm and Liljedahl is horribly disfigured by a chintzy section of Bruno Nicolai's otherwise ravishing score. The film is at its best whenever Christopher Lee's oracular Dolmance appears with his attendant "disciples of the divine Marquis." Eugénie describes them as "the man in the red coat and all his terrible friends," and their deceptively elegant home-invasion tactics reach a grisly end with the murder of Mme and the flight of Eugénie into the sand dunes. There, Franco has her encounter a desolate graveyard straight out of *Nosferatu* and subside naked beside a gibbet-mounted bell echoing *Vampyr*.

Over in Italy, the fading of the country's Gothic strain was accompanied by a chic new manifestation of the giallo. Reflecting, like Franco's films for Harry Alan Towers, the heady experimentation of the late 1960s, the convoluted results were shot through with increasingly provocative levels of eroticism and flashy jet-set satire, with the casting of international

Vanessa Redgrave tries to relieve Franco Nero of his porn addiction
in *Un tranquillo posto di campagna* (1968)

names often considered a crucial selling point. These names were guaranteed to lend distinction to the giallo's customary dramatis personae of improbable stick figures – the faithless spouses, feckless actors, terrorised heiresses, beleaguered newly-weds, conflicted captains of industry, and assorted sexual deviants without whom the labyrinthine plots couldn't function.

Leading the way were Jean-Louis Trintignant and Ewa Aulin, who starred together in Tinto Brass' *Col cuore in gola* (With Heart in Mouth) and Giulio Questi's *La morte ha fatto l'uovo* (Death Laid an Egg), with Gina Lollobrigida thrown in for good measure in the latter. Similarly, Carroll Baker, fresh from playing Jean Harlow in a disastrous Hollywood biopic, was eagerly snapped up by Italian casting directors, who put her into Romolo Guerrieri's *Il dolce corpo di Deborah* (The Sweet Body of Deborah) and the Umberto Lenzi films *Orgasmo* and *Così dolce ... così perverse* (So Sweet ... So Perverse), pairing her with, respectively, Lou Castel, Jean Sorel and Jean-Louis Trintignant. (The still-youthful veteran Ernesto Gastaldi provided the scripts for *Deborah* and *Così dolce*.) Other fashionable names included Haydée Politoff in Giuliano Biagetti's *Interrabang* and Klaus Kinski in Riccardo Freda's *A doppia faccia* (Double Face). Despite these films' ultra-modern gloss and luridly kinky details, the expected reverberations of *Les Diaboliques* can be found in several of them, particularly the three Carroll Baker titles.

Getting right to the heart of the jet-set scene, Brass' *Col cuore in gola* and Freda's *A doppia faccia* even venture to Swinging London; the former, exported as *Deadly Sweet*, revels in an exuberant comic-strip

style inspired by Pop Art, with fumetti artist Guido Crepax providing the storyboards. The same impulse turns Questi's *La morte ha fatto l'uovo* into an unclassifiable oddity, a Marxist parable lumped into the giallo category by many commentators purely for the sake of convenience. Yes, Trintignant fantasises various prostitute killings while plotting to murder his wife (Lollobrigida), but Questi's surrealist imaginings eventually extend to genetically mutated chickens at Lollobrigida's thriving poultry plant – a freakish development that leaves the formula mechanics of the giallo far behind, as does Bruno Maderna's ear-bleeding score and the confrontational editing techniques of Questi's co-writer, Franco Arcalli. The previous year (1966), Questi and Arcalli had subverted the Spaghetti Western in similar style, making the bizarre *Se sei vivo spara* (If You're Alive, Shoot) so outrageously macabre and violent that censors circled over it like famished buzzards. Despite losing a significant amount of weight en route, it was nevertheless exported as *Django Kill!*

Pop Art was also involved in keeping Gothic horror alive, albeit in fashionably mutated form and with examples coming in from some unexpected quarters. Back in June 1965, Elio Petri had directed *La decima vittima* (The Tenth Victim), an inflated adaptation of the Robert Sheckley story *Seventh Victim* that added Pop Art overkill to Sheckley's satire of a future world in which gladiatorial killings have become legal. From modish science fiction Petri moved on to psychological horror with *Un tranquillo posto di campagna* (A Quiet Place in the Country), a project first mooted in 1962 but only shot in April 1968. It was based, rather surprisingly, on Oliver Onions' classic 1911 story *The Beckoning Fair One*, a property formerly coveted by Mario Bava.

"Demented artist Franco Nero turns homicidal as he is hounded by the spirit of a dead girl in a haunted villa," commented *Films in London* on its belated UK release. "Elio Petri directs over-emphatically and kills the early atmosphere of unease which is the film's most successful quality. Vanessa Redgrave has a wretched time as the unfortunate mistress and Ennio Morricone contributes a fetching worry score."[11] Before getting to that 'early atmosphere of unease', however, Petri illustrates Nero's alienation from his vacuous Milanese environment with a jagged nightmare of bondage, porn addiction, consumerism ("I found an underwater television: for scuba diving," says Redgrave), bathroom murders and art installations, in the process leaving the viewer at least as alienated as Nero.

Things pick up in the countryside, where Nero sees his own doppelgänger, reads Edgar Allan Poe, becomes obsessed by an unoccupied villa ("Only death could be quieter than this," mutters the caretaker) and paints the trees red. The house seems bent on driving Redgrave out while Nero hallucinates a red-garbed dead girl from World War II; to find out more he visits her mother in Venice and envisions the old lady as a weirdly articulated, Magritte-style coffin. There follows a brilliant seance sequence in the country villa and a brutal scene in which Nero apparently spades Redgrave to death prior to turning the pretty teenage maid (Rita Calderoni) into a spray-painted artwork. He's finally carted off with a bag over his head and produces vagina-shaped mobiles in a psychiatric clinic. The film looks gorgeous, courtesy of cinematographer Luigi Kuveiller, and remains valuable as a 1968 time-capsule. But its yawn-inducing pretensions – equating Nero's mental breakdown with a similar schism in society – blunt the impact of some otherwise effective nightmare sequences.

Nero's vaginal mobiles were echoed on an epic scale at the beginning of 1969, when writer-director Piero Schivazappa was making the provocative but cumulatively rather boring *Femina ridens* (Laughing Woman). Bringing Pop Art to bear on the then red-hot issue of sexual politics, Schivazappa included a dream sequence in which Philippe Leroy encounters the spread legs of a massive sculpture, strolls into a correspondingly massive vagina dentata and is vomited out as a skeleton. With a shaky hold on his own caricatured masculinity, Leroy's self-absorbed society doctor has imprisoned and tortured Dagmar Lassander as a protest against the encroachment of what was then called Women's Lib. This is the kind of preening dullard who frets that Lassander will reincarnate as "a huge voracious deadly female scorpion," and the film is at its most satisfying when it gradually exposes his raging insecurities, with Lassander becoming paradoxically empowered and Leroy finally drowning just moments after saying "I must have faith in my virility." But the journey there is long and po-faced, with only occasional glimmers of wit – as when the couple, out driving, are halted at a level crossing, Lassander slithers down out of shot, and Leroy daydreams a passing coachload of schoolgirl musicians, all lustily fellating their saxophones.

Leroy's insufferable doctor in *Femina ridens* would no doubt have run screaming from Zbyněk Brynych's 1970 film *Die Weibchen* (Little Women), a Munich-Paris-Rome concoction also known as *Les Mantes religieuses* (The Praying Mantises) and *Femmine carnivore* (Carnivorous Women). With Uschi Glas as the latest customer at an exclusive health spa, this highly coloured satire, complete with absurd sex-farce music by Edgar Wallace composer Peter Thomas, ends with Glas witnessing the bloody buzz-saw dismemberment of Alain Noury. "We keep some bits as souvenirs," explains head doctor Gisela Fischer, whose "museum of stupid men" recalls the pickled penises of the recent short subject *La Fée sanguinaire*. The trigger for Brynych's Grand Guignol comedy was Valerie Solanas' radical-feminist manifesto regarding SCUM (the Society for Cutting Up Men), which duly appears on screen. The result provides a gender-switched echo of Jean Léon's 1964 black comedy *Aimez-vous les femmes?* (Do You Like Women?), in which screenwriters Roman Polanski and Gérard Brach imagined a secret society dedicated to eating an attractive young woman every ninth moon.

Back in 1968, Antonio Margheriti, dormant in horror circles since *I lunghi capelli della morte*, returned to a modified form of Gothic horror with *Contronatura* (Against Nature), interpolating a lesbian subplot but otherwise resisting the new opportunities for sexual excess leapt upon by Jess Franco. Shot as *Trance*, this was an Italian co-production with West Germany and called *Schreie in der Nacht* (Screams in the Night) when released there in May 1969. Working from his own script, Margheriti invoked *The Old Dark House* by sending a bunch of tuxedoed 1920s partygoers to Brighton in the teeth of a raging storm – but not allowing them to reach it. Instead they fetch up at an out-of-commission hunting lodge, where the eerily self-possessed Luciano Pigozzi has them join a seance presided over by his even eerier mother. The seance inevitably exposes a host of guilty secrets, specifically the details behind a double murder for which the peculiar mother and son were unjustly condemned.

"We may get results quickly," murmurs Pigozzi, "but it's also possible that this night will last an eternity." And eternity is what's really at issue, as becomes clear when the mud that stranded the party in the first place suddenly becomes an unstoppable torrent, smashing through the hunting lodge while the supernatural avengers look on serenely. This is a truly powerful image; the cascading river of sludge is an apt metaphor for the vile machinations of the assembled characters and makes for a terrific final tableau. But the film takes an awfully long time getting there, with Riccardo Pallottini's gloomy, blue-tinted photography failing to disguise the essential thinness of Margheriti's claustrophobic set-up. At least Margheriti tries to enliven things by an unusually sophisticated use of flashbacks, one of them artfully framed by close-ups of a spider in its web.

To satisfy the CCC end of the deal, Margheriti cast German favourites Joachim Fuchsberger and Marianne Koch, the latter as a tight-lipped lesbian who goes beyond 'predatory' to full-on rape. At one such heated moment Margheriti cuts to flames in a nearby grate, just as he did in *Danza macabra*. At another, he cuts from Koch eyeing up Helga Anders' pert behind to a close-up of a slavering fox with its tongue hanging out. This just makes one wonder if the 'Against Nature' of the title is meant to apply, not only to murderers, but also to lesbians.

*Contronatura* was an interesting attempt to reinvigorate Italy's Gothic strand, in stark contrast to a June 1969 release so naïve, inept and crude it stood absolutely zero chance of doing so. The first and last assignment for writer-director Ferruccio Casapinta, *La bambola di Satana* (The Devil's Doll) is an unusually tedious reiteration of the 'young heiress threatened in ancestral castle by schemers who want castle for themselves' scenario, with some added rubbish thrown in about a uranium deposit underneath the building. Presumably aware that this was a strictly comic-book concoction, Casapinta opted for a credits sequence composed of photographic panels and engaged as his beleaguered heroine the Neapolitan beauty Erna Schurer, who was used to posing for *Killing*

Locandina artwork (significantly better than the film itself) for *La bambola di Satana* (1969)

and other such *fotoromanzi*. Inspired by a tour of the catacombs, one character says, "You could write a great giallo here" – which only underlines the fact that Casapinta emphatically didn't. Unluckily, Schurer moved on in the autumn of 1969 to Nardo Bonomi's mysterious *Sortilegio* (Spell), which was written by Brunello Rondi, involved Schurer with a Dionysian cult near Lake Castel Gandolfo, and was never released.

## MONSTRUO SAGRADO

In Spain, audience readiness to embrace Paul Naschy's first werewolf foray in *La marca del hombre lobo* had in large part been cultivated by a different filmmaker entirely. For the popular interest in horror and suspense

had been fostered almost single-handedly by Narciso Ibáñez Serrador, and he did it initially via television.

Serrador was the son of the hypnotic Spanish actor Narciso Ibáñez Menta, who had acquired a reputation as a horror specialist in his very first film, the Argentinian production *Una luz en la ventana* (A Light in the Window, 1942). Still in Argentina, father and son were the prime movers behind *Obras maestras del terror* (Masterworks of Terror), a TV series that enjoyed three seasons between 1959 and 1962, together with a film spin-off of the same title in 1960. Where the film focused on three stories by Edgar Allan Poe, the series ranged more widely through the canon of classic horror stories, establishing a successful template that Serrador would pitch to TVE (Televisión Española) on his return to Spain.

The result was *Historias para no dormir* (literally, Stories Not to Sleep By), which ran from 1966 to 1968 prior to a colour revival in 1982. Serrador cast his father in several of the stories and wrote much of the series under the pen name he'd coined back in Argentina – Luis Peñafiel. This little bit of obfuscation did nothing to prevent Serrador's cherubic, bearded features from becoming the undisputed face of horror to millions of Spanish TV viewers. The fact that Alfred Hitchcock's name was later attached to a 1971 print anthology that lifted Serrador's title – *Stories to Stay Awake By* – is instructive. For Serrador had himself cannily adopted the to-camera introductions characteristic of *Alfred Hitchcock Presents*, thereby turning himself into a brand – a brand that resulted in the Hitchcock-style manoeuvre of two *Historias para no dormir* magazines being published simultaneously, one in Barcelona and the other (edited by Serrador himself) in Madrid.

In short, 'Chicho', as he was known, had become, to quote the *Nuevo Fotogramas* reporter Lola Salvador, the 'Monstruo Sagrado de TVE' (TVE's sacred monster).[12] Despite his supremacy, he modestly referred to himself as "a rather chubby fellow who makes scary stuff for Spanish telly," simultaneously pointing out that "Television is the best way to disseminate the genre and give horror real impact, because we don't feel protected there, as we do in the theater or cinema, by the mass audience all around us."[13] Happily, this theory didn't stop him from moving into cinema on the strength of his television success.

The first episode of *Historias para no dormir* was transmitted on Friday 4 February 1966; a similar British anthology, ABC's *Mystery and Imagination*, had begun the previous Saturday. *Mystery and Imagination* would trade in much the same repertoire of high-toned horror classics as its Spanish counterpart and, together with RTF's *Belphégor ou le fantôme du Louvre* in France, the two series typified a renewed interest in Gothic television, manifest across Europe, that helped to rekindle a similar interest among filmmakers.

Just as TVE and ABC developed complementary horror anthologies, so the twin BBC series *Sherlock Holmes* (with Douglas Wilmer, 1965) and *Sir Arthur Conan Doyle's Sherlock Holmes* (with Peter Cushing, 1968) were paralleled in both Germany and Italy. WDR's six-part *Sherlock Holmes* (1967-68) was founded on six of the 12 Wilmer scripts and its Holmes was Erich Schellow – Cushing's 'voice' in the German dubs of *Dracula* and *The Mummy*. The RAI series, also called *Sherlock Holmes*, followed in October-November 1968 and starred Nando Gazzolo – again, Cushing's 'voice' in the Italian dubs of his films. In France, meanwhile, RTF offered a version of Meyrink's *Le Golem*, directed by TV pioneer Jean Kerchbron in February 1967, and two years later RAI treated Italian viewers to a radical, four-part modernisation of the Jekyll and Hyde story; called simply *Jekyll*, it was directed by its star, Giorgio Albertazzi. Confirming the new vogue for Gothic intrigue, RAI then put out Luciano Emmer's *Geminus*, a six-part mystery, starting in August 1969, in which photojournalist Walter Chiari uncovers a subterranean cult in Rome.

It was also in 1969 that 'Chicho' Serrador began shooting his first feature, *La residencia* (The Boarding School), which went into production in the last week of January and was an expanded version of a Juan Tébar script originally submitted for *Historias para no dormir*. The film was conceived quite deliberately as a means of breaching the international market, though in the event AIP entirely fumbled its release in the UK and US, misreading what was obviously a prestige picture as schlock and marketing it as *The House that Screamed*.

Back at home, the film's prestige credentials were themselves controversial, causing a major uproar over the huge budget allocated to it. Though quoted just before production as 27 million pesetas, later estimates headed, perhaps rather fancifully, for nearly twice that figure. Either way, high-class critics foamed

at the mouth over three perceived black marks – (a) Serrador was a debutant, (b) he was an upstart from TV, and (c) worst of all, he specialised in horror. Undaunted, local audiences voted with their feet when the film was released on 12 January 1970, propelling it to a staggering take of nearly 125 million pesetas.

*Turn of the century France. Mme Fourneau runs a Provençal school for 'difficult' girls aged between 15 and 21 – three of whom have mysteriously disappeared in recent months. Soon after the arrival from Avignon of new girl Thérèse, a fourth inmate, Isabelle, goes missing. Isabelle was the confidante of Mme Fourneau's introverted son Louis, whose romantic aspirations are jealously controlled by his mother on the principle that "These girls are poison."*

For exteriors, Mme Fourneau's academy was located in the Comillas region of Cantabria, purporting to be France. Setting the action outside Spain not only placated the 'nasty things don't happen here' attitude of local censors, it also helped give *La residencia* the international flavour that was deemed all-important. To the same end, the film was shot entirely in English (reputedly a first for Spain) and the German star Lilli Palmer was engaged to play the handsome but frosty Mme Fourneau. Having starred in the 1958 version of *Mädchen in Uniform* she was ideal casting for a story in which a familiar stew of girls' school repressions are twisted into a peculiarly sick psycho-thriller.

Girls' schools had appeared in several earlier horror films, notably *The Man Who Turned to Stone* from the USA, Britain's *The Brides of Dracula*, Italy's *Lycanthropus* and the Mexican chiller *Hasta el viento tiene miedo* (Even the Wind is Afraid). Serrador's take on the subject benefits from his expert manipulation of suspense and a hothouse atmosphere of adolescent desire that could be cut with the proverbial knife. It's an atmosphere that, notwithstanding Serrador's international aspirations, had obvious significance for Spanish audiences under Franco. Mme Fourneau is a repressive despot who runs the school with military precision, whether having insubordinates flogged by her toadying head girl Irène (the kind of textbook Little Hitler to be found in any institution) or insisting that the girls retain their nighties even when showering. And, as more pupils disappear, she becomes increasingly isolationist, repeatedly demanding that doors and windows be nailed down. Back at the beginning of the film, Serrador's director credit was tellingly juxtaposed with a shot of the groundsman firmly re-securing the sizable padlock on the school gates, underlining the theme

# LA RESIDENCIA

Spain 1969
UK / US: *The House That Screamed*
Regia Films / Arturo González present an Anabel
  Films production
99 minutes colour
production began 27 January 1969
..............................
Director of Photography: Manuel Berenguer;
Art Director: Ramiro Gómez; Editor:
Mercedes Alonso; Sound: Enrique Molinero,
Luis Castro; Music: Waldo de los Ríos;
Make-up: Carmen Martín; Special Effects:
[Manuel] Baquero; Screenplay: Luis Peñafiel
[Narciso Ibáñez Serrador], based on a story
by Juan Tébar; Producer: Manuel Pérez;
Director: Narciso Ibáñez Serrador

[character names as given on Spanish prints]
Lilli Palmer (Sra Fourneau); Cristina Galbó
(Teresa); John Moulder Brown (Luis); Maribel
Martín (Isabel); Mary Maude (Irene); Cándida
Losada (Srta Desprez); Pauline Challenor
(Catalina); Tomás Blanco (Pedro Baldié);
Víctor Israel (Brechard [groundsman]); Teresa
Hurtado (Andrea); María José Valero (Elena);
Conchita Paredes (Susana); Clovis Dave
(Enrique); Ana María Pol (Claudia); Francisco
Braña [scenes deleted]; María del Carmen
Duque (Julia); Gloria Blanco (Regina); Paloma
Pagés (Cecilia); Juana Azorín (Lucía); Sofía
Casares (Margarita); Elisa Méndez (Maria);
Blanca Sendino (cook); María Elena Arpón
(pupil); Maria Gustaffson (Ingrid)

This disturbing sequence of events, which the viewer follows agog yet
hardly terrified, fails to be 'scary' ... The film is not, as some seem to think,
'horror'. But it's a good picture, entertaining, intriguing and winding up
with a big, truly unexpected surprise ... Also the actors, mostly female,
have been selected with exquisite care. *La Vanguardia* 14 March 1970

The film is shot in the classical manner; it's not intended to be innovative or
make any new discoveries. Do you know what I mean? Like a good foreign
film ... It isn't easy, finding actresses of the ages I needed. We tested around
300 for a total of 20 roles. Some are practically unknown and some will be
a revelation. *Narciso Ibáñez Serrador* [quoted in *Nuevo Fotogramas*, 2 May 1969]

Lilli Palmer investigates her disturbed son's
attic hideaway in *La residencia* (1969)

spectre of sex. Yet, of course, it remains ungovernable
and ever present – in Spain or anywhere else. The
impudent Catherine flouts the rules by removing
her shift in the shower, doing so quite deliberately
to discombobulate the tongue-tied headmistress.
(An abstract fusillade of girlish sighs breaks out
on the soundtrack as Mme Fourneau withdraws in
confusion.) When the loathsome Irène sends out
one of the girls to be serviced by a local boy in the
barn, the others, though engaged in a sewing class,
are clearly aroused by proxy, prompting a rapid-fire
montage of their flickering eyes, tremulous lips,
and a moistened thread being inserted into the eye
of a needle. And Mme Fourneau tells her repressed
16-year-old son that "None of these girls is any
good to you – you need a woman like me" prior to
kissing him full on the lips. At this the screen turns
an irradiated yellow with a sound effect like boiling
acid, offering a new twist on a taboo-breaking scene
featured in Jack Clayton's 1961 film *The Innocents*.

The same film is quoted when Víctor Israel's sinister
groundsman is glimpsed by Thérèse through the
fogged-up window of a greenhouse. That Serrador
was aiming for the kind of stately, high-class horror
exemplified by Clayton's film was confirmed six years

of incarceration. No wonder Mme Fourneau's
under-mistress is moved to remind her that "This is
a boarding school, not a prison."

In battening down the hatches in this way, what
Mme Fourneau is really trying to exclude is the

later when he was working on his second horror picture. "Some great thrillers have been released here without success," he lamented, "like Robert Mulligan's *The Other* and Jack Clayton's *The Innocents*."[14] Yet Serrador wasn't hamstrung by the allusive delicacy of Clayton's film, as becomes clear when the ill-fated Isabelle ventures into the greenhouse at dead of night. With recourse to slow motion and artfully overlapping cross-fades, Serrador turns Isabelle's murder into something disturbingly balletic. Her blood washes over the killer's restraining hand, spatters adjacent petals and finally spews shockingly from her mouth as she hits the floor. The dreamlike horror is intensified by the twinkling sound of a music box, the melody droning slowly downwards as Isabelle's life ebbs away.

Isabelle was the favourite of Mme Fourneau's son, who, as the film progresses, gradually assumes centre stage. Juan Tébar made no bones about his intentions in creating Fourneau and Louis, claiming in *Nuevo Fotogramas* that "The principal theme of *La residencia* is maternal vampirism, a mother's excessive love for her son that could even be seen as compensating for her sexual frustration. This has a lot to do with Hitchcock," he added, pointing out that Oedipus complexes crop up regularly in Hitchcock's work – "not just in *Psycho*, which is the one people always remember."[15] Fair enough, but the fact remains that Louis is an obvious teenage counterpart to *Psycho*'s Norman Bates. With his leanings towards mummification complicated by the fact that mummy is still very much alive, his solution makes for one of the cruellest denouements in the genre, brilliantly staged by Serrador amid the cobwebbed, blue-tinted beams of the boy's attic hideaway as flies buzz oppressively on the soundtrack.

Perhaps the strangest feature of *La residencia* in its latter stages is a further quotation from *Psycho*; the 'heroine transfer' that shifted the focus from Marion Crane to her sister Lila is used here to replace Thérèse with Irène. Yet Irène has been painted all through as a teenage monster, making it hard to muster much sympathy for her as she begins, quite uncharacteristically, to probe Mme Fourneau's guilty conscience. In particular we remember a truly horrific scene in which Irène tortured the hapless Thérèse by baiting her about her mother and forcing her to sing. (Assaultively edited by Mercedes Alonso and brilliantly scored by Serrador's musical associate Waldo de los Ríos, this little tour de force recalls the sadistic military cadets of Volker Schlöndorff's 1965 film *Der junge Törless*.) So our response is maybe rather different to what Serrador intended when we hear the demented Louis telling his mother, "Only the hands were missing. Irène had the same hands as you: slim but strong..."

Presaging the veritable flood of Spanish horror to come in the early 1970s, several other filmmakers ventured cautiously into the field, among them Miguel Iglesias, who completed *Presagio* (Presentiment) at the beginning of September 1969. Having cast María Silva as a beautiful clairvoyant assisting in a murder investigation, Iglesias was keen to confer academic credentials on the result, pointing out that "the crime was based on a real event" and noting that "the marvels enclosed within the human mind"[16] now had college courses devoted to them. And the film itself comes complete with a rubric announcing that 'The parapsychological manifestations shown in this film are scientifically proven'. Maybe Spanish audiences weren't yet ready for a serious look at parapsychology, however – or perhaps they were put off by the talky action and sterile, TV movie look of Iglesias' film, which at times recalls such ITC series as *The Saint* and *The Champions*. Either way, *Presagio* would take nearly two years to win a release in Madrid and four to reach Barcelona. Parapsychologist Sebastián D'Arbó would have better luck when venturing into films in 1980, and he'd borrow that 'scientifically proven' line to advertise at least one of his films.

At the turn of the 1970s, another filmmaker, Juan Logar, showcased the dependable character actor Eduardo Fajardo in a couple of barely seen obscurities, *El perfil de Satanás* (The Profile of Satan) and *Trasplante de un cerebro* (Brain Transplant). The first is a tiresomely pretentious vista of historical evil, morphing the devilish Fajardo from 18th century finery to an SS uniform and then to a contemporary business suit in the blink of an eye, as well as punctuating the turgidly episodic action with offensive stock footage of concentration camps, Biafra, nuclear explosions, even Martin Luther King lying in state. The second involves Frank Wolff implanting the brain of the murdered Simón Andreu into Fajardo's skull, resulting in predictable personality problems that may have reminded the film's handful of viewers of Hammer's *Frankenstein Must Be Destroyed*, which they'd seen as *El cerebro de Frankenstein* just a few months earlier. The result is more engaging than *El perfil*, with pleasant location footage of Sicily and central London, plus a gangster sub-plot that ends with the conflicted Fajardo being put out of his misery by his own surgeon.

Obviously keen on actuality footage, Logar used some genuine brain-probing shots behind the credits (thankfully obfuscated by psychedelic colour-tampering), and by 1973 his mania for quasi-documentary realism would result in an unwatchable 'does exactly what it says on the tin' item called *Autopsia* (Autopsy). But it was through a production predating all these that Logar had an inadvertent impact on Spanish horror. In 1967 he wrote, scored, produced and starred as a grief-crazed Parisian serial killer in a vanity project called *Agonizando en el crimen* (Dying in Crime), which was directed by Enrique López Eguiluz. Further down the cast list, playing a Sûreté detective, was none other than Paul Naschy, who took the opportunity to tell Eguiluz about a script he was working on. Thus had been conceived, in embryo, the game-changer that was the Naschy-Eguiluz collaboration *La marca del hombre lobo*.

## STUDENT UNREST IN SCHLOSS AND CHÂTEAU

In April 1971 the writer-director Hans Wilhelm Geissendörfer got together with Wim Wenders and several others to form Filmverlag der Autoren, indicating that the young independents of 'das neue Kino' were finally ready to take charge of the distribution of their own films. This new movement, which had been coalescing for close to ten years and was to make an international impact similar to France's Nouvelle Vague, aimed to kick over the traces of a commercial industry it considered defunct and to scrutinise the vexed question of Germany's past. In the process various fragments of horror and fantasy emerged, among them the slow descent into madness dramatised in George Moorse's *Lenz* (based on Büchner's 1836 novella), the bizarre echoes of *Freaks* in Werner Herzog's *Auch Zwerge haben klein angefangen* (Even Dwarfs Started Small), and the ill-concealed perversions underlying a so-called utopia in Johannes Schaaf's provocative adaptation of an Alfred Kubin story, *Traumstadt* (Dream City).

For his part, Geissendörfer had made his first film back in 1969. He was 27 and less than two years out of university when the shooting of *Jonathan* was completed on Wednesday 30 April. Narciso Ibáñez Serrador was shooting *La residencia* at much the same time and would go on to invent the Spanish game show *Un, dos, tres*; similarly, Geissendörfer was destined to create Germany's first TV soap opera, *Lindenstraße*. His feature debut, needless to say, gives no indication of this outcome. Resonating through this strange film were several of the most combustible topics of the day – anti-Vietnam activism, the German student movement, a pervasive distrust among young people of their parents' Nazi past. In short, the mood of violent radicalisation that in 1968 had entailed the attempted assassination of student leader Rudi Dutschke and in 1970 would lead to the formation of the Baader-Meinhof group. Yet Geissendörfer chose to set his political parable in the early 19th century,

evoking E T A Hoffmann while very loosely adapting Bram Stoker's *Dracula*.

*The Count and his vampire acolytes preside over a blighted landscape from the vantage point of a massive castle. A young man, Jonathan, is sent on ahead by an elderly resistance leader, charged with infiltrating the castle and finding out as much as he can. Captured and consigned to the dungeons, he's submitted to appalling tortures and only rescued when a full-scale peasant revolt forces the bloodsuckers into the sea.*

*Jonathan* won Geissendörfer the Best New Director award at the 1970 Deutsche Filmpreis ceremony, later picking up some notable plaudits when released in America, from "the most beautiful-looking vampire movie I have seen"[17] to "one of the most entrancing and exquisitely conceived films in my memory."[18] It's certainly arresting in the way it elucidates contemporary concerns in a period context. The lead vampire wears the traditional bat-collared cloak but sports a slicked-down hairdo that no viewer could mistake for anyone other than Adolf Hitler. In one of the film's many serenely extended tracking shots, a group of lordly vampires is seen feasting on various peasants, with one woman pausing to say, "Blood. Good and tasty. Nothing quenches quite like it." And down in the stews yet more peasants are kept in filthy conditions recalling a concentration camp, while the Count's black-clad goons beat up the hero (in a nastily protracted sequence) for all the world like a 19th century version of the SS – or, for that matter, the kind of brutal 1960s police officers protested against by the Sozialistische Deutsche Studentenbund.

Disturbingly, Geissendörfer scores this sequence with the plaintive *Death of Åse* from Grieg's *Peer Gynt*. The majority of the music, however, is by the Viennese jazz musician Roland Kovac, whose jagged guitar licks in the credits sequence – rivetingly strange in themselves – serve notice that this apparently ancient scenario will have a modern resonance. Geissendörfer quickly proves his eye for a striking composition; the opening shot is a tight close-up of a black-gloved hand, complete with a ruby ring, rapping on a door. A surprise defenestration ensues, followed by an eye-catching pietà on the cobbles below as an old lady cradles the dead body. The victim's girlfriend, meanwhile, is seen slumped outside the castle in a blood-spattered white shift, hovered over by three Great Danes as a squad of the Count's militia strides past. Beautifully photographed by Robby Müller, the remainder of the film proves equally riveting, whether trawling through scenes of rural devastation or relishing the Baroque splendours of Schloss Weissenstein at Pommersfelden.

It's here that Geissendörfer stages most of his Stoker-derived scenes. An early vignette in which the chalk-faced Count reveals a ready-made wound on his chest and makes a girl drink from it is a modified Stoker quote. (A few years earlier, in *Dracula Prince of Darkness*, Christopher Lee's Count made the wound from scratch, as per the book, but any imbibing was vetoed by the British censor.) Then, transferring to the castle, the Count is given a few scraps of Stoker dialogue and – in a film first – presents his three brides with a stolen baby in order to divert them from gorging on Jonathan. The distraught mother then appears outside the castle and is hauled off by the 1820s SS. Yet these scraps of the novel seem shoehorned in rather arbitrarily, making little difference to a scenario in which any oppressive vampire overlord would have done just as well.

The film's echoes of older horror films, however, are intriguing. The 'apprentice vampire hunter doing a recce' device recalls Hammer's *Dracula*, while the Count's red-robed cult members, and their screaming panic when finally routed, echo *The Kiss of the Vampire*. Jonathan's stricken fiancée, left behind when he's sent on his mission, is a dead ringer for Hutter's wife in Murnau's *Nosferatu*, the Hoffmann-like atmosphere of which is conjured up at intervals throughout the picture. A more up-to-date reference is to the 1968 release *Witchfinder General*, which Geissendörfer invokes with dungeon scenes more gruelling than anything Michael Reeves could devise. In its rustic verisimilitude, the film also points forward to *Witchfinder*'s 1970 follow-up, *Blood on Satan's Claw*, while the corpse-strewn wastelands surrounding the castle prefigure the plague tableaux staged by Werner Herzog in *Nosferatu Phantom der Nacht*.

Essentially an art film, *Jonathan* is guilty of a few serious longueurs, together with some wilfully obtuse details. The vampires are attended by lilac-clad little girls whose synchronised movements are unintentionally comic, and scenes featuring a wheezing woodland hermit who decorates his shack with inverted crosses are a trial to watch. There's also a peculiar sequence in which a large group of mainly elderly peasants watch a young couple making love; presumably suggesting that the common people in all eras are too entranced by pornography and other distractions to stand up and be counted, it goes on far longer than necessary – though in a weird way it's an interesting echo of Nigel Kneale's 1968 TV play *The Year of the Sex Olympics*. Elsewhere, the film boasts much more gore than the average art-house

## JONATHAN

West Germany 1969
Iduna Film (Munich)
97 minutes colour
production began 10 March 1969

. . . . . . . . . . . . . . . . . . . . . . . . . . . . .

Director of Photography: Robert Müller; Art Director: Hans Gailling; Editor: Wolfgang Hedinger; Sound: Ludwig Probst; Music: Roland Kovac; Make-up: Peter Kraus, Ida Dreissler; Screenplay: Hans W Geissendörfer, based on *Dracula* by Bram Stoker; Executive Producer: Hellmut Haffner; Director: Hans W Geissendörfer

Jürgen Jung (Jonathan); Hans Dieter Jendreyko (Joseph); Paul Albert Krumm (the Count);

Thomas Astan (Thomas); Hertha von Walther (Thomas' mother); Oskar von Schab (professor); Ilona Grübel (Eleonore); Sophie Strehlow (other woman); Henry Liposca (gnome); Ulrike Luderer (gnome girl); Christine Ratej (Elisabeth); Arthur Brauss (Adolf); Hans-Dieter Kerky (Eberhard); Wilfried Klaus (priest); Eleonore Schminke (Lena); Walter Feuchtenberg (Lena's father); Ilse Künkele (Lena's mother); Käthe Tellheim, Monica Teuber (themselves); Gaby Herbst; Michael Hoffmann; Michael Grimm; Bernd Schwamm; Angelika Werner; uncredited: Peter Bauer (young man); Otmar Engel (Count's attendant); Walter Frank; Heidi Hedinger; Peter Heeg (persecutor); Gudrun Gundelach; Alexander May (porter); Willy Schultes

**Right up to the final sequence, in its tangible sense of style, and radical renunciation of outrageous horror effects and heavy-handed sensationalism, Geissendörfer's *Jonathan* attains an artistic quality that enables it to stand beside the classics of the vampire film ... In the process Geissendörfer evidently wants the essence of his parable-style fable to be understood politically.** *Stuttgarter Zeitung* 13 November 1969

**Good vampire films are grim fairy tales for adults. The son of a clergyman, Hans W Geissendörfer has studied the vampire myth with intensive interest, starting with *Nosferatu* by Murnau to Terence Fisher's *Horror of Dracula*. In the disguise of a vampire tale he tries to dramatise the problem of despotism and suppression.** [English-language publicity material reproduced in *German Film News* # 32, 1970]

Ilona Grübel, victim of remorseless Nazi vampires (and their dogs) in *Jonathan* (1969)

patron could stomach, particularly in the climactic battle. According to Geissendörfer, speaking in a DVD supplement, still more was made available for Japanese audiences.

Amid the carnage we encounter various dead pigs, cows and horses – presumably drugged for the occasion. In the dungeon, however, one of the SS creeps repeatedly stamps on a rat, first disabling it and then pulping its head. Depressing that a film advocating freedom from dictatorship should serve up such a revolting instance of animal cruelty.

By late 1971, the echoes of *Dracula* contained in Geissendörfer's first feature were being refined by another debutant director into echoes of a specific film. Niklaus Schilling's *Nachtschatten* (Night Shade) evokes Dreyer's *Vampyr* in several ways, from the hesitant, oneiric tone to the motif of a wandering man perplexed by an enigmatic woman, winding up with a climactic plunge into quicksand recalling the death-by-flour of Dreyer's film.

Dreamlike uncertainty on the Lüneburg Heath: John van Dreelen and Elke Hart in *Nachtschatten* (1971)

A Hamburg music publisher (John van Dreelen), keen to buy a holiday home in the Lüneburg Heath area, becomes hypnotically drawn to the young widow (Elke Hart) who owns the place, with the viewer left unsure as to whether or not he's her dead husband returned. Set against the same forbidding landscapes as Frank Wysbar's *Fährmann Maria*, there are plenty of eerie touches here – a skull-and-crossbones daubed on the side of the man's white Mercedes, a dream in which the woman plucks poppies from the husband's grave, a constant recourse on the soundtrack to Grieg's *Death of Åse*, as in Geissendörfer's film. But Schilling also imposes a somnolent pace, which kills the film.

The German student movement, so vividly present in Geissendörfer's *Jonathan* in coded form, had first made headlines in June 1966, predating the seismic student uprising in France by nearly two years. The French upheaval, as we've seen, was inadvertently reflected in Jean Rollin's debut feature, *Le Viol du vampire*. In his next film, *La Vampire nue* (The Nude Vampire), Rollin came up with a scenario intriguingly at odds with Geissendörfer's approach in *Jonathan*. For Rollin the monstrous capitalists are decidedly human and it's the vampires who represent the brave new world of the counterculture. Yet, coincidentally, the films echo each other via their beach climaxes and similar scenes of a young man cornered in a castle.

Rollin's producer this time round was his distributor friend Jean Lavie; among other new collaborators recruited for *La Vampire nue* were cinematographer Jean-Jacques Renon (who had recently photographed *Hallucinations sadiques*), designer Jio Berk (who had come to Rollin's attention by writing one of the few good reviews of his previous film), and the *Cahiers du Cinéma* critic Michel Delahaye, amusingly cast as an extraterrestrial vampire. Another innovation was the use of Eastmancolor. By his own account, Rollin was aiming "to do something a little more temperate than *Le Viol du vampire*. I wanted to make a well-done, traditional mystery film. Looking back on it now [May 1995], why, it's not a classical film at all! It is exactly the same kind of film as *Le Viol*! Not so delirious maybe, but it has the same spirit. Well, it's a Rollin film."[19]

*Men in animal masks pursue a beautiful woman through darkened streets and eventually shoot her. Having failed to save the woman, Pierre Radamante determines to get to the bottom of the mystery, an enquiry that leads him to his own father. A super-rich entrepreneur, Radamante père is intent on distilling the elixir of immortality from the woman's blood, for she is a vampire. But others of her kind turn up en masse to confound his schemes.*

"The images and dialogues of my films," Rollin wrote in 2004, "attach themselves to the idea that they can become, or are, a cinema of the imaginary ... For me, a cinema which permits these meanderings is the only real cinema."[20] The dreamlike wanderings so prized by Rollin are still present in *La Vampire nue*, but this time they gain impact, paradoxically, from being inserted into a better organised narrative. Abandoning the improvisatory approach of *Le Viol*, Rollin crafted a story that is outstandingly weird – flirting, in fact, with science fiction – but nevertheless hangs together in a style *Le Viol* couldn't manage.

Even so, enigmatic eeriness was Rollin's chief goal and the film's credits sequence plays up to this, showing only a yellow-sleeved, well-manicured hand, sporting a prominent ruby ring and resting on an appropriately inscrutable Sphinx-like statue; it turns out, appropriately, to be Delahaye's hand. (The presence of a ruby ring at this early stage is another odd echo of Geissendörfer's *Jonathan*.)

Rollin's opening scenes, positioned either side of the credits, are riveting in their apparently disconnected strangeness. Accompanied only by a metronomic dripping noise and Yvon Gérault's jagged musique concrète, three white-coated men draw blood from a female subject's inner elbow. The subject is naked but for a blue hood; two of the men wear red hoods, the other a strange, horned animal mask. A series of phials, meanwhile, drain blue, amber, red and lilac fluids into beakers. Then we join a beautiful young woman clad in a diaphanous orange shift; in flight from various other masked men, she's finally shot down on an iron causeway by a man with enormous antlers. The pursuers look like black-turtle-necked mime artists rather than tuxedoed magicians, but Rollin was happy to admit that his inspiration here was Franju's *Judex*.

The climate of mystery is well maintained thereafter, with Rollin's move into colour allowing for a wide range of weird images, notably the colonnaded majesty of the Radamante country seat, swathed in a blue mist. There are a few hiccups along the way, however. A visit to an artist's studio appears to exist only to provide more nudity than sex-hungry punters would otherwise get, and Pierre's discovery of a suicide cult involves a girl shooting herself in the head in the most unconvincing manner imaginable – quite a surprise after the brilliantly executed car chase stunt that featured in *Le Viol*. Similarly clumsy is a scene in which Radamante Senior's concubines – his "two loyal little puppies" – plunge very carefully down a flight of stairs. The puppies are actually Catherine and Marie-Pierre Castel, twin hairdressers who'd just turned 21 at the time and would become totemic presences in Rollin's films. Here they model a fetching if impractical array of spiky fetish gear designed by Jio Berk.

Delahaye's chief vampire is billed as 'Grand Master' and is at one point mistaken by Pierre for a priest. He eventually leads a somnolent swarm of counterculture vampires into Radamante's domain; supremely calm, he takes hold of Radamante's wooden cross, twirls it nonchalantly, then graciously hands it back. Pierre, meanwhile, is transported via a red-curtained proscenium arch to Rollin's trusty Dieppe beach. This is the 'voyage dans la cinquième dimension' (voyage into the fifth dimension) promised in the trailer. There, in as blatant a political statement as possible, the Grand Master tells the older Radamante that "You are the *real* vampire" and forces the monstrous capitalist into the sea. Then, offering a backhanded

## LA VAMPIRE NUE

France 1969
UK / US: **The Nude Vampire**
Films ABC
90 minutes colour
released 20 May 1970
. . . . . . . . . . . . . . . . . . . . . . . . . . . . .
Director of Photography: Jean-Jacques Renon; Art Director: Jio Berk; Sound: Raymond Saint-Martin, Pierre Goumy; Music: Yvon Gerault; Additional Music: François Tusques; Make-up: Carole Fidler; Screenplay: Jean Rollin, Serge Moati [both uncredited]; Director: Jean Rollin

Caroline Cartier (nude vampire); Olivier Martin [Olivier Rollin] (Pierre Radamante); Maurice Lemaître (Georges Radamante); Michel Delahaye (Grand Master); Bernard Musson (Voringe); Jean Aron (Frédor); Ursule Pauly (Solange); Cathy et Pony Tricot [Catherine Castel, Marie-Pierre Castel] (Georges' servants); Paul Bisciglia (valet); Pascal Fardoulis (Robert); Jacques Robiolles (mutant); Elisabeth Suiro; Michelle Watrin; Suzanne Fournier; Nicole Isimat (artist's model); uncredited: R J Chauffard (old man); Ly Lestrong (Ly); Nathalie Perrey (old woman)

Rollin's previous film sought to reinvigorate the classic vampire motifs ... *La Vampire nue*, by contrast, attempts to supersede them, abandoning the theme in favour of that of the mutant. This abandonment ... produces, while viewing the picture, a very curious 'bump' at the very point where the tale ceases to be comprehensible ... and it makes the whole film read like a half-baked political delusion. (Who are these mutants?) *Cahiers du Cinéma* July 1970

In 1967, when we began, there were no French horror films. No producer or distributor in France would take a chance on them ... We were given a simple ultimatum: if you want your film released, we can release it on the sex circuit. They wouldn't think of attempting a pure horror film. But we did attempt to avoid the pornographic; there are no bed scenes in our film.
Jean Rollin [quoted in *Cinefantastique* Fall 1973]

Caroline Cartier in classic candle-bearing pose as *La Vampire nue* (1969)

compliment to the hippy movement that so obviously influenced Rollin in this film, the Grand Master tells us head-on that "Tomorrow, today, at any moment – the day of the mutant will come."

Immediately prior to this, Rollin has created a simple yet striking surrealist image when the fulsome Caroline Cartier emerges from an upright, red-draped magician's cabinet on the shoreline, though this moment was greeted with ribaldry on initial showings. "This is one of the most unusual images of my cinema," Rollin lamented, "and despite the whistling and heckling it remains dazzling for me."[21]

While *La Vampire nue* was being readied for release, there were signs that, despite the angry bewilderment it had induced in audiences, Rollin's previous film was proving influential. Another significant factor was the big impact made at the French box-office by Roman Polanski's *Rosemary's Baby*, which opened in Paris in October 1968. As a result, the small upsurge in French fantastique signalled by *Le Viol du vampire*, *Hallucinations sadiques* and *L'Araignée d'eau* was perpetuated in 1969 by another disparate trio.

*Les Amours particulières* (Private Passions) was directed by Gérard Trembasiewicz and, notwithstanding the glimmerings of pretension contained in it, was exported as the low-grade skin flick it really is under the title *The Room of Chains*. Here, two gay antique dealers retire to the country on regular occasions for voyeuristic perversions in a customised dungeon, where they watch a troglodyte gardener (or something) chastising naked girls chained to pillars. The older dealer also fantasises scenes of a sacrificial subject stretched out nude on an altar with a large snake slithering around between her legs. A fragment of humour surfaces amid the sleaze, when a comely, bra-less victim enthusiastically whips off her top in the local police station to display her non-existent bruises;

LA ROSE ÉCORCHÉE

Another film, another candle-bearer: Olivia Robin in *La Rose écorchée* (1969)

she goes through exactly the same routine later on with a cop up from Paris. The film's dismal level, however, is better demonstrated by one of the local gendarmes, who puzzles over the fact that none of the women was actually violated with the sniggering observation, "I've seen some girls who wouldn't object, no kidding!"

As well as referencing both a cinema and a magazine in its title, Pierre Philippe's *Midi Minuit* (Midday Midnight) displays its horror-fan erudition right from the start, when someone tells the impressionable heroine that "It was a mistake taking you to that Terence Fisher retrospective." Later on, a little girl is briefly seen clutching a Karloff monster doll. Otherwise, this mind-numbing tale of a weird Provençal family beset by 'sadique' murders, committed by a killer wearing the kind of clawed glove popularised by the Congo leopard men, is a chore to sit through. The striking faces on view – Sylvie Fennec's youthful beauty, Béatrice Arnac's exotic femme fatale, Daniel Emilfork's epicene patriarch – are no compensation for the interminable scenes of white-clad figures moving amid the rocky whiteness of Les Baux-de-Provence. Arnac is a sexual sadist in silver lamé, and the eye-catching artworks supposedly concocted by her were actually by Maria Morgan-Snell. Otherwise, the ever-present Mediterranean throb of cicadas induces something akin to catalepsy in record time.

More interesting than either of these was a film made by the 26-year-old writer-director – and horror fan – Claude Mulot, who began shooting *La Rose écorchée* (The Flayed Rose) on 8 May 1969. By June the following year the film was showing at London's Jacey Cinema as *Ravaged*, only appearing in France in September and in the US (as *The Blood Rose*) in October. According to its American publicity, Mulot had created 'The First Sex-Horror Film Ever Made!' In fact he'd cranked out yet another variation on *Les Yeux sans visage*, and to underline the fact he cast the former Dr Orlof, Howard Vernon, as a disgraced surgeon who's blackmailed into reconstructing the fire-ravaged face of a painter's young wife. "The word 'butcher' hurts me," stammers the guilt-ridden Dr Romer, who is privately convinced the operation will fail and, indeed, hangs himself before he can perform it. The policeman dogging Romer's footsteps (well played by Jacques Seiler) is called Inspector Dorsay, in tribute to composer Jean-Pierre Dorsay, whose lushly romantic score is the film's most memorable feature.

There are several indications that Mulot wanted the whole thing to be lushly romantic – Roger Fellous' lighting effects are attractive, Michèle Perello rises from the grave in an arrestingly odd dream sequence, and Olivia Robin drifts with a candelabrum through mist-wreathed ruins in shots that already display the influence of Jean Rollin. (Robin, incidentally, plays Perello's sister, mimicking *Psycho*'s 'puzzled sister investigates' plot.) But vulgarian asides keep crowding in and finally sink the film. Anny Duperey's horror make-up is of Play-Doh ineptitude, her POV shots involve vaseline being loaded onto the lens, and Mulot throws in a couple of fur-clad dwarfs to punch up the exploitation factor. These two are involved in a three-person dungeon scrum that ranks high on the cynicism scale. 'Valérie Boisgel violée par deux nains!' (Valérie Boisgel raped by two dwarfs!) salivated the pressbook.

The artist 'hero', played by Philippe Lemaire, is called Frédéric Lansac, a name subsequently appropriated by Mulot when he moved into directing porn. He used it, for example, on his 1975 film *Le Sexe qui parle*, which became an international hit under the provocative title *Pussy Talk*. Soon after making a half-hearted slasher called *Le Couteau sous la gorge* (The Knife Under the Throat), Mulot drowned in October 1986, aged only 44.

Herbert Fux inflicts hideous torments on Gaby Fuchs in *Hexen bis aufs Blut gequält* (1969)

## CHALK-NOSED WITCHFINDERS AND BARCELONA VAMPIRES

Having been at his most chillingly suave for his weekend visit to the *De Sade 70* set in January 1969, Christopher Lee was back with Harry Alan Towers and Jess Franco in August for *El proceso de las brujas* (The Trial of the Witches), which acquired the catchier title *The Bloody Judge* for export purposes. Shot in Leria, this was Franco's answer to the Michael Reeves classic *Witchfinder General*, which had been released in May 1968 and made a major international impact. Writing, as was his wont, as Peter Welbeck, Towers shifted *Witchfinder*'s action forward a few decades to give a loose account of the fearsome Judge Jeffreys and the Monmouth Rebellion. He clearly lavished some money on the picture too, since Franco manages to stage the kind of reasonably credible battle sequence that the budget-conscious Reeves had been careful to avoid.

On top of this, Towers even squeezed in a few insights into Jeffreys' motivation – more, in fact, than Vincent Price was given in delineating *Witchfinder*'s Matthew Hopkins. Yet these insights aren't especially riveting, leaving Lee to scowl his way through the part while affirming his fanatical belief that witches should be "stamped out like rats in a granary, else we shall never cleanse England of this pestilence." Despite the familiar presence of Howard Vernon in the lower depths (as a leotarded torturer obviously modelled on Boris Karloff in *Tower of London*), *El proceso* is hard to follow and, with Franco's jazzy exuberance thoroughly dampened by the conventional subject matter, it's rather dull to boot. For the German version, however, some

ten minutes of grislier and racier footage were added, much of it focusing on Vernon's perverted practices in the dungeon; this version was retitled *Der Hexentöter von Blackmoor* (The Witch Killer of Blackmoor).

Another *Witchfinder General* variant – conceived, not by Towers, but by an earlier Franco collaborator, Adrian Hoven – was in production at exactly the same time. The film's 'o come all ye sadists' title was *Hexen bis aufs Blut gequält* (Witches Tortured Till They Bleed), though this was modified for export to *Mark of the Devil*. Under this label it was banned in the UK but did terrific business in America, complete with give-away vomit bags and a 'Rated V for Violence' advertising campaign. The beleaguered director was Michael Armstrong, who was presumably selected by Aquila Film because, like *Witchfinder*'s Michael Reeves, he was (a) English, (b) only in his twenties and (c) called Michael.

As well as acting and producing, Hoven also wrote the original script, which he called *The Witch Hunt of Dr Dracula*. Overhauling it completely, Armstrong triggered a running battle between himself, Hoven and Hoven's appointed cinematographer Ernst W Kalinke – a battle resolved when Hoven and his associates took over direction halfway through the schedule. Hypnotised by genuine accounts of ghastly 17th century torture devices, Armstrong determined to cram all of them into his film, resulting in a flat and flavourless parade of barbarities loosely hung around a *Witchfinder*-style romance between an accused serving wench (Olivera Vuco) and a high-minded apprentice witch hunter (Udo Kier). With victims having thumbscrews applied, others sitting bare-arsed on spikes, and still others stretched topless on racks, the film far outstrips *Witchfinder* in grisliness, in the process falling into the predictable trap of condemning centuries-old cruelties while simultaneously revelling in them.

Herbert Lom – fitted, at his own insistence, with a rather conspicuous chalk nose – is the film's Vincent Price substitute, calmly watching a girl's tongue being (unconvincingly) ripped out while telling Kier that "We must never weaken in performing God's work." But the occasional line like this is as far as the film goes in anatomising religious hypocrisy. Perhaps the most effective passages feature, ironically, Adrian Hoven, who cast himself as an aristocratic puppeteer submitted to an insidious water torture when his puppets are assumed to be agents of the Devil. The location was the looming Schloss Moosham near Mauterndorf, and the film certainly looks pretty. But the end result suggests what would later be called 'torture porn' set to a ritzy Euro-lounge score; aptly enough, in 1979 Michael Holm's theme would be echoed by Riz Ortolani for the notorious *Cannibal Holocaust*.

By April 1972 a loose follow-up was in production under the even more offensive title *Hexen geschändet und zu Tode gequält* (Witches Raped and Tortured to Death). This time Hoven was the sole director, shooting once again in the Salzburg area and casting Anton Diffring and Reggie Nalder as the villains; the latter was a carry-over from the first film, though playing a different character. Inept attempts at so-called nunsploitation are added to the mix this time round, indicating that Ken Russell's *The Devils* had come out in the interim, and the grossly misogynist result was exported as *Mark of the Devil Part II*. "Crass, inept and awful, but its intended audience will lap it up, so to speak," opined future director Joe Dante in his *Film Bulletin* review, also describing it as "the sort of entertainment that might have been concocted expressly for an audience of unregenerate Nazi surgeons. (The Argentinian grosses should be worth watching.)" With this waggish judgment Dante was actually being quite prescient, since the natural heirs to these witch-hunting films were the Nazi exploitation pictures that became popular later in the 1970s.

Back in 1969, Christopher Lee's next engagement for Harry Alan Towers was a project that, in the planning stages, meant a great deal to him. *El conde Drácula* (Count Dracula) was originally announced as a multi-million dollar extravaganza with Vincent Price as Van Helsing and Terence Fisher in the director's chair. In the event it became the ninth and last Jess Franco film sponsored by Towers, wrapping on

5 December, two years almost to the day since the first in the sequence had begun shooting. For Lee it offered the opportunity, as he put it in a fan club bulletin in September, "to do Bram Stoker's *Dracula* as he wrote it." But Towers' wayward script and Franco's listless direction squandered the opportunity more comprehensively than anyone could have predicted.

*Jonathan Harker travels to Transylvania to organise Count Dracula's acquisition of a property near London. At Dracula's remote castle Harker is attacked by three vampire women; later, he realises that Dracula, too, is a centuries-old vampire and, in terror, he flings himself from a high window. When he comes to he's in an English clinic run by Professor Van Helsing, who quickly works out that the house next door, Carfax, has a new tenant – the steadily rejuvenating Count Dracula.*

Much of the first half hour of *El conde Drácula* is quite promising. Franco gives Harker's journey to the castle a genuinely dreamlike atmosphere, bathing it in an unearthly blue haze of scudding fogs and ensuring that Dracula (doubling as his own coachman) sees off three accompanying wolves with exactly the sweeping gesture specified by Stoker. Bruno Nicolai's score is also shudderingly effective. The interpolation of jungle sound effects is perplexing, however, as is the use of German Shepherds rather than actual wolves. And, once in the castle, the appearance of a wall-sized mirror, enabling Harker to see at once that Dracula has no reflection, is so egregious a departure from the novel that it's surprising the reverent Lee agreed to play the scene.

Even so, the setting for Harker's post-prandial interview with the Count – a castellated, 16th century chamber in Barcelona's Barrio Gótico – is splendidly atmospheric, with Lee's white-haired Count uttering a string of oracular non-sequiturs in a forlorn, gravelly voice that seems genuinely to issue from the grave. Retiring to the fireside for some martial reminiscences, Lee succeeds admirably in mixing the Count's megalomania with a suppressed vein of melancholy. Particularly resonant is a line penned by Towers rather than Stoker: "I am not young, and yet I am restless."

The appearance of Dracula's three vampire brides, however, is seriously fumbled. They look and sound quite acceptable, yet Harker seems to be unconscious throughout, completely eradicating his confused response to their erotic advances – a Stoker detail one might have expected Franco to revel in. Worse, Dracula's explosive intervention isn't explosive at all; indeed, it announces the strangely enervated directorial style that will predominate in the remainder of the film. Maybe Franco, who not so long before had made a film

Christopher Lee's authentic Count seduces Soledad
Miranda's Lucy Westenra in *El conde Drácula* (1969)

as vital yet disciplined as *Miss Muerte*, felt hamstrung
by the requirements of a straight literary adaptation, or
even intimidated by the responsibility involved. Either
way, from this point on the film sinks like a stone.

It's also at this point that the script abandons all
pretence at fidelity to the novel. In fact, the dubbing
for the German version – *Nachts, wenn Dracula erwacht*
(Nights When Dracula Awakes) – even abandons
the Count's transfer to London, limiting his
globetrotting to Budapest, a sensible move given the
preponderance of palm trees on view. Klaus Kinski is
an excellent Renfield, despite being granted only one
word of dialogue, while Herbert Lom's humourless
Van Helsing is made up to look like a blue-rinsed
version of Lee's Duc de Richleau in the recent
Hammer film *The Devil Rides Out*. Unfortunately,
Soledad Miranda's Lucy behaves like a zombie from
her first entrance, and her nocturnal wander through
Whitby is changed to a shock encounter with Dracula
in a Barcelona colonnade. By the final stages Maria
Röhm's Mina is virtually comatose too – a long way
from the hands-on heroine conceived by Stoker.

## EL CONDE DRÁCULA

Spain-Italy-West Germany-Liechtenstein-UK 1969
Italy: **Il conte Dracula**
West Germany: **Nachts, wenn Dracula erwacht**
UK / US: **Bram Stoker's Count Dracula**
Fénix Films Madrid / Filmar Rome / Corona
Filmproduktion Munich
a Towers of London production [UK, US prints only]
98 ninutes colour
production ended 5 December 1969

. . . . . . . . . . . . . . . . . . . . . . . . . . . . . . .

[credits as given on Spanish prints] Director
of Photography: Manuel Merino; Art
Director: Karl Schneider; Editors: María
Louisa Sorana, G Reinecke; Music: Bruno
Nicolai; Make-up: Gerry Fletcher; Special
Effects: Sergio Pagoni; Screenplay: Peter
Welbeck [Harry Alan Towers, credited on
English-language prints only], Jess Franco,
Augusto Finocchi [on Spanish prints], from
the novel Dracula by Bram Stoker; Producer:
Harry Alan Towers; Director: Jess Franco

Christopher Lee (Count Dracula); Herbert Lom
(Professor Van Helsing); Klaus Kinski (Renfield);
Maria Rohm (Mina Harker); Frederick Williams
(Jonathan Harker); Soledad Miranda (Lucy
Westenra); Jack Taylor (Quincey Morris); Paul
Muller (Dr Seward); uncredited on UK / US
prints: Franco Castellani (warder); Emma Cohen
(vampire bride); Jess Franco (footman at clinic);
Colette Giacobine (Greta); José Martínez Blanco
(fellow passenger); Jeannine Mestre (vampire
bride); Jesús Puente (Home Secretary); Moisés
Augusto Rocha (Home Secretary's footman)

Franco's camera style is a mess – sometimes subjective, sometimes objective
in the same scene – otherwise content to rely on static set-ups and a totally
predictable use of the zoom ... The technical effects are of a standard well
below Hammer's: the disintegration scene is frankly pathetic ... The casting
of Christopher Lee seems a purely exploitative case of 'no show without
Punch'. It is rare that a name actor is so ill-served by a production.
*Films Illustrated July 1973*

I have just returned from Barcelona after two dark and dreadful weeks,
during which time I seldom finished work before 10.00 or 11.00 pm ... The
'producer' is none other than H A Towers Esq. You will therefore immediately
realise that the story has been 'cut down to size', the production value
therefore lessened, and some of the casting based purely on the least
possible financial outlay. *Christopher Lee [fan club letter, dated 6 November 1969]*

Other weirdnesses crop up on all sides. Renfield defenestrates himself (just as Harker did earlier); Van Helsing suffers a stroke and, wheelchair-bound, visits the Home Secretary; Dracula, in a devious move echoing the 1931 film rather than the Stoker book, lures Mina to an opera house via the childish expedient of an anonymous ticket. And, rather than unleash a swarm of Carfax rats on his pursuers as per Stoker, this Dracula animates a bunch of moth-eaten stuffed animals. Fox, warthog, badger, owl, deer, ostrich, raven, even a swordfish – all are quite clearly being joggled towards the camera by an unseen hand, and the result has to be seen to be believed.

Having grown younger on Lucy's blood and therefore looking as darkly Hispanic as almost everybody else in the picture, Lee himself provides the film's only remaining high points. Standing on his London balcony and hissing out malign instructions, he's the very image of Stoker's rejuvenated vampire. And two brief scenes towards the end, with the top-hatted Count accosted by a passing prostitute and himself accosting a Russian sea captain at the quayside, capture the chilly essence of the novel better than any other adaptation. The ending, however, features polystyrene boulders and a climactic disintegration that's unparalleled in its uselessness. "By the last reel even Spanish audiences were howling with laughter,"[22] reported *Variety*. Despite this, the film made over 40 million pesetas in Spain, a tidy sum that presumably compensated Towers for its virtual non-appearance in Britain and America.

Monitoring *El conde Drácula* during production was the young Catalonian filmmaker Pedro Portabella, formerly a member – alongside Vicente Aranda, Jorge Grau, Gonzalo Suárez and others – of the Escuela de Barcelona. The result was an extraordinary avant-garde phantasmagoria called *Cuadecuc Vampír*, 'cua de cuc' meaning 'worm's tail' and thus identifying the film as a poetic addendum to Franco's. With Franco's crew members as much a part of the action as the actors, we're shown stage hands spraying fake fog, exposed arc lights, and Christopher Lee climbing into a coffin attended by a man with a cobweb-making

EL HOMBRE MAS BELLO DEL MUNDO EN LA HISTORIA MAS SOBRECOGEDORA DEL CINE

HELMUT BERGER en EL RETRATO DE **DORIAN GRAY**

T C NC L R CINEMASCOPE
MEDALLA III SEMANA INTERNACIONAL DE CINE FANTÁSTICO Y DE TERROR DE SITGES

MARGARET RICHARD HERBERT ELEONORA LEE · TODD · LOM · ROSSI DRAGO

DIRIGE POR MASSIMO DALLAMANO

*INMINENTE ACONTECIMIENTO EN LAS PANTALLAS DE MADRID Y DEL RESTO DE ESPAÑA*

'The world's most beautiful man in cinema's most horrifying story': Spanish advertising for *Das Bildnis des Dorian Gray* (1969)

machine. The clapperboard, continuity stopwatch, a string-propelled bat and Soledad Miranda's prosthetic neck-wounds all put in appearances. Maria Röhm rehearses in a trendy leopardskin coat, Herbert Lom has his goatee trimmed, and Lee ceremoniously removes his contact lenses and fake fangs. Finally, Portabella ventures into the star's dressing room where, reflected in multiple mirrors, Lee reads the death of Dracula from Stoker's book. Lee's is the only voice in the entire picture. The cumulative effect is of a memorably eerie blurring of fantasy and reality, a film that demystifies the filmmaking process while remaining, in itself, beguilingly mysterious.

Harry Alan Towers, meanwhile, was keeping Jess Franco so busy during this period that he had to hand one of his projects to the Italian director Massimo Dallamano. Having photographed Sergio Leone's two 'Dollars' Westerns, Dallamano had just directed the accomplished semi-giallo *La morte non ha sesso* (Death Has No Gender), exported as *A Black Veil for Lisa* and graced by the unique cast combination of John Mills and Luciana Paluzzi. He'd also made a sex-filled, visually glamorous but fundamentally dreary adaptation of *Venus in Furs* (not to be confused with Franco's contemporaneous film of the same title). For Towers he handled *Das Bildnis des Dorian Gray* (The Picture of Dorian Gray), which featured such Franco and-or Towers regulars as Herbert Lom, Richard Todd, Marie Liljedahl, Maria Röhm and Margaret Lee but gave the title role to Helmut Berger. After London location filming this began studio shooting in the second week of October 1969, just as Franco was starting work on *El conde Drácula*. Lom and Röhm were therefore occupied with both projects simultaneously.

Announced in its own credits sequence as 'a modern allegory based on the work of Oscar Wilde', this ties itself into nonsensical self-reflexive knots when Lom's lordly tempter is accused of peddling "the epigrams of Oscar Wilde, badly edited by Henry Wotton." The film's Swinging London milieu is eye-catching, but thanks to a failure of imagination the same Carnaby Street clothes and accoutrements still hold sway in the latter stages, which are (presumably) set in the

1990s. Curiously, Dallamano features exactly the same drag artist in exactly the same pub as were featured in a British film made at exactly the same time, Alan Gibson's *Goodbye Gemini*. There are a few other intriguing details. The ageless Dorian somehow ends up on the cover of *Cinema X* magazine (which in 1969 was brand new), the story's homoerotic implications aren't dwelt on but are at least acknowledged, and Wotton's early claim that "We degenerate into hideous puppets" is borne out when Dorian's raddled corpse slumps at the foot of the fateful portrait. But no amount of implied oral sex can prevent the bulk of the film from being a boring misfire.

After exchanging lesbian kisses with Margaret Lee in *Dorian Gray*, the distinguished Italian actress Eleonora Rossi Drago went straight to Pesaro, where Sergio Bergonzelli's Italian-Spanish co-production *Nelle pieghe della carne* (In the Folds of the Flesh) started shooting in the first week of November. This one begins in grand style, with a mis-spelt opening rubric, a flash of stock-footage lightning and an unsparing close-up of a laughably poor dummy head purporting to be that of Luciano Catenacci. The camera then pulls back to reveal Rossi Drago, a discarded sword and two traumatised children. This is the primal scene that triggers one of the most hare-brained and crudely strung together of all semi-giallo plots. The action subsequently jumps forward 13 years to find Rossi Drago presiding over a castellated ménage consisting of Pier Angeli and Emilio Gutiérrez Caba (formerly the callow hero of *La llamada*), and further decapitations ensue.

The film's credits sequence mimics those of Roger Corman's Poe pictures, except that here the faux-psychedelic colours just look like an accident in an ice-cream factory. Poor Angeli, required to play a character 14 years younger than herself, is given an old-lady wig to make the job even more difficult, while Rossi Drago's monochrome back-story involves naked women being gassed by Nazis, prefiguring a whole new decade of Nazisploitation tastelessness. The film would qualify as a giallo parody were it not for the fact that it has zero sense of humour, and after a while the only interesting thing about it is Rossi Drago's splendidly Gothic face. Perhaps unsurprisingly, when the film wound up its shooting schedule in January 1970, she opted to retire from the screen altogether.

## JET-SET CREEPS AND A CARBONATED HUSK

In April 1969, Pupi Avati's *Balsamus, l'uomo di Satana* (Balsamus, Satan's Man) was one of 15 Italian films considered for inclusion in the Grand Prix stakes at the Cannes Film Festival. It didn't make the cut, but nevertheless this was a significant achievement for a debutant filmmaker. "With *Balsamus*," Avati explained, "I brought to light the magic, the exorcisms and above all the folk customs of my [home] region, Emilia-Romagna." Giving some indication of the way his bucolic boyhood in World War II shaped his imagination, he also pointed out that "Since we didn't have cinema or television, a 'show' consisted for the most part of going to look at an idiot on display, or deformed people ... It's certainly a bit unhealthy, that kind of curiosity."[23]

*Balsamus* is a bizarre, albeit rather talky, free-for-all in which a dwarfish mountebank (Bob Tonelli), having convinced a rural community that he has magical powers, holes up with various acolytes in a remote mansion and recreates a kind of 18th century salon, right down to the costumes. (Giuseppe Balsamo, Count Cagliostro, was presumably the inspiration.) His final act of hubris involves shooting himself at an outdoor festival; the expected resurrection does not take place, and the film ends on a jubilant note as all the assembled countrymen exit laughing. Absurdist black comedy, rather than horror, is the keynote, as when Balsamus screams "Ascende!" while a fat middle-aged woman struggles unavailingly to shin up a tree. But the regal Gothic beauty of Greta Vaillant is put to good use; especially powerful is a scene in which she writhes naked in a cabinet while being caressed by human hands protruding through its various apertures.

Avati's second film, *Thomas... ...e gli indemoniati* (Thomas and the Possessed), appeared in 1970. Financed by the same Bolognese businessman who backed *Balsamus*, Avati here took as his subject a seven-strong troupe of strolling players who attend a seance at which a small boy, Thomas, is conjured up. The sheer intensity of the seance sequence – with glass tumblers rattling and a childish voice double-tracked over the medium's – is memorable, as is the phantasmagoric train journey the troupe then undertakes to get to their next gig. The eventual performance, with Thomas added to the cast, is prefaced by an astounding scene in which the audience assaults the theatre's metal safety curtain, one of them belabouring it with a detached false leg. Avati had a semi-name at his disposal this time – the British actor Edmund Purdom, whose brief Hollywood celebrity was long past – together with an early performance by the future star Mariangela Melato. Like its predecessor, the film bears witness to the fact that it was Fellini's 8½ that inspired Avati to become a filmmaker. More grotesque than horrific, both films indicated what he might achieve when launching himself into horror full-on.

Mario Bava, meanwhile, was settling back into modified giallo mode after his tilt at the big time with the Dino De Laurentiis extravaganza *Diabolik*. In the last few months of 1969 he dashed off two style-conscious gialli pretty much back-to-back. The first of these, *Un hacha para la luna de miel* (A Hatchet for the Honeymoon), was completed in October at Barcelona's Balcázar Studios; a majority Spanish production, it was written by local horror specialist Santiago Moncada and shown to Italian audiences as *Il rosso segno della follia* (The Red Sign of Madness). The result goes through some familiar *Psycho* paces, with a young man, having suppressed the memory of killing his parents as a boy, chopping up young brides on the principle that "A woman should live only until her wedding night. Love once, and then die." But there are some intriguing variations.

First, the killer isn't a scrawny provincial sad sack like Norman Bates but a chiselled jet-set fashion victim played by the handsome Canadian import Stephen Forsyth. Second, he dispenses at once with any mystery element by regarding himself narcissistically in his shaving mirror and treating us to an inner monologue. "The fact is, I'm completely mad," he confides. Finally, the mummified Mrs Bates of *Psycho* becomes the grimly persistent spectre of the killer's dead wife, who – in a brilliant reversal of the Banquo's Ghost routine parroted by several thousand horror stories – is visible to everyone else but *not* to him. With her chalk face framed by a luscious black mantilla, Laura Betti is a memorably baleful presence, especially when – having finally become visible to her murderer – she assures him that "We'll always be together, at first in the insane asylum and then in Hell, for eternity."

Also worked into the mix is the killer's family business, which, in an echo of Bava's *6 donne per l'assassino*, is a fashion house. As well as manoeuvring the viewer into the equivocal position of rooting for a self-regarding psychopath, Bava also throws in a couple of blatantly Freudian asides – the domineering wife crushes a grape, the psycho husband squishes an egg. The film may not qualify as top-flight Bava, but it still abounds in diverting touches, including multiple

Gérard Tichy, Laura Betti and crazed leading man Stephen Forsyth advertising *Un hacha para la luna de miel* (1969), distributed in Italy as 'The Red Sign of Madness'

reflections in the sheen of Forsyth's trademark cleaver and a splendid suspense set-piece in which the wife, expiring on an upper stairway, drips blood almost, but not quite, onto the head of an inquisitive police inspector.

Rounding off the decade and seeing in the new one, Bava's next film, *5 bambole per la luna d'agosto* (Five Dolls for an August Moon), made it into *Variety*'s 'Italian Films Shooting' digest on 10 December 1969 – albeit erroneously listed, Spaghetti Western style, as 'Five Dollars for an August Moon'. For this one, Bava was by his own account a last-minute replacement, doing all he could to gild a script that he absolutely loathed. Touches of desperation are visible right from the off; a boringly protracted party sequence sees Bava going into masturbatory zoom-lens overdrive as Edwige Fenech's Marie and various other jet-set creeps gyrate for what seem like hours.

Some unspecified scientific formula is up for grabs and, in the tradition of *Ten Little Indians*, people inevitably start to get killed in rapid succession. The production design (by Giuseppe Aldrovandi and Giulia Mafai) is nothing short of luscious, and Bava throws in a few grace notes of his own – a cheque for a million dollars nestling in Fenech's red lingerie, Fenech strung to a tree with a butcher knife buried deep in the same brassiere, a fight on one floor sending a horde of plastic spheres cascading down the stairs and into the blood-clouded bath of yet another victim, and above all the drolly ghoulish spectacle of the titular five 'dolls' (ie, corpses) dangling in the freezer in the kind of plastic shrouds familiar from *Terrore nello spazio*. But the film itself fails to hang together, and in 1971, interviewed in *Horror # 13*, Bava told future director Luigi Cozzi that *5 bambole* was his worst film.

Neither of these new gialli performed well at the Italian box-office, with *5 bambole* compounding the problem by failing to gain distribution in the USA. Indeed, it was made to look even more threadbare on its release in February 1970 by a film that came out in Italy only five days later.

The 29-year-old Dario Argento, former film critic of the Rome daily *Paese Sera*, had crowned a busy screenwriting career by sharing a story credit with Bernardo Bertolucci on Sergio Leone's epic Western *C'era una volta il West* (Once Upon a Time in the West). The announcement of his directorial debut, *L'uccello dalle piume di cristallo* (The Bird with the Crystal Plumage), followed in May 1969, though in the event it didn't start shooting until 25 August. The result was a ghoulish thriller so breathtakingly well made it seemed to bear the mark of a seasoned virtuoso rather than an untried beginner, with a combination of formal elegance and primal violence that added up to a local box-office take of some 1.6 billion lire. With that kind of success, Argento's debut single-handedly engineered a madly productive upsurge in the giallo sub-genre.

Rosita Torosh falls prey to a Rome serial killer in *L'uccello dalle piume di cristallo* (1969)

With a rather loose foundation in Fredric Brown's story *The Screaming Mimi*, Argento concocted a classic 'undecided witness' narrative in which an American writer in Rome reports a violent assault to the police but is dogged by the feeling that a small detail about what he saw has eluded him. With a rash of serial killings under way, the writer, Sam (Tony Musante), and his British girlfriend Julia (Suzy Kendall) discover that a grisly painting is the key to the mystery, the resolution of which indicates that Sam entirely misinterpreted what he saw in the first place.

The film is saddled with a traditionally dull police investigation, and the expository ending is lame in the extreme, but elsewhere Argento's precocious brilliance, abetted by Vittorio Storaro's glamorous cinematography and Ennio Morricone's seductive score, is evident in almost every frame. Having begun with a playful allusion to *Les Diaboliques* (the killer's black-gloved hands typing a cryptic message during the credit titles), he moves on to a canteen of murder weapons being methodically interleaved with red velvet, the kind of fetishistic detail that was to become an Argento trademark. Entrapment is the key-note of the crucial assault scene, with the impotent Sam sandwiched between glass partitions in the vestibule of an art gallery and entirely unable to provide help. So ingenious a set-piece is a tough act to follow, but Argento subsequently offers a nastily sadistic murder and a brilliant nocturnal pursuit in which the saturnine killer Reggie Nalder (previously an assassin in Hitchcock's *The Man Who Knew Too Much*) is made conspicuous by a bright yellow blouson jacket.

This tense sequence winds up with Sam's unscheduled visit to a convention for retired pugilists. The film is leavened with several other shafts of humour, as when Sam explains that he came to Europe on the advice of a friend: "Peace, tranquillity – that's Italy. Nothing ever happens in Italy." *L'uccello* also establishes the question marks that Argento would persistently place over gender, with a conspicuously clueless male 'hero', a traumatised female 'villain', even an identity parade in which a suspect called Luigi Rubatelli appears under a movie-star alias. "How many times do I have to tell you?" complains Enrico Maria Salerno's testy police inspector. "Ursula Andress belongs with the transvestites, not the perverts."

In 1970, Argento's debut was as coolly up-to-the-minute a product as any filmgoer could wish, yet it was marketed in Germany, thanks to the co-production involvement of CCC, as a continuation of their hackneyed Bryan Edgar Wallace series. The same would apply to Argento's second film, *Il gatto a nove code* (The Cat o' Nine Tails), which began production in September 1970. This one defaults to a conventional murder-mystery puzzle, without the intimations of horror that were threaded through *L'uccello*, and Argento would later more or less disown the film. Even so, it was another major hit and remains an extremely well-oiled thriller, focused on a genetics research institute and featuring some typically powerful Argento set-pieces; an early fatality at a railway station is pulverisingly well done. And, whereas in his previous film Argento had to rely on local names like Umberto Raho to shine in the acting department, here it's his US imports, James Franciscus and Karl Malden, who deliver.

Despite the flood of ultra-modern gialli initiated by Argento, a throwback to Italy's old-fashioned costume Gothics was also concocted at the turn of the new decade – by, curiously enough, a producer-director from Spain. José Luis Merino's *Ivanna* benefited from

## IVANNA

Spain-Italy 1970
Italy: *Il castello dalle porte di fuoco*
UK: *The Killers of the Castle of Blood*
US: *Blood Castle | Scream of the Demon Lover*
Carigliano Film | Prodimex Films Rome |
  Hispamer Films Madrid
98 minutes colour
production began March 1970
· · · · · · · · · · · · · · · · · · · · · · · · · · · · ·
Director of Photography: Emanuele Di Cola;
Art Director: Francesco Di Stefano; Editor:
Sandro Lena; Music: Luigi Malatesta;

Make-up: Bianca Verdirosa; Screenplay:
Enrico Colombo, José Luis Merino;
Director: José Luis Merino

Erna Schurer (Ivanna Rakowsky); Carlos Quiney
(Janos Dalmar); Agostina Belli (Cristiana);
Cristiana Galloni (Olga); Antonio Jiménez
Escribano (Boris, the butler); Mariano Vidal
Molina (police inspector); Enzo Fisichella (Igor
Dalmar); Ezio Sancrotti (rapist); Giancarlo
Fantini (doctor); Franco Moraldi (mayor); Renato
Paracchi (drunk | stenographer)

*Ivanna* is a horror movie directed by the Spaniard J L Merino with an admirable awareness of what he can achieve. The plot isn't very credible, as is the rule in this type of picture … But Merino makes us forget the film's weaknesses thanks to the meticulous scene-setting, the ingenuity of the plot devices and the high calibre of the actors.
*La Vanguardia* 18 February 1972

Shooting in Spain was slow because they work to a different rhythm, but it was very enjoyable. José Luis Merino was a fun-loving guy. He wasn't serious – not like Brunello Rondi, for example – but he was a solid professional. It was good fun and the Spanish actors were very fiery.
*Erna Schurer* [interviewed on the CG Entertainment DVD release of *Le altre*, 2016]

Erna Schurer as the biochemist heroine of *Ivanna* (1970), known in Germany
as 'The Secret of Monte Christo Castle'

added Italian finance and, maybe in deference to this, plays very like something Antonio Margheriti or Ernesto Gastaldi might have concocted. Yet the film's fashionably florid Italian title, *Il castello dalle porte di fuoco* (The Castle with the Gates of Fire), is less appropriate to the finished product – for not only does the short and sweet *Ivanna* have the virtue of being a great deal quicker to type, it also privileges the film's heroine, who is its most interesting character by far. She's played by Erna Schurer, whose credentials included not merely the inept Gothic giallo *La bambola di Satana* but also Nardo Bonomi's unreleased *Sortilegio*.

*Ivanna* was made in March and April 1970, exactly ten years after Bava shot *La maschera del demonio*, and Merino seems to have been fully aware of the tradition in which he was working. The opening credits, for example, are superimposed, as in Bava's *La frusta e il corpo*, over quantities of red plush, with the addition of a classic Gothic signifier – a candelabrum sporting three flickering flames.

> Recently graduated biochemist Ivanna Rakowsky has been contracted to assist Baron Janos Dalmar at his remote castle. She arrives in the locality in the midst of a murder spree, with the locals convinced that the six killings are the work of the Baron himself. Undaunted, Ivanna takes up her post, assisting Janos in his attempts to revive his elder brother Igor, whose corpse – unrecognisably charred – is stored in a bath of hallucinogenic preservatives.

With *Ivanna*, Merino and his Italian co-writer Enrico Colombo took the habitual echoes of *Rebecca* found in Italian horror and resolved them into a lightly disguised adaptation of its 19th century precursor, *Jane Eyre*. The result is an anomaly in that it not only features a strong female lead who's a normal woman rather than one of the remorseless she-devils of yore, but also because it balances her with the kind of Byronic hero-villain that – with the notable exception of Christopher Lee's Kurt Menliff in *La frusta e il corpo* – had largely been avoided in Italian Gothic.

*Ivanna* is a scientist who's every bit the Baron's equal,

sparring with him in several stormy exchanges that in less Gothic circumstances might suit a screwball comedy. She fights off a scurvy rapist even as she arrives at the Baron's castle, and when her employer realises that he's inadvertently engaged a woman he insists doggedly on her contract being honoured. "You asked for a top chemist and that's what you've got," she tells him, later pointing out that "I loathe moral conventions." All in all, Erna Schurer has much more to chew on here than in the terrible *La bambola di Satana*. Yet, unusually liberated though Ivanna may be, the film gives with one hand even as it takes away with the other – for, this being 1970, Schurer is required to be liberated in other ways too. The contradiction couldn't be clearer than when she lolls in bed poring over a scientific text, with her breasts continually escaping from her nightdress. The script also damages her feminist credentials when marriage beckons at the end and she says meltingly, "I've waited for this moment all my life."

Baron Janos, meanwhile, is the textbook aristocratic malcontent, whose smouldering introduction – staged, inevitably, on the castle's main staircase – is accompanied by a flash of lightning and an instantaneous rainstorm. His borderline-misogynist contention that "women are too inquisitive" hides a dark family secret, and in the course of the action his irrational rages are replaced by the compromised broodings of a romantic hero. Carlos Quiney was a dashing Zorro and Robin Hood in various other Merino films and is well cast in this untypical role.

In a masculine variation on Italy's female doppelgänger routine, we're led to believe that Janos is the killer, transformed into a frock-coated monster whose fire-ravaged flesh looks unpleasantly like faecal matter. Ivanna, too – having pondered over a book in the Baron's library called *Licantropus* – comes to the conclusion that Janos suffers from homicidal fugues brought on by the hallucinogens in his laboratory. Yet the killer is a different kind of doppelgänger. It's the Baron's supposedly dead brother Igor, who wears a ghastly black wig in an attempt to mitigate the horror of his appearance and vindictively transfers his guilt onto Janos, maintaining that "The hands were mine but the crimes were yours." He's the Baron's equivalent of Mr Rochester's mad wife in *Jane Eyre*, and Ivanna's glimpse of his plushly furnished quarters in an otherwise decrepit wing of the castle is played for maximum creepiness, especially when a sudden draught snuffs out her upheld candelabrum. No explanation is given, however, for the Baron's strange pretence in the laboratory, where Igor's supposed remains are represented by a carbonated husk floating in a bathtub.

The Baron may not be the "sex-craved deviant" the police suspect him of being, but Igor is more than capable of supplying the vein of sexual aberration so crucial to Italy's traditional Gothics. Repulsed by his own appearance, he's become a death-dealing puritan who kills all the Baron's lovers one by one – notably a naïve servant girl called Cristiana, nicely played by the 22-year-old future star Agostina Belli. Though Igor drugs Ivanna on a nightly basis and stretches her out naked in his private torture chamber, he does so only to worship her "as one does a delicate statue, or a jewel," simultaneously crooning, "You must stay pure, otherwise my revenge will be turned on you."

Emanuele Di Cola's photography is pleasantly subdued and autumnal, making the most of the blue and crimson drapes that cloak the bare walls of Janos' castle, and Merino contrives some arresting shots, as when an eavesdropping housekeeper dominates one side of the frame, staring directly at the viewer while Janos and Ivanna are dwarfed on the left. Unfortunately, the fiery climax fails to work up the excitement it should, and Luigi Malatesta's tremulous music is hackneyed throughout. *Ivanna* survives, however, as an elegant envoi to a style that by 1970 had reached its sell-by date.

Intriguingly, during production of *Ivanna* a Spanish news report pointed out that "José Luis Merino is currently working on a film whose chief character is the celebrated Sherlock Holmes," with *Ivanna*'s Carlos Quiney and Vidal Molina listed as the stars and reference to the fact that "The film is being shot in Italy, but later the team will move to Spain to shoot interiors."[24] The police inspector played by Molina does indeed bear a passing physical resemblance to Holmes, but any actual Holmes connection must have been abandoned at a very early stage – a memo that clearly didn't reach the press office in time.

## POSTED PARTS, THICK SNOW AND INVISIBLE THREATS

By the turn of the 1970s Spain's burgeoning horror boom had been picked up on by several avant-garde filmmakers, who saw in it an opportunity to slip radical statements past the Franco regime. That art and commerce could commingle in this way was exemplified by writer-producer Ricardo Muñoz Suay, whose long career encompassed 1950s neorealism, a producer credit on Buñuel's *Viridiana*, and his espousal of the Escuela de Barcelona. As well as maintaining a weekly column in the popular magazine *Nuevo Fotogramas*, Suay would found the production company Profilmes first thing in 1972, explicitly marketing it as the 'Spanish Hammer'.

In the meantime, various members of the Barcelona School seasoned their pictures with scattered horror elements. The group's defining film, *Fata Morgana*, was made by Vicente Aranda in 1965 and cast debutant Teresa Gimpera (an actress who was herself to jump between art and schlock on regular occasions) as a model marked for death in a surrealist, dystopian future world. The playful Pop Art peculiarities of *Fata Morgana* were abandoned three years later in Aranda's much more sombre second film, *Las crueles* (The Cruel Women), which began production in November 1968 under a title, *El cadáver exquisito* (The Exquisite Cadaver), which the censors wouldn't brook. The result is a really compelling, albeit rather slow, borderline-horror, with Carlos Estrada as a whey-faced publisher who becomes even more so when receiving a severed hand in the post. He subsequently gets a telegram offering him a forearm, though the big shock eventually comes in the form of a neatly boxed-up head.

"In *El cadáver exquisito*," noted the elegant French star Capucine, "I play a mysterious woman dedicated to persecuting a man who was the lover of a female friend who has died because of him. I send him packages containing my friend's remains. A macabre plot, as you can tell. I like the story very much."[25] Looking out haughtily from under the black brim of her hat, Capucine looks absolutely stunning as she plots the publisher's downfall. The dead girl, seen in flashbacks, is played by English actress Judy Matheson, who went on to such low-level British shockers as *Lust for a Vampire* and *Crucible of Terror*, while Teresa Gimpera returns as the publisher's wronged wife. Estrada, meanwhile, is dismissed as "a shadow of a man with nothing inside him" – the theme of male fecklessness being avenged by an aristocratic female would recur in Aranda's next film, a fully fledged vampire story called *La novia ensangrentada* (The Blood Spattered Bride). *Las crueles* boasts a mournful, wintery atmosphere that lingers in the memory, together with a bassoon-driven score by Marco Rossi and the striking image of Matheson's body folded up, naked, in a fridge.

The co-writer of *Fata Morgana* and *Las crueles* was Gonzalo Suárez, whose early 16mm shorts included the weirdly ape-fixated *El horrible ser nunca visto* (The Hideous Unseen Thing). In 1968-69 he directed a couple of aggressively avant-garde features called *El extraño caso del Doctor Fausto* (The Strange Case of Dr Faustus) and *Aoom*, films whose imagistic density and rejection of conventional narrative left most viewers conspicuously cold; in July 1970, the first was denied its scheduled screenings at the Berlin Film Festival and the second was thoroughly savaged at San Sebastián.

*Doctor Fausto* advertised itself as 'el cine de futuro' (the cinema of the future) and 'una película realizada con la técnica de los sueños' (a film made with the technology of dreams). Suárez himself plays Mefistófeles, an emissary of an alien race sent to divert Alberto Puig's scholarly Faust with a riot of bamboozling imagery, ranging from gurgling infants, slithering eels and looming giraffes to Teresa Gimpera reading Iris Murdoch's *The Time of the Angels*. (Emma Cohen, another Barcelona beauty due to appear in her share of Spanish horrors, is also featured.) The bill of fare in *Aoom* is equally head-scratching stuff, including Gila Hodgkinson as a mad, poncho-wearing witch in the woods, Julián Ugarte baying like a dog and drowning a woman in the surf of the Costa Cantábrica, Lex Barker (in his last film) transferring his soul, with much oscillation of the camera, into a child's doll, and Gimpera burying said doll after Luis Ciges has dismembered it. Despite the rough reception accorded both films, Suárez's example was followed by his Barcelona School colleague Jacinto Esteva, whose obscure 1971 film *Metamorfosis* retained Ugarte, Ciges and another *Aoom* cast member, Romy, for a story in which Ugarte's medical foundation creates artificial life.

At the opposite extreme to art-house dabblings in Spanish horror was the influence of Italy's blood-bolted giallo films. Echoes of them were already present in England – with titles ranging from Freddie Francis' *The Psychopath* to Peter Collinson's *Fright* – and France, with Nicolas Gessner's *Quelqu'un derrière la porte* (Someone Behind the Door). (Shot, like *Fright*, at the end of 1970, this one delivers puzzled amnesiac Charles Bronson into the calculating hands of Kentish neurologist Anthony Perkins, with an abundance of foggy Folkestone locations, a nastily convoluted plot and two of the strangest lead performances the new decade had to offer.) Spain, however, was the giallo's most enthusiastic inheritor by far. Among the first Spanish films to pick up on the trend in its late-1960s pomp was Javier Setó's *Viaje al vacío* (Journey to Nowhere), which was released in the same year as Setó's untimely death (1969). Marking the first genre script from Santiago Moncada, this involves Teresa Gimpera in the standard 'trying to drive her husband insane' plot, together with the rather less standard 'having an affair with her husband's twin brother' subplot.

As in Italy, international names were sought after for these films, with US TV star Larry Ward fulfilling the function in Setó's film. On the same principle,

Britain's Michael Craig and Italy's favourite giallo star, Carroll Baker, were imported in August 1970 to star in Eugenio Martín's *La última señora Anderson* (The Last Mrs Anderson), which benefited from another Santiago Moncada script. And in December that year Stephen Boyd and Marisa Mell were in Madrid for a *Vertigo* riff, directed by J A Nieves Conde, called *Marta*. Mid-70s beneficiaries of the trend included Spain's favourite German-born sex symbol, Nadiuska, in Ramón Fernández's *La muerte ronda a Mónica* (Death Haunts Monica) and British actress Gillian Hills in Joan Bosch's *La muerte llama a las 10* (Death Calls at 10). (The latter, incidentally, bore as generic an export title as could be imagined – *The Killer Wore Gloves*.) By that time, however, the industrious Paul Naschy had headlined a number of ersatz gialli, proving that foreign names weren't necessarily de rigueur.

Beyond the area of imitation gialli, perhaps Spain's strangest sex-horror film from the cusp of the 1970s was José Luis Madrid's *El vampiro de la autopista* (The Motorway Vampire), which is also known under the inspired export title *The Horrible Sexy Vampire*.

Spanish sex-horror to usher in a new decade:
*El vampiro de la autopista* (1970)

Here, Waldemar Wohlfahrt is a platinum blond nobleman called Count Oblensky, who becomes involved in a series of murders that have recurred at 28-year intervals, starting in 1886 and culminating in 1970. The perpetrator, though an invisible entity most of the time, is Oblensky's ancestor Baron Winninger (Wolfahrt in a grey wig), who leaves extremely nasty suction wounds on his victims' throats.

Fetchingly shot in the thick snow that carpeted Stuttgart in December 1969, the result is a clumsy, charmless bore that ensures all the victims are bathing and bare-breasted at the moment of attack. The film retains some historical curiosity, however, given that it so flagrantly exploits Wohlfahrt's continental notoriety as the 'motorway vampire' of the title. Apparently a private detective at the time, he had been arrested in July 1966 for the murders of four female hitch-hikers, though he was completely exonerated a mere 12 days later. As well as releasing a single under the name Waldemar el Vampiro, he also ploughed his compensation money into the production of *El vampiro de la autopista*. Changing his name thereafter to Wal Davis, he made another dozen films, among them five for Jess Franco and a 1973 Hispanic giallo called *El pez de los ojos de oro* (The Fish with Golden Eyes).

Yet more of Germany's turn-of-the-decade snow was visible in two wildly contrasting films. Helmut Förnbacher's *Beiß mich Liebling!* (Bite Me, Darling!), with Eva Renzi, Barbara Valentin and Brigitte Skay among its assembled beauties, is a generic Munich sex-comedy about a provincial postman (Amadeus August) getting his leg over with Olympian regularity. Somewhat jarringly, Förnbacher shifts focus in the final third to a local psychiatrist whose Dracula lineage shows through after death. For British actor Patrick Jordan, accustomed to playing policemen and other small roles in his homeland, the fanged therapist, Dr von der Wies, constituted a rather surprising lead. The film itself, however, must have appeared pretty tame by comparison to Ernst Hofbauer's *Schulmädchen-Report: Was Eltern nicht für möglich halten* (Schoolgirl Report: What Parents Don't Consider Possible), which was produced by Barbara Valentin's old mentor, Wolf C Hartwig, and on its release a couple of months after *Beiß mich Liebling!* unleashed a slew of copycat sex films.

The third snow-covered title from this period was Jess Franco's first film of the 1970s. Leaving Harry Alan Towers behind but continuing to enjoy the greater freedom available to him outside Spain, Franco had only recently wrapped *El conde Drácula* when he journeyed to Paris and Berlin for yet another Marquis de Sade project. Starting in January 1970 and co-produced by his old colleagues at Eurociné, *Eugénie* is one of Franco's strongest films, with its atmospheric, white-blanketed landscapes – both urban and bucolic – providing a chilly introduction to a new decade of otherwise feverish Euro-exploitation.

With Soledad Miranda's Eugénie in thrall to the Sadean theories of her scholarly stepfather Albert Radeck (Paul Muller), *Eugénie* achieves a real sense of the tipping point between intellectual decadence and full-on murderous perversion. The effect is made all the more powerful by the luxuriously chic trappings of Franco's turn-of-the-'70s interiors, a colour-coded sumptuousness carefully contrasted with the wet and wintery exteriors. The couple (and yes, they do become a couple) add to their Leopold and Loeb-style murder spree a penchant, *Peeping Tom* style, for filming their crimes; it's one such film that plays out under the opening credits as the killers' journalistic nemesis watches in eerily unmoved silence. This strange character is played by Franco himself, explaining self-reflexively that "A writer needs to dip into genuinely extravagant characters to give texture to his own."

The next murder is lent a sickly sense of farce by the extravagantly red 'gear' worn by Albert and Eugénie as they corner a nude Belgian glamour model (Alice Arno). The second is even queasier, with a guileless hitchhiker (Greta Schmidt) coaxed

Mod murderess Soledad Miranda in the Marquis de Sade adaptation *Eugénie* (1970)

into a drinking game prior to a 'play dead' session in which Eugénie (naked but for a single shiny boot) straddles her and Albert smothers the victim with an alcohol-soaked handkerchief. Eight unseen murders intervene, but the film's third act loses interest thanks to Eugénie's romance with a comically self-important young jazz trumpeter (Andrés Monales), who predictably falls prey to the jealous stepfather in an unconvincing throat-slashing sequence. Even so, Franco's trademark nightclub scenes – with the killers sitting watchfully in an all-pervading amber glow – are memorably sinister, as is the lizard-eyed control Muller exercises over his devoted charge. Miranda herself is a bewitching presence, and Franco's camera offers a fetishised tribute to her from beginning to end.

Initiated in autumn 1969 but still being shot in fits and starts as *Eugénie* took shape was *Les Cauchemars naissent la nuit* (Nightmares Come at Night), a self-financed Franco project in which Miranda and Monales play peripheral roles and centre stage goes to Diana Lorys (eight years after her appearance in Franco's *Gritos en la noche*), cast as a fragmenting stripper, Anna, who becomes involved with a psychic vampire called Cynthia (Colette Giacobine). The acting is excellent (the dependable Paul Muller is the equivocal psychiatrist on the case), the lesbian encounters are the strongest Franco had yet filmed, the bloodily oneiric visions experienced by Lorys are mesmerisingly strange, but everything grinds to a halt for a seven-minute strip sequence demonstrating the "lascivious moves" that attracted Cynthia in the first place. The result was seen in Belgium in 1973 and then presumed lost for some 30 years.

During this wildly prolific period Franco may or may not have been aware of a backhanded compliment paid him by Eurociné's Marius Lesoeur. The compliment was Lesoeur's appropriation of Franco's Dr Orloff character for a French-Spanish co-production directed by Pierre Chevalier in April 1970. It was a backhanded one because the end product was far cruder than even Franco's most slapdash efforts.

*Orloff et l'homme invisible* (Orloff and the Invisible Man) is set, very shakily, in the Napoleonic period, with Orloff creating an invisible man whom he considers the forerunner of a master race. Yet when the young hero (Paco Valladares) flings some flour about, we realise Orloff has actually created a transparent ape, which is anticlimactically killed by maddened Alsatians while Orloff's château is 'consumed' by the most half-hearted conflagration in cinema history. Prior to this, the invisible ape has inevitably committed invisible rape. "I was curious to see how the invisible man would behave with a human female," Orloff blandly explains. Camille Sauvage's bizarre, finger-snapping score retains interest, while the indefatigable Howard Vernon – back in his old Orloff role – manages to be fascinatingly odd even in garbage like this.

In fact, Chevalier's film was effectively Vernon's third, rather than second, Orloff. Santos Alcocer's Hispamer production El enigma del ataúd (The Coffin Mystery) reached Barcelona in February 1969, having played in Paris as Les Orgies du Dr Orloff in March 1967. The film's uncredited co-producers, Eurociné, also ensured that it became Le orge nere del Dr Orloff in Italy and Die Folterkammer des Doktor Orloff in Germany. Yet, despite the advertised orgies and torture chambers, Vernon's character wasn't originally Orloff at all, just the standard-issue dying man in yet another retread of the 'will reading in an old dark house' plot. Strangely enough, when Franco himself revived Orloff early in 1973, he did so in the similarly underwhelming Los ojos del doctor Orloff (The Eyes of Dr Orloff), in which Orloff, played now by William Berger, became an ambiguous psychiatrist in a hackneyed 'wheelchair-bound heiress in peril' scenario. Subsequent home video releases tried to curry interest by using the expanded title Los ojos siniestros del doctor Orloff, but to no avail. As Stephen Thrower aptly puts it, "With neither sexual frankness nor improvisational delirium to recommend it, The Sinister Eyes of Dr Orloff plummets like a stone to the nethermost regions of the Franco filmography."[26]

## THE BALL OF BAD TASTE

In Italy, the dawn of the 1970s saw numerous attempts to fit the old Gothic conventions to the new commercial imperatives of sex and violence, though nothing emerged that was as sleekly provocative as Franco's Eugénie. Frequently the results were graceless mish-mashes with no other aim than to expose as much female flesh as possible, though Italy certainly wasn't alone in this clodhopping approach to the new freedoms.

As early as 1969, however, Mario Caiano, sometime director of Amanti d'oltretomba, bucked the trend by concocting two relatively refined hybrids. In mid-April he started shooting the German co-production Komm, süßer Tod (Come Sweet Death), plunging Claudine Auger and Tony Kendall into an oneiric, and eventually murderous, 'Lustschloss' presided over by Christine Kaufmann and the distinguished Austrian star O W Fischer (in his last film). Emphasising the erotic angle, the result came out in Italy as Lovebirds Una strana voglia d'amare (Lovebirds – A Strange Feeling like Love). Caiano went straight from this into Ombre roventi (Burning Shadows), a more lavish affair that transported Miss Italia 1966, Daniela Giordano, to Cairo, allowing Caiano to echo the Marrakech of Hitchcock's The Man Who Knew Too Much in several bustling marketplace scenes. The occult business is less persuasive, with Giordano selected as a reincarnation of Isis by a cult of dodgy hippies and finally realising that her mentor, William Berger, is none other than Osiris – something the viewer cottoned onto the minute he made his entrance and said "Immortals do exist." Giordano is frequently naked, the locations are gorgeous, but the end product is strangely inert.

The same mix of erotica with garbled occult trimmings appeared in Oscar Brazzi's 1970 film Il sesso del diavolo (Trittico), which never does tell us what sex the Devil is, though it certainly focuses on a 'triptych' of mysterious faces sculpted by the deceased mistress of an Istanbul dreamhouse. Assembled there are former heart-throb Rossano Brazzi (the director's elder brother) and the beautiful women in his life, Sylva Koscina and Maitena Galli; the latter is nude or nearly nude almost throughout. Also present is a sombre housekeeper (Güzin Özipek) who bewitches Koscina via the ritualistic use of scorpions. The exotic backdrop, the belly dancers and discothèques, recall Ombre roventi, though in most other respects – travelogue visuals, zoom-happy camera, dabs of lesbianism, scorpions, Istanbul – the film resembles Vampyros Lesbos, a Jess Franco item made at much the same time. The plot is nothing, but as a dream of designer decadence, with '1970' stamped all through it, the film has some wistful charm. Stelvio Cipriani's funky score features a great many comic boings, as if he were sending the whole thing up – as well he might.

Extending the appeal of exotic erotica, Piero Vivarelli's Il dio serpente (The Snake God, 1970) not only yielded a smash No 1 single (Augusto Martelli's Djamballà) but also helped inaugurate a sub-genre trading on the prurient appeal of inter-racial sex, generally in travelogue-friendly Caribbean locations and with a few token voodoo trimmings thrown in. Among its tackier successors were Osvaldo Civirani's Il pavone nero (The Black Peacock, 1975) and Joe D'Amato's Papaya dei Caraibi (Caribbean Papaya, 1978), films known otherwise by the racier titles Voodoo Sexy and Papaya Love Goddess of the Cannibals.

That the Italian censor hadn't entirely relaxed his vigilance was made clear, however, by Filippo Walter Ratti's La notte dei dannati (The Night of the Damned), which shortly before Christmas 1971 gave rise to a strange incident in a cinema in Genoa. At a screening "attended by around 50 people, mostly men," it was noticed that "The film was in English and was therefore incomprehensible to them."[27] Stopping the show, the projectionist explained that the film wasn't just in the wrong language but was also 'too erotic'. It was later clarified that "La notte dei dannati exists in two versions, one of them Italian, duly censored for Italian screens, the other in English and aimed at screens elsewhere. The distributor made the mistake of mixing up the reels."

Ratti's film features Pierre Brice as a glamorous, pipe-smoking journalist who receives a distress call from a castellated, consumptive-looking friend. (He may as well be called Roderick Usher and makes his plea via a cryptic sequence of Baudelaire quotes.) It transpires that the ailing friend is married to a lesbian witch with fake claws, handy for bloodily scoring the naked breasts of her victims. Brice finally routs her with a cry of "strega maledetta!" (damned witch!), whereupon she ages via lap-dissolve to a Muppet-like crone mask, entailing a special 'truccatore strega' credit for make-up man Rino Carboni. The film has its atmospheric moments, notably when Brice uncovers the key to the mystery behind a skein of cobwebs, but its Gothic throwback status, pleasant in itself, is compromised by the lesbian ceremonials, which are wreathed in blue-tinted dry ice and, in the export version at any rate, go on for what seem like hours.

The oddest thing about Ratti's film is the decision by composer Carlo Savina to recycle a warbly pop song he'd previously used in Amando de Ossorio's *Malenka*. It's similar to the *Strange Love* ditty featured in the contemporaneous Hammer film *Lust for a Vampire*, and was hardly worth including in one film, let alone two. As for Ratti, the year after *La notte* he made a film that ran into yet more censorship problems. *I vizi morbosi di una governante* (The Morbid Vices of a Housekeeper) – a clunky giallo featuring such staples as illicit drugs and uprooted eyeballs – took some four years to get a release, losing a significant amount of sexually explicit footage in the process. (English-speaking audiences only got

Erotic reveries for Rosalba Neri in *La bestia uccide a sangue freddo* (1971), issued in Germany as 'The Compulsive Killer'

to see it as a 1996 video release called *Crazy Desires of a Murderer*.) It was all a very long way from Ratti's charming *Christmas Carol* adaptation from 1953, *Non è mai troppo tardi* (It's Never Too Late). It also marked the end of his directorial career.

In addition to the erotic-horror mix, traces of Gothic and-or its near-relation, the giallo, bled through into other genres too. Mario Monicelli, for example, was the sophisticated master of waspish social comedies like *Casanova '70*, but in 1969 he made an ill-received body-count farce called *To', è morta la nonna!* (Oh, Grandma's Dead!), focusing on a self-devouring upper-class family whose fortune is founded, appropriately, on pesticide. Some eight months after the Monicelli film appeared, Alfio Caltabiano gave Italian cinemagoers the chance to see a cult of skull-masked diabolists in an otherwise innocuous swashbuckler called *Una spada per Brando* (A Blade for Brando). Horror archetypes also found their way into Franco Brocani's combined underground film and endurance test, *Necropolis*, with giallo and Spaghetti Western regular Bruno Corazzari turning up as Frankenstein's monster and Warhol 'superstar' Viva playing Countess Báthory. And in 1971 a newer archetype, the Bava-style ghost girl, appeared to Erna Schurer and Wolfgang Hillinger, playing a childless couple holidaying on the Corsican coast in Marcello Avallone's dream-within-a-dream conundrum *Un gioco per Eveline* (A Game for Eveline).

Given the enormous impact made by the coffin-fixated Franco Nero in *Django*, the Spaghetti Western proved an even better fit for horror trappings, all the more so when the search began for outré new adornments to help prolong the form's life. A spate of poisonings and a brace of Wild West witches featured in what was probably the first such hybrid, *Giunse Ringo e ... fu tempo di massacro* (Ringo Arrived and ... It Was Massacre Time), which was begun by writer-director Mario Pinzauti in 1966 but not issued until 1970. Similarly, the robotic, black-clad avenger (Anthony Steffen) in Sergio Garrone's *Django il bastardo* (Django the Bastard, 1969) may just possibly be a dead man, an ambiguity perpetuated by Clint Eastwood in the 1972 classic *High Plains Drifter*. Arguably the grimmest entry of all – Klaus Kinski's demonic pursuit of vengeance in the 1969 film *E Dio disse a Caino...* (And God Said to Cain) – was directed by Gothic specialist Antonio Margheriti.

By January 1971 Kinski was at the familiar Castello Chigi in Castel Fusano, sleepwalking his way through Fernando Di Leo's *La bestia uccide a sangue freddo* (The Beast Kills in Cold Blood). The fact that Massimo Pupillo's *5 tombe per un medium* had been shot at the same location exactly six years before (followed six months later by another Pupillo film, *La vendetta di Lady Morgan*) adds a curious piquancy to this rather sedately demented film, which illustrates in extremely graphic terms how, at the dawn of a new decade, sleaze had suddenly become an inescapable selling point. As so often in the past, we have the black-masked, black-cloaked marauder (rather a splay-footed one in this instance); we have the arbitrary Iron Maiden; we have the protracted stalkings; we have the assemblage of shifty characters confined at a single location. (A women-only mental home, as it happens, complete with extremely handy, ornamental murder weapons mounted on virtually every wall.) Now, however, we also have copious nudity; laboriously extended lesbian liaisons; even, in the version augmented with hardcore inserts, probing labial close-ups during the various masturbation scenes.

For what it's worth, Di Leo's film is campily self-aware sleaze rendered with crystalline gloss, courtesy of cinematographer Franco Villa. It also boasts the smouldering Rosalba Neri, advancing nude on a hulking gardener in the greenhouse and teasing him with a line Barbara Steele never thought of in *Amanti d'oltretomba*: "I'll uproot all your plants." The film's best-known English-language title is *Slaughter Hotel*, though in one of its several French manifestations it acquired a title that rather mournfully recalled the Italian Gothics of a former era – *Les Insatisfaites poupées érotiques du docteur Hichcock* (The Frustrated Sex Dolls of Dr Hichcock). Needless to say, there is no character of that name in the Italian and English versions.

Arguably the most bizarre Italian entry in this period not only heralded the return of an old horror hand but also brought a youthful beauty called Rita Calderoni to the fore. In 1970, two years after being spray-painted by Franco Nero in Elio Petri's *Un tranquillo posto di campagna*, Calderoni plunged headlong into the demented world of Renato Polselli. By this time Polselli's early horrors, *L'amante del vampiro* and *Il mostro dell'opera*, appeared impossibly quaint, despite their forward-looking intimations of voyeuristic sleaze. It took the anarchic atmosphere of the late 1960s to fully liberate Polselli's wilder

Rita Calderoni reflected in the knife edge of *La verità seconda Satana* (1970)

impulses, allowing him to mix sex war and class war in a mind-boggling chamber piece called *La verità secondo Satana* (The Truth According to Satan).

During production in September 1970 the word 'vangelo' (gospel) stood in place of 'verità', and it was under this original title that the film got the cineromanzi treatment, with a wealth of saucy stills, in a June 1971 issue of *Cinestop*. The neutered 'verità' title only turned up when the film was belatedly released nearly a year later. It then became clear that the only remnants it contained of Polselli's ageing Gothics were the casting of *L'amante* veteran Isarco Ravaioli and a tediously overlong dance sequence – though, this being 1970, the dancers are nude save for spray paint and psychedelic appliqués. Aged only 19 during shooting, Calderoni is a titled beauty whose doltish older boyfriend (Ravaioli) has apparently killed himself, an event misinterpreted by a theatrical neighbour as murder. "Enjoy yourself, if you can, at the ball of bad taste," says Calderoni, and as the mad neighbour's blackmail plot intensifies the viewer is left to do exactly that.

Polselli makes enjoyment rather difficult, however, by indulging an outrageously mannered performance from Sergio Ammirata as the crazed neighbour, Tortoletto, who among other torments decorates Calderoni's naked body with raw meat and has a hungry Alsatian lick it all off. Calderoni's Diana is clearly intended as a 'rich bitch' hate figure, especially in her high-handed treatment of a black lesbian lover (Marie-Paul Bastin), but everything around her is so ridiculously over-egged she comes off as an identification figure instead. Stuck with what is effectively a three-hander stage play, Polselli dresses up the remainder with stock footage of falling bombs and such, trying to lend political weight to a story whose actual purpose, if any, is hard to discern.

Despite the aggressive modernity of Polselli's film and others like it, there were a few directors who were willing, like José Luis Merino in *Ivanna*, to make a Canute-like effort to prolong the life of costume Gothic. In 1971, for example, Leopoldo Savona signed his name to a handsomely appointed, and commendably brief, item called *Byleth Il demone dell'incesto* (Byleth, Demon of Incest), in which the American actor Mark Damon returned to the genre for the first time since Bava's *I tre volti della paura* eight years before.

Apart from the threadbare 1972 giallo *La morte scenda leggera* (Death Falls Lightly), Savona was otherwise a specialist in pepla and Westerns, yet he brings a great deal of elegance and poise to this lone foray into horror. In fact, there's a bit too much poise; not a great deal happens and the going is slow. There are some artful highlights, however, as when the young Duke Lionello (Damon) argues with his sister Barbara (Claudia Gravy) in an ornamental maze, aptly reflecting the inescapability of their problem – namely, his unquenchably incestuous passion for her and the fact that she's just got married. He's also a voyeur, bringing in the requisite amount of sex and nudity, and may also be the murderer who's been killing local women with an odd, three-bladed weapon. Indeed, the film begins with an unlucky prostitute (Karin Lorson)

Come-hither advertising for *Byleth Il demone dell'incesto* (1971), released in France as 'Sexual Demons'

shrinking from Savona's oncoming camera in an apt quote from *Peeping Tom*.

But the compromises an old-style Gothic was required to make by 1971 are clearly visible in Savona's best scene, where Lionello advances by candlelight into a shadowy lumber room and looks through various dusty artefacts that belonged to his late father. In concert with cinematographer Giovanni Crisci and, particularly, composer Vassil Kojucharov, Savona works up a bewitching atmosphere here. Yet everything suddenly stops for an abrupt cut to a bare-arsed serving wench (Marzia Damon) putting on her stockings, after which Savona cuts back just as abruptly to Lionello poring over the recovered documents. The ending, too, is bungled. That the 'demon' haunting Lionello is his own sexual repression, manifesting itself in bloody murders,

has been powerfully conveyed. Yet, after the camera-spinning final consummation between brother and sister, his woodland confrontation with Byleth (who, of course, is his doppelgänger) is a damp squib and runs slap bang into the end title.

## SOME DREAMY FEAR

In 1970, the rapid erosion of censorship brought with it a sudden influx of lesbian vampires. Eroticism had always been more frankly handled on the continent than in the UK, yet the climate was changing to such a degree that it was Britain's Hammer Film Productions that was responsible for kick-starting the trend, putting *The Vampire Lovers* into production in the third week of January. The bloodsucker here, as *New York Times* critic A H Weiler put it, "entices and destroys a couple of guys, but only because they're in her way en route to those gorgeous girls."[28]

The film was based on J S Le Fanu's *Carmilla*, a source handled more reticently by Roger Vadim in 1960 and Camillo Mastrocinque in 1963. Hammer had a brazenly exploitative sequel, *Lust for a Vampire*, in production by July 1970, and as of September the trend had even reached the USA, with *Variety* announcing a forthcoming production from Corman graduate Stephanie Rothman called *Blood Lovers*. This became *The Velvet Vampire*, a film that featured a comely seductress called Diane Le Fanu who meets her victims at the so-called Stoker Gallery. 'She's waiting to love you ... to death' leered the posters when the film went out alongside *Scream of the Demon Lover* – the grievously shortened US edit of *Ivanna*.

Inevitably, the equivocal business of equating lesbians with vampirism wasn't confined to Britain and America; almost as inevitably, it was Jess Franco who initiated the trend in mainland Europe. While juggling *Eugénie* and *Les Cauchemars naissent la nuit* in the first few months of 1970, Franco entered into a new agreement with Artur Brauner of CCC, embarking on the first of several Brauner-sponsored projects in the last week of April. Though a Spanish-West German co-production, the resultant film would only make it to Spanish cinemas in 1974 in an emasculated cut entitled *Las Vampiras* (The Vampire Women). The German version was as distinctive a combination of horror and erotica as Franco had yet contrived, a languid sex reverie bearing probably his most famous title – *Vampyros Lesbos*.

> Linda Westinghouse is an estate agent who dreams of a beautiful woman and then sees her in the flesh – as a performer in an erotic nightclub act. Summoned to Anatolia by the Countess Nadine Carody, Linda sees her yet again – for performer and Countess are one and the same. The business under discussion concerns the legacy of Count Dracula, but when Linda submits to Nadine's bite she loses her memory and is taken to an Istanbul clinic run by Dr Eldon Seward.

Just in the course of that 80-word synopsis the bare bones of Stoker's *Dracula* can be discerned quite clearly – bare bones that are acknowledged in the film's German subtitle, *Erbin des Dracula* (Heiress of Dracula). Presumably close kin to Lucy Westenra, Linda Westinghouse is also a Jonathan Harker surrogate, seeming to know her client's face, as Stoker put it, "in connection with some dreamy fear." The clinic she's admitted to – run, inevitably, by a certain Dr Seward – is also home to a female Renfield, Agra, who insists that "My friend is the Queen of the Night." Further echoes weave in and out of the film, making it clear that, less than five months after completing the stodgily straightforward adaptation that was *El conde Drácula*, Franco felt free to kick back and give his subversive imagination free rein.

Unencumbered by the compromises attendant on the previous film, Franco gives centre stage this time to his erstwhile Lucy, the scintillating Soledad Miranda. This Countess, incongruously named Nadine, may well be one of the three vampire brides who aroused Harker's "dreamy fear" in the novel; in a spellbinding monologue, she explains how Dracula rescued her from rape in a long-ago war zone, after which she became "the woman who made his life worth living." This vampire, however, conveys what Stoker's Van Helsing called the "beauty and fascination of the wanton Un-Dead" not from a supine position "in a tomb fretted with age and heavy with the dust of centuries" but from a recliner next to a glittering swimming pool in the so-called Kadidados Islands, wearing only a skimpy white bikini and the largest sunglasses imaginable. Her equivalent to Dracula's "The night air is chill, and you must need

to eat and rest" is similarly iconoclastic. "You must be tired," she smiles. "Would you like a swim before we get down to business?"

Dr Seward, too, is given a complete make-over. Dennis Price, who came direct to the film from the Elstree set of Hammer's *The Horror of Frankenstein*, was 54 at the time and more closely approximated Van Helsing than his eager young student. Yet this is a conniving, manipulative version of Van Helsing who admits in his diary that "I can barely resist the temptation to cross over into the dark world of the supernatural." Despite these aspirations, he proves no match for the Countess, who has her faithful manservant strangle the doctor on the central staircase of his own clinic. That manservant is called Morpho, initiating Franco's playful habit of interweaving characters from his own mythology with figures drawn, however randomly, from other areas of literature and pop culture – a habit that would reach Byzantine levels of complexity in future films. In the same vein, the film offers not one but two replays of the fetishistic nightclub performance already seen in *Miss Muerte* and *Necronomicon*.

The alluring Mediterranean heat haze of *Vampyros Lesbos* induces a cloying sense of languid dislocation, the kind of spell-stopped living death usually represented by ice-cold castles and subterranean crypts. Franco's woozy atmosphere of abandonment and surrender is founded on a repeated sequence of abstract images – scorpions, butterflies, blood running down glass, and Nadine with a red scarf streaming provocatively from her throat. Manuel Merino's photography of the film's exotic locations (ranging from Alicante and Barcelona to Istanbul) repositions *Dracula* as a luxury 1970s travelogue, an effect enhanced by Franco's opportunist emphasis on whatever architectural oddities come his way. An indoor ceiling tapestry, for example, exudes a mass of crimson fronds like writhing blood vessels. The spell is only broken by the hotel room in which Nadine seduces Ewa Strömberg's apprehensive Linda, a room so comically bland and functional it suggests the kind of production-line porn that *Vampyros Lesbos* otherwise stands apart from.

There are a few other 'made at speed' gaffes, notably the identical audience that apparently attends separate burlesque performances. Another disruption to the mood is provided by Franco himself, who plays a sleazy hotel porter who's not only the mad Agra's husband but also a serial killer. The glimpses we get of his basement torture chamber are a poor match for the oneiric mood of the rest of the film, as if Franco was aware that *Vampyros Lesbos* was short on conventional horror and needed a bit of beefing up. In the end he's inventively bow-sawed to death by the imperilled Linda, but the metal rod she subsequently hammers into Nadine's left eye is more in tune with the film's thoroughgoing modernisation of traditional Gothic.

The schedule for *Vampyros Lesbos* coincided exactly with another film for Artur Brauner, *Sie tötete in*

## VAMPYROS LESBOS

Spain-West Germany 1970
Spain: *Las Vampiras*
West Germany: *Vampyros Lesbos Erbin des Dracula*
Fénix Film Madrid / CCC Filmkunst Berlin / Tele-Cine Film-und Fernsehproduktion Berlin
89 minutes colour
production began 27 April 1970
. . . . . . . . . . . . . . . . . . . . . . . . . . . . .
Director of Photography: Manuel Merino; Editor: María Luisa Soriano [Spanish prints], Clarissa Ambach [German prints]; Music: Manfred Hübler and [on German prints] Siegfried Schwab, [on Spanish prints] David Kunne [Jess Franco]; Make-up: Paloma

Fernández; Story and Screenplay: Jess Franco and [credited on Spanish prints only] Jaime Chávarri; Executive Producer: Artur Brauner [uncredited]; Producers: Arturo Marcos Tejedor [Spanish prints], Karl-Heinz Mannchen [German prints]; Director: Jess Franco

Soledad Miranda (Countess Nadine Carody); Ewa Strömberg (Linda Westinghouse); Dennis Price (Dr Eldon Seward); Heidrun Kussin (Agra); José Martínez Blanco (Melnick); Andrés Monales (Omar); Paul Muller (Dr Steiner); Michael Berling (Morpho); Jess Franco (Mehmet); uncredited: Beni Cardoso (Mehmet's victim);

Franco fails to fulfil expectations ... With so much concern over camera angles, focusing, characterisations, lighting and decor, the film becomes pretentious. The original raw horror, the impact – through which blood and eroticism take on an unexpected dimension – has become too refined. The meticulous treatment of detail renders the production dull. It ceases to be entertaining. *Terror Fantastic* November 1973

*Vampyros Lesbos* has a certain charm and mystique, and of course the presence of Soledad, which is highly important. The supporting actors are great too, but other than that it doesn't have much. Artur Brauner came to see the first assembly, when we had just four or five reels ready, and he loved the fact that there was virtually no dialogue in the first half hour.
Jess Franco [quoted in *Cinefantástico y de terror español 1900-1983*, 1999]

*Ekstase* (She Killed in Ecstasy); by this stage, making two films simultaneously was just business as usual for the multi-tasking Franco. Here he contrived a loose remake of *Miss Muerte*, with Fred Williams as a fashion-plate scientist whose hormone research is mocked by four of his peers – Franco regulars Howard Vernon, Ewa Strömberg and Paul Muller, plus Franco himself. Vernon calls Williams' work "an infringement of the Hippocratic oath," a relatively mild charge given that eventually the quartet say the young doctor deserves to be killed. He kills himself as it turns out, whereupon his young wife (Soledad Miranda) determines to avenge him. This bewitching young woman kills, all right, but hardly in ecstasy; the film is so soaked in death and despair that the provocative title proves a misnomer.

Though the set-up is rivetingly done, the film begins to falter just when it should fire on all cylinders – ie, when the murders get under way. Miranda encounters Vernon in the middle of a newspaper interview, listening to his fascist musings about modern youth prior to ensnaring him in a hotel bedroom and removing his penis (off camera) – an action better suited to a 'rape revenge' narrative. Strömberg, being female, gets away with some nude Sapphic embraces recalling *Vampyros Lesbos* and a highly unconvincing death by inflatable pillow, made all the more unconvincing by the corpse's tumultuous breathing in close-up. And Miranda's protracted stalking of Muller, which could have worked up a real feeling of dread given the excellent acting and Franco's clever staging, is comprehensively ruined by the hopelessly unsuitable Manfred Hübler-Siegfried Schwab score. (Hübler and Schwab's work, though engagingly funky in itself, was also out of place in *Vampyros Lesbos*.) The whole thing is rounded off with a drearily staged 'plunging car' anti-climax, leaving only a few scattered Franco touches to linger in the memory – a lesbian clinch shot through a glass of sherry, or a thread of blood from Muller's mouth trailing down Miranda's thigh.

The most memorable feature of both *Vampyros Lesbos* and *Sie tötete*

A bloody consummation for Soledad Miranda and Ewa Strömberg in *Vampyros Lesbos* (1970)

in *Ekstase* remains Soledad Miranda herself. *Die Teufel kam aus Akasava* (The Devil Came from Akasava), a cheerfully illogical spy romp fraudulently 'based' on a non-existent Edgar Wallace story, was her eighth film with Franco in not much more than 12 months. (The first, *Sex Charade*, appears to be lost; another, *Juliette*, was never completed.) Sadly, not long after finishing *Akasava* she was killed, aged 27, in a Costa del Sol car crash on 18 August 1970. Billed as Susann Korda in all but one of her Franco films (reputedly to keep her parents in the dark regarding their erotic content), she nevertheless owes her posthumous fame to these ramshackle fever dreams. Indeed, her hypnotically Gothic presence is second only to that of Barbara Steele.

## JUST AN OUTMODED CHARACTER

Franco's *Sie tötete in Ekstase* and *Vampyros Lesbos* both concluded on 4 June 1970. By 7 July the Belgian director Harry Kümel had started production on *Les Lèvres rouges* (The Red Lips) in Ostend and Brussels. Kümel had acquired a significant reputation with shorts like *Anna la Bonne* and *De Grafbewaker* (The Cemetery Keeper), based, respectively, on Cocteau and Kafka, plus a 1968 feature debut, *Monsieur Hawarden*, that he dedicated to Josef von Sternberg. But, as an outspoken opponent of Belgium's snobbish critical establishment and the high-minded interference of the Belgian Ministry of Culture, his next move was to create a collision between art and exploitation that was designed to confound all standard forms of categorisation.

On the principle that "Sex was coming up quickly, along with violence, horror and chic arty-arty," he decided that "We are going to do something nasty."[29] He took as his subject a modern incarnation of the Countess Erszébet Báthory, whose influence on Euro horror stretched back at least as far as Freda's *I vampiri*. (And Kümel's was to be by no means the last word on the subject; by the end of July Hammer would be making a straight historical version of her story called *Countess Dracula*.) Aiming high, Kümel contacted the noted surrealist Jean Ferry, whose screen collaborators had included Luis Buñuel, Marcel Carné, Henri-Georges Clouzot and Louis Malle; most recently he'd co-written Georges Franju's Zola adaptation *La Faute de l'abbé Mouret* (The Sin of Father Mouret) and Patrick Ledoux's Franco-Belgian 'megalomaniac film director' drama *Klann – grand guignol*. Faced with Kümel's outline, Ferry acclaimed it as "la grande libération!"[30] and augmented it with some of the most quotable dialogue in the genre.

Kümel's film predictably made little impression in Belgium, but it scored heavily in Paris, London and particularly New York. The English-language title during production was *The Promise of Red Lips*, but it was as *Daughters of Darkness* that it grossed nearly $47,000 in its first ten days in New York, as well as earning from British critic Dilys Powell the remarkable sobriquet "the best of modern Gothic."[31]

*The Countess Báthory and her younger companion Ilona have passed through Nice, Monte Carlo and Bruges and are now staying in what the Countess calls a "sinister, deserted caravanserai" in off-season Ostend. The hotel's concierge is convinced the Countess previously stayed there in 1930 – looking exactly as she does now. The only other guests are Stefan Chilton and his new bride Valerie, whom the Countess proceeds to split asunder by means of the seductive Ilona.*

To indicate that *Les Lèvres rouges* was rarefied art-pulp of a high order, Kümel was particularly careful in his choice of leading players. For Stefan he initially thought of the British actor Malcolm McDowell, but was rebuffed. This disappointment was a blessing in disguise, since the US actor John Karlen stepped into the breach, bringing with him all the pulpy associations of *Dark Shadows*, the daytime vampire soap opera he was currently starring in. As for the Countess, the entire production was predicated on the availability of French art-house icon Delphine Seyrig, whose eternal return to grandiose old-world hotels had been signalled as far back as Resnais' *L'Année dernière à Marienbad*.

Added to these exemplars of pulp and art were Danielle Ouimet (Miss Quebec 1966) and the German sex symbol Andrea Rau. Another German actor, Paul Esser, was engaged to play Pierre, the sad-eyed concierge. Cleverly underplaying half-parodic lines like "It's rather dead around here this time of the year," he also gets to stammer out his conviction that "The Countess Báthory stayed at this hotel 40 years ago."

As noted above, Kümel was well aware that "sex was coming up quickly" – and it comes up immediately in the film itself, with a sex scene for Karlen and Ouimet directly after the opening credits. The midnight blue of the sky outside, the confined space of a wagon-lit on a hurtling train, the fetishistic emphasis on tinkling glasses, a champagne bucket and the bride's corsage; all these suggest the jet-set chic of a James Bond film. Yet the sex is clumsy and desperate, the music underlining this with strings suggestive of anxiety rather than swooning romance. Moments later comes a curious Valerie-Stefan exchange: "Do you love me?" "No." Stefan's subsequent remarks, among them his assurance to Valerie that she's "the most

"Slightly sad, slightly mysterious..." Delphine Seyrig as Countess Báthory in *Les Lèvres rouges* (1970)

## LES LÈVRES ROUGES

Belgium-France-West Germany 1970
France: *Le Rouge aux lèvres*
West Germany: *Blut an den Lippen*
UK / US: *Daughters of Darkness*
Showking Films Brussels / Maya Films Paris /
Roxy Film Munich / Ciné Vog Films Brussels
100 minutes colour
production began 7 July 1970
. . . . . . . . . . . . . . . . . . . . . . . . . . . . . . . .
Director of Photography: Eduard van der
Enden; Art Director: Françoise Hardy; Editor:
Magda Reypens; Sound: Jacques Eippers;

Music: François de Roubaix; Make-up: Ulli
Ullrich; Special Effects: Eugène Hendrickx,
Thierry Hallard; Screenplay: Pierre Drouot,
Jean Ferry, Harry Kümel, in association with
Jo Amiel; Producers: Henry Lange, Paul
Collet; Director: Harry Kümel

Delphine Seyrig (Countess Báthory); John Karlen
(Stefan); Danielle Ouimet (Valerie); Andrea Rau
(Ilona); Paul Esser (Pierre); Fons Rademakers
('Mother'); Georges Jamin (former detective);
Joris Collet (Mother's butler)

I cannot quite think of anyone trash-oriented enough to tolerate, let alone revel in, *Daughters of Darkness* … Kümel has managed to get Delphine Seyrig for this movie. Weep for her. Acclaimed actresses have, of course, come to horror films in their maturity, but the exquisite Miss Seyrig simply landed in a horror of a movie. *New York* 7 June 1971

I was strolling through Brussels and my eye fell upon a shop window, in which I saw a booklet about Countess Báthory. I bought it and told my friends, "Here's your subject." But they were afraid it would cost way too much … So I told them we could make a modern version, in which we show that the Countess is still alive. We wrote the story in three days. That's it.
*Harry Kümel [quoted in Flesh and Blood Autumn 1996]*

(To represent this establishment, Kümel created a brilliantly atmospheric synthesis of the Thermae Palace in Ostend, mainly for exteriors, and the Hotel Astoria in Brussels, exclusively for interiors.) When a newspaper announces 'De Vampire van Brugge', together with details of the three young women killed there in the last week, Stefan decides at once that a daytrip to Bruges would be the perfect honeymoon diversion. He proceeds to drool quite openly over their providential sighting of a fourth victim, and when the disconcerted Valerie points this out he says blandly, "We're getting to know each other..." Stefan also seems curiously reluctant to phone his aristocratic mother with news of his marriage. In one of the film's best jokes, we finally discover that 'mother' is a controlling middle-aged queen, ripely played by the celebrated Dutch director Fons Rademakers. Rouged and powdered like a corpse, he responds to the news of Stefan's elopement with the splendid line, "What you did wasn't foolish, Stefan. It was merely unrealistic."

For her part, Valerie is a very recognisable archetype, the woman who learns extremely quickly that the man she's married is a cold-eyed sadist but who shows a masochistic unwillingness to desert him. Until, that is, the Countess intervenes. Lit and costumed like Marlene Dietrich in an old von Sternberg picture, Seyrig's Countess is a perfectly preserved relic of the 1930s demi-monde, sporting a blonde Marcel

adorable girl in all Switzerland," can't help but ring false after this anxious prologue. Clearly these two are a long way from the standard horror-movie newly-weds; David Manners and Jacqueline Wells in *The Black Cat* were never like this.

That Stefan and Valerie represent fertile ground for an ambiguous interloper like the Countess becomes even clearer once they've settled in at their hotel.

wave and, at the climax, a silver lamé sheath that shimmers like a minor constellation. Showing not merely self-awareness but also a firm grasp of genre conventions, she describes herself as "an outmoded character, nothing more. You know – the beautiful stranger, slightly sad, slightly mysterious, that haunts one place after another..." Preening herself like a cat, she ascribes her youthful appearance to "a very strict diet [and] lots of sleep," musing later that "A woman will do anything to stay young." Seyrig's wonderfully mellifluous voice suggests an aristocratic languor at intriguing odds with the Countess' carefully calculated schemes. Immediately spotting the canker at the heart of the newly-weds' union and correctly identifying that canker as Stefan, she uses Ilona as an alluring means of separating the couple.

Just as the Countess recalls Marlene Dietrich, so Ilona is clearly modelled on another pre-war screen icon, Louise Brooks; in this way Kümel gives a slyly sophisticated nod to the vampiric immortality conferred on film stars of any era. Stefan and Valerie are no match for this stylish pair, and when the Countess gets Valerie to herself she issues a feminist manifesto that was nothing if not topical at the turn of the 1970s. "He dreams of making out of you what every man dreams of making out of every woman," she says. "A slave. A thing. An object for pleasure."

One small glitch in the Countess' plan involves the unanticipated death of Ilona – staged quite brilliantly by Kümel in the black-tiled bathroom of the Hotel Astoria's Royal Suite. Even so, it ensures the Countess' total dominance over the compromised Stefan and leads to a grim nocturnal burial in the sand dunes at De Panne. The contest for ownership of Valerie is resolved at a highly charged dinner, during which the Countess lights black candles while Stefan, almost comically underdressed in a brief red dressing gown, tells her that "It's finished. You hear me? Finished. I am a man and she is mine." Rather satisfyingly, it's Stefan who's actually finished – dispatched with a domed glass dish cover that, having broken in two over his face, somehow manages to slice through his wrists. Whereupon the camera spirals ceiling-wards to catch him in cruciform pose, with the women attached hungrily to each arm and Kümel fading tantalisingly, as he does several times in the film, to red rather than black.

"It was just a question of getting a young and beautiful couple to fuck as much as possible," Kümel once observed, "with a maximum of bloody scenes in between. A real commercial machine!"[32] Yet with *Les Lèvres rouges* he crafted one of the most lusciously realised of all vampire pictures, adding to gorgeous music, art direction and cinematography a generous ration of Low Countries surrealism. (As in the work of Jean Rollin, echoes of Paul Delvaux and René Magritte are well to the fore.) In places the film also recalls Vadim's *...Et mourir de plaisir*. A tiny speck of rouge, for example, is left at the corner of Valerie's mouth when the Countess kisses her, while shuddering harps are added to the foreboding mix of cello and cimbalom in François de Roubaix's unforgettable score.

Perhaps with touches like this in mind, Howard Thompson of the *New York Times* hailed Kümel's film as "far and away the most artistic vampire shocker since the Franco-Italian *Blood and Roses* ten years ago." Commending Kümel's knack for "gliding silkenly into horror," he also called the picture "subtle, stately, stunningly colored and exquisitely directed"[33] – a summation that, with a film this good, can't really be improved upon.

## CRUSHED-VELVET GOTHIC

Four weeks after Harry Kümel began shooting *Les Lèvres rouges* in Belgium, Jean Rollin started production in France on his third vampire film – a film that, like Kümel's, introduced a newly-wed couple to a lordly female vampire, though to very different effect. Having worked with Sam Selsky and Jean Lavie on his first two features, for this one Rollin gained the patronage of Monique Natan, whose company Les Films Modernes had recently co-produced the Alain Jessua film *Jeu de massacre* (The Killing Game). Yet Jessua's Pop Art black comedy, in which married cartoonists Jean-Pierre Cassel and Claudine Auger attach themselves to a psychotic Neuchâtel fantasist, was a far cry from the project proposed by Rollin. Even so, Natan was so enthused by *Le Frisson des vampires* (The Thrill of the Vampires) that she actually collaborated with Rollin on the script.

> Ise and Antoine are a honeymooning couple en route to a château belonging to Ise's cousins. On arrival, however, they discover that the cousins died – or at any rate were buried – the previous day. Leaving Antoine's conjugal hopes unsatisfied, Ise is seduced in an adjoining graveyard by a vampire woman called Isolde. Finally the two dandified cousins appear. Formerly vampire hunters, they have now become vampires themselves...

Making the most of an empty castle near Soissons in Picardy, Rollin concocted for *Le Frisson* as dense an agglomeration of Gothic imagery as he'd yet attempted. Flaming sconces abound, skulls and dwarfish mummies reside in ornamental niches, even the bridal chamber features a demonic sculpture

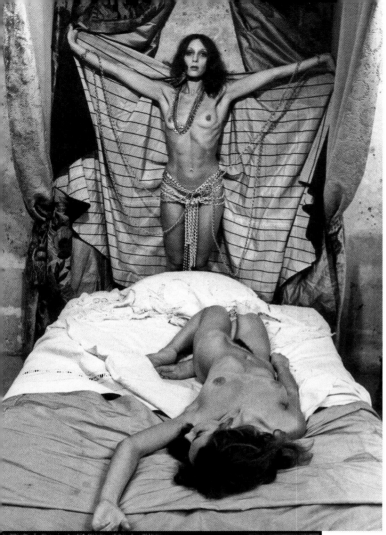

Dominique Toussaint overwhelms Sandra Julien on the marital bed in *Le Frisson des vampires* (1970)

perched above a fish tank that houses a grinning skull. The newly-weds ascend the castle steps exactly like David Manners and Helen Chandler in the 1931 *Dracula*. A pair of ethereal servant girls bear flickering candelabra down the same steps and head for a looming gateway. Rather improbably, the innocent bride spends the first 20 minutes in her white wedding dress, finally stepping out of it to reveal, even more improbably, that she has nothing on underneath. She's then enfolded by Isolde beneath a cruciform monument in the cemetery and slumps decorously, still naked, onto a grave. All this is lustrously conveyed by Jean-Jacques Renon's sumptuous cinematography and the grotesque minutiae of Michel Delesalles' decor.

David Pirie has pointed out that in purely narrative terms the film is strikingly similar to the 1962 Hammer film *The Kiss of the Vampire*, though adding the obvious proviso that in Rollin's hands the results are entirely different. Indeed, Hammer's Dr Ravna and his followers would never dream of discoursing on their condition at such improvisatory length, and in such comically pretentious terms, as the two vampire cousins do here. (This section, with the two men echoing each other's gestures and behaving almost like a comic cross-talk act, is likely to test the patience of even the most sympathetic viewer.) Nor would Ravna's disciple Tania ever dream of erupting dramatically from inside a grandfather clock, something that comes quite naturally to Isolde. This would be one of Rollin's most effective surrealist strokes were it better staged; even the lithe cabaret dancer Dominique Toussaint, cast as Isolde, has a bit of difficulty emerging from the thing. Sadly, laughter is also the natural reflex when Isolde makes another of her outré entrances – down the chimney.

These are small blemishes, however, in an otherwise beguiling canvas. Perhaps Rollin's masterstroke in making *Le Frisson* was to apply to the undead a kind of hippy chic, creating a crushed-velvet Gothic that's obviously dated but still ravishing to the eye. Isolde looks like a gaunt mediaeval sorceress reimagined by fashion monolith Biba, while the two

# LE FRISSON DES VAMPIRES

France 1970
UK: *Sex and the Vampire*
Les Films Modernes / Les Films ABC
90 minutes colour
production began 3 August 1970

· · · · · · · · · · · · · · · · · · · · · · · · · · · ·

Director of Photography: Jean-Jacques Renon; Art Director: Michel Delesalles; Editor: Olivier Grégoire; Assistant Editor: Catherine Horvath; Sound: Jean-Paul Loublier; Costumes: Nathalie Perrey; Music: Groupe Acanthus; Make-up: Eric Pierre;

Screenplay and Production: Jean Rollin, Monique Natan [both uncredited]; Director: Jean Rollin

Sandra Julien (Ise); Jean-Marie Durand (Antoine); Jacques Robiolles (2nd vampire [Hermann]); Michel Delahaye (1st vampire [William]); Marie-Pierre [Castel], Kuelan Herce (maids); Nicole Nancel (Isabelle); Dominique [Toussaint] (Isolde); uncredited: Michel Delesalles (staked vampire); Jean-Noël Delamare, Eric Pierre, Jean-Jacques Renon (pall-bearers)

The title is significant: in *Le Frisson des vampires* the 'thrill' in question isn't just a thrill of horror. With this third film, Jean Rollin slips back into the vein of erotic vampirism ... It's amusing, but it's a kind of humour that's lost on the initiates. *Télérama* 9 May 1971

What I do emphasise is an approach that is slightly surrealistic. For example, in *Le Frisson des vampires* we have a vampire woman who appeared a few times in the script. It fascinated me to try to make her appearances in the film as strange as possible: she appears from within a clock striking midnight, and in one scene comes down through the chimney like a Santa Claus.
Jean Rollin [quoted in *Cinefantastique* Fall 1973]

foppish cousins – one of whom is the critic Michel Delahaye, returning from *La Vampire nue* – have trouble controlling their purple flares when a wind blows up on Dieppe beach at the end. In an echo of the spiky fetish gear worn by the Castel twins in Rollin's previous film, Isolde uses her lance-like nipple covers to dispose of Isabelle, the cousins' former paramour. Indeed, she impales Isabelle's *own* nipples on them – a transgressive image that, again, isn't as well executed as it might be. The viewer, meanwhile, is left to ponder whether the likeness of the three women's names (Isolde, Isabelle, Ise) is meant to indicate that they're facets of the same triangular personality, though in the end this point goes unelucidated in the intoxicating pile-up of weird imagery.

Parts of the film explicitly recall the Belgian surrealist Paul Delvaux, famous for his crepuscular yet lily-white nudes, invariably surrounded by classical architecture and attended, in some instances, by skeletons. But Rollin goes out of his way in the pre-credits sequence to tip his hat to Universal, with a sepia funeral for the as-yet-unrisen cousins that features a careful composition of four male pall-bearers, three female mourners and two coffins. In a nifty transition, a tolling bell then gives place to resonating electric guitars (courtesy of a group of teenage Prog Rockers called Acanthus) and a blue fog rises up behind the blood-red titles.

Elsewhere, Rollin manages a careful balance of comedy and tragedy. "We were surprised to hear of your deaths," Ise tells her cousins as they sit down to dinner, adding, "Your reappearance is even more surprising." Yet at the end, when Ise and the cousins are magically extinguished by the dawn, a genuinely desolate note is struck; as seagulls scream in alarm, poor Antoine runs madly under the cliff edge, repeatedly yelling "Ise, je t'aime!" As for Isolde, she's already expired on the castle steps, having been forced to suck blood from her own wrist – "a precise and evocative image," as Pirie puts it, "of the circularity and futility of physical appetite."[34]

Forming a parochial contrast to the erotic reveries of Rollin, Jean-Louis van Belle's *Le Sadique aux dents rouges* (The Sadist with Red Teeth) was made as the 1960s faded and 1970 began, anticipating the medical vampirism of George Romero's *Martin* by six years. For a long time, however, *Le Sadique* meant little more to British horror fans than a tantalising poster featured in Barrie Pattison's 1975 book *The Seal of Dracula*. 'Un film de SEX HORREUR' screamed the tag-line, though Pattison's own estimate – "Cut-price vampires, none too professional in their presentation"[35] – was less enticing. And, between its lashings of poster-paint

blood, ludicrously gnomic dialogue and heroine Jane Clayton's English-accented French, the film is indeed a pretty gruelling experience.

"Gore is very trendy these days," observes a chirpy shop assistant. "People love horror." Her customer promptly selects a set of comedy fangs from the display and bites her to death. Perpetrator of the so-called 'Paris joke-shop murder case' is gloomy Daniel (played by future director Daniel Moosmann), who inadvertently drank blood when involved in a car crash and now suffers from delusions of vampirism. A scientist, journalist and police inspector are on his trail (all for self-interested reasons of their own) and the action winds up when "fang boy" attends a Louis XVI costume ball, with van Belle putting a counterculture spin on the masques previously featured in *…Et mourir de plaisir*, *The Kiss of the Vampire* and *Dance of the Vampires*.

The film's budget surrealism represents Daniel's tottering psyche via intercut monochrome footage of typhoons, landslides, collapsing buildings and nuclear blasts, and a scene of Parisian pedestrians walking backwards is at first eerily effective – until one notices that all the shopfronts are reversed too. Because Daniel and his British girlfriend work in an advertising agency, van Belle takes the opportunity to show a fulsome nude model having red paint massaged into her breasts. And there are signs, too, that van Belle is as much a humorist as a surrealist. The time-honoured "I won't bite" gag is used not once but twice, Raymond Legrand's overbearing score is better suited to a sex comedy, and some kind of Lord of Evil emerges from behind a hypnotist's wardrobe to reveal a pier-end make-up and a 'finger in the electric socket' hairdo. But the film falls flat either way.

A more plausible Parisian psychopath appeared in Paul Vecchiali's *L'Étrangleur* (The Strangler), which was shot in August 1970 and cast Jacques Perrin as a pretty-boy serial killer who targets only the sad and-or suicidal, maintaining that "I'm doing these women a service." Exceptionally acted, the film examines his weird relationships with the ex-Resistance cop on his trail (Julien Guiomar) and a strangely doting young woman (played by Perrin's sister, Eva Simonet). As well as recalling Michael Powell's *Peeping Tom*, Vecchiali also anticipates Hitchcock's *Frenzy* (the killer is a market-stall fruiterer), though the film only rises to a horror crescendo when the tear-stained boy walks the Paris streets at night and witnesses – or merely imagines? – an appalling series of muggings and murders. This truly nightmarish sequence is made all the queasier by a jaunty stretch of Roland Vincent's excellent score. One of the assaults, incidentally, is undergone by a topless Sandra Julien, who filmed this blink-and-you'll-miss-it role while starring in *Le Frisson des vampires* for Jean Rollin.

Another *Le Frisson* cast member, Jacques Robiolles, moved from playing Julien's long-haired vampire cousin to making poetic 16mm experiments of his own, notably the 1973 film *Le Train de Transylvanie* (The Transylvania Train). Other filmmakers ventured into the territory opened up by Rollin with an eye much more firmly fixed on commercial success. A touch of Rollin is discernible, for example, in Bruno Gantillon's *Morgane et ses nymphes* (Morgana and Her Nymphs). But only a touch, for the film plays more like a feature-length remake of Vadim's *Metzengerstein* (the first instalment of the Poe anthology *Histoires extraordinaires*), except with the horror content siphoned out and a truckload of naked lesbianism pumped in.

Again we have a mediaeval netherworld in which all the lolling, colour-coded decadence is obviously a countercultural pipe dream, plus plenty of twinkling harps, truly ravishing cinematography (by Jean Monsigny) and an imposing sorceress brooding over the proceedings; this time she's plucked from Arthurian legend and played by the gravely beautiful Dominique Delpierre. The 13th century Château de Val at Lanobre looks extremely fetching, but when two modern young women pass into "the realm of the fairies, a place only children can find," the narcoleptic non-intrigues that ensue aren't even enlivened by the presence of a conniving, rather distinguished-looking dwarf (Alfred Baillou).

Gantillon's film began shooting on 4 May 1970; the final days of its six-week schedule thus crossed over with the first week of a British film called *Virgin Witch*, which began on 8 June. The two make an interesting study in the stark difference between French and British approaches to the new witchy-softcore subgenre. The Surrey shenanigans typify the tawdry, sniggering and unflatteringly photographed Anglo approach to the proverbial tee, whereas the pretty and po-faced *Morgane* features zero sniggering and sex scenes that are scrupulously decorous. Sadly, Jean-Claude Morlot's contemporary estimate was pretty accurate: "The fantasy element here is used as little more than a pretext for presenting sapphic scenes, and Bruno Gantillon fails to make anything more of it."[36]

*Morgane et ses nymphes* was a professionally crafted commercial proposition, designed to exploit the new, countercultural interest in esoteric religions while also satisfying the many punters interested only in seeing pretty hippies take their tops off. Other entrants in this burgeoning new field proceeded from much hazier, often semi-professional terrain, among them two occult-inflected films from writer-director Mario Mercier. Having made a mid-1960s featurette called *Les Dieux en colère* (The Angry Gods), Mercier's feature debut, *La Goulve*, duly appeared in July 1972 – and, for all its amateurish crudities, it weaves quite an intriguing spell. A persecuted little boy, Raymond, is taken in by an elderly sorcerer and enquires about the identity of "la dame aux serpents" in one of the old man's pictures. It turns out to be La Goulve, feminine (in Mercier's lexicon, at any rate) of ghoul – an otherworldly being called upon by the adult Raymond to "make Agnès unable to live without me." Agnès is a comely local girl who, alongside Raymond's cousin Nadine and La Goulve herself, spends much of her screen time naked.

Raymond's ritual to summon La Goulve involves a cock being killed on camera for real, an unedifying moment that co-exists with languorous scenes of La Goulve rubbing breasts with Nadine. (The film's producer and co-director, Bepi Fontana, was apparently responsible for the more exploitable material.) La Goulve is a golden-skinned beauty with snakes slithering out of her hair and parallel sets of suckers down each flank; she compels Nadine to dance naked on a nest of vipers and, when the girl cuts herself with broken glass, heals the wounds by sending cheesy lightning bolts from her fingertips. She neglects to do so, however, when the girl climactically cuts her throat. Agnès, meanwhile, is discovered in the swamps by her boyfriend, having been reduced to just a floating face and a mop of hair festooned with snakes – a striking nightmare image accompanied by suitably eerie washes of musique concrète. By this stage, Mercier appears to have entirely forgotten his protagonist, Raymond, which is probably just as well given that he's a robotic, sulky, lank-haired goon who feels the need to rape Agnès even after calling on supernatural aid.

Abandoning Fontana, Mercier went on alone with another wild and woolly collision of the occult with the counterculture, though a considerably less engaging one. *La Papesse* (The High Priestess) was scrutinised by French censors in August 1974 and met with a predictably scandalised response. The lisping title character, Geziale, is played by a bona-fide practitioner also called Geziale; surveying her assembled acolytes, she announces her "mission to pave the way for the oncoming reign of women of all races, who will do their work in the Age of Aquarius." Feminist though this might sound, Mercier's exploration of what Geziale calls "this evolution of humanity" involves heaps of raincoat-friendly female nudity and also a couple of nasty rape scenes.

The victim is the same woman in each case. She's played by the indefatigable Lisa Livane, who at other times is chained up naked in a pig pen, fed a black Communion wafer while tied to cross-beams, molested by a green-faced, long-taloned bird man in a cave, and finally savaged by a coal-black dog. At the climax Geziale herself, having donned lethal black talons of her own, is forced to gyrate semi-naked for a very long time and is then ritualistically taken from behind. Many of the celebrants, like Geziale, were apparently the real thing, and most of the male ones are Christ lookalikes (or Charles Manson lookalikes, depending on your point of view). Yet again a cock is killed on camera; snakes are also much in evidence, as in *La Goulve*, and Mercier even contrives a fake ejaculation. (It jets in rather comically from screen right and, coupled with bird blood, makes up a ceremonial cocktail.) At one point, too, a pair of clueless petty criminals pass through, as if wandering in from another film entirely – a Jean Rollin film, in fact.

## VAMPIRES ANCIENT AND MODERN

While Franco, Kümel and Rollin were making their offbeat vampire pictures in 1970, debutant Italian director Corrado Farina was at work on a film that, like Hans W Geissendörfer's *Jonathan*, used Stoker's *Dracula* as a springboard for a political message – but located it, unlike *Jonathan*, firmly in the modern day.

In ...*Hanno cambiato faccia* (...They've Changed Face), young-ish executive Alberto is invited to meet one Giovanni Nosferatu, the all-powerful business magnate who runs not just the company but also, it seems, most of Italy. This involves a trip to a remote mountain village that Farina plays for maximum atmospheric chills; indeed, the bleak slate-greyness of the environment is almost palpable. ("Is it always so foggy in these parts?" Alberto asks a creepily taciturn gas station attendant.) After this the *Dracula* motifs come thick and fast, with Alberto arriving at a baronial estate where no bird sings, a simultaneously cheery and chilly host appearing at the top of the stairs and saying "Welcome to my house," and a chalk-faced secretary claiming that she and her boss "don't differentiate between the present and the past." This ambiguous secretary is called Corinna, which – significantly or otherwise – is a conflation of Corrado Farina.

Farina's chosen means of satirising capitalism is the hollow world of advertising, one he knew well given his background in corporate filmmaking. Inane jingles assail Alberto even when he takes a shower, and in the third act the traditional gathering of the Satanists is supplanted by a high-powered

Francesca Modigliani, denied admittance to the HQ of vampire capitalists in ...*Hanno cambiato faccia* (1970)

meeting of Nosferatu's top aides; a cardinal is included and monochrome pastiches of Godard and Fellini are among the commercials on display. (The bespectacled, lab-coated gent showing off an LSD aerosol, and calling Nosferatu "the name we trust," is Farina himself.) Finally, having visited a subterranean crypt and found a sarcophagus indicating that his host died in 1801, Alberto realises that "Myths don't die, they become transformed. You've changed faces, but you carry on drinking people's blood."

The idea of a venal elite quelling the proles with force-fed advertising recalls Nigel Kneale's *The Year of the Sex Olympics*, while the 'vampire as capitalist' motif would reappear in Hammer's *The Satanic Rites of Dracula*. Farina's film has trouble maintaining the atmospheric highs of its first act, but it's consistently intriguing and very well acted (by Adolfo Celi, Giuliano Disperati, Geraldine Hooper and Francesca Modigliani). In August 1971 it won a well-deserved Golden Leopard at the Locarno Film Festival.

Geraldine Hooper also turned up briefly in Tonino Cervi's *Le regine* (The Queens), playing one of several satanic emissaries who describe themselves – in an explicit reference to the advertising industry – as "hidden persuaders." Starting production on 15 June 1970, this Italian-French co-production was perfectly positioned to comment on the counterculture of the day – and to compose a mournful elegy for it. To quote the subtitle, it's a *favola thrilling* (thrilling fairy tale) in which a young hippy (Ray Lovelock) is ensnared by three beautiful women at their impossibly chic woodland hideaway. In the persons of Haydée Politoff, Ida Galli and Silvia Monti, they're a three-strong distillate of Italian Gothic's traditional devouring female; they also conform to the 'feminine evil comes in threes' template of *Macbeth* and *Dracula*. Lovelock is lured into making love with all three, after which they transform into back-combed homicidal harpies and are congratulated on their success by a cigar-chewing Devil (Gianni Santuccio), who pointedly blows hellish smoke onto a flower.

"I'm just looking for a new world," explains Lovelock. "A world without selfishness, without egotism, without violence." These are the very attributes most highly prized by the Devil, of course, who frets that "These individuals with their new ideas [ie, hippies] are influencing the whole world." The film is an obvious but alluring parable about the way in which the establishment inevitably contains and commodifies countercultural movements, with a soaring seagull in a blue sky and a baleful owl in a nocturnal tree symbolising the opposing forces. It's also the kind of 90-minute time-capsule that carries a 'casa di moda' (fashion house) credit attributed, rather vaguely, to 'Carnaby Street'. It's just unfortunate that beautiful women are identified as the agents through which freedom is suppressed. That rather stark title, incidentally, was expanded for export to *Queens of Evil*.

The modernisations of the vampire myth proposed by Franco, Kümel, Rollin, Farina and Cervi may have varied in sophistication but all five were a million miles removed from the dismal vampire comedy that got under way in Austria in October 1970. Former Jess Franco associate Pier A Caminnecci was the producer of *Gebissen wird nur nachts* (Bitten Only at Night), which returned him to the imposing Burg Kreuzenstein, the castle

Pia Degermark under threat in the woeful West German sex comedy *Gebissen wird nur nachts* (1970)

he'd used three years earlier for the equally appalling *Im Schloß der blutigen Begierde*. The unit decamped to Burg Liechtenstein, however, for the film's climactic party sequence, a riot of bare boobs and plastic fangs that would give rise to an alluring export title – *The Vampire Happening*. To direct, Caminnecci hired none other than Freddie Francis, presumably on the strength of his 1968 Hammer horror *Dracula Has Risen from the Grave*. And to star Caminnecci selected his own fiancée, Pia Degermark, who'd won

Best Actress at Cannes for Bo Widerberg's tragic romance *Elvira Madigan*.

The cripplingly overlong result, in which a Hollywood film star returns to her ancestral castle to find she's the living image of her vampiric great-grandmother, doesn't have a laugh in it. The tone is that of a German sex comedy, with a gay air steward being symbolically hanged, a bare-arsed vampire monk struggling to get at various bare-breasted over-age schoolgirls, and a family retainer saying "I'm getting completely mixed up" prior to breaking the fourth wall with "I'll bet you are, too." The vampire's name, Clarimonde, is an odd echo of Théophile Gautier's classic story *La Morte amoureuse*, and Ferdy Mayne – whose Count von Krolock had been such a bloodcurdling presence in Polanski's *Dance of the Vampires* – crops up at a late stage as Dracula himself. Though he ends up rushing back to his helicopter with his trousers round his ankles, Mayne at least gets the film's one and only witty line. Demurring at being given his full title, he says, "Why so formal? Call me Christopher. I'm sure he won't mind."

In 1970, equally dismal films were available from Spain. Paul Naschy's third werewolf project, for example, was lumbered with a director – J M Zabalza – who in later years was likened by Naschy to the notoriously inept Edward D Wood Jr. In *La furia del hombre lobo* (Fury of the Wolf Man), Daninsky has been cursed while in Tibet, giving him the opportunity to bed his faithless wife and simultaneously savage her in his werewolf form. Venturing into the rain, he's electrocuted by a fallen pylon and delivered into the hands of an unscrupulous scientist, Ilona Alman (Perla Cristal), who claims to be able "to vary the genotype of an individual to create a being in the laboratory." Rejected experimental subjects, including various dozy hippies, throng the lower depths together with a mysterious figure in a Phantom of the Opera mask. Other incoherent features include a couple of walled-up corpses, a lab assistant being strangled by a sentient plant, and a genuine touch of perversity when Ilona whips the chained wolf man as a prelude to sex. But the film is a total mess, enlivened only by Naschy's typically vigorous werewolf workouts, culminating in a battle royal between Daninsky and his newly lycanthropic wife.

When *La furia* was belatedly unleashed on Spanish audiences in February 1972, critic Pedro Yoldi was perplexed. "We find ourselves faced with a film," he wrote, "which relates many things yet finishes by explaining none of them."[37] Viewer puzzlement, and disappointment, must have been all the more pronounced given that *La furia*'s vastly superior follow-up, *La noche de Walpurgis* (Walpurgis Night), had already been on release for ten months and had notched up a highly impressive 30 million pesetas.

*In search of the tomb of the notorious 15th century sorceress Wandesa Dárvula de Nádasdy, students Elvira and Genevieve are put up at the remote home of Waldemar Daninsky – unaware that he is a werewolf. When Wandesa is providentially resurrected, she quickly turns Genevieve into a vampire and plots to invoke the Devil himself on Walpurgis Night. As Elvira falls in love with him, the fatalistic Waldemar determines to foil Wandesa's schemes.*

Shot in November 1970 as the maiden production of Plata Films, *La noche de Walpurgis* was made in collaboration with the West German company Hi-Fi Stereo 70, which had also co-financed Naschy's debut, *La marca del hombre lobo*. The potential revealed in that film – and subsequently squandered in the childish convolutions of *Los monstruos del terror* and *La furia del hombre lobo* – was at last fulfilled in *La noche de Walpurgis*. The film marked the Gothic horror debut of the 64-year-old Argentinian director León Klimovsky, whose flair for moody visuals elevated it far beyond the script's ragbag collection of exploitable ingredients. Those ingredients, however, were formidable enough in themselves to make the film an influential blueprint for the rising tide of Spanish horror that followed it.

The ingredients include Naschy himself, still at this early stage a rather bovine presence in human form but a splendidly feral lycanthrope when required. We also get a decent amount of throat-ripping (with Daninsky

nonchalantly dropping hunks of flesh from his slavering jaws), arterial blood spraying down onto Marisa Tovar's bare breasts (a detail inevitably withheld from Spanish audiences at the time) and an eye-catching array of atmospheric locations (the usual suspects: Navacerrada, El Cercón, San Martín

## LA NOCHE DE WALPURGIS

Spain-West Germany 1970
West Germany: *Nacht der Vampire*
UK: *Shadow of the Werewolf*
US: *The Werewolf's Shadow / The Werewolf vs the Vampire Woman*
Plata Films Madrid / Hi-Fi Stereo 70 Munich
87 minutes colour
in production November 1970
......................................
Director of Photography: Leopoldo Villaseñor; Art Director: Ludwig Orny; Editor: Antonio Gimeno; Sound: José María San Mateo; Music: Antón García Abril; Make-up: José Luis Morales; Special Effects: Antonio Molina; Screenplay by: Jacinto Molina [Paul Naschy],

Hans Munkel; Dialogue [English-language version]: Dick Randall; Producer: Salvadore Romero [uncredited]; Director: León Klimovsky

Paul Naschy (the wolf man [Waldemar Daninsky]); Patty Shepard (Wandesa); Gaby Fuchs (Elvire); Bárbara Capell (Genevieve Bennett); Andrés Resino (Inspector Marcel); Yelena Samarina (Elizabeth Daninsky); Julio Peña (Dr Hartwig, pathologist); José Marco (Pierre); Betsabé Sharon [Betsabé Ruiz] (barmaid [Pierre's mistress]); Barta Barri (Muller); Luis Gaspar (bereaved man with knife); Ruperto Ares; Marisa Tovar (woodland victim); uncredited: Eduardo Chappa (beggar / monster)

Klimovsky skilfully exploits today's extensive technical resources and gives the story a very stately and sombre narrative rhythm ... The film is punctuated by continuous shocks and shrieks of surprise. But it's also true that some viewers treat it as a joke, greeting the 'terrifying' tricks with loud laughter and derisive comments. Skilled use of colour and a hellish soundtrack, all shivery and scratchy, provide an effective complement to the mind-boggling plot. *La Vanguardia* 22 July 1971

Before filming began somebody from Hispamex phoned to warn me that the producer wanted to replace me with some other blue-eyed boy wonder (I had a strong suspicion that this was Máximo Valverde) – or that, at the very least, the new fellow would play the human Waldemar while I would be left with the part of the lupine Waldemar. Logically, this state of affairs didn't appeal one little bit to the Germans and they soon put a halt to the scheme.
*Paul Naschy [Memorias de un hombre lobo, 1997]*

"Satan's favourite mistress." Patty Shepard as the Blood Countess of *La noche de Walpurgis* (1970)

de Valdeiglesias). On top of all this we have German actress Barbara Capell modelling the regulation baby-doll nightie and a climactic dust-up between Waldemar and Wandesa that quotes fulsomely from Naschy's beloved urtext, *Frankenstein Meets the Wolf Man*. The mixture proved irresistible to local audiences at the time; as a Madrid critic put it in May 1971, "Nobody will feel short-changed by the accumulation of terrifying incidents in the script."[38] Two years later, the same accumulation proved eminently resistible to Britain's *Monthly Film Bulletin*, in which David McGillivray noted that "The plethora of spectral manifestations fails to provide even the cheapest of thrills."[39]

Maybe it was the script's extremely tenuous relationship with logic and motivation that proved the stumbling block to Anglo-Saxon eyes. But a film like *La noche de Walpurgis* requires the viewer to leave such earthbound considerations at the box-office, with the lushly rendered horror highlights justifying themselves on their own terms without regard to plot or character. Certainly, the reliance on spooky and-or bloody set-pieces leaves Naschy's rather listless bits of connective plot tissue looking unusually threadbare; poor Andrés Resino, playing Elvira's original boyfriend, has such a dull part that most of it was sensibly lopped from the export edit. And the film loses momentum just when it should start gripping like a vice – in the third act build-up to the final confrontation.

But in the meantime there's plenty to enjoy, starting with a bracing pre-credits sequence in which Daninsky is accidentally revived in a morgue. The credulous police inspector and sceptical pathologist in this scene are played by two of Spanish horror's most ubiquitous character actors, Barta Barri and Julio Peña. The latter is given the splendid line, "I'm going to take out those two silver bullets, and I can assure you our Mr Daninsky will be as dead as ever…"

Another familiar face – a strikingly dramatic one, and soon to be put to use in several Jess Franco films – is that of Yelena Samarina, who passes through as Daninsky's deranged sister, a character never referred to in Naschy's werewolf saga before or since. After a handful of scenes, she succumbs to the vampires and her own brother is forced to stake her and lop off her head before she can regenerate, with a sadly inadequate dummy filling in for Samarina. That she never comes back as a vampire is perhaps a shame, though Klimovsky certainly makes great use of the two at his disposal.

With lengthy fangs positioned either side of her two front teeth rather than where her canines are, Capell's Genevieve acquires something of a Bugs Bunny aspect but is otherwise a bewitching presence, advancing on Elvira through inexplicable indoor ground fog and telling her, "I'm happy. It's beautiful, Elvira. Join me … and you'll know what pleasure is." When Elvira dreams of a double-attack by Genevieve and the risen Wandesa, the pair fill an ornate goblet with her blood and then, in one of Klimovsky's most memorable inspirations, waltz together through the fog until magically vanishing from view. Wandesa Nádasdy, we're told, was "Satan's favourite mistress" and lived from 1452 to 1480. She's pretty clearly Naschy's version of the ever-reliable Countess Erzsébet Báthory (whose married name was Nádasdy) and is beautifully embodied by the sepulchral Patty Shepard. Klimovsky teasingly uses her enormous, veiled head-dress to obscure the details of her attacks, as well as creating indelible imagery by rendering most of her appearances (and those of the vampirised Genevieve too) in eerie slow-motion.

Among *La noche*'s other peculiarities is a pervert handyman (José Marco) who serves no particular purpose other than to lie in apparent death with a ripped throat and a visibly pulsing neck, a capering zombie monk called Baptiste who is dispatched with almost comical ease, and a briefly glimpsed barmaid (Betsabé Ruiz) who is upstaged by multiple bottles of a drink that was almost omnipresent in Italian gialli of the period, J&B Scotch. Wandesa's resurrection is remarkably similar to Mircalla's in the recent Hammer film *Lust for a Vampire* (though it was almost certainly too soon for Klimovsky to have seen a film made only four months earlier), and Antón García Abril's bodeful score would be recycled the following year in Amando de Ossorio's *La noche del terror ciego*.

# FROM LEFT BANK BEDSIT TO BLACK FOREST CHÂTEAU

In France, recent features like *Le Sadique aux dents rouges* and *L'Étrangleur* paved the way for a far more sustained Parisian nightmare in 1971.

*Le Seuil du vide* (Threshold of the Void) was a pet project of the 25-year-old writer-director Jean-François Davy, who had garnered valuable pre-production publicity for the film in the penultimate number of *Midi-Minuit Fantastique*. He had first read Kurt Steiner's novel back in April 1969, when the book was already 13 years old. (It had been published in Fleuve Noir's 'Collection Angoisse' line – the same series that later accommodated Jean Redon's *Les Yeux sans visage*.) Soon enough, Steiner himself, under his real name of André Ruellan, was helping Davy with the script, and by February 1970 the distinguished producer Mag Bodard was sufficiently interested to ask for

Dominique Erlanger emerges from the ink of the unconscious in *Le Seuil du vide* (1971)

some test footage to be shot. This Davy did, with Juliette Villard cast as Steiner's fragmenting heroine, but finance for a full feature remained elusive. When Villard died in March 1971, Davy turned to another actress, Dominique Erlanger. The completed, full-length version of *Le Seuil du vide* therefore opens with two title cards – the first indicating that Erlanger won the Best Actress award at the Trieste Festival, the second dedicating the film 'à Juliette Villard'.

*Reeling from a sundered relationship, young artist Wanda Leibowitz journeys from Strasbourg to Paris and is befriended at the Gare de l'Est by an elderly lady called Léonie Galois. Offering Wanda a room at 44 Rue de Verneuil, and at an extremely favourable rent, Léonie specifies only that a locked door in the room should never be opened. On arrival, Wanda finds that the room is triangular and wastes little time in unlocking the forbidden door...*

Davy, too, wastes little time in establishing Wanda as a woman who's dislocated in every sense. Right at the beginning she turns to camera, wet-faced, as an Air France jet carries her former lover to some unspecified location. Moments later, on the train to Paris, she's luckless enough to be hit with a 75-franc penalty fare. Her downward spiral only intensifies as the picture goes on, and that Dominique Erlanger won an award for playing Wanda is easy to understand, given that her soulful presence anchors the action and confers on it an understated poignancy rare in the genre. Wanda is a damaged person who shows flashes of gaiety and good humour in the earlier part of the film before her spirit is thoroughly crushed, and her very identity stolen, by the highly peculiar conspiracy that's mobilised against her.

The nature of the conspiracy shows that, by the early 1970s, Steiner's novel had come to seem prescient, for the theme of a younger generation oppressed by their elders was almost inescapable in the horror pictures of the day. Here, as in the American film *The Brotherhood of Satan* (1969) and Britain's *Nothing But the Night* (1972), old people don't merely oppress the young but actually absorb them. The process begins when Wanda is befriended in a terminus café by the faux-solicitous Léonie, who gently deplores Wanda's "trendy trousers" (ie, flared jeans) but offers the rootless girl a second-floor bedsit in the Seventh Arrondissement. (The scene plays rather like the meeting between Boris

## LE SEUIL DU VIDE

France 1971
US: *The Threshold of the Void*
Neyrac Films
76 minutes colour
produced spring 1971

Director of Photography: Louis Soulanes; Art Director and Costumes: Jean Claude Philippe; Editor: Nicole Gauduchon, Cécile Decugis; Sound: Gérard Barra; Music: Jack Arel; Screenplay: Alain Gerber, André Ruellan, Jean-François Davy, based on the novel by Kurt Steiner [André Ruellan]; Producer: Guy Neyrac; Director: Jean-François Davy

Dominique Erlanger (Wanda Leibowitz); Jean Servais (De Gournais); Pierre Vaneck (Dr Liancourt); Odette Duc (Léonie Galois); Catherine Rich (Mona); Michel Lemoine (Franck); Georgette Anys, Liza Braconnier, Jean Droze (train passengers); Arlette Emery (nurse); Adrien Forge (doctor); Phillippe Gasté (artist in café); Karine Jeantet (sales girl in boutique); Yvon Lec (old man in dream); Roger Lumont (ticket inspector); Claude Melki (barman); Paul Pavel (taxi driver); André Tomasi (waiter); uncredited: Jean-François Davy (second artist in café), Nathalie Perrey (woman in Métro carriage); Roland Topor (man in Métro carriage)

**This French fantasy item is well-directed and acted but story never comes across to audience so that when it's all over, they're baffled. More's the pity, because dream sequences are well handled and some of the fantasy points filmically effective ... Dominique Erlanger does a fine job of thesping as the young girl, and carries the pic through almost single-handed.**
*Variety 27 October 1971*

**The project has attracted almost universal support, yet still the financiers are sceptical ... If I can't persuade a producer once and for all, I'll produce *Le Seuil du vide* myself, because I'm convinced of its commercial possibilities – and that the French public is absolutely ready for this kind of story.**
*Jean-François Davy [quoted in Midi-Minuit Fantastique October 1970]*

Karloff and Ian Ogilvy in a West London Wimpy Bar in the 1967 film *The Sorcerers*.) Subsequently, Léonie's strict instructions not to open the mysterious door are clearly designed as a lure; the old lady is obviously well aware that telling a child not to do something is a guarantee of the child going ahead and doing it. She's also familiar, presumably, with the fable of temptation represented by Bluebeard's closet.

Thus tempted, Wanda opens the door on – nothingness. The void of the title is a simple but effective optical trick, and the inky blackness proves irresistible to this woman-in-flux. She even purchases an extra-strong industrial lamp so that she can move her easel into the abyss and coax her surreal paintings direct from her unconscious. This is creepy enough, but Davy does a brilliant job of ratcheting up the weirdness each time Wanda ventures in. First, the void appears enshrouded in mist, through which looms Léonie's enlarged face; later, Wanda has a vision of her own doppelgänger, grinning fixedly in a velvet gown. The feeling of an eerie extra-dimensional limbo is brilliantly conveyed. Eventually the 'room' inducts her into a solarised, psychedelic park, where she meets a decrepit old man who has dreamed his way into the void and lets her know exactly what kind of danger she's in.

This is just one of several splendidly surrealist touches, though Davy reserves his big set-piece for a weird costume ball at which Wanda, wearing the velvet gown she previously envisioned, meets the secret society that's bent on entrapping her. It's led by Léonie's saturnine nephew, a gallery owner played with just the right touch of sophisticated, hard-to-define threat by the Belgian star Jean Servais. After this comes the classic film noir scenario of the girl-whom-nobody-will-believe, with Wanda admitted to hospital and sounding like a lunatic when she makes the entirely accurate observation, "I'm young! They're going to steal my body and replace it with an old one..."

Davy relates all this with smooth and unhurried economy, the film clocking in at a lean and sprightly 76 minutes; only Servais' oddly truncated first scene appears to have suffered from Davy's rigorous streamlining. Erlanger, meanwhile, charts Wanda's disintegration quite beautifully. Visibly debilitated by each visit to the vampire void, she ends up as a twitching, wild-eyed wreck in a corner café. (Davy's pre-production mission statement began with the line, "More than love and death, it's ageing that gives the human condition a tragic quality."[40]) The change in Wanda's personality is announced when she buys a slightly unflattering wig – one of several details that recall Roland Topor's 1964 novel Le Locataire chimérique (The Illusory Tenant), a property later filmed by Roman Polanski. In fact, the channel of influence seems to have flowed in the opposite direction. Topor had provided the illustrations in 1963 for Kurt Steiner's book Manuel du Savoir-Mourir, so it seems more than likely that he was remembering Steiner's Le Seuil du vide when writing Le Locataire chimérique. Acknowledging this, Topor turns up briefly in Davy's film as a creepy man encountered by Wanda on the Métro.

In addition to its other virtues, the film serves as a beguiling time-capsule of 1971 Paris, with Wanda's perambulations accompanied, in Jack Arel's highly eclectic score, by flute-heavy Prog Rock. We also get some lingering reverberations of May 1968,

particularly when Davy himself appears as a louche café philosopher who tells Wanda that "La solution c'est la révolution." There's a nice irony, too, in the fact that the climactic soul-transference takes place at the corner of Rue de Verneuil, a fashionable Left Bank address better known at the time for harbouring various celebrity couples (Serge Gainsbourg and Jane Birkin, Juliette Gréco and Michel Piccoli). Better still, the ending carries a real charge of tragic melancholy, as Wanda (now played by the wizened Odette Duc) sits sprawled by the boulangerie, desperately clutching a Teddy bear – the last vestige of her former life – and looking across at Léonie, standing impassively on the opposite pavement and now played by the fresh-faced Dominique Erlanger.

Sadly, Davy's excellent film, though well received at Sitges and Trieste, languished unreleased until March 1974 – demonstrating pretty clearly the low regard in which French fantastique was still held. To make ends meet, Davy embarked on a series of sex comedies, starting with Bananes mécaniques (Clockwork Bananas) in 1973.

Sitting beside Roland Topor in Le Seuil's Métro scene, incidentally, is Nathalie Perrey. Continuity supervisor on Davy's film, she was to increasingly devote herself to a long working relationship, in various capacities, with Jean Rollin. Among the first of her Rollin titles was Vierges et vampires (Virgins and Vampires), a 1971 production which reunited Rollin with Sam Selsky (producer, three years previously, of Le Viol du vampire). Eventually released under the more elegiac title Requiem pour un vampire (Requiem for a Vampire), this is another visually striking distillate of Rollin's now-familiar obsessions, despite a complete absence of beach scenes. Indeed, Rollin gets by without dialogue for well over 40 minutes.

Another of Rollin's recurring girl duos, Marie and Michelle (Marie-Pierre Castel, Mireille Dargent), begin the film by trading pot shots from a getaway car while escaping a New Year's Eve party dressed as clowns. The opening credits play out over a ravishingly yellow expanse of corn field, the girls traversing it as Pierre Raph's oboes, gongs and keyboards resonate ominously on the soundtrack, then they reappear at the gates of an imposing castle loaned to Rollin by the Duchesse de la Roche-Guyon. For some unexplained reason Marie and Michelle now have fake bats attached to their throats; descending to the lower depths, they recoil in horror from a worm-eaten cadaver hanging in irons.

As usual, Rollin isn't much interested in obligatory horror trimmings like this; the waxy severed arms that project from the stonework and the cowled skeletons that surround the organ-playing Erica (Dominique

Mireille Dargent,
"lost for eternity"
in the elegiac
*Requiem pour un
vampire* (1971)

Toussaint) are similarly desultory. His real enthusiasm is reserved for the dissonant clash of imagery as the lordly Erica, dressed in the brocaded purple velvet of an 18th century male exquisite, is followed onto the screen by a couple of feral, fur-clad troglodyte goons. Here, too, come the first scraps of dialogue. "We got lost," murmurs Marie. "Lost for eternity," replies an older, whip-wielding woman called Louise (Louise Dhour). And, as the sex-crazed goons sexually molest a couple of naked, manacled girls at wearisome length, Rollin offers a transgressive image that even Jess Franco might have envied, panning down one of the captives' bodies to reveal a squeaky bat roosting in her pubic hair.

Though in control of the semi-vampirised Erica, the exhausted-looking 'vieux vampire' (Michel Delesalle) admits that "My powers are too ancient" to fully convert Marie and Michelle. He therefore suicidally entombs himself with the devoted Erica and the film comes to a nebulous but undeniably mournful close. Disregarding the crude dungeon sex scenes (scenes that were apparently forced on Rollin, in any case), the naïve power of Rollin's imagery in *Requiem* substantiates his claim that the film "could be a children's film made by children."[41]

It was becoming clear by now that one of the strengths of Rollin's curious films was the recurrence of the same names behind the camera, Nathalie Perrey included. Another regular contributor was the Belgian production designer Jio Berk, who, having worked on *La Vampire nue*, would miss out on both *Le Frisson des vampires* and *Requiem pour un vampire* prior to rejoining

Rollin in 1973 for *Les Démoniaques*. In the meantime, however, he designed a homegrown Belgian horror in summer 1971 for the Brussels company Cetelci.

Presumably aware of Harry Kümel's achievement with *Les Lèvres rouges*, Cetelci enlisted Italian expertise courtesy of co-production partners Delfino Film. They also engaged veteran filmmaker André Hunebelle to act as consultant to director Jean Brismée, who was making what turned out to be his first and only feature. The result, *La Plus longue nuit du diable* (The Devil's Longest Night), was profitably exported as *Devil's Nightmare* and provided a splendid showcase for the alluring Erika Blanc.

> Together with their tour guide, six tourists are obliged to stay the night at the forbidding Black Forest castle of a former Nazi called Baron von Runberg. Emerging from his alchemical laboratory, the Baron explains over dinner that his family suffers from a curse dating back to the 12th century – a curse that turns all its eldest daughters into devouring succubi. Moments later, a beautiful young woman called Hilse turns up on the doorstep.

*La Plus longue nuit du diable* is populated by all the usual types common to 'old dark house' pictures. Unusually, however, it attempts to confer allegorical significance on them by invoking the Seven Deadly Sins. The film remains a body-count exploitation picture, with an especially confused ending, so any hoped-for microcosm of the human condition doesn't really pan out. Even so, it's diverting to sort through

Jacques Monseu struggles to resist the succubus charms of Erika Blanc in *La Plus longue nuit du diable* (1971)

Attempts at allegory notwithstanding, *La Plus longue nuit* is one of those delirious Euro-horrors of the period that seems to have everything – a ritzy score from Alessandro Alessandroni (complete with a breathy Morricone-style vocalist), a mix-and-match multi-national cast, an unconvincing and laboriously extended lesbian interlude, and a surfeit of elaborate settings, from an alchemical lab in the basement to a torture chamber in the attic. There's also an eye-catching range of 1970s hot pants and catsuits on view; in the fashion-conscious era of Biba, the film's costume designer is called simply Blanda. Even the Devil himself pops up, stoking a roadside bonfire at the beginning and making a phoney deal with the young seminarist at the end. Better still, he's played by the uniquely cadaverous Daniel Emilfork.

Best of all is a demonic female lead who seems to have stepped straight out of the glossy pages of *Nova*. As Hilse, Erika Blanc makes a thoroughly bewitching centrepiece, flashing her copper-coloured hair and Terry-Thomas tooth-gap prior to turning into a remorseless succubus whose flesh tones range from grey to green – and whose mere presence makes red roses turn black. Especially memorable is her look of utter contempt as the money-mad wife sifts through the gold dust in the Baron's laboratory, while her facial contortions as each victim expires indicate something of the pain she experiences in liquidating them.

As a welcome bonus, we're also given the traditional Grade-A actor muddling his way through arrant exploitation, in this case Jean Servais, erstwhile star of Jules Dassin's *Rififi* and coming hot-foot from his brief but scary turn in *Le Seuil du vide*. His role here is the exact opposite of his baleful gallery owner in the Davy film. "My main pleasure has been in searching for philosophical truths," the Baron says unhappily, a line in perfect accord with the affecting, spaniel-eyed resignation Servais brings to the character. The Baron has good reason to look sad; in a sepia-toned

## LA PLUS LONGUE NUIT DU DIABLE

*Belgium-Italy 1971*
*Italy: La terrificante notte dei demonio*
*US: The Devil's Nightmare*
*Cetelci (Brussels) / Delfino Film (Roma)*
*89 minutes colour*
*in production July 1971*

· · · · · · · · · · · · · · · · · · · · · · · · · · · ·

[credits as given on Belgian prints] Director of Photography: André Goeffers; Art Director: Jio Berk; Editor: P Panos; Sound: Jacques Eippers, Henri Morel; Costumes: Ballerina, Blanda; Music: Alessandro Alessandroni; Make-up: Duilio Giustini, Nancy Baudoux; Special Effects: Paul Defru; Screenplay: Patrice Rhomm, based on an original story by Pierre-Claude Garnier [as Charles Lecocq] and

Patrice Rhomm; Artistic Supervisor: André Hunebelle; Producer: Charles Lecocq [Pierre-Claude Garnier]; Director: Jean Brismée;

Erika Blanc (Hilse Müller); Jean Servais (Baron von Runberg); Daniel Emilfork (Satan); Lucien Raimbourg (Mr Mason); Jacques Monseu (Sorel, the seminarist); Colette Emmanuelle (Nancy Foster); Ivana Novak (Corinne); Shirley Corrigan (Régine); Frédérique Hender (Greta, the young midwife); Lorenzo Terzon (Howard Foster); Christian Maillet (Max Duchard, the tour guide); Maurice de Groote (Hans, the butler); Yvonne Garden (Martha, the housekeeper); Carol Ken (journalist)

OK for undemanding addicts; sufficiently unusual to appeal to slightly more demanding addicts who are on the lookout for something different ... It makes a change to meet a succubus instead of a vampire, and once the story really gets going there is a baroque splendour about the killings that goes a long way towards making up for the fact that the pace is slow and the dubbing mediocre. *CinemaTV Today* 16 September 1972

The producer came to Rome and said, "There is a scene that is not written in the script. It's a lesbian scene." Well, it is very soft, isn't it? But it was still very difficult for me to do ... It's strange because, watching the film on DVD the other day, in the beginning ... I suddenly saw myself looking down the aisle of the bus to see what the director was doing and they left that in – which was a mistake. *Shirley Corrigan* [quoted in *The Dark Side* August 2008]

the prospective victims – philandering husband, avaricious wife, slobbish tour guide, indolent sexpot, acquisitive sexpot, tetchy old man and priggish seminarist – and identify them as, respectively, Lust, Greed, Gluttony, Sloth, Envy, Anger and Pride.

World War II prologue, he killed his new-born child to avert the family curse – unaware that his elder brother Rudolf had already sired a daughter by the limping housemaid. That the film begins with a baby being stabbed in its cradle is an indication of the transgressive extremes to which film producers were being pushed by 1971. Inevitably, the scene contributes to an uncertainty of tone, given that the remainder of the film plays out as a lurid horror-comic.

Some of the comedy remains extremely droll, however. The Baron's former adjutant, Hans, has become his butler; he has a prominent bullet wound in his temple and is played by the splendidly sinister Belgian opera singer Maurice de Groote. Showing the visitors to their bedrooms, Hans recites a hilarious litany of the various horrors committed in them – a prince and princess having their throats cut in 1436, an exorcist butchered in 1575, a ghastly defenestration in 1738. (To add to the misery, the Baron later points out that his own brother "was burned alive in his tank at Stalingrad.") The comic tone later embraces kitsch, with the enticing Hilse appearing repeatedly in the seminarist's bedroom, challenging his Catholic rectitude by wearing skimpier clothes on each occasion.

The film's raison d'être, of course, is the sequence of killings that kicks in during the third act. All are well contrived, particularly a show-stopping scene of the grasping Nancy being sucked down into a gilded quicksand. Similarly impressive is the attic set-piece reserved for randy Howard and man-eating Corinne. Hilse wrestles the former onto a guillotine, while the latter recoils, screaming blue murder, into an Iron Maiden. The downward flash of the guillotine blade forms an amusing optical 'wipe', removing Hilse's white nightie and reinstating her trademark black catsuit. And the syrupy puddle of orange blood that seeps out of the Iron Maiden recalls not only the Massimo Pupillo film *Il boia scarlatto*, but also the gruesome Bram Stoker story *The Squaw*.

In 1972 the French paperback series 'Bibliothèque de l'étrange' kicked off with a novelisation of the film by its co-writer Patrice Rhomm. Using the film's alternative title *Au Service du diable* (In the Devil's Service), Rhomm revealed that the Baron's domain is called Wahlentod – ie, 'choose death'. A small but telling detail that might have enriched an already engaging film.

By May 1975 Rhomm was making a film of his own called *Draguse ou Le Manoir infernal* (Draguse or the Infernal House). This French-Swiss co-production shows a flash of wit right at the beginning, with Olivier Mathot musing in voice-over that "Some people encounter Ursula Andress or Brigitte Bardot in their dreams. Me, I get to meet a fanatic who thinks she's Nostradamus. And I've no way of waking up..." The remainder, however, devolves into a tedious semi-sex farce with occult trimmings. Mathot is a historian who, having been cajoled into writing an erotic novel ("Only sex sells nowadays"), holes up in a ghostly house and is granted visions of the saucy encounters that previously took place there. The portmanteau format, which only supervenes about halfway through, recalls the British film *The House that Dripped Blood*, while Mathot's predicament seems like a grindhouse prefiguration of *Sérail*, an arthouse enigma made six months after Rhomm's film. Neither of these pictures, however, offers the unedifying spectacle of Monica Swinn's nude succubus, Draguse, masturbating with a femur.

## FOUR SCORPIONS IN A WOMAN'S SKIN KILL MULTIPLE TIMES

When making *La Plus longue nuit du diable*, Erika Blanc was fresh from performing an eye-popping striptease in Emilio Miraglia's splendidly titled but otherwise uninspired *La notte che Evelyn uscì dalla tomba* (The Night Evelyn Came Out of the Grave). Emerging arse-first from a coffin, she blows out artfully arranged candles and inflames the desires of mad English aristocrat Anthony Steffen. Part of a fiendish (and increasingly mildewed) plot to drive Steffen insane with supposed visions of his dead wife, Blanc expires at the end when repeatedly stabbed by Marina Malfatti, herself awash with poisoned champagne.

Miraglia's film was typical of a provocative new strain of giallo that emerged in the early 1970s, films residing, as Tim Lucas has observed, "very much

Marina Malfatti struggles against strychnine poisoning in the Gothic giallo *La notte che Evelyn uscì dalla tomba* (1971)

within that druggy period ... when the foibles of human perception seemed poised to overtake graphic violence as the major tenet of that sub-genre, and when young filmmakers rejected watertight mystery to drown in liberating excess (nudity, kinky sex, directorial flourishes)."[42] The several other examples of the type graced by Blanc's sensual presence range from Renzo Russo's threadbare *La rossa dalla pelle che scotta* (The Red Headed Corpse, 1972) to Sauro Scavolini's oneiric *Amore e morte nel giardino degli dei* (Love and Death in the Garden of the Gods), both released in the second half of 1972.

Out at the same time, though Blanc-free, was another Emilio Miraglia film in which, again, the supposed phantom is called Evelyn. In *La dama rossa uccide sette volte* (The Lady in Red Kills Seven Times), Barbara Bouchet and Marina Malfatti are embroiled in a series of bloody murders, the most startling of which involves an asylum escapee falling chin-first onto a spiked railing. Like Miraglia's previous film, *La dama rossa* inhabits the Gothic sub-section of the giallo, with a climax (Bouchet assailed by slithering rats in a rapidly water-filling crypt)

Julián Ugarte, Edwige Fenech and Ivan Rassimov trapped in 'a labyrinth of terror, madness, witchcraft and death' in *Tutti i colori del buio* (1971)

straight out of *The Perils of Pauline*. The film also echoes *La Plus longue nuit du diable* in its garbled story of an ancient curse visited on the daughters of an aristocratic German family.

In the wake of Dario Argento's crystal plumage, the giallo was enjoying an explosion of popularity, giving rise to a long series of stylish but increasingly mechanical thrillers. Sergio Martino proved himself one of the most accomplished directors in the field with *Lo strano vizio della Signora Wardh*, which he started shooting in August 1970.

Here, Mrs Wardh's 'strange vice' is glossed by her sadistic ex-lover as "a blood fetish that turns her on." Ernesto Gastaldi's script tells an unusually coherent story of a woman apparently under threat from Vienna's resident razor killer but in fact the victim of the three conspiratorial men in her life. Martino, meanwhile, sets out his stall with a fusillade of eye-catching effects. The beauteous Mrs Wardh, for example, fantasises being ravished in a rain-lashed forest or

being lightly scored with a broken bottle in an eerily shadowed limbo. Elsewhere there's a shower murder, a black-gloved stalker in an underground car park, lizards in the dark and a bleeding body in a bathtub, plus a splendid set-piece in which a rush to rescue the heroine from a gas-filled kitchen is orchestrated by her steadily faltering heartbeat. On top of all this there's a blackmailer who rather improbably demands 20,000 shillings when what he means is £1000, together with a ravishing abundance of location filming when the action moves to the coast near Barcelona.

For his three subsequent gialli, all scripted by Gastaldi, Martino retained the four leading players of *Mrs Wardh* in various permutations. In March 1971 George Hilton and Alberto de Mendoza were enlisted for *La coda dello scorpione* (The Scorpion's Tail). Later that year Martino cast Edwige Fenech, Ivan Rassimov and Hilton again in *Tutti i colori del buio* (All the Colours of the Dark), and by July 1972 Fenech and Rassimov were working on *Il tuo vizio è una stanza chiusa e solo io ne ho la chiave* (Your Vice is a Locked Room and Only I Have the Key). This last, however, reserved its leading roles for two other giallo regulars, with Luigi Pistilli and Anita Strindberg scheming each other's deaths in a story very loosely modelled on Poe's *The Black Cat*.

Of these films *Tutti i colori del buio* is arguably the most alluring, containing as it does a crazed agglomeration of psychedelic effects to illustrate Fenech's mounting paranoia, not forgetting a satanic cult that pushes the film closer to supernatural horror than the average giallo. (Working from yet another Gastaldi script, Martino's avowed influence was the Polanski hit *Rosemary's Baby*.) The cult leader is Julián Ugarte, the trimly goateed Spanish actor familiar from *Malenka* and *La marca del hombre lobo*; he starts by drinking the blood of a sacrificed dog prior to a kaleidoscopic ravishment of Fenech that composer Bruno Nicolai overlays with the wailings of the damned. "The dreams I have are like horror stories," Fenech complains, and to prove the point Martino comes up with such arresting tableaux as an elderly couple frozen in death over their breakfast newspapers.

For British viewers, the film is also distinguished by its locations, with Hilton and Fenech residing at Putney's Kenilworth Court and the cult itself located at Wykehurst Park in West Sussex. (The latter would subsequently be used in the British chillers *Demons of the Mind* and *The Legend of Hell House*.) As a result, the usual giallo incomprehensibility is further bolstered by geographical craziness. At one point Fenech flees the remorseless Ivan Rassimov by taking the tube from Aldwych to Holland Park (just one stop, apparently), then she steps more or less directly into Bishops Park in Putney – the same riverside location, incidentally, that four years later would see a momentous meeting between Gregory Peck and Patrick Troughton in *The Omen*.

Of Martino's star names, George Hilton and Edwige Fenech, in particular, were to become totemic figures in the bloodstained landscape of the giallo, appearing together, for example, in Giuliano Carnimeo's one-and-only entry into the field, the Gastaldi-scripted *Perché quelle strane gocce di sangue sul corpo di Jennifer?* (What Are Those Strange Drops of Blood on Jennifer's Body?). Shot in January 1972, this one had its typically extravagant title moderated for export to *The Case of the Bloody Iris*. In an indication of the way these films were 'exported' on several levels other than mere distribution, Carnimeo's opening elevator murder was fulsomely quoted in Brian De Palma's 1980 smash *Dressed to Kill*.

For his part, Dario Argento followed up *Il gatto a nove code* with a much more macabre murder-mystery, *4 mosche di velluto grigio* (Four Flies on Grey Velvet), which he started shooting in mid-July 1971. Here, rock drummer Roberto Tobias (Michael Brandon) corners a stalker in a derelict theatre and apparently kills him, triggering off a series of murders that also involves his porcelain-delicate wife Nina (Mimsy Farmer). Along the way there are several touches of the sexual confusion that was to become more and more prevalent in later Argento films, among them a housemaid who looks like a man and a female killer brought up as a boy, together with a gay man in the traditionally 'straight' role of private detective. This character – though pointedly introduced while doing some interior decorating and even more pointedly meeting his end in a public lavatory – transcends the threatened gay stereotype purely because he's so engagingly played by Jean-Pierre Marielle, whose casting was a happy outcome of the film's half-French status.

In addition to sexual ambiguity, the film is fuller than ever of Argento's stylistic wizardry. A dazzling credits sequence, for example, alternates views of a redly palpitating heart with a mosquito being smartly squished between Roberto's cymbals. Later, Roberto is plagued by nightmare visions of a public execution in which the head only flies off the fourth time we see it, and poor Francine Racette bumps vertiginously down a flight of stairs as a butcher knife plunges smoothly towards her screaming face. Argento also pays explicit homage to Jacques Tourneur's *The Leopard Man* in a horribly suspenseful sequence in which the maid (Marisa Fabbri) finds herself trapped in an after-hours public park. A bizarre visit to the 'Fifth International Exhibition of Funerary Arts' yields a wryly self-reflexive allusion to "all these worms making a living out of death," and Argento rounds the whole thing off with a charmingly ridiculous plot twist based on the idea that "the last image seen by the victim before death is retained for several hours on the retina." But Argento's final burst of visual audacity – a slow-motion car smash filmed with a 1000-fps camera – falls strangely flat.

Few gialli could match Argento's skin-crawling imagery in *4 mosche* of a doll-masked photographer lurking in the shadows of a theatre box, but there was seemingly no stopping them, with the films on offer ranging from the elegant and well-crafted to the bloody and blatantly exploitative. *La tarantola del ventre nero* (The Black Belly of the Tarantula), directed by Paolo Cavara in May 1971, is a splendid example of the former type, boasting a series of paralysis murders at an exclusive health spa (including notably grisly deaths for Barbara Bouchet and Barbara Bach), a typically seductive Ennio Morricone score, a dazzling rooftop chase sequence, and an excellent performance from Giancarlo Giannini as the conflicted policeman hero. It also works a smart variation on the usual routine, replacing the killer's regulation black leather gauntlets with a nastily transparent pair of masseur's gloves.

Though exported as plain *Torso*, Sergio Martino's *I corpi presentano tracce di violenza carnale* (1972) announces its membership of the second group via its original title, which translates as 'The Corpses Show Signs of Sexual Violence'. Actually, rape isn't on the agenda of this particular killer; instead, his infantile rationale is spelt out in words that parallel the treatment within the film itself of its outstandingly beautiful, but apparently disposable, actresses. "They were only dolls," he gabbles, "stupid dolls made out of flesh and blood ... I hacked them to pieces like dolls." Accordingly, the film, co-written by Ernesto Gastaldi, contains a bona-fide low point in cynical misogyny when a bare-breasted woman (Conchita Airoldi) is brutally strangled in a welter of mud. Bare breasts were clearly *Torso*'s raison d'être, and there's certainly no shortage of them in the finished product. Suzy Kendall remains clothed, however, even during a moderately

EL VICIO ES COMO UNA
JAULA CON LA PUERTA
ABIERTA....
DE LA QUE, UNA VEZ
DENTRO, NADIE DESEA
SALIR.

"Edgar Allan Poe"

FLORINDA BOLKAN
JEAN SOREL
STANLEY BAKER,
LEO GENN
en

UN REPTIL
CON PIEL DE MUJER

Escrita y dirigida por LUCIO FULCI · EN TECHNICOLOR

For reasons of their own, the Mexican distributors of *Una lucertola con la pelle di donna* (1970) advertised the film with a Poe quote

good-value cast matching giallo regulars Jean Sorel and Alberto de Mendoza with Elsa Martinelli and the dazzling, double-faced Marisa Mell, Fulci crafted one of the most alluring of all Swinging Sixties time-capsules – but with only some gloating views of a decomposing corpse to indicate his late-70s destiny as Italy's uncontested gore maestro. There were several more such indications, however, in the exceptional film that followed. *Beatrice Cenci* was a 16th century historical subject (previously filmed by Riccardo Freda in 1956), boasting scenes of brutally realistic torture in which Fulci indulged his anti-clericalism. Shot in August 1969, by 13 December it was being described in *La Stampa* as a "giallo storico (un po' sexy)" – a slightly sexy historical giallo.

suspenseful third act in which she's trapped alone with the killer in a remote clifftop mansion.

Having made provocative British films like *The Penthouse* and *Up the Junction*, Kendall's stint in Argento's *L'uccello dalle piume di cristallo* led first to *Torso* and then to Umberto Lenzi's *Spasmo*. The latter, which started shooting under the Pink Floyd-like title *Dark Shadow on the Moon* at Halloween 1973, features Robert Hoffman as an unknowing homicidal maniac and Ivan Rassimov as his saturnine brother, who sublimates the same tendencies by puncturing various eerie-looking female mannequins. As well as being rather boring, *Spasmo* sets itself off from the pack by featuring virtually nothing in the blood and breasts department. The following year Lenzi rectified this apparent oversight in the inane *Gatti rossi in un labirinto di vetro*, in which a group of tourists in Barcelona, augmented by *Torso*'s John Richardson, are victimised by a red-garbed, eye-removing serial killer. In the USA that intriguing title 'Red Cats in a Glass Labyrinth' became simply *Eyeball*.

Another key contributor to this halcyon period for the giallo was Lucio Fulci. Having helped devise the story for Riccardo Freda's *A doppia faccia*, Fulci went to San Francisco in December 1968 – then riding high as a film location thanks to the recent release of the Peter Yates thriller *Bullitt* – to direct *Una sull'altra* (One on Top of the Other), a glamorous *Vertigo* variant exported as *Perversion Story*. With terrific work from cinematographer Alejandro Ulloa and composer Riz Ortolani, plus a

Fulci's next giallo, *Una lucertola con la pelle di donna* (A Lizard in a Woman's Skin), took him to London in September 1970. There, cinematographer Luigi Kuveiller made the most of some arresting location work while Fulci engaged the services of top-flight local actors like Stanley Baker, Leo Genn and Basil Dignam. (The latter, perplexingly, goes uncredited.) It's Genn who comes up with an especially astute suggestion when analysing the ordeal undergone by his beautiful daughter (Florinda Bolkan): "I wonder if someone's trying to drive her out of her mind?" He's wrong, as it turns out, though it doesn't make much difference; like so many gialli, *Una lucertola* is a complete dead loss as a whodunit. Instead the viewer merely settles back and enjoys Fulci's unfettered artistry in hurling nightmare visions at the beleaguered Bolkan, among them white-faced nudes in an asylum corridor, zombie-like creatures sitting in judgment, and (bizarrely) a giant goose soaring after her in pursuit. Climactically, she repeatedly stabs Anita Strindberg with a paper knife. But did she dream it or actually do it?

Venturing much further with *Una lucertola* into the horror territory that would later become his stock in trade, Fulci garnishes a protracted chase sequence shot at Alexandra Palace with several grisly asides. Bolkan, for example, is attacked by a very persistent cloud of bats in an organ loft and – even more randomly – stumbles into a laboratory featuring four gruesomely vivisected dogs. (In the film, this gratuitously nasty moment is never alluded to again, but it was certainly alluded to by Italian authorities after the film's release. Special effects man Carlo Rambaldi reportedly had to bring his fake dogs into court to prevent Fulci from being tried for animal cruelty.) Beyond these freakishly unmotivated set-pieces, the viewer is left with one of Ennio Morricone's most seductive lounge scores, a typically riveting performance from Stanley Baker, and a narrative attitude towards hippies and the counterculture that's unenlightened to say the least.

It would be tempting to call Fulci's next giallo a rush job, given that it started shooting on 12 May 1972 and was in Italian cinemas by late September. But it comes across as anything but. Filmed in Monte Sant'Angelo in Apulia, *Non si sevizia un paperino* (Don't Torture a Duckling) is unusual in its emphasis, not on vapid jet-setters, but on an atavistic rural community disrupted by a rash of child murders. Brunello Rondi's *Il demonio* seems to have been an influence, with a police inspector musing that "We can build motorways but we can't overcome ignorance and superstition." Prime suspect is a so-called 'witch' (Bolkan again), who is killed by several local men in a truly brutal scene made even nastier by incongruous rock music issuing from a nearby car radio. Fulci assembles his ingredients with a masterful hand – Bolkan's crudely fashioned effigies of the children, tracker dogs scouring a muddy forest in pouring rain, and a glamorous but decidedly equivocal heroine (Barbara Bouchet) who takes an unhealthy interest in little boys. The film is overlong, however, and an exciting clifftop climax is made ridiculous when the real killer takes a dive; the graphic destruction of a totally unconvincing doll is shown in ill-advised detail on the downward plunge.

True to his anti-Catholic bent, a priest looms large in Fulci's film, and the same is true of *Cosa avete fatto a Solange?* (What Have You Done to Solange?), which Massimo Dallamano shot in London in September-October 1971. Here, Dallamano brings unwonted style to a story focused on British schoolgirls being stabbed in their vaginas. Added to the cast so the film could be marketed in Germany as an Edgar Wallace picture, Joachim Fuchsberger and Karin Baal may well have wondered at the boundaries of taste that had been broken in the ten years since their last joint-appearance in a Wallace film, *Die toten Augen von London*. Just as luckless a schoolgirl as she was in Spain's *La residencia*, Cristina Galbó puzzles, Argento style, over exactly what she saw when vaguely witnessing one of the murders, only to get murdered herself before the halfway point. The film has lots of nice views of South Kensington, Fuchsberger is very good indeed, and Dallamano even conjures a borderline-tragic ending

when the traumatised killer is revealed – quite a suprising development for a film predicated on dead teenagers with knives between their thighs.

## BLOOD CAKE AND MEAT SOUP
In 1971, those ubiquitous Spanish faces Romy, Julián Ugarte and Luis Ciges – all three of them veterans of Suárez's *Aoom* and Esteva's *Metamorfosis* – cropped up in yet another avant-garde item, *Pastel de sangre* (Cake of Blood).

This is a portmanteau in which the four stories – or slices – are entirely discrete, with no connecting material whatsoever. The first one, José María Vallés' *Tarota* (Tarot), cooks up some beguiling mediaeval atmosphere as Ugarte, playing an itinerant Bergmanesque knight, stumbles across an undead beauty in a ruined church and is apparently converted by her into a baby. The rebirth theme leads into Emilio Martínez-Lázaro's utterly inert *Victor Frankenstein*, in which creator instructs creation to "slash throats and tear off limbs" but nothing nearly so arresting actually takes place. Francesc Bellmunt's much more engaging *Terror entre cristianos* (Terror Among the Christians) has a Roman senator venturing into a Celtic wood and falling prey to vampires; a beetle traverses his cloak when he indulges his new appetite the next day. Finally, Jaime Chávarri's *La danza* (The Dance) is a murky home-invasion scenario in which the credulous Ciges is cajoled by Romy's spectral husband (José Lifante) into killing her, after which all three dance their way into the closing credits. Sadly, the cumulative effect of *Pastel de sangre* is severely compromised by that disastrous second segment.

The four stories in *Pastel de sangre* were the work of industry newcomers. Around the same time, another young filmmaker, the Basque director Eloy de la Iglesia, was making a much more substantial contribution to what might loosely be termed the art-house end of Spain's horror boom. He set his films apart with the use of political themes that, though veiled, are nevertheless comprehensible – and also by insisting on conventionally gripping thriller scenarios.

Not merely gay but also a fully paid-up member of the Communist Party, Iglesia made his first big impact in 1969 with the controversial drama *Algo amargo en la boca* (Something Bitter in the Mouth). Attracted to stories of marginalised characters, he went on to make four deeply subversive pictures in little more than two years, all of which seem just as hard-hitting in the 21st century. "Conscious," as he put it, "that I live in a society full of repressed people," Iglesia explained in a 1973 interview that "These [four] stories can be reduced to one – a story about death, love and a peculiar 'voyeurism' where characters constantly watch each other, pursue each other. I relate my obsessions through a prism of repression."[43]

Only 26 when he made the first of these films, Iglesia enlisted something of a horror specialist as his co-writer on all four. Antonio Fos had already scripted León Klimovsky's *Ella y el miedo* (Ella and Fear, 1964) and Alfonso Brescia's Italian-Spanish-Moroccan co-production *Il tuo dolce corpo da uccidere* (Your Sweet Body to Kill, 1970), murder-mysteries echoing *The Spiral Staircase* and *Les Diaboliques* respectively. He would subsequently write another giallo for Brescia, the provocatively titled *Ragazza tutta nuda assassinata nel parco* (Completely Naked Girl Murdered in the Park, 1973), as well as collaborating with Eugenio Martín, Klimovsky again and, eventually, Paul Naschy.

The first of Iglesia's quartet, *El techo de cristal* (The Glass Ceiling), finished shooting in the last week of June 1970. During the credits sequence, the camera prowls around the desolate-looking exterior of an apartment building, with footfalls crunching on gravel, birds twittering gaily and dogs panting thirstily in an outdoor cage. It's a disconcerting opening, though the apparently derelict building turns out to be fully tenanted; in fact, its equivocal landlord (Dean Selmier) calls it "the house of lonely wives." Among them is Marta (Carmen Sevilla), who in her isolation begins to suspect that her upstairs neighbour, Julia (Patty Shepard), has murdered her husband.

If Iglesia intended the house as a microcosm of modern Spain, it's a relentlessly grim one, featuring boorish macho seducers as well as lonely wives, carnivorous pigs as well as panting dogs and, in the basement, a furnace described as "a miniature gate of Hell" and a woodpile concealing a foul-smelling dead rat. There's also a resident voyeur whose presence is indicated by sudden still-frames of the unaware women, all of them accompanied by an ominous clicking sound. (At one point, the culprit quotes Godard's dictum that "Cinema is truth 24 times per second.") The whole stew of unhealthy ingredients comes to a head in Marta's grisly nightmare sequence, complete with cut-throat razors, severed fingers, a grey face submerged in sludge-like offal, and a dead man folded up in a fridge – this last explicitly recalling the frigidaired Judy Matheson in Aranda's *Las crueles*. The nocturnal climax includes a stalker sporting giallo-style black gloves and a twist ending compounded of both *Les Diaboliques* and *Strangers on a Train*. Throughout, Iglesia makes great use of the forbiddingly beautiful features of Patty Shepard, who at the time was between Paul Naschy engagements on *Los monstruos del terror* and *La noche de Walpurgis*.

Iglesia's next project focused on a reluctant serial killer and began shooting in mid-August 1971 as *Auténtico caldo de cultivo*. The 'genuine meat soup' of the title had a political double-meaning, in that it could also be translated as 'genuine breeding ground' – strongly suggesting that the repressive Spain of the Franco era was a crucible for madness, murder and, for most average citizens, marginalisation. Though the title was later changed to the more innocuous *La semana del asesino* (The Week of the Killer), the finished film still ran into major censorship difficulties, with up to 100 cuts being insisted on. And there was worse to come. In 1983 the film was featured on a list of 72 supposed 'Video Nasties' concocted by self-appointed moral guardians in the UK. It was made conspicuous by its ridiculous, and inaccurate, English-language title *The Cannibal Man*, not to mention truly frightful footage of cows having their throats slit in an abattoir. Otherwise, the film is a really gripping art-house allegory of early 1970s Spain, with squalour and insanity encroaching, concealed corpses piling up, and (again) the stench becoming overpowering.

> Slaughterhouse worker Marcos is on a night out with his fiancée Paula when he accidentally kills a taxi driver. When Paula insists on reporting the matter to the police, he panics and strangles her. Four more killings ensue and the bodies are stashed in Marcos' bedroom, though he removes parts of them for disposal at the meat-processing plant. Unknown to him, a cultivated gay man, Néstor, is monitoring his every move – with binoculars.

When 40-year-old Vicente Parra made *La semana del asesino*, the glamour of an old-style matinée idol still clung to him thanks to his role as Alfonso XII in a couple of florid royal romances made in the late 1950s. Affirming his commitment to changing his image, he actually served as associate producer on the Iglesia film. Indeed, there can have been few more radical image-changes in cinema history, with Iglesia converting Parra from the noble king of popular cinematic memory into a tragically conflicted working-class loser, embroiling him in a relentlessly grim scenario involving not merely murder and mutilation but also a heavy dose of sexual ambiguity. In doing so Iglesia was making a sardonic comment on the fragility – deep-rooted but swaggeringly concealed – of Spain's macho culture.

Marcos is a pitiful figure from the start. We learn very quickly that he is inured to institutionalised violence (he munches nonchalantly on a sandwich as blood from inverted cows froths into a nearby floor grille), and we soon realise just how cowardly and shiftless he is in his personal relationships. After muttering various evasions regarding his commitment to Paula, he makes out with her in the back of a cab and arouses the anti-permissive fury of the driver. "I don't run a bordello," the driver fumes. "What are you, some kind of homosexual?" replies Marcos (a remark that will gain in significance as the film progresses), after which he's ejected onto the pavement and clubs the cabbie with a stone. This unthinking flurry of violence is relatively minor given the intensity of the murder scenes that follow.

Marcos lives in a humble isolated bungalow on a piece of arid wasteland symbolically overlooked by swanky high-rise apartment blocks. There, Iglesia piles on the claustrophobia with an oppressive sound mix that recalls Polanski's *Repulsion* just as much as the accumulating victims do. A clock ticks conspicuously as Marcos and Paula make love, with the screen whiting out at the moment of orgasm; then the clock starts up again, unnaturally loud, as he simultaneously kisses and throttles her. Iglesia's brutal exchange of massive close-ups – their interlocked lips, Marcos' strangling thumbs – is the cue for a rapid spiral into madness and despair, with the sweaty atmosphere of oppression encircling not just Marcos but also the viewer.

Soon enough Marcos' younger brother Esteban, his fiancée Carmen and Carmen's inquisitive father join Paula in the bedroom mortuary, while Marcos stockpiles ineffective air-freshener and neighbourhood dogs begin to snuffle at his door. Iglesia doesn't skimp on the horror of these killings, either – the brother is brained with a wrench, Carmen has her throat cut *extremely* slowly and the investigative father gets a cleaver in the face. To add to the horror, the story takes on a Sweeney Todd aspect via Marcos' disposal of body parts at the meat factory.

Marcos' crimes are born of his pathological fear of the police, a fear many Spaniards could empathise with at the time, and one of the film's most powerful scenes shows Marcos and Néstor being quizzed by policemen at a late-night café. Realising Néstor lives in the expensive new tower blocks, the officers waive the

requirement to see his ID but they cut the nervy working-class Marcos no such slack. The final section of the film is devoted to the two men's burgeoning relationship, an equivocal attraction which the confused Marcos never fully comprehends. Having taken time out, in a grippingly suspenseful sequence,

## LA SEMANA DEL ASESINO

Spain 1971
West Germany / UK: *The Cannibal Man*
US: *The Apartment on the 13th Floor*
José Truchado PC
104 minutes (Spain) 98 minutes (export) colour
production began 16 August 1971

...........................

Director of Photography: Raúl Artigot;
Editor: Joe Louis Matesanz; Music:
Fernando G Morcillo; Make-up: Gregorio
Mendiri; Special Effects: [Manuel]
Baquero; Screenplay: Eloy de la Iglesia,
Antonio Fos; Dialogue for English version:

Robert H Oliver; Producer: José Truchado;
Director: Eloy de la Iglesia

Vicente Parra (Marcos); Emma Cohen (Paula);
Eusebio Poncela (Néstor); Vicky Lagos (Rosa);
Lola Herrera (Carmen); Charly Bravo (Esteban);
Manuel Clavo (Tipo); Antonio Corencia, Antonio
Fernández del Real, Ángel Blanco (factory
workers); José Franco (shopkeeper); Rafael
Hernández (Agustín); Emilio Hortela; Goyo Lebrero
(taxi driver); Ismael Merlo (personnel officer);
Antonio Orengo (waiter); Fernando Sánchez Polack
(Señor Ambrosio); Valentín Tornos (worker)

**Grisliness, morbidity and psychological suspense go hand in hand ... [but] in terms of demonstrating Spanish cinema's capacity for addressing the thriller genre, the film ranks below [Iglesia's] El techo de cristal. And that's a shame, because, technically, Eloy de la Iglesia has constructed the picture well, knowing how to move the camera, succeeding in capturing little details (humdrum as well as dramatic), and obtaining scenes of considerable depth.** ABC Sevilla 5 May 1972

*La semana del asesino is a genuinely sincere film in which I try to show myself as I am, launching myself head-on against all those obstacles that are already too tedious to discuss. Obviously I've made other films too, but those were cynical juggling exercises where I tried, in part, to disguise my own shamelessness. Eloy de la Iglesia [quoted in Nuevo Fotogramas 2 March 1973]*

Vicente Parra wonders what to do with the remains of Lola Herrera and Charly Bravo
in *La semana del asesino* (1971)

to sleep with and murder an affectionate waitress, Marcos gets a glimpse of how the other half lives when visiting Néstor's plush high-rise apartment. He also gets a crumb of genuine comfort. Néstor, who has witnessed all Marcos' crimes from on high, tells him, "You're alone and you're sad and you need some help."

Disingenuously, Iglesia and co-writer Fos assured the censors that Néstor was emphatically *not* homosexual, when of course he clearly is. Iglesia capitulated to pressure, however, by finally having Marcos call the police and confess to his half-dozen murders. Despite this last-minute adulteration, *La semana del asesino* is a tough-to-watch but extraordinarily powerful film. Even at the time, reviewer Ángeles Masó conceded that "it turns out to be a picture of some importance ... in the currently much-promoted genre of cinematografía sangrienta."[44] In particular, the image of Esteban and Carmen tucked up neatly in bed amid a welter of blood and buzzing flies is arguably the most macabre vignette the Spanish horror boom produced.

By May 1972, when *La semana* opened, Iglesia was shooting *Nadie oyó gritar* (No One Heard the Scream), a film that begins with a funkily fashionable credits sequence suggestive of a super-sophisticated romantic comedy. What develops is anything but. A prologue composed of London location work features a Piccadilly hoarding for Hitchcock's newly released *Frenzy*, which is appropriate given that Iglesia's film is a really brilliant psychological thriller in Hitchcock mode. Uniting the popular stars of his previous films, Carmen Sevilla and Vicente Parra, Iglesia cast them as the only residents of another of those swanky Spanish apartment blocks. There, Sevilla's Elisa stumbles upon Parra's Miguel as he disposes of his wife's body down the elevator shaft.

The rootless Elisa, supported by an older London sugar daddy and herself supporting a beau 20 years her junior, is forced into half-fascinated complicity with a failed writer who suggests that her assistance is "the standard thing any good neighbour would do."

There are a couple of quotes from *Psycho* – the corpse is concealed in a shower curtain and for an agonising moment it fails to sink when dumped in a lake – but Iglesia's main concern is to show the various levels of entrapment, social and sexual, in which these characters find themselves. And in the last ten minutes he springs a truly startling twist, bringing with it yet deeper entrapment. Iglesia also features his trademark homoeroticism via 21-year-old Tony Isbert, cast as Sevilla's young lover and modelling some barely-there swimwear.

By now Iglesia's films had made sufficient impact to invite parody, as when a note from the 1972 Berlin Film Festival, reprinted in the letters section of *Nuevo Fotogramas* on 7 July, was waggishly signed 'Un asesino de cristal con algo dulce en el techo' (A Glass Killer with Something Sweet on the Ceiling), thus amalgamating three Iglesia titles into one. The fourth in Iglesia's loose horror quartet sported an array of titles that were almost as bizarre. Originally called *La agonía del siglo XX* (The Death Throes of the 20th Century), it went on release as *Una gota de sangre para morir amando* (A Drop of Blood to Die Loving). Ignoring its classy export title *Murder in a Blue World*, the film's US distributor called it *Clockwork*

The kiss of death for US imports Sue Lyon and Chris Mitchum in *Una gota de sangre para morir amando* (1972)

*Terror*, acknowledging Iglesia's many playful references to Stanley Kubrick's *A Clockwork Orange*, a film so controversial it had been banned in Spain. Unfortunately, Iglesia's detractors on home ground acknowledged these echoes in a different way, contemptuously referring to the film as 'La mandarina mecánica' (The Clockwork Tangerine). By February 1973 Iglesia was forced to write an explanatory article called 'Mi película es un homenaje a Kubrick, nunca un plagio' (My Film is a Tribute to Kubrick, Not a Rip-Off).[45]

Having played *Lolita* ten years before, Iglesia's star, Sue Lyon, was herself a Kubrick reference, a point made explicit in the film when blood spatters onto a copy of Nabokov's original novel. Even more explicit is an early scene in which, just moments after a TV announcer has trailed a screening of *A Clockwork Orange*, a family is assaulted in their home by a brutal gang of whip-cracking leather boys. The film is garnished with dystopian glimpses of the future only a step or two removed from Iglesia's present, particularly via inane commercials for 'sexy' underwear and blue-tinted alcoholic drinks. But it only gets into its stride, cooking up a great deal of character-based tension, when Lyon's poised young nurse is blackmailed by one of the youthful thugs (Chris Mitchum), for she's actually a scalpel-wielding serial killer who maintains glibly that "They were all dead before I killed them." Her doctor boyfriend (Jean Sorel) is working on imposing conformity via electro-shock therapy, and when Mitchum is subjected to it the film spirals to a predictably bloody conclusion. Iglesia's satirical point is eventually blunted by over-length, but at least there's a really shattering coda in which supposedly re-conditioned criminals start butchering each other over a high-class dinner table.

In March 1973 Iglesia was announced by Lotus Films as the man behind their next project, *The Mummy's Secret*. This was a curious clash, given that at the time Lotus were making a Paul Naschy vehicle called *La venganza de la momia* (The Vengeance of the Mummy). For whatever reason, Iglesia's take on the mummy went unmade. Presumably still smarting from the 'plagiarism' controversy stirred up by the Kubrick-isms of *Una gota de sangre*, from this point on he left the field of avant-garde horror to others.

## WELL-HEELED YET WAXY

Having made the Western *Roy Colt & Winchester Jack* in 1970, Mario Bava returned to horror in January the following year with a film that pushed the envelope in terms of gruesome spectacle – and which was to be seen under a bewildering multiplicity of titles. The original treatment was called *Odore di carne* (Stench of Flesh), yet the working title was *Così imparano a fare i cattivi* (Thus We Learn to Commit Evil). It was seen at the fourth Sitges Festival in October 1971 as *Antefatto* (Before the Fact), winning the Best Special Effects prize, and subsequently, under the same title, at the first Avoriaz Festival in February 1973. In the meantime, the film had been released in Italy as *Ecologia del delitto* (Ecology of Murder) and *Reazione a catena* (Chain Reaction), not faring particularly well under either title. In other territories, it became, among other things, *Carnage*, *Bloodbath*, *A Bay of Blood* and – surely one of the greatest of all exploitation titles – *Twitch of the Death Nerve*. For simplicity's sake we'll call it *Antefatto* here, if only because it takes up less space.

With *Antefatto* Bava provided a complete blueprint for a long stream of US slasher films by the simple expedient of stripping away the giallo's pretence of plot and just going for broke with a series of hideous murders. (Carlo Rambaldi did the effects.) The characters are almost entirely negligible, especially a quartet of irritating teens riding around in a dune buggy; the only exceptions are Luigi Pistilli and former *Thunderball* star Claudine Auger, playing a husband-and-wife team scheming to get their hands on an inheritance. Bava shows something of his old flair in a shadowy opening, in which the great Isa Miranda is shockingly dispatched and her wheelchair spokes slowly stop turning as her life ebbs out. Elsewhere, ugly zooms supervene as machetes plunge through faces and slice through necks; a squid writhes on a waterlogged corpse and two of the teens are skewered à deux while having sex, with the body count hitting 13 in total. Based on its pervasive influence, *Antefatto* has since become Bava's most overrated film. Significantly, its US distributor later had a hand in financing the 1980 release *Friday the 13th*, which came out, oddly enough, a fortnight after Bava's death. The rest is history.

By the first week of October 1971, Bava had been coaxed over to Austria by independent producer Alfredo Leone for a German-Italian co-production that saw him back on form. Working from a script by the US screenwriter Vincent Fotre, Bava was here handling a project as backward-looking as *Antefatto* was forward-looking; indeed, its echoes of the 1953 classic *House of Wax* inspired Leone to court that film's star, Vincent Price, for the title role – *Baron Blood*. The part eventually went to an old colleague of Price's from Orson Welles' Mercury Theatre Company, Joseph Cotten.

*Peter Kleist arrives in Austria to inspect his ancestral castle, the gloomy Schloss des Teufels. Former home of the notorious 16th century sadist Baron Otto von Kleist, it's in the process of being renovated as a tourist attraction. Assisting on site is architecture student Eva Arnold, who is recruited by Peter to join him in a ritual involving an ancient parchment. Inscribed on it is a witch's incantation for reviving Baron Otto.*

"We all want to know where we come from, and from whom," says Antonio Cantáfora's clean-cut Peter on arriving in Vienna. Like the characters played by Basil Rathbone in *Son of Frankenstein* and Richard Carlson in *The Maze*, Peter is one of those cosmopolitan types who makes a foolhardy return to the haunted Europe of his ancestors. It's a plot device perfectly attuned

Franco Tocci
shadows tiny
Nicoletta Elmi in
the German-Italian
chiller *Baron Blood*
(1971)

## BARON BLOOD

*West Germany-Italy 1971*
*Italy: Gli orrori del castello di Norimberga*
*Dieter Geissler Filmproduktion / Euro America*
  *Produzioni Cinematografiche*
*98 minutes colour*
*production began 2 October 1971*
. . . . . . . . . . . . . . . . . . . . . . . . . . . .
Director of Photography: Antonio Rinaldi
and [uncredited] Mario Bava; Art Director:
Enzo Bulgarelli; Editor: Carlo Reali; Sound:
Carlo Tarchi; Music: Stelvio Cipriani; Music
[English-language version]: Les Baxter;
Make-up: Silvana Petri; Special Effects:

Franco Tocci; Screenplay: Vincent Fotre;
English-language version: William A
Bairn; Producer: Alfredo Leone; Director:
Mario Bava

Joseph Cotten (Alfred Becker); Elke Sommer (Eva
Arnold); Massimo Girotti (Dr Karl Hummel);
Rada Rassimov (Christina Hoffmann); Antonio
Cantáfora (Peter Kleist); Humi [Umberto]
Raho (police inspector); Dieter Tressler (Mayor
Dortmundt); Luciano Pigozzi (Fritz); uncredited:
Nicoletta Elmi (Gretchen); Gustavo De Nardo
(Dr Hesse); Franco Tocci (Baron Otto)

**Told in accordance with all the conventions common to this type of picture
– full of worthwhile cues for suspense and packing an effective charge of
terror – the film showcases, albeit in a minor key, the detailed and expert
direction of Mario Bava, whose unmistakable style is evident in his beautiful
scene-setting.** *Cineinforme July 1972*

**Not only was the setting [Burg Kreuzenstein in Lower Austria] fabulous, but
it was furnished from top to bottom with precious antiques. I remember there
was one chair valued at over half a million dollars! When I told Mario we had
made a deal for the castle, he threw his arms around me and kissed me. He
was beside himself, imagining all the ways he could shoot that castle and
everything in it.** *Alfredo Leone [quoted in Lucas, Mario Bava: All the Colors of the Dark, 2007]*

to the time-honoured Gothic theme of ancient,
atavistic horrors reaching from the past to envelop
the living, and in *Baron Blood* the living inhabit just as
contemporary a world as the soulless money-grabbers
of *Antefatto*. To emphasise this collision of ancient

and modern the action opens with Peter ensconced
in a luxurious Pan Am 747, echoing the beginning
of Vadim's *...Et mourir de plaisir*. By coincidence, over
in the UK Hammer used a soaring airliner to mark
the transition from Victorian London to its mod
equivalent in *Dracula A.D. 1972* – a film that began
shooting just five days ahead of Bava's.

In dragging the mouldering horrors of the Gothic
past into the groovy present, *Baron Blood* offered
Bava the chance to reconnect with his own Gothic
antecedents, resulting in self-referential quotes
ranging from the presence of old hands like Luciano
Pigozzi and Gustavo De Nardo to the revived Baron
hauling himself into view exactly as Javutich did in
*La maschera del demonio*. Bava also had the chance
to stage a couple of really stunning resurrection
sequences. Because Peter's ancient parchment contains
a counter-incantation in addition to the Baron-
summoning one, he's sufficiently blasé to tell Eva that
they'll be able to "put the old boy back where he came
from. I mean, if we don't dig him, we'll ditch him."
In response, the camera spirals mockingly around the
castle's gloomy rafters. Suffused in cold tones of blue,
Bava's sedate tours of the castle's cavernous spaces
expertly indicate a lurking, unseen presence.

Their first attempt having been a scary near-miss, the couple go through the same routine the next night, only now, in a neat quote from *Casting the Runes*, the Baron is canny enough to send the parchment, with its counter-incantation, whirling into the fire. He then announces his return in grand style with a pool of blood that seeps under the oaken door; the quote this time is from Jacques Tourneur's 1943 film *The Leopard Man*. The film's other quotes, mandated by the script, are from *House of Wax* – a disfigured, slouch-hatted silhouette lurches in nocturnal pursuit of the heroine and strings up a venal entrepreneur in the castle's echoing stairwell, while the thing's presentable alter ego, apparently wheelchair-bound, rises triumphantly to his feet at the end.

Always at home with a set-piece, Bava gives all three of these scenes a bravura touch. Eva is pursued from the supposedly safe haven of the Studentenheim into a dense fog pierced by unearthly stripes of blue and amber light. The Baron's contempt for the modernisation of his stronghold is symbolised by the businessman's use of a newly installed Coca-Cola dispenser moments before his demise, and that final wheelchair-rising triggers a barnstorming climax in the castle's torture chamber.

The Baron's alter ego is a well-heeled yet waxy-looking character called Alfred Becker, who buys up the castle on the death of the entrepreneur and lovingly restores all its more mediaeval features, notably a defaced portrait of the Baron that was previously consigned to a cobwebbed lumber room in the lower depths. That Becker and the Baron are one and the same is made glaringly obvious from Becker's first appearance, gliding through an auction room with seemingly supernatural ease moments before Bava reveals that he's in a wheelchair. Though Joseph Cotten has some agreeably sinister moments, it seems a shame the role didn't go to Massimo Girotti. Distinguished star of Visconti's *Ossessione* and Pasolini's *Teorema*, Girotti has the right kind of baleful good looks yet is cast instead as Peter's scholarly uncle.

*Baron Blood* has its problems. Peter's frankly unhealthy interest in his demonic ancestor is never properly explored, and Rada Rassimov's powerful presence as an otherworldly medium is confined rather wastefully to the third act. The film isn't really much more than a by-the-book compendium of genre clichés, yet Bava handles them so masterfully they appear fresh. As an index of the film's success, you need only look at Bava's splendidly atmospheric use of his main location, Burg Kreuzenstein – the same castle that in two earlier films, *Im Schloß der blutigen*

*Begierde* and the vampire comedy *Gebissen wird nur nachts*, was given no atmosphere whatsoever.

Bava and *Baron Blood*'s producer, Alfredo Leone, had first met at the end of 1968 when Leone was called in to shore up Bava's embattled sex comedy *Quante volte... quella notte* (How Many Times... That Night). As it turned out the film was banned in Italy, only appearing there in 1972 and taking even longer to reach the USA under the title *Four Times That Night*. Chairman of Italy's censor board at the time was Bava's old colleague Riccardo Freda, who thought nothing of suppressing one Bava film while doing his best to emulate another.

Freda's *Trágica ceremonia en villa Alexander* (Tragic Ceremony at Villa Alexander) was a majority Spanish co-production that, when released in Italy just before Christmas 1972, was lumbered with a ridiculously cumbersome, poliziotteschi-style title: *Estratto dagli archivi segreti della polizia di una capitale europea* (Extracted from the Secret Archives of a European Capital's Police Force). For export it acquired the more user-friendly title *Tragic Ceremony*, highlighting a major set-piece apparently modelled on the go-for-broke gore highlights of Bava's *Antefatto*. Here, US import Camille Keaton is rescued from a satanic ritual in an amazingly overwrought splurge of cathartic violence – one celebrant's head is split down the middle, another is chopped off, yet another is ventilated with a bullet, and burnings and defenestrations are thrown in for good measure.

The scene is really a showcase for Carlo Rambaldi's special effects, which are a good deal cruder than the ones he provided for *Antefatto*. A TV news report rather tastelessly compares the massacre to the Manson murders, with a guitar left at the scene leading the authorities to assume hippies must have been involved. Sadly, Freda's old knack for Gothic atmosphere only comes out when Keaton makes her way, candelabrum in hand, past lightning-lit suits of armour and down a blue-tinted staircase with billowing drapes. The story involves a group of kids constantly running out of gas in an entirely unconvincing Chelsea, and their repetitive comings-and-goings are likely to exasperate even the most indulgent viewer. The whole thing builds up to a bathroom throat-slashing and the image of Spanish favourite Tony Isbert with a blue-painted face, but the journey is barely worth it. The remainder of the cast reveals yet another echo of *Antefatto*, with cult leader Luigi Pistilli partnered once again by a glamorous *Thunderball* veteran – Luciana Paluzzi this time, rather than Claudine Auger.

Pistilli, who in the early 1970s became as familiar a face in the giallo mode as he had previously been in

Spaghetti Westerns, was featured in another December 1972 release, Romano Scavolini's *Un bianco vestito per Marialé* (A White Dress for Marialé). Falling firmly into the 'weird' sub-category of the giallo, this has Paolo (Pistilli) keeping his delicate wife Marialé (Ida Galli) under virtual house arrest in his villa – actually the ever-reliable Castello Borghese at Artena. The arrival of a bunch of *Ten Little Indians*-style guests, covertly invited by Marialé, is the cue for a decadent and increasingly deranged house party reflecting the 'let it all hang out' ethos of the times. A splendid basement set-piece, lit by blue lightning and racked by the unceasing boom of thunder, reveals a set of cobwebbed mannequins, but the ensuing carnivalesque soirée fails to sustain interest despite the amount of self-consciously provocative material shoehorned into it. The film (shot by Scavolini himself) is a luscious-looking affair, and the third act murders, including a nasty razor-slashing and a very thorough savaging-by-dogs, are briskly done. The concluding question mark – was the killer the husband or the wife? – is effective too.

## OLD GOATS FROM BEYOND THE GRAVE

Two days after Mario Bava began shooting *Baron Blood*, Amando de Ossorio started production on what would turn out to be one of Spain's most distinctive contributions to the genre – albeit one filmed in Portugal. Like Bava's film, this was another explosive fusion of ancient and modern in which ghastly revenants visit a hideous revenge on the feckless representatives of the Age of Aquarius.

Having been kicking his heels since the production of *Malenka* in 1968, Ossorio had finally persuaded producers Salvadore Romero and José Antonio Pérez Giner to put ten million pesetas behind a script of his called *El terror ciego* (The Blind Terror). They'd resisted initially because Ossorio had contrived all-new monsters that didn't have the bonus of audience familiarity. Further hedging their bets, they evaded Franco-ist supervision by changing the setting from Ossorio's native Galicia to the more innocuous Portugal. "I was told," Ossorio explained 20-odd years later, "that if I did a movie with the dead coming out of their graves at night in a place that was then being promoted by [cabinet minister Manuel] Fraga as a tourist attraction, they would ban me." The title, he added, was expanded to *La noche del terror ciego* because Romero "had just had a huge hit with *La noche de Walpurgis* and would've added 'la noche' to any script he was offered."[46] The export title, however, abandoned 'The Night of Blind Terror' in favour of the much more alluring *Tombs of the Blind Dead*.

*Heading into the countryside with her boyfriend Roger and former girlfriend Bette, Virginia escapes the claustrophobic ménage by literally jumping off the train. Noticing where she alighted, the driver pointedly fails to respond to Roger's use of the Emergency Stop alarm. Bedding down for the night in a ruined monastery, Virginia is unaware that the surrounding graves are giving up their dead – blind, and bloodthirsty, Knights Templar.*

'They return from the Middle Ages, sightless and thirsting for innocent blood.' So ran one of the film's recommended tag-lines, neatly encapsulating the atavistic dread inspired by Ossorio's creations. (And they really *were* his creations: he not only designed their wizened faces but even sculpted them.) Rising remorselessly from their ankh-adorned tombs and closing with diabolical purpose on their victims, these Templars are brilliantly designed to resemble Mrs Bates from *Psycho* with added facial hair, making them look like devilish old goats from beyond the grave. Better still, Ossorio mounts them on zombie steeds and has them swirl after their quarry in otherworldly slow motion – to stunning effect. And they're accompanied by pseudo-Gregorian *musique concrète* that's chilling in itself. The chanted phrase here, incidentally, is 'Pérez Giner' run backwards – a backhanded compliment, of sorts, to one of the film's executive producers.

Ossorio was insistent that "the Templars are mummies on horseback, not zombies,"[47] though he conceded that they're "closely related to the vampires of myth." He also denied that they were in any way derived from two stories, *El miserere* and *El monte de las ánimas*, written in 1862 by Gustavo Adolfo Bécquer – though why he wished to negate a rare instance of a Spanish horror film using a Spanish literary source is unclear. Whatever their origins, the Templars had the extraordinary virtue in the early 1970s of invoking a crumbling past while representing a still-repressive present. As mediaeval warrior-monks they aptly reflected General Franco's manipulation of the Catholic church, which had given its blessing to the Civil War by labelling Franco's struggle a crusade.

Hence Ossorio's splendid opening, in which Pablo Ripoll's camera prowls a set of gloomy monastic ruins prior to an abrupt cut to bikini-clad young women disporting themselves at an ultra-modern swimming pool. This, of course, is the burgeoning permissive society against which the Templars will rise up, and when one of those young women is consigned to the morgue, the silent Templars find a more than adequate modern-day spokesman in the revoltingly prurient stretcher bearer who delivers her there.

Railway worker José Camoiras falls victim to the revived Knights Templar in *La noche del terror ciego* (1971)

"They're all asking for it," he says leeringly. "The way they dress, it's like they *want* to be bitten. And this one's *sensational*…"

If this was quite a radical conceit to slip past the regime's censors, it's obfuscated somewhat by the commercial necessity Ossorio felt to lard *La noche* with pretty much everything from the exploitation recipe book he could muster. Introduced after 25 minutes and not seen again for another 45, the Templars' show-stopping appearances are separated by a misty-eyed lesbian flashback (scored with some really grisly lounge music), a fairly token resurrection for the first victim, a gruelling rape sequence, even a spirited cat fight that breaks out at a nail-bitingly inopportune moment towards the end. On top of this there's a gruesome mediaeval section detailing the Templars' torture of an improbably tan-lined young peasant girl. The skin-slashing sadism on view here is no less nasty for looking so plasticine-fake, but at least the tableau informs us that the torturers had their eyes pecked out by crows for their sins. The sacrificial victim is Britt Nichols, a Portuguese beauty who would move straight on to Jess Franco's *Christina princesse de l'érotisme*.

More skittishly, Ossorio makes Bette into a businesswoman whose mannequin factory is tellingly positioned next door to the morgue. This plot point

## LA NOCHE DEL TERROR CIEGO

Spain-Portugal 1971
Portugal: *A noite do terror cego*
UK: *Tombs of the Blind Dead*
US: *The Blind Dead*
Plata Films Madrid / Interfilme Lisbon
101 minutes colour
production began 4 October 1971
. . . . . . . . . . . . . . . . . . . . . . . . . . . .
Director of Photography: Pablo Ripoll; Art Director: Jaime Duarte De Brito; Editor: José Antonio Rojo; Sound: José María San Mateo, Luis Castro; Music: Antón García Abril; Make-up: José Luis Campos; Special Effects: José Gómez Soria; Screenplay: Amando de Ossorio; English adaptation:

Robert H Oliver [Dick Randall]; Executive Producer: Salvadore Romero; Producer: José A Perez Giner; Director: Amando de Ossorio

Lone Fleming (Bette Turner); César Burner (Roger Whelan); María Elena Arpón (Virginia White); José Thelman (Pedro Candal); María Silva (María); Rufino Inglés (Inspector Oliveira); Verónica Llimera (Nina); Simón Arriaga (morgue keeper); Francisco Sanz (Professor Candal); Juan Cortés (coroner); Andrés Speizer [Antonio Spitzer] (Officer Marcos); Antonio Orengo (train driver); José Camoiras (train engineer); uncredited: Britt Nichols (sacrificial victim)

Scenes of opening tombs, mummified corpses advancing to the sound of Gregorian chants, and cannibalism abound … Ossorio also includes some gratuitous eroticism. Technical and acting credits are good. The locations are well captured. Despite its excesses, *La noche del terror ciego* will interest and entertain those viewers who ask for nothing more, thus fulfilling the purpose for which it was made – to divert a wide audience by means of terror. *ABC Sevilla* 11 March 1973

You know, it was creepy but fascinating because it was such hard work for Amando. You could say in this film he didn't direct us, his actors, too much because he knew he could rely on us, so he was all the time working with the Templars. The costumes were so heavy and it was hot … He never tired. You could see how he loved it. Lone Fleming [quoted in *Delirium* April-May 2014]

seems to have been included purely to facilitate some Bava-style lighting reminiscent of *6 donne per l'assassino*. (More literal-minded than Bava, Ossorio is careful to have Roger query the red glow pulsing over Bette's corridor of mannequins, prompting a rational explanation involving a neon factory on an upper floor.) Curious asides like this help sustain interest while the viewer recovers from the initial manifestation of the Templars – a galloping, twilight pursuit of Virginia that remains one of the great set-pieces of Spanish horror, containing, as British trade critic Marjorie Bilbow put it at the time, "all the qualities of those nightmares in which you try to run but find your feet won't obey you."[48]

The site of the Templars' resurrection was a cunning combination of two of Spain's most popular horror locations – Madrid's Monasterio del Cercón and a similar ruin, Santa María de Valdeiglesias, at Pelayos de la Presa. The film returns to both sites for a stunning climax in which Bette and Roger team up with a sweaty local smuggler called Pedro and his hardbitten moll, María. Pedro is the resident rapist, defiling Bette just moments after she's revealed that, heterosexually speaking, she's a virgin. Ugly though this scene is, it has a pay-off of sorts when, moments later, Pedro is gruesomely snuffed out by the Templars. María Silva, cast as María, no doubt recalled being chewed on by the sightless Morpho in Franco's *Gritos en la noche* exactly ten years before. Here, her uncontrolled shrieks cause the blind Templars to look up from beneath their grime-caked cowls – a sudden show of interest that's truly blood-curdling. In another masterstroke (this one derived, presumably, from Edgar Allan Poe), Bette cannily bites her lip for silence but suddenly realises, as the camera pulses inexorably towards her heaving breast, that her very heartbeat is enough to give her away.

The whole thing ends with a really grim mini-apocalypse set on board a moving steam train. Ossorio is unafraid to show a mother's blood drizzling onto a little girl's face, and Lone Fleming – an engaging heroine throughout – goes from trauma to shrieking insanity in the style patented by Hilary Dwyer in *Witchfinder General*. Ossorio admitted that his unresolved freeze-frame ending was necessitated by the budget running out. It's just as well it did, however, since the film's impressive local take of 27 million pesetas inspired no fewer than three sequels.

The first of these, *El ataque de los muertos sin ojos* (Attack of the Eyeless Dead), reached Spanish cinemas in October 1973. It gets off to a good start when the first Templar we see, in a mediaeval flashback, is the monolithic Jess Franco regular Luis Barboo. What's immediately puzzling, however, is Ossorio's tendency, which will continue throughout the series, of moving the goalposts regarding the Templars'

back-story. Here, they have their eyes burned out by enraged villagers, rather than being hanged and bird-pecked as in the first film. Furthermore, the site of their 20th century depredations turns out to be a still-thriving village called Bouzano rather than the totally derelict settlement of Berzano. The location was actually El Vellón, which lent its main square to some exciting scenes of panicked villagers being surrounded and hacked down by mounted skeletons.

The occasion is a fête dedicated to Bouzano's age-old triumph over the Templars, which is complicated by the village idiot's decision to sacrifice a local girl and thus raise the monsters once again. Strangely, these Templars show no interest in drinking their victims' blood; vengeful wielding of broadswords seems to content them. Despite such anomalies, Ossorio repeats several of the first film's high points – mainly via recycled footage of the Templars' tomb-grating resurrection – and also some of its low points, including a last-minute attempted rape. Our hero is the granite-jawed Tony Kendall, who doggedly keeps on his suede-and-sheepkin overcoat throughout the climactic siege, which blatantly parrots *Night of the Living Dead*. He's in Bouzano to organise the festive fireworks (an echo, perhaps, of Vadim's *...Et mourir de plaisir*) and at the end he makes his way with Esperanza Roy past hordes of strangely immobile Templars. At cock crow they simply fold up and collapse, presumably because the blood sacrifice was only effective for a single night.

In the meantime Ossorio indulges in some satire at the expense of local government, notably a venal mayor (Fernando Sancho) who's so revoltingly self-interested he sends a little girl among the Templars as a decoy. Loreta Tovar tries to make her escape on one of the Templars' steeds, just as María Elena Arpón did in the first film. Here, though, Tovar gets the splendid line "It's a dead horse" and proves it by removing its mouldering hood. Somewhere along the line, however, the otherworldliness of the first film eludes Ossorio. Where the Templars were, arguably, under-used in their first showcase, here we're given plenty of Templar action – but perhaps just a little too much.

## ENCLOSED WORLDS

In November 1971, Mathieu Carrière – fresh from starring in Jacques Doniol-Valcroze's ponderous SF drama *L'Homme au cerveau greffé* (The Man with the Transplanted Brain) – was one of four headline stars in a picture that was anything but ponderous. Harry Kümel had been planning a film version of Jean Ray's 1943 novel *Malpertuis* for over two years; indeed, his 1970 vampire film, *Les Lèvres rouges*, had been slotted in merely as an interim project, its international success helping to make *Malpertuis* a reality. Armed with the substantial sum of 30 million Belgian francs, Kümel matched Carrière with the British TV star Susan Hampshire, French stage luminary Michel Bouquet and, to play the monstrous patriarch at the centre of the action, none other than Orson Welles. The result was crudely recut by United Artists for its Cannes premiere in May 1972, but, even when restored by Kümel to its intended form and supplemented with the subtitle *Histoire d'une maison maudite* (Story of a Cursed House), it proved as big a flop as Kümel's previous film had been a hit.

*Jan is on shore leave when he gets into a brawl at the raucous Venus Bar. Recovering consciousness, he finds himself in Malpertuis, a labyrinthine mansion presided over by his ailing uncle, Cassavius. Among Cassavius' crazed hangers-on are Jan's sister Nancy and the captivating Euryale, with whom Jan becomes smitten. When Cassavius dies, his will stipulates that, in order to collect their share, the assembled retinue should remain exclusively inside Malpertuis for the rest of their lives.*

The Flemish version of *Malpertuis* begins with a tight close-up on John Tenniel's 1871 illustration of the Jabberwock, accompanied by Alice's confounded words from *Through the Looking-Glass*: "It seems very pretty but it's rather hard to understand! Somehow it seems to fill my head with ideas – only I don't exactly know what they are!" Then an ominous chord ushers in both Georges Delerue's sublime score and the opening credits. The radically different United Artists version plays the credits over René Magritte's contemplative 1948 painting *La Mémoire* and concludes them with a quote from *Macbeth*: "It is a tale / Told by an idiot, full of sound and fury, / Signifying nothing."

UA couldn't have more forcefully indicated their lack of faith in the ramshackle beast that is *Malpertuis* if they'd tried. (Was Kümel himself the idiot they had in mind?) Kümel's version, by contrast, invites viewers to share Alice's awareness of the beauty in horror, as well as tipping them off from the outset that *Malpertuis* will be a riot of surrealist signs and symbols that they must piece together as best they can.

Amid the intense concentration of images, Kümel occasionally throws in a straightforward in-joke, as when Jan discovers that his childhood home has made way for a shop whose windows bear the legend 'H Dickson & H Dickson'. (Harry Dickson was the

## MALPERTUIS

*Belgium-France-West Germany 1971*
US: **The Legend of Doom House**
SOFIDOC Brussels / Société d'expansion du
Spectacle Paris / Les Productions Artistes
Associés Paris / Artemis Berlin
125 minutes colour
production began 1 November 1971
· · · · · · · · · · · · · · · · · · · · · · · · · · ·
Director of Photography: Gerry Fisher; Art
Director: Pierre Cadiou de Condé; Editor:
Richard Marden; Sound: Jacques Eippers;
Music: Georges Delerue; Make-up: Odette
Van der Greyn, Xlaudine Thyrion, John
O'Gorman; Special Effects: Michel Bernard,
Jean Pecriaux; Screenplay: Jean Ferry,
from the novel by Jean Ray; Producers:

Pierre Levie, Paul Laffargue; Director:
Harry Kümel

Orson Welles (Cassavius); Susan Hampshire
(Nancy / Euryale / Alice / nurse / Charlotte);
Michel Bouquet (Charles Dideloo); Mathieu
Carrière (Jan); Jean-Pierre Cassel (Lampernisse);
Daniel Pilon (Mathias Crook); Walter Rilla
(Eisengott); Dora van der Groen (Sylvie Dideloo);
Charles Janssens (Philarète); Sylvie Vartan
(Bets); Jet Naessens (Eléonore); Cara Van Wersch
(Rosalie); Jenny Van Santvoort (Elodie); Fanny
Winkler (Mother Griboin); Robert Lussac [as Bob
Storm] (Griboin); Edouard Ravais (Doucedame);
Gella Allaert (Gerda); Hugo Dellas (Hans);
Cyriel Van Gent (fat man)

From the beautiful novel by Jean Ray (maybe his masterpiece), Harry Kümel has made a diligent, weighty film adaptation, underlining his characters with such broad strokes that they're reduced to caricatures from who knows what expressionist nightmare ... With plenty of dimly lit corridors, red drapes, creaking doors, unnecessary dolly shots and misused angles, Kümel manages to imprison us in a fantasy just as unconvincing as *Lèvres rouges*.
*Les Lettres françaises* 14 June 1972

As with *Daughters of Darkness*, I had devised a set where the demiurge character [Cassavius] was reflected in Nazi colours – red, black and white. Welles produced his own costume, a green dressing gown. My cameraman, Gerry Fisher, reassured me he could make the green look black. Then Welles wanted to use a putty hooked nose. Everyone told me not to argue with him, though I won over a terrible wig he had brought.
*Harry Kümel [quoted in* Sight and Sound *August 2002]*

Mathieu Carrière and Susan Hampshire, enclosed in the labyrinthine domain of *Malpertuis* (1971)

'American Sherlock Holmes' so popular in France and Belgium, whose most imaginative adventures had all been written by *Malpertuis* author Jean Ray.) These opening scenes are beguilingly strange, with Jan being tailed through the deserted streets of Ghent by Diderloo, a weasely little man in a Magritte-style bowler. The eerie emptiness of these sequences is thrillingly displaced by the bustling melée that is the Venus Bar, with the bewitching French pop star Sylvie Vartan taking centre stage in a cabaret set-piece Jess Franco could never have afforded in his wildest dreams. And then we're precipitated into the perplexing domain that is Malpertuis, various translations of which are offered to us by its bizarre inmates, ranging from "house of evil" and "house of damnation" to the emphatic pronouncement that "This house is Hell and Cassavius is the Devil!"

At first we're inclined to scoff, specifically at the fact that Jan, who sustained an extremely bloody head wound at the Venus, wakes up in Malpertuis without a scratch. Kümel will explain this in the first of several last-reel twists, but in the meantime we're encouraged to look upon Malpertuis, in the time-honoured tradition of all the best Old Dark Houses, as a twisting, many-levelled representation of the unconscious. The hallucinatory atmosphere is intensified by the ravishing imagery provided by Kümel's British cinematographer Gerry Fisher, especially when we enter the inner sanctum occupied by the bed-ridden Cassavius. Fisher's wide-angle view emphasises the theatrical sweep of red plush that frames Cassavius' massive bed, which seems to occupy a proscenium arch of its own within his cavernous quarters.

It's here that *Malpertuis* really begins to grip, thanks to Kümel's brilliant staging of the hysteria and fainting fits among the gathered cronies as Cassavius outlines the terms of his will. Curiously, Orson Welles' sprawling patriarch is perhaps the scene's least compelling ingredient. Handsomely remunerated for just three days' work, Welles proved difficult in the extreme – and in his Toad of Toad Hall make-up and self-imposed chalk nose he doesn't really seem worth the effort. On top of this, at 56 he was far too young for the role. John Huston, who was also considered, would have been a much more interesting choice.

The acting honours go instead to Michel Bouquet – whose Diderloo swarms all over Susan Hampshire's coldly seductive Alice with the words "I'm the creep that you do it with!" – and to Charles Janssens' Philarète, a berserk taxidermist in Cassavius' employ whose big scene might well be the best in the film. As Jan surveys the immobilised bats, apes and birds in Philarète's attic, the madman observes that "All the things here are attempts to create new life. As you can see, it all went wrong..." Explaining that "Life isn't worth living if you've not got anything to stuff," he eventually attempts to put out Jan's eyes in paroxysms of sadistic excitement. As with Kümel's previous film, the dialogue for *Malpertuis* was by Jean Ferry, and Jannssens makes the most of such juicy, Sweeney Todd-like lines as "Your skin would be a pleasure to flay!"

As well as recalling Sweeney Todd, Philarète is also reminiscent of Dr Pretorius from James Whale's *Bride of Frankenstein*, a film quoted again when unseen rats in the lower depths are given ridiculously cartoon-like voices. Between them, Philarète and the chattering rats set up Jan's shock discovery of a bloodied baby's hand in a rat trap; this not only gives rise to disturbing questions about the grisly work being done in Cassavius' name but also acts as a cue for a rising tide of horror imagery. Cassavius is found preserved in stone inside his sarcophagus, Diderloo is brutally defenestrated by a cowled femme fatale, a bundle of knitting is flung to the floor and becomes a mass of writhing snakes, and the family members eventually advance, zombie-like, on Jan in a sequence explicitly recalling *Night of the Living Dead*. Here, an elderly retainer belches flame onto Jan's upheld crucifix, instantaneously melting the tiny Christ.

Finally, it's revealed that the house's inmates are Greek gods imprisoned by Cassavius long ago and fitted with Flemish bodies by the industrious Philarète. The fire-breather, for example, is Vulcan, while the rat-fancying Lampernisse turns out to be Prometheus, leading to a really horrible scene in which a plunging eagle rips out his intestines. For her part, the gorgeous green-eyed Euryale announces that "My name is Gorgon. I am Love. I am Death." Making a big impact in no fewer than five different roles, Susan Hampshire brought over her own make-up artist, John O'Gorman, from the UK, while 'her' nude scene as Alice is as blatant a piece of body-doubling as you'll ever see. Kümel, of course, was only interested in swathing the statuesque model's face in darkness, placing her in a blue- and purple-draped chamber and thus reproducing one of Paul Delvaux's creepy midnight nudes.

Ultimately, it's hard to resist the conclusion that for Kümel *Malpertuis* was an indulgent folly from which his international career never recovered. For every bewitching moment – as when Gerry Fisher is let loose in the mist-shrouded environs of the 12th century abbey at Villers-la-Ville – there's another in which the narrative flails in head-scratchingly indecipherable directions, and at a cumulative length, in Kümel's preferred cut, of two hours. The irony is that *Les Lèvres rouges*, which to Kümel was nothing more than a piece of stop-gap trash, remains a far

Gianni Garko tries to escape backwoods Yugoslavia
in La notte dei diavoli (1971)

tighter and more compelling work of art than his
surrealist dream project.

In December 1971, while Kümel was shooting
*Malpertuis*, a very different but equally isolated family
was taking shape in a highly accomplished Italian
shocker called La notte dei diavoli (Night of the Devils).
Despite the abundant promise of his 1960 film *Il
mulino delle donne di pietra*, director Giorgio Ferroni had
spent the intervening years well away from the horror
field, instead making pepla and Spaghetti Westerns
with such crowd-pleasing stalwarts of those genres as
Gordon Scott and Giuliano Gemma. Venturing back
into what was by now Mario Bava territory, he found
himself presiding over a new adaptation of an Aleksey
Tolstoy story previously handled by Bava himself in
I tre volti della paura.

*Confined to a psychiatric hospital, successful
businessman Nicola recalls the horrifying events that
befell him while en route to a meeting in Zehdenick.
Having crashed his car in backwoods Yugoslavia, he
sought shelter with local patriarch Gorca Ciuvelak, who
had buried his brother that same day. When Gorca
determined to confront and destroy a local witch, he was
given a strict time limit by his eldest son Jovan, with
dire consequences promised should he exceed it...*

## LA NOTTE DEI DIAVOLI

Italy-Spain 1971
Spain: **La noche de los diablos**
UK / US: **Night of the Devils**
Filmes Cinematografica / Due Emme
    Cinematografica Rome / Copercines Madrid
91 minutes colour
production began December 1971

. . . . . . . . . . . . . . . . . . . . . . . .

Director of Photography: Manuel Berenguer;
Art Directors: Eugenio Liverani, Cubero-
Galicia; Editor: Gianmaria Messeri; Music:
Giorgio Gaslini; Make-up: Massimo Giustini
[Italian prints]; Adolfo Ponte, A Mecacci
[Spanish prints]; Special Effects: Rambaldi
[Italian prints], Baquero [Spanish prints];

Screenplay: Romano Migliorini, Gianbattista
Mussetto, Eduardo M Brochero; Story:
Eduardo M Brochero, based on a story
[Sem'ya vurdalaka] by A Tolstoi [uncredited
on Spanish prints]; Producer: Eduardo
Manzanos; Director: Giorgio Ferroni

Gianni Garko (Nicola); Agostina Belli (Sdenka);
Roberto Maldera (Jovan); Cinzia De Carolis
(Irina); Teresa Gimpera (Elena); William Vanders
(Gorca Ciuvelak); Umberto Raho (Dr Tosi);
Luis Suárez (Vlado); Sabrina Tamborra (Mira);
Rosita Torosh (nurse); Stefano Oppedisano (male
nurse); uncredited on Spanish prints: Maria
Monti (the witch)

Eeeek! This is one of the rare occasions when I wish I didn't have a good
visual memory for screen images ... However, said she wiping the cold
sweat from her brow, I must praise the special effects as being especially
effective. The plot moves slowly; the acting is unremarkable; and very little
suspense mileage is got out of the family's awareness of their danger. But
the plodding pace is hypnotically effective in establishing an atmosphere
of brooding doom. CinemaTV Today 20 January 1973

Displaying all the usual defects of a low-budget horror quickie – careless
direction, mechanical performances, some obtrusively unconvincing
day-for-night sequences – Night of the Devils provides little in the way of
style to compensate for a story which staggers dully from one
bloodthirsty set-piece to another. Monthly Film Bulletin February 1973

For the lead in La notte dei diavoli, Ferroni was given
another star of Spaghetti Westerns, Gianni Garko.
Garko's Nicola is a rugged 30-something very different
to the Brylcreemed pretty boy used by Bava eight years
before. His clothes, as the Yugoslavian hospital staff
point out, are part English, part Italian and all classy.

Yet his money has been made from lumber export and he ventures out on his travels in a chunky sheepskin jacket, details suggesting that he might still, at heart, be a man of the land. He turns out, though, to be no less out of his depth among the Ciuvelak family as, say, a pampered art dealer would be. Nicola is defiantly of 1971, and the contrast with the seemingly backward Ciuvelaks is a major source of the film's queasy power.

In the first quarter-hour Ferroni indulges in some grandstanding gore effects; lovingly concocted by effects maestro Carlo Rambaldi, these too are very much of 1971. They're there not just to keep the gorehounds happy but also to misdirect them, for Ferroni is going to rely on atmosphere for the bulk of the film prior to finally unleashing Rambaldi again in the third act. Representing Nicola's nightmare visions while under psychiatric observation, these rapid-fire effects range from maggots rioting in the orifices of a grinning skull, a woman's face being bloodily shot away in an inky limbo and a white-robed cultist pulling out a still-pulsing heart in extreme close-up.

After this grisly prologue, Nicola's ordeal, unspooling in flashback, boasts plenty of outré details to disconcert the viewer – details made all the more disquieting by the fact that Nicola's hospitalisation puts us firmly in 'unreliable narrator' territory. The portents of dread are expertly accumulated. Stranded in the woods, Nicola is drawn by strangely elongated cries to a tumbledown ruin – only to find it empty save for a severed, and flayed, bull's head. His first sight of the Ciuvelaks consists of two very spooky, doll-clutching kids, Mira and Irina, contemplating him from a window; these children hardly need to become vampires in order to chill the blood. That the family is trapped in a kind of 19th century time-warp is made clear in several ways, some innocuous (the beautiful daughter, Sdenka, claims never to have seen a television), others less so. Why, for example, do they fearfully bar all the doors and windows prior to sitting down to dinner? And why did it take them a month before they got around to burying Gorca's deceased brother?

While these troubling questions linger in the mind, Ferroni ratchets up the tension with a scene of the white-faced witch visiting the dead man's grave at dead of night. Having reportedly had an illicit hold over him in life, she now unearths one of his exquisite wood carvings from the topsoil prior to cutting her hand and drizzling blood onto the funerary flowers. Later, Ferroni cuts away from the confrontation between the witch and the stake-wielding Gorca to contemplate the same carving lying discarded on a bed of straw. He shows no such reticence on Gorca's return, however. Toting the witch's severed hand (supplanting the bandit's head favoured by Bava), Gorca soon shows his true colours and is himself staked by Jovan, whereupon Ferroni dwells on a messy head-collapsing effect for well over a minute. "Putrefaction is the main visual motif," opined the *Monthly Film Bulletin*, adding sniffily that "the film is unlikely in the end to satisfy either the horror enthusiast or the latent sadist."[49]

After this it remains only for the Ciuvelaks to devour each other in as downbeat, and grisly, a finale as Italian horror had yet achieved. We've already caught a nasty whiff of child abuse on hearing that Gorca bribed his little niece, Mira, not to talk about his nocturnal excursions with her sister. Now the children's glamorous young mother, Elena, is attacked by little Irina, who causes massive bleeding with just one brief bite prior to scoring bloody rents across Elena's exposed breasts. This nasty mother-daughter assault, an obvious nod to a similar scene in *Night of the Living Dead*, became the film's main advertising image, while the casting of the ubiquitous Teresa Gimpera as Elena is one of several indications that Ferroni's film was a Spanish co-production.

With both children giggling happily from atop a woodpile, the transformed Elena subsequently tries to attack Nicola in his stalled car, losing a handful of fingers when he slams the door against her. And the return to the hospital brings with it a resolution of the burgeoning Nicola-Sdenka romance that's as brutal as they come. Ferroni's crescendo of paranoid horror is splendidly sustained, and the film itself – bolstered by Giorgio Gaslini's excellent score and Manuel Berenguer's delicate Scope photography – is ripe for reappraisal as a small classic of Italian horror.

Agostina Belli, the beautiful Sdenka in Ferroni's film, had done her time in Italian horror already, moving from the previously discussed *Ivanna* to Luigi Bazzoni's *Giornata nera per l'ariete* (Black Day for Aries). Starring Franco Nero and exported as *The Fifth Cord*, the latter is a standard-issue 'burned-out reporter strives to exonerate himself' giallo lent unusual distinction by the brilliant music and cinematography of Ennio Morricone and Vittorio Storaro respectively. After *La notte dei diavoli* Belli went straight into Edward Dmytryk's *Bluebeard*, a French-German-Italian folly that began shooting in Budapest on 16 January 1972. Here she was just one of several beauties – Virna Lisi, Nathalie Delon, Raquel Welch, Karin Schubert, Marilù Tolo, Sybil Danning – dancing attendance on a grizzled Richard Burton, whose Baron Kurt von Sepper really *does* have a blue beard. (Mathieu Carrière, late of *Malpertuis*, is also featured.) A flying

British actress Shirley Corrigan caught in the toils of *Doctor Jekyll y el hombre lobo* (1971)

ace in the Great War, Burton's Baron has graduated to quasi-Nazi status, mummifying his venerated mama and sublimating his impotence by killing the guest wives in elaborate but listlessly staged ways. Though he claimed to be channelling Vincent Price, Burton has none of that actor's extravagant brio, helping the intended black comedy to fall resoundingly flat.

## GENUINELY EXPORTABLE

In March 1972 a *Nuevo Fotogramas* gossip column pointed out what was by then an incontrovertible fact: "It seems that there's one facet of Spanish cinema that, despite everything, remains genuinely exportable." The choice of film to illustrate this fact, however, was perhaps not a propitious one. "*Necrophagus*, the Michael Skaife film that won an award at the fourth Semana Internacional de Cine Fantástico y de Terror in Sitges, has been acquired by the American company Independent-International Pictures Corporation for exhibition in a chain of 5000 cinemas ... And given that so far only the films of Jesús Franco have proved viable abroad, we wouldn't be far wrong in saying that the horror genre is our only exportable one. Amen."[50]

That 5000-venue estimate was, hardly surprisingly, somewhat wide of the mark. Retitled *Graveyard of Horror*, Skaife's debut film reportedly only played on TV in the USA. Skaife was actually Miguel Madrid; he'd acted in a couple of Jess Franco films and indeed turns up briefly in *Necrophagus* as a skull-fondling character called Mr Skaife. Distinguished by snowy Spanish vistas doubling as Scotland but utterly disfigured by

editing so cack-handed it has to be seen to be believed, the film is an incoherent mess, with repeated shots of pulsing grave earth counting as the only glimmers of imagination in the entire enterprise. Experimenting on himself, an eminent scientist has been reduced to "nothing but putrefying flesh, that's all – trying desperately to make something of his rotting body." Now he conducts cannibalistic forays from the local graveyard, his presence indicated only by close-ups of fuzzy ginger eyebrows prior to a last-minute reveal of a truly risible humanoid vegetable. The film's screening at Sitges in October 1971 was reportedly attended by plenty of noisy protests and walk-outs, a melée that only intensified when Madrid was inexplicably awarded the Best Director prize, tying with Janusz Majewski, director of the Polish film *Lokis*.

A few weeks after *Necrophagus* made its tumultuous debut at Sitges, León Klimovsky began shooting his second Paul Naschy collaboration. Filmed in November-December 1971, *Doctor Jekyll y el hombre lobo* (Dr Jekyll and the Werewolf) is a genuinely lunatic Naschy scenario that transplants Waldemar Daninsky from backward-looking Transylvania to moderately Swinging Soho. In it, the Transylvanian honeymoon of Shirley Corrigan's Justine is abruptly terminated when her older husband (José Marco) falls prey to local thugs. Rescuing her, Daninsky introduces Justine to an elderly local sorceress archly named Uzvika Báthory (Elsa Zabala). After trouble with torch-wielding villagers, including Uzvika's rather arbitrary decapitation, Daninsky decamps with Justine to her native England. There, Jack Taylor's Jekyll descendant proposes turning Daninsky into Mr Hyde in the hope that the werewolf taint and the Hyde persona will somehow cancel each other out.

The wet and dismal London location shooting throws up some incidental pleasures one doesn't expect from a Spanish werewolf shocker, among them a glimpse of Great Windmill Street's saucy Cameo Moulin cinema and Jekyll's Golders Green HQ at Manor House Hospital, adorned with a plaque reading 'Biological Researchs Clinic' [sic]. This is the setting for an inspired scene in which Daninsky is trapped in a malfunctioning lift at a predictably inopportune moment, which is bad news for the young nurse sharing the confined space with him. Other diverting touches include Justine's nicely lit corridor-wandering in Daninsky's so-called Castillo Maldito, the wolfish Daninsky looking down shame-faced when she spies him from an upper window, and his climactic transformation in a strobe-pulsing West End discothèque.

Though for this film Daninsky's unwanted hair has turned a rather fetching strawberry blond, the werewolf business looks more than ever like kids' stuff, especially by comparison to Naschy's grinning, and genuinely disquieting, Hyde. Lank-haired, green-skinned, golden-eyed, he wakes on the operating table with a cry of "Set me free. My blood is boiling!" He then kits himself out in Victorian garb and heads for Soho, insisting that "I need pleasure! I need women! Lots and lots of women!" Vying with him in villainy is Jekyll's glamorous and thoroughly insane assistant Sandra (ripely played by Mirta Miller), who looks properly formidable when looming over Daninsky in syringe-toting, camera-hogging close-up. A further touch of class is provided by Antón García Abril's avant-garde score, which alternates between eerie electronics and ritzy jazz for a conspicuously grim Soho strangling. The result is an engagingly ridiculous hybrid, and Naschy's Hyde is creepy enough to make one wish that, on this occasion, he could have dumped Daninsky altogether.

Naschy's prodigious work-load in the early 1970s went well beyond his affectionate recreation of

famous monsters; a few Hispanic imitations of Italy's giallo films were thrown into the mix too. The first of these, made in June 1971, was José Luis Madrid's *Jack el destripador de Londres* (Jack the Mangler of London); like *Doctor Jekyll y el hombre lobo*, this one enjoyed a certain amount of location work in London's West End. It benefits from a convincingly damp Soho opening, modelled carefully on that of Michael Powell's *Peeping Tom*. A subjective camera prowls rain-streaked Piccadilly and a prostitute says sunnily, "You wanna make it?" – a 1970s update of Brenda Bruce's stone-faced *Peeping Tom* line, "It'll be five quid." Straight afterwards, however, we're given the first of several childishly gruesome murder sequences – childish in part because of the risibly unconvincing 'knife into plasticine' effects common to so many continental horrors of the period.

In a nice touch, the plummy cop on the case, charmingly played by Renzo Marignano, rejoices in the name Cuthbert Campbell. The modern-day Ripper he seeks – not played by Naschy, incidentally – keeps body parts in jars in his Sussex bolt-hole;

Seventies Soho depicted as a hotbed of serial killings in *Jack el destripador de Londres* (1971)

a head in a hatbox is also featured, and connoisseurs will be diverted by a nocturnal fight scene in which decidedly un-English cicadas can be heard resonating in the background. After this spirited start, Naschy would indeed be the killer in a humdrum Berlin-set giallo shot early in 1972 – a José Luis Madrid reunion called *Los crímenes de Petiot* (The Crimes of Petiot) – after which he would graduate to three further imitation gialli in 1973.

Whether they featured Paul Naschy or not, the exact nationality of some of Spain's quasi-gialli is something of a grey area, given the complex co-production deals involved. A Spanish-Italian film like *Detrás del silencio* (Behind the Silence, 1972) is generally taken to be Italian, given the presence of Umberto Lenzi as director – in which case we should properly call it *Il coltello di ghiaccio* (Knife of Ice). Yet it appears to have been a majority Spanish production, in common with a sister film made by the same producers at the same time – *La mansión de la niebla* (The House of the Fog), which was directed by a

Spaniard, Francisco Lara Polop. In Italy this one was known, more luridly, as *Quando Marta urlò dalla tomba* (When Marta Screamed from the Tomb).

In the first of these, the ubiquitous Carroll Baker is a victimised mute woman recalling Dorothy McGuire in *The Spiral Staircase*, though Lenzi's actual model was, by his own admission, the victimised blind woman played by Mia Farrow in the 1970 film *Blind Terror*. The abundant fog in Lenzi's film was siphoned over into Polop's much more interesting *La mansión de la niebla*, which also picked up several of the same cast members. A highly atmospheric replay of the 'disparate dodgy characters stranded in an old dark house' routine, this one borrows explicitly from Antonio Margheriti's *Contronatura* via several flashbacks to a high-society ball. Sadly, it never quite lives up to one character's claim that "I keep having the sensation that we've crossed the frontier between the real and the unreal." Indeed, it promises vampire matriarchs and ghostly chauffeurs yet defaults to giallo convention with a disappointingly earthbound resolution. Even so, the ending is corpse-strewn and features especially well-acted death scenes for character stalwarts Eduardo Fajardo, Alberto Dalbes and Jorge Rigaud. It's also almost certainly the only continental horror film to feature the fruity tones of British cabinet minister William Whitelaw – discussing the Northern Ireland problem in a radio broadcast.

So ingrained was Spain's horror boom by this stage that another Spanish-Italian offering – a vaguely kinky family drama, spiced up in its latter stages by some giallo-style throat-slashings – could be passed off in 1971 under the supremely misleading title *La casa de las muertas vivientes* (The House of the Living Dead Women). Here, writer-director Alfonso Balcázar gives the standard-issue 'new wife in peril' plot a pleasing sheen that echoes US TV movies of the period. But before the killings kick in the only interest arises from the prolific Teresa Gimpera, peering at a skewered butterfly through a magnifying glass in the 'enlarged eye' style patented by Peter Cushing.

One of Balcázar's co-writers on *La casa*, José Ramón Larraz, was at the time enjoying a directorial career in England, crafting a distinctive brand of crepuscular eroticism in the giallo-tinted titles *Whirlpool* and *Deviation*. Though these were made with Danish and Swedish money respectively, by mid-1973 Larraz had embarked on a genuinely British item called *Scream and Die!*, which was swiftly followed by the Anglo-Belgian co-production *Symptoms* and then in March 1974 by the enduring British cult film *Vampyres*.

Between *Deviation* and *Scream and Die!*, however, Larraz went back to Spain at the very end of 1971 to make *La muerte incierta* (The Unconfirmed Death), following this in mid-1972 with *Emma 'puertas oscuras'* (Emma 'Dark Doorways'). In both cases the leading ladies were British. Playing a young bride in 1930s India in *La muerte incierta*, Mary Maude was familiar from Serrador's *La residencia*, and Susanna East, who not long before had been hung on a meat hook in the UK psycho-shocker *The Fiend*, was herself the aggressor in *Emma*, playing a mentally unstable teen in contemporary London.

*La muerte incierta* entirely wastes Rosalba Neri, cast as a barely glimpsed concubine who returns to haunt her steadily disintegrating former lover (Antonio Molino Rojo) when he remarries. Larraz contrives an eerie nocturnal glimpse of her in a mirror, as well as a couple of surprisingly well-staged tiger attacks (in one of which it's clearly the lycanthropic Neri who does the initial mauling). There are also traces of incestuous desire as the young bride surrenders to her conniving stepson (Raffaele Curi). But the rest is slow-going and overly reliant on stock footage, much of it clearly African rather than Indian.

As *Emma*, East is knocked down on the King's Road in Chelsea and then taken in by the ex-psychiatrist responsible (Perla Cristal). Having killed the woman's husband with scissors and the woman herself with a razor, she falls in with a couple of kinky hippies and stalks them in an abandoned hotel. The shocking suddenness of the scissor attack points forward to *Symptoms* and an outburst of doves in the hotel prefigures *Scream and Die!* Otherwise, *La muerte incierta* and *Emma* contain very little of the dreamlike intensity that characterises Larraz' British films, as if Larraz needed the strangeness of a foreign environment to fully engage his imagination.

## WE'RE BRITISH, YOU KNOW!

While José Larraz decamped to the UK for his most interesting productions (and eventually settled comfortably in Tunbridge Wells), there were two instances during this period of Spanish companies joining forces with British ones to craft, in the first instance, an uneasily paedophilic sex shocker and, in the second, a delightful SF-Gothic hybrid. Arising from the British companies Leisure Media and Leander Films pooling resources with Madrid Eguiluz Films, James Kelly's *Night Hair Child* started shooting on 14 December 1971 and was known in Spain as *Diabólica malicia* (Diabolical Malice). With an obviously psychotic Mark Lester (then 13, and horribly miscast) groping and generally drooling over his father's new wife (29-year-old Britt Ekland), the result is as cumulatively ridiculous as it is creepily distasteful. Because the

British titans Peter Cushing and Christopher Lee with Spanish stalwarts Julio Peña and (in the crate) Víctor Israel in *Pánico en el Transiberiano* (1971)

The second of these collaborations, directed by Eugenio Martín and divided between Granada Films (Spain) and Benmar Productions (UK), is a very different story, with much unbridled lunacy to commend it and a final seal of quality bestowed by the importation of a couple of genre titans. Bringing Peter Cushing and Christopher Lee to Madrid's Estudios 70 complex shortly before Christmas 1971 was an astonishing coup for producer Bernard Gordon, who – like the film's writers, Arnaud d'Usseau and Julian Zimet – was a fugitive from the Hollywood Blacklist. It was a coup brought about on behalf of a film advertised during production as both *Horror Express* and *La plaga* (The Plague); on release, it would retain the *Horror Express* title for export purposes but became *Pánico en el Transiberiano* (Panic on the Trans-Siberian Express) in Spain. Long before Cushing and Lee came on board, the film had been conceived purely as a means of squeezing more value from two splendid model trains built for Bernard Gordon's previous production, *Pancho Villa*.

## PÁNICO EN EL TRANSIBERIANO

Spain-UK 1971
UK / US: **Horror Express**
Granada Films / Benmar Productions
90 minutes colour
production began 6 December 1971
. . . . . . . . . . . . . . . . . . . . . . . . . . . .
Director of Photography: Alejandro Ulloa;
Art Director: Ramiro Gómez; Editor: Robert
Dearberg; Sound: Antonio Illán; Music: John
Cacavas; Make-up: Julián Ruiz; Special Effects:
Pablo Pérez; Contact Lenses: Óptica Cottet
(Madrid); Screenplay: Arnaud D'Usseau and
[uncredited on Spanish prints] Julian Halevy,
from an original story by Eugenio Martín;
Associate Producer: Gregorio Sacristán;
Producer: Bernard Gordon [uncredited on
Spanish prints]; Director: Eugenio Martín

Christopher Lee (Professor Alexander Saxton);
Peter Cushing (Dr Wells); Alberto de Mendoza
(Pujardov); Telly Savalas (Captain Kazan);
Silvia Tortosa (Irina Petrouski); Julio Peña
(Inspector Mirov); Jorge Rigaud (Count
Petrouski); Ángel del Pozo (Yevtuchenko); Víctor
Israel (Maletero [baggage man]); Helga Liné
(Natasha); Alice Reinheart (Miss Jones); José
Jaspe (Konev); Vicente Roca (stationmaster);
Juan Olaguivel (creature); José Canalejas
(Russian guard); Barta Barri (1st telegraph
operator); Fernando Villena (2nd telegraph
operator); José Marco (Vorkin); only credited on
English-language prints: Peter Beckman; Faith
Clift (American woman); Hiroshi Kitatawa
(Krasinsky); Allen Russell

**Using the immortal Peter Cushing and Christopher Lee as indispensable elements in the fabric, Martín has succeeded in making a very interesting film ... in which the atmosphere is a marvel of realism. The two 'sacred monsters', Cushing and Lee, are surrounded by a highly effective ensemble in which Alberto de Mendoza's mystical character is a stand-out ... A quality film, without the shrill effects so common in the genre.** Cineinforme June 1973

**When I made *Horror Express* I was under a three-movie contract with Phil Yordan, although he had somebody else [Bernard Gordon] fronting this project, and the picture was made as an Anglo-Spanish co-production. That's how Peter Cushing and Christopher Lee came to be involved ... It went down really well abroad, but nobody thought much of it here. The Spanish critics reviewed it following their usual negative criteria.** Eugenio Martín [quoted in Fangoria September 1999]

*1906. British anthropologist Alexander Saxton has discovered what he theorises to be the Missing Link, preserved in ice in a Manchurian cave. Transferring it to the Trans-Siberian Express, he doesn't reckon with the professional curiosity of rival anthropologist Dr Wells, whose meddling inadvertently leads to the thawed-out creature's escape. Boiling its victims' brains in order to absorb their knowledge, it turns out to be playing host to an alien life form that got into it two million years ago...*

*Pánico en el Transiberiano* opens with snowy mountain vistas filmed, not in Sichuan, but near Puerto de Navacerrada, giving the film a bit of breadth before train-bound claustrophobia sets in. The first of many genre-literate quotations is sprung upon the viewer almost at once, with Lee's Professor Saxton peering into a demonic, ice-bound face recalling the

film's budget was topped up by Italian and German sources, foreign markets credited Andrea Bianchi as director purely for quota purposes – though later Bianchi films like *Malabimba* and *Le notti del terrore* would, coincidentally or otherwise, touch on similar themes.

imprisoned monster of *Frankenstein Meets the Wolf Man*. The story that develops rapidly recasts the revived ape man as red herring rather than missing link. Once the creature has been gunned down, the alien intelligence within it has the opportunity to inhabit several rather more sophisticated humans, turning the film into a riff on John W Campbell's 1938 novella *Who Goes There?*

As well as echoing *The Thing from Another World* (the 1951 film version of Campbell's story), screenwriters d'Usseau and Zimet grafted their shape-shifting alien onto the kind of exotic train scenario set in stone by the 1932 film *Rome Express*. Their consistently witty and inventive script therefore abounds in eclectic characters – a silky Mata Hari-style spy, a truculent police inspector, a Polish Count and his doe-eyed young Countess, a wholly unexpected bunch of third act Cossacks, even a wild-eyed Rasputin lookalike. The latter, splendidly played by Alberto de Mendoza, is a highly unlikely spiritual adviser to the Count and at one point, in explicit reference to one of Christopher Lee's most memorable Hammer showcases, is referred to as a mad monk.

Pride of place, however, goes to Cushing and Lee, both of whom are at their considerable best. Seeing Lee in a Spanish film isn't unduly startling, of course, but the sight of Cushing – well known for his resistance to working outside the UK – sharing scenes with such staples of Euro-horror as Mendoza, Helga Liné, Jorge Rigaud, Víctor Israel and Julio Peña is an absolute treat. It's Peña, as the impressively mutton-chopped Inspector Mirov, who shares the film's classic exchange. Himself the alien's host by this stage, he tries to put the two anthropologists off the scent by suggesting that *they* might be infected. In affronted reply, Cushing is granted the immortal line, "Monster? We're British, you know!"

The film's gentle satire of Englishmen abroad presents the two leads as carefully contrasted intellectual adventurers, owing something to Holmes and Watson but also to the Charters and Caldicott characters immortalised by Basil Radford and Naunton Wayne in *The Lady Vanishes*. Cushing is on thoroughly mischievous, birdlike form as Dr Wells, relishing absurd lines like "Is Professor Saxton's fossil still at large?" and even attempting a little romance with the sumptuous Liné. Lee's haughty persona is seen at its most relaxed and effective as Saxton, all the more so for his willingness to have it punctured here and there by well-timed humour. He gets to utter the generic line "It's alive!" not once but twice, and at the end he shoots and slices his way through hordes of reactivated zombie Cossacks with great aplomb,

eventually joining Cushing for a thrilling finale which is a cliffhanger in the most literal sense.

The film has an eerily memorable score by John Cacavas and is expertly directed by Eugenio Martín, who keeps things moving at a breathless pace while emphasising a wealth of lustrous cinematography and production design. And as the narrative rockets to its close it keeps throwing up ever more bizarre details. The victims' drained brains, for example, lose their characteristic convolutions (becoming, as Cushing's female assistant puts it, as "smooth as a baby's bottom"), while fluid from the ape's extracted eyeball discloses absurd prehistoric views predicated on the hoary idea – used just recently in Argento's *4 mosche di velluto grigio* – that "The creature's visual memory is located not in the brain, but in the eye itself." The premise, meanwhile, alludes not just to *Who Goes There?* but also Nigel Kneale's *Quatermass and the Pit* (primitive man mentally controlled by extraterrestrials), while providing a curious foretaste of *The Creeping Flesh*, the film that Cushing and Lee would move onto at Shepperton in February 1972. There, intriguingly, it's Cushing, not Lee, who makes a stunning anthropological discovery and it's Lee's meddling, rather than Cushing's, that accidentally releases the evil.

Bolstering its constantly evolving storyline with plenty of gruesome deaths, grisly autopsies, rampaging zombies and even an uninhibited last-minute turn from Telly Savalas, *Pánico en el Transiberiano* earned over 26 million pesetas at the Spanish box-office (having cost $350,000 to make) and took plenty more worldwide. "A very distinguished horror film," enthused *La Vanguardia* when it appeared at the 1972 Sitges Festival, "which is on a higher technical level than many of the pictures we see these days, while just to mention the players is to grasp the film's success: Christopher Lee, Peter Cushing, Telly Savalas. And an actor of cherished memory, Julio Peña, who died this year … Eugenio Martín comes out of the venture with flying colours."[51] The film was especially warmly received in Britain, where trade critic Marjorie Bilbow came up with a memorable endorsement: "Gothic horror on wheels, lightly sprinkled with in-jokes for the benefit of British audiences who can enjoy the understated wit with which Christopher Lee and Peter Cushing portray stiff-upper-lipped Englishmen coping with a lot of hysterical foreigners."[52]

Getting those two actors together in Madrid was a mark of just how far Spanish horror had come in the last few years, and the film containing them endures as a bona-fide classic of the form.

# Part Five

Hospital zombies
José Ruiz Lifante
and Vito Salier collar
Jeannine Mestre in
*No profanar el sueño
de los muertos* (1974)

## *Rites of Blood* 1971-1975

The early 1970s saw the horror market heading inexorably towards over-saturation. The amount of horror on offer was tough for distributors to keep up with, never mind potential audiences. It was an explosion of activity that could be traced all the way back to a couple of American films made in the summer of 1967, films whose impact was still reverberating several years on. Theoretically, Roman Polanski's *Rosemary's Baby* and George Romero's *Night of the Living Dead* couldn't have been more dissimilar – one a glossy big-budget chiller from Paramount, the other a grimy and conspicuously gruesome independent made for peanuts around Pittsburgh. Yet in their different ways they both tapped into the generational turmoil of the period, with an up-and-coming actor selling his wife's womb to a gaggle of elderly Satanists in the first instance and resurrected corpses feasting on their former loved ones in the second. On a more practical level, they had inspired a vogue for Devil worship and risen-dead scenarios that paved the way for the seismic impact of *The Exorcist* at the turn of 1974.

Satanic rites and mouldering zombies may have been the favoured sub-genres worldwide in the early 1970s, but the period was marked by a degree of eclecticism that no doubt added to distributor bewilderment. In Spain, for example, a new company, Profilmes, came into being with the express purpose of feeding the international demand for horror, enlisting such genre specialists as Paul Naschy and Amando de Ossorio to that end, but a host of virtually unclassifiable items could be found lurking at the fringes of the genre, among them horror-comedies both lame (Manuel Esteba's *Horror Story*, 1972) and fetchingly bizarre (Julio Pérez Tabernero's *Sexy Cat*, also 1972). The same year, the exigencies of international co-production saw Spain's premier art-house producer, Elías Querejeta, entering into an extremely combustible partnership with Wim Wenders, leading light of 'das neue Kino', to make a high-toned if rather stodgy version of Hawthorne's *The Scarlet Letter*. Known in Spain as *La letra escarlata* and in Germany as *Der scharlachrote Buchstabe*, the film recreated 17th century Salem on Spanish soil and backed Austrian star Senta Berger with such familiar faces as Yelena Samarina and Alfredo Mayo.

With so much genre material on offer, whether highbrow or lowbrow or somewhere in between, it was an opportune moment for the arrival of Spain's first magazine dedicated to horror and fantasy. The inaugural issue of *Terror Fantastic* in October 1971 featured a gruesome cover shot culled from Mario Bava's *Antefatto*, together with a special feature devoted to Boris Karloff, a retrospective on Tod Browning's *Freaks* and a review section by Juan Tébar, co-writer of *La residencia*. Under the stewardship of Pedro Yoldi, *Terror Fantastic* survived until November 1973, when the 26th issue went out under the abbreviated title *Terror*. Dealing not just with cinema but also literature and even 'Teatro-Terror', the magazine handled local output but the editorial emphasis was by no means parochial. Indeed, its eight Hammer covers considerably outnumbered the handful of issues emblazoned with Paul Naschy, Soledad Miranda and the Blind Dead.

*Terror Fantastic* appeared in the wake of a French magazine that had arisen in a very different milieu. Coinciding exactly with the final issue of *Midi-Minuit Fantastique*, a new genre journal called *L'Écran Fantastique* commenced publication in December 1970 – and at the time of writing it's still going. With its first issue examining such disparate personalities as Roger Corman, Basil Rathbone and Inoshiro Honda, the magazine was the brainchild of 22-year-old Alain Schlockoff, who had previously been involved with a journal called *Horizons du Fantastique* and whose new venture was touted

A backwoods ordeal for newly-weds Ana Belén and Víctor Manuel in *Morbo* (1971)

as the magazine of the L'Association Promotion du Fantastique. By May 1972 Schlockoff's promotional zeal was such that he'd set up the first Festival International du Film Fantastique et de Science-fiction, staging it at the Théâtre des Amandiers in Nanterre. For the time being, however, there still wasn't a great deal of specifically French fantastique to promote.

## HIS AND HERS

In addition to luring Peter Cushing and Christopher Lee into local studios, the Spanish horror boom continued to throw up its fair share of art-house provocations and bottom-of-the-barrel no-hopers. Chief among the first group was Gonzalo Suárez's

*Morbo*, a title carefully poised between 'morbid curiosity' and 'sexual arousal'. With this project, Suárez, still reeling from the reception accorded his impenetrable art films *El extraño caso del Doctor Fausto* and *Aoom*, went to the woods around Santa Cristina d'Aro in September 1971, intent on proving that he could make a film of symbolic weight that also qualified as a gripping thriller. And he succeeded.

Arresting the viewer's attention at once with the creepy image of red-eyed rats nosing their way around a tattered reproduction of the Mona Lisa, Suárez proceeds to weave a very nasty web of disquiet around a pretty pair of newly-weds (Ana Belén and Víctor Manuel) who, for unspecified reasons, decide to spend their honeymoon in a rather uninviting forest clearing. The web is slow to form, with some improbable philosophising impeding its progress, but the atmosphere created is eerily effective. A dead sheep intrudes on the couple's idyll, then a black caterpillar winds itself around the bride-and-groom figurines from their wedding cake, and finally one of their pet hamsters inexplicably eats its companion's head. Jacques Denjean's score is lounge music ruptured by electronic disturbances, and Suárez's nocturnal views of the couple's camper van, hedged about by inky darkness, look back to the previous year's exploitation hit *Count Yorga Vampire* while anticipating such films as *Vampyres*, *Long Weekend* and *The Hills Have Eyes*.

"I've always been upset," says the bride, "by people who spy on other people's pleasure." As the couple's relationship implodes, voyeurism turns out to be a key theme, just as it was in Eloy de la Iglesia's contemporary thrillers – a theme given added weight, perhaps, by the furtive prurience forced upon Spaniards by censorship. The source of the trouble turns out to be a weird couple resident in a derelict mansion, with the male half played by Michael J Pollard. He may have been Oscar-nominated a few years before for *Bonnie and Clyde*, but if Suárez had hoped to charm US viewers by casting Pollard he would have done better to give him a role lasting more than five minutes. Dragging Pollard all the way to the Costa Brava seems in retrospect like a ridiculous indulgence, particularly when a similarly offbeat local actor – Antonio Iranzo, say – would have filled the bill just as well.

Sexual politics of a more deadbeat, dunderheaded kind was available in J M Zabalza's El misterio de Cynthia Baird (The Mystery of Cynthia Baird), which is a bottom-of-the-barrel dweller if ever there was one. Apparently filmed in just 24 hours and being readied for release as early as April 1972, the result seems to have remained unseen for some 13 years. Zabalza was the director so roundly lambasted by Paul Naschy for his inept work on La furia del hombre lobo, and in El misterio he conforms to type with a film that for much of its length might as well be a two-hander stage play.

Simón Andreu and Susan Taff are illicit lovers whose discussion of the sex war is interrupted when Taff looks too long at a reproduction of Goya's 'Saturn Devouring His Son'. Hearing the Berlioz composition Symphonie fantastique, together with a voice saying "Transform into what you really are," she grows fangs and launches herself at Andreu, after which he goes through exactly the same process. Then, after a brief detour to the monastic ruins at Valdeiglesias, they finally work out that they both died back in April 1852. All this, stultifying as it is, just about justifies the film's alternative title, El retorno de los vampiros (The Return of the Vampires). Finally, a resourceful private eye (Guillermo Méndez) engages in an axe fight with Andreu, impaling him and later lopping off Taff's head. After this unwonted piece of action there follows an outstandingly lame Diaboliques-style twist and this extremely boring piece shudders to a halt.

The combination of vampirism and sexual politics was the catalyst for a much more distinguished film made just before Zabalza's and also featuring Simón Andreu as the male lead. Following up on Fata Morgana and Las crueles, writer-director Vicente Aranda focused on a newly-wed couple superficially similar to the one featured in Suárez's Morbo, which was a curious coincidence given that both directors were erstwhile shining stars of the Barcelona School. Aranda, however, threw in his lot with the horror boom much more uncompromisingly than Suárez, crafting a gore-strewn parable of female emancipation and giving it one of the genre's most memorable titles – La novia ensangrentada (The Blood Spattered Bride).

While prepping this film in December 1971, Aranda announced that Patty Shepard was to play the central role. Yet when production began the following month, she had been supplanted by the English actress Alexandra Bastedo, who was soon to become a Spanish favourite as plain 'La Bastedo'. Shepard is said to have regretted appearing in Klimovsky's La noche de Walpurgis, so she presumably didn't fancy playing another lesbian vampire.

*The newly married Susan arrives at her husband's ancestral home and quickly tires of the seemingly non-stop demands for sexual satisfaction thrust upon her. The upper floors are lined with portraits of the husband's male ancestors; the female portraits are hidden from view in a basement lumber room. One of them represents Carmila Karstein but the face has been cut out. That doesn't stop the 205-year-old Carmila from appearing to Susan and guiding her vengeful hand.*

In making La novia ensangrentada, Aranda anticipated by several months a similar move by his old Barcelona School confrere Jorge Grau, who in the summer of 1972 made a horror picture of his own with a rather similar title – Ceremonia sangrienta (Bloody Ceremony). Where Grau focused on a female monster from history (Erzsébet Báthory), Aranda turned to one from literature, very loosely adapting Le Fanu's already much adapted Carmilla. Crucially, both directors questioned exactly how monstrous their protagonists really were. In Aranda's case, Carmilla Karnstein – or Carmila Karstein, as he calls her – is presented as an agent of revenge for an oppressed section of society, just as Christopher Lee's vampire Count proved an equivocal force for liberation in the 1969 Hammer production Taste the Blood of Dracula.

It's tough to define Carmila in precise terms, however, for the film's chief fascination lies in establishing exactly where Aranda stood. Concocting a film that he frankly admitted was a means of getting himself out of financial difficulties, Aranda seems to have deliberately left the story open to different interpretations. As a result, it was possible for a 1980s critic to gloss the 'parable of female emancipation' referred to above as the exact opposite – as an invitation to share in "macho man's anxiety in the face of lesbianism."[1] Craftily playing across to two different audiences, Aranda was able to have his cake and eat it too. As well as offering women the cathartic vision of Susan and Carmila's grisly anti-macho murder spree, he also gave their penis-led menfolk the consolation of seeing the killers very comprehensively wiped out by the young husband in the final reel.

Intriguingly, the husband is never named; he's called simply 'He', a character designation that seems to mark him out as the enemy. Or maybe Aranda intended 'He' to stand for embattled blokes everywhere, heroically holding out against (literally) castrating harpies? But 'He' is so utterly bland, boorish and brutal that it's impossible not to root for the beautiful avengers. 'He' is a man whose chauvinism is so ingrained it appears entirely unthinking; for him, dragging his wife by her hair, caveman-style, is part of

Alexandra Bastedo presents the impassive Maribel Martín with an elegant castration tool in *La novia ensangrentada* (1972)

a supposedly affectionate game. Similarly, when he discovers an old bone and speculates that it might be Carmila's "delicate forearm," he immediately snaps it in two. His other female ancestors are viewable only by torchlight in the darkened cellar to which they've been condemned, an extremely powerful reference to women's invisibility in an oppressively macho culture.

Carmila, who is reputed to have "killed her husband on her wedding night … because he tried to make her do unspeakable things," is given plenty of livid rhetoric to push Susan towards vengeance. Amid nocturnal Gothic arches, she tells her that "Your sanctuary has been ravaged; your shrine stained, corrupted, grossly invaded" – prior to mounting an invasion of her own by sinking her teeth into the girl's throat. The forces ranged against the women are represented by 'He', of course, but also by his doltish groundsman and almost comically sceptical doctor. The latter, having dismissed Carmila as "flesh and blood: a paranoiac pervert," pays a terrible price for his complacency.

Unfortunately, the film is more memorable for the themes it touches on than for its entertainment value. It's about 15 minutes too long and suffers from a very odd and rather hokey score by Antonio Pérez Olea. As if to keep himself amused as the 102 minutes roll on, Aranda throws in various phallic symbols here and there. Susan's wedding veil gets snagged on an ornamental cannon at the beginning, and towards the end even a silhouetted castle window looms phallically as the doctor watches the two women "howling like cats in heat." Aranda also incorporates occasional reminders that he was an art-house director; not too many Spanish horrors of the period invoke Plato and Jung, for example. He shows off his knowledge of exploitation too, utilising a famous image from Russ Meyer's *Cherry, Harry & Raquel!* for *La novia*'s most surrealist moment – when 'He' discovers Carmila inexplicably buried under the local beach, clearing away the sand to reveal only her bare breasts and snorkel-fitted face.

## LA NOVIA ENSANGRENTADA

Spain 1972
UK / US: **The Blood Spattered Bride**
Morgana Films
101 minutes colour
production began January 1972

. . . . . . . . . . . . . . . . . . . . . . . . . .

Director of Photography: Fernando Arribas; Designer: Juan Alberto Soler [uncredited]; Editor: Pablo G del Amo; Sound: Jesús Ocaña, Luis Castro [both uncredited]; Music: Antonio Pérez Olea; Make-up: Cristóbal Criado; Special Effects: Antonio Molina [uncredited]; Based on *Carmila* [sic] by Sheridan Le Fanu; Executive Producer: José López Moreno; Writer-Producer-Director: Vicente Aranda

Simón Andreu ('he'); Maribel Martín (Susan); Alexandra Bastedo (Carmila-Mircala); Dean Selmier (doctor); Ángel Lombarte (caretaker); Montserrat Julió (housekeeper); Rosa María Rodríguez (Carol, their daughter)

Photography, production design, special effects and music are on the level of the worst León Klimovsky picture … The film's only real interest is as another example of how far the faux-intellectual [Barcelona] movement has collapsed, and of how its directors, when aiming their films at a mass audience, lapse into the gruesome and grotesque. *ABC Sevilla* 30 September 1972

*La novia ensangrentada* can be considered a made-to-order movie. Given that I'm also the producer, this might seem like a contradiction in terms. The explanation is that, in order to sort out some boring accounts with a producer I'd got mixed up with, it became essential to make a film that was accepted for distribution in advance. The script was written in two weeks and … the conditions imposed were an important part of the process.
*Vicente Aranda [quoted in Nuevo Fotogramas 7 July 1972]*

At moments like this, Alexandra Bastedo clearly disdained a body-double, unlike her co-star Maribel Martín, whose copious nude scenes are rather obviously performed by someone else. Aranda had been instructed to cram in certain commercial elements and minor matters like a 17-year-old star unwilling to appear nude weren't about to stop him. The other big commercial consideration, of course, was blood, which Aranda provides in veritable rivers, whether in the form of knife-plunging castrations or the apocalyptic climax in which Carmila's sarcophagus, and its two naked occupants, are blasted to kingdom come. Sadly, Aranda also indulges the Spanish penchant for animal cruelty by showing a fox, caught in a trap, being shot to death on camera. Inevitably, Carmila herself gets caught in the same trap later on.

As for that ending – it's somewhat depressing that the particular man the women are after succeeds in eluding and finally killing them, though maybe in this Aranda was demonstrating that a monstrously powerful patriarchy is proof even against supernatural threats. And an undead lesbian murderess is hardly a positive emblem of female liberation anyway. But, with male chauvinism of all kinds being given a long overdue jolt by a newly mobilised feminist movement, it was a confused and hysterical time. And perhaps that's the chief value of *La novia ensangrentada* – as a confused and hysterical time-capsule.

*La novia* seems to have stirred up strong feelings – mainly negative ones – in the people participating in it. Indeed, in later years both Aranda and Bastedo conspicuously omitted it from the filmographies contained on their personal websites. Maybe this isn't so startling in Aranda's case, given that his subsequent career brought him, among other garlands, a Goya award and a Palme d'Or nomination. Yet Bastedo's omission of the film is more telling, particularly since she happily listed a number of other Spanish horrors. Maybe, when the film finally reached the UK in 1980, she'd been stung by Eric Braun's scathing review in *Films and Filming*, which he rendered in verse and concluded like this: "And as for Bastedo, a girl I admire – / One more Les vampire and she may have to retire."[2]

Among the Spanish horrors that Bastedo did include in her filmography was León Klimovsky's 1973 film *Odio mi cuerpo* (I Hate My Body), a Swiss co-production that allegorised the battle of the sexes in far more brazen terms than *La novia*. Here, Bastedo is the subject of a brain transplant conducted by mad German surgeon Narciso Ibáñez Menta. The donor is a dead playboy and 'her' subsequent problems include gloating over other women's breasts and resisting the advances of lascivious men. (In the latter scenes Bastedo is supplanted, to comical, surreal and instructive effect, by her male self, Manuel de Blas.) When Bastedo's perceived gender makes her unable to reclaim the donor's top-flight engineering post, she ends up in the sex industry, with a colleague (Eva León) telling her that men "talk about sexual equality, equality of opportunity. But it's all a dirty lie. The world is theirs." These points, effective in themselves, co-exist rather uneasily with a host of exploitative details. The surgeon, who we're told in passing used to work in the concentration camps, is torched by Bastedo, who subsequently horsewhips the surgeon's partner (Gemma Cuervo), digs up the donor, blackmails his widow (María Silva), and is finally raped and accidentally killed by sailors.

Yet all this appears to have been less offensive to Bastedo than the vampire allegory of *La novia ensangrentada*. Both Bastedo and Aranda are now dead, so we'll never know their reasons for expunging *La novia* from their résumés. But the impulse to efface certain films from history was by no means unique to them. Another example of selective amnesia proving a boon to artistic snobbery was provided by the second-tier Hollywood star Joseph Cotten. The filmography contained in his memoirs makes no distinction between the 1971 Italian films *Lady Frankenstein* and *Baron Blood* – both are omitted entirely. A later title, Sergio Martino's 1978 extravaganza *L'isola degli uomini pesce* (Island of the Fish Men), also failed to make the cut. This rather engaging adventure film contains occasional dashes of horror, together with a brief turn from Cotten as the 1890s Dr Moreau type responsible for the titular mutations. But with such a tawdry title it clearly stood no chance of being listed alongside such imperishable Hollywood classics as *Citizen Kane* and *Airport '77*.

## LOZOYA ZOMBIES AND FUMETTI FRANCO

Helga Liné and Julio Peña, fresh from falling prey to an alien intelligence in *Pánico en el Transiberiano*, moved straight on to Paul Naschy's latest project, *El espanto surge de la tumba* (Horror Rises from the Tomb). Filmed at Naschy's own estate in Lozoya during the wintery February of 1972, this was the first horror picture from Profilmes, a Barcelona company, founded by Ricardo Muñoz Suay and José Antonio Pérez Giner, that would in due course make a further seven Naschy vehicles as well as a few Amando de Ossorio titles.

It also marked the feature debut of director Carlos Aured, León Klimovsky's assistant on *La noche de Walpurgis*, who got the job, according to Naschy, "because Klimovsky couldn't do it." Naschy also maintained that "I wrote the script in one night. They asked me to write the script at four o'clock in the afternoon, and if I hadn't written it so quickly the film might never have been done."[3] Though sounding like one of Naschy's tall tales, this one was independently corroborated by Aured. And that Profilmes really meant business where horror was concerned was indicated by the bullish tag-line: 'El cine de terror, superado en el más espeluznante filme' (Horror cinema outclassed in the most bloodcurdling movie).

Cristina Suriani succumbs to undead seducers Paul Naschy and Helga Liné in *El espanto surge de la tumba* (1972)

*France, 1454. Depraved warlock Alaric de Marnac and his wicked consort Mabille de Lancré are brutally put to death, both pronouncing dire curses on the men responsible. Nearly 520 years later, Alaric's descendant, Hugo, is cajoled into attending a seance, where he learns that Alaric's remains are buried on the family's country estate. Enlisting the aid of his friends Maurice, Paula and Silvia, he decides to dig them up...*

As well as imagining a sulphuric necromancer based on the presumed 15th century child killer Gilles de Rais, Naschy topped and tailed his script for *El espanto* with magpie quotations from *La maschera del demonio* and *Night of the Living Dead*. But for his central setpiece he cheerfully recycled something a bit less high-profile. The 1958 Universal potboiler *The Thing that Couldn't Die* featured the living head of a Devil-worshipping associate of Sir Francis Drake being unearthed on a California farm. Transplanting the action to 1970s France, Naschy inserts a baleful inscription into the rusty old trunk containing de Marnac's head. Perfectly encapsulating the warlock's monstrous sense of droit de seigneur, it reads: "My nourishment will come from the human heart. Red, palpitating and lowly..."

How de Marnac arrived at his headless state is made clear in a really splendid pre-credits sequence. Snow-covered peaks, a serenely babbling brook, the two Satanists transported to their doom on a cart pulled by a team of oxen – the atmosphere is chilly, sombre and almost palpable. Composer Carmelo Bernaola adds peculiar little squalls of percussion to the seething denunciations uttered by Alaric and Mabille, after which the former is smartly decapitated and Mabille is strung upside down, naked, with her exact fate left unclear as the blood-red titles roll in.

It's clear at once, from the first scene in his first film, that Aured had a flair for rendering highly wrought melodrama in serene, stately, low-key images, and the effect is much enhanced by the immediate contrast with contemporary Paris, where Hugo and his bland friends indulge in the familiar 'let's have a seance' routine. That Hugo is boorish as well as bland is confirmed when Julio Peña, playing a committed spiritualist, enthuses about caressing

# EL ESPANTO SURGE DE LA TUMBA

Spain 1972
US: **Horror Rises from the Tomb**
Profilmes
95 minutes colour
production began February 1972
. . . . . . . . . . . . . . . . . . . . . . . . . . . .
Director of Photography: Manuel Merino; Set Designer: Gumersindo Andrés; Chief Editor: Javier Morán; Music: Carmelo A Bernaola; Key Make-up: Julián Ruiz; Make-up: Romana G Escribano; Special Effects: Antonio Molina; Screenplay: Jacinto Molina [Paul Naschy]; Executive Producers: Ricardo Muñoz Suay, José Antonio Pérez Giner; Director: Carlos Aured

Paul Naschy (Hugo, Armand and Alaric de Marnac); Emma Cohen (Elvire); Vic Winner [Víctor Alcázar] (Maurice and André Roland); Helga Liné (Mabille de Lancré); Cristina Suriani (Paula); Betsabé Ruiz (Silvie); Luis Ciges (older thief); Julio Peña (Jean); María José Cantudo (Chantal); Juan Cazalilla (Gaston, Elvire's father); Francisco Llinás (younger thief); Ramón Centenero (André Govar, head vigilante); Montserrat Julió (Jean's wife); Francisco Nieto (Ibea); Elsa Zabala (Mme Irina Komarova); Esther Santana (victim); uncredited: José Marco (sentencing herald)

Blood, terror and – laughter in the film on show at the Capitol [Barcelona] ... Yet it must be admitted that the screenwriter's imagination is considerable. Plenty of emotions are stirred up. And in some places a climate of mystery has been created from the fumes of the supernatural. But, as so often with films of this type, the dialogue is poor and barely sustains the plot.
*La Vanguardia* 20 July 1973

We filmed at Paul's home, but he was so immersed in the picture he hadn't time to worry about the minor infelicities of the house and furniture ... My mind was split between two contradictory thoughts. On the one hand I felt it was the best movie in the world and that the film industry would fall at my feet. On the other, I was plagued by doubts, thinking that maybe I needed more budget, time, experience and talent. *Carlos Aured* [quoted in *Quatermass* Autumn 2002] the bust of Allan Kardec at Père-Lachaise cemetery. "Spiritualism," sneers Hugo, "is an old wives' tale made up by a bunch of con artists to fleece people." He also dismisses the credulous Silvia and Paula as "superstitious scared old ladies."

Obviously he's due for some eye-opening kind of comeuppance, and the process begins when he and his friends drive off into the mountains in Hugo's Mercedes. Amid plenty of unfaked sleet and snow, the foursome are set upon by bandits. That rough justice of a distinctly 15th century kind is still alive and well is demonstrated by a group of local vigilantes; rescuing Hugo and co, they shoot the first bandit (having first cut off his ear as a memento) and hang the second.

At the de Marnac estate, the chest in which Alaric's head is stored initially proves impossible to open, with Aured using a nicely unnerving high-angle shot from a crumbling archway as Hugo, Maurice and a bunch of workmen puzzle over the problem. Aured also stages an especially effective murder, with one of the workmen (Luis Ciges), possessed by Alaric's spirit, scything a girl to death on the kitchen table. Apart from a grisly slit-throat prosthetic, Aured makes do with nothing more than a low-level view of the victim's twitching feet as plates crash to the floor and her hair cascades into shot. We're then transported to the pink-tinted subterranean vault in which Alaric's head is preserved, his eyes flickering in response to the cry of a bat and a discreet little wisp of smoke issuing from his bloodied neck as it's reattached to his body. Then, once Silvia has been bloodily sacrificed to facilitate the resurrection of Mabille, Naschy and the smouldering Helga Liné make a splendidly baleful pair of villains as they gloat hungrily over an old man's extracted heart.

In the film's third act Naschy throws everything into the mix, including a Romero-style zombie siege (complete with the risen dead recoiling from flaming furniture on the patio) and the two resurrected diabolists seducing and killing various neighbourhood juves. Hugo is rather unexpectedly killed off, leaving Naschy with just the Alaric role and entrusting the routing of the villains to the beautiful Emma Cohen, who stoutly insists that "Good always triumphs over evil, and we have faith." Despite this conviction, the mood at the end, as Cohen wanders off amid flecks of snow to cast a sacred talisman into a lake, is distinctly bleak and non-celebratory. El espanto surge de la tumba has its crudities and a few outright absurdities, but Aured's spirited staging – and the deliciously diabolical combination of Naschy and Liné – make it arguably Naschy's most entertaining vehicle of all, a small classic of fantaterrorífico Español.

While Naschy went from strength to strength, Jess Franco continued on his idiosyncratic and wildly productive course. In 1971 he'd contributed threadbare fag ends to two popular West German franchises – Der Todesrächer von Soho (The Deadly Avenger of Soho) in the Bryan Edgar Wallace series, and Dr M schlägt zu (Dr M Strikes Back), a film that for German audiences obfuscated the antagonist's name, despite its proud display in the Spanish title: La venganza del Doctor Mabuse (The Revenge of Dr Mabuse). Then, moving beyond his Artur Brauner association, Franco made Christina princesse de l'érotisme (Christina, Princess of Eroticism) under his own banner, Prodif Ents.

Shot late in 1971 but kept under wraps until appearing at the Cannes Film Market in 1973, Christina is one of Franco's most beguiling films. It has its share of blood and brazen nudity, plus – if you're watching a 1981 re-release called Une Vierge chez les morts vivants (A Virgin Among the Living Dead) – some of the most comically ineffective zombies on record. (Jean Rollin was the reluctant director drafted in by Eurociné to shoot this crudely appended extra footage.) But in its original form it's a coldly measured, even mesmerising reflection on death, with the rootless Christina (Cristine von Blanc) visiting a remote Portuguese house occupied by "my uncle, my aunt and some weirdos." She's twice told by the locals, however, that the house is completely empty, and from this and other hints we gather that she's caught in the same deathly limbo occupied by Candace Hilligoss in the 1961 classic Carnival of Souls.

Into this flimsy fabric Franco weaves numerous surrealist details. The predatory Carmencé (Britt Nichols) is seen cutting a naked blind girl (Linda Hastreiter) with scissors and crooning, "There's nothing like the taste of blood." Christina sits becalmed in a dining room amid a pervasive buzzing of flies; her uncle (Howard Vernon) leads the household in a strange bout of laughing hysterics when pointing out, like Dracula, that "We're seldom hungry, hardly ever," and Christina's errant father (Paul Muller) is found hanged before being drawn into final darkness by the so-called Guardian of the Night (Anne Libert). The appearance in Christina's bedroom of a large ebony phallus apparently seals her fate, and Franco achieves a real sense of spell-stopped suspension as that fate unravels. First there's an extraordinary sacrificial set-piece for the nude Guardian and Christina, then a poetic coda as the Guardian leads the entire cast into a lily-covered lake that presumably signifies death. Some Franco scholars have theorised that the whole film was Franco's traumatised response to the premature passing of Soledad Miranda.

Around this time Franco also entered into partnership with the French producer Robert de Nesle. This was the point, roughly speaking, when Franco began to immerse himself so wholeheartedly in the screen's new freedoms that the elegance of his former work began to appear less and less frequently. The de Nesle arrangement resulted initially in three films that offer wildly transmogrified takes on the screen's traditional monsters, transporting them to craggy Portuguese locations into the bargain. Franco's self-confessed influence in all three was the staccato rhythm of comic books, so it seems reasonable to look upon them as a 'fumetti Franco' triptych.

The first, *Dracula contre Frankenstein* (Dracula versus Frankenstein), was shot (like *Christina*) in November 1971 and has plenty of wintery atmosphere. It's otherwise surprisingly dull for a film whose opening titles promise 'a fight between two Titans of Death'. What this boils down to is an arbitrary, last-minute dust-up between Frankenstein's monster and a putty-nosed werewolf, an echo of *Frankenstein Meets the Wolf Man* that positions the film as an update of Universal's 1940s monster-mashes. In appearance, Fernando Bilbao's monster vaguely resembles the old Universal design, though his facial scarring seems to have been applied with lipstick and his prosthetic chin comes visibly unglued on several occasions.

That Franco was aware of the more contemporary Hammer and AIP product is evident from the bleeding eyes sported by vampires Howard Vernon

Anne Libert falls victim to *La Fille de Dracula* (1972)

and Britt Nichols (quoting *Dracula Has Risen from the Grave*) and a bludgeoning home-invasion attack by Vernon and Paca Gabaldón that echoes *The Return of Count Yorga*. Dennis Price, himself a Hammer echo thanks to his recent appearance in *Twins of Evil*, is here reduced to frowning hard while someone else speaks Rainer von Frankenstein's thoughts in voice-over. Proposing to create an "Army of Shadows, invincible and indestructible," he sends the monster to abduct a Titian-haired nightclub singer (Josyane Gibert). The nightclub scene is a Franco staple, of course (though here it's very lame indeed), and Franco quotes himself again when the kidnapped Gibert is stretched out, Orlof style, on Frankenstein's slab. Her blood is piped

into a jar, appearing to drown a struggling bat (this is played for real), whereupon Vernon's Dracula is magically revived.

Franco can still tweak the imagination in unexpected ways, notably when the hulking Morpho (Luis Barboo) drives up in a sleek Mercedes-Benz to reveal Frankenstein, fur-hatted and puffy-faced, and Dracula, top-hatted and green-skinned, sitting cosily in the back seat. Recalling Franco's liaison with Harry Alan Towers, great chunks of the score are lifted from *Justine* and *El conde Drácula*, while the empty Cascais castle investigated early on by Dr Jonathan Seward (Alberto Dalbes) is familiar from *El proceso de las brujas*; it was to be much utilised by Franco in the 1971-72 period.

Second in the sequence, *La Fille de Dracula* (Dracula's Daughter), followed at the beginning of 1972 and is so catatonically paced it makes its companions seem like models of drive and economy. In Franco's usual self-referential way, it functions as a loose remake of the ten-year-old *La mano de un hombre muerto*, foregrounding a rash of provincial murders and with composer Daniel White taking over the role of under-suspicion aristocrat from Howard Vernon. Vernon is still present, however, sitting up arthritically in his casket as a Dracula even more enervated than his turn in *Dracula contre Frankenstein*. How the Count got into this story is anybody's guess, particularly since he makes his abode in, puzzlingly, Castle Karlstein. Vernon gets to chew on a topless victim in his coffin – his helper, the ubiquitous Britt Nichols, tactfully closes the lid on them – and he's finally killed when Alberto Dalbes hammers a chisel through his forehead. Nichols and Anne Libert have two laboriously extended lesbian encounters, with White's uncharacteristically terrible music applying a rinky-dink misterioso cue to vast close-ups of Nichols' nipples and Libert's pubic hair. All in all the material is so wafer-thin the film outstays its welcome within Reel One.

Franco shot the third of these films, *Les Expériences érotiques de Frankenstein* (The Erotic Experiences of Frankenstein), in the spring of 1972, opting for a monster painted silver (Bilbao again) and re-casting Vernon as a revived and thoroughly malevolent Cagliostro. The latter may as well be called Caligari, given the inevitable missions of murder on which the monster is sent. Cagliostro, it transpires, wants to achieve dominion by mating the monster with a female creation of his own, but to do so he needs the beauteous head of Mme Orloff (Nichols again) and the help of Frankenstein's daughter Véra (Beatriz Savón).

At the outset, Dennis Price's Frankenstein (now called Matias Artur rather than Rainer) succeeds in infusing speech into the monster via some form of head drill; its first words are, understandably, "My head hurts." No sooner has this miracle been achieved than Frankenstein is killed by Cagliostro's minion, a blind, partially feathered bird woman called Melisa (Anne Libert). Thereafter Véra revives her pasty-faced father on a regular basis, with poor Price twitching extravagantly on his slab in much the same way as the monster and his female counterpart do in other scenes. (Nichols twitches nude in the French cut.) Finally he revives spontaneously, tries to strangle Dalbes' Dr Seward and has sulphuric acid thrown on him by the trusty Inspector Tanner (Daniel White). Ridiculously, Frankenstein instantaneously loses his head and one hand while Seward is completely unharmed.

Despite moments like this, the film is too clumsily slung together to make the most of its authentically bonkers plot. There are, however, two genuinely arresting sequences bearing the true Franco stamp, with Cagliostro summoning the so-called Panthos race to witness, first, Mme Orloff's decapitation and, second, her union with the monster. (Surprisingly for Franco, the consummation never actually takes place.) In their winding sheets and crude skull masks these weird revenants point forward to the British film *The Monster Club* but are far more chilling. Libert's Melisa is a surprisingly effective creation too, reminiscent of Olga Baclanova in M-G-M's *Freaks* and sporting far fewer feathers for French audiences. In Spain, incidentally, the film was lumbered with a title, *La maldición de Frankenstein* (The Curse of Frankenstein), that was hardly original.

Another de Nesle production followed straight afterwards. *Les Démons* (The Demons) gave Franco the opportunity to retread ground already well covered in *El proceso de las brujas* three years before, with the saturnine Cihangir Gaffari taking over from Christopher Lee as Judge Jeffreys. Gaffari pledges, as before, to be working "for King and God and Britain" in locations that couldn't look more Portuguese if they tried. But Franco contrives some arresting moments, as when a wart-faced witch breaks the fourth wall by suddenly turning to camera and spitting out the words "Kill me! I don't care. The Devil will take you all!" Franco also involves the fugitive Anne Libert in

a subplot lifted from *Justine* and, to wind things up, Britt Nichols reduces Karin Field, Alberto Dalbes and finally Gaffari to pathetic anatomy-class skeletons just by kissing them. Dalbes, incidentally, having played Dr Seward in Franco's two Frankenstein films, is cast here as a character called Renfield.

Where Franco's previous Jeffreys project had taken *Witchfinder General* as its model, *Les Démons* is clearly a film made in the wake of Ken Russell's *The Devils*; it even has pretty much the same title. Sex-crazed nunsploitation is accordingly well to the fore and yields ever-diminishing returns. The film has a bigger budget than Franco was used to by this time and boasts glamorous cinematography by Raúl Artigot. But all this counts for very little when what seems like the 558th lesbian and-or masturbation scene comes round. When Franco holds up a reasonably coherent and involving story to show us an actress with her nose wedged in another actress' posterior, we're watching him hurtling straight for the career nadir dubbed by Tim Lucas 'the Porno Holocaust years'.[4]

Cihangir Gaffari and Raúl Artigot were also involved in *El monte de las brujas* (The Witches' Mountain), the latter as writer-director rather than cinematographer. Though made in summer 1972 and scheduled for Sitges that year, Artigot's film only appeared in the festival's 1973 line-up, whereupon it was apparently censored into incomprehensibility. The surviving version is indeed mystifying, with Patty Shepard accompanying Gaffari on a mountainous photojournalism assignment and running into a coven of witches. The ominous signs en route range from weird choral music and a stone-deaf innkeeper (Víctor Israel) to an ambiguous old lady (Ana Farra) who refers to the contents of her cauldron as "just some home remedies." The climax features a bunch of undulating young witches who look just like Pan's People, and the outcome is predictably grim for both Shepard and Gaffari. Artigot explained that he had deliberately shot the film "in a little region well known for its 'witchy' background, though if you're at all interested in the place you'll discover a truly impressive tradition: Asturias."[5] The journey there, however, is long, laborious and singularly uneventful.

## A NOBLE BLOOD LINE

After the Paul Naschy vehicle *El espanto surge de la tumba*, Profilmes engaged León Klimovsky to direct the second of four horror pictures made by the company in 1972. In Profilmes' usual tub-thumping style, the result was advertised with the line 'Las alucinaciones del cine de terror se superan en este espectaculo impresionante' (The hallucinations of horror cinema are outdone in this awesome spectacle). *La saga de los Drácula* (The Dracula Saga) was written by Emilio Martínez Lázaro and Juan Tébar under the collective pseudonym Lazarus Kaplan, whose script shows signs of having been intended as a wry-faced pastiche of the whole Dracula business – though the uneven result suggests Klimovsky was either unaware of this intent or unsympathetic to it.

> *Transylvania, late 19th century. Berta is four months' pregnant and travelling with her husband Hans to visit her grandfather, Count Dracula. Unknown to Berta, he died in 1860 and is now a vampire, as are the three beautiful women in his entourage – wife Munia, plus nieces Xenia and Irina. The Count is delighted at the prospect of a Dracula heir, as Valerio, his only son, is a Cyclopean mutant of whom he's deeply ashamed.*

*La saga de los Drácula* remains historically significant for two reasons. It was the first film to pick up on the unconvincing theory put forth in a newly published book called *In Search of Dracula* – namely, that Stoker's Count was based directly on the 15th century Wallachian voivode Vlad III. Pre-publication, Christopher Lee had appeared in a Swedish documentary of the same title in September 1971, but *La saga* was the first fiction film to espouse the idea. (It was swiftly followed by another Spanish entry, *El gran amor del conde Drácula*, then by a Dan Curtis TV movie made in 1973.) Secondly, *La saga* gave the monolithic Narciso Ibáñez Menta the opportunity to commit his extraordinary interpretation of Count Dracula to film. He'd played the role back in 1970 in an Argentinian TV series called *Otro vez Drácula* (Dracula Once Again); in *La saga* he offers a Count far truer to Stoker than the irrelevant Vlad theorising, a Dracula that ranks not far behind Christopher Lee's as the best on film.

La saga announces its gently iconoclastic intentions from the outset. An optically fogged nightmare sequence discloses an extremely strange, snickering werebat creature, equal parts

ridiculous and genuinely nasty. (Sadly, this singular monstrosity is never encountered again.) Then we see a coach thundering across a sparkling, sun-drenched

## LA SAGA DE LOS DRÁCULA

Spain 1972
US: **Death, Death, Death** / *The Dracula Saga* Profilmes
92 minutes colour
produced summer 1972
. . . . . . . . . . . . . . . . . . . . . . . . . . . .
Photography and Colour Effects: Francisco Sanchez; Set Designer: Gumersindo Andrés; Editor: Antonio Ramírez; Sound: José María San Mateo; Music of Johann Sebastian Bach; Mood music and Organ: Daniel J White, A Ramírez Ángel; Make-up: Miguel Sesé; Special Effects: Amobac; Story and Screenplay: Lazarus Kaplan [Emilio Martínez Lázaro, Juan Tébar]; Executive

Producer: Ricardo Muñoz Suay, José Antonio Perez Giner; Director: León Klimovsky

Tina Sainz (Berta); Tony Isbert (Hans); Narciso Ibáñez Menta (Conde Drácula); Helga Liné (Munia); María Kosti (Xenia); Cristina Suriani (Irina); J J Paladino (Gabor); Henry Gregor (Dr Karl); Mimi Muñoz (Sra Petruscu); Betsabé Ruiz (Stilla); Luis Ciges (lay preacher); Elsa Zabala (Sra Gastrop); Javier de Rivera (Gert); Fernando Villena (Sergei); Ramón Centenero (one-eyed villager); Pepe Riesgo (constable); Ingrid Rabel (gypsy woman); Manuel Barrera (gypsy); uncredited: Marisa Tovar (woodland victim)

Hispanic horror cinema, imaginative and always ready to demolish the myths in apparently arbitrary fashion while preserving the foundations on which they're based, has here achieved, thanks to the good offices of Klimovsky, a film that pays no heed whatever to the purity of the vampire legend ... [It's] weakened only by Tony Isbert's feeble performance, the incessant whining melodramatics of Tina Sainz, and the flimsiness of the dialogue.
*Terror Fantastic November 1973*

I made my debut in a film directed by Ana Mariscal [*El paseíllo*, 1968] ... Then I did theatre ... and then several horror films, films that young people these days like a lot. They gave a tribute to me at a festival recently; all the fans were young. If I were to go back to horror movies now I'd like to be the vampire, with plenty of special effects. *María Kosti [quoted in La Razón (Madrid) 26 July 2012]*

Narciso Ibáñez Menta, Tina Sainz and a bloodthirsty baby adorned the Profilmes pressbook for *La saga de los Drácula* (1972)

landscape rather than a mist-shrouded nocturnal one, and when the journey is terminated it isn't because of a superstitious driver (he doesn't seem particularly bothered) but because the fearful horses simply refuse to go on. The damsel inside the coach, Berta, isn't merely in distress but also pregnant, and several of the locals at the nearest hostelry seem to be disabled in some way; even the doctor gets about on crutches.

Sadly, these details, weird as they are, remain just details, for Klimovsky has trouble infusing life into these opening scenes. Part of the problem is the bland young leads, Tina Sainz and Tony Isbert, who look decidedly uncomfortable in their off-the-peg period costumes. Once they reach Berta's ancestral castle, Klimovsky tries to curry interest by filming their arrival through a screen of what looks like burlap; the effect is merely distracting and crops up, more and more damagingly, at regular intervals thereafter. And bona-fide boredom sets in as the couple explore the atmosphere-free castle interiors. Attended by a major-domo who looks more like a 1970s DJ than a Victorian retainer, they finally sit down to a meal of conspicuously rare beef and red wine that's suspiciously thick and syrupy. The 'inadvertent blood-drinking' gag would be repeated later in the year in the British film *The Vault of Horror*.

Finally, however, Ibáñez Menta and his female followers turn up and the interest quickens. Here is a Dracula 'saga' reconfigured as domestic soap opera, with the elderly patriarch lamenting the inter-breeding that has tainted his family while Munia, Xenia and Irina – memorably played by Helga Liné, María Kosti and Cristina Suriani – seduce anybody who crosses their path. In one especially bizarre throwaway moment, the whole brood gets together to form a string quartet.

Fitted with a white widow's peak and an impressive false nose, the 60-year-old Ibáñez Menta embodies "the eternal melancholy that we suffer" without any of the sentimental straining-after-effect that was to mar subsequent Draculas. Despite the enervation of his line, this Dracula is still a masterful presence, especially when turning from a portrait of Vlad III and telling Berta that "Our skin is like ancient parchment, without those variations that give life to human faces" – passing a candle under his own face to emphasise the point. The voice is sonorous yet world-weary and his stare is exactly the "blaze of basilisk horror" specified by Stoker. He has a full beard rather than just a military moustache, but otherwise this is Stoker's Dracula to the life; it's just a pity Ibáñez Menta never had the opportunity to appear in a straightforward adaptation. Indeed, the only mis-step in *La saga* is attributable to the costume designer rather than Ibáñez Menta – the occasional use of a cloak with a bat collar

so improbably huge it crosses the line into camp.

*La saga* has its moments, however, notably when the voracious Munia seduces the by-no-means unwilling Hans and Klimovsky cuts to an extremely creepy shot of Dracula and the rest of his household looking on approvingly from a distant staircase. The retainer (J J Paladino) finally thrusts a comely local wench (Betsabé Ruiz) into an attic room for an assignation with "the one member of the family you've yet to meet" – it's the freakish little Valerio, of course, and in the bloody aftermath the Count's no-nonsense approach to corpse disposal is expressed in the line "Get that garbage out of the castle." And Tina Sainz finally comes into her own when, in a mixture of *Rosemary's Baby* and *Witchfinder General*, Berta's sanity snaps and she descends to the crypt for a post-natal killing spree.

Unfortunately, intriguing though much of it is, *La saga* is entirely lacking in suspense or even rhythm. In particular, the bold use of Bach harpsichord concertos in lieu of a score gives the film a decorously embalmed quality. This may have been part of the point, but it makes the experience of watching it almost as inert as the Count's faltering blood line.

León Klimovsky handled vampires a second time the same year, though the much more energetic *La orgía nocturna de los vampiros* (The Vampires' Night Orgy) was made for producer José Frade rather than Profilmes. This one has the requisite coachload of 1970s Spaniards taking an emergency detour to the conspicuously wet and dismal Tolnia – unmarked on any map, lorded over by a Countess and a squire, and otherwise populated by snaggle-toothed yokels.

The gloom of the place is beautifully captured by veteran cinematographer Antonio L Ballesteros (his only contribution to Spain's horror boom), and Klimovsky contrives some exceptional set-pieces – Indio González being surrounded by the villagers at dead of night, a gang of previously unseen vampires suddenly sitting up in the coach to which they've lured two other victims, and finally a remarkable expansion of an early scene in *Night of the Living Dead*, with hero Jack Taylor and heroine Dyanik Zurakowska trying to escape and the getaway car being assailed by hordes of hungry locals. Helga Liné's smouldering Countess, meanwhile, seduces an *Othello*-reciting young teacher and then flings him over a balcony to the waiting vampires – an undignified end in any circumstances, but particularly since he's only wearing Y-fronts.

The film was written by Antonio Fos and Gabriel Moreno Burgos, who had just scripted the less fantastical *Nadie oyó gritar* for Eloy de la Iglesia. A severed finger duly turns up on a dinner plate (something of a Fos speciality), and a few cannibal gags are thrown in to add flavour. ("In no other place will you find a roast like this," smirks José Guardiola's squire.) In a further echo of earlier Fos scripts, Taylor is frankly presented as a Peeping Tom, with no apparent damage to his hero status. It's possible, too, that the film is saying something characteristically unsavoury about 1970s Spain; take away the vampire angle and it's just another bourgeois nightmare of being stranded among in-bred hicks. Looked at in this light, the slate village of Patones de Arriba is a splendidly primitive location, though the lowering atmosphere is regularly disrupted by some of the most inappropriately funky music cues ever chosen for a Spanish horror film.

In a sure sign of market saturation, *La orgía nocturna de los vampiros* was joined on Spain's production schedules by the very similarly titled *La orgía de los muertos* (Orgy of the Dead), which José Luis Merino made in June 1972. In particular, Dyanik Zurakowska might have been forgiven for a bit of confusion here, given that she did heroine duty in both films. This time she's the daughter of unscrupulous scientist Gérard Tichy, whose necromantic turn-of-the-century experiments have been sponsored by a deceased nobleman whose funeral gets the film off to a delightfully gloomy start. There's the vaulted sepulchre, the sudden storm, the mourners (even the priest) all fleeing through torrential rain – and finally a dead redhead dangling from a tree, thus providing the film's most evocative export title, *The Hanging Woman*. Thereafter, the Scottish highland setting – actually the Lleida Pyrenees – is milked for maximum atmosphere, with the aristocrat's boorish nephew (Stelvio Rosi) inheriting the estate and finding it replete with secret passages and, latterly, a bunch of reanimated corpses.

Like his previous Italian-Spanish co-production, *Ivanna*, this one was written by Merino in cahoots with Enrico Colombo. With no script input for a change, Paul Naschy pops up in a role that, though secondary, is certainly eye-catching. First seen observing the funeral like Dwight Frye's Fritz in *Frankenstein*, he later looms up outside a window just like Bela Lugosi's Ygor in *Son of Frankenstein*. Also called Ygor, this particular gravedigger is an out-and-out necrophile. In an extraordinary sequence, the beautiful young widow (Maria Pia Conte) summons him with incense and then, to get him going, dresses herself in a winding sheet. A sperm-dripping candle is prominent in the frame as he nuzzles her breasts, after which he goes guiltily down to the stews, kisses various corpses and reassures them that "You are the only ones I love." He later makes a pleasingly robotic zombie and is submitted to an extremely nifty decapitation.

Paul Naschy as a necrophile gravedigger turned zombie in *La orgía de los muertos* (1972)

Among the other zombies is Carlos Quiney, formerly the Byronic master in *Ivanna* but here a surly butler. The film boasts an exciting cemetery pursuit, a brilliant seance sequence in which the dead nobleman returns, even an absurd love-making scene in which Rosi and Pia Conte revolve in space. But perhaps its chief charm is, unusually, its English dub track. Rome's veteran ADR director Nick Alexander had a whale of a time here, adapting the dialogue into a series of waggish one-liners, ranging from "I'm afraid we'll just have to start looking for a new butler" to "By Gad: ladies' underwear. The scoundrel!" Best of all, Pasquale Basile's pipe-smoking police detective informs Rosi at a late stage that "Your story about the walking dead will never stand up."

By the summer of 1972 Profilmes' third horror picture of the year was under way, bringing back Paul Naschy for another of his garbled but engaging 'anything goes' concoctions. Klimovsky's *La rebelión de las muertas* (Uprising of the Zombie Women) is nominally set in England, with travelogue views of Piccadilly Circus thrown in to dupe the unwary, and casts Naschy in no fewer than three roles. He's a glamorous Indian guru, he's the guru's disfigured brother, and he's a horned Devil in a dream sequence.

Helga Liné and Tony Kendall (aka Luciano Stella) in Profilmes'
fourth horror project, *Las garras de Lorelei* (1972)

The brother is using voodoo to raise an army of
female zombies with a view to avenging himself on
various colonial types. "You, the living dead, slaves to
my will," he exults, "will be the executioners of your
own families." But a critique of colonialism, as was
featured in José Larraz's *La muerte incierta*, was clearly
the last thing on Naschy's mind; the avenger turns out
to have triggered the whole sorry story by raping and
killing an Englishwoman.

Naschy shows off his erudition in his usual
scattershot style, invoking voodoo spirit Baron
Samedi one minute, British serial killer John Christie
the next. The blue-faced zombie women have a few
show-stopping moments, arising in a morgue and
killing the attendant with his own beer can, or smiling
seraphically when the cops pump bullets into them.
Juan Carlos Calderón's ritzy score, though frequently
off-kilter, accompanies their final contortions with
a pleasing slur of backwards guitar. And there's
plenty for gorehounds to savour, from an axe in
one character's face to someone else's head falling
off. The messy narrative, in which nominal hero Vic
Winner (aka Víctor Alcázar) is given almost nothing
to do, is tolerable enough until an out-of-left-field
twist involving the soon-to-be ubiquitous María Kosti,
whose character has until then barely figured.

Profilmes' fourth and final horror project in their
1972 production schedule was *Las garras de Lorelei*
(The Claws of the Lorelei), which involved the Barcelona
company in a co-production deal with Madrid's
CC Astro outfit. Here, Amando de Ossorio moved from
the risen Knights Templar to a historical-mythological
theme that was potentially just as fruitful – the
Rhine legendry surrounding a fatally alluring female
water spirit. Unfortunately, the production was too
impoverished to do justice to Ossorio's idea, and to
make matters worse he lumbered himself with a very
silly science-fiction angle.

Subjecting a (visibly rubberised) severed hand to
the "photochemical action" of simulated moonlight,
a dodgy professor (Ángel Menéndez) reproduces the
terrible transformation undergone by the beautiful
Lorelei. The square-jawed hero, Sigurd (Tony
Kendall), is decidedly unimpressed but nevertheless
takes away a radioactive dagger with which to combat
the creature. When confronted by Lorelei and her
whip-wielding henchman (Luis Barboo), the now
dagger-less professor has no option but to pour acid
on himself in a laughably poor effects sequence.
Venturing into Lorelei's submarine stronghold –
actually the trusty monastery at Valdeiglesias – Sigurd
sees the fabled treasure of the Nibelungen. Lorelei,
meanwhile, rationalises her inescapable compulsion
to transform into a scaly monster and extract the
hearts of young women with a line suggestive of a
much better film. "Would you accuse a panther, or
a volcano, of being cruel?" she asks him.

Well aware of the exploitation commitments
incumbent on him, Ossorio sets much of the action
in a girls' school, allowing plenty of scope for
swimming pool scenes. Much more imposing than
any of the giggling bikini girls is the 40-year-old
Helga Liné. Winding up a busy year in Spanish horror,
she looks magnificent as the human Lorelei, though
her cloaked, reptilian alter ego is a bona-fide joke.
The rest of the film allows gun-toting Kendall to
model a wide range of denim ensembles, and – more
importantly – features a series of attack scenes staged
by Ossorio with eye-popping ferocity. The best of
these comes right at the beginning, with a young
bride-to-be (Betsabé Ruiz) succumbing to a window-
smashing beast assault in a welter of pre-credits gore.

While Spanish horror attracted such disparate
contributors as Klimovsky, Fos, Merino and Ossorio,
perhaps the strangest figure on the scene was
writer-director José María Oliveira, who appears to
have had a didactic purpose in concocting both
*Las flores del miedo* (The Flowers of Fear, 1972) and
*Los muertos, la carne y el diablo* (The Dead, the Flesh and
the Devil, 1974). As well as being head of the Spanish
branch of the William Morris agency, Oliveira was
even more intimately connected – via his American
wife, Patricia Wright – to the Church of Jesus Christ
of Latter-day Saints. Wright was duly cast in her
husband's first film as a retired medium investigating
the work of a fear-researching psychologist (Fernando
Hilbeck) and in the second as a murdered woman
who returns to her devoutly Christian husband (Carlos
Estrada). The explicitly religious insistence on the

afterlife in Oliveira's films has led to speculation that they were, at least in part, Mormon-sponsored; whatever the truth of this, between them they made fewer than ten million pesetas. Unencumbered by Mormon baggage, the young parapsychologist Sebastián D'Arbó would fare far better in the early 1980s with three afterlife-focused films of his own.

## TEEN TRAUMA AND IMMIGRANT LABOUR

In spring 1972, a long-gestating script co-written by Luis Buñuel and Jean-Claude Carrière finally went into production as an Italian-French-German concoction called *Il monaco*. Known in France as *Le Moine*, this was an adaptation of *The Monk*, Matthew Lewis' scandalously anti-clerical Gothic shocker from 1796. Long a pet project of Buñuel's, the film ended up being directed by Ado Kyrou, author of *Le Surréalisme au cinéma*, and in his hands it became very dull indeed. Franco Nero's errant Ambrosio looks like a famished wolf, while Nathalie Delon, as the blonde sorceress who seduces him to the dark side, performs some eye-catching rituals. There are also several arrestingly odd moments, such as a goat wandering down the aisle during one of the monk's sermons and a final shot in which the monk steps straight from the dungeons of the Inquisition onto the balcony of St Peter's, having apparently morphed into a 1970s Pope. Elsewhere, interest is only kept alive by Nicol Williamson's monied Duke, who is supremely affable yet reveals his true colours with nauseating lines like "It's incredible how rapidly these women age. At nine they're already hags."

While *Il monaco* was in production, Luis Buñuel's son Juan was making his first feature in France. The intriguingly titled *Au Rendez-vous de la mort joyeuse* (At the Meeting with Joyous Death), which for the younger Buñuel came after a lengthy apprenticeship not only to his father but also to Louis Malle, was shot in May-June 1972 at the isolated Château du Petit Chevincourt in Saint-Rémy-lès-Chevreuse. Written in collaboration with Pierre-Jean Maintigneux, the film explores a topic rarely touched on back then but since exploited many times – a poltergeist outbreak apparently triggered by a pubescent girl. Competing with such titles as *Malpertuis*, *La saga de los Drácula* and *Lady Frankenstein*, it won Buñuel the Best Director award at the 1973 Sitges Festival. For his part, Maintigneux wrote a novelisation that duly appeared in Galliera's short-lived 'Bibliothèque de l'étrange' series.

Accompanied by their 14-year-old daughter Sophie and much younger son Dominique, illustrator Marc Villiers and his wife, feminist writer Françoise, move to a secluded country house in Île-de-France that has been empty for eight years. A series of inexplicable disturbances – from overturning paint pots to full-on blizzards of animated furniture – eventually drives them away, whereupon a TV crew moves in for the purposes of a paranormal documentary. But Sophie comes back...

## AU RENDEZ-VOUS DE LA MORT JOYEUSE

France-Italy 1972
US: **Expulsion of the Devil**
Les Productions Artistes Associés Paris / PEA Produzioni Europee Associati Rome / Télécip Paris
90 minutes colour
production began 15 May 1972

............................

Director of Photography: Ghislain Cloquet; Art Director: Robert Clavel; Editor: Geneviève Vaury; Sound: Jean-Louis Ducarme; Music: selections from Vieuxtemps, Beethoven, and Ouazana / Festi aka 'Bloc Note'; Make-up: Loan N'guyen; Special Effects:

Pierre Durin; Screenplay: Juan Buñuel, Pierre-Jean Maintigneux; Executive Producer: Robert Velin; Director: Juan Buñuel

Françoise Fabian (Françoise); Jean-Marc Bory (Marc); Yasmine Dahm (Sophie); Jean-Pierre Darras (Peron [TV director]); Claude Dauphin (Father d'Aval); Michel Creton (Leroy); Gérard Depardieu (Beretti); André Weber (Kleber); Renato Salvatori (Henri); Toni Librizzi (Mario Santini; Loris Baccheschi; Pascale Ange; Corinne Armand; Monique Berardi; Sylvie Bourgoin; Corinne Deforges; Nadia Di Bert; Brigitte Toutain; Mimi Young

I'd venture to say that this *Rendez-vous*, likable and promising though it may be, is nevertheless a missed appointment ... The film can be watched with pleasure yet resists analysis. Juan Buñuel, whose direction is adroit and smooth enough, is undoubtedly a better filmmaker than writer. Should it please Satan that he dedicates himself to fantasy, we'd be delighted – provided he has good material. *Écran March 1973*

For me it remains a love story between a house and a girl. The house isn't sentient; it's a force. The little girl isn't 'aware' either. You could say, if you like, that she's a medium. She's unafraid, looking at everything calmly because children accept things that adults don't. Maybe subconsciously she wishes harm on all the people who push her around ... But don't look for logic. The illogical is my logical. *Juan Buñuel [quoted in Télérama 3 February 1973]*

Father and daughter (Jean-Marc Bory and Yasmine Dahm) contemplate a supposedly peaceful Île-de-France château in *Au Rendez-vous de la mort joyeuse* (1972)

The film's tone is at first bucolic and restful, with an establishing shot of the house succeeded by a 360° pan that circles right back to it, after which the credits play out over an equally sedate 360° pan in the opposite direction. Sophie does a drawing of the façade but adds the ivy that she thinks would give it real character, while her father theorises that the house, though antique-looking, might only be as old as he is – 38. ("In those days, people danced the fox trot in places like this.") In the kitchen, touches of tension are discernible between the rather unmotivated Marc and more dynamic Françoise, whereupon a tub of sludge-like grey-green paint tips over of its own accord.

In due course the manifestations become considerably more dramatic. When Sophie stumbles upon her parents making love, bedroom windows shatter and Buñuel contrives a really striking shot of Sophie standing calmly at the end of a darkened corridor as glass and other oddments spray in. The next day she surveys an alfresco family group through a broken window pane, implying that the family's difficulties go deeper than previously suspected. The screw tightens further when Marc finds a pile of mud (or worse) slathered across his latest illustration. Later, husband and wife are kissing on the lawn when the birds suddenly stop singing and an outdoor drinks table flings itself backwards through the French windows and smashes up the drawing room. A raffish family friend arrives and maybe gets to the heart of the matter when looking at Sophie and saying "This little girl is turning into a woman." Then, after he's been brutally assaulted by kitchen appliances, the family do the sensible thing that so few families do in films of this type – they leave.

As the TV crew moves in the film inevitably shifts gears, yet already Buñuel has left us with a host of tantalising questions, mainly focused on Sophie's role in the disturbances. She's prone to extremely strange behaviour – venturing into the woods, for example, and cementing a couple of snails together while encircling them with a filthy length of rope and covering them with leaves. Yet the serene circularity of Buñuel's opening view of the house suggests that history might be repeating itself, with the house as focal point of numerous disturbances down the years. According to Maintigneux's novelisation, "some unknown force, diabolically intelligent and extremely observant, lives in these old walls."[6] And the film's poster depicts Sophie with much of her hair replaced by a mane of ivy – the very ivy she feels the house lacks. So perhaps Sophie and the house are in some way indivisible? Needless to say, Buñuel is at pains to

clarify none of these puzzles, and in the film's final phase things only get weirder.

At nightfall, the investigative TV types, among them smooth presenter Jean-Pierre Darras and youthful sound guy Gérard Depardieu, are supplemented – in a wildly out-of-left-field development – by Claude Dauphin's elderly curé, who turns up with an entire troop of Girl Scouts in tow. The girls' bizarre recitation of Sacchini's *Chimène, ou Le Cid* helps trigger off a final outburst of freakishness in which several of those present seem to will their own deaths. Sophie, meanwhile, is reflected in a mirror by an ambiguously smiling doppelgänger that fails to match her movements. It's in this section that Buñuel also brings an undercurrent of aberrant sexuality to the surface, with the TV men spotting the priest in bed with two of his charges (it turns out to be a collective hallucination) and the presenter resisting Sophie's precocious advances only to end up pinned to his bed by a revolting counterpane of viscous mud – or, as before, something worse.

Tellingly, it's only Marc who pursues Sophie back to the house in this second phase of the film; her mother, Françoise, is excluded. We remember, however, that she was at work on a manuscript called 'Modern Woman: Sexual Object or Liberated Human Being?' And at the end there is a liberation of sorts when Sophie returns to the house alone, watches it becoming magically overgrown with the ivy she always wanted, then steps serenely inside. Preserving its secrets, the film benefits from a suitably unreadable performance from the teenage model Yasmine Dahm and from Buñuel's expertly sustained climate of low-tech eeriness.

Another French film in 'disturbed teen' mode, though dealing with delusional sociopathy rather than poltergeist activity, was Joël Séria's *Mais ne nous délivrez pas du mal* (But Deliver Us Not from Evil). Made early in 1970, this one became something of a scandal, finding itself suppressed for several months prior to making a belated splash at Cannes in 1971. Loosely based on New Zealand's Parker-Hulme murder case of 1954, it focuses on two teenage girls who turn to vandalism and eventually murder. "Let the other cretins devote themselves to virtue," one of them writes in her diary. "We shall dedicate our lives to Satan." Unfortunately, Séria has trouble maintaining viewer interest in these repugnant creatures for over 100 minutes, and only a bizarre scene in which they sit in their underwear with a bemused middle-aged man (Bernard Dhéran) works up the kind of queasy disquiet that should have characterised the whole film; indeed, he ends up trying to have sex with one of them and gets murdered. Elsewhere, Anne

Alain Delon
confronts Annie
Girardot with the
grisly secrets of his
laboratory annex in
*Traitement de choc*
(1972)

and Lore (Jeanne Goupil and Catherine Wagener),
having listened sneeringly to a nose-blowing priest
sermonising about cinema and TV being "vehicles of
depravity and degradation," kill a couple of birds in
scenes that look distressingly unfaked.

Picked up at Cannes by the maverick Soho distributor
Antony Balch, Séria's film, retitled *Don't Deliver Us from
Evil*, duly opened in January 1972 at the Jacey Cinema
in Piccadilly, with a typically brazen Balch poster
proclaiming it 'The French Film Banned in France!'
In a long history of provocative programming Balch's
masterpiece came round in February 1975, when he put
out his latest French acquisition under the come-hither
title *Doctor in the Nude*. This was actually Alain Jessua's
*Traitement de choc* (Shock Treatment), which had been a
big hit in French cinemas two years earlier and boasted
two of France's biggest stars on the billboards – Annie
Girardot and Alain Delon. For UK filmgoers these
were unusual names to see attached to what sounded,
thanks to Balch, like a low-level British sex farce.

*When 38-year-old Hélène Masson books in at Dr Devilers'
isolated health clinic, she finds that the well-heeled
patients form a self-satisfied community of sorts, based,
as one of them puts it, on "a kind of complicity." The
doctor's rejuvenation therapy, she's told, derives from live
blood cells extracted from sheep embryos. She wonders,
however, why so many of the Portuguese servants seem
listless – and why several of them disappear altogether.*

## TRAITEMENT DE CHOC

France-Italy 1972
Italy: *L'uomo che uccideva a sangue freddo*
UK: **Doctor in the Nude**
US: **Shock Treatment**
Lira Films Paris / AJ Films Paris / Medusa
  Distribuzione Rome
91 minutes colour
production began 17 August 1972

. . . . . . . . . . . . . . . . . . . . . . . . . . . .

Director of Photography: Jacques Robin; Art
Director: Constantin Mejinsky; Supervising
Editor: Hélène Plemiannikov; Sound:
William [Robert] Sivel; Music: René Koering,
Alain Jessua; Make-up: Louis Bonnemaison,
Michel Deruelle; Special Effects: André
Pierdel, Louis Assola; Screenplay: Alain
Jessua; Screenplay Collaborator: Roger
Curel; Producers: Raymond Danon, Jacques
Dorfmann; Director: Alain Jessua

Alain Delon (Dr Devilers); Annie Girardot
(Hélène Masson); Robert Hirsch (Jérôme
Savignat); Michel Duchaussoy (Dr Bernard);
Jean-François Calvé (René Gassin); Gabriel
Cattand (De Boissière); Jeanne Colletin
(Camille Giovanelli); Robert Party (Colonel de
Riberolles); Jean Roquel (Marcel Lussac); Roger
Muni (Paul Giovanelli); Lucienne Legrand (Lise
de Riberolles); Anne-Marie Deschodt (Henriette
Lussac); Salvino Di Pietra; Gabriella Cotta
Ramusino; Nicole Gueden (restaurateur's wife);
François Landolt; Jean Leuvrais (Commissioner
Jean Loubet); Guy Saint Jean (restaurateur);
Anna Gaylor (Mlle Denise); Jurandir Craveiro
(Manoel); Joao Pareira López (Joao); Alvaro
Luis Carrasquinha; Mauricette Pierson; Firmin
Pisias (nurse); uncredited: Jacques Santi
(Le Quérec)

Alain Jessua's intriguing film ... is a particularly adroit shocker, all the
better for having a quality cast, including the ageless Alain Delon and the
sympathetic Annie Girardot ... Basically, it is Hammer horror. But it is that
touch of class which rivets the attention. Wild horses wouldn't have dragged
me away from it before the grim final scene. *Daily Mail* 15 February 1975

After *La Planète bleue* [an aborted project] I was really exhausted so I spent
a week in thalassotherapy. While I was there I had the idea of turning
the experience into a horror film set in a health clinic ... *Traitement de choc*
incorporates a lot of black humour, which is a great way to make your
point while also entertaining your audience.
*Alain Jessua* [quoted by Newwavefilm.com September 2014]

Rejuvenation fantasies had a long Hollywood pedigree
when Jessua started shooting *Traitement de choc* on
the Breton island of Belle-Île-en-Mer in August 1972.
Whether in silent-era whimsies like *The Young Diana* or

*Vanity's Price*, or drive-in 1950s schlock like *The Wasp Woman* and *The Leech Woman*, female protagonists were the norm in 'elixir of youth' dramas, and 20 years after Jessua's film the tradition was upheld in the high-gloss horror-comedy *Death Becomes Her*. Yet by writing about recognisable people, and by adding a political dimension, Jessua diverted the standard narrative well away from whimsy, comedy and schlock. Indeed, his satirical commentary on the unreasoning thirst for eternal youth would be exceeded in gorge-heaving grossness only by Fruit Chan's 2004 film *Dumplings*.

Just as *Dumplings* would use China's one-child policy as a controversial starting point, Jessua focused on the recent peak in Portuguese immigration to France, which in the late 1960s had been bringing in some 80,000 newcomers annually, resulting in a 1971 Franco-Portuguese agreement limiting the yearly intake to 65,000. The aptly named Dr Devilers' solution to the problem is based, rather vaguely, on his experiences in the Amazon. The doctor is still relatively young, so we presume he learned his trade from all the ageing Nazi doctors reputed to have holed up in South America. Yet Hélène finds an ancient volume on his glimmering shelves that includes an illustration of Amazonian natives eviscerating an explorer at the stake, suggesting Devilers' models are considerably older. "Nothing has changed in our society," he explains. "Just like the primitives, we sacrifice the weak."

Inscrutably played by Delon, Devilers is a character rich in associations, recalling France's real-life monkey-gland guru, Dr Serge Voronoff, one minute, and echoing the devious Squire Hamilton from the 1965 film *The Plague of the Zombies* the next. (Devilers' Amazon connections are similar to Hamilton's formative experiences in Haiti, while the doctor's illegal Portuguese immigrants are paralleled by Hamilton's unpaid workforce of Cornish zombies.) And Jessua has fun by slipping in a few indications that Devilers' contempt for humanity extends even to the bourgeois patients who constitute his livelihood. "I returned to all these arseholes," he sneers, "and now I find myself dependent on them."

*Traitement de choc* is a classic conspiracy thriller, expertly controlled by Jessua but really 'sold' by the sincerity of Annie Girardot's extraordinary lead performance. "For the first time in my life," she muses, "I feel my age," and later she has a muted but deeply poignant monologue about looking at herself in the mirror in the wake of being jilted. "A woman doing her make-up is half-blind," she reflects. "It's like putting a watch together."

Despite this introspective mood Hélène proves admirably alert to the accumulation of sinister portents surrounding her. The signs are small at first, from the antiseptic 'script' parroted by the clinic's staff, complete with repeated references to the island's microclimate, to an unsteady Portuguese waiter pitching, salver and all, into the swimming pool. (The waiting staff last year, one of the patients observes, were Spanish and "kept dropping like flies.") The real escalation of the horror is triggered by Hélène's gay friend Jérôme; movingly played by Robert Hirsch, he's become addicted to Devilers' treatment but can no longer afford it, rapidly disintegrating and ending up broken at the foot of a cliff. When a Portuguese boy called Joâo is reported to have left the island, Devilers is given the splendidly ambiguous line "I was the one who saw him off," after which Hélène spirals inexorably into the 'heroine whom no one believes' mode beloved of film noir.

As well as co-writing the film's memorably eccentric score, Jessua's greatest moments in *Traitement de choc* involve a strange kind of euphoria that in the climax lapses into hard-to-watch hysteria. An extraordinary sauna sequence, followed by an almost orgiastic frolic in the surf, requires most of the cast to strip off completely – including Delon, thereby justifying the ridiculous English title imposed on the film by Antony Balch. And the final confrontation between Hélène and Devilers – in which nameless fluids froth from glass tubes and something even worse is suspended in the doctor's laboratory annex – is played in all-stops-out fashion by Girardot and Delon, with Hélène's shrieks really coming from the gut as she launches herself vengefully at Devilers.

Jessua's film is also interesting in that it conforms to the 'something in the air' rule that crops up so often in the film industry. On 5 September 1972 – less than three weeks after *Traitement de choc* started production – Richard Fleischer began work in Los Angeles on *Soylent Green*, in which Charlton Heston traces a brand of synthetic food to an extremely unpleasant source. Anticipating both films, in June Riccardo Ghione was making *Vampire 2000*, a memorably kitsch black comedy in which well-heeled husband and wife Enzo Tarascio and Marina Malfatti drain the blood of hippies, prostitutes and other 'riff raff' for use on the black market; the film reached cinemas under the more elaborate title *Il prato macchiato di rosso* (The Blood Stained Lawn). On a similar wavelength but coming a bit late to the party, Rod Hardy's 1979 film *Thirst* involves an Australian retreat in which humans are bled like cattle for the benefit of vampires. Yet none of these films is as icily effective as Jessua's.

Juan Buñuel, meanwhile, moved from *Au Rendez-vous de la mort joyeuse* to a grotesque fantasy more in line with the work of his revered father Luis, casting Catherine Deneuve as a writer with magical powers in *La Femme aux bottes rouges* (The Woman with Red Boots). Then in December 1974 he started shooting a grimly realistic mediaeval subject called *Leonor*, a French-Italian co-production numbering Jean-Claude Carrière and Bernardino Zapponi among its writers. Here, Michel Piccoli is Richard, an aristocratic widower who replaces the dead Leonor (Liv Ullman) with the 19-year-old Caterina (Ornella Muti) – until he's given the chance, ten years after her departure, to bring Ullman back to life. This would rank as the only film version of one of Ludwig Tieck's Gothic tales were it not for the fact that recent scholarship has re-assigned its 1823 source, *Laßt die Todten ruhen* (Wake Not the Dead), to Tieck's contemporary, Ernst Raupach.

Buñuel focuses less on the spectral reawakening of Leonor and more on the obsessive state of mourning that, as the original story puts it, cuts off the bereaved Richard from the living. As a result, the ambiguous sorcerer who comes to Richard's aid – introduced in the story in paragraph six – doesn't show up in the film until close to the 50-minute mark. Prior to that, the tone is set by the keening wind that whistles through the film's arid mountain landscapes, a chilly mood of desolation that's underlined when Richard kills the horse responsible for crushing his wife and, in discreet long shot, collapses despairingly against the castle gate. Later, indifferent to the youthful Caterina, he falls into drunken dissipation with his fellow feudal knights. Leonor, meanwhile, passes silently before him in a colonnade, subsequently appearing (in a shot reminiscent of Jack Clayton's *The Innocents*) on the opposite side of a babbling stream.

So far Leonor is just a ghost-like memory; when she returns for real she takes Richard's sage old apothecary aside and says, "Would you do me a great favour? Make me a very strong perfume." That she has become a sort of vampire is alluded to merely via her scarlet dress and the long black cloak in which she envelops her small victims – and by the disturbing fact that the killings reawaken her sex drive. A local girl accused of the 13 child murders is, not burned, but actually exploded at the stake, after which the film stutters to a rather anti-climactic close when Richard makes the self-sacrificing decision to end Leonor's new life. But it's brilliantly acted, beautifully photographed (Luciano Tovoli) and scored (Ennio Morricone), and makes Buñuel's subsequent defection to TV seem regrettable.

## ANOTHER BLOODY COUNTESS

In January 1970 the Milanese beauty Lucia Bosé turned 39. Formerly one of the most striking faces of Italian neo-realism, before even that she'd been winner of the 1947 Miss Italia contest. (The runners-up that year were Gianna Maria Canale and Gina Lollobrigida.) By the turn of the 1970s Bosé had acquired a regal, and slightly glacial, maturity that was well-suited for commanding female leads in horror films.

Lucia Bosé and American import Farley Granger were the draws in *Qualcosa striscia nel buio* (1970)

The first of four projects to exploit this started shooting in May 1970. Sadly, the splendid title of Mario Colucci's *Qualcosa striscia nel buio* (Something Crawling in the Dark) isn't quite matched by its plot, which is yet another retread of the 'ill-assorted bourgeois creeps stranded in a remote house' routine, and a rather laboured one at that. Indeed, Margheriti's *Contronatura* may well have been on Colucci's mind when writing it. It begins, however, with one of the truly great opening lines, as Giacomo Rossi Stuart surveys the encroaching storm and tells Bosé, "Helen certainly chose a grand night to unveil her new nose." The remainder involves a supposed haunting and a couple of brief possessions, all of which turn out to be nonsensical, given that the earthbound resolution involves a wanted killer played by Farley Granger. (Granger, sometime star of a couple of Hitchcock classics and Visconti's *Senso*, was here embarking on a handy sideline in Italian exploitation.) The film is notable, however, for two things – the one-and-only acting performance of the brilliant composer Angelo Francesco Lavagnino, and a highly effective seance sequence in which Rossi Stuart is extremely creepy when briefly infiltrated by a dead woman.

Bosé also presided at a seance – several, in fact – in Giulio Questi's extraordinary *Arcana*, which started shooting in the star's native Milan on 21 June 1971. Bosé's phoney medium in this bizarre curio is mother to an unnamed son (Maurizio Degli Eposti) who is genuinely psychic and also seriously deranged. Conducting arcane rituals involving string, photographs and donkey teeth, he causes plates to fly around, playing cards to lay themselves and flowers to wilt. He also cuts the maternal breast, trains a gang of neighbourhood children to attack a well-heeled homosexual, and garlands the city streets with decorative mobiles. The film is full of fascinating images (a donkey being winched up a wall, a gaggle of Milanese weirdos licking door frames), the precise meaning of which remains just out of reach. The military's climactic gunning-down of all and sundry in the street promises some enlightenment, but then the credits roll. Early on Bosé points out that "Illnesses are always expelled from the mouth," setting up the film's pièce de résistance – a scene in which, unfaked, she throws up several leaping frogs. An acting feat that definitely qualifies as above and beyond the call of duty.

In due course Bosé would appear as a callous upper-class wife in a Spanish curio called *Manchas de sangre en un coche nuevo* (Blood Stains in a Brand-New Car), discussed on page 306. In the meantime, she was the main attraction in a Spanish-Italian co-production called *Ceremonia sangrienta* (Bloody Ceremony), which started shooting in July 1972 and was the first of two notable horror pictures made by the Catalan writer-director Jorge Grau. A former member, like Vicente Aranda, of the Barcelona School, Grau had received some pretty remarkable

plaudits for his art films in the previous decade, notably *Noche de verano* (Summer Night) and *Una historia de amor* (A Love Story). As things turned out, *Ceremonia sangrienta*, though conceived as another art film, actually marked Grau's move into commercial cinema, resulting in a snobbish perception among his peers that he had 'sold out'.

> *Cajlice, 1807. Amid a rash of bloody murders, the corpse of a dead doctor is dug up and put on trial for vampirism. In this irrational atmosphere, Erzsébet, the local Marquesa, is reminded by her housekeeper of an ancestor who devised a unique means of preserving her youth. In order to follow suit, Erzsébet persuades her sadistic husband, Karl, to take advantage of the panic by killing a number of neighbourhood girls…*

Grau took as his subject the ever-popular Blood Countess, with Valentine Penrose's 1962 book *Erzsébet Báthory La Comtesse sanglante* as a loose foundation. He'd spent several years trying to get the project off the ground and at one point was told that Hammer Films had expressed an interest. Grau heard nothing further until Peter Sasdy's *Countess Dracula* began shooting at Pinewood in July 1970. Though irritated by this 'coincidence', Grau nevertheless conceded that the existence of a Hammer version of the story helped to finally get *Ceremonia sangrienta* into production two years later.

That the film originated as a personal project is obvious from the start. Despite plenty of visceral detail, it's a sombre and thoughtful affair, boasting a sophisticated focus on Erzsébet's insecurity and accumulated guilt together with a sardonic critique of the mob mentality that holds sway directly outside her castle. This is crystallised in the opening minutes, with the Marques, Karl, looking down from a high window

*Milanese seances are among the many bizarre ingredients of* Arcana *(1971)*

at a strange nocturnal ritual he refers to as "the test of the horse" – wherein the villagers use a naked virgin astride a horse to locate the grave of a suspected vampire. (The Swedish drama-documentary *In Search of Dracula*, shot the previous year, reconstructed this

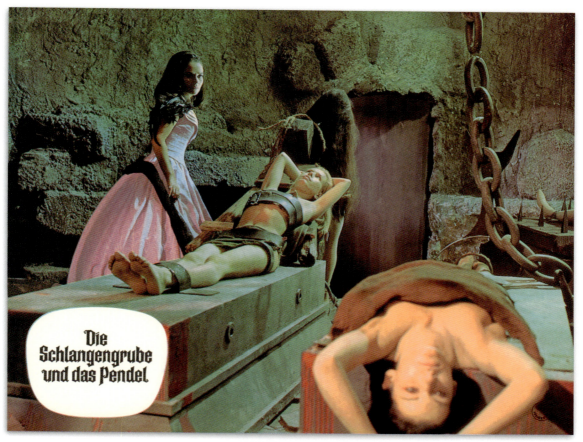

Die
Schlangengrube
und das Pendel

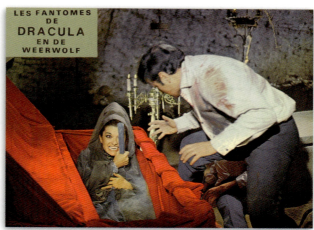

LES FANTOMES
DE
DRACULA
EN DE
WEERWOLF

TOP: Karin Dor encounters two of Graf Regula's dozen dead virgins in *Die Schlangengrube und das Pendel* (1967)

ABOVE: Brand-new horror star Paul Naschy finishes off Aurora de Alba in *La marca del hombre lobo* (1968)

LEFT: Paul Albert Krumm and Eleonore Schminke re-enact a classic Bram Stoker tableau in *Jonathan* (1969)

ABOVE LEFT: Italian poster for the half-Spanish Gothic throwback *Ivanna* (1970)

ABOVE: *Les Lèvres rouges* (1970) – 'The Belgian film that triumphed in New York, London and Paris!!!'

BELOW: A 'sex horreur' oddity from France – *Le Sadique aux dents rouges* (1970)

ABOVE: Candle-bearing maids Marie-Pierre Castel and Kuelan Herce in a hand-tinted publicity handout for *Le Frisson des vampires* (1970)

LANCASTER FILMS présente

# LA NUIT
# DES PETRIFIES

Interdit aux moins de 13 ans

Visa N° 4.684

ABOVE: Lorenzo Terzon loses his head to Erika Blanc in *La Plus longue nuit du diable* (1971)

LEFT: Spanish advertising for the rip-roaring 'alien on a train' adventure *Pánico en el Transiberiano* (1971), aka *Horror Express*

FAR LEFT, ABOVE: A typically weird assemblage observes Mathieu Carrière and Susan Hampshire in *Malpertuis* (1971)

FAR LEFT, BELOW: Four stages of putrefaction for Roberto Maldera in *La notte dei diavoli* (1971)

ABOVE: Centrespread of the Spanish pressbook for
*El ataque de los muertos sin ojos* (1973), featuring Tony Kendall,
Esperanza Roy, José Thelman, Maria Nuria, Luis Barboo,
Fernando Sancho – and, of course, the Blind Dead

LEFT AND BELOW: Oddball vampires young and
old – Nicholas Ney in *La llamada del vampiro* (1972)
and Howard Vernon in *Dracula contre Frankenstein* (1971)

LA LLAMADA DEL
VAMPIRO

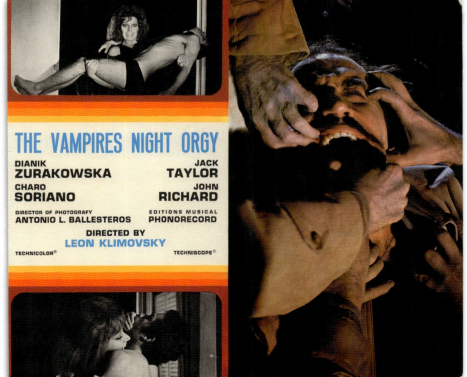

RIGHT:
The Spanish
*Exorcist* variant
*Alucinaciones* was
released as *El juego
del diablo* (1974)

FAR RIGHT, ABOVE:
Christopher Lee
went to Paris for
the droll vampire
comedy *Dracula
père et fils* (1976)

FAR RIGHT, BELOW:
The children
of Almanzora
accumulate an
arsenal in *¿Quién
puede matar a un
niño?* (1975)

BELOW:
Shelley Winters
stumbles on the
dragged-up and
defenestrated
Roman Polanski in
*Le Locataire* (1975)

ABOVE: Jessica Harper falls among diabolists in *Suspiria* (1976)

LEFT: Mariana Karr in a very similar predicament in *Escalofrío* (1977)

BELOW LEFT: Klaus Kinski in repose as *Nosferatu Phantom der Nacht* (1978)

BELOW: Captain Haggerty, first of the many cannibalistic ghouls encountered in *Zombi 2* (1979)

TOP: Cinzia Monreale contemplates 'The Beyond' in ...E tu vivrai nel terrore! L'aldilà (1980)

ABOVE: Julia Saly victimises Azucena Hernández in El retorno del hombre lobo (1980)

RIGHT: Catriona MacColl, trapped under Dr Freudstein's memorial slab in Quella villa accanto al cimitero (1981)

FAR RIGHT: Veronica Moriconi fronted the Italian export pressbook for the haunting 'K-zone' thriller Zeder (1982)

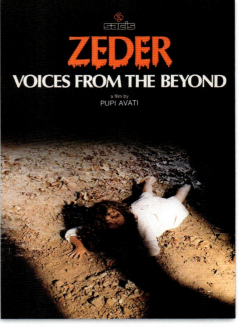

ZEDER
VOICES FROM THE BEYOND
a film by
PUPI AVATI

Lucia Bosé's forlorn Marquesa with medical man
Silvano Tranquilli in *Ceremonia sangrienta* (1972)

ritual with a naked female; here it's
a naked boy.) As Karl gloats from on
high, his neglected wife anxiously
scrutinises herself in a hand mirror
and applies cold cream to her face.
This cosmetic death mask is paralleled
below by the shrouded features of the
unearthed 'vampire', who is efficiently
staked by an ascetic-looking little
man in John Lennon-style granny
glasses – Grau's nod, perhaps, to the
bespectacled fanatic played by Michael
Gothard in *The Devils*.

Concocted by Grau and Juan
Tébar with the Italian writer Sandro
Continenza, the script is immaculate
in its research and erudition. The
accused corpse, for example, is given
the name Peter Plogojowitz (as per
a notorious vampire case in 1720s Serbia) and an
enlightened judge, horrified by the arcane proceedings,
quotes Voltaire's words to the effect that real vampires
live in palaces rather than cemeteries. Other folkloric
tidbits include a servant girl folding the vampire's
blood into dough to create vampire-repellent bread;
later we hear of the same girl using pigeons' blood
to firm her breasts. The erudition elsewhere is of a
more playful variety, with character names alluding
to Sheridan Le Fanu (Silas, Carmila) and even a neck-
braced magistrate unmistakably addressed as Helsing.

Thanks to Grau, the film is visually eloquent too.
This isn't just a matter of his atmospheric deployment
of real locations, including the use of the Palacio de
Goyeneche in Nuevo Baztán as the courthouse in
which the vampire trial takes place. It also extends to a
number of truly powerful images with which he points
up his main theme. Having manoeuvred
a flaxen little girl into cutting herself, the Marquesa is
seen in a mirror, smearing her cheeks with blood and
even tentatively licking some of it. Grau then cuts to a
shot of Erzsébet snipping off the head of a red rose in
the castle grounds. Later, her husband's pretensions
to refinement, which include rhapsodic sessions on
the clavichord, are undercut by a view of his bloodied
hands staining the ivory keyboard. In the first blood-
bathing scene, the camera tracks unfussily from
Erzsébet in her tub to the image of the naked, inverted
donor in a cheval glass. For the second bloodbath,
an artfully contrived hole in the ceiling siphons the
blood direct from a butchered girl in the attic, tactfully

## CEREMONIA SANGRIENTA

Spain-Italy 1972
Italy: **Le vergini cavalcano la morte**
UK / US: **The Legend of Blood Castle**
X Films (Madrid) / Luis Films (Rome)
102 minutes colour
production began July 1972

. . . . . . . . . . . . . . . . . . . . . . . . . . . . .

Directors of Photography: Fernando
Arribas, Oberdan Troiani; Art Director:
Cruz Baleztena; Editor: Pedro del Rey;
Sound: José María San Mateo; Music: Carlo
Savina; Make-up: Carlos Paradela; Special
Effects: Basilio Cortijo; Screenplay: Jorge
Grau, Juan Tébar, Sandro Continenza;
Story by: Jorge Grau; Executive Producer:
José María González Sinde; Director:
Jorge Grau

Lucia Bosé (Erzebeth Báthory); Espartaco Santoni
(Karl Ziemmer); Ewa Aulin (Marina); Ana Farra
(Nodriza); Lola Gaos (Carmilla); Enrique Vivó
(mayor); Ángel Menéndez (magistrate); Franca Grey
(Nadja); Raquel Ortuño (Irina); María Vico (Maria
Plojovitz); Silvano Tranquilli (doctor); Adolfo Thous
(judge); Ismael García Romen (captain); Loreta
Tovar (Sandra); Ghika (Inge); Miguel Buñuel
(secretary); Fabián Conde (constable); Estanis
González (innkeeper); Antonio Puga (Claus);
Francisco Agostín (postman); Antonio De Mossul
(falconer); Rafael Vaquero (painter); Roberto
Daniel (Plojovitz); Ángel Rodal (young Mario);
Juan José Otegui (servant); Mari Paz Ballesteros
(maid); Sergio Alberti (sergeant); Sofía Nogueiras
(Laura); Kino Pueyo (boy at inn); Fernando De
Bran (rector); Rafael Frías (boy on horse)

**Jorge Grau – one of the enfant terribles of the defunct 'nuevo cine catalán'
– follows an increasingly commercial, and less artistically valid, path. From
personal works he has moved on to a horror co-production ... Inexplicably,
when called on to 'solve' a simple horror picture this niche director and
severe critic appears more inexpert than an Ossorio or Klimovsky.**
ABC Sevilla 2 June 1974

It started in Czechoslovakia at the festival in Karlovy Vary. Someone told
me the story of Countess Báthory and it made a great impression on me.
It seemed like a feminine version of *Faust* ... When I returned to Spain,
I wanted to make a film of it, not necessarily a horror film but a human
drama. But the producers saw it as a horror film and wouldn't accept my
justification that it was an intimate drama. *Jorge Grau [quoted in Shivers July 2000]*

removing the victim from Erzsébet's sight. And, again,
our view of Erzsébet is actually a mirror reflection.

By moving the action forward a couple of centuries
and focusing on a descendant of the original Erzsébet,
Grau shrewdly dodges the necessity to portray a
650-victim murder spree and is also able, despite her
heinous crimes, to show some compassion towards his

protagonist. The cruel-yet-slightly-mournful good looks of Lucia Bosé made her a perfect fit for this role, with added piquancy arising from her real-life reputation as a former beauty queen. In a scene modelled on Richard III's visitation from "the souls of all that I had murder'd," she reaches a grand apotheosis when haunted in her boudoir by the worm-eaten visages of her victims. "They've come for me," she babbles. "They're watching. They want their blood back..."

Grau's sympathy for the modern Erzsébet is made possible by the foregrounding of her philandering, self-absorbed husband Karl; an obvious sadist even when indulging in falconry, he was based by Grau on Gilles de Rais (a contemporary of the original Countess) and it is he who does the actual murders. After a leisurely first half in which the two plots (the frustrated Marquesa and the ridiculous vampire trial) co-exist rather uneasily, the film packs in plenty of grisly action in the second, but at the expense of a strange lurch in the narrative, meaning that we have to take it on trust that Karl has faked his own death and is now committing his crimes under the guise of a vampire.

This lurch may have been brought about by front-office interference; as Grau lamented a few years later, "*Ceremonia sangrienta* was massacred. It passed through numerous hands, with each producer ordering it according to his own taste ... It was a very difficult shoot."[7] Whatever the truth may be, the lurch remains symbolic of an extremely classy film that's divided rather uneasily between art and exploitation. Even so, it ends on another of Grau's stunning images, with the camera panning past a sea of untouched, flyblown dinner plates to the incarcerated Marquesa regarding her image again, itself worm-eaten by now. Her final imprisonment, appropriately enough, is in a mirror.

Espartaco Santoni, the playboy actor cast by Grau as Erzsébet's husband, had previously taken the lead in another Spanish-Italian co-production, *Las amantes del diablo* (The Devil Lovers), and here there's no uncertainty as to which side of the art-exploitation divide we're on. Given that Santoni also co-wrote and co-produced the film – and that it includes numerous

The ubiquitous Teresa Gimpera in *Las amantes del diablo* (1970), known in Italy as 'The Diabolical Gathering'

references to his good looks, plenty of Naschy-style opportunities to bed beautiful women, and an impressive range of medallions and Nehru jackets for him to wear – it seems likely that this was, at least in part, a vanity project. He plays Nescu, a mesmeric misogynist guru whose father was regularly whipped by his faithless wife and eventually hanged himself. Now Nescu selects the beautiful Krista Nell as the latest subject of his vengeful satanic rites, which take place in the usual castellated haunt at Valdeiglesias. Films in which the Byronic villain is introduced in red Speedos while water-skiing in Marbella are not common, but *Las amantes* dawdles dispiritedly to an extremely underwhelming conclusion. Even the presence of Teresa Gimpera as Nescu's confederate fails to enliven proceedings.

*Las amantes del diablo* was directed in October 1970 by the veteran filmmaker José María Elorrieta, who was inspired to make a couple of considerably more threadbare horrors in its wake. *La llamada del vampiro* (The Call of the Vampire) returned Elorrieta to the castle at Valdeiglesias and begins in high style, with the rampaging Loreta Tovar bloodily staked even before the credits roll. The vampires here, in a novel touch, are activated only on nights of the full moon, and the chief one is an unprepossessing, straggle-haired young aristocrat played by Nicholas Ney. The medical investigators are Diana Sorel and Elorrieta's daughter Beatriz, whose intellectual credentials don't exempt them from appearing in baby-doll nighties and hot pants respectively. The latter becomes vampirised and plucks the stake from Tovar's chest, after which they flounce about in the nocturnal slow-motion patented by *La noche de Walpurgis*. The dialogue is stilted, the patchwork of library music absolutely awful, and the ending wildly incoherent. In the export version the action is also impeded by a surprisingly explicit lesbian scene.

Having dealt with satanic cults and moon-influenced vampires, Elorrieta moved on in 1972 to a more straightforward stalker scenario with *El espectro del terror* (The Spectre of Terror), this time employing his son Javier to co-write some original music. Elorrieta retained Nicholas Ney, here billed as Aramis Ney, casting him as a sweaty, chainsmoking hippy who relentlessly pursues the glamorous Maria Perschy. In a nod to Italian gialli, he drinks J&B Scotch while watching girls gyrating at a disco. He also strangles Betsabé Ruiz with her own tights and immerses her in acid, finally throttling May Heatherly with a telephone cord – unsuccessfully, as it turns out. Again, Elorrieta struggles to make much of this hand-me-down situation, even when Ney is plagued by the sounds of an air-raid in his head and a vision of cockroaches crawling among his bed sheets.

While directing this unofficial trilogy, Elorrieta also co-wrote something called *Escalofrío diabólico* (Devilish Shiver). This one plays like a sister film to *Las amantes del diablo* and *La llamada del vampiro*, not just because of the Elorrieta connection, but also because it's yet another film shot at the trusty castillo at San Martín de Valdeiglesias. (Watching these films back to back, the recurrence of identical interiors and exteriors becomes almost comical.) For its weirdest scenes it also ventures into the area's equally familiar ruined monastery, where a mute butler (José Villasante) pirouettes with a mannequin while fantasising a living partner. For the rest, it's a limply executed saga of sibling rivalry, fake satanic rites and (as in *Las amantes*) water-skiing, enlivened only by the luminous Patty Shepard. The credited director and co-writer is Spaghetti Western star George Martin, who also appears briefly in a couple of terrible wigs – though it could well be that Elorrieta had a hand in the directorial department too.

## WATCHFUL CATS, SMIRKING DEVILS AND COPULATING CORPSES

'Eclectic' is a good word for the wide range of Italian genre product in the early 1970s.

Among the most unusual projects was *Addio fratello crudele* (Goodbye, Cruel Brother), which Giuseppe Patroni Griffi completed in March 1971. A sumptuous but overblown adaptation of a 17th century incest-revenge tragedy by John Ford, this imported its young leads, Charlotte Rampling and Oliver Tobias, from the UK while retaining Ford's original title – *'Tis Pity She's a Whore* – for export purposes. By June of the same year Riccardo Freda was in Dublin for a rather dull, vitriol-throwing giallo called *L'iguana dalla lingua di fuoco* (The Iguana with the Tongue of Fire), while Aldo Lado was in an equally unconventional location, Prague, for the far more interesting *La corta notte delle bambole di vetro* (The Short Night of Glass Dolls), in which the deceased Jean Sorel rewinds a convoluted

Germany's Doris Kunstmann with Britain's Jane Birkin in the Italian-French-German thriller *La morte negli occhi del gatto* (1972)

puzzle from a prone position on a mortician's slab. A few months later Mario Caiano was on the island of Elba, concocting an oneiric psychological thriller called *L'occhio nel labirinto* (The Eye in the Labyrinth), in which the plucky but credulous Rosemary Dexter is faced with a Grade-A gaggle of oddballs, among them Adolfo Celi, Alida Valli, Sybil Danning and Horst Frank's severed head.

The tough-to-decipher action and 'strange people in an enclosed space' theme of Caiano's film were echoed by two veterans of Italian horror in 1972. British star Jane Birkin arrived in Rome in the first week of February to start work on *La morte negli occhi del gatto* (Death in the Cat's Eyes), with which Antonio Margheriti returned to the 1920s setting and claustrophobic mood of *Contronatura*. He also returned to Castello Massimo at Arsoli, where he'd shot *I lunghi capelli della morte* in 1964, as well as returning, in a more general sense, to the kind of 'old dark house' mystery-thrillers that had been popular on Broadway between the wars. In fact, he may have had a specific one in mind – Ralph Spence's *The Gorilla*. A large circus ape, James, is in residence at the castle seat of Scotland's daggers-drawn MacGrieff clan, even going so far as to pop its head round the door at dinner. Improbably referred to as an orang-outan by his master, James turns out to be a red herring, having nothing to do with the regulation family curse.

Among the shady 1920s types gathered round the dinner table are Anton Diffring and Fellini's pretty young *Satyricon* star Hiram Keller. Luciano Pigozzi is also on hand to get killed outside the crypt (arterial poster paint splashes across the wall), with all the fatalities sombrely observed by an omniscient cat – not the sleek black variety you'd expect, but a rather tubby tabby. Between them, Margheriti and cinematographer Carlo Carlini concoct a really handsome-looking film, with striking set-pieces to spare – a rat-chewed cadaver in the basement, a set of bats waggling their ears as Birkin wanders the lower depths, a Bible accidentally tossed into the grate and corrupting amid the flames, a vision of Birkin's mother rising vampire-like from the dead. The Krimi-style atmosphere is engaging, but the film loses points for its garbled plot, the stunt casting of Birkin's partner, Serge Gainsbourg, as a Scottish policeman, and a pervading air – perhaps inevitable in the circumstances – of reheated goods. The illiterate export title, incidentally, was *Seven Deaths in the Cats Eyes*.

By September 1972 Mario Bava was making another film for producer Alfredo Leone, who, having turned to West German co-finance for *Baron Blood* 12 months earlier, was now in partnership with the Spanish entrepreneur José Gutierrez Maesso. As a result, Bava found himself, not in Austria, but in Toledo, Madrid and Barcelona for a film called *Lisa e il diavolo* (Lisa and the Devil). Where Margheriti's latest horror proved garbled purely because of faulty plot mechanics, Bava's new one sought to subject viewers to exactly the kind of disorientating limbo into which its heroine is plunged. That the film anatomised a dream was appropriate, given that it was itself a dream project for Bava, who for once was unfettered by the compromises normally forced upon him. "I gave him all the freedom he wanted," Leone recalled, adding an important caveat: "But that was Bava's problem, you see. Give Bava a restricted budget of $500,000 and he would come back and present you with a brilliant picture. Give him carte blanche and he was in trouble."

> Visiting Toledo, Lisa Reiner is lured by the sound of a music box into a backstreet antiques shop, where she meets a saturnine figure called Leandro. Becoming disorientated and lost, she's rescued at nightfall by the arrival of a looming limousine of pre-war vintage; curiously, its occupants seem at least 40 years out of date, too. When the car breaks down outside a secluded villa, the butler who answers the door is none other than Leandro.

As a sumptuously imagined 'designer' view of the afterlife, *Lisa e il diavolo* is unrivalled. There are crudities along the way, however, and we may as well dispose of them right now. Among them is a comically idiot-proof moment when Lisa first encounters Leandro; we've already seen his image in a church fresco depicting the Devil and really don't need to have the fresco superimposed over the whimsical features of Telly Savalas in order to get the point. Later on, once the horrific set-pieces have (somewhat belatedly) kicked in, we're shown the evergreen Silva Koscina shrinking from a bludgeon-wielding killer with a conveniently subsided gown that almost, but not quite, exposes her breasts. But crass, laugh-out-loud moments like this are happily few and far between. For most of the action Bava and his Spanish cinematographer, Cecilio Paniagua, create a spell-stopped mood that recalls the labyrinthine strangeness of *Operazione paura*.

Though credited just to Bava and Leone, the script for *Lisa* was founded on an original concocted in part by Romano Migliorini and Roberto Natale, the writers of *Operazione paura*. Indeed, among Bava's greatest achievements in the film's first act is the way he gives the spacious, sunlit backstreets and archways of Toledo the same climate of unease exuded by the pokey, night-shrouded streets of the earlier film. It's here that Lisa encounters first Leandro and then the disturbingly lively dummy that he totes around the city. And when Lisa becomes involved in a fumbled romantic tryst with the dummy-given-flesh, we begin to realise that she has entered a different zone in which Leandro is, quite literally, the puppetmaster. Her disorientation (nicely played by Bava's *Baron Blood* lead, Elke Sommer) finds temporary relief when the headlight beams of a vintage car pierce the gathering darkness. We know, of course, that this providential rescue will only drag her still deeper into metaphysical waters, and in the meantime we puzzle over why the well-heeled couple played by Eduardo Fajardo and Sylva Koscina look as if they've stepped out of the 1920s.

Just as the Leandro role was taken by US import Telly Savalas, so Leone had similarly big plans for the other characters. As Bava biographer Tim Lucas has pointed out, Louis Jourdan was approached to play the amorous living doll and Bette Davis and Anthony Perkins were in line for the funereal mother and son who inhabit the out-of-time villa. In the end Leone went with Espartaco Santoni, Alida Valli and Alessio Orano, with Santoni the very image of a self-absorbed Latin lover, Valli explicitly recalling the mad Baroness Graps from *Operazione paura*, and Orano boasting incipient-werewolf good looks reminiscent of Hammer-era Oliver Reed. Though Santoni is initially encountered outdoors, it's these three that form the boxed-in family unit encountered by Lisa, with the boy, Maximillian, contemplating their cosmopolitan visitors and claiming that "My world instead is the very configuration of this villa."

Trying to configure this oneiric space for themselves, the audience is faced with further puzzles. Whose footsteps can be heard pacing above the visitors' heads? Who or what is concealed behind lacy

Elke Sommer,
immersed in the
disorientating limbo
of *Lisa e il diavolo*
(1972)

drapes in the ornate chamber Maximillian retires to?
And why is it Lisa's face that stares out from a vintage
photo he finds concealed in a dust-covered book?

Leandro, meanwhile, dances attendance on both
family and guests at dinner, memorably wheeling in
a gâteau "with chocolate sprinkles" and appearing
unruffled when a bottle of wine gets smashed. The
image of his impish features, reflected in a puddle
of red liquid on the floor, signals pretty clearly that
blood is soon to flow, and it duly does. (This powerful
'face in pool of blood' image would resurface,
incidentally, in the final moments of Dario Argento's
*Profondo rosso*.) Savalas' fish-out-of-water presence
is itself a disorientating feature in this strange
ménage; he not only has a devilish twinkle in his
eye but also a lollipop in his mouth, an affectation
Savalas took so much to heart that he recycled it the
following year when cast by Universal Television
as *Kojak*. Here, his cheerfully unconventional Grim
Reaper presides in workaday shirt-sleeves over a huge
collection of the dummies so dear to Bava. Later on
he's the centrepiece of a brilliant sequence in which
Paniagua's gliding camera confers solemnity on
an absurd funeral procession, with the murdered
chauffeur gracelessly laid out on the dessert trolley.

This is the crazed, Pythonesque domain of Kümel's
*Malpertuis* converted into a much more sombre distillate
of damned souls, and when the killings crowd in
Bava manages some scenes of really eye-popping
violence while somehow preserving the film's po-faced
mood. Fajardo's character, for example, is pulverised

## LISA E IL DIAVOLO

*Italy-Spain-Monaco* 1972
*Spain: El diablo se lleva a los muertos*
*UK / US: Lisa and the Devil*
Leone International (Rome) / Tecisa (Madrid) /
Roxy Film (Monaco)
95 minutes colour
production began 18 September 1972

Director of Photography: Cecilio Paniagua;
Art Director: Nedo Azzini; Editor: Carlo
Reali; Music: Carlo Savina; Make-up:
Franco Freda; Special Effects: Franco Tocci;

Screenplay: Roberto Natale, Giorgio Monlini,
Mario Bava, plus [on Spanish prints only]
Leonardo Martín, Jose G Maesso; Producer:
Alfredo Leone; Director: Mario Bava

Telly Savalas (Leandro); Elke Sommer (Lisa
Reiner / Elena); Silva Koscina (Sophia Lehar);
Alessio Orano (Maximillian); Alida Valli
(Countess); Gabriele Tinti (George); Kathy
Leone (tourist); Espartaco Santoni (Carlos);
Eduardo Fajardo (Francis Lehar); Franz Von
Treuberg (antiquarian)

The Devil (currently so fashionable) plays an important role, and the expert
direction of a reputable genre name like Mario Bava, ably assisted by an
impeccable technical team, ensures an interesting picture. Furthermore, the
actors are top rank … The film manages to entertain; it's a simple consumer
product … and since it fulfils its primary objectives we shouldn't ask for
anything more. *Cineinforme April 1975*

When I was playing Lisa, I approached her story totally as a dream … The
amazing thing is, Mario would never direct me. He would say, at the most,
"Do it as you always do it, Elke – do it as you feel it." Technically, he was
a genius with the lighting, with creating the environment. The morbidity
of the environment was enough to induce your performance, even without
direction. *Elke Sommer [quoted in Lucas, Mario Bava: All the Colors of the Dark, 2007]*

by his own vintage car no fewer than six times, and
moments later Koscina's head is pulped extremely
comprehensively by an unseen assailant. The climax,
however, is simultaneously far calmer and infinitely
more disturbing. Apparently taking inspiration from
the same Gilles de Rais story on which Mino Guerrini
based *Il terzo occhio*, Bava has the pathetic Maximillian
try to have sex with the insensible Lisa on a bed also
occupied by the skeletal husk of a lost lover.

On this cue the impotent boy goes berserk, with
Bava staging a stunning tableau in which he's faced

by a dinner table of lolling corpses, the skeleton lover at the centre and a maggot-writhing wedding cake positioned in front of her. The subsequent apparition of his murdered mother – with the dead-eyed Valli floating implacably towards Max and us – is among the most coldly frightening things Bava ever filmed. And the resolution acquires a genuinely tragic aura, as Lisa emerges naked from the now shattered villa the following morning and is taken by neighbourhood children for a ghost, quite accurately as it turns out. The coda, apparently added to the script at Leone's suggestion, seems to offer another of those cruelly deceptive reprieves, with Lisa rushing to Barcelona Airport and climbing aboard an eerily deserted 747. The pay-off here is predictable but extremely powerful.

Sadly, Bava's film – elegant, stately, unashamedly inscrutable – proved to be the wrong picture at the wrong time. Maesso's involvement ensured a belated release in Spain, where a modified cut entitled *El diablo se lleva los muertos* (The Devil Carries Off the Dead) hit Barcelona in November 1974 and Madrid the following March. But Leone found he couldn't sell it anywhere else. As a result, some 18 months after the main shoot he reconvened Bava and Sommer, threw in Robert Alda, and filmed various scenes in which a possessed Lisa has intermittent visions of the previously shot action, meanwhile squirming in a hospital bed and puking green goo at her priestly new co-star.

In seeking to ensure a profit by aping William Friedkin's *The Exorcist*, the resulting compromise – entitled *La casa dell'esorcismo* (The House of Exorcism) – was hardly unique. Even so, the use of Stravinsky's *Rite of Spring* over the opening credits is its least disconcerting distortion of the original by far. Elsewhere there's frog vomiting (of the faked variety, unlike Lucia Bosé's amazing display in *Arcana*), projectile serpents, exploding Bibles, a well-staged but inconclusive climax, and some memorable dialogue, as when Lisa spits the following at her TV movie-smooth exorcist: "There's your fucking daily bread. Eat it! Eat it like you did those whores' cunts before you became a priest." That Bava was thoroughly crestfallen by this desecration of his film goes without saying. The original *Lisa e il diavolo* would surface in due course, but not until many years after his death.

US advertising for the hallucinatory curio *Macchie solari* (1974)

At the beginning of 1973, while hopes were still high for *Lisa*, Corrado Farina, director of the striking vampire parable *...Hanno cambiato faccia*, was crafting a weird netherworld of his own in *Baba Yaga*, which turned out to be his second and final feature. This Italian-French co-production started shooting on 3 January with Anne Heywood cast as the title character; she pulled out, however, a few days before she was due to start filming and was hurriedly replaced by giallo regular Carroll Baker.

Sadly, neither Baker nor her mod antagonist Isabella de Funès are well cast, the first as a Slavic witch resurfacing in 1970s Milan, the second as the angular heroine, Valentina, made famous by the erotic fumetti of Guido Crepax. On top of this, the film was gracelessly recut by its producers, doing damage that Farina was only able to put right for a 2009 DVD release. The action begins arrestingly with an anti-American 'happening' that's broken up by Farina himself, playing an Italian policeman. (Tellingly, he doubles as a cat-stroking SS officer in Valentina's nightmares.) And there's a pleasantly storm-laden climax in Baba Yaga's villa, where Valentina tells her "I have no intention of making love with an old dyke like you," a creepy doll in dominatrix gear takes human form as Ely Galleani, and the witch finally plunges through an extra-dimensional hole in the floorboards. But the middle sections are occupied, not only by Farina's sincere but clunky efforts to replicate Crepax's comic-strip style, but also by his trademark satire of the advertising industry, which in this film becomes very tedious very quickly.

Amid this slew of product, Armando Crispino directed a couple of giallo-inflected horrors – or horror-inflected gialli, depending on how you look at them – that are more notable for bizarre content than entertainment value. In late August 1971 he started shooting *L'etrusco uccide ancora* (The Etruscan Kills Again) with the benefit of no fewer than three US-friendly names in the cast – Alex Cord, Samantha Eggar and John Marley. Here, an archaeological dig triggers a series of killings, the first a double-murder in which young lovers are comprehensively bludgeoned in a welter of gore. There's plenty of attractive location photography in

Teresa Gimpera as the wordless but imposing vampire queen of *La tumba de la isla maldita* (1972)

Spoleto, together with the requisite bottles of J&B Scotch hidden among the protagonist's effects and the usual parade of stick-figure caricatures, usefully codified in the dialogue as "paranoid conductor" (Marley), "drunken archaeologist" (Cord) and "faggot choreographer" (Horst Frank). But the whole film turns on the fraudulent suggestion that the ancient Etruscan is indeed killing again, when in fact the killer is the statutory misogynist creep who describes one victim as "dirty, like my mother. Like all women."

Crispino began shooting his second horror picture, *Macchie solari* (Sun Spots), on 15 July 1974, with Mimsy Farmer as a young doctor working in a morgue while a rash of inexplicable suicides is under way. Unfortunately, having crafted a really extraordinary six-minute introduction, Crispino defaults to the same sluggish pace and narrative uncertainty that marred *L'etrusco*. An opening montage of suicides, brutal and uncompromising, is succeeded by Farmer's truly grim hallucinations in the morgue, which include grinning corpses hopping off their slabs and copulating on the floor. In this kind of environment, it's hardly surprising when a white-coated attendant feels up a naked female cadaver and drools "Jesus, what a waste of natural talent," later trying to rape Farmer prior to getting a fork in his face. The extreme morbidity in which *Macchie solari* is steeped extends to a highly unpleasant exhibition of genuine crime-scene photos – images whose use appears utterly meretricious

when the plot dwindles into some off-the-peg rubbish about Ray Lovelock seeking an inheritance and lining up Farmer and Barry Primus as his final victims. The film's export version, incidentally, carries an incorrect copyright date of 1973 and the alternative title *Autopsy*.

## GOTHIC SURVIVALS

Having starred in *Byleth* in 1971, Mark Damon made two further Gothic throwbacks the following year, in the first of which he played, as in *Byleth*, a brother lusting after his sister, while in the second he was cast rather neatly as twin brothers.

The Spanish modern-dress thriller *La tumba de la isla maldita* (The Tomb on the Accursed Island) started shooting on 26 May 1972 in Istanbul, with Julio Salvador – writer the same year of the dismal *El secreto de la momia egipcia* – occupying the director's chair. Damon is joined here by two other US names, Andrew Prine and the ubiquitous Patty Shepard, and their easy, practised interplay makes the film very watchable despite its no-surprises plot. The plot, in fact, appears to have been lifted – in part and uncredited – from a turn-of-the-century short story by F G Loring called *The Tomb of Sarah*. Prine is an engineer investigating his archaeologist father's death, unaware that the affable American helping him (Damon) was responsible for that death by dropping several tons of sarcophagus on the old man. Prine's raising of the sarcophagus inevitably raises its beautiful occupant,

Mark Damon does battle with the fanged Xiro Papas in *Il plenilunio delle vergini* (1972)

## IL PLENILUNIO DELLE VERGINI

Italy 1972
US: *The Devil's Crypt / The Devil's Wedding Night*
Virginia Cinematografica
82 minutes colour
in production autumn 1972

· · · · · · · · · · · · · · · · · · · · · · · · · ·

Director of Photography: Aristide Massaccesi; Art Director: Carlo Gentili; Editors: Piera Bruni, Gianfranco Simoncelli; Sound: Franco Rucci, Manlio Urbani; Music: Vasil Kojucharov; Make-up: Liliana Dulac;

Story and Screenplay: Walter Bigari [Walter Brandi], Paolo Solvay [Luigi Batzella]; Executive Producer: Ralph Zucker; Director: Paolo Solvay [Luigi Batzella]

Mark Damon (Karl and Franz Schiller); Rosalba Neri (Countess Dracula); Esmerelda Barros (Lara); Francesca Romana Davila (Tanya); Xiro Papas (the vampire monster); Sergio Pislar (Franz Schiller [stand-in]); Gengher Gatti (the mysterious man); Giorgio Dolfin, Stefano Oppedisano (villagers)

When we last saw her, Sara Bay [ie, Rosalba Neri] was busy testing the sexual potency of the monster she created as Lady Frankenstein. Now, as Countess Dracula in this new, rather drab European job, she is still concerned with undressing her victims ... Mark Damon works up a good sweat in a dual role ... and it is often difficult to tell which Mark is which. Miss Bay, however, stands out. *Cinefantastique* Fall 1974

I wasn't really proud of the picture, but I had the chance to play twins and that was fun. I think all actors want to do that at some point ... I'm really amazed that anyone still cares about that movie. In fact, with all of those films, it blows my mind to learn that many of them are considered cult classics.
Mark Damon [quoted in *Fangoria* July 2015]

Priestess of Vampires comes across as a rather stately Rose Bowl Pageant Queen,"[8] noted Robert L Jerome at the time, with some justification. Gimpera does, however, have some weirdly affecting moments as she stirs into life and gulps reviving air with a kind of orgasmic hunger. The film has plenty of atmosphere, too, though much of it is vitiated by underwhelming music. It also appears to have had bits and pieces of extra footage, directed by the American actor Ray Danton, appended for US release.

Later in 1972, Damon was in Italy for a film that owed its chief inspiration to a spate of recent, sexed-up Hammer titles from the UK. With *Il plenilunio delle vergini* (Full Moon of the Virgins), producer Ralph Zucker was returning to Gothic horror for the first time since the 1965 duo *5 tombe per un medium* and *Il boia scarlatto*, in the process giving a sly nod to a 1971 potboiler directed by Mel Welles. For, having played the seductive title role in Welles' *Lady Frankenstein*, Rosalba Neri here progressed, quite naturally, to playing none other than Countess Dracula.

*Karl Schiller proposes to visit Transylvania in search of the fabled Ring of the Nibelungen, arming himself against vampires with a talisman given him on an Egyptological dig. Having purloined the talisman, Karl's louche brother Franz gets to the Carpathians before him and learns from a local barmaid that the so-called 'night of the virgin moon' is imminent. Franz then sets out for the castle Karl specified, but unfortunately neglects to take the talisman with him...*

The film's co-writer and production manager was Walter Brandi, who had been a cast member in Zucker's previous Gothics and before that, of course, was the vampire figure in *L'amante del vampiro* and *L'ultima preda del vampiro*. Brandi's third vampire film, *La strage dei vampiri*, had featured Luigi Batzella in the Van Helsing role; ten years on, Brandi and Batzella were reunited on *Il plenilunio*, with Batzella promoted to the director's chair. The result is a film that takes the erotic content of its early 1960s forebears and places it front and centre, with plentiful nudity not just from the titular virgins but also the smouldering Neri.

a 13th century French queen called Hannah – which is good news for the Devil-worshipping Damon as he feels Hannah's evil dominion will sanction the illicit feelings he has for his sister (Shepard).

"She's in that tomb, fangs and all, ready to go after 700 years," scoffs the super-rational Prine at the beginning, though by the end he's leading a gung-ho lynch mob against the glamorous vampire. Hannah is played by another ubiquitous beauty, Teresa Gimpera, though she spends much of her limited screen time in wolf form and says not a word throughout. "With her tiara and faintly ridiculous medieval attire, the High

Batzella has to get through a few formalities beforehand, however, among them a bracingly psychedelic credits sequence and some faux-scholarly exposition involving not one but two Mark Damons. Cast as twins whose similarity extends to an identical over-use of mascara, Damon is introduced as Karl, musing on the existence of an all-powerful ring while poring over dusty volumes in an anachronistic pair of spectacles. Further confusion of the 'when is this set?' variety arises on Franz's entrance. Referring to Poe's *The Raven* and Wagner's *Ring* cycle as if they were exact contemporaries, Franz also introduces the first of several echoes of Hammer films. "I dare say it must be quite valuable," he says of the fabled ring. "Invaluable," replies Karl, the exchange quoting Terence Fisher's *The Devil Rides Out* almost verbatim. That Batzella and co were also aware of Hammer's more recent lesbian vampire films becomes clear when Karl proposes to lodge the ring in the so-called Karnstein Museum of Archaeology.

The film then gets into gear with Franz's hell-for-leather ride into the Carpathians and a broodingly familiar shot of the trusty Castello di Balsorano. In contrast to the tousled academic Karl, Franz is a dissipated wastrel whose slicked-back hair and ashen complexion make his Transylvanian fate seem like a foregone conclusion. His encounter with Neri's seductive Countess has its fair share of diverting moments, together with a surprising amount of playfully literate dialogue. "Perhaps the legend of this castle is having a deleterious effect on your reason," the Countess muses, "or a stimulating effect on your fancy." Later, responding to Franz's queries regarding her robotic handmaiden Lara, she points out that "When I first met her I told her she had the aura of a zombie. Unfortunately she has no sense of humour." She also claims to have bought Castle Dracula on the cheap thanks to its baleful reputation, but in fact she was the late Count's consort and is bent on reincarnating him in the body of poor Franz.

The process begins with a love-making scene in which Neri is shot in a shimmering soft-porn halo; at the end of it she turns, rather disconcertingly, into a weirdly shrieking bat. (That this is a giant bat is later confirmed by some charmingly crude back-projection when the thing rears up in front of the plucky barmaid.) When Karl arrives in search of his brother, Batzella lets rip with the first of the film's two bravura set-pieces. Succumbing to drug-induced hysterics, the Countess, Karl and Lara loom laughingly into camera as a vision unfolds before us of the Countess' rejuvenation routine. The spectacle of Neri rising from her casket – her naked body slathered in blood and

wreathed in plumes of smoke – betrays the influence of Hammer's 1970 production *Countess Dracula*, but betters its instruction to such a degree that Ingrid Pitt's bloodbath seems negligible by comparison.

Batzella's second major set-piece harks back to another Hammer title, *Twins of Evil*, though it begins on a thrillingly Wagnerian note of its own. Ascending to the battlements, the Countess apparently orchestrates the lightning with her glow-in-the-dark ruby ring, thereby summoning five blank-faced virgins from the neighbouring village. The ensuing ceremonial is straight out of *Twins of Evil*, with cowled Satanists gathering for the "black feast" and bad twin Karl telling good twin Franz that "I want you to be my best man" when the wedding draws near. Batzella outstrips *Twins* by showing arterial blood splashing over the breasts of all five sacrificial victims, after which the Countess rises from her throne and floats to the window as if drawn there by the blue glow of the full moon. With a climax featuring decapitations galore and an ending that's fashionably downbeat, *Il plenilunio* scores, in its best moments, as a cheerfully absurd and lusciously upholstered tour de force.

The lustrous photography in Batzella's film was the work of Aristide Massaccesi, who served the same year, not just as cinematographer, but also as co-writer and director of a peculiar Gothic conundrum called *La morte ha sorriso all'assassino* (Death Smiles on a Murderer). "I was trying to evoke a certain atmosphere in that film,"[9] Massaccesi recalled 20-odd years later. He didn't let on exactly *what* atmosphere, though it's safe to assume it was an atmosphere of

Klaus Kinski as a short-lived, and superfluous, medical researcher in *La morte ha sorriso all'assassino* (1972)

disorientation. Set in 1909, the film begins with a shifty-looking doctor (Klaus Kinski) sliding his tie-pin into a beautiful patient's right eye without any ill effect. Kinski shares top billing with the gamine Swedish starlet Ewa Aulin but in fact he throws the film off balance. Claiming to "possess the secret of life itself," he's garrotted in his moment of triumph, with the corpse he's revived expiring at the same time he does. Kinski's scenes, few though they are, obfuscate a story that's already clouded enough by Massaccesi's elliptical flashback structure. Remove Kinski from the equation and you have a fascinating tale of undead vengeance, with Aulin dogging the footsteps of the man responsible for her death.

The man is Giacomo Rossi Stuart, whose presence underlines the film's indebtedness to Bava's *Operazione paura*. Having pursued himself around Villa Graps in the earlier film, here he's pursued by Aulin around a graveyard in a really brilliant sequence that climaxes with Rossi Stuart falling prey, not to Aulin, but to his resurrected daughter-in-law (Angela Bo). Bava is also recalled in Aulin's two-faced performance (at one point the camera goes into strobing overdrive, flashing between her smiling pixie face and the mouldering reality), but Poe references predominate, with *The Black Cat*, *The Masque of the Red Death*, *Ligeia* and *The Cask of Amontillado* all stirred into the mix. Berto Pisano's exceptional score adds weirdly slurred strings to a mesmerising funeral set-piece, and only a rather lame twist ending disappoints. There's plenty of softcore sex and over-the-top gore effects too, anticipating Massaccesi's future career as Joe D'Amato, under which pseudonym he became the notorious purveyor of, on the one hand, hardcore porn and, on the other, several crudely unappealing splatter films.

Klaus Kinski was also the draw in two films made back-to-back by writer-director Sergio Garrone late in 1973. Like the Massaccesi film and the three Damon vehicles, these items – *La mano che nutre la morte* (The Hand that Feeds the Dead) and *Le amanti del mostro* (The Monster's Lover) – ignored the rising tide of gialli in favour of rather stiffly realised Gothic settings. Reaching Italian cinemas in April and May 1974 respectively, their extreme similarity has caused confusion ever since.

The first is the better of the two, with a veiled figure using some kind of tuning fork to control a lumbering killer while hissing out the baleful instruction "I want another one." The figure turns out to be Tanja, fire-ravaged wife of Kinski's mild-mannered Dr Nijinski; in yet another blatant reprise of *Les Yeux sans visage*, she tells a stranded newly-wed that "I need a face. Yours!" Carlo Rambaldi's make-up

effects in the grafting scenes are truly gruesome, but unfortunately these sections are completely ruined by Kinski's non-appearance in them, forcing Garrone to use a half-glimpsed stand-in instead. Even so, when Kinski does appear he's typically good value, particularly when addressing his dying words to an impassive doll called Anjuska.

Featuring the same actors and locations and even one of the same murders, *Le amanti del mostro* is a sequel of sorts but, sadly, it's also a deadening plod. This time Kinski seems to be playing the son-in-law of Dr Nijinski, rapidly getting the cobwebbed basement lab up and running and as a result becoming a Jekyll-Hyde figure; the POV shots during his neighbourhood killing spree come in handy given that, again, Kinski appears to have absented himself from a large part of the shoot. Scenes of the post-kill Kinski lurching bug-eyed through the woods are diverting enough, but the rest of the film is grievously padded. Among the other returning actors is the Turkish star Ayhan Işik, whose presence indicates a reportedly rather fraught co-production deal with Turkey.

## DR ORLA'S PRIMORDIAL SECRET

"It took them a long time to get into the genre but now our film producers don't know how to get out," commented Spanish film correspondent 'Jordan' in early June 1972. "Horror movies are ten a penny in Spain. They're all doing it: Klimovsky, Jess Frank [Franco], José Luis Merino, who's shooting *La orgía de los muertos*, Tulio Demicheli, currently filming *Ella (La Muerte)*, newcomer Raúl Artigot who will do *La montaña del diablo* [ie, *El monte de las brujas*], Jorge Grau, preparing *Los vampiros* [ie, *Ceremonia sangrienta*], and José Larraz, who's soon to start work on *Puertas oscuras* [ie, *Emma*]. And joining them is Javier Aguirre, who's working on two screenplays in collaboration with thriller 'specialist' Paul Naschy, titled nothing less than *La noche de todos los horrores* and *El gran amor del conde Drácula*. May you be thoroughly frightened."[10]

Though a bit off-beam regarding Demicheli's *Ella* (less horror, more a psychological drama featuring an attempted murder), Jordan was otherwise spot on in his analysis of the hydra-like proliferation of Spanish horror. Once the scripts were ready to go, the two Aguirre-Naschy collaborations mentioned by Jordan would be duly announced in *Variety* in mid-September, though by this time *La noche de todos los horrores* (The Night of All the Horrors) had become *El jorobado de la morgue* (The Hunchback of the Morgue). A third Aguirre horror included in the announcement, *El retorno de la Duquesa Drácula* (The Return of Duchess Dracula), never made it in front of the cameras.

The two films that did get made were a result of Naschy's short-lived association with the new-to-horror director Javier Aguirre, and both of them were in the can by the end of the year. For *El gran amor del conde Drácula* (The Great Love of Count Dracula), Janus Film succeeded in casting Haydée Politoff, gamine star of Éric Rohmer's *La Collectioneuse*, who arrived in Madrid on 2 September and claimed that "I love horror ... I saw some Paul Naschy films in Italy, and he's a great genre specialist."[11] Recalled Naschy decades later, "To tell the truth, we didn't get on too well and filming love scenes with her was none too easy."[12] Despite this problem, the film remains significant as the first to reconfigure Dracula as a romantic hero, or at least to attempt to do so. The shooting of Dan Curtis' TV movie version of the original novel, complete with bogus scenes involving the Count's mediaeval amours, was over six months away.

Paul Naschy stakes himself in a fit of pique in *El gran amor del conde Drácula* (1972)

Yet the story, concocted as usual by Naschy himself, is a stop-start affair in which Dracula spends the first two acts disguised as a hospitable sort called Dr Wendell Marlow. The film also suffers from a confusion of intent, with maudlin shots of tears rolling down Dracula's face competing with some of the most outrageous soft-porn interludes yet featured in a Spanish horror. Elsewhere the pace is sluggish and the period clothing straight from the Spaghetti Western costume basket, but Aguirre keeps interest alive with some genuinely oneiric tableaux. The opening, with a couple of light-fingered delivery men coming to grief in Dracula's basement, involves one of the men getting an axe in his head and tumbling repeatedly down a flight of stairs, in slow motion to boot, throughout the credits sequence. As a young doctor and four beautiful women travel by coach through the forest, the trees turn to negative in the style of *Nosferatu*. Dracula's first attack is rendered as a solarised dream in which blue blood drips from his mouth onto the victim's breasts. And love-making, seen in a mirror, reveals the winsome Politoff but not Naschy's passionate Dracula.

Most striking of all are Rosanna Yanni, Ingrid Garbo and Mirta Miller (the latter deputising for the originally announced María Elena Arpón). These three, flouncing and occasionally even vaulting towards their victims in oscillating slow motion, are as formidable a trio of *Penthouse*-style vampire women as the cinema has produced. A scene in which Garbo and Miller initiate the supine Yanni, one at each side of her throat, pushes the eroticised combination of blood and breasts about as far as it can go. Amid all this, Naschy's Dracula is somewhat upstaged. He's a good-looking but rather stolid figure, communicating mainly in telepathic voice-over, presiding over a blood resurrection obviously lifted from Hammer's *Lust for a Vampire*, and telling Politoff that "It's not the first time that a vampire has loved a daughter of man." In the end, he petulantly stakes himself when she balks at joining him in eternity. Just like his idol Lon Chaney Jr, Naschy is a poor fit for the role, and to disguise this he resorts, very obviously, to posing rather than acting.

As 1972 wound down, producer Francisco Lara Polop and director Javier Aguirre moved straight from *El gran amor* to *El jorobado de la morgue*, with the titular hunchback of the morgue being played, inevitably, by Naschy. This turned out to be the second and last horror picture for Aguirre, who, having outlined his avant-garde theories in the 1971 book *Anti-cine*, took on commercial projects purely to help finance his experimental films. Having garnished *El gran amor* with an array of arty, eye-catching visual effects, in *El jorobado* he entirely excluded such flourishes,

# EL JOROBADO DE LA MORGUE

Paul Naschy as the troglodyte anti-hero of *El jorobado de la morgue* (1972)

*Spain 1972*
*UK / US: The Hunchback of the Morgue*
*Eva Film / F Lara Polop*
*82 minutes colour*
*in production December 1972*
..........................................

Director of Photography: Raúl Pérez Cubero;
Art Directors: Jaime Pérez Cubero, José
Luis Galicia; Editor: Petra de Nieva; Music:
Carmelo Bernaola; Make-up: Miguel Sesé;
Special Effects: Pablo Pérez; Screenplay:
Jacinto Molina [Paul Naschy], Javier
Aguirre, Alberto S Insúa; Story by: Jacinto
Molina [Paul Naschy]; Producer: Francisco
Lara Polop; Director: Javier Aguirre

Paul Naschy (Gotho); Rossana [Rosanna] Yanni
(Elke); Vic Winner [Víctor Alcázar] (Tauchner);
Alberto Dalbes (Dr Orla); Maria Perschy
(Frieda); Maria Elena Arpón (Ilse); Manuel de
Blas, Antonio Pica (police inspectors); Joaquín
Rodríguez 'Kinito' (Hans Burgher); Adolfo
Thous; Ángel Menéndez (police commissioner);
Fernando Sotuela (Udo); Antonio Ramis;
Alfonso de la Vega; Sofía Casares; Antonio
Mayans (Hans' drinking companion); Susan
Taff (nurse); José Luis Chinchilla; Richard
Santis; Iris André; Ingrid Rabel; Francisco
Javier Martín 'Blaki' (Dr Orla's butler); Susana
Latour; Dani Card; Saturno Cerra; Júlio Martín;
Victoria Ayllón

> El jorobado de la morgue is ... smoothly plotted and carried through
> with excellent technique and an unerring visual instinct ... The film is
> entertaining and even exciting at times, never, of course, losing sight of
> the audience it's aimed at. Headlining the cast is Paul Naschy ... Equally
> noteworthy is a dazzling contribution from the alluring Rossana [sic] Yanni.
> *La Vanguardia 29 November 1973*

> My characters are 'different' – marginalised creatures that can't be
> integrated into everyday life and have no option but to die. Like Gotho, the
> repulsive and semi-subnormal hunchback in *El jorobado de la morgue*; where
> else can he take refuge but in the lower depths? These beings are forced to
> hide in crypts, dungeons, castles – dismal places, set apart – because they're
> rejected by the normal world. *Paul Naschy [quoted in Quatermass Autumn 2002]*

the slavering tag-line 'Cuerpos mutilados, crimenes
horrendos y, tras ellos, la mente perturbado de un
maniaco asesino' (Mutilated corpses, horrendous
crimes and, behind them, the disturbed mind of
a maniacal killer).

> Austria, 1972. Hunchbacked morgue attendant Gotho
> undergoes constant abuse from the locals but finds comfort
> in his terminally ill childhood friend Ilse. On her death,
> he snaps and kills a couple of fellow morgue workers.
> Pursued by the police, he seeks help from research scientist
> Dr Orla. His funding having been cut, Orla relocates
> his laboratory to Gotho's subterranean hideaway, then
> promises Gotho that he will bring Ilse back to life.

Again eschewing Spanish settings for fear of
censorship, Naschy set his latest fantasy in the
mediaeval city of Feldkirch, the residents of
which presumably didn't object to the place being
represented as home to homicidal hunchbacks and
primordial slime-creatures. Arguably worse than
either of these are the ghastly local children and
even ghastlier trainee doctors who make Gotho's
life unbearable. After much generic wenching and
boozing in the local Bierkeller, one of them staggers

responding to the outrageous extremes of Naschy's
latest scenario with bludgeoning Grand Guignol
vigour. In the same vein, Eva Film's publicists showed
they knew how to lure an audience, coming up with

out into the cobbled streets and is promptly murdered by the embittered Gotho. We're then treated, back at the morgue, to some charming views of Gotho chopping off his head, hands and feet. In typically head-scratching Naschy style, this is the character we're expected to sympathise with throughout the remainder of the film. Yet, such is the artless sincerity of Naschy's performance, we actually do.

The combination of cloying sentiment with levels of gore that, for the time, were pretty extreme is the raison d'être of this utterly deranged film. Devoted to María Elena Arpón's wilting Ilse, Gotho turns up at her hospital room with a small bunch of flowers only to find that she's died. In no time at all a couple of male nurses suggest looting her corpse, enraging Gotho so much he decapitates one and disembowels the other. In a delightfully unexpected development, he then delivers Ilse's body to a full-fledged Gothic dungeon some 25 meters below street level. This dismal space, with a retinue of cowled skeletons worthy of a German Krimi, apparently dates back to the Crusades, was repurposed by the Inquisition and most recently concealed persecuted Jews during the war. (The underground hideaway with its Jewish back-story was almost certainly Naschy's nod to the 1944 hunchback film *La torre de los siete jorobados*.) It's here, in the film's most notorious scene, that Gotho, discovering a horde of rats feasting on Ilse's face, vengefully puts them to the torch. Yes, the flaming rats were real, and to make matters worse the footage is repeated later on.

The film really gets into gear when Gotho hooks up with Dr Orla, who modestly tells him that "The most insignificant people can still be useful to science and mankind; they merely have to allow themselves to be guided by a true leader." Orla entices Gotho with the prospect of somehow creating a 'new' Ilse, but what he's actually working on is a huge jar of tripe-like, greyly pulsing entrails, to which he feeds severed human heads acquired by Gotho. Transferred to a secure cell, the rapidly growing thing wails and gnashes its teeth like the closeted monster in the 1959 film *The Brain That Wouldn't Die*, requiring a steady stream of young females as nourishment. Bizarrely, Orla theorises that the creature is a 'primordial', privy to "all the secrets of previous civilisations," and references H P Lovecraft's Necronomicon to underline his point.

Naschy's fondness for lachrymose anti-heroes made his self-casting as Gotho a foregone conclusion. Yet, effective though he is in the role, it could be argued that he has the film stolen from him by the Argentinian actor Alberto Dalbes. Embroiled at the time in a run of a dozen Jess Franco films, Dalbes is the dapper Dr Orla – a character whose name is suspiciously similar to Franco's Dr Orloff and who, in 1940s Hollywood, would have been perfect for Bela Lugosi or Lionel Atwill. "Impossible is a word that should form no part of a scientist's vocabulary," he says, handily indicating his Napoleonic levels of vainglory. His own vocabulary is peppered with standard epithets from the Lugosi-Atwill phrasebook. "For the first time in history we have the opportunity to create artificial life," he enthuses, later revealing his true Nazi colours when telling the local reform school superintendent that his subjects are drawn from her establishment because "The girls there are garbage and no one will miss them." Faced with juicy ravings of this sort, Dalbes takes the counterintuitive tack of playing Orla entirely deadpan, relying on his personal charisma to sell the role. And it works a treat.

*El jorobado de la morgue* is full of the expected illogicalities, particularly when Gotho earns the love, physical as well as emotional, of Rosanna Yanni's gorgeous Elke – yet still remains mystifyingly hell-bent on resurrecting Ilse. The barnstorming climax finally introduces us to Orla's pleasingly ridiculous humanoid tripe-thing, but is otherwise ineptly staged. (Notice the half-hearted way in which Orla, in tribute to Atwill's Dr Bohmer in *The Ghost of Frankenstein*, is slammed against a bank of sparking machinery.) But none of this matters in a film that draws so much energy from its own absurdity that it has become a bona-fide trash classic.

Both *El gran amor del conde Drácula* and *El jorobado de la morgue* were showcased in April 1973 at Alain Schlockoff's second Convention Française du Cinéma Fantastique in Paris, where Naschy won an award and rubbed shoulders with such genre luminaries as Terence Fisher and Peter Cushing. When arriving at the convention, Naschy had recently polished off *La venganza de la momia* (The Vengeance of the Mummy), his penchant for playing famous monsters having made it inevitable that he would one day add the mummy to his CV as well. He'd been beaten to the punch, however, by a couple of other Spanish-made mummies, both of them conspicuously lacking in the trademark bandages.

Shot in April 1972, Alejandro Martí's *El secreto de la momia egipcia* (The Secret of the Egyptian Mummy) was a French co-production and is mainly distinguished by an obsessional emphasis on irradiated yellows, with French beaches, cornfields, marshes and haylofts all echoing the golden robes of the titular mummy. For variety, the sexagenarian character star Jorge Rigaud (here granted top billing for a change) wears a sky-blue frock coat to match his patrician mane of

Frank Braña encounters a lively severed hand in
*El secreto de la momia egipcia* (1972)

hair. There are a few scraps of charming stop-motion animation here; Rigaud's mummy-reviving scientist inexplicably turns a cane into a writhing snake and, later, the mummy's severed hand comes back to skittering life. There's also a strange quote from Guy de Maupassant's 1883 story *La Main*, when the hand, chained to a wall, is seen being energetically whipped by Rigaud. Unfortunately, the mummy itself is both vampire and sex offender, so the film rapidly collapses into a tediously repetitive round of sexual sadism inflicted on various abducted wenches. The inspired export title was *Love Brides of the Blood Mummy*.

The other 'rival' mummy appeared in *Vudú sangriento* (Bloodthirsty Voodoo). Shot in November-December 1971 as *Vudú loa* (Voodoo Spirits), this one was directed by Manuel Caño and was a collaboration between producer José Antonio Pérez Giner and a Miami film company. The outstandingly inept result eventually gets to Port au Prince but otherwise confines its resurrected Caribbean priest to the hold of a cruise ship. Among the grisly 'delights' on display are Eva León in blackface, a collection of risibly unconvincing severed heads, and a rushed climax in which the prune-faced mummy (Aldo Sambrell) and his reincarnated love (León) are flamethrowered à deux. The only fragment of wit in the whole boring stodge comes when the mummy attributes his perfect English to "three centuries of museums." By the time the film reached America in 1974, it had picked up the catchpenny title *Voodoo Black Exorcist*, though Sambrell's character is neither an exorcist nor (properly speaking) black.

Surprisingly, the script for *Vudú sangriento* was by the normally exemplary Santiago Moncada, who continued his detour into schlock with another US co-production directed by Manuel Caño, *El pantano*

*de los cuervos* (The Swamp of the Ravens). Amid a superfluity of circling buzzards, this film features no ravens whatsoever, though this doesn't stop the youthful Dr Frosta (Ramiro Oliveros) from offering garbled quotes from *The Raven* as he struggles to resurrect the dead in his run-down Ecuadorean shack. There are a few memorable images here, notably a slew of experimental subjects bobbing up to their necks in a nearby swamp. But the execution is otherwise cack-handed in the extreme. "Science demands many victims to advance itself" insists Frosta generically, one of them being his insubordinate girlfriend Simone (Marcia Bichette), who he prefers having sex with when she's dead. Cast as a slightly more efficient police inspector than the one he played in *Vudú sangriento*, the ubiquitous Fernando Sancho has his breakfast in the presence of a severed hand and later stands by while an unfaked autopsy takes place – a bad-taste low point in Spanish horror.

## MONCADA MANIA

By late 1972, Spain's horror boom was entrenched enough, and its scope wide enough, to allow for some intriguing juxtapositions. Ace screenwriter Santiago Moncada, for example, could turn from an abysmal piece of junk like *Vudú sangriento* and hand one of his scripts to none other than Juan Antonio Bardem. As one of the most significant oppositional filmmakers during the Franco era, Bardem had co-written Spain's breakthrough post-war film, *¡Bienvenido Mister Marshall!* (Welcome, Mr Marshall!), in 1952; after this he directed the social-realist classic *Muerte de un ciclista* (Death of a Cyclist), though he was a political prisoner at the time of its award-winning debut at Cannes. He was also looked upon as a mentor by the young Jess Franco, having employed him as an assistant on several 1950s titles, including *Ciclista*.

Embracing the horror genre, in August 1972 Bardem began work at Barcelona's Isasi Studios on a Moncada-scripted film called *La corrupción de Chris Miller* (The Corruption of Chris Miller). Enjoying a princely budget of some 55 million pesetas, it was also shot on location in Santander and at a private house loaned to the producers by the Condesa de San Martín de Hoy. Announced under the title YY (presumably in reference to chromosomes), the project was intended as an image-changing vehicle for former child star Marisol, who had been Spain's equivalent to Hayley Mills in a long series of 1960s hits. Her co-stars were to be Britain's Malcolm McDowell and America's Anne Bancroft, though, in the event, some very short-notice re-casting resulted in Barry Stokes and the French icon Jean Seberg being engaged instead.

British fashion designer Ruth Miller is taking a break at her Cantabrian country home with her half-Spanish stepdaughter Chris; both of them nurse bitter feelings towards Chris' long departed father. Into their midst comes a young British backpacker called Barney, who becomes Ruth's handyman and lover. In the meantime, a serial killer is at large – and, when Barney is summarily thrown out by Ruth, a family of five is slain the same night.

Moncada's basic plot – the claustrophobic lives of two obsessional women being disrupted by a mysterious male stranger – was hardly new. In mainstream climes it had formed the basis of Mark Rydell's D H Lawrence adaptation *The Fox*, while for horror fans it was recognisable from the two film versions of Emlyn Williams' play *Night Must Fall*. The same template had been followed in 1970 by an obscure British film called *The Night Digger*, which Moncada may well have seen and been influenced by. (His next script, *La campana del infierno*, would also incorporate a few *Night Digger* details.) Yet Moncada's script works enough twisted variations on the formula, and Bardem's realisation of them is so powerful, that *La corrupción de Chris Miller* survives as one of Spain's classiest and most effective horror films. Apparently a psychological thriller, it's decorated by extremely strong Grand Guignol details, enough to pitch it into horror territory and make the stated profession of Chris' absentee father – as a 'Petit Guignol' Punch 'n' Judy man – seem like an inside joke.

The weirdness quotient starts high and stays that way. In a riveting pre-credits sequence, musical comedy star Perla (Perla Cristal) is trying to get rid of a persistent lover, whom she's apparently been putting up for a fortnight. (This fact will later serve to implicate the itinerant Barney, though it's actually a bit of a cheat given the film's third act twist.) Bizarrely, the lover makes his entrance dressed as Charlie Chaplin's Little Tramp. The impersonation is hardly on the level of Gloria Swanson's in *Sunset Blvd*, but he proves horribly proficient as a murderer, subsequently escaping into the Cantabrian rain and tossing his Chaplin mask, like a loathsome, sloughed-off skin, into the mud. Appearance and reality are instantly called into question as the credits – accompanied by Waldo de los Ríos' memorably doom-laden score – roll in.

We learn later, via a news report, that Perla's most famous number was called 'Charlie', making a gruesome kind of sense of this opening vignette. In the meantime we've been introduced to Ruth and Chris, the former maintaining grimly that "Men don't love: they

# LA CORRUPCIÓN DE CHRIS MILLER

Spain 1972
UK / US: **The Corruption of Chris Miller**
alternative US: **Behind the Shutters** / **Sisters of Corruption**
a Xavier Armet production
107 minutes colour
production ended early November 1972
. . . . . . . . . . . . . . . . . . . . . . . . . . . . .
Director of Photography: Juan Gelpí; Art Director: Ramíro Gómez; Editor: Emilio Rodríguez; Sound: Jorge Sangenís, Taffy Haines; Music: Waldo de los Ríos; Make-up: Julián Ruiz, Antonio Florido; Special Effects:

Antonio Parra, Antonio Bueno; Screenplay: Santiago Moncada; Executive Producer: Xavier Armet; Director: Juan Antonio Bardem

Marisol (Chris Miller); Jean Seberg (Ruth Miller); Barry Stokes (Barney Webster); Perla Cristal (Perla); Rudy Gaebel (Luis); Gérard Tichy (police superintendent); Alicia Altabella (Adela, mother); Mariano Vidal Molina (Ernesto, father); María Bardem (María, daughter); Juan Bardem (Pedro, elder son); Miguel Bardem (Tin, small son); Gustavo Re (shopkeeper); Carl Rapp (television announcer); Goyo Lebrero (farmer); Antonio Parra (postman)

*La corrupción de Chris Miller* marks the consecration of Marisol, actress ... Screenwriter Santiago Moncada has cunningly constructed a story that assails the viewer with a brutal and violent lash from the moment it starts. The unease spreads through the auditorium even before the credit titles begin ... The example of Peckinpah arises in the viewer's mind ... [in] a Spanish film of international standing. ABC Madrid 20 May 1973

It's so difficult to remove an image from people's heads, you know? There are still people who write to me and say that I must keep on doing those [light musical] movies. Even so, there's no new image for Marisol ... If I've seemed a little absent in recent years it's because I've been doing something that a fault in my personality, together with disproportionate fame, prevented me from doing before: living. Marisol [quoted in ABC Madrid 24 November 1972]

Striking Spanish artwork for the gruesome Marisol vehicle
*La corrupción de Chris Miller* (1972)

possess, they injure, they invade." For her part, Chris is plagued by subliminal flashes of a grunting weightlifter – flashes that are cleverly built up during the course of the film to finally reveal that as a schoolgirl she was raped in a shower cubicle by this perspiring monstrosity. In a slightly hokey development, her shower trauma has given her a pathological terror of rain, making Cantabria a far from ideal holiday destination. Yet it was no doubt chosen for this very purpose by the embittered and calculating Ruth, who, to avenge herself on the missing father, does everything she can to disturb the girl while making extravagant, verging on Sapphic, demonstrations of affection.

Through the sheets of persistent rain advances the ambiguous Barney, who immediately throws this strange ménage into disarray, first by standing naked before Ruth in the stables and then by asking her, over breakfast, the leading question, "Maybe you can think of something I can do around here?" To maximise the ensuing sexual tensions, Moncada made a crucial adjustment to the *Night Must Fall* model, making both women, not just the younger one, beddable as well as biddable.

And the pressure-cooker is just about ready to burst when Bardem blindsides the viewer with two brilliantly staged, and unflinchingly brutal, set-pieces. The rain turns to a rumbling nocturnal storm as a killer in a sodden sou'wester and raincoat sets about an entire family with a scythe; in a subversive touch, a little boy (the fifth and final victim) mistakes the killer for a monk. Back at Ruth's holiday home, there follows an agonisingly extended murder sequence, slathered in the blood artfully withheld in the previous scene, in which multiple stab wounds are climaxed by the overturning of a grandfather clock. Nigel Burrell, in the 2005 book *Hispanic Horrors*, has astutely observed that this scene almost certainly influenced a similarly extreme set-piece in José Larraz's British shocker *Vampyres*.

Seething with off-colour sexual politics, *Chris Miller* is masterfully handled by Bardem and exceptionally acted by the glacial Seberg and feline Marisol. As Barney, Barry Stokes arguably lacks the dangerous edge that might have made the film's middle section more compelling – though, five years later, this didn't stop Norman J Warren from casting him in yet another 'two women intruded on by one man' scenario, *Prey*.

When *Chris Miller* finished filming in the first week of November 1972, Santiago Moncada's next script, *A las tres te mato otra vez* (At Three O'Clock I'll Kill You Again), was just two months away from going into production. It included a plum role for the exceptional character star

Alfredo Mayo, who not too long before had appeared in the rubbishy, Moncada-scripted *Vudú sangriento*. But again, as with *Chris Miller*, the result – retitled *La campana del infierno* (The Bell from Hell) – was about as far from the trash end of Spain's horror market as it was possible to get. Directed by Claudio Guerín, the film has since become notorious for the tragedy that took place on Friday 16 February 1973 – the day earmarked as the last in Guerín's shooting schedule.

In the Plaza del Tapal in Noya, the asymmetrical church of San Martín had been balanced by the crew with a second belltower, from which the 34-year-old director fell 60 feet to his death. "It's unknown as yet whether it was due to vertigo, a fainting fit or from tripping on his long coat tails," reported *Nuevo Fotogramas*. "But it's true. Claudio Guerín died, crushed against the cobbles of a small Galician town square on the edge of the Atlantic."[13] A *Vanguardia* report the day after the tragedy pointed out that "News of the young filmmaker's death has made a deep impression on everyone in the Spanish film industry."[14] Amidst lurid speculation about a local legend wishing death on anyone who augmented the church with another belfry, the film's remaining shots were completed, uncredited, by *Chris Miller*'s director, Juan Antonio Bardem.

*Juan has been in a psychiatric facility for three years, having attempted to rape his cousin Teresa. Released on probation, he takes a job as a slaughterman at an abattoir – purely for research purposes, given that he's planning to avenge himself on his Aunt Marta, who committed him, and her three daughters, one of whom is Teresa. A local builder, meanwhile, is refurbishing the belltower of the local church...*

After a notable TV career, Guerín was perceived as an up-and-coming art-house talent, having won awards for the 1969 portmanteau film *Los desafíos* (The Challenges). Alfredo Mayo had also picked up an award for *Los desafíos*, and indeed would win another for his excellent performance in *La campana del infierno*. Also in Guerín's new film were the formidable Swedish star Viveca Lindfors and the young heart-throb Renaud Verley, the latter satisfying the French end of Hesperia Films' co-production deal.

Verley's cold-eyed presence was crucial in another way too, for in scripting *La campana* Moncada had moved on to another fruitful sub-genre. Foregrounding the kind of seriously disturbed young man popularised by *Psycho* and since exploited in such films as *Twisted Nerve* and *You'll Like My Mother*, he also gave the young man a Ducati motorbike, a detail from *The Night Digger* that hadn't made it into *La corrupción*

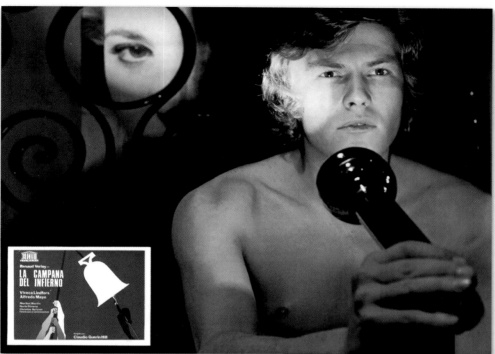

Sadistic practical joker with murder in mind: Renaud Verley in *La campana del infierno* (1973)

*de Chris Miller.* Yet Moncada was a master at putting new twists on old formulae, and the result is a film that combines surrealism, well-judged humour and genuine horror to tremendous effect.

As in *Chris Miller*, the action begins with a young man in a mask, though this time it's a plaster life-mask and we actually see it under construction. For a long time this opening scene floats strangely, disturbingly, in the back of the viewer's mind, not revealing its secrets until a full-size mannequin of Juan is briefly glimpsed in a basement crate; it's this same mannequin that will play a robotic, and borderline ridiculous, role in the film's finale. In the meantime, Juan is discharged from the clinic, exchanges some puzzling words with a bearded sage in the woods, hears a haunting schoolchildren's refrain of *Frère Jacques* that will persist throughout the film, and finally arrives at his late mother's home in driving rain. (Again echoing *Chris Miller*, rain and storm are recurrent motifs.) These curious, apparently disconnected vignettes are assembled by Guerín to ensure maximum disorientation, after which he hits the viewer hard with Juan's revolting spell at an abattoir.

These scenes go far beyond even the horrific actuality footage captured by Eloy de la Iglesia for *La semana del asesino*, and they'll deter a great many viewers from staying with the film. Clearly shot in a real slaughterhouse, they're distinct from the kind

## LA CAMPANA DEL INFIERNO

Spain-France 1973
France: **La cloche de l'enfer**
UK / US: **The Bell of Hell**
Hesperia Films Madrid / Les Films de la Boétie Paris
106 minutes colour
production began 3 January 1973
. . . . . . . . . . . . . . . . . . . . . . . . . . . . .
Director of Photography: Manuel Rojas; Art Director: Eduardo Torre de la Fuente; Editor: Magdalena Pulido; Sound: Tomás Barrio, Luis Castro; Music: Adolfo Waitzman; Make-up: Julián Ruiz; Special Effects: Baquero; Screenplay and Adaptation:

Santiago Moncada; Producer: Claudio Guerín Hill; Director[s]: Claudio Guerín Hill, Juan Antonio Bardem [completion]

Renaud Verley (Juan); Viveca Lindfors (Marta); Alfredo Mayo (Don Pedro); Maribel Martín (Esther); Nuria Gimeno (Teresa); Christine Betzner [Cristine von Blanc] (María); Saturno Cerra (shepherd); Nicole Vesperini (Pedro's wife); Erasmo Pascual (priest); Antonio Puga, Juan Cazalilla, Tito García (huntsmen); Rosetta Vellísca (shepherd's daughter); Ángel Blanco; Susana Latour

The film is a complex and twisted drama that works madness, greed, sadism and death into a delirious, almost apocalyptic carousel ... Taking the viewer from shock to shock and surprise to surprise, Claudio Guerín has lent unexpected conviction to the manoeuvrings and compulsions of this little world – a reflection or paradigm of deranged humanity. The script, by Santiago Moncada, is extremely rich in incident, many of them, such as the finale, literally hair-raising. *La Vanguardia* 2 October 1973

This film ... is of mixed genres. I don't think you can assign any film to a particular genre these days. What genre would you say *Frenzy* belongs to? I'd say the Hitchcock genre. *La campana del infierno* has a somewhat magical atmosphere, it has suspense, it has eroticism. There are symbols because that's the only means of expression we have. But I don't believe in messages and stuff like that. *Claudio Guerín* [quoted posthumously in *Nuevo Fotogramas* 2 March 1973]

of animal cruelty exploited in Italian films; these animals weren't being killed purely for the sake of the film. And yet, in the name of the queasiest kind of verisimilitude imaginable, leading man Renaud Verley is in there doing the job his character is meant to do.

This section leads to a bitterly effective juxtaposition. A delicate white carnation sits in a vase on the cashier's desk as he asks, "Why do you want to leave?" Replies Juan, "I've learned enough."

Given what we already know of Juan's antipathy towards his aunt and cousins, this is among the most bowel-loosening lines in the genre. For the time being, however, Juan is presented as little more than a conspicuously cruel practical joker. Encountering Mayo's venal building contractor for the first time, Juan teases him with a story about his three cousins, suggesting they're dead and are likely to return home any moment through a fog-shrouded doorway. As well as indicating Juan's familiarity with the Saki story *The Open Window*, this scene is a magical little intermingling of comedy and creepy atmospherics, and it's echoed in more ribald fashion by a very funny scene in which the builder, Pedro, is tricked into holding Juan's penis at a urinal.

The remainder of the film abounds in arresting imagery. As Aunt Marta, Lindfors' marvellously Gothic face is a striking image in itself, and in the storm-racked latter stages Guerín echoes Juan's plastered features from the opening with a lightning-bolt reveal of the lumpen horror that is Marta's face after a sustained bee attack. (In a puzzling lapse of continuity, the acromegalic swellings are improbably reduced the very next morning.) Elsewhere, Guerín films a rape scene from the looming vantage point of a vase of red roses and through the prism of a transparent coffee table; the complex interplay of emotions on Nuria Gimeno's face suggests the influence of the highly controversial rape in Sam Peckinpah's recently released *Straw Dogs*. And in a subversive detail recalling the use of monks in *Chris Miller*, Juan is assured by Pedro that "You'll be one of the counterweights" when the new bell is installed in the local church. Finally, the brilliantly orchestrated climax sees Pedro venturing into Juan's darkened home (complete with its robotic harpsichords and strange menagerie of animals), only to become intimately acquainted with the fish tank.

Supplementing the works of Eloy de la Iglesia, Vicente Aranda and Jorge Grau, *La corrupción de Chris Miller* and *La campana del infierno* offered further proof that, under the auspices of Spain's apparently disreputable horror boom, art-house directors could sign their names to brilliantly confected thrillers. A different kind of proof – and a very different kind of film – was provided by Guerín's old associate Víctor Erice, who had part-directed *Los desafíos* with Guerín and two others in 1969. On 12 February 1973 (just four days prior to Guerín's death), Erice began shooting *El espíritu de la colmena* (The Spirit of the Beehive) in Segovia. A slow but mesmerising contemplation of the malaise afflicting Spain in the aftermath of the Civil War, this pivots on an itinerant screening of James Whale's *Frankenstein* and the profound effect it has on a six-year-old girl. In the end she imagines a lakeside meeting with the Monster himself; as well as sporting an excellent reproduction of the classic Karloff make-up, he also looks curiously like her remote and cerebral father.

*El espíritu* has since been enshrined in Spain as maybe the country's best ever film – and yet it might never have been made were it not for the period's horror vogue. As Erice explained, "I had presented various projects to Elías Querejeta [producer of *Los desafíos*], until one day I suggested doing a film on Frankenstein and he accepted."[15] The film even went into production, according to trade papers of the day, as plain *Frankenstein*.

## NOT FROM THE VALLEY
On 24 February 1973, just over a week after the tragedy that curtailed *La campana del infierno*, shooting was completed on *Una vela para el diablo* (A Candle for the Devil). Like Vicente Aranda's *La novia ensangrentada*, this was a José López Moreno production; also like *La novia*, it was a film that couched its horror highlights in weighty, provocative themes. Here, however, the filmmakers' standpoint is clear as day, requiring no great effort at interpretation. The screenplay was by Antonio Fos, whose association with Eloy de la Iglesia was just winding up around this time. Indeed, *Una vela* plays rather like one of the Iglesia films but with the censor-baiting themes placed front and centre rather than operating slyly in the subtext. To make the film as hard-hitting as possible, Moreno bypassed art-house auteurs of the Aranda and Iglesia type, instead engaging the seasoned exploitation director Eugenio Martín, who had displayed an expert grasp of Gothic horror in *Pánico en el Transiberiano*.

*Looking forward to catching up with her sister May, British tourist Laura Barkley arrives at a boarding house run by spinster sisters Marta and Verónica – unaware that they accidentally killed May just moments before. Marta, in particular, is appalled by the scantily clad trippers swarming into town, and proceeds to murder three other people before turning her attention to the dangerously inquisitive Laura...*

*Una vela para el diablo* is a film that sets out its thematic stall with uncluttered ease in its first few minutes. Composer Antonio Pérez Olea gives us cheerful Pan pipes and folksy, rippling guitars as a BEA plane soars aloft, the unsuspecting Laura sitting inside with a Spanish guidebook in her lap. Then, in the kitchen of the fateful guest house, Marta brings the upbeat music to a brutal stop with a heavy cleaver blow. Hacking her way through a knotty joint, she complains that "This lamb isn't from the valley. It smells different." Grandmother, apparently, made a point of using only local produce – "but," Marta adds, "times were different then." She also inveighs against "half-naked tourists" while Verónica timidly points out how much money the tourists bring in.

Fos and Martín leave us in no doubt that what we have here is a microcosm of a country only recently revolutionised by the economic miracle of tourism, struggling to digest the new sexual freedoms, yet still wedded, particularly in rural areas, to Catholicism and other atavistic ways of thinking. Passing through the guest house (its corridors decorated with plenty of religious statuary), the sisters find their latest guest sunbathing topless on the roof terrace. Hurled down the stairs, the girl's head slams through a stained glass window, prompting Marta to a lunatic leap of logic. "She killed herself," she mutters. "She has been punished by God. We were his hand of justice." Organ music bursts out, the body is covered up, and Laura raps on the street door. All this in under eight minutes.

Marta, unsurprisingly, is a hypocrite as well as a religious maniac. When she spies on local youths swimming naked, the only penis we're shown is a hairless one belonging to the single pre-pubescent in the group. In expiation, she takes her departure through the lacerating branches of a thorn bush. Then, having washed away the stigmatic blood, she goes to her boudoir and puts on the pink dress she was wearing when she was jilted long ago. The man, of course, went off instead with just the kind of 'floozy' she now avenges herself on.

To play Laura, Martín cast Judy Geeson, familiar from such British shockers as *Berserk* and *Fear in the Night*. (Calling her "la Mireille Darc británica" and noting her desire to do better and better work, *Nuevo Fotogramas* cynically pointed out that "this film is unlikely to do much to crystallise her

hopes."[16]) Geeson's role is subordinate, however, to the truly meaty ones played by Esperanza Roy and Aurora Bautista. Roy was well known for appearing in several lowbrow 'Landismo' comedies starring Alfredo Landa, so the role of the submissive Verónica was a canny change of pace. Bautista, meanwhile, had starred as Juana la Loca in the Franco-sanctioned 1948 epic *Locura de amor* (Mad from Love), first in a long line of asexual historical heroines that she subverted with the selfless surrogate mother of the 1964 film *La tía Tula* (Aunt Tula). *Una vela* completed this subversion of her old image, twisting the themes of unrequited love and sexual

## UNA VELA PARA EL DIABLO

Spain 1973
UK: *A Candle for the Devil*
US: *It Happened at Nightmare Inn*
Vega Films / Mercofilms / Azor Films
87 minutes colour
production began 22 January 1973

. . . . . . . . . . . . . . . . . . . . . . . . . . . . .

Director of Photography: José F Aguayo; Art Director: Adolfo Cofiño; Editor: Pablo G Del Amo; Sound: José María San Mateo; Music: Antonio Pérez Olea; Make-up: Cristóbal Criado; Special Effects: Pablo Pérez;

Screenplay: Eugenio Martín, Tony [Antonio] Fos; Executive Producer: José López Moreno; Director: Eugenio Martín

Judy Geeson (Laura Barkley); Aurora Bautista (Marta); Esperanza Roy (Verónica); Vic Winner [Víctor Alcázar] (Eduardo); Lone Fleming (Helen Miller); Blanca Estrada (Norma); Charley Piñeiro (Luis); uncredited on English-language prints: Fernando Hilbeck (mayor); Diego Hurtado (Pablo); Montserrat Julió (Beatriz); Loreta Tovar (May); Fernando Villena (doctor)

**A new, blood-spattered picture from Spain. But not just another. Because Eugenio Martín's film is well worthwhile ... [with] fluid direction, convincing acting and a gripping plot. Una vela para el diablo has depth ... [and] sufficient quality to place it at the top of our current film output.**
*La Vanguardia* 12 October 1973

**That was a picture with a message. Antonio Fos' script denounced religious fanaticism, but the film was totally ruined by the censors. We were set to show the picture at Cannes, but Franco's people demanded no fewer than 30 cuts! After that we couldn't get any overseas sales, and the deals that we had already set up fell through.** *Eugenio Martín [quoted in Fangoria September 1999]*

Britain's Judy Geeson takes a traumatic trip to Grazalema in *Una vela para el diablo* (1973)

repression into a character who coldly says of her first victim, "Years ago that shameless girl would've been burned alive in the public square" – and clearly believes that the old ways were the best.

The sisters' victims are played by a range of horror regulars – Loreta Tovar, Lone Fleming (who had recently become Eugenio Martín's wife), Víctor Alcázar (one of the few men in an otherwise female-focused film) and Blanca Estrada. In a disturbing scene, the latter is killed in full view of her squalling baby, while Alcázar – in a plot development borrowed from *Psycho* – poses as Geeson's husband to help solve the mystery. Fos throws in some authentic grisliness in the closing stages; an eyeball discovered on a dinner plate simultaneously recalls the British legend of Sweeney Todd and the body parts Fos had written into his *Iglesia* scripts, while Estrada's cyclopean head rising to the surface of a massive wine barrel echoes the face-in-sludge seen in Iglesia's *El techo de cristal*.

Though the film ends rather too abruptly, it's smoothly directed by Martín and is picturesquely set in the cloisters at El Paular and among the white-walled houses of Grazalema – the latter location chosen, as Martín put it, "because it was well known for its religious processions, where all the zealots come out in the streets like things possessed."[17] Most memorably, *Una vela* enshrines a truly scary performance from Bautista.

Elsewhere in Spain, Paul Naschy's workload, always intense, was particularly onerous in 1973. In February he was playing a possibly psychotic drifter in *Los ojos azules de la muñeca rota* (Blue Eyes of the Broken Doll), directed by Carlos Aured for Profilmes. Here, an eye-removing serial killer is abroad in rural France, and Naschy is upstaged by the three weird but sexy sisters (Diana Lorys, Eva León and Maria Perschy) who give him shelter. The killings are gruesome, with disembodied eyes floating down into belljars in their wake, and Aured makes fetishistic use of the prosthetic arm worn by Lorys when Naschy, inevitably, makes love with her. (He ticks León off his list, too.) Adding to the allure of a good-looking film is a funky but (as was his wont) wholly inappropriate score by Juan Carlos Calderón.

Not yet done with Hispanic giallo imitations, within six months Naschy had dashed off two more. Javier Aguirre's *El asesino está entre los trece* (The Killer is One of the Thirteen) followed in April and is a rather dreary retread of the standard *Ten Little Indians* plot, with Jack Taylor, Patty Shepard and Simón Andreu among the usual ill-fated house guests. Equally uninspiring, León Klimovsky's *Una libélula para cada muerto* (A Dragonfly for Each Corpse) was made for Profilmes in July with its eye on the poliziotteschi end of the market, casting

Naschy as a reactionary, cigar-chomping Milanese cop on the trail of a serial killer sporting conspicuously crimson flares. The always watchable Erika Blanc gets to do some proactive detection of her own, but the trade-off is that she has to do it topless – though not for Spanish audiences, of course.

Becoming increasingly clogged, the Spanish horror market in the mid-1970s was by no means confined to just zombies, serial killers and subterranean necrophiles. There were also a few post-apocalyptic dramas stirred into the mix. In summer 1973 writer-director José Ulloa made *El refugio del miedo* (Refuge of Fear) for Profilmes, in which two married couples – Fernando Hilbeck and Patty Shepard plus the real-life married couple Craig Hill and Teresa Gimpera – hole up in a claustrophobic New York bunker after a nuclear disaster. Other Hispanic post-apocalypses included Angelino Fons' *La casa* (The House) and León Klimovsky's *Último deseo* (Last Will). In the first, Carlos Estrada, Helga Liné and Antonio Cantáfora are among the various survivors, with the titular, inescapable house turning out to be a get-away-from-it-all spaceship. The second, co-written by Vicente Aranda and exported as *The People Who Own the Dark*, has Alberto de Mendoza, Paul Naschy, Julia Saly, Maria Perschy and Teresa Gimpera (again) being besieged by blinded survivors in a ham-fisted retread of *I Am Legend*.

Made in April 1973, *Último deseo* was ready, with amazing speed, for a showcase at the Cannes Film Market the following month. Also on show there was the film Paul Naschy made immediately before *Último deseo*. Carlos Aured's *La venganza de la momia* (The Vengeance of the Mummy) is an especially good-looking entry in the Naschy canon, with luscious cinematography (Francisco Sànchez) and conspicuously lavish sets and costumes (Gumersindo Andrés, Antonio Muñoz). In it, Naschy plays the monstrous pharaoh Amenhotep, performing a gruesome blood sacrifice to ensure his immortality within the first few minutes. As his beautiful consort Amarna, Rina Ottolina is seen stretched out on a chaise just like Elizabeth Taylor in the famous poster for *Cleopatra* – or, for that matter, Amanda Barrie in the parodic poster for *Carry On Cleo*. Flashing forward to 19th century London, expedition sponsor Sir Douglas (Eduardo Calvo) indulges in romantic reminiscences (scored, bizarrely, with Carlo Rustichelli's music from *La frusta e il corpo*) prior to engaging the shifty Assad Bey (Naschy again) to decode the various findings in Amenhotep's tomb.

"It's paradoxical that we, the native Egyptologists," muses Bey, "have to travel around the world to study our own civilisation." It's a telling observation, but elsewhere, unfortunately, a whiff of racism attaches to the half-Egyptian, half-English character of Sir Douglas' daughter Helen (Ottolina again), who is said to harbour "undoubted atavism." She is, of course, the reincarnation of Amenhotep's former love, and when Amenhotep himself (Naschy yet again) is up and about he proves an unusually remorseless mummy. He squishes a museum attendant's head and thinks nothing of mashing the faces of three supine sacrificial maidens when they turn out not to be Amarna; all these atrocities feature oodles of nasty but unconvincing eyeball ejaculate.

A head-lopping mediaeval prologue to the werewolf saga *El retorno de Walpurgis* (1973)

Naschy's half-charred mummy still has a mouldy cloth binding his mouth shut (though this doesn't stop him talking), while his bejewelled appearance is at pleasing variance to the plainer look of previous rampaging mummies. The ubiquitous Helga Liné is a smoulderingly equivocal presence as Bey's concubine Zanufer, and Aured works up some foggy atmosphere in waterfront scenes seemingly modelled on Hammer's *The Curse of the Mummy's Tomb*. But the period detail is betrayed by a view of Tower Bridge flanked by modern buildings, and the ending – in which Helen, having been kissed by the mummy, becomes a mummy herself – is a nice idea poorly executed.

Naschy moved on in June 1973 to Juan Fortuny's dreadful Eurociné gangster thriller *Las ratas no duermen de noche* (Rats Don't Sleep at Night), which would be exported variously as *Crimson* or *The Man with the Severed Head*. Here, Naschy is reprieved from death, in a nod to old Hollywood melodramas like *Black Friday*, by receiving part of the brain matter of an even nastier gangster, inevitably inheriting "the same perverse desires." In a nod to Hammer's Frankenstein series, the professor responsible has useless hands, entrusting the intricate work to his beautiful wife (Silvia Solar). A severed head is packaged in pink ribbon, Evelyne Scott stubs out cigarettes on poor Gilda Arancio, and Naschy himself ends up sprawled over barbed wire with a bandage round his head and a syringe in his back.

Curiously, half the cast of *Las ratas no duermen de noche* – though not Naschy – had just appeared in Jordi Gigó's *La perversa caricia de Satán* (The Wicked Caresses of Satan). Production on this one was noted by *Variety* in May 1973, with the finished product finally being exported under the lame alternative title *Devil Kiss*. Gigó works every possible permutation into his trashy

scenario – a vengeful seeress (Silvia Solar) who claims to "all but live in the other world," a midget assistant, a midnight exhumation, a bald-headed zombie given life by a mixture of science and black magic, the usual ration of unappealing sex scenes. Gigó enlivens the opening with a funky fashion show staged in the bowels of a French château (playing the compère himself), but the rest of the film is deadeningly slow.

While acting in *Las ratas no duermen de noche* in June 1973, Paul Naschy was also making a sixth showcase for his beloved Waldemar Daninsky. Like *La venganza de la momia*, *El retorno de Walpurgis* (Return to Walpurgis) was directed by Carlos Aured for Lotus Films, though for this project Lotus raised extra funds from the Mexican company Escorpión. As well as his fondness for appearing in werewolf make-up, Naschy was never happier, it seems, than when wearing mediaeval plumed helmets. This entry, accordingly, kicks off with Irineus Daninsky lopping off Barna Báthory's head, after which he institutes a mass hanging of witches from the castle drawbridge and has Elizabeth Báthory herself burned at the stake. María Silva utters the usual indignant curses and the credits roll in.

The remainder of the action is set in the 19th century and by and large is much less impressive. The doughty Waldemar is seduced by two unscrupulous women – one of whom puts the gypsy bane of lycanthropy on him – but finds solace with an accommodating nice one (Fabiola Falcón). The film is half over by the time Naschy gets to do his werewolf stuff, attacking a farm girl and later putting paid to a hapless trio of travelling players. Amid the ludicrous gore effects are a few interesting touches – villagers removing the victims'

Knights Templar on the Costa Blanca: the striking climax of *El buque maldito* (1973)

"The sacrificial rites convert the victims into leopard women," Simón Andreu's hardbitten guide tells Jack Taylor's cerebral expedition leader. When these fetching lady vampires, with their back-combed hair, leopard-skin bikinis and billowing capes, are seen in slow-motion stalking mode à la Ossorio's Blind Dead, the effect is risible rather than otherworldly. Even so, there are a few effective moments in this racist exploitation hash, as when native zombies sit up in their rubble graves as a short-skirted blonde photographer (Loreta Tovar) wanders nearby, with only the clink of disturbed stones audible on the soundtrack. A third victim (María Kosti) is battened on by both Rey and Tovar, one on either side, with blood pouring down her baby doll nightie and dripping down her legs. Finally, there's the predictable downbeat wrap-up – a fourth heroine (Kali Hansa) says "I'm all right now" in the rescue jeep prior to revealing fangs of her own.

Also in 1973, Ossorio made a third Blind Dead film, *El buque maldito* (The Cursed Ship), in which he relocated the Templars to an ancient vessel that exists, with a nod to the Bermuda Triangle, in another dimension. In a further nod – this time to the mythical Flying Dutchman – we're told the ship's original captain was called Hollander. Unfortunately, these scraps are about as interesting as the film gets. Ossorio starts with a couple of bikini models lost at sea, then sends in such reliables as Jack Taylor and Maria Perschy to rescue them. Also present is Carlos Lemos, formerly the sage professor of *La llamada*. A professor once again, here he's given a great deal of indigestible blather to speak, inspiring Perschy to quip, "He's seen too many horror films!"

Though pumped for maximum, mist-wreathed creepiness by Ossorio, the shipboard setting necessarily deprives the creatures of their show-stopping forays on slow-motion horses. A grim scene in which they drag Bárbara Rey into the hold contains a single shot – an ankle-grabbing moment in which a skeletal hand is juxtaposed with white platform heels – that neatly sums up the culture clash that animated the first Blind Dead film. And at the very end Ossorio rallies with a marvellous scene of the Templars emerging from the sea and advancing across a Costa

eyeballs to ensure they don't reincarnate, Waldemar himself with his wolf's head sprouting incongruously from a wing collar and frock coat. There's also a satanic ceremony in which the Devil, got up for some reason like a street mime artist in black leotard and face stocking, appears to take a naked gypsy disciple from the rear. But Naschy seems to have been mainly concerned with crafting a romantic melodrama, and here and there – notably in a lushly scored waterfall interlude – he succeeds. But the film, exported as *Curse of the Devil*, is otherwise strangely inert.

Amid this tidal wave of product, Amando de Ossorio was reduced to the level of *La noche de los brujos* (The Night of the Sorcerers), a cut-price, cliché-ridden jungle melodrama produced at Ballesteros Studios in 1973. Set, according to an opening title card, in 'Bumbasa 1910', the action here gets off to a rip-roaring start, with a white woman (Bárbara Rey) having her clothes whipped off (literally) by African voodoo celebrants, after which she's beheaded and native girls daub themselves in her blood. A bunch of pith-helmeted would-be rescuers then blast the whole tribe to kingdom come, whereupon the woman's severed head sprouts instant vampire fangs and shrieks exultantly at the viewer as the credits crash in. This is very much a 'follow that' opening, and in response Ossorio merely repeats the same routine throughout the remainder of the film. In addition to the expected abundance of blood and breasts, this involves a move from 1910 to 1973 and from the soundstage of the prologue to location shots taken at Aldea del Fresno's Safari Madrid attraction.

Blanca beach in silent pursuit of our oblivious heroes. It's too little too late, however, for *El buque maldito* is hamstrung, not only by utterly pathetic model shots of the titular ship, but also a lethargic lack of incident that kills viewer involvement stone dead.

## GALL BLADDERS AT CINECITTÀ

As noted above, Rosalba Neri's sumptuous Countess Dracula in *Il plenilunio delle vergini* was a logical riposte to her previous turn as Baroness Frankenstein. The film in question, *La figlia di Frankenstein* (The Daughter of Frankenstein), started shooting on 2 March 1971 and was the first of a curious little cluster of Italian Frankenstein pictures. Financed in part by Roger Corman's New World operation, *La figlia* was directed by Corman alumnus Mel Welles and exported as *Lady Frankenstein*. The tag-line was inspired in its sleazy conjunction of sex and horror – "Only the monster she made could satisfy her strange desires!"

Unfortunately, the film itself is a rhythmless, atmosphere-free bore, with a hulking monster sporting a pitifully poor make-up and no discernible personality. Surveying it on the operating table, Joseph Cotten's Baron calls it "such a grotesque dream. Or perhaps – perhaps he shall be a nightmare." Fresh from facing off against Vincent Price in *The Abominable Dr Phibes* at Elstree, Cotten looks as if he's undergoing a nightmare of his own in these low-rent surroundings, though he's crushed to death by his creation a mere 40 minutes in and leaves the remainder of the action to his devoted assistant Paul Muller and decidedly perverse daughter, played by Neri. The monster – in green smock, brown corduroys and regulation bovver boots – stomps around the countryside dumping naked girls into rivers. Neri, meanwhile, plans a much more sophisticated creature, transplanting Muller's brain into the fetching body of an idiot handyman (Marino Masé). A scene in which Neri sits astride Masé, coming to orgasm as Muller smothers the prostrate boy, carries the kind of transgressive charge more appropriate to a Jess Franco film. (And, with Franco regular Muller involved, the impression seems all the more pronounced.) The rest, however, is distinguished only by some impressively baronial interiors.

The original story for *Lady Frankenstein* was provided by the American wheeler-dealer Dick Randall, who the following year produced a mutant hybrid of his own called *Terror! Il castello delle donne maledette* (Terror! The Castle of Accursed Women). Exported under the outrageous exploitation title *Frankenstein's Castle of Freaks*, this was one of several cheapskate items churned out by Randall in Italian exile. In 1970 he showcased Victor Buono as a sausage-making Sweeney Todd

surrogate in Guido Zurli's bloodless black comedy *Lo strangolatore di Vienna* (The Strangler of Vienna), and the following year he regressed Rosalba Neri to a 16th century past life, pairing her with the cloak-twitching Edmund Purdom in Paolo Lombardo's leaden Gothic snooze *L'amante del demonio* (The Demon's Lover). Then, either side of *Frankenstein's Castle of Freaks* Randall produced Ferdinando Merighi's fleabitten giallo *Casa d'appuntamento* (The Appointed House), better known by its racier export title *The French Sex Murders*, and cast Daniela Giordano as a gaol bird under threat from puritanical cultists in William Rose's listlessly executed *La casa della paura* (The House of Fear).

*Frankenstein's Castle of Freaks* went into production on 16 December 1972 and its director credit was attributed, rather mysteriously, to the well-known dubbing director Robert H Oliver. The childishly nonsensical result makes *Lady Frankenstein* look like an unsung masterpiece. Here, Rossano Brazzi's Frankenstein – unaccountably styled as a Count rather than Baron – experiments on a local Neanderthal, dubbing him Goliath. Frankenstein's dwarf assistant, played by Michael Dunn, instructs a second Neanderthal in how to commit rape with the repugnant line, "Watch me. I'm going to teach you the pleasures of life." Goliath kills not only Frankenstein but also his manservant (Luciano Pigozzi) and the other Neanderthal, and police commissioner Edmund Purdom wraps things up with the profound observation that "There's a bit of a monster in all of us, especially where there's fear." Simonetta Vitelli, meanwhile, is yet another daughter of Frankenstein, hot on the heels of Rosalba Neri in *Lady Frankenstein* and Beatriz Savón in Franco's *Les Experiences érotiques de Frankenstein*.

Joseph Cotten expires in the arms of Rosalba Neri in *La figlia di Frankenstein* (1971)

For the 3'10" Michael Dunn, who less than ten years before had received Tony and Oscar nominations, *Frankenstein's Castle of Freaks* immediately followed the November 1972 filming of *The Mutations* at Pinewood. There, he was front man for a group of "special sideshow attractions," yet Dick Randall contrived to give him an even more humiliating role than that. By the end of June 1973 he was in Asturias for a reunion with *Mutations* star Donald Pleasence in Gonzalo Suárez's peculiar crime melodrama *La loba y la paloma* (The Wolf and the Dove), and in late August he died in a Knightsbridge hotel, aged 38.

Another *Frankenstein's Castle of Freaks* cast member, Gordon Mitchell, was lumbered with a negligible part as 'Count' Frankenstein's strong-arm flunkey, yet in Mario Mancini's contemporaneous *Frankenstein '80* he was cast as Frankenstein himself. Known in production as *Mosaico*, this one strongly suggests that Dick Randall had a hand in all these sexed-up Italian Frankensteins, given that Robert H Oliver was once again attached to the film's English dub and that Mario Mancini had served as cinematographer on *Frankenstein's Castle of Freaks*.

Not to be confused with either the old Boris Karloff vehicle *Frankenstein 1970* or the later Alain Jessua comedy *Frankenstein 90*, *Frankenstein '80* is set (presumably) in 1980, with disgraced surgeon Otto Frankenstein stealing a revolutionary new transplant serum to help perfect a patchwork creature he calls Mosaic. In a clever touch, 'mosaic' is also the word applied by our journalist hero (John Richardson) to the mystery he has to elucidate. The film's first two thirds are quite cleverly plotted, if one can see past a series of sleazily sexualised killings, including Mosaic's grimly extended rape-murder of a naked prostitute. But, after Frankenstein himself has been chopped up by his creation, the final act devolves into a dull police run-around, with Mosaic strangling a stripper in her dressing room and bludgeoning a male Grand Prix spectator at a urinal. The film dwells obsessively on bloodily extracted organs, while Mosaic (Xiro Papas) is surely the first Frankenstein monster to undergo a testicle transplant.

Featured in *Frankenstein '80* as a conspicuously helpless heroine was Dalila Di Lazzaro, who went on in March 1973 to play a beautiful Frankenstein monster in a film that took the obsession with extracted organs to farcical extremes. The lineage of *Flesh for Frankenstein* stretched right back to Roman Polanski's plan to make a 3-D horror picture. When this didn't work out, Polanski proposed to use 3-D in his sex comedy *Che?* (What?) – which, as it turned out, went ahead in September 1972 without 3-D. But the film's producer,

Carlo Ponti, was sufficiently taken with the process to decide it would be perfect for a Frankenstein film.

"Polanski thought that I, for some reason, would be a natural person to make a 3-D film about Frankenstein," writer-director Paul Morrissey recalled some 20 years later. "I thought it was the most absurd offer I could ever imagine."[18] Even so, in response to Ponti's offer Morrissey duly turned up at Cinecittà, intent on making the film in the improvisatory style he'd perfected for the transgressive Andy Warhol-sponsored features *Flesh*, *Trash* and *Heat*. This plan was rapidly abandoned, but Morrissey's membership of the Factory ménage meant that both *Flesh for Frankenstein* and its companion piece *Blood for Dracula* would be saddled with a Warhol possessory credit in their US advertising. Warhol himself happily admitted that his involvement in the films was pretty much zero. "I go to the parties," he said.[19]

> The youthful Baron Frankenstein proposes to create a master race – "something," as he puts it, "that will represent the finest feature of the Serbian ideals." To make sure his "male zombie" is prepared to procreate with the female one, he decapitates a young patron of the local whorehouse, unaware that the boy, Sacha, was only there by accident and in fact wanted to become a monk. Meanwhile, the Baron's bored wife (who is also his sister) takes Sacha's priapic friend, Nicholas, as a lover...

In stark contrast to his underground Warhol trilogy, at Cinecittà Morrissey was able to make the most of the top-flight Italian expertise Ponti had laid on for him. The film looks marvellous, from Luigi Kuveiller's fetching cinematography to the lavish production design of Enrico Job, who turns Frankenstein's laboratory into a massive, stone-flagged amphitheatre and inlays other parts of the castle with Klimt-style gold leaf. On top of this, Carlo Rambaldi's special effects range from deliberately ropey, as in the Baron's use of a huge pair of secateurs to relieve Sacha of his (patently fake) head, to convincingly nightmarish, as when Frankenstein's children are besieged by bats in a darkened cellar – the same bats, presumably, that Rambaldi had flung at Florinda Bolkan in *Una lucertola con la pelle di donna*.

The children, Erik and Monica, are central to the film's promisingly creepy opening, in which they methodically eviscerate and then guillotine a doll. (Italian veteran Antonio Margheriti was charged with shooting this opening and also the bat sequence, inspiring Ponti, with Italian quota regulations in mind, to credit him as director of the whole film in Italy – a misattribution that has caused widespread confusion

Udo Kier, Arno Juerging, Joe Dallesandro (suspended)
and Dalila Di Lazzaro (eviscerated) in the splattery
climax of *Flesh for Frankenstein* (1973)

ever since.) Later we see the children
spying on their mother's indiscretions and
their father's grisly experiments through
the distorting prism of a clouded mirror,
and later still they play a crucial role in
the film's grimly downbeat ending. The
actors, Marco Liofredi and Nicoletta Elmi,
are serenely spooky in themselves, and
crucially, apart from two reluctant uses of
the word "No" by Erik, they remain eerily
silent. The adult cast members, by contrast,
gab away non-stop. And unfortunately
what they say is utter rubbish.

The film is clearly the quintessence
of camp, so to carp about Morrissey's
consciously absurd dialogue may seem
redundant. But he doesn't have the comic
invention to sustain this torrent of archly
nonsensical verbiage over an entire film.
Giggling over Frankenstein's references to
non-existent body parts (nasum, manus,
seminal vectical) can only go so far before
severe viewer fatigue sets in. Though
a native New Yorker, Morrissey was a
devotee of Britain's Carry On films, finally
offering a disastrous tribute to them in his
1977 folly *The Hound of the Baskervilles*. But
in *Flesh for Frankenstein* it's obvious already
that he's no Talbot Rothwell, writer not
just of the later Carry Ons but also the three 'Up' films
starring Frankie Howerd, a series explicitly referenced
in Morrissey's working title, *Up Frankenstein*.

The Baron's famous line, "To know death, Otto,
you have to fuck life in the gall bladder," has a
certain lunatic splendour, and there's also a glimmer
of drollery at the dinner table, when Frankenstein
surveys his two creations and sheepishly admits
to his incredulous wife that "They have some
interesting medical problems." Beyond that, however,
wit is in painfully short supply. It's also tough to
remain engaged with a trash aesthetic that requires
competent actors to act badly, the better to integrate
with incompetent ones who can't help it. It's the
kind of thing that's fine for maybe two minutes in an
undergraduate revue sketch. Yet, by intercutting them
with other sequences, Morrissey allows the lab scenes
between Udo Kier's barking-mad Baron and Arno
Juerging's craven Otto to drag on and on and on. As
*New York Times* critic Nora Sayre put it at the time, "this
*Frankenstein* drags as much as it camps."[20]

## FLESH FOR FRANKENSTEIN

*Italy-France* 1973
*Italy: Il mostro è in tavola ... barone Frankenstein*
*France: Chair pour Frankenstein*
US: *Andy Warhol's Frankenstein*
*Compagnia Cinematografica Champion / Jean*
*Yanne & Jean Pierre Rassam Productions*
95 minutes colour and 3-D
production began 20 March 1973

Director of Photography: Luigi Kuveiller;
Production Designer: Enrico Job; Editors:
Franca Silvi and [credited on English-language
prints only] Jed Johnson; Sound: Carlo
Palmieri, Roberto Arcangeli; Music: Claudio
Gizzi; Make-up: Mario Di Salvio; Special Effects:
Carlo Rambaldi; Screenplay: Paul Morrissey
[English-language prints]; Tonino Guerra
[Italian prints]; Producer: Andrew Braunsberg;
Director credited on Italian prints: Antonio
Margheriti; Director: Paul Morrissey

Joe Dallesandro (Nicholas); Monique van Vooren
(Baroness Katrin Frankenstein); Udo Kier (Baron
Frankenstein); Arno Juerging (Otto); Dalila Di
Lazzaro (female monster); Srdjan Zelenovic (male
monster); Nicoletta Elmi (Monica); Marco Liofredi
(Erik); Liu Bosisio (Olga); Fiorella Masselli (large
prostitute); Cristina Gaioni (Nicholas' girlfriend);
Rosita Torosh (Sonia); Carla Mancini (farmer);
Imelde Marani (blonde prostitute)

The opening stages bumble along in turgid fashion with stilted dialogue
woodenly delivered. Then it develops into an admixture of eroticism
with the surgical stuff. The final phases become gory, gut-spilling and
distinctly messy, finishing up with a pile of miscellaneous corpses.
The 3-D presentation darkens the colour but, obviously, heightens
the effect. If you like the effect, of course. *Films Illustrated* March 1975

I thought *Frankenstein* is absurd and with the 3-D system it's even more
absurd. This was my reason for doing the film. I figured this could be really
unusual because I saw 3-D as a way to make the absurd world of horror even
more bizarre and amusing. I got my biggest laughs when using the 3-D.
Paul Morrissey [quoted in *Shivers* October 2002]

The real comedy comes from what, in 1973, was a new source – extravagantly ridiculous body-parts splatter. And in this department nobody could accuse the film of lack of invention, particularly with the bonus of 3-D to brazenly thrust or dangle blood-dripping organs in the audience's face. Morrissey later complained that the dismemberments in both this and *Blood for Dracula* were ripped off by another group of British comedians when they made the 1974 film *Monty Python and the Holy Grail*. Quite apart from the fact that neither of Morrissey's films had been seen in the US or UK when *Holy Grail* was in preparation, he was forgetting that the Monty Python team were among the true pioneers of comedy-splatter courtesy of their 'Sam Peckinpah's Salad Days' sketch, shot as far back as January 1972. Indeed, when Sacha's headless trunk staggers about, squirting torrentially from the neck, or Frankenstein loses one of his own hands and flings it vengefully at Nicholas, the action conforms exactly to the Python script specification, "a volcanic quantity of blood geysers upwards."[21]

The film is not without grace notes, notably the broad fascist caricatures represented by the Baron and Baroness, plus Claudio Gizzi's lushly swooning music during the gruesome operation scenes. (He also uses an excerpt from Wagner's *Tannhäuser*, in perfect accord with Frankenstein's Nazi rhetoric.) The obvious homoeroticism of the Baron's scheme is evident even in his references to Serbia's proud antecedents in Ancient Greece, and the gall bladder scene – in which he fists the already sentient female creation through a stomach aperture – carries a queasily pornographic charge that really was a first. Finally, the pile-up of corpses at the end achieves an almost Jacobean grandeur, with the revived Sacha echoing Karloff's "We belong dead" when he announces robotically, "I must be dead."

## VIRGINS' BLOOD AT FRASCATI

*Flesh for Frankenstein* was accompanied by more than just the sexed-up versions of the story discussed above. With Hammer Films drawing their main monster franchises to a close at the end of 1972 with *Frankenstein and the Monster from Hell* and *The Satanic Rites of Dracula*, it seemed as if open season had suddenly been declared on these durable Gothic archetypes. On 15 March 1973, just five days before Morrissey began shooting at Cinecittà, a massive Anglo-American TV movie, *Dr Frankenstein*, started at Pinewood. Retitled *Frankenstein the True Story*, it anticipated *Flesh*'s homoerotic tone and was as splattery as US network TV allowed. Then on 30 April, just a few weeks before Morrissey's *Blood for Dracula* was due to

begin, a *Dracula* TV movie, directed by Dan Curtis and starring Jack Palance, began at Shepperton; exactly three months later, at Elstree, none other than David Niven took on the role in the clumsy comedy *Vampira*. There was clearly something in the air. But none of its emanations was as bizarre as the Morrissey duo.

Carlo Ponti's prescription for Morrissey's films involved a combined 15-week schedule with a week off for Easter. Crucially, with *Blood for Dracula* Morrissey retained the services, not just of leading men Udo Kier, Joe Dallesandro and Arno Juerging, but also composer Claudio Gizzi, production designer Enrico Job and cinematographer Luigi Kuveiller, though this time he dispensed with 3-D.

Neither *Flesh* nor *Blood* would come out in Italy until well after the first of them had made a box-office killing in the USA under the misleading title *Andy Warhol's Frankenstein*. (Its success, as Peter Nicholls amusingly puts it, "had something to do with rendering splatter movies acceptable to fashionable persons."[22]) When they finally did appear they were fitted with appropriately quirky Italian titles. *Il mostro è in tavola ... barone Frankenstein* (The Monster is Served ... Baron Frankenstein) presumably alludes to the film's dinner table sequence, but otherwise doesn't make a great deal of sense. Yet *Dracula cerca sangue di vergine ... e morì di sete!!!* gets right to the heart of the matter, meaning 'Dracula is Searching for Virgins' Blood ... and He's Dying of Thirst!!!'

> Given the scarcity of virgins in 1930s Romania, Count Dracula is reduced to preserving his youth via make-up and hair dye. Seriously ill, he is transported to Italy by his faithful servant Anton, who introduces him to the eccentric Marchese Di Fiore and his English wife. The couple's villa is in disrepair and their fortunes at a low ebb, but two of their four daughters are eminently marriageable. Thanks to the Di Fiores' randy Communist handyman Mario, they are emphatically not virgins, however.

Despite making the films back to back, Morrissey came up with a much more interesting take on Dracula than he did on Frankenstein. Where the first film gets by on uber-splatter and screeds of mock-Nazi speechifying, *Blood for Dracula* creates mood and atmosphere, jettisoning little of the camp artificiality of its forebear yet somehow currying sympathy for Dracula's wretched condition, and even for the absurdly vainglorious aristocrats he encounters in Italy.

Morrissey also takes the unfocused working-class disgruntlement of the Nicholas character from *Flesh* and converts his *Blood* counterpart, Mario, into a full-on Communist. In doing so he succeeds in making *Blood* into a genuine comedy. The deadpan Noo Yawk line readings of Warhol's beefcake superstar, Joe Dallesandro, are invaluable in this regard. "Right now he's a disgusting person with money," he says of Dracula at one point. "After the Revolution he'll be a disgusting person with no money."

Elsewhere, Morrissey wrings laughs from the dissonant clash of competing accents in the film, but more importantly from his characteristic habit of casting non-actors. Sometimes the results are excruciating. Gil Cagné, the celebrated Max Factor make-up artist, plays a moody local who directs Anton to the Di Fiores and his screen time is mercifully brief. But the former model Maxime McKendry is very funny as the enervated Marchesa. Her monotone English RP is perfectly adapted to featherbrained observations about "deadly pale" vegetarians and also to her climactic horror on catching Mario deflowering her youngest child: "My God, you're just an employee! How dare you put my daughter into such an unfortunate position?" Morrissey also prevailed on two distinguished actor-directors to make brief appearances. Roman Polanski is a surly manure-spreader encountered by Anton in the local inn (with Polanski's regular associates Gérard Brach and Andrew Braunsberg visible in the same scene), while Vittorio De Sica's sprightly Marchese, rolling his guest's name around his tongue, proclaims that "There are wine tasters and name tasters. Yes. 'Dra-cu-la' – just the right amount of orient and occident, of reality and fantasy..."

For all the absurd comedy, the film's tone is essentially mournful. During the credits sequence Udo Kier's Dracula blackens his Warhol-like white hair with paint; he does so in front of a mirror that doesn't even register him, and the mood of desolation is beautifully underscored by Gizzi's plangent theme. Later he embarks for Italy in a Lancia sedan whose roof rack is adorned not just with the regulation coffin but also a wheelchair. Morrissey originally intended to cast Srdjan Zelenovic, *Flesh*'s male monster, in the Dracula role, but

# BLOOD FOR DRACULA

Italy-France 1973
Italy: *Dracula cerca sangue di vergine ... e morì di sete!!!*
France: *Du Sang pour Dracula*
US: *Andy Warhol's Dracula*
Compagnia Cinematografica Champion / Jean Yanne & Jean Pierre Rassam Productions
108 minutes colour
production began 20 May 1973
............................

Director of Photography: Luigi Kuveiller; Production Designer: Enrico Job; Editors: Jed Johnson, Franca Silvi; Sound: Carlo Palmieri, Roberto Arcangeli; Music: Claudio Gizzi; Make-up: Mario di Salvio; Special Effects: Carlo Rambaldi; Screenplay: Paul Morrissey; Producer: Andrew Braunsberg; Director credited on Italian prints: Antonio Margheriti; Director: Paul Morrissey

Joe Dallesandro (Mario Balato); Udo Kier (Dracula); Vittorio De Sica (Marchese Di Fiore); Arno Juerging (Anton); Maxime McKendry (Marchesa Di Fiore); Milena Vukotic (Esmeralda); Dominique Darel (Saphiria); Stefania Casini (Rubinia); Silvia Dionisio (Perla); Inna Alexeieuna; Gil Cagne (man with rifle in trattoria); Emi Califri; Eleonora Zani; [uncredited] Roman Polanski (games-playing man in trattoria)

The laughs in *Blood for Dracula* flow as freely as the blood: Dracula himself is sinister and languid; his faithful manservant Anton shares Valentino's hot, darting glances; Roman Polanski – uncredited – makes a brief appearance as a local yokel ... Probably this is Andy Warhol's most commercial film: no freaky transvestites as far as I could discern. *Films Illustrated* May 1975

On the last day of shooting *Frankenstein* Paul Morrissey came in and said, "Well, I guess I have a German Dracula." I said, "Who?" He said, "You. But I want you to lose ten kilos." Well, there was only one week before we started shooting, so I really did starve myself ... and that's why I'm sitting in a wheelchair in *Dracula*: because I really couldn't stand up any more. I was really weak – which I liked. *Udo Kier* [quoted in *Video Watchdog Special Edition* 1995-96]

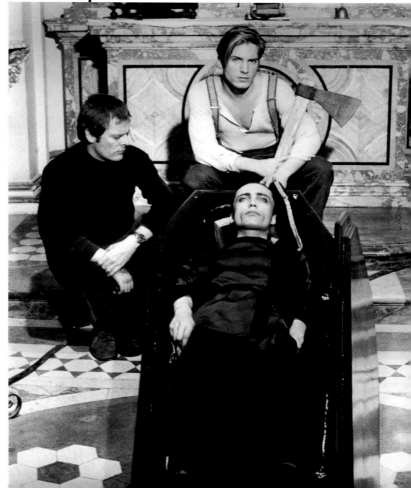

Writer-director Paul Morrissey with stars Joe Dallesandro and Udo Kier during production of *Blood for Dracula* (1973)

arguably neither actor was really old enough for the kind of sunset ennui implied by the script; a male equivalent of Sylvia Miles' raddled starlet from *Heat* might have been closer to the mark. Kier rises to the occasion, however, when thrashing insanely in his en suite bathroom, projectile-vomiting into the tub and lamenting that "Ze blood of zese whores is killing me!" Having trained his unwavering camera on Dallesandro shooting up heroin in *Trash*, Morrissey makes the equation of vampirism with drug addiction in *Blood for Dracula* the film's most disturbing feature.

Morrissey presses a number of other buttons in the film, appealing to the 1970s nostalgia craze, for example, with his hazy scenes of lesbian sisters kissing each other as soft dance music issues from a gramophone. He makes no allowances, however, for leftist sensibilities, weaving a Chekhovian twilight around Dracula while presenting his socialist opponent as a penis-led brute. "I'd like to rape the hell out of her," Mario says of the Di Fiores' 14-year-old daughter – and he actually does so as the film hastens to its barnstormingly bloody conclusion. Morrissey also makes terrific use of his prime location, the Villa Parisi in Frascati, a house whose potential had been investigated in numerous earlier films. Indeed, in *Il terzo occhio* Olga Solbelli took a tumble down exactly the same marble staircase on which Arno Juerging's Anton meets his end here.

With all these proliferating Frankensteins and Draculas, it was hardly surprising that comic versions also cropped up, among them a simple-minded 1975 release called *Frankenstein all'italiana*. As well as deriving its title from a string of fashionable 1960s comedies which advertised their topics – amore, matrimonio, adulterio etc – as 'Italian style', this one owed its very existence to the success of the ingenious Mel Brooks parody *Young Frankenstein*. With a pie-faced erotomaniac monster lusting after future *Playboy* model Jenny Tamburi, this was the last film for Armando Crispino, who had recently made the distinctive and intensely strange *Macchie solari*. In later years he expressed a certain amount of embarrassment over *Frankenstein all'italiana*, which seems reasonable given that it's the kind of film in which the monster announces its existence by resonantly breaking wind.

Irksome vampire comedy, meanwhile, was available not just from Italy but also Spain and Germany. In Spain, *Esos crueles y sanguinarios vampiros* (Those Cruel and Bloodthirsty Vampires) went out in mid-November 1974 under the adjusted title *Las alegres vampiras de Vögel* (The Genial Vampires of Vögel). Shot in February, its original director, José María Elorrieta, died in harness and was replaced by his protégé, and the film's co-writer, Julio Pérez Tabernero. With a plot recycling the 'entertainers stranded at scary castle' template of Italy's *L'ultima preda del vampiro* and jokes never rising above the "I only drink sangría" level, the film is notable for the presence of Juan Antonio Patiño, billed under his noble moniker of Marqués de Toro and cast as another aristocrat – el conde Erik Draculter [sic].

Tabernero's film was swiftly followed by three similarly inane comedies in 1975, though all three were delayed in release. Juan Fortuny's *El pobrecito Draculín* (Poor Draculín) focuses on Dracula's son (Joe Rigoli), and Carlos Benpar's *El jovencito Drácula* (Young Dracula) on his grandson, played by Benpar himself. (As a mark of his ubiquity, the bug-eyed character actor Víctor Israel appears in both these films, in the latter as Renfield.) By contrast, Jorge Darnell's *Tiempos duros para Drácula* (Hard Times for Dracula) features the Count himself in the person of hatchet-faced José Lifante, whose indignities include losing a fang, appearing in a toothpaste commercial and, perhaps worst of all, going to see Franco's *El conde Drácula*. The title, of course, is a Spanish variant on Steno's 1959 comedy *Tempi duri per i vampiri*.

Steno's former assistant, Lucio Fulci, was at work in May 1975 on *Il cav. Costante Nicosia demoniaco, ovvero: Dracula in Brianza* (The Honorable Demonic, Costante Nicosia, or: Dracula in Brianza). Here, a toothpaste magnate (Lando Buzzanca) goes on a business trip to Romania and is bedded by a gay vampire, Count Dragulescu (John Steiner). The businessman's initial rapture on arrival at the lightning-racked castle ("Transylvania, mon amour!") changes to homophobic panic on his return to civilisation, when his imagined blood lust is sublimated by, among other things, biting his wife's bare arse in a bubble bath. (The wife is Sylva Koscina, linking the film right back to *Tempi duri per i vampiri*.) The castle section includes a dinner table scene in which everyone, three of the Count's female acolytes included, is naked, but it runs for less than 15 minutes. The remainder is a sexed-up social comedy in which Fulci was marking time between his early gialli and subsequent notoriety as a gore maestro.

After Fulci's film, Germany finally got in on the act. *Lady Dracula* was produced in Vienna in December 1975, with such Edgar Wallace veterans as director Franz Josef Gottlieb, cinematographer Ernst W Kalinke and comic actor Eddi Arent involved. Mimicking Hammer's *Dracula A.D. 1972*, this one transitions from 1876 to 1976 via a building site crane. The prologue is dominated by a non-speaking, dog-growling Graf Dracula who preys on pre-teen schoolgirls; the role was played by slumming Hollywood star Stephen Boyd some 18 months before his untimely death. His coffin disintegration is halfway decent, and his pretty 1970s descendant, Evelyne Kraft, mounts some surprisingly ferocious attacks in her position as a funeral parlour beautician. The rest is witless West German comedy of the conveyor-belt variety. A stark contrast came in from Belgium in the shape of Maurice Rabinowicz's avant-garde film *Le Nosferat* "*Les eaux glacées du calcul égoiste*", which viewed the myth through a political lens. As president of the jury at the 1976 Sitges Festival, Terence Fisher was exposed to Rabinowicz's 'icy waters of self-interested calculation' and may well have been thoroughly bemused.

## ALL-NUDE NETHERWORLD VISIONS

By 1972 Jean Rollin was contemplating a departure from his fetching lady vampires, though he little guessed how unwelcome this deviation from his established norm would be.

Just as Jess Franco had waded into metaphysical waters the previous year with *Christina princesse de l'érotisme*, so Rollin, inspired by the work of 19th century poète maudit Tristan Corbière, created a deathly limbo of his own in *La Rose de fer* (The Iron Rose). The whiff of morbidity that permeates this film is visible right from the start, when a no-nonsense opening credit dedicates the proceedings to the actor R J Chauffard. As well as playing the 'old man' who

Françoise Pascal at the Cimetière de la Madeleine in *La Rose de fer* (1972)

had ushered people into a red-curtained netherworld in *La Vampire nue*, Chauffard had also written a Rollin profile for *Midi-Minuit Fantastique* in 1970. His early death in October 1972 was followed a scant six months later by *La Rose de fer*'s catastrophic debut at Alain Schlockoff's second Convention Française du Cinéma Fantastique in April 1973, where Rollin's funereal tone poem was rejected in no uncertain terms.

This time the portal to the netherworld isn't a proscenium arch; it's a humble crypt in the crumbling magnificence of the Cimetière de la Madeleine at Amiens. Rollin strands the beautiful Karine (Françoise Pascal) there, alongside a boorish young beau (Hugues Quester), and goes all out for macabre atmosphere. Pascal appears nude in a brief detour to the director's favoured beach location, but otherwise the film eschews not merely conventionalised horror

trappings but also the erotic content that was by this time Rollin's signature. Even when the couple make out in an open pit filled with bones and skulls, the action remains remarkably chaste.

Very little happens in *La Rose de fer* but Rollin nevertheless achieves his trademark quota of striking imagery – a rusting locomotive in a pall of icy mist, Karine obscuring her face by positioning a mouldering skull in front of it, a mordant cut from the lovers' embrace to an ornamental Cupid with its head missing. Arguably the most haunting images, however, come early, with a documentary-style montage of the more decrepit sections of Amiens. By the end, Karine's long night in the cemetery has turned her wits, causing her to promise the boy "all the happiness in the world – Death" prior to consigning him to a well-deserved premature burial. She eventually descends in her turn, closing the iron doors on a world in which she sees those above ground as dead and only the suffocating lovers as really alive.

Netherworld visions were also available in Italy, colourfully incomprehensible rather than coldly contemplative and with the beautiful and copiously nude Rita Calderoni for a centrepiece. Renato Polselli's *Riti, magie nere e segrete orge nel Trecento* (Rituals, Black Magic and Secret Orgies in the 1300s) was made in 1971 but only came out in January 1973. Polselli's working title, *La reincarnazione*, was retained when the film was exported as *The Reincarnation of Isabel*, but the Italian title better exploited the rumbustious mediaeval ribaldry of the 'Decamerotico' genre inadvertently set in train by Pasolini's *Il Decameron*.

The action here kicks off in some studio limbo where red-leotarded goons remove the heart from a sacrificial maiden, squeeze it like a sponge into goblets and pour the reviving blood over the bolt-upright corpse of 14th century witch Isabella Drupel (Calderoni). A flashback to her execution plays out like *Witchfinder General*, with her distraught lover (Mickey Hargitay) wailing on the sidelines as flames encroach around her – though *Witchfinder* didn't include the fetishistic detail of a crummy special-effects stake being bloodily hammered in between the victim's bare breasts. The present-day action is equally indecipherable, with Calderoni returning as Isabella's reincarnation,

Laureen, and the 20th century Hargitay identifying himself as, bizarrely, Count Dracula. (Is this granite-jawed '70s swinger just a deluded idiot? Or is this to be counted as yet another Dracula film?) A tiresome comedy character, Steffy (Stefania Fassio), describes vampires as "dead scary" prior to a sudden splurge of vampire rapes, unedifyingly intercut with Steffy's exertions in a supposedly comical threesome.

Two scenes, however, stand out from the ramshackle, faux-surrealist dross. The first is a self-reflexive replay of Polselli's *L'amante del vampiro*, with Christa (Christa Barrymore) experiencing her own funeral and her cries being steadfastly ignored by a malevolent gravedigger. In the second, two beautiful and barely clothed young women are pursued around a crumbling village and poked with sticks by a pack of elderly accusers, a set-piece made all the more bizarre by the way day turns to night and back again in consecutive shots.

A second netherworld nightmare came Rita Calderoni's way in 1974, though Luigi Batzella's *Nuda per Satana* (Nude for Satan) was apparently so poorly attended on its release in October that it was rapidly pulled from distribution. In contrast to his far superior *Il plenilunio delle vergini*, Batzella was here at the mercy of his own garbled script, relying on the usual 'dream logic' get-out clause to excuse a trashy story in which Calderoni and the impenetrably bovine Stelio Candelli become trapped with doppelgängers of themselves in an isolated castle. This was the Castello di Monte San Giovanni Campano in Frosinone, which Batzella no doubt remembered from the 1961 filming of *La strage dei vampiri*, in which he played the resident vampire expert.

Off-the-scale histrionics: Christa Barrymore and Rita Calderoni in *Delirio caldo* (1972)

As well as their own doppelgängers, Calderoni and Candelli also meet Giuseppe Mattei's totally uncharismatic Devil figure, who comes out with the usual Dracula phrases ("Please consider this house as your own") together with comically petulant outbursts like "I've never had such noisy guests as you two." In a reprise of Moa Tahi's predicament in *Il boia scarlatto*, Calderoni finds herself in a giant web occupied by a monstrous spider clearly made out of an egg box, while Candelli's double tells him that "Alienated in a

lost dimension, you finally found yourself." All ends in a fiery ceremony in which everyone – the women, anyway – gets, as advertised, nude for Satan.

No amount of faux-arty camera wobbling could help Batzella disguise the fact that his new film was complete nonsense, and from here it was just a short step to directing conspicuously horrible Nazi exploitation pictures. In the meantime, however, he made a rare reappearance as an actor in a shockingly dull 1975 potboiler called *La sanguisuga conduce la danza* (The Bloodsucker Leads the Dance). Writer-director Alfredo Rizzo had acted in both *L'ultima preda del vampiro* and *Il boia scarlatto*, and here borrowed the basic situation of those films, stranding a quartet of hard-up actresses (rather than showgirls or fashion models) in a remote castle. Stranded with them are such familiar faces as Giacomo Rossi Stuart, Luciano Pigozzi and Femi Benussi, trapped in a script that abounds in appalling lines like "The world is a stage but sometimes it isn't," "This room has been empty for a long time, just like my life" and – in one of several softcore lesbian interludes – "Feel them; feel how hard they are." Nominally set in 1902 Ireland, it finally gets round to a rash of bloody decapitations and has a dreadful synth score by Marcello Giombini.

As for the indefatigable Rita Calderoni, she and her *Reincarnation of Isabel* co-star, Mickey Hargitay, subsequently appeared in another febrile Renato Polselli film. The convoluted 1972 giallo *Delirio caldo* (Hot Delirium) polishes off its first victim (Stefania Fassio) in a conspicuously nasty waterfall strangling within its first five minutes. Hargitay is a doctor assisting a couple of fashion-victim police inspectors to solve a spate of murders. He's also "a husband who is useless as a man" and turns out – no surprise – to be the black-gloved killer. Or rather, he's one of three black-gloved killers climactically revealed in a barking-mad finale in which Hargitay, Calderoni and Christa Barrymore vie with each other in a crescendo of off-the-scale histrionics. The murders are as leeringly sexualised as the market by then demanded (Katia Cardinali, for example, is submitted to a brutal flogging-smothering-defenestration in a bathroom), while the presence of British bobbies is the sole indication that the film is set in England.

In 1973 Polselli made another demented sex-horror hybrid, *Mania*. In November of that year a typically salacious photo-digest of the film appeared in *Cinesex Mese*, extracts from which are tantalisingly preserved on Johan Melle's excellent 'Euro Fever' blog. Tantalisingly because, after the film's brief exposure in Italian cinemas, it vanished into total obscurity for over 30 years; in May 2007, some seven months after Polselli's death, an emasculated print was discovered and screened at Rome's Cineteca Nazionale as part of a season devoted to 'il cinema psicotronico di Renato Polselli'. After which it promptly disappeared from view yet again. For the record, the film involved a *Diaboliques*-style plot in which a supposedly dead scientist (Brad Euston) stages hallucinatory visions of his walking corpse to avenge himself on his erring wife (Eva Spadaro). As with all his 1970s work, Polselli signed this one with the pseudonym Ralph Brown, and the surviving trailer certainly whets the appetite.

With its roster of lesbianism, snakes, maggots, masturbation and throat-slashings, *Mania* is likely, when unearthed, to prove much more arresting than the rank-and-file Italian horrors from this period. A good example is Angelo Pannacciò's sedentary sex-horror hodgepodge, *Il sesso della strega* (Sex of the Witch). This is a sexed-up 'heirs squabbling over the will' mystery in which a Worcestershire patriarch's dying inner monologue, pouring scorn on his vacuously youthful descendants, takes up much of the opening reel. His valet and maid, meanwhile, are in the family chapel, having sex astride his as-yet-unoccupied sarcophagus. The subsequent killing spree boasts a few artful moments, but the resolution (a local witch has been switching the sex of one of the characters to create a vessel for her murderous revenge) is a garbled mess.

Coming up for inspection by Italian filmgoers in March 1974, the traditional old dark house of Pannacciò's film was thoroughly upstaged by a more fertile breeding ground for unleashed sexuality and unrestrained torture – convents, generally of the mediaeval variety. Mixing together Ken Russell's *The Devils* with a large helping of the Decamerotico and 'women in prison' sub-genres, nunsploitation had already found its way into Jess Franco's *Les Démons*, after which its anti-Catholic fervour was co-opted by Italy's Domenico Paolella for the 1973 releases *Le monache di Sant'Arcangelo* (The Nuns of Sant'Arcangelo) and *Storia di una monaca di clausura* (Story of a Cloistered Nun). The former, featuring conspicuously ghastly Inquisition torments and the star duo of Anne

Heywood and Ornella Muti, acquired a prurient export title – *The Nun and the Devil* – recalling the sub-genre's most venerable ancestor, the 'possessed nuns' segment of Benjamin Christensen's 1921 film *Häxan*.

As entries in the 'erotico-conventuale' strand proliferated, Gianfranco Mingozzi offered a curious art-exploitation hybrid in 1974 called *Flavia la monaca musulmana* (Flavia the Muslim Nun). Exported as *Flavia the Heretic*, this boasts a commanding performance from Florinda Bolkan as a proto-feminist 15th century Saint Joan figure whose vengeful collusion with the Saracens results in her being skinned alive; it also benefits from terrific music and cinematography by Nicola Piovani and Alfio Contini. Despite flabby battle scenes, Mingozzi's depressing message about the persistence of patriarchy is put across with unflinching brutality, proving that nunsploitation could occasionally be channelled, however imperfectly, towards serious themes.

## ZOMBIES EL GRECO

In June 1973 director Jorge Grau, working once again with his *Ceremonia sangrienta* co-writer Juan Tébar, started shooting a loose but highly effective Guy de Maupassant adaptation called *Pena de muerte* (Death Penalty). Here, Fernando Rey is a French judge, given to fussily adjusting his Légion d'honneur rosette, whose Galician vacation is dogged by killings echoing those of a presumed killer he sent to the guillotine. In a particularly grim vignette, Rey leads the Guardia Civil, headed by the ubiquitous José Lifante, to the isolated scene of a triple murder. Later, we're given courtroom flashbacks in which Rey pompously pronounces that "All the magistrates and lawyers, and I imagine to a certain extent the public, will have heard about the double personality," not realising as yet that he's talking about himself. There's an echo here, not just of de Maupassant, but also that ancient German property *Der Andere*.

In the midst of this scrupulously sober anti-capital punishment treatise, Grau amuses himself with random close-ups of sea food prior to including a bizarre lobster-eating contest undertaken by women in bikinis at a swank hotel. Whatever these strange asides might mean, he was probably a great deal less amused when Independent-International Pictures got hold of the film and marketed it in the US under the ridiculous title *Violent Blood Bath*.

After *Pena de muerte*, Fernando Rey joined Sue Lyon, Gloria Grahame and Julián Ugarte in mid-October 1973 for the filming of José María Forqué's quasi-giallo intrigue *Tarots – Detrás de las cartas el diablo* (Tarot – The Devil Behind the Cards). Grau, meanwhile, was approached by the Italian producer Edmondo Amati in early 1974 about directing a zombie film. Announced in *Variety* as *Valley of the Dead*, the result would subsequently acquire a bewildering galaxy of titles. To Grau and his countrymen it was known as *No profanar el sueño de los muertos*, to Amati and his it was *Non si deve profanare il sonno dei morti* – in both cases, a sombre injunction not to profane the sleep of the dead. The alternative Spanish title was *Fin de semana para los muertos* (Weekend for the Dead), while Italy had the more gnomic *Da dove vieni?* (Where Do You Come From?). In the UK, where the film is set, it went out under the splendid title *The Living Dead at Manchester Morgue*, while the American release boasted a rather clever adaptation of the original 'Do Not Profane the Sleep of the Dead' title – *Let Sleeping Corpses Lie*. The others are too many to enumerate; together with the profusion of titles applied to Mario Bava's *Antefatto*, they could probably fill a small book by themselves.

A few years before, Grau had tried to interest Amati in financing *Ceremonia sangrienta*, only to be told the producer would prefer something more like George Romero's *Night of the Living Dead*. With *No profanar* Amati's preoccupation remained the same; his idea was merely to replicate the Romero film in full blood-dripping colour. (Indeed, on Amati's schedule at the same time as *No profanar* was an opportunist clone of *The Exorcist* called *L'anticristo*.) But Grau's background as a member of La Escuela de Barcelona made him determined to put his own auteurist stamp on an otherwise exploitative project. And, thanks to Amati, he had a remarkably generous budget of 30 million pesetas with which to do so – "an exorbitant figure for a Spanish film,"[23] as *Film Guía* complained on the film's release. Technically it was a majority Italian film, of course, yet in an important sense *Film Guía* was right – for Grau succeeded so well in making the film his that it seems thoroughly Spanish from first frame to last.

*George Meaning and Edna Simmons are providentially brought together in the Lake District when Edna reverses her Mini Cooper over George's Norton motorcycle. Later, Edna's brother-in-law, Martin, is killed by a recently deceased tramp called Guthrie, and George begins to suspect that Guthrie and others have been revived by ultrasonic waves emitted by agricultural machinery. George also has to cope with a sustained case of police persecution from a disbelieving Irish cop called Sergeant McCormick.*

True to Amati's prescription, *No profanar* has no shortage of offal-chewing, eye-gouging and even breast-ripping, but thanks to Grau it also abounds in images and (especially) sounds that create a lingering atmospheric chill unknown to most splatterfests. "The voice of the dead," he noted later, "came to me after much reflection"[24] – and the stertorous death-rattle he came up with is a highly disturbing presence throughout the film. Just as conscientiously, Grau presided over a series of in-depth zombie 'workshops' for his half-dozen rejuvenated corpses and coaxed extremely persuasive performances from his three leads – Italian heart-throb Ray Lovelock, Spanish ingenue Cristina Galbó and fading Hollywood star Arthur Kennedy.

Of these, Galbó had just lost her husband, the German actor Peter Lee Lawrence, and Grau later admitted that "in some ways I took advantage of her state of mind and let her express her real horror of death."[25] As for the 60-year-old Kennedy, Grau tapped into the actor's own disenchantment by suggesting McCormick was the kind of policeman whose ambitions to become a government big shot had gone unfulfilled. "When he met me he realised that it wasn't any old film, that for me every scene was important," Grau recalled, "and that awoke in him the reflexes of a man of the theatre."[26] The result is a really blistering portrayal of an old-school reactionary – and, as an added refinement, Kennedy recycled the Irish accent he'd used just a few months previously in Ira Levin's horrific Broadway play *Veronica's Room*.

Grau signs his name on the film from the very first sequence, in which George leaves his Deansgate art gallery and the camera settles contemplatively on an abstract painting depicting a helmeted, amber-hued head. It's here, too, that we first hear the unearthly rasping sounds that will predominate later on. George's motorbike tour of the city – cleverly intercut with restful views of the countryside he's headed for – includes zombie-like Mancunian bus queues, a dead sparrow in the gutter, commuters in white anti-pollution masks, factory chimneys belching smoke, even a female streaker launching herself from the doorway of Manchester Cathedral. (This last detail, inevitably, was cut from Spanish prints.) This gripping montage of dehumanisation, set to Giuliano Sorgini's bongo-driven theme, was also Grau's way of satisfying Edmondo Amati's strange fixation on Manchester. In truth, Grau sneakily picked up some of his shots in Sheffield; either way, the sequence introduces the powerful ecology angle that was Grau's chief contribution to the script.

Though shot in the Peak District, the bulk of the film is set in the Lake District, and it's here that George encounters Edna in a proverbial 'meet cute'situation. No romance develops from this spiky

Cemetery ghoul
Gengher Gatti
chews on a
policeman's
internal organs in
*No profanar el sueño
de los muertos* (1974)

introduction, however; indeed, in an astute analysis of the contradictions of the counterculture, the apparently freethinking George is just as patronising to Edna as the loathsome Sergeant McCormick is intolerant of both of them. Then Grau pulls off a stunning sequence in which the waterlogged Guthrie emerges from the River Dove and assails Edna in her fragile Mini Cooper. With his black hair and beard and strangely soulful expression, the veteran Anglo-Spanish actor Fernando Hilbeck resembles a cadaverous El Greco martyr. George, meanwhile, gets his first look at a radioactive pest-control contraption at a nearby farm, sagely advising the farmer to "Keep the insects and parasites nature's given you."

The ensuing carnage gave special make-up artist Giannetto De Rossi the chance to rehearse effects he'd later perfect in several Lucio Fulci films. To showcase De Rossi's work, Grau selected a Hathersage graveyard and a hospital in Cheadle as the exteriors for two further set-pieces, both of them brilliantly sustained. In the crypt, Guthrie confers a weirdly Messianic benediction on his fellow corpses by daubing reviving blood on their eyelids; driven out of the crypt, the three intelligent zombies lay siege with anything at their disposal, including uprooted crosses and massive headstones. In the hospital, even new-born babies appear to be homicidally affected by the surrounding radiation, while the zombie roster is supplemented by a half-naked male sporting a head

## NO PROFANAR EL SUEÑO DE LOS MUERTOS

*Italy-Spain* 1974
Italy: **Non si deve profanare il sonno dei morti**
UK: **The Living Dead at Manchester Morgue /
The Living Dead**
US: **Breakfast at the Manchester Morgue / Don't
Open the Window / Let Sleeping Corpses Lie**
Flaminia Produzioni Cinematografiche Rome /
Star Film Madrid
94 minutes colour
in production April-May 1974

Music: Giuliano Sorgini; Special Effects:
Giannetto De Rossi, Luciano Bird; Screenplay:
Sandro Continenza, Marcello Coscia; Producer:
Edmondo Amati; Director: Jorge Grau

Ray Lovelock (George); Cristina Galbó (Edna);
Arthur Kennedy (Sgt McCormick); Aldo Massasso
(Kinsey); Giorgio Trestini (Craig); Roberto Posse
(Benson); José Ruiz Lifante (Martin); Jeannine
Mestre (Katie); Gengher Gatti (Keith, zombie);
Fernando Hilbeck (Guthrie, zombie); Vera Drudi
(Mary, zombie); Vicente Vega (Dr Duffield), Paco
Sanz (Perkins); Paul Benson (Wood); Anita Colby
(nurse); Joaquín Hinojosa (autopsy zombie); Vito
Salier (naked zombie); Isabel Mestre (telephonist)

Lighting Cameraman: Francisco Sempere;
Production Designer: Carlo Leva; Editor:
Vincenzo Tomassi; Sound: Antonio Cardenas,
Nick Alexander [English-language dub];

**Grau has crafted his scenes with the atmosphere of fantastical terror the subject demands. The Spanish director maintains a good pace ... [and] the actors move with ease ... Objections to Grau's film: in my view there is excessive repetition in the macabre scenes. Too much living-dead action. But, taken all in all, I would insist on the film's achievement as a model of horror filmmaking.** La Vanguardia 2 October 1974

**When I read the script, it seemed so well-written, so clean, so good, but what I did was to introduce my vision of things. The ecological theme seemed a good idea to Sandro [Continenza] and he altered the script a little; he didn't need to do much to it. It's something which we are seeing today – mad cows in England, contaminated chickens in Belgium. We are poisoned by a progress which doesn't consider the consequences.** Jorge Grau [quoted in Shivers July 2000]

bandage reminiscent of the chin-support worn by Marley's Ghost. In between these two sequences, an extremely nifty plot complication convinces McCormick that George and Edna aren't just hippies but Manson-style Satanists. That McCormick is so persuasive a monster isn't just down to Kennedy; it also gains impetus from Grau's memories of the Fascist policemen of his Catalan youth. No wonder George snaps out his arm at McCormick with an acid cry of "Heil Hitler!"

Oddly, one of the chief delights of the film for English-speaking viewers is entirely lost in the Italian and Spanish versions. ADR guru Nick Alexander was an Englishman and, as with the earlier La orgía de los muertos, deserves credit for his charmingly idiomatic adaptation of the film's dialogue. As a result, this peculiar Hispanic view of Northern England abounds in quotable lines. "The dead don't walk around," maintains George, "except in very bad paperback novels." McCormick rounds splenetically on George with "You're all the same, the lot of you, with your long hair and faggot clothes." And a Lancashire farmer, admiring his futuristic machinery, tells George that "It's killed every bloody insect round 'ere, except for you." Those last two lines, of course, indicate the theme of generational conflict so endemic to horror pictures of the period. In a cleverly adapted echo of Night of the Living Dead, the conflict is carried here to its logical conclusion – but not without a delightful little twist that very satisfyingly wipes the triumphant sneer off McCormick's face.

With its combination of razor-sharp intelligence and industrial-strength gore, Grau's film was an unusual offering to come from a Spanish director, though there were a few similarly intriguing oddities on view in the mid-1970s. Chief among them was Manchas de sangre en un coche nuevo (Blood Stains in a Brand-New Car), which was written and directed by TV stalwart Antonio Mercero.

Mercero had been responsible for a well-nigh perfect short horror film, running a crisp 36 minutes, called La cabina (The Cubicle), which was shot in July 1972 and first seen on television shortly before Christmas. Here, the gifted comic character actor José Luis López Vázquez enters a conspicuously red telephone kiosk in Madrid's Plaza de Arapiles only to find he can't get out. The development of the situation, winding all the way from semi-farcical befuddlement to extremes of claustrophobic terror, is brilliantly contrived, winning several awards for Vázquez and an International Emmy for the film itself. So when Mercero came to make Manchas de sangre late in 1974, it was natural that he should turn once more to Vázquez to play the lead.

The screenplay for Mercero's new venture sprang from an idea just as starkly simple as that of La cabina. No longer the hapless Everyman victim, Vázquez is now self-satisfied art restorer Ricardo Cariedo,

who takes his sleek new Volvo for its first spin and comes upon an overturned car on a deserted country road. Worried about besmirching his beautiful white upholstery, he ignores the pathetic pleas of the driver and his eight-year-old son and drives on. Moments later the other car explodes. A more potent scenario for an exploration of gnawing guilt – with all the implications that might have for a country whose Fascist regime was soon to end – could hardly be imagined. And it's brilliantly developed by Mercero via an unmistakable allusion to Lady Macbeth's obsessional lament of "Will these hands ne'er be clean?" For Ricardo soon finds persistent blood spots manifesting themselves in the Volvo and on his hands. He's clearly a despicable character, yet Vázquez somehow makes us feel for him as his life rapidly implodes.

Manchas de sangre boasts some splendid set-pieces, in particular a scene echoing La cabina in which Ricardo and his mistress María (May Heatherly) find themselves trapped on the highway behind a tow-truck, from which the mangled hulk of the fateful car tauntingly dangles. And the phantom blood spots are memorably accompanied on the soundtrack by a subdued heartbeat and stertorous breathing. But the general impression is that an extremely good short film (like La cabina) is struggling to get out of a sprawling 90-minute format. The critique of bourgeois callousness is fleshed out via Ricardo's regal wife Eva (Lucia Bosé), but her friendship with a predatory art collector doesn't really go anywhere, except to a rather boring party sequence. The film is at its best when Ricardo fusses about "absolute cleanliness and order" and enthuses over his new car's illuminated seatbelts, and particularly when Eva coldly pronounces that she would have responded to the crash victims just as her husband did.

Another Iberian curio from 1974 was Miguel Madrid's El asesino de muñecas (The Doll Killer); in the garish yet essentially conservative world of Spanish fantaterrorífico, an unashamedly gay horror film was presumably the last thing anyone expected to encounter. A long way from the subtle homoeroticism of Eloy de la Iglesia, Madrid's film focuses on a scrawny young psychopath called Paul (David Rocha). Brought up initially as a girl, he now adopts a black wig and an effeminate mask in order to murder women whom he finds canoodling in public spaces. (One of them, brutally decapitated, is pregnant.) Anticipating the American shockers Tourist Trap and Maniac, Paul surrounds himself with dolls and showroom dummies, performing mock-surgery on them to assuage his disappointment at flunking his medical exams. He rejects the advances of his aristocratic employer (Helga Liné) but takes an interest in her underage daughter (Inma de Santis) when a mannequin likeness of her is constructed. He also befriends a small boy, with a scene of 'innocent' horseplay by an ornamental stream unmistakably staged to look like paedophile anal rape.

The confusion of intent in *El asesino de muñecas* is off the scale; though clearly a repugnant figure, the frequently naked Paul is photographed with plenty of erotic emphasis and is presumably meant to be a misunderstood hero. Though billing himself as Michael Skaife, Madrid shows up in person right at the beginning, for all the world as if he were a 'personality' director rather than the man who made the 1971 abomination *Necrophagus*. He dismembers a child's doll prior to offering a few prefatory words, not one of which elucidates what on earth he was getting at with *El asesino*.

Yet the film exercises a strange fascination. A credits sequence set in a mannequin factory benefits from Alfonso Santisteban's memorably funky theme, all Philly strings and *Shaft*-style guitar licks. The supposed setting in Montpellier is constantly betrayed by extended views of Gaudi's unmistakable Barcelona architecture. Paul's nightmares of doll-strangulation are surreal enough, but even in the 'real' scenes we're given such oddities as Paul's mother slapping him with a skinned rabbit. A rock band turns up, playing alfresco while two girls indulge in proto-robot dancing; one of them is subsequently stabbed in the crotch, another gets a billhook in the head. Madrid even finds room for a cameo from Antonio Ráfales Gil, long-time director of the Sitges Festival – presumably out of gratitude for the inexplicable award *Necrophagus* received there in 1971.

## ACID BATHS AND DEPRAVED WRECKERS

In June 1973 the US sales agent for Ulli Lommel's *Die Zärtlichkeit der Wölfe* (The Tenderness of the Wolves) tried to sell the film in *Variety* as "Fassbinder's Romantic Shocker with the Werewolf Thrill ... a German pic in the good gory German tradition of Fritz Lang's M with Kurt Raab in the role that made Peter Lorre famous."[27] The crassness of this effort to sex up Lommel's grim and despairing film is hard to beat. Produced by the provocative wunderkind of 'das neue Kino', Rainer Werner Fassbinder, it cast Raab as Fritz Haarmann, a German descendant of Sweeney Todd whose homosexual-paedophile serial murders are overlooked (and, by implication, sanctioned) by society at large. Raab also wrote the film and is its

David Rocha ('in the nude') and Inma de Santis star 'in a case of sexual split personality': *El asesino de muñecas* (1974)

most memorable feature by far; as British critic Tom Hutchinson put it at the time, "Raab manifests his creation with one of the most unpleasant projections of greasy evil that I have seen on the screen: all Auschwitz in a man's eyes."[28]

The range of Europe's other 'true crime' horrors is quite narrow, stretching from high-end titles like Robert Siodmak's *Nachts, wenn der Teufel kam* (Nights When the Devil Comes, 1957), Claude Chabrol's *Landru* (1962) and Robert Hossein's 1964 film *Le Vampire de Düsseldorf* (The Vampire of Düsseldorf, with Hossein himself as Peter Kürten) right up to Gerald Kargl's cult Austrian film *Angst* (1983). Over in Italy, the formidable Shelley Winters was the wartime 'soap-maker of Correggio' in Mauro Bolognini's outstandingly weird *Gran bollito* (Big Stew, 1977), which counts among its oddities the spectacle of Max von Sydow playing one of the killer's spinster victims.

Showcased at Cannes in May 1974, Francis Girod's French-Italian-German co-production *Le Trio infernal* (The Infernal Trio) dramatised a 1920s Aix-en-Provence murder case in the gorge-rising style of a skittish black comedy. In league with a pair of beautiful German sisters (Romy Schneider and Mascha Gonska), Michel Piccoli is a small-town big shot who works multiple insurance scams by marrying the women to about-to-expire old men. He also shoots two troublesome accomplices (in one case, the bullet passes through the victim's copy of *Le Petit Marseillais* and into his right eye), and the film pauses for an enormously protracted disposal-of-the-bodies sequence complete with gas masks, sulphuric acid, bath tubs, and bucket after bucket of human glop being carried into the grounds. All this accompanied by a gaily eccentric score from the ubiquitous Ennio Morricone.

Girod's film was one of several early 1970s titles in which Michel Piccoli very thoroughly subverted his suave persona, whether reverting to caveman cannibalism in Claude Faraldo's *Themroc*, eating himself to death in Marco Ferreri's *La Grande bouffe* (Blow-Out) or devoting himself to an inflatable sex doll in Luis García Berlanga's *Grandeur nature* (Life Size). And soon afterwards came Piccoli's obsessive mediaeval lord in Juan Buñuel's *Leonor*. As one of France's most compelling actors, he'd certainly come a long way since the 1951 curio *Torticola contre Frankensberg*.

The generously budgeted gloss of *Le Trio infernal* set it apart from other French shockers of the period. Jean Rollin, for example, continued to operate at a virtually subterranean level. Still smarting from the catastrophe of *La Rose de fer*, on 16 July 1973 he began shooting a film so fraught that he was briefly hospitalised on its completion. Devised under the more gender-specific title *Les Diablesses* (The She-Devils), and billed in its opening credits as 'Un film expressioniste de Jean Rollin', *Les Démoniaques* (The Demonic Ones) enabled him to reference the Hollywood swashbucklers he'd adored as a boy. The result is very much a film of two halves, with the first devoted to a quartet of depraved 19th century wreckers vaguely echoing the Fritz Lang film *Moonfleet*, and the second to a bungled revenge exacted by their most recent victims, who are the kind of ethereal female twins familiar from so many Rollin films.

Joelle Coeur goes 'to the sexual outer limits' in *Les Démoniaques* (1973), known in Italy as 'The Island of the She Demons'

Though ramshackle, *Les Démoniaques* contains the usual ration of startling imagery – Joëlle Coeur, as a remorseless female wrecker called Tina, standing naked on a hulking rock formation etched against the night sky, or the twins staggering uncertainly across a nocturnal beach studded by the decomposing skeletons of wrecked ships. But there's a fair amount of crudity to counterbalance the poetry, particularly in over-extended wenching scenes at a grotesque local tavern. (Revealing their mutual love of Belgian fantasist Jean Ray, these scenes play like Rollin's cash-strapped version of Harry Kümel's *Malpertuis*.) Similarly, the initial rape of the twins is no less gloatingly unpleasant for being so ineptly staged. Yet the sustained weirdness of the second half builds up a fascinating momentum, with Pierre Raph's exceptional score (his last for Rollin) adding sonorous death drums to the twins' exploration of the nearby "cursed ruins". There they find an incarcerated demon (or something), whose camp attire makes him look like the ultimate medallion man – until, that is, he shows off his improbably tan-lined buttocks while deflowering them both amid the crumbling masonry.

Rollin's varying effects certainly keep the viewer alert. For some reason he uses a Ronald McDonald-style red-wigged clown as one of the medallion man's benevolent gaolers, and he has Tina kill a local seeress in surely the most perfunctory 'axe in the back' scene in cinema history. But then he unleashes an astounding scene in which the twins will various ecclesiastical effigies to rain down around the traumatised Tina, afterwards showing the twins themselves being tethered to the ribs of the skeletal ships as if being tied to the tracks in an old-style melodrama. These are genuinely bizarre visions that could have come from no other director.

In 1974, Joëlle Coeur, so memorable in *Les Démoniaques*, was showcased by writer-director-star Michel Lemoine in *Les Week-ends maléfiques du Comte*

Zaroff (The Evil Weekends of Count Zaroff). Also known as *Sept filles pour un sadique* (Seven Women for a Sadist), this is an eroticised riff on the human-hunting Zaroff character from Richard Connell's 1924 short story *The Most Dangerous Game*, with Lemoine as a sadist-in-waiting descendant of the original Zaroff.

The film won Philippe Théaudière a Best Cinematography award at Sitges, but only after a gap of several years in which it was effectively banned in France. Quite why is unclear, given that the action is pretty evenly divided between Théaudière's ravishing views of Zaroff's château, a small-ish amount of softcore sex (ritzily scored by Eurovision Song Contest stalwart Guy Bonnet), and a heavy dose of charmingly pretentious dialogue, as when Zaroff tells his new secretary that "Our newly liberated instincts assert and unfetter themselves to the rhythm of profound vibrations that spread throughout our bodies." Elsewhere, Lemoine throws in some in-jokes (a soon-to-be victim lies in bed reading a paperback reprint of Guy Endore's *The Werewolf of Paris*) and an effectively doom-laden ending, in which Zaroff pursues a ghostly vision (Coeur) into a crypt and becomes sealed in with her skeleton.

Lemoine was an old associate of Jess Franco, having appeared in *Necronomicon* and a couple of Franco's other 1967 productions, and for *Les Week-ends* he invited along the faithful Franco mascot Howard Vernon, top-billing him as Zaroff's malevolent, rollneck-sweatered manservant. Curiously, Vernon had recently played Zaroff himself in another lubricious spin on *The Most Dangerous Game*. Shot in April 1973 for Robert de Nesle, Franco's *La Comtesse perverse* (The Perverse Countess) matches Vernon with the statuesque Alice Arno, whose naked Countess Ivanna Zaroff hunts down the similarly naked Sylvia (Lina Romay) with a bow and arrow. These Zaroffs are cannibals as well as human hunters; according to the Count, Sylvia is "dumb but most definitely juicy." The film is beautifully photographed by Gérard Brissaud and benefits from an oneiric sea voyage undertaken by Kali (Kali Hansa), but beyond that it bears all the hallmarks of a reputed five-day

shoot. It eventually collapses altogether under the dead weight of various sex scenes, in one of which Kali is raped by the Zaroffs but nevertheless brought noisily to orgasm. Here, just 12 years after his elegant Orlof in *Gritos en la noche*, Vernon gets to show off his 65-year-old testicles on Franco's behalf.

Made at the same time as *La Comtesse perverse*, *Plaisir à trois* (Pleasure for Three) was also for de Nesle and returned Franco to the Sadean arena of *Philosophie dans le boudoir*, this time with Alice Arno and Robert Woods as the psychotic sexual sophisticates and Tania Busselier as their innocent target, plus the added bonus of a basement gallery of petrified former conquests. Having decamped to Madeira in July 1973, Franco then made something a bit less in his usual line. In *Al otro lado del espejo* (On the Other Side of the Mirror), Emma Cohen's loathsome and probably incestuous father (Howard Vernon) destroys her happiness by calculatedly hanging himself on her wedding day. Escaping to Lisbon, she works as

Howard Vernon's Count Zaroff contemplates Alice Arno's deceased Countess in *La Comtesse perverse* (1973)

a jazz pianist, auditions for a production of *Medea* and finally, in a familiar Franco gesture, murders playboy Philippe Lemaire by sliding a knife, matador-style, into the back of his neck during sex. Franco goes all out for dreamlike disorientation here, but apart from Cohen's sad-eyed performance the result is unengaging. Amazingly, the French version, *Le Miroir obscène* (The Obscene Mirror), replaced the father's suicide with that of an incestuous lesbian sister (Lina Romay) – a character completely absent from the Spanish cut.

Arguably the most bizarre film of the 11 shot by Franco in 1973 was a Spanish production called *La noche de los asesinos* (The Night of the Assassins) – bizarre, paradoxically, because of its complete exclusion of Franco's trademark bizarrerie. Dashed off in November, this is a standard-issue 'old dark house' murder mystery, convoluted, illogical, rather dull, and prefaced with the mind-boggling credit, 'Based on *The Cat and the Canary* by Edgar Allan Poe'. With the Costa Blanca doubling as 19th century Louisiana, it boasts the usual skull-masked murderer (quite an effective one), Luis Barboo dropping his stone-faced shtick and energetically gurning instead, and Yelena Samarina's splendidly sinister housekeeper going up in flames in a sequence that fully exposes the paucity of Franco's resources. It also features a supposed Scotland Yard man (Alberto Dalbes) having the effrontery to tell the local police inspector, "We're in zombie country, and don't you forget it."

## BLUE MIST AND MARAUDING CRABS

Taking shape in the closing months of 1973, with further bits of filming to come in 1974, was one of Jess Franco's best-known films, this one a French-Belgian co-production for his old associates at Eurociné. *La Comtesse noire* (The Black Countess) would sire more variants even than Franco was used to, with titles ranging from *Female Vampire* and *Erotikill* to *The Bare Breasted Countess* (a cut-to-bits, 59-minute edit for UK release). Franco himself initiated the confusion by filming standard blood-sucking scenes for a 'horror' version and others, intended for a softcore 'erotic' variant, in which the titular Countess goes after whatever sexual emissions she can gulp down. Yet another version would surface with non-Franco hardcore material added, called *Les Avaleuses* (The Swallowers) for French patrons and *Lüsterne Vampire im Spermarausch* (Lustful Vampires in a Sperm Frenzy) for Germany. Forty years on, it's the 'erotic' version that has become the standard one.

Interleaving interminable sex scenes with 'lonely vampire' philosophising that redefines the term half-baked, *La Comtesse noire* starts with one of Franco's most iconic scenes. Set to a plangent Daniel White theme, Franco's new muse, 19-year-old Lina Romay, strides through the encroaching blue mist of a spindly forest, clad only in a cloak, heavy belt and knee-high boots; coming into tight close-up, she allows Franco's camera to travel downwards and lose itself in her pubic hair. Unfortunately, Franco's pube-probing camera style recurs throughout the film (as it would through much of his subsequent career) and rapidly becomes at least as wearisome as the undead ennui of the protagonist.

Mute and therefore limited to a sullen pout and fathomless stare, Romay is the Countess Irina Karlstein, beautiful perpetrator of a grisly murder spree on Madeira. Franco himself, playing the seedy local coroner, explains that her first victim "was bitten in the middle of an orgasm, and the vampire sucked his semen and his life away." (Examining a female victim, Jean-Pierre Bouyxou's Dr Orloff concludes that "The two canines have pierced the lips and deformed the clitoris.") Among the film's peculiarities, Romay turns into a seagull rather than a bat, making ridiculous flapping movements with her cloaked arms to indicate flight, and as her ultimate victim she takes an endlessly pontificating writer played by Jack Taylor. "As she approached," he muses, "her diaphanous body seemed to become more and more unreal." Far from diaphanous, Romay writhes uninhibitedly throughout, terminating proceedings with the unedifying spectacle of Taylor being fellated to death.

Of the other Franco titles whose shooting straddled 1973 and 1974, *Les Nuits brûlantes de Linda* (The Hot Nights of Linda) is far grimmer than its racy title suggests. Here, the faithful Paul Muller (playing, as he did in *Eugénie*, a character called Radeck) suffers necrophile visions of Lorna, the dead wife he murdered, while presiding over a benighted household enclosing the ubiquitous Alice Arno and Lina Romay. The shooting of this one took Franco to Paris early in 1974, where he proceeded to set up a couple of threadbare films whose titles made them sound like rip-offs of *The Exorcist*, the no-holds-barred horror picture that at the time was electrifying the world. In fact, they were nothing of the sort. One of them was for Robert de Nesle, the other for Eurociné, and in both cases funds were clearly at a record low.

In the Eurociné title, *Exorcisme*, Franco skulks his way through Paris backstreets in the role of a pint-sized religious maniac called Vogel, offering salvation to promiscuous women via "the exorcism ritual of the early Inquisition" – ie, by sticking a knife in them and (in one instance) hauling out a heap of slithering entrails. "I was expelled from the priesthood," he

Nausea sexualis: Pamela Stanford as the
malign interloper of Lorna... l'exorciste (1974)

complains, sounding very like one of
Bela Lugosi's excommunicated mad
scientists. "Those idiots thought I was
too severe." Shot for the most part
in poky little offices and fly-blown
attic rooms, *Exorcisme* is bisected by a
prolonged orgy of flabby celebrants
that's an even tougher watch than
the material either side of it; to give
Franco his due, the scene was forced
on him by Eurociné. There's the
usual roster of intertextual references
too, from a police inspector called
Tanner to an introductory torture
floorshow. And, as so often, the film
put forth numerous variants, among
them *Sexorcismes*, a hardcore version in
which, according to Stephen Thrower, Franco himself
participates "in shots that brook no argument about
stand-ins or stunt doubles."[29] Later still, in 1979, a
re-cut version called *El sádico de Notre Dame* (The Sadist
of Notre Dame) featured sufficient unique material to
qualify as a separate film.

Intertextuality is also a feature of *Lorna... l'exorciste*
(Lorna... the Exorcist), which utilises a malevolent
central figure who might, or might not, be the
character previously played by Janine Reynaud in
*Necronomicon*. Despite the title, Lorna is in fact about as
far from an exorcist as it's possible to get. Also known
in its native France as *Les Possédées du diable* (Women
Possessed of the Devil), it's as repugnant and weirdly
powerful a film as Franco ever devised, telling a story of
extraordinary mythic power in graphically transgressive
images that even he would find hard to top.

> *Monied entrepreneur Patrick Mariel owes his success to
> a pact he made, 19 years earlier, with an ageless witch
> called Lorna Green. Now, with his daughter Linda's
> 18th birthday coming up, he suddenly switches the
> family festivities from Saint-Tropez to the Camargue.
> There, to his horror, he finds that Lorna is waiting
> to claim the girl's soul. Though admitting to being
> "sterile, like all who come from Beyond," Lorna
> nevertheless considers herself Linda's spiritual mother...*

The first words spoken in *Lorna... l'exorciste* are
given to Lina Romay, with the over-privileged Linda
complaining that "I'm so bored." Given that the
viewer has just been subjected to ten minutes of Linda
and Lorna in languorous lesbian congress (a scene

## LORNA... L'EXORCISTE

France 1974
US: **Linda**
Comptoir Français du Film Production (Paris)
90 minutes colour
in production April 1974
. . . . . . . . . . . . . . . . . . . . . . . . . . . .
Director of Photography: Étienne
Rosenfeld; Editor: Gerard Kikoïne; Music:
André Benichou, Robert de Nesle; Make-
up: Catherine Demesmeaker; Screenplay,
Adaptation and Dialogue: Nicole Franco;

Producer: Robert de Nesle; Director:
Jess Franco

Pamela Stanford (Lorna Greene); Guy Delorme
(Patrick Mariel); Lina Romay (Linda Mariel);
Jacqueline Laurent (Marianne Mariel); Howard
Vernon (Mauricius); Bigotini (manager of the
Frantel Hôtel); Catherine Laferrière (Marielle);
uncredited: Ramón Ardid (male nurse and hotel
receptionist); Jess Franco (doctor); Caroline
Rivière (woman on yacht)

**How far can Jesús Franco sink? Given that each film of his represents a
new debasement, don't be surprised by the cheapness, the vulgarity,
the salaciousness and, worse, the profound foolishness of this latest
production. Here ... in a loose 'remake' of *Necronomicon* Franco is incapable
of coaxing anything even remotely attractive from the pretentious settings
or the profuse and frequently pataphysical dialogue.** *Image et Son* February 1975

**I think from the beginning Jess tried to make me in the way of Soledad
Miranda ... But I'm not Soledad, I'm Lina. I never met Soledad personally.
She was dead when I met Jess. But I think Jess, in me, was thinking
of me as the second part of Soledad. But after a time, when I had more
experience, he allowed me to be myself.**
Lina Romay [quoted in Greaves / Collins, *The Lina Romay File*, 1997]

that, given later developments, we must assume is a
premonitory daydream), it's tempting to think that
Franco was pulling the viewer's leg with this line. But
it's unlikely that his self-reflexivity, rampant though it
generally was, extended to mockery of the prolonged
sex scenes he found so fascinating.

Yet even here, as Linda nuzzles Lorna's pubic
hair at graphically unproductive length, there's
something unmistakably 'off'. Why, for example, is
Lorna wearing a corkscrew blonde wig and wildly
exaggerated green eye make-up, making her resemble
an unholy fusion of Harpo Marx and Ultra Violet?
Franco is operating here at a level beyond that of mere

turn-on; there's an undercurrent of unease behind the sexual couplings that by the film's end will amount to nausea. Looking like a less prepossessing version of Peter Finch, leading man Guy Delorme is by no means a natural for closely observed sex scenes; the off-putting quality of these couplings recalls another 1974 film, José Larraz's *Vampyres*, but in Franco's case the hard-to-watch quality appears to be deliberate. A miasmic fog of sexual disgust hovers over the entire film, and it reaches critical mass with two scenes in which Patrick's wife, Marianne, exudes scuttling green crabs from, apparently, her vagina.

Franco needed a way-beyond-his-budget special effect here if this infestation was to be convincing; as things are, it's equally plausible that Lorna has merely caused crabs to appear magically on Marianne's pubis rather than having her actually 'birth' them. Either way, if Franco's competitive streak was piqued by the pubic bat featured in Rollin's *Requiem pour un vampire*, there can be little doubt that he outdid Rollin with this outrageous image of venereal horror. Patrick's immediate impulse is to sweep away the proliferating crustaceans and crush them underfoot, though this doesn't prevent Marianne from dying during the second outbreak. The horror is all the more powerful because the Mariels have been credibly presented as a genuine family unit. When Marianne tells Patrick that "Whatever happens, nothing can destroy our love," she really seems to mean it.

Incredibly, the marauding crabs, ghastly as they are, turn out to be just a curtain-raiser for the climactic mother-transfer represented by Lorna's seduction of Linda. "You were born from my desire," she tells Linda prior to offering her nipple to the younger woman, who sucks on it with the goggle-eyed intensity of a new-born baby. Lorna then deflowers her with a monstrous dildo and licks the virgin blood off it in unflinching close-up.

In this and all her other scenes, Pamela Stanford's inscrutable Lorna makes Patrick's contention that "Faust was just a figment of a writer's imagination" seem patently absurd. Haunting seaside resorts and preying on vulnerable young women, she superficially resembles a Warhol-flavoured twist on Delphine Seyrig's Countess from *Les Lèvres rouges*, but in Franco's scenario her baleful influence becomes considerably nastier. The borderline-misogynist message is that Lorna is a kind of Typhoid Mary responsible for the transmission of feminine evil. Once she's been shot to death by the vengeful Patrick, her spirit possesses the doe-eyed Linda. Showering in front of her father, she looks at him with a newly sexualised impudence prior to seducing a Lorna-obsessed mad woman in

a neighbouring clinic. She finally entices Patrick himself in the 'nude but for thigh boots' style of *La Comtesse noire*, eventually sliding a knife into the back of his neck in a direct quote from *Necronomicon* and *Al otro lado del espejo*.

The diseased ambience of *Lorna... l'exorciste* makes it arguably Franco's most extreme distillate of sex and horror, yet he still finds room for some characteristic touches of eccentricity. Though persistently nude, the mad woman (Catherine Laferrière) is clearly another of his Renfield surrogates, with Franco himself playing her ineffectual psychiatrist. Elsewhere, a gently comical hotel porter persistently mispronounces Patrick's surname as Mariol rather than Mariel, the trusty Howard Vernon crops up as a Morpho-type in Lorna's service (assaulting Patrick with an exotic sea-shell as if it were a knuckle duster), and André Bénichou, well known at the time for the 1970 album *Jazz Guitar Bach*, provides a hauntingly spidery score. Franco's flashback recreation of 1955 is laughably unconvincing, but in both the past and present-day action he makes unsettling use of his chief location. In the not-quite-completed resort of La Grande-Motte, Jean Balladur's architectural ziggurats complement the uncanny atmosphere of the film quite perfectly.

Among the film's French press notices, the reviewer for *Positif* – waggishly signing himself Pisanus Fraxi, after the Victorian pornographer – gave with one hand even as he took away with the other. Noting that "The first sequence is the strongest, with an evocative power unusual in this kind of film," he ended by saying that "the remainder is a mess, devoid of any stylistic quality or even the slightest credibility."[30] Reviews of this kind did nothing to impede Franco's workaholic progress, of course. Indeed, by the time it came out he had made four further films featuring the combustible *Lorna* combination of Lina Romay and Pamela Stanford, on top of which he would make no fewer than eight pictures in 1975. Up-front titles like *Lady Porno*, *Shining Sex* and *Die Sklavinnen* (The Girl Slaves) gave a pretty good idea of their content.

# HOUSE OF THE SCREAMING CHILD

In September 1974 Dario Argento was in Turin, a favoured city that he'd used in several earlier films, to shoot his fifth feature, *Profondo rosso* (Deep Red). The year before he'd given out conflicting signals regarding his identification with the giallo sub-genre, at first seeming to embrace it – as presenter-producer of RAI TV's four-part anthology *La porta sul buio* (The Door into Darkness) – before appearing to reject it with *Le cinque giornate* (The Five Days), a costume

David Hemmings makes a macabre discovery at the
'villa del bambino urlante' in *Profondo rosso* (1974)

comedy-drama set in the 1840s. The film's failure
focused his mind, unsurprisingly, on reasserting his
dominance in the giallo field.

Argento's previous gialli had sparked off a trend by
referencing animals in their titles; so, having alluded
to birds, cats and flies, Argento's initial idea was to
call this new one *La tigre dai denti a sciabola* (The Sabre-
Toothed Tiger). The eventual title hinted at something,
literally, much deeper. In portraying the labyrinthine
maze into which an Englishman abroad is plunged
after witnessing a hideous murder, Argento seemed to
be suggesting in *Profondo rosso* that all life is stained red
by a pervasive, and largely malign, irrationality. And in
the process he came up with a film that transcended
the giallo to become a horror masterpiece.

*Marc Daly, a British jazz pianist and teacher resident
in Italy, witnesses the brutal cleaver murder of
Lithuanian psychic Helga Ulmann. In the aftermath
he becomes convinced the police have disturbed the
lay-out of the victim's apartment; something he
saw there but can't quite recall seems to be missing.
Investigating the murder with unorthodox reporter
Gianna Brezzi, he realises that the so-called 'House of
the Screaming Child' in Via Susa might hold the key...*

# PROFONDO ROSSO

Italy 1974
UK / US: **Deep Red**
*alternative US:* **The Hatchet Murders**
*Seda Spettacoli Produzione for Rizzoli Films*
126 minutes colour
production began 9 September 1974
. . . . . . . . . . . . . . . . . . . . . . . . . . . . .
Director of Photography: Luigi Kuveiller;
Production Designer: Giuseppe Bassan; Editor:
Franco Fraticelli; Sound: Mario Faraoni,
Nick Alexander [English-language dub];
Music: Giorgio Gaslini, performed by Goblin;
Make-up: Giuliano Laurenti; Special Effects:
Germane Natali, Carlo Rambaldi; Screenplay:
Dario Argento, Bernardino Zapponi; Producer:
Salvatore Argento; Director: Dario Argento

David Hemmings (Marc Daly); Daria
Nicolodi (Gianna Brezzi); Gabriele Lavia
(Carlo); Macha Méril (Helga Ulmann); Eros
Pagni (Superintendent Calcabrini); Giuliana
Calandra (Amanda Righetti); Piero Mazzinghi
(Bardi); Glauco Mauri (Professor Giordani);
Clara Calamai (Marta, Carlo's mother); Aldo
Bonamano (Carlo's father); Liana Del Balzo
(Elvira, Righetti's maid); Vittorio Fanfoni
(cop taking notes); Dante Fioretti (police
photographer); Geraldine Hooper (Massimo
Ricci); Iacopo Mariani (young Carlo); Furio
Meniconi (Rodi); Fulvio Mingozzi (Agent
Mingozzi); Lorenzo Piani (fingerprint cop);
Salvatore Puntillo (Fabbroni); Piero Vida
(hungry cop); Nicoletta Elmi (Olga Rodi)

**The Italian whiz-kid of suspense, Dario Argento, exhibits the kind of
up-and-down quality that ultimately made the career of Mario Bava so
disappointing. This is his new low, a sloppy blood and gore fest involving
David Hemmings in an obsessive search for whodunit.** *Cinefantastique* Fall 1976

**I was aware that it was a love story and love stories have a long life. The crew
put considerable effort into their work and it was a film in which both Dario
and I expressed ourselves to the full ... At that time Dario was walking on air
and re-emerging from the disappointing experience of** *Le cinque giornate* **with
a new-found optimism ...** *Profondo rosso* **is, in every respect, Dario's happiest
film.** Daria Nicolodi [quoted in Palmerini / Mistretta, *Spaghetti Nightmares*, 1996]

At the beginning of *Profondo rosso*, Marc calls a jazz
rehearsal to a halt by describing the music as "Too
formal. It should be trashier." His desire for something
more untrammelled, more hectic and unpredictable
will be answered in nightmarish style once he's seen

a cleaver bisecting Helga Ulmann's head, yet the man himself is no wild man of jazz. Indeed, in his discreetly stylish Sartoria Russo clothing he's as off-handedly elegant as the film that contains him, and as the action develops he also begins to seem just a little prissy, especially when attributing his jumpiness, rather self-consciously, to artistic temperament.

To destabilise this likable but somewhat complacent Englishman, Argento has recourse not just to horror but also, unusually for him, comedy. Sadly, Eros Pagni's philistine police inspector – who, when informed that Marc is a musician, effectively says "Why don't you get a proper job?" – isn't funny in the slightest. But Argento makes quite an engaging stab at screwball comedy via Marc's burgeoning relationship with the cheroot-smoking Gianna, who cuts him down to size in several ways, from besting him in an arm-wrestling contest to putting him into the sunken passenger seat of her decrepit Fiat 500. These two, whose 'meet cute' moment takes place within sight of Helga's butchered body, are charmingly played by David Hemmings and Daria Nicolodi, making the viewer breathe a sigh of relief when both of them survive, however traumatised, to the end credits.

When making *Profondo rosso*, Hemmings was fresh from playing a loathsome young Zaroff type in José María Forqué's Spanish-Venezuelan co-production *No es nada, mamá, sólo un juego* (It's Nothing, Mama, Just a Game). For Argento's film he was a canny casting choice twice over – (a) because he's so good and (b) because of the Antonioni connections he brought to the project. Exactly eight years prior to starting *Profondo rosso*, he had completed work on Antonioni's hyper-fashionable *Blow Up*, in which he starred as a Swinging Sixties photographer who can't be quite certain of what he's photographed when apparently witnessing a murder in a South London park. Problems of perception are central, too, to *Profondo rosso*, in which Marc feels certain that the vital clue he can't recall was vested in a painting; it turns out to have been a reflection in a mirror, a reflection that Argento, playing fair, actually shows to the sharp-eyed viewer in the traumatic murder-aftermath. Elegantly closing the circuit of Marc's faulty perceptions, Argento concludes the film with a shot of Marc reflected in an unfathomable pool of the killer's blood.

Helga Ulmann's perceptions don't involve her eyes but are nevertheless far more acute than Marc's. Her fateful theatre appearance, where she inadvertently signs her own death warrant by revealing a psychic link with the killer, is staged with superlatively unruffled finesse, the kind of finesse that makes it obvious that Argento had hit an imaginative peak with this film. As Luigi Kuveiller's camera probes its way through the foyer of Turin's historic Teatro Carignano, the rear-stalls curtains are magically drawn apart to permit us inside an auditorium that redefines the term 'red plush'; at the end of the scene the curtains swoosh back again, as if to emphasise that what we've just seen is a self-contained play-within-a-play. Yet, paradoxically, there's nothing remotely artificial about Helga's performance, with Macha Méril lending the role such intensity that we never once wonder if she's a charlatan. The same intensity carries over into Helga's apartment, where she goes to answer the door but recoils, as if electrocuted, from the bad vibes invested in the door handle. The killer crashes in, the cleaver flashes down and the viewer is left agog by one of Argento's most pulverising murder scenes.

In the street outside, Argento indulges a couple of his most striking visual conceits. During the murder, the unknowing Marc and his dissipated friend Carlo converse outside a brightly lit yet strangely sombre-looking diner modelled exactly on Edward Hopper's 1942 painting *Nighthawks*. After the killing, Carlo tells Marc that "Sometimes what you actually see and what you imagine get mixed up in your memory like a cocktail" – and he does so while standing at the opposite end of a massive, reclining figure in Turin's Piazza CLN, one of two 1930s statues sculpted by Umberto Baglioni. The figure's restful pose contrasts tellingly with the tense conversation going on between the tiny figures at either side of it. Between them, these haunting Hopper and Baglioni references hint at a kind of urban alienation that, in Argento's universe, produces crazed cleaver killers.

The same mood of nocturnal angst informs Marc's protracted investigation of the 'villa del bambino urlante', which was actually another Turin landmark, an Art Nouveau mansion designed by Pietro Fenoglio at the turn of the century. Examining the interior by torchlight, Marc chips away at a wall to uncover a child's drawing of a Christmas murder, a mural so artlessly hideous it qualifies as a macabre work of art. Later he enthusiastically demolishes a false wall to disclose the murder scene itself – the looming grandfather clock, the cobwebbed Christmas tree, the shrieking, desiccated cadaver. All this is brilliantly scored with an agitated kind of mutant funk by the Prog Rock group Goblin. (In another attempted Antonioni reference, this time to *Zabriskie Point*, Argento initially approached Pink Floyd to score the film.) Yet one of the most disturbing features of the sequence is a seemingly minor one – when a small sheet of glass falls on Marc's head, we're reminded of the shattered window pane that attended Helga's demise.

This is just one of numerous, destabilising echoes studded throughout the film. A draught of water regurgitated by Helga is echoed by the spittle drool of Amanda, the second victim, and by the killer's beige vomit at the end. A doll with a missing head prefigures not only the killer's fate but also the bizarre, tuxedoed mini-robot that launches itself at Giordani, the third victim. A mynah bird impaled on a knitting needle recalls a similarly pinioned lizard, while Marc being blasted by a malfunctioning coffee machine sets us up for a horrendous scene in which Amanda is scalded to death in a red-hot bath tub. A bead of sweat rolling, in massive close-up, down Marc's temple presages the rivulets of condensation in Amanda's boiling bathroom. And, strangest of all, Marc's joking reference to piano-playing as a symbolic means of "bashing his [father's] teeth in" pays off in horrific style when Giordani's teeth are repeatedly smashed against a mantelpiece and then a table top.

Whether the viewer is conscious of them or not, the cumulative effect of these echoes is to suggest some supernatural intelligence controlling a universe that otherwise seems cruelly irrational. The supernatural aura woven around the killer devolves into an earthbound yet still hair-raising solution; only in his subsequent film would Argento go the whole supernatural hog.

In the meantime, the breathtaking sweep of *Profondo rosso* incorporates various charmingly off-kilter details, several of them related to the ill-fated Carlo, his lover and his mother. In a nod to the sexual confusion that crops up time and again in Argento's films, Carlo turns out to be the same person who, in an eerie opening flashback, we took to be a little girl; his male lover, Massimo, is subsequently played by an actress (Geraldine Hooper). And Carlo's mother Marta is introduced to us, rather endearingly, in a small pastiche of *Sunset Blvd*. Constantly referring to Marc as an engineer rather than a pianist, she at first appears merely daffy, with Argento inserting an explicit reference to Norma Desmond when the camera examines the photos commemorating her faded theatrical past. Just as Billy Wilder featured real photos of Gloria Swanson, so Argento used real photos of Clara Calamai, the long-retired actress venerated for such wartime titles as Visconti's *Ossessione*. That this gently absurd figure makes a truly bloodcurdling contribution to the film's finale is the icing on the cake.

Indeed, other gialli of the period had no hope of measuring up. The inexorable slide into witless sleaze was accelerated by Andrea Bianchi's *Nude x assassino*, which began shooting in February 1975 and would

Giallo favourite Edwige Fenech in the 1975 sleazefest *Nude x assassino*, aka *Nude per l'assassino*

be exported under the slightly elaborated title *Strip Nude for Your Killer*. This one begins with a botched abortion, moves on to a 'sex in the sauna' interlude reminiscent of the kind of grubby sex comedies then coming out of the UK, has a repulsively chauvinist 'hero' (Nino Castelnuovo) who refers to Femi Benussi as "first-class merchandise," features a woman having her ears clipped off in an underground car park and various other victims subjected to genital mutilations, and of course parades the usual cast of giallo stereotypes bearing no relation whatsoever to human beings. Poor Edwige Fenech, still game and fetching, recalls the giallo's palmier days but ends up fending off Castelnuovo's attempts at anal sex; this dismal fade-out was presumably intended to be amusing. The only feature of the film that rises above the garbage level is Berto Pisano's mesmeric score, which echoes the modish sound of US funk producers like Norman Whitfield and Gamble & Huff.

The jungle of mid-70s gialli also harboured Tano Cimarosa's *Il vizio ha le calze nere* (Vice Wears Black Stockings), a shabby sex fest numbering Dagmar Lassander and Magda Konopka among its high-class lesbian razor fodder. Slightly more engaging, Mario Moroni's *Ciak si muore* (Clap, You're Dead) is an arch account of murders on a horror movie set, with the 'clap' referring to a clapperboard. Other notable entries include Luigi Cozzi's efficient murder-swapping tale *L'assassino é costretto ad uccidere ancora* (The Killer Must Kill Again), Duccio Tessari's low-key amnesiac murder-mystery *L'uomo senza memoria* (The Man Without a Memory), co-written by Ernesto Gastaldi, and the absurdly convoluted *Diaboliques-*

style plot of Francesco Degli Espinosa's *Giochi erotici di una famiglia per bene* (Erotic Games of a Respectable Family), which was scripted by none other than Renato Polselli. And a continuing pleasure of the mode was the sight of bemused English-speaking guest stars struggling their way through thoroughly alien material, among them Britain's Francis Matthews as the journalist hero of Stelvio Massi's *5 donne per l'assassino* (Five Women for the Killer) and America's Robert Webber as a dyspeptic cop in Maurizio Pradeaux's Greek co-production *Passi di morte perduti nel buio* (Death's Footsteps Lost in Darkness).

## THE EXORCIST MADE THEM DO IT

Two faded Hollywood stars are conferring together in a sunlit Italian colonnade. Arthur Kennedy, sporting a dog collar, looks up at the lanky Mel Ferrer as the latter asks, "In your opinion, does the Devil exist?" "There's no doubt about it," Kennedy replies earnestly. "The Pope himself reaffirmed it recently. And not as a *concept* of evil, but as a real presence."

This exchange from Alberto De Martino's 1974 film *L'anticristo* (The Antichrist) was typical of many such dialogue scenes in the Devil-obsessed mid-1970s. For the film was just one of many that aped William Friedkin's *The Exorcist*, a massively controversial Warner Bros shocker that became a worldwide phenomenon on its US release on Boxing Day 1973. The film had started shooting back on 14 August 1972 and was three months into its seven-month schedule when Pope Paul VI made an influential speech entitled 'Confronting the Devil's Power' on 15 November – a speech in which he stated unequivocally that "this

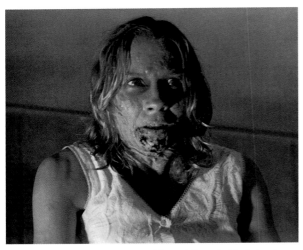

Juliet Mills as a levitating vessel of demonic forces in *Chi sei?* (1974)

dark disturbing being exists and ... is still at work with his treacherous cunning."

With its graphic content and blasphemous utterances, *The Exorcist* changed the horror landscape almost overnight. It finally made it across the Atlantic in mid-March 1974, when it opened in London, and on this cue copycat films started proliferating in amazing numbers, despite the fact that there were still several months to go before the film reached the continent. "Having one version of *The Exorcist* was bad enough," scowled US critic Reynold Humphries, "but two, or three – or who knows how many will be made? – is becoming positively antisocial."[31]

First into the race, with pretty mind-boggling speed, was a West German item called *Magdalena, vom Teufel besessen* (Magdalena, Possessed by the Devil), which reached local cinemas on 22 May 1974 – a full four months before *The Exorcist* itself did. Advertised as 'Ein wahrhaft ungeheuerlicher Film' (a truly super-scandalous film) and beginning with an on-screen quote from the above-mentioned Papal speech, this was directed by Walter Boos, the man responsible for a dozen *Schulmädchen-Report* films, together with various other titles of the Lederhosen slap 'n' tickle variety. Put in charge of a film in which a Munich schulmädchen becomes demonically possessed, he goes through all the expected paces with more sleaze than inspiration. Frequently nude and followed by a pervasive buzzing of flies, Magdalena (Dagmar Hedrich) breaks a would-be rapist's arm, throws the school's lumber-ridden attic into poltergeisted chaos, replicates the slit pupils of her feline familiar, and climactically runs amok with an axe, screaming "I'll kill you all in the name of the Devil!" Forced to recite the Lord's Prayer, she vomits a small snake, thus expelling the demon. Predictably, the ensuing snake-stomping is done for real.

It was unusual for Italian filmmakers to be beaten to the punch in the rip-off stakes, but, making up for lost time, two such films kicked off in Rome in early May. Ovidio G Assonitis began shooting *Chi sei?* (Who Are You?) on the 6th, while Alberto De Martino's *L'anticristo* started production just one week later, on the 13th. Not long afterwards, going in front of the cameras in June, came Mario Gariazzo's *L'ossessa* (The Possessed). Despite the fact that Friedkin's original wouldn't make it into Italian cinemas until October, an all-new filone had been detected and the vein would be tapped relentlessly for several years to come.

Of these films, *Chi sei?* was turned into a major US smash by the Atlanta huckster Edward L Montoro, who titled it *Beyond the Door* and was subject to a failed plagiarism suit by Warner Bros. The British actress

Juliet Mills shoulders much of the weight here, turning in a really bravura performance as Jessica, a San Francisco housewife who undergoes an inexplicable, and remarkably rapid, pregnancy. She has two children already – little Ken and his older sister Gail, whose self-conscious '70s patois includes such gems as "Man, if you don't stop crying you're gonna have a real bad trip." The first signs of demonic possession include Jessica flinging an ash tray at a transparent fish tank (the exploding shards and fluttering fish make for an arresting slow-motion visual), after which, in a direct quote from *The Innocents*, she plants a lingering kiss on little Ken's lips. Then comes a splendidly well-realised set-piece in which the children's den is poltergeisted by suddenly animated dolls. In the next room, Jessica's head turns virtually 360° – displaying a triumphant rictus that's arguably more disturbing than anything in *The Exorcist*.

Jessica's husband Robert is played by Gabriele Lavia, just a few months before having his head squished by a lorry in Argento's *Profondo rosso*. There's a glimmer of a feminist subtext when Jessica rounds on him with the line "You don't give me room to breathe. Never! Never!" But this is rapidly forgotten when an undead Satanist, Dimitri, comes on the scene. Jessica's former lover, he has to ensure she comes to term in order to prolong his existence. Richard Johnson, making an Italian horror film for the first time since *La strega in amore* eight years earlier, brings an engaging hangdog desperation to this conflicted character, finally realising that the Devil has pulled a fast one on him and that his life will end anyway.

Whether vomiting green sludge, telekinetically flinging Robert all over the bedroom, or snickering evilly with a crown of electrodes on her head, Mills' Jessica is a sight to behold in the film's concluding scenes. Yet Assonitis' debt to *The Exorcist* is really just a matter of puke-spattered incidentals, together with the expected ration of speaking in tongues. To bulk up the story *Chi sei?* throws *Rosemary's Baby* in there too and takes the intriguing step of making the demonic vessel the placid mother rather than the pre-teen daughter.

The set-up in *L'anticristo* is rather different, with the wheelchair-bound Carla Gravina regressing to a past life when her patrician father (Mel Ferrer) proposes to remarry. De Martino's realisation of this one is strictly at the 'high-gloss trash' end of the market, with a wide range of baronial interiors and glamorous photography by Aristide Massaccesi (known latterly as Joe D'Amato). An early highlight is Gravina's ridiculous dream of sexed-up demonic initiation; complete with rutting green-skinned couples, Gravina being fed a torn-off toad's head, and a goat having

its anus licked (in long shot), this green-tinged nightmare could have come direct from a Renato Polselli film.

In tone and texture, *L'anticristo* resembles one of the vacuous Hollywood disaster movies of the period, though it doesn't have quite enough slumming US guest stars to make the parallel complete. (Of those that do show up, Arthur Kennedy coupled this assignment with another Edmondo Amati production shot at Cinecittà at the same time, Jorge Grau's *No profanar el sueño de los muertos*.) De Martino serves up a variety of exploitable ingredients – Gravina setting Kennedy's prayer book on fire, spitting green bile in Alida Valli's face, bombarding exorcist George Coulouris with poltergeisted 7" singles, levitating out of a window in one of several very poor effects sequences, and – in a comedy masterstroke – causing Ferrer's animated cravat to start throttling him. There's also a rain-lashed climax set in the Colosseum. Yet the end result is extraordinarily boring, made watchable only by Gravina's demented performance. At the height of her possession, she looks strangely similar to Johnny Rotten, who in October 1976, just six months after the British release of *L'anticristo*, would snarl "I am an Antichrist" in the punk anthem 'Anarchy in the UK'.

Very much the runt of this initial litter is Gariazzo's *L'ossessa*, in which art student Stella Carnacina is possessed by means of a suspiciously life-size 15th century sculpture of a crucified robber. She immediately institutes a masturbation marathon, tries to seduce her father with the excuse that "incest is only an invention of the priests," and develops grisly stigmata in her hands and feet. Luigi Pistilli's taciturn exorcist is called in and, having resisted her comically

"I am an Antichrist." Carla Gravina anticipates Johnny Rotten in *L'anticristo* (1974)

unsubtle advances, finally gives up his life in freeing her. She vomits out the demon via the regulation streams of green goop and, without further ado, the end credits crash in.

Gariazzo tries to justify his numerous soft-porn interludes via Catholic imagery of a very specific kind; the girl's naked mother writhes in ecstasy under her sleazy lover's hail of rose stems, preparing the way for a scene of Pistilli vigorously flagellating himself and finally for Carnacina flogging him at the climax with a heavy chain. But the film is disfigured by a nasty early example of a synth score (Marcello Giombini, a specialist in both liturgical and electronic music, was the composer) and remains memorable only for a couple of satanic hallucinations. In one of these the Devil (Ivan Rassimov) crucifies Carnacina in a subterranean grotto – hence the stigmatic wounds that so puzzle her doctors. The other, echoing a famous scene in Karl Freund's The Mummy, is creepily well realised, with Carnacina absorbed by a painting as the fateful sculpture stirs gradually into life behind her. Departing from Freund, Gariazzo then has the risen Rassimov tear off Carnacina's dress, whip off his loin cloth and take her on the floor as the now-unoccupied cross bursts into hellish flames.

As well as entailing the production of tailor-made rip-offs, the Exorcist-obsessed atmosphere of the mid-1970s extended to the repurposing of films that had nothing whatever to do with The Exorcist. Even a grimly serious Spanish drama set in a women's mental hospital, Rafael Moreno Alba's 1971 film Las melancólicas (The Unhappy Women), found itself exported to America as Exorcism's Daughter and France as La Fille de l'exorciste. Lucio Fulci's Non si sevizia un paperino, meanwhile, appeared in France as La Longue nuit de l'exorcisme, and Mario Bava's Lisa e il diavolo was bastardised for US and UK release as House of Exorcism. Similarly, Mario Siciliano's clunky Italian-Spanish-Mexican co-production Malocchio (Evil Eye), in which Jorge Rivero's dreams of a satanic cult trigger a murder spree, had its title adjusted for Mexican audiences to Más allá del exorcismo (Beyond Exorcism).

Rivero's psychiatrist in Malocchio was played by the minor Hollywood name Richard Conte, who followed his role in The Godfather with a string of Italian exploitation films prior to his death in April 1975. Another of Conte's Italian projects was a bona-fide Exorcist rip-off called Un urlo dalle tenebre (A Shriek from the Darkness), which began shooting on 11 November 1974 and would be attributed to Angelo Pannacciò – though the real director, apparently, was future pornographer Franco Lo Cascio. Echoing Chi sei?, Un urlo was known during filming by the ridiculous

English-language title Who Are You, Satan? – a self-answering question if ever there was one. Eventually exported under the inspired exploitation title Naked Exorcism, it involves an androgynous, boggle-eyed teenage boy (Jean-Claude Verne) becoming possessed by an 18th century succubus (Mimma Monticelli), calling his mother (Françoise Prévost) a "lecherous sow" and flinging her down the stairs, causing poltergeist havoc with tennis rackets and bed linen, and finally vomiting blood at a crucifix flourished in front of him by Conte's late-arriving exorcist. "I spit on you and all your mumbo-jumbo" is as abusive as the boy gets.

For Pannacciò the Exorcist template was clearly just a peg to hang plenty of '70s sleaze on, and the same is true of Diabolicamente... Letizia (Diabolically... Letizia), which Salvatore Bugnatelli directed in December 1974. Here, Franca Gonella is a 23-year-old schoolgirl who induces erotomania in the household of her aunt and uncle (Magda Konopka and Gabriele Tinti), laughs insanely throughout, occasionally transforms into a bearded monkey demon, and is apparently being controlled by a skull-masked man straight out of a German Krimi. The poltergeist activity here involves slightly mobile cushions and ash trays, while the major 'horror' set-piece is Konopka's vision of Gonella's severed head under the bedclothes.

In 1975 The Exorcist even inspired a local spoof, with Ciccio Ingrassia (the lanky one from the old comedy team of Franco e Ciccio) going solo as writer-director-star of L'esorciccio, a project duly exported as The Exorcist Italian Style. But it wasn't just Italian filmmakers who fell over themselves in the rush to rip off The Exorcist; Spanish ones were swept up in the copycat excitement too. By mid-November 1974, writer-director Joan Bosch and writer-star Paul Naschy were making Exorcismo (Exorcism), in which Naschy's dog-collared hero steps in when young Mercedes Molina graduates from standard-issue loathsome little creep to full-fledged demonic vessel. Various murder victims are found with their heads on back to front, British bobbies break up a satanic ritual in a subterranean grotto (replete with the kind of full-frontal female nudity that was withheld from Spanish audiences), and Naschy himself hallucinates toads and snakes prior to doing battle with a maddened Alsatian when the entity shifts hosts.

Naschy claimed to have written the script several years in advance of The Exorcist, but the third act is a fairly pitiful Exorcist rehash distinguished only by some quite good horror make-up applied to Molina. That the film is a fearful reflection on modern youth is made obvious when the resident police inspector equates streaking (!) with Devil worship, and even Naschy's apparently enlightened cleric points out that

"Leila was always a little difficult. And you know how young girls are today. They have a concept of liberty which isn't always nice." Reflecting on dialogue of this kind, Andy Willis has suggested that "*Exorcismo* can be read as a clear warning to Spanish society, and in particular the young, about the choices they might make as Franco's death approached and the future of Spain became increasingly uncertain."[32] Unfortunately, such speculations are far more interesting than the film itself, which is a paralysing bore.

The reactionary sentiments of *Exorcismo* obviously struck a chord, however, given its impressive take of nearly 36 million pesetas. Yet exactly similar views expressed in Amando de Ossorio's *La endemoniada* (The Devil-Possessed) – as a police commissioner puts it, "Young people nowadays are bored with just sex and drugs; they're liable to turn to any strange rituals" – resulted in a more modest take of under 13 million. Made, according to Ossorio, in just eight days, *El endemoniada* has its share of leaden dialogue scenes but rates much higher than *Exorcismo* thanks to Ossorio's characteristic fusillade of exploitation highlights.

A pubescent girl (Marián Salgado) is infiltrated by the spirit of a bald-headed necromantic crone when the latter defenestrates herself in a police station. Little Susan takes on the expected filthy tongue –

Pressbook art for the Spanish *Exorcist* variant *La endemoniada* (1974)

"Why don't you go fuck your boyfriend and leave me alone?" she says to her concerned nanny, as well as calling a conflicted priest "a goddam queer." More surprisingly, she metamorphoses from time to time into a pint-sized version of the old witch, complete with warts and a prominent bald spot; she looks simultaneously ghastly and ridiculous. In this guise she echoes *Dracula* by crawling down a wall face-first and also emasculates the above-mentioned boyfriend. Ossorio's unenlightened message is that gypsies are at the root of the problem, though the film benefits from a tragic ending and a creepily minimalist score from the pop duo Víctor y Diego. Ossorio claimed to have had nothing to do with the casting; whoever did deserves points for the opportunistic use of Salgado, who had recently voiced Linda Blair in the Spanish dub of *The Exorcist*.

Spain's third *Exorcist* clone in 1974, Jorge Darnell's *El juego del diablo* (The Game of the Devil), was produced under the more nondescript title *Alucinaciones* (Hallucinations). Here, 15-year-old Inma de Santis is profoundly affected by a creepy exhibit in a waxworks museum and proceeds to switch off a hospitalised little boy's life-support, fling her mother over a minstrel's gallery, and string up an old retainer's Dalmatian, causing the owner to have a heart attack. All this is pretty predictable, and the film is further hamstrung by a female therapist (María del Puy) given to uttering vacuous platitudes like "The human brain is still an impenetrable labyrinth." Even so, Darnell manages some genuinely eerie visions of the animated waxwork (played by the uniquely gaunt Catalan actor José Lifante), who appears to the girl beside a swimming pool that simultaneously sprouts groping hands from its unruffled surface; the same hands reach out, *Repulsion* style, from her bedroom wall at the end. Despite a plangent score by José Nieto and attractive photography from José Luis Alcaine, the film is otherwise unmemorable – except, perhaps, for its inexplicable emphasis on eels, stuffed piranha and, during a holiday trip to Peñíscola, whole heaps of dead fish in the market.

In the first two months of 1975, writer-director Augusto Fernando was in Lisbon to make a Portuguese co-production called *El espiritista* (The Spiritualist), the title an obvious nod to the all-powerful *El exorcista*. In fact, the film bears little relation to *The Exorcist*, focusing instead on a devious, well-heeled and frequently shirtless medium called Alberto Ramos (Vicente Parra), who doubles as a photographer of saucy photo-spreads. The action begins with a gloomy seance in which two of the female attendees become so transported they rip open their tops and ecstatically fondle their breasts, but too much of the remainder is padded out with disco dancing in nightclubs, guitar-twanging floorshows at chic restaurants, scenic wanders round fishing ports, and laboured discussions of parapsychology at the dinner table.

Even so, the film does give Parra fanciers the opportunity, not only to see him in paisley Y-fronts, but also to relish a bravura scene in which the yowling of a phantom cat, unleashed at a second seance, pursues Ramos home. Stripped to the waist and repeatedly yelling "Maldito," he's thrice given a bloody nose by a formless entity (forcing Parra to indulge in a great deal of 'beaten up by the invisible man' acting) and finally crawls sobbing to a domestic altar prior to vengefully trashing it. The yowling manifests itself even when Ramos is called to account in court, entailing his final exit in a straitjacket. The concluding shot of Lisbon traffic – in which the unearthly yowling blends artfully with the wail of police sirens – is imaginative but also cacophonous.

## BBC BOFFINS AND FEMALE FRAGMENTATION

Amid all this feverish exploitation, the most measured and cerebral of Italy's *Exorcist*-flavoured films took director Massimo Dallamano to Umbria in October 1974. Known in production as *La bambina e il suo diavolo* (The Little Girl and Her Devil), Dallamano's film boasted UK and US imports in the shape of Richard Johnson and Joanna Cassidy, the former fresh from *Chi sei?* The eventual release title was *Il medaglione insanguinato* (The Blood-Stained Medallion), with a superfluous *Perché?!* (Why?!) added in parentheses. The intended export title was *Emily* – echoing such crudely fashioned *Exorcist* rip-offs as William Girdler's *Abby* – but in the end this was supplanted by, among others, *The Night Child*.

These adjustments were fair enough, given that Dallamano's film is the kind of straightforward possession story that was prevalent well before *The Exorcist* was even thought of. Even so, in acknowledgment of *Exorcist* fever a written postscript was added to the film, quoting Pope Paul's momentous 1972 speech to the effect that the Devil "is the hidden enemy."

*Widower and BBC documentarist Michael Williams journeys to Spoleto with his daughter Emily and her nanny Jill. He's preparing a film about representations of the Devil in art and is intrigued by a slide inadvertently sent to him by the Contessa Cappelli. The painting it depicts is subsequently found in a derelict villa – but, unknown to Williams, the 200-year-old events conveyed in the painting have already been appearing in Emily's vivid nightmares...*

*Il medaglione insanguinato* opens with a lovely bit of dramatic irony – ironic because pretty much all viewers, even those new to the film, will have a shrewder idea of what's in store than our poor BBC hero does. Cosily ensconced in his London home and projecting slides of his chosen diabolical artworks, Williams finds among them a family snap featuring his wife Lisa and daughter Emily. "That slide hardly belongs among my demons," he smiles. That he's likely to be tragically wrong is indicated almost at once by Emily's nightmare vision of her mother's recent death, with Lisa gesticulating despairingly from an upper window while wreathed in flames.

In the wake of Lisa's death, the film's tragic scheme is set in train by a cursed medallion originally belonging to Lisa and subsequently passed on to Emily. That the script's family dynamic works so well can be credited to an unusually strong cast. Emily is ideally embodied by ten-year-old Nicoletta Elmi and Richard Johnson is particularly good as the blinkered Williams. Warm enough at first glance, he later shows an intransigent streak when blithely returning to Spoleto despite Emily's protestations that "I hate that place." As a direct consequence the film's climax, played out in the impressively storm-lashed villa, concludes with a downbeat double-death tableau recalling the 1971 Hammer film *Hands of the Ripper*.

For an item thrown onto the blood-soaked exploitation market of the mid-1970s, Dallamano's film is unusually reticent, with Lisa's fiery demise counting as its horror highlight. There's a bit of blood in the above-mentioned climax, but otherwise we're left with Ida Galli's Jill being prodded over a precipice with a croquet mallet and being carried over surging rapids. Sadly, both Lisa and Jill's death scenes involve pitifully poor process work, and the low level of the effects is maintained by the strange, borderline comical, ectoplasmic blob that shows up on Williams' film of the fateful painting. All three effects drain the film of credibility at crucial moments, and they seem especially puzzling given that Dallamano clearly considered the alluring look of his film all-important.

When making *Il medaglione insanguinato* Dallamano's most recent release was *La polizia chiede aiuto* (The Police Appeal for Help), a grimly down-to-earth giallo marketed overseas as *What Have They Done to Your Daughters?* With its abused and murdered 15-year-old girls, not forgetting severed heads tumbling out of car boots, the film fell as much into the workaday poliziotteschi bracket as the giallo category, giving little scope for alluring photography. So with *Il medaglione insanguinato* Dallamano embraced the opportunity to create some really lustrous, otherworldly visuals.

The film's location work in London is pretty functional, taking in Heathrow Airport and BBC Television Centre, as well as suggesting, in a typically puzzling bit of geographical misdirection, that St Pancras Station is south of Westminster Bridge.

But it's in the middle-Italy strangeness of Spoleto that Dallamano's real visual flair comes through. In tandem with cinematographer Franco Delli Colli, he creates a crumbling nocturnal dreamscape explicitly recalling Bava's *Operazione paura*. En route to his first interview with the Countess, Williams meets a three-legged dog and later an old man with cataracts, both encounters frowned down upon by the shadowy arches of Spoleto's narrow back streets. The Countess herself is seen with the fateful painting superimposed over her face by the light of her projector beam – as precise a symbol of the past intruding into the present as could be wished – and the abandoned room in which the painting resides is a small masterpiece of eerily diffused light and dust-gathering artefacts. As for the painting itself, it's an unusually convincing creation, peopled by Goya-style grotesques and presided over by the crimson embrace of a grinning Satan.

Let loose in Spoleto, Williams' antiquarian zeal echoes M R James, while his scrutiny of the Thomas à Becket fresco in the Church of Saints John and Paul nods respectfully to Nicolas Roeg's *Don't Look Now*. Among the film's other peculiarities is some gentle satire at the expense of the BBC – "All my documentaries are boring," Williams tells a colleague, "that's why I work here" – together with numerous appearances from J&B Scotch, the drink that enjoyed ample screen time in more giallo pictures than it's possible to count.

By the time she made *Il medaglione insanguinato*, Nicoletta Elmi was already Italian cinema's premier spooky child, given her appearances in *Baron Blood*, *Flesh for Frankenstein*, *Profondo rosso* and others. Along with Lila Kedrova and Ida Galli, she was one of three *Il medaglione* cast members who, some six months earlier, had appeared in a peculiar psychological horror called *Le orme* (Footsteps). Directed by Luigi Bazzoni in April 1974 and gorgeously shot on Turkish locations by Vittorio Storaro, this has Florinda Bolkan as an interpreter whose intensifying nightmares of a disastrous space mission cause her to lose her job. Her exile in a strange coastal resort called Garma throws up the possibility of a red-wigged doppelgänger having got there several days before her, as well as involving her with an ambiguous young biologist played by British import Peter McEnery. The film is beautifully scored by Nicola Piovani, and only the fleeting views of

## IL MEDAGLIONE INSANGUINATO (PERCHE?!)

*Italy 1974*
UK / US: **The Cursed Medallion**
*alternative US:* **The Night Child** / **Together Forever**
*Fulvio Lucisano presents*
*90 minutes colour*
*production began 22 October 1974*

. . . . . . . . . . . . . . . . . . . . . . . . . . . . .

Director of Photography: Franco Delli Colli; Art Director: Luciano Puccini; Editor: Antonio Siciliano; Sound: Luciano Wellish; Music: Stelvio Cipriani; Make-up: Dante Trani; Optical Effects: Biamonte Cinegroup; Screenplay: Franco Marotta, Massimo

Dallamano, Laura Toscano; Producers: Fulvio Lucisano, William Reich; Director: Massimo Dallamano

*Richard Johnson (Michael Williams); Joanna Cassidy (Joanna Morgan); Ida Galli (Jill Perkins); Nicoletta Elmi (Emily Williams); Lila Kedrova (Contessa Cappelli); Edmund Purdom (doctor); Riccardo Garrone (police inspector); Dana Ghia (Emily's mother [Lisa]); Eleonora Morana (the Contessa's maid); uncredited: Aristide Caporale (Nazareno); Peter Cartwright (minister at funeral); Tom Felleghy (BBC producer)*

**Italian-English production [sic] about a possessed pubescent girl, directing her demonic powers against the other women in her father's life. Some nice incestuous innuendo, and lots of professional polish, but [it] lacks inspiration. It's hack work ultimately.** *Cinefantastique* Spring 1976 [complete review]

[Argento's] *Deep Red* is without any doubt the best thing I've ever done ... The other film I often recall with deep emotion is *The Cursed Medallion*, in which I got to play one of the protagonists for the very first time in my career. Massimo Dallamano, the director, was a very talented and visionary artist, and he helped me exploit all the power and passion I had invested in my character. Nicoletta Elmi [quoted in *Fangoria* January 1996]

Nicoletta Elmi as the traumatised pre-teen heroine of *Il medaglione insanguinato (Perche?!)* (1974)

Klaus Kinski in Bolkan's monochrome dreams – far too distractingly iconic a face to be subordinated to so insignificant a role – disrupts the dread-inducing sense of déjà vu perfected by Bazzoni. The elliptical result is about as far from the *Exorcist* mania then gripping Italian producers as it's possible to get.

In the mid-1970s the Italian industry had no shortage of psychological horrors focused on fragmenting young women, quite apart from the proliferating riffs on *The Exorcist* dealt with above. Among the examples on offer were Roberto Mauri's *Madeleine ... anatomia di un incubo* (Madeleine ... Study of a Nightmare), with Camille Keaton dreaming of pregnancy and pursuit by fright-wigged witches, and Marcello Andrei's *Un fiocco nero per Deborah* (A Black Ribbon for Deborah), in which psychic Marina Malfatti undergoes a pregnancy transfer from a dead woman. But perhaps the most beguiling reality vs fantasy fever dream was *Il profumo della signora in nero* (The Perfume of the Lady in Black), which Francesco Barilli began shooting on 9 July 1973, plunging US import Mimsy Farmer into a convoluted nightmare of rape, matricide and, finally, cannibalism. The key to the nightmare is provided in an early discussion of African witch doctors, helping to make sense of a mind-boggling climactic tableau of mass organ-eating.

In the meantime, Farmer's porcelain beauty, Mario Masini's sumptuous cinematography and another bewitching score from Nicola Piovani sustain interest as Barilli echoes not only *Repulsion* but also *Rosemary's Baby*. Bava's *Operazione paura* is in there too, when Farmer is visited by her creepy, eight-year-old self in the person of Lara Wendel. Scattered references to *Alice in Wonderland* try the viewer's patience, but *Il profumo* is otherwise a mesmerising watch with plenty of ghoulish surprises. Typical is an off-hand moment in which we see a kindly white-haired widower (Mario Scaccia) feeding his cats a heap of raw meat featuring a human finger. It's the kind of grisly touch that makes one look for the name of Antonio Fos in the writing credits; but no, the film was co-written by Barilli and Massimo D'Avak.

Richard Johnson and Joanna Cassidy in *Il medaglione insanguinato*, Peter McEnery in *Le orme*, Camille Keaton

in *Madeleine*, Mimsy Farmer in *Il profumo della signora in nero* – these international names provided yet more examples of Italian filmmakers reaching out, not always successfully, to export audiences. And of course there were plenty of others. In 1974, for example, fashion photographer turned film director Daniele Pettinari showcased the Yugoslavian star Bekim Fehmiu as the 18th century occultist *Cagliostro*, while Mario Lanfranchi's *Il bacio* (The Kiss) imported Martine Beswick, Vladek Sheybal and Brian Deacon from the UK to appear in an adaptation of a classic Carolina Invernizio story from 1886.

The novel had previously been filmed in 1917 and 1949, but Lanfranchi's version was unfortunate in that it went into production in January 1974, just one month after Carlo Infascelli started work on an adaptation of his own at Villa Parisi. Having got in first, Infascelli was able to use Invernizio's full title – *Il bacio di una morta* (The Kiss of a Dead Woman). Despite this, the Infascelli version settles for romantic melodrama, albeit romantic melodrama briefly enlivened by a premature burial. Lanfranchi, by contrast, had the bonus of Pupi Avati as co-screenwriter, lending to Invernizio's convoluted intrigue a beguiling mood of Venetian diabolism. The result is an entertainment so sumptuous it comes as no surprise that Lanfranchi was responsible for bringing grand opera to Italian television back in the mid-1950s.

Ancestral werewolf, ridiculous make-up: Annik Borel as *La lupa mannara* (1975)

Bringing to bear all the personal magnetism familiar from such titles as *Dr Jekyll & Sister Hyde* and *Seizure*, Beswick is an exotic temptress called Nara who ensnares a young Count (Maurizio Bonuglia) and connives in the apparent poisoning of his bride (Eleonora Giorgi). Advertised with mock-Alfons Mucha posters, Nara's smouldering nightclub act pays tribute to Bob Fosse's *Cabaret*, with a white-faced MC announcing the star attraction as a "mysterious virgin of the night." An even more recent release, Nicolas Roeg's *Don't Look Now*, was the source of a spellbinding sequence in which Bonuglia pursues his wife's black-draped ghost through the streets of Venice, with the beckoning fair one finally turning out to be an insanely jeering old woman. There are also occult rituals in the basement, presided over by the imposing Valentina Cortese, with a red-robed Cardinal and a tuxedoed androgyne among the celebrants. The whole thing winds up with a dramatic courtroom scene in which the defeated Nara screams her conviction that "The Countess is dead!" – despite the fact that the 'dead' woman has put in a personal appearance. The film also benefits from lavish interiors shot at Rome's Villino Crespi, previously used in Bava's *Lisa e il diavolo*.

Foreign names were to be found in the bottom-of-the-barrel sector too. By 1975, former muscleman and Colorado native Gordon Mitchell, a ubiquitous figure in continental films, had hit rock-bottom with Alessandro Santini's *La pelle sotto gli artigli* (The Skin Under the Claws), a zero-budget murder spree even tattier and tawdrier than Mitchell's previous mad scientist vehicle, *Frankenstein '80*. Tawdry is also the ideal description for Rino Di Silvestro's *La lupa mannara* (The She-Wolf), which reached Italian cinemas in March 1976 and tastelessly resorted to teen sex abuse as its plot motor. As a result, French actress Annik Borel turns throat-rippingly feral whenever sexually aroused, with a slaveringly realised gang rape leading to a third-act rape-revenge scenario. The ancestral horror of a female werewolf is only seen in an opening flashback; it's Borel again, sporting a tufty leotard, pooch nose, rabid drool, and inflated nipples. The film's true epitaph, however, may well be an unplanned moment later on, when Borel eavesdrops on Dagmar Lassander and Osvaldo Ruggieri making love. As she moves her nightie aside and starts masturbating, a fly buzzes in and briefly settles on the nylon. After *La lupa mannara*, Di Silvestro's move into Nazi exploitation was a natural progression, of sorts.

## A CHOICE OF TEMPLARS

Over in Spain, Paul Naschy and León Klimovsky were reunited at the end of May 1974 for an earthy mediaeval romp called *El mariscal del infierno* (The Marshal of Hell). This was ostensibly an old-fashioned swashbuckler full of Robin Hood-style hijinks. Yet Naschy couldn't help himself; his Gilles de Lancré is "a brave and noble soldier" who degenerates into "a bloodthirsty and sadistic monster" in patented Gilles de Rais style, his scheming consort (Norma Sebre) is a dead ringer for Lady Macbeth, and a freshly severed head speaks to him, or so he thinks, with instructions direct from the Devil. Promising him "science's most occult secrets," a phoney alchemist (Eduardo Calvo) demands virgins' blood as ingredient number one, so Sandra Mosarowsky is duly sacrificed while strangely farting synthesisers burble away on the film's patchwork library soundtrack.

Paul Naschy undergoes multiple piercings in *El mariscal del infierno* (1974)

De Lancré's end – pierced by multiple arrows – is a blatant quote from Kurosawa's 1956 *Macbeth* adaptation *Throne of Blood*, though elsewhere Klimovsky's attempts to craft sword-clanging action scenes in the old Hollywood style are a bit listless. Guillermo Bredeston is an extremely personable hero, however, and *El mariscal del infierno* is an engaging, though schizophrenic, divertissement.

Shooting at the same time, and again featuring Sandra Mosarowsky, was a much less interesting offering, this one produced by Maximiliano Pérez Flórez' Maxper outfit – the company that had launched the Paul Naschy phenomenon with *La marca del hombre lobo*. Pedro Luis Ramírez started shooting *El colegio de la muerte* (The School of Death) at Ballesteros Studios on 1 June 1974, mixing scraps of *La residencia*, *Ivanna* and (for the film's climactic face-peeling 'reveal') *House of Wax* into a somnolently paced saga of London's Saint Elizabeth Refuge in 1899. This establishment's "three most cherished rules [are] silence, discipline and obedience" – hardly surprising, given that its girlish inmates are routinely passed on to a hideously disfigured ex-con brain specialist, Dr Kruger, who converts them into mindless sex slaves for sale to jaded aristocrats. Despite this, the film, unusually for the period, features zero in the way of nudity and extravagant gore, with Ramírez trowelling on plenty of blue-tinted fog instead. Mosarowsky proves an engaging heroine but Dean Selmier, cast as the supposedly heroic Dr Brown, merely mopes his way through the proceedings.

It was also in mid-1974 that a long-gestating Paul Naschy project suffered a serious setback. The script for *El monte de las ánimas* (The Mountain of Souls) was based by Naschy on the Gustavo Adolfo Bécquer story of the same title, together with a couple of related Bécquer tales, and had been entrusted to the British director John Gilling, famous for various Hammer classics and by then living in retirement in Spain. Gilling's nationality was a bone of contention with local unions, however, and on 29 May *Variety* reported that the project had been "nixed by Spanish Cine Syndicate, though formerly [the] green light had been given. Producer Juan José Porto sez he'll appeal the decision with union prez Juan Antonio Bardem. Item has been repeatedly postponed."[33]

Yet by the time Naschy returned from that year's Sitges Festival early in October, he found that the Gilling problem had been sorted out, the film was under way, and that Gilling had had the script radically overhauled. Not only that: he had decreed that Naschy himself shouldn't appear in it. By the time the film came out at Easter 1975 – under a different Bécquer title, *La cruz del diablo* (The Devil's Cross) – Naschy had been forced to threaten legal action in order to keep his name on the credits, though he regretted doing so when finally seeing it. "It was a terrible film," he insisted, attributing its failure to the "two arseholes" that produced it (Porto and Enrique Herreros Jr) and to Gilling himself, who in his opinion "didn't believe in horror. It was just another film for him; there was no passion, there was nothing there."[34]

Naschy's estimate can be attributed to a perfectly understandable combination of wounded pride and molten indignation. But even looked at more objectively, there's little doubt that *La cruz del diablo* falls some way short of its aspirations.

*Late-Victorian London. Hashish-smoking writer Alfred Dawson is bedevilled by dreams of a beautiful woman being pursued by the Knights Templar. When his Spanish sweetheart María presents him with a copy of Bécquer's Leyendas, he notices an illustration in it exactly paralleling his dream. He then learns that his sister Justine has had a miscarriage. Going to Madrid to be with her, he discovers that she's been found murdered at the foot of the Mountain of Souls.*

When the film opened at Madrid's Roxy-B on 29 March 1975, it had the distinction of being attended by all eight of its top-billed actors. The poster, which rather cheekily framed Conrad Veidt's terrified *Caligari* face within an enormous cross, promised that Bécquer's 'prodigiosa sensibilidad' (prodigious sensitivity) would give viewers 'el auténtico sabor del miedo' (the authentic taste of fear). This high claim wasn't supported by the Madrid edition of *ABC*, whose critic described the film as "insufficiently Latinised" and a "completely failed test but worth some sympathy for the attempt."[35]

Gilling's film seems to have been tripped up, not by a lack of feeling for such uniquely Spanish source material, but by a more generalised listlessness that contrasts vividly with the well-honed vigour of such Gilling oldies as *The Flesh and the Fiends* and *The Plague of the Zombies*. And yet *La cruz* begins with an explicit reference to the latter film; in a precise fusion of Spanish and British horror traditions, the hero's dream of a young woman being surrounded by equestrian Knights Templar recalls not only Ossorio's Blind Dead films but also a scene in *Plague* in which the heroine is chased down by red-jacketed fox hunters. Sadly, the excitement level rarely rises above this rousing pre-credits sequence, a problem attributable, in part, to a too-reverent attitude to the literary source. Ossorio's take on Bécquer, Gilling seems to say, reduced a national poet to pulp; this film, though in some respects just as loose an adaptation, will be a scrupulously elegant tribute to Bécquer in all departments.

And so it is, but the penalty is a talky script, a stately pace, and a rigorous exclusion of sex and violence that makes the film seem positively squeamish when lined up against its peers. Exemplifying this tendency is frightened maidservant Inés (Silvia Vivo), whose attempt to undress in front of the hero is curtailed by that noble fellow, after which she's killed by a black-masked interloper in perhaps the quickest and easiest strangulation on record. Elsewhere there's an unconvincing severed head flung at the camera but not much else. The biggest disappointments of all are the Templars themselves, who barely feature anyway but when they do can't hold a candle to Ossorio's indelible creations. Naturally the film wasn't about to imitate the EC Comics-style visages perfected by Ossorio, but the make-up department needed to come up with something far better than the crude masks that are dimly discernible under these Templars' cowls.

In the film's favour, it occasionally boasts a kind of hazy beauty courtesy of cinematographer Fernando Arribas, who seems to have gone all out for dusty, soft-focus Victoriana. The desolate locations – Batres,

Adolfo Marsillach and Mónica Randall, manipulative private secretary and manipulated mistress respectively in *La cruz del diablo* (1974)

Talamanca de Jarana, Escalona – are atmospherically rendered too, and Gilling crafts some arresting images, as when a coach thunders past a horse's skull, abandoned at the roadside and looming massively into camera. Perhaps Gilling's best scene follows Alfred's unhappy arrival in Madrid, when he dreams of his casketed sister and sees her using blood from a livid neck wound to daub a telltale 'XIII' on his palm. To unlock the meaning of this, a lengthy quest supervenes, undertaken by Alfred, his fiancée, his shifty brother-in-law and the latter's even shiftier amanuensis. During this, the script arbitrarily disposes of an actress as formidable as Carmen Sevilla by having María break her ankle and being packed off home before the third act kicks in.

The men then enter an immaculate but lonely villa occupied by Beatriz and Iñigo, a young couple last seen in a 1390s flashback. The latter has a nice response to receiving unexpected guests – "One waits for months and years; they turn into centuries" – and the film builds to a satisfyingly cruel twist when Alfred realises that everything has been illusory and he's in the frame for several murders. Leading up to this, however, the film has made surprisingly little of Alfred's hashish intake and his possibly unreliable perceptions. Worse still, actor-playwright Adolfo Marsillach – playing the repugnant, wheedling and eventually demonic amanuensis – starts out strong but is rapidly defeated by the one-note requirements of the script. All in all, Spanish critic Tomás Fernández Valenti was exaggerating – but not, perhaps, by much – when he asserted that "*La cruz del diablo* will probably be remembered as the greatest missed opportunity in the history of cine fantástico español."[36]

Having played the phantom Beatriz in *La cruz del diablo*, Emma Cohen's next horror assignment was León Klimovsky's beguiling *El extraño amor de los vampiros* (The Strange Love of the Vampires). Here, she brings an affecting undertow of fatalism to a terminally ill heroine called Catherine, who gravitates towards the local vampire Count on the principle that "I too am condemned." Co-written, like *La cruz*, by Juan José Porto, the film begins with a solarised credits sequence accompanied by jagged rock guitar – a misleading intro for a romantic melodrama set firmly in the 19th century. The film's cowled vampires go on a violent nocturnal rampage that Klimovsky cleverly

## LA CRUZ DEL DIABLO

Spain 1974
US: **Cross of the Devil**
Bulnes SA [uncredited]
92 minutes colour
in production October 1974

[Paul Naschy], inspired by the stories of Gustavo Adolfo Bécquer; Producer: Diego G Sempere; Director: John Gilling

Director of Photography: Fernando Arribas; Art Director: José Ma Tapiador; Editor: Alfonso Santacana; Sound: Manuel Ferreiro; Music: Ángel Arteaga; Make-up: Cristóbal Criado; Special Effects: Pablo Pérez; Screenplay: Juan José Porto, Jacinto Molina

Carmen Sevilla (María); Adolfo Marsillach (César del Río); Emma Cohen (Beatriz); Ramiro Oliveros (Alfred Dawson); Eduardo Fajardo (Enrique Carrillo); Mónica Randall (Justine); Tony Isbert (Iñigo de Ataide); Fernando Sancho (Ignacio); Silvia Vivó (Inés); Eduardo Calvo (prison governor); Pascual Hernández (policeman); Antonio Ramis (servant); Mariano Cristóbal (coachman)

In principle the idea of resurrecting old legends to make a horror film is sound. The trouble is that, even though he's familiar with this type of film and known for his connections with Hammer, the British company that has built its success on precisely this genre, Gilling settles for a conventional treatment ... Without a doubt the film's best features are its atmosphere, which is at times very effective, and above all the photography by Fernando Arribas. *La Vanguardia* 17 May 1975

It was all Spanish, cast, crew and subject, and was one of my most enjoyable experiences ... I think the movie was a little highbrow for the general public, although it was very well received by the press ... Paul Naschy wanted to play the lead in the film but Paul, though he is a great 'horror' exponent, is not my idea of a leading man. I am afraid he was very upset and I am sorry to have disappointed him. John Gilling [quoted in *Little Shoppe of Horrors* April 1978]

intercuts with Catherine and the Count conversing in a blindingly white castle boudoir. The next night the villagers go on a rampage of their own, hammering spikes into the creatures' foreheads, while the Count, having left it too late to vampirise the ailing Catherine, sorrowfully steps out into the morning sun.

*El extraño amor* is realised with all Klimovsky's usual dash, particularly in a wild vampire party that comes complete with an inverted victim dangling from a winch. There's also a memorable vignette in which Catherine's vampire sister (Amparo Climent) advances across a bed of mist, only to be repelled by a cross scored into Catherine's window pane. Interestingly, Catherine's attraction to the dark side sets up an explosive generational clash with her straitlaced father (Manuel Pereiro), who just happens to be the chief vampire hunter. But the Count himself lets the side down. He has a nice line in cynical bon mots like "The world is cruel, as are so many of those who infest it." But, as played by Carlos Ballesteros, he looks more like a *Come Dancing* contestant than a mesmeric undead overlord.

Klimovsky's film was first shown at the Sitges Festival at the beginning of October 1975. Also on the bill was Paul Naschy's last werewolf film of the decade, directed, not by Klimovsky or Carlos Aured, but by Miguel Iglesias. *La maldición de la bestia* (The Curse of the Beast) was also Naschy's final Profilmes engagement. "Profilmes could have been the Spanish Hammer," Naschy reflected later, "but they didn't last many years longer. It was a shame."[37]

Even so, *La maldición* starts in truly stunning style. In a snowy wasteland three explorers are shockingly set upon by an anthropoid Yeti, after which the fanged Daninsky snarls his way through the lurid opening credits prior to an establishing shot of Big Ben accompanied by a bagpipe-wheezing rendition of *Scotland the Brave*. This is clearly going to be Euro-exploitation of a particularly unhinged variety, and the film does not disappoint. After the comparative dullness of *El retorno de Walpurgis*, Naschy obviously decided to go for broke with his harebrained script, mixing up a Himalayan expedition, not just with the Yeti, but also with a gang of sadistic Tibetan bandits

and a family of cannibalistic, cave-dwelling lady lycanthropes. He also retained Mercedes Molina, who had just played the possessed teen in *Exorcismo*, casting her this time as Daninsky's love interest.

The outrageous result could easily have been advertised in the tub-thumping style of old Hollywood B-movies. 'See! A cannibal wolf-woman take a dagger between her naked breasts!' 'See! The snarling Waldemar Daninsky frustrate the designs of not one but four would-be rapists!' 'See! A character waggishly called Larry Talbot impaled on an enormous stake!' 'See! Verónica Miriel having the skin flayed from her back by the evil Silvia Solar!' 'See! The bare-arsed girl slaves taking their revenge!' 'See! Luis Induni made-up to look like Attila the Hun and falling into a pit of spikes!' And so on and so forth. In the midst of all this engaging lunacy the Val d'Aran and Montseny Massif make reasonably acceptable substitutes for the Himalayas, with a few moments of genuine atmosphere smuggled in – as when Daninsky seeks refuge in a cave system bathed in an amber glow with lavender highlights.

At Sitges *La maldición* formed part of a roster that also included Freddie Francis' dreary British entry *Legend of the Werewolf*, which must have appeared even drearier by comparison to the Naschy gorefest. Released as *Night of the Howling Beast* in the US, *La maldición* was later, inexplicably, branded a Video Nasty under its British title, *The Werewolf and the Yeti*.

Waldemar Daninsky departed the scene only temporarily in *La maldición de la bestia*, but another set of monsters – the same ones recently appropriated in *La cruz del diablo* – were about to bow out altogether.

'Two battling, bloodthirsty beasts in a savage fight to the death.' Mercedes Molina and Paul Naschy in *La maldición de la bestia* (1975)

Released in August 1975, *La noche de las gaviotas* (The Night of the Seagulls) was the fourth and last of Amando de Ossorio's Blind Dead films, effectively picking up where the previous entry, *El buque maldito*, left off. Last seen rising from the waves of the Costa Blanca, the ghastly Knights Templar have now relocated to the mediaeval castle at Tossa de Mar on the Costa Brava. And yet again Ossorio modifies their back-story, this time making them a French branch of the Templars and supplying a Lovecraftian sea god for them to worship.

Borrowing further from Lovecraft, Ossorio glosses the titular seagulls as the migrant souls of the Templars' sacrificial victims, and he conjures some genuinely haunting scenes of black-clad Spanish matrons leading maidens in white along the water's edge to the appointed place. Occurring over a seven-night period every seven years, these sacrifices have apparently taken place for centuries. The fearful community that condones them is actually Patones de Arriba, last seen in Klimovsky's *La orgía nocturna de los vampiros* and here decorated with fishing nets to fool us into thinking the seaside castle is just next door.

"The horsemen of the sea," as they're evocatively called, still look great as they thunder through the surf towards their tethered victims. And Ossorio wrings plenty of atmosphere from a scene in which our heroes – Víctor Petit, María Kosti and Sandra Mosarowsky – make their escape on three of the Templars' steeds, which gallop in otherworldly slow motion even when ridden by humans. The film is a significant improvement on *El buque maldito*, yet it can't conceal the fact that, after four instalments, the Templars' repertoire is a decidedly limited one. This time the action devolves into another *Night of the Living Dead*-style siege, though Ossorio tries to ring the changes by introducing various outré details – a fleet of stunningly slow-moving crabs that consume the sacrificial remains, or the pints of blood that gush (inexplicably) from the Templars' eye sockets when they expire. But the real ace up his sleeve this time is Julia Saly – by far the best of all the Templars' many sacrificial victims, she replaces the usual sadistic-erotic posturing with a brilliantly convincing display of real panic and fright. We even get to see a small tear rolling from one of her dead eyes as those geriatric crabs move in.

*La noche de las gaviotas* made nearly 20 million pesetas less than the film that started it all, *La noche del terror ciego*. Though the law of diminishing returns eventually snuffed them out, Ossorio's Blind Dead remain, alongside Franco's Dr Orlof and Naschy's Waldemar Daninsky, the classic monsters of Spain's horror boom, and are arguably the most grimly powerful of the lot. It's just a shame that the resources available to Ossorio were so limited; as a contemporary British critic said of their first (and best) showcase, "The sightless dead who stalk through this roughly confected cut-price offering look as if they belong in classier company."[38] Their impact, however, is indisputable, with obvious tribute being paid to them in films as diverse as Roy Ward Baker's *The Legend of the 7 Golden Vampires* (1973) and John Carpenter's *The Fog* (1979).

Ossorio himself remained unsatisfied. "In my opinion, the ideas were much better than the finished products," he lamented, referring not just to the Blind Dead but to his whole output. "When I see them finished, it isn't really how I dreamed them. I wouldn't recommend any of my films."[39] Even so, in 1993 it was reported that Ossorio was trying to get a fifth Blind Dead project into production.

Sandra Mosarowsky is led to sacrifice in *La noche de las gaviotas* (1975), known in Germany as 'The Bloody Assizes of the Undead Horsemen'

Unfortunately, *El Necronomicon de los templarios* (The Templars' Necronomicon) never made it.

## THE BECKONING FAIR ONE

In January 1975, writer-director Serge Leroy was in Normandy to make a French-Italian co-production called *La Traque* (The Pursuit). Here, a visiting Englishwoman (Mimsy Farmer) is raped by a weekend huntsman in Normandy and finds the remainder of the hunting party, led by Jean-Pierre Marielle and Michel Lonsdale, closing ranks against her on the principle that "A team is a team." In as crushing a conclusion as can be imagined, her pursuers, all of them well-heeled and thoroughly corrupt small-town big-shots, get away with it because "We're the kind of people who don't easily arouse suspicion." A really grim outdoor thriller, expertly made and acted (and imitated ad nauseam since), *La Traque* isn't quite a horror film, though Leroy's insight into the misogynist mindset of the French upper-middle classes is quite horrifying enough.

In making an effective thriller complete with social satire and a sensitive approach to a serious subject, Leroy stood apart from the 'anything goes' trend of the period, a trend that, on 30 April 1975, led President Giscard d'Éstaing to more or less abolish film censorship in France. A few weeks later Jean Rollin's latest vampire film came out and, despite an abundance of nudity, sank like a stone. Some 20 years later, Rollin observed that this period "was a disaster for those of us who were producing 'B' movies, because the cinemas which usually ran our films suddenly stopped and started running the far more explicit and profitable porno films. When *Deep Throat* and its host of imitators arrived on the scene, it hit the exploitation industry hard, and it hasn't recovered to this day. In fact, I doubt if it ever will."[40]

In a changed climate that saw even the time-honoured Midi-Minuit switching to sex films, Rollin included in *Lèvres de sang* (Lips of Blood) an elegiac scene in which his hero visits the Cinéma Le Mexico, a Paris establishment previously immortalised in Godard's *Les Carabiniers* and Jessua's *Jeu de massacre*. Self-reflexively, display posters lure us into thinking that *La Vampire nue* is playing, though the Rollin film we actually see is *Le Frisson des vampires*. The cinema's switch to hardcore programming reportedly took place the very week after Rollin had filmed there.

*At a party celebrating the launch of a new perfume, the 30-something Frédéric is profoundly affected by the product's advertising art, which depicts a desolate castle overlooking the sea. It triggers a cloudy memory of his encounter there, aged 12, with a mysterious young woman. Trying to identify the place, he embarks on a strange nocturnal odyssey, dogged at various stages by an inscrutable gunman, a quartet of female vampires, and the obstructive machinations of his own mother...*

The shooting of *Lèvres de sang* entailed what, by then, Rollin must have considered the requisite ration of disasters, including a disappearing backer (necessitating the reduction of a four-week schedule to just three) and a drama on his beloved Dieppe beach, when he was knocked out by, appropriately, a coffin and nearly drowned. On this occasion, however, the familiar desolation of Dieppe's shoreline wasn't Rollin's only obeisance to childhood nostalgia, for he also incorporated scenes at the aquarium in the Trocadéro, scenes in which a pursuing hitman briefly turns this most evanescent of Rollin films into a Hitchcock-style 'wrong man' thriller. Yet, on closer examination, even the premise of the film bears a Hitchcockian stamp. It's the kind of scenario in which the protagonist pulls at a few random threads and eventually unravels a sinister conspiracy.

In this instance, the threads are like gossamer, as is confirmed when our hangdog hero moves among the glitterati at the perfume launch and one of the guests sagely observes that "Scents are like memories. The person evaporates, but the memory remains." Tellingly, it's at exactly this moment that the troubled Frédéric catches sight of the advertisement that will decide his fate. In answer to his queries, Frédéric's disingenuous mother claims that his vague recollection of the castle has no basis in reality, but he persists in thinking that it's not "just a vision from my childhood dreams."

To illustrate the wavering line between dream, memory and reality, Rollin came up with some of the eeriest tableaux of his career, starting with Frédéric's visit to the Mexico. There, the action of *Le Frisson* plays out on the screen and a woman, Jennifer, appears in the aisle, equal parts beautiful and unreadable as she hovers serenely under the 'exit' sign. Moments later, Frédéric rushes outside (into the persistent rain that apparently plagued the entire shoot) and sees her again. A classic image of the 'beckoning fair one', she's framed this time by the prison-like outer doors of the Montmartre cemetery. Frédéric's eyes, meanwhile, are brimming with tears.

That Jennifer, prior to relocating to the elaborate necropolis at Montmartre, should first appear to the adult Frédéric in the so-called 'dream palace' of a cinema (for all that this particular one looks more like an old-fashioned fleapit) is a typically poetic Rollin touch, and it's followed by an extraordinary descent into urban desolation as Frédéric ventures into the back streets of Belleville. Papered-over shop fronts, bricked-up windows, high picket fences, beetling bare walls – all these are weirdly illuminated in a style dating back to *La Vampire nue* but brilliantly perfected here by debutant cinematographer Jean-François Robin. The mood is intensified, too, by the extended funeral dirge that is Didier William Lepauw's score.

It's here that Frédéric starts being shadowed by four vampire women (two of them played by Rollin's faithful Castel twins, who appear this time without eyebrows). These creatures seem to have been liberated from the cemetery by the triggering of his childhood memories. Their first new victim, incidentally, is Rollin himself, drooling blood in slumped stupefaction as the quartet drift past. A later victim, in a splendidly comic scene, is a self-satisfied psychiatrist, who is pondering using ECT on Frédéric when he realises, too late, that his nurses are actually the Castel twins in disguise.

Because of the budgeting fiasco, Rollin had to translate some of the action into reported speech, though in the case of the mother's tremulous final monologue – explaining exactly what kind of link Jennifer has to Frédéric – the results are made riveting by a long-held close-up on Nathalie Perrey's mournful face. Perrey and our hero, Jean-Loup Philippe, are both excellent; the fact that one was a mere seven years older than the other only intensifies the bizarrely dislocated atmosphere. Philippe had appeared, uncredited, as a young doctor in the later stages of Rollin's *Le Viol du vampire* seven years before, and the artless dedication he brings to Frédéric's quest takes on an extra dimension when you notice that he collaborated with Rollin on the script for *Lèvres de sang*.

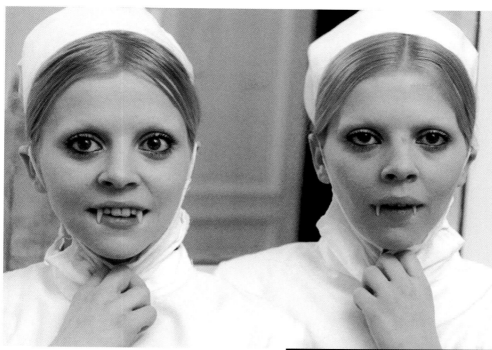

The Castel twins, Catherine and Marie-Pierre, as toothy psychiatric nurses in *Lèvres de sang* (1975)

The action eventually shifts to one of Rollin's typically evocative locations, this time the ruined, mediaeval hulk of the Château Gaillard in Upper Normandy. After a round of stakings and burnings for the attendant vampires, Frédéric and Jennifer end up naked on Rollin's ubiquitous beach. Explaining that "You had to remember me before I could appear to you," Jennifer bites him and he confesses joyfully that "I'm just starting to live." The conclusion, in which the couple sail into infinity in a waterborne coffin for two, has an absurd romantic sweep that maybe only Rollin could have achieved, or attempted.

The film is compromised here and there by a few minor concessions to soft porn. There's a lengthy photographic session featuring a nude model in leather boots, after which the photographer (played by porn actress Martine Grimaud) gets naked too. But *Lèvres de sang* is otherwise a bewitchingly strange rumination on a vanished childhood, with a spell-stopped atmosphere that is entirely unique. Nobly, Rollin allowed the film's young producer, Jean-Marc Ghanassia, to claw back some of the money he'd lost by creating a new film that spliced some of Rollin's footage with newly shot hardcore material; the euphonious title was *Suce moi, vampire* (Suck Me, Vampire).

Ignored in the stampede to soak up hardcore porn, the woozy eroticism of Rollin's original *Lèvres de sang* was an unfortunate victim of the unprecedented

## LÈVRES DE SANG

*France 1975*
US: *Lips of Blood*
*Off Productions / Scorpion V / Nordia Films*
*88 minutes colour*
*visa date 27 May 1975*

............................

Director of Photography: Jean-François Robin; Art Director: Alain Pitrel; Editor: Olivier Grégoire; Sound: Gérard Tilly; Music: Didier William Lepauw; Make-up: Éric Pierre; Screenplay: Jean Rollin; Adaptation: Jean Rollin, Jean-Loup Philippe; Dialogue: Jean-Loup Philippe; Director: Jean Rollin

Jean-Loup Philippe (Frédéric); Annie Brilland [Annie Belle] (Jennifer); Nathalie Perrey (Frédéric's mother); Martine Grimaud (photographer); Catherine and Marie-Pierre Castel (vampire twins); Hélène Maguin (blonde vampire); Anita Berglund (brunette vampire); Claudine Beccarie (Claudine); Béatrice Harnois (nude model); Sylvia Bourdon; Mireille Dargent; Paul Bisciglia (psychiatrist); Willy Braque (assassin); Julien Etchevery; Serge Rollin (Frédéric as a child); uncredited: Jean Rollin (cemetery caretaker)

Sleeping Beauty, the vampire version. Or how a young man will brave a thousand dangers to go to a ruined castle and wake up a young girl who, sad to say, has been vampirised. Amour fou is the key in a mutual passion for bloody kisses in the hollow of the neck. Scenario incoherent, dialogue ridiculous, actors even more so. *Télérama* 23 June 1975

I was the lead, the vampire girl ... I remember being put in a casket; it gave me the shivers. I was 17 ... Jean Rollin was a good director, very talented in my view. He was continually urged by the producers ... to put at least one or two hardcore scenes in his films ... Luckily *Lèvres de sang* wasn't made for the porno circuits, it was a straight horror film. Annie Belle [quoted in Gomarasca, *99 Donne: Stelle e stelline del cinema italiano*, 1999]

relaxations in censorship. After it, Rollin would hit upon a different means of attracting audiences, hardly a new one but certainly pretty novel in France – gore, and lots of it. Because the same thinking applied elsewhere, especially in Italy, the run-up to the 1980s would take place in a veritable welter of blood and body parts.

# Part Six

Coldly beautiful: Brigitte Lahaie as the Glam Reaper of *Fascination* (1979)

# *New Worlds of Fear* 1975-1983

By the mid-1970s a select few film titles had become emblematic of the extreme material that was beginning to find its way into cinemas – or sometimes not. Banned, cut, execrated, and subject to innumerable column inches of controversy, their titles alone bore the fragrance of forbidden fruit. The appearance in 1971 of *The Devils*, *A Clockwork Orange* and *Straw Dogs* ushered in, within just a few years, such combustible successors as *Last Tango in Paris*, *The Exorcist* and *The Texas Chain Saw Massacre*.

For indelibly repellent content, however, none of these films even came close to *Salò o le 120 giornate di Sodoma* (Salò, or the 120 Days of Sodom), the film that Pier Paolo Pasolini completed shortly before his violent death in November 1975. Relocating the Marquis de Sade's original to Salò in the latter part of World War II, the film contemplates Italy's Fascist past – and by implication its consumerist present – through the prism of four repugnant grandees and the 18 young people they round up, incarcerate, sexually abuse, torture and finally kill. With a literal feast of excrement acting as a mere prelude to scalping, nipple-burning, eye-gouging and

tongue-lopping, Pasolini's cold-eyed analysis of power and powerlessness was, inevitably, subject to numerous bans all over the world.

The boundaries of taste were breached with abandon by filmmakers with far less lofty intentions than Pasolini. This, after all, was the decade when supposed prestige pictures like Liliana Cavani's *Il portiere di notte* (The Night Porter, 1973) and Tinto Brass' *Salon Kitty* (1975) helped to trigger off a rash of crudely sadistic Nazi exploitation films, a genre known in Italy, where it was particularly popular, as 'sadiconazista'.

One of the decade's many other indicators of the collapse of censorship restrictions came from Switzerland, a country that had so far been extremely reticent where horror was concerned. There, a company called Monarex, set up in Schwanden by the German producer Christian Nebe, started out in fairly innocuous style before plunging mid-decade into the kind of extremism characteristic of the 1970s. In 1969 the company collaborated on a trashy but tame, half-American horror-comedy called *Guess What Happened to Count Dracula?*, also making it available in a much raunchier version called *Does Dracula Really Suck?* Then in 1973 Monarex co-financed three films by the American sexploitation guru Joseph W Sarno. One of these was a dreary Gothic potboiler called *Der Fluch der schwarzen Schwestern* (The Curse of the Black Sisterhood), exported as *The Devil's Plaything*. In it, the baleful Nadia Henkowa is head of a cult of lesbian Satanists, pledged to "bridge the gulf of darkness that separates the living from the undead" by resurrecting a 400-years-dead vampire called Baroness Varga. With the vapid Swedish sex kitten Marie Forså chief among the innocents falling into the cult's hands, the film is a listless sex-horror that borrows from Rollin, Franco and Hammer while entirely failing to be either sexy or horrific.

Nothing unusual there; the 1970s were full of similarly unstimulating hotchpotches. A few years later, however, Monarex's 1976 schedule included yet another vampire film, but this time a graphic study of necrophilia showing just how far the 'anything goes' approach had gone. Marijan Vajda's *Mosquito der Schänder* (Mosquito the Violator) used the recent Kuno Hofmann case as the foundation for an unrelentingly grim study of a deaf-and-dumb misfit (Werner Pochath) who becomes, in the words of a disbelieving cemetery guard, "a regular 20th century vampire." The film faithfully chronicles his descent into madness, using a two-pronged pipette to suck the blood from (presumably unembalmed) corpses, popping out their eyeballs, disinterring the body of a truly ridiculous neighbourhood flower child, and finally killing a couple of live specimens he finds canoodling in a car.

*Mosquito* rates uncomfortably high for sleaze, thanks chiefly to a really nasty (and ineptly staged) flashback of the young malcontent being beaten by his father and forced to watch his very young sister being sexually abused. There's also a scene in which the unnamed protagonist is given a lesbian floorshow by a couple of prostitutes, a slavering vignette that far exceeds any possible plot justification. As for Vajda's supposedly taboo-busting necrophile horrors, they're severely complicated by the corpses themselves, which are played either by laughably obvious dummies or by actresses unable to control their gulping and eyelash-fluttering reflexes.

In Britain, the local censor board rejected Pasolini's *Salò* outright in January 1976 and was then faced with Vadja's film and Pete Walker's homegrown *Schizo* in October. Having demanded cuts in both prior to rating them 'X' just ten days apart, BBFC chief James Ferman later bracketed the two films together as examples of irresponsible attitudes towards mental illness. Retitled *Bloodlust*, Vadja's film had been submitted

to the censor by the venerable Butchers Film Distributors, which seemed strangely appropriate.

## WISH YOU WEREN'T HERE

Among the oddest emanations of the mid-1970s was Peter Patzak's West German-Austrian co-production *Parapsycho Spektrum der Angst* (Parapsycho – Spectrum of Fear), which was a three-part portmanteau purporting to take parapsychology seriously while offering lashings of fashionable eroticism. To the first end, a teleprinter hammers out the opening credits for each story while quoting big chunks from *Time* magazine's 'The Psychics' issue of March 1974. To the latter end, Marisa Mell's body-double disrobes in the first story, Mascha Gonska obliges in the second (just as she recently had in *Le Trio infernal*), and former *Golden Shot* hostess Alexandra Drewes-Marischka spends almost the entirety of story three completely nude. Despite the obvious exploitation, the film has a chilly air of urban dislocation that lingers in the memory, together with a few bits of striking imagery – from a sparrow hurling itself at a mirror to a cheaply staged but still startling car accident and a dismal scene of a woman lying dead on a wet Munich pavement.

The first story, *Reinkarnation*, involves a family man enjoying a night of love with the cloche-hatted Mell, prior to discovering, via lipstick and fingerprints on a china cup, that she died decades before. *Metempsychose* has William Berger as a pathologist whose affair with a student (Gonska) ends in her very nasty wrist-slitting suicide, after which her spirit, embarrassingly, inhabits the pathologist's daughter (played by Berger's own daughter Debbie). Finally, Mathieu Carrière is an evil Pop artist in the longest story, *Telepathie-Hypnose*, using his mental powers to enslave pretty newly-weds in a repeated pattern that

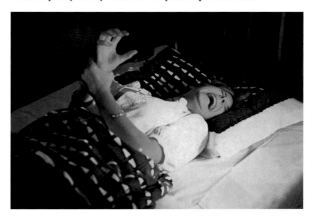

In the throes of possession: Debra Berger in the *Metempsychose* story contained in *Parapsycho Spektrum der Angst* (1974)

always seems to end with his victims defenestrating themselves. The atmosphere cooked up by Patzak in all three instances is only compromised by the tediously reiterated use of Beethoven's *Für Elise* in story one and by what looks hideously like a genuine autopsy in story two.

Released in May 1975, Patzak's film traded on the way the paranormal had well and truly invaded the popular consciousness by the mid-1970s, an invasion exemplified by the international spoon-bending notoriety of Uri Geller. The demon fixation engendered by *The Exorcist* was still in full swing too, prompting Hammer into the tortuous development of *To the Devil a Daughter*, a Dennis Wheatley adaptation that finally went before the cameras on 1 September 1975. Directed by Peter Sykes, this extremely disquieting study of a defrocked priest (Christopher Lee) seeking to create an avatar of Astaroth was a co-production with the West German company Terra Filmkunst. The German side of the deal brought not only some shimmering Munich locations but also a local co-star – Nastassja Kinski, teenage daughter of old horror hand Klaus. In due course the film was released in Germany as *Die Braut des Satans* (Satan's Bride).

Over in Spain, TVE giant Narciso Ibáñez Serrador had his mind on a different horror trend, finally getting round to starting his second feature film on 4 September and, in doing so, tapping into a rush of recent films expressing a queasy ambivalence towards children – from the rustic teen diabolists of Britain's *Blood on Satan's Claw* to the fanged mutant baby of America's *It's Alive*. His new film, shot as *Los niños* (The Children), also provided a memorably grim apostrophe to Spain's 1970s tourist bonanza.

In the six years since completing *La residencia*, Serrador had scored a massive TV hit with the 1972-73 game show *Un, dos, tres* (One, Two, Three), another series of which would kick off while *Los niños* was being readied for release under the more provocative title *¿Quién puede matar a un niño?* (Who Can Kill a Child?). Though one of the most expertly crafted horror-thrillers ever made in Spain, it didn't quite live up to Serrador's rather high-flown ambitions for it, ambitions reflected in the po-faced poster tag-line, 'Una película en defensa de los niños del mundo' (A film in defence of the world's children). This failure may have been due to the rather confused signals given out by the film, the actual plot of which presents children as robotic, remorseless killers. Either way, *Quién puede* certainly didn't fail on any other level; indeed, it made a tidy amount of money. Though Spain's horror boom was by now nearing its end, it was still sufficiently robust to guarantee Serrador an impressive take of over 63 million pesetas.

*Having left their two children in England, Tom and the pregnant Evie are on holiday in Spain. On a trip to the island of Almanzora, which Tom last visited 12 years before, they're puzzled by the preponderance of rather surly local children and the apparently total absence of adults. They only become alarmed, however, when they witness a little girl bludgeoning an elderly man to death with his own walking stick...*

For British holidaymakers, the 1970s package-tour explosion had its fair share of attendant horrors (particularly the 'not quite finished yet' hotels of popular legend), all of them ripe for the farcical treatment provided in the 1972 film *Carry On Abroad*. Of course, the Carry On team didn't venture beyond the Pinewood car park in creating the mythical Hispanic resort of Elsbels, whereas another sex comedy, the Anglo-Spanish co-production *Spanish Fly*, was shot on Menorca just a couple of months before Serrador's film, complete with charming scenes of local children massed on a hillside preparatory to going on an insect hunt. *Quién puede* also features swarms of children lined up on a hillside, but needless to say there's nothing charming about this particular gathering. And Serrador wasn't content with just Menorca as a location, adding to it Sitges and Almuñecar and, to represent Almanzora itself, the tiny Toledo community of Ciruelos.

Part of the film's genius, in fact, lies in the way Serrador and cinematographer José Luis Alcaine exploit precisely the kind of sun-kissed travelogue visuals that presumably lured Tom and Evie abroad in the first place. But the horrors awaiting them on Almanzora go well beyond the standard jerry-built inconveniences, leaving Tom to wrestle with the unenviable question posed by the film's title: who can kill a child? In the UK, incidentally, that title was given a slight tweak to make it even more brutally confrontational, becoming *Would You Kill a Child?*

Using his customary Luis Peñafiel pseudonym, Serrador adapted the screenplay, somewhat loosely, from the Juan José Plans novel *El juego de los niños* (The Children's Game). And in realising his own script, Serrador lays the accumulation of ominous portents before us with an almost offhand expertise. Just before Tom and Evie arrive in the coastal resort of Benavis, a flaxen child discovers the body of a woman, with livid rents in her neck, washed up in the surf – a native of the nearby Almanzora, as we later surmise. Serrador also lends a strange emphasis to a street celebration in which happy children go through the traditional routine of puncturing a dangling piñata, a routine that will turn horrific when we see the imaginative way in which the Almanzora children have adapted it. There's

Out of their depth
on Almanzora:
Lewis Fiander and
Prunella Ransome
in ¿Quién puede matar
a un niño? (1975)

also a strangely tremulous night-time conversation
between Tom and Evie, revealing that Tom originally
recommended aborting the baby that Evie is carrying,
with their trip to Spain designed as a means of getting
their marriage back on track after this crisis.

To play Tom and Evie, Serrador imported Lewis
Fiander and Prunella Ransome from the UK, and
they're just right; they have the slightly overcooked
look common to hapless British tourists and
are ordinary enough to fully engage the viewer's
sympathy. (Serrador reportedly wanted Anthony
Hopkins to play Tom and was disappointed by
Fiander's performance, although it's extremely hard
to understand why.) Evie finally agrees with Tom –
that Benavis is "too noisy: too many people" – and
they set sail for Almanzora with Evie uttering the
classic line, "Oh, I think we're going to enjoy it there!"

On arrival, the ominous portents, naturally enough,
become more ominous still. A sulky little boy, fishing
at the quayside, slams his wicker bait basket shut
when Tom tries to look inside. (What was in it? we
wonder later.) The Plaza Mayor is entirely deserted,
product at the abandoned ice-cream stand has turned
to liquid, and the wall-mounted rotisserie in the local
café is still, eerily, turning. A strange girl appears
behind the café's beaded curtains and, accompanied
by weird synth sounds and the unborn child's

## ¿QUIÉN PUEDE MATAR A UN NIÑO?

Spain 1975
UK: *Would You Kill a Child?*
US: *Island of the Damned*
Penta Films
90 minutes colour
production began 4 September 1975

. . . . . . . . . . . . . . . . . . . . . . . . . . . .

Director of Photography: José Luis
Alcaine; Art Director: Ramiro Gómez;
Editors: Juan Serra, Antonio Ramírez de
Loaysa; Sound: Julio Calvo, Sebastián
Cabezas; Music: Waldo de los Ríos; Make-
up: Fernando Florido; Special Effects:
Juan Antonio Balandín; Screenplay: Luis
Peñafiel [Narciso Ibáñez Serrador],
based on the novel *El juego de los niños*
by Juan José Plans; Executive Producer:

Manuel Salvador; Director: Narcisco
Ibáñez Serrador

Lewis Fiander (Tom); Prunella Ransome (Evelyn);
Antonio Iranzo (father at Fonda la Estrella);
Miguel Narros (coastguard captain); Ma Luisa
Arias; Luis Ciges (Enrique, boat-hire man); Marisa
Porcel (mother on other side of the island);
Juan Cazalilla (tourist information official);
Antonio Canal; Aparicio Rivero; Fabián Conde
(camera salesman); Andrés Gómez; María Druille
(daughter at Fonda la Estrella); Lourdes de la
Cámara, Roberto Nauta, José Luis Romero, Javier
de la Cámara, Marián Salgado, Cristina Torres,
Luis Mateos, Adela Blanco, Juan Carlos Romero,
Julio Jesús Parra, Carlos Parra, Juan Antonio
Balandín [Jr], Pedro Balandín (the children)

In this film by Narciso Ibáñez Serrador innocence and savagery are
combined and hurtle us towards a frightening abyss ... Serrador gave
notice of his ability to make viewers shudder in his previous work,
*La residencia*. This new effort, which is on an entirely different theme,
produces, arguably, a deeper shock. *Blanco y negro* (Madrid) 8 May 1976

What I tried to do with *Los niños* was to make a quality horror film without
clichés, a movie that, when people see it, they'll realise that the story could
have been done in an awfully gimmicky way – with blood, with lynchings,
with dismemberment – because all of that is in the script. But what
happened was, I tried to reach for a more subliminal kind of terror.
*Narciso Ibáñez Serrador* [quoted in Nuevo Fotogramas 13 February 1976]

heartbeat, applies her ear to Evie's pregnant belly.
Finally comes confirmation of what we've already
guessed. In the local supermarket, Tom's denim
flares and sneakers pad past in the background as

Serrador shows us, foregrounded in the parallel aisle, a woman's dead and possibly ravished corpse. No special fanfare, and certainly no shock-horror music sting; just the unhurried, offhand expertise referred to above, and the effect is quite chilling.

The remainder of the film suffers a brief credibility gap when Tom, having just witnessed the children's grisly piñata game, leaves Evie alone among the rattan furniture of a hotel vestibule in order to go exploring upstairs. Otherwise the action is exemplary, building steadily to two astonishing climaxes. First, the children lay siege to the local police station in which the couple have barricaded themselves; here Serrador reveals his indebtedness to both *The Birds* and *Night of the Living Dead*, but adds a uniquely gruelling coda involving Evie's unborn child – proving, if nothing else, that it would have been sensible to abort it after all. Finally, the grief-numbed Tom, in a sublimely moving early-morning set-piece, confronts the gathered children with a machine gun, after which his desperate last stand at the quayside has to be seen to be believed. Throughout, Waldo de los Ríos' tinkling nursery-rhyme score adds immensely to the overall effect.

Along the way Serrador inserts a few peculiar scraps of Spanish satire. When Tom stammers out a strange recollection of having seen *La dolce vita* and mentions that it was directed by Fellini, Evie replies, "Italian? Of course. A Fascist, just like Mussolini." After this cleverly displaced reference to General Franco, Serrador provocatively sets one of the children's nastiest crimes in a church, with the boys plucking off the clothes of a dead Dutch woman sprawled beside the font. The only false note comes right at the beginning, with an embarrassingly meretricious montage of grisly newsreel footage that purports to provide a rationale for the children's rebellion by suggesting, absurdly, that children have always come off worst in global conflicts. Happily, this epic eight-minute misjudgment can easily be skipped by those watching on DVD or Blu-ray.

As well as being a sizable hit in Spain, the film also had great things predicted for it as an export. Calling it "just off-beat enough and sufficiently ingenious that it could prove a blockbuster in all markets," *Variety* announced that "This is probably the hottest, most sellable film to come out of Spain for years."[1] These predictions weren't quite borne out, maybe because AIP got hold of the film for US distribution and slapped it with the lame title *Island of the Damned*.

In doing so, AIP were making a crass appeal to cinemagoers with long memories, echoing the 1960 'alien kids' hit *Village of the Damned*. Indeed, the combustible idea of children turning homicidal

wasn't quite new; when Serrador was making his film, *Peopletoys* (aka *Devil Times Five*), made in California back in February 1973, was still a recent memory. Subsequently, Stephen King wrote the 1977 short story *Children of the Corn*, a 2008 British film called *The Children* reheated the idea, and finally a 2012 Mexican remake of Serrador's film reverted to the title of the original novel. But no one has done it better than Serrador.

It was while Serrador's film was in post-production, in late November 1975, that Generalísimo Francisco Franco, after 36 years in power, finally died. Under a newly installed king, Juan Carlos I, the momentous period of 'transición', by which a Catholic military dictatorship became a secular democratic state, was overseen by prime minister Adolfo Suárez. Among the reforms that ensued were considerable relaxations in censorship of the arts, a circumstance that might have been thought a boon to Spain's horror fraternity. Yet it didn't quite work out that way, as we shall see.

## ABSOLUTELY DEAD STILL

After the intimations of *Through the Looking-Glass* contained in Jean-François Davy's *Le Seuil du vide*, similar Lewis Carroll echoes cropped up in several other French films of the early 1970s, though few with the nightmarish tone indulged by Davy.

Among the writer-directors invoking Carroll's transmogrified Alice was Alain Robbe-Grillet. Venerated architect of the so-called nouveau roman (new novel) in the 1950s, Robbe-Grillet had moved from scripting Resnais' *L'Année dernière à Marienbad* to directing half-a-dozen films of his own. Amid the hints of the supernatural found in such titles as *L'Immortelle* (The Immortal Woman, 1962), the increasing emphasis throughout these pictures was on Robbe-Grillet's fantasies of domination and submission – fantasies so extreme that towards the end of his life he would be referred to by literary critic Frédéric Beigbeder as 'Gilles de Rais-Grillet'.[2] Such fantasies were well to the fore in *Glissements progressifs du plaisir* (Successive Slidings of Pleasure), which Robbe-Grillet made in summer 1973 and subsequently turned into a hybrid form of his own invention – a ciné-roman. It was in this guise that he called his transgressive heroine (who goes unnamed in the film itself) Alice.

Ambiguity and an utter disavowal of linear narrative – founding principles of the nouveau roman – are the shifting sands on which Robbe-Grillet builds a long series of slippery, surreal images. Vaguely identifying its incarcerated, doe-eyed heroine (Anicée Alvina) as a sorceress, the film gives us fragmented glimpses of her impassive rebellion against male authority figures (judicial, clerical), and the key note throughout is sexual sadism. A broken bottle, Exhibit A in a murder investigation, is symbolically housed in a box lined with red silk; the heroine creates a sort of modern art-miscarriage when slathering Olga Georges-Picot's naked body in egg yolks and red cordial; a mannequin with added pubic hair and multiple bleeding gashes is chained to a bed-frame on a beach; martyred nudes are tethered in the stews with stripes and brands and bites. There's even a dash of nunsploitation, a sub-genre at that point just getting into gear in Italy – the very country where, reportedly by order of the Vatican, Robbe-Grillet's film was most thoroughly suppressed.

This, of course, was a thrilling vindication for Robbe-Grillet, who knew exactly the well-heeled demographic that would patronise his avant-garde provocations most avidly. "Good middle-class people do not dare see an erotic film," he maintained. "But if, on the other hand, they have a cultural alibi by saying, 'Oh, it's an Alain Robbe-Grillet film,' they go, but for unspoken reasons."[3]

Where French invocations of *Alice's Adventures in Wonderland* and *Through the Looking-Glass* were concerned, the real art-house succès d'éstime was Jacques Rivette's *Céline et Julie vont en bateau* (Céline and Julie Go Boating) – released, like Robbe-Grillet's film, in 1974. By plunging his heroines into an alternate reality, and placing a modified haunted house at the centre of the surrealist action, Rivette established a template that would be followed by his former Nouvelle Vague colleagues Louis Malle and Claude Chabrol. Malle's *Black Moon* – which places 15-year-old British actress Cathryn Harrison in a post-apocalyptic mansion and confronts her with, among other things, a heavily symbolic unicorn – started production in November 1974, while Chabrol's *Alice ou la dernière fugue* (Alice or the Final Flight) followed in September 1976, submitting the Dutch sex symbol Sylvia Kristel to a death reverie in a haunted estate. In the interim, writer-director Eduardo de Gregorio made *Sérail* in December 1975, coolly observing the gradual collapse of a British novelist (Corin Redgrave) when domiciled in a devouring Gothic château presided over in turn by Bulle Ogier, Marie-France Pisier and Leslie Caron. Significantly, Ogier and Pisier had previously appeared in Rivette's *Céline et Julie*, a film that de Gregorio co-wrote.

The most digestible of these labyrinthine narratives – which acknowledges its *Looking-Glass* derivation even in its heroine's name, Alice Carroll – is the Chabrol film, a picture so firmly in the 'fantastique' bracket it came as a disagreeable surprise to longtime Chabrol followers. Here was a director fêted for a series of queasy anatomisations of the bourgeoisie conceived with

spider-like, often Hitchcockian cunning, most famously his 1969 study of a Dordogne serial killer, *Le Boucher* (The Butcher). Yet here he was making a film in which Kristel flees from her boorish husband and fetches up in a mysterious country house whose saturnine butler (Jean Carmet) points out that "We don't attach much importance to time here." Kristel's attempted flight from the house is attended by a scattering of dead sparrows, her reading matter includes a very carefully selected copy of Borges' magic-realist *Ficciones*, and it becomes obvious very quickly that she's trapped in the kind of inescapable domain familiar from Kümel's *Malpertuis* and Bava's *Lisa e il diavolo*.

Given Kristel's notoriety as *Emmanuelle*, Chabrol takes the opportunity to throw in an entirely unnecessary full-frontal scene. Otherwise, the film occupies a kind of airless atmosphere all its own, with its circular pattern of non-incident much enriched by Chabrol's regular composer Pierre Jansen and also by a really singular casting coup – the way Chabrol positions the smoothly immaculate youth of Kristel against the wizened octogenarian visage of Charles Vanel. Vanel crops up a couple of times as the avuncular master of the house, eventually explaining to the puzzled Kristel that "This is the place where souls arise from Hell and take on human form. Amusing, isn't it?" Chabrol opened the film with a written dedication 'à la mémoire de Fritz Lang', who had just died. As for Chabrol's vague foundation in Lewis Carroll, this was amusingly nailed by British critic Michael Darvell, who pointed out that the story "takes off from a young woman's involvement in a car crash, making it rather more of an *Alice Through the Windscreen*."[4]

Sylvia Kristel, trapped in the airless atmosphere of *Alice ou la dernière fugue* (1976)

# LE LOCATAIRE

Apartment dwellers Jo Van Fleet and Lila Kedrova, plus policeman Jean-Pierre Bagot, watch a suicidal display in *Le Locataire* (1975)

France 1975
UK / US: **The Tenant**
Marianne Productions
126 minutes colour
production began 14 November 1975

. . . . . . . . . . . . . . . . . . . . . . . . . . . . . .

Director of Photography: Sven Nykvist; Production Designer: Pierre Guffroy; Editor: Françoise Bonnot; Sound: Jean-Pierre Ruh, Robert Rietty [English-language dub]; Music: Philippe Sarde; Make-up: Didier Lavergne; Optical Effects: Jean Fouchet; Screenplay: Gérard Brach, Roman Polanski, based on the novel *Le Locataire chimérique* by Roland Topor; Producer: Andrew Braunsberg; Director: Roman Polanski

Roman Polanski (Trelkovsky) [uncredited]; Isabelle Adjani (Stella); Melvyn Douglas (Monsieur Zy); Jo Van Fleet (Mme Dioz); Bernard Fresson

(Scope); Shelley Winters (the concierge); Lila Kedrova (Mme Gaderian); Claude Dauphin (husband at accident); Claude Piéplu (neighbour); Rufus (Georges Badar); Romain Bouteille (Simon); Jacques Monod (café owner); Patrice Alexsandre (Robert); Jean-Pierre Bagot (policeman); Josiane Balasko (office worker); Michel Blanc (Scope's neighbour); Florence Blot (Mme Zy); Louba Chazel [Louba Guertchikoff] (wife at accident); Jacques Chevalier (patron); Jacky Cohen (Stella's friend); Alain David [David Gabison] (witness at accident); Bernard-Pierre Donnadieu (bar waiter); Alain Frerot (beggar); Raoul Guylad (priest); Eva Ionesco (Bettina Gaderian); Gérard Jugnot (office clerk); Héléna Manson (head nurse); Maïté Nahyr (Lucille); André Penvern (café waiter); Gérard Pereira (drunk); Dominique Poulange (Simone Choule); Arlette Reinberg (tramp); Jacques Rosny (Jean-Claude); Serge Spira (Philippe); Vanessa Vaylord (Martine); François Viaur (police sergeant)

Polanski, like a terrier with a particularly juicy bone, worries his story half to death ... The internal logic without which such a phantasmagoria can never work is fatally loosened in the cumulative effort to give us the creeps. But it is still, at the very least, a superior horror story. One to be remembered rather better, perhaps, for its parts than as a whole.
*The Guardian 26 August 1976*

The book was so French, and I decided right from the start that it must be kept Parisian and not [be] adapted for the States ... Those Parisian circles of bourgeois apartments, there are just such places. And yes, the world is quite hostile, particularly to strangers, to people who are in any way different than the rest. The French do not like being the object of satire, especially from an outsider. *Roman Polanski* [quoted in *Cinefantastique* Winter 1977]

Redirecting claustrophobic narratives like Chabrol's into the path of true nightmare, Roman Polanski concocted a picture that strongly recalled Davy's *Le Seuil du vide*, though with a male protagonist rather than a female one. In autumn 1975, Polanski was resident in Paris and hadn't made a film in very nearly two years. But the last one, *Chinatown*, had been a major hit. Recalling a novel that had first been offered to him a decade earlier, Polanski put in a call to Paramount on 2 October and pitched an adaptation of Roland Topor's *Le Locataire chimérique*. A mere six weeks elapsed before production began at Studios d'Épinay.

Topor's book – which, as noted earlier, appears to have been much influenced by the novel on which *Le Seuil du vide* was based – was duly adapted with scrupulous fidelity by Polanski and his old collaborator Gérard Brach. One of their few notable changes was to remove the 'chimérique' (illusory) tag from the tenant of the title, calling their film merely *Le Locataire* (The Tenant). Coincidentally, the Topor original was first published in 1964, the year in which Polanski and Brach had concocted *Repulsion*, a film with a very similar scenario of mental disintegration in an enclosed apartment. In the interim Polanski had made *Rosemary's Baby*, exchanging the South Kensington apartment block of *Repulsion* for a Manhattan brownstone. Now that this recurrent theme was transferred yet again, this time to a singularly inhospitable Paris immeuble, Polanski was ready to give the scenario its most disconcerting expression yet.

*Paris, 1975. Trelkovsky is an expatriate Pole who's set his heart on an unappetising apartment at 39 Rue de Calais. The previous tenant, Simone Choule, recently defenestrated herself but Trelkovsky seems unfazed; indeed, he visits this complete stranger in hospital and in the process meets her grieving friend Stella. When Simone dies he finally moves in. But he quickly feels oppressed – not just by his crotchety neighbours, but also by the dead woman's pervasive spirit.*

For many critics, Polanski's third indulgence of what might loosely be termed his apartment complex was one indulgence too many, providing an excellent opportunity to indulge their own condescensing attitude towards horror films. "*The Tenant* might have made a decent little 20-minute sketch for one of those British horror anthology films in which Christopher Lee, Peter Cushing and Vincent Price pick up a little loose change," wrote an American critic. "As a film by Polanski, it's unspeakably disappointing."[5] Exactly the same sentiment was expressed in the UK, with one reviewer lamenting the film's descent into "horror movie hysteria" and concluding that "The effects might have seemed quite good in a Hammer movie, but from a director of Polanski's reputation one hopes for more."[6] In retrospect, these judgments seem not just snobbish but inexplicable, for in this film Polanski crafted one of the truly great explorations of middle-class paranoia.

Though closely based on someone else's novel, the film's setting was obviously meaningful for Polanski. Not only had he lived in a very similar Paris apartment in the early 1960s, he'd also been confined, 20 years before, to a four-family ground-floor flat in the Krakow ghetto. The genteel squalor of the building itself was therefore crucial to the film's effect, with nearly a quarter of Polanski's $2.2 million budget allotted to a massive set built at Épinay, which was photographed in suitably gloomy hues by Ingmar Bergman's collaborator, Sven Nykvist. Also crucial was the casting of Trelkovsky – and, in taking on the role himself, Polanski couldn't have chosen better. As well as being adept at cringe-inducing comedy (the attempts of this well-meaning misfit to control an overflowing bin bag or remove dog dirt from his shoe

recall Stan Laurel), he also spirals into cross-dressing madness with aplomb, helping to paper over a mid-film transition that's otherwise a little too abrupt.

To play the weird denizens of Trelkovsky's building, Polanski engaged an eye-catching trio of ageing Hollywood names – Melvyn Douglas as waspish landlord Monsieur Zy, Shelley Winters as the blowsy concierge, and Jo Van Fleet as a chalk-faced Little Hitler called Mme Dioz. In Trelkovsky's final breakdown, he confuses Douglas' wizened face with that of his French contemporary Claude Dauphin, who pops up briefly as a well-meaning Paris motorist. And at the opposite end of the film the main theme is explicitly announced when Héléna Manson appears briefly as a hatchet-faced nurse – pretty much the same role she played 32 years earlier in Clouzot's paranoid classic *Le Corbeau*.

It's at the hospital that Trelkovsky meets the traumatised Stella (an early showcase for the 20-year-old Isabelle Adjani). The mummified Simone is conspicuously missing a front tooth and, in response to their well-wishing, she lets out several prolonged and truly bloodcurdling screams. After this, Polanski tightens the screw on viewer discomfort by playing much of the action for a queasy kind of black comedy. But the image of the bandaged Simone, recalling both Franju's *Les Yeux sans visage* and the latterday Hammer horror *Blood from the Mummy's Tomb*, continues to nag at the back of the viewer's mind. Then comes Simone's funeral, bringing with it Trelkovsky's first hallucination, in which the presiding minister waxes lyrical about putrefaction and tells his listeners that "The graveyard is where you belong."

Having moved in to Simone's flat, Trelkovsky makes several ominous discoveries, among them Simone's missing tooth embedded in the living room wall and the fact that the other tenants stand "absolutely dead still" in the communal lavatory for hours at a time. He also picks up hints about the dead woman's preoccupations. Through these we begin to realise that the film is a sardonic exercise in the possession theme that was so popular in the 1970s. Polanski gives no special emphasis to the Nefertiti busts decorating the apartment, or the copy of Théophile Gautier's *Le Roman de la momie* that Simone left behind at a friend's place. These Egyptological hints (not present in Topor's novel) only become concrete when Trelkovsky receives a postcard intended for Simone – a postcard purchased "from the Egyptian department at the Louvre" – and Polanski finally grants us a close-up of the upright sarcophagus depicted on it.

With soul transmigration (Egyptian or otherwise) on the agenda, the word 'tenant' begins to take on a terrible double-meaning, as becomes clear when Trelkovsky, succumbing to a fever-dream, staggers down the corridor to the lavatory. The wall is covered in carefully chiselled hieroglyphs, and when Trelkovsky looks out of the window he sees himself staring back from his apartment. Returning there, he makes his way through bizarrely enlarged furniture to the window, where he sees Simone, swathed in bandages, staring back from the lavatory. Deftly unwinding herself, she grins toothlessly in Trelkovsky's direction in arguably the most disturbing use of the doppelgänger motif cinema has to offer.

Though the film is about 20 minutes too long, Polanski's strange details sustain interest, notably a series of extremely ominous, and entirely unexplained, posters dotted around Paris; bearing the slogan 'La Peinture lure' (The Painting Lure), they were created by Roland Topor himself. Polanski also ensures that the action builds to a terrifying and tragically inevitable climax. Here, Trelkovsky makes his last defiant gesture while imagining the communal courtyard as a gilded auditorium, complete with opera glasses, exclusive boxes and yards of red plush. In the bloody aftermath he visualises Monsieur Zy and Mme Dioz as scaly, tongue-lashing demons, though Polanski is careful to note that the real Zy is solicitously holding out a blanket and the supposedly Nazi old lady is weeping into her handkerchief.

There follows an oneiric coda in which Trelkovsky and Simone fuse identities in the very hospital where they first encountered each other. "So he was she all along, or she was already he, or he turned out to be she, or she he. Or something,"[7] quipped the young novelist, and temporary film critic, Martin Amis. Resolutely inscrutable, Polanski merely zooms into the black hole of his own screaming mouth to emphasise the inscrutability of the self – upon which the Paramount logo reappears and the game is over.

In mid-April 1976, some six months after Polanski began shooting Le Locataire, Alain Resnais started production on Providence. Questions of identity, and the slippage between fantasy and reality, are prominent here too, with the claustrophobic paranoia of Trelkovsky paralleled by a dark night of the soul for septuagenarian British novelist Clive Langham. The film is named after the ivy-covered Gothic mansion in which Langham lives; actually the venerable Château de Montméry near Limoges, it looms large in the film's final act, when the family members who have peopled Langham's nocturnal reveries turn up for real and prove to be far better adjusted than their grotesque fantasy counterparts.

'Providence' might also refer to the home town of the American fantasist H P Lovecraft, about whom Resnais long cherished a desire to make a documentary. Far more than the drifting maybe-ghosts of L'Année dernière à Marienbad, Providence therefore includes an abundance of horrific imagery, demonstrating what Langham calls the "revolution inside my head" and "how darkness creeps into the blood." David Warner is one of several fur-faced victims of hypertrichosis, with werewolfism explicitly invoked; the suicidal Elaine Stritch is discovered floating in a bath of blood; Dirk Bogarde drives down eerie thoroughfares in what appears to be a police state; an autopsy is observed in hideous detail, and fragmented memories of the Holocaust seem to lap at the edges of Langham's imaginings. Even Bogarde's mid-life good looks are given a ghoulish tinge. Unfortunately, the dialogue by British playwright David Mercer becomes more and more gnomic and indigestible as the film goes on. Finally, Langham (played with typically mellifluous charm by John Gielgud) scrutinises a new novel by one of his rivals and twice refers to him as "old bumface." In a neat in-joke, the back-jacket author photo of old bumface is actually David Mercer.

## SACRED MONSTERS IN PARIS

Back in February 1973, Christopher Lee had been president of the jury at the first Festival International d'Avoriaz du Film Fantastique, subsequently lamenting to his fan club that Mario Bava should have sunk to the exploitative level of Antefatto, which, along with titles like Duel, Themroc and Silent Running, was one of the films on show. Lee also claimed to have been offered several new projects while in Avoriaz, among them something called Tendre Dracula ou les confessions d'un buveur de sang (Tender Dracula, or the Confessions of a Blood Drinker) for Alain Robbe-Grillet. Robbe-Grillet went on instead to make Glissements progressifs du plaisir, which has mysterious puncture marks on Olga Georges-Picot's throat but otherwise gives no indication of being made by someone who shortly beforehand was contemplating a Dracula picture.

Maybe Lee was getting his projects (and directors) mixed up. Either way, just 12 months after Lee's stint at Avoriaz, his old co-star Peter Cushing found himself starring opposite Alida Valli in a film called – you guessed it – Tendre Dracula, for untried filmmaker Pierre Grunstein. In this, the sight of Cushing taking Miou-Miou over his knee and spanking her – though pretty startling to the more shockable Cushing fans – certainly wouldn't have been strong enough for a self-proclaimed sadist like Alain Robbe-Grillet.

Also known as La Grande trouille (The Big Fright), this began shooting on 11 February 1974 and for

Peter Cushing tips
a wink to his film
industry guests in
*Tendre Dracula* (1974)

Cushing came between *The Legend of the 7 Golden Vampires* in Hong Kong and *The Ghoul* at Pinewood. That he found this bizarre project puzzling is almost a certainty, though it was also flattering in a garbled sort of way, for it conferred on him the semi-autobiographical honour previously accorded Boris Karloff in *Targets* and Vincent Price in *Madhouse*. For Cushing is McGregor, a mad actor of Scottish descent who dresses in sacramental robes and tells his screenwriter guests that "It takes more than drama courses and actors' workshops to become a high priest of horror." Despite his resolve to focus on romance in future, McGregor seems half convinced that he's a vampire; the film itself doesn't resolve this question or indeed any other. There are scraps of half-baked philosophy, bits of sex farce, musical interludes (as when Miou-Miou and Nathalie Courval, both naked, burst into excruciating song), some misplaced sadism (though not on the Robbe-Grillet level), and fragments of off-kilter comedy from Bernard Menez. The film makes zero sense from start to finish, and Cushing's uncertainty is betrayed by a few uncharacteristic bursts of shouting.

Even so, the Cushing in-jokes are engaging (a scrapbook of his own movie stills, a prominently displayed poster for *The Brides of Dracula*), and there's a genuinely atmospheric flashback in which Cushing plays McGregor's grizzled grandfather and tries to prevent his grandson from joining a troupe of strolling players. Cushing also gives tremulous life to lines that may have struck him at the time as prophetic, among them "Horror is dead and, being dead, it can no longer frighten anyone."

Despite the shambles that was *Tendre Dracula*, not forgetting the parade of farcical entries from Spain, Italy and Germany considered on page 300, it was France that finally came up with a vampire comedy that was intelligent, funny and, yes, even spooky. En route from Belgravia to Beverly Hills in March 1976, Christopher Lee paused in Paris to star in Édouard Molinaro's *Dracula père et fils* (Dracula Father and Son). Shot over an eight-week period at the Studios de Billancourt, the film was based on a 1970 novel, *Paris-vampire*, by Claude Klotz. In due course Klotz would be César-nominated for co-writing Patrice Leconte's wistful classic *Le Mari de la coiffeuse* (The Hairdresser's Husband). His skittish vampire novel, meanwhile, had been reissued by Le Livre de poche under its film title, with Lee on the cover, clutching a conspicuously large baby and looking characteristically sombre. Yet in the film itself he's at his most relaxed and playful.

## DRACULA PÈRE ET FILS

France 1976
US: *Dracula and Son*
Gaumont International / Production 2000
96 minutes colour
production began 16 March 1976

Director of Photography: Alain Levent; Art
Directors: Jacques Bufnoir, Gérard Viard;
Editors: Robert and Monique Isnardon;
Sound: Daniel Brisseau; Music: Vladimir
Cosma; Make-up and Hair: Alex and
Monique Archambault; Screenplay: Alain
Godard, Jean-Marie Poiré and Édouard
Molinaro, based on the novel *Paris-vampire*
by Claude Klotz; Producer: Alain Poiré;
Director: Édouard Molinaro

Christopher Lee (the Count); Bernard Menez
(Ferdinand Pointevin); Marie-Hélène Breillat
(Nicole Clément); Bernard Alane (Jean, Nicole's
boyfriend); Catherine Breillat (Herminie
Pointevin); Raymond Bussières (unemployed
morgue man); Mustapha Dali (Khaleb);
Jean-Claude Dauphin (Christea Polanski); Xavier
Depraz (vampire manservant); Anna Gaël (Miss
Gaylor); Claude Génia (Marguerite); Gérard
Jugnot (factory boss); Jean Lescot (man bitten
by Herminie); Anna Prucnal (Suzanna Podesti,
film star); Albert Simono (coffin vendor); Arlette
Balkis (Nicole's concierge); Geoffrey Carey
(British film director); Lyne Chardonnet (nurse);
Robert Dalban (Hôtel George V concierge); Carlo
Nell (Count's French chauffeur); Guy Piérauld
(vagrant); Jean-Marie Arnoux (morgue worker);
Jacques Boudet (Henri Verneuil, film director);
Véronique Dancier (younger prostitute); Jean-
François Dérec (Antoine, caretaker); Louise
Dhour (Marlene, older prostitute); Cédric
Dumond (Ferdinand aged five); Patrick Feigelson
(soldier); Jacques Galland (orgy motorist);
Jean-Pierre Garrigues (film producer); Jean-Yves
Gautier (ad agency boss); Jacqueline Hopstein
(old woman with cart); Colin Mann (Englishman
in bed); Henry Pillsbury (bearded trawler man);
Pierre-Olivier Scotto (waiter); Jean-Louis Tristan
(apologetic police inspector); Dominique Zardi
(policeman); uncredited: Marthe Villalonga
(woman in Métro mirror)

This film is a torrent of hilarious gags. To see Christopher Lee-Dracula
(superb and fascinating) turning down a TV toothpaste commercial, or
a famished Bernard Menez breaking a tooth on a frozen cadaver in the
morgue: believe me, it's irresistible! And the film often surpasses mere
comedy to attain the level of fable, frequently bitter: the difficulty, in 1976,
of being a vampire in a world of sharks. *Télérama* 18 September 1976

I was convinced that any adaptation [of the book] would only be interesting
if the Dracula role was played, not by some French comic actor like Jean
Lefebvre, but by a specialist … Naturally, Christopher Lee came to mind … The
problem was that he didn't want to play Dracula. Molinaro persuaded him by
saying it would be a high-class comedy like Polanski's *Dance of the Vampires*.
Bernard Menez [quoted in *Le Figaro* 12 June 2015]

Christopher Lee admires Marie-Hélène Breillat's graceful throat in *Dracula père et fils* (1976)

Born in 1784, Ferdinand is a decidedly reluctant
vampire. Nearly 200 years later he has yet to claim
a victim, despite the exasperated exhortations of
his imposing father, the Count. Driven from their
Transylvanian castle by the Communist takeover, the
two become separated in transit. Ferdinand ends up
among Arab immigrants in Paris, while the Count
becomes a fêted horror star in a London film studio.

"It required some courage to take on a genre that's
somewhat despised by French producers," noted
French critic Michel Lengliney when the film came
out, accompanying this trenchant observation with a
quote from Molinaro himself: "I've always dreamed of
making a fantasy film because it was through fantasy
that I first discovered the cinema and fell in love with
it."[8] Though best known at the time for his work with
the star comic Louis de Funès, Molinaro is in no hurry
to get round to the comedy; instead he pastes on plenty
of Gothic atmosphere in an opening reel that echoes
the introduction to Hammer's *The Brides of Dracula*.

The credits having been relayed through the vellum
leaves of an ancient candlelit book, cinematographer
Alain Levent creates a suitably atmospheric twilight
haze as a gaggle of 18th century travellers are involved
in a coach crash. "This is the land of the vampires,"
stammers the doe-eyed heroine, whereupon another
coach appears and a sinister man in a tricorn hat
announces that "The Count cannot wait to meet
his fiancée." In a neat reversal of
expectations, it's only when the haughty
Lee shows up that the comedy kicks in.
He's given a grand entrance, emerging
through a massive door that's decorated
with a bronze effigy of himself. At his first
courtly utterance of "Welcome, my dear,"
his comely guest (Catherine Breillat)
passes out on the spot.

Intriguingly, the character is at no point
called Dracula, nor does he conform to
the standard Dracula image. In brocaded
frock coat, lacy jabot and lengthy grey
wig, Lee's Count looks curiously like the
French star Michel Piccoli – who, by a
bizarre coincidence, had supplied Lee's
voice in the French release of his previous
vampire comedy, *Tempi duri per
i vampiri*. Happily, for *Dracula père et fils*
Lee speaks in beautifully nuanced French
of his own, whether patiently informing
his mirror-gazing bride that "You'll never
see yourself again; it's one of the little
inconveniences of our kind" or, decades

later, telling his adult son that "I refuse to feed you out of a bottle for the rest of your life!"

Previously paired with Peter Cushing in *Tendre Dracula*, Bernard Menez appears far more skilled as a comic actor in this more coherent context, handling some pretty obvious gags (eg, calling his exploitative boss a vampire) with aplomb. Even so, he looks sufficiently lean and hungry to make Ferdinand's furtive visits to Paris morgues and blood banks more genuinely sinister than perhaps Molinaro intended. The humour, however, remains pleasantly grim. Ferdinand breaks a fang on a stiffened corpse and, having accidentally smashed a bottle of blood, he's forced by an irate nurse to give blood himself. ("If my father could see me now," he laments. "The shame!") Elsewhere, Molinaro uses Ferdinand's predicament to satirise France's contemptuous attitude towards ghettoised immigrants, while using the Count's situation as a means of gently satirising Lee himself. Having made 'The Man from Transylvania' in London, he travels to Paris to make 'Les Amours du vampire' and is providentially reunited with Ferdinand at the airport. The idea of a vampire covertly becoming a movie star, already used in *The House that Dripped Blood* in 1970, would be recycled in the 1999 film *Shadow of the Vampire*.

Charming and sumptuous-looking though the film is, it maybe overreaches itself when the archetypal contest between father and son devolves into a battle for the affections of Nicole, a young advertising executive who tries to interest the Count in advertising Permadent toothpaste. (As noted above, the toothpaste commercial gag had previously appeared in *Tiempos duros para Drácula*.) Nicole is played by Marie-Hélène Breillat, sister of Catherine Breillat – thus facilitating the cheesy old 'reincarnation of the vampire's lost love' scenario that's used with a straight face in some other Dracula films. This 1970s ad agency subplot recalls a previous Parisian vampire film, *Le Sadique aux dents rouges*, and Albert Simono, who was a white-coated doctor in *Le Sadique*, turns up here in a very amusing cameo as a perplexed coffin salesman. Another familiar face is Jean Rollin regular Louise Dhour, who passes through as an over-ripe prostitute.

Though Molinaro is eventually defeated by the bedroom farce convolutions of the final reel, *Dracula père et fils* remains valuable for Lee's grey-faced triumph as the Count. He's not only drolly funny but also fully substantiates Nicole's claim that "You can read all the woes of the world in his face." Lee claimed at the time that "By doing this [film] I can close the door very firmly on the vampire."[9] And he did so in style.

Style, unfortunately, was of no consequence to the film's US distributor, who was also unimpressed,

presumably, by the film's box-office success in France. Calling the film *Dracula and Son*, Quartet Films Inc added a juvenile cartoon prologue, lopped the running time to 80 minutes and dubbed over a stream of dismally unfunny wisecracks, ending up with an atrocious bastardisation all their own.

## IN SPAIN AND OUT

In mid-May 1976, the Italian star Daniela Giordano arrived in Madrid to start work on *Inquisición* (Inquisition), a historical horror that marked the directorial debut of Paul Naschy. As he did when signing his scripts, he would use his real name, Jacinto Molina, in this new capacity. Venturing into the nasty witch-hunting sub-genre initiated by the Michael Reeves masterpiece *Witchfinder General*, Naschy's research involved consulting the distinguished Basque anthropologist Julio Caro Baroja. Yet the film's supposedly high-toned credentials were entirely bypassed when it came to advertising it.

Already, Naschy's previous horror, *La maldición de la bestia*, had been trumpeted with the decidedly unlovely tag-line, '¡¡Maravillosas mujeres sometidas a sádicas torturas!!' (Wondrous Women Subjected to Sadistic Tortures!!). And when *Inquisición* finally made it to Spanish cinemas in late April 1977, it too was advertised with a line seemingly pitched at a relatively small demographic of sexual sadists: 'Las más crueles suplicios sexuales en el cuerpo de una mujer' (The cruellest sexual tortures [inflicted] on a woman's body).

> South-western France in the late 16th century. As plague rages nearby, Grand Inquisitor Bernard de Fossey arrives in Perignac with two colleagues. Though convinced that "the Evil One tends to employ women for his dark deeds," he's immediately smitten by Catherine, one of the mayor's three daughters. When Catherine's fiancé Jean is murdered, she resorts to a dream potion provided by a local sorceress and is granted a vision of the man responsible – de Fossey.

"We were told," reported a gossip columnist when covering the film's start-of-shooting party, "that *Inquisición* has nothing to do with horror but will be based on genuine history."[10] Inevitably playing de Fossey himself, Naschy's chief inspiration appears to have been Pierre de Lancré, a French witchfinder of Basque extraction whose surname he'd already used in *El espanto surge de la tumba* and *El mariscal del infierno*. Indeed, the film boasts a patina of genuine antiquity, with art director Gumersindo Andrés turning in tremendous work and Spanish locations like Abadía and Colmenar Viejo giving a convincing impression of

Daniela Giordano dedicates herself to dark forces in *Inquisición* (1976)

# INQUISICIÓN

Spain 1976
US: **Inquisition**
Ancla Century Films / Anubis Films
86 minutes colour
production began mid-May 1976

.......................................

Director of Photography: Miguel F Mila;
Art Directors: Augusto Fenollar,
Gumersindo Andrés; Editor: Soledad
López; Sound: Enrique Molinero, Luis
Castro; Music: Máximo Baratas; Make-up:
Fernando Florido; Special Effects: Pablo
Pérez; Executive Producer: Roberto P Moreno;

Writer-Director: Jacinto Molina
[Paul Naschy]

Paul Naschy (Bernard de Fossey / Satan);
Daniela Giordano (Catherine); Mónica Randall
(Madeleine); Ricardo Merino (Nicolas Rodier);
Tony Isbert (Pierre Burgot); Juan Luis Galiardo
(Jean Duprat); Antonio Casas (Arman, Catherine's
father); Julia Saly (Elvire); Antonio Iranzo
(Rénover); Eduardo Calvo (Émile, the surgeon);
Tota Alba (Mabille); María Salerno; Eva León
(Pierril Fillé); Loreta Tovar (Odile Dufrain); Jenny
O'Neil, Isabel Luque (lady's maids); Belén Cristino

**A gruesome story set in 16th century France, in which the love affair between a young witch and an inquisitor serves as a pretext for scenes of nudity and crude eroticism, marinated with 'Devil worship' and inquisitorial ravings.**
ABC Sevilla 24 April 1977

> My favourite film is Inquisition, directed by Paul Naschy. Because, finally, mine was a real concrete character and because I liked the story. I hoped with this film to do another step toward good quality of films … Unfortunately, Inquisition was not sold in Italy and my agent at that time was not smart enough to take advantage of the success of Inquisition in Spain. We knew about the success of the film only one year later.
> Daniela Giordano [quoted in *The Spaghetti Western Database* 8 April 2013]

old France. But the 'has nothing to do with horror' line was completely disingenuous, as readers of that gossip column were probably aware even at the time. Horror was meat and drink to Naschy and, accordingly, the film's very first shot discloses a mouldering, worm-eaten skeleton dangling from a tree, with half-a-dozen other skeletal husks scattered at its feet and a cart rolling by filled with plague victims.

Later, Naschy is careful to introduce the hallucinogenic potion administered by the old sorceress, Mabille; that way he's able to indulge in a couple of the fantastical set-pieces he so adored. Both are studiedly theatrical, existing in some empty, black-edged space suffused with red drapery and with roiling white fog underfoot. First a horned Belphegor, with red light bulbs for eyes, scores Catherine's cheek with his claws, then the red-robed Devil himself (Naschy in a dual role) watches dispassionately as a naked girl has her throat cut.

These visions can be glossed as just that – visions – but their illusory quality doesn't alter the fact that Naschy portrays witchcraft as a genuine force resorted to by "desperate unfortunates in their revolt against hunger and sickness, misery and tyranny." This was ground already covered by the British directors Michael Reeves, Michael Armstrong and Ken Russell, all of whom stressed the fact that witchcraft was itself an illusion – merely a pious pretext for opportunist, state-sanctioned sadists to get their kicks by terrorising young women. But Naschy wants to have his cake and eat it too. He wants to show the venal hypocrite de Fossey poring over his personal copy of the *Malleus Maleficarum* as if it were his own special brand of pornography. ("There exist 72 infernal princes," he drools, "who hold command over 7000 demons...") But Naschy also wants to show his heroine, Catherine, dedicating herself to those demons in order to destroy the Inquisitor.

The result is a fatal rupture in audience identification. Catherine is a wronged woman and de Fossey a torturing monster, but we're also encouraged to see them as a conniving enchantress and a man 'ensnared' by a woman's witchy wiles. Perhaps a different director would have tried to straighten out this fundamental confusion. Or perhaps not. By 1976 Naschy was a bona-fide 'brand' and his expertise was unquestioned.

Another thing Naschy wanted to show was Daniela Giordano in the nude as she goes about her ritualistic invocations. Nudity abounds elsewhere too, and it's strictly of the top-shelf exploitation variety. Very early on we see a nubile nude covered in hideous plague sores (an image catering to a very specific taste); later we see plenty of rack-stretched girls with perfectly plucked armpits, all of whom are coated in sweat that's really *Penthouse*-style baby oil. One of them even has one of her nipples clipped off with giant pincers. Needless to say, this kind of slavering sadism does little to support Naschy's claims to historical seriousness.

*Inquisición* has other problems, chief among them love scenes between Catherine and Jean that were presumably intended as chivalric romance of a peculiarly Hispanic sort; unfortunately they just come over as sappy soap opera. Yet, confused script notwithstanding, the film is lavishly appointed, efficiently directed and contains a few genuinely striking compositions. Mabille's hut, in particular, is an intricately designed space that teems with arcane detail and is worthy of Benjamin Christensen's silent drama-documentary *Häxan*. It's also pleasant to spend time with familiar character actors like Julia Saly, Antonio Iranzo, Eduardo Calvo, Antonio Casas and Tota Alba. Of these, Iranzo had recently been one of only two adults encountered on Almanzora in Serrador's *¿Quién puede matar a un niño?* (and in the process he made the most of one of the film's best scenes), and Alba had played the grotesque witch in Ossorio's *La endemoniada*, making her an obvious choice to play Mabille.

By the time *Inquisición* reached Spanish cinemas in May 1977, the former flood of indigenous horror had slowed to a mere trickle, so Naschy's film didn't have a great deal of competition in emerging as the year's most successful local shocker. Following close behind it, however, was *Pecado mortal* (Mortal Sin), a debut feature from Miguel Ángel Díez in which Naschy had a cameo role as a passing police inspector. A lame retread of the old 'male stranger intrudes into cloistered lives of three strange women' routine (which Naschy himself had gone through not

long before in *Los ojos azules de la muñeca rota*), the film came out in July and owed much of its success to the post-Franco opportunity to uncover acres of nudity, almost exclusively female. The opportunity would be seized upon all the more avidly when Adolfo Suárez's government formally abolished censorship on 11 November, a liberating measure that brought with it an enticing new certificate, with a flood of pictures bearing the come-hither legend 'clasificada S'.

The following month Spanish filmgoers were presented with a new horror picture, Miguel Iglesias' *Desnuda inquietud* (Naked Anxiety), which cast the German-born softcore queen Nadiuska as a suspected witch. Reincarnated from an Aztec original, she captivates amateur parapsychologist Ramiro Oliveros but is chiefly required to strip off, as the Profilmes publicists put it, for 'the most risqué scenes yet seen in Spanish cinema'. In practice, however, the 'S' certificate, and the swarm of sex films it unleashed, was instrumental in further diminishing public interest in homegrown horror; after so many years, the genie was out of the bottle and for a while sex, not horror, was considered the only worthwhile selling point. As a result, León Klimovsky's *Tres días de noviembre* (Three Days in November), completed at the beginning of April 1976 but unreleased until February the following year, played to only middling houses. Which was a shame, given Klimovsky's smooth development of a Luis Murillo story in which paraplegic Maribel Martín is delivered to a clinic run by an insane, white-coated 'fear therapist', played with all his customary suavity by Narciso Ibáñez Menta.

Unfazed, Paul Naschy made his second film as writer-director-star in November 1977. This was *El huerto del francés* (The Frenchman's Garden), a soberly effective dramatisation, co-written with the redoubtable Antonio Fos, of a conspicuously grim murder spree from Spain's rural past, ending with a double-execution at Halloween 1906. Naschy is the serial-killing mastermind, a supposed Frenchman murdering for profit and depositing his victims beneath the tomato plants adjacent to his Peñaflor tavern. (Much of the film was shot on the actual locations.) Naschy took third billing on the advertising to the beauteous duo of José María Cantudo and Agata Lys. 'Face to face, the two most exciting women in Spanish cinema!' leered the posters, as well as itemising the film's come-hither ingredients as 'Sexo... Amor... Sadismo... Homosexualidad'. In the finished film, however, it's the luminous Julia Saly who's the woman to watch. Naschy also cast two distinguished veterans of *La marca del hombre lobo*, Carlos Casaravilla and José Nieto; he bludgeons the second of these very comprehensively with a mallet.

The following year, Naschy infused a great deal more fun into one of his most accomplished films, casting himself as a sociopathic 16th century vagabond in El caminante (The Traveller). Taking on a naïve young servant called Tomás (David Rocha), Leonardo cheats, whores and murders his way to the top and back again, finally identifying himself as "the Devil in the flesh." Naschy made a similar pronouncement ten years previously in La marca del hombre lobo, only this time he really means it. To emphasise the point, Alejandro Ulloa's handsome cinematography bathes Naschy in a hellish red for all his most diabolical manoeuvres.

The film's cynical view of the human race is crystallised in the wanderer's contention that "The past was no better, nor will the future be," whereupon he gives the boy a nightmare vision consisting of 21st century newsreel footage. Despite these baleful asides, the film backpedals on horror. It achieves, instead, the whimsical flavour of a rural folk tale, even breaking out into Benny Hill-style fast motion

Afternoon tea for Dr Orloff: Klaus Kinski as Jack the Ripper – Der Dirnenmörder von London (1976)

during a skirt-chasing spell in a brothel. The script (co-written by novelist Eduarda Targioni) abounds in crude but eminently quotable one-liners, as when Leonardo expresses wonderment at the money an obese nobleman is prepared to pay for sex with Tomás. "No arsehole on Earth is worth a hundred ducats," he muses, adding craftily, "Come to think of it, no friendship is worth a hundred ducats either..." Simultaneously relaxed and swashbuckling, Naschy has never looked more like a leading man than here.

While Naschy remained firmly wedded to Spain, Jess Franco continued his unpredictable adventures well away from it. Hooking up in the mid-1970s with the Swiss producer Erwin C Dietrich, he turned out a steady stream of 'women in prison' sexploiters but also Das Bildnis der Doriana Gray (The Picture of Doriana Gray) and Jack the Ripper – Der Dirnenmörder von London (Jack the Ripper – the Harlot Killer of London). The first of these, also known as Die Marquise von Sade, is an enervated revision of Vampyros Lesbos, with Monica Swinn interviewing the reclusive millionairess Lina Romay, whose identical twin sister is incarcerated in an asylum (proprietor: Dr Orloff). Awash in tediously extended (and, in the hardcore version, conspicuously ugly) sex scenes, this one writes its own epitaph when the millionairess claims that her life is "an eternal to-and-fro between lethal boredom and wild desire."

Shot in June 1976, the Ripper project promised much; with Franco at the helm and Klaus Kinski in the title role, one might reasonably have expected sparks to fly. But they stubbornly don't. Effectively a remake of Gritos en la noche (the Ripper is here called Dr Dennis Orloff), the film feels embalmed by an excess of period detail that isn't even convincing; the ballerina heroine, for example, wears modern leotards and leg-warmers. Yet for British viewers the attempts to make Zürich look like 1880s London are consistently entertaining. A lop-sided street sign reading 'St Petersburgh Place' is rendered in the municipal style of the 1970s, a proudly displayed Royal Cypher reads ER rather than VR, and the Schanzengraben (into which plenty of bloody body parts are dumped) doesn't stand a chance of looking like the Thames.

In addition to pumping oodles of dry ice across his locations, Franco introduces the faithful Lina Romay via a close-up of her bare arse. Channelling Linda Darnell in John Brahm's Hangover Square, she's a music-hall chanteuse who falls foul of the Ripper in a public park, and her death, though laughably synthetic, is authentically revolting. Haunted by memories of a prostitute mother, this Ripper has a penchant not just for rape but also for cutting women's breasts off in his Botanical Gardens hideaway. A sage old blind man suggests that "He suffers from the particular kind of madness that borders on genius" and nominates him as "more victim than executioner." It would be tough for any actor to embody this contradiction in a picture as flat and flavourless as this, and Kinski (who filmed all his scenes in just seven days) walks through with every sign of indifference bordering on contempt.

Later in 1976, again for Dietrich, Franco returned to nunsploitation with one of his best-looking films, *Die Liebesbriefe einer portugiesischen Nonne* (Love Letters of a Portuguese Nun). Here, Susan Hemingway is a type familiar from Franco's De Sade adaptations – the guileless 17th century teen who is inducted into a convent full of Devil worshippers. Franco skewers religious hypocrisy with infectious abandon, especially via the loathsome zealots played by William Berger and Ana Zanatti, but he's less persuasive when presenting the Devil himself in the guise of Herbert Fux. Taking the girl ritualistically from behind, Fux is dressed in the kind of folkloric cloak and hood that Paul Naschy's Satan had recently worn in *Inquisición* – the same look, roughly speaking, adopted by Henry Irving's Mephistopheles back in the 1880s. Irving and Naschy, however, weren't lumbered with an absurd rubber uni-horn pasted to their foreheads. Fux had previously played Satan, incidentally, in *Der Teufel in*

Ulla Berkévicz as the shockingly abused avenger of *Geburt der Hexe* (1977)

*Miss Jonas*, a limp softcore response – directed by Erwin Dietrich himself – to the hardcore landmark *The Devil in Miss Jones*.

Theoretically in the same sphere as Franco's *Liebesbriefe* film, though in fact a million miles removed, was a Swiss-German item called *Geburt der Hexe* (Birth of the Witch) – co-produced, curiously enough, by an old Franco associate called Karl-Heinz Mannchen. This was made by the celebrated theatre director Wilfried Minks in 1977, though it would remain unseen until 1980. Beginning with a 'young man ploughing a field' vignette recalling the British film *Blood on Satan's Claw*, Minks' film develops into a sombre and extremely compelling portrait of Middle Ages barbarity, with Minks himself playing the oppressive overlord and Minks' then-wife Ulla Berkévicz as a young woman who, after suffering gang rapes and other atrocities, turns to witchcraft. The bleak landscapes are beautifully rendered by cinematographer Jochen Richter and Minks' observation of arcane ritual is second to none – vultures roosting on branches as the overlord receives tribute in the marketplace, the woman hammering new nails into an effigy of Christ on the cross, and the duplicitous priest leading the villagers in a mountaintop ritual at least as weird as the one in Brunello Rondi's *Il demonio*. Berkévicz's ferociously committed performance is remarkable, and the conclusion – in which the overlord is overthrown at the expense of the woman's martyrdom – is grimly powerful.

As an art-house parable of social revolution Minks' film would make a neat, albeit rather depressing, double-feature with Hans W Geissendörfer's *Jonathan*. For the hardiest souls of all, a third film to add to the bill might be Mark Rissi's *Die schwarze Spinne* (The Black Spider), a 1983 release that, somewhat surprisingly, became one of the most successful Swiss films of the decade. Adapting Jeremias Gotthelf's classic 1842 novella (previously filmed in Germany in 1920), Rissi concedes centre stage to the formidable Christine (splendidly played by Beatrice Kessler), who misguidedly calls on the Devil to assist the local farmers in appeasing their feudal lord – but the Devil's kiss implants a hideous running sore on her cheek, which puts forth legs and becomes a plague-bearing tarantula. Rissi's climactic scenes of the creature attaching itself to a jester's cap and bells, or alighting on the bald head of the terrified overlord, or advancing across the white counterpane of a baby in its crib, are truly alarming. Rissi also imposes a modern, and rather less effective, frame on Gotthelf's story, with a bunch of junkies breaking into a chemical laboratory to the strains of an up-to-the-minute score by the Swiss electronic trio Yello. The hazmat-suited functionaries here are reminiscent of Romero's *The Crazies* and Cronenberg's *Rabid*.

## VOICE FROM THE GRAVE

Back in December 1972, Nicolas Roeg had begun shooting an Anglo-Italian co-production called *Don't Look Now*, in which a profoundly bereaved young couple (Julie Christie, Donald Sutherland) are set down amid the spectral desolation of out-of-season Venice when the husband is commissioned to restore an old church. With Roeg staining his elliptical narrative in premonitory daubs of blood red and the psychic-yet-blinkered hero hastening to a truly appalling fate, the film is as powerful a distillate of tragic inevitability as the cinema has achieved, a point not lost on the more ambitious of Italy's indigenous filmmakers. The choice of Venice as the setting for Mario Lanfranchi's *Il bacio* in early 1974 was almost certainly prompted by *Don't Look Now*, and two years later the Roeg film's growing reputation seems to have been the spur behind a couple of Italian quasi-ghost stories also set there.

Marcello Aliprandi directed *Un sussurro nel buio* (A Whisper in the Dark) at the nearby Villa Condulmer in February 1976, with John Phillip Law and Nathalie Delon as the well-heeled parents of a 12-year-old boy whose imaginary friend, Luca, might be the shade of a deceased elder brother. According to little Martino, Luca claims that "The scariest thing about death is finding yourself in a place full of horrible people." A therapeutic father-and-son trip to Venice avails nothing so a peculiar child psychiatrist is called in and promptly gets electrocuted in his bath. (Fernando Rey was announced for this rather negligible role but Joseph Cotten stepped in at the last minute.) Aliprandi teases the viewer as to Luca's culpability or otherwise; Claudio Cirillo's camera, meanwhile, caresses the fog and snow of the haunted estate and Pino Donaggio's score provides an elegiac accompaniment. But the melancholy tone eventually turns soporific, and the

Tongue-lolling insanity in a Venetian attic: Vittorio Gassman
in *Anima persa* (1976)

ending – an exorcism of sorts, in which Delon merely opens the gates and lets Luca out – is a damp squib.

In May of the same year Dino Risi was in Venice to direct an Italian-French co-production – again involving a phantom brother – called *Anima persa* (Lost Soul). Adapting a 1966 Giovanni Arpino novel, Risi moved the setting from Turin and devised a tremendous central role of the Jekyll-Hyde variety for the magnificent Vittorio Gassman. Temporarily domiciled in a haunted Venetian palazzo with a couple of distant relatives, 19-year-old art student Tino (Danilo Mattei) is perplexed by the stiff-backed Fabio (Gassman) and his downtrodden young wife Sofia (Catherine Deneuve), as well as being intrigued by a host of Gothic signifiers, among them piano music at dead of night and a concealed upper room. "Don't ever go up there," he's warned. "The staircase is rotten."

Fabio is an immaculately dressed, Strindberg-quoting misogynist, proud of his German ancestry and regularly reciting from Goethe and Hölderlin. His own pronouncements are eminently quotable, whether he's dismissing 1970s youth as "rootless vagabonds, victims of their own hair" or lamenting that "Churches are deserted. Only cinemas are full." It's quickly revealed that the upper room harbours a rouged, tongue-waggling madman – Fabio's entomologist brother, who fell prey to delusions of his face slipping off. The crumbling house looms over the canals just as Poe's House of Usher loomed over its tarn, husband and wife refer to themselves as decaying corpses lashed together for eternity, and the outcome regarding the 'Professor' upstairs isn't hard to work out. The resolution nevertheless acquires tragic stature, in part through Francis Lai's mournful music but mainly through Gassman's moving performance. Risi and Gassman had won several awards for a previous Arpino adaptation, *Profumo di donna* (Scent of a Woman). Puzzlingly, *Anima persa* received not a single nomination.

While Dino Risi was making *Anima persa*, Pupi Avati was shooting *La casa dalle finestre che ridono* (The House with Laughing Windows) in his native Emilia-Romagna. Though some way from Venice, Avati still managed to incorporate an echo of *Don't Look Now*, in that his guileless protagonist has been engaged to restore a fresco in a local church. In fact, the theme of the past intruding into the present via the restoration of ancient artefacts was an old one in Italian Gothic, with the professional heroes of *La cripta e l'incubo*, *La vendetta di Lady Morgan* and *Un angelo per Satana* all engaged in such work, together with the more recent example of amateur David Hemmings chipping away at a concealed mural in Argento's

*Profondo rosso*. Avati's restorer was played by Lino Capolicchio, a David award-winner for De Sica's *Il giardino dei Finzi Contini* (The Garden of the Finzi-Continis), and the heroine by the 20-year-old future screenwriter Francesca Marciano.

> *Emilia-Romagna, circa 1950. Stefano, engaged to restore two occluded figures in a church fresco of Saint Sebastian, learns that the artist, Buono Legnani, was known as 'the Painter of the Agonies' and that he set fire to himself nearly 20 years before. Looking into the matter with a young teacher called Francesca, he begins to suspect that Legnani's two crazed sisters might still be alive. He's also taken by an alcoholic taxi driver to a mass grave containing Legnani's former subjects...*

Avati's film starts with an amber-tinged flashback that's as grisly as it is unsettling. A suspended, half-naked young man is repeatedly stabbed by a pair of white-robed aggressors against what looks like a shore line – though, given the creepy obfuscation of the image, it could just as easily be a painted backdrop *depicting* a shore line. Later we'll realise that we're seeing a tableau vivant recreating Saint Sebastian's martyrdom, in which butcher knives substitute for arrows and the blood and death are very real. The imagery is accompanied by an outstandingly unpleasant voice-over in which the deceased artist croons obsessively about his "colours" – which, among other things, "are smooth like syphilis." Steeped in as-yet-unspecified perversions, this repulsive voice will return later on via a vintage tape recorder discovered by Stefano; this 'voice from the grave' motif recalls the 1965 Gothic 5 *tombe per un medium* and brings the appalling Legnani vividly, frighteningly alive.

As Stefano begins to realise that something about his latest assignment is very wrong, Avati introduces us to an intriguing range of well-realised characters, sketching in a rural milieu that recalls the Southern Gothic of Tennessee Williams – this despite La casa's northern setting and a tone of arid cold rather than sweltering heat. In a satirical touch, Stefano's employer – the sharp-suited big

shot in this small-town atmosphere – is a midget. (He's played by regular Avati collaborator Bob Tonelli.) The young caretaker of the local church appears to be the generic 'village idiot', while the outgoing teacher, who reportedly "gives it away to the whole town," welcomes Stefano warmly as "a new face in this shit hole." A conspicuously impatient town archivist explains to Stefano that Legnani immolated himself on 4 June 1931, while a limping hotel maid maintains sourly that "Our last tourists were those German bastards in the '40s." And the town's affable

## LA CASA DALLE FINESTRE CHE RIDONO

Italy 1976
UK: *The House with Laughing Windows*
AMA Film
110 minutes colour
produced May-June 1976

· · · · · · · · · · · · · · · · · · · · · · · · · · · · ·

Director of Photography: Pasquale Rachini; Art Director: Luciana Morosetti; Editor: Giuseppe Baghdighian; Sound: Enrico Blasi; Music: Amedeo Tommasi; Make-up: Giovanni Amadei; Special Effects: Giovanni Corridori; Screenplay: Pupi Avati, Antonio Avati, Gianni Cavina, Maurizio Costanzo; Story: Pupi Avati, Antonio Avati; Producers:

Gianni Minervini, Antonio Avati; Director: Pupi Avati

Lino Capolicchio (Stefano); Francesca Marciano (Francesca); Gianni Cavina (Coppola); Giulio Pizzirani (Antonio Mazza); Bob Tonelli (Solmi); Vanna Busoni (teacher); Pietro Brambilla (Lidio); Ferdinando Orlandi (police captain); Andrea Matteuzzi (Poppi); Ines Ciaschetti (concierge); Pina Borione (Laura Legnani); Flavia Giorgio; Arrigo Lucchini (shopkeeper); Carla Astolfi (hotel maid); Luciano Bianchi (archivist); Tonino Corazzari; Libero Grandi; uncredited: Eugene Walter (priest)

**Rendered with a fine if not original brush, the film's progress is slow and even wearisome here and there, but this defect rewards us with a genuine atmosphere of distress and decay, eventually taking root in the church and adjoining rectory, and even more so with a surprise ending that might be signed by a master of the genre.** *La Stampa* 21 August 1976

**The hero must be an ordinary person. Lino Capolicchio in** *La casa dalle finestre che ridono* **and Gabriele Lavia in** *Zeder* **are normal young men caught up in a hellish intrigue ... The danger doesn't come from normal killers but from hypotheses that are patently absurd. What I like more than anything is to succeed in frightening, in terrifying the viewer through events and situations that are totally unbelievable.** *Pupi Avati* [quoted in *Video Watchdog* Jan-Feb 1991]

Lino Capolicchio unknowingly walks over an Emilia-Romagna mass grave in *La casa dalle finestre che ridono* (1976)

restaurateur is married to a wraith-like woman in Victorian garb, whose extensive collection of Legnanis includes a self-portrait in which the painter's ugly male face is affixed to a naked female body.

These characters are all exceptionally well acted, as is Stefano himself and the doe-eyed new teacher he falls in love with, although Francesca Marciano's corkscrew curls constitute one of a handful of slip-ups in post-war period detail. Marciano was cast, incidentally, only at the last minute, the role having originally been earmarked for the American actress Taryn Power. An American who *did* get into the film was the expatriate polymath Eugene Walter. Credited not as an actor but as 'consulenza speciale' (special consultant), his casting as the local priest was presumably a sly nod to his Mother Superior in Fellini's *Giulietta degli spiriti* (Juliet of the Spirits). His creepily ambiguous character in the Avati film is first seen buttoning up his cassock, a moment echoed at the very end when – in a concluding twist that would be up there with *Les Diaboliques* were the film better known – he makes a point of unbuttoning it.

The atmosphere of parochial weirdness is built up of numerous incidental details – a polluted lagoon in which the eels are long gone, a fridge that's empty save for a colony of snails, a murdered friend of Stefano whose coffin is sealed up with a live mouse inside, and a local shopkeeper who explains that muriatic acid is a big seller because "They spill it on the faces of their husbands' lovers." The film's mood of unease is much enhanced by our impression that Avati, himself a local, knew this milieu well; also by Pasquale Rachini's chilly location photography in such places as Malalbergo, Comacchio and Minerbio. When there was talk of a millennial remake, the initial idea, soon abandoned, was to move the action to America. "The story's impact is strong because of its particular location and Italian sensibility," Avati observed. "I've now realised the madness in shifting it away from its origins."[11]

Though guilty of slight overlength, *La casa* is an expertly suspenseful film. Avati's elegant understatement cultivates a climate of all-pervasive dread while somehow co-existing with some of the nastiest, most winceable stabbings yet seen in a continental horror film. It's also an outstandingly cruel picture, with the details of Legnani's hideous crimes, conducted in incestuous cahoots with his monstrous sisters, fully bearing out the perverted intimations of his voice-over. The film is frequently characterised as a giallo, though this designation seems a poor fit for a subdued story that hovers throughout on the verge of the supernatural. Indeed,

one of Avati's creepiest scenes involves Stefano's initial discovery of the tape. Attempting to plug in the tape recorder, he short-circuits the entire room. Yet the tape, and that voice, starts up anyway.

## CLOYING BEAUTY AND UNRELENTING ASSAULT

As Pupi Avati completed work in Emilia-Romagna, Dario Argento was preparing his most ambitious project yet, one which would add to the otherworldly reverberations of *Profondo rosso* the hair-raising impact of a full-blown supernatural assault. *Suspiria* began production at the end of July 1976, representing a plunge into vibrantly coloured irrationality drawn in part from Thomas de Quincey's 1840s anthology *Suspiria de Profundis* and in part from tales of a satanic arts academy confided to co-writer Daria Nicolodi by her grandmother. Numerous other influences were brought into play – the naïve trickery of Georges Méliès, the jagged abstractions of *Caligari*, the occultist underpinnings of the Rudolf Steiner schools, Disney's *Snow White and the Seven Dwarfs* and the rarefied realm of fairy tales generally. Taking nearly 1.5 billion lire, the result slightly outdid *Profondo rosso* at the Italian box-office, as well as making a significant impact internationally.

*American ballet student Suzy Bannion travels to Freiburg to take up her place at the celebrated Tanz-Akademie. Arriving in the teeth of a raging storm, she witnesses another student, Pat, fleeing the place in terror. Unable to gain entrance, Suzy returns the following morning, only to be told by vice-directress Mme Blanc and her baleful assistant, Miss Tanner, that Pat was horribly murdered during the night. Several more deaths ensue before Suzy unravels the truth about the establishment.*

Promoting the film in Britain, EMI's production notes placed Argento himself front and centre. "With *Suspiria* he pushes the farthest boundaries of suspense into new worlds of heart-stopping fear, riveting audiences with scenes of incredible power through his use of sound, music, decor, lighting and special effects," enthused the copywriter. "More than a film to see, *Suspiria* is a film to *experience*, and for lovers of cinematic suspense and shock *Suspiria* may prove the most harrowing shocker ever filmed."

This reads, of course, like the usual hyperbole – and yet it's highly unlikely that any contemporary audience members would have accused that copywriter of exaggeration. Indeed, they may well have seen something quite astute, rather than hyperbolic, about the itemisation of the weapons in Argento's arsenal

Alida Valli and Joan Bennett, consumed in the apocalyptic whirlwind of *Suspiria* (1976)

and above all in the description of the film as an experience. For Argento abandons the narrative niceties of conventional build-up and development by thoroughly immersing the viewer in acute disquiet and outright terror within moments of the film beginning. The film's first 15 minutes are a nightmarish descent into a maelstrom few horror pictures could even aspire to, never mind equal. The initial intimations of dread are expertly laid out – the sickly neon daubs of red, green and blue at the airport, the odd emphasis on the automatic exit doors as Suzy approaches them, and the exaggerated hydraulic hiss as they part, causing her lilac scarf to dance briefly in the blowback. Then comes the elemental onslaught of a truly ferocious nocturnal thunderstorm.

With apparently off-hand strokes, Argento succeeds in investing every detail of Suzy's journey with malefic import. The weirdly taciturn taxi driver, the low-level susurrations of the score (from which the word "Witch!" suddenly rings out), the forest of limbless white trees, and finally the astonishing crimson and gold façade of the Tanz-Akademie. (This, incidentally, was an exact replica, built at Rome's De Paolis Studios, of the 16th century Haus zum Walfisch in Freiburg.) There follows a masterpiece of misdirection, with Argento abandoning Suzy to focus instead on the fleeing Pat. The process by which Pat, having sought sanctuary at a Studentenheim almost as weirdly imposing as the Akademie, is savagely murdered and finally plunges through a multi-coloured skylight – while the face and body of her helpless friend Sonia are bisected by the falling debris – is certain to pulverise any normally constituted viewer into virtual insensility, and all within the first quarter-hour.

Crucial to the effect is Argento's seamless integration of a shattering score by his *Profondo rosso* collaborators, Goblin. Though the band members have since cited the usual Prog suspects like Yes, King Crimson and ELP as influences, the sheer, demented assaultiveness

## SUSPIRIA

*Italy 1976*
*SEDA Spettacoli Rome*
*98 minutes colour*
*production began 28 July 1976*
. . . . . . . . . . . . . . . . . . . . . . . . . . . .
Director of Photography: Luciano Tovoli;
Production Designer: Giuseppe Bassan;
Editor: Franco Fraticelli; Sound: Mario
Dallimonti, Nick Alexander [English-
language dub]; Music: Goblin; Make-up:
Pierantonio Mecacci; Special Effects:
Germano Natali; Screenplay: Dario
Argento, Daria Nicolodi; Producer: Claudio
Argento; Director: Dario Argento

Jessica Harper (Suzy Bannion); Stefania Casini
(Sara); Flavio Bucci (Daniel); Miguel Bosé
(Mark); Alida Valli (Miss Tanner); Joan Bennett
(Mme Blanc); Barbara Magnolfi (Olga); Susanna
Javicoli (Sonia); Eva Axén (Pat); Rudolf Schündler
(Professor Milius); Udo Kier (Professor Frank
Mandel); Margherita Horowitz (teacher); Jacopo
Mariani (Albert); Fulvio Mingozzi (taxi driver);
Franca Scagnetti (Albert's governess [1st servant]);
Renato Scarpa (Professor Verdegast); Serafina
Scorcelletti (2nd servant); Giuseppe Transocchi
(Pavlo); Renata Zamengo (Caroline); Alessandra
Capozza, Salvatore Capozza, Diana Ferrara, Cristina
Latini, Alfredo Raino, Claudia Zaccari (dancers)

**There are few moments of relaxation in this horribly effective fantasy thriller which puts the nerves to a severe test. The gory ravings of Brian De Palma seem almost reserved next to these blood-spattered displays. Consciously exploiting all the ingredients of the genre, Dario Argento nevertheless succeeds in distilling disquiet and inventing a modern, baroque style that owes much to the musical soundtrack.** *Télérama 21 May 1977*

I thought and still think that *Suspiria* was a great pop opera. We needn't have spoken in the film, we could have sung. It was all so closely tied up to the suggestiveness of the images and the colours ... Also, there was this unusual music, this great baroque setting: the girls, the dancing school, the whispering, the chattering, the noises. It was a great opera!
*Stefania Casini [quoted in Palmerini / Mistretta, Spaghetti Nightmares, 1996]*

of the *Suspiria* soundtrack recalls a 1969 track by White Noise called *Black Mass: An Electric Storm in Hell*. (Fragments of the White Noise track appeared in the late Hammer title *Dracula A.D. 1972*, and there all similarities between the two films end.) But the power of the opening, together with the remainder of *Suspiria*, isn't just a matter of coshing the viewer over the head with a screeching soundtrack and high-octane violence. For Argento unsettles the viewer, too, with an almost subliminal recourse to rhyming imagery – the irradiated red that ties together the Flughafen, the Akademie and the Studentenheim; the strange fluttering of Suzy's scarf, of Pat's towel, and of the black lingerie billowing outside her bathroom window; the pulsing redness of a diamond-shaped elevator indicator and the pulsing blood from Pat's exposed heart as a knife stabs into it in ghastly close-up.

The accumulation of sinister portents is reactivated, in a lower key, when Suzy finally enrols at the Akademie the morning after Pat's death. Argento had initially envisaged the pupils as children, and even with adult actresses in the roles the impression of guileless innocents at the mercy of decadent, self-interested, ageless diabolists is vividly conveyed. The toothy grin with which Alida Valli's quasi-Nazi Miss Tanner greets Jessica Harper's huge-eyed Suzy is matched for hard-to-pinpoint unease by a peculiar moment of appraisal as Joan Bennett's regal Mme Blanc looks the new arrival up and down. Completing the effect are an apparently asexual, flaxen-haired little boy in Edwardian Sunday Best, together with a grotesque, lumbering giant who, according to Miss Tanner, has "looked very handsome ever since he got those false teeth."

And, as the skin crawls at these gathering intimations of dread, the eye is ravished by Giuseppe Bassan's extraordinary art direction, with decorative features ranging from angular stabbing shapes and Escher-like puzzles to the serpentine, free-flowing Art Nouveau of Mme Blanc's inner sanctum. In an alluring fusion of ancient and modern, Luciano Tovoli's photography took advantage of the newly invented Steadicam (an Italian first), simultaneously luxuriating in the about-to-be-discontinued lustre of Technicolor processing. Ranging from red to green through blue and finally deep black, Tovoli's colours lend an oneiric yet hard-edged intensity to Argento's remaining set-pieces. A swarm of maggots rains down from a blue-tinted attic and later the same evening the stertorous snoring of the unseen directress issues from behind red-stained curtains. Suzy's friend Sara plunges into a greenish chamber bulging with razor wire, and shortly before that the

school's blind pianist, Daniel, becomes stranded in Munich's eerily deserted Königsplatz, with looming blocks of darkness separating the glimmering Palladian façades, whereupon his guide dog suddenly leaps up to rip out his throat.

In a clever touch, Daniel's dark glasses fall off in death, finally revealing his eyes; later, Sara's corpse is discovered with large pins thrust through its eyeballs, suggesting that these sight-impaired victims have bequeathed the task of seeing through the Akademie's machinations to the resourceful Suzy. And Daniel's demise is given added intensity by the astounding scene that precedes it, in which Miss Tanner screamingly ejects the recalcitrant pianist from the rehearsal room. This scene, in which Valli's gimlet-eyed ferocity is truly a sight to behold, was reportedly among the casualties when the film lost five minutes for its original US release.

Amid the sustained and ultra-modern cacophony of this intensely imagined film, Argento nevertheless contrived to plant numerous playful references to the past. The bitchy Olga, for example, sports a coiled hairdo like Theda Bara, while a sinister doctor ministering to Suzy is called Verdegast (recalling Bela Lugosi in *The Black Cat*). Daniel's demise in Königsplatz incorporates a discreet nod to the Sidney Hayers film *Night of the Eagle*, Suzy and Sara's queasy swimming pool interlude is reminiscent of *Cat People*, and Suzy's climactic invasion of the witches' citadel reveals a tell-tale dint in an old lady's bed akin to *Psycho*. Then, as the Akademie finally implodes like Poe's House of Usher, Suzy is seen hurtling past billowing drapes like Gloria Stuart in *The Old Dark House*.

Some of Argento's casting choices also indicated his willingness to reference the past. Fritz Lang, for example, is invoked via two of his former associates. Rudolf Schündler, over 40 years after appearing in *Das Testament des Dr Mabuse*, appears briefly as a white-haired academic who assures Suzy that witches "are malefic, negative and destructive," able to "change the course of events, and people's lives, but only to do harm." And Joan Bennett, star of four Lang films in the 1940s, utters Mme Blanc's practised platitudes in a smooth, robotic, resistless tone, her white face, piercing blue eyes and red lips suggesting an embalmed Princess Margaret.

These nostalgic touches notwithstanding, on release in 1977 the film's dazzling mixture of cloying beauty and unrelenting assault made it seem aggressively and invigoratingly modern – an untrammelled plunge into the unconscious such as cinemagoers had never seen. *Suspiria* also elevated Argento to superstar status among horror fans at a single stroke. Looked at some four decades on, it's significant for yet another reason – not just as a rare instance of a horror film predicated entirely on its female characters, but also for its complete exclusion of the soft-porn voyeurism that had become almost de rigueur among its peers.

While Argento's 16-week *Suspiria* schedule wore on, Lucio Fulci was making a tentative return to horror, having done nothing in the genre – apart from a negligible vampire comedy – since *Non si sevizia un paperino* in 1972. He began shooting *Sette note in nero* (Seven Notes in Black) on 4 October 1976, and in a self-referential touch he began the action in exactly the way *Non si sevizia* ended – with a comically unconvincing dummy smashing its blood-spattered way down a cliff edge.

This time it's a flashback to 1959 and the suicide of Jennifer O'Neill's mother at the White Cliffs of Dover. Eighteen years later and O'Neill has visions of a ghastly murder prior to, *Profondo rosso* style, finding human remains behind a bricked-up wall; the location is a dilapidated Italian country house belonging to her husband (Gianni Garko). Exported as *The Psychic*, the film looks extremely glamorous and ends with a blatant quote from Poe's *The Black Cat*, but the pace is sluggish and Fulci permits such glaring continuity gaffes as Ida Galli's Marcel wave disappearing in virtually the blink of an eye. However, the fact that the villainous Gabriele Ferzetti falls to his death in an under-renovation church, and that O'Neill's visions turn out to predict the future rather than recollect the past, indicates that, for Italian horror, 1976 ended as it began – with distinct echoes of *Don't Look Now*.

## MORE OMINOUS THAN THE OMEN

In October 1977 Francesco Barilli, director four years previously of *Il profumo della signora in nero*, made his second and final feature, an Italian-Spanish concoction called *Pensione paura* (Hotel Fear). Spanish audiences saw it under the more hard-hitting title *La violación de la señorita Julia* (The Rape of Miss Julia); the gruelling

Leonora Fani, centrepiece of the Italian locandina for *Pensione paura* (1977)

rape in question, committed by a Brylcreemed, peacock-strutting World War II gigolo and abetted by his middle-aged mistress, finally tips the guileless heroine over the edge on which she's been tottering for over an hour. As Julia, the excellent Leonora Fani holds this curiously affecting film together, trying to keep her late mother's hotel going with a minimum of guests, simultaneously waiting in vain for her errant father "to appear on the horizon, tall as the clouds."

Most of the rootless punters have sex on their minds and none survives to the end credits. Though not quite a horror film (and certainly not the giallo some commentators claim it to be), *Pensione paura* is nevertheless a mesmerising study of a young woman's mental disintegration (clearly a Barilli speciality), and is graced by an exceptional Adolfo Waitzman score.

By the late 1970s Italy's bona-fide gialli were long past their heyday but still reasonably numerous. Titles ranged from Ferdinando Baldi's *Nove ospiti per un delitto* (Nine Guests for a Killing), in which Arthur Kennedy is the island patriarch in yet another *Ten Little Indians* scenario, to the cynical social satire of Luigi Zampa's *Il mostro* (The Monster) and the voyeuristic weirdness of Giuliano Petrelli's unclassifiable thriller *L'occhio dietro la parete* (The Eyes Behind the Wall). Among other interesting titles, Flavio Mogherini's *La ragazza dal piagama giallo* (The Girl in the Yellow Pyjamas) not only contrived to get the word 'giallo' into its title but also made the interesting experiment of transplanting the form to Australia.

In the same period (1977-78), debutant director Antonio Bido came up with a pair of heavily Argento-inspired thrillers, *Il gatto dagli occhi di giada* (The Cat with Jade Eyes) and *Solamente nero* (Only Darkness), exported as *The Cat's Victims* and *The Bloodstained Shadow* respectively. The former has a score by a Goblin-soundalike ensemble called Trans Europa Express, plus a story pivoting, unusually, on memories of Nazi collaboration during the war. *Solamente nero* involves a murder spree on a Venetian island (the atmospheric location was Murano) and boasts striking performances from Craig Hill and Juliette Mayniel. The ESP-gifted hero is Lino Capolicchio from Avati's *La casa dalle finestre che ridono*, again playing a character called Stefano, and that Bido's title – also translatable as 'Pure Black' – was intended to recall Argento's *Profondo rosso* goes without saying.

The main prop used to shore up the giallo's waning popularity was, inevitably, sleaze, and plenty of it. Perhaps the most emblematic title in this respect was Giulio Berruti's *Suor omicidi* (Killer Nun), in which the formidable Anita Ekberg is Sister Gertrude, chief suspect in a murder spree set in a French mental home run by nuns, with Alida Valli, Massimo Serrato and Joe Dallesandro also involved. Similarly, Enzo Milioni's *La sorella di Ursula* (Ursula's Sister) wallows in a ton of near-the-knuckle sex together with an Amalfi-stalking serial killer whose weapon of choice is a wooden dildo. A similar instrument figures largely in Alberto Negrin's 'threatened schoolgirls' thriller *Enigma rosso* (Red Puzzle), which was exported as *Rings of Fear*. By 1979, Gianni Martucci's oddly spelt *Trhauma* marked a minor turning point of sorts, in that its story (of a deformed killer avenging a childhood trauma) was modelled unmistakably on recent US slashers – thus reversing the channel of influence that had brought those slashers into being in the first place.

Amid all this sleaze the giallo's originator, Mario Bava, was more than ever a man out of his time. Yet in 1977, aged 62, he made a brave attempt at crafting a contemporary supernatural thriller; the result, *Schock*, would turn out to be his final feature. Hamstrung by a paltry budget and a conspicuous lack of the visual sumptuousness that was Bava's trademark, the film nevertheless makes the most of an intriguing story about a woman haunted by a former husband but maybe – like Nevenka in *La frusta e il corpo* – bedevilled by her own murderous guilt. Bava announces the transition from past to present in style, with a screen-filling cobweb being pulled aside to reveal a hideous set of brown-and-orange sofas. The house which Dora and her new husband Bruno are renovating is the same

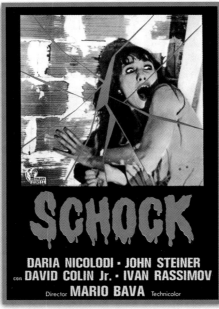

Daria Nicolodi, cover star of the Spanish pressbook for *Schock* (1977)

one in which the former husband, Carlo, apparently killed himself. Now, Dora's ghastly little son, Marco, shows signs of channelling the dead man's spirit.

A queasy kind of horror is conjured up from the boy's precocious displays, whether lying on top of his mother on the lawn or gloating over her as she takes a shower. When Dora and Bruno make love on those grisly sofas, a huge ornamental hand, positioned on a display shelf above them, shifts ever so slightly, as if disturbed by the malign energy of the boy upstairs. ("Pigs!" he seethes repeatedly.) Moments like this are masterfully contrived, and the same applies to a couple of shock appearances from the deceased Carlo and a barnstorming climax in which Bruno hacks down a *Profondo rosso*-style wall before getting pick-axed for his pains. But other scenes are less persuasive. A 'laughing' piano lid in one of Dora's nightmares was an effect best unattempted, and when Dora runs into the garden and succumbs to the old 'stepping on a rake' gag, the phantom hand that claws at her ankle is equally cheesy. Even so, Daria Nicolodi is particularly good when Dora lapses finally into madness, with Bava signalling her breakdown by sending that ornamental hand crashing off its perch.

The film reached Italian audiences in August 1977 prior to coming out in the UK (as *Shock*) exactly three years later, by which time Bava had been dead for four months. "Small but stylish,"[12] was the verdict of one British critic, and in that word 'small' resides the film's failure. Bava's son Lamberto (who reportedly directed about a quarter of the film) was keenly aware of the need for his father to compete with Dario Argento's 'bells and whistles' school of Italian horror, but so claustrophobically tiny a canvas wasn't the way to do it.

Cast here as Marco, David Colin Jr had previously played Juliet Mills' little son in *Chi sei?* Because that film had been marketed in the US as *Beyond the Door*, Colin Jr's presence in *Schock* allowed it to be released to American patrons under the ignominious title *Beyond the Door II*. Yet *Schock*'s 'possessed child' theme had actually been motivated by a more recent satanic smash. The shock waves from *The Exorcist* had barely abated when, in the autumn of 1976, Richard Donner's *The Omen* came on the scene. With the birth of the Antichrist inspiring a rash of wildly imaginative fatalities and the satanic sprog eventually gaining cynical entrée to the White House, the film inevitably initiated an *Omen*-flavoured replay of the *Exorcist* mania of 1974. Again, it was the Italians who plunged into the fray most wholeheartedly – albeit not quite as rapidly as in the old days.

Pier Carpi's laughable *Un'ombra nell'ombra* (A Shadow Within the Shadow) accordingly went into production on 3 January 1977, with a disco-flavoured Devil cult spawning an ungovernable teenage girl who evades all attempts at exorcism and, in the fade-out, sets her sights on St Peter's in Rome. (The actress in question, Lara Wendel, was alarmingly young at the time, though this didn't exempt her from full-frontal nudity, including a climactic confrontation with her equally nude 46-year-old 'mother', Anne Heywood.) By the time this one finished on 25 February, Ugo Liberatore's *Nero veneziano* (Venetian Black) had started in Venice. This plays for two-thirds of its length like a reasonably competent *Don't Look Now* wannabe, with a blind boy afflicted by ghastly visions, mainly of rioting worms. The Antichrist business comes in so late it suggests a finished script being opportunistically *Omen*-skewed at the very last minute, culminating in the familiar pay-off, "The son of Evil has made his kingdom on Earth." Rena Niehaus is the girl who makes it possible, and the film's most transgressive image involves a baby being thrown at a wall of spikes. Pino Donaggio's score, by contrast, is beautiful.

Alberto De Martino, director in 1974 of *L'anticristo*, got in on the act too, starting work on *Holocaust 2000* in Tunis on 2 May. If *L'anticristo* felt like one of the disaster movies of the mid-1970s, *Holocaust 2000* confirms the impression, with a plot hinging on a proposed nuclear reactor in the Middle East and a slew of slumming guest stars – Simon Ward, Agostina Belli, Anthony Quayle, Adolfo Celi, Virginia McKenna, Alexander Knox. Right at the top is Kirk Douglas, who was presumably aware that Charlton Heston and several other names had turned down the lead in *The Omen* and wasn't about to make the same mistake.

Douglas' hardhearted industrialist maintains that "scientific progress today is like a truck without brakes hurtling downhill," though his self-possession slips when he begins to suspect that his own son, archly named Angel, might be the spawn of Satan. Mixing up topical environmental issues with the expected parade of grisly 'accidental' deaths, the film boasts a weirdly transparent lunatic asylum and a

nightmare sequence featuring a seven-headed Hydra. Advertised on release as being 'more ominous than *The Omen*', it was also one of the period's very few continental co-productions with the UK. Another, Jack Gold's *The Medusa Touch*, was Anglo-French and began exactly a week after *Holocaust 2000*, on 9 May 1977. Known in France as *La Grande menace* (The Great Threat), this too picks up on the 1970s disaster movie vibe, with Richard Burton as a stone-faced man who can 'will' catastrophes from his hospital bed and Lino Ventura as the equally stone-faced cop on the case. Again, this extremely efficient thriller – less demented than *Holocaust 2000* but more engaging – has the expected horde of guest stars, with names like Alan Badel, Marie-Christine Barrault and *The Omen*'s Lee Remick representing just the tip of the iceberg.

Films like *Holocaust 2000* and *The Medusa Touch* were sprawling and expensive. That *Omen* clones could be more claustrophobic, and therefore considerably cheaper, was demonstrated by writer-director Giulio Petroni. Coming a bit late to the party, Petroni's Italian-Spanish co-production *La profezia* (The Prophecy) started production in January 1978 and on release sported the more provocative title *L'osceno desiderio* (Obscene Desire). To complicate matters further, for advertising purposes it gained the subtitle *Le pene nel ventre* (The Pains in the Belly), while in Spain it was called plain *Poseída* (Possessed). The stomach pains belong to Marisa Mell, an American newly-wed in Italy who only becomes pregnant in the latter stages, after a long stretch in which the film seems like little more than a Mills & Boon romance garnished with occasional spooky touches and plenty of artfully lit softcore sex. There are also a few inexplicable prostitute murders

Kirk Douglas throttles Simon Ward in the spawn-of-Satan epic *Holocaust 2000* (1977)

thrown in, with the culprit dismissing the victims as "nothing but soulless animals." This makes the denouement a bit tricky, given that it's the killer who joins forces with a youthful exorcist in order to drive out the son of Satan before it can be born.

These two also indulge in a modified replay of *The Omen*'s 'decomposing jackal in the grave' routine, learning the details of a family curse by unearthing a human skeleton with a skeletal baby still nestling within its stomach cavity. Unfortunately, the exorcist, as played by Lou Castel, must be the most wearily inexpressive on record; he also turns out to be the most easily discouraged. After plenty of big talk along the lines of "Satan isn't invincible: I'll drive him out of her body," he places a communion wafer on Mell's tongue, whereupon she spits it out and laughs at him, causing him to dash off in alarm and get flattened by a passing lorry. Mell's laughing fit, by the way, is one of the best there is, up there with Stan Laurel in *Way Out West* and Freda Jackson in *The Brides of Dracula*. It's much more diverting than the token ending, in which she gets on a plane with the newborn and a satanic conspirator murmurs, "A lovely boy like that is just what America needs." Petroni's co-writer, incidentally, was old hand Piero Regnoli, whose experience in Italian horror wound all the way back to *I vampiri*.

The 'cheap versus expensive' response to *The Omen* was perpetuated in two other 1978 productions, Silvio Amadio's threadbare *Il medium* (The Medium) and Giulio Paradisi's comically inflated *Stridulum*. In the first a US musician's five-year-old son is the demonic vessel in a dreary scenario reportedly inspired by the hack director Demofilo Fidani, who had by then changed course and become a medium. The second, shot in Atlanta and exported as *The Visitor*, is a film of such extravagant lunacy that it could never be accused of dreariness. An unclassifiable freak that expended $3 million on its cosmic clash between Good and Evil, it was produced by Ovidio G Assonitis, who, as director, had already been responsible for the *Exorcist* clone *Chi sei? Stridulum* accordingly borrows its demonic eight-year-old girl (Paige Conner) from both *The Exorcist* and *The Omen* while otherwise looting from *Close Encounters of the Third Kind* and a host of other hits. Among the girl's transgressions, she says "Go fuck yourself" to old-time Hollywood guest star Glenn Ford, who soon afterwards has his eyes pecked out by a falcon. *Damien Omen II*, with its sustained raven attack, came out during the film's production, which might account for this particular atrocity.

There are several other perplexed-looking US names involved (Mel Ferrer, Shelley Winters, Sam Peckinpah), while the venerable John Huston is described by Lance Henriksen as "the oldest babysitter I've ever seen." He's nothing of the sort, of course. He's a Godlike emissary "from another time, another place, beyond human knowledge and understanding," and at the very beginning he shares an extraordinary face-off with a ghoulishly snow-caked little girl in a psychedelic desert. From here to its climactic invasion of rapier-beaked comedy pigeons, *Stridulum* is a head-scratching epic of self-important grandiosity, even boasting a couple of brief appearances from Franco Nero, cast as an extradimensional Jesus Christ in a blonde wig. Revived in 2013, the film gained belated cult recognition as, to quote *The Village Voice*, "a Euro-American science fiction horror clusterfuck"[13] of the first magnitude.

## 'S' FOR SATANIC

Spain, too, made several contributions to the *Omen*-inspired sub-genre, though massive expense of the *Stridulum* variety wasn't required in the heyday of the 'S' certificate, when the single ingredient guaranteed to fill Spanish cinemas was copious nudity. The 'S' may have stopped the horror boom dead in its tracks, with Spaniards preferring to see films like Carlos Aured's *¡Susana quiere perder ... eso!* (Susana Wants to Lose ... It!) rather than the kind of stuff Aured used to make with Paul Naschy. But, with *The Omen* giving rise to an interest in Devil scenarios, the obvious answer was to fuse horror and 'S'-style sex far more provocatively than was previously possible.

This so-called 'destape' period (literally, 'stripping away') brought with it the expected avalanche of sleaze, including José Antonio Barrero's 1978 serial killer story *La sombra de un recuerdo* (The Shadow of a Memory), which gave Spanish audiences the chance to see nasty, protracted sex scenes in which the female partner gets strangled but the sex carries on. The period also brought many uninhibited actresses to prominence, among them Blanca Estrada, who in September 1976 appeared topless on the cover of *Nuevo Fotogramas* under the self-explanatory banner 'Blanca se destapa' (Blanca is Stripped Bare). By January 1977 she was making Carlos Puerto's *El francotirador* (The Sniper), starring opposite Paul Naschy and appearing nude into the bargain. Given that General Franco is the proposed target of Naschy's grief-crazed gunman in this controversial thriller, the title enshrines a rather nifty play-on-words.

Puerto's next film, *Escalofrío* (Shiver), featured neither Naschy nor Estrada. Made in three weeks at the end of 1977 under the auspices of producer Juan Piquer Simón, it was made possible by the huge success of Simón's *Viaje al centro de la tierra* (Journey

Carlos Castellano embedded among other frozen items in *Escalofrío* (1977)

to the Centre of the Earth), which was co-written by Puerto and had recently earned nearly 200 million pesetas. The provocative 'S' rating slapped onto *Escalofrío*, based on its abundance of sex-saturated satanic orgies, ensured a mighty domestic take, for a horror picture, of nearly 99 million pesetas. Ironically, this was more than any title from the recently curtailed boom period apart from Serrador's *La residencia*.

> *December 1977. Andrés and Ana are a young couple expecting a baby in around five months' time. Having attended a Madrid matinée of Star Wars they're accosted on the way home by another couple, Bruno and Berta. Bruno regales Andrés with tales of their schooldays together, though Andrés can't quite recall him – probably because Bruno is approximately 15 years his senior. Despite this anomaly, the younger couple make the fateful decision to join Bruno and Berta for dinner at their country home...*

That Puerto proposed to earn his 'S' certificate is evident even in the film's pre-credits sequence, in which a bald-headed mediaeval friar ravishes a copiously naked young woman on a satanic altar, eventually pulling out a sacrificial knife – holding it, perhaps unsurprisingly, with a rather unsteady hand. (According to Puerto, this prologue was added purely because the film had come in at too short a length.) The credits then play out over a sprinkling of crimson

## ESCALOFRÍO

Spain 1977
US: **Don't Panic**
Cinevisión / Almena Films
82 minutes colour
in production November 1977

Director of Photography: Andrés Berenguer; Editor: Pedro del Rey; Music: Librado Pastor; Make-up: Carmen Martín, Carmen Sánchez; Executive Producers: Alfredo

Casado, Juan Piquer Simón; Writer-Director: Carlos Puerto

Ángel Aranda (Bruno); Sandra Alberti (Berta); Mariana Karr (Ana); José María Guillén (Andrés); Luis Barboo (gatekeeper); Manuel Pereiro (friar in prologue); José Pagán (doctor); Isidro Luengo, Ascensión Moreno (neighbours); Carlos Castellano (vagrant); uncredited: Fernando Jiménez del Oso (himself); Juan Piquer Simón (cultist)

That a film presenting a grisly catalogue of black magic and Satanism should induce public hilarity shows all too clearly the uselessness of the filmmakers' efforts ... Sandra Alberti and Marian Karr vie with each other to see which one can undress in the shortest time. But we get the impression that the 'S' is now just a publicity gimmick, deemed essential by producers to ensure the marketability of their merchandise. *La Vanguardia* 9 August 1978

The basic principle of the story was that it had to be an 'S' film ... He [Juan Piquer Simón] wasn't a tyrant, but he was capricious, selfish and stingy ... I recently had the chance to see the film again and noticed numerous errors that could have been rectified with a second take ... Simón was on my back throughout the three weeks of filming. Imagine the pressure; I had no time, no money, no freedom. *Carlos Puerto [quoted in La Abadía de Berzano 7 May 2010]*

blood spots, after which we're introduced to the rather bland but nonetheless likable Andrés and Ana. As a preface to their protracted nightmare they go to see *Star Wars*, which, we notice, is into its fourth week in Madrid. This eccentric little detail is introduced just before the tone darkens – almost imperceptibly at first – with the arrival of Bruno and Berta.

Bruno's obviously bogus story about shared schooldays (a scam echoed many years later in Dominick Moll's exceptional French thriller *Harry,* un ami qui vous veut du bien) is followed by the worryingly long drive to Bruno and Berta's country house. Is there any significance, we wonder, in the alliterative nature of the couples' names (AA, BB)? Have the younger couple convinced themselves to follow the older one merely out of misplaced politeness, or does their slightly precarious social standing make them an easy mark for the more prosperous Bruno and Berta? ("Well, they seem very nice," Ana rationalises, "and we've nothing else to do.") While we ponder these things, the house suddenly looms up, announced by a flurry of autumn leaves and photographed by Andrés Berenguer in memorably bleak, wintery tones. Then we recognise the monolithic gatekeeper as none other than Luis Barboo, a baleful presence familiar from any number of Jess Franco films – and our profound misgivings are confirmed.

What follows contains its fair share of clichés – a storm sets in, making departure inadvisable, and the following morning the young couples' car, predictably, won't start. The ominous portents aren't exactly subtle either. The evening has barely begun, for example, when Ana stumbles upon Berta guzzling dog food off the kitchen work surfaces. (Unfazed, Berta merely produces a large knife and says, "Get the cheese.") But the climate of weirdness is expertly sustained, leavened by a few shafts of social comedy courtesy of the younger couples' growing discomfiture, particularly when Bruno touches the wound on his temple and discusses a failed suicide attempt.

A session round a Ouija board throws up yet more uncomfortable truths and it's decided that Andrés and Ana should stay the night. Puerto, meanwhile, laces the action with plenty of visual oddities – hellish flames leaping in the grate, Ana's descent amid bolts of blue lightning to the kitchen, a portrait of Jesus that steadily corrupts and then bursts into flame, a creepy Victorian doll that, echoing Argento's Profondo rosso, perambulates into Ana's bedroom under its own steam. And the sex entails a writhing foursome at the fireside with multiple permutations. Bruno and Berta slather themselves in baby oil scooped from a sawn-off skull and make disconcerting dog noises while coupling. Maybe they're channelling the other couples' Alsatian, Blackie – which, unknown to its owners, has been killed in the grounds.

For all its blatant exploitativeness, Escalofrío remains an engaging exercise in claustrophobic terror, boasting committed performances from the four leads and a genuinely sadistic punchline when Andrés and Ana finally get back to their apartment. By this time they've discovered Blackie strung up in the kitchen, both Bruno and Berta have died and come to

life again, a dead vagrant has turned up in the freezer cabinet, and that ghastly doll has had its head blown off in a shower of blood. Now, in an obvious nod to Rosemary's Baby, the elderly couple next door tell them that "We've got a few friends round for dinner." Even the resurrected Blackie joins in the resultant carnage.

In a standard dodge followed by skin flicks throughout the ages, the film's Spanish release was prefaced by a 'legitimising' talk from a sober-sided pundit. In this case it was the bearded TV personality Fernando Jiménez del Oso, who as a writer had collaborated, ten years previously, with Narciso Ibáñez Serrador on the second season of Historias para no dormir. Here, in a prologue apparently directed by Juan Piquer Simón rather than Puerto, he discourses on Satanism as a symptom of a jaded society. "Our most advanced cities harbour hundreds of satanic sects," he says. "It remains a dangerous game because evil is a force that actually exists – and, once unleashed, it may be impossible to control."

What certainly seemed impossible to control in the wake of General Franco's death was the inexorable rise of the 'S' certificate, giving plenty of scope for further cocktails of horror and so-called 'blandiporno'. In 1979, for example, Carlos Puerto returned with a low-key chiller called La capilla ardiente (The Burning Shrine), a Spanish-Mexican affair co-scripted by horror veteran Eugenio Martín. This one hung around unreleased till January 1981, finally revealing itself as a rather glum supernatural saga, filmed in hazy brownish hues, of two sisters vying for the same mediumistic young man. Mourning an earlier, now-deceased lover, the younger sister rips open her nightie even before the credits roll; his ghost shows up, an otherworldly orgasm sweeps over her and her assembled make-up bottles quiver in preternatural sympathy. The remainder includes such quaint features as iris-effect fades, together with a monochrome flashback to the sisters' killing and disposal of the lover, an attempted strangulation in a padded cell, and a fumbled last-minute revelation of a bedside shrine to the lovers' severed head. The film vaguely recalls Mario Bava's Schock while anticipating Lamberto Bava's Macabro, but it carries none of the lurid force of Escalofrío.

Even so, by the turn of the decade the Spanish exploitation industry had changed, courtesy of the 'S' certificate, to such a radical degree that José Larraz's latest film could contain the immortal line, "Spread your legs wider so that the goat can enter you." The events of Los ritos sexuales del diablo (The Sexual Rites of the Devil) take place in September 1981, though it was made a year earlier and carries a copyright date ascribed to Larraz personally. Despite this, his director credit is given as Joseph Braunstein, indicating, as he later admitted, that he was ashamed of the film.

Known for export purposes under the more anodyne title *Black Candles*, *Los ritos* is basically a heavy-duty sex film, with the satanic rites thrown in for purely decorative purposes. Set near London, it's the usual 'ensnaring young innocent into participating in depraved ceremonials' saga, topped off with a stunningly limp ending of the 'it was all a dream – or was it?' variety. Among the 'highlights' is a scene of a turncoat domestic having a sword slammed up his rear-end, but the gobsmacking centrepiece is the coupling of a horned goat and a nubile celebrant in the stables. Naked save for white stockings and suede boots, the girl certainly gives it her all but the goat seems strangely underwhelmed. (Presumably because it was doped.) Appropriately, the satanic high priest (Manuel Gómez-Álvarez) sports a goatee, while Helga Liné – still resplendent at 48 – happily participates in topless scenes but leaves the more graphic intimacies to a body-double. A few lonely scraps of Larraz stylishness survive amid the sleaze, and the result raked in an impressive 33 million pesetas.

In this new 'S'-flavoured context, other entries included Manuel Esteba's *Sexo sangriento* (Bloodthirsty Sex), which coupled former Naschy co-star Mirta Miller with a crotch-stabbing serial killer, and the expected contributions from Jess Franco, who, not unnaturally, had gravitated back to Spain now that his Generalísimo namesake was dead. Franco's 1979-81 output (comprising 16 films) included two new riffs on the Marquis de Sade, *Sinfónia erótica* and *Eugénie: Historia de una perversión*, plus a Canary Islands showcase for Ajita Wilson called *Macumba sexual*. This is an 11-years-on voodoo version of *Vampyros Lesbos*, with the transsexual Wilson describing herself as "an unspeakable dream" and "a black woman with an undefined sexuality," later expiring while Lina Romay gives her enthusiastic cunnilingus. Franco himself plays his usual 'pervert on the sidelines' role. Indeed, by this time, 20 years after he created Dr Orlof, Franco had followed his idiosyncratic path so single-mindedly that 'pervert on the sidelines' was pretty much exactly how his detractors looked upon him.

By November 1982, anyone going to see *Secta siniestra* (Sinister Sect) might reasonably have thought

Clasificada S: devilish goat congress for Paola Matos in *Los ritos sexuales del diablo* (1980)

the form had reached its definitive nadir – unless they also happened to catch *Morbus*, an atrocious piece of junk issued the same month. The former, directed by Ignacio F Iquino, is a comically overwrought affair in which Emma Quer is "inseminated with the Devil's sperm" by a Satan-worshipping gynaecologist (he has a tell-tale goatee, of course) and watched over by a demonically beautiful midwife played by Concha Valero. The new-born Antichrist is a Kewpie doll with tiny horns and bursts into flames when faced with a cruciform tree branch. As for the incomprehensible proceedings in Ignasi P Ferre's *Morbus*, they involve comedy cunnilingus in a morgue, an all-nude satanic ceremony broken up by half-hearted zombies, and some truly unedifying two-shots of the boggle-eyed Víctor Israel gurning over a suspended victim's pubic hair. Illustrating the predominance of the 'S' film, it was proudly advertised as 'Eróticas orgías de sexo y terror, formando una mezcla explosiva y pornográfica' (erotic orgies of sex and horror forming an explosive and pornographic cocktail).

## LIVING DEATH AND MOUNTAIN PEAKS

In late 1977 Jean Rollin found himself in the mountainous expanses of the Massif Central, making up to the youthful producer Jean-Marc Ghanassia for the financial catastrophe that was *Lèvres de sang*. His brief was to make something in tune with the 1970s fad for disaster movies; though the budget allotted him (one million francs) was much better than usual, it certainly wasn't enough to emulate something

Paul Bisciglia,
Marie-Georges
Pascal and Brigitte
Lahaie in the
Massif Central
for *Les Raisins de
la mort* (1978)

## LES RAISINS DE LA MORT

France 1978
US: *The Grapes of Death*
Rush Production / Films ABC / Off Production
90 minutes colour
produced winter 1977-78; visa date 25 May 1978
. . . . . . . . . . . . . . . . . . . . . . . . . .
Director of Photography: Claude Becognée;
Editors: Christian Stoianovich, Dominique
Saintcyr; Sound: Gérard Barra; Music:
Philippe Sissmann; Make-up and Special
Effects: Alfredo Tiberi, Raphael Marongiu,
Yannick Josse; Screenplay: Jean Rollin,
Jean-Pierre Bouyxou; Adaptation and

Dialogue: Jean Rollin, Christian Meunier;
Producer: Claude Guedj; Director: Jean Rollin

Marie-Georges Pascal (Élisabeth); Félix Marten
(Paul); Serge Marquand (Lucien); Mirella Rancelot
(Lucie); Patrice Valota (Pierre); Patricia Cartier
(Antoinette, Lucien's daughter); Michel Herval
(Michel); Paul Bisciglia (Lucas); Brigitte Lahaie
(blonde woman); Olivier Rollin (pleading sufferer);
François Pascal (Kowalski); Evelyne Thomas
(Brigitte); Jean-Pierre Bouyxou (man with
scythe); uncredited: Raphael Marongiu (corpse in
wine-press); Jean Rollin (agricultural worker)

In chasing after fashion this film runs out of breath ... The make-up effects
are highly successful and the terror sequences are lacking in neither
savagery nor efficiency. Rollin has developed a real flair for staging
standard scenes of classic horror, but it works to the detriment of what
were his most valuable attributes: raw poetry and a roving imagination.
*Image et Son* September 1978

The shooting of *Les Raisins* was very hard for everyone involved. We were in
a remote mountain region of France. It was incredibly cold and I was freezing;
I only had a thin costume and also some nude scenes. I remember some of the
crew looking at me in a very strange way ... but it was my first chance to work
in a 'normal' film and I was very grateful. It was like walking through a dream.
Brigitte Lahaie [quoted in *Fangoria* January 1996]

like *Earthquake*. Rollin opted instead for a bucolic
apocalypse along the lines of George Romero's 1972
shocker *The Crazies*, collaborating with Jean-Pierre
Bouyxou on a story that had one of France's most
lucrative industries as its chief villain. In a waggish
nod to the John Steinbeck classic *The Grapes of Wrath*,
Rollin called the film *Les Raisins de la mort* (The Grapes
of Death). And, in redefining zombies as living people

corrupted by a ghastly infection, Rollin anticipated
such 21st century films as *28 Days Later*.

*Elisabeth is en route to Roubelais, which she calls "hardly
even a village, just a vineyard with some buildings
round it." Her boyfriend Michel is the local vintner, and
a strange young man whom she meets on the train is
one of his employees. When the boy's face corrupts before
her eyes, Elisabeth pulls the communication cord and
hurriedly disembarks. In the surrounding mountains,
almost everyone she meets is similarly infected –
disfigured, insane and compelled to kill.*

Though Rollin might be thought to have strayed out of
his comfort zone in making a quasi-zombie picture,
it's clear from the opening minutes of *Les Raisins de
la mort* that a few years in the porno wilderness had
done nothing to blunt his flair for eerie atmosphere.
A group of workmen advance on the camera, wearing
face masks and spraying insecticide, while Philippe
Sissman's minimalist score offers serene little synth
blips reminiscent of an electrocardiogram. Rollin
closes in on the face of one such worker, Kowalski,
and emphasises his stertorous breathing as the title
fades up. Moments later, Kowalski falls off his tractor
(the artisan who rushes to help him is Rollin himself),
and the callous Michel orders him back to work with
the assurance that the "completely airtight" masks
will be arriving the next day.

Clearly, the director who put his actors into *Judex*-style animal masks at the beginning of *La Vampire nue* can engender unease just as efficiently with the blandly functional masks of workaday science fiction. The ensuing train sequence is even stronger, with Elisabeth and her friend Brigitte remarking on the fact that they're the only people aboard. Rollin's camera prowls sedately down the train's corridors and we know at once that this can't be quite true. Then something really intriguing happens. Fleeing from the suppurating Kowalski, Elisabeth disappears into a tunnel and crosses a bridge into a mountainous, mist-shrouded region, as if passing from one zone into another. For his part, Kowalski merely sits on the railway tracks and puts his head in his hands. And this was Rollin's masterstroke. For his 'zombies' are actually crazed humans prey to occasional bouts of lucidity, well aware of the horrors they're perpetrating and profoundly affected by them.

Later on, Rollin's emotional approach pays dividends in a scene that outdoes the blood-spouting gore effects of *Flesh for Frankenstein*. (A French gore movie was such an oxymoron at the time that an effects expert had to be called in from Italy.) A beautiful blind girl called Lucie is crucified, topless, to a barn door and then decapitated with a hatchet; the killer is her beloved guardian Lucas. The scene is astounding in its impact. The head doesn't depart Lucie's shoulders without a significant struggle, blood fountains everywhere, and all the while Lucas laughs insanely and sobs "Lucie! Je t'aime, je t'aime!" Then the zombified farm workers close in on Elisabeth through the darkness, bizarrely parroting "Lucie, je t'aime" as they approach. The change of context from the poetic ending of *Le Frisson des vampires* – where the bereft hero yelled "Isle, je t'aime!" to the uncomprehending cliffs at Dieppe – is startling in itself.

Some of the other effects, notably the rivulets of butterscotch pus that run down from a victim's hairline to signify infection, don't work quite as well as Lucie's decapitation; they were apparently compromised by the extreme cold in which the film was made. Elsewhere, Rollin and cinematographer Claude Becognée make capital of the freezing temperatures, turning the peaks and troughs of the Cévennes into a memorably cheerless and desolate environment; characteristically, Rollin dwells lovingly on the ruined, skeletal structures that dot the landscape.

He also has some really good actors at his disposal. Marie-Georges Pascal charts Elisabeth's descent into madness with total conviction, while Brigitte Lahaie – a porn star whom Rollin had recently used in the pseudonymous film *Vibrations sexuelles* – is already quite mad and contributes a nice 'hounds on a leash'

tribute to Barbara Steele's performance in *La maschera del demonio*. And Félix Marten and Patrice Valota are excellent as a couple of gun-toting avengers. Romero-style vigilantes given a Gallic makeover, they discuss the fact that they're "stuck in the middle" between a nuclear plant and a military installation, while the older man claims to have "had this gun since I fought the Germans."

In one of Rollin's queasiest scenes, Elisabeth comes across a rural father and daughter whose unwelcoming surliness recalls Grant Wood's famous painting *American Gothic*. The father pitchforks the girl to death prior to muttering forlornly, "What have I done? This is tearing me apart..." This emotional agony comes full circle at the end, when Elisabeth finally encounters the infected Michel. Though moving, their reunion is given a sardonic twist by Rollin – for Michel is, by his own admission, the duplicitous, corner-cutting vigneron who caused the apocalypse in the first place.

Though Rollin had temporarily set aside his trademark vampires in *Les Raisins de la mort*, other filmmakers were bringing vampires firmly back into fashion – for, after the rash of Dracula projects that had proliferated in 1973, a further eruption followed five years later. First up was *Count Dracula*, a splendid BBC production transmitted just before Christmas 1977, but it was a smash Broadway revival of the 50-year-old stage adaptation that had a predictable effect in Hollywood. As well as being the obvious inspiration for the waggish comedy *Love at First Bite*, which started shooting on 12 June 1978, it also spawned a fully fledged new *Dracula* that went into production on 16 October – almost a year to the day since the Broadway opening. The star, as in the stage show, was Frank Langella.

By a strange coincidence, in mainland Europe the oldest *Dracula* adaptation of all, F W Murnau's *Nosferatu*, was undergoing a fascinating rejuvenation at the hands of Werner Herzog. A leading figure in 'das neue Kino', Herzog had amassed a budget of 2.5 million Deutschmarks from German and French sources and wound up the ten-week schedule of *Nosferatu Phantom der Nacht* (Nosferatu, Night Phantom) on 6 July. His stars were, from France, Isabelle Adjani and, from Germany, the combustible Klaus Kinski, who, after a long career in exploitation, had acquired art-house glamour via Herzog's 1972 breakthrough film *Aguirre, der zorn Gottes* (Aguirre, Wrath of God).

"I feel pretty close to Murnau," Herzog announced. "His *Nosferatu* is the most visionary of all German films. It prophesied the rise of Nazism by showing the invasion of Germany by Dracula and his plague-bearing rats." He also stated his belief that the vampire genre "is one of the very best soils in which cinema could possibly grow, because it has to do with dreams and nightmares and visions and fears."[14]

*Wismar solicitor Jonathan Harker is sent by his certifiable boss, Renfield, to the Transylvanian castle of Count Dracula, an arduous journey that takes a month. As well as being bereft, his wife Lucy is also psychically attuned to the danger Harker finds himself in on arrival. Leaving Harker trapped, Dracula charters a ship to transport his black coffins from Varna to Wismar, unleashing a devastating plague on the city.*

Herzog's reverence for Murnau went hand-in-hand with a pretty outsized arrogance of his own, as when he claimed in the pages of *Der Spiegel* that "Over the next 50 years it will be impossible to make a vampire movie which doesn't relate to my *Nosferatu*."[15] Even so, there can be little doubt that very few horror films begin as arrestingly as Herzog's. The grim assembly of horribly desiccated Mexican mummies from Guanajuato is a masterstroke, given that the camera's dispassionate scrutiny of them establishes an authentic chill of the grave within ten seconds of the film starting. Intensifying that chill is the astonishing music by Popol Vuh, with Robert Eliscu's keening oboe hedged about by Moog synthesisers and the ominous drone of a Munich church choir.

After a premonitory scream from the fearful Lucy, Herzog then executes a restful transition to the canals of Delft (doubling for Wismar) and a shot of kittens playing with a dangling locket – a transition accompanied by a plaintive mixture of sitar, oboe and acoustic guitar. That life's most tranquil and harmonious scenes are nevertheless shadowed by death is made abundantly clear before the action has even begun.

Those kittens are the first of several exact Murnau quotes. The remainder range from Lucy sitting sadly amid headstone-studded dunes to the death ship nosing its way into harbour at journey's end, from a shot of Renfield twitching spasmodically between stone-faced warders to a sailor's feet being nibbled by rats. (The feet were Herzog's own.) These visual references are beautifully done, but the stand-out Murnau moments that Herzog chose to leave out are just as instructive as the ones he left in. The grizzled face of French character actor Jacques Dufilho, as the ship's captain, carries much of the mournful freight required of Dracula's sea voyage, yet he remains conspicuously alone. There's no sign of the mate venturing into the hold, the vampire rising plank-like from his casket, and the traumatised mate flinging himself overboard in response. No doubt

Herzog suspected this material would invite derisive laughter from 1970s audiences, but the plank effect was presumably also excluded because Herzog was aware his remodelled vampire just wasn't frightening enough to sustain such a ghastly moment.

For Kinski's grub-like Dracula resembles Max Schreck's remorseless, insectoid monster not one bit. Of course, the make-up is superficially similar, but this Dracula personifies Fritz Lang's *Der müde Tod* – the weary Death – much more than Murnau's verminous horror. Humanising the vampire was fundamental to Herzog's intentions but it has the unfortunate side-effect of draining Kinski's performance of pity as well as terror. He's among the first in a long line of 'longing for death' Draculas, but it's tough to sympathise with a vampire who comes out with self-absorbed nonsense, masquerading as existential angst, like "The absence of love is the most abject pain." Despite his repugnant appearance, this is as much a 'Dracula made palatable' as Bela Lugosi was when required to deliver such non-Stoker (in fact, anti-Stoker) lines as "To die, to be really dead – that must be glorious." There may be a whiff of Teutonic poetry about a Herzog line like "Time is an abyss a thousand nights deep," but it's really just a short step from this to the kind of Hollywood garbage ("I have crossed oceans of time to find you") uttered by a lachrymose Dracula in Francis Coppola's 1992 version.

Despite the occasional visibility of the Frankenstein's monster bovver boots used to give Kinski some height, this Dracula at least remains a vividly memorable visual image. Yet the best parts of the film don't feature Dracula at all. Bruno Ganz and Isabelle Adjani, for example, are excellent as the Harkers, and in scattered flashes during Jonathan's journey we see as ideal a *Dracula* adaptation as we're likely to get. Harker's prosaic observation in the book – "The impression I had was that we were leaving the West and entering the East" – is given a cosmic makeover here, with a gypsy patriarch claiming that "In the Borgo Pass the light suddenly divides." In a daringly protracted sequence, underscored not by Popol Vuh but by Wagner's roiling prelude to *Das Rheingold*, Herzog actually shows us this as Harker sits among the snow-covered peaks of the High Tatra mountains in Slovakia. The effect is bizarre and spellbinding.

This and many other landscapes in the film are lent a rare beauty by cinematographer Jörg Schmidt-Reitwein, whose pallid, colour-drained approach is echoed in the ghostly faces of Adjani's determined Lucy and Walter Ladengast's dithering Van Helsing. Even the interiors of Castle Pernštejn in Moravia were clearly chosen for their vaulted whiteness, resembling the bleached bone of a well-preserved skull. Among its

Shadowed by plague and pestilence: Isabelle Adjani and Bruno Ganz in *Nosferatu Phantom der Nacht* (1978)

## NOSFERATU PHANTOM DER NACHT

West Germany-France 1978
France: *Nosferatu, fantôme de la nuit*
UK / US: **Nosferatu the Vampire**
Michael Gruskoff presents / Werner Herzog
 Filmproduktion Munich / Gaumont SA Paris
107 minutes colour
production began 1 May 1978
. . . . . . . . . . . . . . . . . . . . . . . .
Director of Photography: Jörg
Schmidt-Reitwein; Production Designer:
Henning von Gierke; Editor: Beate
Mainka-Jellinghaus; Sound: Harald Maury;
Music: Popol Vuh / Florian Fricke, Vokal
Ensemble Gordela (Zinkaro), selections
from Wagner and Gounod; Costumes:
Gisela Storch; Make-up: Reiko Kruk,
Dominique Colladant; Special Effects:
Cornelius Siegel; Producers: Werner
Herzog, Michael Gruskoff; Writer-Director:
Werner Herzog

Klaus Kinski (Count Dracula); Isabelle Adjani
(Lucy Harker); Bruno Ganz (Jonathan Harker);
Jacques Dufilho (ship's captain); Roland
Topor (Renfield); Walter Ladengast (Dr Van
Helsing); Dan van Husen (warden); Jan Groth
(harbourmaster); Carsten Bodinus (Schrader);
Martje Grohmann (Mina); Ryk de Gooyer
(town official); Clemens Scheitz (clerk); Lo
van Hensbergen (harbourmaster's assistant);
John Leddy (1st coachman); Margiet van
Hartingsveld (wench); Tim Beekman (coffin
bearer); uncredited; Attila Árpa (boy violinist);
Roger Berry Losch (sailor); Claude Chiarini,
Bo van Hens Bergen (inspectors); Dominique
Colladant (doctor); Michael Edols (lord); Martin
Gerbl, Walter Saxer, Anja Schmidt-Zäringer,
Gisela Storch (diners); Stefan Husar (2nd
coachman); Johan te Sla (town crier); Beverly
Walker (abbess); Rudolf Wolf (driver of
phantom carriage)

**Murnau's *Nosferatu* haunts our memories. And Werner Herzog toys with those memories even as he successfully denies us a straightforward remake, taking the *Nosferatu* story seriously and not, as per Roman Polanski, as a theme for jokes ... Herzog's realism is that of a visionary, and through the exceptional beauty of his shots the drama of *Dracula* regains a supernatural appearance.** *Le Nouvel Observateur 22 January 1979*

**I never even saw the Murnau film until afterwards. I worked out the make-up with Werner and Reiko [Kruk], the make-up artist. I hate wearing make-up, I never use it – and until one day before shooting the film I only wanted the bald head, the nails and the teeth. I felt myself complete. But Werner persuaded me. He was mad about the ears.** *Klaus Kinski [quoted in Observer Magazine 25 March 1979]*

other curiosities the film numbers Roland Topor's extremely irritating performance as Renfield, who is finally dismissed by Dracula (not before time) with the exasperated instruction, "Go north to Riga." There are also a few Stoker quotes included that show Herzog paid close attention to the book as well as the Murnau film. Dracula, for example, is given some lines about "sunshine and sparkling waters" not heard in any other adaptation, while Lucy, in Dr Seward's absence, is given a variant on his memorable line, "I sometimes think we must be all mad and that we shall wake to sanity in strait-waistcoats."

Herzog's naïve replication of some of the hoariest features of Stoker's tale – notably the superstitious recoil of the Transylvanian peasantry when Dracula's name is mentioned – drew a certain amount of levity from British critics when the film opened in May 1979. "It strikes one pretty forcibly at times that Herzog clearly hasn't seen as many vampire films as we have," wrote one. "He now says he meant us to laugh on occasion. But I don't believe it for an instant."[16] Moments of unintentional comedy notwithstanding, Herzog incorporates a strong vein of Absurdist humour of his own, notably in Van Helsing's fate at the end. After the apocalyptic scenes of plague-ridden St Vitus Dance in the town square at Delft, complete with seething rats and defecating pigs, the old man finally stakes Dracula (who has already been killed by the dawn, anyway) and is apprehended by a pint-sized town official who – given the breakdown of social order – has no idea what to do with him. Though a slightly silly tableau, it's immediately balanced by the infected Harker's resolve to carry on Dracula's unfinished business – a fashionably downbeat ending, but chillingly put across.

In the midst of all this Dracula activity – and presumably with at least one eye on the success of *Love at First Bite* – the Count found himself transposed, once again, to the bizarre world of Bavarian sex comedy, this time in Carl Schenkel's *Graf Dracula in Oberbayern*. Curiously, this film was advertised with the rather fuller title *Graf Dracula (beisst jetzt) in Oberbayern* (Count Dracula Bites in Upper Bavaria Nowadays) prior to reaching US video as *Dracula Blows His Cool*. Here, Gianni Garko opens a disco in the lower depths of his ancestral castle, rousing his lookalike forebear Count Stanislaus and his vampire bride Olivia (Betty Vergès) with funky floor-fillers like *Rock Me, Dracula*. The film reached German cinemas in October 1979, exactly nine years after Freddie Francis had been in Austria to direct *Gebissen wird nur nachts*, aka *The Vampire Happening*. Hippy happenings may have given way to spangled discoramas in the intervening period, but the two films are about equally dispiriting.

Arguably even worse is Boris Szulzinger's excruciating Belgian-French item *Mama Dracula*, which brought Oscar winner Louise Fletcher to Brussels in 1980. Ten years before, Szulzinger had directed *Les Tueurs fous* (The Crazy Killers), applying a coldly horrible touch of social realism to a tale of two homosexual thrill-killers. *Mama Dracula*, by contrast, is a relentlessly camped-up embarrassment. Fletcher's Countess Dracula lives, confusingly, in Báthory Castle and provides a forlorn echo of Delphine Seyrig in *Les Lèvres rouges*. She also parrots Udo Kier when referring to "dusty wolumes" in which she learned about bathing in "the pure blood of young wirgins." Even worse, she's attended by lanky, hook-nosed vampire twins whose witless mugging defies belief. There are several eye-catching Art Nouveau locations here, together with some distinguished contributors – from Britain alone, Szulzinger called on satirist Tony Hendra for script contributions and cult composer Roy Budd to provide the score. But the puerile result doesn't have a laugh in it from beginning to end

As a small footnote, by the beginning of September 1986 Klaus Kinski was making a bogus sequel to

Herzog's film called *Nosferatu a Venezia* (Nosferatu in Venice), a good-looking but incomprehensible Italian project that went through several directors, including Mario Caiano, before its producer, Augusto Caminito, was forced to take the reins. Approaching 60 and as volatile as ever, Kinski refused to reproduce his *Nosferatu* 'look', favouring 1980s Heavy Metal hair extensions over the larval pate seen in Herzog's film.

# DRAUGHTS OF BLOOD AND FLAMES OF HELL

French horror in the late 1970s was as patchy as ever, ranging from the bloodbank-raiding vampires of Wim Lindner's half-Dutch comedy *Bloedverwanten* (Blood Relatives, 1976) to Laurent Boutonnat's untranslatable *Ballade de la féconductrice* (1978). A transgressive story featuring a murderous 'fée maligne' (evil fairy), the latter was advertised at the Cannes Film Market as 'a film fantastique directed by a boy of 17' prior to being booed off.

Jean Rollin, meanwhile, might reasonably have been expected to make another gore movie after the success of *Les Raisins de la mort*. Instead he founded his next project on a hint provided in an 1890s story by the Symbolist poet Jean Lorrain, while appropriating the film's title from a magazine recently inaugurated by the indefatigable Jean-Pierre Bouyxou. Bouyxou's journal, *Fascination*, unearthed fin-de-siècle erotica under the subtitle 'le Musée Secret de l'Érotisme' (the secret museum of eroticism), while Lorrain's story, *Le Verre de sang* (The Glass of Blood), alerted Rollin to the fact that high-society doctors at the turn of the century were apt to prescribe a daily glass of fresh blood to combat tuberculosis. (Lorrain himself was both sufferer and drinker.) Combining these supposedly disparate strands, Rollin embarked on the 12-day shoot for *Fascination* with a skeleton crew and no shooting script.

*April 1905. In flight from a gang of petty criminals whom he's double-crossed, Marc ventures into an enormous château, occupied only by the beautiful Elisabeth and Eva. They are, respectively, companion and lady-in-waiting to the Marquise, Hélène, who's due to return that night with a group of friends. Marc makes love with Eva, thinking he has the upper hand, but when Hélène arrives with her retinue he realises he's been ensnared for a very specific purpose.*

*Fascination* boasts two of Rollin's most indelible images, and the first comes early – two well-heeled women drinking decorously amid the hanging carcasses of an abattoir. The abattoir echoes Lorrain's original story, in which a former actress can't bear the slaughterhouse in which her beloved stepdaughter takes her TB cure, but Rollin repurposes the draughts of blood as a remedy for anaemia. "Drink, my dear," one of the women is assured. "It will bring back your colour." The viewer, meanwhile, is assured that "it's only ox blood," but Rollin's long-held close-up on a pair of incarnadined lips being massaged by a blood-dripping finger indicates that there are murkier cravings to come.

In the meantime we're introduced to a less than alarming gang of thugs. Three men and one woman (plus the equivocal, dandified figure of Marc), they're clearly Rollin's nod to the lawless 'apache' phenomenon that gripped France in 1902 and was immortalised in Jacques Becker's 1951 film *Casque d'or*. Though these apaches are a little too redolent of 1978 to be entirely convincing, they're only really there to manoeuvre Marc into the fateful château – first glimpsed, in an icily effective shot, perched above a mist-shrouded lake behind a screen of beetling trees. "You've stumbled into Elisabeth and Eva's life," Elisabeth tells him, clarifying this with "the universe of madness and death." Though the women subject him to plenty of coquettish mockery, as well as retiring to one of the bedrooms for a prolonged lesbian interlude, Marc remains unfazed, asserting what he presumes is his God-given masculine dominance with the dismissive phrase, "It's not for two little girls like you to lay down the law."

Marc, it quickly transpires, has become embroiled in a class war as well as a sex war. Indeed, his recourse to hollow, low-life gangsterisms (he says "The show's over" no fewer than three times) will prove no match for the aristocratic power of the Marquise and her assembled cult. Similarly, Brigitte Lahaie's Eva is sneeringly described by one of the apaches as a "petite bourgeoise" – but, again, the aristocrat proves more resourceful, skewering him with an ornamental dagger even as she straddles him in the château's outhouses. She then slits the throats of the other two male gangsters with one sweep of a scythe, afterwards pursuing the female apache onto the moated causeway and providing the film with its second indelible image – Eva as a coldly beautiful distillate of sex and death, naked but for a billowing black cloak, red buttoned boots and the monstrous scythe.

As darkness falls the Marquise arrives with her four companions and the film shifts in tone. Hélène is an inscrutable, chalk-faced grandee, surveying Marc through her lorgnettes and saying, "Do you mind if I examine you as if you were my horse?" It quickly becomes obvious that the women

have graduated from ox blood to midnight sacrifices of selected human, and exclusively male, victims. They make an exception, however, for the transgressive Eva. Previously the very image of sexualised Death as she traversed the moat, she now falls prey to her cannibal sisters on the very same causeway. Rollin focuses on this writhing scrum of ravening, barely clad bodies for an absurdly long time, particularly since the carnage is at no point convincing – a failing he would correct a few years later with the flesh-ripping explicitness of *La Morte vivante*. Even so, the film proceeds to a satisfyingly grim endgame when Elisabeth, who has become smitten by Marc, suddenly realises that "The love of blood might be greater than that for the body in which it flows..."

## FASCINATION

France 1979
Consortium Européen Cinematographique / Comex
Productions / Films ABC
80 minutes colour
visa date 20 July 1979

Lara; Writer-Director: Jean Rollin

Director of Photography: Georgie Fromentin; Editor: Dominique Saint-Cyr; Sound: Claude Panier; Music: Philippe d'Aram; Assistant Director: Nathalie Perrey; Producer: Joe De

Franca Mai (Elisabeth); Brigitte Lahaie (Eva); Jean-Marie Lemaire (Marc); Fanny Magier (Hélène); Muriel Montossé (Anita); Sophie Noël (Sylvie); Evelyne Thomas (Dominique); Agnès Bert (fifth cultist); Alain Plumey, Myriam Watteau, Joe De Lara, Jacques Sansoul (apaches); uncredited: Jacques Marbeuf (doctor at abattoir), Nathalie Perrey (aristocrat at abattoir)

**Fascinating, to be sure, but only for its vacuity. A bit of vampirism, a pinch of pornography, three drops of romance, a soupçon of horror: full of good intentions, Jean Rollin tries everything. Too bad: he has a gift for nothing.**
*Télérama* 16 January 1980 [complete review]

**I like *Fascination* very much. It is very close to what I envisioned, very romantic and savage at the same time. It has a truly enigmatic, predatory atmosphere and some great images, such as Brigitte Lahaie wielding the scythe or the opening scene in the slaughterhouse. It's quite arty, and although it is a vampire film it pretty much avoids the pulp ideas which I usually work into my scripts.** Jean Rollin [quoted in *Video Watchdog* January-February 1996]

Brigitte Lahaie, snuffed out by her cannibal sisters in *Fascination* (1979)

Fascination exudes a decadent, autumnal chill much enhanced by Philippe d'Aram's memorable score (his first of several for Rollin) and by an unusually accomplished acting ensemble; arrogantly self-possessed almost to the end, Jean-Marie Lemaire is particularly good as Marc. Perhaps surprisingly, the stately atmospherics of Fascination mesh perfectly with the film's fleshly, exploitable ingredients, which are plentiful. Cinematographer Georgie Fromentin came to the film direct from hardcore titles like Bouyxou's Entrez vite … vite, je mouille! (Put It In Quickly … Quickly, I'm Getting Wet!). But this didn't prevent him from lending Fascination a large measure of painterly beauty.

In Italy, Mario Bava, too, took inspiration from a 19th century French author, in his case Prosper Mérimée. Co-directed by Bava's son Lamberto in the summer of 1978, La Venere d'Ille (The Venus of Ille) was made as part of the RAI television series I giochi del diavolo: storie fantastiche dell'ottocento (Games of the Devil: Fantastic Stories of the 1800s). The Mérimée original, La Vénus d'Ille, was an intriguing choice of source material, having previously been adapted as Die Venus in Austria in 1921 and having served as partial inspiration for Camillo Mastrocinque's Un angelo per Satana 40-odd years later. The Bava version has something of the allusive grace of Lawrence Gordon Clark's M R James adaptations, made earlier in the decade for the BBC. Padded out to 60 minutes with plenty of badminton and epicurean feasting, the film nevertheless gives eerie life to the titular statue and builds to a shadowy bedroom climax that bears the classic Bava stamp, with a foolish bridegroom being enfolded in a bronze embrace as his petrified bride goes insane.

For Bava, the film was another collaboration with Dario Argento's muse Daria Nicolodi, who, as the bride, bears a genuinely disconcerting resemblance to the impassive Venus. Sadly, the film was another instance of the bad luck that dogged Bava in his final years; the series of which it formed a part wasn't transmitted until the summer of 1981, more than a year after his death.

Mario Bava's final work involved a special effects consultancy on Argento's 1979 film Inferno, in which Nicolodi also appeared and (uncredited) co-wrote the script. Appropriately, Bava's duties included the addition of a baleful full moon to a tricked-up New York skyline. The project, on which Lamberto Bava served as assistant director, was budgeted at $3,000,000 and had the benefit of financial input from 20th Century-Fox, who had done very nicely indeed when distributing Suspiria two years before. Inferno, however, wouldn't do nearly so well, in part because Fox declined to release it in the USA, waiting until 1986 before finally dumping it in video stores.

*Having acquired an ancient book called The Three Mothers, Rose Elliott becomes convinced that her New York apartment building is one of the three loci of evil described in it, and writes to her brother Mark, urging him to return from Rome. Sara, a fellow music student of Mark's, reads the letter and, in the course of investigating Rose's claims, is brutally murdered. Arriving in New York, Mark learns that Rose, too, was killed at much the same time…*

Suspiria, of course, had been an imagistic triumph that fell firmly into the 'follow that' category, and in (rather belatedly) following it Argento exchanged Suspiria's hysterical, headlong plunge into nightmare with a somnambulant wallow in stream-of-consciousness dream territory. To give the resultant flow of imagery the barest underpinning of plot, he sketched in a bit more of the arcane imaginings he'd picked up from Thomas de Quincey's Suspiria de Profundis, details only hinted at in Suspiria, indicating that human life is shadowed by a triumvirate of malevolent spirits – Mater Suspiriorum (Mother of Sighs), Mater Tenebrarum (Mother of Darkness) and Mater Lachrymarum (Mother of Tears). Having disposed of the first in Suspiria, he was here moving on to the second. He wouldn't get round to the final instalment, La terza madre (The Third Mother), until late 2006, and was met with critical dismay (even from his keenest supporters) when he did.

Argento also posited three looming homes for the Three Mothers (one of which we have already seen imploding, Usher-style, in Suspiria), and gave them the same architect, Varelli. This character, loosely founded on the mysterious occultist Fulcanelli, is the same person who has been indiscreet enough to write a book about his three maleficent employers. On this slender framework Argento hangs another series of extraordinary set-pieces. This time the oneiric vibrancy of the colours edges towards affectation, prefiguring the self-conscious, candified gloom of 1980s music videos, while Argento displays a riddling disregard for narrative that leaves the viewer no option but to go with the flow. "For him," as Peter Nicholls has put it, "magic is arbitrary and inexplicable. The result is a fragmentation so extreme as to defy analysis of what it all might mean."[17] In other words, dream logic holds sway, and in that regard the film is a truly ingenious contrivance.

Nowhere is this clearer than in the film's first act, in which Irene Miracle's Rose descends into a flooded basement in pursuit of a mislaid key ring. Rarely has the weightless netherworld of the dream state been so persuasively conveyed, with the amber-tinted space disclosing glimpses of waterlogged luxuriance

Gabriele Lavia is disposed of by Mater Tenebrarum in *Inferno* (1979)

along with a sunken portrait of Mater Tenebrarum. Also bobbing into view – in a not-strictly-necessary capitulation to the jump scares of conventional horror – is a tattered corpse that brushes against Rose's feet with horrid persistence.

For the film's score, Argento turned, not to Goblin, but to Keith Emerson, the Prog god cited by Goblin's Claudio Simonetti as an important influence. Emerson scores Rose's quest with a piano motif beguilingly redolent of silent movies, but when Argento moves on to Rome and the similar quest of Eleonora Giorgi's Sara, we're assailed by an atrocious synth transcription of Verdi's *Va pensiero* that has to be heard to be believed. It completely ruins an otherwise compelling taxi ride that exactly parallels a similar scene in *Suspiria*. Here, the blue night sky behind Sara is of stunning beauty, and in front of her sits a neat in-joke in the form of Fulvio Mingozzi, who played the same surly driver in the corresponding *Suspiria* scene. Happily, and to supremely creepy effect, music is entirely absent from Rose's subsequent visit to the Biblioteca Filosofica, which recalls the cloistered atmosphere of such M R James stories as *The Tractate Middoth*. Impressive in its vaulted solemnity, the library yields up a copy of Varelli's foreboding book with dreamlike ease; later, in its lower depths, it discloses a literal Hell's Kitchen with a taloned monstrosity methodically stirring a cauldron.

Argento then dispenses with both Rose and Sara in separate outbursts of shocking violence, after which the equally summary dismissal of Daria Nicolodi's Elise

## INFERNO

USA-Italy 1979
20th Century-Fox Film Corporation / Produzioni Intersound (Rome)
107 minutes colour
production began 21 May 1979
. . . . . . . . . . . . . . . . . . . . . . . . . . .
Director of Photography: Romano Albani; Art Director: Giuseppe Bassan; Editor: Franco Fraticelli; Sound: Francesco Groppioni; Music: Keith Emerson; Make-up: Pierantonio Mecacci; Special Effects: Germano Natali and [both uncredited] Mario Bava, Pino Leoni; Underwater Sequence: Lorenzo Battaglia; Story and Screenplay: Dario Argento and

[uncredited] Daria Nicolodi; Producer: Claudio Argento; Director: Dario Argento

Leigh McCloskey (Mark Elliott); Irene Miracle (Rose Elliott); Eleonora Giorgi (Sara); Daria Nicolodi (Countess Elise Delon-Benaddler); Sacha Pitoëff (Kazanian); Alida Valli (Carol); Veronica Lazar (nurse); Gabriele Lavia (Carlo); Feodor Chaliapin (Varelli); Leopoldo Mastelloni ([John the] butler); Ania Pieroni (musical student); James Fleetwood (cook); Rosario Rigutini (man); Ryan Hilliard (shadow); Paolo Paoloni (music teacher); Fulvio Mingozzi (cab driver); Luigi Lodolo (book binder); Rudolfo Lodi (old man)

*Inferno* is one of those films I wouldn't sit through if I was paid to. Except that I *was* paid to ... This badly dubbed sequel [to *Suspiria*] offers the mixture as before without the style or economy of its predecessor. Buckets of full frontal gore, spooky interiors, an idiotic narrative and a risible script: a shambles of a film, in all senses. *The Guardian* 18 September 1980

It's a very long story with [20th Century-] Fox and what they did to *Inferno*. Halfway through shooting the picture the management at Fox changed and the new management boycotted all the films that were being produced by the previous board. Not only *Inferno* but several others; they didn't want anything to do with them ... It's sad, very sad. *Dario Argento* [quoted in *Fangoria* April 1984]

leaves us with Leigh McCloskey's Mark as a somewhat anodyne identification figure. On arrival at Rose's Manhattan apartment, Mark encounters a selection of its weird inhabitants, including Alida Valli (carried over from *Suspiria*) and the gnarled, wheelchair-bound Feodor Chaliapin Jr. The latter's presence indicates that Argento – having quoted the Val Lewton production *Cat People* in his previous picture – was consciously echoing another Lewton film, *The Seventh Victim*. There, Chaliapin Jr had played a hired assassin in the employ of a coven of Manhattan witches. Here, he turns out to be none other than Varelli himself, communicating by means of an artificial larynx and trying to kill the meddlesome Mark with a hypodermic.

Also memorable is Kazanian, the sinister antique dealer next door, for whom the cadaverous Sacha Pitoëff was a perfect fit. The spectacular sequence in which Kazanian drowns a sackful of cats in Central Park – only to be set upon by a fleet of voracious water rats – was reportedly complicated for the filmmakers by Pitoëff's uninterrupted boozing. On screen the sequence is only complicated by another disastrous passage of Emerson's score, which overlays the rat-nibbling horror with a roistering theme more suitable to a pirate movie.

As the dream flows on, Argento inserts cut-away reminders of the inescapable dominion of death, including a lizard chomping on a butterfly and a cat digesting a mouse. (The latter section, with half the mouse dropping from the cat's jaws, was censored in numerous territories.) He even finds room for further in-jokes, as when a valet solemnly takes the temperature of Elise's bath, reminding us of the scalding horrors of *Profondo rosso*. Argento finally contrives to lower Mark into the depths just as Rose was lowered at the beginning of the film. The ancient motif of the inscrutable Gothic mansion, its various levels mirroring the unconscious mind, has been hinted at already by Elise's reference to the strange pipes that honeycomb the place: "This weird old building is full of secrets like that." Now, Mark enters a crawl-space that leads to a magical set of subterranean chambers, reacquainting him not just with Varelli but also the old man's forbidding nurse (Veronica Lazar). The latter itemises the Latin names of the Three Mothers prior to an electrifying proclamation: "But men call us by a single name, a name which strikes fear into everyone's heart. They call us Death. Death!"

Appropriately, the final hallucinatory revelation is engineered by means of an ornate mirror (Mario Bava was responsible for the effect), after which the expected conflagration winds up with the cowled Death figure, resembling a grinning Grim Reaper from a mediaeval woodcut, standing exultant and unbowed amid the flames. It's a powerful climax to a film whose somnolent pace ranks it lower than *Suspiria*, but which nevertheless features flashes of genuine brilliance.

## ENTRAIL-CHEWING IN THE TROPICS

Fresh from a splendid series of poliziotteschi starring Franco Nero, Enzo G Castellari found himself on the Costa Brava in August 1978, directing a horror picture called *Diabla* (She Devil). "It was a completely Spanish production involving some questionable money," he explained some 15 years later. "I was not very happy to see my name on that picture."[18]

Shown in Castellari's native Italy as *Sensitività*, the film was shot by Alejandro Ulloa in beguiling soft-focus tones at least as hazy as the garbled and frankly incomprehensible plot. Leonora Fani, the impressive heroine of Francesco Barilli's *Pensione paura*, is back, this time as a leatherclad motorcyclist looking for answers about her ancestry and telling people that "I'm interested in ghosts and witches, do you get me?" Under the influence of a baleful, black-veiled forebear called Kyra, she takes four lovers on returning to her hick home town, with three of whom she appears to 'die' at the moment of orgasm, thus precipitating the boys' actual deaths. The sex, accompanied by suitably bass-heavy porn music, was presumably considered more important than the horror; even so, Castellari contrives a terrific shot – straight out of *Carnival of Souls* – in which Kyra is picked out in the headlights of the first victim's car. (As it plunges in flames over a cliff, we're even given a nifty bit of split-screen.) Masturbating on the sidelines during the sex scenes is a wild child (Patricia Adriani) who turns out to be Fani's sister. To break the curse, they indulge in a pretty staggering climactic cat fight, during which they succeed in tearing each other's clothes off.

Castellari claimed that the film was finished off by its Spanish producer (Diego Alchimede); whoever was responsible, its clunky attempts at dreamlike atmosphere are strangely watchable. Even so, the *Diabla* experience convinced Castellari he wasn't a good fit for horror, prompting him, the following year, to turn down a project called *Zombi 2*. He wasn't to know that this film, having been passed on to Lucio Fulci, would trigger the next and most notorious phase in Italian horror.

In true Italian style, this new phase was itself triggered by the success of a foreign film – in this instance, a film made just east of Pittsburgh. To top up the budget for his long-awaited follow-up to *Night of the Living Dead*, writer-director George Romero turned to Dario Argento, granting him in return the right to prepare his own edit for non-English-speaking territories. (For Argento, this side-project was a significant feature of the noticeable two-year gap between the success of *Suspiria* and the production of *Inferno*.) The Argento cut reached Italian cinemagoers as *Zombi* in September 1978, some nine months before Romero's version – *Dawn of the Dead* – opened in the USA.

For producer Fabrizio De Angelis, initiating an indigenous follow-up was an obvious move. Shot

A fatal embrace for Richard Johnson in *Zombi 2* (1979)

in just four weeks in the summer of 1979 and rush-released in the last week of August, *Zombi 2* cost a mere 410 million lire and amassed a worldwide gross of over three billion – this despite the fact that, aside from flesh-ripping zombies, it resembled the Romero film in no way whatsoever. In the US it would become plain *Zombie*, while in the UK it acquired the euphonious title *Zombie Flesh-Eaters* and was released in March 1980, three months ahead of the Romero film. It was also under this title that it became, in due course, an embattled centrepiece of the 'Video Nasties' hysteria.

More importantly, the film reinvented Lucio Fulci as a master of visceral horror, a development he apparently foresaw even before the film was released. "On the day we finished shooting," he recalled in 1991, "I told the crew we had made a horror classic without knowing it."[19] There was clearly no false modesty involved here, yet Fulci turned out to be absolutely right.

*Ann Bolt engages British journalist Peter West to help track down her father. Her fears are made worse by the fact that the missing man's boat has been found derelict in New York harbour, with only a cannibalistic ghoul on board. Heading for the Caribbean island of Matul, they discover that the place is overrun by zombies. Yet their host, a British scientist called Menard, clings stubbornly to the idea that the crisis must have a logical explanation.*

## ZOMBI 2

Italy 1979
UK: **Zombie Flesh-Eaters**
US: **Zombie**
Variety Film
94 minutes colour
production began 11 June 1979

. . . . . . . . . . . . . . . . . . . . . . . . . . . . .

Director of Photography: Sergio Salvati; Production Designer: Walter Patriarca; Editor: Vincenzo Tomassi; Sound: Ugo Celani, Nick Alexander [English-language dub]; Music: Fabio Frizzi, Giorgio Tucci; Make-up and Special Effects: Gianetto De Rossi; Screenplay: Elisa Briganti and [uncredited] Dardano Sacchetti; Producers:

Ugo Tucci, Fabrizio de Angelis; Director: Lucio Fulci

Tisa Farrow (Ann Bolt / Ann Bowles in US version); Ian McCulloch (Peter West); Richard Johnson (Dr David Menard); Al Cliver [Pier Luigi Conti] (Bryan Curt / Brian Hull in US version); Auretta Gay (Susan Barrett); Stefania d'Amario (nurse); Olga Karlatos (Paola Menard); uncredited: Ugo Bologna (Ann's father); Dakkar (Lucas); Ottaviano Dell'Acqua (conquistador zombie); Lucio Fulci (newspaper editor); Franco Fantasia (Father Mattias); Leo Gavero (Fritz); Captain Haggerty (first zombie); James Sampson (coroner); Mónica Zanchi (dying woman)

**Zombi 2 lacks – for all the weaknesses of [George] Romero's film – even a tenth of the minatory charge harboured by Zombies [ie, Dawn of the Dead]. It begins well enough ... But once the island is reached, Lucio Fulci's direction becomes statutory in the extreme, making a hash even of the scene in which the graves yawn (much better done in John Gilling's Plague of the Zombies).**
Monthly Film Bulletin March 1980

**My problem was to write a story having zombies without copying Romero's movie; the script was written in 15 days. Lisa [Briganti] and I thought up an exotic story, as opposed to Romero's urban one ... Also, in Romero's movie the zombies are given a social character, while in ours they are only the dead who have come out of their tombs.** Dardano Sacchetti [quoted in The Dark Side August 1992]

The *Zombi 2* pre-credits sequence lasts barely half a minute but is certainly an attention grabber. Having blasted a zombie's head with no fanfare at all, the silhouetted Dr Menard cues the door, no-nonsense credit titles with the enigmatic line "The boat can leave now. Tell the crew." This first head-blasting is meted out to a risen corpse already shrouded in sacking, ready for burial, but far more graphic eviscerations are to come, courtesy of Giannetto De Rossi's consistently brilliant special make-up effects.

Yet, for all its notoriety, the film is by no means just a gore fest, for Fulci's expert deployment of De Rossi's show-stopping effects is only half the story. The derelict yacht that noses its way into Staten Island waters at the beginning does so in a forlorn shot recalling the arrival of the ghost ship in both versions of Nosferatu, and the remainder of the film boasts a similarly dislocated atmosphere. Matul, for example, is far from a tropical paradise, with Fulci's chilly images ranging from wandering goats, scuttling crabs and wind-agitated dust storms to the the bare boards of a shanty town and the stark, forbidding whiteness of Menard's makeshift hospital; the bleakness is almost palpable. "The best parts of my movies are shot with mystery," Fulci maintained. "I have no idea where that sense of atmosphere comes from, but it appears as if by magic."[20] Wherever it originated, it would prove just as much Fulci's stock in trade as the extravagant splatter in which his films are soaked.

Though Dardano Sacchetti had worked for Fulci before (together with Bava and Argento), the screenplay for Zombi 2 was his first horror script written in collaboration with his wife, Elisa Briganti. In restoring zombies to their traditional setting in the West Indies they opened up the film to some interesting interpretations. Ian Olney, for example, has argued that Zombi 2 "is less a postmodern recycling than a postcolonial revision of Dawn of the Dead … [returning] to the roots of the zombie myth in order to deconstruct it."[21]

That the zombies are largely Caribbean natives, supposedly rebelling against the contemporary descendants of their western exploiters, is an intriguing angle. Certainly, Peter and Ann, and their friends Bryan and Susan, are an uninspiring bunch who amount to little more than Caucasian zombie fodder however the film is interpreted. (The female roles are particularly insipid.) Yet arguably the most memorable of the film's zombie attacks involves, not West Indians, but a group of risen Conquistadores, who emerge from the jungle floor to the electronic strains of Fabio Frizzi's excellent music. One of these, played by actor-stuntman Ottaviano Dell'Acqua, is a worm-eyed monstrosity who would become the film's predominant poster image. He also rips out Susan's throat in an eye-popping welter of pump-action gore.

Whether Spanish or West Indian, De Rossi's zombies return to "the roots of the zombie myth" in more ways than one; resembling humanoid root vegetables, they seem like organic emanations of the very earth in which they were interred. (According to De Rossi, "Fulci and I called them walking flower pots."[22]) These zombies are putrescent works of art, making the thin layer of greenish foundation applied to the Dawn of the Dead zombies look like child's play.

Fulci's scene of the risen Conquistadores is just one dazzlingly confected set-piece in a film replete with them. Though much fêted, the scene in which an aquatic zombie battles a visibly doped-up Tiger shark is limply put together from what was (presumably) insufficient coverage, but the final assault on Menard's infirmary by the zombie hordes is stunningly well sustained. In a largely humourless film, this section also boasts a splendidly funny-horrible detail when the creatures bump blindly against the hospital doors like so many skittles, together with a moving moment in which Brian encounters the resurrected Susan. The film's other pièce-de-résistance has passed into legend. Inaugurating Fulci's fascination for eye trauma, it puts the viewer through protracted agony as Menard's disaffected wife is slowly hauled by her hair towards a jagged splinter protruding from a shattered door. The suspense is set up when the showering Mrs Menard is viewed through a window and a mouldering, blue-tinged hand suddenly attaches itself to the panes. The almost 3-D clarity of this image is a prime example of the way cinematographer Sergio Salvati converts horror into a strange kind of beauty.

Hovering over the action is the ambiguous figure of Dr Menard. Doggedly seeking to rationalise events from the vantage point of his church-cum-hospital, he's played with grizzled resignation by horror veteran Richard Johnson. His name may recall Dr Moreau, but Menard's culpability or otherwise in the zombie uprising is left tantalisingly unclear. Whatever his transgressions may be, he certainly pays for them when a large section of his face is bitten off, with shocking suddenness, in the climactic siege.

Fulci's setting in the Dominican Republic no doubt looked familiar to the massively industrious Joe D'Amato, who made a string of Caribbean sex-horror hybrids at the turn of the 1980s, some of them venturing into hardcore. Titles like Porno Holocaust, Orgasmo nero (Black Orgasm), Sesso nero (Black Sex) and Le notti erotiche dei morti viventi (Erotic Nights of the Living Dead) speak for themselves. As for Zombi 2's producer Fabrizio De Angelis, by the end of 1979 he was back in Santo Domingo and its environs for Marino Girolami's Zombi Holocaust, which retained British actor Ian McCulloch from the Fulci film and made it into Italian theatres in March 1980. Here, a

New York mortuary is the site of various body-part thefts – a plasticine hand is hacked off under cover of night as soon as the credits are over – and the resident professor concludes that "We must have a psychopathic deviant in the hospital." In a predictably racist development, the thefts are traced to cannibal immigrants, leading nurse Alexandra Delli Colli to join anthropologist McCulloch on an expedition to the Caribbean island from which they originated.

The zombies (a few of which sport reasonably imaginative make-ups) only show up after 50 minutes have gone by, too late to save party member Peter O'Neal from having his eyes put out and abdomen torn open by cannibals but just in time to save McCulloch from a similar fate. Conversely, at the end of the film McCulloch and Delli Colli are saved from rampaging zombies by the intervention of the cannibals. By this time we've

Alexandra Delli Colli encounters a maggoty severed head in *Zombi Holocaust* (1979), distributed in Spain as 'Burial Ground of the Zombies'

been introduced to mad scientist Dr Obrero (Donald O'Brien), whose unhinged presence provides this piece of purest catchpenny trash with its only redeeming moments. He's making zombies out of the cannibals for unspecified reasons, and to this end has scalped another party member (Sherry Buchanan) and, in a very nasty scene, severed her vocal chords.

The film boasts some highly quotable dialogue, as when McCulloch calls O'Brien "a bloodthirsty lunatic" and O'Brien spits out in reply, "I could easily kill you now. But I'm determined to have your brain. It will be the culmination of my career!" It also has some grandstanding gore effects, including McCulloch's quick-thinking application of an outboard motor to a beach zombie's head. But it suffers a catastrophic failure in its final moments, fudging its 'consummation devoutly to be wished' climax by withholding from us the final evisceration of Dr Obrero by his cannibal underlings. This in a film that has no other raison d'être but unwithheld eviscerations.

In perhaps the lamest of *Zombi Holocaust*'s many lame moments, Delli Colli asks the rhetorical question "Do you really think we're that much different from savages?" This is an obvious echo of the concluding line in Ruggero Deodato's 1979 film *Cannibal Holocaust*, when a disillusioned anthropologist, nauseated by the raw documentary footage he's just watched, ventures back onto the streets of New York and says to himself, "I wonder who the *real* cannibals are?"

Deodato's film was the most extreme – and, for all its repugnant details, by far the most accomplished – entry in a cannibal cycle that had begun back in 1972 with Umberto Lenzi's *Il paese del sesso selvaggio* (The Land of Savage Sex), exported as *Deep River Savages*. Mixing prurient and unrelentingly violent views of primitive peoples with numerous instances of on-screen animal cruelty, the sub-genre only got into its stride five years later with Deodato's *Ultimo mondo cannibale* (Last Cannibal World), Joe D'Amato's *Emanuelle e gli ultimi cannibali* (Emanuelle and the Last Cannibals) and Sergio Martino's *La montagna del dio cannibale* (The Mountain of the Cannibal God). The last of these made the typically disingenuous promise, in a written prologue, to provide insight into 'immense unexplored areas, shrouded in mystery, where life has remained at its primordial level.'

Old hands Jess Franco and Antonio Margheriti also did time in the genre, directing entries like *El caníbal* and *Apocalisse domani* respectively. The latter, exported as *Cannibal Apocalypse*, is untypical in that it deals not with a jungle expedition but Vietnam vets returning to Atlanta infected with "a form of contagious illness which manifests itself as a kind of rabies." Then at the turn of the 1980s Lenzi attempted to reassert his dominance with the exploitative extremes of two of the sub-genre's most infamous titles, *Mangiati vivi!* (Eaten Alive!) and *Cannibal Ferox*. Cementing their notoriety, in Great Britain the majority of these films would end up on the Department of Public Prosecutions' 1983 list of

'Video Nasties', with only *Ultimo mondo cannibale* and *Mangiati vivi!* somehow escaping the stigma.

But it's Deodato's uncompromising *Cannibal Holocaust* that remains the most disturbingly potent product of the trend, earning from US critic Craig Ledbetter the sobriquet "the *Citizen Kane* of cannibal movies."[23] It begins, as several of these films do, in New York City; among the location shots there's even a briefly glimpsed hoarding for John Badham's about-to-open *Dracula* remake, a film about as far from Deodato's transgressive horrors as it's possible to get. Taking the disappearance in South America of a four-strong documentary crew as its starting point, the action reaches its infamous centrepiece when the crew's undeveloped footage is returned to New York and screened. Nowadays the film can be seen as a forerunner of the 'found footage' mode popularised in 1999 by *The Blair Witch Project*, but it remains more rawly powerful than all its descendants put together.

The scenes of animal cruelty are vile and irredeemable, but the skill with which Deodato orchestrates the crescendo of horror in the film's second half is impossible to deny. The "four brave young Americans" referenced by a TV presenter at the beginning turn out to have been four monstrous young psychopaths, destroying everything in their path on the principle that "We're gonna get an Oscar for this!" In a simple but effective reversal, they're infinitely more depraved than the so-called savages, eventually falling prey to appalling but richly deserved retribution in the final gruelling stages.

Skilful as Deodato's work is (so skilful, indeed, that he was almost imprisoned for what Italian authorities mistakenly assumed was a snuff movie), the film's real stroke of genius is provided by Riz Ortolani's freakishly beautiful music. Ortolani was an appropriate choice; he'd scored several of the meretricious mondo shockumentaries peddled in the 1960s by Jacopetti and Prosperi (including the trend-setting *Mondo cane*), films of which Deodato's was a viciously cynical reductio ad absurdum. And in *Cannibal Holocaust* Ortolani makes even pinball-effect disco syn-drums sound ominous. The climactic immolation of the filmmakers, including emasculation, disembowelment, gang rape and decapitation, is set to a theme of plangently soaring strings that's elegiac, almost serene. The perversely poetic result suggests that we're watching a dramatisation of the human condition at its most basic: just a self-perpetuating round of killing and being killed. And, of course, eaten.

Directly after finishing *Cannibal Holocaust*, Deodato made *La casa sperduta nel parco* (The House on the Edge of the Park) in 19 days during September 1979.

A vacuous home-invasion thriller for the disco era, equal parts lame-brained, mean-spirited and gloatingly sadistic, this showcased the brutish David Hess (formerly the psychotic centrepiece of Wes Craven's 1971 shocker *Last House on the Left*) and beautiful Annie Belle (the wide-eyed revenant from Jean Rollin's *Lèvres de sang*). In Britain the Department of Public Prosecutions lost no time in placing it very firmly on the 'Video Nasties' list.

# A FRIDGE MAGNET AND FIVE CATS

Fourteen years after entering the film industry, Lamberto Bava, son of Mario, was ready to make his feature debut as a director in his own right. *Macabro* accordingly went into production in Salò in mid-December 1979, not long after the younger Bava had finished work on Argento's *Inferno* in his old role as assistant director. Yet *Macabro* would be a very different proposition; eschewing the sprawling metaphysics of *Inferno*, this was an intimate chamber piece written in part by none other than Pupi Avati. And Bava had another ace up his sleeve in his choice of female lead. British actress Bernice Stegers was fresh from starring opposite Marcello Mastroianni in the latest Fellini phantasmagoria, *La città delle donne* (City of Women), and in *Macabro* she lends unusual intensity to what, in its essentials, is a sick joke.

*Having sex with her lover Fred, Jane Baker learns that her small son has been drowned in the bath by his older sister, Lucy. Driving Jane home at high speed, Fred is decapitated in a car crash... A year later, the now-divorced Jane emerges from an institution and moves into the apartment where her trysts with Fred took place. Robert, the young landlord, is blind – and distinctly puzzled by the sounds of ecstasy floating down from above.*

When Bava started shooting *Macabro*, Joe D'Amato's *Buio omega* had been on release in Italy for a month. As studies in necrophilia they couldn't be more different. With Bava exchanging the juvenile entrail-flinging of D'Amato's film for a far more discreet, and cumulatively much more disturbing, approach, *Macabro* trades on a climate of eroticised dread that builds methodically to a predictable but effective pay-off. Unfortunately, when the film came out the pay-off's predictability or otherwise was entirely blown by a 'tell all' trailer, and successive home video releases have repeated this blunder through cover artwork that announces the denouement as clearly as can be.

The set-up is arrestingly done, introducing us to a family situation that's sufficiently dysfunctional without the intrusion of necrophile passions. The blind young man is a repairer of musical instruments, allowing for an outrageous visual gag as he fits interlocking trumpet tubes while listening to Jane's orgasmic moans issuing from the room above. The subsequent drowning of Jane's little boy by her monstrous daughter recalls the 1965 Hammer thriller *The Nanny*, while the theme of parental neglect and guilt vaguely recalls the Ibsen play *Little Eyolf*, in which a baby boy is crippled by falling off a table while his parents are making love. This prologue points forward as well as back, however; the windscreen-piercing method of Fred's demise would be quoted pretty much verbatim in the credits sequence of Neil Marshall's 2005 hit *The Descent*.

Bava's schedule included a three-day stint in New Orleans, yielding location footage that meshes convincingly with claustrophobic interiors devised by Katia Dottori. The intricacy of Dottori's design is seen at its creepiest in the triangular shrine that Jane lights candles to in her new apartment. It's a horrid little artefact, decorated with three photos, a fountain pen, fag ends, buttons, a razor blade and a letter, plus a Visa card, car keys, a passport and even a CND badge. Spoiling the effect a little for English-speaking audiences, there's also a newspaper clipping headed 'atrocius [sic] car accident – victim decapitated'. The shrewdness of the design extends to the conspicuously spartan nature of the ground floor – domain of the blind and ascetic Robert – and the over-ripe, velvety plushness of the erotomaniac's apartment above. Here, Bernice Stegers, in the first of several admirably uninhibited scenes, prostrates herself in a sheer black negligée before the candlelit shrine, while the viewer is left to ponder the significance of the lock she firmly attaches to the fridge in the adjoining kitchen.

Bava has glossed the story – adapted, apparently, from a real New Orleans case that Avati came across in a newspaper – as an allegory of Catholic guilt, in which Jane has to keep her shameful sexual secret firmly under wraps and the mystified Robert has no option but to

close his eyes to the appalling details. The sexual tension between Jane and Robert (excellently played by the Croatian actor Stanko Molnar) is intensified when Jane fails to go through with an attempted seduction, turning instead to her illusory lover with a smouldering cry of "Fred, come in, my darling. You're late." And, with the return of the ghastly 12-year-old daughter, proceedings come to a head in a supremely

## MACABRO

Italy 1980
UK / US: *Macabre*
AMA Film Rome / Medusa Distribuzione
89 minutes colour
production began December 1979
..........................

Director of Photography: Franco Delli Colli;
Art Director: Katia Dottori; Editor: Piera
Gabutti; Sound: Gianni Zampagni; Music:
Ubaldo Continiello; Make-up: Alfonso Cioffi;

Special Effects: Tonino Corridori, Angelo Mattei; Story and Screenplay: Pupi Avati, Roberto Gandus, Lamberto Bava, Antonio Avati; Produces: Gianni Minervini, Antonio Avati; Director: Lamberto Bava

Bernice Stegers (Jane); Stanko Molnar (Robert Duval); Veronica Zinny (Lucy); Roberto Posse (Fred Kellerman); Ferdinando Orlandi (Mr Wells); Fernando Pannullo (Leslie Baker); Elisa Kadiga Bove

That this film is macabre we can all agree. There are the murdered corpses, the perversions related to their deaths, a strong component of fetishism and necrophilia ... But we don't believe it. What we have here is a 'horror story' where the horror arises purely from bad taste ... Madness, death and mystery round off an hour and a half of unadulterated tedium. *La Stampa* 12 August 1980

That whole picture started off by chance. I received a call from Pupi Avati (I didn't know him then), who asked me if I would like to make a film with him. I assumed that I was to be his assistant, but then realised that I was supposed to direct the film. We sat down at a desk and wrote the story 'Avati style' – very hurriedly ... *Macabro* received very good reviews ... [but] didn't have much success with the public.
Lamberto Bava [quoted in Palmerini / Mistretta, *Spaghetti Nightmares*, 1996]

Bernice Stegers surrenders to necrophile erotomania in *Macabro* (1980)

macabre dinner party, complete with a disembodied ear lobe in the soup and Jane's total homicidal meltdown in the aftermath.

Coming on like a kind of fleshly Blanche DuBois, Stegers is exceptional throughout; her off-kilter beauty is perfect for the role and her look of crazed exultation when returning the object of her affection to the freezer isn't easily forgotten. The story is a trifle (it might have been better off at featurette-length, maybe as part of a portmanteau film), but it handles taboo imagery far more elegantly than would be the case when Jörg Buttgereit got round to making the notorious *Nekromantik* and *Nekromantik 2*. And the film even contains a few scraps of off-colour wit, as when Robert receives a phone call from Jane's estranged husband. "If I were you, young man," he's told, "I'd have my head examined."

*Macabro* reached Italian cinemagoers on 17 April 1980, its posters proudly announcing it as 'Il film che ha terrorizzato anche Dario Argento' (the film that even terrified Dario Argento). An older maestro – Lamberto Bava's father Mario – died a week later, on the 25th. The elder Bava was 65 and had been kicking his heels since fulfilling his special effects role on Argento's *Inferno*. Yet just two days before Bava's death *Variety* had reported on Frank Agrama's plans to use

Fabrizio Jovine triggers the horrific events of
*Paura nella città dei morti viventi* (1980)

him as special effects director on the US production *Dawn of the Mummy*. By late May *Variety* finally got round to publishing a Bava obituary, mistitling the majority of his films but acknowledging that horror was "his specialty and he raised it to an art – developing cult stature in Italy, France and other European countries."[24]

When Bava died, his old mentor Riccardo Freda, by then a septuagenarian, was preparing his final film, *Murder Obsession (Follia Omicida)*, which was in production by July. By a strange quirk, John Richardson, who 20 years previously had been the chiselled juve in Bava's debut picture, loomed large in Freda's swansong as a lanky, psychic and now-balding butler. As swansongs go, *Murder Obsession*

isn't too bad – an arrant potboiler, with something of the hothouse atmosphere of a José Larraz film, but rendered by Freda with some nostalgic shafts of his old mastery. In getting a bunch of feckless movie types together at a secluded mansion the story echoes Massimo Pupillo's long-ago *Il boia scarlatto*, and a ridiculous giant spider duly shows up to confirm the impression. A young movie star, pallidly played by Stefano Patrizi, is convinced he killed his father when a child, but after a few unconvincing axe and chainsaw killings he realises he was misled.

The film gave Freda the opportunity to work with Laura Gemser, star of Italy's hydra-headed 'Black Emanuelle' franchise, though Silvia Dionisio is naked just as often. In Dionisio's show-stopping dream sequence, white-cowled mutants puke ecstatically down their fronts, a swirl of autumn leaves turns into a cloud of bats, and Dionisio is confronted by a tree studded with blood-weeping skulls. It's here, too, that the fake spider pops up, together with a real cock that, regrettably, has its head cut off. Disorientatingly, the whole sequence is set to a piano arrangement of Bach's *Jesu, Joy of Man's Desiring*. Otherwise, much of Franco Mannino's score is electronic, as seemed de rigueur after *Suspiria*; also echoing *Suspiria*, Dionisio is pursued through the spindly limbs of a rain-lashed nocturnal forest. The satanic rites featured in the dream sequence turn out to have been real, and Freda, the old provocateur, ends with an incestuous pietà guaranteed to ruffle Catholic feathers. The final shot of all is Dionisio screaming her head off, nostalgically replicating the conclusion of Freda's 1949 film *Il conte Ugolino*.

At the time of Mario Bava's death, Lucio Fulci was making a second horror picture in the aggressively up-to-date style he had introduced in *Zombi 2*. For *Paura nella città dei morti viventi*, however, he went, not to Santo Domingo, but to Savannah, Georgia. The literal title of this one – 'Fear in the City of the Living Dead' – was reduced to plain *Fear* when *Variety* reported on the filming in late April 1980, though for its eventual English-language release it became *City of the Living Dead*. Here, Fulci went all out to stamp his new style – alternately eerie and gob-smackingly visceral – on an otherwise garbled story in which a hollow-eyed priest hangs himself in a Dunwich graveyard and in doing so throws wide the proverbial Gates of Hell.

Fulci's opening scenes here are deliciously chilly. The benighted Father Thomas shambles through like the cemetery ghoul in *Night of the Living Dead*, candles flicker at a far-distant seance in New York City, and a high wind and scudding fogs encircle a young man as he approaches an abandoned house. Thereafter Fulci unleashes a series of stunningly well-realised set-pieces. A young psychic is rescued from premature burial in a Manhattan cemetery by a cigar-chomping reporter who, hair-raisingly, uses a pick-axe to break open the coffin. The dead priest rubs worms in a young woman's face, then, in an unearthly wash of blue light, appears at a car window in a shot explicitly recalling the 1961 chiller *Carnival of Souls*. The girl inside the car weeps blood prior to vomiting up her own intestines and the boy is efficiently de-brained via the back of his head. Later, our heroes are assailed by a really unpleasant blizzard of maggots while a weird young man, roughly equivalent to the village idiot, has an industrial power-drill put through his head by an angry redneck. This particular effect is jaw-dropping in its impact.

The set-pieces, however, are all. The remainder furnishes striking shots of the dead rising amid a huge skein of cobwebs, but has them spontaneously combust in a climax that's not only incomprehensible but also not very exciting. The film marked Fulci's first collaboration with the ethereal British actress Catriona MacColl, whom he'd spotted playing the gender-confused title character in Jacques Demy's *Lady Oscar*. And it drew from Fulci a rather gnomic observation about the startling new idiom he was perfecting. "Violence is Italian art," he maintained. "I find much of what I must film very repugnant but it has to be done. My co-writer Dardano Sacchetti insisted on the many gory moments in *City* to underline his fascist subtext."[25] Britain's brilliantly sardonic Marjorie Bilbow was more down to earth, observing that the film "is outrageous fun for the viewer who is not nauseated beyond endurance by worms and maggots all-alive-o and the sight of squashed brains oozing from crushed skulls. Given a packed house of consenting adults reacting vocally, a good time should be had by all except those who are throwing up."[26]

The film was put before Italian audiences on 11 August 1980; Fulci began shooting his next picture the same day, this time in England. Employing no fewer than five performing felines and making atmospheric use of the Buckinghamshire village of Hambleden, Fulci's latest was called, rather baldly, *Black Cat* – a title that would be used, not just for export, but in Italy itself. This time Fulci cooked up the script in tandem with Biagio Proietti, who back in 1974 had co-written a grim, theatre-set giallo called *L'assassino ha riservato nove poltrone* (The Killer Reserved Nine Seats). More recently he'd been involved in the TV mini-series *I racconti fantastici di Edgar Allan Poe* (The Fantastic Tales of Edgar Allan Poe), whose outré elaborations on Poe made him a good fit for Fulci's take on the same author. Anyone expecting a gritty tale of drink-sodden, axe-wielding domestic abuse, as per Poe, will be confounded by the Proietti-Fulci alternative, in which a mad, beetle-browed medium encounters a feisty female photographer and a motorbike-riding Scotland Yard man.

*A Home Counties village is plagued by a series of grisly fatalities, apparently induced by the malevolent stare of a black cat. The creature belongs to Professor Robert Miles, a reclusive psychic researcher attempting to use technology in contacting the dead. A visiting American, Jill Travers, becomes convinced that Miles is exerting a mesmeric influence over the cat. Yet the animal returns even after Miles has hanged it, prompting him to wall up the troublesome Jill in the cellar...*

As well as utilising the same bucolic village used by Hammer in *The Witches* 14 years previously, Fulci also went to a Hammer star when casting the forbidding Professor Miles. Peter Cushing made plenty of typically fastidious notes on his script – eg, "Play Miles oddly. Slightly mad to start with"[27] – but in the end he opted to appear in a lavish Hallmark version of *A Tale of Two Cities* instead. It's tempting, nonetheless, to imagine that Cushing made his usual dialogue tweaks and that some of them were preserved by Fulci. For Miles pursues his arcane researches on a principle that Cushing, in the years following his wife's death, fully endorsed. "Death is not the end of everything," Miles says, "just the beginning of a new journey."

In Cushing's absence, the Miles role was offered to Donald Pleasence before finishing up as an exceptional showcase for the 56-year-old (but prematurely aged) Patrick Magee, who during filming in August 1980 had just two years left to live. Thanks to such titles as *The Fiend*, *Demons of the Mind* and *Asylum*, he had form where horror was concerned, and in *Black Cat* his rheumy eyes and uniquely cadenced line-readings are a kind of shorthand indicating, from the minute he appears, that Miles is seriously insane. His eyes, in particular, are exploited for all they're

Patrick Magee brings technology to bear on psychic research in *Black Cat* (1980)

## BLACK CAT

*Italy 1980*
US: ***The Black Cat***
*Selenia Cinematografica*
*92 minutes colour*
production began 11 August 1980
. . . . . . . . . . . . . . . . . . . . . . . . . . .
Director of Photography: Sergio Salvati;
Production Designer: Francesco Calabrese;
Editor: Vincenzo Tomassi; Sound: Ugo
Celani, Nick Alexander [English-language
dub]; Music: Pino Donaggio; Make-up:
Franco Di Girolamo; Screenplay: Biagio

Proietti, Lucio Fulci; Story: Biagio Proietti,
freely adapted from Edgar Allan Poe's
short story *The Black Cat*; Producer: Giulio
Sbarigia; Director: Lucio Fulci

Patrick Magee (Professor Robert Miles);
Mimsy Farmer (Jill Trevers); David Warbeck
(Inspector Gorley); Al Cliver [Pier Luigi Conti]
(Sgt Wilson); Dagmar Lassander (Lillian
Grayson); Bruno Corazzari (Ferguson);
Geoffrey Copleston (Inspector Flynn); Daniela
Doria (Maureen)

**Though mis-using Poe's name and telling a rather different story to the one that provided the title, this film is not without a certain charm. Well shot – designed, photographed and edited with care – it's reminiscent of *The Exorcist* at one point (when a species of earthquake makes Mimsy's bed dance), nor does it entirely eliminate the relationship of mutual persecution, characteristic of the original story, between the protagonist and the bewitched cat.** *La Stampa 5 June 1981*

**Patrick Magee was a great actor and I respected him so much ... And Lucio Fulci was a fine craftsman ... Kind of gruff, a little bit on the unsmooth side, but nice and very interesting. I don't think the movie's good at all, it's boring, but the experience was great!** *Mimsy Farmer [quoted in Video Watchdog March-April 2011]*

The film isn't a favourite among Fulci fans, maybe because of its relaxed English vibe and a relative paucity of gaudy eviscerations. But Fulci still manages to perfect his trademark blend of the genuinely eerie and the wince-makingly gory, juxtaposing creepy scenes of Magee advancing, microphone in hand, into mist-wreathed graveyards with various bloody clawings and impalements. There's a highly accomplished suspense sequence in which a neighbourhood drunk is stalked by the cat, with Fulci's low-slung shots of the creature explicitly echoing a similar stalking in the 1943 film *The Leopard Man*. Just as impressive is a show-stopping mid-film inferno that's given a real kick by Dagmar Lassander's highly wrought fear and panic – though compromised later on by a cheesy shot of her face suppurating amid the flames. Fulci also stages a preternatural gale in Farmer's bedroom, with composer Pino Donaggio's agitated strings going full blast, and later assails her with whirling bats in a first-class replay of a scene from *Una lucertola con la pelle di donna*.

The film also has moments of mordant wit, as when David Warbeck's Scotland Yard man points out that the ill-fated drunk "turned himself into shish-kebab," together with the expected ration of clumsiness. A car-crash victim's tombstone, for example, bears an inlaid photo of the dead man (an unheard-of practice in Britain), while one of the uniformed policemen is, for some reason, given a

worth by Fulci, whose ocular fetish here reaches epic proportions. Among other choice moments, Magee confers, eyeball to eyeball, with first Dagmar Lassander and then Mimsy Farmer through a gash in an outhouse door. Elsewhere, even an innocuous vignette of Farmer looking at a crime-scene photo is framed by Fulci so that the photo screens off all but her eyes. The cat too (whose eyes are even yellower than Magee's) gets plenty of the same treatment.

strong Australian accent. Poe's image of the strung-up cat impressed in plaster needed something better than what looks like a bit of chalked-up graffiti, and a shot of paw prints in thickly layered dust – indicating the highly improbable culprit in a fatal locked-room murder mystery – is unintentionally comic.

But, as usual, the climate of weirdness whipped up by Fulci, focused mainly on the nocturnal slinkings of the malignant cat, goes a long way to compensate for a fragmented and unfocused script. Everything falls into place, after a fashion, when the splendidly baleful Magee emerges from cobwebbed shadows to offer the heroine a uniquely garbled explanation. "The beast just understood my suppressed hatred," he growls, "and people's failure to understand the frustration of the solitude I was forced into..." Even so, Peter Cushing's interpretation of Miles – which without a doubt would have been much less heavily sinister – remains one of the most tantalising might-have-beens of Italian horror.

## PARAPSYCHOLOGY AND BEYOND

As the 1980s dawned, there were signs that Spanish horror was picking up slightly after the water-treading of the previous few years. The increased productivity didn't guarantee success, of course, or even, in some cases, visibility.

The 1980 film *Terror en el tren de medianoche* (Terror on the Midnight Train) is a case in point; a promising 'ghost train' scenario co-written by director Manuel Iglesias and horror specialist Antonio Fos, it sank almost immediately into total obscurity. Similarly, *El invernadero* (The Greenhouse), made by Santiago Lapeira in April 1982, involved Ovidi Montllor losing his grip on reality while obsessing over Berta Cabré. The result attracted an absolutely rock-bottom number of paying punters: 480. Conversely, Tomás Aznar's *Más allá del terror* (Beyond Fear) scored a hefty 77 million pesetas by the clever expedient of fusing the out-of-favour cine de terror with the wildly popular cine quinqui – ie, hard-hitting exploitation thrillers revolving around juvenile delinquents. Hence Aznar's conspicuously sleazy home-invasion story being flipped on its head when the invaded old dear turns out to be a diabolist, visiting supernatural vengeance on her loathsome attackers by teleporting them to an extradimensional monastery. Coming from the same company that had previously enjoyed an even bigger hit with *Escalofrío*, Aznar's film came out in August 1980 and was advertised, rather mildly, as 'iiiUn reto a sus nervios!!!' (A challenge for your nerves!!!).

Home invasion also featured in Juan José Porto's *Morir de miedo* (To Die of Fear), a three-handed chamber piece, co-written by *Escalofrío* director Carlos Puerto, in which Mónica Randall and Miguel Ayones are celebrating their anniversary when threatened by psychopath Simón Andreu. An opening rubric declares that 'The day this film began shooting [29 April 1980] Alfred Hitchcok [sic] died. Cinema will never be the same again.' Then, after the final image (which, in true 'S' certificate style, is a close shot of Randall simulating an orgasm), comes a final epigraph, borrowed from Jules Verne: 'Death doesn't destroy, it merely causes invisibility.' With pretensions of this sort on show, it's hardly surprising that Porto's humdrum offering got a kicking in the press; a report from the Sitges Festival, for example, suggested that *Morir de tedio* (To Die of Tedium) would have been a better title.[28]

Porto had been co-author of the groundbreaking 1974 book *Cine de Terror y Paul Naschy*, immediately after which Naschy had branded him an 'arsehole' over his perceived mishandling of *La cruz del diablo* – though this didn't stop Porto from getting a producer credit on three further Naschy vehicles. Porto had also written Miguel Ángel Díez's *Pecado mortal* and co-written two León Klimovsky titles, *El extraño amor de los vampiros* and *Violación fatal*, the latter an accomplished giallo that turned out to be Klimovsky's final film. After *Morir de miedo*, Porto pressed on as writer-director of *Regreso del más allá* (Back of Beyond), a 1982 release in which Ana Obregón succumbs to visions of a murdered family in Granada. Nor was Porto the only veteran of the boom period who kept on going into the 1980s. Eugenio Martín directed the October 1980 release *Aquella casa en las afueras* (That House on the Outskirts), in which the fragmenting Silvia Aguilar's new home turns out to be the sometime clinic where she had an abortion, and Carlos Aured was responsible for casting the evergreen Silvia Tortosa in the maritime body-count shocker *El enigma del yate* (The Riddle of the Yacht), which was a decent-sized hit in November 1983.

Another veteran of palmier days was José Larraz, still resident in Tunbridge Wells but ready to pop back to Spain for various film assignments. In 1979 he had directed Alfredo Landa in *Polvos mágicos* (Magic Powder), a typical 'Landismo' farce in which the naïve lead gets married to a husband-sacrificing satanist called Lucifera. (The title involves a charming pun on the Spanish euphemism for ejaculation.) Larraz followed this in 1981 with a still cruder 'S' certificate sex comedy called *La momia nacional*, adding vampire hookers, a tail-wagging werewolf, comedy splatter and oodles of nudity to the advertised national mummy. "The title was a reference to Franco," he explained

20 years later, "who was mummified – embalmed – after he died. People made jokes about Franco as a mummy, coming back from the grave and so on." Thanks to his producers' cold feet, however, "the film I shot didn't have anything to do with Franco."[29]

The tremendous success of these two films meant that Larraz was suddenly typed, much to his amazement, as a comedy director. In between the two, however, he managed to squeeze in both *Estigma* and *Los ritos sexuales del diablo*, though his disenchantment was quite clear in an interview given in the final week of April 1980, when he'd just started filming *Estigma* (Stigma) in Barcelona. "I'm getting a bit tired of the cinema racket," he sighed. "I'm thinking seriously about dropping direction and devoting myself entirely to drawing. It's a quieter activity."[30] As noted earlier, *Los ritos sexuales del diablo* was a soft-porn throwaway that Larraz preferred to draw a veil over. But, notwithstanding Larraz's jaded attitude going in, *Estigma* came out the other end as a perfectly serviceable thriller, a bit long-winded in its first two acts but ending with an impressive final third that could be a different film entirely.

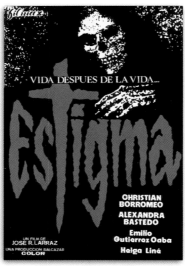

'Life After Life': Spanish pressbook cover for *Estigma* (1980)

Obviously modelled, as Larraz cheerfully admitted, on the Brian De Palma films *Carrie* and *The Fury*, this gloomy tale of reincarnation briefly switched titles during production to *Reencarnación* before reverting to *Estigma*. In it, Larraz ticks off the kinky details expected of him in pretty listless, mechanical style – a teenage boy with lethal psychic powers (Christian Borromeo) who openly salivates over his own mother (Helga Liné), a fearful middle-aged medium (Irene Gutiérrez Caba) who clearly has suppressed longings for the bookseller heroine (Alexandra Bastedo), and in the third act, set in 1880, the boy's former self having sex with his sister (Virginie Blavier). The present-day action only grips when Larraz stages some of his trademark visions, notably of the boy being visited by his nude, blue-skinned victims in a darkened doorway. The 19th century flashback, however, builds to a Lizzie Borden-style triple axe murder and is much more intriguing. This being an Italian co-production, the baronial setting for the flashback, inside and out, is the ever-popular Villa Parisi near Rome, which Larraz and cinematographer Giuseppe Bernardini

make sumptuous use of. The ending, in which Borromeo disposes of the sympathetic Bastedo, stares balefully into a shattered mirror and then lapses into total madness, is powerful too.

Eugenio Martín also ventured into the world of the paranormal, starting production on *Sobrenatural* (Supernatural) in December 1980. Despite Martín's misgivings about the very limited budget allotted to him, *Sobrenatural*, like *Estigma*, is quite an acceptable shocker, foregrounding Cristina Galbó as Julia, a young widow whose loathed husband returns to her in various threatening forms. (The film pre-dated the April 1981 filming of *The Entity*, though not the novel on which Sidney J Furie's film was based.) "May the Lord forgive him for all the evil he has done," mutters elderly housekeeper María (Lola Lemos), adding ominously, "If only he were truly dead…" In a show-stoppingly queasy scene, the dead man has his revenge by sending a poltergeisted electric carving knife after the old lady, who lapses into a coma but still manages to warn Julia to "Get out of this house!"

The pace slows for various po-faced consultations with lab-coated parapsychologists, complete with mutterings about quantum physics and the Tibetan Book of the Dead. But Martín has other set-pieces up his sleeve besides carved-up old ladies. Echoing M R James, the spectre manifests itself as a levitating human shape under a bed sheet. Julia herself levitates in her chair at the inevitable seance, a visiting priest is flung headlong by the entity, and a burned hand reaches for Julia through a smashed windscreen prior to ripping off her car door in a pall of otherworldly fog. Martín even contrives some fetchingly eerie views of limbo. The film winds up with the bizarre spectacle of a crazed Alsatian inadvertently hanging itself on its own leash, and only Carlos Viziello's rather cheesy score, complete with syn-drums, lets the side down.

While Larraz and Martín merely toyed with otherworldly scenarios, a far more rigorous proponent of the subject scored a much bigger success – at least initially. In 1980 the Barcelona parapsychologist Sebastián D'Arbó established his own film company and came up with an Amicus-style anthology called *Viaje al más allá* (Journey to the

Beyond). D'Arbó was the man behind the trailblazing parapsychological magazine *Karma-7* and credited himself in the film, rather grandiloquently, as Prof D'Arbó. He even turns up in person, trimly goateed and highly personable, to explain at the outset that the five segments are genuine case histories – or, as he puts it, "historias auténticas y certificadas." To bolster the air of gravity, an opening rubric dedicates the film 'a la memoria del Dr Josep[h] Banks Rhine, padre de la moderna Parapsicología.' Elsewhere – in story five to be exact – D'Arbó pays tribute to another recently deceased pioneer, showing a man reading a copy of *Dirigido* magazine with a big portrait of Alfred Hitchcock on the front.

The 'cases' in *Viaje al más allá* are usefully signposted in terms of theme. *Caso de aparición* involves a spooky nocturnal hitchhiker, *Caso de posesión* a convent girl who progresses from masturbation to full-on (and mainly naked) possession, and *Caso de premonición* a premonitory dream about a car wreck. After that, two somewhat longer stories involve an injured little boy regressing to a past life in *Caso de reencarnación* and a poltergeist-plagued woman, a seance and a juicy double-murder in *Caso casa encantada* (Case of the Haunted House). In a set-up familiar from any number of inter-war potboilers, the stories are told by five strangers who have been mysteriously invited to a house in the Pyrenees; their host, the cigar-twirling Dr Meinen, turns out to be not quite what he seems and is played by the splendid Narciso Ibáñez Menta. The stories are functionally told and even slightly mundane (this was probably the whole point, of course), though D'Arbó isn't above garnishing the connecting story with lashings of blue-tinted Pyrenean lightning. To restore the sober tone, he signs off with a written quote regarding 'other worlds' from surrealist poet Paul Éluard.

"My plan is to make a trilogy," D'Arbó announced in 1982, "showing in dramatised form the terror caused by certain phenomena in all different parts of the world."[31] Having shot his first film in the Vall de Núria, D'Arbó stuck with mountainous locations for a couple of single-story follow-ups, shooting *El Ser* (The Being, 1982) in the Montseny Massif and *Más allá de la muerte* (Beyond Death, 1986) in La Molina. He

also retained his to-camera introductions and use of portentous epigraphs (with written quotations from Freud in the first film, Einstein in the second), as well as sticking with the faithful Menta for marquee value.

Advertised with the tag-line '¡Su poder estaba por encima de la muerte!' (His power transcended death!), *El Ser* was released in Spain just a few months ahead of Sidney J Furie's *The Entity*. Like Martín's *Sobrenatural*, it tells a very similar, effects-laden story about a young widow (Mercedes Sampietro) beset by paranormal phenomena coming from a predictable source. More bizarrely, D'Arbó founded *Más allá de la muerte* on Mengele's death-camp experiments in defining the afterlife, casting Tony Isbert as a bereaved young man investigating a former SS scientist (Menta, sans hairpiece for a change). This one was trumpeted with the emphatic pronouncement, '¿Es posible viajar al más allá y ... volver? Científicamente: ¡Demostrado!' (Is it possible to travel to the Beyond and ... come back? Scientifically: Proven!).

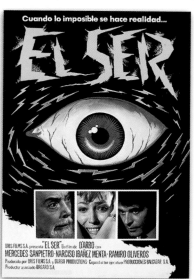

'When the impossible becomes reality': poster for the parapsychological thriller *El ser* (1982)

Sadly, waning public interest in parapsychology was rather cruelly exposed by the box-office performance of D'Arbó's films. Where *Viaje al más allá* scored very nicely with just under 43 million pesetas, *El Ser* dropped to just over 14 million and *Más allá de la muerte* plunged to 4.4 million. In the case of the last film, it may just be that, after sitting through Tomás Aznar's *Más allá del terror*, Juan José Porto's *Regreso del más allá* and D'Arbó's own *Viaje al más allá*, the Spanish public were just sick and tired of films with 'más allá' in the title.

D'Arbó's film career actually predated the three parapsychological projects that he signed as writer-director. Indeed, he had got to know the patrician Menta and his celebrated son, Narciso Ibáñez Serrador, during his early days at Televisión Española, an environment that also introduced him to Tomás Muñoz. In 1975, Muñoz was writer-director of an award-winning 25-minute Poe adaptation called *Valdemar, el homónculus dormido* (Valdemar, the Sleeping Homunculus), which D'Arbó produced. Poe's theme – of a terminally ill man suspended at the moment of death by hypnosis – was of obvious interest to D'Arbó, and the result gained Muñoz an award at that year's Sitges Festival.

## INTERNATIONAL WEREWOLF

Amid these scattered signs of life Paul Naschy, too, was still keeping his hand in, though not to the prolific degree of, say, six years earlier. In the summer of 1980, however, he achieved, along with actress-producer Julia Saly, a film first – a Spanish-Japanese co-production.

El carnaval de las bestias (The Beasts' Carnival) begins as an amusingly clunky gangster thriller, with Naschy as a thoroughly unpleasant mercenary who double-crosses his Japanese paymasters and is pursued by them back to Madrid. (In his usual style, Naschy indicates the change of scene by focusing on an architectural landmark, in this case the Cervantes monument in the Plaza de España.) With echoes of his seven-year-old semi-giallo Los ojos azules de la muñeca rota, the badly wounded Naschy fetches up at the isolated home of a club-footed doctor, whose beauteous daughters – inevitably – vie with each other for the invalid's romantic interest. A black-gloved serial killer appears to be on the loose, not forgetting the apparent ghost of the doctor's late wife, furnishing Saly with a typically compelling cameo.

El carnaval is up there with Naschy's wildest imaginings, complete with narrative gear-changes that can only be described as barking mad. But it certainly holds the attention. Among the gallery of provincial grotesques is a farting padre, a sleazy vet (who gets fed to the doctor's hungry pigs), and finally a bunch of fancy-dressed party guests whose disastrously unfunny byplay almost keelhauls the film just as the climax is in sight. (At least this section yields the charming spectacle of Naschy dressed, extremely convincingly, as Napoléon.) Naschy decorates the rest with plenty of nightmare sequences, love scenes involving no fewer than three nude 20-somethings, and an impudent African housemaid who, in a decidedly unenlightened development, seems to have had a profound effect on the family's culinary habits. Naschy also has his Spanish sweetheart (Azucena Hernández) comment on her Japanese counterpart (Eiko Nagashima) with the unembarrassed line, "All Orientals look the same to me."

On completion of El carnaval, Naschy's new Dálmata outfit went without Japanese assistance for its second production, El retorno del hombre lobo (The Return of the Wolf Man). Now routinely hailed as "nuestro hombre lobo nacional"[32] (our national werewolf), Naschy here resurrected his Waldemar Daninsky character after a five-year hiatus. For this loose retread of the 1970 smash La noche de Walpurgis, Naschy filmed at the Castillo de Belmonte in Cuenca and wisely retained his two most crucial collaborators of the period – Julia Saly and cinematographer Alejandro Ulloa. The budget was unusually generous but the takings (of

nearly 23 million pesetas) weren't enough to justify the expense. As a result, El retorno del hombre lobo was the last Dálmata production.

*Italian students Erika, Barbara and Karin journey to the Carpathians to locate the tomb of the notorious Countess Báthory. Unknown to her friends, Erika is insane; intent on resurrecting the Countess, she does so with the aid of Barbara's blood. What even Erika doesn't know is that (a) the Countess will return as a vampire and (b) her unwilling confederate, Waldemar Daninsky, has also been providentially revived.*

In a market dominated by slasher scenarios and body-horror special effects, the film's underwhelming box-office performance was perhaps a foregone conclusion. For with El retorno del hombre lobo Naschy had crafted a backward-looking Gothic romance in wilful defiance of current trends; to underline its anomalous status, both Joe Dante's The Howling and John Landis' An American Werewolf in London followed it into Spanish cinemas within six months of its release. Yet in retrospect it seems like the old-fashioned classic that Naschy had been working towards for over a decade.

This is not to suggest that El retorno del hombre lobo doesn't have its share of problems. The process – inevitable in a Naschy film – by which the revived Daninsky and winsome Karin fall in love is unfeasibly rapid; indeed, it's passed over entirely and served up as a given. To make matters worse, the 46-year-old Naschy has now reached the point where his love interest (Azucena Hernández again) is over a quarter of a century his junior. Erika, ripely played by Silvia Aguilar, is a self-serving psychopath whose malignance appears entirely motiveless. The patchwork of library music isn't always apt and, more damagingly, Naschy's command of pacing and narrative is all over the place. To keep the plot going, it's shored up with any number of situations that Naschy had exploited time and again, from the 'held up by bandits en route to the castle' gimmick to the 'graverobbers inadvertently reviving the werewolf' routine lifted from Naschy's primal film, Frankenstein Meets the Wolf Man.

Yet the sheer vigour with which the main set-pieces are put together, and the wraparound Gothic luxuriance of cinematography and production design, make it easy to overlook such flaws. Indeed, part of the film's charm arises from Naschy's quixotic determination to turn the clock back, giving the viewer a 'Greatest Hits' gazetteer of time-honoured Daninsky conventions. To this end familiar actors are stirred into the mix as well. The leader of the rape-fixated bandits is the scar-faced Luis Barboo. Beatriz Elorrieta,

A nostalgic
werewolf work-out
for Paul Naschy in
*El retorno del hombre
lobo* (1980)

previously a fetching vampire in her father's 1971
film *La llamada del vampiro*, shows up here as a female
Igor with hideous fire damage to the left side of her
face; in due course she becomes a vampire again. And
lending a seal of distinction to the whole enterprise is
'guest star' Narciso Ibáñez Menta, contributing three
brief scenes as a wheelchair-bound sage who finds out
the hard way just how crazy his star pupil, Erika, really
is. In a delightful affirmation of Daninsky's iconic
status, Menta's lightning-lit study features a triptych
of baleful portraits on one wall – genuine images of
Vlad Dracula and Erzsébet Báthory at either side, with
Daninsky arrogantly positioned in between.

In another familiar Naschy touch, the action begins
with a pre-credits flashback to 16th century Hungary.
Here we see Báthory and Daninsky being arraigned
for their inhuman crimes and hear Julia Saly's
unusually forthright version of the standard 'curse
uttered just before execution' – "You bastards! I shall
return from the ashes and turn your world into an
inferno of blood and death!" Post-credits, a glimpse
of the Trevi Fountain indicates that we've moved to
contemporary Rome, after which Naschy emphasises
the gulf between ancient and modern in a vacuous
swimming pool scene that could have come out of a
slasher film. The two Neanderthals accompanying
Karin and Barbara are unimpressed by Karin's
claim to have "spent many years engaged in serious

## EL RETORNO DEL HOMBRE LOBO

Spain 1980
US: *Night of the Werewolf*
Dálmata Films
92 minutes colour
in production August 1980
. . . . . . . . . . . . . . . . . . . . . . . . . . . . .
Director of Photography: Alejandro Ulloa;
Art Director: Luis Vazquez; Editor: Pedro del
Rey; Sound: José Antonio Bermudez, Luis
Castro; Music: CAM España [library tracks];
Make-up: Ángel Luis de Diego; Special
Effects: Antonio Molina; Screenplay: Jacinto
Molina [Paul Naschy]; Producer: Modesto
Pérez Redondo; Director: Jacinto Molina
Álvarez [Paul Naschy]

Paul Naschy (Waldemar Daninsky); Julia Saly
(Countess Báthory); Silvia Aguilar (Erika);
Azucena Hernández (Karin); Beatriz Elorrieta
(Mircaya); Pilar Alcón (Barbara); Narciso Ibáñez
Menta (professor); Rafael Hernández (Yoyo, small
grave robber); Pepe Ruiz ('preacher' thief); Ricardo
Palacios (Verez, fat grave robber); Tito Garcia
(fat thief); David Rocha (young bandit); Charly
Bravo (bearded bandit); Luis Barboo (scar-faced
bandit); José Riesgo (2nd judge); Manuel Pereiro
(1st judge); Ramón Centenero (sentencing herald);
Alexia Loreta (Kinga); José Thelman (Sandor);
Mauro Rivera (young man at pool); Jose L Baringo
(Renato, 2nd young man at pool); José Cela;
Berto Navarro; José L Chinchilla; José Sacristán

Vampirism and lycanthropy are the elements combined by Naschy in this
picture, with mixed results ... The film offers undeniable formal elegance,
it's been made with means, and Naschy plays it pretty clean, without
surrendering to gore or shock effects. Naschy's naïveté, and his passion for
a character that wouldn't frighten anybody, is something to be grateful for.
*La Vanguardia* 21 April 1981

When I was writing the script I had in mind those privileged individuals who
abuse their power to crush the weak and defenceless ... The superb make-up
was the work of Ángel Luis de Diego, with photography by Alejandro Ulloa. I
really enjoyed making this picture, giving full rein to my love of heavy Gothic
imagery, blended with both real historical detail and unbridled flight of fancy.
Paul Naschy [*Memorias de un hombre lobo*, 1997]

research." (An unlikely story actually, given that
she's only 21.) "Scientists?" one of the boys guffaws.
"You're too beautiful for anything so boring. Come
on, cuties, quit playing at being intellectual." Opposed
to these modern oiks is the old-fashioned chivalry

of the revived Daninsky, who rescues the women from Barboo's bandits and determines to foil his old mistress when Báthory, too, returns from the grave.

Daninsky's werewolf fugues are unusually powerful this time around, even when he plunges through a stained-glass window that's clearly made of paper. The make-up is arguably the best Naschy ever wore, and the final battle with Báthory is thrillingly staged. (Among other things, she psychically levitates a coffin and lobs it at his lupine head.) And the agglomeration of Gothic imagery, much enhanced by Ulloa's earthily subdued colour palette, yields a steady stream of memorable moments – smoke wisping from a corpse's cobwebbed mouth, Báthory's slab floating upwards of its own accord, another tomb literally exploding to disclose her dusty zombie assistant, the vampirised Erika and Barbara floating towards their victims through a screen of cobwebs, the staked Erika writhing and screaming like a petulant, baffled baby. That dusty zombie, incidentally, was prominently featured in the film's advertising but does disappointingly little in the film itself. Julia Saly's Báthory, however, exudes adamantine evil from every pore and is as marvellous a villainess as Spanish horror ever produced. In one remarkably graphic shot her face is entirely obscured by the syrupy blood draining down from a sacrificial victim.

All in all, El retorno del hombre lobo is one of those curious films, like Terence Fisher's Frankenstein and the Monster from Hell, where the producers, ignoring commercial considerations to a virtually suicidal

degree, came up with a nostalgic, and thoroughly engaging, farewell to an entire filmmaking tradition.

When Naschy's latest went on release in 1981, Spanish audiences were still flocking, not to backward-looking werewolf pictures, but to ribald 'S' certificate sex comedies. Of Naschy's trio of student anthropologists in El retorno del hombre lobo, two of them, Azucena Hernández and Pilar Alcón, appeared in another 1981 release, Mariano Ozores' Brujas mágicas (Magical Witches), a sex farce set during a period, the Inquisition, that not long ago had been handled by Naschy with a straight face. The film scored nearly 158 million pesetas, outdistancing El retorno by around 135 million. Hernández and Alcón also appeared in another saucy 1981 smash, José Larraz's above-mentioned El momia nacional, while for the prolific Ozores Brujas mágicas was a sort of follow-up to a blockbuster 'old dark house' burlesque from the previous year, El liguero mágico (The Magic Suspender Belt). Yet the comic werewolves featured in both El momia nacional and El liguero mágico seem to have daunted Naschy not one bit, for the Waldemar Daninsky saga was by no means over.

First, however, he would guy the character at the behest of José Frade, the eclectic producer of both Brujas mágicas and El momia nacional. The aptly titled Christmas 1982 release Buenas noches, Señor Monstruo (Good Night, Señor Monster) was directed by Antonio Mercero of La cabina fame but was strictly for kids, showcasing the flash-in-the-pan pop quartet Regaliz plus Naschy as 'HL' – ie, el hombre lobo.

Bathroom apparitions Charly Bravo and José Sacristán Hernández terrorise Julia Saly in Latidos de pánico (1983)

Among other menaces, Fernando Bilbao got the chance to reprise his Frankenstein's monster, last seen in Jess Franco's monster-mashes of a decade earlier. In his memoirs, Naschy would refer to Regaliz as "a bunch of unbearable child singers" and, comparing himself to Lon Chaney Jr once again, pointed out that "I had been forced into self-parody, although I had to face Regaliz instead of Bud Abbott and Lou Costello. The film angered my fans, who practically accused me of prostituting their beloved Waldemar Daninsky."[33]

As if to make amends, at the end of March 1983 Naschy and producer Julia Saly completed production on a conspicuously grim little film that resurrected the mediaeval warlock Naschy had played to such grand effect in El espanto surge de la tumba. Yet the baleful Alaric de Marnac only really manifests himself at the beginning and end of *Latidos de pánico* (Panic Beats). In the meantime Naschy plays a thoroughly despicable de Marnac descendant, with contemporary Paris handily indicated – as it was in *El espanto* – by lingering shots of the Arc de Triomphe and the Eiffel Tower.

The film begins, however, in suitably Gothic style, with the original de Marnac's naked wife being pursued through a blue-filtered woodland clearing; a dangling skeleton, mist curling through its empty eye sockets, is silent witness to Alaric's brutal murder of the woman with a mace. The Alaric portrait that survives into the 1980s is described as having "a satanic look" but actually appears rather whimsical. Either way, it frowns down approvingly on his descendant's scheme to murder his ailing wife (Saly) and get together with a pert young gold-digger (Pat Ondiviela). Even the wife is savvy enough to invoke *Rebecca*, while Naschy also quotes from *What Ever Happened to Baby Jane?* (the invalid is served something very nasty on a salver) and *Les Diaboliques* (a two-for-the-price-of-one apparition in a bathtub). All this builds to some extremely gruesome murders and then to a splendid twist. Turning on her newly widowed accomplice, the nasty young mistress comes out with the memorable line, "We're both evil. But I'm more evil than you, idiot!"

Her comeuppance echoes the kind of ghostly retribution dealt out in EC Comics, with zombies turning up on a rain-lashed doorstep (rather like George Romero's EC compendium of the year before, *Creepshow*) and Alaric himself finishing her off in the family chapel. Though the film begins and ends with faithless women being comprehensively bludgeoned, the whiff of misogyny seems to be subsumed into an all-embracing contempt for human beings in general – a contempt familiar from Naschy's earlier films *El caminante* and *El carnaval de las bestias*. Only a truly horrible synth score spoils the overall effect.

When *Latidos de pánico* wrapped, Naschy immediately began preparing a film that would bring back Waldemar Daninsky yet again. Not only that: the summer 1983 filming of *La bestia y la espada mágica* (The Beast and the Magic Sword) represented another Japanese co-production for Naschy and executive producer Julia Saly, this time in cahoots with the veteran actor Shigeru Amachi.

Shot in Spain and at Toshiro Mifune's studio in Tokyo, the result was ready for the Brussels International Fantasy Film Festival in November, where it was shown alongside *Latidos de pánico* and garnered Naschy a career award. The scope is wide and the action little short of epic, moving from Irineus Daninsky's fateful beheading of a barbaric

opponent in 938 to 16th century Toledo, where Waldemar determines to seek deliverance from his lycanthropic condition by travelling to Japan. In no time at all a sombre Samurai general is complaining about "the full-moon murderer" while his sage nephew Kian (Amachi) strives to perfect a cure. An amazing series of energetic dust-ups ensues, from Daninsky laying waste to a Kyoto brothel to a sword-flashing ninja ambush in an ornamental pool. When an evil sorceress (Junko Asahina) confines the lupine Daninsky in a cell and unleashes a tiger on him, the resultant battle is a real eye-opener, with Daninsky vomiting tiger's blood to signal his eventual triumph.

The film's fascinating clash of cultures recalls Hammer's Hong Kong collaboration from 1973, *The Legend of the 7 Golden Vampires*, and after so many scenarios dramatising Naschy's obsession with noble families the move to feudal Japan seems entirely fitting. Sadly, a few too many talky scenes push the running time, rather taxingly, towards the two-hour mark. Naschy's werewolf 'look' is different once again; resembling the old Lon Chaney Jr make-up but augmented with ridged brows à la Oliver Reed in *The Curse of the Werewolf*, it's by no means as effective as the version seen in *El retorno del hombre lobo*. Even so, when Kian pronounces Daninsky's epitaph – "The horror of that murderous beast will be lost for eternity in the shadows of forgetfulness" – one can't help feeling that Naschy was being too modest. For, despite his various ups and downs, Daninsky deserves to be remembered as one of the cinema's classic misunderstood monsters.

## NASTIER AND NASTIER

In addition to the numerous cannibal epics itemised above, Britain's 'Video Nasties' list included several examples of an even more disreputable sub-genre. Combining sexploitation and mad science, Italy's lurid Nazi-themed potboilers of the 1970s might have traced their lineage to art-house directors like Visconti, Pasolini and Cavani, but their true home was the grindhouse and their presence on the DPP list a foregone conclusion. The listed titles – *Lager SSadis kastrat kommandantur* (SS Experiment Camp), *L'ultima orgia del III Reich* (The Gestapo's Last Orgy) and *La bestia in calore* (The Beast in Heat) – are pretty representative of the form. The last, directed by Luigi Batzella, remains arguably the most notorious. A scene in which a caged troglodyte bites off a rape victim's pubic mound is a nauseating low point in the kind of violent misogyny that became briefly permissible in the 1970s.

The DPP list was headed – alphabetically, at any rate – by two films directed by the kingpin of Italian exploitation, Joe D'Amato (real name: Aristide

Massaccesi). *Absurd* and *Anthropophagous the Beast* had been dashed off by D'Amato in 1980 under the titles *Rosso sangue* (Blood Red) and *Antropophagus*, both of them comparing very poorly with *Buio omega*, which D'Amato made the previous year. That film – though nauseating enough to make its omission from the DPP list quite a surprise – had at least been competently made.

Of D'Amato's DPP twosome, *Antropophagus* came first, with the towering George Eastman (real name: Luigi Montefiori) co-writing the script in addition to playing the title horror. This modified cannibal film boasts a few spooky moments, particularly in a set of Greek catacombs crammed with skulls, bats and red-eyed rats, but otherwise leaves the viewer stranded with an unspeakably dreary bunch of young tourists headed by *Zombi 2*'s Tisa Farrow. "There's evil on this island," stammers the psychic member of the party, "an evil that won't let us get away." In fact it's a leprous family man-turned-crazed cannibal who has already polished off the indigenous population. Though Eastman is genuinely formidable, D'Amato brings zero tension to the proceedings, only granting gorehounds some relief in the last ten minutes, when the thing chews on a forcibly miscarried foetus prior to making a meal of his own entrails outside Rome's Villino Crespi.

No longer leprous, Eastman reappeared in D'Amato's loose follow-up, *Rosso sangue*, which apes John Carpenter's *Halloween* in its tale of a virtually indestructible killer – hailing, as in *Antropophagus*, from Greece – who terrorises a family and their babysitter in small-town America. This time Eastman's depredations involve inventive use of power drills, bandsaws and pick-axes, with the pièce de résistance reserved for a scene in which he forces a young woman (Annie Belle) head-first into an oven; the killer himself eventually has his eyes put out and his head chopped off. The result is tighter and more eventful than *Antropophagus* but no more engaging. An early victim in *Rosso sangue*, incidentally, is the hapless Michele Soavi, whose directorial debut in 1986, *Deliria*, would be co-written by Eastman and co-produced by D'Amato.

Another D'Amato associate, Bruno Mattei, vied with him as Italy's premier sleaze merchant at the turn of

Margaret Mazzantini surges up blindly from a wine barrel in *Antropophagus* (1980)

the 1980s. After doing time in the mondo and Nazi exploitation genres, Mattei graduated to demented nunsploitation with titles like *L'altro inferno* (The Other Hell, 1980) and thence to the ever-lucrative area of *Zombi 2* rip-offs. *Virus*, also made in 1980, focuses on a New Guinea research centre whose racist answer to Third World starvation – developing a gas that will make native peoples eat each other – inevitably gets out of hand and infects New York City. Though visibly under-budgeted and utterly laughable, the result, retitled *Zombie Creeping Flesh*, duly fetched up on the DPP list. Mattei subsequently turned out the equally risible *Rats – notte di terrore* (Rats – Night of Terror, 1984), a post-apocalyptic scenario which replaces the 'cat bursting out of a zombie' set-piece from *Virus* with a scene in which a rat bursts out of an eviscerated girl.

Mattei's dead hand was then applied to the similarly inept *Zombi 3*, a 1987 *Zombi 2* sequel abandoned by Lucio Fulci when he became ill. The entirely resistible attractions here include an airborne severed head, undead gulls besieging a bus, even an improbably loquacious zombie disc jockey.

In the opportunist world of Italian movie marketing, *Zombi 3* wasn't the first film to lay claim to that title, given that it had already done duty in some territories as an alternative title for Andrea Bianchi's dire *Le notti del terrore* (The Nights of Terror). Dating from 1980 (and known in the USA as *Burial Ground*), this one has clay-faced zombies emerging from Etruscan catacombs and laying siege to a nearby villa, bringing with them the titular 'nigths [sic] of terror', as promised in the so-called 'Profecy [sic] of the Black Spider'. Chief among the villa's occupants are Mariangela Giordano and her highly peculiar pre-teen son (played by the 20-something midget Pietro Barzocchini), for whom zombification brings an opportunity to act out his Oedipal desires by consuming the maternal breast. The film also parrots Fulci's *Zombi 2* as blatantly as possible when a female victim is hauled eyeball-first onto a sliver of broken window-pane.

The screenwriter of Bianchi's film was none other than Piero Regnoli, for whom co-writing Freda's

*I vampiri* and serving as writer-director of *L'ultima preda del vampiro* were presumably distant memories. Also in this period he wrote another Andrea Bianchi item, *Malabimba*, a late-coming *Exorcist* clone (very late – it was shot in March 1979) in which a young woman (Katell Laennec) is possessed by an erotomaniac spirit and has her way with, among others, a glamorous nun played by Mariangela Giordano; unnecessary hardcore inserts were added to spice up an already sex-saturated brew. Three years later a Regnoli-scripted follow-up, *La bimba di Satana*, offered much the mixture as before, including Giordano but omitting the hardcore; directed by Mario Bianchi (no relation), the film was exported as *Satan's Baby Doll*.

Regnoli also wrote Mario Landi's *Patrick vive ancora* (Patrick Still Lives), a phoney sequel to the 1978 Australian film *Patrick*, featuring the requisite coma victim exercising his telekinetic powers from his hospital bed, together with several grossly exploitative details of its own. The long-suffering Mariangela Giordano, for example, receives a poltergeisted rod in one orifice only for it to exit via another. Gabriele Crisanti, producer of all four of these Regnoli-scripted items, was also responsible for Mario Landi's much-banned 1979 shocker *Giallo a Venezia* (Thriller in Venice), which was scripted by Aldo Serio rather than Regnoli. In this one Giordano is tethered naked to a kitchen table and has one of her legs sawn off. That Giordano was Crisanti's girlfriend at the time puts the misogyny underpinning these films into an unusually intimate context.

Yet another Piero Regnoli script became Umberto Lenzi's ridiculous but curiously engaging *Incubo sulla città contaminata* (Nightmare of the Contaminated City). Exported as plain *Nightmare City*, this one showcases a mob of irradiated and disconcertingly fleet-footed quasi-zombies over 20 years before the British classic *28 Days Later*. They're also unusually resourceful, using hatchets, machine guns, knives, chains and even brooms in their blood-drinking killing spree, as well as cunningly disabling a telephone line at one point. "Only bullets damaging the cranium can stop these monsters," concludes a military man, a prescription rendered in simpler, Romero-style terms by a slumming Mel Ferrer as "Aim for the brain." There's some half-baked chatter about "a race of monsters ... created by other monsters" and "the vital cycle of the human race," but the film is really just a non-stop parade of inept gore and make-up effects. (An eye-gouging in a darkened cellar passes muster, but not much else.) And, 20 years after *L'ultima preda del vampiro*, Regnoli is still keen on gyrating dancing girls, with Lycra-clad disco dancers being messily butchered during a live TV broadcast.

Similarly themed, and just as derivative, *Contamination* was directed and co-written by Luigi Cozzi at the beginning of 1980. This one is modelled entirely around the chest-burster sequence in *Alien*, bringing hordes of pod-like Martian eggs to New York City and charting, in splattery detail, the entrail-busting mayhem when they come into contact with human beings. Though amusingly trashy, the action devolves into a dull 007-style conspiracy thriller focused, bizarrely, on a Colombian coffee factory. (The complex recalls the 1950s classic *Quatermass 2* while the hideous 'Alien Cyclops' inside it echoes another, *It Came from Outer Space*.) There are some relishable dialogue gems on offer, ranging from the ridiculous ("Get me out of here! There's an egg!") to the genuinely witty ("Three tons of coffee could make a lot of people very nervous"), and the film also boasts a no-nonsense MIT-educated colonel who happens to be female (Louise Marleau). Cozzi's imported star, incidentally, was Ian McCulloch, who had made *Zombi 2*, *Zombi Holocaust* and *Contamination* in an eight-month period and was bemused to find all three ending up on the DPP blacklist.

Also due to be immortalised on the DPP roster was, perhaps unsurprisingly, Jess Franco, who saw two of his 1980 productions fetch up on the 'prosecuted' part of the list. One was the previously mentioned Eurociné item *El caníbal* (aka *Devil Hunter*), the other was a German slasher picture called *Die Säge des Todes*. This 'does exactly what it says on the tin' title – meaning 'The Saw of Death' – was bypassed for export in favour of the more abstract *Bloody Moon*.

Over 20 years after he produced *Die Nackte und der Satan*, this was Munich mogul Wolfgang C Hartwig's contribution to the box-office bonanza triggered by *Friday the 13th*. Franco's imitation of the new style is so note-perfect and professionally crafted that *Bloody Moon* inevitably becomes inane, inert and flavourless within the first reel. Filmed in Franco's old stamping ground of Alicante, the setting is the so-called 'International Youth-Club Boarding School of Languages' and the student victims are nubile enough to satisfy any slasher fan. Franco puts in a few gags, as when the heroine is seen reading Marc Olden's recent thriller *Poe Must Die* or when a crossword clue is given as "a capital offence ending in 'r'." Whether being threatened by a polystyrene rock or a crazed, knife-wielding language tutor, Olivia Pascal does her best to sell this uninspiring material, though the stand-out moment for gorehounds is the brutal decapitation of Jasmin Losensky with an industrial buzz-saw. Beyond that, the film has plenty to offer students of 1980s disco and fashion, both of which are seen here at their most abysmal.

Yet another title itemised by the DPP, though not actually prosecuted, was Lucio Fulci's third film of 1980. After sleepy Buckinghamshire, his next stop was Louisiana, where *...E tu vivrai nel terrore! L'aldilà* started shooting a mere 12 weeks after *Black Cat* had begun. For the film's UK release in November 1981 its unwieldy title – translating literally as '...And You Will Live in Terror! The Beyond' – was helpfully abbreviated to just *The Beyond*. After a long delay it arrived in America as *7 Doors of Death*, though in both territories the film had to be extensively trimmed. For here Fulci reached the apogee of his new style, combining meandering, metaphysical strangeness with grandstanding set-pieces abounding in blood and viscera.

*Liza Merrill inherits the Seven Gates Hotel in New Orleans and considers it "the first good break" she's had. Soon, however, she learns from a young blind woman, Emily, that back in 1927 the house witnessed the hideous lynching of a diabolist painter called Schweik. Worse, Emily also claims that the hotel is one of the seven gateways to Hell. Liza's friend Dr John McCabe pooh-poohs all this, but events prove him wrong.*

*L'aldilà* dramatises the thin membrane separating the living from the dead in free-flowing images that pay only the scantest heed to narrative logic. Even the fact that Liza's hotel renovations have (presumably) triggered the hellish manifestations is something we're left to work out for ourselves. The events are hung loosely around an ancient tome called the Book of Eibon, but this plot point is so arbitrary it seems as elusive as everything else in the film. Anchoring the action, however – and serving as suitably bewildered audience surrogates – are Fulci's English-speaking leads, porcelain beauty Catriona MacColl and square-jawed doctor David Warbeck, who struggle to remain rational even as they're assailed by shambling, shoe-gazing zombies. MacColl, in particular, is excellent. Though mainly required to fulfil the hackneyed role of beautiful screamer, she comes across as a real person throughout, regardless of a script that has her refer to "her good English breeding" while claiming to have "lived in New York all my life."

Oneiric levels of narrative uncertainty aside, the film's horror highlights are as extravagantly gruesome as Fulci's fans by this time expected. The 1920s prologue features a nasty lynching in which the frightful wounds inflicted by a chain are no less grisly for being rendered in sepia. Moving into vivid colour, a woman's face is dissolved by acid in extremely elaborate rainbow hues, the detritus lapping at her little daughter's feet in a huge crescent of yoghurt-like foam. An incapacitated architect is feasted on by a horde of flesh-hungry tarantulas, a scene made weirdly powerful by the irrational sound effects accompanying the spiders as they march towards him. (Less effective is the mixture of real with ridiculously fake tarantulas and the obviously wax head they burrow into.) And, in the mortuary climax, a face blown off with a single bullet counts as Gianetto De Rossi's pièce de résistance.

Fulci also works witty reverses on situations from his own *Zombi 2*. A woman's eyeball is popped out from behind rather than skewered face-on, while the resurrected Schweik – a grimly powerful, clay-faced figure – does battle with a dog rather than a shark, after which the dog tears out its mistress' throat. That one, of course, is a quote from Argento's *Suspiria*, but here we get the refinement of the dog ripping her ear off too. Throughout, the effects emphasise putrescent rot and rivers of (often inexplicable) vomit, an emphasis echoed by the putrid water of an abandoned bathtub, the wet and muddy walls of the hotel's basement, and the fetid sewer water in the lower depths.

Yet Fulci balances these visceral horrors with the eerie asides characteristic of him. He makes brilliantly atmospheric use of his main location, the Frank Otis House east of Madisonville, behind the windows of which huge shadows lurch clumsily to indicate that the dead have resumed their dominion. And the nearby causeway at Lake Pontchartrain lends its vanishing-point strangeness to Liza's first encounter with the spectral Emily and her faithful dog, Dickie – a scene suggestive of the otherworld to which Emily belongs, and which Fulci reportedly improvised more or less on the spot.

John and Liza's climactic battle with hospital zombies – in which nude autopsy subjects arise en masse and all telephone lines turn out, appropriately, to be dead – ends with our heroes struggling down a spiral staircase and emerging, miraculously, in the hotel basement they escaped from several minutes before. As in Bava's *Operazione paura*, John and Liza are clearly caught on some unending cosmic treadmill. "Impossible, impossible," John stammers as they stumble through a thick pall of mist and gain unexpected access to the so-called "sea of darkness." And here Warbeck and MacColl round out their performances with discreetly differentiated responses to this chilling endgame – the man aghast at the collapse of his materialist illusions, the woman quietly resigned on having her darkest suspicions confirmed.

"The idea of the characters walking into the greyness of Hell itself at the climax is quite a nice one," noted David Quinlan in 1981, "but, like so many other things in the film, it's too crudely realised."[34] Crude or otherwise, Fulci's realisation of the Beyond

Catriona MacColl seized by a horde of hospital revenants in E tu vivrai nel terrore! L'aldilà (1980)

is refreshingly different. The word 'greyness' indicates that this is no roiling sulphurous pit – as seen, for example, in the British film *Tales from the Crypt* – but an ashen landscape studded with calcified bodies, rather as if the devastation of Pompeii had been transferred to a Louisiana basement. And, suddenly, Fulci's narrative incoherence makes perfect sense. With the protagonists trapped for eternity in a mist-wreathed limbo, the film succeeds all too well in reproducing the awful circularity of a nightmare.

## STRANGE CASES

When the comedy veteran Steno began directing Paolo Villaggio and Edwige Fenech in *Il Dottor Jekyll Jr* on 4 December 1978, very nearly 20 years had passed since he'd made the comic vampire film *Tempi duri per i vampiri*. But any contemporary suspicions that Italian horror had come full circle were quickly confounded when Lucio Fulci's groundbreaking *Zombi 2* preceded Steno's film into release (by a week) in August 1979. By that time the Steno picture had been retitled *Dottor Jekyll e gentile signora* (Dr Jekyll and the Gracious Lady), offering patrons an elementary reversal – a despicable Jekyll descendant becoming benevolent on exposure to the famous potion.

## E TU VIVRAI NEL TERRORE! L'ALDILÀ

Italy 1980
UK: **The Beyond**
US: **Seven Doors of Death**
Fulvia Film
88 minutes colour
production began 20 October 1980

Director of Photography: Sergio Salvati; Design: Massimo Lentini; Editor: Vincenzo Tomassi; Sound: Ugo Celani, Enzo Diliberto; Music: Fabio Frizzi; Make-up: Maurizio Trani; Special Effects and Make-up created by: Giannetto De Rossi; Special Effects: Germano Natali; Screenplay: Dardano Sacchetti, Giorgio Mariuzzo, Lucio Fulci; Story: Dardano Sacchetti; Producer: Fabrizio De Angelis; Director: Lucio Fulci [Lewis (or Louis) Fuller on US prints]

Katherine [Catriona] MacColl (Liza Merrill); David Warbeck (Dr John McCabe); Cinzia Monreale (Emily); Antoine Saint Jean (Schweik); Veronica Lazar (Martha); Anthony Flees (Larry); Giovanni De Nava (Joe); Al Cliver [Pier Luigi Conti] (Dr Harris); Michele Mirabella (Martin Avery); Giampaolo Saccarola (Arthur); Maria Pia Marsale (Jill); Laura De Marchi (Mary Ann); uncredited: Lucio Fulci (town clerk)

The indefatigable Lucio Fulci ... has a very distinctive, if not unique, way of messing with his characters' heads, practising this art with nauseating glee. The spécialité maison of this upright and highly honourable apprentice pastry-cook is disfigurement. It is his favourite dish. He excels in it ... Too bad that, film after film, there's always just the one dish on the menu. Certainly he's perfected it but it gets old very quickly. *Cahiers du Cinéma* November 1981

What I wanted to get across with that film was the idea that all of life is often really a terrible nightmare and that our only refuge is to remain in this world but outside time. In the end, the two protagonists' eyes turn completely white and they find themselves in a desert where there's no light, no shade, no wind – no nothing. I believe, despite my being Catholic, that they reached what many people imagine to be the Afterworld.
*Lucio Fulci [quoted in Palmerini / Mistretta, Spaghetti Nightmares, 1996]*

The turn of the 1980s saw several other indications of the shape-shifting potential of Stevenson's *Strange Case of Dr Jekyll and Mr Hyde*. In March 1980, for example, Oliver Reed was in Hollywood for an irreverent farce called *Dr Heckyl and Mr Hype*. This was followed by a sober BBC reassessment of the original novella that reached British viewers in November, with Reed's fellow Swinging Sixties survivor, David Hemmings, in the leads. By that time, however, the Polish filmmaker Walerian Borowczyk was in London to make arguably the strangest Stevenson adaptation of all.

Long resident in France, Borowczyk had made his first international impact as an animator, though by the time Jekyll and Hyde came round he'd become notorious for live-action features in which the 'male gaze' of conventional erotica was given a unique gloss of painterly precision, equal parts antiquarian-academic and provocateur-skittish. Two short films, *La Marée* (The Tide) and *La Bête de Gévaudan* (The Beast of Gévaudan), intended for an in-development anthology called *Contes immoraux* (Immoral Tales), had appeared at the London Film Festival back in November 1973, with the explicitness of *Gévaudan*, in particular, causing widespread consternation. In the event, it wasn't included among the four stories featured in *Contes immoraux*, instead being recycled as a horny dream sequence in a full-length feature called simply *La Bête*. The French tag-line made no bones about the feature version's content: 'Pour la première fois au cinéma les amours monstrueuses et charnelles de la femme et la Bête' (For the first time on film, the monstrous and carnal love life of woman and beast).

In its short form, the film was inspired, as its title made clear, by the French legend of the Beast of Gévaudan; the fleshed-out version was loosely founded on Prosper Mérimée's novel *Lokis*, a subject previously filmed in 1970 by another Pole, Janusz Majewski. Repurposed as the rape fantasy of an American heiress who's poised to marry the lycanthropic scion of a demented French family, Borowczyk's dream sequence focuses on an 18th century ancestor (Sirpa Lane) who is waylaid by a bear-like creature with a face like a musk rat and a member like an ever-spurting champagne bottle. That the woman begins to enjoy the experience, and eventually shags the beast to death, is just the politically incorrect icing (so to speak) on a patently ridiculous cake. Playing like a Benny Hill chase sketch, with tinkling Scarlatti harpsichords replacing the crazed strains of *Yakety Sax*, the sequence prompted one British critic to formulate the conundrum that would come to define Borowczyk's career – "Is it art or pornography?"[35]

The conundrum was relevant to the completed *Contes immoraux* too, which included a 35-minute vignette featuring Paloma Picasso as Erzsébet Báthory, whose naked victims are herded up en masse on the assurance that "Happy are those who please the Countess." The nude girls' screaming fever of avarice

as they clutch and tear at the Countess' luxurious robes is powerfully realised, but the best thing about this otherwise slightly boring episode comes straight after the statutory blood-bathing sequence. It's the little twinge of disgust shown by the Countess' pretty page (Pascale Christophe), who has presided impassively over the bathroom proceedings and will subsequently go to bed with her mistress prior to betraying her to the authorities. On the belated UK release of *Contes immoraux* in 1977, the Báthory story was aptly singled out by Clancy Sigal as "a concentration camp nightmare with a sexual veneer."[36]

When he got round to Jekyll and Hyde in late 1980, Borowczyk had made *Interno di un convento*, an artful contribution to Italy's nunsploitation cycle exported as *Behind Convent Walls*, and was fresh from a radical new version of Wedekind's *Lulu*, first fruit of a partnership with the French producers Robert Kruperberg and Jean-Pierre Labrande. Udo Kier – Paul Morrissey's Baron Frankenstein and Count Dracula – popped up at the end as Jack the Ripper and was subsequently cast in the twin leads of another Kruperberg-Labrande production, a film known during shooting as *Le Cas étrange de Dr Jekyll et Miss Osbourne* (The Strange Case of Dr Jekyll and Miss Osbourne).

According to Borowczyk expert Daniel Bird, the director's impudent claim was that he had found the original, unexpurgated manuscript of Stevenson's story, the manuscript that Stevenson's wife, the real-life Fanny Osbourne, had reputedly put to the torch in a fit of disgust. Of course, Borowczyk had found nothing of the sort, but as an indication that his film was to transgress the boundaries of all previous adaptations, coaxing to the surface all the fouler implications of Stevenson's published version, his playful little confabulation was a PR masterstroke. Spoiling the effect, the film's French distributors released the film as *Dr Jekyll et les femmes* (Dr Jekyll and the Women), not only to underline Borowczyk's reputation for arty soft-porn but also, presumably, to remind punters of *Dracula et les femmes*, the local title for Hammer's *Dracula Has Risen from the Grave*.

*While celebrating his engagement to Fanny Osbourne, Dr Henry Jekyll defends his theory of what he calls "transcendental medicine" against the pooh-poohing of his older associate, Dr Lanyon. Soon enough, the household is disrupted by several appalling crimes, including a pubescent ballerina being raped to death, a young man being fatally sodomised in the attic, and an elderly General being pierced with multiple arrows. As Fanny discovers, the key to the horror lies in her fiancé's bathroom...*

Isabelle Cagnat
in flight from the
remorseless Mr
Hyde in Dr Jekyll
et les femmes (1980)

That Borowczyk's take on the story is to be more uncompromising than any other is indicated at once by his choice of Stevenson's most disturbing vignette – the brutalisation of a little girl – as a nightmarish jumping-off point. The streets are suffused a funereal blue, the soundtrack resonates to the eerie synthesiser drone of electronic music pioneer Bernard Parmegiani, and in one stunning shot, when the terrified girl pauses briefly in her flight, Borowczyk recalls the window-gazing ghost children of Mario Bava. Giving notice of the depravity to come, a rending-petticoats sound effect suggests that this Hyde would have progressed to necrophile child abuse were he not disturbed at his work by a passing prostitute.

From this outdoors atrocity Borowczyk moves to the decorous interior that is to dominate the remainder of the film, introducing a gaggle of late-Victorian grotesques reminiscent of the venal French oddballs assembled for *La Bête*. Also recalling *La Bête*, a whiff of Luis Buñuel attaches to the subsequent dinner party sequence, in which the diners' faux-intellectual conversation is so seriously unengaging Borowczyk takes the wise precaution of interleaving the blather with premonitory flashes of the horrors to come – Fanny savagely stabbing her mother; a *La Bête*-style monster phallus ready for rear entry; the black maid, inverted and bloodied, dangling naked.

Sadly, Borowczyk's trademark fetishisation of antiquarian bric-à-brac, lingering fascinatedly over phonographs and lab equipment and such, did not translate into an interest in actors. Indeed, it quickly becomes clear that, once he'd assembled a set of suitably quirky faces, Borowczyk felt his task was

## DR JEKYLL ET LES FEMMES

*France-West Germany 1980*
UK: **The Blood of Dr Jekyll**
US and alternative UK: **Bloodbath of Doctor Jekyll**
*Robert Kuperberg, Jean-Pierre Labrande present*
*92 minutes colour*
*production began mid-November 1980*
.....................................
*Director of Photography: Noël Véry;*
*Supervising Editor: Khadicha Bariha;*
*Sound: Gérard Barra; Music: Bernard*
*Parmegiani; Make-up: Christine Fornelli;*
*Special Effects: Crescendo Productions;*
*Based on Strange Case of Dr Jekyll and*
*Mr Hyde by Robert Louis Stevenson;*
*Producers: Robert Kuperberg, Jean-Pierre*

*Labrande; Art Director and Writer-*
*Director: Walerian Borowczyk*

*Udo Kier (Dr Henry Jekyll); Marina Pierro*
*(Miss Fanny Osbourne); Patrick Magee*
*(General Carew); Gérard Zalcberg (Mr Hyde);*
*Howard Vernon (Dr Lanyon); Clément Harari*
*(Revd Guest); Jean Mylonas (Jekyll's notary);*
*Gisèle Preville (Mrs Jekyll); Eugène Braun*
*Munk (Enfield); Louis Michel Colla (Mr Maw);*
*Catherine Coste (Katherine Enfield); Rita Maiden*
*(Lady Osbourne); Michèle Maze; Agnès Daems*
*(Charlotte Carew); Magali Noaro (Victoria*
*Enfield); Dominique Andersen; Isabelle Cagnat*
*(child victim); uncredited: Michael Levy (Poole)*

**Blood of Dr Jekyll ... has sneaked covertly into London as if in a dirty raincoat and is in fact a high and gamey masterwork by Walerian Browczyck [sic]** (of *Blanche* and *Story of Sin*). **This thunderously dotty farrago of swords and arrases and secret panels and blood rites ... is vivacious, atonal and unforgettable, like a meeting of minds between *Lulu* and *Dracula*.**
*Financial Times 17 February 1984*

I began this movie with two British cameramen ... but after three days I'd had just about enough. I'm used to working fast and concentrated, and their working techniques didn't blend well with mine. The shooting took about four weeks, but it would have taken four months to have it shot by Englishmen! But I must say, they were very good.
*Walerian Borowczyk [quoted in Video Watchdog Special Edition 1994]*

complete. As a result, even horror veterans like Patrick Magee and Howard Vernon, together with the baby-faced Udo Kier, are made to seem rudderless and fatally unsure of what they're doing. Magee came to the film direct from his creepy performance in Fulci's *Black Cat*, and his splenetic General Carew is very funny indeed when he mutters "Really terribly, terribly sorry" after accidentally killing the Jekyll family's groom. But at other moments he's forced to just go through the mad-eyed Magee-style motions, especially in a totally unmotivated scene in which he manhandles Marina Pierro's Fanny. Indeed, at the dinner table Borowczyk makes the elementary mistake of introducing Magee's famous voice – disembodied and therefore impossible to assign to anyone in particular – long before introducing Magee himself.

The first half of the film nevertheless includes some telling details, as when the assembled grandees are shown the splintered cane that killed the little girl and proceed to fondle it on a person-by-person basis. And, once the dreary dinner party is out of the way, Borowczyk wastes little time in ratcheting up Hyde's perverted stream of atrocities. As the veteran of any number of Jess Franco films, Vernon no doubt had a feeling of déjà vu while contemplating the dead ballerina's exposed and blood-smeared pudenda, noting the gory exit wound in her belly and telling us that the offending phallus was approximately six centimetres in diameter and 35 in length.

If this isn't nasty enough, Hyde then informs the tethered General that "You will live long enough to witness things no one has ever dared to show you" and proceeds to violate the General's more-than-willing teenage daughter. Even here, however, we're given the absurdity of the General's bonds only being applied to his shoulders (making them completely ineffective, if only the General thought to struggle out of them), followed by a predictable scene in the aftermath in which the inflamed old man tans his daughter's bare arse with the same rope. Eventually the General is shot to death with his own poisoned arrows – though Borowczyk does a poor job of disguising the fact that Magee was obviously unavailable that day, his place being taken by a twitching body-double.

Apart from the hazily diffused photography by Noël Véry and the obvious provocations of Hyde's escalating sex crimes, there's nothing in the film to really make the viewer sit up until well after the halfway point. Here, however, Borowczyk hits us with an astounding scene in which Fanny spies on Jekyll as he transforms into Hyde. (Though cast as both Jekyll and Hyde, Udo Kier was disappointed to be denied Hyde in the end, a role which, for logistical reasons, Borowczyk assigned to the extremely creepy Gérard Zalcberg.) Emphasising the duality in all of us, Borowczyk frames alternating slivers of Fanny's face between two concealing chests of drawers – an image so powerful he pressed it into service for the film's French poster. And what Fanny sees is genuinely imaginative and disturbing. Sloshing about in a bathtub of what may as well be amniotic fluid, Jekyll eventually submerges and, with magical simplicity, reappears as Hyde.

"Each experience costs me five years of life," Jekyll later explains, and we puzzle briefly over the credulity-busting regularity with which Jekyll undergoes the (rather lengthy) process during this single nocturnal binge. But the scene is so weirdly mesmerising it becomes the undoubted centrepiece of the film, and is given added resonance for Borowczyk followers by its echoes of the Báthory bloodbath featured in Contes immoraux.

The scene is rivalled only by the dazzling conflagration of the ending, in which Fanny undergoes the process too and joins Hyde in an exhilarating orgy of destruction, trashing virtually every sacred cow held dear by Victorian society and eventually escaping in a closed carriage. The wild and revolutionary rush on which the film ends makes it easy to overlook the nasty implications of Fanny's transformation. Having contradicted the usual one-man-for-both-roles practice by casting a separate actor as Hyde, Borowczyk sticks with just Marina Pierro for the transmogrified Fanny, nor does he supply her with the shaved eyebrows and pinhead peculiarity of Hyde. It seems that, for Borowczyk, a beautiful woman need only be given orange contact lenses in order to become an avatar of evil. And, in this scenario, evil is indeed what lies beneath; if the couple's final blow-out appears liberating, it should be remembered that Hyde's sex crimes make him unmistakably monstrous.

Despite confusions of intent, Dr Jekyll et les femmes remains a genuinely iconoclastic work, fully bearing out Borowczyk's claim in 1985 that "Genre films disgust me. Nauseating repetitions of the same old thing – that, for me, is pornography."[37] Having concluded his remarks with the categorical statement that "I have a great aversion to being labelled," this unique stylist nevertheless discovered that labels have a tendency of sticking. In May 1986, less than 18 months after publication of that interview, he began shooting his penultimate film – an enervated soft-porn sequel called Emmanuelle 5.

Dr Jekyll et les femmes was by no means the only turn-of-the-decade cult curio on offer as the 1980s came into view. In Iván Zulueta's Spanish oddity Arrebato (Rapture), a crazed underground filmmaker (Will More) is subsumed by his own work in an updated echo of Poe's 'canvas-as-vampire' story The Oval Portrait. (One of Zulueta's mid-1960s student films was an Oval Portrait adaptation called Ágata, and to judge from Arrebato he was also familiar with de Maupassant's 'stealth vampire' story Le Horla.) There are a number of eccentric touches here to point up the fact that film is just as addictive a substance as the heroin the three principals constantly shoot up. A daffy aunt suggests that the filmmaker's director friend (Eusebio Poncela) should cast the long-dead Alan Ladd in his new project, a schlock horror called *Hombres lobos*. A fetishistic tour of Madrid cinemas in the summer of 1979 reveals hoardings for, among others, *The Humanoid*, *Oliver's Story*, *The Deer Hunter*, *Phantasm* and *Superman*. And Cecilia Roth does an elaborate Betty Boop floorshow in front of a blank screen.

But that's as engaging as the film gets. There are creepy details – a doll with eyes that light up, for example – and the interest quickens (at a very late stage) when the callow avant-gardiste is warned that his film means to "devour you like a praying mantis." But having the camera focus on people under its own steam and literally 'disappear' them is just risible; the idea, of people being permanently translated from a 'real' into a 'film' zone, is much more striking than the jump-cut execution. And Zulueta – whose own heroin addiction helped to terminate his film career at this point – was no doubt well aware he was writing *Arrebato*'s epitaph when the demented filmmaker describes his life as "a massive wank without a climax."

The same judgment can be applied to another film of which obsession was the key note. Shot in Berlin in the summer of 1980, Andrzej Zulawski's French-German co-production *Possession* sprang from Zulawski's own marriage break-up, conjuring slimily sexual nightmare visions from the trauma rather as David Cronenberg did, in similar circumstances, in *The Brood*. But where Cronenberg created a genre classic, Zulawski concocted a barely watchable stew of unmediated mad-eyed acting and dialogue so laughably pretentious one has to check that the film isn't a parody.

As the sundered couple, Isabelle Adjani and Sam Neill pitch their performances on a note of raving hysteria from first to last, and where Heinz Bennent, as Adjani's epicene lover, is coming from is anybody's guess. Adjani has a subway miscarriage in which rivers of slimy goo are exuded, for some reason, from her shoulders. And her congress with a man-sized octopoid monster (designed by Carlo Rambaldi) is preceded by a couple of halfway effective scenes in which two gay detectives (Carl Duering and Shaun Lawton) encounter the thing in turn. (Duering's horrified response: "Was ist?" Lawton's: "Mein Gott!") The thing eventually morphs into a Neill doppelgänger, which, like Adjani's, has green rather than blue eyes, after which the action resolves itself via an incomprehensible espionage subplot. Released in the UK in June 1982 at its full, endurance-test length of over two hours, it was aptly dismissed by critic Al Clark. "*Possession* defines new heights

Adulation turns murderous for Desirée Nosbusch and Bodo Steiger in *Der Fan* (1981)

in awfulness, with a plotline staggering under the increasing weight of ludicrous incident," he wrote. "The slurping tentacular creature ... is, by comparison with the surrounding mess, quite engaging."[38]

Yet another brooding portrait in obsession, Eckhart Schmidt's *Der Fan* (The Fan), was shot in Munich at the end of 1981 and is perhaps most valuable now as a snapshot of the post-punk music scene dubbed Neue Deutsche Welle. At the time, however, it stirred up plenty of local controversy with its story of tunnel-visioned Simone (played by 16-year-old model Desirée Nosbusch) plotting to ensnare the pop star of her dreams, 'R', who's played by the genuine article – Bodo Steiger of the group Rheingold. Watching him being interviewed on TV by former film star Joachim Fuchsberger, Simone wonders "if he'll give me the sign I asked for." Even when he doesn't, she remains convinced that "I can put meaning into [his] life."

When they finally can have sex and R snubs her in the aftermath, she kills him and, still naked, chops him up with an electric carving knife as tears roll gently down her face. (Happily, sound effects do most of the work during this gruelling sequence.) Having licked his blood off the kitchen floor, she finally reduces him to a bag of powdered bone, then returns to her parents sporting the bald head characteristic of the female mannequins used in R's pop videos. Stephen Bissette was bang on when describing this cold and rather repellent film as "a slow, static, talky, calculated, tortuously obsessive and horribly sterile experience – but if you get caught up in its spell, you'll never forget it."[39] Schmidt's film also indicates that electric carving knives were suddenly the domestic weapon of choice in three separate countries, given their wince-making use in France's *Possession*, Spain's *Sobrenatural* and, later, another French film, *Le Démon dans l'île*. All this carnage presumably derived from Marco Ferreri's 1976 release *La Dernière femme* (The Last Woman), in which Gérard Depardieu climactically emasculates himself with a similar device. The real pioneer, however, was Capucine in *Las crueles*, way back in 1968.

## DR FREUDSTEIN WILL SEE YOU NOW

While all these obsessive and frankly unapproachable films were in the works, actor-writer-director Jean-Pierre Mocky was preparing *Litan*, a picture that packs in, if possible, more high-octane weirdness than *Dr Jekyll et les femmes*, *Arrebato*, *Possession* and *Der Fan* put together. Back in 1964 Mocky had made *La Grande frousse* (The Big Fright), turning a Jean Ray novel into a macabre farce with the help of such distinguished actors as Bourvil, Jean-Louis Barrault and Victor Francen. Later on, Mocky restored various scenes cut by meddlesome producers and had the film reissued under Ray's original title, which he'd always favoured, *La Cité de l'indicible peur* (The City of Unspeakable Fear). Now, shooting in the French commune of Annonay early in 1981, he made the extraordinary *Litan* on his own terms.

In the Jean Ray adaptation, the bizarre community investigated by Bourvil's all-at-sea police inspector had been called Barges, echoing the French word corresponding with 'barmy'. In *Litan*, the titular mountain community is piously referred to by the Mayor as "cette ville fleuri" (this flowery town), but it's actually consumed in sheets of rain and mist. The character roughly corresponding to the old Bourvil role is a middle-aged geologist played by Mocky himself and called Jock (a conflation of Jean-Pierre Mocky). Arriving in Litan on its annual day devoted to the dead, Jock and his girlfriend Nora (Marie-José Nat) find themselves surrounded and eventually pursued by skull-masked celebrants, pig-masked thugs, robot-masked red-jacketed musicians, rampaging Boy Scouts, and squiggly little water-borne organisms that instantly dissolve people on contact.

"As a child," Mocky pointed out, "I was terrified of the death masks people decked themselves out with in my home, over in Slovenia."[40] That childhood trauma was the film's starting point seems to make sense, unlike the film itself, which is truly a one-of-a-kind item saturated in soft-focus photography and selections from Shostakovich. The film's subtitle – only on the posters, not the print – is *La Cité des spectres verts* (The City of Green Ghosts), which makes no more sense than anything else given the pronounced lack of greenery and the slightly cheesy special effects that make the squiggly things electric-blue. But the film's bizarre progress culminates in a small but genuine frisson – when a

dead Boy Scout, experimented on by a mad scientist, informs him telepathically that "We're dreaming your life. And when the dream stops, you die."

In March 1981, while Mocky was finishing work in Annonay, Lucio Fulci was in the USA yet again – this time in the Massachusetts environs of Concord and Scituate – for a film that began life as an Elisa Briganti outline called *La notte dell'inferno* (The Night of Hell) before acquiring the splendid working title *Freudstein*. The film eventually became known as *Quella villa accanto al cimitero* (The House by the Cemetery), a title frankly designed to remind Italian viewers of Tobe Hooper's *Eaten Alive*, which they'd seen as *Quel motel vicino alla palude* (That Motel Near the Swamp). The last of Fulci's three collaborations with female lead Catriona MacColl, the result is, if anything, even more loosely scripted and wilfully perplexing than the first two. Yet it remains memorable for one truly formidable creation – an undead, cellar-dwelling abomination called Dr Jacob Freudstein.

*New York researcher Dr Norman Boyle brings his wife Lucy and small son Bob to a remote New England house, proposing to spend the winter. The house was previously tenanted by Norman's colleague Dr Peterson, who committed suicide there after reportedly murdering his mistress. Bob quickly establishes psychic contact with a dead little girl called Mae, while Lucy, removing a hallway rug, finds a dust-clogged funerary slab marked Freudstein.*

Early on, Paolo Malco's Norman surveys Oak Mansion – a property better known to the locals as "the Freudstein house" – and airily describes it as having "shades of Walden pond." This brief spot of Massachusetts literacy is pleasantly ironic; we know already that the Boyles' retreat is unlikely to echo the idyllic dream of 19th century self-sufficiency embodied in Thoreau's *Walden*, even before we suspect the awful truth – that a character struck off the medical register in 1879 is still on the premises 102 years later. The film's other attempts at literacy are less persuasive. The action concludes with a written inscription attributed to Henry James but which is actually unadulterated Fulci: 'No one will ever know whether children are monsters or monsters are children.' This bogus attempt to link the relationship between little Bob and the ghostly Mae to *The Turn of the Screw* is hard to substantiate in the film itself, recalling the phoney attempts to lend films literary pedigree that characterised Italian horror 20 years before.

*Variety* was closer to the mark when referring to the film as "prolific Italian director Lucio Fulci's riposte to Stanley Kubrick's hit *The Shining*."[41] To this one might add such recent US hits as *Burnt Offerings*, *The Amityville Horror* and the whole spate of slasher pictures kicked off by *Halloween*. Indeed, the pre-credits sequence is pure *Halloween*, though draped by Fulci in the kind of crepuscular Gothic trappings he relished. The very first shot is of a tombstone, with a benighted dog howling mournfully on the soundtrack. Moving from ancient convention to contemporary cliché, we next see a bare-breasted girl in the gloom of the Freudstein house; inevitably, she's already lost track of the boy she's just made love with. In a neat reference to the ending of his previous film, in which our heroes were admitted to Hell via a spiral staircase, Fulci films the girl through a skein of cobwebs stretched across an identical set of steps. The film's subsequent references to *The Shining* are less successful, if only because Mae's interaction with Bob is arbitrarily developed; also, perhaps, because Bob himself is far creepier than Mae.

The Boyles' holiday home is situated in a fictional New England community called New Whitby (presumably a reference to *Dracula*), though the actual location was on the Ellis Estate in the coastal town of Scituate. (The same house turned up again, to much less effect, in Umberto Lenzi's 1988 release *Ghosthouse*, aka *La casa 3*.) Fulci lends the house his customary

dollops of spooky atmosphere, simultaneously making it the site of some staggeringly gruesome set-pieces. Echoing Fulci's own *Una lucertola con la pelle di donna*, a bat attaches itself to Lucy's hair prior to embedding itself in Norman's hand, with blood

## QUELLA VILLA ACCANTO AL CIMITERO

*Italy 1981*
UK / US: **The House by the Cemetery**
*Fulvia Film*
*87 minutes colour*
*production began 11 March 1981*
. . . . . . . . . . . . . . . . . . . . . . . . . . . . .
Director of Photography: Sergio Salvati; Production Designer: Massimo Lentini; Editor: Vincenzo Tomassi; Sound: Ugo Celani; Music: Walter Rizzati; Make-up: Gianetto De Rossi, Maurizio Trani; Special Effects: Gino De Rossi, Giorgio Mariuzzo, Lucio Fulci;

Story: Elisa Livia Briganti; Producer: Fabrizio De Angelis; Director: Lucio Fulci

*Katherine [Catriona] MacColl (Lucy Boyle); Paolo Malco (Dr Norman Boyle); Ania Pieroni (Anne); Giovanni Frezza (Bob Boyle); Silvia Collatina (Mae Freudstein); Dagmar Lassander (Laura Gittleson); Giovanni De Nava (Dr Jacob Freudstein); Daniela Doria (first female victim); Giampaolo Saccarola (Daniel Douglas); Carlo De Mejo (Mr Wheatley); John Olson; Elmer Johnson; Ranieri Ferrara; Teresa Rossi Passante (Mary Freudstein); uncredited: Lucio Fulci (Professor Muller)*

Fulci, our homegrown impersonator of 'Gothic' cinema, shows off his personal prowess in conferring visual flair on a mind-boggling horror saga ... The monster, thanks to the make-up plastered over the real face of actor Giovanni De Nava, is horrendous beyond imagining ... Seeing children mixed up in so ghastly and oppressive a horror story will probably induce perplexity and discomfort, sooner than pity, in the majority of viewers. *La Stampa* 18 August 1981

I don't really have to do anything too horrible in these movies. As the heroine I'm mainly running around screaming and nothing too hideous happens to me, and certainly I don't get my eyes poked out or anything, thank God. So from my point of view it was really a kind of challenge to play these parts because I had to explore my own sense of fear. *Catriona MacColl [quoted in The Dark Side February 1996]*

DAS HAUS AN DER FRIEDHOFMAUER

Giovanni De Nava looms over Giovanni Frezza in the appalling basement of *Quella villa accanto al cimitero* (1981)

spraying all over the kitchen (and Bob) as Norman struggles to prise it off. Later, Dagmar Lassander's pragmatic estate agent is trapped in the maw of Freudstein's commemorative slab when it suddenly splits open under her feet; her body is subsequently penetrated three times by Freudstein's poker as her screams compete with the killer's sexually gratified heavy breathing.

The film has the expected ration of narrative loose ends, notably a creepily beautiful babysitter whose motivations (prior to losing her head in the basement) make no sense whatever. But Fulci's staging, Sergio Salvati's autumnal photography and above all the towering figure of Dr Freudstein offer ample compensation. The most intense scenes in the film take place in Freudstein's cellar, reflecting a vivid childhood memory of co-screenwriter Dardano Sacchetti. Despite the presence of a token test-tube or two, Freudstein's subterranean laboratory more closely resembles a torture chamber or charnel house.

As spindly yet terrifying as Max Schreck's *Nosferatu*, the man himself reveals a hideous visage closer to some distorted root vegetable than anything human, and there's a highly suggestive moment when, having been stabbed by Norman, his body disgorges a torrent of maggots mixed with revolting faecal matter. Intentional or not, there's an echo here of the strange scene in Stoker's *Dracula* when the Count's punctured body bleeds gold coins. If Dracula stands for blood-sucking capitalism, it's clear from Freudstein's outpourings that he represents the more basic bodily functions, together with the final corruption to which all of them are subject. He seems, in fact, like an unstoppable symbol of Fate itself, particularly in his slow but sure assault on the Boyle family at the end. Accompanied by the eerie, subdued sobbing of children (presumably a psychic echo of Freudstein's former victims), these climactic scenes represent a sustained crescendo of terror that approaches genius.

"Those movies were both very good," noted Fulci's producer, Fabrizio De Angelis, of their last two pictures together. "Fulci really was the best director for that sort of subject. The films had lots of atmosphere and tension."[42] Sadly, it was at precisely this moment that Fulci's hot streak was definitively snuffed out. Originally due to be shot in April 1981

Spanish poster for the Americanised body-count shocker *Mil gritos tiene la noche* (1982), known for export as *Pieces*

by Ruggero Deodato, *Lo squartatore di New York* (The New York Ripper) eventually fell to Fulci and began shooting in the last week of August. This is a police-procedural giallo in which the cynicism of the sub-genre is pushed to new extremes. The film is a vivid time-capsule of Times Square in all its sleazy, porn-era pomp, but the murders, rendered in repugnant detail, entailed bans in several territories.

English actor Jack Hedley was recruited to take top billing as the regulation hypocritical and fagged-out NYPD detective, and his splendidly jaded face sustains interest – though not his voice, which was supplied by an ADR artiste. Another voice is described by a garrulous elderly lady early in the film as "The strangest voice I ever heard – sort of like a duck." Yes, it's the killer himself, whose bizarre choice of diction is explained at the end in a typically harebrained giallo resolution. As a result, the film moved Chas Balun to invoke the Marx Brothers. "One can *almost* summarily dismiss the clunky plotting, regressive world view, mean-spirited misogyny and sleazy sexual sadism," he wrote in 1989, "but no one can let Fulci off the hook for featuring a psychopathic killer who quacks like a duck! I mean, a wolverine, donkey, chihuahua or parakeet even, but why a duck?"[43]

## HUMAN JIGSAWS AND ACTION PAINTINGS

While Lucio Fulci was putting Jack Hedley through his paces in NYC, Spain too was producing its share of imitation slasher pics. Among them were two films that were so unsuccessful they racked up a puny take, collectively, of around five million pesetas. Silvio F Balbuena's *Escrito en la niebla* (Written in the Fog) echoed *Psycho* in having its boy protagonist kill his mother's lover; as an adult (played by Terpy Ibir, who also wrote the script) he anticipates *Psycho II* by reactivating a diner and snuffing out the waitresses. Naschy veterans Jack Taylor and Mirta Miller, meanwhile, were the chief attractions in Francisco Rodríguez Gordillo's stultifyingly boring *El cepo* (The Snare), in which Taylor is a two-faced doctor-huntsman, Miller the on-the-make Parisian call girl he takes in, and Gordillo the guilty party in that he includes no worthwhile slasher set-pieces whatsoever.

This was a mistake emphatically avoided in Juan Piquer Simón's Mil gritos tiene la noche (The Night Has a Thousand Screams), an outrageous gorefest that also featured the indefatigable Taylor and was exported under the enticing title Pieces. Starting from a 'count the anachronisms' pre-credits sequence set in 1942 Boston, in which May Heatherly receives four axe blows to the head from her ten-year-old son, this leaps forward four decades to a Boston college beset by a rash of chainsaw killings. Among the highlights are shots of the silhouetted killer lurking outside a disco-aerobics class, the entirely unmotivated nocturnal appearance of a demented Kung Fu practitioner, and a waterbed killing in which Simón contrives a poor imitation of the 'knife going from back of the head through mouth' effect so recently staged by Fulci in the Freudstein House.

Amid all this horror we're given precisely three suspects together with an extraordinary histrionic outburst from undercover policewoman Lynda Day George. "The lousy bastard was in there killing her!" she screams. "Bastard! Bastard! BASTARD!" That killer silhouette is frequently shown with the chainsaw in an obviously erectile position, a self-conscious touch echoed by the amazing ending, in which the patchwork woman created by the killer suddenly lurches into life and gouges the young hero's private parts. The boy has been a cocksure little creep and serial seducer throughout, though this pleasant piece of poetic justice would make more sense in a film that didn't rejoice quite so much in showing topless girls being chased around locker rooms. In any case, the 'grasp from the grave' kicker is an obvious steal from Carrie, while the 'perfect woman being pieced together' scenario is an equally obvious lift from La residencia.

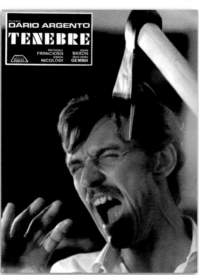

A hatchet in the head for John Steiner in Tenebre (1982)

Known in production as Jigsaw, Pieces began shooting on 15 February 1982 and was a uniquely garbled meeting of some major exploitation minds. The US producers comprised longtime huckster Dick Randall and a newer face, Steve Friday the 13th Minasian, while the English-language script was by Randall and John Shadow. (The latter was Ewa Aulin's British ex-husband and not, as many have assumed, a pseudonym for Joe D'Amato, whose involvement in the film was nil.)

During production, Simón was planning a modern-dress 3-D extravaganza called Las nuevas aventuras del Dr Jekyll y Mr Hyde (The New Adventures of Dr Jekyll and Mr Hyde), which eventually, perhaps mercifully, fell by the wayside. In the meantime, Pieces made nearly 62 million pesetas in Spain and over $2 million in the USA, where it was distributed by Edward L Montoro and graced with the ingenious tag-line 'You Don't Have to Go to Texas for a Chainsaw Massacre'.

Prominent components of Pieces are the above-mentioned, and entirely unconvincing, 1940s flashback, a murderer with a shoe fetish and an absurd scene in which a girl has both her arms sawn off in an elevator, entailing industrial quantities of ejaculatory gore. Coincidentally, variations on all three can be found in Dario Argento's Tenebre (Darkness), which began shooting on 3 May the same year and would reach English-speaking audiences under the Latinised title Tenebrae. In Argento's hands the stiletto-related psychic trauma involves a contemptuous teenage girl rather than the dead mother of Pieces, and the blood-pumping severed arm set-piece is staged in a scrupulously white bourgeois home. The tone is also quite different for the simple reason that a master magician was calling the shots, rather than a bludgeoning journeyman like Juan Piquer Simón. Yet the outrageous wall-spraying gore of the Argento scene, apparently intended as an action-painting tribute to Jackson Pollock, derives quite clearly from the same source as Pieces – the comedy bloodletting perfected by Paul Morrissey and borrowed by him from Monty Python's Flying Circus.

Of course, the similarities between Pieces and Tenebre end there, for the Argento film is a chic, alluring and cleverly constructed masterwork by comparison to the lumpen, meat-and-potatoes stodge of Pieces. Yet it remains disappointing that Argento, thoroughly drained by the difficulties involved in filming Inferno, should revert so squarely to his non-supernatural giallo roots. Luckily, the mundane murder-mystery at the heart of Tenebre is carried by Anthony Franciosa, whose delightfully engaging performance as US thriller writer Peter Neal is brim-full of the art that conceals art. (He's ably backed up, too, by another old US hand, John Saxon, back in an Italian giallo exactly 20 years after

Lara Lamberti encounters a blade in the dark in *La casa con la scala nel buio* (1982)

of unsuspecting women in their own home, a shattering sequence in which Lara Wendel is pursued by a terrifyingly persistent Doberman, and the storm-racked denouement in which all is revealed and almost everybody killed. Argento is also confident enough to introduce some intriguingly self-reflexive touches, notably a novelist hero who quotes Conan Doyle and a woman journalist who, quoting Argento's own detractors, denounces Neal's new book as "a sexist novel" and "hairy macho bullshit." The woman (Mirella D'Angelo) is a lesbian – or, in the killer's parlance, a "filthy slimy pervert" – and of course gets horribly murdered.

Later in 1982, Lamberto Bava channelled his experience on *Tenebre* (on which he served as assistant director) into a proposed giallo TV series, concocted by the tireless Dardano Sacchetti and Elisa Briganti, that was rejected for excessive violence. Recut as a feature film, it was called *La casa con la scala nel buio* (The House with the Dark Stairway) and exported as *A Blade in the Dark*. The result, perhaps inevitably, is seriously over-long and also limited in scope. The central character is a young composer, holed up in the countryside and working on a horror film, and the only other people involved are those unlucky enough to work for or visit him, all of whom are picked off one by one by the usual mystery assailant.

Unfortunately, the action is dogged by an all-pervading 1980s blandness, cued, perhaps, by the hero's truly horrible sweaters. The plot pivots on the usual theme of, as one character puts it, "childhood trauma turning a normal person into a monster," together with the equally standard complication of gender confusion. But there are still some effective moments. The protracted dragging of an early victim's corpse into the shrubbery is grimly done, a 'staring eye' quotation from *The Spiral Staircase* makes a red herring of the resident handyman, another victim is submitted to a thoroughly brutal head-banging and throat-slashing in a shimmering bathroom, and the female film director is inventively strangled with her own celluloid.

Bava's film wasn't the only giallo of the period to forsake an intended TV audience and move to theatres instead. Nestore Ungaro's *L'isola del gabbiano* (Seagull Island), in which blind girls are the fetishised victims, was a UK co-production, hence the casting of Prunella Ransome, Jeremy Brett and Nicky Henson. Also diverted to cinemas was Sergio Martino's *Assassinio al cimitero etrusco* (Murder in the Etruscan Cemetery), which owed its script to another veteran, Ernesto Gastaldi, but remains a dreary shadow of a not-great-anyway film directed by Armando Crispino some ten years earlier, *L'etrusco uccide ancora*. In an attempt to

appearing in the very first, *La ragazza che sapeva troppo*.) Neal's latest novel, hailed as "le giallo dell'anno," has been # 1 in Italy for 12 weeks, but the celebrations turn sour when a beautiful young shoplifter (Ania Pieroni) is discovered with her throat slashed and large chunks of Neal's novel crammed into her mouth.

*Tenebre* certainly sets up a fascinating dichotomy in its opening moments – a disconcerting credits sequence set against infernal flames and accompanied by a vocodered voice repeatedly hissing "paura" (fear), immediately followed by a Kennedy Airport intrigue that sets up Neal as a Cary Grant-type in a pastiche Hitchcock thriller. But the dichotomy is never really developed, Argento focusing instead on his bravura set-pieces and as outrageously bloody a climax as he'd yet devised. In the meantime, the acting is decidedly variable. Poor Daria Nicolodi, so good in *Profondo rosso* and *Schock*, is all at sea here in a dull second-banana role. And the interesting British actor John Steiner is only on hand to play a sketchily drawn gay TV personality who gets a hatchet in the head.

But those set-pieces really are stunning – the famous Louma crane shot that stalks a couple recall the giallo's exotic heyday, this one was known for export purposes as *Scorpion with Two Tails*.

Among the theatrical features that recorded the last gasps of the giallo's popularity were Carlo Lizzani's clever, stage-derived chamber piece *La casa del tappeto giallo* (The House of the Yellow Carpet), which benefits from the mesmerisingly sinister presence of the great Swedish actor Erland Josephson, and Ovidio G Assonitis' halfway decent *There Was a Little Girl*, an 'evil twin' slasher that, under its UK title *Madhouse*, ended up on the 'Video Nasties' roster. A murderous twin of the Siamese variety featured in Alberto De Martino's *Extrasensorial* (aka *Blood Link*), a double-showcase for oddball US actor Michael Moriarty. Of Moriarty's fellow cast members, Cameron Mitchell was an old hand in Italian sleaze; grande dames Geraldine Fitzgerald and Virginia McKenna somewhat less so.

## GALLIC GORE

In France, the Christmas 1980 release *Les Charlots contre Dracula* may have brought joy to followers of the titular Monkees-style pop group but probably not to horror fans. Fortunately, the grisly example of Rollin's *Les Raisins de la mort*, together with the arrival of Lucio Fulci's Italian zombies, hadn't gone unnoticed by the very few fringe filmmakers willing to venture into the disreputable field of 'ciné-bis'.

One such was writer-director Raphaël Delpard, whose *La Nuit de la mort!* (The Night of Death!) was a Halloween 1980 release coupling cannibalistic OAPs with a so-called 'Golden Needle Killer'. Made with no budget to speak of but a certain amount of dash and wit (starting with the titular pun on 'la nuit de l'amour'), Delpard's film is set in an isolated old people's home in Senlis run by a handsome 50-something woman called Hélène Robert (Betty Beckers). Yet none of the tenants looks a day over 70 and they get through nurses at the rate of one every two months. Like all the others, the latest recruit, Martine (Isabelle Goguey), is an orphan. Surveying the looming hulk on her arrival, she murmurs, "I don't think I'll last very long here..." And how right she turns out to be.

Goguey is an engaging heroine and Beckers a commanding villainess, always reserving the heart for herself whenever a new nurse is to be eviscerated and telling her tenants that "Without me you'd all be rotting in your coffins!" When a faded newspaper clipping indicates that Hélène was a 20-year-old beauty queen in 1886, poor Martine has to take up pen and paper in order to work out that her boss must be 114. (A similarly absurd moment occurs in the latterday Hammer film *Dracula A.D. 1972*.) Other humorous touches are more calculated, as when

Martine expresses a liking for The Bee Gees and the cultured Hélène gasps, "Spare me the mediocrity." The gore effects, including bloody organs being scooped out of a naked but obviously vinyl torso, are elementary and the body-count climax rather listlessly staged, though Delpard compensates with a very nifty twist to usher in the end credits. The film is exactly the kind of formula shocker parodied so carefully in Ti West's 2008 hit *The House of the Devil*, though in theme it harks back to such French titles as Jessua's *Traitement de choc* and Rollin's *Fascination*.

Also in 1980, Rollin himself was given just two weeks to make *La Nuit des traquées* (The Night of Hunted Women) and the threadbare facilities of an after-hours Paris office block to do it in. In the first week of June the result was announced for Sitges alongside such titles as Lamberto Bava's *Macabro* and Riccardo Freda's yet-to-be-completed *Murder Obsession* (*Follia Omicida*), duly appearing at the festival early in October. Producer Monique Samarcq had been responsible for a couple of porn films, so *La Nuit des traquées* has its share of de rigueur sex scenes. But it's otherwise an eerily off-kilter addition to Rollin's work.

The focus is on Brigitte Lahaie once more, this time as a beautiful amnesiac, Elisabeth, who falls for a guileless young man (Vincent Gardère) only to be forcibly readmitted to a strange hospital by an icily bureaucratic doctor (Bernard Papineau). "You can see the Arc de Triomphe from the top floor," we're told, placing Rollin's mournful conspiracy narrative right at the heart of Paris. His antiseptic rendering of the location, however, recalls the municipal blandness of David Cronenberg's Canadian films *Rabid* and *The Brood*, with Elisabeth's fellow amnesiacs drifting sadly through the corridors like living dead.

"The only thing left for us to do is to touch our bodies," mutters Elisabeth's friend Catherine (played by Lahaie's fellow porn star Cathy Stewart). "It's our only pleasure. The only one we don't forget." Having spoken the line that allowed the film to be made, Catherine puts out her eyes with scissors when she thinks (mistakenly) that Elisabeth has forgotten her. Rollin also stages a rape scene in which the opportunistic perpetrator is hammered gruesomely to death during the act, his poster-paint blood splashing all over the naked victim. But for all the film's low-budget crudities, and a perfunctory suggestion that radiation poisoning is at the root of the mass memory loss, the overall mood is elegiac and weirdly haunting, particularly when Elisabeth and her mortally wounded beau stagger listlessly across a causeway and into the closing credits.

After this, Rollin inherited a Jess Franco project that Franco had reneged on directing at the very last minute; for *Le Lac des morts vivants* (Lake of the Living Dead), Rollin was credited by Eurociné as J A Lazer. "What can I tell you?" he said in 1993. "I didn't care what name they used as long as it wasn't Rollin."[44] In fact the pseudonym also encompassed Rollin's co-director Julian de Laserna, though neither man could save the project from becoming an utter fiasco.

Recycling the 'aquatic Nazi zombies' premise of Ken Wiederhorn's 1975 picture *Shock Waves*, the film is set in a French town in the mid-1950s, presided over by mayor Howard Vernon and subject to an influx of apparently time-travelling volleyball players in hotpants and a '70s camper van. Also present are dead Nazis in green face-paint whose effects make-up falls off under the slightest stress. The film's other hilarities are manifold – a soldier in a WWII flashback who leaps heroically into shot only to fall flat on his face, a lake that comes complete with plainly visible swimming-pool viewing ports, a peerless air-raid scene in which we're shown no aircraft whatever, and on and on. There's also one classic line of dialogue. "Let's split!" a cop tells his superior. "Shit, let's get away from this heap of hicks!" The senior cop, by the way, is Rollin, acting under his own name. The film itself became *Zombie Lake* in the USA and *Zombies' Lake* in Britain.

Recovering from this dismal experience, Rollin – recalling, perhaps, that his last successful film, *Les Raisins de la mort*, had also been France's first gore movie – concocted a new scenario with unprecedented opportunities for bloodshed. Unfortunately, the gore effects for *La Morte vivante* (The Living Dead Girl) would be somewhat hit-and-miss. The appointed effects artist, Benoît Lestang, was to be fêted in future years but at this point was only 17 and still feeling his way. And of course there were all the usual financial horrors complicating the shoot at Châtillon-sur-Seine in July 1982. Even so, Rollin succeeded in conjuring up the same elegiac quality that so distinguished *Lèvres de sang* and *Fascination*.

*The 20-year-old Catherine Valmont died over two years ago but rises from her tomb as a result of a chemical accident. Dispatching the three workmen responsible, she wanders catatonically to her family seat, now empty save for an after-hours estate agent and her lover, both of whom she also kills. Her friend Hélène is racked with guilt about reneging on their childhood vow to die together – and, becoming aware of Catherine's blood lust, she goes about supplying her with suitable victims.*

That elegiac quality takes a while to manifest itself, however. The action begins, in an unmistakable echo of *Les Raisins de la mort*, with atonal music, SF-style

'radiation' sound effects and a view of some kind of power plant. "The whole idea of the chemical waste was not very good," Rollin later admitted. "It was just thrown in for better or worse."[45] The 'ill-fated looters in a crypt' scenario reworks the ever-reliable prologue to *Frankenstein Meets the Wolf Man*, and the limitations of Lestang's gore effects are immediately apparent courtesy of a plasticine eye-gouging for one victim and some rubbery acid-scarring for another. The third, however, is convincingly stabbed in the throat by the impassive Catherine, who uses her death-lengthened fingernails for the purpose. The first and third of these unfortunates, incidentally, were played by Rollin's horror-scholar chums Jean-Pierre Bouyxou and Alain Petit.

Rollin was required to satisfy seekers after flesh as well as blood, hence the graceless gropings indulged in shortly afterwards by a pretty young estate agent and her plug-ugly boyfriend. Hearing piano notes and venturing out to investigate, the boy returns with a gaping neck wound that squirts unfeasible amounts of blood all over the screaming girl's bare breasts and face. Yes, it's the torrential 'facial' beloved of hardcore directors, suitably adapted to fit the Freudian dictum that blood and semen are synonymous in the unconscious mind. And, sure enough, a mock-penetration follows when Catherine does her fingernail move again, this time into the girl's neck; the victim staggers out and collapses, naked and slathered in blood, on the château's stone steps. Crude and bludgeoning though it is, this scene scores high for outrageous Grand Guignol excess, though Rollin will outstrip it before the film's end.

Elsewhere, he infuses *La Morte vivante* with his trademark blend of memory and mystery, dreams and displacement. In her ancestral château, the somnambulant Catherine hovers by a long-neglected rocking horse, later holding a childhood photo in her bloodily taloned hands, the image causing tears to run down her face. The other girl in the picture, Hélène, now in her mid-twenties, shows up and is granted no gradual realisation of her friend's condition; after all, Catherine is seated naked at the piano with blood and corpses everywhere. Clutching at the music box that has stirred memories in both of them, Catherine lets out a very startling moan of despair that signals her gradual return to sentience. Yet, as Hélène becomes more and more obsessed with preserving her friend, she devolves into an intriguing haze of denial. Looking at the pair of them in a mirror, she says pleadingly, "Give me a sign – anything. I can't stand this indifference. It's as if you were dead..."

In this state, Hélène becomes a calculating procuress prefiguring the Julia character in Clive Barker's

Françoise Blanchard
as the mournful
zombie protagonist
of *La Morte vivante*
(1982)

1986 film *Hellraiser*. Yet much the queasiest of these procurement scenes harks back quite deliberately to Franju's *Les Yeux sans visage*. Like Juliette Mayniel before her, Fanny Magier is lured to an out-of-the-way château and given a glass of port; having thrown her to the ravenous Catherine in the crypt, Hélène blocks her ears to the screams as a cloud of doves (descendants of the ones liberated by Édith Scob in the Franju film) bursts upwards in alarm. The ironic process at work here – with the beautiful zombie becoming revolted by the horror around her while the human plunges ever deeper into conscienceless insanity – is played out with tremendous intensity by Françoise Blanchard and the Italian actress Marina Pierro, the latter fresh from Borowczyk's *Dr Jekyll et les femmes*.

Before the women's amour fou finally reaches its self-devouring crescendo, there are some peripheral flies in the ointment – notably a bizarre spot of community dancing in the nearest village and a subplot involving a pair of irksome American tourists. At least these two are given eye-catching ends (the woman turned into a living torch, the man axed in the head) just before the final reckoning on the steps of the château. Gore wasn't something Rollin relished, but he set aside his misgivings here for a cannibal climax given added impact by the tragic dead end the childhood friends have reached. "Hélène, I am your death," Catherine breathes. On this cue, and with the château illuminated by the eerie nocturnal light

## LA MORTE VIVANTE

France 1982
Films ABC / Films Aleriaz / Films du Yaka /
Sam Selsky
92 minutes colour
production began July 1982
...........................
Director of Photography: Max Monteillet;
Editor: Janette Kronegger; Sound: Henri
Graff, Jacky Dufour; Music: Philippe d'Aram;
Make-up: Eric Pierre; Special Effects:
Benoît Lestang; Screenplay: Jean Rollin;
Adaptation: Jean Rollin, Jacques Ralf;
Dialogue: Jacques Ralf; American Version:
Gregory Heller; Producer: Sam Selsky
[uncredited]; Director: Jean Rollin

Marina Pierro (Hélène); Françoise Blanchard
(Catherine Valmont); Mike Marshall (Greg);
Carina Barone (Barbara Simon); Fanny Magier
(motorist victim); Patricia Besnard-Rousseau
(estate agent victim); Véronique Pinson (tethered-
to-pillar victim); Sandrine Morel (child Catherine);
Delphine Laporte (child Hélène); Jean Cherlian
(acid-burned burglar), Jean-Pierre Bouyxou
(eyes-gouged burglar), Alain Petit (neck-stabbed
burglar); Jacques Marbeuf (MC at village dance);
Sam Selsky (American buyer); Lise Overman;
Laurence Royer; Véronique Carpentier; Jean Hérel
(irate father); Dominique Treillou; L'Orchestre 'Les
Stars Fire' with Anita (The Fireflies); uncredited:
Jean Rollin (stallholder); Mrs Selsky (buyer's wife)

It's easy to see how such American zero budgeters as *Goregasm* and *Cannibal Hookers* have been influenced by Rollin's work, but far more fascinating to recognise themes that later form the basis of the *Hellraiser* and *Return of the Living Dead* films cropping up here. One small grouse – Rollin leaves the lesbian implications of Pierro's feelings for her ghoulfriend regrettably (and uncharacteristically) underdeveloped.
The Dark Side June 1995 [review of British VHS premiere]

I think there are some very good things in it. Of course, we had to make certain commercial concessions … I like very much the part in which the living dead girl returns to the castle and finds all these toys and telephones her friend. It was interesting to do that. Maybe we should have enlarged this part.
Jean Rollin [quoted in *Video Watchdog* January-February 1996]

familiar from so many Rollin films, Hélène willingly surrenders to Catherine's appetite amid veritable rivers of blood and viscera. Though not for weak stomachs, this is one of the most shattering climaxes in the genre.

Shot in May-June 1982, just before *La Morte vivante*, Alain Robbe-Grillet's *La Belle captive* (The Beautiful

Anny Duperey ministers to accident victims Jean-Louis Foulquier and Michèle Moretti in *Le Démon dans l'île* (1982)

Captive) added an angelic vampire seductress (Gabrielle Lazure) and a leatherclad Angel of Death (Cyrielle Claire) to an avant-garde replay of the Ambrose Bierce chestnut *An Occurrence at Owl Creek Bridge*. The film is a sort of companion piece to Robbe-Grillet's same-titled 1975 novel, a copy of which is seen lurking in a wardrobe as our wishy-washy, trenchcoated protagonist (Daniel Mesguich) makes his way to his predestined end. Several René Magritte canvases, together with Édouard Manet's iconic firing squad, are restaged in the course of this odyssey, and Robbe-Grillet creates some arresting moments as inexplicable thunderclaps ring out over sunlit beaches. There are also a few scraps of wit in the dialogue, as when the vampire girl's mediumistic father recalls that "I was at the cinema last week and in the intermission I found I was seated next to Marcel Proust."

There are plenty of cinematic as well as literary allusions, such as the recycling from Herzog's *Nosferatu* of the brooding prelude to Wagner's *Das Rheingold* and the presence of a sinister barman, explicitly recalling Kubrick's *The Shining*. Returning the compliment, it's possible that Kubrick borrowed *La Belle captive*'s cabal of castellated upper-class decadents for his final film, *Eyes Wide Shut*. The deathly leatherclad biker echoes both Cocteau's *Orphée* and the British portmanteau *Tales from the Crypt*, and the vampire girl certainly looks fetching as she swirls around in a diaphanous white gown amid yards of red plush. But the jumble of bizarre signs and portents is betrayed by a pace that's merely somnambulant rather than oneiric; also, presumably, by a straitened budget. Despite the best

efforts of cinematographer Henri Alekan (who nearly 40 years before had shot *La Belle et la Bête* for Cocteau), the end result seems like *L'Année dernière à Marienbad* – the film Robbe-Grillet wrote for Alain Resnais back in 1961 – reconfigured as a slightly tatty 1980s rock video.

For all the high weirdness of Robbe-Grillet's film, maybe the most unusual French genre picture of the early 1980s was *Si j'avais 1000 ans* (If I Had a Thousand Years), the only feature made by writer-director Monique Enckell. Having won a screenplay prize at the Avoriaz Festival in 1981, Enckell began shooting the film in February 1982, with Klaus Maria Brandauer cast opposite former Nouvelle Vague star Marie Dubois. The fact that Brandauer isn't in the finished film gives some indication of what was reportedly an extremely difficult shoot.

Enckell's premise here vaguely recalls Amando de Ossorio's Blind Dead films – a Breton island, cursed 1000 years before when the locals resisted delivering a pregnant woman to the squire for execution, is now haunted by five Celtic knights on horseback, demanding a sacrifice but only appearing, as a title screen poetically puts it, in the 'jours sombres de novembre' (the dark days of November). The mournful atmosphere conjured up by Enckell and cinematographer Étienne Szabo is really the whole show, but since the miasmic beach sequences, shot around the port town of Saint-Cast-le-Guildo, bring to mind *Nosferatu* and *Vampyr*, the atmosphere is on the highest level. A lake shimmering in a grotto lit by innumerable candles, fog scudding over marshes as silhouetted horsemen appear on the horizon, a cloaked figure passing through a cruciform-studded graveyard under a storm-threatening sky – the damp and the chill is almost palpable. The plangent score by Breton harp virtuoso Alan Stivell is effective too. Sadly, the finished film, though an official selection at Cannes, failed to get a theatrical release.

Another offshore setting featured in *Le Démon dans l'île* (The Demon on the Island), which Francis Leroi made in Barfleur and adjoining Normandy locations in October 1982. This one has Anny Duperey as a doctor from the mainland setting up shop on the titular island and tangling with the existing GP, a creepily dapper fellow played by the former Nouvelle Vague icon Jean-Claude Brialy. The first two-thirds are devoted to a series of horrible accidents with household implements. The mayor has trouble with a disposable razor within the first minute, and thereafter the wince factor is well and truly tweaked by rebellious coffee-makers, electric carving knives, ovens and – nastiest of all – a motorised teddy bear that shoves one of its drum sticks into a little girl's eye. Though a specialist in sex films, Leroi proved himself a dab hand in the unfamiliar area of amputations, picking up the Prix du Suspense at the 1983 Avoriaz Festival.

The cause of all the horror – a weird child with an enlarged cranium and awesome telekinetic powers – is cleverly revealed in the darkened aisles of an after-hours supermarket. The dapper doctor has been experimenting on the child and, in the final showdown, explains blandly that "What I'm doing is for the good of humanity. Understanding the mechanisms of the brain by means of my own brain is much more exciting than treating lumbago." The creepy kid (Cyrille Mans-Palevodi) isn't given much opportunity to engage our sympathy prior to committing telekinetic suicide, so the film's success rests largely on the excellent performances of Duperey and Brialy. Even so, the action winds up with a memorably outré pay-off; what happens to the mad doctor at the child's mist-wreathed graveside has to be seen to be believed.

At the opposite end of the scale to Leroi and his kind was the burgeoning community of gore fans who were getting ready to put their money where their Super 8 cameras were, chief among them an accountant called Norbert Moutier. In 1982 Moutier, publisher of the fanzine *Monster Bis*, situated a masked backwoods axe murderer in Orléans forest, included such genre aficionados as the above-mentioned Alain Petit and *Mad Movies* founder Jean-Pierre Putters among his victims, and called the truly indescribable result *Ogroff*. Climaxing with a bunch of zombies surging up from the killer's cellar and advancing on Orléans, together with a quick cameo from the too-indulgent Howard Vernon as a vampire Cardinal, the film was reissued as *Mad Mutilator* and acquired a cult following among adherents, like Moutier himself, of the extremest depths of ciné-bis.

Amid all this activity, Raphaël Delpard, writer-director of *La Nuit de la mort!*, re-emerged with a gnomic curio called *Clash*, which premiered at Avoriaz in January 1984. Dedicated, according to a title screen, 'to my dearest and very much missed Betty Beckers' (star of Delpard's previous horror, who had died in December 1982), this has a young woman retiring to a decommissioned mannequin factory to stand guard over a cache of smuggling money given to her by a treacherous boyfriend.

Delpard, who told so engagingly straightforward a story in *La Nuit*, here trots through as many surrealist psychosexual clichés as he can muster, with the woman going steadily stir-crazy and reliving primal horrors from her childhood in a fragmented narrative held together only by the valiant performance of Catherine Alric. A mysterious man (Pierre Clémenti)

yodels a great deal, weeps blood and is described by Alric as "a real nutcase," Alric becomes increasingly panicked and gets trapped in her own sleeping bag, a little girl reaches for a massively enlarged light switch, and the film's handful of gore effects are handled by the 18-year-old Benoît Lestang. The result – a French-Yugoslavian co-production shot in Zagreb – is a kind of cash-strapped re-run of the surrealist 'fragmenting female' narratives that were popular in France some ten years earlier. It's also, unfortunately, a wearisome snooze, and not long afterwards Delpard retired from filmmaking to become a noted historian.

## REALMS BEYOND

In 1981, Jess Franco – having recently walked away, as noted above, from an atrocious Euterpé project about Nazi zombies called *Le Lac des morts vivants* (Lake of the Living Dead) – proceeded, perversely, to make an atrocious Euterpé project about Nazi zombies called *L'Abîme des morts vivants* (Oasis of the Living Dead). Here, Franco's characteristic travelogue longueurs, as the so-called action moves from jungle to desert and then to interminable tours of mosque and marketplace, entirely squander the film's potential for trashy fun and convert it into an 82-minute endurance test, with only a brief, atmospheric shot of zombies on a sand dune, lit by a blazing sunset, to even hint at his former flair. At the end the absurd hero, who has been searching listlessly for Nazi treasure, is asked whether he found what he was looking for and replies, fatuously, "I mainly found myself" – pompous icing on the cake for one of Franco's most abysmal efforts. Incredibly, for the Spanish market Franco made an alternative version of this farrago, with different actors, called *La tumba de los muertos vivientes* (The Tomb of the Living Dead).

Though the end products continued to deteriorate, Franco was still filming at a phenomenal pace, and in 1982 he added *El siniestro Dr Orloff* (The Sinister Dr Orloff) and *La mansión de los muertos vivientes* (The Mansion of the Living Dead) to his overstuffed horror portfolio. In the first the septuagenarian Howard Vernon is back as Orloff, but the focus is on new Franco regular Antonio Mayans as Orloff's son Alfred, who indulges in the usual prostitute-killing routine in the hope of resurrecting his mother. In the second Lina Romay and other topless waitresses strut naked around a Gran Canaria beach, have plenty of lesbian sex, and encounter Franco's utterly feeble versions of the monastic revenants created by Bécquer and immortalised in Ossorio's Blind Dead films. In both cases, the impression of recycled goods, and of an out-of-inspiration director who just has to keep filming in the way a shark has to keep swimming, is hard to resist.

Confirming this estimate, in 1983 Franco made *El hundimiento de la casa Usher* (The Fall of the House of Usher), in which Vernon is the 100-year-old Dr Usher (or Dr Russia as the dubbing actors call him), frankly admitting to his apprehensive visitor (Mayans) that "I am a sadist." Lina Romay is on hand of course, Olivier Mathot turns up as the blind Morpho, Franco's regular composer, Daniel White, passes through as family physician Dr Seward, and the splicing in of monochrome footage from *Gritos en la noche* (a good 15 minutes' worth) has a two-fold effect – (a) it confirms to attentive Franco followers that this Usher is actually Orloff in disguise, and (b) it underlines how precipitously Franco had fallen since that trailblazing title of 1961. Though the film was retitled *Revenge in the House of Usher* for export, there is indeed a 'fall' in the closing minutes, and it's every bit as ineffective as the film's straitened budget would lead you to expect.

Though the budgets accorded Lucio Fulci by producer Fabrizio De Angelis were much higher than anything Franco could expect, Fulci was nevertheless on a similar downward slide, and it wasn't arrested by *L'occhio del male* (The Evil Eye), which he began shooting in late March 1982. Subsequently acquiring the inexplicable release title *Manhattan Baby*, this one begins in Egypt and periodically returns to it via the pulsing blue eye of an amulet that gives access to "the infernal gate of Time and Space." This whole section was apparently a late addition to the Sacchetti-Briganti script, included to give the film a bit of epic sweep; majestically captured by cinematographer Guglielmo Mancori, the scenes certainly succeed in that regard. Yet it's obvious that the desert vistas, scuttling scorpions and inscrutable Sphinx are really there to evoke (unbelievable as it may seem) a truly feeble Egyptological box-office bomb of the period called *The Awakening*, together with somewhat older items like *Damien Omen II* and *The Exorcist*.

*Peyton Place* veteran Christopher Connelly is the token US lead, convinced that he's found "the key to mysteries that have stymied cryptologists for years" but temporarily losing his sight when exposed to the eye's cheesy blue laser beams. Returning to New York, he doesn't realise his little daughter has custody of the baleful amulet, though in the final scene he exorcises

the evil by the anticlimactic expedient of throwing it in the river. He's been advised to do this by a mystical antiques vendor archly called Adrian Marcato, whose name is a truly puzzling reference to *Rosemary's Baby*. But he doesn't do it soon enough for Marcato's purposes, given that the latter has already fallen prey to a last-minute gore sequence in which a bunch of visibly wire-borne stuffed birds come to life and peck him to death. This idea failed laughably when used by Jess Franco in *El conde Drácula*, and it's just as stupid here; worse, it's the only trademark splatter sequence Fulci has to offer this time round. The script is an enervated trifle and Fulci – all out of imagination by this stage – resolutely fails to bring it to life.

In the early 1980s, Fulci's steadily deteriorating films were among the glossiest examples of a genre that could still boast an extraordinarily wide reach. The florid, and occasionally gruesome, supernatural romance *Fantasma d'amore* (Ghost of Love, 1981), showcasing the ultra-glamorous combination of Marcello Mastroianni, Romy Schneider and Wolfgang Preiss with director Dino Risi and writer Bernardino Zapponi,

Night terrors for Brigitta Boccoli in *Manhattan Baby* (1982), seen in America as *Eye of the Evil Dead*

was a world away from the flyblown zombie hardcore porn of Joe D'Amato's *Orgasmo esotico* (Exotic Orgasm, 1982). Also available were a couple of good-natured comedies starring Renato Pozzetto – *Mia moglie è una strega* (My Wife's a Witch, 1980) and *La casa stregata* (The Haunted House, 1982), with glamorous co-stars in Eleonora Giorgi and Gloria Guida respectively. Other attractions included the Piedmontese haunted house featured in Carlo Ausino's rubbishy *La villa delle anime maledetti* (The Villa of Damned Souls, 1982), a plague-ridden mutant running amok in Tonino Ricci's supposedly English-set *Bakterion* (aka *Panic*, 1982), and the rampaging animals unleashed on Frankfurt in Franco Prosperi's *Wild Beasts* (1983) – a rare foray into the 'nature's revenge' sub-genre with enough animal abuse to remind us that, 20 years earlier, Prosperi had helped popularise the mondo mode.

Rising well above the dismal level of these films was the latest work from Pupi Avati. Immediately after crafting the 'laughing windows' of his masterful 1976 shocker *La casa dalle finestre che ridono*, Avati had made *Tutti defunti... tranne i morti* (All Dead ... Except

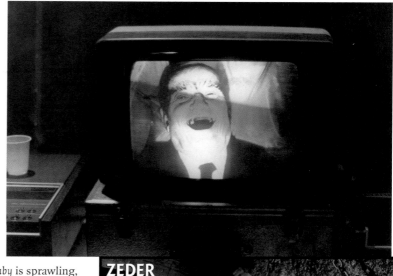

A ghastly resurrection caught on video:
Aldo Sassi in the elegantly chilling *Zeder* (1982)

the Dead); an anarchic body-count comedy set in an old dark Emilia-Romagna house, it sprang from Avati's decision that "I didn't want to follow one horror film with another identical one. So I decided to poke fun at the genre and play around with it."[46] By the summer of 1982, however, he was ready to return to the profoundly chilling ambience of *La casa*. In preparation while Lucio Fulci was making *Manhattan Baby* in New York, *Zeder* dealt with a concept vaguely similar to Fulci's so-called 'infernal gate'. And yet the result is as tightly wound, cunningly plotted and elegantly directed as *Manhattan Baby* is sprawling, incoherent and unmotivated.

> *Author of two unpublished novels, Stefano is working on a third when his wife Alessandra presents him with a secondhand electric typewriter. Having found a cryptic text preserved on the ribbon, Stefano's quest to unlock the mystery takes him from Bologna to Rimini and finally the Etruscan necropolis near Comacchio. In the process he uncovers a conspiracy regarding so-called K-zones — "areas suspended in a time-lock, where it's possible to bring those buried there back from the beyond..."*

In shooting *Zeder* Avati focused, as usual, on his native Emilia-Romagna but also ranged as far afield as Chartres in the Loire valley. The inspiration behind the film was the mysterious French alchemist Fulcanelli, previously referenced (as Varelli) in Argento's *Inferno*. Working on the screenplay with his brother Antonio and their usual collaborator Maurizio Costanzo, Avati made an important adjustment, changing Fulcanelli's mastery of alchemical enigmas into an investigation into the secret of eternal life. The result, like *La casa dalle finestre che ridono*, is a film predicated on atavistic, slow-burning dread rather than extremes of gross-out horror.

That Avati's distinctive flair hadn't deserted him since 1976 is made immediately clear in the opening reel, which is set, like *La casa*, in the 1950s. It's 1956, to be precise; the setting is a dilapidated mansion in Chartres that seems to groan and tremble while shedding various bits of crumbling masonry. There's an old lady inside and another old lady outside, one of whom will be swiftly dispatched. From giving us a brief glimpse of her autopsy Avati moves on to a bizarre

## ZEDER

Italy 1982
US: *Revenge of the Dead*
AMA Film / RAI Radiotelevisione Italiana
100 minutes colour
production began 19 July 1982
. . . . . . . . . . . . . . . . . . . . . . . . . . .
Director of Photography: Franco Delli Colli;
Art Directors: Giancarlo Basili, Leonardo
Scarpa; Editor: Amedeo Salfa; Sound: Raffaele
De Luca; Music: Riz Ortolani; Make-up:
Alfonso Cioffi; Screenplay: Pupi
Avati, Maurizio Costanzo, Antonio Avati;
Story: Pupi Avati; Producers: Gianni
Minervini, Antonio Avati with the collaboration
of Enea Ferrario; Director: Pupi Avati

Gabriele Lavia (Stefano); Anne Canovas
(Alessandra); Paola Tanziani (Gabriella Goodman);
Cesare Barbetti (Dr Meyer); Bob Tonelli (Mr
Big); Ferdinando Orlandi (Giovine); Enea Ferrario
(Mirko); John Stacy (Professor Chesi); Alessandro
Partexano (Lieutenant Silvestri); Marcello Tusco
(Dr Melis); Aldo Sassi (Don Luigi Costa); Veronica
Moriconi (young Gabriella); Enrico Ardizzone
(Benni); Maria Teresa Toffano (Anna); Andrea
Montuschi (Inspector Bouffet); Adolfo Belletti
(Don Emidio); Paolo Bacchi (Mr Big's secretary);
Giuseppina Borione (Helena); Imelde Marani
(nurse); Gianluigi Gaspari; Carlo Schincaglia;
Luciano Bianchi; Pino Tosca; Giovanni Bussadori;
Sergio Lama; Giuseppe Lentini; Giancarlo Bandini

*Zeder* **is a mild excursion into supernatural horror by noted Italian filmmaker Pupi Avati ... Acceptably English-dubbed and more interesting than most horror films of late,** *Zeder* **fails to deliver the shocks and thrills that have become de rigueur in the genre. There is some gore, but credit Avati with trying to tell a story rather than simply build up a body count.** *Variety* 12 June 1985

**I think the idea of placing a video camera in a coffin represents a form of extreme violence. That's the sect's 'sin'. Nothing is more indecent than spying on what happens after one is buried, during death. That's the most vulgar thing there is, the very lowest.** Pupi Avati [quoted in *Video Watchdog* Jan-Feb 1991]

ritual in the mansion's cellar, in which a girl of about 14 is being used to locate a concealed grave rather as a pig is used to sniff out truffles. The sound of stertorous breathing fills the house and the floorboards split open of their own accord. The girl, Gabriella, escapes with a seriously maimed leg and the chief researcher, Dr Meyer, consults a dusty wallet that was found in the grave. Examining a Vatican Archive pass stashed inside it, he announces excitedly: "We've found Paolo Zeder. A K-zone. He stumbled across a K-zone..."

This opening scores high for crepuscular atmosphere and also for audience mystification. The need to make sense of these bizarre events places the viewer in much the same position as the driven Stefano, whose zeal to get to the bottom of the K-zone conspiracy begins to resemble a death wish, leading his wife to denounce him as "a crazy, selfish nut." For Stefano, the mystery begins in Bologna, where Alessandra decorates her anniversary gift with flowers, inadvertently suggesting a well-kept grave. "The typewriter that you saw in the film," Avati explained, "is the very one I use to write my scripts and which I bought secondhand from one of my musician friends. One evening while trying it out I said to myself: let's see what Amadeo (the previous owner) wrote..."[47] From this humdrum circumstance Avati created the fascinating idea of a typewriter ribbon acting like a palimpsest, disclosing a faded message that isn't humdrum in the slightest: "The barriers of death shall at last be destroyed."

Avati's hero shares the same name, Stefano, as the hero of his previous horror film. Yet, unlike the soft and amiable Lino Capolicchio, Gabriele Lavia's Stefano is a haggard and high-strung obsessive even before the mystery starts deepening, making him a less-than-engaging protagonist. But the ball-of-twine intrigue that develops is sufficiently gripping to negate this problem. The hints are brilliantly laid out, from a scene in an indoor swimming pool, vaguely recalling Jacques Tourneur's *Cat People*, in which the lights go out and Stefano is surrounded by more of that stertorous breathing, to a visit to the Vatican Archive in which a haunted-looking woman of about 40, with a conspicuous limp, presents her identity card to the dog-collared attendant. The woman, who of course is Gabriella, is also seen re-visiting Chartres, where she joins the now white-haired Dr Meyer in consulting a sceptical big shot. The latter, played by Avati regular Bob Tonelli, pours cold water on their K-zone research by reminding them that death is "an indispensable process" and that "a demise isn't a treatable malady, it's a pure end."

The brief glimpse we're given here of Chartres Cathedral forms a pleasing contrast to the abandoned building in Emilia-Romagna that Stefano finally identifies as the heart of the conspiracy. It's actually the skeletal remains of the Colonia Varese outside Milano Marittima, a Fascist hulk whose empty spaces and mouldering corridors form the perfect setting for Avati's denouement.

Recalling his childhood, Avati pointed out that "I spent every summer on the Adriatic, and the huge Fascist buildings that were broken into by gangs of kids reminded me of ant hills, which terrified me."[48] The one stumbled on by Stefano, we're informed, was a Nazi prison during the war before becoming a kids' holiday camp and more recently a nudist colony. Now a French company proposes to turn it into a 1000-room hotel, but for the time being it's the site of a scientific investigation into its ancient heritage as a K-zone. To that end, a recently deceased priest called Luigi Costa – the original owner of Stefano's fateful typewriter – has been buried there and his coffin fitted with a video camera. Stefano's climactic encounter in the control room, where multiple TV monitors relay to him the hideous spectacle of the toothless, beetle-browed Costa stirring into life and laughing triumphantly, induces a genuine frisson.

In addition to its considerable virtues as a carefully crafted and unusually thoughtful thriller, *Zeder* is also interesting as yet another example of the 'something in the air' principle – Stephen King's novel *Pet Sematary*, with its very similar theme, was published just a few months after the film came out. On top of this, *Zeder*'s deployment of science as a means of investigating the afterlife recalls the work of Nigel Kneale, simultaneously anticipating the horrific 'ghost on video' imagery of Japan's *Ringu* by some 15 years.

## EIGHTIES AND AFTER

Perhaps inadvertently, Avati's *Zeder* contains an image so appropriate to the time in which it was made that it seems to apply a stylish and dread-inducing full-stop to the 20-odd years of Italian horror that preceded it. Relayed via the grainy fuzz of television monitors, the glimpse we're given of a restless corpse with a video camera installed in its coffin is a potent one given the role that television and, increasingly, video was playing in the Italian industry's terminal decay.

The competitive allure of home entertainment was to finally sweep all before it in the 1980s, with the figures speaking for themselves. The 1970s total of 2087 Italian films tumbled, in the following decade, to just 1148, with something like 4000 cinemas closing between 1980 and 1989, and admissions of 95 million in 1989 comparing poorly, to say the least, with the post-war peak of 819 million in 1955. Of that 95 million, noted the *New York Times*, "only 22 million tickets, less than one in four, were for Italian movies. American films accounted for most of the rest."[49] In this context the head of steam provided by Fulci's *Zombi 2* seemed already like Italian horror's last gasp, albeit a dazzling one. In the scramble for the last remaining punters, producers were turning to new catchpenny filoni, notably a stream of violent action movies of the post-apocalyptic or Vietnam Vet variety inspired by *Mad Max 2* and the Rambo film *First Blood*. Jack-of-all-trades Antonio Margheriti, for example, was responsible for a 1983 war picture exported as *Last Blood*.

The rise of VHS, meanwhile, offered a temporary reprieve via straight-to-video productions, as was recalled by John Steiner, the British actor who starred in Mario Bava's final feature, *Schock*, and many other Italian films. "The movie business was changing profoundly," he noted, adding that "the video market suddenly sprang up and I started working like crazy, from 1982 up to '85. In '86, again, the video market fell out."[50] As well as keeping Italians at home rather than in cinemas, video had a different effect on the reputation of the Italian industry overseas. In Britain, as already noted, Italian exploitation titles loomed large on the roster of proscribed films dubbed, by both Westminster and tabloid hysterics, 'Video Nasties'.

Struggling against adverse circumstances, Italian horror died a rapid death in the latter part of the 1980s, with the elegantly maintained dread of Avati's *Zeder* proving in short supply and only a small number of notable titles holding up the slide. Even Lucio Fulci proved incapable of replicating the intriguing combination of metaphysical strangeness and unflinching gore that stamped his 1979-81 output. Indeed, he dwindled through a frugally budgeted and disastrously uninspired series of 1980s projects, from a lycra-and-ankle-warmers NY giallo called *Murderock Uccide a passo di danza* (Murder Rock Kills to a Dance Step, 1984) to such comprehensive misfires as *Aenigma* (1986), the above-mentioned *Zombi 3* (1987), *Un gatto nel cervello* (A Cat in the Brain, 1989) and *Demonia* (1990).

Fiorenza Tessari in extremis in *Phenomena* (1984)

Dario Argento was still riding high, but stylish curiosities like *Phenomena* (1984) and *Opera* (1987) nevertheless sowed the seeds of his own precipitous decline in the following decade.He also produced and co-wrote Lamberto Bava's 1985 film *Dèmoni* (Demons), an Americanised monsterfest, self-reflexively set in a Berlin cinema, that made well over four billion lire. (Nicoletta Elmi, the spooky child of several 1970s horrors, here graduated to playing an usherette beleaguered by possessed Heavy Metal teens.) The film sired a quickly hatched Bava sequel called *Dèmoni 2... l'incubo ritorna* (Demons 2... The Nightmare Returns) and a predictable rip-off from Marcello Avallone called *Spettri* (Spectres). In 1989

Bava would transplant the juvenile teensploitation of *Dèmoni* onto a made-for-TV retread of his father's *La maschera del demonio*, resulting in a gauche and graceless hybrid of old and new.

In addition to the 'Demons' titles, Dario Argento was also involved in co-writing and producing the more sedate and cerebral Michele Soavi films *La chiesa* (The Church, 1988) and *La setta* (The Sect, 1990). Soavi bookended these two with *Deliria* in 1986 and *Dellamorte Dellamore* in 1993, sprightly and imaginative divertissements that suggested Soavi might be a contender. Yet, beyond TV projects, his directorial career more or less ended after *Dellamorte Dellamore*. The ailing Lucio Fulci, in the meantime, was pinning his hopes on a loose, hi-tech retread of *House of Wax* called *MDC Maschera di cera* (MDC Wax Mask), which finally went into production in July 1996, a few months after Fulci's death, with Sergio Stivaletti (special effects man for Argento, Bava and Soavi) stepping in as director. In this climate, a masterful 16th century mystery like Pupi Avati's *L'arcano incantatore* (The Arcane Enchanter, 1995), with its beguiling litany of "ghosts, exorcisms and demonic hand-lettered books ... ghostly little girls giggling behind doors, a severed hand inside a glass reliquary, midnight reburial of corpses and the like,"[51] was a rare bird indeed.

A similar decline was initiated in Spain by legislation. The arrival, in December 1982, of a socialist government under Felipe González brought with it many liberalising measures but also a complete wipe-out of low-level film production via the so-called Decreto Miró (Miró Decree). Film and TV director Pilar Miró, having been put in charge of the cinema section of González's Ministry of Culture, diverted advance subsidies to 'quality' pictures and in the process the number of Spanish films produced dwindled significantly. The 1982 total of 146, for example, was down to 69 a mere five years later, while in the same period public indifference to high-toned films ensured that domestic revenue from homegrown product was almost halved.

Though giving a start to such major names as Fernando Trueba and Pedro Almodóvar, the Miró Decree also attempted to kick over the traces of the shameful

Brigitte Lahaie disposes of Daniel Beretta in *Les Prédateurs de la nuit* (1987)

'secret' of all those recent 'S' films and, indeed, of Paul Naschy's noble werewolf and other supposedly lowbrow monsters. The Franco regime had done its best to present a state-sanctioned view of Spanish culture, ruthlessly suppressing genre production for decades prior to allowing the presence of lycanthropes so long as they were clearly signposted as non-Spanish. Now the unloved werewolves had apparently been shown the door once and for all. As well as calling Miró's measures "infamously biased," Naschy was fond of quoting the veteran actress-filmmaker Ana Mariscal, who pointed out that "The Franco regime eliminated artists by firing squad. Now we have a more refined and cruel way of getting rid of them."[52] Even so, in 1987 Naschy contrived to make a self-referential horror show called *El aullido del diablo* (The Howl of the Devil). Matched with genre regulars Howard Vernon and Fernando Hilbeck, plus British beauty Caroline Munro, Naschy cast himself here as a crazed old actor, facilitating nostalgic turns as Mr Hyde, Quasimodo, Fu Manchu, Frankenstein's monster, the wolf man and several others. The result was barely released.

By the end of 1987 Caroline Munro and Howard Vernon, together with other horror veterans like Brigitte Lahaie and Anton Diffring, were appearing in Jess Franco's *Les Prédateurs de la nuit* (The Night Predators). With a decent budget provided by French

video mogul René Chateau, Franco here regained some of his old brio, transplanting *Les Yeux sans visage* (yet again) to an ambience of glamorous 1980s tat. Vernon passes through as a certain Dr Orloff, and the grisly result, exported as *Faceless*, was one of Franco's last films to be released theatrically. The remainder of his output was devoted to fan-financed, shot-on-video curiosities like *Marie-Cookie and the Killer Tarantula*, *Lust for Frankenstein* and *Killer Barbys vs Dracula*.

Other veterans making last-gasp contributions included Amando de Ossorio, with the laughable monster movie *Serpiente de mar* (Sea Serpent, 1984), and José Larraz, with the cack-handed haunting *Descanse en piezas* (Rest in Pieces, 1987) and the enervated slashers *Al filo del hacha* (Edge of the Axe, 1988) and *Deadly Manor* (1990), a quartet of films that between them offered roles to such familiar faces as Gérard Tichy, Víctor Israel, Jack Taylor, Patty Shepard, Fernando Bilbao, Tony Isbert and Conrado San Martín. The indefatigable Juan Piquer Simón also persevered with such Americanised gorefests as *Slugs, muerte viscosa* (Slugs: Slimy Death, 1987), *La grieta* (The Rift, 1989) and *La mansión de los Cthulhu* (Cthulhu Mansion, 1991), the last a career low for the British star Frank Finlay. Younger filmmakers, meanwhile, provided early signs of the millennial revival that was to follow, with scattered cult titles like Agustí Villaronga's claustrophobic and highly controversial *Tras el cristal* (Behind the Glass, 1985), Bigas Luna's cunningly interactive *Angustía* (Anguish, 1986), for which he won a Goya award, and the anarchic Yuletide exuberance of Álex de la Iglesia's *El día de la bestia* (Day of the Beast, 1995).

Naschy then returned as Waldemar Daninsky, in an interestingly minimal make-up but with correspondingly minimal screen time, in Francisco Ródriguez Gordillo's 1996 damp squib *Licántropo*, after which Pilar Miró tried to make amends for her damaging 'decree' by nominating Naschy for an honorary Goya award. She died in 1997, however, and the proposal was forgotten. Naschy himself died, aged 75, in November 2009, some nine months after Jess Franco received an honorary Goya. Wheelchair-bound at the time of the awards ceremony, Franco died four years later, at 82.

In France and Germany, too, this was a fallow period, with only isolated outbreaks of horror as the 20th century wound down. French offerings encompassed spectral rape fantasy (Pierre B Reinhard's *Ghost Soldier*, 1981), witty monster parody (Alain Jessua's *Frankenstein 90*, 1984) and gore-strewn in-utero possession (Alain Robak's *Baby Blood*, 1989), together with a couple of self-reflexive, end-of-the-decade oddities from Jean Rollin, *Perdues dans New York* (Lost in New York) and

*Killing Car*. Germany, meanwhile, ranged from the Munich suicide house of Dominik Graf's *Das zweite Gesicht* (The Second Face, 1982) to the artificially created women of both Georg Tressler's *Sukkubus* (1987) and Eckhart Schmidt's Hoffmann adaptation *Der Sandmann* (The Sand Man, 1992). There was also the Bayerischer Filmpreis awarded to debutant director Robert Sigl for the evanescent coming-of-age Gothic, *Laurin* (1988), a film so entrancing in its studied echoes of Murnau and others that its dreary synth score (typical of the period) seems doubly regrettable. In addition there was the berserk East-West satire of Christoph Schlingensief's *Das deutsche Kettensägenmassaker* (The German Chainsaw Massacre, 1990) and an underground horror scene that threw up such taboo-busting provocations as Jörg Buttgereit's *Nekromantik* (1987).

These slim pickings, characteristic not just of mainland Europe but also of the UK's horror output, were a far cry from the halcyon period that had stretched from the late 1950s to the early 1980s. The dominance of slickly commodified Hollywood horror in the wake of such global hits as *A Nightmare on Elm Street*, *House* and *Fright Night* – hits characterised by a teen-pleasing combination of shape-shifting special effects and wink-tipping facetiousness – proved a force that most European producers felt unequal to competing with. But as the more vacuous Hollywood formulae began to loosen their grip in the 1990s, there were signs of a revival in other parts of the world. Though by no means recapturing the dominance of previous eras, Germany and Italy enjoyed modest 21st century resurgences. Spain and France, however, experienced a truly remarkable genre renaissance, with the former gaining an international reputation for cerebral hauntings and the latter for eye-popping extremes of gruesomeness.

Amid these (entirely unexpected) rivers of mean-spirited Gallic gore, Jean Rollin resurfaced with wistful echoes of an earlier age. In the summer of 1995 he directed a screen adaptation of his recent novel *Les Deux orphelines vampires* (The Two Orphan Vampires), a film that initiated a quartet of final features, culminating 14 years later with *Le Masque de la Méduse* (The Mask of Medusa). Together with the two films that intervened – *La Fiancée de Dracula* (The Fiancée of Dracula) and *La Nuit des horloges* (Night of the Clocks) – these were poetic meditations on Rollin's back catalogue, with the nostalgic re-use of themes, images, settings and actors. Much of *Le Masque*, for example, was played out on the stage of the Théâtre du Grand Guignol and in the leafy avenues of the cemetery at Père Lachaise. The first had featured heavily in Rollin's debut, *Le Viol du vampire*, over 40 years earlier. The second, having

provided a forlorn Gothic backdrop in several of his films, went on to become Rollin's last resting place when he died, aged 72, in December 2010.

In the brutal and uncompromising context of 21st century horror, these last, autumnal Rollin films were not, of course, calculated to be commercial heavy-hitters. They were elaborate valentines to his fans and nostalgic recreations of a style that was long past. They were typical of a director whose work had been among the most distinctive products of a golden age of horror cinema, a golden age that also boasted the very different but equally striking Gothic landscapes of Riccardo Freda, Mario Bava, Jess Franco, Narciso Ibáñez Serrador, Jorge Grau, Lucio Fulci and many more.

Coupled with the earlier golden age experienced in the silent era, the heyday of European horror was responsible for a genuinely macabre procession of ghoulish creatures – the loathsome Caligari and his doctor descendants Ood, Orlof, Hichcock and Freudstein; the elongated talons of Graf Orlok, the possessed hands of Paul Orlac, the lethal fingernails of Miss Muerte and the skeletal grasp of the Blind Dead; the multiple faces of Christiane Génessier, the flaxen shade of Melissa Graps and the centuries-old ennui of Countess Báthory; the petrified exhibits of Count Drago, the ungovernable werewolf fugues of Waldemar Daninsky and the gore-soaked torture chambers of Baron Blood, right up to the obscene cackling of Luigi Costa in his camera-fitted casket. These and other baleful characters were emanations from the most elegant of nightmares. Inevitably, these mad doctors, fatal women, bloodthirsty revenants and misunderstood monsters had plenty of brothers and sisters who sprang direct from the darkest depths of exploitation, but in this respect European horror, like horror cinema generally, was only following the example of the original Gothic fictions, which, as noted right at the beginning of this book, were written by Grub Street hacks as well as high-minded poets.

When that *Monthly Review* critic, assessing *Feudal Tyrants* at the height of the Gothic craze in 1807, complained about "the direful croaking of this German raven," he was reckoning without horror's deep-rooted allure and the cathartic release it can offer when the constraints of realism have exhausted their appeal. With the direful croakings of France, Italy and Spain added to those of the German raven, European filmmakers between the end of World War I and the dawn of the 1980s added a special kind of lustre – by turns shadowy and poetic, gaudy and transgressive – to that deep-rooted allure. They also came up with some of the wildest and most memorable releases from realism the cinema has ever devised.

# Source Notes

## Introduction

1   Agnes Smith, *The Screen in Review: Critical Comment on Recent Releases*, Picture-Play Magazine vol 14 # 4, June 1921

2   quoted in BR, *Comes Stravinsky to the Film Theater*, Musical America 16 April 1921; reproduced in Julie Hubbert, *Modernism at the Movies*, The Musical Quarterly vol 88 # 1, Spring 2005

3   quoted in Angela Wright, *Gothic Fiction*, London 2007

4   Barbara Steele, Foreword, in Antonio Bruschini, *Horror all'italiana 1957-1979*, Firenze 1996

## Part One – *Warning Shadows*

1   Lotte H Eisner, *L'Écran démoniaque*, Paris 1952; UK reprint: *The Haunted Screen*, London 1969

2   Gaumont advertisement featured in *Motion Picture News*, The New York Clipper 19 October 1912

3   Hanford C Judson, *The Lunatics*, The Moving Picture World vol 20 # 1, 4 April 1914

4   unsigned review of *Der Golem*, Der Kinematograph # 421, 20 January 1915

5   *Illustrierter Film-Kurier* # 9 (1919); quoted in John T Soister, *Conrad Veidt On Screen: A Comprehensive Illustrated Filmography*, Jefferson NC 2002

6   quoted in David Robinson, *BFI Film Classics: Das Cabinet des Dr Caligari*, London 1997

7   ibid

8   unsigned review of *Das Cabinet des Dr Caligari*, The Screen, New York Times 4 April 1921

9   Gilbert Seldes, *Movies for the Millions: An Account of Motion Pictures, Principally in America*, London 1937

10   Robinson, op cit

11   Siegfried Kracauer, *From Caligari to Hitler: A Psychological History of the German Film*, Princeton 1947

12   quoted in Eisner, op cit

13   Carlos Clarens, *An Illustrated History of the Horror Film*, New York 1967

14   Kracauer, op cit

15   Béla Balász, *Der sichtbare Mensch*, Halle 1924; quoted in Kracauer, op cit

16   Fritz Arno Wagner, *I Believe in the Sound Film*, Film Art # 8, 1936; quoted in Kracauer, op cit

17   Heinz Michaelis, [review of *Orlacs Hände*], Film-Kurier # 28, 2 February 1925

18   Paul Rotha, *The Film Till Now*, London 1930; revised edition 1967

19   Clarens, op cit

20   Gilbert Seldes, *The Path of the Movies*, The Nation 29 April 1925; reprinted in *Cinema Nation: The Best Writing on Film from The Nation 1913-2000*, New York 2000

21   unsigned review, *The Man Who Cheated Life*, National Board of Review Magazine February 1929

22   quoted in Henry Nicolella and John T Soister, *Many Lives: The Horror and Fantasy Films of Paul Wegener*, Duncan 2012

23   quoted in Theodore Strauss, *The Return of the Somnambulist*, New York Times 12 May 1940

24   Rotha, op cit

25   Kracauer, op cit

26   Michael Powell, *A Life in Movies: An Autobiography*, London 1986

27   H G Wells, *Metropolis – the Silliest Film*, New York Times 17 April 1927

28   quoted in Eisner, op cit

29   quoted in Robinson, op cit

30   Jean Cocteau, *Two Screenplays*, London / New York 1968 (translator Carol Martin-Sperry)

31   Carl Theodor Dreyer, *Four Screenplays*, London 1970 (translator Oliver Stallybrass)

32   'Magnus', *Pictures: Unheimliche Geschichten*, Variety 27 September 1932

33   Bosley Crowther, *The Living Dead*, New York Times 17 December 1940

34   Graham Greene in *The Spectator* 1 May 1936; reprinted in *The Pleasure Dome: The Collected Film Criticism 1935-40*, London 1972

35   David Stewart Hull, *Film in the Third Reich: A Study of the German Cinema 1933-1945*, Berkeley and Los Angeles 1969

36   J C Trewin, *The Turbulent Thirties: A Further Decade of the Theatre*, London 1960

37   Peter Galway, [review of *Le Joueur d'échecs*], New Statesman and Nation 18 March 1939

38   quoted in Kevin Brownlow, *The Parade's Gone By...*, London 1968

39   Bosley Crowther, *Tale of Supernatural*, New York Times 8 April 1947

40   Elizabeth M Harris, *The Foreign Film: 1946 and in the Future*, Film Review [volume three], London 1946

41   Richard Winnington, *Love Eternal*, News Chronicle 16 February 1946

42   Ivan Butler, *The Horror Film*, London / New York 1967

43   Evelyn Ehrlich, *Cinema of Paradox: French Filmmaking Under the German Occupation*, New York 1985

44   Jean Cocteau, *La Belle et la Bête: Journal d'un film*, Paris 1946 / *Beauty and the Beast: Diary of a Film*, London 1950 (translator Ronald Duncan)

45   Marcel and Hélène Oms, *Entretien avec Gaston Bonheur sur La Fiancée des ténèbres*, Les Cahiers de la cinémathèque # 16, January 1975

46   H Saenz Guerrero, *El año cinematográfico en Barcelona*, La Vanguardia 2 January 1945

47   Tennessee Williams, *A Movie by Cocteau...*, New York Times 5 November 1950

48  Marina Warner, *La Belle et la Bête*, in *Gothic The Dark Heart of Film: A BFI Compendium*, London 2013
49  Virginia Graham, *Cinema: Orpheus (Rialto)*, *The Spectator* 1 June 1950
50  Elizabeth Frank, [review of *Orphée*], *News Chronicle* 27 May 1950
51  unsigned, *Alraune: A bisserl was Obszönes*, *Der Spiegel* 3 December 1952
52  unsigned, *Neu in Deutschland: Alraune*, *Der Spiegel* 5 November 1952

## Part Two – *Experiments in Evil*

1  Kingsley Amis, *Dracula, Frankenstein, Sons & Co*, *The Observer Magazine* 8 July 1968
2  François Truffaut, *Une Certaine Tendance du cinéma français*, *Cahiers du Cinéma* # 31, January 1954
3  Bosley Crowther, *Wages of Fear has premiere at Paris [Theatre]*, *New York Times* 17 February 1955
4  R D Smith, *Vulgar, nasty – and French*, *Tribune* 16 November 1955
5  Carlos Clarens, *An Illustrated History of the Horror Film*, New York 1967
6  Ivan Butler, *The Horror Film*, London / New York 1967
7  unsigned preview, *A Diabolical Horror Film*, *Life* 19 March 1956
8  Dilys Powell, *Films: Horror Corner*, *Sunday Times* 4 December 1955
9  unsigned review of *Les Diaboliques*, *Cinema: Current and Choice*, *Time* 19 December 1955
10  ibid
11  contemporary review in *Los Angeles Herald-Examiner*, quoted in Stephen Rebello, *Alfred Hitchcock and the Making of Psycho*, London 1990
12  'from our own correspondent: Paris Feb 8', *Suspense on the Screen: A Horrifying New Murder Mystery*, *The Times* 9 February 1955
13  quoted in Éric Poindron, *Riccardo Freda: Un pirate à la caméra*, Lyon 1994
14  quoted in Michel Caen and Jean-Claude Romer, *Riccardo Freda (entretien)*, *Midi-Minuit Fantastique* # 7, September 1963
15  unsigned, *French Exhibs Oppose Distrib of TV-Made Pic*, *Variety* 26 October 1960
16  quoted in Jean-Luc Godard, *Jean Renoir and Television*, in *Godard on Godard*, London 1972 (translator Tom Milne)
17  Kim Newman, *Opinion*, *Shivers* # 97, June-July 2002
18  Raymond Durgnat, *Franju*, London 1967
19  John Braine, *This One is Revolting*, *Daily Express* 29 January 1960
20  quoted in Durgnat, op cit
21  unsigned, *Kinsey*, *Der Spiegel* 5 September 1956
22  quoted in *Sittenfilme: Der Wäsche-Kodex*, *Der Spiegel* 6 May 1959
23  unsigned, *Le Mort dans le filet*, *Cinéma 61* # 56, May 1961
24  Ado Kyrou, *Mort dans le filet*, *Positif* # 39, May 1961
25  unsigned review of *Caltiki il mostro immortale*, *Schermi* 19 December 1959
26  Riccardo Freda, Foreword, in Tim Lucas, *Mario Bava: All the Colors of the Dark*, Cincinnati 2007
27  unsigned review of *Tempi duri per i vampiri*, *Intermezzo* 15 December 1959
28  quoted in Antonio Bruschini, *Renato Polselli: Vampires, Witches, and Mad Loves*, in *Horror all'italiana 1957-1979*, Firenze 1996
29  Ernesto Gastaldi, *Voglio entrare nel cinema: Storia di uno che ce l'ha fatta*, Milan 1991
30  Truffaut, op cit
31  David Pirie, *The Vampire Cinema*, London 1977
32  Michel Caen, *Moulin des supplices*, *Midi-Minuit Fantastique* # 3, October 1962
33  quoted in Ornella Volta, *Mario Bava (entretien)*, *Positif* # 138, May 1972
34  J-P Török, *Le Cadavre exquis: Le Masque du démon*, *Positif* # 40, July 1961
35  John Trevelyan, *What the Censor Saw*, London 1973
36  Antonio Bruschini, *Mario Bava: Maestro of the Macabre*, in *Horror all'italiana*, Firenze 1996
37  'l.p.', *Fumetto dell'orrore con un falso gorilla*, *La Stampa* 29 November 1960
38  Kim Newman, *Edgar Wallace: Your Pocket Guide to the Rialto Krimi Series*, *Video Watchdog* # 134, September 2007
39  Pierre Macabru, *La Chambre ardente*, *Combat* 13 April 1962
40  unsigned review of *La Chambre ardente*, *Le Canard enchaîné* 6 April 1962
41  quoted in Durgnat, op cit
42  unsigned review of *Gritos en la noche*, *Shorter Notices*, *Monthly Film Bulletin* June 1963
43  Alain Le Bris, *Jack l'éventreur*, *Midi-Minuit Fantastique* # 2, August 1962
44  quoted in Ed Senior, *Witchmaster: Forty Years in Another Town*, *Shock Xpress* vol 2 # 2, Winter 1987
45  quoted in Alan Upchurch, Tim Lucas and Luigi Boscaino, *Raptus: The Making of The Horrible Dr Hichcock*, *Video Watchdog* # 49, January-February 1999
46  Caen and Romer, op cit
47  Upchurch, Lucas and Boscaino, op cit
48  Eugene Archer, *A Pair of Films*, *New York Times* 3 December 1964
49  'Donald', *Estreno de las películas El empleo, La cara del terror y Una isla con tomate*, *ABC Madrid* 30 October 1962
50  quoted in Mike Hodges, *Riding the Horror Express*, *Fangoria* # 186, September 1999
51  Caen and Romer, op cit
52  Philip Strick, *Science Fiction Movies*, London 1976

## Part Three – *Angels for Satan*

1  F Maurice Speed, *The Year in the Cinema / Foreign Films*, *Film Review 1962-1963*, London 1962
2  Jean-André Fieschi, *Histoire extraordinaire*, *Cahiers du Cinéma* May-June 1965
3  quoted in Peter Blumenstock, *Margheriti: The Wild, Wild Interview*, *Video Watchdog* # 28, May-June 1995
4  ibid
5  PJD [Peter John Dyer], *Film Reviews: Night is the Phantom*, *Daily Cinema* 27 January 1965
6  quoted in Tim Lucas, *What Are Those Strange Drops of Blood in the Scripts of Ernesto Gastaldi?*, *Video Watchdog* # 39, May-June 1997
7  Christopher Lee, *Tall, Dark and Gruesome: An Autobiography*, London 1977
8  ibid
9  quoted in Lucas, op cit

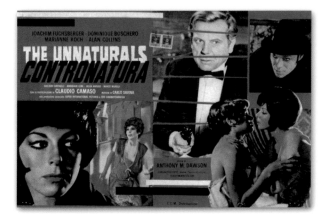

10 James Powers, Film Reviews: Blood and Black Lace, Hollywood Reporter 11 June 1965

11 Antonio Bruschini, Mario Bava: Maestro of the Macabre, in Horror all'italiana, Firenze 1996

12 Jim Barden, Horror-for-Fun Pays Off, Daily American 30-31 August 1964

13 Graham Clarke, Reviews: The Castle of the Living Dead, Kinematograph Weekly 24 February 1968

14 quoted in Christopher S Dietrich and Peter Beckman, Karma, Catsup & Caskets: The Barbara Steele Interview, Video Watchdog # 7, September-October 1991

15 quoted in John Martin, Blood on the Daisies, The Dark Side # 48, August 1995

16 quoted in Lucas Balbo, I Talked with a Zombie: The Forgotten Horrors of Massimo Pupillo, in Shock Xpress: The Essential Guide to Exploitation Cinema, London 1996

17 quoted in Robert Skotak, Worlds, Wars & Wonders: The Amazing Career of Ib J Melchior, Filmfax # 62, August-September 1997

18 Jeffrey Frentzen, It! The Terror from Beyond the Planet of the Vampires, Cinefantastique vol 8 # 4, Summer 1979

19 Philip Strick, Retrospective: Planet of the Vampires, Monthly Film Bulletin vol 53 # 625, February 1986

20 AS, Andalucía: El sonido de la muerte, ABC Andalucía 14 January 1967

21 Sidney Pink, So You Want to Make Movies: My Life as an Independent Film Producer, Sarasota 1989

22 AS, Estreno de las películas El tesoro de Makuba y La isla de la muerte, ABC Andalucía 1 April 1967

23 Graham Clarke, Kine Booking Guide, Kinematograph Weekly 25 November 1967

24 quoted in Alberto Farina, D'Amato Ketchup, Shivers # 22, August 1992

25 unsigned, La ragazza del boia, La Stampa 10 July 1965

26 quoted in Antonio Bruschini, Massimo Pupillo: Sadistic Hangmen and Avenging Ghosts, in Horror all'italiana, Firenze 1996

27 quoted in Mark Kermode and Alan Jones, Steele and Lace, The Dark Side # 11, August 1991

28 'Byro' (Stuart Byron), Kill, Baby... Kill, Variety 30 October 1968

29 quoted in Christian Kessler, Un sogno chiamato Erika, Amarcord vol 3 # 12, March-April 1998

30 quoted in Franco Piccinini, Si gira a Fino Mornasco in una storica villa: La lunga notte di Veronique, La Stampa 5 May 1966

# Part Four – *Nights of the Devil*

1 John Trevelyan, What the Censor Saw, London 1973

2 quoted in Hans Königstein, Aus der Fabrik des Bösen II, Film vol 5 # 12, December 1967

3 unsigned, Film neu in Deutschland: Greuel in Grüften, Der Spiegel 22 May 1967

4 Ralf Klee and Broder-Jürgen Trede, Kinogeschichte: Im Bann des Killer-Froschs, Der Spiegel 4 September 2009

5 Steven Erlanger, May 1968 – a watershed in French life, New York Times 30 April 2008

6 Barrie Pattison, The Seal of Dracula, London 1975

7 Juan José Porto and Ángel Falquina, Cine de Terror y Paul Naschy, Madrid 1974

8 Paul Naschy, Crónica de las tinieblas: Frankenstein y el hombre lobo, Cinerama # 93, July-August 2000

9 Nigel Andrews, Feature Films: Marca del hombre lobo, La (Hell's Creatures), Monthly Film Bulletin vol 39 # 459, April 1972

10 Paul Naschy, Memorias de un hombre lobo, Madrid 1997 (translator Mike Hodges)

11 unsigned, West End Opinion: The Rest, Films in London # 52, 30 May-12 June 1971

12 Lola Salvador, Narciso Ibáñez Serrador – 'Monstruo Sagrado' de TVE rueda La Residencia, Nuevo Fotogramas # 1072, 2 May 1969

13 quoted in Juan Montserrat, Terror, Terror, Terror, con 'Chicho' Ibáñez Serrador, Nuevo Fotogramas # 1173, 9 April 1971

14 quoted in Rosa Montero, La vuelta de 'Chicho', Nuevo Fotogramas # 1426, 13 February 1976

15 quoted in Lola Salvador, Dickens, Hitchcock y ... Juan Tébar, Nuevo Fotogramas # 1072, 2 May 1969

16 quoted in Del Arco, Mano a mano: Miguel Iglesias, La Vanguardia 25 December 1969

17 Roger Greenspun, Vampires of Jonathan Strike a Metaphoric Blow Against Fascism, New York Times 16 June 1973

18 Alan Kriegsman in The Washington Post, title and date unknown

19 quoted in Peter Blumenstock, Jean Rollin Has Risen from the Grave!, Video Watchdog # 31, January-February 1996

20 Jean Rollin, introduction to Alternative Europe: Eurotrash and Exploitation Cinema since 1945, New York 2004

21 Jean Rollin and Peter Blumenstock, Virgins and Vampires, Villingen-Schwenningen 1997

22 'Besa', Film Reviews: El conde Drácula, Variety 7 April 1970

23 quoted in Pupi Avati: Two Interviews, Video Watchdog # 3, Jan-Feb 1991; translated by Alan Upchurch from a Giuseppe Salza interview featured in L'Écran Fantastique # 36, July-August 1983

24 unsigned, Una película española sobre Sherlock Holmes, La Vanguardia 7 April 1970

25 quoted in E Vila-Matas, Encuentro con Capucine, Nuevo Fotogramas # 1049, 22 November 1968

26 Stephen Thrower (with Julian Grainger), Murderous Passions: The Delirious Cinema of Jesús Franco, London 2015

27 unsigned, Insolita censura in un cinematografo di Genova: Operatore sospende la proiezione perché il film è 'troppo erotico', La Stampa 19 December 1971

28 A H Weiler, Vampire Story with a New Angle Appears at the Penthouse, New York Times 4 February 1971

29 quoted in David Soren, Unreal Reality: The Cinema of Harry Kümel, Columbia 1979

30 quoted in David Thompson, Auteur of Darkness, Sight and Sound August 2002

31 Dilys Powell, [review of Daughters of Darkness], Sunday Times 12 September 1971

32 quoted in Ernest Mathijs, The Cinema of the Low Countries, New York 2004

33 Howard Thompson, Film: Artistic Vampires, New York Times 29 May 1971

34 David Pirie, The Vampire Cinema, London 1977

35  Pattison, op cit
36  Jean-Claude Morlot, *Impossible is Not French*, *Cinefantastique* vol 3 # 1, Fall 1973
37  Pedro Yoldi in *Terror Fantastic* # 6, March 1972
38  unsigned review of *La noche de Walpurgis*, *El Pueblo* 25 May 1971
39  David McGillivray, *Feature Films: Nacht der Vampire (Shadow of the Werewolf)*, *Monthly Film Bulletin* vol 40 # 474, July 1973
40  Jean-François Davy and André Ruellan, *Présentation du Seuil du vide*, *Midi-Minuit Fantastique* # 23, October 1970
41  Rollin and Blumenstock, op cit
42  Tim Lucas, *Video Tapevine*, *Video Watchdog* # 23, May-July 1994
43  quoted in Fernando Lara, Diego Galán and Ramón Rodríguez, *Eloy de la Iglesia y la violencia*, *Triunfo* 22 September 1973; reproduced in Antonio Lázaro-Reboll, *Spanish Horror Film*, Edinburgh 2012
44  Ángeles Masó, *Música, Teatro y Cinematografía: La semana del asesino*, *La Vanguardia* 9 June 1972
45  Eloy de la Iglesia, *Mi película es un homenaje a Kubrick, nunca un plagio*, *Nuevo Fotogramas* # 1272, 2 March 1973
46  quoted in Josu Olano and Borja Crespo, *Amando de Ossorio: Entrevista*, in *Cine fantástico y de terror español 1900-1983*, San Sebastián 1999
47  quoted in Jan van Genechten (editor), *Fandom's Film Gallery* # 3, July 1978
48  Marjorie Bilbow, *The New Films: Tombs of the Blind Dead*, *Cinema TV Today*, 2 June 1973
49  Nigel Andrews, *Feature Films: Notte dei Diavoli, La (Night of the Devils)*, *Monthly Film Bulletin* vol 40 # 469, February 1973
50  unsigned, *Actualidad Barcelona: Terror exportable*, *Nuevo Fotogramas* # 1220, 3 March 1972
51  Ángeles Masó, *Sitges: En el transiberiano un monstruo cobra vida por obra de Eugenio Martín*, *La Vanguardia* 5 October 1972
52  Marjorie Bilbow, *The New Films: Horror Express*, *CinemaTV Today* 16 March 1974

# Part Five – *Rites of Blood*

1  Phil Hardy (editor), *The Aurum Film Encyclopedia: Horror*, London 1985
2  Eric Braun, *The Blood Spattered Bride*, *Films and Filming* April 1980
3  quoted in Cathal Tohill, *Return of El Hombre Lobo!*, *The Dark Side* # 41, August-September 1994
4  Tim Lucas, *How to Read a Franco Film*, *Video Watchdog* # 1, Summer 1990
5  quoted in [unsigned] *Raúl Artigot: director de El monte de las brujas*, *Terror Fantastic* # 26, November 1973
6  Pierre J Maintigneux, *Au Rendez-vous de la mort joyeuse* [Bibliothèque de l'étrange # 8], Paris 1973
7  quoted in TD, *El último opus de Jorge Grau: Los españoles podemos hacer el mejor cine erótico del mundo*, *Nuevo Fotogramas* # 1440, 21 May 1976
8  Robert L Jerome, *Short Notices: Crypt of the Living Dead*, *Cinefantastique* vol 4 # 1, Spring 1975
9  quoted in John Martin, *Man of a Thousand Pseudonyms*, *The Dark Side* # 53, January-February 1996
10  'Jordan', *Acontecimientos del cine español: Mas vampiros*, *La Vanguardia* 7 June 1972
11  'V', *La musa de Eric Rohmer en La Colecionista, en Madrid*, *La Vanguardia* 3 September 1972
12  Paul Naschy, *Memorias de un hombre lobo*, Madrid 1997 (translator Mike Hodges)
13  Claudi Montañá, *Claudio Guerín una esperanza rota*, *Nuevo Fotogramas* # 1272, 2 March 1973
14  Cifra, *Claudio Guerín ha muerto*, *La Vanguardia* 17 February 1973
15  quoted in Peter Besas, *Behind the Spanish Lens: Spanish Cinema under Fascism and Democracy*, Denver 1985
16  unsigned, *Judy, la rubia, cine-stopista en España*, *Nuevo Fotogramas* # 1272, 2 March 1973
17  quoted in Mike Hodges, *Riding the Horror Express*, *Fangoria* # 186, September 1999
18  quoted in Paul Talbot, *Monsters for Morrissey: The Making of Andy Warhol's Frankenstein & Dracula*, *Video Watchdog* # 28, May-June 1995
19  ibid
20  Nora Sayre, *Screen: Butchery Binge*, *New York Times* 16 May 1974
21  *The Complete Monty Python's Flying Circus: All the Words Volume 2*, London 1989
22  Peter Nicholls, *Fantastic Cinema: An Illustrated Survey*, London 1984
23  unsigned review, *No profanar el sueño de los muertos*, *Film Guía* # 11, December 1975-January 1976
24  quoted in Perry Martin and R J Gallentine, *Jorge Grau: Director of Manchester Morgue*, *Video Watchdog* # 66, December 2000
25  quoted in Josephine Botting, *Catalonian Creeps*, *Shivers* # 79, July 2000
26  ibid
27  *Zaertlichkeit der Woelfe: Fassbinder's Romantic Shocker with the Werewolf Thrill*, full-page ad in *Variety* 27 June 1973
28  Tom Hutchinson, *Blood Curdling*, *Sunday Telegraph* 9 May 1976
29  Stephen Thrower (with Julian Grainger), *Murderous Passions: The Delirious Cinema of Jesús Franco*, London 2015
30  PF ('Pisanus Fraxi'), *Possédées du diable*, *Positif* # 166, February 1975
31  Reynold Humphries, *Short Notices: Antichristo 1974* [sic], *Cinefantastique* vol 4 # 4, Winter 1976
32  Andy Willis, *Paul Naschy, Exorcismo and the Reactionary Horrors of Spanish Popular Cinema in the Early 1970s*, in *European Nightmares: Horror Cinema in Europe since 1945*, New York 2012
33  unsigned item in *International Soundtrack*, *Variety* 29 May 1974
34  quoted in Cathal Tohill, *Return of El Hombre Lobo!*, *The Dark Side* # 41, August-September 1994
35  LLS, *Flojo ensayo de terror a la española: La cruz del diablo*, *ABC* (Madrid) 2 April 1975
36  Tomás Fernández Valenti, *Antología del cine fantástico español: La cruz del diablo*, in *Quatermass* # 4/5, autumn 2002
37  Naschy, op cit
38  Richard Combs, *Feature Films: Noche del terror ciego, La (Tombs of the Blind Dead)*, *Monthly Film Bulletin* vol 40 # 474, July 1973

39  speaking in *Amando de Ossorio o último Templario* [TV documentary], Xosé Zapata / Lorelei Producciones 2001
40  quoted in Darren Ross, *Lust at First Bite*, *The Dark Side* # 22, July 1992

# Part Six – *New Worlds of Fear*

1  'Besa', *Film Reviews: Quién puede matar a un niño?*, *Variety* 5 May 1976
2  Frédéric Beigbeder, *Gilles de Rais-Grillet*, *Lire* November 2007
3  quoted in Anthony N Fragola and Roch C Smith, *The Erotic Dream Machine: Interviews with Alain Robbe-Grillet on His Films*, Carbondale 1992
4  Michael Darvell, *Made But Not Shown – The Movies You May Never See*, in *Film Review 1977-78*, London 1977
5  Roger Ebert, [review of *The Tenant*], *Chicago Sun-Times* 27 September 1976
6  Ian Cameron, *High Rent*, *The Spectator* 18 September 1976
7  Martin Amis, *Socket to Her*, *New Statesman* 27 August 1976
8  Michel Lengliney, *Dracula père et fils: Droles de vampires*, *Télérama* 18 September 1976
9  quoted in [unsigned] *Christopher Lee plays Dracula for the last time ... again!*, *Cinefantastique* vol 5 # 4, Spring 1977
10  unsigned, *Agenda: Una película sobre la Inquisición*, *Blanco y Negro* (Madrid), 15 May 1976
11  quoted in Alan Jones, *Enchanter of the Dark: director Pupi Avati*, *Shivers* # 80, August 2000
12  F Maurice Speed, *Film Review 1981-1982*, London 1981
13  Alan Scherstuhl, *1979's Astounding Sci-Fi Horror Mess The Visitor is in Theaters At Last*, *The Village Voice* 5 November 2013
14  quoted in Mike Bygrave and Joan Goodman, *The Return of Old Red Eyes*, *The Observer Magazine* 25 March 1979
15  quoted in Wolfgang Limmer, *Leben eines Untoten*, *Der Spiegel* 15 January 1979
16  Derek Malcolm, *Laughter in the Teeth of Misfortune*, *The Guardian* 17 May 1979
17  Peter Nicholls, *Fantastic Cinema: An Illustrated Survey*, London 1984
18  quoted in Peter Blumenstock and Christian Kessler, *Enzo G Castellari Part 2*, *European Trash Cinema* vol 2 # 10, 1994
19  quoted in Alan Jones, *Master of Maggot Mayhem*, *The Dark Side* # 9, June 1991
20  ibid
21  Ian Olney, *Euro Horror: Classic European Horror Cinema in Contemporary American Culture*, Bloomington 2013
22  quoted in John Martin, *Who is Giannetto De Rossi?*, *The Dark Side* # 42, October-November 1994
23  Craig Ledbetter, *Video Around the World: Venezuela*, *Video Watchdog* # 7, September-October 1991
24  unsigned, *Obituaries*, *Variety* 23 May 1980
25  quoted in Jones, *Master of Maggot Mayhem*, op cit
26  Marjorie Bilbow, *The New Films: City of the Living Dead*, *Screen International* 1 May 1982
27  quoted in David Miller, *The Complete Peter Cushing*, London 2005
28  J Sandoval, *La noche al día: Otoño*, *La Vanguardia* 11 October 1980
29  quoted in Maitland McDonagh, *Profile: Señor Splatter*, *Gorezone* # 17, Spring 1991
30  quoted in Bonet Mojica, *Rueda un filme a Barcelona: José Ramón Larraz, el mirón que no quiso ir a Hollywood*, *La Vanguardia* 26 April 1980
31  quoted in Sara Maso, *El Ser, terror psicológico*, *La Vanguardia* 16 September 1982
32  Sandoval, op cit
33  Paul Naschy, *Memorias de un hombre lobo*, Madrid 1997 (translator Mike Hodges)
34  David Quinlan, *Background: The Beyond*, *Films Illustrated* # 123, December 1981
35  Derek Malcolm, [review of *Immoral Tales*], *The Guardian* 29 November 1973
36  Clancy Sigal, *High Porn*, *The Spectator* 28 May 1977
37  quoted in Susan Adler, *Enticements to Voyeurism*, *Cinema Papers* # 50, February-March 1985
38  Al Clark, *The Films: Possession*, in *The Virgin Film Yearbook 1983*, London 1982
39  Stephen Bissette, *Der Fan / Trance* (1980?), *European Trash Cinema* vol 1 # 2-3, unknown date
40  quoted in Pierre Tchernia (editor), *80 grands succés du cinéma fantastique*, Brussels 1988
41  'Lor', *Film Reviews: House by the Cemetery*, *Variety* 11 April 1984
42  quoted in Martin Coxhead, *Where De Angelis Fears to Tread*, *The Dark Side* # 27, December 1992
43  Chas Balun, *Piece o' Mind: Bravo, Fulci!*, *Gorezone* # 10, November 1989
44  quoted in Peter Blumenstock, Christian Kessler and Michael Nagenborg, *The Jean Rollin Interview*, *European Trash Cinema* vol 2 # 8, 1993
45  quoted in Peter Blumenstock, *Jean Rollin Has Risen from the Grave!*, *Video Watchdog* # 31, January-February 1996
46  quoted in Jones, *Enchanter of the Dark*, op cit
47  quoted in *Pupi Avati: Two Interviews*, *Video Watchdog* # 3, Jan-Feb 1991; translated by Alan Upchurch from a Lorenzo Codelli interview featured in *L'Écran Fantastique* # 36, July-August 1983
48  ibid
49  Clyde Haberman, *Italy's Movie Industry Falls on Hard Times*, *New York Times* 27 December 1990
50  quoted in Tim Lucas, *Mario Bava: All the Colors of the Dark*, Cincinnati 2007
51  Deborah Young, *Film Review: The Arcane Enchanter*, *Variety* 22 April 1996
52  quoted in Naschy, op cit

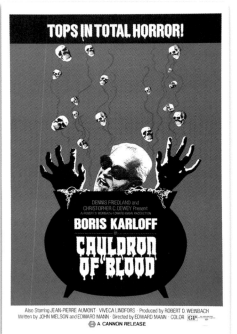

The posthumously released Boris Karloff vehicle *El coleccionista de cadáveres* (1967) was exported as, among other things, *Cauldron of Blood*

# Title Index

Film titles are given in bold type; television productions in italics; plays, novels, short stories etc in regular type.
Numerals in bold type indicate illustrations. Numerals followed by an asterisk refer to the 16 pages of colour illustrations, while ep1 and ep2 indicate stills contained in the front and back endpapers.

# Alternative Titles

Listed below are films shown theatrically with alternative titles, excluding those already alluded to in the text. Retitlings for video and-or TV are not included.

- Alraune (1927) : A Daughter of Destiny (US)
- Alraune (1952) : Unnatural (US)
- Las amantes del diablo : Feast of Satan (US)
- L'arcidiavolo : The Devil in Love (US)
- Baba Yaga : The Devil Witch (US)
- Beiß mich Liebling! : Love Vampire Style (UK)
- Das Bildnis des Dorian Gray : Dorian Gray (UK, US)
- El buque maldito : Horror of the Zombies (US)
- Buio omega : aka Buried Alive (US)
- La casa de las muertes vivientes : The Night of the Scorpion (US)
- Chi sei? : The Devil Within Her (UK)
- La coda dello scorpione : The Case of the Scorpion's Tail (US)
- Contronatura : The Unnaturals (US)
- De Sade 70 : Philosophy in the Boudoir (UK), Eugenie… the Story of Her Journey into Perversion (US)
- La donna del lago : The Possessed (US)
- La endemoniada : Demon Witch Child (US)
- Ercole al centro della terra : Hercules in the Haunted World (US)
- L'Éternel retour : Love Eternal (UK)
- L'etrusco uccide ancora : The Dead Are Alive (US)
- El extraño amor de los vampiros : The Night of the Walking Dead (US)
- Der Frosch mit der Maske : Face of the Frog (US)

- Las garras de Lorelei : The Lorelei's Grasp (US)
- La Goulve : Erotic Witchcraft (UK, US)
- Un hacha para la luna de miel : Blood Brides (UK)
- Harry, un ami qui vous veut du bien : Harry, He's Here to Help (UK), With a Friend Like Harry… (US)
- Häxan : Witchcraft Through the Ages (UK, US)
- Holocaust 2000 : The Chosen (US)
- Il mio amico Jekyll : My Friend, Dr Jekyll (US)
- La isla de la muerte : Island of the Doomed (US)
- L'isola degli uomini pesce : Island of Mutations (UK), Screamers (US)
- J'Accuse (1937) : That They May Live (US)
- Der junge Törless : Young Torless (UK, US)
- La lupa mannara : Werewolf Woman (UK, US)
- Malenka : Fangs of the Living Dead (US)
- La mansión de la niebla : Maniac Mansion (US)
- El mariscal del infierno : Devil's Possessed (US)
- Los monstruos del terror : Dracula versus Frankenstein (UK), Assignment Terror (US)
- Nella stretta morsa del ragno : Web of the Spider (US)
- Nero veneziano : Damned in Venice (US)
- Night Hair Child : Night Child (US)
- No es nada, mamá, sólo un juego : Lola (US)
- La notte che Evelyn uscì dalla tomba : The Night She Rose from the Tomb (UK)
- Nude … si muore : The Young, the Evil and the Savage (US)
- Un'ombra nell'ombra : Ring of Darkness (US)
- Opera : Terror at the Opera (UK, US)
- La orgía de los muertos : Bracula, the Terror of the Living Dead! (UK)

- Orloff et l'homme invisible : Secret Love Life of the Invisible Man (US)
- L'ossessa : The Sexorcist, The Tormented, Enter the Devil (all US)
- La Papesse : A Woman Possessed (US)
- Phenomena : Creepers (US)
- I pianeti contro di noi : Hands of a Killer (UK)
- Plaisir à trois : How to Seduce a Virgin (UK)
- El proceso de las brujas : Night of the Blood Monster (US)
- La rebelión de las muertas : Vengeance of the Zombies (US)
- Requiem pour un vampire : Caged Virgins (US)
- El sonido de la muerte : The Sound of Horror (US)
- La strangolatore di Vienna : The Mad Butcher (US)
- Lo strano vizio della Signora Wardh : Next! (US), aka Blade of the Ripper
- Der Student von Prag (1926) : The Man Who Cheated Life (US)
- Tarots – Détrás de las cartas el diablo : The Magician (UK)
- Tempi duri per i vampiri : Uncle Was a Vampire (US)
- Tras el cristal : In a Glass Cage (US)
- La tumba de la isla maldita : Hannah Queen of the Vampires, Crypt of the Living Dead (US)
- Tutti i colori del buio : They're Coming to Get You (US)
- L'uccello dalle piume di cristallo : The Gallery Murders (UK)
- La última señora Anderson : The Fourth Victim (US)
- Das Verrätertor : Traitor's Gate (UK, US)
- Violación fatal : aka Trauma
- Zombi Holocaust : Doctor Butcher M.D. (US)

DRACULA
im Schloß des
Schreckens

Ein wahrhaft ungeheuerlicher Film
Magdalena-
vom Teufel
besessen